Scholarship Handbook

2018

CollegeBoard

Scholarship
Handbook

2018

CollegeBoard

Scholarship Handbook

21st Edition

The College Board, New York

☝ CollegeBoard

The College Board

The College Board is a mission-driven not-for-profit organization that connects students to college success and opportunity. Founded in 1900, the College Board was created to expand access to higher education. Today, the membership association is made up of over 6,000 of the world's leading educational institutions and is dedicated to promoting excellence and equity in education. Each year, the College Board helps more than seven million students prepare for a successful transition to college through programs and services in college readiness and college success — including the SAT® and the Advanced Placement Program®. The organization also serves the education community through research and advocacy on behalf of students, educators, and schools.

For further information, visit www.collegeboard.org.

Editorial inquiries concerning this book should be directed to Guidance Publications, The College Board, 250 Vesey Street, New York, NY 10281; or telephone 800-323-7155.

Copies of this book are available from your local bookseller or may be ordered from College Board Publications, P.O. Box 7500, London, KY 40742-7500. The book may also be ordered online through the College Board Store at www.collegeboard.org. The price is $31.99.

© 2017 The College Board. College Board, ACCUPLACER, Advanced Placement, Advanced Placement Program, AP, CLEP, College-Level Examination Program, CSS/Financial Aid PROFILE, SAT, SpringBoard, and the acorn logo are registered trademarks of the College Board. CSS Profile, My College QuickStart, MyRoad, SAT Preparation Booklet, SAT Preparation Center, SAT Reasoning Test, SAT Subject Tests, The Official SAT Online Course, The Official SAT Study Guide, and The Official Study Guide for all SAT Subject Tests are trademarks owned by the College Board. PSAT/NMSQT is a registered trademark of the College Board and National Merit Scholarship Corporation. All other products and services may be trademarks of their respective owners.

ISBN: 978-1-4573-0927-4

Printed in the United States of America

Distributed by Macmillan. For information on bulk purchases please contact Macmillan Corporate and Premium Sales Department at (800) 221-7945 x5442.

The College Board is committed to publishing in a manner that both respects the environment and helps preserve the Earth's resources. We seek to achieve this through eco-friendly practices, including the use of FSC and recycled paper and biodegradable materials. When you see this symbol, be assured that we are working to reduce our ecological footprint. The interior of this book is made of 100% recycled/30% PCW paper.

Contents

Preface

Searching for scholarships has often been described as looking for a needle in a haystack. There are thousands of award programs available, but the typical student can expect to qualify for only a small number of them. This book is designed to point you toward programs that match your own personal and academic qualifications.

Compiled within this book are detailed descriptions of national and state-level award programs for students seeking an undergraduate degree. All are portable to more than one college or university. Most are available to all undergraduates, but some are restricted to entering freshmen, and others are only for continuing students — sophomores, juniors or seniors. Most awards are only available to U.S. citizens or permanent residents, but some are also available to students in other countries who plan to come to the United States for college.

Not included in this book are scholarships that colleges award directly to their own students, as these are generally awarded upon admission rather than by separate application. Such "inside" scholarships can be found listed in the college profiles in the College Board book *Getting Financial Aid 2018*.

The award program descriptions are based on information provided by the sponsors themselves, in response to the College Board's Annual Survey of Financial Aid Programs, conducted in the spring of 2017. A staff of editors verified the facts for every award program. While every effort was made to ensure that the information is correct and up to date, we urge you to confirm facts, especially deadline information, with the programs themselves. The award programs' websites are the best sources for current information.

We'd like to thank those who worked so hard to bring the *Scholarship Handbook 2018* to press: editors Ariella Gould and Julie Sheib, who researched and compiled the data, and project managers Randy Peery, David Christ and Chris Hagan. We would also like to thank the team of programmers and typesetters at DataStream Content Solutions, LLC, who converted the database into readable pages.

We wish to give special acknowledgment to Renée Gernand, who recently retired. It is with sincere appreciation that we thank for the leadership and service she gave to both the College Board and the entire higher education community.

Tom Vanderberg
Senior Editor, Guidance Publications

How to Use This Book

You may be tempted to go directly to the program descriptions and start browsing, but to get the most out of this book, start by reading the information and advice in the opening pages. They'll help you get a realistic perspective on financial aid and give you useful guidelines for understanding and taking advantage of your college funding options.

Your next step should be to complete the "Personal Characteristics Checklist" on page 13. This will help you think about all the ways you might qualify for scholarships and give you an idea of where you might start looking for awards you can apply for.

Using the eligibility indexes

After your checklist is complete, use the eligibility indexes beginning on page 27 to find the award programs that correspond to your qualifications. You can also use the scholarship search program on www.collegeboard.org. This user-friendly program enables you to search with more criteria and with much greater speed than is possible with print indexes.

Please keep in mind that the eligibility indexes show programs for which *one* of the criteria is covered by the index. Most of these programs have additional requirements, such as financial need (as demonstrated on the FAFSA or CSS/Financial Aid PROFILE®), standardized test scores or GPA.

Corporate/Employer: Listed here are the many companies and businesses that offer scholarships to employees and/or employees' family members. You should check out any company that employs a member of your immediate family.

Disabilities: This category covers students with hearing or visual impairments, physical handicaps or learning disabilities.

Field of Study/Intended Career: This category, by far the longest, identifies broad major and career areas. If you don't see your specific area of interest, look for a more general area into which it might fit. In many cases, these awards require applicants to be already enrolled in college and to have declared a major in the relevant field.

KNOW THE LINGO

You'll find sidebars like this throughout the first part of this book highlighting and defining key terms. There's also a comprehensive glossary beginning on page 21.

1

Gender: Although the vast majority of awards are not gender-specific, there are just under 60 awards in this book exclusively for women, and more than 20 for men only.

International Students: Most awards in this book are available only to U.S. citizens or permanent residents. The programs in this category, however, are open to students from outside the United States.

Military Participation: Many of the awards in this category are for the children, descendants or spouses of members of the military, including the Reserves and National Guard, going back as far as the Civil War.

Minority Status: There are eight groups within this category, representing a wide range of awards.

National/Ethnic Background: The national/ethnic groups in this category are determined by the sponsoring organizations that responded to our annual survey.

Organization/Civic Affiliation: Many membership organizations and civic associations have generous higher education funding programs that are available for their members and/or their members' dependents or relatives. Check to see if any apply to your family.

Religious Affiliation: The 10 denominations in this category represent a broad range but, like the national/ethnic category, are determined by the respondents to our annual survey.

Returning Adult: This category includes awards for undergraduate, graduate and nondegree study. The age qualification varies, but most often is for students 25 years or older.

State of Residence: Each state has several award programs exclusively for state residents. Be sure to examine closely all those listed under your state.

Study Abroad: While most award programs for study abroad are for graduate students, a few are geared for undergraduates, and you will find them listed here.

What's in the program descriptions?

The scholarship programs in this book are organized alphabetically by sponsor within three sections.

The scholarships section covers public and private scholarships and research grants for undergraduates. To be included, a scholarship program must grant at least $250 for the purpose of financing some aspect of higher education: tuition and fees, research, study abroad, travel expenses or other educational endeavors.

KEEP IN MIND

This book does not describe local award programs that are restricted to a single community or school. For information about local programs for which you might qualify, talk to your school counselor or contact your local chamber of commerce.

Also not included in this are scholarships offered by colleges to their own students. For these "inside" awards, you should consult the financial aid offices at the colleges you are considering. Detailed financial aid information for more than 3,000 colleges can also be found in the College Board book *Getting Financial Aid 2018*.

PLANNING AHEAD

Even if you qualify for a scholarship, you won't get it if you don't **apply on time**! Use the **planning worksheet on page 17** to keep track of deadlines, application requirements and notification dates for the programs you've selected.

The internships section covers public and private internships, providing opportunities either to earn money for education or to gain academic credit. To be included, paid internships must pay at least $100 per week and provide a viable path toward a future career. (The ESPN internship is an example of this; the Oscar Mayer Wienermobile is not.)

The loans section covers public and private education loan programs. Many have loan forgiveness options, usually in exchange for public or community service for a certain period of time.

Each program description contains all of the information provided by the sponsor and verified for accuracy by a staff of editors at the College Board. A typical description includes:

Type of award: Whether the award is a scholarship, grant, internship or loan; and whether it's renewable.

Intended use: Tells you the range and limitations of the award, such as level of study, full time or part time, at what kind of institution, and whether in the United States or abroad.

Eligibility: Indicates the characteristics you must have to be considered for an award — for example, U.S. citizenship, specific state of residence, disability, membership in a particular organization or minority status.

Basis for selection: May include major or career interest; personal qualities such as seriousness of purpose, high academic achievement or depth of character; or financial need.

Application requirements: Outlines what you must provide in support of your application, such as recommendations, essay, transcript, interview, proof of eligibility, a résumé or references.

Additional information: Gives you any facts or requirements not covered in the categories above — for example, which test scores to submit, GPA required, whether a particular type of student is given special consideration, when application forms are available, etc.

Amount of award: A single figure generally means the standard amount, but may indicate the maximum of a range of amounts. If a program awards different amounts, the range is provided.

Number of awards: Tells you how many awards are granted by the sponsor.

Number of applicants: Tells you how many students applied the previous year.

Application deadline: The date by which your application must be submitted; some scholarships have two deadlines for considering applications. Note: This information was obtained in spring 2016. Deadlines may have passed or changed. Check the sponsor's website for current deadlines.

Notification begins: The earliest date that an award notification is sent; in some cases, all go out on the same date; in others, notification is on a rolling basis. If there are two application deadlines, there are usually two notification dates.

GOOD TO KNOW

In addition to the eligibility indexes preceding the scholarship descriptions, there are two general indexes in the back of the book that list award programs by sponsor name and program name.

KNOW THE LINGO

Academic internship — An internship where you are not paid for your work, but rather earn college credit.

Paid internship — An internship where you are paid for your work.

Total amount awarded: Tells you how much money is disbursed in the current award year, including renewable awards.

Contact: Gives you all available information on where to get application forms and further information. Where the contact name and address are identical for several different scholarship programs sponsored by the same organization, this information will appear at the end of the last scholarship in that group.

While some descriptions don't include all these details because they were either not applicable or not supplied by the sponsor, in every case all essential information is provided. Readers are urged to verify all information (the sponsor's website is the best source) before submitting applications.

Understanding Financial Aid

You shouldn't count on "outside scholarships" and summer internships like the ones in this book to pay for college. Rather, you should treat them as one possible source of aid, along with federal student aid and the scholarships and work-study jobs offered by colleges. In fact, outside scholarships account for only 6 percent of total student financial aid each year.

In order to get the most out of this book, you should first understand how to apply for the other 94 percent of total aid.

What Is Financial Aid?

Financial aid is money given or loaned to you to help you pay for college. Different forms have different rules. The vast majority of aid comes from the federal government, and most of it consists of loans that you must pay back. However, some aid does not require repayment — which makes it the best kind.

If you qualify for financial aid, your college will put together an aid "package," usually with different types of aid bundled together. Most students qualify for some form of financial aid, so it makes sense to apply for it.

You'll apply for financial aid either at the same time or soon after you apply for admission. You might have to fill out more than one application. At the very least you will fill out the FAFSA, or federal government form, available online at **FAFSA on the Web**. You might also fill out another form, the CSS Profile™, which many colleges require. Some colleges and state aid agencies require their own financial aid forms, too.

The colleges to which you apply will use the forms to figure out what your family can afford to pay and what your "need" is — that is, the difference between what you can pay and what the college actually costs. If the school wants you as a student but sees that you can't handle the whole bill, it will make you a financial aid offer to help you meet your need. If you accept, that financial aid package is your award.

KNOW THE LINGO

Merit aid — Aid awarded on the basis of academics, character or talent.

Need-based aid — Aid awarded on the basis of a family's inability to pay the full cost of attending a particular college.

Non-need-based aid — Aid awarded on some basis other than need or merit, such as grants with eligibility requirements related to field of study or state residence.

You will need to apply for financial aid every year that you are in college, mainly because your family's financial situation changes yearly. As a result, your financial aid package will probably be somewhat different from year to year.

Financial aid is a helping hand, not a free pass. In the United States, everyone has a right to a free public school education, but not to a free college education. The federal government and most colleges agree that students and their parents are the ones most responsible for paying for college. "The primary responsibility of paying for the student's education lies with the student and his or her parents," says Forrest M. Stuart, the director of financial aid at Furman University in Greenville, S.C. "Financial aid comes in to fill that gap, if you will, between what they can afford and what the college costs."

Types of Aid

Financial aid may come in many forms. However, all forms can be grouped into two major categories: gift aid and self-help aid.

Gift Aid

Gift aid is free money, money that you don't have to pay back or work for. Naturally, this is the kind of aid most people want. It can take the form of grants or scholarships.

The terms "grant" and "scholarship" are often used interchangeably to mean free money. But here's the difference: A grant is usually given only on the basis of need, or your family's inability to pay the full cost of college. Scholarships are usually awarded only to those who have "merit," such as proven ability in academics, the arts or athletics. Once you're in college, you may have to maintain a minimum GPA or take certain courses to continue receiving a scholarship.

Self-Help Aid

Self-help aid is money that requires a contribution from you. That can mean paying back the money (if the aid is a loan) or working for the money (if the aid is a work-study job).

The most common form of self-help aid is a loan. A loan is money that you have to pay back with interest. In light of that, you might not consider this aid at all. But it is — a loan means you don't have to pay the full price of college all at once: You can stretch the payments over time, as you would when buying a house or a car. Furthermore, some student loans are subsidized by the federal government, which means you don't have to pay the interest that comes due while you're in college.

Subsidized loans, which are awarded based on need and administered by the college, are the best kind. But you can also take out unsubsidized student loans and parent loans, which are not packaged by most colleges. However, be careful not to take on more debt than necessary. No matter what kind of loan you take out, you will have to pay it back.

GOOD TO KNOW

You'll find a more thorough explanation of student financial aid in the College Board book *Getting Financial Aid 2018,* or in the "Pay for College" articles on collegeboard.org.

Another form of self-help is work-study. This is financial aid in the form of a job. Since you earn the money through your work, this too may not seem like aid. But it is, because the federal work-study program pays most of your wages. And work-study jobs are usually available right on campus, with limits on your hours so that you won't be unduly distracted from studying.

Who Gets Aid?

Grants and loans are not just for the poorest of the poor, nor are scholarships only for the smartest of the smart. The truth about who gets financial aid is somewhat different from what many people think.

Those Who Need It

Most financial aid is based on need, not merit. There is money for merit, but most colleges in the United States focus their financial aid packages on meeting financial need.

However, there is a lot of confusion about what "need" means. "A lot of people think that they either have to be on welfare or Social Security — really poor — to get financial aid, and that's not correct," says Mary San Agustin, director of financial aid and scholarships at Palomar College in San Marcos, Calif. On the other hand, some wealthy families mistakenly think they are needy because their high living expenses leave them little money for college. "It's this expectation of, I pay my taxes, so my kid should be entitled to some federal financial aid regardless of how much money I make," says San Agustin.

Need simply means that your family can't afford to pay the full cost of a particular college. The *amount* of your need will vary from college to college, because it depends on the cost of attending an individual college. Whether your family has need is determined not by whether you think you are rich or poor, but by the financial aid forms you fill out.

Those Who Don't

Despite the overall emphasis on need, many colleges do give away money on the basis of merit. They do this to attract the students they want most, and they may award this money even if it is more than the student needs. However, in many cases, the student both needs the money and has earned it on the basis of merit.

Don't think that only geniuses get merit aid. At many colleges a B average can put you in the running for merit money. Sometimes a separate application for merit aid is required to put you into consideration; sometimes your application for admission is enough. In either case, don't count yourself out by not applying; apply and let the college decide.

Grants are sometimes awarded based on neither need nor merit. For example, you may get a grant if you are in a certain field of study, are a resident of the state, or are a student from the same town as the college.

Part-Time Students

Some kinds of aid are only available to students enrolled in college full time — usually 12 or more credit hours of courses per semester. But part-time students are eligible for some financial aid. For example, federal loan programs require only that students be enrolled at least half time. Also, some employers offer tuition reimbursement benefits to students who work full time and go to college part time.

Where the Money Comes From

Financial aid comes from three basic sources: governments (both federal and state), colleges and outside benefactors.

From the Government

The lion's share of total financial aid awarded to undergraduates comes from the federal government. Almost three-quarters of all such aid is sent from Washington. For undergraduates, the largest chunk of that aid consists of federal loans, which represented 32 percent of all student aid distributed in 2015-2016. The loans take multiple shapes. Perkins loans are subsidized, with the lowest interest rate of any education loan. Stafford loans may be subsidized or unsubsidized. Both Perkins and Stafford loans are for students, but parents may take out a PLUS loan, which is not subsidized, to help pay for their children's education.

The federal government also offers grants, such as the Pell Grant and the Supplemental Educational Opportunity Grant (SEOG). These grants are strictly need based, with no academic criteria. The government also funds the federal work-study program, which provides part-time employment (usually on-campus) and is also strictly need-based.

A much smaller piece of the financial aid pie (6 percent) comes from individual state governments. This is available in the form of grants, scholarships and loans. Most of this aid is for use only at colleges within the state, though a few states offer "portable" aid, which state residents can take with them to a college in another state.

From the College

A great deal of financial aid comes from individual colleges, using their own "institutional" funds. In fact, colleges award nearly half of all grants. Many, though not all, award merit scholarships as well as need-based grants. They may also offer on-campus job opportunities and loans.

Private colleges give more financial aid than public ones, but their tuition is usually higher as well. Public colleges award less aid, but taxpayer support keeps their tuition lower.

Outside Grants and Scholarships

Outside grants and scholarships (what you will find in this book) come from sources other than the college. These sources may include corporations like Coca-Cola or community groups like the Elks Club. Some are well known, such as National Merit Scholarship Corporation, but altogether they are the smallest piece of the financial aid pie: Only 6 percent of all student aid comes from outside sources. Pursue them, but don't expect them to outweigh the other aid you will get.

Bear in mind also that an outside scholarship is unlikely to expand the total aid you receive. If a college has already "met your full need" — that is, offered an aid package that covers the entire difference between what the college costs and what your family is expected to pay — it will not add an outside scholarship to that aid package. Rather, it will use your scholarship to substitute for some other piece of aid in the package. Think of your financial aid package as a barrel: When the barrel is full, no more can be added unless something is taken away. The last thing colleges will take away is whatever sum of money your family is expected to contribute.

How Outside Awards Can Help

Even though outside scholarships rarely decrease the amount that your family is expected to pay out of pocket, it's still very worthwhile to pursue them. Why? Simply put, they expand your options for where you can go to college.

At some colleges, the first things taken away from a full-need package to make room for an outside scholarship are loans. Since that reduces the total amount you will have to pay back later, it makes that college more affordable. (Colleges vary in their policies on how they adjust packages for outside scholarships; you should call or e-mail the financial aid offices at the colleges you're considering to learn about their policies.)

There are also colleges that can't afford to offer every admitted student a financial aid package that meets the student's full need. If, for example, your need is $25,000 at a particular university, and the university's aid office can only offer you a combined total of $23,000 in grants, scholarships, work-study and subsidized federal loans, then there is a $2,000 "gap" in your aid package. Outside scholarships can help fill that gap.

Finally, there may be colleges where you don't have any financial need. For example, if your family's expected contribution to your college costs is $10,000, a state university that costs $10,000 a year to attend couldn't offer you any need-based aid. An outside merit scholarship, in this case, could decrease what your family pays below their expected contribution.

FINANCIAL AID APPLICATION CALENDAR

SOPHOMORE/JUNIOR YEARS

- Talk to your parents about college costs. Have realistic expectations, but understand how financial aid can expand your options.
- Take the PSAT/NMSQT® in October of each year. If you take it as a junior and meet other requirements, you will be entered into National Merit Scholarship Corporation competitions.
- Think about colleges you might want to apply to. If possible, visit some campuses in the spring of your junior year.

- Take the SAT® in the spring of your junior year.
- If you have a job, do your taxes each year (ask your parents for help). Knowing about tax forms and documents will be helpful when you have to fill out financial aid applications.
- Begin searching for scholarships during summer vacation after junior year.

SENIOR YEAR

SEPTEMBER

- Create a list of colleges you want to apply to. **Start a checklist** of their financial aid requirements and deadlines.
- Find out if there will be a **family financial aid night** at your school or elsewhere in your area this fall, and put it on your calendar.
- Start applying for outside scholarship programs. Ask your school counselor about local scholarships offered by groups and businesses in your community.
- **Go to FAFSA on the Web** to create an **FSA ID**. You'll need that to access the FAFSA, which you can submit any time after Oct. 1.

OCTOBER

- **Start working on your FAFSA** and submit it as soon as you can, especially if you are applying to a college under an Early Decision plan.
- If you need to fill out the CSS Profile™, you can do so on the CSS Profile Online Web site starting Oct. 1.

NOVEMBER

- Finalize the list of colleges that you'll apply to regular decision. Make sure you know all the deadlines and priority dates for their financial aid applications.

DECEMBER

- Contact the financial aid office at the colleges on your list to get any **other financial aid forms** they might require.
- Apply for scholarships in time to meet application deadlines.

JANUARY

- **Submit your FAFSA** as soon as you can if you haven't already. Check your college's deadlines and priority dates; some can be as early as Feb. 1.
- Submit any other financial aid forms that may be required. Keep copies.

FEBRUARY

- Correct or update your Student Aid Report (SAR) that follows the FAFSA, if necessary.
- If any special circumstances affect your family's financial situation, alert each college's financial aid office.
- You and your parents should consider filing your income tax returns early this year. Some colleges might want to verify the information on your family's returns before finalizing offers.

MARCH

- As you begin to receive letters of acceptance, check with aid offices to see if additional documentation (such as tax forms) must be submitted.

APRIL

- Compare your financial aid award letters using the online tools at **www.collegeboard.org**.
- Write, e-mail or call the colleges that have offered you aid if you have any questions about the packages they've offered you.
- If you don't get enough aid to be able to attend a college, consider your options, which include appealing the award.

MAY

- Be sure to **accept the aid package** from the college you want to attend by May 1.
- Be sure also to let other schools know you won't be attending.
- Plan now how you will cover your family's out-of-pocket expenses.
- Apply for loans if necessary.

Finding and Applying for Scholarships

While you're researching and applying for colleges, you should also use this book to find scholarships that you qualify for and apply for them. In this chapter you'll find advice, as well as a calendar and worksheets to help keep you on track.

When to Start Looking

It's never too early to start looking for scholarships. There are programs where you begin the work of applying up to a year before the final determination is made. For example, National Merit Scholarship Corporation competitions begin when students take the PSAT/NMSQT® in October of their junior year, and the competitions proceed in several rounds until fall of their senior year. If you're already a senior, though, don't despair — there are plenty of programs for entering freshmen that you can apply for during your senior year.

The best time of the year to research programs is in the summer or early fall. That way you can be sure to find programs before their deadlines have passed, and with enough advance time to prepare a complete, competitive application. Remember that many scholarship programs require you to submit an essay as part of your application, and essays take time to write. Many programs also require recommendations; as a general rule, you should ask for recommendations at least four weeks in advance, and preferably more. Some programs even require you to perform additional academic work outside of school, such as writing a research paper or competing in a science fair.

You should let your school counselor know as early as possible that you're interested in applying for scholarships. He or she can help you think about your strengths as a student, which will make it easier to narrow down your scholarship search. Your counselor will also be able to recommend some programs you should apply for. (See "Thinking Locally" on page 14.)

PLANNING AHEAD

If you haven't already started looking for scholarships, start now. Today. Use this book to find a program you qualify for, and make a note of its application deadline and requirements. Then go to the program's website and download an application.

Playing Catch-Up

If it's already the middle of your senior year, you've probably missed some opportunities to apply for scholarships with October, November and December deadlines. But don't give up yet; there are plenty of scholarships with January, February and March deadlines.

The key to playing catch-up is to start working now, today. Find scholarships where the deadline hasn't passed. Get applications from the sponsors' websites. Talk to your school counselor immediately. The longer you wait, the less likely you are to win any awards.

The good news: Since you're already far into the college application process, you're now a pro at describing yourself to admission committees and scholarship review boards. You also have personal essays, academic writing samples and teacher recommendations ready to go.

Choosing Where to Apply

There are so many scholarships, grants, fellowships, internships, fee waivers, work-study jobs and low-interest loans available for college-level study that just looking at the options can be daunting. (This book alone describes over 2,400 national and state-level programs.) Fortunately, there are some easy ways to narrow the field of potential programs down to the ones where you have a good chance of winning an award.

The personal characteristics checklist on the next page highlights some of the common eligibility criteria for scholarship programs. You're not likely to find a scholarship that's targeted to every one of your characteristics, but you can use your answers on the checklist as a starting point for finding programs. The eligibility indexes starting on page 27 will help you quickly match your characteristics to programs.

You'll probably find a few scholarship programs that match your characteristics. If you find a lot, you should consider narrowing your search — applying for scholarships is a lot of work! It's far better to send in four high-quality applications to programs that closely match your characteristics and interests than to send 16 hurried applications to a wide variety of programs.

PERSONAL CHARACTERISTICS
CHECKLIST

Are you **male** or **female**?

What is your **state of residence**?

Do you have a **learning or physical disability**? Many scholarships are offered to those who are disabled in any way, but some are for those with a specific disability.

Military service is the basis of many scholarships. Many of these awards are not just for those who have worn a uniform, but also for their spouses and children, or even descendants of a veteran. Talk to your family about its military history (was Grandpa in the Vietnam War?) Be sure to find out what branch of the military your family members served in, and, if possible, which unit(s) they served in.

List any family history of military service here:

You'll find scholarships for students with **minority status**, (e.g., African American, Alaska Native), and also for students with a particular **nationality or ethnic background** (e.g., Chinese, Greek).

If you belong to a minority, list it here:

List your ethnic and/or national origin(s) here:

What, if any, is your **religious affiliation**?

Are you an **international student** (a citizen of a foreign country, including Canada, seeking to study in the United States)?

The largest category of scholarships and internships is for students planning to study a particular college major (e.g., math, English, a foreign language) or prepare for a particular career (e.g., law, education, aviation). Even if you are "undecided" at this point, you should list all the **majors/careers** you are leaning toward.

☐ Do you want to **study abroad**? There are scholarships to help you pay for it — check here to remind yourself to seek them out.

"Returning adult" refers to students who have been out of high school a year or more before entering college. If that's you, look for scholarships designed to encourage your pursuit.

Years out of high school:

Your age:

Do you or any members of your family belong to a **national or local organization** or **civic association** (e.g., Kiwanis, Rotary, Elks Club)? Many such groups offer scholarships to members and/or their families. List here any that apply:

Employers and corporations often offer scholarship benefits to employees and/or their families. List the companies that you or someone in your family works for here:

Narrowing Your Search

If you're having trouble narrowing down your scholarship search, consider the following:

How many applicants are there each year? Some of the better-known programs (such as the Coca-Cola Scholars Program) see hundreds of applicants for every award they give out! It can't hurt to apply for these programs, but you shouldn't invest so much effort in applying for them that you miss out on smaller programs where your chances may be better.

Is this really for me? If you couldn't get through *Atlas Shrugged* the first time, don't force yourself to read it and write an essay on its philosophical meaning for the Ayn Rand Institute contest — even if you're a great English student. Focus instead on programs that appeal to you or sound like fun.

Can I live with the strings attached? Many scholarship and internship programs have service requirements. Most notably, the Reserve Officers Training Corps (ROTC) program requires cadets to become military reserve officers upon graduation. And some summer internships will require you to move to another city.

KEEP IN MIND

Don't let your scholarship search overshadow your other responsibilities and application requirements. You still need to do well in school, get your college applications in on time, and submit the FAFSA and other financial aid forms by your colleges' priority dates.

Thinking Locally

This book contains national and statewide financial aid programs offered by government agencies, charitable foundations and major corporations. But there are also thousands of small scholarship programs offered on a local level by civic clubs, parishes, memorial foundations and small businesses.

In many cases, these programs award just a few hundred dollars — enough to buy a semester's worth of textbooks. But since they are offered on a local level, your chances of receiving an award are much higher than they are for the big national competitions. So it pays to look for local scholarships.

Your school counselor may have files of local scholarship programs. There may even be a scholarship designated for graduates of your high school — you'll never know until you ask. You should also check with employers (either your parents' or your own); your church, temple or mosque; and any civic clubs that your family members are involved in.

Avoiding Scholarship Scams

The Federal Trade Commission (FTC) developed Project $cholar$cam to alert students and families about potential scams and how to recognize them. Here are the FTC's seven basic warning signs:

- "This scholarship is guaranteed or your money back."
- "You can't get this information anywhere else."
- "May I have your credit card/bank account number to hold this scholarship?"
- "We'll do all the work for you."

GOOD TO KNOW

For more information about scholarship scams, visit the FTC's website at **www.ftc.gov**.

- "The scholarship will cost some money."
- "You've been selected by a national foundation to receive a scholarship."
- "You're a finalist" in a competition you never entered.

Remember that no one can guarantee that you'll receive a grant or scholarship, and that you will have to do the work of submitting applications to be considered. Don't pay money for a service without a written document saying what you'll get for your money and what the company's refund policies are. And never, ever give your credit card number, Social Security number or bank account information to someone who called you unsolicited.

Applying for Scholarships

This may mean not only filling out a form but also compiling supporting documents, such as transcripts, recommendations and an essay. Or you might need to provide evidence of leadership, patriotism, depth of character, desire to serve, or financial need. Get to know the requirements of each scholarship as early as possible so you can do any necessary extra work on time.

A few pointers to remember:

Apply early! Apply as early as possible to scholarship programs. If you can, do it in the fall of your senior year, even if the deadlines aren't until February or March. Very often, scholarship programs will have awarded all their funds for the year on a first-come, first-served basis before their stated deadline.

Follow directions. Read instructions carefully and do what they say. Scholarship programs receive hundreds and even thousands of applications. Don't lose out because of failure to submit a typewritten essay versus a handwritten one if required, or to provide appropriate recommendations. If you have a question about your eligibility for a particular scholarship or how to complete the application, contact the scholarship sponsors.

Be organized. It's a good idea to create a separate file for each scholarship and sort them by their due dates. Track application deadlines and requirements. Store in one place the different supporting documents you may need, such as transcripts, standardized test scores and letters of recommendation.

Check your work. Proofread your applications for spelling or grammar errors, fill in all blanks and make sure your handwriting is legible.

Keep copies of everything. If application materials get lost, having copies on file will make it easier to resend the application quickly.

Reapply. Some programs only offer money for the first year of college, but others must be renewed each subsequent year.

SCHOLARSHIP APPLICATION PLANNER

	PROGRAM 1	PROGRAM 2	PROGRAM 3
PROGRAM/SPONSOR	WyzAnt Scholarship	Young Naturalist Awards	Town Bank
ELIGIBILITY REQUIREMENTS	Essay contest	Academic merit	Need, local residency
TYPE OF AWARD	Scholarship	Scholarship	Internship
AMOUNT OF AWARD	$10,000, $3,000, $2,000	$50 to $2,500	$2,500
CAN BE USED FOR	Any expense	Any expense	Any expense
CAN BE USED AT	Any 4-yr college	Any college	In-state colleges
DEADLINE	May 1	Mar. 1	April 1
FORMS REQUIRED	Online application	Web form	Application (includes need analysis)
TEST SCORES REQUIRED	None	None	SAT
ESSAY OR ACADEMIC SAMPLE	300-word essay	Essay, research project	None required
RECOMMENDATIONS	None	None	One teacher (Mr. Filmer), Local branch manager
NOTIFICATION BEGINS	May 15	Not sure	May 15
REQUIREMENTS TO KEEP AFTER FRESHMAN YEAR	One-time payment only	One-time payment only	Based on performance during internship

For a blank version of this worksheet that you can photocopy for your own use, see the next page.

SCHOLARSHIP APPLICATION PLANNER

	PROGRAM 1	PROGRAM 2	PROGRAM 3
PROGRAM/SPONSOR			
ELIGIBILITY REQUIREMENTS			
TYPE OF AWARD			
AMOUNT OF AWARD			
CAN BE USED FOR			
CAN BE USED AT			
DEADLINE			
FORMS REQUIRED			
TEST SCORES REQUIRED			
ESSAY OR ACADEMIC SAMPLE			
RECOMMENDATIONS			
NOTIFICATION BEGINS			
REQUIREMENTS TO KEEP AFTER FRESHMAN YEAR			

Sources of Information About State Grant Programs

Alabama

Alabama Commission on
  Higher Education
P.O. Box 302000
Montgomery, AL 36130-2000
334-242-1998
www.ache.state.al.us

Alaska

Alaska Commission on
  Postsecondary Education
P.O. Box 110505
Juneau, AK 99811
800-441-2962
www.acpe.alaska.gov

Arizona

Arizona Department of Education
1535 West Jefferson Street
Phoenix, AZ 85007
800-352-4558
www.azed.gov

Arkansas

Arkansas Department of Higher
  Education
423 Main Street, Suite 400
Little Rock, AR 72201
501-371-2000
www.adhe.edu

California

California Student Aid Commission
P.O. Box 419026
Rancho Cordova, CA 95741-9026
888-224-7268
www.csac.ca.gov

Colorado

Colorado Department of Education
201 East Colfax Avenue
Denver, CO 80203
303-866-6600
www.cde.state.co.us

Connecticut

Connecticut Office of Higher
  Education
450 Columbus Boulevard
Hartford, CT 06103-1841
860-947-1800
www.ctohe.org

Delaware

Delaware Higher Education Office
The Townsend Bldg.
401 Federal St., Suite 2
Dover, DE 19901-3639
302-735-4000
www.doe.k12.de.us

District of Columbia

Office of the State Superintendent
  of Education
810 First Street, NE, 9th Floor
Washington, DC 20002
202-727-6436
www.seo.dc.gov

Florida

Florida Department of Education
Office of Student Financial
  Assistance
325 W. Gaines Street, Suite 1514
Tallahassee, FL 32399
888-827-2004
www.floridastudentfinancialaid.org

Georgia

Georgia Student Finance Commission
2082 East Exchange Place
Tucker, GA 30084
800-505-4732
www.gsfc.org

Hawaii

Hawaii State Department
  of Education
1390 Miller Street
Honolulu, HI 96813
808-586-3230
www.hawaiipublicschools.org

Idaho

Idaho State Department of Education
650 West State Street
P.O. Box 83720
Boise, ID 83720-0027
800-432-4601
www.sde.idaho.gov

Illinois

Illinois Student Assistance
  Commission
1755 Lake Cook Road
Deerfield, IL 60015-5209
800-899-4722
www.isac.org

Indiana

State Student Assistance
  Commission of Indiana
101 West Ohio Street, Suite 300
Indianapolis, IN 46204
888-528-4719
www.in.gov/ssaci

Iowa

Iowa College Student
  Aid Commission
430 East Grand Avenue, FL 3
Des Moines, IA 50309
877-272-4456
www.iowacollegeaid.gov

Kansas

Kansas Board of Regents
1000 SW Jackson Street, Suite 520
Topeka, KS 66612-1368
785-430-4240
www.kansasregents.org

Kentucky

KHEAA Student Aid Branch
100 Airport Road
Frankfort, KY 40602-0798
800-928-8926
www.kheaa.com

Louisiana

Louisiana Office of Student
    Financial Assistance
P.O. Box 91202
Baton Rouge, LA 70801-9202
800-259-5626
www.osfa.la.gov

Maine

Finance Authority of Maine
Education Assistance Division
5 Community Drive
Augusta, ME 04332-0949
800-228-3734
www.famemaine.com

Maryland

Maryland Higher Education
    Commission
Office of Student Financial
    Assistance
6 N. Liberty St.
Baltimore, MD 21201
800-974-0203
www.mhec.state.md.us

Massachusetts

Massachusetts Department of
    Higher Education
Office of Student Financial
    Assistance
One Ashburton Place
Boston, MA 02108
617-391-6070
www.osfa.mass.edu

Michigan

Michigan Higher Education
    Assistance Authority
Office of Scholarships and Grants
P.O. Box 30462
Lansing, MI 48909-7962
888-447-2687
www.michigan.gov/mistudentaid

Minnesota

Minnesota Office of Higher Education
1450 Energy Park Drive, Suite 350
St. Paul, MN 55108-5227
800-657-3866
www.ohe.state.mn.us

Mississippi

Mississippi Office of Student
    Financial Aid
3825 Ridgewood Road
Jackson, MS 39211-6453
800-327-2980
www.mississippi.edu/riseupms

Missouri

Missouri Department of
    Higher Education
205 Jefferson Street
P.O. Box 1469
Jefferson City, MO 65102-1469
800-473-6757
www.dhe.mo.gov

Montana

Montana Board of Regents
P.O. Box 203201
2500 Broadway Street
Helena, MT 59620-3201
406-444-6570
http://mus.edu/board

Nebraska

Coordinating Commission for
    Postsecondary Education
P.O. Box 95005
Lincoln, NE 68509-5005
402-471-2847
www.ccpe.nebraska.gov

Nevada

Nevada Department of Education
700 East Fifth Street
Carson City, NV 89701
775-687-9200
www.doe.nv.gov

New Hampshire

New Hampshire Postsecondary
    Education Commission
101 Pleasant Street
Concord, NH 03301-3860
603-271-3494
www.education.nh.gov/highered

New Jersey

HESAA Grants & Scholarships
P.O. Box 540
Trenton, NJ 08625-0540
800-792-8670
www.hesaa.org

New Mexico

New Mexico Higher Education
    Department
2044 Galisteo Street
Santa Fe, NM 87505
505-476-8400
www.hed.state.nm.us

New York

New York State Higher Education
    Services Corporation
99 Washington Avenue
Albany, NY 12255
888-697-4372
www.hesc.ny.gov

North Carolina

North Carolina State Education
    Assistance Authority
P.O. Box 14103
Research Triangle Park, NC 27709
919-549-8614
www.ncseaa.edu

North Dakota

North Dakota University System
10th Floor, State Capitol
600 East Boulevard Ave, Dept. 215
Bismarck, ND 58505-0230
701-328-2960
www.ndus.edu

Ohio

Ohio Board of Regents
25 South Front Street
Columbus, OH 43215
614-466-6000
www.ohiohighered.org

Oklahoma

Oklahoma State Regents for
    Higher Education
Tuition Aid Grant Program
655 Research Parkway, Suite 200
Oklahoma City, OK 73104
405-225-9100
www.okhighered.org

Oregon

Oregon Student Assistance
    Commission
1500 Valley River Drive, Suite 100
Eugene, OR 97401
800-452-8807
www.oregonstudentaid.gov

Pennsylvania

Pennsylvania Higher Education
   Assistance Agency
P.O. Box 8157
Harrisburg, PA 17105-8157
800-692-7392
www.pheaa.org

Puerto Rico

Departmento de Educacion
P.O. Box 190759
San Juan, PR 00919-0759
787-759-2000
www.de.gobierno.pr

Rhode Island

Rhode Island Higher Education
   Assistance Authority
560 Jefferson Boulevard, Suite 100
Warwick, RI 02886-1304
800-922-9855
www.riheaa.org

South Carolina

South Carolina Commission on
   Higher Education
1122 Lady Street, Suite 300
Columbia, SC 29201
803-737-2260
www.che.sc.gov

South Dakota

South Dakota Department
   of Education
Office of Finance and Management
800 Governors Drive
Pierre, SD 57501
605-773-3134
www.doe.sd.gov

Tennessee

Tennessee Student Assistance
   Corporation
404 James Robertson Parkway,
Suite 1510, Parkway Towers
Nashville, TN 37243-0820
800-342-1663
www.tn.gov.collegepays

Texas

Texas Higher Education
   Coordinating Board
   Student Loan Program
P.O. Box 12788
Austin, TX 78711-2788
800-242-3062
www.hhloans.com

Utah

Utah Higher Education
   Assistance Authority
P.O. Box 145110
Salt Lake City, UT 84114-5110
877-336-7378
www.uheaa.org

Vermont

Vermont Student Assistance
   Corporation
P.O. Box 2000
Winooski, VT 05404
800-642-3177
www.vsac.org

Virginia

State Council of Higher Education
   for Virginia
101 North 14th Street, 10th Fl.
James Monroe Building
Richmond, VA 23219
804-225-2600
www.schev.edu

Washington

Washington Student Achievement
   Council
917 Lakeridge Way SW
Olympia, WA 98502
(360) 753-7800
www.wsac.wa.gov

West Virginia

West Virginia Higher Education Policy
   Commission
1018 Kanawha Boulevard East,
   Suite 700
Charleston, WV 25301
304-558-2101
www.wvhepc.com

Wisconsin

Wisconsin Higher Educational
   Aids Board
P. O. Box 7885
Madison, WI 53707-7885
608-267-2206
www.heab.state.wi.us

Wyoming

Wyoming Department of Education
2300 Capitol Avenue
Hathaway Building, Second Floor
Cheyenne, WY 82002-2060
307-777-7675
www.edu.wyoming.gov

Guam

University of Guam
Student Financial Aid Office
UOG Station
Mangilao, GU 96923
671-735-2288
www.uog.edu

Virgin Islands

Financial Aid Office, Virgin Islands
   Board of Education
60B, 61, & 62 Dronningens Gade
P.O. Box 11900
St. Thomas, VI 00801
340-774-4546
www.myviboe.com

Glossary

ACT. A college admission test given at test centers on specified dates. Please visit the organization's website for further information.

AP (Advanced Placement Program). An academic program of the College Board that provides high school students with the opportunity to study and learn at the college level. AP offers courses in 38 subjects, each culminating in an AP Exam. High schools offer the courses and administer the exams to interested students. Most colleges and universities accept qualifying AP Exam scores for credit, advanced placement, or both.

Associate degree. A degree granted by a college or university upon completion of a two-year, fulltime program of study or its part-time equivalent.

Bachelor's, or baccalaureate, degree. A degree received after the satisfactory completion of a four- or five-year, full-time program of study (or its part-time equivalent) at a college or university. The bachelor of arts (B.A.), bachelor of science (B.S.), and bachelor of fine arts (B.F.A.) are the most common bachelor's degrees.

CB code. A four-digit College Board code number that students use to designate colleges or scholarship programs to receive their SAT score reports.

Community/junior college. A two-year college. Community colleges are public, whereas junior colleges are private. Both usually offer vocational programs as well as the first two years of a four-year program.

Competition. An award based upon superior performance in relation to others in the competition. This book lists competitions based upon artistic talent, writing ability and other demonstrable talents.

Cooperative education (co-op). A career-oriented program in which students alternate between class attendance and employment in business, industry or government. Co-op students usually receive both academic credit and payment for their work. Five years are normally required for completion of a bachelor's degree, but that includes about a year's practical work experience.

Credit Hour. The standard unit of measurement for a college course. Each credit hour requires one classroom hour per week.

CSS code. A four-digit College Board number that students use to designate colleges or scholarship programs to receive their CSS Profile information. A complete list of all CSS codes can be viewed at the CSS Profile section on collegeboard.org.

CSS/Financial Aid PROFILE (CSS Profile). A Web-based application service offered by the College Board and used by some colleges, universities and private scholarship programs to award their private financial aid funds. Students complete the application online at collegeboard.org. The CSS Profile is not a federal form and may not be used to apply for federal student aid.

Curriculum Vitae (CV). A type of résumé, from the Latin for "the course of one's life." Typically, a CV is used by applicants for fellowships or grants, or jobs in higher education, the sciences, or in a research capacity. The CV is typically longer than a résumé, and provides details about papers published, research conducted and more.

Dependents. Generally speaking, people who are dependent upon others (parents, relatives, a spouse) for food, clothing, shelter, and other basics. For purposes of getting federal financial aid, such students are either under the age of 24, attend an undergraduate program, are not married, do not have children of their own, are not orphans or wards of the court, or veterans of the active-duty armed services.

EFC (Expected Family Contribution). The total amount students and their families are expected to pay toward college costs out-of-pocket for one academic year.

FAFSA (Free Application for Federal Student Aid). A form completed by all applicants for federal student aid. In many states, completion of the FAFSA is also sufficient to establish eligibility for state-sponsored aid programs. There is no charge for completing the FAFSA, and you can file it any time after October 1 of the year before the academic year for which you are seeking aid (e.g., after October 1, 2017, for the academic year 2018–19)

Federal code number. A six-digit number that identifies a specific college to which students want their FAFSA submitted. Also known as the Title IV number.

Federal Direct Loan Program. A program whereby participating schools administer federal loans that students and parents borrow directly from the U.S. Department of Education. Direct loans include the subsidized and unsubsidized Federal Stafford Loan, PLUS Loan, and Loan Consolidation programs.

Federal student aid. A number of programs sponsored by the federal government that award students loans, grants or work-study jobs for the purpose of meeting their financial need.

Federal Work-Study Program. A campus-based financial aid program that allows students to meet some of their financial need by working on or off campus while attending school.

Financial aid. Money awarded to students to help them pay for college. Financial aid comes in the form of scholarships, grants, loans, and work-study opportunities.

Financial aid package. The total financial aid offered to a student by a college, including all loans, grants, scholarships and work-study opportunities.

Financial need. The difference between the total cost of attending a college and a student's expected family contribution (EFC).

Free Application for Federal Student Aid. See *FAFSA*.

Full-time status. Enrollment at a college or university for 12 or more credit hours per semester. Students must be enrolled full time to qualify for the maximum award available to them from federal grant programs.

GED (General Educational Development). A series of tests that individuals who did not complete high school may take through their state education system to qualify for a high school equivalency certificate.

Gift. Financial aid in the form of scholarships or grants that do not have to be repaid.

Grade Point Average (GPA). A system used by many schools for evaluating the overall scholastic performance of students. Grade points are determined by first multiplying the number of hours given for a course by the numerical value of the grade and then dividing the sum of all grade points by the total number of hours carried. The most common system of numerical values for grades is A = 4, B = 3, C = 2, D = 1, and E or F = 0.

Graduate study. A program leading to an advanced degree (master's, doctoral, or professional) following a bachelor's degree.

Grant. A financial aid award that is given to a student and does not have to be paid back. The terms "grant" and "scholarship" are often used interchangeably, but often grants are awarded solely on the basis of financial need, while scholarships may require the student to demonstrate merit.

Half-time status. Enrollment at a college or university for at least six credit hours per semester, but less than the 12 credit hours required to qualify as full time. Students must be enrolled at least half time to qualify for federal student aid loan programs.

High school transcript. A formal document that shows all classes taken and grades earned in high school.

Independent student. Generally includes students who are either 24 years old, married, a veteran or an orphan, a ward of the court, certified as homeless or have legal dependents (not including spouse).

Internship. Any short-term, supervised work, usually related to a student's major, for which academic credit is earned. The work can be full or part time, on or off campus, paid or unpaid.

Loan. Money lent with interest for a specified period of time. This book includes several loan programs; some forgive the loan in exchange for public service, such as teaching in a rural area.

Major. The subject area in which students concentrate, or specialize, during their undergraduate study. At most colleges, students take a third to a half of their courses in their chosen major; the rest of their course work is devoted to core requirements and electives.

Merit aid. Financial aid awarded on the basis of academic qualifications, artistic or athletic talent, leadership or similar traits. Financial need may or may not be an additional requirement.

Need-based aid. Financial aid given to students who have demonstrated financial need, calculated by subtracting the student's expected family contribution from a college's total cost of attendance.

Nomination. Being named as a candidate for an award or scholarship. Some scholarship programs require that a teacher or principal nominate students as applicants, and do not invite applications from students.

Non-need-based aid. Financial aid awarded without regard to the student's demonstrated ability to pay for college.

Outside resources. Student financial aid granted by a source other than the college. Examples include scholarships from private foundations, employer tuition assistance and veterans' educational benefits.

Part-time status. Enrollment at a college or university for 11 or fewer credit hours per semester.

Pell Grant. A federally funded and administered need-based grant to undergraduate students. Congress annually sets the dollar range; for 2017-18 the maximum award is $5,920. Eligibility for Pell Grants is based on a student's expected family contribution, the total cost of attendance at the college, and whether the student is attending the college full time or part time.

Perkins Loan. A federally funded, need-based, low-interest student loan. Repayment does not begin until after graduation, and payments may be deferred for periods of service in the military, Peace Corps or other approved organizations. The loan may be totally forgiven if the student enters a career of service as a public health nurse, law enforcement officer, public school teacher or social worker.

Permanent resident. A non-U.S. citizen who has been given permission to make his or her permanent home in the United States.

PLUS (Federal Parents' Loan for Undergraduate Students). A federal direct loan program that permits parents of undergraduate students to borrow up to the full cost of education, less any other financial aid the student may have received.

Portfolio. A collection of a student's work that demonstrates skills and accomplishments. Portfolios may be physical or digital. Academic portfolios can include student-written papers and projects, and art portfolios can include created objects, such as paintings, photography, fashion illustrations and more. Some scholarship programs request a portfolio.

Priority date. The date by which an application must be received to be given the strongest possible consideration. After that date, applicants are considered on a first-come, first-served basis.

PROFILE. See *CSS Profile.*

PSAT/NMSQT® (Preliminary SAT/National Merit Scholarship Qualifying Test). A comprehensive program that helps schools put students on the path to college. The PSAT/NMSQT is administered by high schools to sophomores and juniors each year in October and serves as the qualifying test for scholarships awarded by the National Merit Scholarship Corporation.

Renewable. A scholarship or loan that can be renewed after the first award. Typically students have to apply annually in order to receive the funds after the first year.

Residency requirements. The minimum amount of time a student is required to have lived in a particular state or community in order to be eligible for scholarship, internship or loan programs offered to such residents.

ROTC (Reserve Officers' Training Corps). Programs conducted by certain colleges that prepare students to become military officers while they attend college. There are both scholarship and nonscholarship programs available for each branch: Army, Navy, Air Force, and Marines (the Coast Guard and Merchant Marine do not sponsor ROTC programs). While in college, students take some military courses each year for credit and attend training sessions. After college they must complete a period of service in the military.

Room and board. The cost of housing and meals for students who reside on campus and/or dine in college-operated meal halls.

SAT. A college admission exam that tests reading, writing, language, and mathematics skills. It is given on specified dates throughout the year at test centers in the United States and other countries. The SAT is used by most colleges and sponsors of financial aid programs.

SAT Subject Tests. Admission tests in specific subjects that are given at test centers in the United States and other countries on specified dates throughout the year. The tests are used by colleges for help in both evaluating applicants for admission and determining course placement and exemption of enrolled first-year students.

Scholarship. A type of financial aid that doesn't have to be repaid. Scholarships may be based on need, on need combined with merit, or solely on the basis of merit or some other qualification, such as minority status. See also *Grant*.

Section 529 plans. State-sponsored college savings programs commonly referred to as "529 plans" after the section of the Internal Revenue Code that provides the plan's tax breaks. There are two kinds: college savings plans; and prepaid tuition plans, in which parents can pay in advance for tuition at public institutions in their state of residence.

Self-help aid. Student financial aid, such as loans and jobs, that requires repayment or employment.

SEOG (Federal Supplemental Educational Opportunity Grant Program). A federal program that provides need-based grants of up to $4,000 a year for undergraduate study. Each college is given a certain total amount of SEOG money each year to distribute among their financial aid applicants and determines the amount to which the student is entitled.

Stafford Loan. A federal direct loan program that allows students to borrow money for educational expenses. *Subsidized* Stafford loans are based on need; the federal government pays the interest while the student is in college, and repayment does not begin until after graduation. *Unsubsidized* Stafford loans are not based on need; anyone may apply for one regardless of their ability to pay for college. For both programs, the amounts that may be borrowed depend on the student's year in school.

Student expense budget. A calculation of the annual cost of attending college that is used to determine your financial need. Student expense budgets usually include tuition and fees, books and supplies, room and board, personal expenses and transportation. Sometimes additional expenses are included for students with special education needs, students who have a disability, or students who are married or have children.

Student's contribution. The amount you are expected to pay toward college costs from your own income and assets, as opposed to your parents'.

Subsidized loan. A need-based student loan for which the federal or state government pays the interest on the loan while the student is in college. See also *Unsubsidized loan*.

Supplemental Educational Opportunity Grant. See *SEOG*.

Taxable income. Income earned from wages, salaries and tips, as well as from interest income, dividends, alimony, estate or trust income, business or farm profits, and rental or property income. Some scholarship awards must be reported as taxable income.

Title IV code. See *Federal code number*.

Transcript. A copy of a student's official academic record listing all courses taken and grades received.

Tuition. The price of instruction at a college. Tuition may be charged per term or per credit hour.

Undergraduate. A college student in the freshman, sophomore, junior or senior year of study, as opposed to a graduate student who has earned an undergraduate degree and is pursuing a master's, doctoral or professional degree.

Unmet need. The difference between a student's total available resources and the total cost of attendance at a specific institution.

Unsubsidized loan. An education loan that is not based on need, and therefore not subsidized by the government; the borrower is responsible for accrued interest throughout the life of the loan. See also *Subsidized loan*.

Vocational program. An education program designed to prepare students for immediate employment. These programs usually can be completed in less than four years beyond high school and are available in most community colleges, career colleges, and vocational-technical institutes.

Work-Study. An arrangement by which a student combines employment and college study. The employment may be an integral part of the academic program (as in cooperative education and internships) or simply a means of paying for college. See also *Federal Work Study Program*.

Eligibility Indexes

Corporate/ Employer

Disabilities

Hearing impaired

Learning disabled

Physically challenged

Visually impaired

Field of Study/ Intended Career

Agricultural science, business, and natural resources conservation

Field of Study/Intended Career: Agricultural science, business, and natural resources conservation

Architecture and design

Area and ethnic studies

Arts, visual and performing

Biological and biomedical sciences

Biological and physical sciences

Business/management/administration

Communications

Computer and information sciences

Education

Engineering and engineering technology

Eligibility Indexes

English and literature

Foreign languages

Health professions and allied services

Eligibility Indexes

Tolliver Annual Nursing
Scholarship, 404
Tyson Foods Intern Program, 678
U.S. Army/ROTC Nursing
Scholarship, 616
Vet Tech AND Other Veterinary
Support Careers Electric Dog Fence
DIY Scholarship, 272
Virginia's Nurse Practitioner Nurse
Midwife Scholarship, 627
Walter and Marie Schmidt
Scholarship, 508
The William R. Goldfarb Memorial
Scholarship, 186
Wilma Motley Memorial California
Merit Scholarship, 86
The Wilse Morgan WX7P Memorial
ARRL Northwestern Division
Scholarship Fund, 186
ZendyHealth Med Tech
Scholarship, 645

Home economics

Academy of Nutrition and Dietetics
Graduate, Baccalaureate or
Coordinated Program
Scholarships, 81
Al Schulman Ecolab First-Time
Freshman Entrepeneurial
Scholarship, 470
American Chemical Society Scholars
Program, 101
American Society for Enology and
Viticulture Scholarship
Program, 188
Bern Laxer Memorial
Scholarship, 380
Bob Zappatelli Memorial
Scholarship, 380
Chefs of Louisiana Cookery
Scholarship, 381
Christian Wolffer Scholarship, 381
The Cynthia E. Morgan Memorial
Scholarship Fund, 262
Dairy Student Recognition
Program, 458
Dean Foods Company
Scholarship, 299
Deseo at the Westin Scholarship, 382
DMI Milk Marketing
Scholarships, 458
Foth Production Solutions, LLC
Scholarship, 300
Hormel Foods Corporation
Scholarship, 301
Iager Dairy Scholarship, 458
Institute of Food Technologists
Freshman Scholarship, 285
Institute of Food Technologists
Undergraduate Scholarship, 285
Kikkoman Foods, Inc.
Scholarship, 302
Kildee Scholarship, 458
New Mexico Allied Health Student
Loan-for-Service Program, 687
NPFDA Foundation Scholarship, 469

Paradise Tomato Kitchens
Scholarship, 465
The Peter Cameron/Housewares
Charity Foundation
Scholarship, 384
Peter Kump Memorial
Scholarship, 384
Rose Acre Farms Scholarship, 305
Scholarship for Foodservice
Communication Careers, 370
Targeting Excellence Scholarship, 588
Tyson Foods Intern Program, 678
USDA/1890 National Scholars
Program, 619
Wells Fargo Scholarship, 307

Law

Adam Kutner's Helping Future
Lawyers Scholarship, 83
American Bar Foundation Summer
Research Diversity Fellowships in
Law and Social Sciences for
Undergraduate Students, 648
American Society of International
Law Internships, 650
The Ankin Law Offices College
Scholarship, 201
Auto Accident Scholarship, 645
Benson And Bingham First Annual
Scholarship, 224
Bick Bickson Scholarship, 323
Brandner Scholarship, 230
Cantor Crane Personal Injury Lawyer
Scholarship Fund, 240
Cogburn Law Offices Adversity
Scholarship, 250
Congressional Institute
Internships, 652
Constitutional Officers Association of
Georgia, Inc. Scholarship, 258
Dairy Student Recognition
Program, 458
Genentech, Inc. Internship
Program, 657
George T. Bochanis Law Offices
College Scholarship, 405
Gordon Law Group Need-Based
Scholarship, 317
Groth Law Firm Scholarship, 319
Horizons Scholarship, 641
Horizons-Michigan Scholarship, 641
Johnson Controls Co-op and
Internship Programs, 661
Keller Law Offices Scholarship for
Higher Education, 393
Law Office of Matthew L Sharp
Need-Based Scholarship, 425
Mainor Wirth Injury Lawyers
Need-Based Scholarship, 417
Naqvi Injury Law Scholarship, 441
NASA Space Grant Wisconsin
Consortium Undergraduate
Research Program, 451
New Leader Scholarship, 77
Peck Law Firm Scholarship, 512
The Reeves Law Group
Scholarship, 536

Rosengren Kohlmeyer Law Office
Scholarship, 539
Schechter, McElwee, Shaffer and
Harris Aspiring Law Student
Scholarship, 542
Sony Credited Internship, 676
Spence Reese Scholarship, 230
Strom And Associates Need-Based
Scholarship, 581
Taradash Law Firm Scholarship, 587
Tyson Foods Intern Program, 678
U.S. Senate Member Internships, 678
Water Companies (NJ Chapter)
Scholarship, 455
Zinda Law Group Scholarship, 645

Liberal arts and interdisciplinary studies

AFSCMA/UNCF Union Scholars
Program, 649
American Bar Foundation Summer
Research Diversity Fellowships in
Law and Social Sciences for
Undergraduate Students, 648
Charles L. Hebner Memorial
Scholarship, 267
Community Scholarship Fund, 324
Feminism & Leadership
Internship, 656
Harriet Irsay Scholarship, 116
J. Paul Getty Multicultural
Undergraduate Summer Internships
at the Getty Center, 659
National Federation of the Blind
Scholarships, 460
National Junior Classical League
Scholarship, 469
Pulliam Journalism Fellowship, 658

Library science

ALISE Bohdan S. Wynar Research
Paper Competition, 218
ALISE Research Grant, 219
ALISE/ProQuest Methodology Paper
Competition, 219
Guggenheim Museum Internship, 675
Kennedy Library Archival
Internship, 660
Museum Coca-Cola Internship, 667
Roosevelt Archival Internships, 657

Mathematics

Actuarial Diversity Scholarships, 82
Aerospace Undergraduate STEM
Research Scholarship Program, 450
AFCEA ROTC Scholarship, 205
AFCEA Scholarship for Underserved
Students (HBCU), 205
AFCEA War Veterans/Disabled War
Veterans Scholarship, 205
AfterCollege STEM Inclusion
Scholarship, 87
Ahmad-Sehar Saleha Ahmad and
Abrahim Ekramullah Zafar
Foundation, 500

Military science

Mortuary science

Philosophy, religion, and theology

Protective services

Social sciences and history

Trade and industry

Eligibility Indexes

Gender

Female

Male

International Student

Military Participation

Air Force

Reserves/National Guard

Minority Status

African American

Alaskan native

American Indian

Asian American

Hispanic American

Mexican American

Native Hawaiian/Pacific Islander

OCA-AXA Achievement Scholarships, 493
OCA/UPS Foundation Gold Mountain College Scholarship, 494
Office of Hawaiian Affairs Higher Education Scholarship Program, 343
Philippine Nurses' Association Scholarship, 345
Rosemary & Nellie Ebrie Fund, 346
STEM Bridge Scholarship, 451
Steven R. Nelson Native Educator Scholarship Program, 275
The Tang Scholarship, 553
TechChecks Business Leadership Scholarship, 588
Technical Minority Scholarship, 644
Tennessee Minority Teaching Fellows Program, 690
Weisman Scholarship, 258

Puerto Rican

Actuarial Diversity Scholarships, 82
AFSCMA/UNCF Union Scholars Program, 649
American Association of Advertising Agencies Multicultural Advertising Intern Program, 647
American Chemical Society Scholars Program, 101
American Institute of Certified Public Accountants Scholarship for Minority Accounting Students, 116
American Meteorological Society/Industry Minority Scholarship, 169
Brown and Caldwell Minority Scholarship Program, 233
California Teachers Association Martin Luther King, Jr., Memorial Scholarship, 238
CCNMA Scholarships, 243
The Chesapeake Energy Scholarship, 263
Colgate Bright Smiles, Bright Futures Minority Scholarships, 84
Connecticut Minority Teacher Incentive Grant, 256
Diversity Internship Program, 677
The EDSA Minority Scholarship, 402
El Café del Futuro Scholarship Essay Contest, 236
Fifth Third Bank of Central Indiana Scholarship, 463
Gates Millennium Scholars Program, 311
GE Foundation/LULAC Scholarship Program, 406
HACU (Hispanic Association of Colleges and Universities) Scholarships, 113
The Hyatt Hotels Fund for Minority Lodging Management Students Competition, 112
Indiana Minority Teacher & Special Education Services Scholarship, 580

INROADS Internship, 659
J. Paul Getty Multicultural Undergraduate Summer Internships at the Getty Center, 659
Jackie Robinson Foundation Mentoring and Leadership Curriculum, 377
James E. Webb Internship Program for Minority Undergraduate Seniors and Graduate Students in Business and Public Administration, 672
Jose Marti Scholarship Challenge Grant Fund, 290
Kansas Ethnic Minority Scholarship, 391
The Lagrant Foundation Scholarship Program, 400
Latin American Educational Scholarship, 404
Leonard M. Perryman Communications Scholarship for Ethnic Minority Students, 614
Los Padres Foundation College Tuition Assistance Program, 411
Los Padres Foundation Second Chance Program, 412
Louis Carr Summer Internship, 661
Minority Teacher Education Scholarship Program/Florida Fund for Minority Teachers, Inc., 290
Minority Teachers of Illinois Scholarship, 368
Morgan Stanley Richard B. Fisher Scholarship Program, 439
NABA National Scholarship Program, 453
The Prospanica Foundation Scholarship, 528
STEM Bridge Scholarship, 451
TechChecks Business Leadership Scholarship, 588
Technical Minority Scholarship, 644
Weisman Scholarship, 258
Wisconsin Minority Teacher Loan Program, 692

National/ethnic background

Arab

Helen Abbott Community Service Awards, 203

Armenian

AGBU International Scholarships, 206
Armenian General Benevolent Union Performing Arts Fellowships, 206
Edward Hosharian Scholarship, 276

Chinese

Cynthia Kuo Scholarship, 550
Thz Fo Farm Fund, 348

Greek

PanHellenic Scholarship Awards, 511

Italian

Alphonse A. Miele Scholarship, 612
College Scholarship Program, 253
DiMattio Celli Family Study Abroad Scholarship, 612
Ella T. Grasso Literary Scholarship, 612
Henry Salvatori Scholarship, 570
Italian Catholic Federation Scholarship, 375
Major Don S. Gentile Scholarship, 612
Maria and Paolo Alessio Southern Italy Scholarship, 611
Sant'Anna Institute-Sorrento Lingue Scholarship, 571
Sons of Italy General Scholarship, 571
Sons of Italy Italian Language Scholarship, 571
Sons of Italy National Leadership Grant, 571
Theodore Mazza Scholarship, 613
William C. Davini Scholarship, 613

Japanese

Ventura County Japanese-American Citizens League Scholarships, 625

Jewish

Charles Kosmutza Memorial Grant, 387
Jewish War Veterans of the United States of America Bernard Rotberg Memorial Scholarship, 388
Leon Brooks Memorial Grant, 388
Max R. & Irene Rubenstein Memorial Grant, 388
Robert and Rebecca Rubin Memorial Grant, 388
Seymour and Phyllis Shore Memorial Grant, 389

Polish

Massachusetts Federation of Polish Women's Clubs Scholarships, 398
The Polish American Club of North Jersey Scholarships, 398
The Polish National Alliance of Brooklyn, USA, Inc. Scholarships, 398

Swiss

Sonia Streuli Maguire Outstanding Scholastic Achievement Award, 586
Swiss Benevolent Society Medicus Student Exchange, 586
Swiss Benevolent Society Pellegrini Scholarship, 586

Welsh

Organization/civic affiliation

American Indian Science & Engineering Society

American Legion

American Legion Auxiliary

American Legion South Carolina Auxiliary Scholarship, 159
American Legion South Dakota Auxiliary Scholarships, 160
American Legion South Dakota Auxiliary Senior Member Scholarship, 160
Anna Gear Junior Scholarship, 163
Children of Warriors National President's Scholarship, 164
Della Van Deuren Memorial Scholarship, 121
Dr. Kate Waller Barrett Grant, 164
Elsie B. Brown Scholarship Fund, 150
Florence Lemcke Memorial Scholarship, 165
Grace S. High Memorial Child Welfare Scholarship Fund, 151
Laura Blackburn Memorial Scholarship, 134
Lucille Ganey Memorial Scholarship, 122
Marguerite McAlpin Nurse's Scholarship, 165
Marion J. Bagley Scholarship, 151
Mary Barrett Marshall Student Loan Fund, 683
Nannie W. Norfleet Scholarship, 154
Ruby Paul Campaign Fund Scholarship, 147
Spirit of Youth Scholarship, 157
Susan Burdett Scholarship, 165
Thelma Foster Junior American Legion Auxiliary Members Scholarship, 160
Thelma Foster Senior American Legion Auxiliary Member Scholarship, 161
Wilma D. Hoyal/Maxine Chilton Memorial Scholarship, 119
Wisconsin American Legion Auxiliary H.S. & Angeline Lewis Scholarship, 121
Wisconsin American Legion Auxiliary Merit & Memorial Scholarship, 121

American Legion, Boys State

American Legion Iowa Outstanding Citizen of Boys State Scholarship, 130
American Legion Maryland Boys State Scholarship, 135
American Legion New Hampshire Boys State Scholarship, 148
Lillie Lois Ford Boys' Scholarship, 141

American Legion/Boys Scouts of America

American Legion Wisconsin Eagle Scout of the Year Scholarship, 167

Boy Scouts of America

American Legion Illinois Boy Scout Eagle Scout Scholarship, 127

Boy Scouts of America, Eagle Scouts

American Legion Eagle Scout of the Year, 144
American Legion Iowa Boy Scout of the Year Scholarship, 130
American Legion Tennessee Eagle Scout of the Year Scholarship, 161
American Legion Vermont Eagle Scout of the Year, 162

First Catholic Slovak Ladies Association

First Catholic Slovak Ladies Association Scholarship Program, 287

Golf Course Superintendents Association of America

GCSAA Legacy Awards, 279, 316
GCSAA Scholars Competition, 279, 317
GCSAA Student Essay Contest, 317

Harness Racing Industry

Harness Tracks of America Scholarship Fund, 320

International Union of EESMF Workers, AFL-CIO

Bruce van Ess Scholarship, 376
James B. Carey Scholarship, 376
Sal Ingrassia Scholarship, 376
Willie Rudd Scholarship, 376

Learning for Life

Captain James J. Regan Memorial Scholarship, 408
Sheryl A. Horak Law Enforcement Explorer Scholarship, 408

New York State Grange

Caroline Kark Scholarship, 482
Grange Denise Scholarship, 482
Grange Student Loan Fund, 688
Grange Susan W. Freestone Education Award, 482
June Gill Nursing Scholarship, 482

Polish National Alliance of Brooklyn

The Polish National Alliance of Brooklyn, USA, Inc. Scholarships, 398

Reserve Officers Training Corps (ROTC)

Kansas ROTC Service Scholarship, 392

Screen Actor's Guild

John L. Dales Standard Scholarship, 543
John L. Dales Transitional Scholarship, 543

Society of Physics Students

Herbert Levy Memorial Scholarship, 564
Peggy Dixon Two-Year Scholarship, 564
Society of Physics Students Future Teacher Scholarship, 566
Society of Physics Students Leadership Scholarship, 566
Society of Physics Students Summer Internship Program, 675

Society of Women Engineers

SWE Scholarships, 569

Soil and Water Conservation Society

Donald A. Williams Soil Conservation Scholarship, 570
Melville H. Cohee Student Leader Conservation Scholarship, 570

Sons of Norway

Astrid G. Cates Scholarship Fund and Myrtle Beinhauer Scholarship, 571
King Olav V Norwegian-American Heritage Fund, 572
Nancy Lorraine Jensen Memorial Scholarship, 572

United States Association of Blind Athletes

I C You Foundation Valor Achievement Award, 616

United Transportation Union

United Transportation Union Insurance Association Scholarship, 617

Religious Affiliation

Christian

Cynthia Kuo Scholarship, 550
Next Generation Christian Leaders Scholarship, 433
Young Christian Leaders Scholarship, 644

Horatio Alger Delaware Scholarship Program, 357

I Matter Scholarship, 626

Kent Nutrition Group, Inc. Scholarship, 302

Michael Birchenall Scholarship Fund, 534

Moody's Mega Math M3 Challenge, 438

Sonia Streuli Maguire Outstanding Scholastic Achievement Award, 586

Swiss Benevolent Society Pellegrini Scholarship, 586

Welsh Society of Philadelphia Undergraduate Scholarship, 632

District of Columbia

American Legion District of Columbia National High School Oratorical Contest, 124

DC Tuition Assistance Grant Program (DCTAG), 272

Denny's Hungry for Education Scholarship, 415

Diverse Minds Writing Challenge, 223

Horatio Alger District of Columbia, Maryland and Virginia Scholarship Program, 357

Lisa Higgins-Hussman Foundation Scholarship, 610

Michael Birchenall Scholarship Fund, 534

Moody's Mega Math M3 Challenge, 438

The Paula Kovarick Segalman Family Scholarship Fund For ALS, 97

Florida

Academic Common Market, 576

Access to Better Learning and Education (ABLE) Grant Program, 288

American Legion Florida Auxiliary Department Scholarships, 125

American Legion Florida Auxiliary Memorial Scholarship, 125

American Legion Florida Eagle Scout of the Year, 124

American Legion Florida General Scholarship, 124

American Legion Florida High School Oratorical Contest, 125

The Andersons, Inc. Scholarship, 297

Animal Health International Scholarship, 297

The ARRL Earl I. Anderson Scholarship, 174

Bern Laxer Memorial Scholarship, 380

Birdsong Peanuts Scholarship, 298

Children of Florida UPS Employees Scholarship, 390

CSX Scholarship, 462

Cumberland Farms Believe and Achieve Scholarship Program, 262

Dana Campbell Memorial Scholarship, 382

Denny's Hungry for Education Scholarship, 415

Disaster Preparation Scholarship, 546

Fastline Publications Scholarship, 463

Florida Bright Futures Scholarship Program, 288

Florida Department of Education Florida Incentive Scholarship Program, 289

Florida First Generation Matching Grant Program, 289

Florida Public Postsecondary Career Education Student Assistance Grant Program, 289

Florida Scholarship Program, 246

Florida Scholarships for Children and Spouses of Deceased or Disabled Veterans, 289

Florida Student Assistance Grant (FSAG) Program, 290

Florida Work Experience Program, 290

Gulf Coast Hurricane Scholarships, 567

IRARC Memorial, Joseph P. Rubino, WA4MMD, Scholarship, 180

Jim Dodson Law Scholarship for Brain Injury Victims & Their Caregivers, 389

Jose Marti Scholarship Challenge Grant Fund, 290

King Ranch Scholarship, 303

Mahindra USA Women in Ag Scholarship, 303

Mary McLeod Bethune Scholarship, 290

MetLife Foundation Scholarship, 303

Minority Teacher Education Scholarship Program/Florida Fund for Minority Teachers, Inc., 290

Moody's Mega Math M3 Challenge, 438

The North Fulton Amateur Radio League Scholarship Fund, 182

NTA Florida Scholarship, 604

The Orlando HamCation Scholarship, 182

Pumphrey Law Scholarship, 529

Salute to Education Scholarship, 541

Southern Nursery Association Sidney B. Meadows Scholarship, 548

State University System of Florida Theodore R. and Vivian M. Johnson Scholarship, 390

Tennessee Valley Interstellar Workshop Scholarship Program, 593

University Tutoring Support Scholarship, 266

Visit Orlando/James Beard Scholarship, 386

The Wayne Nelson, KB4UT, Memorial Scholarship, 185

William L. Boyd, IV, Florida Resident Access Grant (FRAG) Program, 291

Georgia

The 5 Strong Scholarship Foundation, 79

Academic Common Market, 576

American Legion Georgia Auxiliary Past Presidents Parley Nurses Scholarship, 126

American Legion Georgia Oratorical Contest, 125

American Legion Georgia Scholarship, 125

Animal Health International Scholarship, 297

ASHRAE Region IV Benny Bootle Scholarship, 191

Birdsong Peanuts Scholarship, 298

The Charles Clarke Cordle Memorial Scholarship, 176

Cheryl Dant Hennesy Scholarship, 461

Constitutional Officers Association of Georgia, Inc. Scholarship, 258

CSX Scholarship, 462

Dana Campbell Memorial Scholarship, 382

Denny's Hungry for Education Scholarship, 415

The Eugene Gene Sallee, W4YFR, Memorial Scholarship, 178

Fastline Publications Scholarship, 463

Georgia Hope Grant - GED Recipient, 311

Georgia Hope Grant - Public Technical Institution, 312

Georgia Hope Scholarship - Private Institution, 312

Georgia Hope Scholarship - Public College or University, 312

Georgia Student Finance Commission Public Safety Memorial Grant, 312

Georgia Tuition Equalization Grant, 313

Greenhouse Scholars Program, 319

The Gwinnett Amateur Radio Society Scholarship, 179

Horatio Alger Georgia Scholarship Program, 358

Mahindra USA Women in Ag Scholarship, 303

MetLife Foundation Scholarship, 303

Monty's Food Plant Company, 464

Moody's Mega Math M3 Challenge, 438

Move on When Ready, 313

NASA Space Grant Georgia Fellowship Program, 442

The North Fulton Amateur Radio League Scholarship Fund, 182

PAGE Foundation Scholarships, 527

Rose Acre Farms Scholarship, 305

The Southeastern DX Club Scholarship Fund, 184

Southern Nursery Association Sidney B. Meadows Scholarship, 548

Student Aid Foundation Loan, 689

TAG Education Collaborative Web Challenge Contest, 586

Idaho

Illinois

Eligibility Indexes

Maryland

Academic Common Market, 576
American Legion Maryland Auxiliary
Past Presidents Parley
Scholarship, 136
American Legion Maryland Auxiliary
Scholarship, 136
American Legion Maryland Boys
State Scholarship, 135
American Legion Maryland Oratorical
Contest, 135
American Legion Maryland
Scholarship, 136
Applebee's/The Rose Group
Hospitality Scholarship, 533
CSX Scholarship, 462
The Cynthia E. Morgan Memorial
Scholarship Fund, 262
Dana Campbell Memorial
Scholarship, 382
Diverse Minds Writing
Challenge, 223
Edward T. Conroy Memorial
Scholarship Program, 418
Farmers Mutual Hail Insurance
Company of Iowa Scholarship, 300
The Gary Wagner, K3OMI,
Scholarship, 179
Horatio Alger District of Columbia,
Maryland and Virginia Scholarship
Program, 357
Horticultural Research Institute
Carville M. Akehurst Memorial
Scholarship, 361
Howard P. Rawlings Guaranteed
Access Grant, 419
Kent Nutrition Group, Inc.
Scholarship, 302
Letitia B. Carter Scholarship, 533
Lisa Higgins-Hussman Foundation
Scholarship, 610
Mahindra USA Women in Ag
Scholarship, 303
Marcia S. Harris Legacy Fund
Scholarship, 534
Maryland Delegate Scholarship, 419
Maryland Educational Assistance
Grant, 419
Maryland Jack F. Tolbert Memorial
Grant, 419
Maryland Part-Time Grant
Program, 420
Maryland Senatorial Scholarship, 420
Maryland Tuition Waiver for Foster
Care Recipients, 420
Michael Birchenall Scholarship
Fund, 534
Monty's Food Plant Company, 464
Moody's Mega Math M3
Challenge, 438
The Paula Kovarick Segalman Family
Scholarship Fund For ALS, 97
Southern Nursery Association Sidney
B. Meadows Scholarship, 548
Welsh Society of Philadelphia
Undergraduate Scholarship, 632

Massachusetts

Agnes M. Lindsey Scholarship, 421
American Legion Department of
Massachusetts Oratorical
Contest, 136
American Legion Massachusetts
Auxiliary Past Presidents Parley
Scholarship, 137
American Legion Massachusetts
Auxiliary Scholarship, 137
American Legion Massachusetts
General and Nursing
Scholarships, 137
Androscoggin Amateur Radio Club
Scholarship, 174
The Byron Blanchard, N1EKV
Memorial Scholarship Fund, 175
Categorical Tuition Waiver, 421
Cru Restaurant Scholarship, 381
Cumberland Farms Believe and
Achieve Scholarship Program, 262
DCF Foster Child Tuition Waiver and
Fee Assistance Program, 421
The Dr. James L. Lawson Memorial
Scholarship, 178
Foster Child Grant Program, 422
Garden Club Federation of
Massachusetts, 308
Gear Up Scholarship Program, 422
Henry David Thoreau
Foundation, 352
High Technology Scholar/Intern
Tuition Waiver Program, 422
Incentive Program for Aspiring
Teachers, 422
John and Abigail Adams
Scholarship, 422
Joint Admissions Tuition Advantage
Waiver Program, 423
Kent Nutrition Group, Inc.
Scholarship, 302
Living the Dream Scholarship, 411
LSP Association Scholarship
Fund, 415
Mahindra USA Women in Ag
Scholarship, 303
Massachusetts Cash Grant
Program, 423
Massachusetts Christian A. Herter
Memorial Scholarship Program, 423
Massachusetts Federation of Polish
Women's Clubs Scholarships, 398
Massachusetts Gilbert Matching
Student Grant, 423
Massachusetts MASSgrant
Program, 424
Massachusetts Math and Science
Teachers Scholarship, 424
Massachusetts No Interest Loan, 685
Massachusetts Part-Time Grant
Program, 424
Massachusetts Public Service Grant
Program, 424
Moody's Mega Math M3
Challenge, 438
NEBHE's Tuition Break Regional
Student Program, 478

The New England FEMARA
Scholarship, 182
NTA Massachusetts Scholarship, 604
OMEGA: Opportunities for
Multigenerational Engagement,
Growth, and Action, 88
One Family Scholars Program, 499
Paul Tsongas Scholarship
Program, 424
PHCC of Massachusetts Auxiliary
Scholarship, 522
September 11, 2001 Tragedy Tuition
Waiver Program, 425
Stanley Z. Koplik Certificate of
Mastery Tuition Waiver
Program, 425
Timothy and Palmer W. Bigelow, Jr.
Scholarship, 362
Valedictorian Tuition Waiver
Program, 425
Yankee Clipper Contest Club Youth
Scholarship, 186

Michigan

American Legion Michigan Auxiliary
Medical Career Scholarships, 138
American Legion Michigan Auxiliary
Memorial Scholarship, 138
American Legion Michigan Auxiliary
National President's
Scholarship, 138
American Legion Michigan Oratorical
Contest, 137
The Andersons, Inc. Scholarship, 297
The ARRL Earl I. Anderson
Scholarship, 174
Beck's Hybrids Scholarship, 461
Children of Veterans Tuition
Grant, 428
David Arver Memorial
Scholarship, 90
Disability Attorneys of Michigan
Scholarship, 270
Earl R. Sorensen Memorial
Scholarships, 299
Farmers Mutual Hail Insurance
Company of Iowa Scholarship, 300
Fastline Publications Scholarship, 463
Guy M. Wilson Scholarship, 138
Horizons-Michigan Scholarship, 641
Hormel Foods Corporation
Scholarship, 301
I Matter Scholarship, 626
Kent Nutrition Group, Inc.
Scholarship, 302
Mahindra USA Women in Ag
Scholarship, 303
MetLife Foundation Scholarship, 303
Michigan Society of Professional
Engineers Scholarships for High
School Seniors, 429
Michigan Tuition Grant, 429
Michigan Tuition Incentive
Program, 429
Midwest Student Exchange
Program, 430

Eligibility Indexes

Oklahoma

Oregon

Pennsylvania

Tennessee

Texas

Eligibility Indexes

Utah

Vermont

Virgin Islands

Virginia

Washington

West Virginia

Wisconsin

Wyoming

Study Abroad

Scholarships

1-800 Hansons

1-800 Hansons Scholarship Program

Type of award: Scholarship.
Intended use: For full-time at vocational, 2-year, 4-year or graduate institution.
Application requirements: 1000-1500 word essay.
Additional information: Must have a minimum 3.3 GPA. For more details and essay prompt, visit website.

Amount of award:	$500-$5,000
Number of awards:	8
Application deadline:	October 31
Notification begins:	November 30
Total amount awarded:	$10,000

Contact:
1-800 Hansons
977 East 14 Mile Road
ATTN: Hansons Scholarship Program c/o Brian E
Troy, MI 48083
Web: www.hansons.com/Scholarship.htm

10,000 Degrees

10,000 Degrees Undergraduate Scholarships

Type of award: Scholarship, renewable.
Intended use: For full-time undergraduate study at accredited 2-year or 4-year institution in United States.
Eligibility: Applicant must be residing in California.
Basis for selection: Applicant must demonstrate financial need.
Application requirements: Essay. FAFSA.
Additional information: Must be resident of Marin, Sonoma, Vallejo, Richmond, or Ringgold counties. Must be enrolled for minimum of twelve units per term. Applicants automatically considered for six other scholarships ranging from $500-$5,000. Students seeking teaching credentials with an interest in working with children over 5 years old also eligible. Awards and amounts may vary. Visit Website for more information.

Amount of award:	$500-$5,000
Number of awards:	20

Contact:
10,000 Degrees
1650 Los Gamos Drive
Suite 110
San Rafael, CA 94903
Phone: 415-451-4240
Web: www.10000degrees.org/students/scholarships/undergraduate-scholarships

New Leader Scholarship

Type of award: Scholarship.
Intended use: For full-time sophomore, junior, senior or graduate study at postsecondary institution. Designated institutions: University of California, Berkeley, California State University East Bay, San Francisco State University, San Jose State University, Sonoma State University.
Eligibility: Applicant must be residing in California.
Basis for selection: Major/career interest in economics; health sciences; law; medicine; psychology; social work or sociology. Applicant must demonstrate financial need, high academic achievement, leadership and service orientation.
Application requirements: Interview, recommendations, essay, transcript. Financial statement.
Additional information: Preference given to recent immigrants and students of color. Applicants do not need to be Marin County residents to apply. Applicants should demonstrate commitment to giving back to their communities and plan to pursue career in public, legal, psychological, health, or social services. Graduate students may be considered if they have received scholarship as undergraduate and are attending California public universities. See Website (www.goldmanfamilyfund.com) for more information. Minimum 3.5 GPA. Consideration will be given to students with a GPA of 3.2 - 3.49 under special circumstances. Awards and amounts may vary.

Amount of award:	$8,000
Application deadline:	March 10

Contact:
10,000 Degrees
New Leader Scholarship
781 Lincoln Avenue, Suite 140
San Rafael, CA 94901
Phone: 415-459-4240
Fax: 415-459-0527
Web: www.newleaderscholarship.org, www.10000degrees.org

10x Digital

10x Digital Marketing Scholarship

Type of award: Scholarship.
Intended use: For full-time undergraduate study.
Eligibility: Applicant must be high school senior.
Basis for selection: Major/career interest in marketing.
Application requirements: Essay. 500 word essay on your choice of provided topics.
Additional information: Must major (or plan to major) in a field related to digital marketing.

Number of awards:	1
Application deadline:	June 30
Total amount awarded:	$1,000

Contact:
Web: www.10xdigitalinc.com/digital-marketing-scholarship/

1199SEIU Benefit Funds

Joseph Tauber Scholarship

Type of award: Scholarship, renewable.
Intended use: For full-time undergraduate or non-degree study at accredited vocational, 2-year or 4-year institution in or outside United States.
Basis for selection: Applicant must demonstrate financial need.
Application requirements: Proof of eligibility. CSS profile.
Additional information: Applicant must be dependent of eligible member of 1199SEIU. Minimum award is $750 each year for full-time students. Must be receiving family coverage (Wage or Eligibility Class One) through benefit fund. Apply for pre-screening by deadline date; applications sent to qualified candidates. Visit Website for updates. Must apply for renewal. Amount of award varies.

Amount of award:	$750
Number of awards:	3,000
Number of applicants:	6,000
Application deadline:	January 31
Notification begins:	November 1
Total amount awarded:	$4,500,000

Contact:
1199SEIU Child Care Funds Joseph Tauber Scholarship Program
330 West 42nd Street, 18th Floor
New York, NY 10036-6977
Phone: 646-473-8999
Fax: 646-473-6949
Web: www.1199seiubenefits.org/funds-and-services/child-care-funds/youth-programs/jts

123Writings

123Writings Scholarship Writing Contest

Type of award: Scholarship, renewable.
Intended use: For full-time undergraduate or graduate study at accredited vocational, 2-year, 4-year or graduate institution.
Application requirements: Essay.
Additional information: How to apply:. Like 123Writings on Facebook or follow on Twitter. Share the post about writing contest. Choose the topic from the list on official website. Send your completed essay to Writingcontest@123writing.com. Eligible applicants are ready for essay writing as a competition.

Amount of award:	$1,500-$2,500
Number of awards:	3
Application deadline:	August 20
Notification begins:	September 1
Total amount awarded:	$6,000

Contact:
123Writings
Civic Center
Miami, FL 33136
Phone: 877-752-5255
Web: 123writings.com/writing-contest

1SEO Digital Agency

1SEO Digital Agency Scholarship Program

Type of award: Scholarship.
Intended use: For undergraduate study at 2-year or 4-year institution in United States.
Eligibility: Applicant must be at least 17, no older than 100, high school senior. Applicant must be U.S. citizen residing in Delaware, New Jersey or Pennsylvania.
Basis for selection: Major/career interest in marketing; business or communications.
Application requirements: Record a 2-5 minute video explaining how internet marketing (SEO, PPC, Email Marketing, Social Medica, Content Marketing) impacts you on a daily basis (creativity is encouraged). Video must be uploaded to YouTube. Title of video must read: [Student's Name] - 1SEO.com Digital Agency Scholarship Application. Description must read: [Very brief description of yourself/ video] [Link to 1SEO.com]. Applicant must "like" the 1SEO.com Digital Agency Facebook page. Applicant must fill out basic information in a brief application found on the scholarship page.
Additional information: Funds can be used for Study Abroad. Our committee will consist of five judges who will base their decision on creativity, drive, and storytelling through each submission. All enties must comply with the application process.

Amount of award:	$1,000
Number of awards:	1
Application deadline:	May 31
Notification begins:	June 16
Total amount awarded:	$1,000

Contact:
1SEO Digital Agency
1414 Radcliffe Street
#301
Bristol, PA 19007
Phone: 215-407-5674
Web: https://1seo.com/scholarship/

1st Marine Division Association

1st Marine Division Association Scholarship

Type of award: Scholarship, renewable.
Intended use: For full-time undergraduate study at accredited vocational, 2-year or 4-year institution in United States.
Eligibility: Applicant must be U.S. citizen. Applicant must be dependent of disabled veteran or deceased veteran who served in the Marines. Must have served specifically in any unit part of, attached to, or in support of 1st Marine Division.
Basis for selection: Applicant must demonstrate depth of character and seriousness of purpose.
Application requirements: Essay, proof of eligibility. Veteran sponsor's DD214 if available (if not, applicant must complete Standard Form 180). Death certificate or affidavit proving veteran's 100 percent and permanent disability. Copy of

applicant's birth certificate. Photograph. See Website for other required information.
Additional information: Number of awards varies. Visit Website for application deadline and details.

Amount of award:	$1,750
Total amount awarded:	$36,750

Contact:
1st Marine Division Association
403 North Freeman Street
Oceanside, CA 92054
Phone: 760-967-8561
Fax: 760-967-8567
Web: www.1stmarinedivisionassociation.org/Scholarships.html

280 Group

280 Group Product Management Scholarship

Type of award: Scholarship.
Intended use: For undergraduate or graduate study at 2-year, 4-year or graduate institution in or outside United States or Canada.
Basis for selection: Major/career interest in business or economics.
Application requirements: Essay. 1,000 word essay to be completed with application.
Additional information: Must have a minimum 2.5 GPA. Included in the scholarship is full tuition for the 280 Group's product management class. Student may take class at any of the in-person locations within one year of award. No travel, lodging or other expenses will be reimbursed. See website for locations and dates.

Amount of award:	$500
Number of awards:	5
Application deadline:	November 15
Notification begins:	December 31
Total amount awarded:	$2,500

Contact:
280 Group
142B S Santa Cruz Avenue
Los Gatos, CA 95030
Phone: 1-408-834-7518
Web: https://280group.com/contact/280-group-product-management-scholarship/

The 5 Strong Scholarship Foundation

The 5 Strong Scholarship Foundation

Type of award: Scholarship, renewable.
Intended use: For full-time undergraduate study at 4-year institution. Designated institutions: Bethune Cookman University, Alabama A&M University, Langston University, and The University of Arkansas Pine Bluff.
Eligibility: Applicant must be at least 17, no older than 20. Applicant must be residing in Georgia.

Additional information: Minimum 2.5 GPA. Must reside in metropolitan Atlanta area (Fulton, Cobb, Clayton, DeKalb, Gwinett counties). Must attend bi-monthly 5 strong college prep and development sessions. Application can be found online.

Amount of award:	$6,000-$10,000
Number of awards:	20
Application deadline:	December 20
Notification begins:	January 10

Contact:
Phone: 770-873-6621
Web: www.5strongscholars.org

A Place for Mom

Senior Care Innovation Scholarship

Type of award: Scholarship.
Intended use: For undergraduate or graduate study at accredited 2-year, 4-year or graduate institution.
Basis for selection: Major/career interest in gerontology; medicine; nursing; social work or sociology.
Application requirements: Essay.
Additional information: Five $1,000 scholarships available for students studying gerontology, medicine, nursing, social work, sociology or long-term care administration.

Amount of award:	$1,000
Number of awards:	5
Number of applicants:	500
Application deadline:	April 15

Contact:
A Place for Mom
701 5th Avenue
Suit 3200
Seattle, WA 98104
Phone: 866-333-7935
Web: www.aplaceformom.com/scholarship

Abbie Sargent Memorial Scholarship Fund

Abbie Sargent Memorial Scholarship

Type of award: Scholarship, renewable.
Intended use: For undergraduate or graduate study at postsecondary institution.
Eligibility: Applicant must be residing in New Hampshire.
Basis for selection: Major/career interest in agriculture. Applicant must demonstrate financial need, high academic achievement and depth of character.
Application requirements: Recommendations, essay, transcript. Recent photo.
Additional information: Recipient may attend out-of-state university. Preference given to those involved in agriculturally related studies. Send SASE for application or download from Website. Number of awards varies.

Amount of award:	$400-$1,000
Number of applicants:	8
Application deadline:	March 15
Notification begins:	June 1

Contact:
Abbie Sargent Memorial Scholarship
Attn: Diane Clary, Treasurer
295 Sheep Davis Road
Concord, NH 03301
Phone: 603-224-1934
Web: www.nhfarmbureau.org

AbbVie

AbbVie Cystic Fibrosis Scholarship

Type of award: Scholarship.
Intended use: For undergraduate or graduate study at vocational, 2-year, 4-year or graduate institution in or outside United States.
Eligibility: Applicant must be physically challenged. Applicant must be U.S. citizen or permanent resident.
Additional information: Intended for exceptional students living with cystic fibrosis. It is not necessary for applicants to have taken, currently take, or intend to take in the future, any medicine or product marketed by AbbVie, and this will not be a consideration in the recipient selection criteria. Forty AbbVie CF Scholars will be selected to receive $3,000 for use during the academic year based on their outstanding academic record, extracurricular activities, and creativity. Each scholar will also be given the opportunity to compete for one of two Thriving Student Scholarships (based on level of study) for a total amount of $25,000 each. In celebration of the 25th anniversary of the scholarship program, AbbVie is introducing a new award category - the Blogger's Choice Award - which provides each scholar with an additional opportunity to be awarded a total amount of $25,000.

Amount of award:	$3,000-$25,000
Number of awards:	40
Number of applicants:	250
Application deadline:	May 24
Total amount awarded:	$186,000

Contact:
AbbVie
1 North Waukegan Road
North Chicago, IL 60064
Phone: 847-937-6477
Fax: 847-937-1418
Web: www.abbviecfscholarship.com

Abe Voron Committee

Abe Voron Scholarship

Type of award: Scholarship.
Intended use: For full-time junior, senior or graduate study at 4-year or graduate institution. Designated institutions: BEA Institutional Member schools.
Basis for selection: Major/career interest in radio/television/film. Applicant must demonstrate high academic achievement, depth of character and seriousness of purpose.

Application requirements: Recommendations, essay, transcript.
Additional information: Award intended for study in radio only. Should be able to show evidence of potential to be outstanding electronic media professional. Application available from campus faculty or online.

Amount of award:	$3,000
Number of awards:	3
Application deadline:	October 10
Total amount awarded:	$9,000

Contact:
Broadcast Education Association (BEA)
1771 N Street, N.W.
Washington, DC 20036-2891
Phone: 202-429-3935
Web: www.beaweb.org

Abrahamson & Uiterwyk Scholarship Essay Contest

Abrahamson & Uiterwyk Scholarship Essay Contest

Type of award: Scholarship.
Intended use: For freshman study at vocational, 2-year, 4-year or graduate institution.
Eligibility: Applicant must be at least 18. Applicant must be U.S. citizen.
Application requirements: Explain the importance of creating a Family Safety Contract. For example, why should there be an agreement with children and their parents on safety issues? What topics should be covered? Tell us about a specific instance you or someone in your family would have benefitted from discussing safety and making a plan. Did you rear end someone as a result of distracted driving? Were you ashamed or scared to tell your parents? Were you aware of proper steps to take after being in an accident? Create a mock Family Safety Contract that you believe would help families discuss common safety issues and set guidelines for acceptable and unacceptable behaviors. For example, having a list that starts with I will or I will not followed by actions that either promote or compromise safety. The essay must be at least 500 words and no longer than 750 words. Only one essay per student is allowed to be entered.
Additional information: Send a scanned, signed copy of the application in by e-mail.

Number of awards:	1
Application deadline:	July 31
Notification begins:	August 15
Total amount awarded:	$1,500

Contact:
Abrahamson & Uiterwyk Injury Law Firm
2639 McCormick Drive
Clearwater, FL 33759
Phone: 727-725-9411
Web: www.theinjurylawyers.com/scholarship/

Absolute Dental

Absolute Dental's Dentists of the Future Scholarship

Type of award: Scholarship.
Basis for selection: Major/career interest in dentistry. Applicant must demonstrate financial need.
Additional information: To help students pursuing a career in Dentistry. 3.0+ GPA and pursing a dental related degree. Apply on website or download PDF and submit. Application deadline is 06/15 and notifications will be made over summer prior to new school year.

    Amount of award: $2,000
    Number of awards: 1
    Application deadline: June 15
Contact:
ABSOLUTE DENTAL
526 South Tonopah Dr. Suite #200
Las Vegas, NV 89106
Phone: 702-739-3082
Web: www.absolutedental.com/dentists-scholarship-program

Academy of Interactive Arts & Sciences

Mark Beaumont Scholarship Fund

Type of award: Scholarship.
Intended use: For full-time sophomore, junior, senior or graduate study in United States.
Basis for selection: Major/career interest in business. Applicant must demonstrate financial need, depth of character, leadership and service orientation.
Application requirements: Recommendations, transcript, proof of eligibility. Verification of enrollment. Two-page letter including information about your studies and how they will benefit the game industry and statement addressing service, leadership, character, and financial need.
Additional information: Minimum 3.3 GPA. Must intend to enter game industry in the area of business. Possible career paths include, but are not limited to: executive leadership, law, marketing, public relations, business development. Deadline in summer. Notifications begin in August.

    Amount of award: $2,500
    Number of awards: 2
    Total amount awarded: $5,000
Contact:
Academy of Interactive Arts & Sciences
Web: www.interactive.org/foundation/scholarships.asp

Randy Pausch Scholarship Fund

Type of award: Scholarship.
Intended use: For full-time sophomore, junior, senior or graduate study at accredited postsecondary institution in United States.
Basis for selection: Major/career interest in music; arts, general or computer graphics. Applicant must demonstrate financial need, depth of character, leadership and service orientation.

Application requirements: Recommendations, transcript, proof of eligibility. Two-page letter including information about your studies and how they will benefit the game industry and statement addressing service, leadership, character, and financial need.
Additional information: Minimum 3.3 GPA. Must intend to enter game industry as developer of interactive entertainment. Possible career paths include, but are not limited to: art, animation, programming, engineering, game direction, game design, sound design, music composition. Deadline in summer. Notifications begin in August.

    Amount of award: $2,500
    Number of awards: 2
    Application deadline: April 28
    Total amount awarded: $5,000
Contact:
Academy of Interactive Arts & Sciences
Web: www.interactive.org/foundation/scholarships.asp

Academy of Nutrition and Dietetics

Academy of Nutrition and Dietetics Graduate, Baccalaureate or Coordinated Program Scholarships

Type of award: Scholarship, renewable.
Intended use: For full-time junior, senior or graduate study at accredited 4-year or graduate institution. Designated institutions: ACEND-accredited/approved dietetics education programs.
Eligibility: Applicant must be U.S. citizen or permanent resident.
Basis for selection: Major/career interest in dietetics/nutrition. Applicant must demonstrate high academic achievement and seriousness of purpose.
Application requirements: Recommendations, proof of eligibility. GPA documentation signed by academic advisor.
Additional information: Applicant must be a member of the Academy of Nutrition and Dietetics. Number and amount of awards varies. Minority status considered. Must demonstrate or show promise of being a valuable, contributing member of the profession. See Website for more information and application.

    Amount of award: $500-$3,000
    Number of applicants: 500
    Total amount awarded: $264,000
Contact:
Academy of Nutrition and Dietetics
Education Programs
120 South Riverside Plaza, Suite 2000
Chicago, IL 60606-6995
Phone: 800-877-1600
Web: www.eatright.org/students/careers/aid.aspx

ACFE Foundation

Ritchie-Jennings Memorial Scholarship

Type of award: Scholarship.
Intended use: For full-time undergraduate or graduate study at accredited 4-year institution.

Basis for selection: Major/career interest in criminal justice/law enforcement; accounting; business or finance/banking.
Application requirements: Recommendations, essay, transcript. Applicant must include three letters of recommendation, preferably one from a certified fraud examiner.
Additional information: Award includes one-year ACFE Student Associate membership. Deadline in early February. Notifications of awards begin in end of April. Visit Website for additional information.

Amount of award:	$1,000-$10,000
Number of awards:	30
Number of applicants:	150
Notification begins:	April 15
Total amount awarded:	$53,000

Contact:
ACFE Foundation Scholarships Program Coordinator
The Gregor Building
716 West Avenue
Austin, TX 78701-2727
Phone: 800-245-3321
Fax: 512-276-8127
Web: www.acfe.com/scholarship.aspx

Active Renter Property Management

Active Renter Property Management Entrepreneur Scholarship

Type of award: Scholarship.
Intended use: For full-time freshman or sophomore study at accredited 2-year or 4-year institution in United States.
Eligibility: Applicant must be high school senior. Applicant must be residing in Arizona.
Application requirements: Essay, transcript. Respond to five essay questions on the application. 1: Describe your business. 2: Discuss how your business is innovative or promotes innovation. 3: Explain how you provide exemplary customer service and give a specific example of a time you gave a customer outstanding service. 4: Discuss how you believe your business functions to improve society. 5: Describe your plans for the future of your business.
Additional information: Minimum 3.5 GPA. Must either be a high school senior or a student currently attending a University or College in Maricopa County with 60 credits or less. Applicant must have run his or her own business for at least one year. The applicant must provide supporting evidence of this business (e.g., marketing materials, a product, a customer reference, etc.).

Number of awards:	1
Application deadline:	January 15
Notification begins:	April 1
Total amount awarded:	$1,000

Contact:
Active Renter Property Management
1428 East Northern Avenue
Phoenix, AZ 85020
Phone: 602-635-1063
Fax: 602-635-4286
Web: www.activerenter.com/scholarship

Activia

Activia Training Annual Scholarship Award

Type of award: Scholarship, renewable.
Intended use: For undergraduate or graduate study at 2-year, 4-year or graduate institution in United States.
Eligibility: Applicant must be at least 16. Applicant must be U.S. citizen or permanent resident.
Additional information: Two scholarship awards of $750 each year, awarded in November and May. One video submission will receive $500, and an essay submission will receive $250. Full details and application can be found on website.

Amount of award:	$250-$500
Number of awards:	4
Application deadline:	October 31, April 30
Total amount awarded:	$1,500

Contact:
Web: https://www.activia.co.uk/scholarship-us

The Actuarial Foundation

Actuarial Diversity Scholarships

Type of award: Scholarship, renewable.
Intended use: For full-time undergraduate or graduate study at accredited 2-year, 4-year or graduate institution.
Eligibility: Applicant must be Alaskan native, African American, Mexican American, Hispanic American, Puerto Rican, American Indian or Native Hawaiian/Pacific Islander. Applicant must be U.S. citizen, permanent resident or international student.
Basis for selection: Major/career interest in insurance/actuarial science or mathematics. Applicant must demonstrate high academic achievement.
Application requirements: Recommendations, essay, transcript, proof of eligibility. SAT/ACT scores.
Additional information: Must have at least one birth parent who is Black/African American, Hispanic, Native American, or Pacific Islander. Applicant must be admitted to institution offering actuarial science program or courses that will prepare student for actuarial career. Minimum 3.0 GPA. Minimum 28 ACT math score or 600 SAT math score. International students must have F1 visa. Visit Website for application, deadline, and more information.

Amount of award:	$1,000-$4,000
Number of awards:	30
Application deadline:	May 1
Notification begins:	August 5

Contact:
The Actuarial Foundation
Actuarial Diversity Scholarship
475 North Martingale Road, Suite 600
Schaumburg, IL 60173-2226
Phone: 847-706-3535
Web: www.actuarialfoundation.org/programs/actuarial/scholarships.shtml

Actuary of Tomorrow Stuart A. Robertson Memorial Scholarship

Type of award: Scholarship.
Intended use: For full-time sophomore, junior or senior study at accredited 4-year institution in United States.
Basis for selection: Applicant must demonstrate high academic achievement.
Application requirements: Recommendations, essay, transcript.
Additional information: Minimum 3.0 GPA. Major/career interest: Mathematics, Statistics and Actuarial Science. Must have successfully completed two actuarial exams. Must pursue course of study leading to career in actuarial science. Visit Website for essay topic and application.

Amount of award:	$9,000
Number of awards:	2
Application deadline:	June 1
Notification begins:	August 1
Total amount awarded:	$18,000

Contact:
The Actuarial Foundation
Attn: Actuary of Tomorrow Scholarship
475 North Martingale Road, Suite 600
Schaumburg, IL 60173-2226
Phone: 847-706-3535
Web: www.actuarialfoundation.org/programs/actuarial/scholarships.shtml

Curtis E. Huntington Memorial Scholarship

Type of award: Scholarship.
Intended use: For full-time senior study at 4-year institution.
Eligibility: Applicant must be U.S. citizen or permanent resident.
Basis for selection: Major/career interest in insurance/actuarial science. Applicant must demonstrate high academic achievement and leadership.
Application requirements: Recommendations, essay, transcript, nomination by professor.
Additional information: Minimum 3.0 GPA. Applicant must have passed at least one actuarial examination. Application is available on Website. Immediate relatives of members of the Board of Trustees of the Actuarial Foundation or boards of affiliated organizations are not eligible to apply. Limit one application per school.

Amount of award:	$2,000
Application deadline:	June 16
Notification begins:	August 21

Contact:
The Actuarial Foundation
475 North Martingale Road, Suite 600
Schaumburg, IL 60173-2226
Phone: 847-706-3535
Fax: 847-706-3599
Web: www.actuarialfoundation.org/programs/actuarial/scholarships.shtml

Acuity Training

Acuity Training Scholarship for Outstanding Leadership

Type of award: Scholarship.
Intended use: For undergraduate or graduate study at 2-year, 4-year or graduate institution.
Application requirements: To enter upload your video to YouTube and put "Acuity Training Scholarship Program" as the title. You should also provide a link to this page inside the description area. When you have completed all of those steps, email scholarships@acuitytraining.co.uk and provide the link to the video. You should also include the following information: your full name, telephone number and mailing address, the name of the school you attend (If you have been accepted but haven't started yet that counts), proof that you are a student of the school you specified, and your area of study.
Additional information: Students who wish to apply should create a three to four minute video discussing the merits of leadership. Include one or more of the following ideas: A) What is leadership? Why is it valuable and how can it be developed? What is the difference between leadership, management and assertiveness? B) Examples of how and when you have shown leadership and the benefits that have flowed from that, and C) The importance of leadership qualities in the 21st century workplace.

Number of awards:	1
Application deadline:	December 31
Notification begins:	January 15
Total amount awarded:	$500

Contact:
Web: www.acuitytraining.co.uk/scholarships/

Adam S. Kutner's & Associates

Adam Kutner's Helping Future Lawyers Scholarship

Type of award: Scholarship.
Basis for selection: Major/career interest in law. Applicant must demonstrate financial need.
Additional information: To help students pursuing a career in Law. 3.0+ GPA and pursing a Law related degree. Apply on website or download PDF and submit. Application deadline is 06/15 and notifications will be made over summer prior to new school year.

Amount of award:	$2,500
Number of awards:	1
Application deadline:	June 15

Contact:
Adam S. Kutner & Associates
1137 South Rancho Dr #150A
Las Vegas, NV 89102
Phone: 702-739-3082
Web: www.askadamskutner.com/adam-kutner-scholarship-program

ADHA Institute for Oral Health

ADHA Institute for Oral Health Scholarship for Academic Excellence

Type of award: Scholarship.
Intended use: For full-time sophomore, junior or senior study at accredited 2-year or 4-year institution in United States.
Basis for selection: Major/career interest in dental hygiene. Applicant must demonstrate high academic achievement.
Additional information: Applicant must have completed minimum one year dental hygiene curriculum; may apply during first year. Minimum 3.5 GPA in dental hygiene. Must be member of ADHA or Student ADHA.

Amount of award:	$1,000
Number of awards:	5
Application deadline:	February 1
Notification begins:	July 1

Contact:
ADHA Institute for Oral Health
Scholarship Award Program
444 N. Michigan Ave., Suite 3400
Chicago, IL 60611
Phone: 312-440-8900
Web: www.adha.org/scholarships-and-grants

Carol Bauhs Benson Scholarship

Type of award: Scholarship.
Intended use: For full-time undergraduate certificate, sophomore, junior, senior or post-bachelor's certificate study at accredited 2-year institution in United States.
Eligibility: Applicant must be residing in Wisconsin, South Dakota, Minnesota or North Dakota.
Basis for selection: Major/career interest in dental hygiene. Applicant must demonstrate financial need and high academic achievement.
Application requirements: Recommendations, essay. FAFSA.
Additional information: Must have completed one year in a dental hygiene curriculum by award year; may apply during first year. Must be active ADHA or Student ADHA member with minimum 3.5 GPA in dental hygiene. Download application from Website. All applications must be typed. Applying to more than one scholarship may void application.

Amount of award:	$1,000
Number of awards:	1
Application deadline:	February 1
Notification begins:	July 1

Contact:
ADHA Institute for Oral Health
Scholarship Award Program
444 N. Michigan Ave., Ste. 3400
Chicago, IL 60611-3980
Phone: 312-440-8900
Web: www.adha.org/scholarships-and-grants

Colgate Bright Smiles, Bright Futures Minority Scholarships

Type of award: Scholarship, renewable.
Intended use: For full-time undergraduate certificate, sophomore, junior or senior study in United States.
Eligibility: Applicant must be Asian American, African American, Mexican American, Hispanic American, Puerto Rican or American Indian.
Basis for selection: Major/career interest in dental hygiene. Applicant must demonstrate financial need and high academic achievement.
Application requirements: Recommendations, essay. FAFSA.
Additional information: Applicant must be member of ADHA or Student ADHA. Men considered a minority in this field and encouraged to apply. Applicant must have completed at least one year of certificate-level dental hygiene program; may apply during first year. Minimum 3.5 dental hygiene GPA. Download application from Website. All applications must be typed. Applying to more than one scholarship may void application.

Amount of award:	$1,250
Number of awards:	2
Application deadline:	February 1
Notification begins:	July 1

Contact:
ADHA Institute for Oral Health
Scholarship Award Program
444 N. Michigan Ave., Suite 3400
Chicago, IL 60611-3980
Phone: 312-440-8900
Web: www.adha.org/scholarships-and-grants

Crest Oral-B Dental Hygiene Scholarship

Type of award: Scholarship.
Intended use: For full-time sophomore, junior or senior study at accredited 4-year institution in United States.
Basis for selection: Major/career interest in dental hygiene. Applicant must demonstrate financial need, high academic achievement and seriousness of purpose.
Application requirements: Recommendations, essay. FAFSA.
Additional information: Applicant must have completed minimum one year dental hygiene curriculum; may apply during first year. Minimum 3.5 GPA in dental hygiene. Must demonstrate intent to encourage professional excellence and scholarship, promote quality research, and support dental hygiene through public and private education. Must be member of ADHA or Student ADHA. Download application from Website. All applications must be typed. Applying to more than one scholarship may void application. Amount of award varies.

Amount of award:	$1,000
Number of awards:	2
Application deadline:	February 1
Notification begins:	July 1

Contact:
ADHA Institute for Oral Health
Scholarship Award Program
444 N. Michigan Ave., Suite 3400
Chicago, IL 60611-3980
Phone: 312-440-8900
Web: www.adha.org/scholarships-and-grants

Dr. Esther Wilkins Scholarship

Type of award: Scholarship.
Intended use: For full-time sophomore, junior, senior or post-bachelor's certificate study at accredited 2-year or 4-year institution in United States.
Basis for selection: Major/career interest in dental hygiene. Applicant must demonstrate financial need and high academic achievement.
Application requirements: Essay. FAFSA.

Additional information: Awarded to applicants pursuing additional degree necessary for career in dental hygiene education. Applicants must have completed an entry-level dental hygiene program. Must be active ADHA or Student ADHA member with minimum 3.5 GPA. Download application from Website. All applications must be typed. Applying to more than one scholarship may void application. Amount of award varies.

Amount of award:	$1,000
Number of awards:	1
Application deadline:	February 1
Notification begins:	July 1

Contact:
ADHA Institute for Oral Health
Scholarship Award Program
444 N. Michigan Ave., Ste. 3400
Chicago, IL 60611-3980
Phone: 312-440-8900
Web: www.adha.org/scholarships-and-grants

Hu-Friedy/Esther Wilkins Instrument Scholarships

Type of award: Scholarship.
Intended use: For full-time undergraduate certificate, sophomore, junior or senior study at accredited 2-year or 4-year institution in United States.
Basis for selection: Major/career interest in dental hygiene. Applicant must demonstrate financial need and high academic achievement.
Application requirements: FAFSA.
Additional information: Must have completed one year of dental hygiene curriculum by award year; may apply during first year. Must be active ADHA or Student ADHA member with minimum 3.0 dental hygiene GPA. Download application from Website. Award given as $1,000 worth of Hu-Friedy dental hygiene instruments. All applications must be typed. Applying to more than one scholarship may void application.

Amount of award:	$1,000
Number of awards:	5
Application deadline:	February 1
Notification begins:	July 1

Contact:
ADHA Institute for Oral Health
Scholarship Award Program
444 N. Michigan Ave., Suite 3400
Chicago, IL 60611-3980
Phone: 312-440-8900
Web: www.adha.org/scholarships-and-grants

Karla Girts Memorial Community Outreach Scholarship

Type of award: Scholarship.
Intended use: For full-time undergraduate certificate, sophomore, junior or senior study at accredited 2-year or 4-year institution in United States.
Basis for selection: Major/career interest in dental hygiene. Applicant must demonstrate financial need and high academic achievement.
Application requirements: Recommendations, essay. FAFSA. Additional essay required.
Additional information: Applicants must display a commitment to improving oral health within the geriatric population. Must have completed one year in a dental hygiene curriculum by award year; may apply during first year. Must be active ADHA or Student ADHA member with minimum 3.0

dental hygiene GPA. Download application from Website. All applications must be typed. Applying to more than one scholarship may void application. Amount of award varies.

Amount of award:	$2,000
Number of awards:	2
Application deadline:	February 1
Notification begins:	July 1

Contact:
ADHA Institute for Oral Health
Scholarship Award Program
444 N. Michigan Ave., Suite 3400
Chicago, IL 60611-3980
Phone: 312-440-8900
Web: www.adha.org/scholarships-and-grants

Sigma Phi Alpha Certificate/ Associate Scholarship

Type of award: Scholarship.
Intended use: For full-time sophomore, junior, senior or post-bachelor's certificate study at accredited vocational or 2-year institution in United States.
Basis for selection: Major/career interest in dental hygiene. Applicant must demonstrate high academic achievement.
Additional information: Applicant must have completed minimum one year dental hygiene curriculum; may apply during first year. Minimum 3.5 GPA in dental hygiene. Must be member of ADHA or Student ADHA. Applicant's school must have active chapter of the Sigma Phi Alpha Dental Hygiene Honor Society.

Amount of award:	$1,000
Number of awards:	1
Application deadline:	February 1
Notification begins:	July 1

Contact:
ADHA Institute for Oral Health
Scholarship Award Program
444 N. Michigan Ave., Suite 3400
Chicago, IL 60611
Phone: 312-440-8900
Web: www.adha.org/scholarships-and-grants

Sigma Phi Alpha Undergraduate Scholarship

Type of award: Scholarship.
Intended use: For full-time undergraduate certificate, sophomore, junior or senior study at accredited 2-year or 4-year institution in United States. Designated institutions: Schools with active chapter of Sigma Phi Alpha Dental Hygiene Honor Society.
Basis for selection: Major/career interest in dental hygiene. Applicant must demonstrate financial need and high academic achievement.
Application requirements: Recommendations, essay. FAFSA.
Additional information: Must be current or potential member of Sigma Phi Alpha. Minimum 3.5 GPA in dental hygiene. Must be member of ADHA or Student ADHA. Must have completed at least one year of dental hygiene program. Visit Website for application. All applications must be typed. Applying to more than one scholarship may void application. Amount of award varies.

Amount of award:	$1,000
Number of awards:	1
Application deadline:	February 1
Notification begins:	July 1

Scholarships

Contact:
ADHA Institute for Oral Health
Scholarship Award Program
444 N. Michigan Ave., Suite 3400
Chicago, IL 60611-3980
Phone: 312-440-8900
Web: www.adha.org/scholarships-and-grants

Wilma Motley Memorial California Merit Scholarship

Type of award: Scholarship.
Intended use: For full-time sophomore, junior, senior or graduate study at accredited 2-year, 4-year or graduate institution in United States.
Basis for selection: Major/career interest in dental hygiene. Applicant must demonstrate high academic achievement and leadership.
Application requirements: Recommendations, essay.
Additional information: Awarded to individuals pursuing associate/certificate in dental hygiene, baccalaureate degree, degree completion in dental hygiene, Registered Dental Hygienist in Alternative Practice (RDHAP), master's or doctorate degree in dental hygiene or related field. Applicants must either be a resident of California or attending a dental hygiene program in California. Must have completed one year in a dental hygiene curriculum by award year; may apply during first year. Must be active ADHA or Student ADHA member with minimum 3.5 GPA. Download application from Website. All applications must be typed. Applying to more than one scholarship may void application. Amount of award varies.

Amount of award:	$2,000
Number of awards:	3
Application deadline:	February 1
Notification begins:	July 1

Contact:
ADHA Institute for Oral Health
Scholarship Award Program
444 N. Michigan Ave., Ste. 3400
Chicago, IL 60611-3980
Phone: 312-440-8900
Web: www.adha.org/scholarships-and-grants

AEL and Pepperdine University

AEL Collegiate Essay Contest

Type of award: Scholarship.
Intended use: For full-time undergraduate study at 2-year or 4-year institution in United States.
Eligibility: Applicant must be U.S. citizen.
Application requirements: Essay. Essay must be between 1,500 and 2,000 words in length, typed and double-spaced. After completion, it should be emailed to AEL@pepperdine.edu by the deadline date. In addition, each student must submit a brief biography.
Additional information: Essay prompt and full details can be found on the web site.

Amount of award:	$1,000-$2,500
Number of awards:	3
Application deadline:	June 30
Total amount awarded:	$5,000

Contact:
Pepperdine University
24255 Pacific Coast Highway
Malibu, CA 90263-4786
Phone: 310-506-7273
Web: infoguides.pepperdine.edu/AEL

AFSA Scholarship Programs

Air Force Sergeants Association Scholarship, Airmen Memorial Foundation, and Chief Master Sergeants of the Air Force Scholarship Programs

Type of award: Scholarship.
Intended use: For full-time undergraduate study at accredited postsecondary institution in United States.
Eligibility: Applicant must be single, no older than 23. Applicant must be dependent of active service person or veteran in the Air Force. May be dependent of retired member as well. Dependents of members of the Air National Guard or Air Force Reserve also eligible.
Basis for selection: Applicant must demonstrate high academic achievement, depth of character and leadership.
Application requirements: Recommendations, essay, transcript, proof of eligibility.
Additional information: Applicant must be under 23 years of age as of August 1 of award year. Applications available January 1 to March 31. Amount of award varies. See Website for application and eligibility requirements.

Amount of award:	$1,000-$3,000
Number of awards:	46
Number of applicants:	287
Application deadline:	March 31
Notification begins:	July 1
Total amount awarded:	$74,000

Contact:
AFSA Scholarship Programs
Attn: Brandon Alsobrooks, Scholarship Coord.
5211 Auth Road
Suitland, MD 20746
Phone: 301-899-3500 ext. 230
Web: www.hqafsa.org

After School Athlete

After School Athlete Scholarship

Type of award: Scholarship.
Intended use: For freshman, sophomore or junior study at accredited vocational, 2-year or 4-year institution.
Eligibility: Applicant must be high school senior. Applicant must be U.S. citizen.
Basis for selection: Applicant must demonstrate seriousness of purpose and service orientation.

Number of awards:	1
Application deadline:	May 1
Notification begins:	June 1
Total amount awarded:	$250

Contact:
After School Athlete
16810 104th Avenue
Renton, WA 98055
Web: http://www.afterschoolathlete.com/scholarships/

AfterCollege

AfterCollege Business Student Scholarship

Type of award: Scholarship, renewable.
Intended use: For full-time undergraduate or graduate study at accredited 2-year, 4-year or graduate institution.
Basis for selection: Major/career interest in business; accounting; economics; business/management/administration; human resources; public relations; advertising or finance/banking. Applicant must demonstrate high academic achievement.
Additional information: Minimum 3.0 GPA. Quarterly deadlines: 3/31; 6/30; 9/30; 12/31. Winners notified 30 days after scholarship deadline. AfterCollege profiles are used as criteria to select recipients.

Amount of award:	$500
Number of awards:	4
Number of applicants:	453
Application deadline:	March 31, June 30
Total amount awarded:	$2,000

Contact:
AfterCollege
98 Battery Street
Suite 502
San Francisco, CA 94111
Phone: 415-263-1300
Web: acdc.mx/acschools

AfterCollege Nursing Student Scholarship

Type of award: Scholarship.
Intended use: For undergraduate or graduate study at accredited 2-year, 4-year or graduate institution.
Basis for selection: Major/career interest in nursing.
Application requirements: Transcript. AfterCollege profile, including a brief Personal Statement, and unofficial transcript.
Additional information: Minimum 3.0 GPA required. Quarterly deadlines: 3/31; 6/30; 9/30; 12/31. One scholarship will be awarded each deadline, and students may re-apply. Open to currently enrolled students who are seeking a baccalaureate, master's or doctoral degree in nursing; special consideration will be given to students in a graduate program with the goal of becoming a nurse educator; students completing an RN-to-BSN or RN-to-MSN program; and those enrolled in an accelerated program.

Amount of award:	$500-$2,000
Number of awards:	4
Application deadline:	March 31, June 30

Contact:
AfterCollege
98 Battery Street
Suite 502
San Francisco, CA 94111
Phone: 415-263-1300
Fax: 415-263-1307
Web: acdc.mx/acschools

AfterCollege Sales & Marketing Student Scholarship

Type of award: Scholarship.
Intended use: For full-time undergraduate or graduate study at accredited 2-year, 4-year or graduate institution.
Basis for selection: Major/career interest in marketing.
Additional information: Minimum 3.0 GPA. Quarterly deadlines: 3/31; 6/30; 9/30; 12/31. Winners notified 30 days after scholarship deadline. AfterCollege profiles are used as criteria to select recipients.

Amount of award:	$500-$2,000
Number of awards:	4
Application deadline:	March 31, June 30

Contact:
AfterCollege
98 Battery Street
Suite 502
San Francisco, CA 94111
Phone: 415-263-1300
Web: acdc.mx/acschools

AfterCollege STEM Inclusion Scholarship

Type of award: Scholarship.
Intended use: For full-time undergraduate or graduate study at accredited 2-year, 4-year or graduate institution.
Basis for selection: Major/career interest in science, general; technology; engineering or mathematics.
Additional information: Minimum 3.0 GPA. Applicant must be from a group underrepresented in their field of study. Underrepresented groups may be defined by: gender, race, ethnic background, disability, sexual orientation, age, socio-economic status, nationality, and other non-visible differences. Quarterly deadlines: 3/31; 6/30; 9/30; 12/31. Winners notified 30 days after scholarship deadline. AfterCollege profiles are used as criteria to select recipients.

Amount of award:	$500-$500
Number of awards:	4
Application deadline:	March 31, June 30
Total amount awarded:	$2,000

Contact:
AfterCollege
98 Battery Street
Suite 502
San Francisco, CA 94111
Phone: 415-263-1300
Web: acdc.mx/acschools

AfterCollege Succurro Scholarship

Type of award: Scholarship.
Intended use: For full-time undergraduate or graduate study at accredited 2-year, 4-year or graduate institution.
Additional information: Minimum 2.5 GPA. Quarterly deadlines: 3/31; 6/30; 9/30; 12/31. Winners notified 30 days

after scholarship deadline. AfterCollege profiles are used as criteria to select recipients.

Amount of award:	$500-$500
Number of awards:	4
Application deadline:	March 31, June 30
Total amount awarded:	$2,000

Contact:
AfterCollege
98 Battery Street
Suite 502
San Francisco, CA 94111
Phone: 415-263-1300
Web: acdc.mx/acschools

AfterCollege/AACN Nursing Student Scholarship

Type of award: Scholarship.

Intended use: For full-time undergraduate or graduate study at accredited 4-year or graduate institution. Designated institutions: AACN member institutions.

Basis for selection: Major/career interest in nursing. Applicant must demonstrate high academic achievement.

Application requirements: Essay.

Additional information: Minimum 3.0 GPA. Quarterly deadlines: 3/31; 6/30; 9/30; 12/31. Winners notified 30 days after scholarship deadline. Special consideration will be given to students in a graduate program with the goal of becoming a nurse educator; students completing an RN-to-BSN or RN-to-MSN program; and those enrolled in an accelerated program.

Amount of award:	$2,500
Number of awards:	4
Application deadline:	March 31, June 30
Total amount awarded:	$10,000

Contact:
AfterCollege
98 Battery Street
Suite 502
San Francisco, CA 94111
Phone: 415-263-1300
Web: acdc.mx/acschools

NSA Electrical Engineering Student Scholarship

Type of award: Scholarship, renewable.

Intended use: For full-time undergraduate or graduate study at accredited 2-year, 4-year or graduate institution.

Eligibility: Applicant must be U.S. citizen.

Basis for selection: Major/career interest in engineering, electrical/electronic. Applicant must demonstrate high academic achievement.

Additional information: Minimum 3.0 GPA. Quarterly deadlines: 3/31; 6/30; 9/30; 12/31. Winners notified 30 days after scholarship deadline. AfterCollege profiles are used as criteria to select recipients.

Amount of award:	$500
Number of awards:	4
Number of applicants:	264
Application deadline:	March 31, June 30
Total amount awarded:	$4,000

Contact:
AfterCollege
98 Battery Street
Suite 502
San Francisco, CA 94111
Phone: 415-263-1300
Web: acdc.mx/acschools

NSA Mathematics & Computer Science Student Scholarship

Type of award: Scholarship.

Intended use: For full-time undergraduate or graduate study at accredited 2-year, 4-year or graduate institution.

Eligibility: Applicant must be U.S. citizen.

Basis for selection: Major/career interest in computer/information sciences or mathematics. Applicant must demonstrate high academic achievement.

Additional information: Computer engineering majors also eligible. Minimum 3.0 GPA. Quarterly deadlines: 3/31; 6/30; 9/30; 12/31. Winners notified 30 days after scholarship deadline. AfterCollege profiles are used as criteria to select recipients.

Amount of award:	$500
Number of awards:	4
Number of applicants:	357
Application deadline:	March 31, June 30
Total amount awarded:	$4,000

Contact:
AfterCollege
98 Battery Street
Suite 502
San Francisco, CA 94111
Phone: 415-263-1300
Web: acdc.mx/acschools

AgeLab

OMEGA: Opportunities for Multigenerational Engagement, Growth, and Action

Type of award: Scholarship.

Intended use: For full-time undergraduate study at 2-year or 4-year institution. Designated institutions: School in Connecticut, Maine, Massachusetts, New Hampshire, Rhode Island, or Vermont.

Eligibility: Applicant must be high school junior or senior. Applicant must be residing in Vermont, Connecticut, New Hampshire, Maine, Massachusetts or Rhode Island.

Application requirements: Recommendations, essay, research proposal. Applicants must be anticipating completion of a high school diploma at the time of application and planning to pursue a degree at an accredited US post-secondary institution. One letter of recommendation attesting to an applicant's contributions to generational engagement and connection must accompany the application, the letter should come from either the student group advisor or from a representative of the organization serving older adults.

Additional information: Notification date is May. One letter of recommendation attesting to an applicant's contributions to generational engagement and connection must accompany the application, the letter should come from either the student group advisor or from a representative of the organization serving older adults. More information about the scholarship is in the website http://agelab.mit.edu/about-omega-scholarships.

Amount of award:	$1,000-$1,000
Number of awards:	3
Number of applicants:	2
Application deadline:	March 31
Total amount awarded:	$6,000

Contact:
AgeLab
77 Massachusetts Avenue
E90-9071F
Cambridge, MA 02139
Phone: 617-253-3506
Web: http://agelab.mit.edu/about-omega-scholarships

AHIMA Foundation

AHIMA Student Merit Scholarships

Type of award: Scholarship.
Intended use: For full-time undergraduate or graduate study at accredited 2-year, 4-year or graduate institution.
Basis for selection: Major/career interest in information systems; health services administration or health-related professions. Applicant must demonstrate high academic achievement, seriousness of purpose and service orientation.
Application requirements: Recommendations, transcript. Enrollment verification form.
Additional information: Applicant must be member of AHIMA and enrolled in an undergraduate CAHIIM-accredited health information administration or health information technology program or a national accredited graduate level program. Minimum 3.5 GPA. Applicants must be actively enrolled in a minimum of six credit hours. Must have completed twenty-four credit hours toward a degree (graduate applicants can include undergraduate credit hours), and have at least six credit hours remaining after award date. Award is $1,000 for associate's degree, $1,500 for bachelor's degrees, $2,000 for master's degrees, and $2,500 for doctoral degrees. Apply online.

Amount of award:	$1,000-$2,500
Number of awards:	58
Number of applicants:	215
Application deadline:	September 30
Notification begins:	November 30
Total amount awarded:	$91,500

Contact:
AHIMA Foundation
233 North Michigan Avenue, 21st Floor
Chicago, IL 60601-5809
Phone: 312-233-1585
Web: www.ahimafoundation.org/Scholarships/
MeritScholarships.aspx

Air Force Aid Society

General Henry H. Arnold Education Grant

Type of award: Scholarship.
Intended use: For full-time undergraduate study at accredited vocational, 2-year or 4-year institution in or outside United States.

Eligibility: Applicant must be spouse of active service person or deceased veteran who serves or served in the Air Force. Applicant may also be dependent child of active, retired or deceased Air Force service member. Veteran status alone not eligible. Sponsoring member must be active duty, retired due to length of service, retired Reserve with 20-plus qualifying years of service, or deceased while on active duty or in retired status. Dependent children of Title 32 AGR performing full-time active duty service are also eligible.
Basis for selection: Applicant must demonstrate financial need and high academic achievement.
Application requirements: Proof of eligibility.
Additional information: Minimum 2.0 GPA. Deadline in March.

Amount of award:	$500-$4,000
Number of awards:	3,000
Number of applicants:	4,000
Notification begins:	June 1
Total amount awarded:	$6,000,000

Contact:
Air Force Aid Society
Education Assistance Department
241 18th Street South, Suite 202
Arlington, VA 22202
Phone: 703-972-2647
Web: www.afas.org

Air Force/ROTC

Air Force/ROTC Four-Year Scholarship (Types 1, 2, and 7)

Type of award: Scholarship.
Intended use: For freshman study at accredited 4-year institution in United States.
Eligibility: Applicant must be at least 17, no older than 27, high school senior. Applicant must be U.S. citizen.
Basis for selection: Applicant must demonstrate high academic achievement and leadership.
Application requirements: Interview, transcript. SAT/ACT Scores, Transcript and Counselor Form, Physical Fitness Test, Activity Sheet, and Interview (if you meet eligibility requirements).
Additional information: Recipients agree to serve four years' active duty. Minimum 3.0 GPA. At least 26 ACT or 1180 SAT excluding writing tests. Opportunities available in any major. Applicants must not be enrolled in college full-time prior to application. Type 1 provides full tuition, most fees, $900 for textbooks, and is awarded mostly to technical fields. Type 2 provides tuition, most fees up to $18,000, $900 for textbooks per year. Type 7 provides tuition and fees up to the equivalent of the in-state rate, $900 for books. Scholarship board decides which type is offered. For all scholarships, amount of stipend is based on student's academic year. Apply online.

Amount of award:	Full tuition
Application deadline:	January 12

Contact:
Air Force/ROTC
High School Scholarship Section
551 E. Maxwell Blvd.
Maxwell AFB, AL 36112-5917
Phone: 866-423-7682
Web: www.afrotc.com

Air Traffic Control Association, Inc.

Air Traffic Control Full-Time Employee Student Scholarship

Type of award: Scholarship.
Intended use: For freshman, sophomore, junior, graduate or non-degree study at accredited postsecondary institution.
Eligibility: Applicant or parent must be employed by Aviation industry. Applicant must be returning adult student.
Basis for selection: Major/career interest in aviation. Applicant must demonstrate financial need.
Application requirements: Recommendations, essay, transcript.
Additional information: Applicant must work full-time in aviation-related field and be enrolled in coursework designed to enhance air traffic control or aviation skills. Must have minimum 30 semester or 45 quarter hours still to be completed before graduation. Award amount determined by ATCA Scholarship Program Board of Directors. Visit Website for application.

   Number of awards: 1
   Application deadline: May 1
Contact:
Air Traffic Control Association, Inc.
Attn: Scholarship Fund
1101 King Street, Suite 300
Alexandria, VA 22314
Phone: 703-299-2430
Fax: 703-299-2437
Web: www.atca.org

Air Traffic Control Non-Employee Student Scholarship

Type of award: Scholarship.
Intended use: For freshman, sophomore, junior or graduate study at accredited 4-year or graduate institution.
Basis for selection: Major/career interest in aviation. Applicant must demonstrate financial need.
Application requirements: Recommendations, essay, transcript.
Additional information: Must have minimum 30 semester hours or 45 quarter hours still to be completed before graduation. Number of awards varies based on funding. Visit Website for application.

   Application deadline: May 1
Contact:
Air Traffic Control Association, Inc.
Attn: Scholarship Fund
1101 King Street, Suite 300
Alexandria, VA 22314
Phone: 703-299-2430
Fax: 703-299-2437
Web: www.atca.org

Buckingham Memorial Scholarship

Type of award: Scholarship, renewable.
Intended use: For freshman, sophomore, junior or graduate study at accredited 4-year or graduate institution in United States.
Eligibility: Applicant or parent must be employed by Aviation industry. Applicant must be U.S. citizen.

Basis for selection: Major/career interest in aviation. Applicant must demonstrate financial need.
Application requirements: Recommendations, essay, transcript.
Additional information: Must be child of a person serving, or having served, as an air traffic control specialist. Must have minimum of 30 semester or 45 quarter hours to be completed before graduation. Number of awards varies based on funding. Visit Website for application.

   Application deadline: May 1
Contact:
Air Traffic Control Association, Inc.
Attn: Scholarship Fund
1101 King Street, Suite 300
Alexandria, VA 22314
Phone: 703-299-2430
Fax: 703-299-2437
Web: www.atca.org

Gabe A. Hartl Scholarship

Type of award: Scholarship.
Intended use: For freshman, sophomore, junior or graduate study at accredited 2-year, 4-year or graduate institution. Designated institutions: FAA-approved institutions.
Basis for selection: Major/career interest in aviation. Applicant must demonstrate financial need.
Application requirements: Recommendations, essay, transcript.
Additional information: Must have minimum of 30 semester or 45 quarter hours to be completed before graduation. Must be enrolled in air traffic control curriculum. Number of awards varies based on funding. Visit Website for application.

   Application deadline: May 1
Contact:
Air Traffic Control Association, Inc.
Attn: Scholarship Fund
1101 King Street, Suite 300
Alexandria, VA 22314
Phone: 703-299-2430
Fax: 703-299-2437
Web: www.atca.org

Aircraft Electronics Association Educational Foundation

David Arver Memorial Scholarship

Type of award: Scholarship, renewable.
Intended use: For full-time undergraduate study at accredited vocational or 2-year institution.
Eligibility: Applicant must be residing in Wisconsin, Michigan, Iowa, South Dakota, Minnesota, Kansas, Indiana, Nebraska, Illinois, North Dakota or Missouri.
Basis for selection: Major/career interest in aviation; aviation repair or electronics. Applicant must demonstrate high academic achievement, depth of character and seriousness of purpose.
Application requirements: Recommendations, essay, transcript, proof of eligibility.

Additional information: Minimum 2.5 GPA. Awards are announced at AEA Annual Convention and Trade Show each spring. Visit Website for more information.

Amount of award:	$1,000
Number of awards:	1
Application deadline:	February 15
Notification begins:	April 1
Total amount awarded:	$1,000

Contact:
Aircraft Electronics Association Educational Foundation
3570 NE Ralph Powell Road
Lee's Summit, MO 64064
Phone: 816-347-8400
Fax: 816-347-8405
Web: www.aea.net/educationalfoundation

Dutch and Ginger Arver Scholarship

Type of award: Scholarship, renewable.
Intended use: For full-time undergraduate study at accredited vocational, 2-year or 4-year institution.
Basis for selection: Major/career interest in aviation; electronics or aviation repair. Applicant must demonstrate high academic achievement, depth of character and seriousness of purpose.
Application requirements: Recommendations, essay, transcript, proof of eligibility.
Additional information: Minimum 2.5 GPA. Awards are announced at AEA Annual Convention and Trade Show each spring. Visit Website for more information.

Amount of award:	$1,000
Number of awards:	1
Application deadline:	February 15
Notification begins:	April 1
Total amount awarded:	$1,000

Contact:
Aircraft Electronics Association Educational Foundation
3570 NE Ralph Powell Road
Lee's Summit, MO 64064
Phone: 816-347-8400
Fax: 816-347-8405
Web: www.aea.net/educationalfoundation

Field Aviation Co. Inc. Scholarship

Type of award: Scholarship, renewable.
Intended use: For full-time undergraduate study at accredited vocational, 2-year or 4-year institution.
Basis for selection: Major/career interest in aviation; aviation repair or electronics. Applicant must demonstrate high academic achievement, depth of character and seriousness of purpose.
Application requirements: Recommendations, essay, transcript, proof of eligibility.
Additional information: Minimum 2.5 GPA. Awards are announced at AEA Annual Convention and Trade Show each spring. Visit Website for more information.

Amount of award:	$1,000
Number of awards:	1
Application deadline:	February 15
Notification begins:	April 1

Contact:
Aircraft Electronics Association Educational Foundation
3570 NE Ralph Powell Road
Lee's Summit, MO 64064
Phone: 816-347-8400
Fax: 816-347-8405
Web: www.aea.net/educationalfoundation

Garmin Scholarship

Type of award: Scholarship, renewable.
Intended use: For full-time undergraduate study at accredited vocational, 2-year or 4-year institution.
Basis for selection: Major/career interest in aviation; aviation repair or electronics. Applicant must demonstrate high academic achievement, depth of character and seriousness of purpose.
Application requirements: Recommendations, essay, transcript, proof of eligibility.
Additional information: Minimum 2.5 GPA. Awards are announced at AEA Annual Convention and Trade Show each spring. For more information, visit Website.

Amount of award:	$2,000
Number of awards:	1
Application deadline:	February 15
Notification begins:	April 1
Total amount awarded:	$2,000

Contact:
Aircraft Electronics Association Educational Foundation
3570 NE Ralph Powell Road
Lee's Summit, MO 64064
Phone: 816-347-8400
Fax: 816-347-8405
Web: www.aea.net/educationalfoundation

Johnny Davis Memorial Scholarship

Type of award: Scholarship, renewable.
Intended use: For full-time undergraduate study at accredited vocational, 2-year or 4-year institution.
Basis for selection: Major/career interest in aviation; aviation repair or electronics. Applicant must demonstrate high academic achievement, depth of character and seriousness of purpose.
Application requirements: Recommendations, essay, transcript, proof of eligibility.
Additional information: Minimum 2.5 GPA. Awards are announced at AEA Annual Convention and Trade Show each spring. Visit Website for additional information.

Amount of award:	$1,000
Number of awards:	1
Application deadline:	February 15
Notification begins:	April 1
Total amount awarded:	$1,000

Contact:
Aircraft Electronics Association Educational Foundation
3570 NE Ralph Powell Road
Lee's Summit, MO 64064
Phone: 816-347-8400
Fax: 816-347-8405
Web: www.aea.net/educationalfoundation

L-3 Avionics Systems Scholarship

Type of award: Scholarship, renewable.
Intended use: For full-time undergraduate study at accredited vocational, 2-year or 4-year institution.

Basis for selection: Major/career interest in aviation; aviation repair or electronics. Applicant must demonstrate high academic achievement, depth of character and seriousness of purpose.

Application requirements: Recommendations, essay, transcript, proof of eligibility.

Additional information: Applicant may be high school senior. Minimum 2.5 GPA. Awards are announced at AEA Annual Convention and Trade Show each spring. Visit Website for more information.

Amount of award:	$2,500
Number of awards:	1
Application deadline:	February 15
Notification begins:	April 1
Total amount awarded:	$2,500

Contact:
Aircraft Electronics Association Educational Foundation
3570 NE Ralph Powell Road
Lee's Summit, MO 64064
Phone: 816-347-8400
Fax: 816-347-8405
Web: www.aea.net/educationalfoundation

Lee Tarbox Memorial Scholarship

Type of award: Scholarship, renewable.

Intended use: For full-time undergraduate study at accredited vocational, 2-year or 4-year institution.

Basis for selection: Major/career interest in aviation; aviation repair or electronics. Applicant must demonstrate high academic achievement, depth of character and seriousness of purpose.

Application requirements: Recommendations, essay, transcript, proof of eligibility.

Additional information: Minimum 2.5 GPA. Awards are announced at AEA Annual Convention and Trade Show each spring. Visit Website for additional information.

Amount of award:	$2,500
Number of awards:	1
Application deadline:	February 15
Notification begins:	April 1
Total amount awarded:	$2,500

Contact:
Aircraft Electronics Association Educational Foundation
3570 NE Ralph Powell Road
Lee's Summit, MO 64064
Phone: 816-347-8400
Fax: 816-347-8405
Web: www.aea.net/educationalfoundation

Lowell Gaylor Memorial Scholarship

Type of award: Scholarship, renewable.

Intended use: For full-time undergraduate study at accredited vocational, 2-year or 4-year institution.

Basis for selection: Major/career interest in aviation; aviation repair or electronics. Applicant must demonstrate high academic achievement, depth of character and seriousness of purpose.

Application requirements: Recommendations, essay, transcript, proof of eligibility.

Additional information: Minimum 2.5 GPA. Awards are announced at AEA Annual Convention and Trade Show each spring. Visit Website for more information.

Amount of award:	$1,000
Number of awards:	1
Application deadline:	April 1
Notification begins:	April 1

Contact:
Aircraft Electronics Association Educational Foundation
3570 NE Ralph Powell Road
Lee's Summit, MO 64064
Phone: 816-347-8400
Fax: 816-347-8405
Web: www.aea.net/educationalfoundation

Mid-Continent Instrument Scholarship

Type of award: Scholarship, renewable.

Intended use: For full-time undergraduate study at accredited vocational, 2-year or 4-year institution.

Basis for selection: Major/career interest in aviation; electronics or aviation repair. Applicant must demonstrate high academic achievement, depth of character and seriousness of purpose.

Application requirements: Recommendations, essay, transcript, proof of eligibility.

Additional information: Minimum 2.5 GPA. Awards are announced at AEA Annual Convention and Trade Show each spring. Visit Website for more information.

Amount of award:	$1,000
Number of awards:	1
Application deadline:	February 15
Notification begins:	April 1
Total amount awarded:	$1,000

Contact:
Aircraft Electronics Association Educational Foundation
3570 NE Ralph Powell Road
Lee's Summit, MO 64064
Phone: 816-347-8400
Fax: 816-347-8405
Web: www.aea.net/educationalfoundation

AJ Madison

AJ Madison $1000 Scholarship

Type of award: Scholarship.

Intended use: For full-time undergraduate or graduate study at accredited 4-year or graduate institution in United States.

Eligibility: Applicant must be at least 18. Applicant must be U.S. citizen, permanent resident or international student.

Application requirements: Must be a legal resident of the United States or hold a valid student visa. Essay Topic: In 300 words or less, how have you demonstrated leadership, both in and out of school and how has this helped better your school or community?

Additional information: Email application must include: Full Name, Address, Phone, School Name, GPA, Date of Birth. More information found on webpage.

Amount of award:	$1,000
Number of awards:	1
Application deadline:	December 1
Notification begins:	December 15
Total amount awarded:	$1,000

Contact:
AJ Madison
3605 13th Avenue
Brooklyn, NY 11218
Web: https://www.ajmadison.com/learn/aj-madison-1000-scholarship/

Alabama Commission on Higher Education

Alabama Education Grant Program

Type of award: Scholarship, renewable.
Intended use: For undergraduate study at 2-year or 4-year institution. Designated institutions: Private institutions: Amridge University, Birmingham-Southern College, Concordia College, Faulkner University, Huntingdon College, Judson College, Miles College, Oakwood University, Samford University, South University, Spring Hill College, Stillman College, United States Sports Academy, University of Mobile.
Eligibility: Applicant must be residing in Alabama.
Application requirements: Proof of eligibility.
Additional information: For use at private institutions. For more information, contact financial aid office of participating colleges.

   Amount of award: $1,200

Contact:
Alabama Commission on Higher Education
Phone: 334-242-1998
Fax: 334-242-0268
Web: www.ache.alabama.gov

Alabama National Guard Educational Assistance Program

Type of award: Scholarship, renewable.
Intended use: For undergraduate or graduate study at postsecondary institution. Designated institutions: Public institutions in Alabama.
Eligibility: Applicant must be U.S. citizen residing in Alabama. Applicant must be in military service in the Reserves/National Guard. Must be active member in good standing with federally recognized unit of Alabama National Guard.
Application requirements: Proof of eligibility.
Additional information: Award to be used for tuition, books, fees, and supplies (minus any federal veterans benefits). Applications available from Alabama National Guard units. Funds are limited; apply early.

   Amount of award: $25-$1,000

Contact:
Alabama Commission on Higher Education
Phone: 334-242-1998
Fax: 334-242-0268
Web: www.ache.alabama.gov

Alabama Student Assistance Program

Type of award: Scholarship, renewable.
Intended use: For full-time undergraduate study. Designated institutions: Eligible Alabama institutions.
Eligibility: Applicant must be residing in Alabama.

Basis for selection: Applicant must demonstrate financial need.
Application requirements: Proof of eligibility. FAFSA.
Additional information: Students urged to apply early. Applications available at college financial aid office.

   Amount of award: $300-$2,500

Contact:
Alabama Commission on Higher Education
Phone: 334-242-1998
Fax: 334-242-0268
Web: www.ache.alabama.gov

Police/Firefighters' Survivors Educational Assistance Program

Type of award: Scholarship, renewable.
Intended use: For undergraduate study at vocational, 2-year or 4-year institution. Designated institutions: Public institutions in Alabama.
Eligibility: Applicant must be residing in Alabama. Applicant's parent must have been killed or disabled in work-related accident as firefighter or police officer.
Application requirements: Proof of eligibility.
Additional information: Grant covers full tuition, mandatory fees, books, and supplies. Also available to eligible spouses.

   Amount of award: Full tuition

Contact:
Alabama Commission on Higher Education
P.O. Box 302000
Montgomery, AL 36130-2000
Phone: 334-242-2273
Fax: 334-242-0268
Web: www.ache.alabama.gov

Alabama Department of Postsecondary Education

Alabama Institutional Scholarship Waivers

Type of award: Scholarship, renewable.
Intended use: For freshman or sophomore study at accredited 2-year institution. Designated institutions: Alabama public 2-year community or technical colleges.
Eligibility: Applicant must be U.S. citizen or permanent resident.
Basis for selection: Applicant must demonstrate high academic achievement.
Additional information: Focus of scholarship is determined by each institution. Application deadlines printed on application forms. Award may be renewed if student demonstrates academic excellence. Contact individual institutions for scholarship/waiver requirements. Number and amount of awards vary. Visit Website for participating institutions.

Contact:
Department of Postsecondary Education
P.O. Box 302130
Montgomery, AL 36130-2130
Phone: 334-293-4557
Fax: 334-293-4559
Web: www.accs.cc

Alabama Junior/Community College Athletic Scholarship

Type of award: Scholarship, renewable.
Intended use: For freshman or sophomore study at 2-year institution. Designated institutions: Alabama public 2-year community colleges.
Eligibility: Applicant must be U.S. citizen or permanent resident.
Basis for selection: Competition/talent/interest in athletics/sports, based on athletic ability determined through tryouts.
Additional information: Renewal dependent on continued athletic participation. Contact individual institutions for specific requirements and amount of awards. Number of awards available varies by sport. Visit Website for participating institutions.
Contact:
Department of Postsecondary Education
P.O. Box 302130
Montgomery, AL 36130-2130
Phone: 334-293-4500
Fax: 334-293-4559
Web: www.accs.cc

Alabama Department of Veterans Affairs

Alabama G.I. Dependents' Scholarship Program

Type of award: Scholarship, renewable.
Intended use: For undergraduate study at postsecondary institution. Designated institutions: Alabama public institutions.
Eligibility: Applicant must be residing in Alabama. Applicant must be dependent of disabled veteran, deceased veteran or POW/MIA; or spouse of disabled veteran, deceased veteran or POW/MIA. Veteran must have served for at least 90 days continuous active federal duty, be rated with at least a 20% service-connected disability and must have resided in the state of Alabama for at least one year prior to enlistment or be rated with a 100% service connected disability and be a permanent resident of the State of Alabama for at least 5 years immediately prior to application for program.
Application requirements: Proof of eligibility.
Additional information: Children of veterans must submit application before their 26th birthday. In certain situations a child or stepchild may be eligible up to the age of 30. Spouses of veterans have no age limit, but must not be remarried. Award for five academic years for children and three academic years for spouses (or part-time equivalent); covers tuition, textbooks, and laboratory fees. No application deadline. There is no restriction on the number of eligible dependents under the veteran.

Amount of award:	Full tuition
Number of applicants:	3,126
Total amount awarded:	$30,094,787

Contact:
Alabama Department of Veterans Affairs
P.O. Box 1509
Montgomery, AL 36102-1509
Phone: 334-242-5077
Fax: 334-353-4078
Web: www.va.alabama.gov/scholarship.htm

Alaska Commission on Postsecondary Education

Alaska Education Grant

Type of award: Scholarship.
Intended use: For undergraduate study at vocational, 2-year or 4-year institution in United States. Designated institutions: Alaska institutions.
Eligibility: Applicant must be U.S. citizen or permanent resident residing in Alaska.
Basis for selection: Applicant must demonstrate financial need.
Application requirements: FAFSA.
Additional information: Applicants must be eligible for federal Title IV aid. To apply, student must complete FAFSA between January 1 and June 30 each year.

Amount of award:	$500-$3,000
Application deadline:	June 30

Contact:
Alaska Commission on Postsecondary Education
P.O. Box 110505
Juneau, AK 99811-0505
Phone: 800-441-2962
Fax: 907-465-5316
Web: acpe.alaska.gov

Alaska Performance Scholarship

Type of award: Scholarship.
Intended use: For undergraduate study at postsecondary institution in United States. Designated institutions: Any participating college or university in Alaska.
Eligibility: Applicant must be high school senior. Applicant must be residing in Alaska.
Basis for selection: Applicant must demonstrate financial need and high academic achievement.
Application requirements: FAFSA.
Additional information: Application is the Free Application for Federal Student Aid (FAFSA). Complete FAFSA as early as possible after January 1 of the year you plan to attend school. Minimum 2.5 GPA. Award amount dependent upon academic performance, ACT and/or SAT scores, and WorkKeys scores. Visit Website for eligibility requirements and additional information,

Amount of award:	$2,378-$4,755
Application deadline:	June 30

Contact:
Alaska Commission on Postsecondary Education
P.O. Box 110505
Juneau, AK 99811-0505
Phone: 800-441-2962
Fax: 907-465-5316
Web: acpe.alaska.gov

Alaska CyberKnife

Medical Exploration Scholarship

Type of award: Scholarship.
Intended use: For undergraduate or graduate study at vocational, 2-year, 4-year or graduate institution.
Eligibility: Applicant must be high school senior.

Application requirements: Essay Prompt: "How will you use your education to create a stronger local economy?"
Additional information: Minimum 3.0 GPA. Application can be found on web site.

Number of awards:	1
Application deadline:	June 15
Total amount awarded:	$2,500

Contact:
Web: http://alaskacyberknife.com/alaska-cyberknife-scholarship/

Alexander Graham Bell Association for the Deaf and Hard of Hearing

AG Bell College Scholarship Awards

Type of award: Scholarship.
Intended use: For full-time undergraduate or graduate study at accredited 4-year or graduate institution in or outside United States.
Eligibility: Applicant must be hearing impaired.
Basis for selection: Applicant must demonstrate high academic achievement.
Application requirements: Recommendations, essay, transcript, proof of eligibility. Unaided audiogram or CI programming report.
Additional information: Applicant must have bilateral hearing loss in the moderate to profound range, diagnosed before the fourth birthday. Must use listening and spoken language as primary form of communication, and be accepted or enrolled in mainstream college/university. Number of awards granted varies. Visit Website for additional eligibility criteria, application, and deadlines.

Amount of award:	$1,000-$10,000
Number of awards:	20
Number of applicants:	124
Total amount awarded:	$100,000

Contact:
AG Bell College Scholarship Program
3417 Volta Place, NW
Washington, DC 20007-2778
Phone: 202-337-5220
Web: www.agbell.org/ScholarshipProgram/

Alexia Foundation

Alexia Foundation Grant and Scholarship

Type of award: Scholarship.
Intended use: For full-time undergraduate or graduate study in or outside United States or Canada.
Basis for selection: Competition/talent/interest in photography.
Application requirements: Essay. 750-word proposal and 25-word summary, resume, portfolio of 10 to 20 photographs.
Additional information: Awards and amounts may vary yearly. Students who have completed more than three internships or who have a year of full-time professional experience are not eligible. Application must be submitted online. Check Website for number of awards available, deadlines, and additional information.

Amount of award:	$1,500-$28,000
Number of awards:	5

Contact:
Mike Davis/The Alexia Competition
Phone: 315-443-7388
Web: www.alexiafoundation.org

AlgaeCal

AlgaeCal Health Scholarship

Type of award: Scholarship, renewable.
Intended use: For full-time undergraduate or graduate study at vocational, 2-year, 4-year or graduate institution.
Eligibility: Applicant must be at least 18, no older than 100.
Application requirements: Essay. Applicants must be currently attending a post-secondary institute in the United States or Canada. Essay:. 750 words describing "If you could, what, if any, changes to programs, policies, and education etc, would you implements for the general health/well being of the average modern person?"
Additional information: Open to students in the United States and Canada. How to submit:. All applications should be sent to scholarships@algaecal.com. We accept only online applications during the initial application phase.

Amount of award:	$1,000-$1,000
Number of awards:	1
Number of applicants:	50
Application deadline:	June 30
Notification begins:	August 31
Total amount awarded:	$1,000

Contact:
AlgaeCal Philip Wong
401-1250 Homer Street
Vancouver, BC, V6B 1C6
Phone: 1-877-916-5901
Fax: 604-899-4572
Web: https://www.algaecal.com/expert-insights/algaecal-scholarships/

Alliance for Young Artists and Writers

Scholastic Art Portfolio Gold Award

Type of award: Scholarship.
Intended use: For undergraduate study at postsecondary institution.
Eligibility: Applicant must be high school senior.
Basis for selection: Competition/talent/interest in visual arts, based on originality, level of technical proficiency, and emergence of personal style or vision. Major/career interest in arts, general.
Application requirements: Portfolio, essay. Signed registration form, artist's statement. Portfolio must contain eight digital works uploaded online.
Additional information: Deadline varies by region. Contact sponsor or visit Website for more information.

Amount of award:	$10,000
Number of applicants:	4,500

Contact:
Alliance for Young Artists & Writers
Scholastic Art & Writing Awards
557 Broadway
New York, NY 10012
Phone: 212-343-7729
Fax: 212-389-3939
Web: www.artandwriting.org

Scholastic Art Portfolio Silver With Distinction Award

Type of award: Scholarship.
Intended use: For undergraduate study at postsecondary institution.
Eligibility: Applicant must be high school senior.
Basis for selection: Competition/talent/interest in visual arts, based on originality, level of technical proficiency, and emergence of personal style or vision. Major/career interest in arts, general.
Application requirements: Portfolio, essay. Signed registration form, artist's statement. Portfolio must contain eight digital works uploaded online.
Additional information: Students nominated for scholarships offered by participating higher education institutions. Deadline varies by region. Contact sponsor or visit Website for more information.

Amount of award:	$1,000
Number of applicants:	4,500

Contact:
Alliance for Young Artists & Writers
Scholastic Art & Writing Awards
557 Broadway
New York, NY 10012
Phone: 212-343-7700
Fax: 212-389-3939
Web: www.artandwriting.org

Scholastic Photography Portfolio Silver Award

Type of award: Scholarship.
Intended use: For undergraduate study at postsecondary institution.
Eligibility: Applicant must be high school senior.
Basis for selection: Competition/talent/interest in writing/journalism, based on originality, level of technical proficiency, and emergence of personal style or vision. Major/career interest in arts, general; journalism; literature; theater arts or English.
Application requirements: Portfolio. Signed registration form. For writing, writer's statement. Portfolio must contain three to eight works. Excerpts from longer works permitted. Entry form must be signed by student's parent and teacher, counselor, or principal.
Additional information: Students nominated for scholarships offered by participating higher education institutions. Deadline varies by region. Application fee varies by location and may be waived. Contact sponsor or visit Website for more information.

Amount of award:	$1,000
Number of applicants:	900

Contact:
Alliance for Young Artists & Writers
Scholastic Art & Writing Awards
557 Broadway
New York, NY 10012
Phone: 212-343-7729
Fax: 212-389-3939
Web: www.artandwriting.org

Scholastic Writing Portfolio Gold Award

Type of award: Scholarship.
Intended use: For undergraduate study at postsecondary institution.
Eligibility: Applicant must be high school senior.
Basis for selection: Competition/talent/interest in writing/journalism, based on originality, level of technical proficiency, and emergence of personal voice or style. Major/career interest in English; journalism; literature or theater arts.
Application requirements: Portfolio. Writer's statement. Portfolio must contain three to eight works in any category demonstrating diversity and talent. Excerpts from longer works permitted. Entry form must be signed by student's parent and teacher, counselor, or principal.
Additional information: Deadline varies by region. Application fee varies by location and may be waived. Contact sponsor or visit Website for more information.

Amount of award:	$10,000
Number of applicants:	900

Contact:
Alliance for Young Artists & Writers
Scholastic Art & Writing Awards
557 Broadway
New York, NY 10012
Phone: 212-343-7700
Fax: 212-389-3939
Web: www.artandwriting.org

AllTheRooms

Room to Travel - Study Abroad Scholarship

Type of award: Scholarship, renewable.
Intended use: For at accredited 2-year or 4-year institution in United States.
Eligibility: Applicant must be U.S. citizen or permanent resident.
Application requirements: Essay. University students enrolled in or enrolling in a study abroad program with their university must submit a 600-800 worded essay on what inspires them to travel and the benefits they stand to gain from their study abroad experience.
Additional information: Scholarship can only be used for abroad study.

Amount of award:	$1,000-$1,000
Number of awards:	1
Application deadline:	August 1
Notification begins:	August 30
Total amount awarded:	$1,000

Contact:
AllTheRooms
712 5th Avenue
New York, NY 10019
Web: http://alltherooms.com/w/room-to-travel-scholarship

Alpha Beta Gamma International Business Honor Society

Alpha Beta Gamma National Scholarship

Type of award: Scholarship.
Intended use: For full-time junior or senior study at accredited 4-year institution. Designated institutions: Participating four-year colleges.
Basis for selection: Major/career interest in business; business, international; business/management/administration; accounting or computer/information sciences. Applicant must demonstrate high academic achievement and leadership.
Application requirements: Recommendations. Copy of ABG diploma.
Additional information: Must be initiated member of Alpha Beta Gamma. Awarded to enrollees of two-year schools who have been accepted at four-year schools to pursue baccalaureate degree in business or related professions. Some colleges have minimum GPA requirement. Amount of award varies by institution.

Amount of award:	$500-$8,100
Number of awards:	300
Number of applicants:	400
Total amount awarded:	$600,000

Contact:
Alpha Beta Gamma Scholarship Committee
75 Grasslands Road
Valhalla, NY 10595
Web: www.abg.org

Alpha Mu Gamma, the National Collegiate Foreign Language Honor Society

Alpha Mu Gamma Scholarships

Type of award: Scholarship.
Intended use: For full-time undergraduate, graduate or postgraduate study at 2-year, 4-year or graduate institution.
Basis for selection: Major/career interest in foreign languages. Applicant must demonstrate high academic achievement and seriousness of purpose.
Application requirements: Recommendations, essay, transcript. Photocopy of applicant's AMG full member certificate.
Additional information: Applicant must be full member of Alpha Mu Gamma. Three $1,000 awards granted for study of any foreign language; one $500 award for study of Esperanto or Spanish; one $500 award for study of any foreign language.

May apply unlimited number of times. National office will not send out applications; forms must be requested from advisor of local AMG chapter.

Amount of award:	$500-$1,000
Number of awards:	4
Number of applicants:	25
Application deadline:	February 1
Notification begins:	April 1
Total amount awarded:	$4,000

Contact:
Advisor of local Alpha Mu Gamma chapter.
Web: www.lacitycollege.edu/academic/honor/amg/homepage.html

ALS Association

The Paula Kovarick Segalman Family Scholarship Fund For ALS

Type of award: Scholarship.
Intended use: For full-time undergraduate study at accredited vocational, 2-year, 4-year or graduate institution in United States.
Eligibility: Applicant must be U.S. citizen residing in Virginia, District of Columbia or Maryland.
Basis for selection: Applicant must demonstrate financial need.
Application requirements: Essay, transcript. Two letters of recommendation (personal and academic).official transcript. A 500-word essay describing how ALS has impacted him/her.
Additional information: Residents of Washington DC, Maryland, or Virginia. Applicant must have an annual household income of less than $50,000. Applicant must have a parent or legal guardian currently battling ALS or who has passed away from the disease. All scholarship info on eligibility, requirements, and application process included in ALS website.

Amount of award:	$25,000
Number of awards:	1
Application deadline:	May 1
Notification begins:	August 1
Total amount awarded:	$25,000

Contact:
ALS Association
7507 Standish Place
Rockville, MD 20855
Phone: 240-238-9057
Fax: 301-978-9854
Web: http://webdc.alsa.org/site/PageNavigator/DC_Chapter/DC_6_Paula_Segalman_Scholarship.html

Alumnae Panhellenic Association of Washington, D.C.

Alumnae Panhellenic Association Women's Scholarship

Type of award: Scholarship, renewable.
Intended use: For sophomore, junior, senior or graduate study at 4-year or graduate institution.

Scholarships

Eligibility: Applicant must be female.

Basis for selection: Based on sorority involvement. Applicant must demonstrate high academic achievement and service orientation.

Application requirements: Recommendations, essay, transcript.

Additional information: Applicant must be member in good standing of sorority of National Panhellenic Conference and live or attend school in Washington, D.C., metro area. Send email for application request. Deadline in February or March. Amount and number of awards varies.

Number of awards:	3
Number of applicants:	20
Total amount awarded:	$2,550

Contact:
Alumnae Panhellenic Association of Washington, DC
Candice Marshall, Vice President
19621 Galway Circle #301
Germantown, MD 20874
Web: www.dcalumnaepanhellenic.shutterfly.com

Alzheimer's Foundation of America

AFA Teens for Alzheimer's Awareness College Scholarship

Type of award: Scholarship.

Intended use: For freshman study at accredited 4-year institution.

Eligibility: Applicant must be high school senior. Applicant must be U.S. citizen or permanent resident.

Application requirements: Essay, proof of eligibility. 200-word or less autobiography. Two copies of 1,200 to 1,500 word essay based on topic on Website. Entire submission fastened with paper clip.

Additional information: Must be current high school junior or senior planning to enter college. First place: $5,000; second place: $2500; third place: $1000; honorable mention: $500. Winners must agree to have name and city published, have essay published on AFA Teens Website, provide AFA with photo for publicity purposes, and be available for interviews with media. Proof of college registration and U.S. citizenship required upon selection.

Amount of award:	$500-$5,000
Number of awards:	15
Number of applicants:	10
Application deadline:	February 15
Notification begins:	April 15
Total amount awarded:	$15,000

Contact:
Alzheimer's Foundation of America
Attn: AFA Teens College Scholarship
322 Eighth Avenue, 7th Floor
New York, NY 10001
Phone: 866-232-8484
Web: www.afateens.org

Ambrosia Treatment Center

We Do Recover

Type of award: Scholarship.

Intended use: For full-time undergraduate or graduate study at 2-year, 4-year or graduate institution.

Eligibility: Applicant must be at least 18.

Application requirements: Essay. Share a positive story of your or a loved one's recovery from drug addiction or alcoholism. Winner will be selected based on the most shares on Facebook or Linkedin. Submit a 1,000 written story, a 1-2.5 minute video, and 2+ images of yourself.

Amount of award:	$500
Number of awards:	3
Application deadline:	July 31
Total amount awarded:	$1,500

Contact:
Ambrosia Treatment Center
5220 Hood Road
Palm Beach Gardens, FL 33418
Phone: 561-578-9964
Web: https://www.ambrosiatc.com/we-do-recover/?ambTRK=PR

AMBUCS

AMBUCS Scholars-Scholarship for Therapists

Type of award: Scholarship.

Intended use: For full-time junior, senior or master's study at accredited 4-year or graduate institution in United States. Designated institutions: Schools with programs accredited by appropriate health therapy association.

Eligibility: Applicant must be U.S. citizen.

Basis for selection: Major/career interest in occupational therapy; physical therapy or speech pathology/audiology. Applicant must demonstrate financial need, depth of character and service orientation.

Additional information: Award amount typically maximum $1,500, but one additional two-year award of $6,000 offered. Students must apply online; no paper applications accepted. Applicants may print online enrollment certificate. Additional documentation, including prior year's 1040 tax form, requested if applicant is selected as semifinalist.

Amount of award:	$500-$6,000
Number of applicants:	1,267
Application deadline:	April 15
Notification begins:	June 20
Total amount awarded:	$150,000

Contact:
AMBUCS Resource Center
P.O. Box 5127
High Point, NC 27262
Phone: 336-852-0052
Fax: 336-852-6830
Web: www.ambucs.org

American Alpine Club

Arthur K. Gilkey Memorial/Bedayn Research Grants

Type of award: Research grant.
Intended use: For undergraduate or graduate study.
Basis for selection: Major/career interest in science, general; biology; environmental science; forestry or atmospheric sciences/meteorology.
Application requirements: Research proposal. Curriculum vitae with biographical information.
Additional information: Research proposals evaluated on scientific or technical quality and contribution to scientific endeavor germane to mountain regions. Research focus may vary yearly; contact organization before applying. Applications available from Website; must be submitted via email. Number of awards varies.

Amount of award:	$250-$1,000
Number of applicants:	25
Application deadline:	January 15
Notification begins:	March 15
Total amount awarded:	$8,880

Contact:
American Alpine Club
710 Tenth Street
Suite 100
Golden, CO 80401
Phone: 303-384-0110
Fax: 303-384-0111
Web: www.americanalpineclub.org/grants

American Association for Cancer Research

Gary J. Miller Undergraduate Prizes for Cancer and Cancer-Related Biomedical Research

Type of award: Scholarship.
Intended use: For full-time undergraduate study at 4-year institution.
Basis for selection: Competition/talent/interest in science project. Major/career interest in biochemistry; biology; chemistry; pharmacy/pharmaceutics/pharmacology; microbiology; engineering, chemical; epidemiology; oncology or science, general.
Additional information: Applicants compete in the annual Undergraduate Student Caucus and Poster Competition, where applicants exhibit a scientific poster concerning cancer or cancer-related biomedical research. First prize receives $1,500 in funding to support cost of participation in the next AACR Annual Meeting. Second place receives $300; third place receives $200. All applicants receive complimentary registration to the AACR Annual Meeting, where the competition takes place. Application deadline and Abstract submission deadlines in March. Visit Website for dates and details.

Amount of award:	$200-$1,500
Number of awards:	5
Number of applicants:	85

Contact:
American Association for Cancer Research
615 Chestnut Street, 17th Floor
Philadelphia, PA 19106-4404
Phone: 215-440-9300
Fax: 215-440-9412
Web: www.aacr.org/USCPC

Thomas J. Bardos Science Education Awards for Undergraduate Students

Type of award: Research grant.
Intended use: For full-time junior study at 4-year institution.
Basis for selection: Major/career interest in biochemistry; biology; chemistry; pharmacy/pharmaceutics/pharmacology; microbiology; science, general; epidemiology or oncology. Applicant must demonstrate high academic achievement.
Application requirements: Recommendations, essay.
Additional information: Two-year award consists of $1,500 per year for travel expenses and registration fee waiver for AACR annual meeting. Selection based on qualifications and interest in research, mentor references, and selection committee's evaluation of potential professional benefit. Applicants not yet committed to cancer research welcome; those studying molecular biology and genetics or pathology also eligible. Awardees must attend scientific sessions at AACR meeting for at least four days and participate in required activities. Must submit two comprehensive reports each year. Contact AACR or visit Website for more information and deadline.

Amount of award:	$3,000
Number of awards:	10
Number of applicants:	75

Contact:
American Association for Cancer Research
615 Chestnut Street, 17th Floor
Philadelphia, PA 19106-4404
Phone: 215-440-9300
Fax: 215-440-9412
Web: www.aacr.org/Bardos

American Association for Geodetic Surveying

AAGS Joseph F. Dracup Scholarship Award

Type of award: Scholarship, renewable.
Intended use: For undergraduate study at 4-year institution.
Basis for selection: Major/career interest in surveying/mapping. Applicant must demonstrate high academic achievement and seriousness of purpose.
Application requirements: Recommendations, essay, transcript, proof of eligibility.
Additional information: Applicant must be member of AAGS. Preference will be given to applicants with significant focus on geodetic surveying. Students may also be enrolled in degree program related to surveying, such as geomatics or survey engineering. Visit Website for deadlines and additional information.

Amount of award:	$2,000
Number of awards:	1
Total amount awarded:	$2,000

Contact:
NSPS and AAGS Scholarships
5119 Pegasus Court
Suite Q
Frederick, MD 21704
Phone: 240-439-4615
Fax: 240-439-4952
Web: www.nsps.us.com

American Association of Geographers

Anne U. White Fund

Type of award: Research grant, renewable.
Intended use: For non-degree study.
Basis for selection: Major/career interest in geography.
Application requirements: Research proposal.
Additional information: Fund enables Association of American Geographers member to engage in useful field study jointly with his/her partner. Must have been member for at least two years at time of application. Report summarizing results and documenting expenses underwritten by grant must be submitted within 12 months of receiving award.

Amount of award:	$1,500
Number of awards:	2
Application deadline:	December 31
Notification begins:	March 1

Contact:
American Association of Geographers
1710 16th Street, NW
Washington, DC 20009-3198
Phone: 202-234-1450
Fax: 202-234-2744
Web: www.aag.org/grantsawards

Darrel Hess Community College Geography Scholarship

Type of award: Scholarship, renewable.
Intended use: For freshman or sophomore study at 2-year institution in United States.
Basis for selection: Major/career interest in geography. Applicant must demonstrate financial need and high academic achievement.
Application requirements: Recommendations, essay, transcript.
Additional information: Applicants eligible if currently enrolled in a U.S. community college, junior college, city college, or similar two-year educational institution at the time of submission of application. Applicant must have completed at least two transfer courses in geography and plan to transfer to a four-year institution as a geography major during the coming academic year. AAG membership strongly encouraged, but not required.

Amount of award:	$1,000
Number of awards:	4
Application deadline:	December 31

Contact:
American Association of Geographers
1710 16th Street, NW
Washington, DC 20009-3198
Phone: 202-234-1450
Fax: 202-234-2744
Web: www.aag.org/grantsawards

Marble-Boyle Award

Type of award: Scholarship, renewable.
Intended use: For full-time senior study at accredited postsecondary institution in United States or Canada.
Basis for selection: Major/career interest in computer/information sciences or geography.
Application requirements: Recommendations, essay, transcript. Cover letter.
Additional information: Applicant must demonstrate reasonable intent to embark upon a career or further education that will make use of joint geographic science and computer science knowledge. AAG membership strongly encouraged, but not required. Award consists of $1000 cash prize and $200 credit for books published by the ESRI Press. ESRI will provide priority consideration to awardees interested in participating in ESRI Summer Intern Program. Awardees also eligible to compete for an additional research fellowship award offered biannually by MicroGIS Foundation for Spatial Analysis (MFSA).

Amount of award:	$1,000
Number of awards:	3
Application deadline:	October 15

Contact:
American Association of Geographers
1710 16th Street, NW
Washington, DC 20009-3198
Phone: 202-234-1450
Fax: 202-234-2744
Web: www.aag.org/grantsawards

American Association of University Women San Jose

San Jose Local Scholarships for Women

Type of award: Scholarship, renewable.
Intended use: For junior or senior study at accredited 4-year institution in United States.
Eligibility: Applicant must be female. Applicant must be U.S. citizen or permanent resident residing in California.
Basis for selection: Applicant must demonstrate high academic achievement.
Additional information: Minimum 3.0 GPA. Must have a permanent home address in Campbell, Milpitas, San Jose, or Santa Clara, California. Number and amount of scholarships awarded depends upon funds available. Eligibility includes completion of two full years at an accredited college or university. Application available on Website March 1st. Deadline in early April. Visit Website for specific dates.

Amount of award:	$1,000-$2,500
Number of awards:	12
Number of applicants:	20
Application deadline:	April 15
Notification begins:	March 1
Total amount awarded:	$18,000

Contact:
American Association of University Women San Jose
Grace O'Leary
1128 Sterling Gate Drive
San Jose, CA 95120-4246
Phone: 408-294-2430
Web: www.aauwsanjose.org

American Board of Funeral Service Education

American Board of Funeral Service Education National Scholarship

Type of award: Scholarship.
Intended use: For full-time undergraduate study at 2-year or 4-year institution in United States.
Eligibility: Applicant must be U.S. citizen or permanent resident.
Basis for selection: Major/career interest in mortuary science. Applicant must demonstrate financial need, high academic achievement, depth of character, leadership and seriousness of purpose.
Application requirements: Recommendations, essay.
Additional information: Student must have completed at least one semester (or quarter) of study in funeral service or mortuary science at an education program accredited by American Board of Funeral Service Education. Visit Website for more information and application. Extracurricular activities are considered for eligibility. Number of awards varies.

Amount of award:	$250-$1,000
Number of applicants:	200
Application deadline:	March 1, September 1
Notification begins:	May 1, November 1
Total amount awarded:	$25,000

Contact:
American Board of Funeral Service Education
Attn: Scholarship Committee
3414 Ashland, Suite G
St. Joseph, MO 64506
Phone: 816-233-3747
Fax: 816-233-3793
Web: www.abfse.org

American Center of Oriental Research

Jennifer C. Groot Fellowship

Type of award: Research grant.
Intended use: For undergraduate or graduate study.
Eligibility: Applicant must be U.S. citizen or Canadian citizen.

Basis for selection: Major/career interest in archaeology; Middle Eastern studies; ancient Near Eastern studies or ethnic/cultural studies.
Application requirements: Proof of acceptance on archaeological fieldwork in Jordan.
Additional information: Applicant must be accepted as staff member on archaeological project in Jordan with ASOR/CAP affiliation. Award used only for travel to project site in Jordan.

Amount of award:	$1,500
Number of awards:	3
Number of applicants:	15
Application deadline:	February 1
Notification begins:	April 15
Total amount awarded:	$3,600

Contact:
American Center of Oriental Research
Fellowship Committee
656 Beacon Street
Boston, MA 02215-2010
Phone: 617-353-6571
Fax: 617-353-6575
Web: www.bu.edu/acor

American Chemical Society

American Chemical Society Scholars Program

Type of award: Scholarship, renewable.
Intended use: For full-time at accredited 2-year or 4-year institution in United States.
Eligibility: Applicant must be African American, Mexican American, Hispanic American, Puerto Rican or American Indian. Applicant must be U.S. citizen or permanent resident.
Basis for selection: Major/career interest in chemistry; biochemistry; engineering, chemical; materials science; environmental science; forensics or food science/technology. Applicant must demonstrate financial need, high academic achievement, leadership, seriousness of purpose and service orientation.
Application requirements: Recommendations, transcript. SAR. ACT/SAT scores (for high school applicants).
Additional information: Other chemically-related majors also eligible. Minimum 3.0 GPA. Must be planning career in chemical sciences (pre-med, pharmacy, nursing, dentistry, veterinary medicine programs not eligible). African American, Hispanic, or American Indian students who are high school seniors, college freshman, college sophomores, or college juniors are eligible.

Amount of award:	$1,000-$5,000
Number of awards:	120
Number of applicants:	400
Application deadline:	March 1
Notification begins:	November 1
Total amount awarded:	$1,000,000

Contact:
ACS Scholars Program
1155 16th Street, NW
Washington, DC 20036
Phone: 800-227-5558 ext. 6250
Fax: 202-872-4361
Web: www.acs.org/scholars

American Classical League

Arthur Patch McKinlay Scholarship

Type of award: Scholarship.
Intended use: For non-degree study.
Basis for selection: Major/career interest in classics or education. Applicant must demonstrate financial need.
Application requirements: Recommendations. Study program proposal, including budget.
Additional information: Must be current member of American Classical League and for three years preceding application. Must be planning to teach classics in elementary or secondary school in upcoming school year. May apply for independent study program funding or support to attend American Classical League Institute for first time. Number of awards varies year to year.

Amount of award:	$1,500
Number of applicants:	14
Application deadline:	January 15

Contact:
American Classical League Scholarship Awards
Miami University
422 Wells Mill Drive
Oxford, OH 45056
Phone: 513-529-7741
Fax: 513-529-7742
Web: www.aclclassics.org

Maureen V. O'Donnell/Eunice C. Kraft Teacher Training Scholarships

Type of award: Scholarship.
Intended use: For junior, senior or graduate study at 4-year or graduate institution.
Basis for selection: Major/career interest in education or classics.
Application requirements: Recommendations.
Additional information: Must be member of ACL. Must be training for certification to teach Latin and have completed a substantial number of these courses. Must wait at least three years before reapplying. Number of awards varies.

Amount of award:	$1,000
Number of applicants:	14
Application deadline:	January 15

Contact:
The American Classical League
Miami University
422 Wells Mill Drive
Oxford, OH 45056
Phone: 513-529-7741
Fax: 513-529-7742
Web: www.aclclassics.org

American College of Musicians

National Guild of Piano Teachers $200 Scholarship

Type of award: Scholarship.
Intended use: For undergraduate, graduate or non-degree study.
Basis for selection: Major/career interest in music.
Application requirements: Nomination by piano teacher, who must be member of National Guild of Piano Teachers. Copies of ten inner report cards and stubs.
Additional information: Award to be used for piano study. Student must have been national winner for ten years, Paderewski Medal winner, and Guild High School Diploma recipient.

Amount of award:	$200
Number of awards:	150
Application deadline:	September 15
Notification begins:	October 1

Contact:
American College of Musicians
Scholarship Committee
P.O. Box 1807
Austin, TX 78767-1807
Phone: 512-478-5775
Web: www.pianoguild.com

National Guild of Piano Teachers Composition Contest

Type of award: Scholarship.
Intended use: For undergraduate, graduate or non-degree study.
Basis for selection: Competition/talent/interest in music performance/composition, based on composition for solo keyboard and keyboard ensemble.
Application requirements: Manuscript of composition.
Additional information: Teacher must be member of National Guild of Piano Teachers. Compositions rated on imagination, originality, and skill. Entry fees vary according to classification of student and length of composition. See Website for specific details.

Application deadline:	November 8

Contact:
American College of Musicians
P.O. Box 1807
Austin, TX 78767-1807
Phone: 512-478-5775
Web: www.pianoguild.com

American Council of Engineering Companies

ACEC Scholarship

Type of award: Scholarship, renewable.
Intended use: For junior, senior, master's or doctoral study at 4-year or graduate institution. Designated institutions: ABET-accredited engineering programs.
Eligibility: Applicant must be U.S. citizen.
Basis for selection: Major/career interest in engineering. Applicant must demonstrate high academic achievement and seriousness of purpose.
Application requirements: Recommendations, essay, transcript.
Additional information: Applicants may also be seeking a degree from an accredited land-surveying program. Submit application through respective state member organization. Deadline date, number and amount of awards varies. Visit Website for deadlines and more information.

Number of applicants:	19
Application deadline:	March 6

Contact:
American Council of Engineering Companies
1015 15th Street, NW
8th Floor
Washington, DC 20005-2605
Phone: 202-347-7474
Fax: 202-898-0068
Web: www.acec.org/getinvolved/scholarships.cfm

American Council of the Blind

Floyd Qualls Memorial Scholarship

Type of award: Scholarship, renewable.
Intended use: For full-time undergraduate or graduate study at accredited postsecondary institution in United States.
Eligibility: Applicant must be visually impaired.
Basis for selection: Applicant must demonstrate high academic achievement, depth of character and leadership.
Application requirements: Interview, recommendations, essay, transcript, proof of eligibility.
Additional information: Applicant must be legally blind in both eyes. One award each for an entering freshman, other undergraduate, graduate, and vocational student, plus one discretionary award. Number of awards may vary.

Amount of award:	$3,500
Number of awards:	5
Number of applicants:	200
Application deadline:	March 1
Notification begins:	May 15
Total amount awarded:	$28,250

Contact:
American Council of the Blind
6300 Shingle Creek Parkway
Suite 195
Brooklyn Center, MN 55430
Phone: 612-332-3242
Fax: 763-432-7562
Web: www.acb.org

American Dental Assistants Association

Juliette A. Southard/Oral-B Laboratories Scholarship

Type of award: Scholarship.
Intended use: For undergraduate study.
Basis for selection: Major/career interest in dental assistant. Applicant must demonstrate high academic achievement.
Application requirements: Recommendations, essay, transcript, proof of eligibility.
Additional information: Scholarships open to high school graduates and GED certificate holders. Must be ADAA member. Applicants must be enrolled in dental assisting program or be taking courses applicable to furthering career in dental assisting. Visit Website for application. All forms must be submitted via email.

Amount of award:	$750
Number of awards:	10
Number of applicants:	30
Application deadline:	March 15
Total amount awarded:	$7,500

Contact:
American Dental Assistants Association
35 East Wacker Drive
Suite 1730
Chicago, IL 60601-2211
Phone: 312-541-1550
Fax: 312-541-1496
Web: www.dentalassistant.org

American Federation of State, County and Municipal Employees

AFSCME Family Scholarship

Type of award: Scholarship, renewable.
Intended use: For full-time undergraduate study at accredited 2-year or 4-year institution.
Eligibility: Applicant must be high school senior.
Application requirements: Recommendations, essay, transcript, proof of eligibility. SAT or ACT scores.
Additional information: Scholarships open to children and financially dependent grandchildren of active or retired full dues-paying AFSCME members. Students at two-year institutions must intend to transfer to four-year institution.

Amount of award:	$2,000
Number of awards:	10
Number of applicants:	650
Application deadline:	December 31
Notification begins:	March 31
Total amount awarded:	$20,000

Contact:
AFSCME Family Scholarship Program
Attn: AFSCME Advantage
1625 L Street, NW
Washington, DC 20036-5687
Phone: 202-429-5066
Web: www.afscme.org/family

Jerry Clark Memorial Scholarship

Type of award: Scholarship, renewable.
Intended use: For full-time junior study at accredited 4-year institution.
Basis for selection: Major/career interest in political science/government; sociology; communications or ethnic/cultural studies. Applicant must demonstrate high academic achievement.
Application requirements: Transcript, proof of eligibility.
Additional information: Scholarships open to children and financially dependent grandchildren of AFSCME members. Applicant must be a current college sophomore. Winners given opportunity to intern at International Union headquarters in Political Action department. Minimum 2.5 GPA.

Amount of award: $5,000
Number of awards: 2
Number of applicants: 30
Application deadline: April 30
Notification begins: August 1
Total amount awarded: $10,000
Contact:
Jerry Clark Memorial Scholarship Program
AFSCME, Attn: Political Action Department
1625 L Street, NW
Washington, DC 20036-5687
Phone: 202-429-1250
Web: www.afscme.org

American Fire Sprinkler Association

AFSA $20,000 High School Scholarship Contest

Type of award: Scholarship.
Intended use: For freshman study at accredited vocational, 2-year or 4-year institution in United States.
Eligibility: Applicant must be high school senior. Applicant must be U.S. citizen or permanent resident.
Basis for selection: For each question answered correctly, applicant receives one entry into drawing for $2,000 scholarship.
Application requirements: Applicant is to read essay on Website, fill out registration information, and take ten-question multiple choice open book test.
Additional information: Scholarship payable to winner's college, university, or certified trade school. Relatives of AFSA staff or board members not eligible. No phone calls or emails. Visit Website for more information and to enter.

Amount of award: $2,000
Number of awards: 10
Number of applicants: 60,000
Application deadline: April 7
Notification begins: April 16
Total amount awarded: $20,000
Contact:
American Fire Sprinkler Association
Web: www.afsascholarship.org

AFSA $5,000 Second Chance Scholarship Contest

Type of award: Scholarship.
Intended use: For undergraduate or graduate study at accredited vocational, 2-year, 4-year or graduate institution in United States.
Eligibility: Applicant must be high school senior. Applicant must be U.S. citizen or permanent resident.
Basis for selection: For each question answered correctly, applicant gets one entry into drawing for one of five $1,000 scholarships.
Application requirements: Applicant must read essay on Website, complete registration page, and take ten-question open book multiple choice test.
Additional information: Must have high school diploma, GED, or equivalent. Relatives of AFSA staff or board members not eligible. No phone calls or emails. Entries will be accepted

until 12:00 pm CDT August 26. Visit Website for more information and to enter.

Amount of award: $1,000
Number of awards: 5
Number of applicants: 35,000
Application deadline: August 30
Total amount awarded: $5,000
Contact:
American Fire Sprinkler Association
Web: www.afsascholarship.org

American Floral Endowment

American Florists' Exchange Scholarship

Type of award: Scholarship, renewable.
Intended use: For junior or senior study at 4-year institution.
Eligibility: Applicant must be U.S. citizen or permanent resident.
Basis for selection: Major/career interest in agriculture. Applicant must demonstrate high academic achievement.
Application requirements: Recommendations, transcript.
Additional information: Minimum 3.0 GPA. Must be resident or attending college in California and majoring in agriculture with an emphasis on a future in floriculture.

Amount of award: $1,500-$2,000
Number of awards: 1
Number of applicants: 1
Application deadline: May 1
Total amount awarded: $2,000
Contact:
American Floral Endowment
1001 North Fairfax St
Suite 201
Alexandria, VA 22314
Phone: 703-838-5211
Fax: 703-838-5212
Web: www.endowment.org

Ball Horticultural Company Scholarship

Type of award: Scholarship.
Intended use: For junior or senior study at accredited 4-year institution in United States.
Eligibility: Applicant must be U.S. citizen or permanent resident.
Basis for selection: Major/career interest in horticulture. Applicant must demonstrate high academic achievement.
Application requirements: Recommendations, transcript.
Additional information: Intended for students pursuing career in commercial floriculture. Submit transcript and letters of recommendation via e-mail. Submit applications on the Website.

Amount of award: $500-$800
Number of awards: 1
Number of applicants: 1
Application deadline: May 1
Notification begins: January 1
Total amount awarded: $800

Contact:
American Floral Endowment
Attn: AFE Scholarship Applications
1601 Duke Street
Alexandria, VA 22314
Phone: 703-838-5211
Fax: 703-838-5212
Web: http://endowment.org/scholarships/

Bioworks/IPM Sustainable Practices Scholarship

Type of award: Scholarship, renewable.
Intended use: For sophomore, junior or senior study at 2-year or 4-year institution.
Eligibility: Applicant must be U.S. citizen or permanent resident.
Basis for selection: Applicant must demonstrate high academic achievement.
Application requirements: Recommendations, transcript.
Additional information: Applicant should major or show a career interest in floriculture, specifically in furthering the use of Integrated Pest Management (IPM) or sustainable practices. Minimum 3.0 GPA. Email is preferred method for submitting transcript and letters of recommendation. Submit applications via the Website.

Amount of award:	$1,000-$1,200
Number of awards:	1
Number of applicants:	1
Application deadline:	May 1
Notification begins:	January 1
Total amount awarded:	$1,100

Contact:
American Floral Endowment
1601 Duke Street
Alexandria, VA 22314
Phone: 703-838-5211
Fax: 703-838-5212
Web: www.endowment.org

Bud Olman Memorial Scholarship

Type of award: Scholarship, renewable.
Intended use: For sophomore, junior or senior study at accredited postsecondary institution in United States.
Eligibility: Applicant must be U.S. citizen or permanent resident.
Basis for selection: Major/career interest in horticulture. Applicant must demonstrate high academic achievement.
Application requirements: Recommendations, transcript.
Additional information: For students pursuing a career in growing bedding plants. Minimum 3.0 GPA. Email is preferred method for submitting transcript and letters of recommendation. Submit applications via the Website.

Amount of award:	$500
Number of awards:	1
Number of applicants:	1
Application deadline:	May 1
Notification begins:	January 1
Total amount awarded:	$500

Contact:
American Floral Endowment
1601 Duke Street
Alexandria, VA 22314
Phone: 703-838-5211
Fax: 703-838-5212
Web: www.endowment.org

Earl Dedman Memorial Scholarship

Type of award: Scholarship.
Intended use: For full-time sophomore, junior or senior study at accredited 4-year institution in United States.
Eligibility: Applicant must be U.S. citizen or permanent resident residing in Wyoming, Oregon, Montana, Idaho or Washington.
Basis for selection: Major/career interest in horticulture. Applicant must demonstrate high academic achievement.
Application requirements: Recommendations, transcript.
Additional information: Minimum 3.0 GPA. Career interest in becoming a greenhouse grower required. To apply for this scholarship, applicant must have interest in greenhouse production and potted plants. Applicant must be from the Northwestern area of the U.S. Number and amount of scholarships vary. Submit applications via the Website.

Amount of award:	$1,500-$2,000
Number of awards:	1
Number of applicants:	1
Application deadline:	May 1
Notification begins:	January 1
Total amount awarded:	$1,800

Contact:
American Floral Endowment
1601 Duke Street
Alexandria, VA 22314
Phone: 703-838-5211
Fax: 703-838-5212
Web: http://endowment.org/scholarships/

Harold Bettinger Memorial Scholarship

Type of award: Scholarship.
Intended use: For full-time sophomore, junior or senior study at accredited 4-year institution in United States.
Eligibility: Applicant must be U.S. citizen or permanent resident.
Basis for selection: Major/career interest in horticulture; business or marketing. Applicant must demonstrate financial need and high academic achievement.
Application requirements: Recommendations, transcript.
Additional information: Minimum 3.0 GPA. To apply for this scholarship, applicant's major or minor must be in business and/or marketing with intent to apply it to a horticulture-related business. Amount of award varies. Submit applications via the Website.

Amount of award:	$1,500-$2,000
Number of awards:	1
Number of applicants:	1
Application deadline:	May 1
Notification begins:	January 1
Total amount awarded:	$1,800

Contact:
American Floral Endowment
1601 Duke Street
Alexandria, VA 22314
Phone: 703-838-5211
Fax: 703-838-5212
Web: www.endowment.org

Jacob Van Namen Marketing Scholarship

Type of award: Scholarship.
Intended use: For sophomore, junior or senior study at accredited 2-year or 4-year institution in United States.
Eligibility: Applicant must be U.S. citizen or permanent resident.
Basis for selection: Major/career interest in marketing or agribusiness. Applicant must demonstrate financial need and high academic achievement.
Application requirements: Recommendations, transcript.
Additional information: Minimum 3.0 GPA. Applicant must have interest in agribusiness marketing and distribution of floral products. Number and amount of awards vary.

Amount of award:	$800-$1,200
Number of awards:	1
Number of applicants:	1
Application deadline:	May 1
Notification begins:	January 1
Total amount awarded:	$1,000

Contact:
American Floral Endowment
1601 Duke Street
Alexandria, VA 22314
Phone: 703-838-5211
Fax: 703-838-5212
Web: www.endowment.org

James Bridenbaugh Memorial Scholarship

Type of award: Scholarship.
Intended use: For sophomore, junior or senior study at accredited postsecondary institution.
Eligibility: Applicant must be U.S. citizen or permanent resident.
Basis for selection: Major/career interest in horticulture. Applicant must demonstrate high academic achievement.
Application requirements: Recommendations, transcript.
Additional information: For students pursuing career in floral design and marketing of fresh flowers and plants. Minimum 3.0 GPA. Email is preferred method for submitting transcripts and letters of recommendation. Submit applications via the Website.

Amount of award:	$500
Number of awards:	1
Number of applicants:	1
Application deadline:	May 1
Notification begins:	January 1
Total amount awarded:	$500

Contact:
American Floral Endowment
Attn: AFE Scholarship Applications
1601 Duke Street
Alexandria, VA 22314
Phone: 703-838-5211
Fax: 703-838-5212
Web: www.endowment.org

J.K. Rathmell, Jr. Memorial Scholarship for Work/Study Abroad

Type of award: Scholarship.
Intended use: For full-time junior, senior or graduate study at accredited 4-year or graduate institution outside United States.
Eligibility: Applicant must be U.S. citizen or permanent resident.
Basis for selection: Competition/talent/interest in study abroad. Major/career interest in horticulture or landscape architecture. Applicant must demonstrate financial need, high academic achievement, depth of character and seriousness of purpose.
Application requirements: Recommendations, transcript. Letter of invitation from host institution abroad.
Additional information: Minimum 3.0 GPA. Applicants must plan work/study abroad and submit specific plan for such. Preference given to those planning to work or study for six months or longer. Must have interest in floriculture, ornamental horticulture, or landscape architecture. Number and amount of awards vary.

Amount of award:	$2,500-$3,500
Number of awards:	1
Number of applicants:	1
Application deadline:	May 1
Notification begins:	January 1
Total amount awarded:	$3,100

Contact:
American Floral Endowment
1601 Duke Street
Alexandria, VA 22314
Phone: 703-838-5211
Fax: 703-838-5212
Web: www.endowment.org

John L. Tomasovic, Sr. Scholarship

Type of award: Scholarship, renewable.
Intended use: For sophomore, junior or senior study at accredited postsecondary institution.
Eligibility: Applicant must be U.S. citizen or permanent resident.
Basis for selection: Major/career interest in horticulture. Applicant must demonstrate financial need and high academic achievement.
Application requirements: Recommendations, transcript.
Additional information: For horticulture students with financial need. 3.0-3.5 GPA required. Email is preferred method for submitting transcript and letters of recommendation. Submit applications via the Website.

Amount of award:	$500-$1,000
Number of awards:	1
Number of applicants:	1
Application deadline:	May 1
Notification begins:	January 1
Total amount awarded:	$900

Contact:
American Floral Endowment
1001 North Fairfax St.
Suite 201
Alexandria, VA 22314
Phone: 703-838-5211
Fax: 703-838-5212
Web: www.endowment.org

Johnson-Carlson Non-Traditional Scholarship

Type of award: Scholarship.
Intended use: For full-time undergraduate or graduate study at accredited 4-year or graduate institution in United States.
Eligibility: Applicant must be returning adult student. Applicant must be U.S. citizen or permanent resident.

Basis for selection: Major/career interest in horticulture. Applicant must demonstrate financial need and high academic achievement.

Application requirements: Recommendations, transcript.

Additional information: Specific interest in bedding plants or floral crops required. Must be re-entering school after a minimum three-year absence. Number and amount of awards vary. Submit applications via the Website.

Amount of award:	$800-$1,200
Number of awards:	1
Number of applicants:	1
Application deadline:	May 1
Notification begins:	January 1
Total amount awarded:	$1,000

Contact:
American Floral Endowment
1001 North Fairfax Street
Suit 201
Alexandria, VA 22314
Phone: 703-838-5211
Fax: 703-838-5212
Web: www.endowment.org

Julio and Sarah Armellini Scholarship

Type of award: Scholarship, renewable.

Intended use: For sophomore, junior or senior study at 4-year institution.

Eligibility: Applicant must be U.S. citizen or permanent resident.

Application requirements: Recommendations, transcript.

Additional information: Must have an interest in the marketing or distribution of floral products. Visit Website for additional information.

Amount of award:	$500-$2,000
Number of awards:	1
Number of applicants:	1
Application deadline:	May 1
Total amount awarded:	$1,000

Contact:
American Floral Endowment
1001 North Fairfax St
Suite 201
Alexandria, VA 22314
Phone: 703-838-5211
Fax: 703-838-5212
Web: www.endowment.org

Long Island Flower Grower Association (LIFGA) Scholarship

Type of award: Scholarship, renewable.

Intended use: For sophomore, junior or senior study at 2-year or 4-year institution. Designated institutions: Institutions in the Long Island/New York area.

Basis for selection: Major/career interest in horticulture. Applicant must demonstrate high academic achievement.

Application requirements: Recommendations, transcript.

Additional information: For students pursuing a career in ornamental horticulture. Minimum 3.0 GPA. Email is preferred method for submitting transcript and letters of recommendation. Submit applications via the Website.

Amount of award:	$1,000-$1,500
Number of awards:	1
Number of applicants:	1
Application deadline:	May 1
Notification begins:	January 1
Total amount awarded:	$1,000

Contact:
American Floral Endowment
1601 Duke Street
Alexandria, VA 22314
Phone: 703-838-5211
Fax: 703-838-5212
Web: www.endowment.org

Markham-Colegrave International Scholarship

Type of award: Scholarship.

Intended use: For sophomore, junior, senior or graduate study at accredited 2-year, 4-year or graduate institution in United States or Canada.

Eligibility: Applicant must be U.S. citizen, permanent resident or Canadian citizen.

Basis for selection: Major/career interest in horticulture or marketing. Applicant must demonstrate financial need and high academic achievement.

Application requirements: Recommendations, transcript.

Additional information: Minimum 3.0 GPA. Must have interest in studying horticulture marketing through international travel. Operates in conjunction with the David Colegrave Foundation in London, England. Scholarship is part of annual exchange of students between U.S. and Europe, alternating between the two countries. U.S. students should apply in even number years (i.e. 2012, 2014, etc.). Number and amount of awards vary. Submit applications via the Website.

Amount of award:	$3,000-$4,000
Number of awards:	1
Number of applicants:	1
Application deadline:	May 1
Notification begins:	January 1
Total amount awarded:	$3,500

Contact:
American Floral Endowment
1001 North Fairfax Street
Suit 201
Alexandria, VA 22314
Phone: 703-838-5211
Fax: 703-838-5212
Web: www.endowment.org

Mike and Flo Novovesky Scholarship

Type of award: Scholarship, renewable.

Intended use: For sophomore, junior or senior study at accredited postsecondary institution.

Eligibility: Applicant must be U.S. citizen or permanent resident.

Basis for selection: Major/career interest in horticulture. Applicant must demonstrate financial need and high academic achievement.

Application requirements: Recommendations, transcript.

Additional information: For married students with financial need. Minimum 2.5 GPA. Email is preferred method for submitting transcript and letters of recommendation.

Scholarships

107

Amount of award:	$1,000-$1,500
Number of awards:	1
Number of applicants:	1
Application deadline:	May 1
Total amount awarded:	$1,000

Contact:
American Floral Endowment
1601 Duke Street
Alexandria, VA 22314
Phone: 703-838-5211
Fax: 703-838-5212
Web: www.endowment.org

National Greenhouse Manufacturing Association (NGMA) Scholarship

Type of award: Scholarship, renewable.
Intended use: For sophomore, junior or senior study at accredited 4-year institution.
Eligibility: Applicant must be U.S. citizen or permanent resident.
Basis for selection: Major/career interest in horticulture or bioengineering. Applicant must demonstrate high academic achievement.
Application requirements: Recommendations, transcript.
Additional information: Minimum 3.0 GPA. Email is preferred method for submitting transcript and letters of recommendation. Submit applications via the Website.

Amount of award:	$500-$750
Number of awards:	1
Number of applicants:	1
Application deadline:	May 1
Notification begins:	January 1
Total amount awarded:	$500

Contact:
American Floral Endowment
1601 Duke Street
Alexandria, VA 22314
Phone: 703-838-5211
Fax: 703-838-5212
Web: www.endowment.org

Seed Companies Scholarship

Type of award: Scholarship, renewable.
Intended use: For junior or senior study at accredited postsecondary institution.
Eligibility: Applicant must be U.S. citizen or permanent resident.
Basis for selection: Major/career interest in horticulture. Applicant must demonstrate high academic achievement.
Application requirements: Recommendations, transcript.
Additional information: For students pursuing a career in the seed industry. Minimum 3.0 GPA. Email is preferred method for submitting transcript and letters of recommendation.

Amount of award:	$2,000-$2,500
Number of awards:	1
Number of applicants:	1
Application deadline:	May 1
Notification begins:	January 1
Total amount awarded:	$2,300

Contact:
American Floral Endowment
1001 North Fairfax St
Suite 201
Alexandria, VA 22314
Phone: 703-838-5211
Fax: 703-838-5212
Web: www.endowment.org

Vocational (Bettinger, Holden and Perry) Memorial Scholarship

Type of award: Scholarship.
Intended use: For full-time undergraduate certificate, freshman, sophomore or non-degree study at accredited vocational or 2-year institution in United States.
Eligibility: Applicant must be U.S. citizen or permanent resident.
Basis for selection: Major/career interest in horticulture. Applicant must demonstrate financial need and high academic achievement.
Application requirements: Recommendations, transcript.
Additional information: Minimum 3.0 GPA. Must intend to become floriculture grower or greenhouse manager. Number and amount of awards vary.

Amount of award:	$1,000-$1,500
Number of awards:	1
Number of applicants:	1
Application deadline:	May 1
Notification begins:	January 1
Total amount awarded:	$1,100

Contact:
American Floral Endowment
1601 Duke Street
Alexandria, VA 22314
Phone: 703-838-5211
Fax: 703-838-5212
Web: www.endowment.org

American Foundation for the Blind

Delta Gamma Foundation Florence Margaret Harvey Memorial Scholarship

Type of award: Scholarship.
Intended use: For undergraduate or graduate study at accredited postsecondary institution in United States.
Eligibility: Applicant must be visually impaired.
Basis for selection: Major/career interest in education, special or rehabilitation/therapeutic services.
Application requirements: Recommendations, essay, transcript, proof of eligibility.
Additional information: Applicant must be legally blind and studying in field of rehabilitation and/or education of blind or visually impaired persons.

Amount of award:	$1,000
Number of awards:	1
Application deadline:	May 31
Total amount awarded:	$1,000

Contact:
American Foundation for the Blind Scholarship Committee
Attn: Tara Annis
1000 5th Avenue, Suite 350
Huntington, WV 25701
Phone: 800-232-5463
Web: www.afb.org/scholarships.asp

The Gladys C. Anderson Memorial Scholarship

Type of award: Scholarship.
Intended use: For undergraduate or graduate study at 2-year, 4-year or graduate institution.
Eligibility: Applicant must be visually impaired. Applicant must be female.
Basis for selection: Competition/talent/interest in music performance/composition. Major/career interest in music.
Application requirements: Recommendations, essay, transcript, proof of eligibility. Music performance on CD.
Additional information: Applicant must be legally blind and studying classical or religious music. Visit Website for deadline.

Amount of award:	$3,500
Number of awards:	1
Application deadline:	April 1

Contact:
American Foundation for the Blind
Attn: Tara Annis
1000 5th Avenue, Suite 350
Huntington, WV 25701
Phone: 800-232-5463
Web: www.afb.org/scholarships.asp

The Paul and Helen Ruckes Scholarship

Type of award: Scholarship, renewable.
Intended use: For full-time undergraduate or graduate study at accredited postsecondary institution in United States.
Eligibility: Applicant must be visually impaired.
Basis for selection: Major/career interest in engineering; computer/information sciences; physical sciences or life sciences.
Application requirements: Recommendations, essay, transcript, proof of eligibility.
Additional information: Applicant must be legally blind.

Amount of award:	$1,000
Number of awards:	1
Application deadline:	May 31
Total amount awarded:	$1,000

Contact:
American Foundation for the Blind Scholarship Committee
Attn: Tara Annis
1000 5th Avenue, Suite 350
Huntington, WV 25701
Phone: 800-232-5463
Web: www.afb.org/scholarships.asp

R.L. Gillette Scholarship

Type of award: Scholarship, renewable.
Intended use: For full-time undergraduate study at accredited 4-year institution in United States.
Eligibility: Applicant must be visually impaired. Applicant must be female.
Basis for selection: Major/career interest in literature or music.

Application requirements: Recommendations, essay, transcript, proof of eligibility. Creative writing sample or performance tape/CD not to exceed 30 minutes.
Additional information: Applicant must be legally blind.

Amount of award:	$1,000
Number of awards:	2
Application deadline:	May 31
Total amount awarded:	$2,000

Contact:
American Foundation for the Blind Scholarship Committee
Attn: Tara Annis
1000 5th Avenue, Suite 350
Huntington, WV 25701
Phone: 800-232-5463
Web: www.afb.org/scholarships.asp

The Rudolph Dillman Memorial Scholarship

Type of award: Scholarship.
Intended use: For full-time undergraduate or graduate study at accredited postsecondary institution in United States.
Eligibility: Applicant must be visually impaired.
Basis for selection: Major/career interest in education, special or rehabilitation/therapeutic services.
Application requirements: Recommendations, essay, transcript, proof of eligibility.
Additional information: Applicant must be legally blind and studying in field of rehabilitation and/or education of blind or visually impaired persons.

Amount of award:	$2,500
Number of awards:	4
Application deadline:	May 31
Total amount awarded:	$10,000

Contact:
American Foundation for the Blind Scholarship Committee
Attn: Tara Annis
1000 5th Avenue, Suite 350
Huntington, WV 25701
Phone: 800-232-5463
Web: www.afb.org/scholarships.asp

American Ground Water Trust

Amtrol Scholarship

Type of award: Scholarship.
Intended use: For full-time freshman study at 4-year institution.
Eligibility: Applicant must be high school senior. Applicant must be U.S. citizen or permanent resident.
Basis for selection: Major/career interest in geology/earth sciences; engineering, environmental; environmental science; natural resources/conservation or hydrology. Applicant must demonstrate high academic achievement, leadership, seriousness of purpose and service orientation.
Application requirements: Recommendations, essay, transcript. Description of completed high school science project involving ground water resources or of non-school work experience related to environment and natural resources.
Additional information: Applicant must be entering field related to ground water, e.g. geology, hydrology, environmental

science, or hydrogeology. Minimum 3.0 GPA required. Visit Website for application procedure and forms.

Amount of award:	$1,500
Number of awards:	2
Number of applicants:	40
Application deadline:	June 1
Notification begins:	August 15
Total amount awarded:	$3,000

Contact:
American Ground Water Trust Scholarship
50 Pleasant Street, Suite 2
Concord, NH 03301-4073
Phone: 603-228-5444
Fax: 603-228-6557
Web: www.agwt.org

Baroid Scholarship

Type of award: Scholarship.
Intended use: For full-time freshman study at accredited 4-year institution.
Eligibility: Applicant must be high school senior. Applicant must be U.S. citizen or permanent resident.
Basis for selection: Major/career interest in engineering, environmental; geology/earth sciences; environmental science or natural resources/conservation. Applicant must demonstrate high academic achievement, leadership, seriousness of purpose and service orientation.
Application requirements: Recommendations, essay, transcript. Description of previously completed high school science project involving ground water resources or of non-school work experience related to environment and natural resources.
Additional information: Must be entering field related to ground water, e.g. hydrology or hydrogeology. Minimum 3.0 GPA. Visit Website for application procedure and forms.

Amount of award:	$2,000
Number of awards:	1
Number of applicants:	40
Application deadline:	June 1
Notification begins:	August 15
Total amount awarded:	$2,000

Contact:
American Ground Water Trust Scholarship
50 Pleasant Street, Suite 2
Concord, NH 03301-4073
Phone: 603-228-5444
Fax: 603-228-6557
Web: www.agwt.org

Thomas M. Stetson Scholarship

Type of award: Scholarship.
Intended use: For full-time undergraduate study at accredited 4-year institution in United States. Designated institutions: Colleges and universities located west of the Mississippi River.
Eligibility: Applicant must be high school senior. Applicant must be U.S. citizen or permanent resident.
Basis for selection: Major/career interest in environmental science; natural resources/conservation or science, general. Applicant must demonstrate high academic achievement.
Application requirements: Recommendations, essay.
Additional information: Applicant must intend to pursue career in ground water related field. Minimum 3.0 GPA. Visit Website for application procedure and forms.

Amount of award:	$2,000
Number of awards:	1
Number of applicants:	40
Application deadline:	June 1
Notification begins:	August 15
Total amount awarded:	$2,000

Contact:
American Ground Water Trust
50 Pleasant Street
Concord, NH 03301
Phone: 603-228-5444
Fax: 603-228-6557
Web: www.agwt.org

American Helicopter Society

Arizona Chapter Vertical Flight Engineering Scholarship

Type of award: Scholarship.
Intended use: For full-time undergraduate or graduate study. Designated institutions: Schools of engineering in Arizona.
Basis for selection: Major/career interest in aviation or engineering. Applicant must demonstrate high academic achievement.
Application requirements: Recommendations, transcript. Resume.
Additional information: Award for students who demonstrate an interest in pursuing engineering careers in the fixed wing, rotorcraft, or VTOL aircraft industry. Recipients also receive one-year membership in AHS.

Amount of award:	$1,500-$3,000
Number of awards:	4
Application deadline:	October 10
Notification begins:	November 26

Contact:
Friedrich Straub
The Boeing Company
Mail Stop M530-B229, 5000 East McDowell Road
Mesa, AZ 85215-9797
Phone: 480-891-6058
Web: www.vtol.org/education/vertical-flight-foundation-scholarships

Vertical Flight Foundation Scholarship

Type of award: Scholarship.
Intended use: For full-time junior, senior, master's or doctoral study at accredited postsecondary institution.
Basis for selection: Major/career interest in aerospace; aviation or engineering. Applicant must demonstrate high academic achievement, depth of character and seriousness of purpose.
Application requirements: Recommendations, essay, transcript. Resume.
Additional information: Must demonstrate career interest in vertical flight engineering. Minimum 3.0 GPA required, 3.5 recommended. Number of awards varies based on funding.

Scholarships

Amount of award:	$1,000-$5,000
Number of applicants:	62
Application deadline:	February 1
Notification begins:	April 15
Total amount awarded:	$50,000

Contact:
The Vertical Flight Foundation
217 North Washington Street
Alexandria, VA 22314-2538
Phone: 703-684-6777
Fax: 703-739-9279
Web: www.vtol.org/education/vertical-flight-foundation-scholarships

American Hellenic Educational Progressive Association Educational Foundation

AHEPA Educational Foundation Scholarships

Type of award: Scholarship.
Intended use: For full-time undergraduate or graduate study at accredited postsecondary institution.
Basis for selection: Applicant must demonstrate high academic achievement and service orientation.
Application requirements: Recommendations, transcript. Photo, financial information (when applicable).
Additional information: Applicant must be of Greek descent, or member/child of member (in good standing) of AHEPA, Daughters of Penelope, Sons of Pericles, or Maids of Athena. Minimum 3.0 GPA. High school seniors eligible to apply. Visit Website for details and application.

Amount of award:	$2,000
Application deadline:	March 31

Contact:
AHEPA Educational Foundation
1909 Q Street N.W., Suite 500
Washington, DC 20009
Phone: 202-232-6300
Fax: 202-232-2140
Web: www.ahepa.org

American Hotel & Lodging Educational Foundation

American Express Scholarship Competition

Type of award: Scholarship, renewable.
Intended use: For undergraduate study at accredited 2-year or 4-year institution.
Basis for selection: Major/career interest in hotel/restaurant management or hospitality administration/management.
Application requirements: Essay, transcript.
Additional information: Must work a minimum of 20 hours a week at hotel and have 12 months of hotel experience. Hotel

must be member of American Hotel & Lodging Association. Dependents of hotel employees may also apply. Award must be used in hospitality management degree program. Visit Website to download application or apply online.

Amount of award:	$500-$2,000
Number of applicants:	20
Application deadline:	May 1
Notification begins:	July 15
Total amount awarded:	$11,000

Contact:
American Hotel & Lodging Educational Foundation
1201 New York Avenue, NW
Suite 600
Washington, DC 20005-3931
Phone: 202-289-3180
Fax: 202-289-3199
Web: www.ahlef.org

American Hotel & Lodging Educational Foundation Incoming Freshman Scholarship Competition

Type of award: Scholarship.
Intended use: For full-time freshman study at 2-year or 4-year institution.
Eligibility: Applicant must be U.S. citizen or permanent resident.
Basis for selection: Major/career interest in hotel/restaurant management or hospitality administration/management. Applicant must demonstrate high academic achievement.
Additional information: Award must be used in hospitality management program. Minimum 2.0 GPA. $1,000 awards go to Associate majors, $2,000 to Baccalaureate majors. Preference will be given to high school graduates of the Hospitality and Tourism Management Program (HTMP) or the Lodging Management Program (LMP). Visit Website to download application or apply online.

Amount of award:	$1,000-$2,000
Number of applicants:	158
Application deadline:	May 1
Notification begins:	July 15
Total amount awarded:	$35,000

Contact:
American Hotel & Lodging Educational Foundation
1250 I Street
NW Suite 1100
Washington, DC 20005-3931
Phone: 202-289-3180
Fax: 202-289-3199
Web: www.ahlef.org

Ecolab Scholarship Competition

Type of award: Scholarship.
Intended use: For full-time undergraduate study at 2-year or 4-year institution in United States.
Basis for selection: Major/career interest in hotel/restaurant management or hospitality administration/management.
Application requirements: Essay, transcript.
Additional information: Award must be used in hospitality management program. Applicant must maintain minimum 12 credit hours. Visit Website to download application or apply online.

Amount of award:	$1,000-$2,000
Number of applicants:	620
Application deadline:	May 1
Notification begins:	July 15
Total amount awarded:	$23,000

Contact:
American Hotel & Lodging Educational Foundation
1201 New York Avenue, NW
Suite 600
Washington, DC 20005-3931
Phone: 202-289-3181
Fax: 202-289-3199
Web: mpoinelli@ahlef.org

The Hyatt Hotels Fund for Minority Lodging Management Students Competition

Type of award: Scholarship, renewable.
Intended use: For junior or senior study at 4-year institution.
Eligibility: Applicant must be Alaskan native, Asian American, African American, Mexican American, Hispanic American, Puerto Rican, American Indian or Native Hawaiian/Pacific Islander. Applicant must be U.S. citizen or permanent resident.
Basis for selection: Major/career interest in hotel/restaurant management or hospitality administration/management.
Application requirements: Essay, transcript.
Additional information: Award must be used in hospitality management program. Must be enrolled in at least 12 credit hours for upcoming fall and spring semesters, or just fall semester if graduating in December. Visit Website to download application or apply online.

Amount of award:	$2,000
Number of applicants:	102
Application deadline:	May 1
Notification begins:	July 15
Total amount awarded:	$36,000

Contact:
American Hotel & Lodging Educational Foundation
1201 New York Avenue, NW
Suite 600
Washington, DC 20005
Phone: 202-289-3180
Fax: 202-289-3199
Web: www.ahlef.org

American Indian College Fund

Full Circle/TCU Scholarship Program

Type of award: Scholarship.
Intended use: For undergraduate or graduate study at accredited vocational, 2-year, 4-year or graduate institution in United States. Designated institutions: TCU Scholarship Program - Tribal Colleges and Universities only. Full Circle Scholarship Program - Any not-for-profit vocational schools/colleges/universities (including TCUs),
Eligibility: Applicant must be Alaskan native or American Indian.
Basis for selection: Most scholarships are merit-based but some are based on financial need.

Application requirements: Transcript, proof of eligibility. Applicant must be a citizen of the United States or Canada. Students must complete online application. Must provide Tribal ID document/proof of descendency. Must be registered as an enrolled member of a federal or state recognized tribe, or a descendant of at least one grandparent or parent who is an enrolled tribal member; Alaska Natives may use Native Corporation membership.

Amount of award:	$1,000-$18,000
Number of awards:	6,578
Number of applicants:	10,985
Application deadline:	May 31
Total amount awarded:	$7,781,005

Contact:
American Indian College Fund
8333 Greenwood Blvd
Denver, CO 80221
Phone: 303-426-8900
Fax: 303-426-1200
Web: http://collegefund.org/student-resources/scholarships/scholarship-programs/

American Indian Science & Engineering Society

A.T. Anderson Memorial Scholarship

Type of award: Scholarship.
Intended use: For full-time undergraduate or graduate study at accredited 2-year, 4-year or graduate institution in United States.
Eligibility: Applicant or parent must be member/participant of American Indian Science & Engineering Society. Applicant must be Alaskan native, American Indian or Native Hawaiian/Pacific Islander. Must be member of American Indian tribe or be at least 1/4 American Indian/Alaskan Native blood.
Basis for selection: Major/career interest in science, general; engineering; medicine; natural resources/conservation; mathematics; physical sciences or technology. Applicant must demonstrate high academic achievement, depth of character, leadership, seriousness of purpose and service orientation.
Application requirements: Recommendations, essay, transcript, proof of eligibility. Resume, proof of tribal enrollment or ancestry.
Additional information: Must be AISES member. Minimum 3.0 GPA. Undergraduate student award $1,000; graduate student award $2,000. Deadline is in mid-May. Membership and scholarship applications available on Website.

Amount of award:	$1,000-$2,000
Number of awards:	80
Number of applicants:	200
Notification begins:	October 1
Total amount awarded:	$85,000

Contact:
AISES Scholarships
P.O. Box 9828
Albuquerque, NM 87119-9828
Phone: 702-552-6123
Fax: 505-765-5608
Web: www.aises.org/scholarships

Burlington Northern Santa Fe Foundation Scholarship

Type of award: Scholarship, renewable.
Intended use: For full-time freshman study at accredited 4-year institution in United States.
Eligibility: Applicant or parent must be member/participant of American Indian Science & Engineering Society. Applicant must be Alaskan native, American Indian or Native Hawaiian/ Pacific Islander. Must be member of American Indian tribe or be at least 1/4 American Indian/Alaskan Native blood. Applicant must be high school senior. Applicant must be U.S. citizen residing in South Dakota, Texas, Minnesota, Washington, Kansas, Arizona, Oklahoma, California, Oregon, Montana, New Mexico, Colorado or North Dakota.
Basis for selection: Major/career interest in science, general; engineering; mathematics; physical sciences; medicine; natural sciences; business; health services administration; technology or education. Applicant must demonstrate financial need, high academic achievement, depth of character, leadership, seriousness of purpose and service orientation.
Application requirements: Recommendations, essay, transcript, proof of eligibility. Resume, proof of tribal enrollment or ancestry.
Additional information: Applicant must be AISES member. Minimum 2.0 GPA. Award is renewable for four years (eight semesters) or until degree obtained, whichever comes first, assuming eligibility maintained. Deadline is in mid-May. Membership and scholarship applications available on Website.

Amount of award:	$2,500
Number of awards:	5
Number of applicants:	60
Notification begins:	October 1
Total amount awarded:	$12,500

Contact:
AISES Scholarships
P.O. Box 9828
Albuquerque, NM 87119-9828
Phone: 702-552-6123
Fax: 505-765-5608
Web: www.aises.org/scholarships

Intel Scholarship

Type of award: Scholarship.
Intended use: For full-time undergraduate or graduate study at accredited 2-year, 4-year or graduate institution.
Eligibility: Applicant or parent must be member/participant of American Indian Science & Engineering Society. Applicant must be Alaskan native, American Indian or Native Hawaiian/ Pacific Islander.
Basis for selection: Major/career interest in computer/ information sciences; engineering, computer; engineering, electrical/electronic; engineering, chemical or materials science. Applicant must demonstrate high academic achievement.
Application requirements: Recommendations, essay, transcript, proof of eligibility. Certificate of Indian Blood or proof of tribal enrollment document. Resume.
Additional information: Minimum 3.0 GPA. Must be a member of an American Indian tribe or be considered American Indian by the tribe which affiliation is claimed or have at least 1/4 American Indian blood; or be at least 1/4 Alaskan Native or considered to be an Alaskan Native by an Alaskan Native group to which affiliation is claimed. Must be a member of AISES. To obtain an AISES membership, visit Website. Deadline is in mid-May. Award is $5,000 for undergraduates; $10,000 for graduates.

Amount of award:	$5,000-$10,000
Number of awards:	7
Number of applicants:	100
Notification begins:	October 1

Contact:
AISES Scholarships
P.O. Box 9828
Albuquerque, NM 87119-9828
Phone: 702-552-6123
Fax: 505-765-5608
Web: www.aises.org/scholarships

American Institute for Foreign Study

Diversity Abroad Achievement Scholarship

Type of award: Scholarship.
Intended use: For undergraduate study at postsecondary institution in Argentina, Australia, Austria, Brazil, Chile, Costa Rica, Czech Republic, England, France, Ghana, Greece, India, Ireland, Italy, New Zealand, Russia, South Africa, Spain, Turkey. Designated institutions: AIFS programs.
Basis for selection: Competition/talent/interest in study abroad. Applicant must demonstrate high academic achievement and leadership.
Application requirements: Recommendations, essay, transcript.
Additional information: Minimum 3.0 GPA. Must be involved in multicultural/international activities. Scholarship offered to student from under represented group. Number of awards varies. Application deadlines are April 15 for fall and September 15 for spring.

Amount of award:	$5,000
Number of applicants:	55
Application deadline:	April 15, October 1
Notification begins:	November 1, May 15
Total amount awarded:	$20,000

Contact:
AIFS College Division
1 High Ridge Park
Stamford, CT 06905
Phone: 800-727-2437
Fax: 203-399-5597
Web: www.aifsabroad.com

HACU (Hispanic Association of Colleges and Universities) Scholarships

Type of award: Scholarship.
Intended use: For undergraduate study in Argentina, Australia, Austria, Brazil, Chile, Costa Rica, Czech Republic, England, France, Germany, Ghana, Greece, India, Ireland, Italy, New Zealand, Russia, South Africa, Spain, Turkey. Designated institutions: HACU member institutions.
Eligibility: Applicant must be Mexican American, Hispanic American or Puerto Rican.
Basis for selection: Competition/talent/interest in study abroad. Applicant must demonstrate high academic achievement and leadership.

Application requirements: Recommendations, essay, transcript.

Additional information: Scholarship intended for use at AIFS programs. Applicant must be involved in multicultural/international activities. Deadlines are March 1 for summer, April 15 for fall, and September 15 for spring. Award amount is up to half of the AIFS all-inclusive program fee for summer and semester programs.

Number of awards:	3
Number of applicants:	50
Application deadline:	April 15
Notification begins:	April 1, May 15
Total amount awarded:	$25,000

Contact:
AIFS College Division
1 High Ridge Park
Stamford, CT 06905
Phone: 800-727-2437
Fax: 203-399-5597
Web: www.aifsabroad.com

International Semester Scholarship

Type of award: Scholarship.

Intended use: For undergraduate study in Argentina, Australia, Austria, Brazil, Chile, Costa Rica, Czech Republic, England, France, Germany, Ghana, Greece, India, Ireland, Italy, New Zealand, Russia, South Africa, Spain, Turkey. Designated institutions: AIFS programs.

Basis for selection: Competition/talent/interest in study abroad. Applicant must demonstrate high academic achievement and leadership.

Application requirements: Recommendations, essay, transcript. Disciplinary clearance.

Additional information: Minimum 3.0 GPA. Must be involved in multicultural/international activities. Award amount is $500 for summer and $1,000 for semester program. Number of awards varies. Application deadlines are March 1 for summer, April 15 for fall, and September 15 for spring.

Amount of award:	$500-$1,000
Number of awards:	130
Number of applicants:	450
Application deadline:	September 15, April 15
Notification begins:	November 1, May 15
Total amount awarded:	$105,000

Contact:
AIFS College Division
1 High Ridge Park
Stamford, CT 06905
Phone: 800-727-2437
Fax: 203-399-5597
Web: www.aifsabroad.com

NAFEO (National Association for Equal Opportunity in Higher Education) Scholarships

Type of award: Scholarship.

Intended use: For undergraduate study in Argentina, Australia, Austria, Brazil, Chile, Costa Rica, Czech Republic, England, France, Ghana, Greece, India, Ireland, Italy, New Zealand, Russia, South Africa, Spain, Turkey. Designated institutions: HCBUs or PBIs.

Eligibility: Applicant must be African American.

Basis for selection: Competition/talent/interest in study abroad. Applicant must demonstrate high academic achievement and leadership.

Application requirements: Recommendations, essay, transcript.

Additional information: Scholarship intended for use at AIFS programs. Applicant must be involved in multicultural/international activities. Deadlines are April 15 for fall and September 15 for spring. Award amount is up to half of the AIFS all-inclusive program fee for semester programs.

Number of awards:	2
Number of applicants:	30
Application deadline:	April 15, September 15
Notification begins:	May 15, November 1
Total amount awarded:	$20,000

Contact:
AIFS College Division
1 High Ridge Park
Stamford, CT 06905
Phone: 800-727-2437
Fax: 203-399-5597
Web: www.aifsabroad.com

American Institute of Aeronautics and Astronautics

AIAA Foundation Undergraduate Scholarship

Type of award: Scholarship, renewable.

Intended use: For full-time sophomore, junior or senior study in United States.

Basis for selection: Major/career interest in aerospace; engineering; mathematics or science, general. Applicant must demonstrate high academic achievement.

Application requirements: Recommendations, essay, transcript.

Additional information: Minimum 3.3 GPA. Must be AIAA member to apply. Not open to members of any AIAA national committees or subcommittees. Applicants must reapply for renewal.

Amount of award:	$2,500
Number of awards:	11
Number of applicants:	58
Application deadline:	January 31
Notification begins:	June 15
Total amount awarded:	$17,500

Contact:
AIAA Student Programs - Scholarships
1801 Alexander Bell Drive
Suite 500
Reston, VA 20191-4344
Phone: 703-264-7500
Web: www.aiaa.org

American Institute of Architects

AIA/AAF Minority/Disadvantaged Scholarship

Type of award: Scholarship, renewable.

Intended use: For full-time freshman or sophomore study at accredited postsecondary institution in United States.

Designated institutions: NAAB-accredited institutions.

Eligibility: Applicant must be high school senior. Applicant must be U.S. citizen or permanent resident.

Basis for selection: Major/career interest in architecture. Applicant must demonstrate financial need.

Application requirements: Recommendations, essay, transcript, proof of eligibility, nomination by high school guidance counselor, architect, or other individual who can speak to student's aptitude for architecture. Drawing.

Additional information: Check Website for deadline. Open to high school seniors, community college students and college freshmen who plan to enter programs leading to professional degree in architecture. Students who have completed full year of undergraduate course work not eligible. Visit Website for additional information.

Amount of award:	$3,000-$4,000
Number of awards:	5
Number of applicants:	120
Total amount awarded:	$20,000

Contact:
The American Institute of Architects
1735 New York Avenue, NW
Washington, DC 20006-5292
Phone: 800-242-3837
Fax: 202-626-7547
Web: www.aia.org/education/AIAB081881

American Institute of Architects New Jersey

AIA New Jersey Scholarship Foundation

Type of award: Scholarship, renewable.

Intended use: For full-time sophomore, junior, senior, master's or first professional study at accredited postsecondary institution. Designated institutions: Architectural schools.

Eligibility: Applicant must be residing in New Jersey.

Basis for selection: Major/career interest in architecture. Applicant must demonstrate financial need, high academic achievement, depth of character and seriousness of purpose.

Application requirements: $5 application fee. Portfolio, essay, transcript. FAFSA.

Additional information: Non-New Jersey residents attending architecture school in New Jersey also eligible. Applicant must have completed at least one year of architectural school at an accredited architecture program. Number of awards and amounts may vary. Deadline May or June. Visit Website for more information.

Amount of award:	$3,000-$6,000

Contact:
AIA New Jersey Scholarship Foundation, Inc.
Attn: Christine Miseo, AIA
205 Mt. Pleasant Avenue
East Hanover, NJ 07936
Phone: 973-533-0002
Fax: 908-725-7957
Web: www.aia-nj.org

American Institute of Certified Public Accountants

Accountemps Student Scholarship

Type of award: Scholarship.

Intended use: For full-time sophomore, junior, senior or graduate study at postsecondary institution in United States. Designated institutions: AACSB- and/or ACBSP-accredited institutions.

Eligibility: Applicant must be U.S. citizen or permanent resident.

Basis for selection: Major/career interest in accounting. Applicant must demonstrate financial need, high academic achievement, leadership and service orientation.

Application requirements: Recommendations, essay, transcript. Resume.

Additional information: Must be AICPA student affiliate member. Applicants may also study accounting-related fields, and must exhibit strong commitment to becoming a licensed CPA professional. Applicants must have completed at least thirty semester hours, including at least six hours in accounting. Students selected to advance to second round selections notified in May. Award recipients must commit to performing eight hours of CPA-related community service per semester. AICPA and RHI/Accountemps staff and family members are ineligible. Scholarship Open Date: January 1. Scholarship Close Date: April 1.

Amount of award:	$2,500
Number of awards:	10
Number of applicants:	400
Application deadline:	April 1
Notification begins:	August 1
Total amount awarded:	$25,000

Contact:
AICPA Accountemps Student Scholarship
Samantha Mitchell
220 Leigh Farm Road
Durham, NC 27707
Phone: 919-402-2161
Fax: 919-419-4705
Web: www.thiswaytocpa.com/accountemps

AICPA Foundation Two-Year Transfer Scholarship

Type of award: Scholarship.

Intended use: For junior or senior study at 4-year institution.

Basis for selection: Major/career interest in accounting.

Application requirements: Resume.

Additional information: Minimum 3.0 GPA. Applicants must have earned an associate's degree in business, accounting, finance, or economics with a declared intent to major in accounting at a four-year institution.

Amount of award:	$1,000
Number of awards:	5
Application deadline:	April 1

115

Contact:
AICPA Foundation Two-Year Transfer Scholarship
Samantha Mitchell
220 Leigh Farm Road
Durham, NC 27707
Phone: 919-402-2161
Fax: 919-419-4705
Web: https://thiswaytocpa.com/education/scholarship-search/

American Institute of Certified Public Accountants Scholarship for Minority Accounting Students

Type of award: Scholarship, renewable.
Intended use: For full-time undergraduate or graduate study at postsecondary institution.
Eligibility: Applicant must be Alaskan native, Asian American, African American, Mexican American, Hispanic American, Puerto Rican, American Indian or Native Hawaiian/Pacific Islander. Applicant must be U.S. citizen or permanent resident.
Basis for selection: Major/career interest in accounting. Applicant must demonstrate high academic achievement, leadership and seriousness of purpose.
Application requirements: Recommendations, essay, transcript, proof of eligibility. Resume.
Additional information: Applicants must have completed at least 30 semester hours or equivalent of college work, with at least six hours in accounting. Applicants must be enrolled as accounting major, taxation major, finance major, or other related field and must exhibit strong commitment to becoming a licensed CPA professional. Application must be submitted online. Recipients must complete eight hours of community service per semester. Scholarship Open Date: January 1. Scholarship Close Data: April 1.

Amount of award:	$5,000
Number of awards:	80
Number of applicants:	300
Application deadline:	April 1
Notification begins:	August 1
Total amount awarded:	$240,000

Contact:
AICPA Minority Scholarship Program
Samantha Mitchell
220 Leigh Farm Road
Durham, NC 27707
Phone: 919-402-2161
Fax: 919-419-4705
Web: www.thiswaytocpa.com/minorityscholarship

American Institute of Polish Culture

Harriet Irsay Scholarship

Type of award: Scholarship.
Intended use: For full-time undergraduate or graduate study in United States.
Eligibility: Applicant must be U.S. citizen or permanent resident.
Basis for selection: Major/career interest in communications; education; film/video; history; humanities/liberal arts; international relations; journalism; polish language/studies;

public relations or music. Applicant must demonstrate high academic achievement.
Application requirements: $10 application fee. Recommendations, essay, transcript. Detailed resume or CV, 700-word article on any subject about Poland.
Additional information: Application available on Website. Preference given to American students of Polish heritage.

Amount of award:	$1,000
Number of awards:	15
Application deadline:	June 28
Notification begins:	August 9

Contact:
The American Institute of Polish Culture Scholarship Applications
1440 79th Street Causeway
Suite 117
Miami, FL 33141-3555
Phone: 305-864-2349
Fax: 305-865-5150
Web: www.ampolinstitute.org

American Legion

American Legion Pennsylvania High School Oratorical Contest

Type of award: Scholarship.
Intended use: For undergraduate study at postsecondary institution.
Eligibility: Applicant must be enrolled in high school. Applicant must be U.S. citizen or permanent resident residing in Pennsylvania.
Basis for selection: Competition/talent/interest in oratory/ debate, based on language style, voice, diction, delivery, originality, logic, breadth of knowledge, application of knowledge about topic, and skill in selecting examples and analogies.
Additional information: Awards: First place, $7,500; second place, $5,000; third place, $4,000. Contact local American Legion Post for details and application.

Amount of award:	$4,000-$7,500
Number of awards:	3
Application deadline:	January 1
Total amount awarded:	$16,500

Contact:
American Legion Pennsylvania
Scholarship Secretary
P.O. Box 2324
Harrisburg, PA 17105-2324
Phone: 717-730-9100
Web: www.pa-legion.com

American Legion Alabama

American Legion Alabama Oratorical Contest

Type of award: Scholarship.
Intended use: For undergraduate study at postsecondary institution.

Eligibility: Applicant or parent must be member/participant of American Legion. Applicant must be enrolled in high school. Applicant must be U.S. citizen residing in Alabama.
Basis for selection: Competition/talent/interest in oratory/debate, based on language style, voice, diction, delivery, originality, logic, breadth of knowledge, application of knowledge about topic, and skill in selecting examples and analogies.
Application requirements: Proof of eligibility.
Additional information: First place, $3,000; second place, $2,000; third place, $1,000. State finals held in March. Send business-size SASE for application.

Amount of award:	$1,000-$3,000
Number of awards:	3
Total amount awarded:	$6,000

Contact:
The American Legion, Department of Alabama
P.O. Box 1069
Montgomery, AL 36101-1069
Phone: 334-262-6638
Web: www.americanlegionalabama.org

American Legion Alabama Scholarship

Type of award: Scholarship, renewable.
Intended use: For undergraduate study at postsecondary institution.
Eligibility: Applicant or parent must be member/participant of American Legion. Applicant must be U.S. citizen or permanent resident residing in Alabama. Applicant must be descendant of veteran; or dependent of veteran during Korean War, Persian Gulf War, WW I, WW II or Vietnam.
Application requirements: Recommendations, transcript, proof of eligibility. SAT/ACT scores.
Additional information: Four-year scholarships at Alabama colleges. Children and grandchildren of U.S. military veterans may apply. Send business-size SASE for application or download online.

Amount of award:	$850
Number of awards:	130
Application deadline:	April 1
Total amount awarded:	$110,500

Contact:
The American Legion, Department of Alabama
P.O. Box 1069
Montgomery, AL 36101-1069
Phone: 334-262-6638
Web: www.americanlegionalabama.org

American Legion Alabama Auxiliary

American Legion Alabama Auxiliary Scholarship

Type of award: Scholarship, renewable.
Intended use: For undergraduate study at postsecondary institution. Designated institutions: Alabama state-supported colleges.
Eligibility: Applicant or parent must be member/participant of American Legion Auxiliary. Applicant must be U.S. citizen or permanent resident residing in Alabama. Applicant must be

descendant of veteran; or dependent of veteran during Grenada conflict, Korean War, Lebanon conflict, Panama conflict, Persian Gulf War, WW I, WW II or Vietnam.
Application requirements: Proof of eligibility.
Additional information: Four-year scholarships at Alabama colleges. Previous one-year scholarship recipients can reapply. Grandchildren of veterans also eligible. Also applicable for descendants/dependents of veterans of Operation Desert Shield/Storm. Send SASE for application.

Amount of award:	$850
Number of awards:	40
Application deadline:	April 1
Total amount awarded:	$34,000

Contact:
American Legion Auxiliary, Department of Alabama
120 North Jackson Street
Montgomery, AL 36104
Phone: 334-262-1176

American Legion Alaska

American Legion Alaska Oratorical Contest

Type of award: Scholarship.
Intended use: For undergraduate study at postsecondary institution.
Eligibility: Applicant or parent must be member/participant of American Legion. Applicant must be enrolled in high school. Applicant must be U.S. citizen or permanent resident residing in Alaska.
Basis for selection: Competition/talent/interest in oratory/debate, based on language style, voice, diction, delivery, originality, logic, breadth of knowledge, application of knowledge about topic, and skill in selecting examples and analogies.
Application requirements: Proof of eligibility.
Additional information: Awards: First place, $3,000; second place, $2,000; third and fourth place, $1,000. Must be high school student attending Alaska accredited institution. Must participate in local speech contests. Contest begins in November.

Amount of award:	$1,000-$3,000
Number of awards:	4
Total amount awarded:	$7,000

Contact:
American Legion, Department of Alaska
Department Adjutant
1550 Charter Circle
Anchorage, AK 99508
Phone: 907-278-8598
Fax: 907-278-0041
Web: www.alaskalegion.org

Richard D. Johnson Memorial Scholarship

Type of award: Scholarship.
Intended use: For undergraduate study at vocational, 2-year or 4-year institution.
Eligibility: Applicant or parent must be member/participant of American Legion. Applicant must be high school senior. Applicant must be residing in Alaska.

Scholarships

Basis for selection: Applicant must demonstrate financial need, high academic achievement, seriousness of purpose and service orientation.
Application requirements: Recommendations, essay, transcript.
Additional information: Minimum 2.0 GPA.

Amount of award:	$1,000
Application deadline:	March 30

Contact:
American Legion Western District Postsecondary Scholarship
1550 Charter Circle
Anchorage, AK 99508
Phone: 907-488-5310
Fax: 775-201-1107
Web: www.alaskalegion.org

American Legion Alaska Auxiliary

American Legion Alaska Auxiliary Scholarship

Type of award: Scholarship.
Intended use: For freshman study at postsecondary institution.
Eligibility: Applicant or parent must be member/participant of American Legion Auxiliary. Applicant must be at least 17, no older than 24, high school senior. Applicant must be U.S. citizen or permanent resident residing in Alaska. Applicant must be dependent of veteran during Grenada conflict, Korean War, Lebanon conflict, Panama conflict, Persian Gulf War, WW I, WW II or Vietnam.
Application requirements: Proof of eligibility.
Additional information: Scholarship to apply toward tuition, laboratory, or similar fees. Must not have attended institution of higher education.

Amount of award:	$1,500
Application deadline:	March 15

Contact:
American Legion Auxiliary, Department of Alaska
P.O. Box 670750
Chugiak, AK 99567
Web: www.alaskalegionauxiliary.org

American Legion Arizona

American Legion Arizona Oratorical Contest

Type of award: Scholarship.
Intended use: For undergraduate study at postsecondary institution.
Eligibility: Applicant or parent must be member/participant of American Legion. Applicant must be enrolled in high school. Applicant must be U.S. citizen or permanent resident residing in Arizona.
Basis for selection: Competition/talent/interest in oratory/debate, based on language style, voice, diction, delivery, originality, logic, breadth of knowledge, application of knowledge about topic, and skill in selecting examples and analogies.

Additional information: Awards: First place, $1,500; second place, $800; third place, $500. For students enrolled in accredited Arizona high schools.

Amount of award:	$500-$1,500
Number of awards:	3
Application deadline:	January 1
Total amount awarded:	$2,800

Contact:
American Legion Arizona, Oratorical Contest
4701 North 19th Avenue, Suite 200
Phoenix, AZ 85015-3799
Phone: 602-264-7706
Fax: 602-264-0029
Web: www.azlegion.org/programs

American Legion Arizona Auxiliary

American Legion Arizona Auxiliary Health Care Occupation Scholarship

Type of award: Scholarship.
Intended use: For undergraduate or post-bachelor's certificate study at accredited vocational, 2-year or 4-year institution. Designated institutions: Arizona tax-supported institutions.
Eligibility: Applicant or parent must be member/participant of American Legion Auxiliary. Applicant must be U.S. citizen residing in Arizona.
Basis for selection: Major/career interest in health-related professions; health sciences or physical therapy. Applicant must demonstrate financial need, high academic achievement, depth of character and seriousness of purpose.
Application requirements: Recommendations, essay, transcript. Photograph of self.
Additional information: Must be resident of Arizona at least one year. Preference given to immediate family members of veterans.

Amount of award:	$500
Application deadline:	May 15

Contact:
American Legion Auxiliary, Department of Arizona
4701 North 19th Avenue, Suite 100
Phoenix, AZ 85015-3727
Phone: 602-241-1080
Fax: 602-604-9640
Web: www.aladeptaz.org

American Legion Arizona Auxiliary Nurses' Scholarship

Type of award: Scholarship.
Intended use: For sophomore study. Designated institutions: Arizona institutions.
Eligibility: Applicant or parent must be member/participant of American Legion Auxiliary. Applicant must be U.S. citizen residing in Arizona.
Basis for selection: Major/career interest in nursing.
Application requirements: Recommendations, essay, transcript. Photograph of self.
Additional information: Must be pursuing RN degree. Must be Arizona resident for at least one year. Preference given to immediate family members of veterans.

Amount of award: $600
Application deadline: May 15
Contact:
American Legion Auxiliary, Department of Arizona
4701 North 19th Avenue, Suite 100
Phoenix, AZ 85015-3727
Phone: 602-241-1080
Fax: 602-604-9640
Web: www.aladeptaz.org

Wilma D. Hoyal/Maxine Chilton Memorial Scholarship

Type of award: Scholarship.
Intended use: For full-time sophomore, junior or senior study. Designated institutions: University of Arizona, Arizona State University, Northern Arizona University.
Eligibility: Applicant or parent must be member/participant of American Legion Auxiliary. Applicant must be U.S. citizen residing in Arizona.
Basis for selection: Major/career interest in political science/government; education, special or public administration/service. Applicant must demonstrate financial need, high academic achievement, depth of character and seriousness of purpose.
Application requirements: Recommendations, transcript. Resume.
Additional information: For second-year or upper-division full-time students. Three $1,000 awards payable to three designated institutions in Arizona. Applicant must be state resident at least one year. Preference given to immediate family members of veterans.

Amount of award: $3,000
Number of awards: 3
Application deadline: May 15
Contact:
American Legion Auxiliary, Department of Arizona
4701 North 19th Avenue, Suite 100
Phoenix, AZ 85015-3727
Phone: 602-241-1080
Fax: 602-604-9640
Web: www.aladeptaz.org

American Legion Arkansas

American Legion Arkansas Oratorical Contest

Type of award: Scholarship.
Intended use: For undergraduate study at postsecondary institution.
Eligibility: Applicant or parent must be member/participant of American Legion. Applicant must be high school sophomore, junior or senior. Applicant must be U.S. citizen or permanent resident residing in Arkansas.
Basis for selection: Competition/talent/interest in oratory/debate, based on language style, voice, diction, delivery, originality, logic, breadth of knowledge, application of knowledge about topic, and skill in selecting examples and analogies.
Application requirements: Proof of eligibility.
Additional information: Oratorical Contest, State Division: first place, $2,000; second place, $1,500; third place, $1,000. Must apply to local Post.

Amount of award: $1,000-$2,000
Number of awards: 3
Application deadline: January 1
Total amount awarded: $4,500
Contact:
American Legion Arkansas
Department Adjutant
P.O. Box 3280
Little Rock, AR 72203
Phone: 501-375-1104
Fax: 501-375-4236
Web: www.arlegion.org

American Legion Coudret Trust Scholarship

Type of award: Scholarship.
Intended use: For undergraduate study at postsecondary institution.
Eligibility: Applicant or parent must be member/participant of American Legion. Applicant must be residing in Arkansas.
Basis for selection: Applicant must demonstrate depth of character, patriotism and seriousness of purpose.
Application requirements: Recommendations, essay, transcript, proof of eligibility. Photograph.
Additional information: Must be child, grandchild, or great-grandchild of American Legion member. Must have either received high school diploma or be graduate of two-year AR institution by time of award.

Amount of award: $2,000
Number of awards: 4
Application deadline: March 15
Total amount awarded: $8,000
Contact:
American Legion Arkansas
Department Adjutant
P.O. Box 3280
Little Rock, AR 72203
Phone: 501-375-1104
Fax: 501-375-4236
Web: www.arlegion.org

American Legion Arkansas Auxiliary

American Legion Arkansas Auxiliary Scholarships

Type of award: Scholarship.
Intended use: For undergraduate study at postsecondary institution.
Eligibility: Applicant or parent must be member/participant of American Legion Auxiliary. Applicant must be high school senior. Applicant must be U.S. citizen residing in Arkansas. Applicant must be descendant of veteran; or dependent of veteran during Grenada conflict, Korean War, Lebanon conflict, Panama conflict, Persian Gulf War, WW I, WW II or Vietnam.
Basis for selection: Applicant must demonstrate financial need, high academic achievement, depth of character, leadership and patriotism.
Application requirements: Recommendations, essay, transcript, proof of eligibility. SAT/ACT scores.

Additional information: Academic Scholarship: one $1,000; Nurse Scholarship: one $500. Awards paid half first semester, half second semester. Student must be Arkansas resident attending Arkansas school. Include name of high school and SASE with application request.

Amount of award:	$500-$1,000
Number of awards:	2
Application deadline:	March 1
Total amount awarded:	$1,500

Contact:
American Legion Auxiliary, Department of Arkansas
Department Secretary
1415 West 7th St.
Little Rock, AR 72201
Phone: 501-374-5836
Web: www.auxiliary.arlegion.org

American Legion Auxiliary

American Legion Auxiliary Girls State Scholarship

Type of award: Scholarship.
Intended use: For at 2-year or 4-year institution.
Eligibility: Applicant must be female, high school junior.
Basis for selection: Applicant must demonstrate high academic achievement, depth of character and leadership.
Application requirements: $275 application fee. Has to attend Girls State in Mississippi.
Additional information: Must be keenly interested in government and current events, have high moral character, show strong leadership abilities. Must have completed Girls State program in its entirety. Scholarships are won by being elected a City Mayor, Party Whip, top 8 State positions, good citizenship, or delegate to Girls Nation. Some scholarships are chosen as to community service, need, and academic awards.

Amount of award:	$250-$2,500
Number of awards:	40
Application deadline:	May 15

Contact:
American Legion Auxiliary
P.O. Box 1382
Jackson, MS 39215-1382
Phone: 601-353-3681
Web: https://www.alaforveterans.org/ALA-Girls-State/

American Legion Auxiliary Department of Connecticut

American Legion Auxiliary Department of Connecticut Memorial Education Grant

Type of award: Scholarship.
Intended use: For undergraduate study at vocational, 2-year or 4-year institution.
Eligibility: Applicant or parent must be member/participant of American Legion Auxiliary. Applicant must be at least 16, no older than 23. Applicant must be residing in Connecticut.

Basis for selection: Applicant must demonstrate financial need.
Application requirements: Recommendations, essay, transcript, proof of eligibility.
Additional information: Candidate must be Connecticut resident and child of veteran; child/grandchild of Connecticut American Legion or American Legion Auxiliary member (no residency required); or member of Connecticut ALA or Sons of the American Legion (no residency required).

Amount of award:	$500
Number of awards:	4
Application deadline:	March 1
Total amount awarded:	$2,000

Contact:
American Legion Auxiliary, Department of Connecticut
P.O. Box 266
Rocky Hill, CT 06067-0266
Phone: 860-616-2343
Fax: 860-616-2342
Web: www.ct.legion.org

American Legion Auxiliary Department of Connecticut Past Presidents Parley Education Grant

Type of award: Scholarship, renewable.
Intended use: For undergraduate study at vocational, 2-year or 4-year institution.
Eligibility: Applicant or parent must be member/participant of American Legion Auxiliary. Applicant must be at least 16, no older than 23.
Basis for selection: Applicant must demonstrate financial need.
Application requirements: Recommendations, essay, transcript, proof of eligibility.
Additional information: Preference given to child or grandchild of ex-servicewoman who is a CT American Legion or American Legion Auxiliary member of at least three years or who was a member for the three years prior to her death. Second preference to child or grandchild of CT American Legion, American Legion Auxiliary, or Sons of American Legion member of at least three years, or who was a member for three years prior to death.

Amount of award:	$500
Number of awards:	4
Application deadline:	March 1
Total amount awarded:	$2,000

Contact:
American Legion Auxiliary, Department of Connecticut
P.O. Box 266
Rocky Hill, CT 06067-0266
Phone: 860-616-2343
Fax: 860-616-2342
Web: www.ct.legion.org

American Legion Auxiliary Department of Tennessee

Vara Gray Scholarship Fund

Type of award: Scholarship.
Intended use: For undergraduate study at vocational, 2-year or 4-year institution.

Eligibility: Applicant must be high school senior. Applicant must be residing in Tennessee. Applicant must be dependent of veteran.
Application requirements: Recommendations, essay, nomination by local American Legion Auxiliary Unit.
Additional information: There are three (3) Vara Gray Scholarships that are offered annually, (one in each division of Tennessee - East, West, and Middle) in the amount of $500 each by the American Legion Auxiliary Department of Tennessee. For more information on how to apply, please email the address above.

Amount of award:	$500
Number of awards:	3
Application deadline:	March 1
Total amount awarded:	$1,500

Contact:
American Legion Auxiliary Department of Tennessee
104 Point East Drive
Nashville, TN 37216
Phone: 615-226-8648
Fax: 615-226-8649

American Legion Auxiliary Department of Wisconsin

American Legion Auxiliary Past Presidents' Parley Scholarship

Type of award: Scholarship.
Intended use: For undergraduate study at accredited vocational, 2-year or 4-year institution.
Eligibility: Applicant or parent must be member/participant of American Legion Auxiliary. Applicant must be residing in Wisconsin. Applicant must be descendant of veteran; or dependent of veteran or deceased veteran; or spouse of veteran or deceased veteran. Grandchildren or great-grandchildren of veterans eligible if Auxiliary member.
Basis for selection: Major/career interest in nursing. Applicant must demonstrate financial need and high academic achievement.
Application requirements: Recommendations, essay, transcript, proof of eligibility.
Additional information: Minimum 3.5 GPA. Award may be used for nursing school, Registered Nurse program, or course of study for health career.

Amount of award:	$1,000
Number of awards:	2
Application deadline:	March 15

Contact:
American Legion Wisconsin Auxiliary
Department Secretary
P.O. Box 140
Portage, WI 53901-0140
Phone: 608-745-0124
Fax: 608-745-1947
Web: www.amlegionauxwi.org

Della Van Deuren Memorial Scholarship

Type of award: Scholarship.
Intended use: For undergraduate study.

Eligibility: Applicant or parent must be member/participant of American Legion Auxiliary. Applicant must be residing in Wisconsin. Applicant must be descendant of veteran; or dependent of veteran; or spouse of veteran or deceased veteran.
Basis for selection: Applicant must demonstrate financial need and high academic achievement.
Application requirements: Recommendations, essay, transcript, proof of eligibility.
Additional information: Applicant's mother or applicant must be member of a Wisconsin American Legion Auxiliary. Minimum 3.5 GPA. Applicant's school need not be in Wisconsin.

Amount of award:	$1,000
Number of awards:	2
Application deadline:	March 15
Total amount awarded:	$2,000

Contact:
American Legion Wisconsin Auxiliary
Department Secretary
P.O. Box 140
Portage, WI 53901-0140
Phone: 608-745-0124
Fax: 608-745-1947
Web: www.amlegionauxwi.org

Wisconsin American Legion Auxiliary H.S. & Angeline Lewis Scholarship

Type of award: Scholarship.
Intended use: For undergraduate or graduate study at accredited postsecondary institution.
Eligibility: Applicant or parent must be member/participant of American Legion Auxiliary. Applicant must be residing in Wisconsin. Applicant must be descendant of veteran; or dependent of veteran; or spouse of veteran or deceased veteran. Applicant must be direct descendent, wife or widow of a veteran.
Basis for selection: Applicant must demonstrate financial need and high academic achievement.
Application requirements: Recommendations, essay, transcript, proof of eligibility. Applicant must be resident of Wisconsin unless he/she is a member of the Wisconsin American Legion Family.
Additional information: Minimum 3.5 GPA. One award for graduate study; three awards for undergraduate study.

Amount of award:	$1,000
Number of awards:	4
Application deadline:	March 15
Total amount awarded:	$4,000

Contact:
American Legion Wisconsin Auxiliary
Department Secretary
P.O. Box 140
Portage, WI 53901-0140
Phone: 608-745-0124
Fax: 608-745-1947
Web: www.amlegionauxwi.org

Wisconsin American Legion Auxiliary Merit & Memorial Scholarship

Type of award: Scholarship.
Intended use: For undergraduate study.

Eligibility: Applicant or parent must be member/participant of American Legion Auxiliary. Applicant must be residing in Wisconsin. Applicant must be descendant of veteran; or dependent of veteran; or spouse of veteran or deceased veteran. Applicant must be direct descendent, wife or widow of a veteran.

Basis for selection: Applicant must demonstrate financial need and high academic achievement.

Application requirements: Recommendations, essay, transcript, proof of eligibility. Applicant must be resident of Wisconsin unless he/she is a member of the Wisconsin American Legion Family.

Additional information: Minimum 3.5 GPA.

Amount of award:	$1,000
Number of awards:	7
Application deadline:	March 15
Total amount awarded:	$7,000

Contact:
American Legion Wisconsin Auxiliary
Department Secretary
P.O. Box 140
Portage, WI 53901-0140
Phone: 608-745-0124
Fax: 608-745-1947
Web: www.amlegionauxwi.org

American Legion California

American Legion California Oratorical Contest

Type of award: Scholarship.
Intended use: For undergraduate study at postsecondary institution.
Eligibility: Applicant must be enrolled in high school. Applicant must be U.S. citizen or permanent resident residing in California.
Basis for selection: Competition/talent/interest in oratory/debate, based on language style, voice, diction, delivery, originality, logic, breadth of knowledge, application of knowledge about topic, and skill in selecting examples and analogies.
Additional information: Students selected by schools to participate in district contests, followed by area and departmental finals. Awards: First place, $1,200; second place, $1,000; third to sixth place, $700 each. Contact local Post for entry.

Amount of award:	$700-$1,200
Number of awards:	6
Total amount awarded:	$5,000

Contact:
American Legion California
401 Van Ness Avenue, Room 117
San Francisco, CA 94102-4587
Phone: 415-431-2400
Fax: 415-255-1571
Web: www.calegion.org

American Legion California Auxiliary

American Legion California Auxiliary General Scholarships

Type of award: Scholarship.
Intended use: For freshman study at postsecondary institution. Designated institutions: California colleges and universities.
Eligibility: Applicant or parent must be member/participant of American Legion Auxiliary. Applicant must be residing in California. Applicant must be dependent of veteran.
Basis for selection: Applicant must demonstrate financial need.
Application requirements: Recommendations, transcript, proof of eligibility. Cover letter.
Additional information: One $2,000 scholarship; four $1,000 scholarships; three $500 scholarships. Applications must be submitted to local Unit. Applicant may also be Girl Scout, child of American Legion member or child of Sons of Legion member.

Amount of award:	$500-$2,000
Number of awards:	8
Total amount awarded:	$7,500

Contact:
American Legion Auxiliary, Department of California
War Memorial Building
401 Van Ness Avenue, Room 113
San Francisco, CA 94102-4586
Phone: 415-861-5092
Fax: 415-861-8365
Web: www.calegionaux.org

Lucille Ganey Memorial Scholarship

Type of award: Scholarship.
Intended use: For undergraduate study. Designated institutions: Stephens College, Missouri.
Eligibility: Applicant or parent must be member/participant of American Legion Auxiliary. Applicant must be high school senior. Applicant must be residing in California. Applicant must be dependent of active service person or veteran during Grenada conflict, Korean War, Lebanon conflict, Panama conflict, Persian Gulf War, WW I, WW II or Vietnam.
Additional information: Awarded annually to California high school senior who will attend Stephens College in Missouri. California students already attending Stephens College in Missouri also eligible. See Website for application. Applications must be submitted to local Unit.

Amount of award:	$500
Number of awards:	1
Application deadline:	March 16
Total amount awarded:	$500

Contact:
American Legion Auxiliary, Department of California
War Memorial Building
401 Van Ness Avenue, Room 113
San Francisco, CA 94102
Phone: 415-861-5092
Fax: 415-861-8365
Web: www.calegionaux.org

American Legion Colorado

American Legion Colorado National High School Oratorical Contest

Type of award: Scholarship.
Intended use: For undergraduate study at postsecondary institution.
Eligibility: Applicant must be enrolled in high school. Applicant must be residing in Colorado.
Basis for selection: Competition/talent/interest in oratory/ debate, based on language style, voice, diction, delivery, originality, logic, breadth of knowledge, application of knowledge about topic, and skill in selecting examples and analogies.
Additional information: Awards: First place, $1,250; second place, $750; third place, $500. Apply at local Post.

Amount of award:	$500-$1,250
Number of awards:	3
Total amount awarded:	$2,500

Contact:
American Legion, Department of Colorado
7465 East First Avenue, Suite D
Denver, CO 80230
Phone: 303 366-5201
Fax: 303 366-7618
Web: www.coloradolegion.org

American Legion Colorado Auxiliary

American Legion Colorado Auxiliary Department President's Scholarship

Type of award: Scholarship.
Intended use: For undergraduate study at postsecondary institution.
Eligibility: Applicant or parent must be member/participant of American Legion Auxiliary. Applicant must be high school senior. Applicant must be residing in Colorado. Applicant must be dependent of veteran during Grenada conflict, Korean War, Lebanon conflict, Panama conflict, Persian Gulf War, WW I, WW II or Vietnam.
Additional information: One $1,000 award and two $500 awards.

Amount of award:	$500-$1,000
Number of awards:	3
Application deadline:	March 11
Total amount awarded:	$2,000

Contact:
American Legion Auxiliary, Department of Colorado
7465 East First Avenue, Suite D
Denver, CO 80230
Web: www.alacolorado.com

American Legion Colorado Auxiliary Department President's Scholarship for Junior Auxiliary Members

Type of award: Scholarship.
Intended use: For undergraduate study at postsecondary institution.
Eligibility: Applicant or parent must be member/participant of American Legion Auxiliary. Applicant must be high school senior. Applicant must be residing in Colorado. Applicant must be Colorado Junior Auxiliary member.

Amount of award:	$1,000
Number of awards:	1
Application deadline:	March 11
Total amount awarded:	$1,000

Contact:
American Legion Auxiliary, Department of Colorado
7465 East First Avenue, Suite D
Denver, CO 80230
Web: www.alacolorado.com

American Legion Colorado Auxiliary Past Presidents Parley Nurse's Scholarship

Type of award: Scholarship.
Intended use: For undergraduate study at accredited 2-year or 4-year institution.
Eligibility: Applicant or parent must be member/participant of American Legion Auxiliary. Applicant must be residing in Colorado. Applicant must be veteran; or dependent of veteran; or spouse of veteran during Grenada conflict, Korean War, Lebanon conflict, Panama conflict, Persian Gulf War, WW I, WW II or Vietnam.
Basis for selection: Major/career interest in nursing.
Additional information: Number and amount of awards vary.

Amount of award:	$500-$1,000
Application deadline:	April 15

Contact:
American Legion Auxiliary, Department of Colorado
7465 East First Avenue, Suite D
Denver, CO 80230
Web: www.alacolorado.org

American Legion Connecticut

American Legion Connecticut National High School Oratorical Contest

Type of award: Scholarship.
Intended use: For undergraduate study at postsecondary institution.
Eligibility: Applicant must be no older than 19, enrolled in high school. Applicant must be residing in Connecticut.
Basis for selection: Competition/talent/interest in oratory/ debate, based on language style, voice, diction, delivery, originality, logic, breadth of knowledge, application of

123

knowledge about topic, and skill in selecting examples and analogies.

Additional information: Awards: First place, $1,500; second, $1,000; third to seventh place, $500. Contest open only to students attending Connecticut high schools. Contact high school for more information.

Amount of award:	$500-$1,500
Number of awards:	7
Total amount awarded:	$5,000

Contact:
American Legion, Department of Connecticut
Department Oratorical Chairman
P.O. Box 208
Rocky Hill, CT 06067
Phone: 860-436-9986
Web: www.ct.legion.org

American Legion Delaware Auxiliary

American Legion Delaware Auxiliary Past Presidents Parley Nursing Scholarship

Type of award: Scholarship.
Intended use: For undergraduate study at postsecondary institution.
Eligibility: Applicant or parent must be member/participant of American Legion Auxiliary. Applicant must be residing in Delaware. Applicant must be dependent of veteran.
Basis for selection: Major/career interest in nursing.
Application requirements: Essay.
Additional information: Must be the child, grandchild, or great grandchild of a veteran. Essay theme changes annually.

Amount of award:	$300
Number of awards:	1
Application deadline:	February 28
Total amount awarded:	$300

Contact:
American Legion Auxiliary, Department of Delaware
Attn: Tina Washington
25109 Prettyman Rd.
Georgetown, DE 19947

American Legion District of Columbia

American Legion District of Columbia National High School Oratorical Contest

Type of award: Scholarship.
Intended use: For undergraduate study at postsecondary institution.
Eligibility: Applicant must be no older than 19, enrolled in high school. Applicant must be U.S. citizen or permanent resident residing in District of Columbia.

Basis for selection: Competition/talent/interest in oratory/debate, based on language style, voice, diction, delivery, originality, logic, breadth of knowledge, application of knowledge about topic, and skill in selecting examples and analogies.
Application requirements: Proof of eligibility.
Additional information: Awards: First place, $1,500; second place, $500; third place, $300; fourth place, $100.

Amount of award:	$100-$800
Number of awards:	4
Total amount awarded:	$1,600

Contact:
The American Legion, Department of DC
1325 D St. SE
Suite 202
Washington, DC 20003
Phone: 202-362-9151
Fax: 202-362-9152

American Legion Florida

American Legion Florida Eagle Scout of the Year

Type of award: Scholarship.
Intended use: For undergraduate study at accredited postsecondary institution in United States.
Eligibility: Applicant or parent must be member/participant of American Legion. Applicant must be male, enrolled in high school. Applicant must be residing in Florida.
Application requirements: Transcript, proof of eligibility.
Additional information: Applicant must have earned Eagle Award and religious emblem, must be a high school student and Florida resident, must be in a troop chartered to an American Legion Post or the son/grandson of a Legion Member or parent eligible to join the American Legion Department of Florida. Awards: First place, $2,500; second place, $1,500; third place, $1,000; fourth place, $500.

Amount of award:	$500-$2,500
Number of awards:	4
Application deadline:	March 1
Total amount awarded:	$5,500

Contact:
American Legion Florida, Department Headquarters
P.O. Box 547859
Orlando, FL 32854-7859
Phone: 407-295-2631
Web: www.floridalegion.org

American Legion Florida General Scholarship

Type of award: Scholarship.
Intended use: For undergraduate study at accredited postsecondary institution in United States.
Eligibility: Applicant or parent must be member/participant of American Legion. Applicant must be high school senior. Applicant must be residing in Florida. Must be child, grandchild, great-grandchild, or legally adopted child of member in good standing of American Legion Florida, or of a deceased U.S. veteran who would have been eligible for membership.
Application requirements: Proof of eligibility.

Additional information: Awards: First place, $2,500; second place, $1,500; third place, $1,000; fourth to seventh place, $500. Student must be senior attending Florida high school. Parents must be Florida residents.

Amount of award:	$500-$2,500
Number of awards:	7
Application deadline:	March 1
Total amount awarded:	$7,000

Contact:
American Legion Florida, Department Headquarters
P.O. Box 547859
Orlando, FL 32854-7859
Phone: 407-295-2631
Web: www.floridalegion.org

American Legion Florida High School Oratorical Contest

Type of award: Scholarship.
Intended use: For undergraduate study at postsecondary institution.
Eligibility: Applicant or parent must be member/participant of American Legion. Applicant must be enrolled in high school. Applicant must be residing in Florida.
Basis for selection: Competition/talent/interest in oratory/debate, based on language style, voice, diction, delivery, originality, logic, breadth of knowledge, application of knowledge about topic, and skill in selecting examples and analogies.
Additional information: Awards: First place, $2,500; second place, $1,500; third place, $1,000; fourth to sixth place, $500. Parents must be Florida residents.

Amount of award:	$500-$2,500
Number of awards:	6
Application deadline:	December 1
Total amount awarded:	$6,500

Contact:
American Legion Florida, Department Headquarters
P.O. Box 547859
Orlando, FL 32854-7859
Phone: 407-295-2631
Web: www.floridalegion.org

American Legion Florida Auxiliary

American Legion Florida Auxiliary Department Scholarships

Type of award: Scholarship, renewable.
Intended use: For undergraduate study at vocational, 2-year or 4-year institution.
Eligibility: Applicant or parent must be member/participant of American Legion Auxiliary. Applicant must be residing in Florida. Must be child or stepchild of honorably discharged U.S. military veteran and sponsored by local Auxiliary Unit.
Basis for selection: Applicant must demonstrate high academic achievement.
Application requirements: Recommendations, essay, transcript, proof of eligibility. Income tax forms.
Additional information: Up to $2,000 for four-year university; $1000 for junior colleges and vocational schools. Must maintain minimum 2.5 GPA.

Amount of award:	$1,000-$2,000

Contact:
American Legion Auxiliary, Department of Florida
Department Secretary
P.O. Box 547917
Orlando, FL 32854
Fax: 407-293-7411
Web: www.alafl.org

American Legion Florida Auxiliary Memorial Scholarship

Type of award: Scholarship, renewable.
Intended use: For full-time undergraduate study at vocational, 2-year or 4-year institution.
Eligibility: Applicant or parent must be member/participant of American Legion Auxiliary. Applicant must be residing in Florida. Must be member or daughter/granddaughter of member with at least three years membership in FL unit.
Basis for selection: Applicant must demonstrate high academic achievement.
Application requirements: Recommendations, essay, transcript, proof of eligibility. Income tax forms.
Additional information: Up to $2,000 for four-year university; $1,000 for junior colleges and vocational schools. Must maintain minimum 2.5 GPA.

Amount of award:	$1,000-$2,000
Application deadline:	February 1

Contact:
American Legion Auxiliary, Department of Florida
Department Secretary
P.O. Box 547917
Orlando, FL 32854
Fax: 407-293-7411
Web: www.alafl.org

American Legion Georgia

American Legion Georgia Oratorical Contest

Type of award: Scholarship.
Intended use: For undergraduate study.
Eligibility: Applicant or parent must be member/participant of American Legion. Applicant must be residing in Georgia.
Additional information: Awards: First place, $1,300; second place, $900; third place, $650; fourth place, $450.

Amount of award:	$450-$1,300
Number of awards:	4

Contact:
American Legion, Department of Georgia
3035 Mt. Zion Rd
Stockbridge, GA 30281-4101
Phone: 678-289-8883
Web: www.galegion.org

American Legion Georgia Scholarship

Type of award: Scholarship.
Intended use: For undergraduate study at postsecondary institution.
Eligibility: Applicant or parent must be member/participant of American Legion Auxiliary. Applicant must be high school

senior. Applicant must be residing in Georgia. Applicant must be dependent of veteran or deceased veteran.
Additional information: Applicant must be outstanding student endorsed by post and high school principal. Must be child or grandchild of veteran member of Georgia Legion.

Amount of award:	$1,000
Number of awards:	6
Total amount awarded:	$6,000

Contact:
American Legion Georgia, Department Headquarters
3035 Mt. Zion Road
Stockbridge, GA 30281-4101
Phone: 678-289-8883
Web: www.galegion.org

American Legion Georgia Auxiliary

American Legion Georgia Auxiliary Past Presidents Parley Nurses Scholarship

Type of award: Scholarship.
Intended use: For undergraduate study at 2-year or 4-year institution.
Eligibility: Applicant or parent must be member/participant of American Legion Auxiliary. Applicant must be residing in Georgia. Applicant must be dependent of veteran or deceased veteran. Must be sponsored by local Auxiliary Unit.
Basis for selection: Major/career interest in nursing.
Application requirements: Proof of eligibility.
Additional information: Number and amount of scholarships determined by available funds.

Application deadline: June 1
Contact:
American Legion Georgia Auxiliary, Department Headquarters
3035 Mt. Zion Road
Stockbridge, GA 30281-4101
Phone: 678-289-8446
Web: www.galegionaux.org

American Legion Hawaii

American Legion Hawaii Oratorical Contest

Type of award: Scholarship.
Intended use: For undergraduate study at postsecondary institution.
Eligibility: Applicant must be enrolled in high school. Applicant must be residing in Hawaii.
Basis for selection: Competition/talent/interest in oratory/debate, based on language style, voice, diction, delivery, originality, logic, breadth of knowledge, application of knowledge about topic, and skill in selecting examples and analogies.
Additional information: Awards: First place, $1,000; second place, $500; third place, $100; fourth place, $50. Contest normally held in February.

Amount of award:	$50-$1,000
Number of awards:	4
Total amount awarded:	$1,650

Contact:
American Legion Hawaii, Department Headquarters
612 McCully Street
Honolulu, HI 96826
Phone: 808-946-6383
Fax: 808-947-3957
Web: www.americanlegionhawaii.org

American Legion Idaho

American Legion Idaho Oratorical Contest

Type of award: Scholarship.
Intended use: For undergraduate study at postsecondary institution.
Eligibility: Applicant must be enrolled in high school. Applicant must be residing in Idaho.
Basis for selection: Competition/talent/interest in oratory/debate, based on language style, voice, diction, delivery, originality, logic, breadth of knowledge, application of knowledge about topic, and skill in selecting examples and analogies.
Additional information: Awards: First place, $750; second place, $500; third place, $250; fourth place, $100. Visit Website for more information.

Amount of award:	$100-$750
Number of awards:	4
Total amount awarded:	$1,600

Contact:
American Legion Idaho, Department Headquarters
901 Warren Street
Boise, ID 83706
Phone: 208-342-7061
Fax: 208-342-1964

American Legion Idaho Scholarships

Type of award: Scholarship.
Intended use: For undergraduate study at postsecondary institution.
Eligibility: Applicant or parent must be member/participant of American Legion. Applicant must be residing in Idaho.
Application requirements: Proof of eligibility.
Additional information: Grandchildren of American Legion members and children/grandchildren of American Legion Auxiliary members in Idaho also eligible. Scholarships determined annually. See Website for more information.

Application deadline: July 1
Contact:
American Legion Idaho, Department Headquarters
901 Warren Street
Boise, ID 83706
Phone: 208-342-7061
Fax: 208-342-1964

American Legion Idaho Auxiliary

American Legion Idaho Auxiliary Nurse's Scholarship

Type of award: Scholarship.
Intended use: For undergraduate study at 2-year or 4-year institution.
Eligibility: Applicant must be at least 17, no older than 35. Applicant must be residing in Idaho. Applicant must be veteran; or dependent of veteran.
Basis for selection: Major/career interest in nursing.
Application requirements: Recommendations, transcript, proof of eligibility. Financial statement, photograph.
Additional information: Grandchildren of veterans also eligible. Submit application to local Auxiliary Unit.

Amount of award:	$1,000
Application deadline:	May 15

Contact:
American Legion Idaho Auxiliary, Department Headquarters
905 Warren Street
Boise, ID 83706-3825
Phone: 208-342-7066
Web: www.idahoala.org

American Legion Illinois

American Legion Illinois Boy Scout Eagle Scout Scholarship

Type of award: Scholarship.
Intended use: For undergraduate study at postsecondary institution.
Eligibility: Applicant or parent must be member/participant of Boy Scouts of America. Applicant must be high school senior. Applicant must be residing in Illinois.
Basis for selection: Competition/talent/interest in writing/journalism.
Application requirements: Proof of eligibility. 500-word essay on American Legion, Americanism, and Boy Scout programs.
Additional information: Boy Scout Scholarship: $700. Runner-up awards: $200. Contact American Legion Department of Illinois, Post, County, District, or Division for application.

Amount of award:	$200-$700
Number of awards:	3
Application deadline:	April 15

Contact:
American Legion, Department of Illinois
c/o Boy Scout Committee
2720 E. Lincoln St.
Bloomington, IL 61704
Phone: 309-663-0361
Web: www.illegion.org

American Legion Illinois Oratorical Scholarship Program

Type of award: Scholarship.
Intended use: For undergraduate study at accredited vocational, 2-year or 4-year institution.
Eligibility: Applicant must be enrolled in high school. Applicant must be U.S. citizen or permanent resident residing in Illinois.
Basis for selection: Competition/talent/interest in oratory/debate, based on language style, voice, diction, delivery, originality, logic, breadth of knowledge, application of knowledge about topic, and skill in selecting examples and analogies.
Application requirements: Proof of eligibility.
Additional information: Contest begins in January and starts at Post level, continuing to District level, to Division level, to Department level. Awards: First place, $2,000; second place, $1,500; third place, $1,200; fourth and fifth place, $1,000. First place winner of Department will proceed to national competition. Contact local Post or Department Headquarters.

Amount of award:	$1,000-$2,000
Number of awards:	5
Application deadline:	January 31
Total amount awarded:	$6,700

Contact:
American Legion, Department of Illinois
2720 E. Lincoln St.
Bloomington, IL 61704
Phone: 309-663-0361
Web: www.illegion.org

American Legion Illinois Scholarships

Type of award: Scholarship.
Intended use: For at accredited vocational, 2-year or 4-year institution.
Eligibility: Applicant or parent must be member/participant of American Legion. Applicant must be high school senior. Applicant must be residing in Illinois.
Basis for selection: Applicant must demonstrate financial need and high academic achievement.
Application requirements: Proof of eligibility.
Additional information: Grandchildren of American Legion members also eligible.

Amount of award:	$1,000
Number of awards:	20
Application deadline:	March 15

Contact:
American Legion, Department of Illinois
2720 E. Lincoln St.
Bloomington, IL 61704
Phone: 309-663-0361
Web: www.illegion.org

American Legion Illinois Auxiliary

American Legion Illinois Auxiliary Ada Mucklestone Memorial Scholarship

Type of award: Scholarship.
Intended use: For undergraduate study at postsecondary institution.

Eligibility: Applicant must be residing in Illinois. Applicant must be descendant of veteran; or dependent of veteran during Grenada conflict, Korean War, Lebanon conflict, Panama conflict, Persian Gulf War, WW I, WW II or Vietnam.

Basis for selection: Applicant must demonstrate financial need, high academic achievement, depth of character and leadership.

Application requirements: Recommendations, essay, transcript, proof of eligibility. Copy of parents' most recent federal income tax return.

Additional information: Must be a high school senior or graduate of accredited high school. For first time post-secondary education only. May also be a grandchild or great-grandchild of eligible veteran. Must be a resident of Illinois or a member in good standing of The American Legion Family, Department of Illinois. Nursing majors not eligible. Unit sponsorship required. Contact local Unit for application.

Amount of award:	$1,000
Application deadline:	March 15

Contact:
American Legion Auxiliary, Department of Illinois
2720 E. Lincoln St.
Bloomington, IL 61704
Phone: 309-663-9366
Web: www.ilala.org

American Legion Illinois Auxiliary Special Education Teaching Scholarships

Type of award: Scholarship.

Intended use: For sophomore or junior study at 4-year institution.

Eligibility: Applicant must be residing in Illinois. Applicant must be veteran or descendant of veteran; or dependent of veteran during Grenada conflict, Korean War, Lebanon conflict, Panama conflict, Persian Gulf War, WW I, WW II or Vietnam.

Basis for selection: Major/career interest in education, special. Applicant must demonstrate financial need.

Application requirements: Proof of eligibility.

Additional information: Unit sponsorship required. Contact local Unit for application.

Amount of award:	$1,000
Application deadline:	March 15
Total amount awarded:	$1,000

Contact:
American Legion Auxiliary, Department of Illinois
2720 E. Lincoln St.
Bloomington, IL 61704
Phone: 309-663-9366
Web: www.ilala.org

American Legion Illinois Auxiliary Student Nurse Scholarship

Type of award: Scholarship.

Intended use: For undergraduate study at 2-year or 4-year institution.

Eligibility: Applicant must be residing in Illinois.

Basis for selection: Major/career interest in nursing.

Application requirements: Recommendations, essay, transcript, proof of eligibility.

Additional information: Unit sponsorship required. Contact local Unit for application.

Amount of award:	$1,000
Number of awards:	1
Application deadline:	April 10
Total amount awarded:	$1,000

Contact:
American Legion Auxiliary, Department of Illinois
2720 E. Lincoln St.
Bloomington, IL 61704
Phone: 309-663-9366
Web: www.ilala.org

Americanism Essay Contest Scholarship

Type of award: Scholarship.

Intended use: For undergraduate study at postsecondary institution.

Eligibility: Applicant must be enrolled in high school. Applicant must be residing in Illinois.

Application requirements: 500-word essay on selected topic.

Additional information: Award amount depends on placement and grade level. Open to students grade 7-12 enrolled at accredited Illinois junior high and high schools or home schooled. Deadline is first Friday in February. Submit essay to local American Legion Post, Auxiliary Unit, or Sons of American Legion Squadron.

Amount of award:	$100-$1,200

Contact:
American Legion Illinois Auxiliary
2720 E. Lincoln St.
Bloomington, IL 61704
Web: www.illegion.org

Mildred R. Knoles Scholarship

Type of award: Scholarship.

Intended use: For sophomore, junior or senior study at postsecondary institution.

Eligibility: Applicant must be residing in Illinois. Applicant must be veteran or descendant of veteran; or dependent of veteran during Grenada conflict, Korean War, Lebanon conflict, Panama conflict, Persian Gulf War, WW I, WW II or Vietnam.

Basis for selection: Applicant must demonstrate financial need, high academic achievement, depth of character and leadership.

Application requirements: Recommendations, essay, transcript, proof of eligibility. Copy of most recent federal income tax return.

Additional information: Must be resident of Illinois or member in good standing of the American Legion Family, Department of Illinois. Awards: one $1,200; several $800. Unit sponsorship required. Contact local Unit for application. Nursing students not eligible.

Amount of award:	$1,000
Application deadline:	March 15

Contact:
American Legion Auxiliary, Department of Illinois
2720 E. Lincoln St.
Bloomington, IL 61704
Phone: 309-663-9366
Web: www.ilala.org

American Legion Indiana

American Legion Indiana Americanism and Government Test

Type of award: Scholarship.
Intended use: For undergraduate study at postsecondary institution.
Eligibility: Applicant must be high school sophomore, junior or senior. Applicant must be residing in Indiana.
Additional information: Six state winners chosen annually (one male, one female in each grade). Test given during American Education Week in November. Visit Website for local chairperson's contact information.

Amount of award:	$1,000
Number of awards:	6
Total amount awarded:	$6,000

Contact:
American Legion, Department Headquarters
Attn: Americanism Office
5440 Herbert Lord Road
Indianapolis, IN 46216-2119
Phone: 317-630-1391
Fax: 317-237-9891
Web: www.indianalegion.org

American Legion Indiana Eagle Scout of the Year Scholarship

Type of award: Scholarship.
Intended use: For freshman study at postsecondary institution in United States.
Eligibility: Applicant or parent must be member/participant of American Legion. Applicant must be residing in Indiana.
Additional information: Eagle Scout of the Year winner from IN submitted to the National Organization. Indiana awards the state winner a $1,000 scholarship and district winners receive a $200 scholarship. Applicant must attend U.S. postsecondary education institution for advance education beyond high school. Check website for details.

Amount of award:	$200-$1,000
Application deadline:	March 1

Contact:
American Legion, Department Headquarters
Attn: Americanism Office
5440 Herbert Lord Road
Indianapolis, IN 46216-2119
Phone: 317-630-1391
Web: www.indianalegion.org

American Legion Indiana Family Scholarship

Type of award: Scholarship.
Intended use: For undergraduate study at accredited vocational, 2-year or 4-year institution in United States.
Eligibility: Applicant or parent must be member/participant of American Legion. Applicant must be residing in Indiana. Applicant must be child or grandchild of current or deceased member of The American Legion Indiana, American Legion Indiana Auxiliary, or Sons of The American Legion.
Application requirements: Essay, transcript, proof of eligibility.
Additional information: Five $1,500 awards.

Amount of award:	$1,500
Number of awards:	5
Application deadline:	April 1

Contact:
American Legion, Department Headquarters
Attn: Americanism Office
5440 Herbert Lord Road
Indianapolis, IN 46216-2119
Phone: 317-630-1391
Web: www.indianalegion.org

American Legion Indiana Oratorical Contest

Type of award: Scholarship.
Intended use: For undergraduate study at postsecondary institution.
Eligibility: Applicant must be no older than 19, enrolled in high school. Applicant must be residing in Indiana.
Basis for selection: Competition/talent/interest in oratory/debate, based on language style, voice, diction, delivery, originality, logic, breadth of knowledge, application of knowledge about topic, and skill in selecting examples and analogies.
Application requirements: Proof of eligibility.
Additional information: State awards: First place, $3,400; second to fourth place, $1,000. Zone awards: four winners receive $800 each; 7 participants receive $200 each. Must participate in local contests. Competition begins in December.

Amount of award:	$200-$3,400
Number of awards:	15
Total amount awarded:	$11,000

Contact:
American Legion, Department Headquarters
Attn: Americanism Office
5440 Herbert Lord Road
Indianapolis, IN 46216-2119
Phone: 317-630-1391
Web: www.indianalegion.org

American Legion Indiana Auxiliary

American Legion Indiana Auxiliary Past Presidents Parley Nursing Scholarship

Type of award: Scholarship.
Intended use: For undergraduate study.
Eligibility: Applicant or parent must be member/participant of American Legion Auxiliary. Applicant must be female. Applicant must be residing in Indiana.
Basis for selection: Major/career interest in nursing.
Application requirements: Send SASE for application.

Amount of award:	$500
Total amount awarded:	$500

Contact:
American Legion Auxiliary, Department Headquarters
Past Presidents Parley Nursing Scholarship
5440 Herbert Lord Road
Indianapolis, IN 46216-2119
Phone: 317-630-1391
Fax: 317-237-9891
Web: www.aladeptin.org

American Legion Iowa

American Legion Iowa Boy Scout of the Year Scholarship

Type of award: Scholarship.
Intended use: For undergraduate study at postsecondary institution.
Eligibility: Applicant or parent must be member/participant of Boy Scouts of America, Eagle Scouts. Applicant must be male, at least 15. Applicant must be residing in Iowa.
Basis for selection: Applicant must demonstrate service orientation.
Application requirements: Recommendations, transcript, proof of eligibility.
Additional information: Must be registered, active member of Boy Scout Troop, Varsity Scout Team, or Venturing Crew chartered to American Legion Post, Auxiliary Unit, or Sons of American Legion Squadron; or be a registered, active member of Boy Scout Troop, Varsity Scout Team, or Venturing Crew and the son or grandson of an American Legion or Sons of American Legion member. Awards: First place, $2,000; second place, $1,500; third place, $1,000. Awarded on recommendation of Boy Scout Committee to Boy Scout who demonstrates outstanding service to religious institution, school, and community. Must have received Eagle Scout Award.

Amount of award:	$1,000-$2,000
Number of awards:	3
Application deadline:	February 1
Total amount awarded:	$4,500

Contact:
American Legion Iowa, Department Headquarters
720 Lyon Street
Des Moines, IA 50309
Phone: 515-282-5068
Fax: 515-282-7583
Web: www.ialegion.org

American Legion Iowa Oratorical Contest

Type of award: Scholarship.
Intended use: For undergraduate study at postsecondary institution.
Eligibility: Applicant must be enrolled in high school. Applicant must be U.S. citizen or permanent resident residing in Iowa.
Basis for selection: Competition/talent/interest in oratory/debate, based on language style, voice, diction, delivery, originality, logic, breadth of knowledge, application of knowledge about topic, and skill in selecting examples and analogies.
Application requirements: Proof of eligibility.

Additional information: Awards: First place, $2,000; second place, $1,500; third place, $1,000. Must enter Oratorical Contest at local level in September.

Amount of award:	$1,000-$2,000
Number of awards:	3
Total amount awarded:	$4,500

Contact:
American Legion Iowa, Department Headquarters
720 Lyon Street
Des Moines, IA 50309
Phone: 515-282-5068
Fax: 515-282-7583
Web: www.ialegion.org

American Legion Iowa Outstanding Citizen of Boys State Scholarship

Type of award: Scholarship.
Intended use: For undergraduate study at postsecondary institution. Designated institutions: Eligible colleges and universities in Iowa.
Eligibility: Applicant or parent must be member/participant of American Legion, Boys State. Applicant must be male, high school senior. Applicant must be residing in Iowa.
Application requirements: Recommendations.
Additional information: Must have completed junior year in high school to attend Boys State. Awarded on recommendation of Boys State.

Amount of award:	$5,000
Number of awards:	1

Contact:
American Legion Iowa, Department Headquarters
720 Lyon Street
Des Moines, IA 50309
Phone: 515-282-5068
Fax: 515-282-7583
Web: www.ialegion.org

American Legion Iowa Auxiliary

American Legion Department of Iowa Scholarships

Type of award: Scholarship.
Intended use: For undergraduate study at postsecondary institution. Designated institutions: Eligible Iowa postsecondary institutions.
Eligibility: Applicant must be residing in Iowa. Applicant must be veteran or descendant of veteran; or dependent of veteran or deceased veteran; or spouse of veteran or deceased veteran.
Application requirements: Recommendations, essay, transcript, proof of eligibility. Photo of self.

Amount of award:	$300
Number of awards:	10
Application deadline:	May 20
Total amount awarded:	$3,000

Contact:
American Legion Auxiliary, Department of Iowa
Attn: Education Chair
720 Lyon Street
Des Moines, IA 50309
Phone: 515-282-7987
Fax: 515-282-7583
Web: www.ialegion.org/ala

American Legion Iowa Auxiliary Past President's Scholarship

Type of award: Scholarship.
Intended use: For undergraduate study at postsecondary institution.
Eligibility: Applicant must be residing in Iowa. Applicant must be veteran or descendant of veteran; or dependent of veteran or deceased veteran; or spouse of veteran or deceased veteran.
Application requirements: Recommendations, essay, transcript, proof of eligibility. Photo of self.

Amount of award:	$500
Application deadline:	May 20
Total amount awarded:	$500

Contact:
American Legion Iowa Auxiliary
Attn: Education Chair
720 Lyon Street
Des Moines, IA 50309
Phone: 515-282-7987
Fax: 515-282-7583
Web: www.ialegion.org/ala/

Harriet Hoffman Memorial Scholarship

Type of award: Scholarship.
Intended use: For undergraduate study at postsecondary institution. Designated institutions: Eligible Iowa postsecondary institutions.
Eligibility: Applicant must be residing in Iowa. Applicant must be veteran or descendant of veteran; or dependent of veteran or deceased veteran; or spouse of veteran or deceased veteran.
Basis for selection: Major/career interest in education or education, teacher.
Application requirements: Recommendations, essay, transcript, proof of eligibility. Photo of self.

Amount of award:	$500
Number of awards:	1
Application deadline:	May 20
Total amount awarded:	$500

Contact:
American Legion Auxiliary, Department of Iowa
Attn: Education Chair
720 Lyon Street
Des Moines, IA 50309
Phone: 515-282-7987
Fax: 515-282-7583
Web: www.ialegion.org/ala

Mary Virginia Macrea Memorial Scholarship

Type of award: Scholarship.
Intended use: For undergraduate study at postsecondary institution. Designated institutions: Eligible Iowa postsecondary institutions.

Eligibility: Applicant must be residing in Iowa. Applicant must be veteran or descendant of veteran; or dependent of veteran or deceased veteran; or spouse of veteran or deceased veteran.
Basis for selection: Major/career interest in nursing.
Application requirements: Recommendations, essay, transcript, proof of eligibility. Photo of self.

Amount of award:	$500
Number of awards:	1
Application deadline:	May 20
Total amount awarded:	$500

Contact:
American Legion Auxiliary, Department of Iowa
Attn: Education Chair
720 Lyon Street
Des Moines, IA 50309
Phone: 515-282-7987
Fax: 515-282-7583
Web: www.ialegion.org/ala

American Legion Kansas

Albert M. Lappin Scholarship

Type of award: Scholarship.
Intended use: For freshman or sophomore study at accredited vocational, 2-year or 4-year institution. Designated institutions: Eligible colleges, universities, and trade schools in Kansas.
Eligibility: Applicant or parent must be member/participant of American Legion. Applicant must be residing in Kansas.
Application requirements: Recommendations, essay, transcript, proof of eligibility. Income tax forms. Photo of self.
Additional information: High school seniors may also apply. Must be child of member of American Legion Kansas or American Legion Kansas Auxiliary whose parent has been a member for the past three years; or be a child of deceased member of either organization whose dues were paid-up at time of death.

Amount of award:	$1,000
Number of awards:	1
Application deadline:	February 15
Total amount awarded:	$1,000

Contact:
American Legion Kansas
1314 Southwest Topeka Boulevard
Topeka, KS 66612-1886
Phone: 785-232-9315
Web: www.ksamlegion.org

American Legion Kansas Oratorical Contest

Type of award: Scholarship.
Intended use: For undergraduate study at postsecondary institution.
Eligibility: Applicant must be enrolled in high school. Applicant must be residing in Kansas.
Basis for selection: Competition/talent/interest in oratory/debate, based on language style, voice, diction, delivery, originality, logic, breadth of knowledge, application of knowledge about topic, and skill in selecting examples and analogies.
Additional information: State awards: First place, $1,500; second place, $500; third place, $250; and fourth place, $150.

Many Posts, County Councils, and Districts also provide scholarships.

Amount of award:	$150-$1,500
Number of awards:	4
Total amount awarded:	$2,400

Contact:
American Legion Kansas
1314 Southwest Topeka Boulevard
Topeka, KS 66612-1886
Phone: 785-232-9315
Web: www.ksamlegion.org

American Legion Music Committee Scholarship

Type of award: Scholarship.
Intended use: For freshman or sophomore study at accredited vocational, 2-year or 4-year institution. Designated institutions: Eligible Kansas colleges and universities.
Eligibility: Applicant must be residing in Kansas.
Basis for selection: Major/career interest in music. Applicant must demonstrate financial need.
Application requirements: Recommendations, transcript, proof of eligibility. Income tax forms. Photo of self.
Additional information: High school seniors may also apply.

Amount of award:	$1,000
Number of awards:	1
Application deadline:	February 15
Total amount awarded:	$1,000

Contact:
American Legion Kansas
1314 Southwest Topeka Boulevard
Topeka, KS 66612-1886
Phone: 785-232-9315
Web: www.ksamlegion.org

Charles and Annette Hill Scholarship

Type of award: Scholarship.
Intended use: For freshman, sophomore or junior study at postsecondary institution.
Eligibility: Applicant or parent must be member/participant of American Legion. Applicant must be residing in Kansas. Must be descendent of member of American Legion Kansas who has been a member for the past three years; or be descendent of deceased member whose dues were paid-up at time of death.
Basis for selection: Major/career interest in science, general; engineering or business/management/administration. Applicant must demonstrate high academic achievement.
Application requirements: Recommendations, essay, transcript, proof of eligibility. Income tax forms. Photo of self.
Additional information: Minimum 3.0 GPA. High school seniors may also apply.

Amount of award:	$1,000
Number of awards:	1
Application deadline:	February 15
Total amount awarded:	$1,000

Contact:
American Legion Kansas
1314 Southwest Topeka Blvd.
Topeka, KS 66612-1886
Phone: 785-232-9315
Web: www.ksamlegion.org

Dr. Click Cowger Scholarship

Type of award: Scholarship.
Intended use: For freshman or sophomore study at accredited vocational, 2-year or 4-year institution. Designated institutions: Eligible Kansas colleges, universities, and trade schools.
Eligibility: Applicant must be male. Applicant must be residing in Kansas.
Basis for selection: Competition/talent/interest in athletics/sports.
Application requirements: Recommendations, essay, transcript, proof of eligibility. Income tax forms.
Additional information: For current players or those who have played in Kansas American Legion Baseball. High school seniors may also apply.

Amount of award:	$500
Number of awards:	1
Application deadline:	July 15
Total amount awarded:	$500

Contact:
American Legion Kansas
1314 Southwest Topeka Boulevard
Topeka, KS 66612-1886
Phone: 785-232-9315
Web: www.ksamlegion.org

Hugh A. Smith Scholarship

Type of award: Scholarship.
Intended use: For freshman or sophomore study at accredited vocational, 2-year or 4-year institution. Designated institutions: Eligible Kansas colleges, universities, and trade schools.
Eligibility: Applicant or parent must be member/participant of American Legion. Applicant must be residing in Kansas. Applicant must be dependent of veteran or deceased veteran.
Application requirements: Recommendations, essay, transcript, proof of eligibility. Income tax forms. Photo of self.
Additional information: Must be child of member of American Legion Kansas or American Legion Kansas Auxiliary whose parent has been a member for the past three years; or be a child of deceased member of either organization whose dues were paid up at time of death.

Amount of award:	$500
Number of awards:	1
Application deadline:	February 15
Total amount awarded:	$500

Contact:
American Legion Kansas
1314 Southwest Topeka Boulevard
Topeka, KS 66612-1886
Phone: 785-232-9315
Web: www.ksamlegion.org

John and Geraldine Hobble Licensed Practical Nursing Scholarship

Type of award: Scholarship.
Intended use: For freshman study at accredited postsecondary institution. Designated institutions: Kansas accredited schools that award LPN diplomas.
Eligibility: Applicant must be at least 18. Applicant must be residing in Kansas.
Basis for selection: Major/career interest in nursing. Applicant must demonstrate financial need.
Application requirements: Recommendations, transcript, proof of eligibility. Income tax forms, photo of self.

Additional information: One-time award of $300.

Amount of award:	$300
Number of awards:	1
Application deadline:	February 15
Total amount awarded:	$300

Contact:
American Legion Kansas
1314 Southwest Topeka Boulevard
Topeka, KS 66612-1886
Phone: 785-232-9315
Web: www.ksamlegion.org

Rosedale Post 346 Scholarship

Type of award: Scholarship.
Intended use: For freshman or sophomore study at vocational, 2-year or 4-year institution.
Eligibility: Applicant or parent must be member/participant of American Legion. Applicant must be high school senior. Applicant must be residing in Kansas. Applicant must be dependent of veteran or deceased veteran. Must be child of member of American Legion Kansas or American Legion Kansas Auxiliary whose parent has been a member for the past three years; or be a child of deceased member of either organization whose dues were paid up at time of death.
Application requirements: Recommendations, essay, transcript, proof of eligibility. Income tax forms. Photo of self.
Additional information: High school seniors may also apply.

Amount of award:	$1,500
Number of awards:	2
Application deadline:	February 15
Total amount awarded:	$3,000

Contact:
American Legion Kansas
1314 Southwest Topeka Blvd.
Topeka, KS 66612-1886
Phone: 785-232-9315
Web: www.ksamlegion.org

Ted and Nora Anderson Scholarship

Type of award: Scholarship.
Intended use: For freshman or sophomore study at accredited vocational, 2-year or 4-year institution. Designated institutions: Eligible colleges, universities, and trade schools in Kansas.
Eligibility: Applicant or parent must be member/participant of American Legion. Applicant must be residing in Kansas. Applicant must be dependent of veteran or deceased veteran. Must be child of member of American Legion Kansas or American Legion Kansas Auxiliary whose parent has been a member for the past three years; or be a child of deceased member of either organization whose dues were paid up at time of death.
Basis for selection: Applicant must demonstrate financial need.
Application requirements: Recommendations, essay, transcript, proof of eligibility. Photo of self.
Additional information: High school seniors may also apply.

Amount of award:	$500
Number of awards:	4
Application deadline:	February 15
Total amount awarded:	$2,000

Contact:
American Legion Kansas
1314 Southwest Topeka Boulevard
Topeka, KS 66612-1886
Phone: 785-232-9315
Web: www.ksamlegion.org

American Legion Kansas Auxiliary

American Legion Kansas Auxiliary Department Scholarships

Type of award: Scholarship.
Intended use: For full-time freshman study at postsecondary institution. Designated institutions: Kansas institutions.
Eligibility: Applicant must be residing in Kansas. Applicant must be descendant of veteran; or dependent of veteran; or spouse of veteran or deceased veteran.
Application requirements: Recommendations, transcript. SAT/ACT scores.
Additional information: Eight two-year scholarships of $500, payable at $250 per year for two years. Applicants must be entering college for the first time. Spouses of deceased veterans must not be remarried.

Amount of award:	$500
Number of awards:	8
Application deadline:	April 1
Total amount awarded:	$4,000

Contact:
American Legion Kansas Auxiliary
Department Secretary
1314-B Southwest Topeka Boulevard
Topeka, KS 66612-1886
Phone: 785-232-1396
Web: www.kslegionaux.org

American Legion Kentucky

American Legion Kentucky Department Oratorical Awards

Type of award: Scholarship.
Intended use: For undergraduate study at postsecondary institution.
Eligibility: Applicant must be enrolled in high school. Applicant must be residing in Kentucky.
Basis for selection: Competition/talent/interest in oratory/debate, based on language style, voice, diction, delivery, originality, logic, breadth of knowledge, application of knowledge about topic, and skill in selecting examples and analogies.
Additional information: Awards: First place, $2,000; second place, $1,500; third place, $1,000. District winners (11) each receive $200.

Amount of award:	$200-$2,000
Number of awards:	14
Total amount awarded:	$5,800

Contact:
American Legion Kentucky, Department Headquarters
P.O. Box 2123
Louisville, KY 40201
Phone: 502-587-1414
Fax: 502-587-6356
Web: www.kylegion.org

American Legion Kentucky Auxiliary

American Legion Kentucky Auxiliary Mary Barrett Marshall Scholarship

Type of award: Scholarship.
Intended use: For undergraduate study at vocational, 2-year or 4-year institution. Designated institutions: Eligible postsecondary institutions in Kentucky.
Eligibility: Applicant or parent must be member/participant of American Legion Auxiliary. Applicant must be female. Applicant must be residing in Kentucky. Applicant must be descendant of veteran; or dependent of veteran; or spouse of veteran or deceased veteran during Grenada conflict, Korean War, Lebanon conflict, Panama conflict, Persian Gulf War, WW I, WW II or Vietnam.
Application requirements: Proof of eligibility. SASE.

Amount of award:	$1,000
Number of awards:	1
Application deadline:	April 1
Total amount awarded:	$1,000

Contact:
American Legion Auxiliary, Department of Kentucky
P.O. Box 5435
Frankfort, KY 40602
Phone: 502-352-2380
Fax: 502-352-2381
Web: www.kyamlegionaux.org

Laura Blackburn Memorial Scholarship

Type of award: Scholarship.
Intended use: For undergraduate study at postsecondary institution.
Eligibility: Applicant or parent must be member/participant of American Legion Auxiliary. Applicant must be high school senior. Applicant must be residing in Kentucky. Applicant must be descendant of veteran; or dependent of veteran during Grenada conflict, Korean War, Lebanon conflict, Panama conflict, Persian Gulf War, WW I, WW II or Vietnam.
Application requirements: Recommendations, essay, transcript, proof of eligibility. SAT/ACT scores.
Additional information: Must submit application to local American Legion Auxiliary Unit president.

Amount of award:	$1,000
Number of awards:	1
Application deadline:	March 31
Total amount awarded:	$1,000

Contact:
American Legion Auxiliary, Department of Kentucky
P.O. Box 5435
Frankfort, KY 40602
Phone: 502-352-2380
Fax: 502-352-2381
Web: www.kyamlegionaux.org

American Legion Maine

American Legion Maine Children and Youth Scholarship

Type of award: Scholarship.
Intended use: For undergraduate study at accredited postsecondary institution.
Eligibility: Applicant or parent must be member/participant of American Legion. Applicant must be high school senior. Applicant must be residing in Maine.
Basis for selection: Applicant must demonstrate financial need and depth of character.
Application requirements: Recommendations, essay, transcript.
Additional information: High school seniors, college students, and veterans eligible. Students with GED may also apply.

Amount of award:	$500
Number of awards:	7
Number of applicants:	300
Application deadline:	May 1
Total amount awarded:	$3,500

Contact:
American Legion Maine
Department Adjutant, State Headquarters
P.O. Box 900
Waterville, ME 04903-0900
Phone: 207-873-3229
Fax: 207-872-0501
Web: www.mainelegion.org

Daniel E. Lambert Memorial Scholarship

Type of award: Scholarship.
Intended use: For undergraduate study at accredited vocational, 2-year or 4-year institution.
Eligibility: Applicant must be high school senior. Applicant must be U.S. citizen residing in Maine. Applicant must be descendant of veteran; or dependent of veteran.
Basis for selection: Applicant must demonstrate financial need and depth of character.
Application requirements: Recommendations, proof of eligibility.
Additional information: Must be child or grandchild of veteran.

Amount of award:	$1,000
Number of awards:	2
Application deadline:	May 1
Total amount awarded:	$2,000

Contact:
American Legion Maine
Department Adjutant, State Headquarters
P.O. Box 900
Waterville, ME 04903-0900
Phone: 207-873-3229
Fax: 207-872-0501
Web: www.mainelegion.org

James V. Day Scholarship

Type of award: Scholarship.
Intended use: For undergraduate study at vocational, 2-year or 4-year institution.

Eligibility: Applicant or parent must be member/participant of American Legion. Applicant must be high school senior. Applicant must be U.S. citizen residing in Maine.
Basis for selection: Applicant must demonstrate financial need, high academic achievement and depth of character.
Application requirements: Recommendations, essay, proof of eligibility.
Additional information: Must be in top half of graduating class. Grandchildren of current American Legion Post in Maine also eligible.

Amount of award:	$500
Number of awards:	2
Application deadline:	May 1
Total amount awarded:	$1,000

Contact:
American Legion Maine
Department Adjutant, State Headquarters
P.O. Box 900
Waterville, ME 04903-0900
Phone: 207-873-3229
Fax: 207-872-0501
Web: www.mainelegion.org

American Legion Maine Auxiliary

American Legion Maine Auxiliary Presidents Parley Nursing Scholarship

Type of award: Scholarship.
Intended use: For undergraduate study.
Eligibility: Applicant must be residing in Maine. Applicant must be descendant of veteran; or dependent of veteran during WW I or WW II.
Basis for selection: Major/career interest in nursing.
Application requirements: Proof of eligibility.
Additional information: Must be graduate of accredited high school.

Amount of award:	$300
Number of awards:	1
Total amount awarded:	$300

Contact:
American Legion Auxiliary, Department of Maine
Department Secretary
886B Kennedy Memorial Drive
Oakland, ME 04963
Phone: 207-465-4966
Fax: 207-465-4967
Web: www.mainelegion.org

American Legion Maine Auxiliary Scholarship

Type of award: Scholarship.
Intended use: For undergraduate study at vocational, 2-year or 4-year institution.
Eligibility: Applicant must be high school senior. Applicant must be residing in Maine. Applicant must be dependent of veteran.
Basis for selection: Applicant must demonstrate financial need.

Application requirements: Send SASE with application request.

Amount of award:	$300
Number of awards:	2
Application deadline:	April 5
Total amount awarded:	$600

Contact:
American Legion Auxiliary, Department of Maine
Department Secretary
886B Kennedy Memorial Drive
Oakland, ME 04963
Phone: 207-465-4966
Fax: 207-465-4967
Web: www.mainelegion.org

American Legion Maryland

American Legion Maryland Boys State Scholarship

Type of award: Scholarship.
Intended use: For undergraduate study at postsecondary institution.
Eligibility: Applicant or parent must be member/participant of American Legion, Boys State. Applicant must be male, at least 16, no older than 19. Applicant must be residing in Maryland.
Application requirements: Recommendations, transcript.
Additional information: Applicant must be Maryland Boys State graduate.

Amount of award:	$500
Number of awards:	5
Application deadline:	May 1
Total amount awarded:	$2,500

Contact:
American Legion Maryland
Attn: Department Adjutant
101 N. Gay St.
Baltimore, MD 21202-1405
Phone: 410-752-1405
Fax: 410-752-3822
Web: www.mdlegion.org

American Legion Maryland Oratorical Contest

Type of award: Scholarship.
Intended use: For undergraduate study at postsecondary institution.
Eligibility: Applicant must be at least 16, no older than 19. Applicant must be U.S. citizen or permanent resident residing in Maryland.
Basis for selection: Competition/talent/interest in oratory/debate, based on language style, voice, diction, delivery, originality, logic, breadth of knowledge, application of knowledge about topic, and skill in selecting examples and analogies.
Additional information: Awards: First place, $2,500; second place, $1,000; third through seventh place, $500 each. Apply to nearest American Legion Post.

Amount of award:	$500-$2,500
Number of awards:	7
Application deadline:	October 1
Total amount awarded:	$6,000

Contact:
American Legion Maryland
Attn: Department Adjutant
101 N. Gay St.
Baltimore, MD 21202-1405
Phone: 410-752-1405
Fax: 410-752-3822
Web: www.mdlegion.org

American Legion Maryland Scholarship

Type of award: Scholarship.
Intended use: For undergraduate study at postsecondary institution.
Eligibility: Applicant must be at least 16, no older than 19. Applicant must be residing in Maryland. Applicant must be dependent of veteran.
Application requirements: Recommendations, essay, transcript.
Additional information: Applicant must not have reached 20th birthday by January 1 of calendar year application is filed.

Amount of award:	$500
Number of awards:	11
Application deadline:	April 15
Total amount awarded:	$5,500

Contact:
American Legion Maryland
Attn: Department Adjutant
101 N. Gay St.
Baltimore, MD 21202-1405
Phone: 410-752-1405
Fax: 410-752-3822
Web: www.mdlegion.org

American Legion Maryland Auxiliary

American Legion Maryland Auxiliary Past Presidents Parley Scholarship

Type of award: Scholarship.
Intended use: For undergraduate study at 2-year or 4-year institution.
Eligibility: Applicant must be female, at least 16, no older than 22. Applicant must be residing in Maryland. Must be daughter/step-daughter, granddaughter/step-granddaughter, great-granddaughter/step-great-granddaughter of ex-servicewoman or ex-serviceman.
Basis for selection: Major/career interest in nursing. Applicant must demonstrate financial need.
Application requirements: Recommendations.
Additional information: For RN degree only.

Amount of award:	$2,000
Number of awards:	1
Application deadline:	May 1
Total amount awarded:	$2,000

Contact:
American Legion Maryland Auxiliary
Chairman, Past President's Parley Scholarship
1589 Sulphur Spring Road, Suite 105
Baltimore, MD 21227
Phone: 410-242-9519
Fax: 410-242-9553
Web: www.alamd.org

American Legion Maryland Auxiliary Scholarship

Type of award: Scholarship, renewable.
Intended use: For undergraduate study at 2-year or 4-year institution.
Eligibility: Applicant must be female, high school senior. Applicant must be residing in Maryland. Applicant must be dependent of veteran.
Basis for selection: Major/career interest in arts, general; biomedical; business; education; health-related professions; health sciences; physical therapy; physician assistant; public administration/service or science, general. Applicant must demonstrate financial need, depth of character and leadership.
Additional information: Other medical majors eligible. Nursing students not eligible.

Amount of award:	$2,000
Number of awards:	1
Application deadline:	May 1
Total amount awarded:	$2,000

Contact:
American Legion Auxiliary, Department of Maryland
Department Secretary
1589 Sulphur Spring Road, Suite 105
Baltimore, MD 21227
Phone: 410-242-9519
Fax: 410-242-9553
Web: www.alamd.org

American Legion Massachusetts

American Legion Department of Massachusetts Oratorical Contest

Type of award: Scholarship.
Intended use: For undergraduate study at postsecondary institution.
Eligibility: Applicant must be no older than 19. Applicant must be residing in Massachusetts.
Basis for selection: Competition/talent/interest in oratory/debate, based on language style, voice, diction, delivery, originality, logic, breadth of knowledge, application of knowledge about topic, and skill in selecting examples and analogies.
Application requirements: Proof of eligibility.
Additional information: Awards: First place, $1,000; second place, $800; third place, $700; fourth place, $600.

Amount of award:	$600-$1,000
Number of awards:	4
Application deadline:	December 15
Total amount awarded:	$3,100

Scholarships

Contact:
American Legion Massachusetts
Department Oratorical Chair
State House, Room 546-2
Boston, MA 02133-1044
Phone: 617-727-2966
Fax: 617-727-2960
Web: www.masslegion.org

American Legion Massachusetts General and Nursing Scholarships

Type of award: Scholarship.
Intended use: For freshman study at 2-year or 4-year institution.
Eligibility: Applicant or parent must be member/participant of American Legion. Applicant must be residing in Massachusetts. Applicant must be descendant of veteran; or dependent of veteran.
Application requirements: Recommendations, transcript, proof of eligibility.
Additional information: Grandchildren of American Legion Department of Massachusetts members also eligible. General Scholarships: Nine $1,000 awards; ten $500 awards. Nursing Scholarship: One $1,000 award.

Amount of award:	$500-$1,000
Number of awards:	20
Application deadline:	April 1
Total amount awarded:	$15,000

Contact:
American Legion Massachusetts
Department Adjutant
State House, Room 546-2
Boston, MA 02133-1044
Phone: 617-727-2966
Fax: 617-727-2969
Web: www.masslegion.org

American Legion Massachusetts Auxiliary

American Legion Massachusetts Auxiliary Past Presidents Parley Scholarship

Type of award: Scholarship.
Intended use: For undergraduate study at postsecondary institution.
Eligibility: Applicant must be residing in Massachusetts. Applicant must be dependent of veteran or deceased veteran.
Basis for selection: Major/career interest in nursing.
Additional information: Must be child of living or deceased veteran not eligible for Federal or Commonwealth scholarships.

Amount of award:	$200
Number of awards:	1
Total amount awarded:	$200

Contact:
American Legion Massachusetts Auxiliary
Department Secretary
State House, Room 546-2
Boston, MA 02133-1044
Phone: 617-727-2958
Fax: 617-727-0741
Web: www.masslegion-aux.org

American Legion Massachusetts Auxiliary Scholarship

Type of award: Scholarship.
Intended use: For undergraduate study at vocational, 2-year or 4-year institution.
Eligibility: Applicant must be at least 16, no older than 22. Applicant must be residing in Massachusetts. Applicant must be descendant of veteran; or dependent of veteran or deceased veteran during Grenada conflict, Korean War, Lebanon conflict, Panama conflict, Persian Gulf War, WW I, WW II or Vietnam.
Additional information: One $750 award; ten $200 awards.

Amount of award:	$200-$750
Number of awards:	11
Application deadline:	March 1
Total amount awarded:	$2,750

Contact:
American Legion Auxiliary, Department of Massachusetts
Department Secretary
State House, Room 546-2
Boston, MA 02133-1044
Phone: 617-727-2958
Fax: 617-727-0741
Web: www.masslegion-aux.org

American Legion Michigan

American Legion Michigan Oratorical Contest

Type of award: Scholarship.
Intended use: For undergraduate study at postsecondary institution.
Eligibility: Applicant must be no older than 19, enrolled in high school. Applicant must be U.S. citizen or permanent resident residing in Michigan.
Basis for selection: Competition/talent/interest in oratory/debate, based on ability to deliver an 8 to 10-minute speech on the U.S. Constitution.
Additional information: Awards: First place, $1,500; second place, $1,000; third place, $800. Local contest in early February. Contact local American Legion Post for more information.

Amount of award:	$800-$1,500
Number of awards:	3
Total amount awarded:	$3,300

Contact:
Deanna Clark American Legion Michigan
212 North Verlinden Avenue
Ste A
Lansing, MI 48915
Phone: 517-371-4720 ext. 11
Fax: 517-371-2401
Web: www.michiganlegion.org

Guy M. Wilson Scholarship

Type of award: Scholarship.
Intended use: For undergraduate study at 2-year or 4-year institution. Designated institutions: Michigan institutions.
Eligibility: Applicant must be enrolled in high school. Applicant must be residing in Michigan. Applicant must be descendant of veteran; or dependent of veteran or deceased veteran.
Basis for selection: Applicant must demonstrate financial need and high academic achievement.
Application requirements: Transcript, proof of eligibility.
Additional information: Minimum 2.5 GPA. Application should be filed at local American Legion Post.
    Amount of award: $500
    Application deadline: January 14
Contact:
Deanna Clark American Legion Michigan
212 North Verlinden Avenue
Ste A
Lansing, MI 48915
Phone: 517-371-4720 ext. 11
Fax: 517-371-2401
Web: www.michiganlegion.org

William D. & Jewell W. Brewer Scholarship Trusts

Type of award: Scholarship.
Intended use: For undergraduate study at 2-year or 4-year institution.
Eligibility: Applicant must be residing in Michigan. Applicant must be descendant of veteran; or dependent of veteran or deceased veteran.
Basis for selection: Applicant must demonstrate financial need and high academic achievement.
Application requirements: Transcript, proof of eligibility.
Additional information: Minimum 2.5 GPA. Application should be filed at local American Legion Post.
    Amount of award: $500
    Application deadline: January 14
Contact:
Deanna Clark American Legion Michigan
212 North Verlinden Avenue
Ste A
Lansing, MI 48915
Phone: 517-371-4720 ext. 11
Fax: 517-371-2401
Web: www.michiganlegion.org

American Legion Michigan Auxiliary

American Legion Michigan Auxiliary Medical Career Scholarships

Type of award: Scholarship.
Intended use: For freshman study at postsecondary institution. Designated institutions: Michigan institutions.
Eligibility: Applicant must be high school senior. Applicant must be residing in Michigan. Applicant must be descendant of veteran; or dependent of veteran or deceased veteran; or spouse of veteran or deceased veteran during Grenada conflict, Korean War, Lebanon conflict, Panama conflict, Persian Gulf War, WW I, WW II or Vietnam. Applicant must be child, grandchild, great-grandchild, wife, or spouse of honorably discharged or deceased veteran.
Basis for selection: Major/career interest in medicine; physical therapy; respiratory therapy or nursing. Applicant must demonstrate financial need and high academic achievement.
Application requirements: Recommendations, transcript, proof of eligibility. FAFSA or copy of income tax form.
Additional information: Applicants must be pursuing education in medical field. Applications available after November 15. Visit website for details and application.
    Amount of award: $500
    Application deadline: March 15
Contact:
American Legion Auxiliary, Department of Michigan
212 North Verlinden Avenue
Lansing, MI 48915
Phone: 517-267-8809 x21
Fax: 517 371-3698
Web: www.michalaux.org

American Legion Michigan Auxiliary Memorial Scholarship

Type of award: Scholarship, renewable.
Intended use: For undergraduate study at postsecondary institution. Designated institutions: Michigan institutions.
Eligibility: Applicant must be female, at least 16, no older than 21. Applicant must be residing in Michigan. Applicant must be descendant of veteran; or dependent of veteran or deceased veteran during Grenada conflict, Korean War, Lebanon conflict, Panama conflict, Persian Gulf War, WW I, WW II or Vietnam. Applicant must be daughter, granddaughter, or great-granddaughter of honorably discharged or deceased veteran.
Basis for selection: Applicant must demonstrate financial need and high academic achievement.
Application requirements: Recommendations, transcript, proof of eligibility. FAFSA or copy of parents' income tax forms.
Additional information: Must be Michigan resident for at least one year. Visit Website for details and application.
    Amount of award: $500
    Application deadline: March 15
Contact:
American Legion Auxiliary, Department of Michigan
212 North Verlinden Avenue
Lansing, MI 48915
Phone: 517-267-8809 x21
Fax: 517-371-3698
Web: www.michalaux.org

American Legion Michigan Auxiliary National President's Scholarship

Type of award: Scholarship.
Intended use: For undergraduate study at postsecondary institution.
Eligibility: Applicant must be high school senior. Applicant must be residing in Michigan. Applicant must be descendant of veteran; or dependent of veteran during Grenada conflict, Korean War, Middle East War, Lebanon conflict, Panama conflict, Persian Gulf War, WW I, WW II or Vietnam.

Application requirements: Applicant must have completed 50 hours of community service during high school.

Amount of award:	$2,500-$3,500
Number of awards:	1
Application deadline:	March 1

Contact:
American Legion Auxiliary, Department of Michigan
212 North Verlinden Avenue
Lansing, MI 48915
Phone: 517-267-8809 x21
Fax: 517-371-3698
Web: www.michalaux.org

American Legion Minnesota

American Legion Minnesota Legionnaire Insurance Trust Scholarship

Type of award: Scholarship.
Intended use: For undergraduate study at accredited vocational, 2-year or 4-year institution. Designated institutions: Minnesota colleges and universities and institutions in neighboring states with reciprocating agreements.
Eligibility: Applicant or parent must be member/participant of American Legion. Applicant must be U.S. citizen residing in Minnesota. Applicant must be veteran or descendant of veteran; or dependent of veteran.
Basis for selection: Applicant must demonstrate financial need and high academic achievement.
Application requirements: Recommendations, essay, transcript, proof of eligibility.

Amount of award:	$500
Number of awards:	3
Application deadline:	April 1
Total amount awarded:	$1,500

Contact:
American Legion Minnesota
Education Committee
20 West 12th Street, Room 300A
St. Paul, MN 55155-2000
Phone: 866-259-9163
Web: www.mnlegion.org

American Legion Minnesota Memorial Scholarship

Type of award: Scholarship.
Intended use: For undergraduate study at accredited postsecondary institution. Designated institutions: Minnesota colleges and universities and institutions in neighboring states with reciprocating agreement.
Eligibility: Applicant or parent must be member/participant of American Legion. Applicant must be residing in Minnesota.
Basis for selection: Applicant must demonstrate financial need.
Application requirements: Recommendations, essay, transcript, proof of eligibility.
Additional information: Grandchildren of American Legion or American Legion Auxiliary members also eligible.

Amount of award:	$500
Number of awards:	6
Application deadline:	April 1
Total amount awarded:	$3,000

Contact:
American Legion Minnesota
Education Committee
20 West 12th Street, Room 300A
St. Paul, MN 55155-2000
Phone: 866-259-9163
Web: www.mnlegion.org

American Legion Minnesota Oratorical Contest

Type of award: Scholarship.
Intended use: For undergraduate study at accredited postsecondary institution.
Eligibility: Applicant must be enrolled in high school. Applicant must be U.S. citizen or permanent resident residing in Minnesota.
Basis for selection: Competition/talent/interest in oratory/debate, based on language style, voice, diction, delivery, originality, logic, breadth of knowledge, application of knowledge about topic, and skill in selecting examples and analogies.
Additional information: Awards: First place, $1,500; second place, $1000; third place, $700; fourth place, $500.

Amount of award:	$500-$1,500
Number of awards:	4
Application deadline:	December 15
Total amount awarded:	$3,700

Contact:
American Legion Minnesota
Education Committee
20 West 12th Street, Room 300A
St. Paul, MN 55155-2000
Phone: 866-259-9163
Web: www.mnlegion.org

American Legion Minnesota Auxiliary

American Legion Minnesota Auxiliary Department Scholarship

Type of award: Scholarship.
Intended use: For undergraduate study at accredited postsecondary institution.
Eligibility: Applicant or parent must be member/participant of American Legion Auxiliary. Applicant must be residing in Minnesota. Applicant must be descendant of veteran; or dependent of veteran.
Application requirements: Recommendations, essay, transcript.

Amount of award:	$1,000
Number of awards:	7
Application deadline:	March 15
Total amount awarded:	$7,000

Scholarships

Contact:
American Legion Auxiliary, Department of Minnesota
State Veterans Service Building
20 W 12th Street, Room 314
St. Paul, MN 55155-2069
Phone: 651-224-7634
Fax: 651-224-5243
Web: www.mnala.org

American Legion Minnesota Auxiliary Past Presidents Parley Health Care Scholarship

Type of award: Scholarship.
Intended use: For undergraduate study at accredited postsecondary institution.
Eligibility: Applicant or parent must be member/participant of American Legion Auxiliary. Applicant must be residing in Minnesota.
Basis for selection: Major/career interest in health-related professions.

Amount of award:	$1,000
Number of awards:	10
Application deadline:	March 15
Total amount awarded:	$10,000

Contact:
American Legion Auxiliary, Department of Minnesota
State Veterans Service Building
20 W. 12th Street, Room 314
St. Paul, MN 55155-2069
Phone: 651-224-7634
Fax: 651-224-5243
Web: www.mnala.org

American Legion Mississippi Auxiliary

American Legion Mississippi Auxiliary Nursing Scholarship

Type of award: Scholarship.
Intended use: For undergraduate study at accredited postsecondary institution.
Eligibility: Applicant must be high school senior. Applicant must be descendant of veteran; or dependent of veteran during Korean War, Lebanon conflict, Panama conflict, Persian Gulf War, WW I, WW II or Vietnam.
Basis for selection: Major/career interest in nursing.
Additional information: Can be used wherever there is a nursing program, and is available to anyone and any age who has applied for and was accepted in an accredited nursing school. Descendent of a veteran is preferred.

Amount of award:	$1,000
Number of awards:	1
Application deadline:	May 1

Contact:
American Legion Mississippi Auxiliary, Department Headquarters
P.O. Box 1382
Jackson, MS 39215-1382
Phone: 601-353-3681
Fax: 601-353-3682
Web: www.missala.com

American Legion Missouri

American Legion Missouri Commander's Scholarship Fund

Type of award: Scholarship.
Intended use: For full-time undergraduate study at postsecondary institution. Designated institutions: Vocational/technical colleges or universities in Missouri.
Eligibility: Applicant must be residing in Missouri. Applicant must be veteran who served in the Army, Air Force, Marines, Navy or Coast Guard. Applicant must have served in one of the U.S. Armed Forces branches for a minimum of 90 days and received honorable discharge.
Application requirements: Proof of eligibility. Letter of acceptance from college or university.
Additional information: Membership in The American Legion not required.

Amount of award:	$1,000
Number of awards:	2
Application deadline:	April 20
Total amount awarded:	$2,000

Contact:
American Legion Missouri
Attn: Education and Scholarship Committee
P.O. Box 179
Jefferson City, MO 65102-0179
Phone: 800-846-9023
Web: www.missourilegion.org

American Legion Missouri Oratorical Contest

Type of award: Scholarship.
Intended use: For undergraduate study at postsecondary institution.
Eligibility: Applicant must be enrolled in high school. Applicant must be residing in Missouri.
Basis for selection: Competition/talent/interest in oratory/debate, based on language style, voice, diction, delivery, originality, logic, breadth of knowledge, application of knowledge about topic, and skill in selecting examples and analogies.
Application requirements: Proof of eligibility.
Additional information: Awards: First place, $2,000; second place, $1,800; third place, $1,600; and fourth place, $1,400. Awards to be used to defray expenses of higher education.

Amount of award:	$1,400-$2,000
Number of awards:	4
Total amount awarded:	$6,800

Contact:
American Legion Missouri
Department Headquarters
P.O. Box 179
Jefferson City, MO 65102-0179
Phone: 800-846-9023
Web: www.missourilegion.org

Charles L. Bacon Memorial Scholarship

Type of award: Scholarship.
Intended use: For full-time undergraduate study at accredited 2-year or 4-year institution.

Eligibility: Applicant or parent must be member/participant of American Legion. Applicant must be single, no older than 20. Applicant must be U.S. citizen residing in Missouri.
Basis for selection: Applicant must demonstrate financial need.
Additional information: Applicants must be current member of American Legion, American Legion Auxiliary or the Sons of the American Legion, or descendent of any member.

Amount of award:	$500
Number of awards:	2
Application deadline:	April 20
Notification begins:	July 1
Total amount awarded:	$1,000

Contact:
American Legion Missouri
Attn: Education and Scholarship Committee
P.O. Box 179
Jefferson City, MO 65102-0179
Phone: 800-846-9023
Fax: 573-893-2980
Web: www.missourilegion.org

Erman W. Taylor Memorial Scholarship

Type of award: Scholarship.
Intended use: For full-time undergraduate study at accredited 2-year or 4-year institution.
Eligibility: Applicant must be single, no older than 20. Applicant must be U.S. citizen residing in Missouri. Applicant must be descendant of veteran who served in the Army, Air Force, Marines, Navy or Coast Guard. Must be child, grandchild, or great-grandchild of veteran who served 90 or more days of active duty in the Army, Navy, Air Force, Marines, or Coast Guard and has an honorable discharge.
Basis for selection: Major/career interest in education.
Application requirements: Proof of eligibility. Copy of discharge certificate for veteran parent, grandparent; essay on selected topic.

Amount of award:	$500
Number of awards:	2
Application deadline:	April 20
Notification begins:	July 1
Total amount awarded:	$1,000

Contact:
American Legion Missouri
Attn: Education and Scholarship Committee
P.O. Box 179
Jefferson City, MO 65102-0179
Phone: 800-846-9023
Web: www.missourilegion.org

Joseph J. Frank Scholarship

Type of award: Scholarship.
Intended use: For full-time freshman study at accredited postsecondary institution.
Eligibility: Applicant or parent must be member/participant of American Legion. Applicant must be single, no older than 20. Applicant must be residing in Missouri. Applicant must be veteran or descendant of veteran; or dependent of veteran who served in the Army, Air Force, Marines, Navy or Coast Guard. Applicant must have served in one of the U.S. Armed Forces branches for a minimum of 90 days and received honorable discharge.
Application requirements: Proof of eligibility.

Additional information: Applicant must have attended a full session of the American Legion Boys State or Auxiliary Girls State program.

Amount of award:	$500
Number of awards:	5
Application deadline:	April 20
Total amount awarded:	$2,500

Contact:
American Legion Missouri
Attn: Education and Scholarship Committee
P.O. Box 179
Jefferson City, MO 65102-0179
Phone: 800-846-9023
Web: www.missourilegion.org

Lillie Lois Ford Boys' Scholarship

Type of award: Scholarship.
Intended use: For full-time undergraduate study at accredited postsecondary institution.
Eligibility: Applicant or parent must be member/participant of American Legion, Boys State. Applicant must be single, male, no older than 20. Applicant must be residing in Missouri. Applicant must be descendant of veteran who served in the Army, Air Force, Marines, Navy or Coast Guard. Must be child, grandchild, or great-grandchild of veteran who served at least 90 days active duty in Army, Navy, Air Force, Marines, or Coast Guard, and was honorably discharged.
Basis for selection: Applicant must demonstrate financial need.
Application requirements: Proof of eligibility.
Additional information: Must have attended complete session of American Legion Boys State or American Legion Department of Missouri Cadet Patrol Academy.

Amount of award:	$1,000
Number of awards:	1
Application deadline:	April 20
Notification begins:	July 1
Total amount awarded:	$1,000

Contact:
American Legion Missouri
Attn: Education and Scholarship Committee
P.O. Box 179
Jefferson City, MO 65102-0179
Phone: 800-846-9023
Web: www.missourilegion.org

Lillie Lois Ford Girls' Scholarship

Type of award: Scholarship.
Intended use: For full-time undergraduate study at accredited postsecondary institution.
Eligibility: Applicant must be single, female, no older than 20. Applicant must be residing in Missouri. Applicant must be descendant of veteran who served in the Army, Air Force, Marines, Navy or Coast Guard. Must be child, grandchild, or great-grandchild of veteran who served at least 90 days active duty in Army, Navy, Air Force, Marines, or Coast Guard, and was honorably discharged.
Basis for selection: Applicant must demonstrate financial need.
Application requirements: Proof of eligibility.
Additional information: Must have attended complete session of American Legion Auxiliary Girls State or American Legion Department of Missouri Cadet Patrol Academy.

Amount of award:	$1,000
Number of awards:	1
Application deadline:	April 20
Notification begins:	July 1
Total amount awarded:	$1,000

Contact:
American Legion Missouri
Attn: Education and Scholarship Committee
P.O. Box 179
Jefferson City, MO 65102
Phone: 800-846-9023
Web: www.missourilegion.org

M.D. Jack Murphy Memorial Nurses Training Fund

Type of award: Scholarship, renewable.
Intended use: For full-time undergraduate study at 2-year or 4-year institution.
Eligibility: Applicant must be single, no older than 20. Applicant must be residing in Missouri. Applicant must be descendant of veteran who served in the Army, Air Force, Marines, Navy or Coast Guard. Must be child, grandchild, or great-grandchild of veteran who served at least 90 days active duty in Army, Navy, Air Force, Marines, or Coast Guard, and was honorably discharged.
Basis for selection: Major/career interest in nursing. Applicant must demonstrate financial need.
Application requirements: Proof of eligibility.
Additional information: Available to students training to be registered nurses. Applicant must have graduated in top 40% of high school class or have minimum "C" or equivalent standing from last college semester prior to applying for award.

Amount of award:	$750
Number of awards:	1
Application deadline:	April 20
Notification begins:	July 1
Total amount awarded:	$750

Contact:
American Legion Missouri
Attn: Education and Scholarship Committee
P.O. Box 179
Jefferson City, MO 65102-0179
Phone: 800-846-9023
Web: www.missourilegion.org

Shane Dean Voyles Memorial Scholarship

Type of award: Scholarship.
Intended use: For full-time freshman study at accredited postsecondary institution.
Eligibility: Applicant must be single, no older than 20, high school senior. Applicant must be residing in Missouri. Applicant must be descendant of veteran; or dependent of veteran who served in the Army, Air Force, Marines, Navy or Coast Guard. Applicant must have served in one of the U.S. Armed Forces branches for a minimum of 90 days and received honorable discharge.
Basis for selection: Applicant must demonstrate high academic achievement, leadership and service orientation.
Application requirements: Nomination by high school.
Additional information: Each school in Missouri may nominate one student for the award. Nominee selected based on leadership, athletic, and scholastic abilities.

Amount of award:	$750
Number of awards:	1
Application deadline:	April 20
Total amount awarded:	$500

Contact:
American Legion Missouri
Attn: Education and Scholarship Committee
P.O. Box 179
Jefferson City, MO 65102-0179
Phone: 800-846-9023
Web: www.missourilegion.org

American Legion Missouri Auxiliary

American Legion Missouri Auxiliary National President's Scholarship

Type of award: Scholarship.
Intended use: For freshman study.
Eligibility: Applicant or parent must be member/participant of American Legion Auxiliary. Applicant must be residing in Missouri. Applicant must be dependent of veteran.
Additional information: Applicant must be child of veteran who served in the Armed Forces during the eligibility dates of the American Legion. Applicant must complete 50 hours of community service during student's high school years.

Amount of award:	$500
Number of awards:	1
Total amount awarded:	$500

Contact:
American Legion Missouri Auxiliary
600 Ellis Blvd
Jefferson City, MO 65101-2204
Phone: 573-636-9133
Fax: 573-635-3467
Web: www.deptmoala.org

American Legion Missouri Auxiliary Past Presidents Parley Scholarship

Type of award: Scholarship.
Intended use: For undergraduate study at 2-year or 4-year institution.
Eligibility: Applicant must be residing in Missouri. Applicant must be descendant of veteran; or dependent of veteran.
Basis for selection: Major/career interest in nursing.
Application requirements: Recommendations.
Additional information: Applicant must not have previously attended institution of higher learning.

Amount of award:	$500
Number of awards:	2

Contact:
American Legion Missouri Auxiliary
Department Secretary
600 Ellis Blvd
Jefferson City, MO 65101-2204
Phone: 573-636-9133
Fax: 573-635-3467
Web: www.deptmoala.org

American Legion Missouri Auxiliary Scholarship

Type of award: Scholarship.
Intended use: For undergraduate study at postsecondary institution.
Eligibility: Applicant must be high school senior. Applicant must be residing in Missouri. Applicant must be descendant of veteran; or dependent of veteran during Korean War, Lebanon conflict, Panama conflict, Persian Gulf War, WW I, WW II or Vietnam.
Additional information: Applicant must not have previously attended institution of higher learning.

Amount of award:	$500
Number of awards:	2
Application deadline:	March 1
Total amount awarded:	$1,000

Contact:
American Legion Missouri Auxiliary
Department Secretary
600 Ellis Blvd.
Jefferson City, MO 65101-2204
Phone: 573-636-9133
Fax: 573-635-3467
Web: www.deptmoala.org

American Legion Montana Auxiliary

Aloha Scholarship

Type of award: Scholarship.
Intended use: For freshman study at postsecondary institution. Designated institutions: Accredited nursing schools.
Eligibility: Applicant or parent must be member/participant of American Legion Auxiliary. Applicant must be residing in Montana.
Basis for selection: Major/career interest in nursing. Applicant must demonstrate depth of character and leadership.
Application requirements: Recommendations, essay, transcript, proof of eligibility.
Additional information: Grandchildren of Auxiliary members also eligible.

Amount of award:	$400
Number of awards:	1
Application deadline:	April 1

Contact:
American Legion Montana Auxiliary
Department Secretary
P.O. Box 17318
Missoula, MT 59808
Phone: 406-541-8425
Web: mtlegion.org/forms/scholarships.html

American Legion Montana Auxiliary Scholarships (1)

Type of award: Scholarship.
Intended use: For undergraduate study at postsecondary institution.
Eligibility: Applicant must be high school senior. Applicant must be residing in Montana. Applicant must be dependent of veteran.
Basis for selection: Applicant must demonstrate financial need.
Application requirements: Essay, proof of eligibility. 500-word essay on any topic.
Additional information: Applicant must be high school senior or graduate who has not attended college. Must be state resident for at least two years.

Amount of award:	$500
Number of awards:	2
Application deadline:	March 15
Total amount awarded:	$1,000

Contact:
American Legion Montana Auxiliary
Department Secretary
P.O. Box 17318
Missoula, MT 59808
Phone: 406-266-4566
Web: mtlegion.org/forms/scholarships.html

American Legion Montana Auxiliary Scholarships (2)

Type of award: Scholarship.
Intended use: For junior study at postsecondary institution.
Eligibility: Applicant must be residing in Montana. Applicant must be dependent of veteran.
Application requirements: Proof of eligibility. Essay stating interest in issues relating to children and youth.
Additional information: Must have completed sophomore year in college and be going into field relating to children and youth.

Amount of award:	$500
Number of awards:	2
Application deadline:	June 1
Total amount awarded:	$1,000

Contact:
American Legion Montana Auxiliary
Department Secretary
P.O. Box 17318
Missoula, MT 59808
Phone: 406-266-4566
Web: mtlegion.org/forms/scholarships.html

American Legion National Headquarters

American Legion Auxiliary National Presidents Scholarship

Type of award: Scholarship.
Intended use: For undergraduate study at postsecondary institution.
Eligibility: Applicant or parent must be member/participant of American Legion Auxiliary. Applicant must be high school senior. Applicant must be dependent of veteran during Grenada conflict, Korean War, Lebanon conflict, Panama conflict, Persian Gulf War, WW I, WW II or Vietnam.
Basis for selection: Applicant must demonstrate financial need, high academic achievement, depth of character, leadership, patriotism and service orientation.
Additional information: Scholarships awarded annually: five-$3,500; five-$3,000; five-$2,500. Applications available online, from Unit President of Auxiliary in local community, from

Department Secretary, or from National Headquarters. See Website for details.

Amount of award:	$2,500-$3,500
Number of awards:	15
Application deadline:	March 1
Total amount awarded:	$45,000

Contact:
American Legion Auxiliary
8945 North Meridian Street
Indianapolis, IN 46260-1189
Phone: 317-569-4500
Fax: 317-569-4502
Web: www.alaforveterans.org/Scholarships/

American Legion Auxiliary Spirit of Youth Scholarship for Junior Members

Type of award: Scholarship.
Intended use: For undergraduate study at postsecondary institution.
Eligibility: Applicant or parent must be member/participant of American Legion Auxiliary. Applicant must be high school senior. Applicant must be U.S. citizen.
Basis for selection: Applicant must demonstrate financial need, high academic achievement, depth of character, leadership and patriotism.
Application requirements: Proof of eligibility.
Additional information: Must be Junior member of three years standing, holding current membership card. Applications available online, from Unit President of Auxiliary in local community, from Department Secretary, or from National Headquarters. See Website for details.

Amount of award:	$5,000
Number of awards:	5
Application deadline:	March 1
Total amount awarded:	$25,000

Contact:
American Legion Auxiliary
8945 North Meridian Street
Indianapolis, IN 46260
Phone: 317-569-4500
Fax: 317-569-4502
Web: www.alaforveterans.org/Scholarships/

American Legion Eagle Scout of the Year

Type of award: Scholarship.
Intended use: For undergraduate study at accredited postsecondary institution in United States.
Eligibility: Applicant or parent must be member/participant of Boy Scouts of America, Eagle Scouts. Applicant must be male, enrolled in high school. Applicant must be U.S. citizen.
Basis for selection: Applicant must demonstrate depth of character, leadership, patriotism and service orientation.
Application requirements: Recommendations, transcript, proof of eligibility, nomination.
Additional information: Applicant must be registered, active member of Boy Scout Troop, Varsity Scout Team or Venturing Crew AND either (1) chartered to American Legion Post/ Auxiliary Unit or (2) son or grandson of American Legion or Auxiliary member. Awards: One $10,000 Eagle Scout of the Year; three runners-up get $2,500. Scholarships available upon graduation from accredited high school and must be used within four years of graduation date. Request application from State Department Headquarters.

Amount of award:	$2,500-$10,000
Number of awards:	4
Total amount awarded:	$17,500

Contact:
American Legion National Headquarters
Eagle Scout of the Year
P.O. Box 1055
Indianapolis, IN 46206-1055
Phone: 317-630-1200
Fax: 317-630-1223
Web: www.legion.org

American Legion Legacy Scholarship

Type of award: Scholarship, renewable.
Intended use: For undergraduate study at postsecondary institution in United States.
Eligibility: Applicant must be high school senior. Applicant must be residing in Indiana. Applicant must be child (dependent, legally adopted, or from a spouse of prior marriage) of active duty personnel of the U.S. military or National Guard or military reservists who were federalized and died on active duty on or after September 11, 2001.
Application requirements: Transcript, proof of eligibility.
Additional information: Amount and number of awards vary. Previous scholarship recipients may reapply. Visit website for details.

Application deadline:	April 15

Contact:
American Legion National Headquarters
Education Programs Chair
P.O. Box 1055
Indianapolis, IN 46206-1055
Phone: 317-630-1200
Fax: 317-630-1223
Web: www.legion.org

American Legion National High School Oratorical Contest

Type of award: Scholarship.
Intended use: For undergraduate study at postsecondary institution.
Eligibility: Applicant must be no older than 19, enrolled in high school. Applicant must be U.S. citizen or permanent resident.
Basis for selection: Competition/talent/interest in oratory/ debate, based on language style, voice, diction, delivery, originality, logic, breadth of knowledge, application of knowledge about topic, and skill in selecting examples and analogies.
Additional information: Awards: Finalists win $18,000 (first place), $16,000 (runner-up), and $14,000 (third place). Other certified participants who advance beyond first round receive $1,500; those who make it past second round receive additional $1,500. Obtain oratorical contest rules from local Legion Post or state Department Headquarters.

Amount of award:	$1,500-$18,000
Number of awards:	54
Total amount awarded:	$123,000

Contact:
American Legion National Headquarters
Education Programs Chair
P.O. Box 1055
Indianapolis, IN 46206-1055
Phone: 317-630-1200
Fax: 317-630-1223
Web: www.legion.org

American Legion Scholarship for Non-Traditional Students

Type of award: Scholarship.
Intended use: For undergraduate study.
Eligibility: Applicant or parent must be member/participant of American Legion Auxiliary.
Basis for selection: Applicant must demonstrate financial need, depth of character and leadership.
Additional information: Applicant must be a non-traditional student returning to school after some period in which his or her formal education was interrupted or who is just beginning his or her education at a later point in life.

Amount of award:	$2,000
Number of awards:	5
Application deadline:	March 1
Total amount awarded:	$10,000

Contact:
American Legion Auxiliary
8945 North Meridian Street
Indianapolis, IN 46260
Phone: 317-569-4500
Fax: 317-569-4502
Web: www.alaforveterans.org/Scholarships/

Eight and Forty Lung and Respiratory Disease Nursing Scholarship

Type of award: Scholarship.
Intended use: For undergraduate, graduate or non-degree study.
Eligibility: Applicant must be returning adult student.
Basis for selection: Major/career interest in health education; health services administration or nursing.
Application requirements: Proof of eligibility.
Additional information: Applicant must be registered nurse. Program assists registered nurses with advanced preparation for positions in supervision, administration, or teaching. On completion of education, must have full-time employment prospects related to pediatric lung and respiratory control in hospitals, clinics, or health departments. Contact Eight and Forty Scholarship Chairman or the American Legion Education Program for application. Number of awards varies.

Amount of award:	$5,000
Application deadline:	May 15
Notification begins:	July 1

Contact:
American Legion National Headquarters
Eight and Forty Scholarships
P.O. Box 1055
Indianapolis, IN 46206-1055
Phone: 317-630-1200
Fax: 317-630-1223
Web: www.legion.org

Samsung American Legion Scholarship

Type of award: Scholarship.
Intended use: For undergraduate study at postsecondary institution in United States.
Eligibility: Applicant or parent must be member/participant of American Legion. Applicant must be high school junior. Applicant must be descendant of veteran; or dependent of veteran.
Basis for selection: Applicant must demonstrate financial need, high academic achievement and service orientation.
Application requirements: Essay, proof of eligibility.
Additional information: Applicant must have completed American Legion Boys State or Girls State program. Amount and number of awards vary. In 2013, 9 $20,000 and 89 $1,000 scholarships awarded. Visit website for details.

Amount of award:	$1,000-$20,000
Total amount awarded:	$269,000

Contact:
American Legion National Headquarters
Education Programs Chair
P.O. Box 1055
Indianapolis, IN 46206-1055
Phone: 317-630-1200
Fax: 317-630-1223
Web: www.legion.org

American Legion Nebraska

American Legion Nebraska Oratorical Contest

Type of award: Scholarship.
Intended use: For undergraduate study at postsecondary institution.
Eligibility: Applicant or parent must be member/participant of American Legion. Applicant must be enrolled in high school. Applicant must be residing in Nebraska.
Basis for selection: Competition/talent/interest in oratory/debate, based on language style, voice, diction, delivery, originality, logic, breadth of knowledge, application of knowledge about topic, and skill in selecting examples and analogies.
Application requirements: Proof of eligibility.
Additional information: Awards: First place, $1,000; second place, $600; third place, $400; and fourth place, $200. Contact local American Legion post for more information.

Amount of award:	$200-$1,000
Application deadline:	November 1

Contact:
American Legion Nebraska, Department Headquarters
P.O. Box 5205
Lincoln, NE 68505-0205
Phone: 402-464-6338
Fax: 402-464-6330
Web: www.nebraskalegion.net

Edgar J. Boschult Memorial Scholarship

Type of award: Scholarship.
Intended use: For full-time undergraduate study. Designated institutions: University of Nebraska.
Eligibility: Applicant or parent must be member/participant of American Legion. Applicant must be residing in Nebraska.
Basis for selection: Applicant must demonstrate financial need and high academic achievement.
Additional information: Must be student at University of Nebraska with high academic and ROTC standing, or military veteran attending University of Nebraska with financial need and acceptable scholastic standing.

Amount of award:	$500
Number of awards:	4
Application deadline:	March 1

Contact:
American Legion Nebraska, Department Headquarters
P.O. Box 5205
Lincoln, NE 68505-0205
Phone: 402-464-6338
Fax: 402-464-6330
Web: www.nebraskalegion.net

Maynard Jensen American Legion Memorial Scholarship

Type of award: Scholarship.
Intended use: For full-time undergraduate study at vocational, 2-year or 4-year institution. Designated institutions: Nebraska institutions.
Eligibility: Applicant or parent must be member/participant of American Legion. Applicant must be residing in Nebraska. Applicant must be descendant of veteran; or dependent of veteran, deceased veteran or POW/MIA.
Basis for selection: Applicant must demonstrate financial need and high academic achievement.

Amount of award:	$500
Number of awards:	10
Application deadline:	March 1
Total amount awarded:	$5,000

Contact:
American Legion Nebraska, Department Headquarters
P.O. Box 5205
Lincoln, NE 68505-0205
Phone: 402-464-6338
Fax: 402-464-6330
Web: www.nebraskalegion.net

American Legion Nebraska Auxiliary

American Legion Nebraska Auxiliary Graduate Scholarship

Type of award: Scholarship.
Intended use: For graduate study.
Eligibility: Applicant must be residing in Nebraska. Applicant must be descendant of veteran; or dependent of veteran; or spouse of veteran.
Basis for selection: Major/career interest in education, special.

Amount of award:	$200

Contact:
American Legion Nebraska Auxiliary, Department Headquarters
P.O. Box 5227
Lincoln, NE 68505-0227
Phone: 402-466-1808
Web: www.nebraskalegionaux.net

American Legion Nebraska Auxiliary Junior Member Scholarship

Type of award: Scholarship.
Intended use: For undergraduate study at postsecondary institution.
Eligibility: Applicant must be residing in Nebraska.
Additional information: Given to Nebraska's entry for Spirit of Youth Scholarship for Junior member, in event applicant does not win same.

Amount of award:	$200
Application deadline:	March 1

Contact:
American Legion Nebraska Auxiliary
Department Education Chairman
P.O. Box 5227
Lincoln, NE 68505-0227
Phone: 402-466-1808
Web: www.nebraskalegionaux.net

American Legion Nebraska Auxiliary Nurse Gift Tuition Scholarships

Type of award: Scholarship.
Intended use: For undergraduate study.
Eligibility: Applicant must be residing in Nebraska. Applicant must be descendant of veteran; or dependent of veteran; or spouse of veteran.
Basis for selection: Major/career interest in nursing. Applicant must demonstrate financial need.
Application requirements: Recommendations, essay, transcript, proof of eligibility.
Additional information: Awards given as funds permit.

Amount of award:	$200-$400
Application deadline:	March 1

Contact:
American Legion Nebraska Auxiliary, Department Headquarters
P.O. Box 5227
Lincoln, NE 68505-0227
Phone: 402-466-1808
Web: www.nebraskalegionaux.net

American Legion Nebraska Auxiliary Practical Nursing Scholarship

Type of award: Scholarship.
Intended use: For undergraduate study at 2-year or 4-year institution. Designated institutions: Schools of practical nursing.
Eligibility: Applicant must be residing in Nebraska. Applicant must be veteran or descendant of veteran; or dependent of veteran; or spouse of veteran.
Basis for selection: Major/career interest in nursing. Applicant must demonstrate financial need.
Application requirements: Recommendations, transcript, proof of eligibility.

Additional information: Must be Nebraska resident for at least three years, be accepted at school of practical nursing, and be veteran-connected.

    Amount of award: $300
    Application deadline: March 1

Contact:
American Legion Nebraska Auxiliary, Department Headquarters
P.O. Box 5227
Lincoln, NE 68505-0227
Phone: 402-466-1808
Web: www.nebraskalegionaux.net

American Legion Nebraska Auxiliary Student Aid Grant or Vocational Technical Scholarship

Type of award: Scholarship.
Intended use: For undergraduate study at vocational or 2-year institution in United States.
Eligibility: Applicant must be residing in Nebraska. Applicant must be descendant of veteran; or dependent of veteran; or spouse of veteran.
Application requirements: Recommendations, transcript, proof of eligibility.
Additional information: Nursing students not eligible.

    Amount of award: $200-$300
    Application deadline: March 1

Contact:
American Legion Nebraska Auxiliary, Department Headquarters
P.O. Box 5227
Lincoln, NE 68505-0227
Phone: 402-466-1808
Web: www.nebraskalegionaux.net

American Legion Nebraska President's Scholarship

Type of award: Scholarship.
Intended use: For undergraduate study at postsecondary institution.
Eligibility: Applicant must be residing in Nebraska.
Additional information: Given to Nebraska's entry for National President's Scholarship in event applicant does not win same.

    Amount of award: $200
    Application deadline: March 1

Contact:
American Legion Nebraska Auxiliary, Department Headquarters
P.O. Box 5227
Lincoln, NE 68505-0227
Phone: 402-466-1808
Web: www.nebraskalegionaux.net

Averyl Elaine Keriakedes Memorial Scholarship

Type of award: Scholarship.
Intended use: For undergraduate study. Designated institutions: University of Nebraska-Lincoln.
Eligibility: Applicant must be female. Applicant must be residing in Nebraska. Applicant must be descendant of veteran; or dependent of veteran; or spouse of veteran.
Basis for selection: Major/career interest in education or social/behavioral sciences.
Application requirements: Recommendations, transcript, proof of eligibility.

Additional information: Applicant must plan to teach middle or junior high school social studies. Awards given as funds permit.

    Amount of award: $200-$400

Contact:
American Legion Nebraska Auxiliary, Department Headquarters
P.O. Box 5227
Lincoln, NE 68505-0227
Phone: 402-466-1808
Web: www.nebraskalegionaux.net

Roberta Marie Stretch Memorial Scholarship

Type of award: Scholarship.
Intended use: For undergraduate or master's study at 4-year institution.
Eligibility: Applicant must be residing in Nebraska. Applicant must be descendant of veteran; or dependent of veteran; or spouse of veteran.
Application requirements: Recommendations, transcript, proof of eligibility.
Additional information: Preference given to former Nebraska Girls State citizens.

    Amount of award: $400
    Application deadline: March 1

Contact:
American Legion Nebraska Auxiliary, Department Headquarters
P.O. Box 5227
Lincoln, NE 68505-0227
Phone: 402-466-1808
Web: www.nebraskalegionaux.net

Ruby Paul Campaign Fund Scholarship

Type of award: Scholarship.
Intended use: For freshman study at accredited 2-year or 4-year institution.
Eligibility: Applicant or parent must be member/participant of American Legion Auxiliary. Applicant must be high school senior. Applicant must be residing in Nebraska. Must be Legion member, ALA member, Sons of the American Legion member of two years standing, or child, grandchild, or great-grandchild of American Legion or ALA member of two years standing.
Basis for selection: Applicant must demonstrate high academic achievement.
Application requirements: Recommendations, essay, transcript, proof of eligibility.
Additional information: Award varies with availability of funds. Applicant must be state resident for three years. Must have maintained "B" or better during last two semesters of high school. Must be accepted for fall term at college or university. Scholarships exclude applicants enrolled in nursing.

    Amount of award: $100-$300
    Application deadline: March 1

Contact:
American Legion Nebraska Auxiliary, Department Headquarters
P.O. Box 5227
Lincoln, NE 68505-0227
Phone: 402-466-1808
Web: www.nebraskalegionaux.net

American Legion Nevada

American Legion Nevada Oratorical Contest

Type of award: Scholarship.
Intended use: For undergraduate study at postsecondary institution.
Eligibility: Applicant must be enrolled in high school. Applicant must be U.S. citizen or permanent resident residing in Nevada.
Basis for selection: Competition/talent/interest in oratory/ debate, based on language style, voice, diction, delivery, originality, logic, breadth of knowledge, application of knowledge about topic, and skill in selecting examples and analogies.
Additional information: Awards: First place, $500; second place, $300; and third place, $200.

Amount of award:	$200-$500
Number of awards:	3
Application deadline:	January 15
Total amount awarded:	$1,000

Contact:
American Legion Nevada Oratorical Contest
737 Veterans Memorial Drive
Las Vegas, NV 89101
Web: www.nevadalegion.org

American Legion Nevada Auxiliary

American Legion Nevada Auxiliary Past Presidents Parley Nurses' Scholarship

Type of award: Scholarship.
Intended use: For junior study at postsecondary institution.
Eligibility: Applicant must be residing in Nevada. Applicant must be veteran; or dependent of veteran.
Basis for selection: Major/career interest in nursing.
Additional information: $150 for each university. Applicant must have completed first two years of training.

Amount of award:	$150

Contact:
American Legion Nevada Auxiliary
4030 Bobolink Cir.
Reno, NV 89508
Phone: 775-224-0073
Web: www.nevadaauxiliary.com

American Legion Nevada Auxiliary President's Scholarship

Type of award: Scholarship.
Intended use: For undergraduate study at postsecondary institution.
Eligibility: Applicant must be residing in Nevada.
Additional information: President's Scholarship: $300 for winner of Department competition.

Amount of award:	$300
Number of awards:	1

Contact:
American Legion Nevada Auxiliary, Department Secretary
4030 Bobolink Cir.
Reno, NV 89508
Phone: 775-224-0073
Web: www.nevadaauxiliary.com

Silver Eagle Indian Scholarship

Type of award: Scholarship.
Intended use: For undergraduate study at postsecondary institution.
Eligibility: Applicant must be American Indian. Applicant must be U.S. citizen residing in Nevada. Applicant must be child or grandchild of American Indian veteran.

Amount of award:	$200

Contact:
American Legion Nevada Auxiliary, Department Secretary
4030 Bobolink Cir.
Reno, NV 89508
Phone: 775-224-0073
Web: www.nevadaauxiliary.com

American Legion New Hampshire

Albert T. Marcoux Memorial Scholarship

Type of award: Scholarship.
Intended use: For freshman study at accredited postsecondary institution.
Eligibility: Applicant or parent must be member/participant of American Legion. Applicant must be residing in New Hampshire. Must be child of living or deceased New Hampshire American Legion or New Hampshire American Legion Auxiliary member.
Basis for selection: Applicant must demonstrate high academic achievement.
Application requirements: Recommendations, essay, transcript, proof of eligibility. Resume.
Additional information: Must be child of living or deceased New Hampshire Legionnaire or Auxiliary member. Must be graduate of New Hampshire high school and state resident for three years.

Amount of award:	$2,000
Number of awards:	1
Application deadline:	May 1
Total amount awarded:	$2,000

Contact:
American Legion New Hampshire
State House Annex
25 Capitol Street, Room 431
Concord, NH 03301-6312
Phone: 603-271-2211
Web: www.nhlegion.com

American Legion New Hampshire Boys State Scholarship

Type of award: Scholarship.
Intended use: For undergraduate study at postsecondary institution.

Eligibility: Applicant or parent must be member/participant of American Legion, Boys State. Applicant must be male. Applicant must be residing in New Hampshire.
Additional information: Award given to participants of Boys State during Boys State graduation. Award amount varies. Apply during Boys State session.
Contact:
American Legion New Hampshire
State House Annex
25 Capitol Street, Room 431
Concord, NH 03301-6312
Phone: 603-271-2211
Web: www.nhlegion.com

American Legion New Hampshire Department Vocational Scholarship

Type of award: Scholarship.
Intended use: For freshman study at vocational or 2-year institution.
Eligibility: Applicant or parent must be member/participant of American Legion. Applicant must be enrolled in high school. Applicant must be residing in New Hampshire.
Basis for selection: Applicant must demonstrate high academic achievement.
Application requirements: Recommendations, essay, transcript, proof of eligibility.
Additional information: Must be high school student or graduate from New Hampshire school entering first year of higher education in specific vocation; state resident for at least three years.

Amount of award:	$2,000
Number of awards:	1
Application deadline:	May 1
Total amount awarded:	$2,000

Contact:
American Legion New Hampshire
State House Annex
25 Capitol Street, Room 431
Concord, NH 03301-6312
Phone: 603-271-2211
Web: www.nhlegion.com

American Legion New Hampshire Oratorical Contest

Type of award: Scholarship.
Intended use: For undergraduate study at postsecondary institution.
Eligibility: Applicant must be enrolled in high school. Applicant must be residing in New Hampshire.
Basis for selection: Competition/talent/interest in oratory/debate, based on language style, voice, diction, delivery, originality, logic, breadth of knowledge, application of knowledge about topic, and skill in selecting examples and analogies.
Application requirements: Proof of eligibility.
Additional information: Awards: First place, $1,000; second place, $750; third place, $500; fourth place, $250; and four $100 awards.

Amount of award:	$100-$1,000
Number of awards:	8
Total amount awarded:	$2,900

Contact:
American Legion New Hampshire
State House Annex
25 Capitol Street, Room 431
Concord, NH 03301-6312
Phone: 603-271-2211
Web: www.nhlegion.com

Christa McAuliffe Memorial Scholarship

Type of award: Scholarship.
Intended use: For freshman study at accredited 4-year institution.
Eligibility: Applicant must be residing in New Hampshire.
Basis for selection: Major/career interest in education. Applicant must demonstrate high academic achievement.
Application requirements: Recommendations, essay, transcript. Resume.
Additional information: Must be high school student or recent graduate of New Hampshire school entering first year of higher education; state resident for at least three years.

Amount of award:	$2,000
Number of awards:	1
Application deadline:	May 1
Total amount awarded:	$2,000

Contact:
American Legion New Hampshire
State House Annex
25 Capitol Street, Room 431
Concord, NH 03301-6312
Phone: 603-271-2211
Web: www.nhlegion.com

Department of New Hampshire Scholarship

Type of award: Scholarship.
Intended use: For freshman study at accredited 4-year institution.
Eligibility: Applicant or parent must be member/participant of American Legion. Applicant must be enrolled in high school. Applicant must be residing in New Hampshire.
Basis for selection: Applicant must demonstrate high academic achievement.
Application requirements: Recommendations, essay, transcript. Resume.
Additional information: Must be high school student or graduate from New Hampshire school entering first year of higher education; state resident for at least three years.

Amount of award:	$2,000
Number of awards:	2
Application deadline:	May 1
Total amount awarded:	$4,000

Contact:
American Legion New Hampshire
State House Annex
25 Capitol Street, Room 431
Concord, NH 03301-6312
Phone: 603-271-2211
Web: www.nhlegion.com

John A. High Child Welfare Scholarship

Type of award: Scholarship.
Intended use: For freshman study at postsecondary institution.

Eligibility: Applicant must be male, high school senior. Applicant must be residing in New Hampshire.
Basis for selection: Applicant must demonstrate financial need, high academic achievement, depth of character and patriotism.
Application requirements: Recommendations, essay, transcript.
Additional information: Parent must be member of American Legion New Hampshire or American Legion New Hampshire Auxiliary for three consecutive years.

Amount of award:	$2,000
Number of awards:	1
Application deadline:	May 1
Total amount awarded:	$2,000

Contact:
American Legion New Hampshire
State House Annex
25 Capitol Street, Room 431
Concord, NH 03301-6312
Phone: 603-271-2211
Web: www.nhlegion.com

Raymond K. Conley Memorial Scholarship

Type of award: Scholarship.
Intended use: For freshman study at vocational, 2-year or 4-year institution.
Eligibility: Applicant must be high school senior. Applicant must be residing in New Hampshire.
Basis for selection: Major/career interest in rehabilitation/therapeutic services. Applicant must demonstrate high academic achievement.
Application requirements: Recommendations, essay, transcript.
Additional information: Three-year state residency required. Must have at least a "B" average.

Amount of award:	$2,000
Number of awards:	1
Application deadline:	May 1
Total amount awarded:	$2,000

Contact:
American Legion New Hampshire
State House Annex
25 Capitol Street, Room 431
Concord, NH 03301-6312
Phone: 603-271-2211
Web: www.nhlegion.com

American Legion New Hampshire Auxiliary

Adrienne Alix Scholarship

Type of award: Scholarship.
Intended use: For undergraduate study at postsecondary institution.
Eligibility: Applicant or parent must be member/participant of American Legion Auxiliary. Applicant must be returning adult student. Applicant must be residing in New Hampshire.
Application requirements: Recommendations, essay.
Additional information: Must be one of the following: Re-entering work force or upgrading skills; displaced from work force; or recently honorably discharged from military.

Scholarship must be used for a refresher course or to advance applicant's knowledge of techniques needed in today's work force.

Amount of award:	$1,000
Number of awards:	1
Application deadline:	March 15
Total amount awarded:	$1,000

Contact:
American Legion New Hampshire Auxiliary
Department Secretary
121 South Fruit Street
Concord, NH 03301-6312
Web: www.nhlegion.com

American Legion New Hampshire Auxiliary Past Presidents Parley Nurses' Scholarship

Type of award: Scholarship.
Intended use: For undergraduate study at postsecondary institution.
Eligibility: Applicant or parent must be member/participant of American Legion Auxiliary. Applicant must be residing in New Hampshire.
Basis for selection: Major/career interest in nursing. Applicant must demonstrate financial need.
Application requirements: Recommendations, essay, transcript.
Additional information: Applicant must be high school graduate. Children of veteran given preference. One award to Registered Nurse study and one to Licensed Practical Nurse study.

Number of awards:	2
Application deadline:	March 15

Contact:
American Legion Auxiliary, Department of New Hampshire
Department Secretary
121 South Fruit Street
Concord, NH 03301-6312
Web: www.nhlegion.com

Elsie B. Brown Scholarship Fund

Type of award: Scholarship.
Intended use: For freshman study at postsecondary institution.
Eligibility: Applicant or parent must be member/participant of American Legion Auxiliary. Applicant must be residing in New Hampshire. Applicant must be dependent of deceased veteran.
Application requirements: Recommendations, essay, transcript.

Amount of award:	$150
Number of awards:	1
Application deadline:	March 15
Total amount awarded:	$150

Contact:
American Legion New Hampshire Auxiliary
Department Secretary
121 South Fruit Street
Concord, NH 03301-6312
Web: www.nhlegion.com

Grace S. High Memorial Child Welfare Scholarship Fund

Type of award: Scholarship.
Intended use: For undergraduate study at postsecondary institution.
Eligibility: Applicant or parent must be member/participant of American Legion Auxiliary. Applicant must be female. Applicant must be residing in New Hampshire. Daughters of deceased veterans also eligible.
Basis for selection: Applicant must demonstrate financial need.
Application requirements: Recommendations, essay, transcript, proof of eligibility.
Additional information: Applicant must be high school graduate and daughter of Legion or Auxiliary member. Parent must be member of American Legion New Hampshire or American Legion New Hampshire Auxiliary for at least three years.

Amount of award:	$300
Number of awards:	2
Application deadline:	March 15
Total amount awarded:	$600

Contact:
American Legion Auxiliary, Department of New Hampshire
Department Secretary
121 South Fruit Street
Concord, NH 03301-6312
Web: www.nhlegion.com

Marion J. Bagley Scholarship

Type of award: Scholarship.
Intended use: For undergraduate study at accredited postsecondary institution.
Eligibility: Applicant or parent must be member/participant of American Legion Auxiliary. Applicant must be residing in New Hampshire.
Application requirements: Recommendations, essay, transcript.
Additional information: Applicant must be high school graduate (or equivalent) or attending school of higher learning.

Amount of award:	$1,000
Number of awards:	1
Application deadline:	March 15
Total amount awarded:	$1,000

Contact:
American Legion Auxiliary, Department of New Hampshire
Department Secretary
121 South Fruit Street
Concord, NH 03301-6312
Web: www.nhlegion.com

American Legion New Jersey

American Legion New Jersey Department of New Jersey Scholarship

Type of award: Scholarship.
Intended use: For undergraduate study at 4-year institution.

Eligibility: Applicant or parent must be member/participant of American Legion. Applicant must be high school senior. Applicant must be residing in New Jersey.
Basis for selection: Applicant must demonstrate financial need, high academic achievement, depth of character, leadership and seriousness of purpose.
Application requirements: Recommendations, essay, transcript, proof of eligibility.
Additional information: Two $4,000 awards; four $2,000 awards; and two $1,000 awards. Applicant must be natural or adopted child of American Legion, Department of New Jersey member, or of a deceased member if parent was member at time of death. Contact local Post for application.

Amount of award:	$1,000-$4,000
Number of awards:	8
Application deadline:	February 15

Contact:
American Legion, Department of New Jersey
Department Adjutant
135 West Hanover Street
Trenton, NJ 08618
Phone: 609-695-5418
Web: www.njamericanlegion.org

American Legion New Jersey Oratorical Contest

Type of award: Scholarship.
Intended use: For undergraduate study at postsecondary institution.
Eligibility: Applicant must be enrolled in high school. Applicant must be residing in New Jersey.
Basis for selection: Competition/talent/interest in oratory/debate, based on language style, voice, diction, delivery, originality, logic, breadth of knowledge, application of knowledge about topic, and skill in selecting examples and analogies.
Application requirements: Proof of eligibility.
Additional information: Awards: First place, $4,000; second place, $2,500; third place, $2,000; fourth place, $1000; fifth place, $1000. See high school counselor for application.

Amount of award:	$1,000-$4,000
Number of awards:	5
Total amount awarded:	$10,500

Contact:
American Legion New Jersey
135 West Hanover Street
Trenton, NJ 08618
Phone: 609-695-5418
Web: www.njamericanlegion.org

American Legion New Jersey Auxiliary

American Legion New Jersey Auxiliary Department Scholarships

Type of award: Scholarship.
Intended use: For freshman study at 2-year or 4-year institution.
Eligibility: Applicant must be high school senior. Applicant must be residing in New Jersey. Must be child or grandchild of honorably discharged veteran of U.S. Armed Forces.

Additional information: Amount and number of awards vary. Must be New Jersey resident for at least two years.

Contact:
American Legion Auxiliary, Department of New Jersey
Department Secretary
1540 Kuser Road, Suite A-8
Hamilton, NJ 08619
Phone: 609-581-9580
Fax: 609-581-8429
Web: www.alanj.org

American Legion New Jersey Auxiliary Past Presidents Parley Nurses' Scholarship

Type of award: Scholarship.
Intended use: For freshman study at 2-year or 4-year institution.
Eligibility: Applicant must be high school senior. Applicant must be residing in New Jersey. Must be child or grandchild of honorably discharged veteran of U.S. Armed Forces.
Basis for selection: Major/career interest in nursing.
Additional information: Applicant must be enrolled in nursing program. Must be New Jersey resident for at least two years. Award amount varies.

Contact:
American Legion Auxiliary, Department of New Jersey
Department Secretary
1540 Kuser Road, Suite A-8
Hamilton, NJ 08619
Phone: 609-581-9580
Fax: 609-581-8429
Web: www.alanj.org

Claire Oliphant Memorial Scholarship

Type of award: Scholarship.
Intended use: For freshman study at 2-year or 4-year institution.
Eligibility: Applicant must be high school senior. Applicant must be residing in New Jersey. Must be child of honorably discharged veteran of U.S. Armed Forces.
Additional information: Must be New Jersey resident for at least two years. Rules and applications distributed to all New Jersey high school guidance departments.

Amount of award:	$1,800
Number of awards:	1
Application deadline:	April 15
Total amount awarded:	$1,800

Contact:
American Legion Auxiliary, Department of New Jersey
Department Secretary
1540 Kuser Road, Suite A-8
Hamilton, NJ 08619
Phone: 609-581-9580
Fax: 609-581-8429
Web: www.alanj.org

American Legion New Mexico Auxiliary

American Legion New Mexico Auxiliary National Presidents Scholarship

Type of award: Scholarship.
Intended use: For undergraduate study at postsecondary institution.
Eligibility: Applicant must be residing in New Mexico.
Additional information: Awarded to Department winner of National President's Scholarship, if candidate does not win in Division. If candidate does, it will be given to second-place winner in Department.

Amount of award:	$150
Number of awards:	1
Application deadline:	April 1
Total amount awarded:	$150

Contact:
American Legion New Mexico Auxiliary
Attn: National President's Scholarship
1215 Mountain Road, NE
Albuquerque, NM 87102
Phone: 505-247-0400
Web: www.nmlegion.org

American Legion New Mexico Auxiliary Past President's Parley Scholarship for Nurses

Type of award: Scholarship.
Intended use: For undergraduate study at postsecondary institution.
Eligibility: Applicant must be residing in New Mexico.
Basis for selection: Major/career interest in health-related professions; nursing or medicine.
Application requirements: Copy of school registration and letter of request for assistance.

Application deadline:	May 1

Contact:
American Legion Auxiliary, Department of New Mexico
Attn: Nurses Scholarship
1215 Mountain Road, NE
Albuquerque, NM 87102
Phone: 505-247-0400
Web: www.nmlegion.org

American Legion New York

American Legion New York Oratorical Contest

Type of award: Scholarship.
Intended use: For undergraduate study at postsecondary institution.
Eligibility: Applicant or parent must be member/participant of American Legion. Applicant must be no older than 19, enrolled in high school. Applicant must be residing in New York.

Scholarships

Basis for selection: Competition/talent/interest in oratory/ debate, based on language style, voice, diction, delivery, originality, logic, breadth of knowledge, application of knowledge about topic, and skill in selecting examples and analogies.

Application requirements: Proof of eligibility.

Additional information: All orations must be performed from memory. Awards: First place, $6,000; second place, $4,000; third place, $2,500; fourth and fifth place, $2,000. Scholarship payments are made directly to student's college and are awarded over a four-year period. Contact local Post for more information.

Amount of award:	$2,000-$6,000
Number of awards:	5
Total amount awarded:	$16,500

Contact:
American Legion, Department of New York
Department Adjutant
112 State Street, Suite 1300
Albany, NY 12207
Phone: 518-463-2215
Web: nylegion.net

Dr. Hannah K. Vuolo Memorial Scholarship

Type of award: Scholarship.

Intended use: For freshman study at accredited 2-year or 4-year institution.

Eligibility: Applicant or parent must be member/participant of American Legion. Applicant must be no older than 20, high school senior. Applicant must be descendant of veteran.

Basis for selection: Major/career interest in education, teacher.

Additional information: Applicant must be natural or adopted direct descendant of member or deceased member of American Legion, Department of New York.

Amount of award:	$1,000
Number of awards:	1
Application deadline:	May 1
Total amount awarded:	$1,000

Contact:
American Legion, Department of New York
Department Adjutant
112 State Street, Suite 1300
Albany, NY 12207
Phone: 518-463-2215
Web: nylegion.net

James F. Mulholland American Legion Scholarship

Type of award: Scholarship.

Intended use: For freshman study at postsecondary institution.

Eligibility: Applicant or parent must be member/participant of American Legion. Applicant must be high school senior. Applicant must be residing in New York. Applicant must be dependent of veteran.

Basis for selection: Applicant must demonstrate financial need and high academic achievement.

Amount of award:	$500
Number of awards:	2
Application deadline:	May 1
Total amount awarded:	$1,000

Contact:
American Legion, Department of New York
Department Adjutant
112 State Street, Suite 1300
Albany, NY 12207
Phone: 518-463-2215
Web: nylegion.net

New York American Legion Press Association Scholarship

Type of award: Scholarship.

Intended use: For full-time undergraduate study at accredited 4-year institution.

Eligibility: Applicant or parent must be member/participant of American Legion. Applicant must be residing in New York.

Basis for selection: Major/career interest in communications; journalism; graphic arts/design; film/video or radio/television/ film.

Additional information: Applicant must be child of New York Legion or Auxiliary member; Sons of American Legion or American Legion Auxiliary Junior member; or graduate of New York American Legion Boys State or Girls State.

Amount of award:	$1,000
Number of awards:	1
Application deadline:	April 15

Contact:
New York American Legion Press Association
Scholarship Chairman
P.O. Box 650
East Aurora, NY 14052
Web: nylegion.net

American Legion New York Auxiliary

American Legion New York Auxiliary Past Presidents Parley Student Scholarship in Medical Field

Type of award: Scholarship.

Intended use: For undergraduate study at 2-year or 4-year institution.

Eligibility: Applicant must be no older than 19, high school senior. Applicant must be U.S. citizen residing in New York. Applicant must be descendant of veteran; or dependent of veteran during Grenada conflict, Korean War, Lebanon conflict, Panama conflict, Persian Gulf War, WW I, WW II or Vietnam.

Basis for selection: Major/career interest in health-related professions. Applicant must demonstrate financial need, high academic achievement, depth of character, leadership and patriotism.

Application requirements: Essay, transcript.

Additional information: Visit Website for application.

Amount of award:	$1,000
Number of awards:	2
Application deadline:	March 1

Scholarships

Contact:
American Legion New York Auxiliary
112 State Street, Suite 1310
Albany, NY 12207-0003
Phone: 518-463-1162
Web: www.deptny.org

American Legion New York Auxiliary Scholarship

Type of award: Scholarship.

Intended use: For undergraduate study at postsecondary institution.

Eligibility: Applicant must be U.S. citizen residing in New York. Applicant must be descendant of veteran; or dependent of veteran or deceased veteran during Grenada conflict, Korean War, Lebanon conflict, Panama conflict, Persian Gulf War, WW I, WW II or Vietnam.

Basis for selection: Applicant must demonstrate financial need, high academic achievement, depth of character, leadership and patriotism.

Application requirements: Essay, transcript.

Additional information: May use other scholarships. Visit Website for application.

Amount of award:	$1,000
Number of awards:	1
Application deadline:	March 1
Total amount awarded:	$1,000

Contact:
American Legion New York Auxiliary
112 State Street, Suite 1310
Albany, NY 12207-0003
Phone: 518-463-1162
Web: www.deptny.org

American Legion North Carolina

American Legion North Carolina Oratorical Contest

Type of award: Scholarship.

Intended use: For undergraduate study at postsecondary institution.

Eligibility: Applicant must be enrolled in high school. Applicant must be U.S. citizen or permanent resident residing in North Carolina.

Basis for selection: Competition/talent/interest in oratory/debate, based on language style, voice, diction, delivery, originality, logic, breadth of knowledge, application of knowledge about topic, and skill in selecting examples and analogies.

Additional information: Awards: First place, $2,000; second place, $750; third, fourth, and fifth place, $500. Visit Website for more information.

Amount of award:	$500-$2,000
Number of awards:	5
Total amount awarded:	$4,250

Contact:
American Legion North Carolina
Oratorical Contest
P.O. Box 26657
Raleigh, NC 27611-6657
Phone: 919-832-7506
Web: www.nclegion.org

Colon Furr Nursing Scholarship

Type of award: Scholarship.

Intended use: For undergraduate study at 2-year or 4-year institution. Designated institutions: North Carolina schools granting LPN or RN degree.

Eligibility: Applicant must be residing in North Carolina.

Basis for selection: Major/career interest in nursing.

Application requirements: Recommendations, transcript, nomination by North Carolina American Legion Post.

Additional information: Applicant must be accepted or enrolled in a one-year LPN program or a two, three, or four-year RN program. Contact local Post for application.

Amount of award:	$600
Number of awards:	1
Total amount awarded:	$600

Contact:
American Legion North Carolina
P.O. Box 26657
Raleigh, NC 27611-6657
Phone: 919-832-7506
Web: www.nclegion.org

American Legion North Carolina Auxiliary

Nannie W. Norfleet Scholarship

Type of award: Scholarship.

Intended use: For undergraduate study at postsecondary institution.

Eligibility: Applicant or parent must be member/participant of American Legion Auxiliary. Applicant must be high school senior. Applicant must be residing in North Carolina.

Basis for selection: Applicant must demonstrate financial need.

Additional information: Preference given to children of American Legion Auxiliary members.

Amount of award:	$1,000
Number of awards:	1
Total amount awarded:	$1,000

Contact:
American Legion North Carolina Auxiliary, Department Headquarters
P.O. Box 25726
Raleigh, NC 27611
Phone: 919-832-4051
Web: www.nclegion.org

Scholarships

American Legion North Dakota

American Legion North Dakota Oratorical Contest

Type of award: Scholarship.
Intended use: For undergraduate study at postsecondary institution.
Eligibility: Applicant must be high school freshman, sophomore, junior or senior. Applicant must be residing in North Dakota.
Basis for selection: Competition/talent/interest in oratory/debate, based on language style, voice, diction, delivery, originality, logic, breadth of knowledge, application of knowledge about topic, and skill in selecting examples and analogies.
Application requirements: Proof of eligibility. For application, contact local American Legion Post or Department Headquarters after start of school year.
Additional information: State awards: First place, $400; second place, $300; third place, $200; and fourth place, $100. Local contests begin in the fall.
   Amount of award: $100-$400
Contact:
American Legion North Dakota, Department Headquarters
P.O. Box 5057
West Fargo, ND 58078-2666
Phone: 701-293-3120
Fax: 701-293-9951
Web: www.ndlegion.org

Edward O. Nesheim Scholarship

Type of award: Scholarship, renewable.
Intended use: For full-time at accredited vocational, 2-year or 4-year institution.
Eligibility: Applicant must be high school senior. Applicant must be U.S. citizen residing in North Dakota.
Basis for selection: Major/career interest in medicine or agriculture. Applicant must demonstrate financial need and high academic achievement.
Application requirements: Recommendations, essay, transcript, proof of eligibility. Submit the completed application Form. Include an original essay (500-750 words, typed, double spaced, 12 pt font with 1 inch margins) to address the following issues:. What are your educational and career goals. How do you plan to accomplish those goals and what part will your education play in attaining those goals. Where do you plan to continue your education and why did you choose that institution. Briefly discuss your secondary education (coursework, extracurricular activities, sports. Jobs, volunteerism, etc) and how you feel they may or may not have helped you prepare for your choice of college, your life and your career. Provide proof of acceptance into a past secondary institution in North Dakota that grants associate or higher degrees. Include a high school transcript. Include three letters of reference, all from non-family members, and one of which must be from a U.S veteran who served honorably. Provide proof of financial need from the educational institution to be attended.
Additional information: Aplicant must be direct descendent of a U.S veteran. Must be pursuing a degree in some phsae of Agriculture, Nutrition,, or Medicine (Medical Dr, PA, Dentistry, Dental Hygiene, Pharmacy or Chiropractic).

Amount of award: $1,500
Number of awards: 1
Number of applicants: 3
Application deadline: April 15
Total amount awarded: $1,500
Contact:
David Johnson
P.o Box 5057
West Fargo, ND 58078
Phone: 701-293-3120
Fax: 701-293-9951
Web: www.ndlegion.org/wp-content/uploads/2016/04/Nesheim-Memorial-Bio.pdf

Hattie Tedrow Memorial Fund Scholarship

Type of award: Scholarship.
Intended use: For undergraduate study at vocational, 2-year or 4-year institution.
Eligibility: Applicant must be high school senior. Applicant must be residing in North Dakota. Applicant must be descendant of veteran; or dependent of veteran.
Basis for selection: Applicant must demonstrate high academic achievement.
Application requirements: Essay, proof of eligibility. SASE.
Additional information: Number and amount of awards based on availability of funds.
   Amount of award: $2,000
   Application deadline: April 1
Contact:
American Legion North Dakota
Hattie Tedrow Memorial Fund Scholarship
P.O. Box 1055
Indianapolis, IN 46206
Phone: 701-293-3120
Fax: 701-293-9951
Web: www.ndlegion.org

American Legion North Dakota Auxiliary

American Legion North Dakota Auxiliary Past Presidents Parley Scholarship

Type of award: Scholarship.
Intended use: For undergraduate study at 2-year or 4-year institution. Designated institutions: North Dakota hospital and nursing schools.
Eligibility: Applicant or parent must be member/participant of American Legion Auxiliary. Applicant must be residing in North Dakota.
Basis for selection: Major/career interest in nursing.
Additional information: Children, grandchildren or great-grandchildren of American Legion or Auxiliary member in good standing. Must be graduate of North Dakota high school. Apply to local American Legion Auxiliary Unit.
   Amount of award: $350
   Application deadline: May 15

Contact:
American Legion Auxiliary, Department of North Dakota
Chair of Dept. Parley Scholarship Committee
P.O. Box 1060
Jamestown, ND 58402-1060
Phone: 701-253-5992
Web: www.ndala.org

American Legion North Dakota Auxiliary Scholarships

Type of award: Scholarship.
Intended use: For undergraduate study at postsecondary institution. Designated institutions: North Dakota institutions.
Eligibility: Applicant must be residing in North Dakota.
Basis for selection: Applicant must demonstrate financial need.
Additional information: Obtain application from local American Legion Auxiliary Unit.

Amount of award:	$500
Number of awards:	4
Application deadline:	January 15

Contact:
American Legion North Dakota Auxiliary
Department Education Chairman
P.O. Box 1060
Jamestown, ND 58402-1060
Phone: 701-253-5992
Web: www.ndala.org

American Legion Ohio

American Legion Ohio Department Oratorical Awards

Type of award: Scholarship.
Intended use: For undergraduate study at postsecondary institution.
Eligibility: Applicant or parent must be member/participant of American Legion. Applicant must be enrolled in high school. Applicant must be residing in Ohio.
Basis for selection: Competition/talent/interest in oratory/debate, based on language style, voice, diction, delivery, originality, logic, breadth of knowledge, application of knowledge about topic, and skill in selecting examples and analogies.
Additional information: Awards: First place, $2,000; second place, $1000. Additional smaller awards based on number of overall participants.
Contact:
American Legion Ohio
Department Scholarship Committee
P.O. Box 8007
Delaware, OH 43015-8007
Phone: 740-362-7478
Fax: 740-362-1429
Web: www.ohiolegion.com

American Legion Ohio Scholarships

Type of award: Scholarship.
Intended use: For undergraduate study at postsecondary institution.

Eligibility: Applicant or parent must be member/participant of American Legion. Applicant must be residing in Ohio. For Legion members; direct descendants of Legionnaires in good standing; direct descendants of deceased Legionnaires; spouses or children of deceased U.S. military persons who died on active duty or of injuries received on active duty.
Additional information: Number and amount of awards vary. Contact sponsor or visit Website for more information.

Application deadline:	April 15

Contact:
American Legion, Department of Ohio
Department Scholarship Committee
P.O. Box 8007
Delaware, OH 43015-8007
Phone: 740-362-7478
Fax: 740-362-1429
Web: www.ohiolegion.com

American Legion Ohio Auxiliary

American Legion Ohio Auxiliary Department President's Scholarship

Type of award: Scholarship.
Intended use: For freshman study at postsecondary institution.
Eligibility: Applicant or parent must be member/participant of American Legion Auxiliary. Applicant must be high school senior. Applicant must be residing in Ohio. Applicant must be descendant of veteran; or dependent of veteran or deceased veteran during Grenada conflict, Korean War, Lebanon conflict, Persian Gulf War, WW I, WW II or Vietnam.
Additional information: Awards: one $1,500 and one $1,000.

Amount of award:	$1,000-$1,500
Number of awards:	2
Application deadline:	March 1
Total amount awarded:	$2,500

Contact:
American Legion Ohio Auxiliary
Department Secretary
1100 Brandywine Blvd., Suite D
Zanesville, OH 43702-2760
Phone: 740-452-8245
Fax: 740-452-2620
Web: www.alaohio.org

American Legion Ohio Auxiliary Past Presidents Parley Nurse's Scholarship

Type of award: Scholarship.
Intended use: For undergraduate study at 2-year or 4-year institution.
Eligibility: Applicant or parent must be member/participant of American Legion Auxiliary. Applicant must be residing in Ohio. Applicant must be descendant of veteran; or dependent of veteran; or spouse of veteran.
Basis for selection: Major/career interest in nursing. Applicant must demonstrate financial need, high academic achievement, depth of character, leadership, patriotism and seriousness of purpose.
Application requirements: Recommendations, essay, transcript.

Scholarships

Additional information: Number and amount of awards varies annually.

   Application deadline: May 1

Contact:
American Legion Ohio Auxiliary
Department Secretary
1100 Brandywine Blvd., Suite D
Zanesville, OH 43702-2760
Phone: 740-452-8245
Fax: 740-452-2620
Web: www.alaohio.org

American Legion Oregon

American Legion Department Oratorical Contest

Type of award: Scholarship.
Intended use: For undergraduate study at postsecondary institution.
Eligibility: Applicant must be enrolled in high school. Applicant must be U.S. citizen or permanent resident residing in Oregon.
Basis for selection: Competition/talent/interest in oratory/debate, based on language style, voice, diction, delivery, originality, logic, breadth of knowledge, application of knowledge about topic, and skill in selecting examples and analogies.
Application requirements: Proof of eligibility.
Additional information: Awards available for first place through fourth place. Applications available at local high schools.

   Amount of award: $200-$500
   Number of awards: 4
   Application deadline: December 1
   Total amount awarded: $1,400

Contact:
American Legion Oregon
P.O. Box 1730
Wilsonville, OR 97070-1730
Phone: 503-685-5006
Fax: 503-685-5008
Web: www.orlegion.org

American Legion Oregon Auxiliary

American Legion Oregon Auxiliary Department Nurses Scholarship

Type of award: Scholarship.
Intended use: For undergraduate study at accredited 2-year or 4-year institution.
Eligibility: Applicant must be residing in Oregon. Applicant must be dependent of disabled veteran or deceased veteran; or spouse of disabled veteran or deceased veteran.
Basis for selection: Major/career interest in nursing. Applicant must demonstrate financial need, high academic achievement, depth of character, seriousness of purpose and service orientation.

Application requirements: Proof of eligibility.
   Amount of award: $1,500
   Number of awards: 1
   Application deadline: May 15
   Total amount awarded: $1,500

Contact:
American Legion Auxiliary, Department of Oregon
Chairman of Education
P.O. Box 1730
Wilsonville, OR 97070-1730
Phone: 503-682-3162
Fax: 503-685-5008
Web: www.alaoregon.org

American Legion Oregon Auxiliary National President's Scholarship

Type of award: Scholarship.
Intended use: For undergraduate study at postsecondary institution.
Eligibility: Applicant or parent must be member/participant of American Legion Auxiliary. Applicant must be high school senior. Applicant must be residing in Oregon. Applicant must be dependent of veteran during Grenada conflict, Korean War, Lebanon conflict, Panama conflict, Persian Gulf War, WW I, WW II or Vietnam.
Additional information: Three awards in each division of American Legion Auxiliary: First place, $3,500; second place, $3,000; and third place, $2,500.

   Amount of award: $2,500-$3,500
   Number of awards: 15
   Application deadline: March 1
   Total amount awarded: $9,000

Contact:
American Legion Auxiliary, Department of Oregon
Chairman of Education
P.O. Box 1730
Wilsonville, OR 97070-1730
Phone: 503-682-3162
Fax: 503-685-5008
Web: www.alaoregon.org

Spirit of Youth Scholarship

Type of award: Scholarship.
Intended use: For undergraduate study at accredited vocational, 2-year or 4-year institution.
Eligibility: Applicant or parent must be member/participant of American Legion Auxiliary. Applicant must be residing in Oregon. Applicant must be dependent of deceased veteran; or spouse of disabled veteran or deceased veteran.
Additional information: Must be Junior member of the American Legion Auxiliary for past three years and hold current membership.

   Amount of award: $5,000
   Application deadline: March 1

Contact:
American Legion Auxiliary, Department of Oregon
Chairman of Education
P.O. Box 1730
Wilsonville, OR 97070-1730
Phone: 503-682-3162
Fax: 503-685-5008
Web: www.alaoregon.org

American Legion Pennsylvania

Joseph P. Gavenonis Scholarship

Type of award: Scholarship, renewable.
Intended use: For full-time undergraduate study at 4-year institution. Designated institutions: Pennsylvania colleges and universities.
Eligibility: Applicant or parent must be member/participant of American Legion. Applicant must be high school senior. Applicant must be residing in Pennsylvania. Applicant must be child of living member in good standing of Pennsylvania American Legion, or child of deceased Pennsylvania American Legion member.
Basis for selection: Applicant must demonstrate financial need and high academic achievement.
Application requirements: Transcript, proof of eligibility.
Additional information: Award is $1,000 per year for four years; renewal based on grades. Minimum GPA 2.5.

Amount of award:	$1,000
Number of awards:	1
Application deadline:	May 30
Total amount awarded:	$4,000

Contact:
American Legion Pennsylvania
Scholarship Secretary
P.O. Box 2324
Harrisburg, PA 17105-2324
Phone: 717-730-9100
Web: www.pa-legion.com

Robert W. Valimont Endowment Fund Scholarship

Type of award: Scholarship, renewable.
Intended use: For full-time undergraduate study at vocational or 2-year institution.
Eligibility: Applicant must be residing in Pennsylvania. Applicant must be dependent of active service person, veteran or deceased veteran.
Basis for selection: Applicant must demonstrate financial need and high academic achievement.
Application requirements: Proof of eligibility.
Additional information: Parent must be member of American Legion, Pennsylvania. Award is $600 for first year; must reapply for second year. Minimum 2.5 GPA.

Amount of award:	$600
Application deadline:	May 30
Total amount awarded:	$600

Contact:
American Legion Pennsylvania
Scholarship Secretary
P.O. Box 2324
Harrisburg, PA 17105-2324
Phone: 717-730-9100
Web: www.pa-legion.com

American Legion Pennsylvania Auxiliary

Scholarship for Children of Deceased or Totally Disabled Veterans

Type of award: Scholarship, renewable.
Intended use: For undergraduate study at postsecondary institution.
Eligibility: Applicant must be high school senior. Applicant must be residing in Pennsylvania. Applicant must be dependent of disabled veteran or deceased veteran.
Basis for selection: Applicant must demonstrate financial need.
Additional information: Award is $600 per year, renewable for four years.

Amount of award:	$600
Number of awards:	1
Application deadline:	March 15
Total amount awarded:	$2,400

Contact:
American Legion Auxiliary, Department of Pennsylvania
Department Education Chairman
P.O. Box 1285
Camp Hill, PA 17001
Phone: 717-763-7545
Web: www.ala.pa-legion.com

Scholarship for Children of Living Veterans

Type of award: Scholarship, renewable.
Intended use: For undergraduate study at postsecondary institution.
Eligibility: Applicant must be high school senior. Applicant must be residing in Pennsylvania. Applicant must be dependent of veteran.
Basis for selection: Applicant must demonstrate financial need.
Additional information: Award: $600 per year, renewable for four years.

Amount of award:	$600
Number of awards:	1
Application deadline:	March 15
Total amount awarded:	$2,400

Contact:
American Legion Auxiliary, Department of Pennsylvania
Department Education Chairman
P.O. Box 1285
Camp Hill, PA 17001
Phone: 717-763-7545
Web: www.ala.pa-legion.com

American Legion Puerto Rico Auxiliary

American Legion Puerto Rico Auxiliary Nursing Scholarships

Type of award: Scholarship.
Intended use: For undergraduate study at 2-year or 4-year institution. Designated institutions: Eligible institutions in Puerto Rico.

Eligibility: Applicant must be residing in Puerto Rico.
Basis for selection: Major/career interest in nursing.
Application requirements: Interview.
Additional information: Two $250 awards for two consecutive years.

Amount of award:	$250
Number of awards:	2
Application deadline:	March 15

Contact:
American Legion Auxiliary, Department of Puerto Rico
Education Chairman
P.O. Box 11424
Caparra Heights Station, PR 00922-1424

American Legion Rhode Island

American Legion Rhode Island Oratorical Contest

Type of award: Scholarship.
Intended use: For undergraduate study.
Eligibility: Applicant must be enrolled in high school. Applicant must be U.S. citizen or permanent resident residing in Rhode Island.
Basis for selection: Competition/talent/interest in oratory/debate, based on language style, voice, diction, delivery, originality, logic, breadth of knowledge, application of knowledge about topic, and skill in selecting examples and analogies.
Additional information: Awards: First place, $500; second place, $250; third place, $100; fourth place, $50.

Amount of award:	$50-$500
Number of awards:	4
Total amount awarded:	$900

Contact:
American Legion of Rhode Island, Oratorical Contest
1005 Charles Street
North Providence, RI 02904
Phone: 401-726-2126
Fax: 401-726-2464
Web: www.legionri.org

American Legion Rhode Island Auxiliary

American Legion Rhode Island Auxiliary Book Award

Type of award: Scholarship.
Intended use: For undergraduate study at postsecondary institution.
Eligibility: Applicant or parent must be member/participant of American Legion Auxiliary. Applicant must be residing in Rhode Island. Applicant must be descendant of veteran; or dependent of veteran.
Additional information: Award: $500. Must be child or grandchild of veteran.

Amount of award:	$500
Number of awards:	1
Application deadline:	April 1
Total amount awarded:	$500

Contact:
American Legion Auxiliary, Department of Rhode Island
Department Secretary
55 Algonquin Dr.
Warwick, RI 02888
Phone: 401-369-7998
Web: www.rialaux.com

American Legion South Carolina

American Legion South Carolina Department Oratorical Contest

Type of award: Scholarship.
Intended use: For undergraduate study at postsecondary institution.
Eligibility: Applicant must be enrolled in high school. Applicant must be residing in South Carolina.
Basis for selection: Competition/talent/interest in oratory/debate, based on language style, voice, diction, delivery, originality, logic, breadth of knowledge, application of knowledge about topic, and skill in selecting examples and analogies.
Additional information: Awards: First place, $3,500; second place, $2,000; third and fourth place, $500. Distributed over four-year period. Zone Contest winners: four $100 awards.

Amount of award:	$100-$3,500
Number of awards:	8
Application deadline:	January 28
Total amount awarded:	$6,900

Contact:
American Legion South Carolina, Department Adjutant
P.O. Box 3309
Irmo, SC 29063
Phone: 803-612-1171
Fax: 803-213-9902
Web: www.scarolinalegion.org

American Legion South Carolina Auxiliary

American Legion South Carolina Auxiliary Scholarship

Type of award: Scholarship.
Intended use: For undergraduate study at postsecondary institution.
Eligibility: Applicant or parent must be member/participant of American Legion Auxiliary. Applicant must be high school senior. Applicant must be residing in South Carolina.
Additional information: Must be American Legion Auxiliary junior or senior member with at least three consecutive years' membership at time of application. Must have current membership card.

Amount of award:	$500
Number of awards:	2
Application deadline:	April 15
Total amount awarded:	$1,000

Contact:
American Legion Auxiliary, Department of South Carolina
Department Secretary
107 A Legion Plaza Rd.
Columbia, SC 29210
Phone: 803-772-6366
Fax: 803-772-6284
Web: www.aladsc.org

American Legion South Dakota

American Legion South Dakota Oratorical Contest

Type of award: Scholarship.
Intended use: For undergraduate study at postsecondary institution.
Eligibility: Applicant must be enrolled in high school. Applicant must be residing in South Dakota.
Basis for selection: Competition/talent/interest in oratory/debate, based on language style, voice, diction, delivery, originality, logic, breadth of knowledge, application of knowledge about topic, and skill in selecting examples and analogies.
Application requirements: Proof of eligibility.
Additional information: Awards: First place, $1,000; second place, $500; third place, $300; fourth through eighth place, $100. Redeemable within five years of date of award.

Amount of award:	$100-$1,000
Number of awards:	8
Total amount awarded:	$2,300

Contact:
American Legion, Department of South Dakota
Department Adjutant
P.O. Box 67
Watertown, SD 57201-0067
Phone: 605-886-3604
Web: www.sdlegion.org

American Legion South Dakota Auxiliary

American Legion South Dakota Auxiliary Scholarships

Type of award: Scholarship.
Intended use: For undergraduate study at vocational, 2-year or 4-year institution.
Eligibility: Applicant or parent must be member/participant of American Legion Auxiliary. Applicant must be at least 16, no older than 22. Applicant must be residing in South Dakota. Applicant must be dependent of veteran.

Basis for selection: Applicant must demonstrate financial need, high academic achievement, depth of character, leadership and patriotism.
Application requirements: Recommendations, essay, transcript.
Additional information: College scholarships: two $500; vocational scholarships: two $500.

Amount of award:	$500
Number of awards:	4
Application deadline:	March 1
Total amount awarded:	$2,000

Contact:
American Legion South Dakota Auxiliary
129 North Main Avenue
Hartford, SD 57033
Phone: 605-461-3389
Web: www.sdlegionaux.org

American Legion South Dakota Auxiliary Senior Member Scholarship

Type of award: Scholarship.
Intended use: For undergraduate study at vocational, 2-year or 4-year institution.
Eligibility: Applicant or parent must be member/participant of American Legion Auxiliary. Applicant must be residing in South Dakota.
Basis for selection: Applicant must demonstrate financial need, high academic achievement, depth of character, leadership and patriotism.
Application requirements: Recommendations, essay, transcript. Resume.
Additional information: Applicant must have been senior South Dakota American Legion Auxiliary member for three consecutive years including current year.

Amount of award:	$400
Number of awards:	1
Application deadline:	March 1
Total amount awarded:	$400

Contact:
American Legion South Dakota Auxiliary
129 N Main Avenue
Hartford, SD 57033
Phone: 605-461-3389
Web: www.sdlegionaux.org

Thelma Foster Junior American Legion Auxiliary Members Scholarship

Type of award: Scholarship.
Intended use: For undergraduate study at postsecondary institution.
Eligibility: Applicant or parent must be member/participant of American Legion Auxiliary. Applicant must be residing in South Dakota. Must be Junior American Legion member for at least three years, including current year.
Basis for selection: Applicant must demonstrate financial need, high academic achievement, depth of character, leadership and patriotism.
Application requirements: Recommendations, essay, transcript.
Additional information: Must be high school senior or graduate of accredited high school.

Amount of award:	$300
Number of awards:	1
Application deadline:	March 1

Contact:
American Legion South Dakota Auxiliary
129 North Main Avenue
Hartford, SD 57033
Phone: 605-461-3389
Web: www.sdlegionaux.org

Thelma Foster Senior American Legion Auxiliary Member Scholarship

Type of award: Scholarship.
Intended use: For undergraduate study at postsecondary institution.
Eligibility: Applicant or parent must be member/participant of American Legion Auxiliary. Applicant must be residing in South Dakota. Must be senior South Dakota American Legion Auxiliary member for past three years, including current year.
Basis for selection: Applicant must demonstrate financial need, depth of character, leadership and patriotism.
Application requirements: Recommendations, essay.

Amount of award:	$300
Number of awards:	1
Application deadline:	March 1
Total amount awarded:	$300

Contact:
American Legion South Dakota Auxiliary
129 North Main Avenue
Hartford, SD 57033
Phone: 605-461-3389
Web: www.sdlegionaux.org

American Legion Tennessee

American Legion Tennessee Eagle Scout of the Year Scholarship

Type of award: Scholarship.
Intended use: For undergraduate study at postsecondary institution in United States.
Eligibility: Applicant or parent must be member/participant of Boy Scouts of America, Eagle Scouts. Applicant must be male, at least 15, no older than 18, enrolled in high school. Applicant must be residing in Tennessee.
Application requirements: Nomination by Tennessee American Legion.
Additional information: Must be registered, active member of Boy Scout Troop, Varsity Scout Team, or Venturing Crew and either chartered to an American Legion Post, Auxiliary Unit or Sons of American Legion Squadron, or be son or grandson of American Legion or American Legion Auxiliary member.

Amount of award:	$3,000
Number of awards:	1
Total amount awarded:	$3,000

Contact:
American Legion Tennessee
318 Donelson Pike
Nashville, TN 37214
Phone: 615-391-5088
Web: www.tennesseelegion.org

American Legion Tennessee Oratorical Contest

Type of award: Scholarship, renewable.
Intended use: For undergraduate study at vocational, 2-year or 4-year institution in United States.
Eligibility: Applicant must be enrolled in high school. Applicant must be residing in Tennessee.
Basis for selection: Competition/talent/interest in oratory/debate, based on language style, voice, diction, delivery, originality, logic, breadth of knowledge, application of knowledge about topic, and skill in selecting examples and analogies.
Application requirements: Proof of eligibility.
Additional information: Awards: First place, $3,000; second place, $2,000; third place, $1,000. Enter contest through local high school participating in Tennessee Oratorical Contest.

Amount of award:	$1,000-$3,000
Number of awards:	3
Application deadline:	January 1
Total amount awarded:	$6,000

Contact:
American Legion Tennessee
318 Donelson Pike
Nashville, TN 37214
Phone: 615-391-5088
Web: www.tennesseelegion.org

American Legion Texas

American Legion Texas Oratorical Contest

Type of award: Scholarship.
Intended use: For undergraduate study at postsecondary institution.
Eligibility: Applicant must be no older than 18, enrolled in high school. Applicant must be residing in Texas.
Basis for selection: Competition/talent/interest in oratory/debate, based on language style, voice, diction, delivery, originality, logic, breadth of knowledge, application of knowledge about topic, and skill in selecting examples and analogies. Applicant must demonstrate patriotism.
Application requirements: Proof of eligibility.
Additional information: Awards: First place, $2,000; second place, $1,500; third place, $1,000; fourth place, $500. First place winner eligible to enter national contest.

Amount of award:	$500-$2,000
Number of awards:	4
Application deadline:	August 31
Total amount awarded:	$5,000

Contact:
American Legion, Department of Texas
P.O. Box 140527
Austin, TX 78714-0527
Phone: 512-472-4138
Fax: 512-472-0603
Web: www.txlegion.org

American Legion Texas Auxiliary

American Legion Texas Auxiliary General Education Scholarship

Type of award: Scholarship.
Intended use: For undergraduate study at postsecondary institution.
Eligibility: Applicant must be residing in Texas. Applicant must be descendant of veteran; or dependent of veteran during Grenada conflict, Korean War, Lebanon conflict, Panama conflict, Persian Gulf War, WW I, WW II or Vietnam.
Basis for selection: Applicant must demonstrate financial need and depth of character.
Application requirements: Recommendations, transcript. Resume listing statements of financial support from all their sources not listed on the application, extracurricular activities, and honors and awards received.
Additional information: Obtain application from local Unit. Unit sponsorship required.

Amount of award:	$500
Application deadline:	April 1

Contact:
American Legion Auxiliary, Department of Texas
P.O. Box 140407
Austin, TX 78721-0407
Phone: 512-476-7278
Web: www.alatexas.org

American Legion Texas Past Presidents Parley Scholarship

Type of award: Scholarship.
Intended use: For undergraduate study at postsecondary institution.
Eligibility: Applicant must be residing in Texas. Applicant must be descendant of veteran; or dependent of veteran during Grenada conflict, Korean War, Lebanon conflict, Panama conflict, Persian Gulf War, WW I, WW II or Vietnam.
Basis for selection: Major/career interest in medicine; health sciences; health-related professions; medical assistant or nursing. Applicant must demonstrate depth of character and seriousness of purpose.
Application requirements: Recommendations, essay, transcript, proof of eligibility.
Additional information: Applicant must be pursuing career in medical field. Obtain application from local Unit.

Amount of award:	$1,000
Application deadline:	May 1

Contact:
American Legion Auxiliary, Department of Texas
P.O. Box 140407
Austin, TX 78721-0407
Phone: 512-476-7278
Web: www.alatexas.org

American Legion Utah Auxiliary

American Legion Utah Auxiliary National President's Scholarship

Type of award: Scholarship.
Intended use: For undergraduate study at postsecondary institution.
Eligibility: Applicant must be high school senior. Applicant must be residing in Utah. Applicant must be descendant of veteran; or dependent of veteran during Grenada conflict, Korean War, Lebanon conflict, Panama conflict, Persian Gulf War, WW I, WW II or Vietnam.

Amount of award:	$1,500
Number of awards:	1
Application deadline:	February 15
Total amount awarded:	$1,500

Contact:
American Legion Utah Auxiliary
Department Secretary
P.O. Box 148000
Salt Lake City, UT 84114-8000
Phone: 801-539-1011
Web: www.utlegion.org

American Legion Vermont

American Legion Vermont Eagle Scout of the Year

Type of award: Scholarship.
Intended use: For undergraduate study.
Eligibility: Applicant or parent must be member/participant of Boy Scouts of America, Eagle Scouts. Applicant must be male, at least 15, no older than 18, enrolled in high school. Applicant must be residing in Vermont.
Application requirements: Recommendations.
Additional information: Must be registered, active member of Boy Scout Troop, Varsity Scout Troop, or Explorer Post. Awarded for outstanding service to school and community. Applicant must have received Eagle Scout Award.

Amount of award:	$1,000
Number of awards:	1
Application deadline:	March 1
Total amount awarded:	$1,000

Contact:
American Legion of Vermont
Education and Scholarship Committee
P.O. Box 396
Montpelier, VT 05601
Phone: 802-223-7131
Fax: 802-223-0318
Web: www.vtlegion.org

American Legion Vermont National High School Oratorical Contest

Type of award: Scholarship.
Intended use: For undergraduate study at postsecondary institution.

Eligibility: Applicant must be enrolled in high school. Applicant must be U.S. citizen or permanent resident residing in Vermont.
Basis for selection: Competition/talent/interest in oratory/debate, based on language style, voice, diction, delivery, originality, logic, breadth of knowledge, application of knowledge about topic, and skill in selecting examples and analogies.
Additional information: Winner receives $2,000; runners-up, $100. Selection based on prepared oration. Request rules by January 1.

Amount of award:	$100-$2,000

Contact:
American Legion of Vermont
Education and Scholarship Committee
P.O. Box 396
Montpelier, VT 05601-0396
Phone: 802-223-7131
Fax: 802-223-0318
Web: www.vtlegion.org

American Legion Vermont Scholarship

Type of award: Scholarship.
Intended use: For undergraduate study at postsecondary institution.
Eligibility: Applicant must be high school senior. Applicant must be U.S. citizen or permanent resident.
Application requirements: Recommendations, transcript.
Additional information: Awards: Charles Barber, one $1,000 award; Ray Greenwood, one $1,500 award and ten $500 awards. Applicant must be senior at Vermont secondary school; senior from adjacent state whose parents are legal Vermont residents; or senior from adjacent state attending Vermont school.

Amount of award:	$500-$1,500
Number of awards:	12
Application deadline:	April 1
Total amount awarded:	$7,500

Contact:
American Legion of Vermont
Education and Scholarship Committee
P.O. Box 396
Montpelier, VT 05601
Phone: 802-223-7131
Fax: 802-223-0318
Web: www.vtlegion.org

American Legion Virginia

American Legion Virginia Oratorical Contest

Type of award: Scholarship.
Intended use: For undergraduate study at postsecondary institution.
Eligibility: Applicant must be enrolled in high school. Applicant must be residing in Virginia.
Basis for selection: Competition/talent/interest in oratory/debate, based on language style, voice, diction, delivery, originality, logic, breadth of knowledge, application of knowledge about topic, and skill in selecting examples and analogies.

Application requirements: Proof of eligibility.
Additional information: Awards given to first, second, and third-place finishers.

Number of awards:	3
Application deadline:	December 1

Contact:
American Legion Virginia
Department Adjutant
1708 Commonwealth Ave.
Richmond, VA 23230
Phone: 804-353-6606
Fax: 804-358-1940
Web: www.valegion.org

American Legion Virginia Auxiliary

American Legion Virginia Auxiliary Past Presidents Parley Nurse's Scholarship

Type of award: Scholarship.
Intended use: For undergraduate study at postsecondary institution.
Eligibility: Applicant must be U.S. citizen residing in Virginia. Applicant must be descendant of veteran; or dependent of veteran.
Basis for selection: Major/career interest in nursing.
Application requirements: Recommendations, essay, transcript, proof of eligibility.
Additional information: Applicants may be seniors in or graduates of high school, but may not have attended institute of higher education. Previous recipients not eligible. More scholarship information found here: http://www.vaauxiliary.org/site2/wp-content/uploads/2015/05/2016.2017-Medical-Scholarship-Application.pdf.

Amount of award:	$1,000
Application deadline:	March 15

Contact:
American Legion Virginia Auxiliary
Donna J. Ellis, Past President Parleys Chair
328 South 14th Avenue
Hopewell, VA 23860
Phone: 804-355-6410
Web: www.vaauxiliary.org

Anna Gear Junior Scholarship

Type of award: Scholarship.
Intended use: For undergraduate study at postsecondary institution.
Eligibility: Applicant or parent must be member/participant of American Legion Auxiliary. Applicant must be high school senior. Applicant must be residing in Virginia. Must be Junior member of American Legion Auxiliary for three years.
Basis for selection: Applicant must demonstrate leadership and service orientation.
Application requirements: Recommendations, essay.

Amount of award:	$1,000
Number of awards:	1
Application deadline:	May 1
Total amount awarded:	$1,000

Contact:
American Legion Auxiliary, Department of Virginia
Education Chairman
1708 Commonwealth Avenue
Richmond, VA 23230
Phone: 804-355-6410
Web: www.vaauxiliary.org

Children of Warriors National President's Scholarship

Type of award: Scholarship.
Intended use: For undergraduate study at postsecondary institution.
Eligibility: Applicant or parent must be member/participant of American Legion Auxiliary. Applicant must be high school senior. Applicant must be U.S. citizen residing in Virginia. Applicant must be descendant of veteran; or dependent of veteran.
Basis for selection: Applicant must demonstrate financial need, high academic achievement and depth of character.
Application requirements: Recommendations, essay, transcript, proof of eligibility. SAT/ACT scores, FAFSA, verification of 50 hours of voluntary service.
Additional information: One $1,500, $2,000, and $2,500 scholarship awarded. Previous scholarship recipients not eligible.

Amount of award:	$1,500-$2,500
Number of awards:	15
Application deadline:	March 1
Total amount awarded:	$6,000

Contact:
American Legion Virginia Auxiliary
1708 Commonwealth Avenue
Richmond, VA 23230
Phone: 804-355-6410
Web: www.vaauxiliary.org

Dr. Kate Waller Barrett Grant

Type of award: Scholarship.
Intended use: For undergraduate study at accredited vocational, 2-year or 4-year institution.
Eligibility: Applicant or parent must be member/participant of American Legion Auxiliary. Applicant must be high school senior. Applicant must be residing in Virginia. Applicant must be dependent of veteran.
Basis for selection: Applicant must demonstrate financial need, high academic achievement, leadership and service orientation.
Application requirements: Recommendations, essay, transcript.

Amount of award:	$1,000
Number of awards:	1
Application deadline:	March 15
Total amount awarded:	$1,000

Contact:
American Legion Auxiliary, Department of Virginia
Education Chairman
1708 Commonwealth Avenue
Richmond, VA 23230
Phone: 804-355-6410
Web: www.vaauxiliary.org

American Legion Washington

American Legion Washington Children and Youth Scholarship Fund

Type of award: Scholarship.
Intended use: For undergraduate study at accredited vocational, 2-year or 4-year institution. Designated institutions: Eligible institutions in Washington State.
Eligibility: Applicant or parent must be member/participant of American Legion. Applicant must be high school senior. Applicant must be residing in Washington.
Basis for selection: Applicant must demonstrate financial need, leadership and seriousness of purpose.
Application requirements: Recommendations.
Additional information: Must be child of living or deceased member of American Legion Department of Wisconsin or its auxiliary. One $2,500 award and one $1,500 award.

Amount of award:	$1,500-$2,500
Number of awards:	2
Application deadline:	April 1
Total amount awarded:	$4,000

Contact:
American Legion Washington
Chairman, Department of Child Welfare
P.O. Box 3917
Lacey, WA 98503
Phone: 360-491-4373
Fax: 360-491-7442
Web: www.walegion.org

American Legion Washington Department Oratorical Contest

Type of award: Scholarship.
Intended use: For undergraduate study at postsecondary institution.
Eligibility: Applicant must be enrolled in high school. Applicant must be residing in Washington.
Basis for selection: Competition/talent/interest in oratory/debate, based on language style, voice, diction, delivery, originality, logic, breadth of knowledge, application of knowledge about topic, and skill in selecting examples and analogies.
Additional information: State winner receives $2,000 scholarship. Runners-up also receive awards.

Application deadline:	December 15
Total amount awarded:	$5,000

Contact:
American Legion Washington
Chairman, Department of Child Welfare
P.O. Box 3917
Lacey, WA 98503
Phone: 360-491-4373
Fax: 360-491-7442
Web: www.walegion.org

American Legion Washington Auxiliary

American Legion Washington Auxiliary Scholarships

Type of award: Scholarship.
Intended use: For undergraduate study at postsecondary institution.
Eligibility: Applicant must be high school senior. Applicant must be residing in Washington. Applicant must be dependent of disabled veteran or deceased veteran.
Basis for selection: Applicant must demonstrate financial need.
Application requirements: Recommendations, essay, transcript, proof of eligibility.
Additional information: Must be high school senior or high school graduate who has not attended institution of higher learning. Must submit application to Unit chairman.

Amount of award:	$400
Number of awards:	2
Application deadline:	March 1

Contact:
American Legion Washington Auxiliary
P.O. Box 5867
Lacey, WA 98503
Phone: 360-456-5995
Fax: 360-491-7442
Web: www.walegion-aux.org

Dayle and Frances Pieper Scholarship

Type of award: Scholarship.
Intended use: For undergraduate study at postsecondary institution.
Eligibility: Applicant must be residing in Washington. Applicant must be dependent of veteran, disabled veteran or deceased veteran.
Basis for selection: Applicant must demonstrate financial need, high academic achievement, depth of character and leadership.
Application requirements: Recommendations, essay, transcript, proof of eligibility.
Additional information: Must be a dependent of veteran.

Amount of award:	$1,000
Number of awards:	1
Application deadline:	March 15
Total amount awarded:	$1,000

Contact:
American Legion Auxiliary, Department of Washington
P.O. Box 5867
Lacey, WA 98503
Phone: 360-456-5995
Fax: 360-491-7442
Web: www.walegion-aux.org

Florence Lemcke Memorial Scholarship

Type of award: Scholarship.
Intended use: For undergraduate study at 2-year or 4-year institution.

Eligibility: Applicant or parent must be member/participant of American Legion Auxiliary. Applicant must be high school senior. Applicant must be residing in Washington. Applicant must be dependent of veteran or deceased veteran.
Basis for selection: Major/career interest in arts, general; art/art history; architecture; dance; literature; music or theater arts. Applicant must demonstrate financial need and depth of character.
Application requirements: Recommendations, essay, transcript, proof of eligibility.
Additional information: For use in field of fine arts.

Amount of award:	$1,000
Number of awards:	1
Application deadline:	April 25
Total amount awarded:	$1,000

Contact:
American Legion Washington Auxiliary
P.O. Box 5867
Lacey, WA 98503
Phone: 360-456-5995
Fax: 360-491-7442
Web: www.walegion-aux.org

Marguerite McAlpin Nurse's Scholarship

Type of award: Scholarship.
Intended use: For undergraduate or graduate study at postsecondary institution.
Eligibility: Applicant or parent must be member/participant of American Legion Auxiliary. Applicant must be residing in Washington. Applicant must be dependent of veteran, disabled veteran or deceased veteran. Grandchildren of veterans also eligible.
Basis for selection: Major/career interest in nursing. Applicant must demonstrate financial need, high academic achievement and depth of character.
Application requirements: Recommendations, essay, transcript, proof of eligibility.
Additional information: Must submit application to local Unit chairman.

Amount of award:	$1,000
Number of awards:	1
Application deadline:	April 25
Total amount awarded:	$1,000

Contact:
American Legion Washington Auxiliary
P.O. Box 5867
Lacey, WA 98503
Phone: 360-456-5995
Fax: 360-491-7442
Web: www.walegion-aux.org

Susan Burdett Scholarship

Type of award: Scholarship.
Intended use: For undergraduate study at postsecondary institution.
Eligibility: Applicant or parent must be member/participant of American Legion Auxiliary. Applicant must be female. Applicant must be residing in Washington. Applicant must be dependent of veteran, disabled veteran or deceased veteran. Grandchildren of veterans also eligible.
Basis for selection: Applicant must demonstrate financial need, high academic achievement, depth of character and leadership.
Application requirements: Recommendations, essay, transcript, proof of eligibility.

Additional information: Applicant must be former citizen of Evergreen Girls State (WA). Must submit application to local Unit chairman.

Amount of award:	$1,000
Number of awards:	1
Application deadline:	April 25
Total amount awarded:	$1,000

Contact:
American Legion Washington Auxiliary
Education Scholarships
P.O. Box 5867
Lacey, WA 98503
Phone: 360-456-5995
Fax: 360-491-7442
Web: www.walegion-aux.org

American Legion West Virginia

American Legion West Virginia Oratorical Contest

Type of award: Scholarship.
Intended use: For undergraduate study at postsecondary institution.
Eligibility: Applicant must be enrolled in high school. Applicant must be residing in West Virginia.
Basis for selection: Competition/talent/interest in oratory/debate, based on language style, voice, diction, delivery, originality, logic, breadth of knowledge, application of knowledge about topic, and skill in selecting examples and analogies.
Additional information: State winner receives $500 and four-year scholarship to West Virginia University or other eligible state college. Nine district awards of $200; three section awards of $300. Contest is held in January and February. Information may be obtained from local high school or American Legion Post.

Amount of award:	$200-$2,000

Contact:
American Legion West Virginia
State Adjutant
Box 3191
Charleston, WV 25332-3191
Phone: 304-343-7591
Fax: 304-343-7592
Web: www.wvlegion.org

Sons of the American Legion Scholarship

Type of award: Scholarship.
Intended use: For full-time freshman study at postsecondary institution.
Eligibility: Applicant must be residing in West Virginia.
Application requirements: Essay, transcript. Must submit copy of transcript from first college semester to receive award.
Additional information: First place winner: $1,000; second place: $500.

Amount of award:	$500-$1,000
Number of awards:	1
Application deadline:	May 15
Total amount awarded:	$1,000

Contact:
American Legion, Department of West Virginia
State Adjutant
Box 3191
Charleston, WV 25332-3191
Phone: 304-343-7591
Fax: 304-343-7592
Web: www.wvlegion.org

American Legion West Virginia Auxiliary

American Legion West Virginia Auxiliary Scholarship

Type of award: Scholarship.
Intended use: For undergraduate study at postsecondary institution. Designated institutions: West Virginia institutions.
Eligibility: Applicant must be no older than 21. Applicant must be residing in West Virginia. Applicant must be dependent of veteran.
Application requirements: Proof of eligibility.
Additional information: Number and amount of awards varies.

Application deadline:	March 1

Contact:
American Legion West Virginia Auxiliary
HC 60 Box 17
New Martinsville, WV 26155
Phone: 888-604-2242
Web: www.wvaux.org

American Legion Wisconsin

American Legion Wisconsin Baseball Scholarship

Type of award: Scholarship.
Intended use: For undergraduate study at vocational, 2-year or 4-year institution.
Eligibility: Applicant must be residing in Wisconsin.
Basis for selection: Competition/talent/interest in athletics/sports. Applicant must demonstrate financial need.
Application requirements: Nomination by Wisconsin American Baseball Board of Directors.
Additional information: Applicant must be current member of Wisconsin American Legion baseball team. Award rotates yearly from region to region and is awarded at State Convention.

Amount of award:	$500
Number of awards:	1
Total amount awarded:	$500

Contact:
American Legion Wisconsin
Program Secretary
P.O. Box 388
Portage, WI 53901
Phone: 608-745-1090
Fax: 608-745-0179
Web: www.wilegion.org

American Legion Wisconsin Eagle Scout of the Year Scholarship

Type of award: Scholarship.
Intended use: For undergraduate study at postsecondary institution.
Eligibility: Applicant or parent must be member/participant of American Legion/Boys Scouts of America. Applicant must be male, high school senior. Applicant must be residing in Wisconsin.
Basis for selection: Applicant must demonstrate high academic achievement.
Additional information: Applicant must be Boy Scout, Varsity Scout or Explorer. Applicant's group must be sponsored by Legion, Auxiliary, or Sons of American Legion, applicant's father or grandfather must be Legion or Auxiliary member.

Amount of award:	$1,000
Number of awards:	1
Application deadline:	March 1
Total amount awarded:	$1,000

Contact:
American Legion Wisconsin
Program Secretary
P.O. Box 388
Portage, WI 53901
Phone: 608-745-1090
Fax: 608-745-0179
Web: www.wilegion.org

American Legion Wisconsin Oratorical Contest Scholarships

Type of award: Scholarship.
Intended use: For undergraduate study at postsecondary institution.
Eligibility: Applicant must be enrolled in high school. Applicant must be residing in Wisconsin.
Basis for selection: Competition/talent/interest in oratory/debate, based on language style, voice, diction, delivery, originality, logic, breadth of knowledge, application of knowledge about topic, and skill in selecting examples and analogies.
Additional information: Awards: First place, $2,000; second place, $1,500; third place, $1,000. Regional winners receive $1,000; regional participants win $600 each.

Amount of award:	$600-$2,000

Contact:
American Legion, Department of Wisconsin
Program Secretary
P.O. Box 388
Portage, WI 53901
Phone: 608-745-1090
Fax: 608-745-0179
Web: www.wilegion.org

Schneider-Emanuel American Legion Scholarships

Type of award: Scholarship.
Intended use: For undergraduate study at 4-year institution in United States.
Eligibility: Applicant or parent must be member/participant of American Legion. Applicant must be residing in Wisconsin. Applicant must be veteran; or dependent of veteran.
Basis for selection: Applicant must demonstrate financial need, high academic achievement and depth of character.

Application requirements: Recommendations, transcript. ACT scores.
Additional information: Must be current member or child/grandchild of current member of American Legion, Auxiliary/Junior Auxiliary, or Sons of the American Legion, and have membership card at time of application.

Amount of award:	$1,000
Number of awards:	3
Application deadline:	March 1
Total amount awarded:	$3,000

Contact:
American Legion, Department of Wisconsin
Program Secretary
P.O. Box 388
Portage, WI 53901
Phone: 608-745-1090
Fax: 608-745-0179
Web: www.wilegion.org

American Legion Wyoming

American Legion Wyoming E.A. Blackmore Memorial Scholarship

Type of award: Scholarship.
Intended use: For undergraduate study at postsecondary institution.
Eligibility: Applicant or parent must be member/participant of American Legion. Applicant must be residing in Wyoming. Applicant must be dependent of veteran.
Basis for selection: Applicant must demonstrate financial need and high academic achievement.
Application requirements: Recommendations, transcript, proof of eligibility. Resume. Photo.
Additional information: Must be child or grandchild of American Legion member in good standing, or child or grandchild of deceased American Legion member who was in good standing. Must rank in upper 20 percent of high school class.

Amount of award:	$1,000
Number of awards:	1
Application deadline:	May 15
Total amount awarded:	$1,000

Contact:
American Legion Wyoming
Department Adjutant
1320 Hugur Ave.
Cheyenne, WY 82001
Phone: 307-634-3035
Fax: 307-635-7093
Web: www.wylegion.org

American Legion Wyoming Oratorical Contest

Type of award: Scholarship.
Intended use: For undergraduate study at postsecondary institution.
Eligibility: Applicant must be enrolled in high school. Applicant must be U.S. citizen or permanent resident residing in Wyoming.
Basis for selection: Competition/talent/interest in oratory/debate, based on language style, voice, diction, delivery, originality, logic, breadth of knowledge, application of

knowledge about topic, and skill in selecting examples and analogies.

Application requirements: Proof of eligibility.

Additional information: State awards: First place, $500; second place, $400; and third place, $200. District winners also receive awards.

Number of awards:	3
Application deadline:	May 15
Total amount awarded:	$1,450

Contact:
American Legion Wyoming
Department Adjutant
1320 Hugur Ave.
Cheyenne, WY 82001
Phone: 307-634-3035
Fax: 307-635-7093
Web: www.wylegion.org

American Legion Wyoming Auxiliary

American Legion Wyoming Auxiliary Past Presidents Parley Scholarship

Type of award: Scholarship, renewable.

Intended use: For full-time sophomore study at accredited 2-year or 4-year institution. Designated institutions: University of Wyoming or one of Wyoming community colleges.

Eligibility: Preference given to nursing students who are children of veterans.

Basis for selection: Major/career interest in health-related professions; medicine; nursing; occupational therapy; pharmacy/pharmaceutics/pharmacology; physical therapy; respiratory therapy or speech pathology/audiology. Applicant must demonstrate financial need and high academic achievement.

Application requirements: Recommendations.

Additional information: Must have completed one year or two semesters of study. Minimum 3.0 GPA. Preference given to Wyoming residents.

Amount of award:	$300
Number of awards:	1
Application deadline:	June 1

Contact:
American Legion Wyoming Auxiliary
Department Secretary
P.O. Box 2198
Gillette, WY 82717-2198
Phone: 307-686-7137
Web: www.wylegionaux.org

American Medical Technologists

American Medical Technologists Student Scholarship

Type of award: Scholarship.

Intended use: For full-time undergraduate study at accredited postsecondary institution in United States.

Eligibility: Applicant must be U.S. citizen or permanent resident.

Basis for selection: Major/career interest in medical assistant or dental assistant. Applicant must demonstrate financial need.

Application requirements: Recommendations, essay, transcript. W-2 current tax form.

Additional information: Scholarship is available only to high school seniors and graduates studying to become one of the following: medical assistant, dental assistant, medical administrative specialist, medical technologist, medical laboratory technician, medical laboratory assistant, allied health instructor, clinical laboratory consultant, or phlebotomy technician. Award amount may vary. Visit Website for application.

Amount of award:	$500
Number of awards:	5
Number of applicants:	76
Application deadline:	April 1
Total amount awarded:	$2,500

Contact:
American Medical Technologists
10700 West Higgins Road, Suite 150
Rosemont, IL 60018
Phone: 847-823-5169
Fax: 847-823-0458
Web: www.americanmedtech.org

American Meteorological Society

American Meteorological Society Freshman Undergraduate Scholarship Program

Type of award: Scholarship, renewable.

Intended use: For full-time freshman study at accredited 4-year institution in United States.

Eligibility: Applicant must be high school senior. Applicant must be U.S. citizen or permanent resident.

Basis for selection: Major/career interest in atmospheric sciences/meteorology or hydrology. Applicant must demonstrate high academic achievement.

Application requirements: Recommendations, essay, transcript. SAT/ACT scores.

Additional information: Scholarships are renewable for the sophomore year, providing recipient plans to continue studies in the AMS-related sciences. Marine biology majors not eligible. Minimum 3.0 GPA. Deadline is in early February. Award is $2,500 each for freshman and sophomore years.

Amount of award:	$2,500
Number of awards:	14
Number of applicants:	159
Notification begins:	May 1
Total amount awarded:	$5,000

Contact:
American Meteorological Society
Fellowship/Scholarship Program
45 Beacon Street
Boston, MA 02108-3693
Phone: 617-226-3907
Fax: 617-742-8718
Web: www.ametsoc.org

American Meteorological Society Named Undergraduate Scholarship

Type of award: Scholarship.
Intended use: For full-time senior study at accredited 4-year institution in United States.
Eligibility: Applicant must be U.S. citizen or permanent resident.
Basis for selection: Major/career interest in atmospheric sciences/meteorology or hydrology. Applicant must demonstrate high academic achievement and seriousness of purpose.
Application requirements: Recommendations, transcript.
Additional information: Minimum 3.25 GPA. Deadline is in early February. Marine biology majors not eligible. Must be a junior at the time of application. Application can be downloaded or submitted directly online. Number and amount of scholarships vary. Applicants must demonstrate financial need to be eligible for the Schroeder Scholarship. The Murphy Scholarship is awarded to students who, through curricular or extracurricular activities, have shown interest in weather forecasting or in the value and utilization of forecasts. The Glahn Scholarship is for a student who has shown strong interest in statistical meteorology. The Crow Scholarship is for a student who has shown strong interest in applied meteorology. Number and amount of awards varies.

Notification begins:	May 1

Contact:
American Meteorological Society
Fellowship/Scholarship Program
45 Beacon Street
Boston, MA 02108-3693
Phone: 617-226-3907
Fax: 617-742-8718
Web: www.ametsoc.org

American Meteorological Society/ Industry Minority Scholarship

Type of award: Scholarship.
Intended use: For full-time freshman study at accredited 4-year institution in United States.
Eligibility: Applicant must be Alaskan native, Asian American, African American, Mexican American, Hispanic American, Puerto Rican, American Indian or Native Hawaiian/Pacific Islander. Applicant must be high school senior. Applicant must be U.S. citizen or permanent resident.
Basis for selection: Major/career interest in atmospheric sciences/meteorology or hydrology. Applicant must demonstrate high academic achievement.
Application requirements: Recommendations, essay, transcript. SAT or ACT scores.
Additional information: Minimum 3.0 GPA. Deadline is in early February. Award is $3,000 per year for freshman and sophomore years. Award is for minority students who have traditionally been underrepresented in the sciences, especially Hispanic, Native American, and African-American students. Marine biology majors ineligible. Number of awards varies. Visit Website to download application.

Amount of award:	$6,000
Number of applicants:	40
Notification begins:	May 1
Total amount awarded:	$6,000

Contact:
American Meteorological Society
Fellowship/Scholarship Program
45 Beacon Street
Boston, MA 02108-3693
Phone: 617-226-3907
Fax: 617-742-8718
Web: www.ametsoc.org

Father James B. Macelwane Annual Award

Type of award: Scholarship.
Intended use: For undergraduate study.
Eligibility: Applicant must be U.S. citizen or permanent resident.
Basis for selection: Major/career interest in atmospheric sciences/meteorology; oceanography/marine studies or hydrology.
Application requirements: Essay, transcript, proof of eligibility. Original paper plus four photocopies. Letter of application including contact information and stating paper's title and name of university where paper was written. Letter from university faculty stating author was undergraduate when paper was written and indicating elements of paper that are original contributions by the student. Abstract of maximum 250 words describing paper.
Additional information: Award intended to stimulate interest in meteorology among college students through submission of original papers concerned with some phase of atmospheric sciences. Student must have been undergraduate when paper was written. Submissions from women, minorities and disabled students who are traditionally underrepresented in atmospheric and related oceanic and hydrologic sciences encouraged. No more than two students from any one institution may enter papers in any one contest. Visit Website for application and additional information.

Amount of award:	$1,000
Number of awards:	1
Application deadline:	June 12
Notification begins:	September 1
Total amount awarded:	$1,000

Contact:
American Meteorological Society
Macelwane Award
45 Beacon Street
Boston, MA 02108-3693
Phone: 617-226-3907
Fax: 617-742-8718
Web: www.ametsoc.org

American Military Retirees Association

Bernard E. Dillon Vocational Skills Scholarship

Type of award: Scholarship.
Intended use: For undergraduate study at accredited vocational, 2-year or 4-year institution.
Eligibility: Applicant must be U.S. citizen.

Basis for selection: Applicant must demonstrate high academic achievement, depth of character, leadership and service orientation.

Application requirements: Those eligible for a scholarship are current members of AMRA, their spouses and dependent children, and their grandchildren (who can be claimed as dependents on their parents' income tax return).

Additional information: Applicants must be post-high school students attending vocational-technical classes.

Amount of award:	$1,000
Number of awards:	5
Application deadline:	March 1

Contact:
American Military Retirees Association
5436 Peru Street
Suite 1
Plattsburgh, NY 12901
Phone: 800-424-2969
Fax: 519-324-5204
Web: www.amra1973.org

Sergeant Major Douglas R. Drum Memorial Scholarship

Type of award: Scholarship, renewable.

Intended use: For full-time undergraduate study at accredited 2-year or 4-year institution.

Additional information: Must be member or spouse, dependent child, or grandchild of member of American Military Retirees Association. Applications must be submitted electronically via fax or email.

Amount of award:	$1,000-$5,000
Number of awards:	24
Number of applicants:	63
Application deadline:	March 1
Total amount awarded:	$34,000

Contact:
American Military Retirees Association
5436 Peru Street
Suite 1
Plattsburgh, NY 12901
Phone: 800-424-2969
Fax: 518-324-5204
Web: www.amra1973.org

American Museum of Natural History

Young Naturalist Awards

Type of award: Scholarship, renewable.

Intended use: For freshman study.

Basis for selection: Competition/talent/interest in science project.

Application requirements: Essay. Original artwork/ photographs.

Additional information: For students grades 7-12 in the U.S and Canada to plan and conduct scientific investigations and report them in an illustrated essay. Children of Alcoa Corporation or American Museum of Natural History employees or consultants are ineligible. Two winners per grade level receive the following: 7th grade, $500; 8th grade, $750; 9th grade, $1,000; 10th grade, $1,500; 11th grade, $2,000; 12th grade, $2,500. Up to 36 additional finalists receive $50 prize. Deadline in early March. Visit Website for exact date.

Amount of award:	$50-$2,500
Number of awards:	48
Application deadline:	March 1

Contact:
Young Naturalist Awards Administrator
American Museum of Natural History
Central Park West at 79th Street
New York, NY 10024-5192
Phone: 212-496-3498
Web: www.amnh.org/learn-teach/young-naturalist-awards

American Nuclear Society

Accelerator Applications Division Scholarship

Type of award: Scholarship.

Intended use: For full-time junior study at accredited 4-year institution in United States.

Eligibility: Applicant must be U.S. citizen or permanent resident.

Basis for selection: Major/career interest in physics; engineering or materials science. Applicant must demonstrate financial need and high academic achievement.

Application requirements: Recommendations, essay, transcript.

Additional information: Applicant must be an ANS student member. Must be sponsored by ANS organization. Visit Website for application. One request/application covers all Graduate and Undergraduate scholarships; check appropriate boxes on application form. Number of awards varies. Additional consideration given to applicants who are members of an under-represented class (female/minority), and have a record of service to ANS. Recipients will receive $1,000 for their junior year and $1,000 for their senior year for a total award of $2000 over a two-year period.

Amount of award:	$2,000
Application deadline:	February 1

Contact:
American Nuclear Society
555 North Kensington Avenue
La Grange Park, IL 60526
Phone: 708-352-6611
Fax: 708-352-0499
Web: www.ans.org

American Nuclear Society Operations and Power Division Scholarship

Type of award: Scholarship.

Intended use: For full-time junior, senior or graduate study at accredited 4-year or graduate institution in United States.

Eligibility: Applicant must be U.S. citizen or permanent resident.

Basis for selection: Major/career interest in nuclear science or engineering, nuclear.

Application requirements: Recommendations, transcript.

Additional information: Applicant must be an ANS student member enrolled in a program leading to a degree in nuclear science, nuclear engineering or a nuclear related field. Must be sponsored by ANS organization. Must have completed at least two full academic years of four-year nuclear science or engineering program. Visit Website for application. One request/application covers all Graduate and Undergraduate scholarships; check appropriate boxes on application form.

Amount of award: $2,500
Number of awards: 1
Application deadline: February 1

Contact:
American Nuclear Society
555 North Kensington Avenue
La Grange Park, IL 60526
Phone: 708-352-6611
Fax: 708-352-0499
Web: www.ans.org

ANS Decommissioning & Environmental Sciences Division Undergraduate Scholarship

Type of award: Scholarship.
Intended use: For undergraduate study at accredited 4-year institution in United States.
Eligibility: Applicant must be U.S. citizen.
Basis for selection: Major/career interest in engineering, nuclear; environmental science; engineering, environmental or nuclear science.
Application requirements: Recommendations, essay, transcript.
Additional information: Applicant must be enrolled in curriculum of engineering or science associated with decommissioning/decontamination of nuclear facilities, management/characterization of nuclear waste, restoration of environment, or nuclear engineering. If awarded scholarship, student must join ANS and designate DDR Division as one professional division. Awardee must also provide support to DDR Division at next ANS meeting after receiving award (funding provided for travel to meeting, food, and lodging). Visit Website for application.

Amount of award: $2,000
Number of awards: 1
Application deadline: February 1

Contact:
American Nuclear Society
555 North Kensington Avenue
La Grange Park, IL 60526
Phone: 708-352-6611
Fax: 708-352-0499
Web: www.ans.org

ANS Incoming Freshman Scholarship

Type of award: Scholarship.
Intended use: For full-time freshman study at accredited postsecondary institution in United States.
Eligibility: Applicant must be high school senior. Applicant must be U.S. citizen or permanent resident.
Basis for selection: Major/career interest in engineering, nuclear. Applicant must demonstrate high academic achievement.
Application requirements: Recommendations, transcript, proof of eligibility. 500-word essay.
Additional information: For graduating high school seniors who have enrolled in college courses and are pursuing a degree in nuclear engineering or have the intent to pursue a degree in nuclear engineering.

Amount of award: $1,000
Number of awards: 4
Application deadline: April 1

Contact:
American Nuclear Society
555 North Kensington Avenue
La Grange Park, IL 60526
Phone: 708-352-6611
Fax: 708-352-0499
Web: www.ans.org

ANS Undergraduate Scholarships

Type of award: Scholarship.
Intended use: For sophomore, junior or senior study at accredited 4-year institution in United States.
Eligibility: Applicant must be U.S. citizen or permanent resident.
Basis for selection: Major/career interest in nuclear science or engineering, nuclear.
Application requirements: Recommendations, transcript.
Additional information: Maximum of four scholarships for entering sophomores in study leading to degree in nuclear science, nuclear engineering, or nuclear-related field; maximum of 21 scholarships for students who will be entering junior or senior year. Applicant must be an ANS student member and must be sponsored by ANS organization. Visit website for application. One request/application covers all Graduate and Undergraduate scholarships; check appropriate boxes on application form.

Amount of award: $2,000
Application deadline: February 1

Contact:
American Nuclear Society
555 North Kensington Avenue
La Grange Park, IL 60526
Phone: 708-352-6611
Fax: 708-352-0499
Web: www.ans.org

ANS Washington, D.C. Section Undergraduate Scholarship

Type of award: Scholarship.
Intended use: For full-time junior or senior study at accredited 4-year institution in United States.
Eligibility: Applicant must be U.S. citizen or permanent resident.
Basis for selection: Major/career interest in engineering, nuclear.
Application requirements: Recommendations, transcript.
Additional information: Permanent address must be within 100 miles of Washington, DC. Applicant must be an ANS student member enrolled in a program leading to a degree in nuclear engineering, health physics, or nuclear-related studies. Must be sponsored by ANS organization. Visit Website for application. One request/application covers all Graduate and Undergraduate scholarships; check appropriate boxes on application form.

Amount of award: $2,500
Number of awards: 1
Application deadline: February 1

Contact:
American Nuclear Society
555 North Kensington Avenue
La Grange Park, IL 60526
Phone: 708-352-6611
Fax: 708-352-0499
Web: www.ans.org

Charles (Tommy) Thomas Memorial Scholarship

Type of award: Scholarship.
Intended use: For full-time junior or senior study at accredited 4-year institution in United States.
Basis for selection: Major/career interest in nuclear science; engineering, nuclear; environmental science; engineering, environmental; ecology or natural resources/conservation.
Application requirements: Recommendations, transcript.
Additional information: Applicant must be an ANS student member enrolled in a program leading to a degree in nuclear science, nuclear engineering or a nuclear related field. Must be sponsored by ANS organization. Visit Website for application. One request/application covers all Graduate and Undergraduate scholarships; check appropriate boxes on application form.

Amount of award:	$3,000
Number of awards:	1
Application deadline:	February 1

Contact:
American Nuclear Society
555 North Kensington Avenue
La Grange Park, IL 60526
Phone: 708-352-6611
Fax: 708-352-0499
Web: www.ans.org

Delayed Education Scholarship for Women

Type of award: Scholarship.
Intended use: For undergraduate study at accredited 4-year institution in United States.
Eligibility: Applicant must be female, returning adult student. Applicant must be U.S. citizen or permanent resident.
Basis for selection: Major/career interest in nuclear science or engineering, nuclear. Applicant must demonstrate financial need and high academic achievement.
Application requirements: Recommendations, transcript.
Additional information: Must be a mature woman whose undergraduate studies in nuclear science, nuclear engineering, or a nuclear-related field have been delayed. Applicants must check the appropriate box on the Landis Scholarship form. For more information please call the American Nuclear Society scholarship coordinator.

Amount of award:	$5,000
Number of awards:	1
Application deadline:	February 1

Contact:
American Nuclear Society
555 North Kensington Avenue
La Grange Park, IL 60526
Phone: 708-352-6611
Fax: 708-352-0499
Web: www.ans.org

James K. Vogt Radiochemistry Scholarship

Type of award: Scholarship.
Intended use: For full-time junior, senior or graduate study at accredited 4-year or graduate institution in United States.
Eligibility: Applicant must be U.S. citizen or permanent resident.
Basis for selection: Major/career interest in chemistry or nuclear science.
Application requirements: Recommendations, essay, transcript.
Additional information: Applicants must be engaged in proposing to undertake graduate or undergraduate research in radioanalytical chemistry or its applications of nuclear science. Applicant must be an ANS student member and must be sponsored by ANS organization. Visit website for application and requirements. One request/application covers all Graduate and Undergraduate scholarships; check appropriate boxes on application form.

Amount of award:	$3,000
Number of awards:	1
Application deadline:	February 1

Contact:
American Nuclear Society
555 North Kensington Avenue
La Grange Park, IL 60526
Phone: 708-352-6611
Fax: 708-352-0499
Web: www.ans.org

John and Muriel Landis Scholarship

Type of award: Scholarship.
Intended use: For undergraduate or graduate study at accredited 4-year or graduate institution in United States.
Eligibility: Applicant must be U.S. citizen or permanent resident.
Basis for selection: Major/career interest in nuclear science or engineering, nuclear. Applicant must demonstrate financial need.
Application requirements: Recommendations, transcript.
Additional information: Awarded to students with greater than average financial need. Consideration given to conditions or experiences that render student disadvantaged (poor high school/undergraduate preparation, etc.). Applicants should be planning career in nuclear science or nuclear engineering. Qualified high school seniors eligible to apply. Number of awards varies. Visit website for application and requirements. Applicants must check the appropriate box on the Landis Scholarship form.

Amount of award:	$5,000
Number of awards:	9
Application deadline:	February 1

Contact:
American Nuclear Society
555 North Kensington Avenue
La Grange Park, IL 60526
Phone: 708-352-6611
Fax: 708-352-0499
Web: www.ans.org

Joseph Naser (HFICD) Scholarship

Type of award: Scholarship.
Intended use: For undergraduate study at accredited 4-year institution in United States.

Eligibility: Applicant must be U.S. citizen or international student.
Basis for selection: Major/career interest in engineering, nuclear.
Application requirements: Recommendations, transcript. Letter of sponsorship.
Additional information: Must be ANS student member. Scholarship to be used to study technical disciplines involved in nuclear plant instrumentation, controls, and human-machine interface technologies in the context of nuclear power or other nuclear engineering specific applications.

Amount of award:	$2,000
Number of awards:	1
Application deadline:	February 1

Contact:
American Nuclear Society
555 North Kensington Avenue
La Grange Park, IL 60526
Phone: 708-352-6611
Fax: 708-352-0499
Web: www.ans.org

Pittsburgh Local Section Scholarship

Type of award: Scholarship.
Intended use: For full-time junior, senior or graduate study at accredited 4-year or graduate institution in United States.
Basis for selection: Major/career interest in nuclear science or engineering, nuclear.
Application requirements: Recommendations, transcript.
Additional information: Applicant must either attend school in Western Pennsylvania or have some affiliation with the region. Awards are $2,000 for undergraduates and $3,500 for graduate students. Applicant must be an ANS student member enrolled in a program leading to a degree in nuclear science, nuclear engineering or a nuclear related field. Must be sponsored by ANS organization. Visit website for application. One request/application covers all Graduate and Undergraduate scholarships; check appropriate boxes on application form.

Amount of award:	$2,000-$3,500
Number of awards:	2
Application deadline:	February 1

Contact:
American Nuclear Society
555 North Kensington Avenue
La Grange Park, IL 60526
Phone: 708-352-6611
Fax: 708-352-0499
Web: www.ans.org

American Public Power Association

DEED Student Research Grants

Type of award: Research grant.
Intended use: For full-time undergraduate or graduate study at accredited 2-year, 4-year or graduate institution in United States.
Basis for selection: Major/career interest in electronics; engineering, electrical/electronic; engineering, mechanical or energy research.
Application requirements: Transcript.

Additional information: Applicants must complete energy-related research project and be sponsored by DEED member utility. Award also includes up to $1,000 for travel to applicable conferences. Applicants must not be graduating within 12 months of the application deadline.

Amount of award:	$4,000
Number of awards:	10
Application deadline:	February 15, October 15
Total amount awarded:	$40,000

Contact:
American Public Power Association
Attn: DEED Administrator
2451 Crystal Drive, Suite 1000
Arlington, VA 22202
Phone: 202-467-2942
Web: www.publicpower.org

American Quarter Horse Foundation

American Quarter Horse Foundation Scholarships

Type of award: Scholarship, renewable.
Intended use: For full-time undergraduate or first professional study in United States or Canada.
Eligibility: Applicant must be at least 17.
Basis for selection: Applicant must demonstrate financial need and high academic achievement.
Application requirements: Recommendations, transcript, proof of eligibility.
Additional information: Number of scholarships varies. Active membership in either the American Quarter Horse Youth Association or American Quarter Horse Association may be required. Number of awards given varies. Visit website for requirements, deadline, and scholarship criteria.

Amount of award:	$500-$25,000
Number of applicants:	200
Application deadline:	December 1
Notification begins:	May 1
Total amount awarded:	$275,000

Contact:
American Quarter Horse Foundation
Scholarship Office
2601 I-40 East
Amarillo, TX 79104
Phone: 806-378-5029
Fax: 806-376-1005
Web: https://www.aqha.com/foundation/pages/support-scholarships/

American Radio Relay League (ARRL) Foundation, Inc.

The Albert H. Hix, W8AH, Memorial Scholarship

Type of award: Scholarship.
Intended use: For undergraduate study at accredited postsecondary institution. Designated institutions: West Virginia institutions.

Eligibility: Applicant must be residing in West Virginia.
Basis for selection: Competition/talent/interest in amateur radio. Applicant must demonstrate high academic achievement.
Application requirements: Transcript. FAFSA.
Additional information: Minimum 3.0 GPA. Must be amateur radio operator with active General Class license or higher. High school seniors are eligible to apply. Residents of West Virginia Section and school attendance in the West Virginia Section preferred. Visit Website for application.

Amount of award:	$500
Number of awards:	1
Application deadline:	January 31

Contact:
The ARRL Foundation, Inc. Scholarship Program
225 Main Street
Newington, CT 06111
Phone: 860-594-0397
Fax: 860-594-0259
Web: www.arrlf.org

The Alfred E. Friend, Jr., W4CF Memorial Scholarship

Type of award: Scholarship.
Intended use: For undergraduate study at postsecondary institution.
Basis for selection: Competition/talent/interest in amateur radio. Major/career interest in engineering.
Application requirements: Transcript. FAFSA.
Additional information: Must be amateur radio operator with any class of active Amateur Radio license. Visit Website for application.

Amount of award:	$5,000
Number of awards:	1
Application deadline:	January 31

Contact:
The ARRL Foundation, Inc. Scholarship Program
225 Main Street
Newington, CT 06111
Phone: 860-594-0397
Fax: 860-594-0259
Web: www.arrlf.org

The Allen and Bertha Watson Memorial Scholarship

Type of award: Scholarship.
Intended use: For undergraduate study at 4-year institution.
Basis for selection: Competition/talent/interest in amateur radio. Major/career interest in science, general; technology or engineering.
Application requirements: Transcript. FAFSA.
Additional information: Must be amateur radio operator with any class of active Amateur Radio license and reside or attend a college or university in Oklahoma. If no qualified applicant is identified, preference will be awarded to applicants residing or attending a college or university in the ARRL Gulf Division (Texas and Oklahoma). Visit Website for application.

Amount of award:	$500
Number of awards:	1
Application deadline:	January 31

Contact:
The ARRL Foundation, Inc. Scholarship Program
225 Main Street
Newington, CT 06111
Phone: 860-594-0397
Fax: 860-594-0259
Web: www.arrlf.org

Androscoggin Amateur Radio Club Scholarship

Type of award: Scholarship.
Intended use: For undergraduate study at 2-year or 4-year institution.
Eligibility: Applicant must be residing in Vermont, Connecticut, New Hampshire, Maine, Massachusetts or Rhode Island.
Basis for selection: Competition/talent/interest in amateur radio. Major/career interest in computer/information sciences; electronics or engineering, electrical/electronic.
Application requirements: Transcript. FAFSA.
Additional information: Must be amateur radio operator with active Technician Class license or higher. High school seniors are eligible to apply. Offered as either $1,000 award for a 4-year college student or two awards of $500 each for 2-year college students. Related majors also eligible. Visit Website for application.

Amount of award:	$500-$1,000
Application deadline:	January 31

Contact:
The ARRL Foundation, Inc. Scholarship Program
225 Main Street
Newington, CT 06111
Phone: 860-594-0397
Fax: 860-594-0259
Web: www.arrlf.org

The ARRL Earl I. Anderson Scholarship

Type of award: Scholarship.
Intended use: For undergraduate or graduate study at accredited postsecondary institution in United States.
Eligibility: Applicant must be residing in Michigan, Indiana, Illinois or Florida.
Basis for selection: Competition/talent/interest in amateur radio. Major/career interest in engineering, electrical/electronic.
Application requirements: Transcript. FAFSA.
Additional information: Must be amateur radio operator holding any class license. Must be ARRL member. Major may be in other related technical field. Must be attending classes in Illinois, Indiana, Michigan, or Florida. High school seniors eligible to apply. Application may be obtained on Website, and will only be accepted via email.

Amount of award:	$1,250
Number of awards:	3
Application deadline:	January 31

Contact:
The ARRL Foundation, Inc. Scholarship Program
225 Main Street
Newington, CT 06111
Phone: 860-594-0397
Fax: 860-594-0259
Web: www.arrlf.org

ARRL Foundation General Fund Scholarship

Type of award: Scholarship.
Intended use: For undergraduate or graduate study at postsecondary institution.
Basis for selection: Competition/talent/interest in amateur radio.
Application requirements: Transcript. FAFSA.
Additional information: Must hold active Amateur Radio license. Number of awards varies. High school seniors eligible to apply. Application may be obtained on Website, and will only be accepted via email.

  Amount of award: $2,000
  Application deadline: January 31
Contact:
The ARRL Foundation, Inc. Scholarship Program
225 Main Street
Newington, CT 06111
Phone: 860-594-0397
Fax: 860-594-0259
Web: www.arrlf.org

ARRL Foundation PHD Scholarship

Type of award: Scholarship.
Intended use: For undergraduate, graduate or non-degree study at postsecondary institution in United States.
Eligibility: Applicant must be residing in Iowa, Nebraska, Kansas or Missouri.
Basis for selection: Competition/talent/interest in amateur radio. Major/career interest in journalism; computer/information sciences or engineering, electrical/electronic.
Application requirements: Transcript. FAFSA.
Additional information: Must hold active Amateur Radio license. May be child of deceased radio amateur. High school seniors eligible to apply. Application may be obtained on Website, and will only be accepted via email.

  Amount of award: $1,000
  Number of awards: 1
  Application deadline: January 31
  Total amount awarded: $1,000
Contact:
The ARRL Foundation, Inc. Scholarship Program
225 Main Street
Newington, CT 06111
Phone: 860-594-0397
Fax: 860-594-0259
Web: www.arrlf.org

The ARRL Scholarship to Honor Barry Goldwater, K7UGA

Type of award: Scholarship.
Intended use: For undergraduate or graduate study at accredited 4-year or graduate institution in United States.
Basis for selection: Competition/talent/interest in amateur radio.
Application requirements: Transcript. FAFSA.
Additional information: Must hold active Amateur Radio license in any class. High school seniors are eligible to apply. Application may be obtained on Website, and will only be accepted via email.

  Amount of award: $5,000
  Number of awards: 1
  Application deadline: January 31
  Total amount awarded: $5,000

Contact:
The ARRL Foundation, Inc. Scholarship Program
225 Main Street
Newington, CT 06111
Phone: 860-594-0397
Fax: 860-594-0259
Web: www.arrlf.org

The Betty Weatherford, KQ6RE, Memorial Scholarship

Type of award: Scholarship.
Intended use: For undergraduate study at postsecondary institution.
Basis for selection: Competition/talent/interest in amateur radio. Major/career interest in engineering, electrical/electronic.
Application requirements: Transcript. FAFSA.
Additional information: Must be amateur radio operator with any class of active Amateur Radio license. Applicants studying communications engineering also eligible. Visit Website for application.

  Amount of award: $1,000
  Number of awards: 1
  Application deadline: January 31
Contact:
The ARRL Foundation, Inc. Scholarship Program
225 Main Street
Newington, CT 06111
Phone: 860-594-0397
Fax: 860-594-0259
Web: www.arrlf.org

The Bill, W2ONV, and Ann Salerno Memorial Scholarship

Type of award: Scholarship.
Intended use: For undergraduate study at accredited 4-year institution.
Basis for selection: Competition/talent/interest in amateur radio. Applicant must demonstrate financial need and high academic achievement.
Application requirements: Transcript. FAFSA.
Additional information: Minimum 3.7 GPA. Must be amateur radio operator with active Amateur Radio license. High school seniors are eligible to apply. Aggregate income of family household must be no greater than $100,000 per year. Visit Website for application.

  Amount of award: $1,000
  Number of awards: 2
  Application deadline: January 31
Contact:
The ARRL Foundation, Inc. Scholarship Program
225 Main Street
Newington, CT 06111
Phone: 860-594-0397
Fax: 860-594-0259
Web: www.arrlf.org

The Byron Blanchard, N1EKV Memorial Scholarship Fund

Type of award: Scholarship.
Intended use: For undergraduate study at postsecondary institution.
Eligibility: Applicant must be residing in Vermont, Connecticut, New Hampshire, Maine, Massachusetts or Rhode Island.

Basis for selection: Competition/talent/interest in amateur radio.

Application requirements: Transcript. FAFSA.

Additional information: Must be amateur radio operator with any class of active Amateur Radio license and reside in ARRL New England Division. Visit Website for application.

Amount of award:	$500
Number of awards:	1
Application deadline:	January 31

Contact:
The ARRL Foundation, Inc. Scholarship Program
225 Main Street
Newington, CT 06111
Phone: 860-594-0397
Fax: 860-594-0259
Web: www.arrlf.org

The Carole J. Streeter, KB9JBR, Scholarship

Type of award: Scholarship.

Intended use: For undergraduate study at accredited postsecondary institution.

Eligibility: Applicant must be U.S. citizen.

Basis for selection: Competition/talent/interest in amateur radio. Major/career interest in medicine.

Application requirements: Transcript. FAFSA.

Additional information: Must be amateur radio operator with any class of active Amateur Radio license with preference for basic Morse code capability. High school seniors are eligible to apply. Applicants should study medicine or related majors. Visit website for application.

Amount of award:	$1,000
Number of awards:	1
Application deadline:	January 31

Contact:
The ARRL Foundation, Inc. Scholarship Program
225 Main Street
Newington, CT 06111
Phone: 860-594-0397
Fax: 860-594-0259
Web: www.arrlf.org

The Central Arizona DX Association Scholarship

Type of award: Scholarship.

Intended use: For undergraduate study at postsecondary institution.

Eligibility: Applicant must be residing in Arizona.

Basis for selection: Competition/talent/interest in amateur radio. Applicant must demonstrate high academic achievement.

Application requirements: Transcript. FAFSA.

Additional information: Minimum 3.2 GPA. Must be amateur radio operator with active Technician Class or higher license. High school seniors are eligible to apply. Graduating high school students will be considered before current college students. Visit website for application.

Amount of award:	$1,000
Number of awards:	1
Application deadline:	January 31

Contact:
The ARRL Foundation, Inc. Scholarship Program
225 Main Street
Newington, CT 06111
Phone: 860-594-0397
Fax: 860-594-0259
Web: www.arrlf.org

The Challenge Met Scholarship

Type of award: Scholarship.

Intended use: For undergraduate study at accredited vocational, 2-year or 4-year institution.

Eligibility: Applicant must be learning disabled.

Basis for selection: Competition/talent/interest in amateur radio.

Application requirements: Transcript, proof of eligibility. Documentation of learning disability by physician or school. FAFSA.

Additional information: Must be amateur radio operator holding any class license. Preference given to those with documented learning disabilities that put forth effort regardless of resulting grades. High school seniors are eligible to apply. Application may be obtained on Website, and will only be accepted via email. Number of awards varies.

Amount of award:	$500
Application deadline:	January 31

Contact:
The ARRL Foundation, Inc. Scholarship Program
225 Main Street
Newington, CT 06111
Phone: 860-594-0347
Fax: 860-594-0259
Web: www.arrlf.org

The Charles Clarke Cordle Memorial Scholarship

Type of award: Scholarship.

Intended use: For undergraduate or graduate study at postsecondary institution in United States. Designated institutions: Institutions in Alabama or Georgia.

Eligibility: Applicant must be residing in Alabama or Georgia.

Basis for selection: Competition/talent/interest in amateur radio. Major/career interest in electronics or communications. Applicant must demonstrate high academic achievement.

Application requirements: Transcript. FAFSA.

Additional information: Minimum 2.5 GPA. Must hold active Amateur Radio license. Preference to students of majors listed or other related fields. High school seniors are eligible to apply. Application may be obtained from website, and will only be accepted via email.

Amount of award:	$1,000
Number of awards:	1
Application deadline:	January 31
Total amount awarded:	$1,000

Contact:
The ARRL Foundation, Inc. Scholarship Program
225 Main Street
Newington, CT 06111
Phone: 860-594-0397
Fax: 860-594-0259
Web: www.arrlf.org

The Charles N. Fisher Memorial Scholarship

Type of award: Scholarship.
Intended use: For undergraduate or graduate study at accredited postsecondary institution in United States.
Eligibility: Applicant must be residing in California or Arizona.
Basis for selection: Competition/talent/interest in amateur radio. Major/career interest in communications or electronics.
Application requirements: Transcript. FAFSA.
Additional information: Must hold active Amateur Radio license. Major may be in other fields related to those listed. California candidates must reside in Los Angeles, Orange County, San Diego, or Santa Barbara. High school seniors eligible to apply. Application may be obtained on Website, and will only be accepted via email.

Amount of award:	$1,000
Number of awards:	1
Application deadline:	January 31
Total amount awarded:	$1,000

Contact:
The ARRL Foundation, Inc. Scholarship Program
225 Main Street
Newington, CT 06111
Phone: 860-594-0397
Fax: 860-594-0259
Web: www.arrlf.org

The Chicago FM Club Scholarship

Type of award: Scholarship.
Intended use: For undergraduate study at accredited vocational, 2-year or 4-year institution in United States.
Eligibility: Applicant must be U.S. citizen residing in Wisconsin, Indiana or Illinois.
Basis for selection: Competition/talent/interest in amateur radio.
Application requirements: Transcript. FAFSA.
Additional information: Student also eligible if within three months of becoming U.S. citizen. Must be amateur radio operator with Technician Class license or higher. Number of awards varies. High school seniors eligible to apply. Application may be obtained on Website, and will only be accepted via email.

Amount of award:	$500
Application deadline:	January 31

Contact:
The ARRL Foundation, Inc. Scholarship Program
225 Main Street
Newington, CT 06111
Phone: 860-594-0397
Fax: 860-594-0259
Web: www.arrlf.org

The David Knaus Memorial Scholarship

Type of award: Scholarship.
Intended use: For undergraduate study at 2-year or 4-year institution.
Basis for selection: Competition/talent/interest in amateur radio.
Application requirements: Transcript. FAFSA.
Additional information: Must be amateur radio operator with active Amateur Radio license, any class. Preference to resident of Wisconsin. If no applicant identified, preference will be

given to applicant from the ARRL Central Division (Illinois, Indiana, Wisconsin). Visit website for application.

Amount of award:	$1,500
Number of awards:	1
Application deadline:	January 31

Contact:
The ARRL Foundation, Inc. Scholarship Program
225 Main Street
Newington, CT 06111
Phone: 860-594-0397
Fax: 860-594-0259
Web: www.arrlf.org

The Dayton Amateur Radio Association Scholarships

Type of award: Scholarship.
Intended use: For undergraduate study at accredited 4-year institution in United States.
Basis for selection: Competition/talent/interest in amateur radio.
Application requirements: Transcript. FAFSA.
Additional information: Must be amateur radio operator holding any class license. High school seniors are eligible to apply. Application may be obtained on Website, and will only be accepted via email.

Amount of award:	$1,000
Number of awards:	4
Application deadline:	January 31

Contact:
The ARRL Foundation, Inc. Scholarship Program
225 Main Street
Newington, CT 06111
Phone: 860-594-0347
Fax: 860-594-0259
Web: www.arrlf.org

The Don Riebhoff Memorial Scholarship

Type of award: Scholarship.
Intended use: For undergraduate or graduate study at accredited 2-year, 4-year or graduate institution in United States.
Basis for selection: Competition/talent/interest in amateur radio. Major/career interest in international relations. Applicant must demonstrate financial need and high academic achievement.
Application requirements: Transcript. FAFSA.
Additional information: Must be amateur radio operator with Active Technician class license or higher. Preference given to ARRL members and candidates seeking baccalaureate degree or higher. High school seniors are eligible to apply. Application may be obtained on Website, and will only be accepted via email.

Amount of award:	$1,000
Number of awards:	1
Application deadline:	January 31

Contact:
The ARRL Foundation, Inc. Scholarship Program
225 Main Street
Newington, CT 06111
Phone: 860-594-0397
Fax: 860-594-0259
Web: www.arrlf.org

Scholarships

The Dr. James L. Lawson Memorial Scholarship

Type of award: Scholarship.
Intended use: For undergraduate or graduate study at 4-year or graduate institution in United States. Designated institutions: Any institution in New England or New York State.
Eligibility: Applicant must be residing in Vermont, New York, New Hampshire, Connecticut, Maine, Massachusetts or Rhode Island.
Basis for selection: Competition/talent/interest in amateur radio. Major/career interest in communications or electronics.
Application requirements: Transcript. FAFSA.
Additional information: Must be amateur radio operator holding a General Class license or higher. Major may be in other fields related to those listed. High school seniors eligible to apply. Application may be obtained on Website, and will only be accepted via email.

Amount of award:	$500
Number of awards:	1
Application deadline:	January 31
Total amount awarded:	$500

Contact:
The ARRL Foundation, Inc. Scholarship Program
225 Main Street
Newington, CT 06111
Phone: 860-594-0397
Fax: 860-594-0259
Web: www.arrlf.org

The Edmond A. Metzger Scholarship

Type of award: Scholarship.
Intended use: For undergraduate, graduate or non-degree study at 4-year or graduate institution in United States. Designated institutions: Schools in ARRL Central Division (Illinois, Indiana, Wisconsin).
Eligibility: Applicant must be residing in Wisconsin, Indiana or Illinois.
Basis for selection: Competition/talent/interest in amateur radio. Major/career interest in engineering, electrical/electronic.
Application requirements: Transcript. FAFSA.
Additional information: Must be amateur radio operator with active license in any class. Must be American Radio Relay League member. High school seniors eligible to apply. Application may be obtained on Website, and will only be accepted via email.

Amount of award:	$500
Number of awards:	1
Application deadline:	January 31
Total amount awarded:	$500

Contact:
The ARRL Foundation, Inc. Scholarship Program
225 Main Street
Newington, CT 06111
Phone: 860-594-0397
Fax: 860-594-0259
Web: www.arrlf.org

The Eugene Gene Sallee, W4YFR, Memorial Scholarship

Type of award: Scholarship.
Intended use: For undergraduate or graduate study at accredited postsecondary institution in United States.
Eligibility: Applicant must be residing in Georgia.

Basis for selection: Competition/talent/interest in amateur radio. Major/career interest in electronics or communications. Applicant must demonstrate financial need and high academic achievement.
Application requirements: Transcript. FAFSA.
Additional information: Must be amateur radio operator with active Technician Plus or higher class license. Preference given to students with a minimum 3.0 GPA. Major may be in a related field. High school seniors are eligible to apply. Application may be obtained on Website, and will only be accepted via email.

Amount of award:	$500
Number of awards:	1
Application deadline:	January 31
Total amount awarded:	$500

Contact:
The ARRL Foundation, Inc. Scholarship Program
225 Main Street
Newington, CT 06111
Phone: 860-594-0397
Fax: 860-594-0259
Web: www.arrlf.org

The Francis Walton Memorial Scholarship

Type of award: Scholarship.
Intended use: For undergraduate or graduate study at 4-year or graduate institution.
Eligibility: Applicant must be residing in Wisconsin, Indiana or Illinois.
Basis for selection: Competition/talent/interest in amateur radio. Major/career interest in agriculture; electronics; history or communications. Applicant must demonstrate financial need and high academic achievement.
Application requirements: Transcript. FAFSA.
Additional information: Must be amateur radio operator with any active Amateur Radio license class, with preference to applicants that provide documentation of CW proficiency of more than 5 wpm. High school seniors are eligible to apply. Other majors also eligible. Applicant should demonstrate interest in promoting Amateur Radio. Visit website for application.

Amount of award:	$500
Number of awards:	1
Application deadline:	January 31

Contact:
The ARRL Foundation, Inc. Scholarship Program
225 Main Street
Newington, CT 06111
Phone: 860-594-0397
Fax: 860-594-0259
Web: www.arrlf.org

The Fred R. McDaniel Memorial Scholarship

Type of award: Scholarship.
Intended use: For undergraduate or graduate study at 4-year or graduate institution in United States. Designated institutions: Any colleges or universities in FCC fifth call district (Texas, Oklahoma, Arkansas, Louisiana, Mississippi, New Mexico).
Eligibility: Applicant must be residing in Oklahoma, Texas, Mississippi, Arkansas, New Mexico or Louisiana.
Basis for selection: Competition/talent/interest in amateur radio. Major/career interest in electronics or communications. Applicant must demonstrate high academic achievement.

Application requirements: Transcript. FAFSA.

Additional information: Preference for students with minimum 3.0 GPA. Must be amateur radio operator holding General Class license or higher. Major may be in other fields related to those listed. High school students eligible to apply. Application may be obtained from Website, and will only be accepted via email.

Amount of award:	$500
Number of awards:	1
Application deadline:	January 31
Total amount awarded:	$500

Contact:
The ARRL Foundation, Inc. Scholarship Program
225 Main Street
Newington, CT 06111
Phone: 860-594-0397
Fax: 860-594-0259
Web: www.arrlf.org

The Gary Wagner, K3OMI, Scholarship

Type of award: Scholarship.

Intended use: For undergraduate study at accredited 4-year institution.

Eligibility: Applicant must be U.S. citizen residing in Virginia, Tennessee, West Virginia, Maryland or North Carolina.

Basis for selection: Competition/talent/interest in amateur radio. Major/career interest in engineering. Applicant must demonstrate financial need.

Application requirements: Transcript. FAFSA.

Additional information: Must be amateur radio operator with an active Novice Class Amateur Radio License or higher. High school seniors are eligible to apply. Visit website for application.

Amount of award:	$1,000
Number of awards:	1
Application deadline:	January 31

Contact:
The ARRL Foundation, Inc. Scholarship Program
225 Main Street
Newington, CT 06111
Phone: 860-594-0397
Fax: 860-594-0259
Web: www.arrlf.org

The Gwinnett Amateur Radio Society Scholarship

Type of award: Scholarship.

Intended use: For undergraduate study at 4-year institution.

Eligibility: Applicant must be residing in Georgia.

Basis for selection: Competition/talent/interest in amateur radio.

Application requirements: Transcript. FAFSA.

Additional information: Must be amateur radio operator with active Amateur Radio license, any class. Applicants must be residents of Gwinnett County, GA or the state of GA. High school seniors are eligible to apply. Visit website for application.

Amount of award:	$500
Number of awards:	1
Application deadline:	January 31

Contact:
The ARRL Foundation, Inc. Scholarship Program
225 Main Street
Newington, CT 06111
Phone: 860-594-0397
Fax: 860-594-0259
Web: www.arrlf.org

The Henry Broughton, K2AE, Memorial Scholarship

Type of award: Scholarship.

Intended use: For undergraduate or graduate study at accredited 4-year or graduate institution in United States.

Eligibility: Applicant must be residing in New York.

Basis for selection: Competition/talent/interest in amateur radio. Major/career interest in engineering or science, general.

Application requirements: Transcript. FAFSA.

Additional information: Must be amateur radio operator with General Class license. Major may be in other fields similar to those listed. High school seniors are eligible to apply. Applicants must live within 70 miles of Schenectady, New York. May offer additional awards if funding permits. Application may be obtained on Website, and will only be accepted via email.

Amount of award:	$1,000
Number of awards:	1
Application deadline:	January 31

Contact:
The ARRL Foundation, Inc. Scholarship Program
225 Main Street
Newington, CT 06111
Phone: 860-594-0397
Fax: 860-594-0259
Web: www.arrlf.org

The Indianapolis Amateur Radio Association Fund

Type of award: Scholarship.

Intended use: For undergraduate study at postsecondary institution.

Eligibility: Applicant must be residing in Wisconsin, Indiana or Illinois.

Basis for selection: Competition/talent/interest in amateur radio. Major/career interest in engineering, electrical/electronic or computer/information sciences.

Application requirements: Transcript. FAFSA.

Additional information: Must be amateur radio operator with any class of active Amateur Radio license and reside in ARRL Central Division. Visit website for application.

Amount of award:	$1,000
Number of awards:	1
Application deadline:	January 31

Contact:
The ARRL Foundation, Inc. Scholarship Program
225 Main Street
Newington, CT 06111
Phone: 860-594-0397
Fax: 860-594-0259
Web: www.arrlf.org

Scholarships

IRARC Memorial, Joseph P. Rubino, WA4MMD, Scholarship

Type of award: Scholarship.
Intended use: For undergraduate or post-bachelor's certificate study at accredited vocational or 4-year institution.
Eligibility: Applicant must be residing in Florida.
Basis for selection: Competition/talent/interest in amateur radio. Major/career interest in electronics. Applicant must demonstrate financial need and high academic achievement.
Application requirements: Transcript. FAFSA.
Additional information: Minimum 2.5 GPA. Must be amateur radio operator with any active Amateur Radio license class. High school seniors are eligible to apply. Number of awards varies. Visit website for application. Preference given to residents of Brevard County, FL, or any Florida resident. Students enrolled in an electronic technician certification program also eligible.

Amount of award:	$750
Application deadline:	January 31

Contact:
The ARRL Foundation, Inc. Scholarship Program
225 Main Street
Newington, CT 06111
Phone: 860-594-0397
Fax: 860-594-0259
Web: www.arrlf.org

The Irving W. Cook WA0CGS Scholarship

Type of award: Scholarship.
Intended use: For undergraduate or graduate study at 4-year or graduate institution.
Eligibility: Applicant must be residing in Kansas.
Basis for selection: Competition/talent/interest in amateur radio. Major/career interest in communications or electronics.
Application requirements: Transcript. FAFSA.
Additional information: Must hold active Amateur Radio license. Major may be in other fields related to those listed. High school seniors eligible to apply. Application may be obtained on Website, and will only be accepted via email.

Amount of award:	$1,000
Number of awards:	1
Application deadline:	January 31
Total amount awarded:	$1,000

Contact:
The ARRL Foundation, Inc. Scholarship Program
225 Main Street
Newington, CT 06111
Phone: 860-594-0397
Fax: 860-594-0259
Web: www.arrlf.org

The Jackson County ARA Scholarship

Type of award: Scholarship.
Intended use: For undergraduate or graduate study at postsecondary institution.
Basis for selection: Competition/talent/interest in amateur radio.
Application requirements: Transcript. FAFSA.
Additional information: Must be amateur radio operator with active Amateur Radio license, any class. Preference given to applicants from Mississippi. If no applicant is identified, preference will be given to an applicant from the ARRL Delta Division (Arkansas, Louisiana, Mississippi, and Tennessee). Visit website for application.

Amount of award:	$500
Number of awards:	1
Application deadline:	January 31

Contact:
The ARRL Foundation, Inc. Scholarship Program
225 Main Street
Newington, CT 06111
Phone: 860-594-0397
Fax: 860-594-0259
Web: www.arrlf.org

The Jake McClain Driver KC5WXA Scholarship Fund

Type of award: Scholarship.
Intended use: For undergraduate study at postsecondary institution.
Eligibility: Applicant must be residing in Tennessee, Mississippi, Arkansas or Louisiana.
Basis for selection: Competition/talent/interest in amateur radio. Major/career interest in electronics; computer/information sciences or journalism.
Application requirements: Transcript. FAFSA.
Additional information: Must be amateur radio operator with active Technician Class Amateur Radio License or higher and can provide at least one QLSL card received within the past twelve months. Must reside in the ARRL Delta Division. Visit website for application.

Amount of award:	$1,000
Number of awards:	1
Application deadline:	January 31

Contact:
The ARRL Foundation, Inc. Scholarship Program
225 Main Street
Newington, CT 06111
Phone: 860-594-0397
Fax: 860-594-0259
Web: www.arrlf.org

The K2TEO Martin J. Green, Sr. Memorial Scholarship

Type of award: Scholarship.
Intended use: For undergraduate or graduate study at postsecondary institution.
Basis for selection: Competition/talent/interest in amateur radio.
Application requirements: Transcript. FAFSA.
Additional information: Must be amateur radio operator with General Class license or higher. Preference given to student from family of ham operators. High school seniors are eligible to apply. Application may be obtained on Website, and will only be accepted via email.

Amount of award:	$1,000
Number of awards:	1
Application deadline:	January 31
Total amount awarded:	$1,000

Contact:
The ARRL Foundation, Inc. Scholarship Program
225 Main Street
Newington, CT 06111
Phone: 860-594-0397
Fax: 860-594-0259
Web: www.arrlf.org

The L. Phil and Alice J. Wicker Scholarship

Type of award: Scholarship.
Intended use: For undergraduate, graduate or non-degree study at 4-year or graduate institution in United States. Designated institutions: Schools in ARRL Roanoke Division (NC, SC, VA, WV).
Eligibility: Applicant must be residing in Virginia, West Virginia, North Carolina or South Carolina.
Basis for selection: Competition/talent/interest in amateur radio. Major/career interest in communications or electronics.
Application requirements: Transcript. FAFSA.
Additional information: Must be amateur radio operator holding a General Class license or higher. Major may be in other fields related to those listed. High school seniors eligible to apply. Application may be obtained on Website, and will only be accepted via email.

Amount of award:	$500
Number of awards:	1
Application deadline:	January 31

Contact:
The ARRL Foundation, Inc. Scholarship Program
225 Main Street
Newington, CT 06111
Phone: 860-594-0397
Fax: 860-594-0259
Web: www.arrlf.org

The L.B. Cebik, W4RNL, and Jean Cebik, N4TZP, Memorial Scholarship

Type of award: Scholarship.
Intended use: For undergraduate study at 4-year institution in United States.
Basis for selection: Competition/talent/interest in amateur radio.
Application requirements: Transcript. FAFSA.
Additional information: Must be amateur radio operator holding Technician Class license or higher. High school seniors are eligible to apply. Application may be obtained on Website, and will only be accepted via email.

Amount of award:	$1,000
Number of awards:	1
Application deadline:	January 31

Contact:
The ARRL Foundation, Inc. Scholarship Program
225 Main Street
Newington, CT 06111
Phone: 1-860-594-0200
Fax: 860-594-0259
Web: www.arrlf.org

The Louisiana Memorial Scholarship

Type of award: Scholarship.
Intended use: For undergraduate study at 4-year or graduate institution in United States.
Basis for selection: Competition/talent/interest in amateur radio. Applicant must demonstrate high academic achievement.
Application requirements: Transcript. FAFSA.
Additional information: Must be resident of or student in Louisiana. Minimum 3.0 GPA. Must be amateur radio operator holding Technician Class license or higher. High school seniors eligible to apply. Application may be obtained on Website, and will only be accepted via email.

Amount of award:	$750
Number of awards:	1
Application deadline:	January 31

Contact:
The ARRL Foundation, Inc. Scholarship Program
225 Main Street
Newington, CT 06111
Phone: 860-594-0200
Fax: 860-594-0259
Web: www.arrlf.org

The Magnolia DX Association Scholarship

Type of award: Scholarship.
Intended use: For undergraduate study at vocational, 2-year or 4-year institution. Designated institutions: Mississippi institutions.
Eligibility: Applicant must be high school senior. Applicant must be residing in Tennessee, Mississippi, Arkansas or Louisiana.
Basis for selection: Competition/talent/interest in amateur radio. Major/career interest in electronics; communications; computer/information sciences or engineering.
Application requirements: Transcript. FAFSA.
Additional information: Must be amateur radio operator with active Technician Class license or higher. Preference given to graduating high school seniors in Mississippi or Delta Division (Arkansas, Louisiana, Mississippi, and Tennessee) for use at a Mississippi institution. Visit Website for application.

Amount of award:	$500
Number of awards:	1
Application deadline:	January 31

Contact:
American Radio Relay League (ARRL) Foundation, Inc.
225 Main Street
Newington, CT 06111
Phone: 860-594-0397
Fax: 860-594-0259
Web: www.arrlf.org

The Mary Lou Brown Scholarship

Type of award: Scholarship.
Intended use: For undergraduate or graduate study at 4-year institution in United States.
Eligibility: Applicant must be residing in Oregon, Montana, Alaska, Idaho or Washington.
Basis for selection: Competition/talent/interest in amateur radio. Applicant must demonstrate high academic achievement.
Application requirements: Transcript. FAFSA.
Additional information: Minimum 3.0 GPA and demonstrated interest in promoting Amateur Radio Service. Must be amateur radio operator with General Class license. Number of awards varies based on funding. High school seniors eligible to apply. Application may be obtained on Website, and will only be accepted via email.

Amount of award:	$2,500
Application deadline:	January 31

Contact:
The ARRL Foundation, Inc. Scholarship Program
225 Main Street
Newington, CT 06111
Phone: 860-594-0397
Fax: 860-594-0259
Web: www.arrlf.org

Scholarships

The Mississippi Scholarship

Type of award: Scholarship.
Intended use: For undergraduate or graduate study at 4-year or graduate institution in United States. Designated institutions: Schools in Mississippi.
Eligibility: Applicant must be no older than 30. Applicant must be residing in Mississippi.
Basis for selection: Competition/talent/interest in amateur radio. Major/career interest in communications or electronics.
Application requirements: Transcript. FAFSA.
Additional information: Must hold active Amateur Radio license. Major may be in other fields related to those listed. High school seniors eligible to apply. Application may be obtained on Website, and will only be accepted via email.

Amount of award:	$500
Number of awards:	1
Application deadline:	January 31
Total amount awarded:	$500

Contact:
The ARRL Foundation, Inc. Scholarship Program
225 Main Street
Newington, CT 06111
Phone: 860-594-0397
Fax: 860-594-0259
Web: www.arrlf.org

The New England FEMARA Scholarship

Type of award: Scholarship.
Intended use: For undergraduate, graduate or non-degree study at postsecondary institution.
Eligibility: Applicant must be residing in Vermont, Connecticut, New Hampshire, Maine, Massachusetts or Rhode Island.
Basis for selection: Competition/talent/interest in amateur radio.
Application requirements: Transcript. FAFSA.
Additional information: Must be amateur radio operator holding Technical Class license or higher. Number of awards varies based on funding. High school seniors eligible to apply. Application may be obtained on Website, and will only be accepted via email.

Amount of award:	$1,000
Application deadline:	January 31

Contact:
The ARRL Foundation, Inc. Scholarship Program
225 Main Street
Newington, CT 06111
Phone: 860-594-0397
Fax: 860-594-0259
Web: www.arrlf.org

The Norman E. Strohmeier, W2VRS, Memorial Scholarship

Type of award: Scholarship.
Intended use: For undergraduate study at postsecondary institution.
Eligibility: Applicant must be residing in New York.
Basis for selection: Competition/talent/interest in amateur radio. Applicant must demonstrate high academic achievement.
Application requirements: Transcript. FAFSA.
Additional information: Minimum 3.2 GPA. Must be amateur radio operator with active Technician Class Amateur Radio License or higher. Preference given to Western New York

resident. High school seniors are eligible to apply. Preference to high school senior. Applicant must provide documentation of Amateur Radio activities and achievements and any honor from community service. Visit Website for application.

Amount of award:	$500
Number of awards:	1
Application deadline:	January 31

Contact:
American Radio Relay League (ARRL) Foundation, Inc.
225 Main Street
Newington, CT 06111
Phone: 860-594-0397
Fax: 860-594-0259
Web: www.arrlf.org

The North Fulton Amateur Radio League Scholarship Fund

Type of award: Scholarship.
Intended use: For undergraduate study at postsecondary institution.
Eligibility: Applicant must be residing in Puerto Rico, Virgin Islands, Alabama, Georgia or Florida.
Basis for selection: Competition/talent/interest in amateur radio. Major/career interest in engineering or computer/information sciences.
Application requirements: Transcript. FAFSA.
Additional information: Must be a member of ARRL. If no qualified applicant in Georgia, preference will be awarded to applicants from the ARRL Southeastern Division (Alabama, Florida, Georgia, Puerto Rico, and the U.S. Virgin Islands). Award given to applicants regardless of field of study if there are no other qualified applicants.

Amount of award:	$900
Number of awards:	1
Application deadline:	January 31

Contact:
American Radio Relay League (ARRL) Foundation, Inc.
225 Main Street
Newington, CT 06111
Phone: 860-594-0397
Fax: 860-594-0259
Web: www.arrlf.org

The Orlando HamCation Scholarship

Type of award: Scholarship.
Intended use: For undergraduate study at accredited 4-year institution.
Eligibility: Applicant must be U.S. citizen residing in Florida.
Basis for selection: Competition/talent/interest in amateur radio. Major/career interest in radio/television/film or communications.
Application requirements: Transcript. FAFSA.
Additional information: Must be amateur radio operator with any class of active Amateur Radio license. High school seniors are eligible to apply. Preference given to residents of Central Florida (Orange, Seminole, Osceola, Lake, Volusia, Brevard and Polk counties); if no suitable applicant, resident of the State of Florida. Applicant should study a technical field that supports the radio arts. Visit Website for application.

Amount of award:	$1,000
Number of awards:	1
Application deadline:	January 31

Contact:
American Radio Relay League (ARRL) Foundation, Inc.
225 Main Street
Newington, CT 06111
Phone: 860-594-0397
Fax: 860-594-0259
Web: www.arrlf.org

The Outdoor Hams Scholarship

Type of award: Scholarship.
Intended use: For undergraduate study at accredited 2-year or 4-year institution.
Eligibility: Applicant must be residing in North Carolina.
Basis for selection: Competition/talent/interest in amateur radio.
Application requirements: Transcript. FAFSA.
Additional information: One $1,000 award given for a 4-year college or two $500 awards given for a 2-year college. Must be in technical field of study. Must be amateur radio operator with any class of active Amateur Radio license. Preference given to amateur radio operators that incorporate amateur radio into outdoor activities. Visit Website for application.

Amount of award:	$500-$1,000
Application deadline:	January 31

Contact:
American Radio Relay League (ARRL) Foundation, Inc.
225 Main Street
Newington, CT 06111
Phone: 860-594-0397
Fax: 860-594-0259
Web: www.arrlf.org

The Paul and Helen L. Grauer Scholarship

Type of award: Scholarship.
Intended use: For undergraduate or graduate study at 4-year or graduate institution in United States. Designated institutions: Schools in Midwest Division (Iowa, Kansas, Missouri, Nebraska).
Eligibility: Applicant must be residing in Iowa, Nebraska, Kansas or Missouri.
Basis for selection: Competition/talent/interest in amateur radio. Major/career interest in communications or electronics.
Application requirements: Transcript. FAFSA.
Additional information: Must hold active Amateur Radio license in any class. Major may be in other fields related to those listed. High school seniors are eligible to apply. Application may be obtained on Website, and will only be accepted via email.

Amount of award:	$1,000
Number of awards:	1
Application deadline:	January 31
Total amount awarded:	$1,000

Contact:
The ARRL Foundation, Inc. Scholarship Program
225 Main Street
Newington, CT 06111
Phone: 860-594-0397
Fax: 860-594-0259
Web: www.arrlf.org

The Peoria Area Amateur Radio Club Scholarship

Type of award: Scholarship.
Intended use: For undergraduate study at accredited 2-year or 4-year institution.
Eligibility: Applicant must be residing in Illinois.
Basis for selection: Competition/talent/interest in amateur radio.
Application requirements: Transcript. FAFSA.
Additional information: Must be amateur radio operator with active Technician Class license or higher. High school seniors are eligible to apply. Preference given to a resident of Central Illinois in one of the following counties: Peoria, Tazewell, Woodford, Knox, McLean, Fulton, Logan, Marshall or Stark. Visit Website for application.

Amount of award:	$500
Number of awards:	1
Application deadline:	January 31

Contact:
American Radio Relay League (ARRL) Foundation, Inc.
225 Main Street
Newington, CT 06111
Phone: 860-594-0397
Fax: 860-594-0259
Web: www.arrlf.org

The Ray, NØRP, & Katie, WØKTE, Pautz Scholarship

Type of award: Scholarship.
Intended use: For undergraduate study at accredited 4-year institution.
Eligibility: Applicant must be residing in Iowa, Nebraska, Kansas or Missouri.
Basis for selection: Competition/talent/interest in amateur radio. Major/career interest in electronics or computer/information sciences. Applicant must demonstrate financial need.
Application requirements: Transcript. FAFSA.
Additional information: Must be an ARRL member, and an amateur radio operator with active General Class or higher license. High school seniors are eligible to apply. Applicant should be majoring in electronics, computer science or related field. Visit Website for application.

Amount of award:	$500-$1,000
Number of awards:	1
Application deadline:	January 31

Contact:
American Radio Relay League (ARRL) Foundation, Inc.
225 Main Street
Newington, CT 06111
Phone: 860-594-0397
Fax: 860-594-0259
Web: www.arrlf.org

The Richard W. Bendicksen, N7ZL, Memorial Scholarship

Type of award: Scholarship.
Intended use: For undergraduate study at 4-year institution in United States.
Basis for selection: Competition/talent/interest in amateur radio.
Application requirements: Transcript. FAFSA.

Additional information: Must hold active Amateur Radio license. High school seniors eligible to apply. Application may be obtained on Website, and will only be accepted via email.

Amount of award: $2,000
Number of awards: 1
Application deadline: January 31

Contact:
The ARRL Foundation, Inc. Scholarship Program
225 Main Street
Newington, CT 06111
Phone: 860-594-0397
Fax: 860-594-0259
Web: www.arrlf.org

The Rocky Mountain Division Scholarship

Type of award: Scholarship.
Intended use: For undergraduate study at accredited 4-year institution in United States.
Eligibility: Applicant must be U.S. citizen residing in Wyoming, Utah, New Mexico or Colorado.
Basis for selection: Competition/talent/interest in amateur radio.
Application requirements: Recommendations, transcript. FAFSA.
Additional information: Winner also receives one-year ARRL membership if nominee is not an ARRL member. Must be amateur radio operator with active Amateur Radio license, any class. Visit Website for application.

Amount of award: $500
Number of awards: 1
Application deadline: January 31

Contact:
American Radio Relay League (ARRL) Foundation, Inc.
225 Main Street
Newington, CT 06111
Phone: 860-594-0397
Fax: 860-594-0259
Web: www.arrlf.org

The Scholarship of the Morris Radio Club of New Jersey

Type of award: Scholarship.
Intended use: For undergraduate study at 4-year institution.
Basis for selection: Competition/talent/interest in amateur radio.
Application requirements: Transcript. FAFSA.
Additional information: Must be amateur radio operator with active Technician Class or higher license. High school seniors are eligible to apply. Visit Website for application.

Amount of award: $1,000
Number of awards: 1
Application deadline: January 31

Contact:
American Radio Relay League (ARRL) Foundation, Inc.
225 Main Street
Newington, CT 06111
Phone: 860-594-0397
Fax: 860-594-0259
Web: www.arrlf.org

The Six Meter Club of Chicago Scholarship

Type of award: Scholarship.
Intended use: For undergraduate study at accredited postsecondary institution in United States. Designated institutions: Schools in Illinois, Indiana or Wisconsin.
Eligibility: Applicant must be residing in Wisconsin, Indiana or Illinois.
Basis for selection: Competition/talent/interest in amateur radio. Applicant must demonstrate high academic achievement.
Application requirements: Transcript. FAFSA.
Additional information: Must hold active Amateur Radio license. Preference given to applicants with minimum 2.5 GPA. High school seniors eligible to apply. Application may be obtained on Website, and will only be accepted via email.

Amount of award: $500
Number of awards: 1
Application deadline: January 31
Total amount awarded: $500

Contact:
The ARRL Foundation, Inc. Scholarship Program
225 Main Street
Newington, CT 06111
Phone: 860-594-0397
Fax: 860-594-0259
Web: www.arrlf.org

The Southeastern DX Club Scholarship Fund

Type of award: Scholarship.
Intended use: For undergraduate study at postsecondary institution.
Eligibility: Applicant must be residing in Georgia.
Basis for selection: Competition/talent/interest in amateur radio.
Application requirements: Transcript. FAFSA.
Additional information: Must be an active member of an amateur radio club affiliated with the ARRL. If no qualified applicant in Georgia, preference will be awarded to applicants from the ARRL Southeastern Division (Alabama, Florida, Georgia, Puerto Rico, and the U.S. Virgin Islands). Preference given to applicants pursuing engineering or computer science. Visit Website for application.

Amount of award: $500
Number of awards: 1
Application deadline: January 31

Contact:
American Radio Relay League (ARRL) Foundation, Inc.
225 Main Street
Newington, CT 06111
Phone: 860-594-0397
Fax: 860-594-0259
Web: www.arrlf.org

The Ted, W4VHF, and Itice, K4LVV, Goldthorpe Scholarship

Type of award: Scholarship.
Intended use: For undergraduate study at 4-year institution.
Basis for selection: Competition/talent/interest in amateur radio. Applicant must demonstrate financial need and service orientation.
Application requirements: Transcript. FAFSA.

Additional information: Must be amateur radio operator with any active Amateur Radio license class. High school seniors are eligible to apply. Visit Website for application.

Amount of award:	$500
Number of awards:	1
Application deadline:	January 31

Contact:
American Radio Relay League (ARRL) Foundation, Inc.
225 Main Street
Newington, CT 06111
Phone: 860-594-0397
Fax: 860-594-0259
Web: www.arrlf.org

The Thomas W. Porter, W8KYZ, Scholarship Honoring Michael Daugherty, W8LSE

Type of award: Scholarship.
Intended use: For undergraduate study at accredited vocational, 2-year or 4-year institution.
Eligibility: Applicant must be residing in Ohio or West Virginia.
Basis for selection: Competition/talent/interest in amateur radio.
Application requirements: Transcript. FAFSA.
Additional information: Must be amateur radio operator with active Amateur Radio License of Technician Class or higher. High school seniors are eligible to apply. Visit Website for application.

Amount of award:	$1,000
Number of awards:	1
Application deadline:	January 31

Contact:
American Radio Relay League (ARRL) Foundation, Inc.
225 Main Street
Newington, CT 06111
Phone: 860-594-0397
Fax: 860-594-0259
Web: www.arrlf.org

The Tom and Judith Comstock Scholarship

Type of award: Scholarship.
Intended use: For freshman study at 2-year or 4-year institution in United States.
Eligibility: Applicant must be high school senior. Applicant must be residing in Oklahoma or Texas.
Basis for selection: Competition/talent/interest in amateur radio.
Application requirements: Transcript. FAFSA.
Additional information: Must hold active Amateur Radio license. Application may be obtained on Website, and will only be accepted via email.

Amount of award:	$2,000
Number of awards:	1
Application deadline:	January 31
Total amount awarded:	$2,000

Contact:
The ARRL Foundation, Inc. Scholarship Program
225 Main Street
Newington, CT 06111
Phone: 860-594-0397
Fax: 860-594-0259
Web: www.arrlf.org

The Victor Poor W5SMM Memorial Scholarship Fund

Type of award: Scholarship.
Intended use: For undergraduate study at postsecondary institution.
Basis for selection: Competition/talent/interest in amateur radio. Major/career interest in engineering, electrical/electronic.
Application requirements: Transcript. FAFSA.
Additional information: Must be amateur radio operator with active Technician Class Amateur Radio License or higher. Preference given to applicants with a concentration in digital communications. Visit Website for application.

Amount of award:	$2,500
Number of awards:	1
Application deadline:	January 31

Contact:
American Radio Relay League (ARRL) Foundation, Inc.
225 Main Street
Newington, CT 06111
Phone: 860-594-0397
Fax: 860-594-0259
Web: www.arrlf.org

The Wayne Nelson, KB4UT, Memorial Scholarship

Type of award: Scholarship.
Intended use: For undergraduate study at accredited 4-year institution.
Eligibility: Applicant must be U.S. citizen residing in Florida.
Basis for selection: Competition/talent/interest in amateur radio. Major/career interest in engineering; technology; science, general or electronics. Applicant must demonstrate high academic achievement.
Application requirements: Transcript. FAFSA.
Additional information: Minimum 3.0 GPA. Must be amateur radio operator with any class of active Amateur Radio license. High school seniors are eligible to apply. Preference given to residents of Central Florida (Orange, Seminole, Osceola, Lake, Volusia, Brevard and Polk counties); if no suitable applicant, resident of the State of Florida. Visit Website for application.

Amount of award:	$1,000
Number of awards:	1
Application deadline:	January 31

Contact:
American Radio Relay League (ARRL) Foundation, Inc.
225 Main Street
Newington, CT 06111
Phone: 860-594-0397
Fax: 860-594-0259
Web: www.arrlf.org

The William Bennett, W7PHO, Memorial Scholarship

Type of award: Scholarship.
Intended use: For undergraduate study at 4-year institution.
Basis for selection: Competition/talent/interest in amateur radio. Applicant must demonstrate high academic achievement.
Application requirements: Transcript. FAFSA.
Additional information: Minimum 3.0 GPA. Must be amateur radio operator with active General Class license or higher. High school seniors are eligible to apply. Applicants should be residents of the ARRL's Northwest, Pacific or Southwest Divisions. Visit Website for application.

Scholarships

Amount of award:	$500
Number of awards:	1
Application deadline:	January 31

Contact:
American Radio Relay League (ARRL) Foundation, Inc.
225 Main Street
Newington, CT 06111
Phone: 860-594-0397
Fax: 860-594-0259
Web: www.arrlf.org

The William R. Goldfarb Memorial Scholarship

Type of award: Scholarship, renewable.
Intended use: For freshman study at accredited 4-year institution in United States. Designated institutions: Regionally accredited institution.
Eligibility: Applicant must be high school senior.
Basis for selection: Competition/talent/interest in amateur radio. Major/career interest in business; engineering; science, general; computer/information sciences; medicine or nursing. Applicant must demonstrate financial need.
Application requirements: Recommendations, transcript. FAFSA or Student Aid Report.
Additional information: Must hold active Amateur Radio license. Award amount varies based on applicant's qualifications, need, and other funding; $10,000 is the minimum award. Application may be obtained on Website, and will only be accepted via email.

Amount of award:	$10,000
Number of awards:	1
Application deadline:	January 31

Contact:
The ARRL Foundation, Inc. Scholarship Program
225 Main Street
Newington, CT 06111
Phone: 860-594-0397
Fax: 860-594-0259
Web: www.arrlf.org

The Wilse Morgan WX7P Memorial ARRL Northwestern Division Scholarship Fund

Type of award: Scholarship.
Intended use: For undergraduate study at postsecondary institution.
Eligibility: Applicant must be residing in Oregon, Montana, Alaska, Idaho or Washington.
Basis for selection: Competition/talent/interest in amateur radio. Major/career interest in engineering; medicine; science, general or business.
Application requirements: Transcript. FAFSA.
Additional information: Must be amateur radio operator with active General Class Amateur Radio License or higher and reside in the ARRL Northwestern Division. Preference given to applicants with a 3.0 GPA or higher for the academic year immediately prior to application. Visit Website for application.

Amount of award:	$1,000
Number of awards:	1
Application deadline:	January 31

Contact:
American Radio Relay League (ARRL) Foundation, Inc.
225 Main Street
Newington, CT 06111
Phone: 860-594-0397
Fax: 860-594-0259
Web: www.arrlf.org

Yankee Clipper Contest Club Youth Scholarship

Type of award: Scholarship.
Intended use: For undergraduate study at accredited 2-year or 4-year institution in United States.
Eligibility: Applicant must be residing in Vermont, New York, Maine, Pennsylvania, Massachusetts, Connecticut, New Hampshire, New Jersey or Rhode Island.
Basis for selection: Competition/talent/interest in amateur radio.
Application requirements: Transcript. FAFSA.
Additional information: Must be amateur radio operator holding active General Class license or higher. Must be resident of or college/university student in area within 175-mile radius of YCCC Center in Erving, MA. This includes MA; RI; CT; Long Island, NY; and some of VT, NH, ME, PA, and NJ. High school seniors are eligible to apply. Application may be obtained on Website, and will only be accepted via email.

Amount of award:	$1,200
Number of awards:	1
Application deadline:	January 31

Contact:
The ARRL Foundation, Inc. Scholarship Program
225 Main Street
Newington, CT 06111
Phone: 860-594-0397
Fax: 860-594-0259
Web: www.arrlf.org

The Yasme Foundation Scholarship

Type of award: Scholarship, renewable.
Intended use: For undergraduate study at accredited 4-year institution in United States.
Basis for selection: Competition/talent/interest in amateur radio. Major/career interest in science, general or engineering. Applicant must demonstrate high academic achievement and service orientation.
Application requirements: Transcript. FAFSA.
Additional information: Must hold active amateur radio license Technician Class or higher. Preference given to high school applicants in top five to ten percent of class or college students in top ten percent of class. Participation in local amateur radio club and community service strongly preferred. Previous YASME winners must submit new application and transcript each year. Number of awards varies. Application may be obtained on Website, and will only be accepted via email.

Amount of award:	$1,000
Application deadline:	January 31

Contact:
The ARRL Foundation, Inc. Scholarship Program
225 Main Street
Newington, CT 06111
Phone: 860-594-0397
Fax: 860-594-0259
Web: www.arrlf.org

Scholarships

The You've Got a Friend in Pennsylvania Scholarship

Type of award: Scholarship.
Intended use: For undergraduate, graduate or non-degree study at postsecondary institution in United States.
Eligibility: Applicant must be residing in Pennsylvania.
Basis for selection: Competition/talent/interest in amateur radio. Applicant must demonstrate high academic achievement.
Application requirements: Transcript. FAFSA.
Additional information: Must be amateur radio operator with a General Class or Extra Class license. Must be member of American Radio Relay League and maintain an "A" equivalent GPA. High school seniors eligible to apply. Application may be obtained from Website, and will only be accepted via email.

Amount of award:	$2,000
Number of awards:	2
Application deadline:	January 31
Total amount awarded:	$4,000

Contact:
The ARRL Foundation, Inc. Scholarship Program
225 Main Street
Newington, CT 06111
Phone: 860-594-0397
Fax: 860-594-0259
Web: www.arrlf.org

The Zachary Taylor Stevens Scholarship

Type of award: Scholarship.
Intended use: For undergraduate study at accredited vocational, 2-year or 4-year institution in United States.
Eligibility: Applicant must be residing in Michigan, Ohio or West Virginia.
Basis for selection: Competition/talent/interest in amateur radio.
Application requirements: Transcript. FAFSA.
Additional information: Must be amateur radio operator holding Technician Class license or higher. High school seniors eligible to apply. Application may be obtained on Website, and will only be accepted via email.

Amount of award:	$750
Number of awards:	1
Application deadline:	January 31

Contact:
The ARRL Foundation, Inc. Scholarship Program
225 Main Street
Newington, CT 06111
Phone: 860-594-0397
Fax: 860-594-0259
Web: www.arrlf.org

American Respiratory Care Foundation

Jimmy A. Young Memorial Education Recognition Award

Type of award: Scholarship, renewable.
Intended use: For undergraduate study at accredited postsecondary institution.

Basis for selection: Competition/talent/interest in research paper. Major/career interest in respiratory therapy. Applicant must demonstrate high academic achievement.
Application requirements: Recommendations, transcript, proof of eligibility, nomination by school or program representative. Student may initiate request for sponsorship in absence of nomination. Original referenced paper on some aspect of respiratory care.
Additional information: Minimum 3.0 GPA. Award includes coach airfare, one night lodging, and registration for AARC Congress. Preference given to applicants of minority origin. Application available on Website.

Amount of award:	$1,000
Number of awards:	1
Application deadline:	June 15
Total amount awarded:	$1,000

Contact:
American Respiratory Care Foundation
Attn: Education Recognition Award
9425 N. MacArthur Blvd., Suite 100
Irving, TX 75063-4706
Phone: 972-243-2272
Fax: 972-484-2720
Web: www.arcfoundation.org/awards

Morton B. Duggan, Jr. Memorial Education Recognition Award

Type of award: Scholarship, renewable.
Intended use: For undergraduate study at accredited postsecondary institution.
Basis for selection: Competition/talent/interest in research paper. Major/career interest in respiratory therapy. Applicant must demonstrate high academic achievement.
Application requirements: Recommendations, transcript, proof of eligibility. Research paper on some aspect of respiratory care.
Additional information: Applicants accepted from all states, but preference given to applicants from Georgia and South Carolina. Minimum 3.0 GPA. Award includes airfare, one night lodging, and registration for the AARC Congress. Application available on Website.

Amount of award:	$1,000
Number of awards:	1
Application deadline:	June 15
Total amount awarded:	$1,000

Contact:
American Respiratory Care Foundation
Attn: Education Recogniton Award
9425 N. MacArthur Blvd., Suite 100
Irving, TX 75063-4706
Phone: 972-243-2272
Fax: 972-484-2720
Web: www.arcfoundation.org/awards

NBRC/AMP Robert M. Lawrence, MD Education Recognition Award

Type of award: Scholarship.
Intended use: For junior or senior study at accredited 4-year institution.
Basis for selection: Competition/talent/interest in research paper. Major/career interest in respiratory therapy. Applicant must demonstrate high academic achievement.
Application requirements: Recommendations, essay, transcript, proof of eligibility. Original referenced paper on some aspect of respiratory care.

Additional information: Minimum 3.0 GPA. Award includes coach airfare, one night lodging, and registration for AARC Congress. Application available on Website.

Amount of award:	$2,500
Number of awards:	1
Application deadline:	June 15

Contact:
American Respiratory Care Foundation
Attn: Education Recognition Award
9425 N. MacArthur Blvd., Suite 100
Irving, TX 75063-4706
Phone: 972-243-2272
Fax: 972-484-2720
Web: www.arcfoundation.org/awards

American Society for Enology and Viticulture

American Society for Enology and Viticulture Scholarship Program

Type of award: Scholarship, renewable.
Intended use: For full-time at accredited 4-year or graduate institution.
Eligibility: Applicant must be Must be a resident of Canada, Mexico or or the United States.
Basis for selection: Major/career interest in agriculture; food science/technology or horticulture. Applicant must demonstrate high academic achievement.
Application requirements: Recommendations, essay, transcript. Student questionnaire, statement of intent, list of planned courses for upcoming year.
Additional information: Minimum 3.0 overall GPA for undergraduates, 3.2 overall GPA for graduate students. Must reside in North America (Canada, Mexico, or U.S.A.). May be used for full time study with a minimum of junior status for the upcoming academic year. Applicants must be enrolled in major or graduate program emphasizing enology or viticulture, or in curriculum emphasizing science basic to wine and grape industry. Awards vary.

Application deadline:	March 1

Contact:
ASEV Scholarship Committee
P.O. Box 1855
Davis, CA 95617-1855
Phone: 530-753-3142
Fax: 530-753-3318
Web: www.asev.org/scholarship-program

American Society for Microbiology

American Society for Microbiology Undergraduate Research Fellowship (URF)

Type of award: Research grant.
Intended use: For full-time undergraduate study in United States.

Eligibility: Applicant must be U.S. citizen or permanent resident.
Basis for selection: Major/career interest in microbiology. Applicant must demonstrate high academic achievement and seriousness of purpose.
Application requirements: Recommendations, transcript.
Additional information: Applicant must demonstrate strong interest in pursuing graduate career (Ph.D. or M.D./Ph.D.) in microbiology. Students conduct research for a minimum of ten weeks in summer and present results at ASM General Meeting the following year. Fellowship offers up to $4,000 stipend and up to $1,000 to travel to ASM General Meeting (if abstract is accepted). Applicant must have ASM member at home institution willing to serve as faculty mentor. Students may not receive financial support for research from other scientific organizations during fellowship. Faculty member's department chair or dean must endorse research project. Number of awards varies. See Website for application.

Amount of award:	$5,000
Number of applicants:	81
Application deadline:	February 1
Notification begins:	April 15

Contact:
American Society for Microbiology
ASM Undergraduate Research Fellowship Program
1752 N Street, NW
Washington, DC 20036
Phone: 202-942-9283
Fax: 202-942-9329
Web: www.asm.org/students

American Society of Civil Engineers

B. Charles Tiney Memorial ASCE Student Chapter Scholarship

Type of award: Scholarship.
Intended use: For undergraduate study at accredited 4-year institution.
Basis for selection: Major/career interest in engineering, civil. Applicant must demonstrate financial need, high academic achievement and leadership.
Application requirements: Recommendations, essay, transcript. Resume, detailed financial plan.
Additional information: Must be American Society of Civil Engineers member in good standing and be enrolled in ABET-accredited program. Awards and amounts determined annually. Visit Website for deadline and awards.
Contact:
American Society of Civil Engineers
Attn: Honors and Awards Program
1801 Alexander Bell Drive
Reston, VA 20191-4400
Phone: 800-548-2723 ext. 6106
Fax: 703-295-6222
Web: www.asce.org

Eugene C. Figg Jr. Civil Engineering Scholarship

Type of award: Scholarship.
Intended use: For junior or senior study.

Eligibility: Applicant must be U.S. citizen.
Basis for selection: Major/career interest in engineering, civil. Applicant must demonstrate financial need, high academic achievement and leadership.
Application requirements: Recommendations, essay, transcript. Resume, financial plan.
Additional information: Must be American Society of Civil Engineers member in good standing, be enrolled in ABET-accredited program, and have passion for bridges. Recipient eligible to interview for internship opportunity with Figg Engineering Group.

Amount of award:	$3,000
Number of awards:	1
Application deadline:	February 10
Total amount awarded:	$3,000

Contact:
American Society of Civil Engineers
Attn: Honors and Awards Program
1801 Alexander Bell Drive
Reston, VA 20191-4400
Phone: 800-548-2723 ext. 6106
Fax: 703-295-6222
Web: www.asce.org

Freeman Fellowship

Type of award: Research grant.
Intended use: For undergraduate or graduate study.
Basis for selection: Major/career interest in engineering, civil.
Application requirements: Recommendations, essay, transcript, research proposal. One to two-page resume. Detailed financial statement indicating how fellowship will finance applicant's research. Statement from institution where research will be conducted.
Additional information: Applicant must be American Society of Civil Engineers member in good standing. Grants are made toward expenses for experiments, observations, and compilations to discover new and accurate data that will be useful in engineering. Grant may be in form of prize for most useful paper relating to science/art of hydraulic construction. Travel grants available to ASCE members under 45, in recognition of achievement or promise. Visit Website for application and more information.

Amount of award:	$2,000-$5,000
Application deadline:	February 10

Contact:
American Society of Civil Engineers
Attn: Honors and Awards Program
1801 Alexander Bell Drive
Reston, VA 20191-4440
Phone: 800-548-2723 ext. 6106
Fax: 703-295-6222
Web: www.asce.org

John Lenard Civil Engineering Scholarship

Type of award: Scholarship.
Intended use: For junior or senior study at accredited 4-year institution.
Basis for selection: Major/career interest in engineering, civil or engineering, environmental. Applicant must demonstrate financial need, high academic achievement and leadership.
Application requirements: Recommendations, essay, transcript. One-page resume.
Additional information: Must be American Society of Civil Engineers member in good standing, be enrolled in ABET-accredited program, and have demonstrated commitment to either water supply and/or environmental engineering. Awards may vary based on available funds.

Amount of award:	$2,000
Number of awards:	2
Application deadline:	February 10

Contact:
American Society of Civil Engineers
Attn: Honors and Awards Program
1801 Alexander Bell Drive
Reston, VA 20191-4400
Phone: 800-548-2723 ext. 6106
Fax: 703-295-6222
Web: www.asce.org/scholarships/lenard/

Lawrence W. and Francis W. Cox Scholarship

Type of award: Scholarship.
Intended use: For undergraduate study at accredited 4-year institution.
Basis for selection: Major/career interest in engineering, civil. Applicant must demonstrate financial need, high academic achievement and leadership.
Application requirements: Recommendations, essay, transcript. One-page resume, detailed annual budget.
Additional information: Must be American Society of Civil Engineers member in good standing and be enrolled in ABET-accredited program. Awards and amounts may vary based on available funding.

Amount of award:	$5,000
Number of awards:	1
Application deadline:	February 10

Contact:
American Society of Civil Engineers
Attn: Honors and Awards Program
1801 Alexander Bell Drive
Reston, VA 20191-4400
Phone: 800-548-2723 ext. 6106
Fax: 703-295-6222
Web: www.asce.org/scholarships/cox/

Robert B.B. and Josephine Moorman Scholarship

Type of award: Scholarship.
Intended use: For undergraduate study at accredited 4-year institution. Designated institutions: ABET-accredited schools.
Basis for selection: Major/career interest in engineering, civil. Applicant must demonstrate financial need, high academic achievement and leadership.
Application requirements: Recommendations, essay, transcript. Resume, financial plan.
Additional information: Must be American Society of Civil Engineers member in good standing and be enrolled in ABET-accredited program. Awards may vary based on available funds.

Amount of award:	$2,000
Number of awards:	1
Application deadline:	February 10

Contact:
American Society of Civil Engineers
Attn: Honors and Awards Program
1801 Alexander Bell Drive
Reston, VA 20191-4400
Phone: 800-548-2723 ext. 6106
Fax: 703-295-6222
Web: www.asce.org

Samuel Fletcher Tapman ASCE Student Chapter Scholarship

Type of award: Scholarship, renewable.
Intended use: For undergraduate study at accredited postsecondary institution.
Basis for selection: Major/career interest in engineering, civil. Applicant must demonstrate financial need, high academic achievement and leadership.
Application requirements: Recommendations, essay, transcript. Resume, annual budget.
Additional information: Applicant must be enrolled in ABET-accredited program and be member in good standing of local American Society of Civil Engineers student chapter and national society. Membership applications may be submitted with scholarship application. One submission per student chapter. Visit Website for application and more information.

Amount of award:	$3,000
Number of awards:	12
Application deadline:	February 10

Contact:
American Society of Civil Engineers
Attn: Honors and Awards Program
1801 Alexander Bell Drive
Reston, VA 20191-4440
Phone: 800-548-2723 ext. 6106
Fax: 703-295-6222
Web: www.asce.org

Y.C. Yang Civil Engineering Scholarship

Type of award: Scholarship.
Intended use: For junior or senior study.
Basis for selection: Major/career interest in engineering, civil or engineering, structural. Applicant must demonstrate financial need, high academic achievement and leadership.
Application requirements: Recommendations, essay, transcript. Resume, financial plan.
Additional information: Must be student at ABET-accredited institution, an ASCE student member in good standing, and have interest in structural engineering. Awards may vary based on funding.

Amount of award:	$2,000
Number of awards:	2
Application deadline:	February 10

Contact:
American Society of Civil Engineers
Attn: Honors and Awards Program
1801 Alexander Bell Drive
Reston, VA 20191-4400
Phone: 800-548-2723 ext. 6106
Fax: 703-295-6222
Web: www.asce.org

American Society of Heating, Refrigerating, and Air-Conditioning Engineers, Inc.

Alwin B. Newton Scholarship

Type of award: Scholarship.
Intended use: For full-time undergraduate study at accredited 4-year institution in or outside United States. Designated institutions: Schools with ABET-accredited programs.
Basis for selection: Major/career interest in engineering or air conditioning/heating/refrigeration technology. Applicant must demonstrate financial need, high academic achievement, depth of character and leadership.
Application requirements: Recommendations, transcript.
Additional information: For engineering students considering service to heating/ventilation/air-conditioning (HVAC) and/or refrigeration profession. Minimum 3.0 GPA.

Amount of award:	$3,000
Number of awards:	1
Application deadline:	December 1

Contact:
ASHRAE, Inc. - Scholarship Administrator
1791 Tullie Circle, NE
Atlanta, GA 30329-2305
Phone: 404-636-8400
Fax: 404-321-5478
Web: www.ashrae.org/students/page/1271

ASHRAE Engineering Technology Scholarships

Type of award: Scholarship.
Intended use: For full-time undergraduate study at accredited 2-year or 4-year institution. Designated institutions: PAHRA accredited educational organizations with ABET-accredited engineering technology programs.
Basis for selection: Major/career interest in engineering or air conditioning/heating/refrigeration technology. Applicant must demonstrate financial need, high academic achievement, depth of character and leadership.
Application requirements: Recommendations, transcript.
Additional information: For students pursuing bachelor's or associate's degree in engineering technology and intending to pursue career in heating/ventilation/air-conditioning (HVAC) and/or refrigeration profession. Minimum 3.0 GPA.

Amount of award:	$5,000
Number of awards:	3
Application deadline:	May 1

Contact:
ASHRAE, Inc. - Scholarship Administrator
1791 Tullie Circle, NE
Atlanta, GA 30329-2305
Phone: 404-636-8400
Fax: 404-321-5478
Web: www.ashrae.org/students/page/1271

ASHRAE General Scholarships

Type of award: Scholarship.
Intended use: For full-time undergraduate study at accredited 4-year institution in or outside United States. Designated institutions: Schools with ABET-accredited programs.
Basis for selection: Major/career interest in engineering or air conditioning/heating/refrigeration technology. Applicant must demonstrate financial need, high academic achievement, depth of character and leadership.
Application requirements: Recommendations, transcript.
Additional information: For engineering students considering service to heating/ventilation/air-conditioning (HVAC) and/or refrigeration profession. Minimum 3.0 GPA.

Amount of award:	$5,000
Number of awards:	2
Application deadline:	December 1

Contact:
ASHRAE, Inc. - Scholarship Administrator
1791 Tullie Circle, NE
Atlanta, GA 30329-2305
Phone: 404-636-8400
Fax: 404-321-5478
Web: www.ashrae.org/students/page/1271

ASHRAE Memorial Scholarship

Type of award: Scholarship.
Intended use: For full-time undergraduate study at accredited 4-year institution in or outside United States. Designated institutions: Schools with ABET-accredited programs.
Basis for selection: Major/career interest in engineering or air conditioning/heating/refrigeration technology. Applicant must demonstrate financial need, high academic achievement, depth of character and leadership.
Application requirements: Recommendations, transcript.
Additional information: For engineering students considering service to heating/ventilation/air-conditioning (HVAC) and/or refrigeration profession. Minimum 3.0 GPA.

    Amount of award: $5,000
    Number of awards: 1
    Application deadline: December 1
Contact:
ASHRAE, Inc. - Scholarship Administrator
1791 Tullie Circle, NE
Atlanta, GA 30329-2305
Phone: 404-636-8400
Fax: 404-321-5478
Web: www.ashrae.org/students/page/1271

ASHRAE Region IV Benny Bootle Scholarship

Type of award: Scholarship.
Intended use: For full-time undergraduate study at accredited 4-year institution. Designated institutions: Schools with NAAB or ABET-accredited program located within the geographic boundaries of ASHRAE's Region IV (North Carolina, South Carolina, Georgia).
Eligibility: Applicant must be residing in North Carolina, Georgia or South Carolina.
Basis for selection: Major/career interest in air conditioning/heating/refrigeration technology; architecture or engineering. Applicant must demonstrate financial need, high academic achievement, depth of character and leadership.
Application requirements: Recommendations, transcript.
Additional information: Minimum 3.0 GPA. For engineering or architecture students considering service to heating/ventilation/air-conditioning (HVAC) and/or refrigeration profession. Visit www.abet.org and www.naab.org for list of ABET- and NAAB-accredited programs within Region IV.

    Amount of award: $3,000
    Number of awards: 1
    Application deadline: December 1
Contact:
ASHRAE, Inc. - Scholarship Administrator
1791 Tullie Circle, NE
Atlanta, GA 30329-2305
Phone: 404-636-8400
Fax: 404-321-5478
Web: www.ashrae.org/students/page/1271

ASHRAE Region VIII Scholarship

Type of award: Scholarship.
Intended use: For full-time undergraduate study in or outside United States. Designated institutions: Schools with ABET-accredited programs located within the geographic boundaries of ASHRAE's Region VIII (Arkansas, Oklahoma, Mexico, and parts of Louisiana and Texas).
Eligibility: Applicant must be residing in Oklahoma, Texas, Arkansas or Louisiana.
Basis for selection: Major/career interest in engineering or air conditioning/heating/refrigeration technology. Applicant must demonstrate financial need, high academic achievement, depth of character and leadership.
Application requirements: Recommendations, transcript.
Additional information: Minimum 3.0 GPA. For engineering students considering service to heating/ventilation/air-conditioning (HVAC) and/or refrigeration profession. Contact ASHRAE for information regarding Region VIII. Visit www.abet.org for ABET-accredited programs within the region.

    Amount of award: $3,000
    Number of awards: 1
    Application deadline: December 1
Contact:
ASHRAE, Inc. - Scholarship Administrator
1791 Tullie Circle, NE
Atlanta, GA 30329-2305
Phone: 404-636-8400
Fax: 404-321-5478
Web: www.ashrae.org/students/page/1271

Duane Hanson Scholarship

Type of award: Scholarship.
Intended use: For full-time undergraduate study at accredited 4-year institution in or outside United States. Designated institutions: Schools with ABET-accredited programs.
Basis for selection: Major/career interest in engineering or air conditioning/heating/refrigeration technology. Applicant must demonstrate financial need, high academic achievement, depth of character and leadership.
Application requirements: Recommendations, transcript.
Additional information: For engineering students considering service to heating/ventilation/air-conditioning (HVAC) and/or refrigeration profession. Minimum 3.0 GPA.

    Amount of award: $3,000
    Number of awards: 1
    Application deadline: December 1
Contact:
ASHRAE, Inc. - Scholarship Administrator
1791 Tullie Circle, NE
Atlanta, GA 30329-2305
Phone: 404-636-8400
Fax: 404-321-5478
Web: www.ashrae.org/students/page/1271

Frank M. Coda Scholarship

Type of award: Scholarship.
Intended use: For full-time undergraduate study at accredited 4-year institution in or outside United States. Designated institutions: Schools with ABET-accredited programs.
Basis for selection: Major/career interest in engineering or air conditioning/heating/refrigeration technology. Applicant must demonstrate financial need, high academic achievement, depth of character and leadership.
Application requirements: Recommendations, transcript.

Scholarships

Additional information: For engineering students considering service to heating/ventilation/air-conditioning (HVAC) and/or refrigeration profession. Minimum 3.0 GPA.

Amount of award:	$5,000
Number of awards:	1
Application deadline:	December 1

Contact:
ASHRAE, Inc. - Scholarship Administrator
1791 Tullie Circle, NE
Atlanta, GA 30329-2305
Phone: 404-636-8400
Fax: 404-321-5478
Web: www.ashrae.org/students/page/1271

Henry Adams Scholarship

Type of award: Scholarship.
Intended use: For full-time undergraduate study at accredited 4-year institution in or outside United States. Designated institutions: Schools with ABET-accredited programs.
Basis for selection: Major/career interest in engineering or air conditioning/heating/refrigeration technology. Applicant must demonstrate financial need, high academic achievement, depth of character and leadership.
Application requirements: Recommendations, transcript.
Additional information: For engineering students considering service to heating/ventilation/air-conditioning (HVAC) and/or refrigeration profession. Minimum 3.0 GPA.

Amount of award:	$3,000
Number of awards:	1
Application deadline:	December 1

Contact:
ASHRAE, Inc. - Scholarship Administrator
1791 Tullie Circle, NE
Atlanta, GA 30329-2305
Phone: 404-636-8400
Fax: 404-321-5478
Web: www.ashrae.org/students/page/1271

J. Richard Mehalick Scholarship

Type of award: Scholarship.
Intended use: For full-time undergraduate study at accredited 4-year institution in United States. Designated institutions: University of Pittsburgh.
Basis for selection: Major/career interest in engineering, mechanical or air conditioning/heating/refrigeration technology. Applicant must demonstrate financial need, high academic achievement, depth of character and leadership.
Application requirements: Recommendations, transcript.
Additional information: Must have minimum 3.0 GPA. For mechanical engineering students considering service to heating/ventilation/air-conditioning (HVAC) and/or refrigeration profession.

Amount of award:	$3,000
Number of awards:	1
Application deadline:	December 1

Contact:
ASHRAE, Inc. - Scholarship Administrator
1791 Tullie Circle, NE
Atlanta, GA 30329
Phone: 404-636-8400
Fax: 404-321-5478
Web: www.ashrae.org/students/page/1271

Lynn G. Bellenger Scholarship

Type of award: Scholarship.
Intended use: For full-time undergraduate study at accredited 4-year institution.
Eligibility: Applicant must be female.
Basis for selection: Major/career interest in engineering or air conditioning/heating/refrigeration technology. Applicant must demonstrate financial need, high academic achievement, depth of character and leadership.
Application requirements: Recommendations, transcript.
Additional information: Must have minimum 3.0 GPA and/or a class ranking of no less than 30%. For mechanical engineering students considering service to heating/ventilation/air-conditioning (HVAC) and/or refrigeration profession.

Amount of award:	$5,000
Application deadline:	December 1

Contact:
ASHRAE, Inc. - Scholarship Administrator
1791 Tullie Circle, NE
Atlanta, GA 30329
Phone: 404-636-8400
Fax: 404-321-5478
Web: www.ashrae.org/students/page/1271

Reuben Trane Scholarship

Type of award: Scholarship.
Intended use: For full-time undergraduate study at accredited 4-year institution in or outside United States. Designated institutions: Schools with ABET-accredited programs.
Basis for selection: Major/career interest in air conditioning/heating/refrigeration technology or engineering. Applicant must demonstrate financial need, high academic achievement, depth of character and leadership.
Application requirements: Recommendations, transcript.
Additional information: Minimum 3.0 GPA. Award is for two years; $5,000 given at beginning of each year. Must be considering service to heating/ventilation/air-conditioning (HVAC) and/or refrigeration profession.

Amount of award:	$10,000
Number of awards:	4
Application deadline:	December 1

Contact:
ASHRAE, Inc. - Scholarship Administrator
1791 Tullie Circle, NE
Atlanta, GA 30329-2305
Phone: 404-636-8400
Fax: 404-321-5478
Web: www.ashrae.org/students/page/1271

Willis H. Carrier Scholarship

Type of award: Scholarship.
Intended use: For full-time undergraduate study at accredited 4-year institution in or outside United States. Designated institutions: ABET-accredited institutions.
Basis for selection: Major/career interest in engineering or air conditioning/heating/refrigeration technology. Applicant must demonstrate financial need, high academic achievement, depth of character and leadership.
Application requirements: Recommendations, transcript.
Additional information: For engineering students considering service to heating/ventilation/air-conditioning (HVAC) and/or refrigeration profession. Minimum 3.0 GPA.

Amount of award:	$10,000
Number of awards:	2
Application deadline:	December 1

Contact:
ASHRAE, Inc. - Scholarship Administrator
1791 Tullie Circle, NE
Atlanta, GA 30329-2305
Phone: 404-636-8400
Fax: 404-321-5478
Web: www.ashrae.org/students/page/1271

American Society of Interior Designers Foundation, Inc.

American Society of Interior Designers Legacy Scholarship for Undergraduates

Type of award: Scholarship.
Intended use: For junior or senior study at 4-year institution.
Basis for selection: Major/career interest in interior design.
Application requirements: Recommendations, essay, transcript. Portfolio, portfolio description (max. 250 words), list of portfolio components, personal statement with career goals, biographical statement (max. 100 words) and headshot.
Additional information: Deadline in April; visit Website for exact date and additional information.

Amount of award:	$4,000
Number of awards:	1

Contact:
American Society of Interior Designers Foundation, Inc.
Legacy Scholarship for Undergraduates
608 Massachusetts Avenue, NE
Washington, DC 20002-6006
Phone: 202-546-3480
Fax: 202-546-3240
Web: www.asidfoundation.org/SCHOLARSHIPS_and_AWARDS.html

David Barrett Memorial Scholarship

Type of award: Scholarship.
Intended use: For undergraduate or graduate study at 4-year or graduate institution.
Basis for selection: Major/career interest in interior design.
Application requirements: Portfolio, recommendations, essay. Design portfolio containing 8-12 design components with a written description detailing how classical designs and traditional materials are used in each design component.
Additional information: Visit Website for deadline and additional details.

Amount of award:	$12,000
Number of awards:	1
Application deadline:	December 1

Contact:
American Society of Interior Designers Foundation, Inc.
David Barret Memorial Scholarship
1152 15th Street NW, Suite 910
Washington, DC 20005
Phone: 202-546-3480
Fax: 202-675-2345
Web: www.asidfoundation.org/SCHOLARSHIPS_and_AWARDS.html

Irene Winifred Eno Grant

Type of award: Research grant.
Intended use: For undergraduate or graduate study at 4-year or graduate institution.
Basis for selection: Major/career interest in interior design.
Application requirements: Abstract (max. 250 words), explanation of how you intend to use funds (max. 500 words), promotion plan (max. 1000 words), biographical statement and headshot.
Additional information: Awarded to individuals or groups engaged in the creation of an education program(s) or an interior design research project dedicated to health, safety, and welfare. Open to students, educators, interior design practitioners, institutions or other interior-design related groups. Deadline in April; visit Website for exact date and additional information.

Amount of award:	$5,000

Contact:
American Society of Interior Designers Foundation, Inc.
Irene Winifred Eno Grant
608 Massachusetts Avenue, NE
Washington, DC 20002-6006
Phone: 202-546-3480
Fax: 202-546-3240
Web: www.asidfoundation.org/SCHOLARSHIPS_and_AWARDS.html

Joel Polsky Academic Achievement Award

Type of award: Scholarship.
Intended use: For undergraduate or graduate study at postsecondary institution.
Basis for selection: Competition/talent/interest in research paper, based on content, breadth of material, comprehensive coverage of topic, innovative subject matter, bibliography, and references. Major/career interest in interior design.
Application requirements: Photo. Abstract (max. 250 words). Biographical statement. Thesis, dissertation, or research project.
Additional information: Award to recognize outstanding interior design research or thesis project addressing topics such as educational research, behavioral science, business practice, design process, theory, or other technical subjects. Deadline in April; visit Website for exact date.

Amount of award:	$5,000
Number of awards:	1

Contact:
American Society of Interior Designers Foundation, Inc.
Joel Polsky Academic Achievement Award
608 Massachusetts Avenue, NE
Washington, DC 20002-6006
Phone: 202-546-3480
Fax: 202-546-3240
Web: www.asidfoundation.org/SCHOLARSHIPS_and_AWARDS.html

Joel Polsky Prize

Type of award: Scholarship.
Intended use: For undergraduate or graduate study at 4-year or graduate institution.
Basis for selection: Major/career interest in interior design.
Application requirements: Copy of publication or visual communication, description of publication or visual communication (max. 250 words), biographical statement and headshot.

Additional information: Different from the Joel Polsky Academic Achievement Award. Entries should address the needs of the public, designers and students on such topics as educational research, behavioral science, business practice, design process, theory or other technical subjects. Deadline in April; visit Website for exact date and additional information.

Amount of award:	$5,000

Contact:
American Society of Interior Designers Foundation, Inc.
Joel Polsky Prize
608 Massachusetts Avenue, NE
Washington, DC 20002-6006
Phone: 202-546-3480
Fax: 202-546-3240
Web: www.asidfoundation.org/SCHOLARSHIPS_and_
AWARDS.html

American Society of Mechanical Engineers

ASME Society of Hispanic Professional Engineer Scholarships

Type of award: Scholarship.
Intended use: For full-time sophomore, junior, senior or graduate study at accredited 2-year, 4-year or graduate institution in United States.
Eligibility: Membership in Hispanic engineering society. Applicant must be U.S. citizen, permanent resident or F1 Visa residency status.
Basis for selection: The award recipient will be selected on the basis of leadership, scholastic ability, potential contribution to the mechanical engineering profession, and financial need. Volunteer work through at least two societies is highly desirable. Major/career interest in engineering, mechanical. Applicant must demonstrate financial need, high academic achievement and leadership.
Application requirements: Recommendations, essay. Must be a member of both ASME (American Society of Mechanical Engineers) and SHPE (Society of Hispanic Professional Engineers). One to two letters of recommendation.
Additional information: One scholarship for Grad student and one scholarship for undergraduate for study in their sophomore, junior, or senior year of study. Scholarship applies to ABET institutions.

Amount of award:	$5,000
Number of awards:	2
Number of applicants:	2,000
Application deadline:	March 1
Notification begins:	July 1
Total amount awarded:	$10,000

Contact:
American Society of Mechanical Engineers
2 Park Avenue
Fl. 7
New York, NY 10016
Phone: 800-843-2763
Web: www.asme.org/about-asme/scholarship-and-loans/about-asme-scholarships

American Society of Naval Engineers

ASNE Scholarship

Type of award: Scholarship.
Intended use: For full-time senior or graduate study at accredited 4-year or graduate institution.
Eligibility: Applicant must be U.S. citizen.
Basis for selection: Major/career interest in engineering; engineering, civil; engineering, electrical/electronic; engineering, environmental; engineering, marine; engineering, mechanical; engineering, nuclear; engineering, structural or physical sciences. Applicant must demonstrate high academic achievement and seriousness of purpose.
Application requirements: Recommendations, essay, transcript.
Additional information: Graduate applicants must be members of American Society of Naval Engineers. Applicants' major/career interests may also include naval architecture, applied mathematics, aeronautical and ocean engineering, or other programs leading to careers with relevant military and civilian organizations. Financial need may be considered. Award also includes one-year honorary student membership to Society. Deadline varies.

Amount of award:	$3,000-$4,000
Number of awards:	25
Number of applicants:	55
Notification begins:	May 1
Total amount awarded:	$66,000

Contact:
American Society of Naval Engineers (ASNE)
CC: Jared Pierce
1452 Duke Street
Alexandria, VA 22314-3458
Phone: 703-836-6727
Fax: 703-836-7491
Web: www.navalengineers.org/scholarships

American Water Ski Educational Foundation

American Water Ski Educational Foundation Scholarship

Type of award: Scholarship, renewable.
Intended use: For full-time sophomore, junior or senior study at 2-year or 4-year institution.
Eligibility: Applicant must be U.S. citizen.
Basis for selection: Applicant must demonstrate financial need, high academic achievement, depth of character, leadership and seriousness of purpose.
Application requirements: Recommendations, essay, transcript. College freshmen should include both college and high school transcripts. Visit Website for current essay topic.
Additional information: Must be member of USA Water Ski Association.

Amount of award:	$1,500-$3,000
Number of awards:	8
Number of applicants:	25
Application deadline:	March 1
Notification begins:	July 1
Total amount awarded:	$13,500

Contact:
American Water Ski Educational Foundation
1251 Holy Cow Road
Polk City, FL 33868-8200
Phone: 863-324-2472
Fax: 863-324-3996
Web: www.waterskihalloffame.com

American Welding Society Foundation, Inc.

Airgas-Jerry Baker Scholarship

Type of award: Scholarship, renewable.
Intended use: For full-time undergraduate study at postsecondary institution.
Eligibility: Applicant must be at least 18. Applicant must be U.S. citizen or Canadian citizen.
Basis for selection: Major/career interest in welding. Applicant must demonstrate high academic achievement.
Application requirements: Essay.
Additional information: Applicants must have minimum 2.8 overall GPA with 3.0 GPA in engineering courses. Priority given to individuals residing or attending school in Alabama, Georgia, or Florida. Applicant must show interest in welding engineering or welding engineering technology.

Amount of award:	$2,500
Number of awards:	1
Number of applicants:	8
Application deadline:	February 15
Notification begins:	April 1
Total amount awarded:	$2,500

Contact:
AWS Foundation, Inc.
Attn: Scholarships
8669 Doral Boulevard, Suite 130
Miami, FL 33166
Phone: 800-443-9353
Web: scholarship.aws.org

Airgas-Terry Jarvis Memorial Scholarship

Type of award: Scholarship.
Intended use: For full-time sophomore, junior or senior study at 4-year institution in United States or Canada.
Eligibility: Applicant must be at least 18. Applicant must be U.S. citizen or Canadian citizen.
Basis for selection: Major/career interest in welding. Applicant must demonstrate high academic achievement.
Application requirements: Recommendations, essay, transcript, proof of eligibility.
Additional information: Must have interest in pursuing a minimum four-year degree in welding engineering or welding engineering technology. Minimum 2.8 GPA overall, with 3.0 GPA in engineering courses. Priority given to residents of Florida, Alabama, and Georgia. Applicant does not have to be a member of the American Welding Society.

Amount of award:	$2,500
Number of awards:	1
Number of applicants:	8
Application deadline:	February 15
Notification begins:	April 1
Total amount awarded:	$2,500

Contact:
AWS Foundation, Inc.
Attn: Scholarships
8669 Doral Boulevard, Suite 130
Miami, FL 33166
Phone: 800-443-9353
Web: scholarship.aws.org

American Welding Society District Scholarship Program

Type of award: Scholarship.
Intended use: For undergraduate study at accredited vocational, 2-year or 4-year institution in United States.
Eligibility: Applicant must be U.S. citizen.
Basis for selection: Major/career interest in welding. Applicant must demonstrate financial need, high academic achievement, depth of character, leadership and seriousness of purpose.
Application requirements: Recommendations, transcript, proof of eligibility. Personal statement, biography, and photo.

Amount of award:	$200-$3,500
Number of awards:	189
Number of applicants:	436
Application deadline:	March 1
Notification begins:	July 1
Total amount awarded:	$165,000

Contact:
AWS Foundation, Inc.
Attn: Scholarships
8669 Doral Boulevard, Suite 130
Miami, FL 33166
Phone: 800-443-9353
Web: scholarship.aws.org

Arsham Amirikian Engineering Scholarship

Type of award: Scholarship, renewable.
Intended use: For undergraduate study at accredited 4-year institution.
Eligibility: Applicant must be at least 18. Applicant must be U.S. citizen.
Basis for selection: Major/career interest in welding. Applicant must demonstrate financial need and high academic achievement.
Additional information: Minimum 3.0 GPA. Must show interest in pursuing career in the application of the art of welding in civil and structural engineering.

Amount of award:	$2,500
Number of awards:	1
Number of applicants:	21
Application deadline:	February 15
Notification begins:	April 1
Total amount awarded:	$2,500

Contact:
AWS Foundation, Inc.
Attn: Scholarships
8669 Doral Boulevard, Suite 130
Miami, FL 33166
Phone: 800-443-9353
Web: scholarship.aws.org

Scholarships

195

D. Fred and Mariam L. Bovie Scholarship

Type of award: Scholarship, renewable.
Intended use: For full-time undergraduate study at 4-year institution. Designated institutions: The Ohio State University.
Eligibility: Applicant must be U.S. citizen.
Basis for selection: Major/career interest in welding or engineering, electrical/electronic.
Application requirements: Recommendations, essay, transcript, proof of eligibility. Statement of Unmet Financial Need.
Additional information: Award may be renewed for a maximum of four years. Membership in the American Welding Society is not required. Electrical engineering candidates will be considered if there are no qualified welding engineering candidates.

Amount of award:	$3,000
Number of awards:	1
Number of applicants:	9
Application deadline:	February 15

Contact:
AWS Foundation, Inc.
Attn: Scholarships
8669 Doral Boulevard, Suite 130
Miami, FL 33166
Phone: 800-443-9353
Web: scholarship.aws.org

D. Fred and Mariam L. Bovie Technical Scholarship

Type of award: Scholarship, renewable.
Intended use: For undergraduate study at postsecondary institution.
Basis for selection: Major/career interest in welding. Applicant must demonstrate financial need and high academic achievement.
Application requirements: Recommendations, essay, transcript, proof of eligibility. Statement of Unmet Financial Need.
Additional information: Minimum 2.8 GPA. Applicant must be pursuing an associate's degree in welding, with a minimum of a two-year program. Award may be renewed for a maximum of four years. Membership in the American Welding Society is not required.

Amount of award:	$2,000
Number of awards:	1
Number of applicants:	9
Application deadline:	February 15
Total amount awarded:	$2,000

Contact:
AWS Foundation, Inc.
Attn: Scholarships
8669 Doral Boulevard, Suite 130
Miami, FL 33166
Phone: 800-443-9353
Web: scholarship.aws.org

Donald and Shirley Hastings National Scholarship

Type of award: Scholarship, renewable.
Intended use: For undergraduate study at 4-year institution in United States.
Eligibility: Applicant must be at least 18. Applicant must be U.S. citizen.
Basis for selection: Major/career interest in welding. Applicant must demonstrate financial need and high academic achievement.
Additional information: Minimum 2.5 GPA. Must show interest in welding engineering or welding engineering technology. Priority given to Iowa, Ohio, or California residents.

Amount of award:	$2,500
Number of awards:	1
Number of applicants:	21
Application deadline:	February 15
Notification begins:	April 1
Total amount awarded:	$2,500

Contact:
AWS Foundation, Inc.
Attn: Scholarships
8669 Doral Boulevard, Suite 130
Miami, FL 33166
Phone: 800-443-9353
Web: scholarship.aws.org

Donald F. Hastings Scholarship

Type of award: Scholarship, renewable.
Intended use: For sophomore, junior or senior study at 4-year institution in United States.
Eligibility: Applicant must be at least 18. Applicant must be U.S. citizen.
Basis for selection: Major/career interest in welding. Applicant must demonstrate financial need, high academic achievement and seriousness of purpose.
Application requirements: Recommendations, transcript, proof of eligibility.
Additional information: Priority given to residents of Ohio and California. Minimum 2.5 GPA.

Amount of award:	$2,500
Number of awards:	1
Number of applicants:	20
Application deadline:	February 15
Notification begins:	April 1
Total amount awarded:	$2,500

Contact:
AWS Foundation, Inc.
Attn: Scholarships
8669 Doral Boulevard, Suite 130
Miami, FL 33166
Phone: 800-443-9353
Web: scholarship.aws.org

Edward J. Brady Memorial Scholarship

Type of award: Scholarship, renewable.
Intended use: For sophomore, junior or senior study at 4-year institution.
Eligibility: Applicant must be at least 18. Applicant must be U.S. citizen or Canadian citizen.
Basis for selection: Major/career interest in welding or engineering. Applicant must demonstrate financial need, high academic achievement and seriousness of purpose.
Application requirements: Recommendations, essay, transcript, proof of eligibility. Proposed curriculum; brief biography; proof of hands-on welding experience.
Additional information: Interest in pursuing minimum four-year degree in welding engineering or welding engineering technology. Minimum 2.5 GPA.

Amount of award:	$2,500
Number of awards:	1
Number of applicants:	17
Application deadline:	February 15
Notification begins:	April 1
Total amount awarded:	$2,500

Contact:
AWS Foundation, Inc.
Attn: Scholarships
8669 Doral Boulevard, Suite 130
Miami, FL 33166
Phone: 800-443-9353
Web: scholarship.aws.org

Howard E. and Wilma J. Adkins Memorial Scholarship

Type of award: Scholarship, renewable.
Intended use: For full-time junior or senior study at 4-year institution.
Eligibility: Applicant must be at least 18. Applicant must be U.S. citizen.
Basis for selection: Major/career interest in welding. Applicant must demonstrate high academic achievement and seriousness of purpose.
Application requirements: Recommendations, transcript, proof of eligibility.
Additional information: Applicant should have interest in pursuing four-year degree in welding engineering or welding engineering technology. Priority given to residents of Kentucky and Wisconsin. Minimum 3.2 GPA in engineering, scientific, and technical subjects; minimum overall 2.8 GPA.

Amount of award:	$2,500
Number of awards:	1
Number of applicants:	16
Application deadline:	February 15
Notification begins:	April 1
Total amount awarded:	$2,500

Contact:
AWS Foundation Inc.
Attn: Scholarships
8669 Doral Boulevard, Suite 130
Miami, FL 33166
Phone: 800-443-9353
Web: scholarship.aws.org

Jack R. Barckhoff Welding Management Scholarship

Type of award: Scholarship.
Intended use: For junior study at 4-year institution.
Designated institutions: Ohio State University.
Eligibility: Applicant must be U.S. citizen.
Basis for selection: Major/career interest in welding. Applicant must demonstrate high academic achievement.
Application requirements: 300- to 500-word essay.
Additional information: Minimum 2.5 GPA.

Amount of award:	$2,500
Number of awards:	2
Number of applicants:	5
Application deadline:	February 15
Notification begins:	April 1
Total amount awarded:	$5,000

Contact:
AWS Foundation, Inc.
Attn: Scholarships
8669 Doral Boulevard, Suite 130
Miami, FL 33166
Phone: 800-443-9353
Web: scholarship.aws.org

James A. Turner, Jr. Memorial Scholarship

Type of award: Scholarship, renewable.
Intended use: For full-time sophomore, junior or senior study at accredited 4-year institution.
Eligibility: Applicant must be at least 18. Applicant must be U.S. citizen.
Basis for selection: Major/career interest in welding or business/management/administration. Applicant must demonstrate financial need and seriousness of purpose.
Application requirements: Recommendations, transcript, proof of eligibility. Verification of employment, brief biography, financial aid report, proposed curriculum.
Additional information: Must have interest in pursuing management career in welding. Must work minimum ten hours per week at welding store.

Amount of award:	$3,500
Number of awards:	1
Number of applicants:	1
Application deadline:	February 15
Notification begins:	April 1
Total amount awarded:	$3,500

Contact:
AWS Foundation, Inc.
Attn: Scholarships
8669 Doral Boulevard, Suite 130
Miami, FL 33166
Phone: 800-443-9353
Web: scholarship.aws.org

John C. Lincoln Memorial Scholarship

Type of award: Scholarship, renewable.
Intended use: For sophomore, junior or senior study at 4-year institution.
Eligibility: Applicant must be at least 18. Applicant must be U.S. citizen.
Basis for selection: Major/career interest in welding. Applicant must demonstrate financial need, high academic achievement and seriousness of purpose.
Application requirements: Recommendations, transcript, proof of eligibility.
Additional information: Minimum 2.5 GPA. Priority will be given to those individuals residing or attending school in Ohio or Arizona.

Amount of award:	$3,500
Number of awards:	1
Number of applicants:	22
Application deadline:	February 15
Notification begins:	April 1
Total amount awarded:	$3,500

Contact:
AWS Foundation, Inc.
Attn: Scholarships
8669 Doral Boulevard, Suite 130
Miami, FL 33166
Phone: 800-443-9353
Web: scholarship.aws.org

Matsuo Bridge Company Ltd. of Japan Scholarship

Type of award: Scholarship.
Intended use: For junior, senior or graduate study at accredited 4-year or graduate institution in United States.
Eligibility: Applicant must be at least 18.
Basis for selection: Major/career interest in welding or engineering, civil. Applicant must demonstrate high academic achievement.
Application requirements: Recommendations, transcript, proof of eligibility.
Additional information: For students interested in pursuing career in civil engineering, welding engineering, or welding engineering technology. Priority given to applicants residing in California, Texas, Oregon, or Washington. Applicant does not have to be member of American Welding Society but must agree to participate in AWS Foundation or Matsuo Bridge Company sponsored publicity. Minimum 3.0 GPA.

Amount of award:	$2,500
Number of awards:	1
Number of applicants:	21
Application deadline:	February 15
Notification begins:	April 1
Total amount awarded:	$2,500

Contact:
AWS Foundation, Inc.
Attn: Scholarships
8669 Doral Boulevard, Suite 130
Miami, FL 33166
Phone: 800-443-9353
Web: scholarship.aws.org

Miller Electric Manufacturing Company Ivic Scholarship

Type of award: Scholarship, renewable.
Intended use: For undergraduate study at accredited vocational, 2-year or 4-year institution in United States.
Eligibility: Applicant must be U.S. citizen.
Basis for selection: Major/career interest in welding. Applicant must demonstrate depth of character, leadership and seriousness of purpose.
Additional information: Competition based on AWS National Welding Trials and World Skills Competition.

Amount of award:	$10,000
Number of awards:	1

Contact:
AWS Foundation, Inc.
Attn: Scholarships
8669 Doral Boulevard, Suite 130
Miami, FL 33166
Phone: 800-443-9353
Web: scholarship.aws.org

Miller Electric Mfg. Co. Scholarship

Type of award: Scholarship, renewable.
Intended use: For senior study at 4-year institution.

Eligibility: Applicant must be at least 18. Applicant must be U.S. citizen.
Basis for selection: Major/career interest in welding. Applicant must demonstrate high academic achievement.
Additional information: Applicant must show interest in welding engineering or welding engineering technology, and have work experience in the welding equipment field. Applicant must have minimum 3.0 GPA.

Amount of award:	$3,000
Number of awards:	2
Number of applicants:	20
Application deadline:	February 15
Notification begins:	April 1
Total amount awarded:	$6,000

Contact:
AWS Foundation, Inc.
Attn: Scholarships
8669 Doral Boulevard, Suite 130
Miami, FL 33166
Phone: 800-443-9353
Web: scholarship.aws.org

Past Presidents Scholarship

Type of award: Scholarship.
Intended use: For junior, senior, master's or doctoral study at 4-year or graduate institution.
Basis for selection: Major/career interest in welding or engineering. Applicant must demonstrate financial need.
Application requirements: Essay should be 300-500 words.

Amount of award:	$2,500
Number of awards:	1
Number of applicants:	8
Application deadline:	February 15
Notification begins:	April 1
Total amount awarded:	$2,500

Contact:
AWS Foundation, Inc.
Attn: Scholarships
8669 Doral Boulevard, Suite 130
Miami, FL 33166
Phone: 800-443-9353
Web: scholarship.aws.org

Praxair International Scholarship

Type of award: Scholarship, renewable.
Intended use: For full-time sophomore, junior or senior study at 4-year institution.
Eligibility: Applicant must be at least 18. Applicant must be U.S. citizen or Canadian citizen.
Basis for selection: Major/career interest in welding. Applicant must demonstrate financial need, high academic achievement, leadership and service orientation.
Application requirements: Recommendations, transcript, proof of eligibility.
Additional information: Applicant must have interest in pursuing minimum four-year degree in welding engineering or welding engineering technology. Minimum 2.5 GPA.

Amount of award:	$2,500
Number of awards:	1
Number of applicants:	22
Application deadline:	February 15
Notification begins:	April 1
Total amount awarded:	$2,500

Scholarships

Contact:
AWS Foundation, Inc.
Attn: Praxair Scholarship
8669 Doral Boulevard, Suite 130
Miami, FL 33166
Phone: 800-443-9353
Web: scholarship.aws.org

Robert L. Peaslee Brazing Scholarship

Type of award: Scholarship, renewable.
Intended use: For junior or senior study at 4-year institution.
Eligibility: Applicant must be at least 18. Applicant must be U.S. citizen.
Basis for selection: Major/career interest in welding. Applicant must demonstrate high academic achievement.
Application requirements: Recommendations, essay, transcript.
Additional information: Applicant must have 3.0 GPA in engineering courses. Must show interest in pursuing degree in welding engineering or welding technology with emphasis on brazing applications.

Amount of award:	$2,500
Number of awards:	1
Number of applicants:	6
Application deadline:	February 15
Notification begins:	April 1
Total amount awarded:	$2,500

Contact:
AWS Foundation, Inc.
Attn: Scholarships
8669 Doral Boulevard, Suite 130
Miami, FL 33166
Phone: 800-443-9353
Web: scholarship.aws.org

RWMA Scholarship

Type of award: Scholarship.
Intended use: For full-time junior study at 4-year institution.
Eligibility: Applicant must be U.S. citizen or Canadian citizens.
Basis for selection: Major/career interest in welding or engineering. Applicant must demonstrate high academic achievement.
Application requirements: 500-word or less essay.
Additional information: Minimum 3.0 GPA.

Amount of award:	$2,500
Number of awards:	1
Number of applicants:	3
Application deadline:	February 15
Notification begins:	April 1

Contact:
AWS Foundation, Inc.
Attn: Scholarships
8669 Doral Boulevard, Suite 130
Miami, FL 33166
Phone: 800-443-9353
Web: scholarship.aws.org

William A. and Ann M. Brothers Scholarship

Type of award: Scholarship, renewable.
Intended use: For full-time undergraduate study at accredited 4-year institution.

Eligibility: Applicant must be at least 18. Applicant must be U.S. citizen.
Basis for selection: Major/career interest in welding. Applicant must demonstrate financial need and high academic achievement.
Additional information: Applicant must have minimum 2.5 GPA. Priority will be given to those individuals residing or attending schools in Ohio.

Amount of award:	$6,000
Number of awards:	1
Number of applicants:	23
Application deadline:	February 15
Notification begins:	April 1

Contact:
AWS Foundation, Inc.
Attn: Scholarships
8669 Doral Boulevard, Suite 130
Miami, FL 33166
Phone: 800-443-9353
Web: scholarship.aws.org

William B. Howell Memorial Scholarship

Type of award: Scholarship, renewable.
Intended use: For full-time undergraduate study at accredited 4-year institution in United States.
Eligibility: Applicant must be at least 18. Applicant must be U.S. citizen.
Basis for selection: Major/career interest in welding. Applicant must demonstrate financial need and high academic achievement.
Application requirements: Recommendations, transcript, proof of eligibility.
Additional information: Minimum 2.5 GPA required. Priority given to residents of Florida, Michigan, and Ohio. Applicant does not have to be a member of the American Welding Society.

Amount of award:	$2,500
Number of awards:	1
Number of applicants:	26
Application deadline:	February 15
Notification begins:	April 1
Total amount awarded:	$2,500

Contact:
AWS Foundation, Inc.
Attn: Scholarships
8669 Doral Boulevard, Suite 130
Miami, FL 33166
Phone: 800-443-9353
Web: scholarship.aws.org

Americans United for Separation of Church and State

Americans United for Separation of Church and State Essay Contest

Type of award: Scholarship.
Intended use: For full-time undergraduate or graduate study at 2-year, 4-year or graduate institution.

Eligibility: Applicant must be high school junior or senior. Applicant must be U.S. citizen.

Application requirements: Essay. Employees and board members of Americans United for Separation of Church and State, and members of their families, are not eligibles to apply. Students should write 750-1200 words about a potential violation involving one of the following:. The teaching of religiously-based curricula in public schools, which includes inaccurate versions of history based on religious teachings, creationism and climate change denial, and abstinence-only sex education. Mandating students who attend public school to attend assemblies with religious content or to pray. Discriminating against students based on the religion they practice or their choice not to practice. Using religion as an excuse to discriminate against LGBTQ students. After choosing one type of violation to write about, students should explain why this violation encroaches upon the constitutional principle of church-state separation, and tell us how they would solve this problem if it occurred (or has already occurred) in their school; They can reference current events, U.S. history, personal experiences,AU.org, protectthyneighbor.org, or primary sources in their response.

Additional information: For more information about the essay contest go to the website listed.

Amount of award:	$500-$1,500
Number of awards:	3
Number of applicants:	150
Application deadline:	April 15
Total amount awarded:	$3,000

Contact:
Americans United for Separation of Church and State
1310 L Street NW
Suite 200
Washington, DC 20005
Phone: 202-466-3234
Web: www.austudents.org/essaycontest

Amrponix

Ampronix Scholarship Program

Type of award: Scholarship.

Intended use: For full-time undergraduate study at vocational, 2-year, 4-year or graduate institution in United States.

Eligibility: Applicant must be at least 18. Applicant must be U.S. citizen or permanent resident.

Application requirements: Must have performed at least 20 hours of community service in the last year. Submit a photo of something or someone that has inspired you to continue your education and plan your future career.

Additional information: Full details and application found online.

Amount of award:	$500-$1,000
Number of awards:	3
Application deadline:	May 31
Total amount awarded:	$2,250

Contact:
Web: www.ampronix.com/ampronix-college-scholarship

Anchell Workshops

Anchell International Documentary Photography Scholarship

Type of award: Scholarship.

Intended use: For undergraduate or graduate study at accredited vocational, 2-year or 4-year institution.

Application requirements: Essay. Photocopy of a current student ID card. 350 words about your documentary photo project including who, what, where, when, and why must be included.

Additional information: 12 to 20 scanned photos, film or digital, saved 4 to an 8 1/2 x11 in PDF, DOC, DOCX, or JPEG format. The medium of capture is not important. Subject matter should clearly document a person, group of people, place, event, or happening of social relevance. Submitted images should be arranged and presented so they clearly tell the story of what is being documented.

Number of awards:	1
Application deadline:	January 1
Notification begins:	March 1
Total amount awarded:	$1,000

Contact:
Web: http://anchellworkshops.com/scholarship/

Angie DiPietro Attorney At Law

Angie Dipietro Women in Business Scholarship

Type of award: Scholarship.

Intended use: For undergraduate or graduate study at accredited postsecondary institution in United States.

Eligibility: Applicant must be female, high school senior.

Basis for selection: Applicant must demonstrate high academic achievement.

Application requirements: Recommendations, essay, transcript. Unofficial transcript, one letter of recommendation, application cover sheet, application essay, updated resume. Essay topic (500 words): "If you could see one change in gender inequality in your lifetime, what would it be, and why? How do you think this can be achieved?"

Additional information: Minimum 3.0 GPA required. Candidates must possess an interest in business or entrepreneurship, as demonstrated by past and present volunteer, professional, and educational experiences.

Amount of award:	$500
Number of awards:	1
Application deadline:	May 1
Total amount awarded:	$500

Contact:
Angela DiPietro Women in Business Scholarship
110 Baptist Street
Salisbury, MD 21801
Phone: 202-517-0502
Fax: 410-749-5917
Web: marylandcriminallaws.com/scholarship.html

Angie Houtz Memorial Fund

Angie Houtz Scholarship

Type of award: Scholarship.
Intended use: For full-time undergraduate study at 2-year or 4-year institution in United States. Designated institutions: Maryland public institutions.
Eligibility: Applicant must be U.S. citizen, permanent resident or international student.
Basis for selection: Applicant must demonstrate high academic achievement and service orientation.
Application requirements: Recommendations, essay, transcript. List of extracurricular activities, detailed community service information.
Additional information: Minimum 3.0 GPA. Award based on GPA, amount and nature of community service, strength of letters of recommendation, and essay quality. Must have participated in at least 200 hours of community service in the last five years. Must not be related to any member of the Board of Directors. Award amount may vary. Applicant does not have to be a Maryland resident; international students encouraged to apply.

Amount of award:	$3,000
Number of awards:	3
Application deadline:	April 30

Contact:
Angie Houtz Memorial Fund
414 Bottsford Ave
Upper Marlboro, MD 20774
Phone: 240-770-6688
Web: www.theangiefund.com/Scholarship.html

Ankin Law

Undergraduate Need-Based Scholarship

Type of award: Scholarship.
Intended use: For full-time undergraduate study at accredited 2-year or 4-year institution in United States.
Eligibility: Applicant must be high school senior.
Application requirements: Submit a 500-1000 word essay on what you believe is the biggest threat to social justice or public safety and what can be done to limit that threat. The essay should express what you believe is the biggest threat to social safety in the United States.
Additional information: Submit online.

Number of awards:	1
Application deadline:	June 1
Total amount awarded:	$1,500

Contact:
Web: http://ankinlaw.com/aaaa_scholarship/

Ankin Law Office

The Ankin Law Offices College Scholarship

Type of award: Scholarship.
Intended use: For full-time undergraduate study at accredited 2-year or 4-year institution in United States.
Eligibility: Applicant must be U.S. citizen or permanent resident.
Basis for selection: Major/career interest in law. Applicant must demonstrate financial need.
Application requirements: Essay. The applicant must complete an online application and submit an essay addressing the topic: "What effect will driverless, car technology have on personal injury automobile cases?"

Amount of award:	$5,000
Number of awards:	1
Number of applicants:	475
Application deadline:	June 1
Notification begins:	September 1
Total amount awarded:	$5,000

Contact:
Ankin Law Office
620B Academy Drive
Northbrook, IL 60062
Phone: 847-940-4000
Web: http://ankinlaw.com/aaaa_scholarship/

Annie's Homegrown

Annie's Homegrown Sustainable Agriculture Scholarships

Type of award: Scholarship.
Intended use: For full-time undergraduate or graduate study at accredited 2-year, 4-year or graduate institution in United States.
Basis for selection: Major/career interest in agriculture. Applicant must demonstrate high academic achievement.
Application requirements: Recommendations, essay, transcript.
Additional information: Award amount varies. Application and deadline available on Website.

Amount of award:	$2,500-$10,000
Number of awards:	16
Total amount awarded:	$100,000

Contact:
Annie's Homegrown Scholarship
Web: www.annies.com/giving-back/agricultural-scholarships

Annovnce

The Annovnce $500 Scholarship

Type of award: Scholarship, renewable.
Intended use: For undergraduate or graduate study at accredited vocational, 2-year, 4-year or graduate institution.
Eligibility: Applicant must be high school senior.

Application requirements: A quarterly winner will be chosen every quarter. The quarterly winner will be determined by a random drawing, and then contacted directly and announced on social media outlets and email newsletter.

Additional information: Fill out online form up to once per day for chance to win $500. Scholarship is open to all current students and those planning on enrolling in the next 12 months. One winner every quarter. Quarterly winner will be determined by random drawing. One entry per person, but applicants can come back and enter daily.

Amount of award:	$500
Number of awards:	1
Application deadline:	March 31
Notification begins:	April 1
Total amount awarded:	$500

Contact:
Annovnce
P.O. Box 31693
Tucson, AZ 85751
Phone: 520-433-8422
Web: www.Annovnce.com/scholarship

Anthony Mu|fnoz Foundation

Anthony Mu|fnoz Scholarship Fund

Type of award: Scholarship, renewable.

Intended use: For full-time. Designated institutions: Ohio: Art Academy of Cincinnati, Cedarville University, Central State University, Cincinnati Christian University, Cincinnati State, Clark State Community College, College of Mount St Joseph, Miami University, Sinclair Community College, University of Cincinnati, University of Dayton, Wilmington College, Wittenburg University, Wright State University, Xavier University. Kentucky: Georgetown College, Northern Kentucky University, Thomas More College. Indiana: Earlham College, Purdue University College of Technology-Richmond.

Eligibility: Applicant must be high school senior. Applicant must be residing in Ohio, Indiana or Kentucky.

Basis for selection: Applicant must demonstrate financial need, leadership and service orientation.

Application requirements: Essay, transcript. Must have attended High School in these counties by state:. Kentucky: Boone, Bracken, Campbell, Gallatin, Grant, Kenton. Indiana: Dearborn, Franklin, Ohio, Switzerland, Union. Ohio: Brown, Butler, Clermont, Clinton, Greene, Hamilton, Highland, Montgomery, Preble, Warren. Must be a student entering an accredited Tri-State college or university.

Additional information: Must have an ACT composite score of 18 or at least 2.5 minimum GPA. Must have an acceptance letter from your intended College or University. Must declare other financial awards being received. Only renewable if recipient maintains full-time status and cumulative GPA remains above 2.00.

Amount of award:	$20,000
Number of awards:	7
Application deadline:	May 1
Notification begins:	May 31

Contact:
Anthony Munoz Foundation
8919 Rossash Road
Cincinnati, OH 45236
Fax: 513-772-4911
Web: www.munozfoundation.org

Appaloosa Youth Association

Appaloosa Youth Association Educational Scholarships

Type of award: Scholarship, renewable.

Intended use: For full-time undergraduate or graduate study at accredited postsecondary institution in United States.

Eligibility: Applicant must be U.S. citizen or permanent resident.

Basis for selection: Applicant must demonstrate high academic achievement, leadership and service orientation.

Application requirements: Recommendations, essay, transcript, proof of eligibility. Photo. SAT/ACT scores optional.

Additional information: Applicant must be member of Appaloosa Horse Club or Appaloosa Youth Association. Must be involved in the Appaloosa industry and have general knowledge and accomplishments in horsemanship. GPA of 3.5 for one scholarship, GPA of 2.5 for other scholarships. Application available online.

Amount of award:	$1,000-$2,000
Number of awards:	9
Number of applicants:	25
Application deadline:	March 21
Notification begins:	June 1

Contact:
Appaloosa Youth Association Scholarship Committee
2720 Pullman Road
Moscow, ID 83843
Phone: 208-882-5578 ext. 245
Fax: 208-882-8150
Web: www.appaloosa.com

April Cockerham

April Cockerham DREAM Act Scholarship

Type of award: Scholarship.

Intended use: For undergraduate or graduate study at accredited vocational, 2-year, 4-year or graduate institution.

Eligibility: Applicant must be high school senior.

Basis for selection: Applicant must demonstrate high academic achievement.

Application requirements: Essay, transcript. Unofficial transcript, application cover sheet, application essay, updated resume.

Additional information: Minimum 3.0 GPA required.

Amount of award: $500
Number of awards: 1
Application deadline: May 1
Total amount awarded: $500
Contact:
April Cockerham
409 7th Street NW
Washington, DC 20004
Phone: 202-517-0502
Fax: 202-664-1331
Web: thevisafirm.com/scholarship/

Arab American Institute

Helen Abbott Community Service Awards

Type of award: Scholarship.
Intended use: For undergraduate study at accredited vocational, 2-year or 4-year institution.
Eligibility: Applicant must be no older than 30, enrolled in high school. Applicant must be Arab. Applicant must be U.S. citizen or permanent resident.
Basis for selection: Applicant must demonstrate service orientation.
Application requirements: Recommendations, essay, transcript. Resume which indicates a strong interest and commitment to community service, two letters of recommendation, and a no more than 700 word essay on how your field of study is a springboard for a life of community service and what growing up and being an Arab American means to you.
Additional information: Minimum 3.0 GPA. Must be enrolled as an undergraduate in a college or university program; or enrolled in High School. Must be a US citizen or permanent legal resident of Arab descent.
Amount of award: $500-$1,000
Number of awards: 3
Application deadline: March 1
Notification begins: April 30
Total amount awarded: $2,500
Contact:
Arab American Institute Foundation
1600 K Street, NW
Suite 601
Washington DC, DC 20006
Phone: 202-429-9210
Fax: 202-429-9214
Web: www.aaiusa.org/scholarships_aai

The Argenta Reading Series

High School Writing Contest

Type of award: Scholarship.
Intended use: For full-time freshman study at accredited 2-year or 4-year institution in United States. Designated institutions: Must be an Arkansas institution.
Eligibility: Applicant must be high school sophomore, junior or senior. Applicant must be U.S. citizen residing in Arkansas.

Application requirements: Essay. Original creative writing must be submitted. Finalists must read in front of a live audience in North Little Rock, Arkansas on May 27. Essay details are on the website.
Additional information: Applicant must be resident of Arkansas state and intending to go to school at an Arkansas institution.
Amount of award: $1,000-$1,000
Number of awards: 1
Application deadline: April 21
Notification begins: May 1
Total amount awarded: $1,000
Contact:
Argenta Reading Series
4904 Randolph Road
North Little Rock, AR 72116
Phone: 501-831-4950
Web: https://www.argentareadingseries.com/writing-contest

The Ark Law Group

Ark Law Group Fresh Start Scholarship Program

Type of award: Scholarship.
Intended use: For undergraduate or graduate study at 2-year, 4-year or graduate institution.
Application requirements: Essay. 500-1000 word essay answering two questions regarding the American Dream and economic exploitation in home ownership. See website for full questions. Diagrams, schematics, illustrations and photographs may be included as supporting documents.
Additional information: Applications must be submitted by email and must include applicant's name, contact information, institution, major and expected date of graduation/certification and completed essay in Word format.
Amount of award: $1,000
Number of awards: 1
Application deadline: July 31
Contact:
Ark Law Group
Web: www.arklawgroup.com/scholarships

Student Voices Scholarship Program

Type of award: Scholarship.
Intended use: For full-time undergraduate or graduate study at vocational, 2-year, 4-year or graduate institution.
Application requirements: Essay. Essay must be between 500 and 1,000 words.
Additional information: Four awards per year in quarterly essay contests. Due dates and essay topics can be found online.
Number of awards: 1,000
Number of applicants: 200
Contact:
The Ark Law Group
227 Bellevue Way NE
Suite 980
Bellevue, WA 98004
Phone: 800-603-3525
Fax: 888-860-1314
Web: www.arklawgroup.com/scholarships

Arkansas Department of Higher Education

Arkansas Academic Challenge Scholarship

Type of award: Scholarship, renewable.
Intended use: For undergraduate study at postsecondary institution in United States. Designated institutions: Approved Arkansas colleges and universities.
Eligibility: Applicant must be high school senior. Applicant must be U.S. citizen or permanent resident residing in Arkansas.
Basis for selection: Applicant must demonstrate financial need and high academic achievement.
Application requirements: Transcript. ACT scores and FAFSA.
Additional information: Award is renewable up to four years. Eligibility requirements vary and are based on three student categories: Traditional (Incoming Freshman), Current Achievers, and Nontraditional Students. Visit Website for requirements. Applications available online or from the Department of Higher Education.

  Amount of award: $2,000-$5,000
  Application deadline: June 1
Contact:
Arkansas Department of Higher Education
423 Main Street
Suite 400
Little Rock, AR 72201
Phone: 501-371-2000
Web: www.scholarships.adhe.edu

Arkansas Governor's Scholars Program

Type of award: Scholarship, renewable.
Intended use: For full-time undergraduate study at postsecondary institution. Designated institutions: Approved Arkansas colleges and universities.
Eligibility: Applicant must be high school senior. Applicant must be U.S. citizen or permanent resident residing in Arkansas.
Basis for selection: Applicant must demonstrate high academic achievement and leadership.
Additional information: Governor's Distinguished Scholars must have at least 32 ACT or 1410 SAT and minimum 3.5 GPA or have been selected as National Merit or National Achievement Finalist. Governor's Distinguished Scholars receive award equal to tuition, fees, room, and board up to $10,000 per year. Awards renewable up to four years if Distinguished Scholars maintain minimum 3.25 GPA. Visit Website for more information.

  Amount of award: $10,000
  Application deadline: February 1
Contact:
Arkansas Department of Higher Education
Attn: Governor's Scholars Program
423 Main Street, Suite 400
Little Rock, AR 72201
Phone: 501-371-2000
Web: www.scholarships.adhe.edu

Arkansas Law Enforcement Officers' Dependents Scholarship

Type of award: Scholarship, renewable.
Intended use: For undergraduate study at accredited vocational, 2-year or 4-year institution in United States. Designated institutions: Public schools in Arkansas.
Eligibility: Applicant must be U.S. citizen or permanent resident residing in Arkansas.
Basis for selection: Applicant must demonstrate high academic achievement.
Application requirements: Proof of eligibility.
Additional information: Applicant must be dependent or spouse of one of the following who was killed or permanently disabled in line of duty: law enforcement officer; firefighter; sheriff; constable; game warden; certain state highway, forestry, correction, or park employees; EMT; Department of Community Punishment employee. Dependent child applicant may be no older than 23; no age restriction for spouse, but must not be remarried. Award is for tuition, fees, and room and is for up to eight semesters. Must maintain 2.0 GPA. Visit Website for more information and application.

  Amount of award: Full tuition
  Application deadline: June 1
Contact:
Arkansas Department of Higher Education
423 Main Street
Suite 400
Little Rock, AR 72201
Phone: 501-371-2000
Web: www.scholarships.adhe.edu

Arkansas Military Dependents Scholarship Program

Type of award: Scholarship, renewable.
Intended use: For full-time undergraduate study at vocational, 2-year or 4-year institution in United States. Designated institutions: Public schools in Arkansas.
Eligibility: Applicant must be U.S. citizen or permanent resident residing in Arkansas. Applicant must be dependent of disabled veteran or POW/MIA; or spouse of disabled veteran or POW/MIA who served in the Army, Air Force, Marines, Navy, Coast Guard or Reserves/National Guard. Parent/spouse may also have been killed in action or killed on ordinance delivery. All incidents must have occurred while on active duty after 1/1/60. Parent/spouse must be AR resident or must have been at time of enlistment. Dependent must have been born, adopted, or in legal custody of veteran under whom he/she is applying.
Basis for selection: Applicant must demonstrate high academic achievement.
Application requirements: Proof of eligibility.
Additional information: Award for tuition, fees, room, and board. Renewable up to four years. Must maintain 2.0 GPA and complete a minimum 24 semester hours per academic year. Visit Website for more information and application.

  Amount of award: Full tuition
  Application deadline: June 1
Contact:
Arkansas Department of Higher Education
Attn: Military Dependents Scholarship Program
423 Main Street, Suite 400
Little Rock, AR 72201
Phone: 501-371-2000
Web: www.scholarships.adhe.edu

Armed Forces Communications and Electronics Association

AFCEA ROTC Scholarship

Type of award: Scholarship.
Intended use: For full-time sophomore or junior study at accredited 4-year institution in United States.
Eligibility: Applicant must be U.S. citizen.
Basis for selection: Major/career interest in aerospace; engineering; computer/information sciences; education; physics; mathematics; technology; electronics; foreign languages or international studies. Applicant must demonstrate financial need, high academic achievement, depth of character, leadership, patriotism, seriousness of purpose and service orientation.
Application requirements: Recommendations, transcript, nomination by professor of military science, naval science, or aerospace studies or designated commanding officer. Other degree/major interest include: Biometry/Biometrics, Computer Engineering, Computer Forensics Science, Computer Programming, Computer Science, Computer Systems, Cybersecurity, Electrical Engineering, Electronics Engineering, Geospatial Science, Information Science, Information Technology, Information Resource Management, Intelligence, Mathematics, Network Engineering, Network Security, Operations Research, Physics, Robotics Engineering, Robotics Technology, Statistics, Strategic Intelligence, or Telecommunications Engineering.
Additional information: Applicant must be enrolled in ROTC. Majors directly related to support of U.S. national security enterprises with relevance to mission of AFCEA also eligible.

Amount of award:	$2,500-$5,000
Number of awards:	50
Application deadline:	February 17
Notification begins:	June 1
Total amount awarded:	$112,000

Contact:
Armed Forces Communications and Electronics Association
Mr. Fred H. Rainbow
4400 Fair Lakes Court
Fairfax, VA 22033-3899
Phone: 703-631-6149
Fax: 703-631-4693
Web: www.afcea.org/scholarships

AFCEA Scholarship for Underserved Students (HBCU)

Type of award: Scholarship.
Intended use: For full-time sophomore or junior study at accredited 2-year or 4-year institution in United States. Designated institutions: Historically black colleges and universities.
Eligibility: Applicant must be U.S. citizen.
Basis for selection: Major/career interest in aerospace; engineering, electrical/electronic; engineering, computer; information systems; computer/information sciences; physics or mathematics. Applicant must demonstrate financial need, high academic achievement and leadership.
Application requirements: Recommendations, transcript.
Additional information: Distance-learning or online programs affiliated with HCBUs are eligible. Majors directly related to

the support of U.S. intelligence or homeland security enterprises with relevance to the mission of AFCEA are also eligible. Special consideration given to military-enlisted candidates/military veterans.

Amount of award:	$5,000
Number of awards:	2
Application deadline:	May 15

Contact:
AFCEA Educational Foundation
Mr. Fred H. Rainbow
4400 Fair Lakes Court
Fairfax, VA 22033-3899
Phone: 703-631-6149
Fax: 703-631-4693
Web: www.afcea.org/scholarships

AFCEA War Veterans/Disabled War Veterans Scholarship

Type of award: Scholarship.
Intended use: For undergraduate study at 4-year institution in United States.
Eligibility: Applicant must be U.S. citizen. Applicant must be in military service or veteran in the Army, Air Force, Marines, Navy, Coast Guard or Reserves/National Guard.
Basis for selection: Major/career interest in aerospace; engineering, computer; engineering, electrical/electronic; information systems; technology; computer/information sciences; physics; mathematics or education. Applicant must demonstrate high academic achievement.
Application requirements: Recommendations, transcript. Certificate of Service, Discharge Form DD214, or facsimile of candidate's current DoD or Coast Guard Identification Card. Please black out your Social Security Number when submitting.
Additional information: For honorably discharged U.S. military veterans and disabled veterans of the Enduring Freedom (Afghanistan) or Iraqi Freedom operations. Majors directly related to Majors: C4I-related fields related to the mission of AFCEA: Biometry/Biometrics, Computer Engineering, Computer Forensics Science, Computer Programming, Computer Science, Computer Systems, Cybersecurity, Electrical Engineering, Electronics Engineering, Geospatial Science, Information Science, Information Technology, Information Resource Management, Intelligence, Mathematics, Network Engineering, Network Security, Operations, Research, Physics, Robotics Engineering, Robotics Technology, Statistics, Strategic Intelligence, and Telecommunications Engineering. Distance-learning or online programs affiliated with a major U.S. institution are eligible.

Amount of award:	$2,500
Application deadline:	April 15, November 1

Contact:
Armed Forces Communications and Electronics Association
Mr. Fred H. Rainbow
4400 Fair Lakes Court
Fairfax, VA 22033-3899
Phone: 703-631-6138
Fax: 703-631-4693
Web: www.afcea.org/scholarships

Cyber Security Scholarships

Type of award: Scholarship, renewable.
Intended use: For full-time sophomore, junior or graduate study at accredited 2-year, 4-year or graduate institution in United States.
Eligibility: Applicant must be U.S. citizen.

Basis for selection: Major/career interest in computer/information sciences or engineering, electrical/electronic. Applicant must demonstrate financial need, high academic achievement and leadership.
Application requirements: Recommendations, transcript.
Additional information: Minimum 3.0 GPA. Must be pursuing academic degree in cyber security, cyber attack, computer science, information technology, digital forensics, or electronic engineering. Deadline in November.

Amount of award:	$5,000

Contact:
Armed Forces Communications and Electronics Association
Attn: Mr. Fred Rainbow
4400 Fair Lakes Court
Fairfax, VA 22033
Phone: 800-336-4583
Web: www.afcea.org/scholarships

STEM Majors Scholarship

Type of award: Scholarship, renewable.
Intended use: For undergraduate or graduate study at vocational, 4-year or graduate institution.
Eligibility: Applicant must be U.S. citizen.
Basis for selection: Major/career interest in electronics; computer/information sciences; engineering, chemical; technology; information systems; physics or mathematics. Applicant must demonstrate high academic achievement.
Application requirements: Recommendations, transcript.
Additional information: Minimum 3.0 GPA. Must be studying STEM major: Science, Technology, Engineering, or Math. Visit Website for more details.
Contact:
Armed Forces Communications and Electronics Association
Attn: Mr. Fred Rainbow
4400 Fair Lakes Court
Fairfax, VA 22033
Phone: 800-336-4583
Web: www.afcea.org/scholarships

Armenian General Benevolent Union (AGBU)

AGBU International Scholarships

Type of award: Scholarship, renewable.
Intended use: For full-time undergraduate or graduate study at postsecondary institution outside United States or Canada.
Eligibility: Applicant must be Armenian. Applicant must be international student.
Basis for selection: Applicant must demonstrate financial need, high academic achievement and service orientation.
Application requirements: Recommendations, essay, transcript, proof of eligibility. Resume, passport-size photograph. Copy of Bursar's receipt, copy of financial award letter.
Additional information: Minimum 3.5 GPA. Awarded to students of Armenian descent enrolled in institutions in their countries of residence. Some selected fields of graduate study may also be considered. Excludes Armenian citizens studying in Armenia. Deadline is June 1 for study in all countries except Syria and France. Deadline for study in Syria and France is July 15. Number of awards and amounts vary. Not for use in the U.S.

Amount of award:	$3,000
Number of applicants:	603
Application deadline:	June 1, July 15
Notification begins:	October 31
Total amount awarded:	$245,600

Contact:
Armenian General Benevolent Union (AGBU)
55 East 59th Street
7th Floor
New York, NY 10022
Phone: 212-319-6383
Fax: 212-319-6507
Web: www.agbu-scholarship.org

Armenian General Benevolent Union Performing Arts Fellowships

Type of award: Scholarship, renewable.
Intended use: For full-time undergraduate or graduate study in or outside United States.
Eligibility: Applicant must be Armenian.
Basis for selection: Competition/talent/interest in performing arts. Major/career interest in performing arts. Applicant must demonstrate financial need, high academic achievement and service orientation.
Application requirements: Recommendations, essay, transcript, proof of eligibility. Resume, one passport-size photograph, enrollment verification/acceptance letter, bursar's receipt, financial award letter, CD of or link to most current recording (if applicable).
Additional information: Minimum 3.5 GPA. Number of awards varies based on funding. Applicants may be of Armenian descent. Excludes Armenian citizens studying in Armenia. Number of awards varies. Visit Website for more information.

Amount of award:	$2,500-$7,500
Number of applicants:	111
Application deadline:	May 31
Notification begins:	July 31
Total amount awarded:	$234,250

Contact:
Armenian General Benevolent Union
Attn: Scholarship Program
55 E. 59th Street, 7th Floor
New York, NY 10022-1112
Phone: 212-319-6383
Fax: 212-319-6507
Web: www.agbu-scholarship.org

ARMY Emergency Relief

MG James Ursano Scholarship Program

Type of award: Scholarship, renewable.
Intended use: For full-time undergraduate study at accredited postsecondary institution.
Eligibility: Applicant must be single, no older than 23. Applicant must be dependent of active service person, veteran or deceased veteran who serves or served in the Army.
Basis for selection: Applicant must demonstrate financial need, high academic achievement and leadership.
Application requirements: Transcript, proof of eligibility. Student Aid Report (SAR).

Additional information: Applicant must be registered in DEERS. Student Aid Report deadline 5/1. Must maintain 2.0 GPA. Amount of award and number of recipients vary. Application must be submitted via Website; supporting documentation should be emailed.

Amount of award:	$500-$3,500
Number of applicants:	5,300
Application deadline:	May 1
Notification begins:	June 1
Total amount awarded:	$6,000,000

Contact:
ARMY Emergency Relief
MG James Ursano Scholarship Program
200 Stovall Street
Alexandria, VA 22332-0600
Phone: 703-428-0035
Fax: 703-325-7183
Web: www.aerhq.org

Army Women's Foundation

Army Women's Foundation Legacy Scholarship

Type of award: Scholarship, renewable.
Intended use: For full-time undergraduate or graduate study at accredited vocational, 2-year, 4-year or graduate institution.
Eligibility: Applicant must be in military service or veteran; or dependent of active service person or veteran.
Application requirements: Recommendations, essay, transcript. Commander's verification of active duty or qualified documentation of the sponsor or woman's service. Official transcript from college or university. Two letters of recommendation (one must be from a school advisor, counselor, dean of students, professor). Short essay (2 pages or less) highlighting why the recipient should be considered for the scholarship.
Additional information: Must have a 2.5 GPA for community college or certificate program and a 3.0 GPA for the college/university or graduate program. Application can be found on website.

Amount of award:	$1,000-$2,500
Application deadline:	January 15

Contact:
Army Women's Foundation
PO Box 5030
ATTN: Scholarship Committee
Fort Lee, VA 23801
Phone: 804-734-3078
Web: http://awfdn.org/scholarships.shtml

The Art Institutes

Best Teen Chef Culinary Scholarship Competition

Type of award: Scholarship.
Intended use: For undergraduate study at 2-year or 4-year institution in United States. Designated institutions: Art Institute schools offering culinary arts programs.

Eligibility: Applicant must be high school senior. Applicant must be U.S. citizen, Canadian citizen (excluding Quebec).
Basis for selection: Competition/talent/interest in culinary arts, based on meal preparation ability and originality. Major/career interest in culinary arts or hotel/restaurant management. Applicant must demonstrate high academic achievement.
Application requirements: Essay, transcript. Recipe.
Additional information: Award amount varies depending on placement in competition. First-place winner will compete in national event slated for April. Minimum high school GPA of 2.0. Visit Website for deadline and application.

Amount of award:	$1,000-$4,000
Number of awards:	2
Number of applicants:	265
Total amount awarded:	$5,000

Contact:
The Art Institutes
210 Sixth Avenue, 33rd Floor
Pittsburgh, PA 15222-2603
Phone: 888-624-0300
Web: www.artinstitutes.edu or www.culinary.aischolarship.com

Arthur and Doreen Parrett Scholarship Trust Fund

Arthur and Doreen Parrett Scholarship

Type of award: Scholarship, renewable.
Intended use: For full-time sophomore, junior, senior, master's, doctoral or first professional study at accredited postsecondary institution.
Eligibility: Applicant must be residing in Washington.
Basis for selection: Major/career interest in science, general; engineering; dentistry or medicine. Applicant must demonstrate financial need and high academic achievement.
Application requirements: Recommendations, transcript.
Additional information: Applicants must have completed first year of college. Include SASE with inquiries, and information will be forwarded.

Amount of award:	$2,500-$4,000
Number of awards:	10
Application deadline:	January 31

Contact:
Arthur and Doreen Parrett Scholarship Trust Fund
c/o U.S. Bank - Trust Dept.
1420 5th Avenue, Suite 2100
Seattle, WA 98101

The ASCAP Foundation

The Herb Alpert Young Jazz Composer Awards

Type of award: Scholarship.
Intended use: For undergraduate study at postsecondary institution.
Eligibility: Applicant must be no older than 29. Applicant must be U.S. citizen or permanent resident.

Basis for selection: Competition/talent/interest in music performance/composition.

Application requirements: Notated score and CD or cassette of one composition. Biographical information listing music studies, background, and experience. SASE.

Additional information: Number of awards and award amounts vary. Must be under age 30 as of Dec. 31.

Amount of award:	$500-$2,000
Number of awards:	30
Number of applicants:	350
Application deadline:	December 1
Notification begins:	February 15
Total amount awarded:	$40,000

Contact:
Cia Toscanini, The ASCAP Foundation
Young JAZZ Composer Awards
One Lincoln Plaza
New York, NY 10023
Phone: 212-621-6329
Web: www.ascap.com/music-career/support/young-jazz-guidelines.aspx

Morton Gould Young Composer Awards

Type of award: Scholarship, renewable.
Intended use: For non-degree study.
Eligibility: Applicant must be no older than 29.
Basis for selection: Competition/talent/interest in music performance/composition. Major/career interest in music.
Application requirements: Reproduction of original score, biographical and educational information, list of compositions to date, SASE, CD of composition (if available).
Additional information: Number of awards varies. Applicant must not have reached 30th birthday by January 1 and may submit only one composition. International applicants must have student visa.

Amount of award:	$750-$2,500
Number of applicants:	750
Application deadline:	February 15
Notification begins:	May 1
Total amount awarded:	$40,000

Contact:
The ASCAP Foundation Morton Gould Young Composer Awards
c/o Cia Toscanini
One Lincoln Plaza
New York, NY 10023
Phone: 212-621-6329
Web: www.ascap.com/music-career/support/morton-gould-guidelines.aspx

Rudolf Nissim Prize

Type of award: Scholarship.
Intended use: For non-degree study.
Basis for selection: Competition/talent/interest in music performance/composition. Major/career interest in music.
Application requirements: Bound copy of score of one original concert work, composer biography, SASE.
Additional information: Award for work requiring a conductor that has not been performed professionally. Applicant must be concert composer member of ASCAP. Visit Website for specific application requirements and details.

Amount of award:	$5,000
Number of awards:	1
Number of applicants:	230
Application deadline:	November 15
Notification begins:	January 15
Total amount awarded:	$5,000

Contact:
Cia Toscanini
c/o The ASCAP Foundation/Rudolf Nissim Prize
One Lincoln Plaza
New York, NY 10023
Phone: 212-621-6329
Web: www.ascap.com/music-career/support/nissim-guidelines.aspx

ASCO

Industrial Automation Engineering College Scholarships

Type of award: Scholarship.
Intended use: For full-time junior, senior or graduate study at accredited 4-year or graduate institution in United States.
Eligibility: Applicant must be U.S. citizen or permanent resident.
Basis for selection: Major/career interest in engineering; engineering, electrical/electronic or engineering, mechanical. Applicant must demonstrate high academic achievement and leadership.
Additional information: For students planning to pursue careers in industrial automation-related disciplines. Minimum 3.2 GPA. ASCO Numatics employees and their families are ineligible. Notification begins mid-June. Application details and forms available on Website.

Amount of award:	$5,000
Number of awards:	2
Application deadline:	March 31
Total amount awarded:	$10,000

Contact:
ASCO Headquarters
160 Park Avenue
Florham Park, NJ 07932
Phone: 973-966-2000
Fax: 973-966-2628
Web: www.asconumatics.com/scholarship

Asian American Journalists Association

Asian American Journalists Association Print & Online News Grants

Type of award: Scholarship.
Intended use: For full-time undergraduate study.
Eligibility: Applicant must be at least 18.
Basis for selection: Major/career interest in journalism. Applicant must demonstrate financial need and seriousness of purpose.

Application requirements: Recommendations, essay. Resume, proof of age, statement of financial need, and internship verification.

Additional information: Applicant may also be recent college graduate. Must have already secured summer internship at print or online company before applying. Must be committed to AAJA's mission. AAJA membership encouraged for all applicants and required for selected interns. Deadline late-March or mid-April; notification begins February. Visit Website for specific dates. Apply online.

Amount of award:	$500-$1,000
Application deadline:	April 16

Contact:
Asian American Journalists Association
Justin Seiter
5 Third Street, Suite 1108
San Francisco, CA 94103
Phone: 415-346-2051 ext. 107
Fax: 415-346-6343
Web: www.aaja.org

Broadcast News Grants

Type of award: Scholarship.
Intended use: For full-time undergraduate study at 4-year institution.
Eligibility: Applicant must be at least 18.
Basis for selection: Major/career interest in journalism or radio/television/film. Applicant must demonstrate financial need.
Application requirements: Recommendations, essay. Resume, proof of age, statement of financial need, and internship verification. Submit original plus three copies of all materials.
Additional information: Applicant must have already secured summer broadcast internship at TV or radio network, and must be committed to AAJA's mission. AAJA membership encouraged for all applicants and required for awardees. Recent college graduates also eligible. Visit Website for deadline. Apply online.

Amount of award:	$500-$1,000
Application deadline:	April 16

Contact:
Asian American Journalists Association
Justin Seiter
5 Third Street, Suite 1108
San Francisco, CA 94103
Phone: 415-346-2051 ext. 107
Fax: 415-346-6343
Web: www.aaja.org

CIC/Anna Chennault Scholarship

Type of award: Scholarship.
Intended use: For freshman, sophomore, junior or senior study at 4-year institution.
Eligibility: Applicant must be high school senior.
Basis for selection: Major/career interest in journalism. Applicant must demonstrate high academic achievement.
Additional information: The selected student will receive travel, lodging and registration to attend AAJA's national annual convention in August 2015 in San Francisco. Recipients must become AAJA student members. Applicant must demonstrate journalistic ability, commitment to the field of journalism, and sensitivity to Asian American and Pacific Islander issues. Deadline in May.

Amount of award:	$5,000
Number of awards:	1
Application deadline:	April 16
Total amount awarded:	$5,000

Contact:
Asian American Journalists Association
CIC/Anna Chennault Scholarship
5 Third Street, Suite 1108
San Francisco, CA 94103
Phone: 415-346-2051 ext. 107
Fax: 415-346-6343
Web: www.aaja.org

Mary Quon Moy Ing Memorial Scholarship

Type of award: Scholarship.
Intended use: For full-time undergraduate or graduate study at 4-year or graduate institution.
Basis for selection: Major/career interest in journalism. Applicant must demonstrate financial need and high academic achievement.
Additional information: AAJA student membership is encouraged for all applicants and required for the selected scholarship recipients. Visit the Website for additional information.

Amount of award:	$2,000
Number of awards:	1
Application deadline:	April 16
Total amount awarded:	$2,000

Contact:
Asian American Journalists Association
5 Third Street
Suite 1108
San Francisco, CA 94103
Phone: 415-346-2051 ext. 107
Fax: 415-346-6343
Web: www.aaja.org

Stanford Chen Internship Grant

Type of award: Scholarship.
Intended use: For junior, senior or graduate study at 4-year or graduate institution.
Basis for selection: Major/career interest in journalism. Applicant must demonstrate financial need and seriousness of purpose.
Application requirements: Recommendations, essay, proof of eligibility. Resume, statement of financial need, and internship verification. Original plus three copies of all application materials.
Additional information: Applicant must have already secured internship with small- to medium-size media company (print companies with daily circulation under 100,000 and broadcast markets smaller than top 50). Application may be downloaded from Website. AAJA membership is encouraged for all applicants and required for selected recipients. Deadline varies. Visit Website for specific dates.

Amount of award:	$1,750
Number of awards:	1
Application deadline:	April 2
Total amount awarded:	$1,750

Contact:
Asian American Journalists Association
Stanford Chen Internship Grant
5 Third Street, Suite 1108
San Francisco, CA 94103
Phone: 415-346-2051 ext. 107
Fax: 415-346-6343
Web: www.aaja.org

Vincent Chin Memorial Scholarship

Type of award: Scholarship.
Intended use: For full-time undergraduate study at 2-year or 4-year institution.
Basis for selection: Major/career interest in journalism. Applicant must demonstrate financial need, high academic achievement and service orientation.
Additional information: AAJA student membership is encouraged for all applicants and required for the selected scholarship recipients. Visit the Website for additional information.

Amount of award:	$500
Number of awards:	1
Application deadline:	April 16

Contact:
Asian American Journalists Association
5 Third Street
Suite 1108
San Francisco, CA 94103
Phone: 415-346-2051 ext. 107
Fax: 415-346-6343
Web: www.aaja.org

Asian Pacific Community Fund

Chen Foundation Scholarship

Type of award: Scholarship, renewable.
Intended use: For full-time freshman or sophomore study at accredited 2-year or 4-year institution in United States. Designated institutions: California State Universities and California Community Colleges.
Eligibility: Applicant must be high school senior. Applicant must be U.S. citizen or permanent resident residing in California.
Basis for selection: Applicant must demonstrate financial need and service orientation.
Application requirements: Recommendations, transcript. Must have a minimum high scholl cumulative unweighted GPA of 3.0. Recommendation from one person familiar with your community service activities.
Additional information: Must have a household income at or below California State/County income level. Application and complete instructions online.

Amount of award:	$2,000
Number of awards:	10
Number of applicants:	400
Application deadline:	March 29
Notification begins:	June 30
Total amount awarded:	$40,000

Contact:
Asian Pacific Community Fund
1145 Wilshire Boulevard
Suit 105
Los Angeles, CA 90017
Phone: 213-624-6400 ext. 8
Fax: 213-624-6406
Web: http://www.apcf.org/2017-chen-foundation-scholarship-program/

Royal Business Bank Scholarship Program

Type of award: Scholarship.
Intended use: For full-time freshman study at accredited 2-year or 4-year institution in United States. Designated institutions: United States 4-year college, University of California, Nevada Community College.
Eligibility: Applicant must be high school senior. Applicant must be U.S. citizen or permanent resident residing in California or Nevada.
Basis for selection: Applicant must demonstrate financial need and high academic achievement.
Application requirements: Recommendations, transcript. Must provide official high school transcript. Employees of Royal Business Bank and their immediate family members are not eligible to apply. Applicant must be a high school senior entering college in the Fall semester. Recommendation from one person familiar with your community service activities.
Additional information: Must have a household income at or below the County Low Income Level.

Amount of award:	$1,000
Number of awards:	20
Application deadline:	March 29
Notification begins:	December 13
Total amount awarded:	$20,000

Contact:
Asian Pacific Community Fund
1145 Wilshire Boulevard
Suite 105
Los Angeles, CA 90017
Phone: 213-624-6400 ext. 6
Fax: 213-624-6406
Web: www.apcf.org/2017-royal-business-bank-scholarship-program/

Taiwanese American Scholarship Fund Program

Type of award: Scholarship.
Intended use: For full-time freshman or sophomore study at accredited 2-year or 4-year institution in United States.
Eligibility: Applicant must be high school senior. Applicant must be U.S. citizen or permanent resident.
Application requirements: Recommendations, transcript. Three references/recommendations.
Additional information: Must be direct blood descendant of a Taiwanese citizen. Must have a household income at or below the federal/state/county low income level. After receiving award, awardees must submit a short YouTube video. Application online.

Amount of award:	$2,500
Number of awards:	20
Application deadline:	March 29
Notification begins:	June 30

Scholarships

Contact:
Asian Pacific Community Fund
1145 Wilshire Boulevard
Suite 105
Los Angeles, CA 90017
Phone: 213-624-6400 ext. 8
Fax: 213-624-6406
Web: http://tascholarshipfund.org/2017-tasf-scholarship-overview/

Asian Women In Business

Asian Women In Business Scholarship

Type of award: Scholarship.
Intended use: For full-time undergraduate study at 4-year institution in United States.
Eligibility: Applicant must be Asian American or Native Hawaiian/Pacific Islander. Applicant must be female. Applicant must be U.S. citizen or permanent resident.
Application requirements: Recommendations, transcript.
Additional information: Minimum 3.0 GPA. Must have either a leadership role in a community endeavor or a record of entrepreneurial achievement. For the additional $2,500 financial need must be demonstrated by submitting a copy of the most current FAFSA form and the Financial Aid Award Notice from your institution for the academic year. Visit web site for application and complete guidelines.

Amount of award:	$2,500-$5,000
Number of applicants:	120

Contact:
Asian Women In Business
42 Broadway
Suite 1748
New York, NY
Phone: 212-868-1368
Web: www.awib.org/index.cfm?fuseaction=Page.viewPage&pageId=811

ASM Materials Education Foundation

ASM Outstanding Scholars Awards

Type of award: Scholarship, renewable.
Intended use: For full-time sophomore, junior or senior study at accredited 4-year institution in or outside United States.
Basis for selection: Major/career interest in engineering, materials or materials science. Applicant must demonstrate high academic achievement.
Application requirements: Recommendations, essay, transcript. Photograph. Resume optional.
Additional information: May also major in metallurgy or related science or engineering disciplines if applicant demonstrates strong interest in materials science. Must be student member of Material Advantage. International student members may apply. Visit Website for application and full details.

Amount of award:	$2,000
Number of awards:	3
Application deadline:	May 1
Notification begins:	July 15
Total amount awarded:	$6,000

Contact:
ASM Materials Education Foundation
Undergraduate Scholarship Program
9639 Kinsman Road
Materials Park, OH 44073-0002
Phone: 440-338-5151
Fax: 440-338-4634
Web: www.asmfoundation.org

Edward J. Dulis Scholarship

Type of award: Scholarship, renewable.
Intended use: For junior or senior study at accredited 4-year institution in United States or Canada.
Basis for selection: Major/career interest in engineering, materials or materials science. Applicant must demonstrate financial need and high academic achievement.
Application requirements: Recommendations, essay, transcript. Photograph. Resume optional.
Additional information: Applicant may also major in metallurgy or related science or engineering field if interested in materials science. Must be student member of Material Advantage. Visit Website for application and full details.

Amount of award:	$1,500
Number of awards:	1
Application deadline:	May 1
Notification begins:	July 15

Contact:
ASM Materials Education Foundation
Undergraduate Scholarship Program
9639 Kinsman Road
Materials Park, OH 44073-0002
Phone: 440-338-5151
Fax: 440-338-4634
Web: www.asmfoundation.org

George A. Roberts Scholarships

Type of award: Scholarship, renewable.
Intended use: For junior or senior study at accredited 4-year institution in United States or Canada.
Basis for selection: Major/career interest in engineering, materials or materials science. Applicant must demonstrate financial need and high academic achievement.
Application requirements: Recommendations, essay, transcript. Photograph, resume optional.
Additional information: Applicant may also major in metallurgy or related science or engineering field if interested in materials science. Must be student member of Material Advantage. Visit Website for application and full details.

Amount of award:	$6,000
Number of awards:	7
Application deadline:	May 1
Notification begins:	July 15
Total amount awarded:	$42,000

Contact:
ASM Materials Education Foundation
Undergraduate Scholarship Program
9639 Kinsman Road
Materials Park, OH 44073-0002
Phone: 440-338-5151
Fax: 440-338-4634
Web: www.asmfoundation.org

Scholarships

John M. Haniak Scholarship

Type of award: Scholarship, renewable.
Intended use: For junior or senior study at accredited 4-year institution in United States or Canada.
Basis for selection: Major/career interest in engineering, materials or materials science. Applicant must demonstrate financial need and high academic achievement.
Application requirements: Recommendations, essay, transcript. Photograph. Resume optional.
Additional information: Applicant may also major in metallurgy or related science or engineering field if interested in materials science. Must be student member of Material Advantage. Visit Website for application and full details.

Amount of award:	$1,500
Number of awards:	1
Application deadline:	May 1
Notification begins:	July 15

Contact:
ASM Materials Education Foundation
Undergraduate Scholarship Program
9639 Kinsman Road
Materials Park, OH 44073-0002
Phone: 440-338-5151
Fax: 440-338-4634
Web: www.asmfoundation.org

Ladish Co. Foundation Scholarships

Type of award: Scholarship.
Intended use: For sophomore, junior or senior study at accredited 4-year institution. Designated institutions: Wisconsin institutions.
Eligibility: Applicant must be residing in Wisconsin.
Basis for selection: Major/career interest in engineering or materials science. Applicant must demonstrate high academic achievement, depth of character and seriousness of purpose.
Application requirements: Recommendations, essay, transcript. Photograph, resume optional.
Additional information: Applicant must be a Material Advantage student member, and must have intended or declared major in metallurgy, materials science engineering, or related science or engineering disciplines. Visit Website for application and details.

Amount of award:	$2,500
Number of awards:	2
Application deadline:	May 1
Notification begins:	July 15

Contact:
ASM Materials Education Foundation
Undergraduate Scholarship Program
9639 Kinsman Road
Materials Park, OH 44073-0002
Phone: 440-338-5151
Fax: 440-338-4634
Web: www.asmfoundation.org

Lucille & Charles A. Wert Scholarship

Type of award: Scholarship, renewable.
Intended use: For junior or senior study at accredited 4-year institution in United States or Canada.
Basis for selection: Major/career interest in engineering, materials or materials science. Applicant must demonstrate financial need and high academic achievement.
Application requirements: Recommendations, essay, transcript. Photograph, resume optional.

Additional information: Applicant may also major in metallurgy or related science or engineering field if interested in materials science. Must be student member of Material Advantage. Scholarship provides recipient with one-year full tuition up to $10,000. Visit Website for application and full details.

Amount of award:	$10,000
Number of awards:	1
Application deadline:	May 1
Notification begins:	July 15

Contact:
ASM Materials Education Foundation
Undergraduate Scholarship Program
9639 Kinsman Road
Materials Park, OH 44073-0002
Phone: 440-338-5151
Fax: 440-338-4634
Web: www.asmfoundation.org

William Park Woodside Founder's Scholarship

Type of award: Scholarship, renewable.
Intended use: For junior or senior study at accredited 4-year institution in United States or Canada.
Basis for selection: Major/career interest in engineering, materials or materials science. Applicant must demonstrate financial need and high academic achievement.
Application requirements: Recommendations, essay, transcript. Photograph. Resume optional.
Additional information: May also have major in metallurgy or related science or engineering discipline if applicant demonstrates strong interest in materials science. Must be Material Advantage student member. Scholarship provides recipient with one-year full tuition, up to $10,000. Visit Website for application and full details.

Amount of award:	$10,000
Number of awards:	1
Application deadline:	May 1
Notification begins:	July 15
Total amount awarded:	$10,000

Contact:
ASM Materials Education Foundation
Undergraduate Scholarship Program
9639 Kinsman Road
Materials Park, OH 44073-0002
Phone: 440-338-5151
Fax: 440-338-4634
Web: www.asmfoundation.org

ASME Auxiliary, Inc.

Agnes Malakate Kezios Scholarship

Type of award: Scholarship.
Intended use: For full-time senior study at 4-year institution in United States. Designated institutions: Schools with ABET-accredited mechanical engineering programs.
Eligibility: Applicant must be U.S. citizen.
Basis for selection: Major/career interest in engineering, mechanical. Applicant must demonstrate financial need, high academic achievement and depth of character.
Application requirements: Recommendations, transcript.

Additional information: For student in final year of undergraduate program in mechanical engineering. Must be ASME student member. Apply online.

Amount of award:	$3,000
Number of awards:	2
Application deadline:	March 1

Contact:
ASME Auxiliary - Undergraduate Scholarships
Web: www.asme.org/career-education/scholarships-and-grants/scholarship-and-loans

Allen J. Baldwin Scholarship

Type of award: Scholarship.
Intended use: For full-time senior study at 4-year institution in United States. Designated institutions: Schools with ABET-accredited mechanical engineering programs.
Eligibility: Applicant must be U.S. citizen.
Basis for selection: Major/career interest in engineering, mechanical. Applicant must demonstrate financial need, high academic achievement and depth of character.
Application requirements: Recommendations, transcript.
Additional information: For student in final year of undergraduate study in mechanical engineering. Must be ASME student member. Apply online.

Amount of award:	$3,000
Number of awards:	2
Application deadline:	March 1

Contact:
ASME Auxiliary - Undergraduate Scholarships
Web: www.asme.org/career-education/scholarships-and-grants/scholarship-and-loans

Berna Lou Cartwright Scholarship

Type of award: Scholarship.
Intended use: For full-time senior study at 4-year institution in United States. Designated institutions: Schools with ABET-accredited mechanical engineering programs.
Eligibility: Applicant must be U.S. citizen.
Basis for selection: Major/career interest in engineering, mechanical. Applicant must demonstrate financial need, high academic achievement and depth of character.
Application requirements: Recommendations, transcript.
Additional information: For student in final year of undergraduate program in mechanical engineering. Must be ASME student member. Apply online.

Amount of award:	$3,000
Number of awards:	2
Application deadline:	March 1

Contact:
ASME Auxiliary - Undergraduate Scholarships
Web: www.asme.org/career-education/scholarships-and-grants/scholarship-and-loans

Charles B. Scharp Scholarship

Type of award: Scholarship.
Intended use: For full-time senior study at 4-year institution in United States. Designated institutions: Schools with ABET-accredited mechanical engineering programs.
Eligibility: Applicant must be U.S. citizen.
Basis for selection: Major/career interest in engineering, mechanical. Applicant must demonstrate financial need, high academic achievement and depth of character.
Application requirements: Recommendations, transcript.

Additional information: For student in final year of undergraduate program in mechanical engineering. Must be ASME student member. Apply online.

Amount of award:	$3,000
Number of awards:	1
Application deadline:	March 1

Contact:
ASME Auxiliary - Undergraduate Scholarships
Web: www.asme.org/career-education/scholarships-and-grants/scholarship-and-loans

Sylvia W. Farny Scholarship

Type of award: Scholarship.
Intended use: For full-time senior study at 4-year institution in United States. Designated institutions: Schools with ABET-accredited mechanical engineering programs.
Eligibility: Applicant must be U.S. citizen.
Basis for selection: Major/career interest in engineering, mechanical. Applicant must demonstrate financial need, high academic achievement and depth of character.
Application requirements: Recommendations, transcript.
Additional information: For student in final year of undergraduate study in mechanical engineering. Must be ASME student member. Apply online.

Amount of award:	$3,000
Number of awards:	2
Application deadline:	March 1

Contact:
ASME Auxiliary - Undergraduate Scholarships
Web: www.asme.org/career-education/scholarships-and-grants/scholarship-and-loans

ASME Foundation

Allen Rhodes Memorial Scholarship

Type of award: Scholarship.
Intended use: For full-time sophomore, junior or senior study at accredited 4-year institution. Designated institutions: Schools with ABET-accredited programs.
Basis for selection: Major/career interest in engineering, mechanical. Applicant must demonstrate high academic achievement.
Application requirements: Recommendations, essay, transcript.
Additional information: For student with specific interest in oil and gas industry. Preference given to students enrolled at Villanova University. Applicant must be ASME student member in good standing. Mechanical engineering technology and other related majors also eligible. Apply online. Deadline in March.

Amount of award:	$1,500
Number of awards:	1
Total amount awarded:	$1,500

Contact:
ASME
Attn: Beth Lefever
2 Park Avenue
New York, NY 10016-5990
Phone: 800-843-2763
Web: www.asme.org/about-asme/scholarship-and-loans/about-asme-scholarships

American Electric Power Scholarship

Type of award: Scholarship.
Intended use: For full-time junior or senior study at accredited 4-year institution. Designated institutions: Schools with ABET-accredited programs.
Basis for selection: Major/career interest in engineering, mechanical. Applicant must demonstrate high academic achievement.
Application requirements: Recommendations, essay, transcript.
Additional information: Applicant must be American Society of Mechanical Engineers student member in good standing. Preference given to students interested in power engineering or who reside or attend school in American Electric Power service area of Arkansas, Indiana, Kentucky, Louisiana, Michigan, Ohio, Oklahoma, Tennessee, Texas, Virginia, and West Virginia. Apply online. Deadline in March.

Amount of award:	$4,000
Number of awards:	1
Total amount awarded:	$4,000

Contact:
ASME
Attn: Beth Lefever
2 Park Avenue
New York, NY 10016-5990
Phone: 800-843-2763
Web: www.asme.org/about-asme/scholarship-and-loans/about-asme-scholarships

ASME Auxiliary/FIRST Clarke Scholarship

Type of award: Scholarship.
Intended use: For full-time freshman study at accredited 4-year institution. Designated institutions: Schools with ABET-accredited programs.
Eligibility: Applicant must be high school senior.
Basis for selection: Major/career interest in engineering, mechanical. Applicant must demonstrate financial need, high academic achievement and leadership.
Application requirements: Transcript, nomination by ASME member, ASME Auxiliary member, or student member active with FIRST. Financial data worksheet, letter of support, resume.
Additional information: Applicant must be active on FIRST team. One nomination per member. Applicant may also enroll in mechanical engineering technology program. Recipient announced at FIRST National Championship. Visit Website for more information and to download forms.

Amount of award:	$5,000
Application deadline:	March 15

Contact:
ASME
Attn: RuthAnn Bigley
3416 Washington Commons Avenue
Kennesaw, GA 30144
Phone: 212-591-7650
Fax: 770-917-8508
Web: www.asme.org/about-asme/scholarship-and-loans/about-asme-scholarships

The ASME Foundation Hanley Scholarship

Type of award: Scholarship.
Intended use: For full-time sophomore, junior or senior study at accredited 4-year institution. Designated institutions: Schools with ABET-accredited programs.
Basis for selection: Major/career interest in engineering, mechanical. Applicant must demonstrate financial need and high academic achievement.
Application requirements: Recommendations, essay, transcript.
Additional information: Must be American Society of Mechanical Engineers student member in good standing. Apply online. Deadline in March.

Amount of award:	$2,500
Number of awards:	1

Contact:
ASME
Attn: Beth Lefever
2 Park Avenue
New York, NY 10016-5990
Phone: 800-843-2763
Web: www.asme.org/about-asme/scholarship-and-loans/about-asme-scholarships

ASME Foundation Scholar Award

Type of award: Scholarship, renewable.
Intended use: For sophomore, junior or senior study at accredited 4-year institution. Designated institutions: Schools with ABET-accredited programs.
Basis for selection: Major/career interest in engineering, mechanical. Applicant must demonstrate high academic achievement.
Application requirements: Recommendations, essay, transcript.
Additional information: Applicant must be student member of American Society of Mechanical Engineers. Apply online. Deadline in March. Renewable up to a maximum 3 years.

Number of awards:	1
Total amount awarded:	$11,000

Contact:
ASME
Attn: Beth Lefever
2 Park Avenue, 22nd Floor
New York, NY 10016-5990
Phone: 800-843-2763
Web: www.asme.org/about-asme/scholarship-and-loans/about-asme-scholarships

ASME Nuclear Engineering Division (NED) Scholarship

Type of award: Scholarship.
Intended use: For full-time junior or senior study at accredited 4-year institution. Designated institutions: ABET-accredited organizations.
Basis for selection: Based on potential contribution to the nuclear engineering profession. Major/career interest in engineering, nuclear. Applicant must demonstrate financial need, high academic achievement, depth of character, leadership and seriousness of purpose.
Application requirements: Recommendations, essay, transcript.
Additional information: Applicant must be a current ASME student member in good standing, and must demonstrate a

particular interest in the design, analysis, development, testing, operation, and maintenance of reactor systems and components, nuclear fusion, heat transport, nuclear fuels technology, and radioactive waste. Apply online. Deadline in March.

Amount of award:	$5,000
Number of awards:	3
Total amount awarded:	$15,000

Contact:
ASME
Attn: Beth Lefever
2 Park Avenue
New York, NY 10016-5990
Phone: 800-843-2763
Web: www.asme.org/about-asme/scholarship-and-loans/about-asme-scholarships

ASME Power Division Scholarship

Type of award: Scholarship.
Intended use: For full-time sophomore, junior or senior study at accredited 4-year institution. Designated institutions: Schools with ABET-accredited programs.
Basis for selection: Major/career interest in engineering, mechanical. Applicant must demonstrate financial need and high academic achievement.
Application requirements: Recommendations, essay, transcript.
Additional information: Applicant must be American Society of Mechanical Engineers student member in good standing and demonstrate special interest in area of fuels, combustion, or the power industry. Apply online. Deadline in March.

Amount of award:	$3,000
Number of awards:	1
Total amount awarded:	$3,000

Contact:
ASME
Attn: Beth Lefever
2 Park Avenue
New York, NY 10016-5990
Phone: 800-843-2763
Web: www.asme.org/about-asme/scholarship-and-loans/about-asme-scholarships

Frank and Dorothy Miller ASME Auxiliary Scholarships

Type of award: Scholarship.
Intended use: For full-time sophomore, junior or senior study at accredited 4-year institution in United States. Designated institutions: Schools with ABET-accredited programs.
Eligibility: Applicant must be U.S. citizen, permanent resident or Resident of Canada or Mexico.
Basis for selection: Major/career interest in engineering, mechanical. Applicant must demonstrate high academic achievement, depth of character and leadership.
Application requirements: Recommendations, essay, transcript.
Additional information: Applicant must be student member of American Society of Mechanical Engineers. Apply online. Deadline in March.

Amount of award:	$2,000
Number of awards:	2
Number of applicants:	138

Contact:
ASME
Attn: Beth Lefever
2 Park Avenue
New York, NY 10016-5990
Phone: 800-843-2763
Web: www.asme.org/about-asme/scholarship-and-loans/about-asme-scholarships

F.W. Beich Beichley Scholarship

Type of award: Scholarship.
Intended use: For full-time junior or senior study at accredited 4-year institution in United States. Designated institutions: Schools with ABET-accredited programs.
Basis for selection: Major/career interest in engineering, mechanical. Applicant must demonstrate financial need, high academic achievement, depth of character and leadership.
Application requirements: Recommendations, essay, transcript.
Additional information: Applicant must be member of American Society of Mechanical Engineers. Apply online. Deadline in March.

Amount of award:	$3,000
Number of awards:	1

Contact:
ASME
Attn: Beth Lefever
2 Park Avenue
New York, NY 10016-5990
Phone: 800-843-2763
Web: www.asme.org/about-asme/scholarship-and-loans/about-asme-scholarships

Garland Duncan Scholarships

Type of award: Scholarship.
Intended use: For full-time junior, senior or graduate study at accredited 4-year or graduate institution. Designated institutions: Schools with ABET-accredited programs.
Basis for selection: Major/career interest in engineering, mechanical. Applicant must demonstrate financial need, high academic achievement and leadership.
Application requirements: Recommendations, essay, transcript.
Additional information: Applicant must be member of American Society of Mechanical Engineers. Apply online. Deadline in March.

Amount of award:	$5,000
Number of awards:	2
Number of applicants:	138
Total amount awarded:	$10,000

Contact:
ASME
Attn: Beth Lefever
2 Park Avenue
New York, NY 10016-5990
Phone: 800-843-2763
Web: www.asme.org/about-asme/scholarship-and-loans/about-asme-scholarships

John & Elsa Gracik Scholarships

Type of award: Scholarship.
Intended use: For full-time sophomore, junior or senior study at accredited 4-year institution in United States. Designated institutions: Schools with ABET-accredited programs.
Eligibility: Applicant must be U.S. citizen.

Basis for selection: Major/career interest in engineering, mechanical. Applicant must demonstrate financial need, high academic achievement, depth of character and leadership.
Application requirements: Recommendations, essay, transcript.
Additional information: Applicant must be member of American Society of Mechanical Engineers. Apply online. Deadline in March.

Amount of award:	$2,500
Number of awards:	10
Number of applicants:	138

Contact:
ASME
Attn: Beth Lefever
2 Park Avenue
New York, NY 10016-5990
Phone: 800-843-2763
Web: www.asme.org/about-asme/scholarship-and-loans/about-asme-scholarships

John Rice Memorial Scholarship ASME Metropolitan Section

Type of award: Scholarship.
Intended use: For full-time junior or senior study at 4-year institution. Designated institutions: City College/CUNY, College of Staten Island, Columbia University, Cooper Union, Manhattan College, NYC Technology College of City University, Polytechnic Institute of New York University (Brooklyn), SUNY/Maritime College.
Basis for selection: Major/career interest in engineering, mechanical. Applicant must demonstrate high academic achievement, depth of character, leadership and seriousness of purpose.
Application requirements: Recommendations, essay, transcript.
Additional information: Applicant must be a current ASME student member in good standing. Awarded to student attending a school within ASME Met Section. Apply online. Deadline in March.

Amount of award:	$3,000
Number of awards:	1

Contact:
ASME
Attn: Beth Lefever
2 Park Avenue
New York, NY 10016-5990
Phone: 800-843-2763
Web: www.asme.org/about-asme/scholarship-and-loans/about-asme-scholarships

Kate Gleason Scholarship

Type of award: Scholarship.
Intended use: For full-time sophomore, junior, senior or graduate study at accredited 4-year institution in United States. Designated institutions: Schools with ABET-accredited programs.
Eligibility: Applicant must be female.
Basis for selection: Major/career interest in engineering or engineering, mechanical. Applicant must demonstrate financial need.
Application requirements: Recommendations, essay, transcript.
Additional information: Applicant must be American Society of Mechanical Engineers student member in good standing. Visit Website for additional information.

Amount of award:	$3,000
Number of awards:	1
Application deadline:	March 1
Notification begins:	June 15, July 15

Contact:
ASME Foundation
Attn: Beth Lefever
2 Park Avenue
New York, NY 10016-5990
Phone: 800-843-2763
Web: www.asme.org/career-education/scholarships-and-grants/scholarship-and-loans

Kenneth Andrew Roe Mechanical Engineering Scholarship

Type of award: Scholarship.
Intended use: For full-time junior or senior study at accredited 4-year institution in United States. Designated institutions: Schools with ABET-accredited programs or equivalent.
Eligibility: Applicant must be U.S. citizen, permanent resident or resident of Canada or Mexico.
Basis for selection: Major/career interest in engineering, mechanical. Applicant must demonstrate high academic achievement, depth of character and leadership.
Application requirements: Recommendations, essay, transcript.
Additional information: Applicant must be member of American Society of Mechanical Engineers. Apply online. Deadline in March.

Amount of award:	$13,000
Number of awards:	1
Number of applicants:	138

Contact:
ASME
Attn: Beth Lefever
2 Park Avenue
New York, NY 10016-5990
Phone: 800-843-2763
Web: www.asme.org/about-asme/scholarship-and-loans/about-asme-scholarships

Melvin R. Green Scholarships

Type of award: Scholarship.
Intended use: For full-time junior or senior study at accredited 4-year institution. Designated institutions: Schools with ABET-accredited programs.
Basis for selection: Major/career interest in engineering, mechanical. Applicant must demonstrate financial need, high academic achievement and leadership.
Application requirements: Recommendations, essay, transcript.
Additional information: Applicant must be student member of American Society of Mechanical Engineers. Apply online. Deadline in March.

Amount of award:	$4,000
Number of awards:	2
Total amount awarded:	$8,000

Contact:
ASME
Attn: Beth Lefever
2 Park Avenue
New York, NY 10016-5990
Phone: 800-843-2763
Web: www.asme.org/about-asme/scholarship-and-loans/about-asme-scholarships

Stephen T. Kugle Scholarship

Type of award: Scholarship.
Intended use: For full-time junior or senior study at 4-year institution in United States. Designated institutions: Public colleges or universities in District E (Arizona, Arkansas, Colorado, Louisiana, New Mexico, Oklahoma, Texas, Utah, and Wyoming).
Eligibility: Applicant must be U.S. citizen.
Basis for selection: Major/career interest in engineering, mechanical. Applicant must demonstrate high academic achievement.
Application requirements: Recommendations, essay, transcript.
Additional information: Applicant must be American Society of Mechanical Engineers student member in good standing and U.S. citizen by birth. Minimum 3.0 GPA. Students from University of Texas at Arlington not eligible. Apply online. Deadline in March.

Amount of award:	$3,000
Number of awards:	1

Contact:
ASME
Attn: Beth Lefever
2 Park Avenue
New York, NY 10016-5990
Phone: 800-843-2763
Web: www.asme.org/about-asme/scholarship-and-loans/about-asme-scholarships

William J. and Marijane E. Adams, Jr. Scholarship

Type of award: Scholarship.
Intended use: For full-time sophomore, junior or senior study at accredited 4-year institution in United States. Designated institutions: Schools with ABET-accredited programs in California, Nevada, and Hawaii.
Eligibility: Applicant must be residing in California, Hawaii or Nevada.
Basis for selection: Major/career interest in engineering, mechanical. Applicant must demonstrate financial need and high academic achievement.
Application requirements: Recommendations, essay, transcript.
Additional information: Minimum 2.5 GPA. Applicant must be member of American Society of Mechanical Engineers. Award designated for student with special interest in product development and design. Apply online. Deadline in March.

Amount of award:	$3,000
Number of awards:	1

Contact:
ASME
Attn: Beth Lefever
2 Park Avenue
New York, NY 10016-5990
Phone: 800-843-2763
Web: www.asme.org/about-asme/scholarship-and-loans/about-asme-scholarships

Willis F. Thompson Memorial Scholarship

Type of award: Scholarship.
Intended use: For full-time sophomore, junior, senior or graduate study at accredited 4-year institution. Designated institutions: Schools with ABET-accredited programs.

Basis for selection: Major/career interest in engineering, mechanical. Applicant must demonstrate high academic achievement.
Application requirements: Recommendations, essay, transcript.
Additional information: Applicant must be American Society of Mechanical Engineers student member in good standing. Preference given to students who demonstrate interest in advancing field of power generation. Apply online. Deadline in March.

Amount of award:	$4,500
Number of awards:	3
Total amount awarded:	$15,000

Contact:
ASME
Attn: Beth Lefever
2 Park Avenue
New York, NY 10016-5990
Phone: 800-843-2763
Web: www.asme.org/about-asme/scholarship-and-loans/about-asme-scholarships

Associated General Contractors Education and Research Foundation

AGC Education and Research Undergraduate Scholarship

Type of award: Scholarship, renewable.
Intended use: For full-time sophomore, junior or senior study at accredited 2-year or 4-year institution. Designated institutions: ABET- or ACCE-accredited institutions.
Eligibility: Applicant must be U.S. citizen or permanent resident.
Basis for selection: Major/career interest in engineering, civil; engineering, construction or construction.
Application requirements: Recommendations, essay, transcript.
Additional information: Must be enrolled in or planning to enroll in an ABET- or ACCE-accredited full-time, four- or five-year university program of construction or civil engineering. Applications are available July 1 from AGC Website. Seniors with one full academic year of coursework remaining are eligible. Number of awards varies.

Amount of award:	$2,500-$7,500
Number of awards:	100
Application deadline:	November 1
Notification begins:	February 1

Contact:
Association of General Contractors Education and Research Foundation
Attn: Melinda Patrician, Director
2300 Wilson Boulevard, Suite 400
Arlington, VA 22201
Phone: 703-837-5342
Fax: 703-837-5451
Web: www.agcfoundation.org

Scholarships

James L. Allhands Essay Competition

Type of award: Scholarship, renewable.

Intended use: For full-time senior study at accredited 4-year institution. Designated institutions: ABET- or ACCE-accredited universities with construction or construction-related engineering programs.

Basis for selection: Competition/talent/interest in research paper, based on advancement of technological, educational, or vocational expertise in the construction industry. Major/career interest in engineering, civil; engineering, construction or construction.

Application requirements: Essay, proof of eligibility. Essay abstract, letter from faculty sponsor.

Additional information: First prize is $1,000, plus all-expenses-paid trip to AGC convention; winner's faculty sponsor receives $500 and all-expenses-paid trip to convention. Second prize is $500. Third prize is $300. Application material must be emailed. Only five submittals from each college/university are accepted. See Website for essay topic and guidelines.

Amount of award:	$300-$1,000
Number of awards:	3
Number of applicants:	50
Application deadline:	November 15
Total amount awarded:	$2,300

Contact:
AGC Education and Research Foundation
Attn: Melinda Patrician, Director of Programs
2300 Wilson Boulevard, Suite 400
Arlington, VA 22201
Phone: 703-548-3118
Fax: 703-837-5451
Web: www.agc.org

Associated General Contractors of Maine Education Foundation

AGC of Maine Scholarship Program

Type of award: Scholarship.

Intended use: For full-time undergraduate study at accredited postsecondary institution in United States. Designated institutions: Schools in Maine.

Eligibility: Applicant must be U.S. citizen residing in Maine.

Basis for selection: Major/career interest in construction. Applicant must demonstrate financial need and high academic achievement.

Application requirements: Interview, recommendations, essay, transcript.

Additional information: Number of awards varies.

Amount of award:	$1,500-$5,000
Number of applicants:	30
Application deadline:	March 31
Total amount awarded:	$24,000

Contact:
AGC Maine
188 Whitten Road
Augusta, ME 04330
Phone: 207-622-4741
Web: www.agcmaine.org

The Associated Press Television and Radio Association

APTRA-Clete Roberts/Kathryn Dettman Memorial Journalism Scholarship

Type of award: Scholarship.

Intended use: For sophomore, junior, senior or graduate study at 4-year or graduate institution in United States. Designated institutions: Colleges and universities in California, Nevada, Hawaii, Arizona, New Mexico, Idaho, Washington, Colorado, Utah, Montana, Wyoming and Alaska.

Basis for selection: Major/career interest in journalism or radio/television/film. Applicant must demonstrate financial need, high academic achievement and seriousness of purpose.

Application requirements: Essay. May submit examples of broadcast-related work.

Additional information: Open to students pursuing career in broadcast journalism. Applications must be typed and mailed; no emailed or faxed submissions accepted. Visit Website for more information.

Amount of award:	$1,500
Number of awards:	1
Application deadline:	February 20

Contact:
AP West
Chris Havlik
1850 N. Central Avenue, Suite 640
Phoenix, AZ 85004
Phone: 602-417-2405
Web: www.aptra.com/scholar_about.asp

Association for Library and Information Science Education

ALISE Bohdan S. Wynar Research Paper Competition

Type of award: Scholarship.

Intended use: For undergraduate or graduate study.

Basis for selection: Competition/talent/interest in research paper, based on any aspect of library and information science using any methodology. Major/career interest in library science.

Application requirements: Paper must not exceed 35 double-spaced pages with one-inch margins and 12-point font. Two title pages, one with and one without author name(s) and institution.

Additional information: Research papers prepared by joint investigators eligible; at least one author must be member of Association for Library and Information Science Education. Winners expected to present papers at ALISE Annual Conference. Can submit only one paper per competition and may not submit same paper to other ALISE competitions. Paper cannot have been published, though may be accepted for publication. Papers completed in pursuit of master's and doctoral degrees not eligible, though data and spinoffs from such papers are eligible, as are papers generated through other grants and funding. Visit Website for detailed explanation of requirements.

Amount of award:	$2,500
Number of awards:	2
Number of applicants:	7
Application deadline:	July 15
Notification begins:	October 1
Total amount awarded:	$2,500

Contact:
ALISE
65 E. Wacker Place, Suite 1900
Chicago, IL 60601-7246
Phone: 312-795-0996
Fax: 312-419-8950
Web: www.alise.org

ALISE Research Grant

Type of award: Research grant.
Intended use: For non-degree study.
Basis for selection: Major/career interest in library science. Applicant must demonstrate high academic achievement.
Application requirements: Research proposal.
Additional information: Must be member of Association for Library and Information Science Education. Proposal must not exceed 20 double-spaced pages. Award to support research broadly related to education for library and information science. Visit Website for detailed explanation of proposal requirements. More than one grant may be awarded; however, total amount of funding for all grants not to exceed $5,000. Award cannot be used to support doctoral dissertation. Awardee(s) must present preliminary report at ALISE Annual Conference.

Amount of award:	$5,000
Application deadline:	October 1
Total amount awarded:	$5,000

Contact:
ALISE
65 E. Wacker Place, Suite 1900
Chicago, IL 60601-7246
Phone: 312-795-0996
Fax: 312-419-8950
Web: www.alise.org

ALISE/ProQuest Methodology Paper Competition

Type of award: Scholarship.
Intended use: For undergraduate or graduate study.
Basis for selection: Competition/talent/interest in research paper, based on description and discussion of a research method or technique. Major/career interest in library science.
Application requirements: Paper must not exceed 25 double-spaced pages with one-inch margins and 12-point font. Two title pages, one with and one without author name and institution. 200-word abstract.
Additional information: Papers prepared by joint authors eligible; at least one author must be member of Association for

Library and Information Science Education. Papers completed in pursuit of master's or doctoral degrees are eligible, as are papers generated as result of research grant or other source of funding. Papers that stress findings are ineligible. Winners expected to present papers at ALISE Annual Conference. May submit only one paper per competition and may not submit same paper to multiple ALISE competitions.

Amount of award:	$500
Number of awards:	1
Number of applicants:	8
Application deadline:	July 15
Notification begins:	October 1
Total amount awarded:	$500

Contact:
ALISE
2150 N 107th St
Suit 205
Seattle, wa 98133-7246
Phone: 312-795-0996
Fax: 312-419-8950
Web: www.alise.org

Association for Women in Architecture Foundation

Women in Architecture Scholarship

Type of award: Scholarship, renewable.
Intended use: For full-time sophomore, junior, senior or graduate study at 4-year or graduate institution.
Eligibility: Applicant must be female.
Basis for selection: Major/career interest in architecture; interior design; landscape architecture; urban planning; engineering, structural; engineering, civil; engineering, electrical/electronic or engineering, mechanical. Applicant must demonstrate high academic achievement.
Application requirements: Portfolio, recommendations, essay, transcript. SASE.
Additional information: Must be California resident or attending accredited California school to qualify. Students may also be studying land planning or environmental design. Must have completed minimum of 18 units in major by application due date. Applications may be downloaded from Website. Applications due in mid-April; see Website for exact date.

Amount of award:	$1,000
Number of awards:	5
Application deadline:	April 15
Total amount awarded:	$5,000

Contact:
Association for Women in Architecture Foundation
AWAF Scholarship
22815 Frampton Avenue
Torrance, CA 90501-5034
Phone: 310-534-8466
Fax: 310-257-6885
Web: www.awa-la.org/scholarships

Association for Women in Communications

Seattle Professional Chapter Scholarship

Type of award: Scholarship.
Intended use: For junior, senior or graduate study at accredited 4-year or graduate institution in United States. Designated institutions: Washington state colleges.
Eligibility: Applicant must be residing in Washington.
Basis for selection: Major/career interest in communications; journalism; radio/television/film; film/video; graphic arts/design; advertising; public relations or marketing. Applicant must demonstrate financial need and high academic achievement.
Application requirements: Transcript. Cover letter, resume, two work samples.
Additional information: Additional majors may include multimedia design, photography, or technical communication. Selection based on demonstrated excellence in communications and positive contributions to communications on campus or in community. Application deadline March/April; check Website for exact date. Amount and number of awards varies.

Amount of award:	$1,500
Number of awards:	2

Contact:
AWC Scholarships
P.O. Box 60262
Shoreline, WA 98160
Phone: 425-280-1968
Web: www.seattleawc.org

Association of Insurance Compliance Professionals

AICP Scholarship

Type of award: Scholarship, renewable.
Intended use: For full-time sophomore, junior, senior or master's study.
Basis for selection: Major/career interest in business; business/management/administration; economics; finance/banking; insurance/actuarial science; mathematics or statistics. Applicant must demonstrate high academic achievement.
Application requirements: Recommendations, transcript. Resume, short narrative describing current and future interest to pursue education/career in the insurance field.
Additional information: Minimum 3.0 GPA. Applicant must be at least a second-semester sophomore. Applicants with major/career interest in risk management also eligible. Deadline in early June.

Amount of award:	$1,500
Number of awards:	3
Number of applicants:	32
Application deadline:	June 2
Notification begins:	July 15

Contact:
Association of Insurance Compliance Professionals
12100 Sunset Hills Road, Suite 130
Reston, VA 20190
Phone: 703-234-4074
Fax: 703-435-4390
Web: www.aicp.net

Association of State Dam Safety Officials

ASDSO Undergraduate Scholarship

Type of award: Scholarship.
Intended use: For full-time senior study in United States.
Eligibility: Applicant must be U.S. citizen.
Basis for selection: Major/career interest in engineering, civil. Applicant must demonstrate financial need and high academic achievement.
Application requirements: Recommendations, essay, transcript.
Additional information: Must be planning to pursue career related to dam or levee safety. Minimum 2.5 GPA for first three years of college. Winners will also receive travel stipend to attend National Dam Safety Conference.

Amount of award:	$10,000
Number of awards:	3
Number of applicants:	20
Application deadline:	March 31
Notification begins:	July 1
Total amount awarded:	$10,000

Contact:
Association of State Dam Safety Officials
239 South Limestone Street
Lexington, KY 40508
Phone: 855-228-9732
Fax: 859-550-2795
Web: www.damsafety.org

Astanza

Astanza Q-Switched Laser Annual Scholarship

Type of award: Scholarship.
Intended use: For full-time undergraduate study at vocational, 2-year, 4-year or graduate institution.
Eligibility: Applicant must be at least 17. Applicant must be U.S. citizen.
Basis for selection: Major/career interest in physics; biology; engineering; medicine or nursing.
Application requirements: Transcript. Completed application form, scanned acceptance letter to accredited college/university, and scanned recent transcript (either from high school or college). Application e-mail should include a cover letter explaining why you are a good candidate for this scholarship and why you are pursuing an education in your field of choice.
Additional information: Application and guidelines on Website.

Amount of award:	$2,500
Application deadline:	June 30
Notification begins:	July 31
Total amount awarded:	$25,000

Contact:
Astanza
1770 Saint James Place
Houston, TX 77056
Web: www.astanzalaser.com/q-switched-laser-annual-scholarship

AutoInsuranceEZ.com

AIEZ Driver Safety Scholarship Contest

Type of award: Scholarship.
Intended use: For undergraduate study at vocational, 2-year or 4-year institution.
Eligibility: Applicant must be high school senior.
Application requirements: Essay. A 1500 word (or less) essay on driver safety, the specific essay prompt can be found at the website.
Additional information: All entries should be submitted to scholarship@autoinsuranceez.com.

Amount of award:	$1,000
Number of awards:	1
Application deadline:	May 31
Total amount awarded:	$1,000

Contact:
AutoInsuranceEZ.com
Phone: 855-406-0240
Web: www.autoinsuranceez.com/aiez-driver-safety-scholarship-contest/

AvaCare

AvaCare Medical Scholarship

Type of award: Scholarship.
Intended use: For full-time undergraduate study at 2-year, 4-year or graduate institution in United States.
Eligibility: Applicant must be U.S. citizen or permanent resident.
Additional information: Minimum 3.0 GPA. Must have a medical-related major. Applicants must submit a blog post, an image or a short video clip about an inspiring act of kindness. Submissions will be judged on content, creativity and quality of work. The final winner of the scholarship will be chosen based on a combination of AvaCare Medical judges' scores as well as public votes. Full details on website.

Number of awards:	1
Application deadline:	December 15
Total amount awarded:	$1,000

Contact:
AvaCare Medical Judges
1665 Corporate Road West
Lakewood, NJ 08701
Phone: 1-877-813-7799
Fax: 732-813-7798
Web: https://avacaremedical.com/scholarship

Avvo

Avvo Undergraduate/ Pre-law Scholarship

Type of award: Scholarship.
Intended use: For full-time in United States.
Basis for selection: Essay merit.
Application requirements: For students with the desire to attend law school and pursue a law degree to be applied to tuition and school expenses as needed.
Additional information: The Undergraduate/Pre-Law scholarship is open to students intending to pursue a graduate law program, including but not limited to those in an official pre-law program or common pre-law majors such as Political Science, Economics, Accounting or Finance, English, Philosophy, Criminal Justice, Engineering, and Medicine. 2014-15 is the first year of this program.

Amount of award:	$5,000
Number of awards:	1
Application deadline:	January 1

Contact:
Avvo Undergraduate/ Pre-law Scholarship
705 5th Ave S
Seattle, WA 98104
Web: scholarships.avvo.com/undergraduate-pre-law-student-scholarship/

AWeber

The AWeber Developing Futures Scholarship

Type of award: Scholarship.
Intended use: For undergraduate study at 4-year institution.
Application requirements: Complete and submit a 500-700 word essay OR create a video essay no longer than 3 minutes, that answers a prompt. Detailed instructions can be found on the scholarship webpage.

Number of awards:	1
Application deadline:	May 31
Total amount awarded:	$2,500

Contact:
AWeber
1100 Manor Drive
Chalfont, PA 18914
Web: www.aweber.com/email-marketing-scholarship.htm

AXA

AXA Achievement Scholarship

Type of award: Scholarship.
Intended use: For full-time freshman study at accredited 2-year or 4-year institution in United States.
Eligibility: Applicant must be high school senior. Applicant must be U.S. citizen or permanent resident.
Basis for selection: Applicant must demonstrate depth of character and seriousness of purpose.

Additional information: The AXA Achievement Scholarship is awarded to 52 students nationwide - one selected from each state, Washington, D.C. and Puerto Rico. Each state winner receives a scholarship award of $10,000. From that pool of 52 winners, ten are selected as national winners and receive an additional $15,000, bringing the national AXA Achievers' total scholarship awards to $25,000 each.

Amount of award:	$10,000-$25,000
Number of awards:	62

Contact:
Web: https://us.axa.com/axa-foundation/AXA-achievement-scholarship.html

AXA Foundation

AXA Achievement Scholarship

Type of award: Scholarship.
Intended use: For full-time undergraduate study at accredited 2-year or 4-year institution in United States.
Eligibility: Applicant must be high school senior. Applicant must be U.S. citizen.
Application requirements: Recommendations.
Additional information: Fifty-two (52) students will each receive a $10,000 scholarship, One recipient will be selected from each U.S. state, the District of Columbia, and Puerto Rico. From among these 52 recipients, ten (10) will be selected to receive an additional $15,000 scholarship, These national AXA Achievers will each be awarded scholarships totaling $25,000. Approximately 300 students will be selected to receive a $2,500 scholarship, These will be chosen per AXA Advisors branch office, Specific award amount - either $2,500, $10,000 or $25,000 - will be determined by Scholarship America, A student may only receive one AXA-sponsored scholarship, Every AXA Achiever's high school - no matter the amount of their scholarship - will receive a grant of $1,000. Visit Website for more information, application, and deadline date. Questions about the application process may be directed to Scholarship America's toll-free number or by e-mail to axaachievement@scholarshipamerica.org.

Amount of award:	$10,000-$25,000
Number of awards:	52
Number of applicants:	10,000
Application deadline:	December 15
Total amount awarded:	$670,000

Contact:
AXA Achievement Scholarship
Scholarship America
One Scholarship Way
Saint Peter, MN 56082
Phone: 800-537-4180
Web: www.axa-achievement.com

Ayn Rand Institute

Anthem Essay Contest

Type of award: Scholarship.
Intended use: For undergraduate study.
Eligibility: Applicant must be high school freshman or sophomore. Applicant must be residing in Wisconsin, Indiana or Illinois.

Application requirements: Essay between 600 and 1,200 words, typewritten and double-spaced.
Additional information: Rules, guidelines, and topic questions on Website. Award is in cash.

Amount of award:	$500-$2,000
Number of awards:	4
Number of applicants:	13,420
Application deadline:	April 19
Notification begins:	August 3
Total amount awarded:	$3,500

Contact:
Ayn Rand Institute
"Anthem" Essay Contest
P.O. Box 57044
Irvine, CA 92619
Phone: 949-222-6550
Fax: 949-222-6558
Web: www.aynrand.org/students/essay-contests

Atlas Shrugged Essay Contest

Type of award: Scholarship.
Intended use: For undergraduate or graduate study.
Eligibility: Applicant must be high school senior.
Basis for selection: Competition/talent/interest in writing/journalism, based on an outstanding grasp of the philosophic meaning of "Atlas Shrugged."
Application requirements: Essay between 800 and 1,600 words, typewritten and double-spaced. Rules, guidelines, and topic questions on Website.
Additional information: Student must be enrolled in full-time college degree program or 12th grade at time of entry. See Website for rules, guidelines, and topic questions. Award is in cash.

Amount of award:	$50-$20,000
Number of awards:	84
Number of applicants:	1,500
Application deadline:	October 23
Notification begins:	February 1
Total amount awarded:	$35,000

Contact:
The Ayn Rand Institute
Ayn Rand Essay Contest
P.O. Box 57044
Irvine, CA 92606
Phone: 949-222-6550
Fax: 949-222-6558
Web: www.aynrand.org/students/essay-contests

The Fountainhead Essay Contest

Type of award: Scholarship.
Eligibility: Applicant must be enrolled in high school.
Application requirements: Essay between 800 and 1,600 words, typewritten and double-spaced.
Additional information: Rules, guidelines, and topic questions on Website. Award is in cash.

Amount of award:	$50-$10,000
Number of awards:	236
Number of applicants:	3,000
Application deadline:	April 26
Notification begins:	July 26
Total amount awarded:	$43,250

Contact:
Ayn Rand Institute
"The Fountainhead" Essay Contest
P.O. Box 57044
Irvine, CA 92606
Phone: 949-222-6550
Fax: 949-222-6558
Web: www.aynrand.org/students/essay-contests

B'nai B'rith International

Diverse Minds Writing Challenge

Type of award: Scholarship.
Intended use: For undergraduate study.
Eligibility: Applicant must be enrolled in high school.
Applicant must be residing in District of Columbia, New York,
Delaware, New Jersey or Maryland.
Basis for selection: Judging will be based on the following
criteria: creativity, artistic and writing skill, clarity of message,
uniqueness of story topic, understanding for the intended
audience and appropriateness to the contest themes.
Application requirements: Applicants must create a 16 to 24
page children's story, accompanied by full-color illustrations,
that has themes of how tolerance, diversity and inclusion can
improve our world. Submissions must include a cover letter.
Entries may be sent through mail or email. See website for full
rules and details.
Additional information: Applicants must be high school
student residing in one of the following areas, and must meet
the associated deadline: Washington, DC Metro Area - March
18; Atlantic City Electric Region (southern New Jersey) -
March 11; Delmarva Peninsula (Delaware & Maryland) -
March 11; New York - March 25. Three awards per location:
$5000 for first place, $2000 for second place, $1000 for third
place.

Amount of award:	$1,000-$5,000
Number of awards:	12

Contact:
Diverse Minds Youth Writing Challenge
B'nai B'rith International
4605 Lankershim Boulevard, Suite 710
Los Angeles, CA 91602
Phone: 1-323-308-0195
Web: www.bnaibrith.org/diverse-minds.html

Back 2 School Illinois

Back 2 School Illinois College Scholarship Program

Type of award: Scholarship.
Intended use: For undergraduate study at 2-year or 4-year
institution in United States.
Eligibility: Applicant must be high school senior. Applicant
must be U.S. citizen residing in Illinois.
Basis for selection: Applicant must demonstrate high academic
achievement and leadership.
Application requirements: Recommendations, essay,
transcript, proof of eligibility. Applicants must provide an
official high school transcript which includes first semester

senior year grades and standardized test scores. Applicants also
need to provide two letters of recommendation (one from a
community service organization and one from their school), a
description of their community service activities.
Additional information: Must be Illinois Resident. The
Scholarship Program does not accept applications from children
or grandchildren of Back 2 School Illinois Board members or
employees. Applications are available through the program
URL link provided above or here: http://b2si.org/college-sch/ .

Amount of award:	$2,500
Number of awards:	7
Number of applicants:	50
Application deadline:	April 1
Notification begins:	April 15
Total amount awarded:	$17,500

Contact:
Back 2 School Illinois
3959 N Lincoln Avenue
Chicago, IL 60613
Phone: 847-268-3550
Web: http://b2si.org/college-sch/

Bariatric Surgery Source

The Future of Bariatric Surgery Scholarship

Type of award: Scholarship.
Intended use: For undergraduate or graduate study at
accredited vocational, 2-year, 4-year or graduate institution in
United States.
Eligibility: Applicant must be high school senior.
Basis for selection: Major/career interest in medicine.
Application requirements: Recommendations, transcript.
2,000 word essay describing how the field of bariatric surgery
will evolve over the next five years. Two letters of
recommendation.
Additional information: Must be currently majoring in any
medically-related degree or attending any medically-related
certification program. Apply using online application.

Amount of award:	$500-$1,000
Number of awards:	4
Application deadline:	January 1, July 1
Notification begins:	February 1, August 1
Total amount awarded:	$2,000

Contact:
Web: www.bariatric-surgery-source.com/bariatric-surgery-
scholarship.html

Barnett Howard and Williams Law Firm

Military Dependent Scholarship

Type of award: Scholarship.
Intended use: For full-time undergraduate study at accredited
4-year institution.
Eligibility: Applicant must be dependent of active service
person.

Application requirements: Candidates are encouraged to submit a valid dependent ID or DD-214 from one of their parents.

Additional information: Must have a minimum 2.5 GPA. Full details and application on website.

Number of awards:	1
Application deadline:	August 1
Notification begins:	August 15
Total amount awarded:	$500

Contact:

Web: https://www.bhwlawfirm.com/military-dependent-scholarship/

Barry Goldwater Scholarship and Excellence In Education Foundation

Barry Goldwater Scholarship

Type of award: Scholarship, renewable.

Intended use: For full-time junior or senior study at accredited 2-year or 4-year institution in United States.

Eligibility: Applicant must be U.S. citizen, permanent resident or U.S. national.

Basis for selection: Major/career interest in engineering; mathematics; natural sciences or engineering, computer. Applicant must demonstrate high academic achievement and seriousness of purpose.

Application requirements: Recommendations, essay, transcript, nomination by Goldwater faculty representative. Permanent resident nominees must include letter of intent to obtain U.S. citizenship and photocopy of Permanent Resident Card.

Additional information: Bulletin of information, nomination materials, application, and list of faculty representatives available on Website. Applicants must be legal residents of state in which they are candidates. Residents of District of Columbia, Puerto Rico, Guam, American Samoa, Virgin Islands, and Commonwealth of Northern Mariana Islands also eligible. Must have minimum 3.0 GPA and rank in top 25 percent of class. Application deadline in late January or early February; check Website for exact date.

Amount of award:	$7,500
Number of awards:	300
Notification begins:	April 1

Contact:

Barry Goldwater Scholarship and Excellence in Education Foundation
6225 Brandon Avenue
Suite 315
Springfield, VA 22150-2519
Phone: 703-756-6012
Fax: 703-756-6015
Web: https://goldwater.scholarsapply.org

Baurkot & Baurkot

Attorney Raymond Lahoud Scholar Program

Type of award: Scholarship.

Intended use: For sophomore, junior or senior study at 4-year or graduate institution.

Application requirements: Essay, transcript.

Additional information: Minimum 3.0 GPA. For students who wish to pursue a career in the legal profession. Must be enrolled in a 4-year college or university program and about to embark on their sophomore, junior, or senior year; OR be accepted, or already enrolled in an ABA-accredited law school and about to embark on their first, second, or third year of law school.

Amount of award:	$10,000
Number of awards:	5
Application deadline:	March 1
Notification begins:	April 1
Total amount awarded:	$50,000

Contact:

205 South 7th Street
Easton, PA 18042
Web: http://nationalimmigrationlawyers.com/legalscholars/

Benson And Bingham Attorneys At Law

Benson And Bingham First Annual Scholarship

Type of award: Scholarship.

Intended use: For full-time undergraduate or graduate study.

Eligibility: Applicant must be U.S. citizen or permanent resident.

Basis for selection: Major/career interest in law. Applicant must demonstrate high academic achievement.

Application requirements: Essay, transcript, proof of eligibility. Proof of Law School acceptance or attendance must accompany the application.Entrants for our scholarship must submit a minimum of a 600-word typed essay, more information about the essay topic can be found on the Website.

Additional information: Scholarship is for students who are persuing pre-law/law school. Scholarship is indeed available to Pre-Law undergraduates that are accepted to an accredited law school.Applications must be sent to the following email address: scholarship@bensonbingham.com , in the subject line, please reference: Benson & Bingham First Annual Scholarship Application. Questions regarding the application or process may be submitted to : scholarship@bensonbingham.com.

Amount of award:	$2,000-$2,000
Number of awards:	1
Application deadline:	August 31
Notification begins:	August 31
Total amount awarded:	$2,000

Contact:
Benson And Bingham
11441 Allerton Park Drive
Suit 100
Las Vegas, NV 89135
Phone: 858-720-0046
Fax: 702-382-9798
Web: https://www.bensonbingham.com/benson-bingham-first-annual-scholarship

Best Price Nutrition

Best Price Nutrition and Health Scholarship

Type of award: Scholarship.
Intended use: For full-time undergraduate study at 4-year institution.
Additional information: Best Price Nutrition is offering one student a $1,000 paid scholarship towards their academic costs for the 2015 school year. If any alumni wins this scholarship, $1,000 will be given to the school the alumni graduated from. The scholarship is paid to the school of the selected recipient. It will be paid in a one-time amount of $1,000 USD and sent directly to the school's financial aid office to be placed on the student's account. Currently residing in the United States. All eligible participants must be a currently enrolled full-time in college or an alumni. Student must provide the address of the college's Financial Aid Office. Student must provide college student identification number.

Amount of award:	$1,000
Number of awards:	1
Application deadline:	December 31
Total amount awarded:	$1,000

Contact:
Best Price Nutrition and Health Scholarship
5 Earl Court
Woodridge, IL 60517
Phone: 708-478-8143
Web: www.bestpricenutrition.com/scholarship.html

The Best Schools

The Best Schools Online Learning Scholarship

Type of award: Scholarship.
Intended use: For undergraduate or graduate study at accredited vocational, 2-year, 4-year or graduate institution.
Eligibility: Applicant must be at least 18. Applicant must be U.S. citizen or permanent resident.
Application requirements: Essay on the subject: how my online degree can help me achieve my career goals.
Additional information: Minimum 3.0 GPA. Student must be currently enrolled in an accredited online degree program.

Amount of award:	$1,000
Number of awards:	6
Application deadline:	November 1, March 1
Total amount awarded:	$6,000

Contact:
11237 South Forrestville Avenue
Chicago, IL 60628
Web: www.thebestschools.org/online-learning-scholarships/

Best Value

Best Value Education Scholarship

Type of award: Scholarship.
Intended use: For undergraduate or graduate study at vocational, 2-year, 4-year or graduate institution.
Application requirements: Essay prompt: "How will you use your education to create a stronger local economy?"
Additional information: Minimum 3.0 GPA. Application can be found online.

Number of awards:	1
Total amount awarded:	$500

Contact:
Web: www.bestvalueschools.org/best-value-scholarship/

Bethesda Lutheran Communities

Lutheran Student Scholastic and Service Scholarship

Type of award: Scholarship.
Intended use: For full-time freshman, junior or senior study at accredited 4-year institution in United States.
Eligibility: Applicant must be Lutheran.
Basis for selection: Major/career interest in social work; education; psychology; mental health/therapy; education, special; education, early childhood; education, teacher; speech pathology/audiology; occupational therapy or health-related professions. Applicant must demonstrate high academic achievement, seriousness of purpose and service orientation.
Application requirements: Recommendations, essay, transcript, proof of eligibility. Community service hours in support of people with intellectual and developmental disabilities.
Additional information: Applicant must be active member of Lutheran congregation with career objectives in the field of intellectual and developmental disabilities. Minimum 3.0 GPA. Seminary students also eligible to apply.

Amount of award:	$500-$3,000
Number of awards:	2
Number of applicants:	40
Application deadline:	May 1
Notification begins:	June 1
Total amount awarded:	$10,000

Contact:
Bethesda Lutheran Communities
Attn: Pam Bergen
600 Hoffmann Drive
Watertown, WI 53094
Phone: 920-206-4410
Fax: 920-206-7706
Web: www.bethesdalutherancommunities.org

Scholarships

225

The BHW Group

Women in STEM Scholarship

Type of award: Scholarship.
Intended use: For full-time undergraduate or graduate study at vocational, 2-year, 4-year or graduate institution.
Eligibility: Applicant must be female, high school senior.
Basis for selection: Major/career interest in science, general; mathematics; technology or engineering.
Application requirements: Essay. Applicants must write an essay on either of the following topics: Tell us about your favorite app and what you like about it; Tell us about a time an app played a significant role in improving your day. Your essay should be between 500-800 words. Feel free to be as formal or informal as you like. International students can apply if you are attending a US-based school. If your college is outside the US, yo ucannot apply at this time.
Additional information: More information and the application are found on the web page.

Amount of award:	$3,000-$3,000
Number of awards:	1
Number of applicants:	500
Application deadline:	April 17
Notification begins:	May 1
Total amount awarded:	$3,000

Contact:
The BHW Group
6011 W. Courtyard Drive
Suite 410
Austin, TX 78730
Phone: 512-220-0035
Web: https://thebhwgroup.com/scholarship

BioCommunications Association, Inc.

Endowment Fund For Education (EFFE)

Type of award: Scholarship.
Intended use: For full-time sophomore, junior, senior or graduate study at accredited vocational or 4-year institution.
Basis for selection: Major/career interest in arts, general; biomedical; communications or science, general.
Application requirements: Portfolio, recommendations, essay, transcript, proof of eligibility.
Additional information: For students pursuing careers in scientific/biomedical visual communications and scientific/biomedical photography.

Amount of award:	$500
Number of awards:	1
Application deadline:	April 30
Notification begins:	June 1
Total amount awarded:	$500

Contact:
BioCommunications Association, Inc.
220 Southwind Lane
Hillsborough, NC 27278-7907
Phone: 919-245-0906
Web: www.bca.org

Blinded Veterans Association

Kathern F. Gruber Scholarship Program

Type of award: Scholarship, renewable.
Intended use: For full-time undergraduate or graduate study at accredited postsecondary institution in United States.
Eligibility: Applicant must be U.S. citizen. Applicant must be dependent of disabled veteran; or spouse of disabled veteran who served in the Army, Air Force, Marines, Navy or Coast Guard.
Application requirements: Recommendations, essay, transcript.
Additional information: Dependent children, spouses and grandchildren of blinded veterans are eligible to include active duty blinded service members. The number of shcolarships a receipient may receive under this program is limited to four. Notification begins in late June.

Amount of award:	$2,000
Number of awards:	6
Number of applicants:	30
Application deadline:	April 15
Total amount awarded:	$12,000

Contact:
Blinded Veterans Association
125 NW Street 3rd Floor
Alexandria, VA 22314
Phone: 202-371-8880
Fax: 202-371-8258
Web: www.bva.org

Thomas H. Miller Scholarship

Type of award: Scholarship.
Intended use: For full-time undergraduate or graduate study at accredited postsecondary institution in United States.
Eligibility: Applicant must be U.S. citizen. Applicant must be dependent of disabled veteran; or spouse of disabled veteran who served in the Army, Air Force, Marines, Navy or Coast Guard.
Application requirements: Recommendations, essay, transcript.
Additional information: Dependent children, spouses, and grandchildren of blinded veterans are eligible to include active duty blinded service members. Preference given to applicants focusing on the arts. The number of scholarships recipient may receive under this program is limited to four. Notification begins late June.

Amount of award:	$1,000
Number of awards:	1
Number of applicants:	30
Application deadline:	April 21
Total amount awarded:	$1,000

Contact:
Blinded Veterans Association
125 NW Street 3rd Floor
Alexandria, VA 22314
Phone: 202-371-8880
Fax: 202-371-8258
Web: www.bva.org

Scholarships

Blue Kangaroo

Community Activist Scholarship

Type of award: Scholarship.
Intended use: For undergraduate study at accredited 2-year or 4-year institution in United States.
Eligibility: Applicant must be U.S. citizen.
Basis for selection: Applicant must demonstrate service orientation.
Application requirements: Recommendations. Less than 500 word essay describing your accomplishments in helping your community through activism. Photos or a video of your initiative. Letter of recommendation from a professor or community activist board member.
Additional information: Must have a minimum 3.0 GPA. Must participate in a community project or program.

Number of awards:	1
Application deadline:	December 31
Notification begins:	February 1
Total amount awarded:	$1,000

Contact:
Web: www.bluekangaroo.com/page/scholarship

BlueScope Foundation, N.A.

Bluescope Foundation Scholarship

Type of award: Scholarship, renewable.
Intended use: For full-time undergraduate study at accredited 4-year institution.
Eligibility: Applicant must be high school senior.
Basis for selection: Applicant must demonstrate financial need, high academic achievement, depth of character, leadership and service orientation.
Application requirements: Recommendations, essay, transcript. SAT/ACT scores, financial report.
Additional information: Applicant's parent must be employed by BlueScope Steel. Contact human resources office at workplace for information and application. Renewable up to four years.

Amount of award:	$3,000
Number of awards:	12
Number of applicants:	46
Application deadline:	February 15
Notification begins:	April 30
Total amount awarded:	$104,000

Contact:
BlueScope Foundation, N.A.
P.O. Box 419917
Kansas City, MO 64141-6917
Phone: 816-968-3208
Fax: 816-627-8993

BMI Foundation

BMI Founders Award for Radio Broadcasting

Type of award: Scholarship.
Intended use: For undergraduate or graduate study at accredited vocational, 2-year, 4-year or graduate institution in United States.
Eligibility: Applicant must be at least 17, no older than 24.
Basis for selection: Applicant must demonstrate high academic achievement.
Application requirements: Recommendations, essay, transcript. Must provide most recent transcript. One letter of recommendation from a full-time faculty member at their institution. Written submissions must be between 700-1500 words in length. Video submissions must be between six and twelve minutes in length.
Additional information: Minimum 3.0 GPA. Must be currently enrolled; students accepted for future enrollment are NOT eligible. Applicants should retain copies of their entries, as the Foundation will not undertake to return materials. Broadcasting degree candidates with an academic focus in radio broadcasting. Applicable majors include, but are not limited to: Broadcast and Emerging Media, Broadcast Communications, Broadcast Journalism, Broadcasting, Broadcasting and Mass Communications, Electronic Media and Broadcasting, and Radio and Television Broadcast Technology.

Amount of award:	$5,000
Number of awards:	1
Application deadline:	February 1
Total amount awarded:	$5,000

Contact:
BMI Foundation
7 World Trade Center
250 Greenwich Street
New York, NY 10007
Web: www.bmifoundation.org/broadcast

BMI Future Jazz Master Scholarship

Type of award: Scholarship.
Intended use: For full-time undergraduate or graduate study at vocational, 2-year, 4-year or graduate institution.
Eligibility: Applicant must be at least 17, no older than 24.
Application requirements: Applicants are required to submit three recordings (MP3 or MP4 files) of recent performances, at least one of these performed works must be original. There are no limitations to age, style, instrumentation, or voice. Applications will be judged on evidence of talent and potential as a jazz performer and composer.

Amount of award:	$5,000
Number of awards:	1
Application deadline:	February 1
Total amount awarded:	$5,000

Contact:
BMI Foundation
7 World Trade Center
250 Greenwich Street
New York, NY 10007
Web: bmifoundation.org/jazzmaster

Nashville Songwriting Scholarship

Type of award: Scholarship.
Intended use: For undergraduate or graduate study at vocational, 2-year, 4-year or graduate institution in United States.
Eligibility: Applicant must be at least 17, no older than 24.
Application requirements: Scholarship will be awarded for the best original song entry in any of the following genres: Americana, blues, bluegrass, contemporary Christian, country, folk, and roots. Applications must be submitted online. Applicants may submit only one song to the competition. The submitted work must be an original song with lyrics accompanied by whatever instrumentation is chosen by the applicant. Both lyrics and music must be original and not based on any prior work. The entry must be submitted as a MP3 or MP4a file, which should be named only with the title of the song. One copy of the lyrics must also be submitted as a PDF. Neither of these items may indicate the name of the applicant or their school. Applicants should retain copies of their recordings and lyrics since the Foundation will not undertake to return materials. In the case of a joint or co-written song: a) All applicants must meet all eligibility requirements; b) Such a jointly written work will be considered as a single entry; c) Should a jointly written work receive any type of award under this contest, the scholarship will be divided equally between applicants. Applicants must warrant that they have not assigned any rights in the submitted work to a major music publisher or major record label.
Additional information: Must be currently enrolled; students who have been accepted for future enrollment are NOT eligible. In any given year, songwriters who meet the above criteria may apply to either the Nashville Songwriting Scholarship or John Lennon Scholarships competition, but not both.

Amount of award:	$5,000
Number of awards:	1
Application deadline:	February 1
Total amount awarded:	$5,000

Contact:
7 World Trade Center
250 Greenwich Street
New York, NY 10007
Web: www.bmifoundation.org/nashville

BMI Foundation, Inc.

BMI Student Composer Awards

Type of award: Scholarship.
Intended use: For undergraduate or graduate study.
Eligibility: Applicant must be Citizen of a Western hemisphere country.
Basis for selection: Competition/talent/interest in music performance/composition, based on composition of classical music. Major/career interest in music.
Application requirements: PDF scores must be submitted online at website in contact information.
Additional information: Age Eligibility: 27 or younger. Check Website for rules and application. Must be enrolled in public, private, or parochial secondary schools; colleges or conservatories of music; or engaged in private study of music with recognized and established teachers (other than relatives). Visit Website for additional information.

Amount of award:	$500-$5,000
Application deadline:	February 1
Total amount awarded:	$20,000

Contact:
BMI Student Composer Awards
Deirdre Chadwick, Director
7 World Trade Center, 250 Greenwich St.
New York, NY 10007-0030
Web: www.bmifoundation.org/sca

John Lennon Scholarships

Type of award: Scholarship.
Intended use: For undergraduate or graduate study.
Eligibility: Applicant must be at least 17, no older than 25.
Basis for selection: Competition/talent/interest in music performance/composition, based on best song of any genre with original music and lyrics. Major/career interest in music or performing arts.
Application requirements: Music and lyrics of original song on CD or MP3 and three typed lyric sheets.
Additional information: Current students and alumnae at select schools may apply directly to Foundation; others must contact the National Association for Music Education chapter advisor at their college. Visit Website for deadlines, application, and more information.

Amount of award:	$5,000-$10,000
Number of awards:	3
Total amount awarded:	$20,000

Contact:
BMI Foundation, Inc.
John Lennon Scholarship Competition
7 World Trade Center, 250 Greenwich St.
New York, NY 10007-0030
Web: www.bmifoundation.org

PeerMusic Latin Scholarship

Type of award: Scholarship.
Intended use: For undergraduate or graduate study at postsecondary institution in or outside United States.
Eligibility: Applicant must be at least 16, no older than 24.
Basis for selection: Competition/talent/interest in music performance/composition, based on best song or instrumental work in any Latin genre with original music and lyrics. Major/career interest in music.
Application requirements: CD or MP3 of original song and typed lyric sheet. Should not include name of student or school.
Additional information: Applicants studying in Puerto Rico also eligible. Application deadline in February. Check Website for exact date and application.

Amount of award:	$5,000
Number of awards:	1

Contact:
BMI Foundation, Inc.
peermusic Latin Scholarship Competition
7 World Trade Center, 250 Greenwich St.
New York, NY 10007-0030
Web: http://bmifoundation.org/programs/info/peermusic_latin_scholarship

Scholarships

BMW of Freeport

BMW of Freeport Scolarship

Type of award: Scholarship.
Intended use: For freshman study at 4-year institution in United States.
Eligibility: Applicant must be high school senior.
Application requirements: Essay. BMW is considered The Ultimate Driving Machine and BMW of Freeport wants to know what drives you to succeed: In 1,000 to 1,500 words, write about what motivates you to succeed.
Additional information: Must have a minimum 3.0 GPA. Apply via e-mail.

Number of awards:	1
Application deadline:	August 3
Total amount awarded:	$500

Contact:
Web: www.bmwoffreeport.com/bmw-of-freeport-scholarship.html

BOG

The BOG Pest Control Scholarship

Type of award: Scholarship.
Intended use: For full-time undergraduate study at 4-year institution.
Basis for selection: Major/career interest in chemistry; engineering, chemical; biology or environmental science.
Application requirements: Recommendations, essay, transcript.

Number of awards:	1
Application deadline:	March 15
Notification begins:	May 27
Total amount awarded:	$1,000

Contact:
B.O.G Pest Control ATTN: Angela Osborne
645 Central Avenue E
#200
Edgewater, MD 21037
Web: www.bogpestcontrol.com/culture/bog-pest-control-scholarship-fund

Bounce Energy

Be More Scholarship

Type of award: Scholarship.
Intended use: For undergraduate or graduate study at vocational, 2-year, 4-year or graduate institution.
Eligibility: Applicant must be at least 13, no older than 24, high school senior.
Application requirements: Essay. Maximum 500-word essay responding to: "Bounce Energy considers itself to be more than just an electricity company. Going beyond just competitive electricity rates, we also offer customer rewards, community charity support opportunities, and other convenient products and services. Bounce Energy wants to know: how do you consider yourself to be more than just a student?"

Additional information: Must have a minimum 3.0 GPA. Must reside or attend school in Texas.

Amount of award:	$2,500
Number of awards:	3
Application deadline:	June 30
Notification begins:	August 31
Total amount awarded:	$7,500

Contact:
Bounce Energy
12 Greenway Plaza
Houston, TX 77046
Phone: 1-888-452-6862
Web: https://www.bounceenergy.com/scholarships

Box

Box Engineering Diversity Scholarship

Type of award: Scholarship.
Intended use: For full-time sophomore or junior study at accredited 4-year institution in United States.
Eligibility: Applicant must be Alaskan native, African American, Mexican American, Hispanic American or American Indian. Applicant must be female. Applicant must be U.S. citizen.
Basis for selection: Major/career interest in computer/information sciences; engineering or mathematics.
Additional information: Must identify with a minority group underrepresented in tech (female, LGBT, Hispanic, African American, or Native American). Must be a current college sophomore or junior. Must be enrolled in computer science, engineering, information technology, mathematics, or a related major. Must be able to travel to Box Headquarters in Los Altos, CA for the finalist weekend Nov 19-21 (Box will sponsor travel.)

Amount of award:	$4,000-$20,000
Number of awards:	5
Number of applicants:	150
Application deadline:	October 30
Notification begins:	November 20
Total amount awarded:	$36,000

Contact:
Box
4440 El Camino Real
Los Altos, CA 94022
Web: www.boxdiversityscholarship.com/

Boy Scouts of America Patriots' Path Council

Frank D. Visceglia Memorial Scholarship

Type of award: Scholarship, renewable.
Intended use: For full-time freshman study at accredited 4-year institution.
Eligibility: Applicant must be male, high school senior. Applicant must be U.S. citizen or permanent resident residing in New Jersey.

Additional information: Applicant must be an Eagle Scout. Preference given to Scouts whose service projects relate to the environment or economy. Application available online.

Amount of award:	$1,000
Number of awards:	1
Number of applicants:	35
Application deadline:	June 1
Notification begins:	August 1
Total amount awarded:	$1,000

Contact:
The Frank D. Visceglia Memorial Scholarship Program
Attn: Dennis Kohl
1 Saddle Road
Cedar Knolls, NJ 07927
Phone: 973-765-9322
Fax: 973-267-3407
Web: www.advancement.ppbsa.org/scholarship.htm

Boys and Girls Clubs of Greater San Diego

Spence Reese Scholarship

Type of award: Scholarship, renewable.
Intended use: For full-time undergraduate study at accredited 4-year institution in United States.
Eligibility: Applicant must be male, high school senior.
Basis for selection: Major/career interest in engineering; law; medicine or political science/government. Applicant must demonstrate financial need and high academic achievement.
Application requirements: Recommendations, transcript. SAT/ACT scores, college acceptance letter.
Additional information: One award in each of four eligible majors. Award is renewable for four years of study. Application available on Website.

Amount of award:	$4,000
Number of awards:	4
Number of applicants:	40
Application deadline:	April 1
Notification begins:	May 15
Total amount awarded:	$32,000

Contact:
Boys and Girls Clubs of Greater San Diego
Attn: Spence Reese Scholarship Committee
PO Box 178569
San Diego, CA 92177
Phone: 858-866-0591 ext. 201
Web: www.sdyouth.org/scholarships.aspx

Brainly

Brainly Everyone Knows Something Scholarship

Type of award: Scholarship.
Intended use: For freshman study at accredited 2-year or 4-year institution in United States.
Eligibility: Applicant must be at least 16, high school senior. Applicant must be U.S. citizen or permanent resident.

Application requirements: Essay. Answer our short essay question in 250 words or less: How have you helped teach another student and how has that impacted you? Entrants must have a free Brainly account.

Amount of award:	$1,000
Number of awards:	1
Application deadline:	May 31
Notification begins:	June 9
Total amount awarded:	$1,000

Contact:
Brainly
161 Bowery 2nd Floor
New York, NY 10002
Web: https://brainly.com/app/scholarship

Brandner Law Firm

Brandner Scholarship

Type of award: Scholarship.
Intended use: For freshman study at 4-year institution.
Eligibility: Applicant must be at least 17. Applicant must be residing in Louisiana.
Basis for selection: Major/career interest in law. Applicant must demonstrate high academic achievement and leadership.
Application requirements: Essay, transcript. Provide a 500 to 1,400 word essay on the prompt "How have your childhood experiences influenced your desire to pursue a career in law". Essay must be in PDF format with the file name lastname_firstname_blf.pdf. Applicant must have an official copy of their high school transcript.
Additional information: Open to all eligible college or university students in Louisiana. Must be planning to pursue a career as an attourney. Apply online.

Number of awards:	1
Application deadline:	July 31
Notification begins:	December 15
Total amount awarded:	$1,500

Contact:
Brandner Law Firm
610 Baronne St.
3rd floor
New Orleans, LA 70113
Phone: 504-552-5000
Fax: 504-521-7550
Web: www.brandnerlawfirm.com/scholarship/

Brandon Goodman Scholarship

BG Scholarship

Type of award: Scholarship.
Intended use: For undergraduate or graduate study at vocational, 2-year, 4-year or graduate institution.
Eligibility: Applicant must be U.S. citizen or permanent resident.
Basis for selection: Applicant must demonstrate financial need, high academic achievement and service orientation.
Application requirements: Essay.

Additional information: 2.0 minimum GPA. Twelve awards given monthly. Deadline is the last day of the month. Visit Website for application.

Amount of award:	$300
Number of awards:	144
Number of applicants:	7,200
Total amount awarded:	$4,200

Contact:
Brandon Goodman Scholarship
Phone: 949-547-9427
Web: www.bgscholarship.com/scholarship

Breyer Law Offices

Husband and Wife Law Team Arizona Scholarship

Type of award: Scholarship.
Intended use: For undergraduate study at accredited 2-year or 4-year institution.
Eligibility: Applicant must be high school senior. Applicant must be U.S. citizen or permanent resident residing in Arizona.
Application requirements: Essay. In your essay, write about your education goals, and how your education will help you better the Arizona community.
Additional information: Must have a minimum 2.8 GPA. Must be a resident of Arizona.

Number of awards:	1
Application deadline:	April 17
Notification begins:	May 17
Total amount awarded:	$1,000

Contact:
3840 East Ray Road
Phoenix, AZ 85044
Web: www.breyerlaw.com/az-scholarship/

Husband and Wife Law Team Scholarship

Type of award: Scholarship.
Intended use: For freshman study at 2-year or 4-year institution.
Eligibility: Applicant must be high school senior. Applicant must be U.S. citizen or permanent resident.
Application requirements: Transcript. Finalists will be asked to provide transcripts, proof of enrollment, and a copy of photo identification. 1000 word essay question can be found on website.
Additional information: Must have a minimum 2.8 GPA.

Number of awards:	1
Application deadline:	April 17
Notification begins:	May 17
Total amount awarded:	$1,000

Contact:
Breyer Law Offices
2942 North 24th Street
Suite 114
Phoenix, AZ 85016
Web: www.breyerlaw.com/scholarship/

BrightLife Direct

BrightLife Physical Therapist Scholarship

Type of award: Scholarship, renewable.
Intended use: For full-time sophomore, junior or senior study.
Eligibility: Applicant must be enrolled in high school. Applicant must be U.S. citizen.
Basis for selection: Major/career interest in physical therapy or occupational therapy. Applicant must demonstrate high academic achievement.
Application requirements: Recommendations, essay, transcript. Must be enrolled in a program accredited by CAPTE or ACOTE. At least one year of the program must be completed before the application deadline. Completed application. Official transcript, Current curriculum vitae, Proof of enrollment in CAPTE or ACTOE approved course. At least one letter of recommendation (includes the person's name, position, contact information and email). Complete a short essay (must explain why you decided to pursue an education in physical/occupational therapy, and what you hope to accomplish in your career, Essay should be no longer than one page in length).
Additional information: For additional information or to download an application please see: http://www.brightlifedirect.com/brightlife-physical-therapist-scholarship.asp.

Amount of award:	$1,000
Number of awards:	1
Application deadline:	July 14
Notification begins:	August 1
Total amount awarded:	$1,000

Contact:
BrightLife Direct
6925-D Willow Street NW
Washington, DC 20012
Phone: 877-545-8585
Web: www.brightlifedirect.com/brightlife-physical-therapist-scholarship.asp

Brilliant Earth

Brilliant Earth's Social Enterprise Scholarship

Type of award: Scholarship.
Intended use: For full-time undergraduate study at vocational, 2-year or 4-year institution in United States.
Eligibility: Applicant must be at least 16, no older than 22. Applicant must be U.S. citizen or permanent resident.
Application requirements: Essay. Essay of 800 words or less.
Additional information: Visit website for application and essay prompt.

Number of awards:	1
Application deadline:	December 8
Notification begins:	December 9
Total amount awarded:	$1,000

Contact:
26 O'Farrell Street
San Francisco, CA 94108
Phone: 703-596-1353
Web: www.brilliantearth.com/news/scholarship-2016/

BrisDigital

Digital Media and Marketing Scholarship

Type of award: Scholarship, renewable.
Intended use: For undergraduate study at 4-year institution.
Application requirements: Students who are interested in applying are required to compose an article application of up to 1000 words OR publish a video of up to 5 minutes about how you believe furthering your education can help to make the world a better place.
Additional information: Any full time university students at any globally recognized university or college are eligible. Further information can be found on scholarship webpage.

Amount of award:	$1,000
Number of awards:	1
Application deadline:	June 30
Notification begins:	July 10
Total amount awarded:	$1,000

Contact:
BrisDigital
11755 Wilshire Boulevard
Suite 1250
Los Angeles, CA 90025
Phone: 213-438-9509
Web: https://www.brisdigital.com.au/digital-media-marketing-scholarship/

Bristol-Myers Squibb

Bristol-Myers Squibb Scholarship for Cancer Survivors

Type of award: Scholarship.
Intended use: For full-time undergraduate study at accredited vocational, 2-year or 4-year institution.
Eligibility: Applicant must be at least 17, no older than 25, high school senior. Applicant must be U.S. citizen.
Basis for selection: Applicant must demonstrate high academic achievement, depth of character and leadership.
Application requirements: Transcript. Current complete transcript(s) of grades. Unofficial or online transcripts must display student name, school name, grade and credit hours earned for each course, and term in which each course was taken. Completed Applicant Appraisal Form.
Additional information: Applicants must be cancer survivors (diagnosed by a physician as having treatment of cancer and survived). More information about submitting applications can be found on the Website.

Amount of award:	$10,000
Number of awards:	50
Application deadline:	March 31
Total amount awarded:	$500,000

Contact:
Bristol-Myers Squibb Scholarship for Cancer Survivors
One Scholarship Way
St. Peter, MN 56082
Phone: 800-537-4180
Web: https://scholarsapply.org/cancer-survivors

Broadcast Education Association

BEA Founders Award

Type of award: Scholarship.
Intended use: For full-time undergraduate study at 2-year or 4-year institution. Designated institutions: BEA Institutional Member schools.
Basis for selection: Major/career interest in radio/television/film. Applicant must demonstrate high academic achievement, depth of character and seriousness of purpose.
Application requirements: Recommendations, essay, transcript.
Additional information: Preference given to students enrolled in BEA 2-Year/Small College Member Institution or graduates of these programs now enrolled in BEA 4-Year Institution. Should show evidence of potential in electronic media. Application available from campus faculty or on Website.

Amount of award:	$1,500
Number of awards:	2
Application deadline:	October 10
Total amount awarded:	$3,000

Contact:
Broadcast Education Association (BEA)
1771 N Street, N.W.
Washington, DC 20036-2891
Phone: 202-429-3935
Web: www.beaweb.org

Peter B. Orlik Scholarship

Type of award: Scholarship.
Intended use: For full-time junior, senior or graduate study at 4-year or graduate institution. Designated institutions: Scholalrship must be used on a campus that is an institutional member of the Broadcast Education Association.
Eligibility: Applicant must be enrolled in high school.
Application requirements: Recommendations, essay, transcript. Solid GPA is required.The online writable PDF forms ask for personal and academic data and transcripts, broadcast and other experience, a written statement of goals, and supportive statements from two references, one of which must be an electronic media faculty member. Major must be in some aspect of electronic media.
Additional information: Scholarship is for students who are pursuing major in some aspect of electronic media.

Amount of award:	$3,000
Number of awards:	1
Application deadline:	October 11
Notification begins:	November 25
Total amount awarded:	$3,000

Contact:
BEA
613 Kane Street
Mt. Pleasant, MI 48858
Phone: 989-774-3851
Web: www.beaweb.org

Richard Eaton Foundation Award

Type of award: Scholarship.
Intended use: For full-time junior, senior or graduate study at 4-year or graduate institution. Designated institutions: Scholalrship must be used on a campus that is an institutional member of the Broadcast Education Association.
Eligibility: Applicant must be enrolled in high school.
Application requirements: Solid GPA requested. Major must be in some aspect of electronic media.
Additional information: Scholarship is for students who are pursuing major in some aspect of electronic media.

Amount of award:	$3,000
Number of awards:	1
Application deadline:	October 11
Notification begins:	November 25
Total amount awarded:	$3,000

Contact:
BEA
613 Kane Street
Mt. Pleasant, MI 48858
Phone: 989-774-3851
Web: www.beaweb.org

Walter S. Patterson Scholarship

Type of award: Scholarship.
Intended use: For full-time junior, senior or graduate study at 4-year or graduate institution. Designated institutions: BEA Institutional Member schools.
Basis for selection: Major/career interest in radio/television/film. Applicant must demonstrate high academic achievement, depth of character and seriousness of purpose.
Application requirements: Recommendations, essay, transcript.
Additional information: Award intended for study in radio only. Should be able to show evidence of potential in electronic media. Application available from campus faculty or on Website.

Amount of award:	$1,750
Number of awards:	2
Application deadline:	October 10
Total amount awarded:	$3,500

Contact:
Broadcast Education Association (BEA)
1771 N Street, N.W.
Washington, DC 20036-2891
Phone: 202-429-5355
Web: www.beaweb.org

Brown and Caldwell

Brown and Caldwell Minority Scholarship Program

Type of award: Scholarship.
Intended use: For full-time junior, senior or graduate study at accredited 4-year or graduate institution.

Eligibility: Applicant must be Alaskan native, Asian American, African American, Mexican American, Hispanic American, Puerto Rican, American Indian or Native Hawaiian/Pacific Islander. Applicant must be U.S. citizen or permanent resident.
Basis for selection: Major/career interest in engineering, civil; engineering, chemical; engineering, environmental; environmental science; ecology; geology/earth sciences; biology or hydrology. Applicant must demonstrate high academic achievement.
Application requirements: Recommendations, essay, transcript. Resume.
Additional information: Minimum cumulative 3.0 GPA. Must have a declared major in civil, chemical, or environmental engineering, or a major in one of the environmental sciences (ie biology, geology, hydrogeology, or ecology). Scholarship is for Juniors and Seniors in college.

Amount of award:	$5,000
Number of awards:	4
Application deadline:	April 30
Total amount awarded:	$20,000

Contact:
Brown and Caldwell
Attn: HR/Scholarship Program
1527 Cole Boulevard, Suite 300
Lakewood, CO 80401
Web: www.brownandcaldwell.com/scholarships

Dr. W. Wes Eckenfelder Jr. Scholarship

Type of award: Scholarship.
Intended use: For full-time at accredited postsecondary institution.
Eligibility: Applicant must be U.S. citizen or permanent resident.
Basis for selection: Major/career interest in engineering, civil; engineering, chemical; engineering, environmental; environmental science; ecology; geology/earth sciences; hydrology or biology. Applicant must demonstrate high academic achievement.
Application requirements: Recommendations, essay, transcript. Resume.
Additional information: Minimum 3.0 GPA. Must have either a declared major in civil, chemical, or environmental engineering, or an environmental science (ie biology, geology, hydrogeology, ecology). Scholarship is for Juniors and Seniors in college.

Amount of award:	$5,000
Number of awards:	1
Application deadline:	April 30
Total amount awarded:	$5,000

Contact:
Brown and Caldwell
Attn: HR/Scholarship Program
1527 Cole Boulevard, Suite 300
Lakewood, CO 80401
Web: www.brownandcaldwell.com/scholarships

Brown, PC

National Founder's Undergraduate Business Student Scholarship

Type of award: Scholarship.
Intended use: For undergraduate study at 4-year institution in United States.

Eligibility: Applicant must be U.S. citizen.
Basis for selection: Major/career interest in business.
Application requirements: Submit a cover letter by e-mail summarizing interest and experience in entrepreneurship. Cover letter should contain: name, e-mail address, physical address, phone number, university name and location, student ID, GPA, and expected graduation date.
Additional information: Minimum 3.0 GPA. Awarded to a business student with a demonstrated interest in entrepreneurship.

Number of awards:	1
Application deadline:	August 7
Notification begins:	August 18
Total amount awarded:	$500

Contact:
Brown, PC
500 Main Street
Suite 400
Fort Worth, TX 76102
Phone: 817-870-0025
Fax: 817-870-0515
Web: www.browntax.com/National-Founders-Undergraduate-Business-Student-Scholarship.shtml

Brownstone Law

Brownstone Scholarship Program

Type of award: Scholarship.
Intended use: For undergraduate or graduate study at accredited 4-year or graduate institution in United States.
Eligibility: Applicant must be U.S. citizen or permanent resident.
Basis for selection: All scholarships are based on academic performance and for academic purposes. Scholarships are awarded only to students at an accredited academic university, college, or graduate program. On the basis of academic merit and taking into account the overall performance of the essay portion of the Program, along with potential and goals. Brownstone also looks to personal characteristics, as evidence by community participation, vocational interests and outside work or other evidence of self-help. Applicants have no right to appeal a decision regarding the winners of the Program. Applicant must demonstrate high academic achievement.
Application requirements: Online application and 1000 essay on following topic: Whether a 99 year state prison sentence-(without parole)-for a convicted, juvenile African American male is a de facto life-sentence that violates Eighth Amendment or, the due process clause of the Fourteenth Amendment? Essay can be mailed or emailed as a PDF or Word document.
Additional information: Minimum 3.0 GPA required. The scholarship is open to all current full-time and part-time undergraduate and graduate students in an ABA accredited law school or accredited graduate program.

Amount of award:	$1,000
Number of awards:	1
Application deadline:	April 1
Notification begins:	April 30

Contact:
201 North New York Avenue
Suite 200
Winter Park, FL 32789
Phone: 855-776-2773
Web: https://www.brownstonelaw.com/scholarships

Bryant Surety Bonds

Bryant Surety Bonds Scholarships

Type of award: Scholarship.
Intended use: For undergraduate or graduate study at accredited vocational, 2-year, 4-year or graduate institution in United States.
Eligibility: Applicant must be U.S. citizen.
Additional information: One scholarship is provided to the winner of an Essay contest, and one scholarship is provided to the winner of a visual content contest. Essay is 500-2,000 words, and visual content can be an image, infographic, cinemagraph, video, or slides. For prompts and full details, visit Website.

Amount of award:	$1,000
Number of awards:	2
Application deadline:	June 15
Notification begins:	June 30
Total amount awarded:	$2,000

Contact:
Scholarships Department
73 Old Dublin Pike
Suite 10 #306
Doylestown, PA 18901
Web: https://www.bryantsuretybonds.com/bryant-surety-scholarship-opportunities

Builders League of South Jersey

Builders League of South Jersey Scholarship Foundation Scholarships

Type of award: Scholarship, renewable.
Intended use: For full-time freshman study at accredited vocational, 2-year, 4-year or graduate institution.
Eligibility: Applicant must be residing in New Jersey.
Basis for selection: Major/career interest in construction or real estate. Applicant must demonstrate financial need.
Application requirements: Recommendations, transcript. County residency: Residents of Atlantic, Burlington, Camden, Cape May, Cumberland, Gloucester, or Salem counties in New Jersey.
Additional information: Scholarships will be awarded as a tuition payment directly to the institution of higher education. Students may reapply for the scholarship each year, as long as they continue their course of study.

Amount of award:	$1,000-$3,500
Application deadline:	April 28
Notification begins:	June 1

Contact:
Builders League of South Jersey Scholarship Foundation
114 Haddentowne Ct.
Cherry Hill, NJ 08034
Phone: 856-616-8460
Web: www.blsj.com/about/scholarship-foundation.html

Building Industry Association

BIA Cares of San Diego Scholarship

Type of award: Scholarship.

Intended use: For full-time sophomore, junior or senior study at postsecondary institution.

Eligibility: Applicant must be residing in California.

Basis for selection: Major/career interest in engineering, civil; real estate; construction; finance/banking; landscape architecture; engineering, construction; advertising; accounting; architecture or engineering, structural. Applicant must demonstrate financial need, high academic achievement and seriousness of purpose.

Application requirements: Interview, essay, transcript, proof of eligibility.

Additional information: For residents of San Diego who have either graduated from a San Diego County high school or are attending college in San Diego and are interested in careers in the building industry. Also open to students pursuing major/career as developer, contractor, soils engineer, designer, land planner, framer, plumber, electrician, carpenter, city planner, or other related profession. Number and amount of awards varies. See Website for application and deadline.

> **Number of applicants:** 7
> **Total amount awarded:** $15,000

Contact:
Building Industry Association of San Diego
c/o Nancy Diamond
9201 Spectrum Center Blvd., Suite 110
San Diego, CA 92123
Phone: 858-450-1221
Web: www.biasandiego.org/bia-cares

Bureau of Indian Education

Bureau of Indian Education Higher Education Grant Program

Type of award: Scholarship, renewable.

Intended use: For full-time undergraduate study at accredited 2-year or 4-year institution in United States.

Eligibility: Applicant must be American Indian. Member or at least one-quarter degree descendent of member of federally recognized tribe.

Basis for selection: Applicant must demonstrate financial need.

Application requirements: Proof of eligibility.

Additional information: Contacts or inquiries for these funds should be directed to the person's tribal headquarters. The Higher Education scholarships are not awarded through the D.C. offices. Award amount based on student's financial need. No application deadline.

> **Number of awards:** 12,000
> **Total amount awarded:** $25,000,000

Contact:
Bureau of Indian Education
Division of Post Secondary Education
215 Dean A McGee, Suite 610
Oklahoma City, OK 73102
Phone: 405-605-6001
Fax: 405-605-6010
Web: www.bie.edu

Bureau of Indian Education-Oklahoma Area Education Office

Osage Tribal Education Committee Program

Type of award: Scholarship.

Intended use: For undergraduate or graduate study at accredited postsecondary institution in United States.

Eligibility: Applicant must be American Indian. Must be member of Osage Tribe.

Basis for selection: Applicant must demonstrate high academic achievement.

Application requirements: Recommendations, essay, transcript, proof of eligibility. Signed statement of privacy, recent photo, test scores.

Additional information: Minimum 2.0 GPA. Part-time students funded at half rate. Application deadlines: July 1 for fall semester, December 31 for spring semester, and May 1 for summer semester (funds permitting). Contact Oklahoma Area Education Office for application and additional information.

> **Number of applicants:** 204
> **Application deadline:** July 1, December 31

Contact:
Bureau of Indian Affairs - Oklahoma Area Education Office
200 N.W. 4th Street
Suite 4049
Oklahoma City, OK 73102
Phone: 405-605-6051 ext. 304
Web: www.osagetribe.com/education

BuyerSynthesis Inc.

BuyerSynthesis Marketing Research Scholarship

Type of award: Scholarship.

Intended use: For full-time undergraduate study at accredited 4-year or graduate institution.

Eligibility: Applicant must be at least 18, high school senior. Applicant must be U.S. citizen or permanent resident.

Basis for selection: Entries will be judged on: creativity and humor; originality; intellectual content. Major/career interest in marketing; business; economics or social/behavioral sciences.

Application requirements: Pick a current product, service, company, or organization that could benefit from marketing research, and communicate the reasons for your choice in the most interesting, creative and compelling way possible, such as a video (max 4-5 minutes), essay, (3-5 paragraphs), series of photos, or combination of these forms. Include: a picture of the company, product or ad; one-sentence caption from the perspective of the photo subject describing why marketing research is needed; why you think the product/service/advertisement needs marketing research help.

Additional information: See website for full details on how to apply for the scholarship.

Amount of award:	$1,000
Number of awards:	1
Number of applicants:	12
Application deadline:	May 15
Notification begins:	June 15
Total amount awarded:	$1,000

Contact:
BuyerSynthesis Inc.
3700 Quebec Street #100
PMB 105
Denver, CO 80207
Phone: 303-321-9979
Web: www.buyersynthesis.com/blueocean/buyersynthesis-marketing-research-scholarship-rules-of-entry/

Café Bustelo

El Café del Futuro Scholarship Essay Contest

Type of award: Scholarship.
Intended use: For full-time undergraduate study.
Eligibility: Applicant must be Mexican American, Hispanic American or Puerto Rican. Latino descent. Applicant must be U.S. citizen or permanent resident.
Basis for selection: The essay must be submitted on the contest website along with a letter of recommendation and official proof of current enrollment and registration from the college or university being attended. All essays and recommendation letters will be judged by a qualified panel of judges and assigned points based on criteria and point system.
Application requirements: Recommendations. Students should complete all requirements in the online application on the HACE website and, in 800 words or less, write an essay in English or Spanish responding to the following topic: Describe how your Latino heritage, family, and the community in which you grew up have impacted your desire and motivation to obtain a college degree. Additionally, describe what you intend to accomplish with your degree and how you will give back to your community.
Additional information: To be eligible for the 2014 El Café del Futuro Scholarship Essay Contest, students must be 18 years of age or older and of Latino decent, currently enrolled full-time at a college or university and permanent legal residents of the United States.

Amount of award:	$5,000
Number of awards:	9
Application deadline:	January 15
Notification begins:	April 15
Total amount awarded:	$45,000

Contact:
El Café del Futuro Scholarship Essay Contest
5605 NW 82nd Avenue
Doral, FL 33166
Phone: 305-492-2746
Web: www.haceonline.org/café_bustelo_scholarship

California Association of Realtors Scholarship Foundation

C.A.R. Scholarship

Type of award: Scholarship, renewable.
Intended use: For undergraduate or graduate study at 2-year or 4-year institution. Designated institutions: California colleges/universities.
Eligibility: Applicant must be U.S. citizen residing in California.
Basis for selection: Major/career interest in real estate. Applicant must demonstrate financial need and high academic achievement.
Application requirements: Recommendations, essay, transcript, proof of eligibility. Photocopy of valid CA driver's license or ID card.
Additional information: Must be California resident of at least one year before applying. Awarded to all eligible applicants. Students attending two-year colleges receive up to $2,000; four-year college/university students receive up to $4,000. May receive one award per year, maximum two years. Minimum 2.6 GPA. Must have completed minimum 12 college-level course units within last four years; at least two courses in real estate or real-estate related. Must be enrolled in one real estate course at the time of submission of application. Visit Website for application, exact deadlines, and other information.

Amount of award:	$2,000-$4,000

Contact:
California Association of Realtors Scholarship Foundation
525 South Virgil Avenue
Los Angeles, CA 90020-1403
Phone: 213-739-8200
Fax: 213-739-7724
Web: www.car.org/aboutus/carscholarships

California Farm Bureau Federation

California Farm Bureau Scholarship

Type of award: Scholarship, renewable.
Intended use: For full-time undergraduate study at accredited 4-year institution. Designated institutions: Colleges/universities in California.
Eligibility: Applicant must be U.S. citizen residing in California.
Basis for selection: Major/career interest in agriculture; agribusiness; engineering, agricultural or veterinary medicine. Applicant must demonstrate high academic achievement, leadership and seriousness of purpose.
Application requirements: Recommendations, transcript.
Additional information: Must be preparing for career in agricultural industry and a member of the Collegiate Farm Bureau in California. Visit Website for application. Number and amount of awards vary. Notification begins late May/early June.

Number of applicants: 250
Application deadline: March 1
Total amount awarded: $165,750
Contact:
California Farm Bureau Scholarship Foundation
2300 River Plaza Drive
Sacramento, CA 95833
Phone: 916-561-5500
Web: www.cfbf.com/scholarship

California Precast Concrete Association

Mel C. Marshall Scholarship

Type of award: Scholarship, renewable.
Intended use: For undergraduate study at vocational, 2-year or 4-year institution in United States.
Eligibility: Applicant must be residing in California.
Basis for selection: Major/career interest in construction; accounting; information systems; engineering, civil or engineering, structural.
Application requirements: Recommendations, transcript, nomination. Transcript of high school/college grades through the latest grading period with ACT/SAT scores and class standing. Letter of recommendation from the high school or college faculty. Letter of sponsorship from a CPCA member considered to be in good standing (contact the CPCA office if you need help contacting a member).
Additional information: Must have a minimum 2.5 GPA. Student's academic field must be related to the building, construction, or PRECAST concrete industry (can include safety, accounting, IT, etc). Must be a California resident.
Amount of award: $500
Number of awards: 5
Number of applicants: 1
Application deadline: October 30, April 30
Notification begins: November 30, May 30
Total amount awarded: $5,000
Contact:
California Precast Concrete Association
P O Box 417
Rocklin, CA 95677
Phone: 916-259-2629
Fax: 866-831-2790
Web: www.caprecastconcrete.org/scholarship

California Student Aid Commission

Cal Grant A & B Entitlement Award Program

Type of award: Scholarship, renewable.
Intended use: For undergraduate study at postsecondary institution. Designated institutions: Qualifying California postsecondary schools.
Eligibility: Applicant must be high school senior. Applicant must be U.S. citizen or permanent resident residing in California.

Basis for selection: Applicant must demonstrate financial need and high academic achievement.
Application requirements: FAFSA, GPA verification form.
Additional information: Applicants who graduated in the last year and high school graduates transferring from a California community college with a minimum 2.4 GPA are also eligible. Awards given to all eligible applicants. Minimum 3.0 GPA for Cal Grant A; minimum 2.0 GPA for Cal Grant B. Cal Grant A provides tuition and fees. Cal Grant B awards up to $1,473 the first year and $1,473 plus tuition and fees for years two through four. Visit Website or contact CSAC for more details.
Amount of award: $1,473-$12,192
Application deadline: March 2
Notification begins: February 15
Contact:
California Student Aid Commission
Student Support Services Branch
P.O. Box 419027
Rancho Cordova, CA 95741-9027
Phone: 888-224-7268 opt. 3
Fax: 916-464-8240
Web: www.calgrants.org

Cal Grant A and B Competitive Awards

Type of award: Scholarship, renewable.
Intended use: For undergraduate study at postsecondary institution. Designated institutions: Qualifying California postsecondary schools.
Eligibility: Applicant must be U.S. citizen or permanent resident residing in California.
Basis for selection: Applicant must demonstrate financial need and high academic achievement.
Application requirements: FAFSA, GPA verification form.
Additional information: Minimum 3.0 GPA for Cal Grant A; minimum 2.0 GPA for Cal Grant B. Cal Grant A pays tuition and fees. Cal Grant B awards up to $1,473 first year and $1,473 plus tuition and fees for years two through four. Students with no available GPA can submit SAT, ACT, or GED scores. Visit Website or contact CSAC for more details.
Amount of award: $1,473-$12,192
Number of awards: 22,500
Application deadline: March 2, September 2
Notification begins: April 30, October 15
Contact:
California Student Aid Commission
Student Support Services Branch
P.O. Box 419027
Rancho Cordova, CA 95741-9027
Phone: 888-224-7268 opt. 3
Fax: 916-464-8240
Web: www.calgrants.org

Cal Grant C Award

Type of award: Scholarship, renewable.
Intended use: For undergraduate study at vocational or 2-year institution. Designated institutions: Qualifying California postsecondary institutions.
Eligibility: Applicant must be U.S. citizen or permanent resident residing in California.
Basis for selection: Applicant must demonstrate financial need.
Application requirements: FAFSA, GPA verification form.
Additional information: Funding is available for up to two years, and vocational program must be at least four months in length. Visit Website or contact CSAC for more details.

Amount of award:	$547-$2,462
Number of awards:	7,761
Application deadline:	March 2
Notification begins:	May 30

Contact:
California Student Aid Commission
Student Support Services Branch
P.O. Box 419027
Rancho Cordova, CA 95741-9027
Phone: 888-224-7268 opt. 3
Fax: 916-464-8240
Web: www.calgrants.org

California Chafee Grant Program

Type of award: Scholarship, renewable.
Intended use: For undergraduate or graduate study at accredited postsecondary institution.
Eligibility: Applicant must be no older than 21.
Basis for selection: Applicant must demonstrate financial need.
Application requirements: FAFSA, Chafee Need Analysis Report.
Additional information: Must be current or former foster youth from any state attending a California college or current foster youth from California attending any college. Foster youth dependency of the court must have been established between the ages of 16 to 18. Students must maintain satisfactory academic progress. School must report financial need on the Chafee Need Analysis Report. Must not have reached 22nd birthday by July 1st of award year. Must be enrolled at least half-time in course of study lasting at least one academic year. Renewable through 23rd birthday. Apply early.

Amount of award:	$5,000
Number of awards:	3,143
Notification begins:	July 1

Contact:
California Student Aid Commission
Attn: Specialized Programs Operations Branch
P.O. Box 419029
Rancho Cordova, CA 95741-9029
Phone: 888-224-7268
Fax: 916-464-8240
Web: www.chafee.csac.ca.gov

California Child Development Grant Program

Type of award: Scholarship.
Intended use: For undergraduate study at accredited 2-year or 4-year institution. Designated institutions: California postsecondary institutions.
Eligibility: Applicant must be U.S. citizen or permanent resident residing in California.
Basis for selection: Major/career interest in education, early childhood. Applicant must demonstrate financial need.
Application requirements: Recommendations, nomination by postsecondary institution or employing agency. FAFSA.
Additional information: Recipients attending two-year institutions receive up to $1,000 annually; those attending four-year institutions receive up to $2,000 annually. Recipients must maintain at least half-time enrollment in approved course of study leading to Child Development Permit in one of following levels: Teacher, Master Teacher, Site Supervisor or Program Director. Must maintain satisfactory academic progress, meet federal Selective Service filing requirements, and commit to one year of full-time employment in licensed child care center for every year they receive the grant. Deadlines and notification dates vary. Visit Website for application and more information.

Amount of award:	$1,000-$2,000
Number of awards:	100
Number of applicants:	894
Total amount awarded:	$277,000

Contact:
California Student Aid Commission
Attn: Child Development Grant Program
P.O. Box 419029
Rancho Cordova, CA 95741-9029
Phone: 888-224-7268 opt. 3
Fax: 916-464-8240
Web: www.csac.ca.gov

California Law Enforcement Personnel Dependents Grant Program (LEPD)

Type of award: Scholarship, renewable.
Intended use: For undergraduate study at accredited 2-year or 4-year institution. Designated institutions: California postsecondary institutions.
Eligibility: Applicant must be U.S. citizen residing in California. Applicant's parent must have been killed or disabled in work-related accident as firefighter, police officer or public safety officer.
Basis for selection: Applicant must demonstrate financial need.
Application requirements: SAR, birth certificate (not required for spouse), death certificate, findings of Workers' Compensation Appeals Board.
Additional information: Applicant must be dependent or spouse of California peace or law enforcement officer, officer or employee of Department of Corrections or Division of Juvenile Justice in California, or California firefighter, who was killed or 100 percent disabled in performance of duty. Number of awards varies.

Amount of award:	$100-$12,192
Number of applicants:	7
Notification begins:	February 1
Total amount awarded:	$21,460

Contact:
California Student Aid Commission
LEPD Program
P.O. Box 419029
Rancho Cordova, CA 95741-9029
Phone: 888-224-7268 opt. 5
Fax: 916-464-8240
Web: www.csac.ca.gov

California Teachers Association

California Teachers Association Martin Luther King, Jr., Memorial Scholarship

Type of award: Scholarship.
Intended use: For undergraduate or graduate study at accredited postsecondary institution.

Eligibility: Applicant must be Alaskan native, Asian American, African American, Mexican American, Hispanic American, Puerto Rican, American Indian or Native Hawaiian/Pacific Islander. Applicant must be residing in California.
Basis for selection: Major/career interest in education; education, early childhood; education, special or education, teacher. Applicant must demonstrate financial need.
Application requirements: Recommendations, essay, transcript, proof of eligibility.
Additional information: Must be active California Teachers Association (CTA) member, active Student CTA member, or dependent child of an active, retired, or deceased CTA member. Amount of award and number of awards varies. To receive funds, must show proof of registration in approved credential or degree program. Must pursue teaching-related career in public education. Application must be typed and mailed. Check Website for deadline and additional information.

Amount of award:	$4,000
Application deadline:	February 17

Contact:
CTA Scholarship Committee Human Rights Department
c/o Janeya Dawson
P.O. Box 921
Burlingame, CA 94011-0921
Phone: 650-697-1400
Fax: 650-552-5001
Web: www.cta.org/scholarships

CTA Scholarship for Dependent Children

Type of award: Scholarship, renewable.
Intended use: For full-time undergraduate or graduate study at accredited postsecondary institution.
Eligibility: Applicant must be residing in California.
Basis for selection: Major/career interest in education. Applicant must demonstrate high academic achievement, depth of character, leadership, seriousness of purpose and service orientation.
Application requirements: Recommendations, essay, transcript, proof of eligibility.
Additional information: Applicant must be dependent child of active, retired, or deceased member of California Teachers Association. Application deadline between end of January and beginning of February; visit Website for exact date and the most current information. Number of awards varies.

Amount of award:	$3,000-$5,000
Number of awards:	34

Contact:
CTA Scholarship Committee Human Rights Department
c/o Janeya Dawson
P.O. Box 921
Burlingame, CA 94011-0921
Phone: 650-552-5446
Fax: 650-552-5001
Web: www.cta.org/scholarships

CTA Scholarships for Members

Type of award: Scholarship, renewable.
Intended use: For full-time undergraduate or graduate study at accredited postsecondary institution.
Eligibility: Applicant must be residing in California.
Basis for selection: Major/career interest in education; education, early childhood; education, special or education, teacher. Applicant must demonstrate high academic achievement, depth of character, leadership, seriousness of purpose and service orientation.

Application requirements: Recommendations, essay, transcript, proof of eligibility.
Additional information: Applicant must be active member of California Teachers Association (including members working on emergency credential). Application deadline is between end of January and beginning of February; visit Website for exact date and the most up-to-date information. Number of awards varies.

Amount of award:	$3,000
Number of awards:	5
Application deadline:	February 3

Contact:
CTA Scholarship Committee Human Rights Department
c/o Janeya Dawson
P.O. Box 921
Burlingame, CA 94011-0921
Phone: 650-697-1400
Fax: 650-552-5001
Web: www.cta.org/scholarships

GLBT Guy DeRosa Safety in Schools Grant and Scholarship Program

Type of award: Scholarship.
Intended use: For undergraduate or graduate study at 2-year, 4-year or graduate institution.
Application requirements: Essay, proof of eligibility.
Additional information: Awards support projects and presentations that promote understanding and respect for GLBT persons and GLBT educators. Must be active California Teachers Association (CTA) member, active Student CTA member, or a public school student or district nominated by a CTA or SCTA member. Number of awards varies. Both grants and scholarships available. Check Website for deadline and additional information. Application must be typed and mailed.

Amount of award:	$2,000

Contact:
California Teachers Association
Human Rights Department
1705 Murchison Drive
Burlingame, CA 94011-0921
Phone: 650-552-5446
Fax: 650-552-5001
Web: www.cta.org/scholarships

L. Gordon Bittle Memorial Scholarship for SCTA

Type of award: Scholarship, renewable.
Intended use: For full-time undergraduate, graduate or non-degree study at accredited postsecondary institution.
Basis for selection: Major/career interest in education; education, early childhood; education, special or education, teacher. Applicant must demonstrate high academic achievement, depth of character and service orientation.
Application requirements: Recommendations, essay, transcript.
Additional information: Applicant must be active member of Student CTA. Must pursue career in public education. Not available to CTA members currently working in schools. May be enrolled in teacher credential program. Application deadline is between end of January and beginning of February; visit Website for exact date and more information.

Amount of award:	$5,000
Number of awards:	3
Number of applicants:	20

Contact:
CTA Scholarship Committee Human Rights Department
c/o Janeya Dawson
P.O. Box 921
Burlingame, CA 94011-0921
Phone: 650-552-5446
Fax: 650-552-5001
Web: www.cta.org/scholarships

Californians for Population Stabilization

Crowdifornia Essay Writing Competition

Type of award: Scholarship.
Intended use: For full-time undergraduate or graduate study at vocational, 2-year, 4-year or graduate institution.
Eligibility: Applicant must be at least 18. Applicant must be U.S. citizen.
Application requirements: Essay. Essay contest: 500-750 word essay focusing on overpopulation in California and its effects on the environment, the quality of human life, and the benefits that a stabilized population would bring.

Amount of award:	$500-$1,500
Number of awards:	3
Application deadline:	November 30
Notification begins:	December 31
Total amount awarded:	$3,000

Contact:
Californians for Population Stabilization
1129 State Street
Suite 3D
Santa Barbara, CA 93101
Web: Crowdifornia.com

Cantor Law Group

Cantor Crane Personal Injury Lawyer Scholarship Fund

Type of award: Scholarship, renewable.
Intended use: For full-time undergraduate or graduate study at 2-year, 4-year or graduate institution in United States.
Eligibility: Applicant must be at least 18.
Basis for selection: Cantor Crane will use a randomizing algorithm of all eligible entries to determine the winner. The winner will have one year from the date of the award to provide a tuition invoice from the school of their choice. The scholarship award will be in the amount of $1,000 and a check will be sent directly to the college or university that is designated by the winner. Major/career interest in law.
Application requirements: Must fill out the form on website and all required form fields. Your full name, address, phone and email address must be submitted.
Additional information: Must be pursing degree or career in/as: Law, Pre-law, Paralegal.

Amount of award:	$1,000-$1,000
Number of awards:	1
Application deadline:	July 31
Notification begins:	August 21
Total amount awarded:	$1,000

Contact:
Cantor Crane Personal Injury Lawyer Scholarship Fund
1 East Washington Street
Suite 1800
Phoenix, AZ 85004
Web: www.cantorcrane.com/personal-injury-lawyer-student-scholarship-fund

Capital One

Capital One Virginia Military Dependent Scholarship

Type of award: Scholarship.
Intended use: For undergraduate study at accredited 2-year or 4-year institution.
Eligibility: Applicant must be high school senior. Applicant must be U.S. citizen or permanent resident residing in Virginia. Applicant must be dependent of active service person.
Application requirements: Essay. Current High School senior. Attending accredited college or university in the upcoming academic year. Applicant must be a dependent of an active duty Service Member, or dependent of a Service Member in the National Guard or Reserves. GPA and SAT and/or ACT are required.
Additional information: The purpose of this scholarship is to aid and honor talented high school seniors who are dependents of Service Members, and have exemplified excellence through school work and community involvement.

Amount of award:	$5,000-$5,000
Number of awards:	1
Number of applicants:	30
Application deadline:	April 30
Notification begins:	May 31
Total amount awarded:	$5,000

Contact:
Capital One
4881 Cox Road
Glen Allen, VA 23060
Web: https://www.surveymonkey.com/r/N7FGQ2C

Cards Against Humanity

Science Ambassador Scholarship

Type of award: Scholarship, renewable.
Intended use: For undergraduate or graduate study at 4-year institution in United States.
Eligibility: Applicant must be female, enrolled in high school.
Basis for selection: Major/career interest in science, general; engineering; technology or mathematics.
Application requirements: Three minute mini-lecture on a scientific topic, submitted as a public YouTube video link.

Amount of award:	Full tuition
Number of awards:	2
Number of applicants:	1,200
Application deadline:	December 11
Notification begins:	March 27

Contact:
Web: www.scienceambassadorscholarship.org/

Caring.com

Caring.com Student Caregiver Scholarship

Type of award: Scholarship.
Intended use: For undergraduate or graduate study in United States.
Eligibility: Applicant must be U.S. citizen.
Additional information: Students must answer questions about being a caregiver in either the form of an essay or video submission. See website for application and complete details.

Amount of award:	$1,500
Number of awards:	3
Application deadline:	June 30
Notification begins:	February 1

Contact:
Web: www.caring.com/scholarship

Carl's Jr. Restaurants

Carl N. & Margaret Karcher Founders' Scholarship

Type of award: Scholarship.
Intended use: For full-time freshman study at accredited vocational, 2-year or 4-year institution.
Eligibility: Applicant must be no older than 21, high school senior. Applicant must be residing in Utah, Texas, Alaska, Washington, Arizona, Nevada, Oklahoma, California, Oregon, Idaho, New Mexico, Colorado or Hawaii.
Application requirements: Transcript.
Additional information: High school graduates also eligible. Employees, affiliates, and franchisees of Carl Karcher Enterprises, Inc., Scholarship America, affiliated agencies and their immediate families are ineligible. Application available on Website beginning in January. Visit Website for deadline.

Amount of award:	$1,000
Number of awards:	60
Total amount awarded:	$60,000

Contact:
Carl N. & Margaret Karcher Founders' Scholarship
c/o Scholarship America
One Scholarship Way
St. Peter, MN 56082
Phone: 507-931-1682
Web: www.carlsjr.com/scholarship

Carolina Pest Management

Going Green With Carolina Pest Management

Type of award: Scholarship.
Intended use: For full-time undergraduate study at accredited vocational, 2-year, 4-year or graduate institution in United States.
Eligibility: Applicant must be U.S. citizen or permanent resident.
Application requirements: 1,000 to 1,500 word essay.

Number of awards:	1
Application deadline:	February 28
Notification begins:	March 31
Total amount awarded:	$1,000

Contact:
Web: www.carolinapest.com/scholarship/

Casa Circulo Cultural

Community Impact Scholarship Program

Type of award: Scholarship.
Intended use: For full-time freshman study at accredited 4-year institution.
Eligibility: Applicant must be high school senior. Applicant must be residing in California.
Application requirements: Interview, recommendations. Two letters of recommendation. Must write a proposal for a high-impact, community service project, 300-500 words in length.
Additional information: Must have a minimum 3.0 GPA.

Amount of award:	$2,500-$10,000
Number of awards:	5
Application deadline:	January 9
Notification begins:	January 11

Contact:
Casa Circulo Cultural
1757 East Bayshore Road
Redwood City, CA 94063
Web: http://cccisp.org/

Casper

Casper Scholarship Program

Type of award: Scholarship.
Intended use: For full-time freshman study at accredited vocational, 2-year or 4-year institution.
Eligibility: Applicant must be high school senior.
Application requirements: High school academic records and GPA, SAT or ACT scores, and acceptance or admissions offer from your School.
Additional information: Minimum 3.5 GPA. Minimum SAT score of 1800 or ACT score of 26. Available to graduating High School seniors who are enrolling as full-time freshman at any accredited university, college, technical or vocational school. Application and full details on web site.

Number of awards: 1
Application deadline: March 5
Total amount awarded: $2,000
Contact:
Web: https://casper.com/scholarships

Catching the Dream

MESBEC Scholarships

Type of award: Scholarship, renewable.
Intended use: For full-time undergraduate or graduate study at accredited postsecondary institution in United States.
Eligibility: Applicant must be Alaskan native or American Indian. Must be at least one-quarter Native American and enrolled member of federally recognized, state recognized, or terminated tribe. Applicant must be U.S. citizen or permanent resident.
Basis for selection: Major/career interest in mathematics; engineering; science, general; business; education; computer/ information sciences; health sciences or medicine. Applicant must demonstrate high academic achievement, depth of character, leadership, seriousness of purpose and service orientation.
Application requirements: Recommendations, essay, transcript, proof of eligibility.
Additional information: Deadlines are March 15 for summer funding, April 15 for fall, September 15 for spring. MESBEC stands for Math, Engineering, Science, Business, Education, and Computers.

Amount of award: $500-$5,000
Number of awards: 180
Number of applicants: 150
Application deadline: April 15, September 15
Total amount awarded: $300,000
Contact:
Catching the Dream
8200 Mountain Road NE
Suite 203
Albuquerque, NM 87110
Phone: 505-262-2351
Fax: 505-262-0534
Web: www.catchingthedream.org

Native American Leadership in Education Scholarship

Type of award: Scholarship, renewable.
Intended use: For full-time undergraduate or graduate study at accredited postsecondary institution in United States.
Eligibility: Applicant must be American Indian. Must be at least one-quarter Native American and enrolled member of federally recognized, state recognized, or terminated tribe. Applicant must be U.S. citizen or permanent resident.
Basis for selection: Major/career interest in education. Applicant must demonstrate high academic achievement, depth of character, leadership, seriousness of purpose and service orientation.
Application requirements: Recommendations, essay, transcript, proof of eligibility.
Additional information: For students who are paraprofessionals in Indian schools, and who plan to complete their degree in education, counseling, or school administration.

Deadlines are March 15 for summer funding, April 15 for fall, September 15 for spring.

Amount of award: $500-$5,000
Number of awards: 30
Number of applicants: 40
Application deadline: April 15, September 15
Total amount awarded: $100,000
Contact:
Catching the Dream
8200 Mountain Road NE
Suite 203
Albuquerque, NM 87110
Phone: 505-262-2351
Fax: 505-262-0534
Web: www.catchingthedream.org

Tribal Business Management Scholarship

Type of award: Scholarship, renewable.
Intended use: For full-time undergraduate, graduate or postgraduate study at accredited postsecondary institution in United States.
Eligibility: Applicant must be Alaskan native or American Indian. Must be at least one-quarter Native American and enrolled member of federally recognized, state recognized, or terminated tribe. Applicant must be U.S. citizen or permanent resident.
Basis for selection: Major/career interest in business; economics; finance/banking; hotel/restaurant management; accounting; marketing or business/management/administration. Applicant must demonstrate high academic achievement, depth of character, leadership, seriousness of purpose and service orientation.
Application requirements: Recommendations, essay, transcript, proof of eligibility.
Additional information: Scholarships are for fields of study directly related to tribal business development and management. Application deadlines are March 15 for summer semester, April 15 for fall semester, September 15 for spring semester.

Amount of award: $500-$5,000
Number of awards: 15
Number of applicants: 30
Application deadline: April 15, September 15
Total amount awarded: $50,000
Contact:
Catching the Dream
8200 Mountain Road NE
Suite 203
Albuquerque, NM 87110
Phone: 505-262-2351
Fax: 505-262-0534
Web: www.catchingthedream.org

Catholic United Financial

Catholic United Financial Post-High School Tuition Scholarship

Type of award: Scholarship.
Intended use: For undergraduate study at accredited vocational, 2-year or 4-year institution in United States.

Basis for selection: Applicant must demonstrate leadership and service orientation.

Application requirements: Proof of eligibility.

Additional information: Must have been member of Catholic United Financial for two years prior to application deadline. Award is $300 for students attending non-Catholic schools and $500 for those attending Catholic colleges. Visit Website for application. Number of awards varies.

Amount of award:	$300-$500
Number of awards:	461
Number of applicants:	511
Application deadline:	April 30
Notification begins:	February 15
Total amount awarded:	$153,500

Contact:
Catholic United Financial Scholarship Program
3499 Lexington Avenue North
St. Paul, MN 55126
Phone: 651-490-0170
Fax: 651-765-6556
Web: www.catholicunitedfinancial.org

CCNMA: Latino Journalists of California

CCNMA Scholarships

Type of award: Scholarship, renewable.

Intended use: For full-time undergraduate or graduate study at accredited postsecondary institution.

Eligibility: Applicant must be Mexican American, Hispanic American or Puerto Rican.

Basis for selection: Competition/talent/interest in writing/ journalism. Major/career interest in journalism. Applicant must demonstrate financial need, high academic achievement, seriousness of purpose and service orientation.

Application requirements: Interview, recommendations, essay, transcript. Proof of full-time enrollment. Samples of work: newspaper clips, photographs, audio or television tapes.

Additional information: Must be a Latino resident of California attending school in or out of state, or nonresident attending school in California. Number of awards varies.

Amount of award:	$500-$2,000
Number of awards:	6
Number of applicants:	100
Application deadline:	April 1
Notification begins:	June 1
Total amount awarded:	$6,000

Contact:
CCNMA: Latino Journalists of California
725 Arizona Avenue
Suite 406
Santa Monica, CA 90401-1734
Phone: 424-229-9482
Fax: 424-238-0271
Web: www.ccnma.org

Center for Architecture

Center for Architecture Design Scholarship

Type of award: Scholarship.

Intended use: For undergraduate study at accredited postsecondary institution in United States. Designated institutions: New York State institutions.

Eligibility: Applicant must be U.S. citizen, permanent resident or international student residing in New York.

Basis for selection: Major/career interest in architecture; design or engineering. Applicant must demonstrate financial need and high academic achievement.

Application requirements: Recommendations, nomination by dean or chair of school attended. Portfolio. Cover page with full contact information, SASE required if applicants would like work samples returned.

Additional information: Number of awards varies. Applicant may also study related disciplines, including planning, architectural engineering, civil engineering, electrical engineering, environmental engineering, mechanical engineering, structural engineering, architectural design, environmental design, furniture design, industrial design, interior design, landscape design, sustainable design, and urban design. Graduate students eligible if undergraduate degree is in a field other than architecture. Students cannot be nominated for both the CFA Design and Allwork awards.

Amount of award:	$5,000
Application deadline:	March 15

Contact:
Center for Architecture
Attn: CFA Design Scholarship
536 LaGuardia Place
New York, NY 10012
Phone: 212-358-6110
Web: www.cfafoundation.org/cfadesign

Eleanor Allwork Scholarship

Type of award: Scholarship.

Intended use: For undergraduate or graduate study at accredited postsecondary institution. Designated institutions: NAAB-accredited schools in the State of New York.

Eligibility: Applicant must be U.S. citizen, permanent resident or international student residing in New York.

Basis for selection: Major/career interest in architecture. Applicant must demonstrate financial need and high academic achievement.

Application requirements: Portfolio, recommendations, nomination by Dean of architecture school. Cover page with full contact information, SASE required for return of work samples. Must apply both online and hard copy and can be hand-delivered.

Additional information: Applicants must be nominated by the dean or chair of the school of architecture in which they are currently studying in order to apply. Awards and amounts may vary. Multiple awards of up to $7,500 each with the potential of an Honor(s) grant of up to $10,000. Graduate students eligible if from a different undergraduate background and currently completing their first architectural degree. Students cannot be nominated for both the CFA Design and Allwork awards.

Amount of award:	$7,500-$10,000
Application deadline:	March 15

Contact:
Center for Architecture
Attn: Eleanor Allwork Scholarship
536 LaGuardia Place
New York, NY 10012
Phone: 212-358-6133
Web: www.cfafoundation.org/allwork

Walter A Hunt, Jr. Scholarship

Type of award: Scholarship.
Intended use: For freshman study at 4-year institution. Designated institutions: NAAB-accredited school of architecture in New York State.
Eligibility: Applicant must be high school senior. Applicant must be residing in New York.
Basis for selection: Major/career interest in architecture.
Application requirements: Portfolio, recommendations, essay, transcript. Application cover page. College acceptance letter. Students at private, parochial or other schools where tuition is charged are not eligible.
Additional information: Applicant must be attending public school in New York City and must have been accepted to a 5-year Bachelor of Architecture or a 4-year Batchelor of Science in Architecture program at one of the NAAB-accredited Schools of Architecture in New York State. A single award in the amount of $10,000 per year for two years.

Amount of award:	$10,000-$20,000
Number of awards:	1
Application deadline:	May 15
Total amount awarded:	$20,000

Contact:
Center for Architecture
Attn: Walter A. Hunt, Jr. Scholarship
536 LaGuardia Place
New York, NY 10012
Phone: 212-358-6133
Web: www.cfafoundation.org/walter-hunt-scholarship

Center For Cyber Safety and Education

Undergraduate & Graduate Cybersecurity Scholarships

Type of award: Scholarship.
Intended use: For sophomore, junior or senior study at vocational, 2-year, 4-year or graduate institution in or outside United States or Canada.
Eligibility: Applicant must be at least 15, no older than 100.
Basis for selection: Applicants will be scored by members of (ISC)² and scholarship sponsors (if applicable). Scoring will be based upon three categories: Passion, Merit, Financial Need. Major/career interest in computer/information sciences or engineering, computer. Applicant must demonstrate financial need and high academic achievement.
Application requirements: Recommendations, transcript. Required documents: transcripts (unofficial okay until (ISC)² Foundation receives official transcripts from your current or most recent university), one letter of academic recommendation, verification of enrollment or letter from advisor stating you are a student in good standing, resume/CV, and statement of purpose.

Additional information: Must be pursuing a degree with a focus on cybersecurity or information assurance (majors include: Computer Science or Computer Engineering with a security focus; Cybersecurity or Information Assurance). Must have completed at least two semesters an undergraduate degree program by August of the calendar year in which scholarship funding will commence. GPA requirement: 3.0 for undergraduate students, and 3.3 for graduate students. May be attending: on campus or online; full time or part time; in the US or Internationally. May be used for study abroad.

Amount of award:	$1,000-$5,000
Number of awards:	30
Number of applicants:	1,710
Application deadline:	April 20
Total amount awarded:	$100,000

Contact:
Center For Cyber Safety and Education
311 Park Place Boulevard
Suite 400
Clearwater, FL 33759
Phone: 727-493-3587
Fax: 727-489-2803
Web: https://www.isc2cares.org/Scholarships/

Women's Cybersecurity Scholarship

Type of award: Scholarship.
Intended use: For sophomore, junior, senior or graduate study at vocational, 2-year, 4-year or graduate institution.
Eligibility: Applicant must be female, at least 15, no older than 100.
Basis for selection: Applicants will be scored by members of (ISC)² and scholarship sponsors (if applicable). Scoring will be based upon three categories: Passion, Merit, Financial Need. Applicant must demonstrate financial need and high academic achievement.
Application requirements: Recommendations, transcript. Required documents: transcripts (unofficial okay until (ISC)² Foundation receives official transcripts from your current or most recent university), one letter of academic recommendation, verification of enrollment or letter from advisor stating you are a student in good standing, resume/CV, and statement of purpose.
Additional information: Must be pursuing a degree with a focus on cybersecurity or information assurance (majors include: Computer Science or Computer Engineering with a security focus; Cybersecurity or Information Assurance). Must have completed at least two semesters an undergraduate degree program by August of the calendar year in which scholarship funding will commence. Minimum 3.2 GPA. May be attending: on campus or online; full time or part time; in the US or Internationally. May be used for study abroad.

Amount of award:	$1,000-$10,000
Number of awards:	5
Number of applicants:	35
Application deadline:	March 9
Total amount awarded:	$40,000

Contact:
Center For Cyber Safety and Education
311 Park Place Boulevard
Suite 400
Clearwater, FL 33759
Phone: 727-493-3587
Fax: 727-489-2803
Web: https://www.isc2cares.org/Scholarships/

The Center for Reintegration

Lilly Reintegration Scholarship

Type of award: Scholarship.
Intended use: For undergraduate or graduate study at postsecondary institution in United States.
Eligibility: Applicant must be at least 18. Applicant must be U.S. citizen.
Basis for selection: Applicant must demonstrate financial need, high academic achievement, seriousness of purpose and service orientation.
Application requirements: Recommendations, essay, transcript. FAFSA. A copy of desired school's statement of standard costs for tuition, books, lab supplies, and mandatory fees. Signed Personal Consent & Release Form. Self-addressed stamped envelope.
Additional information: Must be diagnosed with bipolar, schizophrenia, schizophreniform disorder, or schizoaffective disorder. Must be currently receiving medical treatment for the disease, including medication and psychiatric follow-up. Must be actively involved in rehabilitative or reintegration efforts, such as clubhouse membership, part-time work, volunteer efforts, or school enrollment. Must have success in dealing with the disease.

Number of awards:	70
Number of applicants:	600
Application deadline:	January 31
Notification begins:	July 1

Contact:
Lilly Reintegration Scholarship
PMB 327
310 Busse Highway
Park Ridge, IL 60068-3251
Phone: 800-809-8202
Web: www.reintegration.com

Central Intelligence Agency

CIA Undergraduate Scholarship Program

Type of award: Scholarship, renewable.
Intended use: For full-time freshman or sophomore study at accredited 4-year institution in United States.
Eligibility: Applicant must be at least 18, high school senior. Applicant must be U.S. citizen.
Basis for selection: Major/career interest in engineering; computer/information sciences; foreign languages; international relations; human resources or finance/banking. Applicant must demonstrate financial need, high academic achievement, depth of character, patriotism and seriousness of purpose.
Application requirements: Recommendations, transcript. SAT/ACT scores, FAFSA or SAR.
Additional information: Applicant may have wide range of majors in addition to those listed. High school applicants must be 18 by April 1 of senior year. Minimum 3.0 GPA; 1500 SAT (1000 Math and Reading, 500 Writing), or 21 ACT required. Household income must not exceed $70,000 for family of four or $80,000 for family of five or more. Scholars work at CIA offices in Washington, D.C. metro area during summer breaks

and receive annual salary in addition to up to $18,000 per school year for tuition, fees, books, and supplies. Must commit to employment with Agency after college graduation for period 1.5 times length of scholarship. Number of awards varies. Apply online. Deadline may vary; check site for exact date.

Amount of award:	$18,000
Application deadline:	October 15

Contact:
Phone: 800-368-3886
Fax: 703-374-2281
Web: www.cia.gov

Centre Technologies

Kathy Pace Technology Scholarship

Type of award: Scholarship.
Intended use: For full-time undergraduate study at accredited vocational, 2-year, 4-year or graduate institution. Designated institutions: Accredited college in Texas or Louisiana.
Eligibility: Applicant must be high school senior.
Basis for selection: Major/career interest in technology.
Application requirements: Two letters or recommendation. Unofficial copy of High School or College Transcript. Personal statement essay: describe what technology means to you and describe how you hope to work with technology in the future (maximum 800 words).
Additional information: Awarded to college student pursuing higher education in a technology related field. Submit application materials by e-mail.

Number of awards:	1
Application deadline:	May 1
Notification begins:	June 1
Total amount awarded:	$5,000

Contact:
480 N. Sam Houston Parkway E
Suite 100
Houston, TX 77060
Phone: 281-506-2480
Fax: 281-763-2353
Web: www.kathypacescholarship.com/

C.G. Fuller Foundation c/o Bank of America

C.G. Fuller Foundation Scholarship

Type of award: Scholarship, renewable.
Intended use: For full-time undergraduate study at 4-year institution. Designated institutions: Colleges and universities in South Carolina.
Eligibility: Applicant must be high school senior. Applicant must be residing in South Carolina.
Basis for selection: Applicant must demonstrate financial need, high academic achievement and leadership.
Application requirements: Recommendations, essay, transcript. Financial statement, copy of parents' most recent 1040 tax return, SAT or ACT scores, high school guidance form.
Additional information: Application must be completed. Applicant must be a current South Carolina resident. Applicant

245

must attend a South Carolina college or university. Applicant must be a high school senior entering their first year of college. SAT score must meet or exceed 1400 (critical reading, math and writing) or, ACT composite score must meet or exceed 24. Adjusted Gross Income of parent(s) or guardian(s) from IRS Form 1040 or 1040A must be $60,000 or less; A complete copy (all pages) of most current filed tax return must accompany the application. Letter of recommendation from your high school guidance counselor (or unrelated equivalent) along with the attached form must be received in a sealed envelope with application or directly from the guidance counselor. All information, as noted on the application, must be received by the appropriate due date or your application may not be considered.

Amount of award:	$1,250-$2,500
Number of applicants:	40
Application deadline:	May 1
Notification begins:	August 1
Total amount awarded:	$10,000

Contact:
U.S. Trust, Bank of America C.G. Fuller Foundation
P.O. Box 448
#SC3-240-04-17
Columbia, SC 29202-0448

CGTrader, Inc.

Annual CGTrader Scholarship

Type of award: Scholarship, renewable.
Intended use: For full-time undergraduate or graduate study at vocational, 2-year, 4-year or graduate institution.
Eligibility: Applicant must be at least 18.
Application requirements: Essay. Write an essay (500-1000 words) on "The future of technology in education" and submit via online form. Applicant must be enrolled full-time at an academic institution for the upcoming academic year.

Amount of award:	$500-$2,000
Number of awards:	3
Application deadline:	June 1
Notification begins:	June 15
Total amount awarded:	$3,000

Contact:
Web: https://www.cgtrader.com/scholarship

ChairScholars Foundation, Inc.

Florida Scholarship Program

Type of award: Scholarship, renewable.
Intended use: For freshman study at postsecondary institution.
Eligibility: Applicant must be physically challenged. Applicant must be residing in Florida.
Basis for selection: Applicant must demonstrate financial need and high academic achievement.
Application requirements: Recommendations, essay, transcript. Recent photograph. Parent's or guardian's federal income tax return. Physician's documentation of disability. Notification of receipt of other scholarships.

Additional information: Open to physically disabled 7th-11th grade students in Florida public schools. Minimum "B" average. Visit Website for details and application.

Application deadline:	April 15
Notification begins:	May 15

Contact:
ChairScholars Foundation, Inc.
16101 Carencia Lane
Odessa, FL 33556
Phone: 813-926-0544
Fax: 813-920-7661
Web: www.chairscholars.org

National ChairScholars Scholarship

Type of award: Scholarship, renewable.
Intended use: For full-time undergraduate study at postsecondary institution.
Eligibility: Applicant must be physically challenged. Applicant must be no older than 21. Applicant must be U.S. citizen or permanent resident.
Basis for selection: Applicant must demonstrate financial need, high academic achievement and service orientation.
Application requirements: Recommendations, essay, transcript. Photograph, parent's IRS Form 1040 from last year, SAT and ACT scores.
Additional information: Applicant must have a serious physical disability but does not have to be confined to a wheelchair. Applicant must be unable to attend college without financial aid; no household income above $85,000. Applicant must have at least a B average. If applicant has obtained any other scholarships already, he or she must inform ChairScholars. Award is renewable up to four years, for maximum $20,000.

Amount of award:	$1,000-$5,000
Number of awards:	15
Number of applicants:	85
Application deadline:	April 15
Notification begins:	May 15
Total amount awarded:	$320,000

Contact:
ChairScholars Foundation, Inc.
16101 Carencia Lane
Odessa, FL 33556
Phone: 813-926-0544
Fax: 813-920-7661
Web: www.chairscholars.org

ChameleonJohn.com

ChameleonJohn.com Student Scholarship

Type of award: Scholarship.
Intended use: For undergraduate or graduate study at vocational, 2-year or 4-year institution in United States.
Additional information: Essay questions and complete rules available on the web site.

Number of awards:	1
Application deadline:	December 15
Total amount awarded:	$2,000

Contact:
Electrim Technologies Corporation 3rd floor
Phone: 415-992-6330
Web: www.chameleonjohn.com/scholarship

Charles & Lucille King Family Foundation, Inc.

Charles & Lucille King Family Foundation Scholarships

Type of award: Scholarship, renewable.
Intended use: For full-time junior or senior study at accredited 4-year institution in United States.
Basis for selection: Major/career interest in communications or radio/television/film. Applicant must demonstrate financial need and high academic achievement.
Application requirements: Recommendations, transcript. Personal statement. Application form with financial information.
Additional information: Download application from Website.

Amount of award:	$3,500
Application deadline:	March 15

Contact:
Charles & Lucille King Family Foundation, Inc.
c/o Charles Brucia & Co.
400 Madison Avenue
New York, NY 10017
Phone: 212-682-2913
Web: www.kingfoundation.org

The Charles A. and Anne Morrow Lindbergh Foundation

Lindbergh Grant

Type of award: Research grant.
Intended use: For undergraduate or non-degree study at postsecondary institution.
Basis for selection: Major/career interest in agriculture; aviation; biomedical; education; environmental science; health sciences or natural resources/conservation.
Application requirements: Research proposal.
Additional information: Applicant research or educational project should address balance between technological advancement and environmental preservation. Citizens of all countries are eligible. Deadline is second Thursday in June.

Amount of award:	$1,000-$10,580
Number of awards:	10
Number of applicants:	200
Notification begins:	April 15

Contact:
The Charles A. and Anne Morrow Lindbergh Foundation
Phone: 763-576-1596
Web: www.lindberghfoundation.org

Charleston Women in International Trade

Charleston Women in International Trade Scholarship

Type of award: Scholarship.
Intended use: For undergraduate study at accredited postsecondary institution in United States.
Eligibility: Applicant must be U.S. citizen residing in South Carolina.
Basis for selection: Applicant must demonstrate financial need and seriousness of purpose.
Application requirements: Recommendations, transcript, proof of eligibility. Two-page (minimum length), double-spaced essay explaining the importance of international trade and state your goals for working in the international business environment. Must also explain why you believe you should be awarded this scholarship. Listing of courses/work experience relevant to interest in international trade; extracurricular activities, civic and community involvement. List of relevant courses/work experience. Financial aid/tuition information.
Additional information: Applicant must be pursuing degree specific to international trade or related course of study. To apply, complete application on Website. Deadline varies yearly, visit Website for date.

Amount of award:	$1,500-$3,000
Number of awards:	4
Total amount awarded:	$6,000

Contact:
Ashley Kutz Kelley, CWIT Awards Chairperson
P.O. Box 31258
Charleston, SC 29417
Phone: 843-577-8678
Web: www.cwitsc.org

Children of Deaf Adults, Inc (CODA)

Millie Brother Scholarship for Hearing Children of Deaf Adults

Type of award: Scholarship, renewable.
Intended use: For at accredited vocational, 2-year, 4-year or graduate institution.
Application requirements: Recommendations, essay, transcript. Only hearing children with at least one deaf parent are elligible for this scholarship. Application package must include: application form, essay, transript, and 2 letters of recommendation. Unofficial transcrips will not be accepted. Essay should be 2 pages double spaced. Essay topics can be found on the scholarship web page.
Additional information: All application packages must be completed and postmarked by the First Friday in April. Application package is not considered submitted until you have received an email confirmation from ouroffice. It can take up to 2 weeks to process your application. Applicants will be notified by July.

Amount of award:	$1,000-$3,000
Number of awards:	5
Number of applicants:	83
Application deadline:	April 7
Total amount awarded:	$9,000

Contact:
CODA International Dr. Jennie E. Pyers
Wellesley College
106 Central St
Wellesley, MA 02481
Phone: 413-650-2632
Fax: 781-283-3730
Web: www.coda-international.org/2017-Scholarship-Application

Choctaw Nation of Oklahoma

Choctaw Nation Higher Education Program

Type of award: Scholarship, renewable.
Intended use: For undergraduate or graduate study at accredited 2-year, 4-year or graduate institution in United States.
Eligibility: Applicant must be American Indian. Must be enrolled member of Choctaw Tribe and have Certificate of Degree of Indian Blood (CDIB) and tribal membership card.
Basis for selection: Applicant must demonstrate high academic achievement.
Application requirements: Transcript. Proof of Choctaw descent. FAFSA. School enrollment verification via submission of class schedule.
Additional information: Program made up of two awards: a grant or a scholarship. Grant is based on financial need; minimum 2.0 GPA required. The scholarship is for applicants with minimum 2.5 GPA. Grant will assist with any unmet need up to award amount. Must reapply for renewal. Number of awards varies. May only receive either grant or scholarship.

Amount of award:	$1,000-$2,000
Number of awards:	5,000
Number of applicants:	5,200
Application deadline:	October 1, March 1

Contact:
Choctaw Nation of Oklahoma
Higher Education Department
P.O. Box 1210
Durant, OK 74702-1210
Phone: 800-522-6170
Fax: 580-924-1267
Web: www.choctawnation.com

Christensen Law

Distracted Driving Awareness Scholarship

Type of award: Scholarship.
Intended use: For undergraduate or graduate study at vocational, 2-year, 4-year or graduate institution in United States.

Application requirements: Essay. Applicants must provide proof of identity and school enrollment. Applicant must include a link to their Facebook or Twitter profile. 1,800 to 2,000 word essay on how drunk driving has impacted applicant's life.

Number of awards:	1
Application deadline:	July 15
Notification begins:	August 15
Total amount awarded:	$2,500

Contact:
Christensen Law Attn: Distracted Driving Scholarship
25925 Telegraph Road
Suite 200
Southfield, MI 48033
Web: https://www.davidchristensenlaw.com/distracted-driving-scholarship/

Christian Record Services

Christian Record Services Scholarship

Type of award: Scholarship, renewable.
Intended use: For full-time undergraduate study at postsecondary institution in United States.
Eligibility: Applicant must be visually impaired.
Basis for selection: Applicant must demonstrate financial need and high academic achievement.
Application requirements: Recommendations. Photo and bio.
Additional information: Applicants must be totally or legally blind. Awardees must reapply yearly.

Amount of award:	$500
Number of awards:	10
Number of applicants:	14
Application deadline:	April 1
Notification begins:	May 15
Total amount awarded:	$5,000

Contact:
Christian Record Services
5900 S 58th Street
Suit M
Lincoln, NE 68516
Phone: 402-488-0981
Fax: 402-488-7582
Web: www.christianrecord.org

Citrix ShareFile

Scholarship for Future Entrepreneurs

Type of award: Scholarship.
Intended use: For undergraduate or graduate study at accredited vocational, 2-year, 4-year or graduate institution in United States.
Application requirements: 600-1000 word essay on the prompt: "Can entrepreneurship be taught? How can colleges better promote and teach entrepreneurship?"

Amount of award:	$2,000-$5,000
Number of awards:	3
Application deadline:	December 1
Notification begins:	January 31
Total amount awarded:	$10,000

Contact:
Web: https://www.sharefile.com/scholarship

CJ Pony Parts

CJ Pony Parts Scholarship Video Contest

Type of award: Scholarship.
Intended use: For full-time undergraduate or graduate study at vocational, 2-year, 4-year or graduate institution in United States.
Eligibility: Applicant must be U.S. citizen or permanent resident.
Basis for selection: Major/career interest in automotive technology.
Application requirements: Short video, under three minutes long, on one of these topics: what it means to live in America, my first memory of a Mustang, how the auto industry changed America, what a Mustang teaches me about life, how a Mustang relates to your field of study (get creative!)
Additional information: Upload your video to YouTube and then email the link before midnight EST on the appropriate deadline.

Amount of award:	$500
Number of awards:	2
Application deadline:	April 15, October 15
Notification begins:	May 1, November 1
Total amount awarded:	$1,000

Contact:
CJ Pony Parts
7461 Allentown Boulevard
Harrisburg, PA 17112
Phone: 1-800-888-6473
Web: www.cjponyparts.com/cj-pony-parts-scholarship-video-contest

Clara Lionel Foundation

Clara Lionel Foundation Global Scholarship Program

Type of award: Scholarship, renewable.
Intended use: For full-time freshman study at accredited 4-year institution in United States.
Eligibility: Applicant must be high school senior. Applicant must be international student.
Additional information: Open to citizens or natives of Brazil, Barbados, Cuba, Haiti, Grenada, Guyana, or Jamaica who are eligible to study in the United States and have been accepted to an accredited four-year college or university in the United States. Applicants must be a first-time college freshman. Students must be eligible to receive funding per the Office of Foreign Assets Control. Renewable up to three years or until a bachelor's degree is earned - renewal is contingent upon maintaining a GPA of 2.5 each semester.

Amount of award:	$5,000-$50,000
Application deadline:	June 10

Contact:
Phone: 507-931-1682
Web: www.scholarsapply.org/claralionelfdn

Clubs of America

Clubs of America Scholarship Award for Career Success

Type of award: Scholarship.
Intended use: For undergraduate study at accredited 4-year institution.
Basis for selection: Applicant must demonstrate high academic achievement.
Application requirements: Essay. Write an essay of no fewer than 600 words about career aspirations and how current course load will help achieve success in careers. Email essay as DOC or PDF attachment. YouTube submissions are optional, although not required. Video should be no longer than 5 minutes (Essays submitted via YouTube must also be submitted in writing).
Additional information: Minimum 3.0 GPA required. The full award amount will be sent directly to the financial aid office of the winning candidates' institution.

Amount of award:	$1,000
Number of awards:	1
Number of applicants:	850
Application deadline:	August 31
Notification begins:	September 30
Total amount awarded:	$1,000

Contact:
Scholarship Dept
484 Wegner Road
Lakemoor, IL 60051
Phone: 815-363-4000
Web: www.greatclubs.com/scholarship-award-for-career-success.asp

The Clunker Junker

Cash for Cars and College

Type of award: Scholarship, renewable.
Intended use: For full-time undergraduate or master's study at vocational, 2-year, 4-year or graduate institution.
Eligibility: Applicant must be at least 18.
Basis for selection: The winner will be selected based on essay quality, grammar and writing style, personality, and thoughtfulness. Major/career interest in automotive technology; engineering or marketing.
Application requirements: Essay. To apply for the scholarship, please write a minimum 500 word essay telling us how you became interested in automotive technology, what your career goals and ambitions are, and why you feel you're the best qualified for this scholarship.

Amount of award:	$1,000
Number of awards:	1
Application deadline:	August 1
Notification begins:	August 7
Total amount awarded:	$1,000

Contact:
The Clunker Junker
11228 77th Street E
Parrish, FL 34219
Phone: 774-314-1825
Web: https://theclunkerjunker.com/cash-for-cars-and-college

CNA PLUS

CNA PLUS ANNUAL SCHOLARSHIP

Type of award: Scholarship, renewable.
Intended use: For full-time undergraduate study at vocational, 2-year or 4-year institution.
Eligibility: Applicant must be at least 18.
Basis for selection: Major/career interest in nursing.
Application requirements: Applicants must create a 3-minute video on the topic of the importance of senior assistance and post it online (YouTube or Vimeo are preferred), then submit the link using the form on the Scholarship page or by email. The video should answer the following question: "Senior care of the future: what can we do to provide better care to our senior citizens?"
Additional information: Applicant must be enrolled in a state-approved CNA training/certification program with a vocational school, community college, university, technical institution, or the Red Cross.

Number of awards:	1
Application deadline:	December 31
Total amount awarded:	$2,000

Contact:
CNA Plus
4283 Express Lane
Suite 392-536
Sarasota, FL 34249
Web: http://cna.plus/scholarship/

The Coca-Cola Foundation

Coca-Cola Community College Academic Team Scholarship

Type of award: Scholarship.
Intended use: For undergraduate study at 2-year or 4-year institution in United States. Designated institutions: Community colleges.
Eligibility: Applicant must be U.S. citizen or permanent resident.
Basis for selection: Applicant must demonstrate high academic achievement, depth of character and service orientation.
Application requirements: Nomination by college at which student is enrolled or is planning to enroll.
Additional information: Must be enrolled at a community college through December 2015. Must be planning to enroll in at least two courses during next term. Children and grandchildren of Coca-Cola employees not eligible. Program administered by Phi Theta Kappa Honor Society. Visit Website for college credit requirements and nomination information.

Amount of award:	$1,000-$1,500
Number of awards:	150
Number of applicants:	1,700
Application deadline:	December 1
Notification begins:	March 1
Total amount awarded:	$187,500

Contact:
Scholarship Operations Department
Phi Theta Kappa Honor Society
1625 Eastover Drive
Jackson, MS 39211
Phone: 800-946-9995
Web: www.coca-colascholars.org or www.ptk.org

Coca-Cola Scholars Program

Type of award: Scholarship, renewable.
Intended use: For full-time undergraduate study at accredited 4-year institution in United States.
Eligibility: Applicant must be high school senior. Applicant must be U.S. citizen or permanent resident.
Basis for selection: Applicant must demonstrate high academic achievement, depth of character, leadership, seriousness of purpose and service orientation.
Additional information: Applicant may also be temporary resident in legalization program, refugee, asylee, Cuban/Haitian entrant, or Humanitarian Parole. Must be attending high school in United States or territories. Minimum 3.0 GPA required at the end of junior year high school. Award is for four years, $2,500 or $5,000 per year. Notification begins December 1 for semifinalists; mid-February for finalists. Children and grandchildren of Coca-Cola employees not eligible.

Amount of award:	$10,000-$20,000
Number of awards:	250
Number of applicants:	75,000
Application deadline:	October 31
Notification begins:	December 5
Total amount awarded:	$3,000,000

Contact:
Coca-Cola Scholars Foundation
Phone: 800-306-2653
Web: www.coca-colascholars.org

Cogburn Law Offices

Cogburn Law Offices Adversity Scholarship

Type of award: Scholarship.
Intended use: For full-time undergraduate study at accredited 2-year or 4-year institution in United States.
Eligibility: Applicant must be U.S. citizen or permanent resident.
Basis for selection: Major/career interest in law. Applicant must demonstrate financial need.
Application requirements: Essay. The applicant must complete an online application and submit an essay or video demonstrating how he or she has overcome great personal adversity.

Amount of award: $5,000
Number of awards: 1
Application deadline: June 1
Notification begins: September 1
Total amount awarded: $5,000
Contact:
Cogburn Law Offices
620B Academy Drive
Northbrook, IL 60062
Phone: 847-940-4000
Web: http://cogburnlaw.com/scholarship/

Collective

Bill Caspare Memorial Fund Scholarship

Type of award: Scholarship.
Intended use: For full-time junior or senior study in United States. Designated institutions: Baruch, Carnegie Mellon, Columbia, Cornell, Dartmouth, Fordham, Hamilton, Haverford, Lehigh, MIT, Montclair, Northeastern, NYU, UPenn, Rutgers, Smith, Stony Brook,Tufts, UVA, Wesleyan, and Yale.
Eligibility: Applicant must be Asian American, African American, Mexican American, Hispanic American, American Indian or Native Hawaiian/Pacific Islander. LGBTQ students elligible. Applicant must be U.S. citizen or permanent resident.
Application requirements: Portfolio, recommendations, essay, transcript. Online application form. Personal statement 1: Why should you be granted the scholarship (limited to 1 page/500 words) Personal statement 2: Why are you pursuing a career in : New Media/Digital Advertising and/or Data Science field? (limited to 1 page/500 words). Current Resume. Three educational and/or professional references. Three examples of work (either school and/or outside project work).
Additional information: Minimum 3.25 GPA. Must be a rising junior or senior at the time of application. Must have an interest in pursuing a career in new media/digital advertising and/or data science. Completed application packets should be sent by e-mail. Application can be found online at link below. Include name and school in the subject line of your e-mail. Please provide documents with a naming structure for easy identification.

Amount of award: $10,000
Number of awards: 2
Application deadline: July 14
Total amount awarded: $20,000
Contact:
Collective
229 West 43rd Street
New York, NY 10036
Web: collective.com/scholarship/

College For All Texans

Texas Educational Opportunity Grant Program

Type of award: Scholarship.
Intended use: For at 2-year institution.
Eligibility: Applicant must be residing in Texas.

Amount of award: $708-$5,486
Application deadline: March 15
Contact:
College For All Texans/DeCha Reid
1200 East Anderson Street
Austin, TX 78752
Phone: 512-427-6393
Web: www.collegeforalltexans.com/apps/financialaid/tofa.cfm?Kind=GS

College Foundation of North Carolina

North Carolina Education Lottery Scholarship

Type of award: Scholarship.
Intended use: For undergraduate certificate study at vocational, 2-year or 4-year institution in United States. Designated institutions: Eligible North Carolina institutions (UNC campuses, community college campuses, independent college campuses and certain private colleges).
Eligibility: Applicant must be U.S. citizen or permanent resident residing in North Carolina.
Basis for selection: Applicant must demonstrate financial need.
Application requirements: FAFSA.
Additional information: Must meet Satisfactory Academic Progress requirements of institution. Eligibility based on same criteria as Federal Pell Grant with one exception: students not eligible for Federal Pell Grant with estimated family contribution of $5,000 or less are eligible for Education Lottery Scholarship. Go to fafsa.gov to fill out application. Must be a North Carolina resident for tuition purposes. Must enroll for at least six credit hours per semester in a curriculum program. Must be admitted, enrolled and classified as an undergraduate student in matriculated status in a degree, certificate or diploma program at eligible North Carolina institutions (UNC campuses, community college campuses).

Amount of award: $100-$3,000
Contact:
College Foundation of North Carolina
Phone: 866-866-2362
Web: https://www.cfnc.org/Gateway?command=SearchBasedPrograms&note=no&type=7

The College Investor

The Side Hustlin' Student Scholarship Opportunity

Type of award: Scholarship.
Intended use: For full-time undergraduate or graduate study at vocational, 2-year, 4-year or graduate institution.
Application requirements: Essay. Applicants must submit a 600+ word essay about how you are earning extra income on the side of going to school, Topics can include anything from how you started a business, to why you decided to get a job, to how your parents encouraged you to work. Essay must be your

own work not previously published on any other website or publication.

Additional information: Applicants must either be enrolled or actively applying for enrollment to an undergraduate or graduate program. Applicants must state the school they are or plan to attend. Applications should be submitted to robert@thecollegeinvestor.com: Please include a name, address, phone number, and headshot to be included with article publication, Please include "Scholarship" in the subject line. Essays will be screened, and the top essays will be published on The College Investor.

Amount of award:	$500-$2,000
Number of awards:	2
Application deadline:	March 31
Notification begins:	July 31
Total amount awarded:	$2,500

Contact:
The College Investor LLC
2514 Jamacha Road
Suit 502, PMB 75
El Cajon, CA 92019
Phone: 858-598-3149
Web: http://thecollegeinvestor.com/18899/side-hustle-student-scholarship-opportunity/

Colonial Ghosts

Colonial Ghosts Marketing Scholarship

Type of award: Scholarship.
Intended use: For full-time undergraduate study at accredited 4-year or graduate institution.
Eligibility: Applicant must be at least 18. Applicant must be U.S. citizen.
Basis for selection: Major/career interest in marketing.
Application requirements: Essay. Application includes a 1,000 word essay explaining your education goals and plans after graduating college. If an honorably discharged veteran, send a copy of your DD-214 with your application and mention it in your essay.
Additional information: Must have a declared major in marketing.

Number of awards:	1
Application deadline:	December 15
Total amount awarded:	$1,000

Contact:
Colonial Ghosts
424 West Duke of Gloucester Street
Williamsburg, VA 23185
Phone: 757-598-1805
Web: https://colonialghosts.com/scholarship/

Colorado Commission on Higher Education

Colorado Student Grant

Type of award: Scholarship.
Intended use: For undergraduate study at postsecondary institution. Designated institutions: Eligible Colorado institutions.

Eligibility: Applicant must be residing in Colorado.
Basis for selection: Applicant must demonstrate financial need.
Application requirements: FAFSA.
Additional information: Contact college financial aid office or visit Website for additional information. International students must be working toward becoming permanent resident of U.S.

Total amount awarded:	$69,381,910

Contact:
Colorado Commission on Higher Education
1560 Broadway
Suite 1600
Denver, CO 80202
Phone: 303-866-2723
Web: highered.colorado.gov

Colorado Work-Study Program

Type of award: Scholarship.
Intended use: For undergraduate study at postsecondary institution. Designated institutions: Eligible postsecondary institutions in Colorado.
Eligibility: Applicant must be residing in Colorado.
Additional information: Part-time employment program for students who need work experience or who can prove financial need. International students must be working toward becoming permanent resident of U.S. Amount of award cannot exceed need. Institutions must award 70% of work-study allocations to students with documented need; remaining 30% may be awarded to students without need. Contact college financial aid office or visit Website for additional information.

Total amount awarded:	$17,581,757

Contact:
Colorado Commission on Higher Education
1560 Broadway
Suite 1600
Denver, CO 80202
Phone: 303-862-3001
Web: highered.colorado.gov

Colorado Council on High School and College Relations

Colorado Council Volunteerism and Community Service Scholarship

Type of award: Scholarship.
Intended use: For full-time freshman study at 2-year or 4-year institution. Designated institutions: Colorado Council member institutions.
Eligibility: Applicant must be high school senior. Applicant must be U.S. citizen or permanent resident residing in Colorado.
Basis for selection: Applicant must demonstrate high academic achievement and service orientation.
Application requirements: Recommendations, essay, transcript.
Additional information: Minimum 2.5 GPA. Must be enrolled full-time at Colorado Council member institution within six months of graduating from high school. Visit Website for full list of Colorado Council member institutions.

Amount of award:	$1,500
Number of awards:	16
Number of applicants:	221
Application deadline:	January 30
Total amount awarded:	$21,000

Contact:
ATTN: Tiffany Anderson CCHS/CR Scholarships Committee
PO Box 718
Denver, CO 80201
Web: www.coloradocouncil.org

Colorado Masons' Benevolent Fund Association

Colorado Masons Scholarship

Type of award: Scholarship, renewable.
Intended use: For full-time undergraduate study at accredited vocational, 2-year or 4-year institution. Designated institutions: Institutions of higher learning in Colorado.
Eligibility: Applicant must be high school senior. Applicant must be U.S. citizen residing in Colorado.
Basis for selection: Applicant must demonstrate financial need, high academic achievement and depth of character.
Application requirements: Interview, recommendations, essay, transcript, proof of eligibility. Letter of acceptance and FAFSA or SAR.
Additional information: Applicant must be graduating senior at public high school in Colorado. Scholarship is renewable for up to four years. Number of awards varies. Visit Website for application and details.

Amount of award:	$7,000
Number of applicants:	456
Application deadline:	March 15
Notification begins:	May 1
Total amount awarded:	$279,000

Contact:
Colorado Masons' Benevolent Fund Association
Scholarship Administrator
2400 Consistory Court
Grand Junction, CO 81501
Phone: 303-290-8544
Web: www.cmbfa.org

Colorado Society of CPAs Educational Foundation

Colorado Society of CPAs General Scholarship

Type of award: Scholarship, renewable.
Intended use: For undergraduate or graduate study at accredited 4-year or graduate institution in United States. Designated institutions: Colorado colleges/universities with accredited accounting programs.
Eligibility: Applicant must be U.S. citizen or permanent resident residing in Colorado.

Basis for selection: Major/career interest in accounting. Applicant must demonstrate high academic achievement.
Application requirements: Essay, transcript.
Additional information: Applicant must be COCPA student member or have submitted new member application. Must have completed six semester/eight quarter hours in accounting. Must be at least half-time student. Applicants should intend to practice the profession of accounting in Colorado. Minimum 3.0 GPA, with 3.25 GPA in accounting. International students must have work visa. Visit Website for application.

Amount of award:	$2,500
Application deadline:	June 1

Contact:
COCPA
7887 E. Belleview Avenue
Suite 200
Englewood, CO 80111-6076
Phone: 303-773-2877
Web: www.want2bcpa.com

Mark J. Smith Scholarship

Type of award: Scholarship.
Intended use: For undergraduate or graduate study at accredited 4-year or graduate institution in United States. Designated institutions: Colorado colleges and universities with accredited accounting programs.
Eligibility: Applicant must be U.S. citizen or permanent resident residing in Colorado.
Basis for selection: Major/career interest in accounting. Applicant must demonstrate financial need and high academic achievement.
Application requirements: Essay, transcript.
Additional information: Applicant must be COCPA student member or have submitted new member application. Special consideration for students from single-parent background or attending college as a single parent. Must have completed six semester/eight quarter hours in accounting. Must be at least half-time student. Applicants should intend to practice the profession of accounting in Colorado. Minimum 3.0 GPA, with 3.25 GPA in accounting. International students must have work visa. Visit Website for application.

Amount of award:	$2,500
Number of awards:	1
Application deadline:	June 1

Contact:
COCPA
7887 E. Belleview Avenue
Suite 200
Englewood, CO 80111-6076
Phone: 800-523-9082
Web: www.want2bcpa.com

Columbus Citizens Foundation

College Scholarship Program

Type of award: Scholarship, renewable.
Intended use: For full-time undergraduate study at accredited 4-year institution in United States or Canada.
Eligibility: Applicant must be high school senior. Applicant must be Italian.

Basis for selection: Applicant must demonstrate financial need, high academic achievement and service orientation.
Application requirements: $30 application fee. Interview, recommendations, essay, transcript. Parent/guardian's most recent state and federal income tax returns, family tree.
Additional information: Applicant must be Italian American. Minimum 3.0 GPA. Family's taxable income must not exceed $25,000 per household dependent. Applicants who reach semifinalist round must travel to New York City for interview at own expense. Applications available on Website in first week of December each year; deadline is in February. Number and amount of awards varies.

Amount of award:	$500-$6,250
Number of awards:	40

Contact:
Columbus Citizens Foundation College Scholarship Program
8 East 69th Street
New York, NY 10021-4906
Phone: 212-249-9923
Fax: 212-517-7619
Web: www.columbuscitizensfd.org

Commerce Bank

Commerce Bank Scholarship Sweepstakes

Type of award: Scholarship.
Intended use: For undergraduate or graduate study at postsecondary institution.
Eligibility: Applicant must be at least 18.
Additional information: Only lawful residents of the United States are eligible to enter and win. Void in NY, RI and FL, and where prohibited by law.

Amount of award:	$1,000
Number of awards:	12
Application deadline:	August 31
Total amount awarded:	$12,000

Contact:
Commerce Bank
811 Main Street KCBC12
Kansas City, MO 64105
Phone: 816-234-7487
Web: www.commercebank.com/scholarship

Community Veterinary Partners

Community Veterinary Partners Scholarship Program

Type of award: Scholarship.
Intended use: For undergraduate or graduate study.
Application requirements: Essay.
Additional information: Applicants must be enrolled at college or university or are actively applying for the following year. Open to both undergraduate and graduate students. Submit 500+ word essay on specified questions found on website.

Amount of award:	$1,000
Number of awards:	2
Application deadline:	April 1, October 1
Total amount awarded:	$2,000

Contact:
Phone: 215-302-3996
Web: https://cvpco.com/community/

Congressional Black Caucus Foundation, Inc.

The CBC General Mills Health Scholarship

Type of award: Scholarship, renewable.
Intended use: For full-time undergraduate or graduate study at accredited vocational, 2-year, 4-year or graduate institution.
Eligibility: Applicant must be U.S. citizen or permanent resident.
Basis for selection: Major/career interest in engineering; health-related professions; medicine or technology. Applicant must demonstrate financial need, high academic achievement, leadership and service orientation.
Application requirements: Recommendations, essay, transcript, proof of eligibility. Copy of Student Aid Report (SAR).
Additional information: Minimum 2.75 GPA. Awards and amounts may vary. Preference given to CBC constituents and African-American students. Deadline in February or March. Visit Website for application and details.

Amount of award:	$2,500
Number of awards:	43

Contact:
CBCF General Mills Health Scholarship Program
Scholarship Management Services
One Scholarship Way
Saint Peter, MN 56082
Phone: 507-931-1682
Web: www.cbcfinc.org

The CBC Spouses Education Scholarship

Type of award: Scholarship, renewable.
Intended use: For full-time undergraduate or graduate study at accredited 4-year or graduate institution in United States.
Eligibility: Applicant must be U.S. citizen or permanent resident.
Basis for selection: Applicant must demonstrate financial need, high academic achievement, leadership and service orientation.
Application requirements: Recommendations, essay, transcript. Resume, recent photo, copy of Student Aid Report (SAR).
Additional information: Minimum 2.5 GPA. Award amount varies. Selection made at district level. Preference given to CBC member constituents. Deadline in late May or early June. Visit Website for application and details.

Contact:
Congressional Black Caucus Foundation
1720 Massachusetts Avenue, NW
Washington, DC 20036
Phone: 202-263-2800
Fax: 202-775-0773
Web: www.cbcfinc.org

The CBC Spouses Heineken USA Performing Arts Scholarship Program

Type of award: Scholarship, renewable.
Intended use: For full-time undergraduate study at accredited 4-year institution.
Basis for selection: Major/career interest in performing arts or music. Applicant must demonstrate financial need, high academic achievement, leadership and service orientation.
Application requirements: Recommendations, essay, transcript, proof of eligibility. Resume, recent photograph, copy of Student Aid Report (SAR), two-minute performance sample.
Additional information: Minimum 2.5 GPA. Check Website for application and details. Deadline in late April or early May.

Amount of award:	$3,000
Number of awards:	10

Contact:
Congressional Black Caucus Foundation
1720 Massachusetts Avenue, NW
Washington, DC 20036
Phone: 202-263-2800
Fax: 202-775-0773
Web: www.cbcfinc.org

The CBC Spouses Visual Arts Scholarship

Type of award: Scholarship.
Intended use: For full-time undergraduate study at accredited 4-year institution in United States.
Basis for selection: Major/career interest in arts, general. Applicant must demonstrate financial need, high academic achievement, leadership and service orientation.
Application requirements: Recommendations, essay, transcript. Recent photo of applicant, resume, copy of Student Aid Report (SAR), up to five artwork samples. High school seniors must submit college acceptance letter.
Additional information: Minimum 2.5 GPA. Deadline in late April or early May. Check Website for application and details.

Amount of award:	$3,000
Number of awards:	10

Contact:
Congressional Black Caucus Foundation
1720 Massachusetts Avenue, NW
Washington, DC 20036
Phone: 202-263-2800
Fax: 202-775-0773
Web: www.cbcfinc.org

Louis Stokes Health Scholars

Type of award: Scholarship.
Intended use: For full-time undergraduate study at vocational, 2-year or 4-year institution.
Eligibility: Applicant must be U.S. citizen or permanent resident.

Basis for selection: Major/career interest in health-related professions. Applicant must demonstrate financial need and high academic achievement.
Application requirements: Recommendations, essay, transcript. Resume, photograph. Student Aid Report.
Additional information: High school seniors also eligible to apply. Minimum 3.0 GPA. For students entering the health workforce. Preference given to students demonstrating an interest in underserved communities. Students currently attending two-year institutions strongly encouraged to apply. Deadline and number of awards may vary. Notification begins six to eight weeks after deadline.

Amount of award:	$4,000-$8,000
Number of awards:	10
Number of applicants:	130
Total amount awarded:	$90,000

Contact:
Congressional Black Caucus Foundation, Inc.
1720 Massachusetts Avenue, NW
Washington, DC 20036
Phone: 202-263-2800
Fax: 202-775-0773
Web: https://cbcfinc.academicworks.com/opportunities/3

Congressional Hispanic Caucus Institute

Congressional Hispanic Caucus Institute Scholarship Awards

Type of award: Scholarship.
Intended use: For full-time undergraduate or graduate study at 2-year, 4-year or graduate institution.
Eligibility: Applicant must be U.S. citizen or permanent resident.
Basis for selection: Applicant must demonstrate financial need, leadership and service orientation.
Application requirements: Recommendations, essay. One-page resume, SAR.
Additional information: Community college students receive $1,000; students enrolled at four-year colleges or universities receive $2,500; students enrolled in graduate programs receive $5,000. Apply online.

Amount of award:	$1,000-$5,000
Number of awards:	150
Application deadline:	April 16

Contact:
Congressional Hispanic Caucus Institute Scholarship
300 M Street, SE
5th Floor, Suite 510
Washington, DC 20003
Phone: 202-543-1771
Fax: 202-546-2143
Web: www.chci.org/scholarships

Connect

Future Leaders of IT Scholarship

Type of award: Scholarship.
Intended use: For undergraduate or graduate study at vocational, 2-year, 4-year or graduate institution.
Eligibility: Applicant must be high school senior.
Basis for selection: Major/career interest in information systems; computer/information sciences or engineering, computer.
Application requirements: Recommendations, essay, transcript. Most recent high school or college transcripts and three letters of recommendation from teachers or counselors required. A 1000 word minimum essay on why you are pursuing a career in information engineering, information management (or related academic discipline) and what you hope to accomplish in your career.
Additional information: High School seniors must provide proof of university or college acceptance.

Number of awards:	1
Application deadline:	December 1
Total amount awarded:	$2,000

Contact:
P.O. Box 204086
Austin, TX 78720
Phone: 800-807-7560
Web: www.connect-community.org/?page=FLIT

Connecticut Building Congress

Connecticut Building Congress Scholarship Fund

Type of award: Scholarship, renewable.
Intended use: For full-time freshman study at accredited 4-year institution in United States.
Eligibility: Applicant must be U.S. citizen residing in Connecticut.
Basis for selection: Major/career interest in construction; construction management; engineering, civil; engineering, electrical/electronic; engineering, environmental; engineering, mechanical; engineering, structural or surveying/mapping.
Application requirements: Essay, transcript. Essay of no more than 500 words which explains how your planned studies will relate to a career in the construction industry. A transcript of your high school grades, including grading scale, class standing, and results of SAT/ACT tests. Copy of student aid report or FAFSA and custodial parent's statement (from the College Board) if applicable.
Additional information: Applications are only accepted from Connecticut-resident students who will be entering college-level programs in architecture, construction-related engineering, construction management, surveying, planning or other courses of study leading to associate, baccalaureate, or masters degrees in the construction field. The scholarships will be given for academic merit, extracurricular activities, potential, and financial need. A high school transcript and essay will need to be submitted. Letters of recommendation are encouraged. Renewal contingent upon grades and college major.

Amount of award:	$500-$2,000
Number of awards:	4
Application deadline:	March 10
Notification begins:	June 1

Contact:
Connecticut Building Congress
500 Purdy Hill Road
Monroe, CT 06468
Phone: 203-452-1331 x108
Fax: 203-268-8103
Web: www.cbc-ct.org/CBC_Scholarship

Connecticut Office of Higher Education

Connecticut Aid to Dependents of Deceased/POW/MIA Veterans

Type of award: Scholarship.
Intended use: For undergraduate or graduate study. Designated institutions: Connecticut public colleges and universities.
Eligibility: Applicant must be U.S. citizen residing in Connecticut. Applicant must be dependent of deceased veteran or POW/MIA; or spouse of deceased veteran or POW/MIA. Death must be service-related. Parent/spouse must have been Connecticut resident prior to enlistment.
Application requirements: Proof of eligibility.
Additional information: Visit Website for more information.

Amount of award:	$800
Number of awards:	5

Contact:
Connecticut Office of Higher Education
61 Woodland Street
Hartford, CT 06105-2391
Phone: 800-842-0229
Fax: 860-947-1310
Web: www.ctohe.org

Connecticut Minority Teacher Incentive Grant

Type of award: Scholarship.
Intended use: For full-time junior or senior study. Designated institutions: Eligible Connecticut colleges and universities.
Eligibility: Applicant must be Alaskan native, Asian American, African American, Mexican American, Hispanic American, Puerto Rican, American Indian or Native Hawaiian/Pacific Islander. Applicant must be residing in Connecticut.
Basis for selection: Major/career interest in education; education, special or education, teacher.
Application requirements: Nomination by college or university's Education Dean, or other appropriate official.
Additional information: Must be enrolled in Connecticut college or university teacher preparation program. Grants up to $5,000/year for two years; loan reimbursement of $2,500/year for up to four years of teaching in Connecticut public school. Visit Website for more information.

Amount of award:	$2,500-$5,000
Number of awards:	45
Number of applicants:	36
Application deadline:	October 1
Total amount awarded:	$150,000

Contact:
Connecticut Office of Higher Education
61 Woodland Street
Hartford, CT 06105-2326
Phone: 860-947-1857
Fax: 860-947-1838
Web: www.ctohe.org

Connecticut Tuition Waiver for Senior Citizens

Type of award: Scholarship.
Intended use: For undergraduate study at 2-year or 4-year institution. Designated institutions: Connecticut public colleges and universities.
Eligibility: Applicant must be returning adult student. Applicant must be U.S. citizen residing in Connecticut.
Application requirements: Proof of eligibility.
Additional information: Waivers approved on space available basis. Apply through financial aid office of institution.

Amount of award:	Full tuition
Number of awards:	1,683
Total amount awarded:	$874,080

Contact:
Connecticut Office of Higher Education
61 Woodland Street
Hartford, CT 06105-2391
Phone: 800-842-0229
Fax: 860-947-1310
Web: www.ctohe.org

Connecticut Tuition Waiver for Veterans

Type of award: Scholarship, renewable.
Intended use: For undergraduate or graduate study. Designated institutions: Connecticut public colleges and universities.
Eligibility: Applicant must be U.S. citizen residing in Connecticut. Applicant must be veteran. Must have been Connecticut resident at time of enlistment. Active members of Connecticut Army or Air National Guard also eligible.
Application requirements: Proof of eligibility.
Additional information: Visit Website for more information.

Amount of award:	Full tuition
Number of awards:	3,228
Total amount awarded:	$4,365,411

Contact:
Connecticut Office of Higher Ed.
450 Columbus Boulevard
Suit 510
Hartford, CT 06103-1841
Phone: 800-842-0229
Fax: 860-947-1310
Web: www.ctohe.org

Connecticut Tuition Waiver for Vietnam MIA/POW Dependents

Type of award: Scholarship.
Intended use: For undergraduate study. Designated institutions: Connecticut public colleges and universities.
Eligibility: Applicant must be U.S. citizen residing in Connecticut. Applicant must be dependent of POW/MIA; or spouse of POW/MIA. Open to spouse or dependent of veteran who is POW/MIA after 1/1/60.
Application requirements: Proof of eligibility.

Additional information: Apply at financial aid office of institution. Awarded through Connecticut public colleges. Visit Website for more information.

Amount of award:	Full tuition

Contact:
Connecticut Office of Higher Ed.
61 Woodland Street
Hartford, CT 06105-2326
Phone: 800-842-0229
Fax: 860-947-1310
Web: www.ctohe.org

Roberta B. Willis Scholarship - Need & Merit-Based Award

Type of award: Scholarship.
Intended use: For freshman study at 2-year or 4-year institution in United States. Designated institutions: Connecticut public and private not-for-profit colleges and universities.
Eligibility: Applicant must be high school senior. Applicant must be U.S. citizen residing in Connecticut.
Basis for selection: Applicant must demonstrate financial need and high academic achievement.
Application requirements: FAFSA.
Additional information: Applicants must rank in the top 20 percentile of their junior year class, and/or have a minimum 1800 SAT score or a minimum 27 ACT score. Applicant must have a federal Expected Family Contribution (EFC) equal to, or below the maximum allowable EFC for the year.

Amount of award:	$500-$5,250
Number of awards:	3,056
Number of applicants:	4,475
Application deadline:	February 15
Total amount awarded:	$6,256,664

Contact:
Connecticut Office of Higher Education
61 Woodland Street
Hartford, CT 06105-2391
Phone: 800-842-0229
Fax: 860-947-1311
Web: www.ctohe.org/SFA/default.shtml

Roberta B. Willis Scholarship - Need-Based Award

Type of award: Scholarship.
Intended use: For undergraduate study at 2-year or 4-year institution in United States. Designated institutions: Connecticut public and private not-for-profit colleges and universities.
Eligibility: Applicant must be U.S. citizen residing in Connecticut.
Basis for selection: Applicant must demonstrate financial need.
Application requirements: FAFSA.
Additional information: Applicant must have a federal Expected Family Contribution (EFC) equal to, or below the maximum allowable EFC for the year. Award amount determined by eligible EFC. Deadline based on college financial aid deadline. Inquire at eligible college or university financial aid offices for more information.

Amount of award:	$500-$4,500

Contact:
Connecticut Office of Higher Education
61 Woodland Street
Hartford, CT 06105-2391
Phone: 800-842-0229
Fax: 860-947-1311
Web: www.ctohe.org

Weisman Scholarship

Type of award: Scholarship, renewable.
Intended use: For full-time junior or senior study. Designated institutions: Eligible Connecticut colleges and universities.
Eligibility: Applicant must be Alaskan native, Asian American, African American, Mexican American, Hispanic American, Puerto Rican, American Indian or Native Hawaiian/Pacific Islander. Applicant must be residing in Connecticut.
Basis for selection: Major/career interest in education or education, teacher.
Application requirements: Nomination by college or university's Education Dean, or other appropriate official.
Additional information: Must be enrolled in Connecticut teacher preparation program and intend to teach math or science in middle or high school. Loan reimbursement up to $2,500 per year for up to four years of teaching science or math in Connecticut public middle or high school. Visit Website for more information and deadline.

Amount of award:	$2,500-$5,000
Number of awards:	2
Number of applicants:	47
Total amount awarded:	$10,000

Contact:
Connecticut Office of Higher Ed.
61 Woodland Street
Hartford, CT 06105-2326
Phone: 800-842-0229
Fax: 860-947-1838
Web: www.ctohe.org

Connecticut Women's Hall of Fame

Eileen Kraus Scholarship

Type of award: Scholarship.
Intended use: For freshman study at 2-year or 4-year institution.
Eligibility: Applicant must be female, high school senior. Applicant must be residing in Connecticut.
Application requirements: Transcript. Two-page essay on the following question: "Among the 115 Inductees of the Hall, who do you find most inspiring, and how do you see the legacy of this woman reflected in your own goals?"
Additional information: Scholarship winner must be able to attend the CWHF 24th Annual Induction Ceremony on November 9, 2017 in Hartford, CT. (Ticket to attend event will be provided. Transportation and other costs are at the expense of the awardee.)

Number of awards:	1
Application deadline:	February 15
Notification begins:	March 31
Total amount awarded:	$5,000

Contact:
Connecticut Women's Hall of Fame
320 Fitch Street
New Haven, CT 06515
Web: cwhf.org/scholarship

ConocoPhillips

U.S. Dependent Scholarship Program

Type of award: Scholarship, renewable.
Intended use: For undergraduate or graduate study at postsecondary institution in United States. Designated institutions: Colorado School of Mines, Kansas State University, Oklahoma State University, Texas A&M University, Texas Tech University, University of Oklahoma, University of Texas at Austin, University of Tulsa, University of Colorado.
Basis for selection: Major/career interest in business; engineering or geology/earth sciences. Applicant must demonstrate high academic achievement.
Additional information: Information and applications can only be obtained from the university directly. http://hr.conocophillips.com/policies-and-programs/financial-assistance/Pages/dependent-scholarship.aspx.
Contact:
ConocoPhillips

Constitutional Officers Association of Georgia

Constitutional Officers Association of Georgia, Inc. Scholarship

Type of award: Scholarship.
Intended use: For full-time undergraduate study at accredited vocational, 2-year or 4-year institution.
Eligibility: Applicant must be enrolled in high school. Applicant must be U.S. citizen residing in Georgia.
Basis for selection: Major/career interest in political science/government; accounting; finance/banking; business or law.
Application requirements: Applicant must present a letter of acceptance or letter of enrollment from a school of accredited higher education located within Georgia (four year college, junior college or technical college) to provide verification of degree field related to government/law enforcement, political science, accounting/finance or business, pre-law. Provide proof of residency in the State of Georgia. Submit a 1,000 word essay. Presenting a COAG scholarship application.
Additional information: You must be seeking an undergraduate degree in a field related to government/law enforcement, political science, accounting/finance, business, or pre-law.

Amount of award:	$500-$1,500
Number of awards:	3
Application deadline:	April 1
Total amount awarded:	$3,000

Contact:
Constitutional Officers Association of Georgia
PO Box 1644
Decatur, GA 30031
Phone: 404-377-1364
Fax: 404-378-7831
Web: www.coag.info/2016-2017-scholarships

Construction Institute of ASCE

CI Construction Engineering Student Scholarship

Type of award: Scholarship.
Intended use: For undergraduate study at 4-year institution.
Basis for selection: Major/career interest in engineering, civil or construction management. Applicant must demonstrate leadership.
Application requirements: Recommendations, transcript. Statement of professional goals, resume.
Additional information: Must be American Society of Civil Engineers member and/or Construction Institute student member in good standing and be enrolled in civil engineering program with concentration in construction engineering or construction management. Preference given to applicants enrolled in programs with an accredited Construction Management program. Award to be paid up to three years until graduation; amount determined by award committee.

Number of awards:	1
Application deadline:	April 1

Contact:
Construction Institute of ASCE
Attn: Construction Scholarship
1801 Alexander Bell Drive
Reston, VA 20191-4400
Phone: 703-295-6390
Fax: 703-295-6222
Web: www.asce.org

Costume Society of America

Adele Filene Student Presenter Grant

Type of award: Scholarship.
Intended use: For full-time undergraduate or graduate study in United States.
Eligibility: Applicant must be U.S. citizen or international student.
Basis for selection: Major/career interest in ethnic/cultural studies; art/art history; arts, general; history or fashion/fashion design/modeling.
Application requirements: One faculty recommendation. Must submit additional essay.
Additional information: Award only for those who have paper or research poster accepted for presentation at National Symposium. Award is for travel expenses to the meeting. Applicant must reside outside 200 mile radius of Symposium site. Must be student member of Costume Society of America.

Major/career interests may include apparel design, historic costume, and fashion merchandising. Number of awards varies.

Amount of award:	$500
Application deadline:	March 1
Notification begins:	April 1

Contact:
Chair, CSA Adele Filene Student Presenter Grant Committee
Attn: Dennita Sewell
1625 North Central Avenue
Phoenix, AZ 85004-1685
Phone: 602-257-1880
Web: www.costumesocietyamerica.com/GrantsAwards/adelefilene.html

Stella Blum Student Research Grant

Type of award: Research grant.
Intended use: For undergraduate or graduate study at accredited vocational, 2-year, 4-year or graduate institution in United States.
Eligibility: Applicant must be U.S. citizen, permanent resident or international student.
Basis for selection: Major/career interest in art/art history; arts, general; history; museum studies or performing arts.
Application requirements: Recommendations, transcript, proof of eligibility. References and written research proposal. The proposal should be typed, double-spaced, no more than 1,000 words. Must also submit a brief abstract, no more than 50 words. Must provide seven copies of all documents. Must also include letters of permission from any research site, museum or library applicant intends to visit for research.
Additional information: Must be member of Costume Society of America. Award is $2,000 for research and $500 for expenses to present at national meeting.

Amount of award:	$2,500
Number of awards:	1
Application deadline:	May 1
Notification begins:	August 15
Total amount awarded:	$2,500

Contact:
Costume Society of America
Attn: Ann Wass, Committee Chair
5903 60th Ave
Riverdale, MD 20737
Phone: 908-359-1471
Fax: 908-450-1118
Web: www.costumesocietyamerica.com/GrantsAwards/stellablum.html

Council on International Educational Exchange

CIEE Academic Excellence Scholarship

Type of award: Scholarship.
Intended use: For full-time undergraduate study at accredited 4-year institution. Designated institutions: CIEE Member or CIEE Academic Consortium Member institutions.
Basis for selection: Competition/talent/interest in study abroad. Applicant must demonstrate financial need and high academic achievement.
Application requirements: Essay, transcript.

Additional information: Available to CIEE Study Center program applicants only. Program application is used in consideration of scholarship applicants. Award is $2000 for winter, $1000 for summer. Visit Website for details and application.

Amount of award:	$1,000-$2,000
Application deadline:	April 1, November 1
Notification begins:	May 1, December 1

Contact:
CIEE
Attn: Scholarship Committee
300 Fore Street
Portland, ME 04101
Phone: 800-40-STUDY
Fax: 207-221-4299
Web: www.ciee.org/study-abroad/scholarships

Jennifer Ritzmann Scholarship for Studies in Tropical Biology

Type of award: Scholarship.
Intended use: For full-time undergraduate study at accredited 4-year institution. Designated institutions: CIEE Study Center program in Monteverde, Costa Rica.
Basis for selection: Competition/talent/interest in study abroad. Major/career interest in biology or ecology. Applicant must demonstrate financial need and high academic achievement.
Application requirements: Essay, transcript.
Additional information: Award is for students applying to the Monteverde, Costa Rica Tropical Ecology and Conservation or the Sustainability and Environment semester programs only. Visit Website for more information.

Amount of award:	$1,000
Number of awards:	2
Application deadline:	April 1, November 1
Notification begins:	May 1, December 1

Contact:
CIEE
Attn: Scholarship Committee
300 Fore Street
Portland, ME 04101
Phone: 800-40-STUDY
Fax: 207-221-4299
Web: www.ciee.org/study/scholarships.aspx

John E. Bowman Travel Grants

Type of award: Scholarship.
Intended use: For full-time undergraduate study at accredited 4-year institution. Designated institutions: CIEE Member or CIEE Academic Consortium member institutions.
Basis for selection: Competition/talent/interest in study abroad. Applicant must demonstrate financial need and high academic achievement.
Application requirements: Essay, transcript.
Additional information: Applicant must participate in CIEE study abroad program in Africa, Asia, Europe, or Latin America. Visit Website for details and application.

Amount of award:	$1,000
Application deadline:	April 1, November 1
Notification begins:	May 1, December 1

Contact:
CIEE
Attn: Scholarship Committee
300 Fore Street
Portland, ME 04101
Phone: 800-40-STUDY
Fax: 207-221-4299
Web: www.ciee.org/study/scholarships.aspx

Kathleen McDermott Health Sciences Scholarship

Type of award: Scholarship.
Intended use: For undergraduate study at postsecondary institution outside United States.
Basis for selection: Competition/talent/interest in study abroad. Major/career interest in public health or nursing. Applicant must demonstrate financial need.
Application requirements: Essay.
Additional information: Applicant must be a public health or nursing major and/or participating in a community public health study abroad program. Award amount varies depending on duration of study and financial need.

Amount of award:	$1,000-$2,500
Application deadline:	April 1, November 1

Contact:
CIEE
Attn: Scholarship Committee
300 Fore Street
Portland, ME 04101
Phone: 800-40-STUDY
Fax: 207-221-4299
Web: www.ciee.org/study-abroad/scholarships

Michael Stohl Scholarship

Type of award: Scholarship.
Intended use: For undergraduate study at postsecondary institution outside United States. Designated institutions: CIEE Member or CIEE Academic Consortium member institutions.
Basis for selection: Competition/talent/interest in study abroad. Applicant must demonstrate financial need.
Application requirements: Essay.
Additional information: Applicant must be non-traditionally aged, first-generation college student from non-traditional background. Must plan to conduct research as part of a study abroad program.

Amount of award:	$1,000-$5,000
Application deadline:	April 1, November 1

Contact:
CIEE
Attn: Scholarship Committee
300 Fore Street
Portland, ME 04101
Phone: 800-40-STUDY
Fax: 207-221-4299
Web: www.ciee.org/study-abroad/scholarships/

Peter Wollitzer Scholarships for Study in Asia

Type of award: Scholarship.
Intended use: For full-time undergraduate study at accredited 4-year institution. Designated institutions: CIEE Academic Consortium Board Member institutions.

Basis for selection: Competition/talent/interest in study abroad. Applicant must demonstrate financial need and high academic achievement.
Application requirements: Essay, transcript.
Additional information: Applicant must participate in a CIEE Study Center program in Asia (includes Cambodia, China, India, Japan, Korea, Taiwan, Thailand, and Vietnam). Applicants also eligible if studying through the University of California Education Abroad Program (EAP) Office. Award amounts vary based on program duration and financial need.

Amount of award:	$1,000-$5,000
Application deadline:	April 1, November 1
Notification begins:	May 1, December 1

Contact:
CIEE
Attn: Scholarship Committee
300 Fore Street
Portland, ME 04101
Phone: 800-40-STUDY
Fax: 207-221-4299
Web: www.ciee.org/study/scholarships.aspx

Robert B. Bailey Scholarship

Type of award: Scholarship.
Intended use: For full-time undergraduate or graduate study at accredited 4-year institution. Designated institutions: CIEE Member or CIEE Academic Consortium member institutions.
Basis for selection: Competition/talent/interest in study abroad. Applicant must demonstrate financial need and high academic achievement.
Application requirements: Essay, transcript.
Additional information: Available to CIEE Study Center applicants only. Must be self-identified as belonging to underrepresented group. Award amounts vary based on program duration and financial need. Program application is used in consideration of scholarship applicants. Visit Website for details and application.

Amount of award:	$1,000-$5,000
Application deadline:	April 1, November 1
Notification begins:	May 1, December 1

Contact:
CIEE
Attn: Scholarship Committee
300 Fore Street
Portland, ME 04101
Phone: 800-40-STUDY
Fax: 207-221-4299
Web: www.ciee.org/study/scholarships.aspx

Courage Kenny Rehabilitation Institute

Courage Center Scholarship for People with Disabilities

Type of award: Scholarship.
Intended use: For full-time undergraduate study at accredited vocational, 2-year or 4-year institution.
Eligibility: Applicant must be visually impaired, hearing impaired or physically challenged. Applicant must be U.S. citizen residing in Minnesota.
Basis for selection: Applicant must demonstrate financial need.

Application requirements: Interview, essay.
Additional information: If not Minnesota resident, student must be participant in Courage Center services.

Amount of award:	$500-$1,000
Number of awards:	30
Number of applicants:	30
Application deadline:	May 31
Notification begins:	July 31
Total amount awarded:	$11,000

Contact:
Courage Kenny Rehabilitation Institute Vocational Services
Attn: Administrative Assistant
3915 Golden Valley Road
Minneapolis, MN 55422
Phone: 763-520-0553
Fax: 763-230-1923
Web: www.couragecenter.org/ContentPages/Resources.aspx

Courage to Grow

Courage to Grow Scholarship

Type of award: Scholarship.
Intended use: For undergraduate or graduate study at vocational, 2-year, 4-year or graduate institution in United States.
Eligibility: Applicant must be U.S. citizen.
Basis for selection: Applicant must demonstrate financial need and high academic achievement.
Application requirements: Essay.
Additional information: High school seniors may also apply. Minimum 2.5 GPA. Program awards one $500 scholarship every month; deadline date is last day of each month. Visit Website for application and details.

Amount of award:	$6,000
Number of awards:	12
Number of applicants:	1,000
Total amount awarded:	$6,000

Contact:
Courage to Grow Scholarship
P.O. Box 2507
Chelan, WA 98816
Phone: 509-731-3056
Web: www.couragetogrowscholarship.com

Crescent Electric Supply Company

Crescent Electric Supply Company Energy Efficient Scholarship

Type of award: Scholarship.
Intended use: For full-time freshman, sophomore or junior study at vocational, 2-year or 4-year institution.
Eligibility: Applicant must be at least 16, no older than 22, high school freshman, sophomore, junior or senior.
Application requirements: Show us how you make an effort to minimize your energy usagge by sharing a photo on Twitter that represents how you reduce your carbon footprint (use the

hashtag #CEscholarship for a chance to win and submit through the form on our website).

Additional information: Visit the company scholarship page and follow directions http://www.cesco.com/content/EnergySaverScholarship .

Amount of award:	$1,000
Number of awards:	1
Application deadline:	August 8
Notification begins:	August 9
Total amount awarded:	$1,000

Contact:
Crescent Electric Supply Company
1225 26th Avenue COURT SW
Cedar Rapids, IA 52404
Phone: 855-999-2372
Web: http://www.cesco.com/content/EnergySaverScholarship

Criminal Defense Incorporated

Criminal Defense Incorporated Scholarship

Type of award: Scholarship.
Intended use: For full-time undergraduate study at accredited 4-year institution.
Eligibility: Applicant must be high school senior. Applicant must be U.S. citizen or permanent resident.
Basis for selection: Applicant must demonstrate high academic achievement.
Application requirements: Transcript, proof of eligibility. Introduction and Short Essay answering prompt on website. Unofficial and Official transcripts. Proof of Enrollment in post secondary education institution. Photo Identification.
Additional information: Minimum 3.0 GPA required. Qualifying students must have demonstrated a meaningful commitment to not only building their own future, but improving the local community as well. Students currently attending a two-year college may apply if they intend to transfer to an accredited four-year college or university.

Amount of award:	$500
Number of awards:	1
Application deadline:	April 15
Notification begins:	June 15

Contact:
Criminal Defense Incorporated
Web: www.criminaldefenseinc.com/scholarship/

Cumberland Farms

Cumberland Farms Believe and Achieve Scholarship Program

Type of award: Scholarship.
Intended use: For undergraduate study at accredited vocational, 2-year or 4-year institution.
Eligibility: Applicant must be high school senior. Applicant must be residing in Vermont, New York, New Hampshire, Connecticut, Maine, Massachusetts, Rhode Island or Florida.

Additional information: Must have a minimum 3.0 GPA. Applicants should reside within a 30 mile radius of a Cumberland Farms store. Intended for seniors in high school.

Amount of award:	$1,000
Number of awards:	130
Application deadline:	December 15
Total amount awarded:	$130,000

Contact:
Phone: 978-468-3076
Fax: 978-526-8206
Web: https://www.cumberlandfarms.com/company/doing-good/believe-achieve

CuraDebt

CuraDebt Scholarship

Type of award: Scholarship, renewable.
Intended use: For undergraduate or graduate study at accredited 2-year or 4-year institution in United States.
Eligibility: Applicant must be high school senior.
Basis for selection: Major/career interest in science, general; engineering; technology or mathematics.
Application requirements: Provide a unique solution to the following issue: "Come up with a unique way to solve the budget deficit through education and empowering our youth." Students can upload a video, write an essay, or create an infographic. Include a cover letter with your name, college, year, graduating year, and major. In the cover letter, explain how you plan to use the scholarship and why you should be selected. For video submissions, provide a link in the cover letter.
Additional information: Graduating high school seniors with a GPA of 3.0 or above are also eligible to apply for the scholarship. Must be pursuing their bachelor's degree in the fields of STEM (science, technology, engineering, and math). Apply via e-mail.

Number of awards:	1
Application deadline:	December 31
Notification begins:	March 1
Total amount awarded:	$500

Contact:
CuraDebt Financial Solutions
4000 Hollywood Boulevard
Hollywood, FL 33021
Phone: 877-850-3328
Web: www.curadebt.com/#applyforscholarship

The Cynthia E. Morgan Memorial Scholarship Fund

The Cynthia E. Morgan Memorial Scholarship Fund

Type of award: Scholarship.
Intended use: For undergraduate or graduate study at accredited vocational, 2-year or 4-year institution. Designated institutions: Maryland vocational school, college, or university.
Eligibility: Applicant must be high school junior or senior. Applicant must be residing in Maryland.

Basis for selection: Major/career interest in medicine; nursing; pharmacy/pharmaceutics/pharmacology; dietetics/nutrition; occupational therapy; physical therapy; physician assistant or speech pathology/audiology. Applicant must demonstrate financial need and high academic achievement.
Application requirements: Essay, transcript, proof of eligibility.
Additional information: Must be first person in immediate family to attend college. Must be entering or planning on entering medical or medical-related field.

Amount of award:	$1,000
Application deadline:	February 25
Notification begins:	March 15

Contact:
The Cynthia E. Morgan Memorial Scholarship Fund
5516 Maudes Way
White Marsh, MD 21162
Web: www.cemsfund.com

Cystic Fibrosis Foundation

Cystic Fibrosis Student Traineeship

Type of award: Research grant, renewable.
Intended use: For full-time senior, master's or doctoral study at accredited 4-year or graduate institution in United States.
Basis for selection: Major/career interest in medical specialties/research.
Application requirements: Recommendations, research proposal.
Additional information: Trainees must work with faculty sponsor on research project related to cystic fibrosis. Applications accepted throughout the year, but should be submitted at least two months prior to anticipated start date of project.

Amount of award:	$1,500

Contact:
Cystic Fibrosis Foundation
Grants & Contracts Office
6931 Arlington Road
Bethesda, MD 20814
Phone: 301-951-4422
Fax: 301-841-2605
Web: www.cff.org/research/forresearchers/fundingopportunities/traininggrants

The Dallas Foundation

The Chesapeake Energy Scholarship

Type of award: Scholarship, renewable.
Intended use: For undergraduate study at accredited vocational, 2-year or 4-year institution.
Eligibility: Applicant must be Alaskan native, Asian American, African American, Mexican American, Hispanic American, Puerto Rican, American Indian or Native Hawaiian/Pacific Islander. Applicant must be high school senior. Applicant must be U.S. citizen or permanent resident residing in Texas.
Basis for selection: Applicant must demonstrate high academic achievement and service orientation.
Application requirements: Recommendations, essay, transcript. FAFSA or SAR.

Additional information: Must be a graduating senior of eligible high schools in Dallas Independent School District. Must be active member of Education is Freedom (EIF Dallas). Must be female or member of minority group. Minimum 3.0 GPA. Must have taken SAT or ACT. Children and grandchildren of Chesapeake Energy employees not eligible. Visit Website for application. Deadline in mid-April.

Amount of award:	$20,000
Application deadline:	April 14

Contact:
The Dallas Foundation
3963 Maple Ave. Ste. 390
Dallas, TX 75219
Phone: 214-741-9898
Web: www.dallasfoundation.org

Dallas Architectural Foundation - Swank Travelling Fellowship

Type of award: Scholarship.
Intended use: For senior or graduate study at accredited postsecondary institution.
Eligibility: Applicant must be U.S. citizen or permanent resident residing in Texas.
Basis for selection: Major/career interest in architecture.
Application requirements: Portfolio, recommendations, essay, transcript. Resume, budget statement.
Additional information: Applicant must be permanent resident of the Dallas-Fort Worth area. Fellowship established to assist architecture students or recent graduates in broadening their architectural knowledge through travel. Funds must be used for travel and study costs, and within the same calendar year. Recipient must agree to present program of results to the Dallas Architectural Foundation board. Visit Website for application.

Amount of award:	$2,000
Number of awards:	1
Number of applicants:	5
Application deadline:	March 27
Total amount awarded:	$2,000

Contact:
Dallas Architectural Foundation
1909 Woodall Rodgers Freeway
Suite 100
Dallas, TX 75201
Phone: 214-742-3242
Web: www.dallascfa.com

The Dallas Morning New Journalism Scholarship

Type of award: Scholarship.
Intended use: For freshman study at 4-year institution.
Eligibility: Applicant must be high school senior. Applicant must be U.S. citizen or permanent resident residing in Texas.
Basis for selection: Major/career interest in journalism. Applicant must demonstrate high academic achievement, leadership and service orientation.
Application requirements: Recommendations, essay, transcript. Two samples demonstrating aptitude for print journalism. Description of community service experience.
Additional information: Must live within Collin, Dallas, Denton, Ellis, Kaufman, Rockwall, or Tarrant counties. Minimum 3.0 GPA. Must show aptitude for print journalism. Visit Website for application and deadline.

Amount of award: $1,500
Number of awards: 3
Application deadline: April 17
Contact:
The Dallas Morning News Journalism Scholarship
c/o The Dallas Foundation
3963 Maple Ave., Suite 390
Dallas, TX 75219
Phone: 214-741-9898
Web: www.dallasfoundation.org

Dr. Dan J. and Patricia S. Pickard Scholarship

Type of award: Scholarship, renewable.
Intended use: For freshman study at 2-year or 4-year institution.
Eligibility: Applicant must be African American. Applicant must be male. Applicant must be residing in Texas.
Basis for selection: Applicant must demonstrate financial need, high academic achievement and service orientation.
Application requirements: Recommendations, essay, transcript. FAFSA or SAR.
Additional information: Must be graduating from high school in Dallas County. Minimum 2.5 GPA. Visit Website for application.

Amount of award: $1,000
Application deadline: April 1
Contact:
The Dallas Foundation
3963 Maple Ave., Ste. 390
Dallas, TX 75219
Phone: 214-741-9898
Web: www.dallasfoundation.org

Dr. Don and Rose Marie Benton Scholarship

Type of award: Scholarship, renewable.
Intended use: For undergraduate or graduate study at accredited postsecondary institution in United States.
Eligibility: Applicant must be residing in Texas.
Application requirements: Nomination by member of the Scholarship Committee at Trinity River Mission.
Additional information: Award amount varies; maximum is $1,500. Number of awards varies. Applicant or parent must be affiliated with Trinity River Mission. Must reside in Dallas county.

Amount of award: $1,500
Number of awards: 3
Application deadline: April 1
Contact:
Trinity River Mission
Marie Rivera, Trinity River Mission
2060 Singleton Blvd., Suite 104
Dallas, TX 75212
Phone: 214-744-6774
Web: www.dallasfoundation.org

Hirsch Family Scholarship

Type of award: Scholarship.
Intended use: For freshman study at accredited vocational, 2-year or 4-year institution in United States.
Eligibility: Applicant must be high school senior.
Basis for selection: Applicant must demonstrate financial need and high academic achievement.

Application requirements: Recommendations, essay, transcript. List of extracurricular activities, community service, and work experience; FAFSA.
Additional information: Applicant must be the dependent child of an active employee of Eagle Materials, Performance Chemicals and Ingredients, The Composites Group, Custom Winder System, Ascend, Lund, JuiceTyme, Highlander Partners and any of their majority-owned subsidiaries. Past recipients are encouraged to apply each year.

Amount of award: $1,000-$6,000
Application deadline: April 15
Contact:
The Dallas Foundation
3963 Maple Ave., Ste. 390
Dallas, TX 75219
Phone: 214-741-9898
Web: www.dallasfoundation.org

Jere W. Thompson, Jr. Scholarship Fund

Type of award: Scholarship, renewable.
Intended use: For full-time junior or senior study at accredited 4-year institution in United States. Designated institutions: Texas institutions.
Eligibility: Applicant must be U.S. citizen or permanent resident residing in Texas.
Basis for selection: Major/career interest in engineering, civil or engineering, construction. Applicant must demonstrate financial need, high academic achievement and seriousness of purpose.
Application requirements: Recommendations, essay, transcript, proof of eligibility. FAFSA or SAR.
Additional information: Applicant must be college sophomore. Award amount varies; maximum is $2,000 per semester, renewable for three additional semesters if student maintains 3.0 GPA and submits grade report within 45 days after the end of the semester. Recipients will be given opportunity for paid internship with one of scholarship's sponsors between junior and senior year. Preference may be given to residents of Collin, Dallas, Denton, or Tarrant counties. Visit Website for program profile and application.

Amount of award: $2,000
Number of awards: 1
Application deadline: February 3
Contact:
The Dallas Foundation
3963 Maple Ave., Ste. 390
Dallas, TX 75219
Phone: 214-741-9898
Web: www.dallasfoundation.org

The Tommy Tranchin Award

Type of award: Scholarship.
Intended use: For non-degree study at postsecondary institution.
Eligibility: Applicant must be physically challenged or learning disabled. Applicant must be high school freshman, sophomore, junior or senior. Applicant must be residing in Texas.
Application requirements: Recommendations, essay. Description and budget for proposed activity.
Additional information: Award for student with physical, emotional, or intellectual disability who wants to participate in an activity that furthers development in an area in which he/she excels or shows promise. Funds may be used for program expenses, travel, other related expenses. Must be high school

student in North Texas. Award is up to $1,500. Visit Website for application.

Application deadline: March 6
Contact:
The Dallas Foundation
3963 Maple Ave., Ste. 390
Dallas, TX 75219
Phone: 214-741-9898
Web: www.dallasfoundation.org

Daniels Fund

Daniels Scholarship Program

Type of award: Scholarship, renewable.
Intended use: For freshman study at accredited 2-year or 4-year institution in United States. Designated institutions: Not-for-profit institutions.
Eligibility: Applicant must be high school senior. Applicant must be U.S. citizen or permanent resident residing in Wyoming, Utah, New Mexico or Colorado.
Basis for selection: Applicant must demonstrate financial need, high academic achievement, depth of character, seriousness of purpose and service orientation.
Application requirements: Interview, recommendations, essay, transcript, nomination. ACT/SAT scores, copies of income tax information, proof of U.S. citizenship.
Additional information: Minimum ACT score: 17. Minimum SAT score: 830. Daniels Scholarship covers unmet needs of the student. Amount is determined after all other financial aid sources and Expected Family Contribution have been applied. Amounts vary. Scholarship can only be used at one of the schools listed on student's application. Apply online. Semifinalists must submit additional materials and go through interview process. Amount of award varies. Deadline in November; notification begins March. Visit Website for more information.

Number of awards:	250
Number of applicants:	2,475
Total amount awarded:	$12,800,000

Contact:
Daniels Fund
101 Monroe Street
Denver, CO 80206
Phone: 303-393-7220
Web: www.danielsfund.org

Data Processing Management Association/ Portland Chapter

DPMA/PC Scholarship

Type of award: Scholarship, renewable.
Intended use: For undergraduate study in United States. Designated institutions: Institutions in Oregon or Washington.
Eligibility: Applicant must be high school senior. Applicant must be residing in Oregon or Washington.

Basis for selection: Major/career interest in computer/ information sciences. Applicant must demonstrate financial need, high academic achievement and seriousness of purpose.
Application requirements: Recommendations, transcript. List and description of past and current IT-related activities, and of IT career goals. Explanation of reasons for applying for scholarship.
Additional information: Applicants must graduate from high school in Oregon or Clark County in Washington. Renewable for $500 each year if awardee maintains a minimum "B" GPA and remains in a technology-related program. Check Website for application deadline.

Amount of award:	$1,000
Number of awards:	1
Number of applicants:	17
Application deadline:	May 31
Notification begins:	June 15
Total amount awarded:	$4,000

Contact:
DPMA/PC Scholarship
Attn: Scholarship Chair
P.O. Box 61545
Vancouver, WA 98660
Fax: 360-816-0235
Web: www.dpmapc.com/scholarship.htm

Daughters of Union Veterans of the Civil War 1861-1865

Grand Army of the Republic Living Memorial Scholarship

Type of award: Scholarship.
Intended use: For sophomore, junior or senior study at accredited 4-year institution in United States.
Eligibility: Applicant must be descendant of veteran during Civil War. Must be lineal descendant of Union Veteran of Civil War of 1861-1865.
Basis for selection: Applicant must demonstrate depth of character, leadership, patriotism, seriousness of purpose and service orientation.
Application requirements: Transcript. Two letters of reference, ancestor's military record.
Additional information: Must be of good moral character and have firm belief in US Government. Must have satisfactory scholastic standing. Request for information and application honored only with SASE. Number of awards varies.

Amount of award:	$200-$500
Application deadline:	April 30
Notification begins:	August 30
Total amount awarded:	$1,500

Contact:
Web: www.duvcw.org

Davidson Institute

Davidson Fellows Scholarship

Type of award: Scholarship.
Intended use: For undergraduate study at accredited postsecondary institution in United States.
Eligibility: Applicant must be U.S. citizen or permanent resident.
Basis for selection: Major/career interest in literature; music; philosophy; mathematics; science, general; technology or engineering.
Application requirements: Two nominator forms. Signed statement of commitment that, if named a Davidson Fellow, the applicant and a parent or guardian will attend the award reception in Washington, D.C.
Additional information: Applicants awarded for accomplishment that is recognized as significant by experts in that field and has a positive contribution to society. Applicant must be 18 or under as of October 1st of the year of application. Applications are accepted in the following categories: science, technology, engineering, mathematics, music, literature, philosophy, and outside the box. Work may be exceptionally creative application of existing knowledge, new idea with high impact, innovative solution with broad-range implications, important advancement that can be replicated and built upon, interdisciplinary discovery, prodigious performance, or another demonstration of extraordinary accomplishment. Application deadline is second Wednesday in February.

Amount of award:	$10,000-$50,000
Number of awards:	20
Notification begins:	July 1
Total amount awarded:	$500,000

Contact:
Davidson Institute for Talent Development
9665 Gateway Drive
Suite B
Reno, NV 89521
Phone: 775-852-3483 ext. 423
Fax: 775-852-2184
Web: www.davidsongifted.org/fellows

Davis-Roberts Scholarship Fund

Davis-Roberts Scholarship

Type of award: Scholarship, renewable.
Intended use: For full-time undergraduate study at 2-year or 4-year institution.
Eligibility: Applicant must be U.S. citizen residing in Wyoming.
Basis for selection: Applicant must demonstrate financial need.
Application requirements: Recommendations, essay, transcript. Applicant's photograph.
Additional information: Applicant must be member of Job's Daughters or DeMolay.

Amount of award:	$300-$1,000
Number of awards:	10
Number of applicants:	12
Application deadline:	June 15
Notification begins:	August 31
Total amount awarded:	$5,000

Contact:
Davis-Roberts Scholarship Fund
c/o Gary D. Skillern
P.O. Box 20645
Cheyenne, WY 82003
Phone: 307-632-0491

The De Moya Foundation

University Tutoring Support Scholarship

Type of award: Scholarship.
Intended use: For full-time undergraduate study at 2-year or 4-year institution in United States.
Eligibility: Applicant must be learning disabled. Applicant must be residing in Florida.
Basis for selection: Major/career interest in engineering, civil or construction management. Applicant must demonstrate financial need.
Application requirements: Recommendations, transcript. Include most recent IRS Income Tax Form, two acacemic letters of reference, transcript, copies of awards or honors, proof of volunteer work, and a copy of college/university acceptance letter or proof of enrollment.
Additional information: Minimum 2.5 GPA. Must be a Florida resident and attend a Florida college/university full time. Must use award towards tutoring support to obtain a college/university degree. Dowload application online. Submit application by e-mail.

Amount of award:	$2,500
Number of awards:	2
Application deadline:	March 1
Total amount awarded:	$5,000

Contact:
Web: tinyurl.com/demoyafoundationscholarships16

Defense Attorney Steve Duckett

Steve Duckett Local Conservation Scholarship

Type of award: Scholarship.
Intended use: For undergraduate or graduate study at accredited vocational, 2-year, 4-year or graduate institution.
Eligibility: Applicant must be high school senior.
Basis for selection: Applicant must demonstrate high academic achievement.
Application requirements: Essay, transcript. Unofficial transcript, application cover sheet, application essay, updated resume. Essay topic (500 words): Explain the candidate's dedication to local conservation and detailing the efforts, past

and current, he or she has made to contribute to conservation and natural preservation efforts.

Additional information: Minimum 3.0 GPA required. Candidates for this scholarship must be able to demonstrate a commitment to environmental conservation using past and present volunteer, professional, and educational experiences.

Amount of award:	$500
Number of awards:	1
Application deadline:	May 1
Total amount awarded:	$500

Contact:
Steve Duckett Local Conservation Scholarship
9119 Church Street
Suite 12
Manassas, VA 20110
Phone: 202-517-0502
Fax: 703-991-0604
Web: www.virginiacriminallaws.com/scholarship.html

Delaware Higher Education Office

B. Bradford Barnes Scholarship

Type of award: Scholarship, renewable.
Intended use: For full-time freshman study at 4-year institution. Designated institutions: University of Delaware.
Eligibility: Applicant must be high school senior. Applicant must be U.S. citizen or permanent resident residing in Delaware.
Basis for selection: Applicant must demonstrate high academic achievement.
Application requirements: Essay, transcript. FAFSA.
Additional information: Must rank in top 25 percent of high school class. Combined score of 1800 on the SAT. Awards full tuition, fees, room, board, and books. Visit Website for deadline.

Amount of award:	Full tuition
Number of awards:	1
Number of applicants:	35

Contact:
Delaware Higher Education Office
John G. Townsend Building
401 Federal Street
Dover, DE 19901
Phone: 302-735-4000
Fax: 302-739-4654
Web: www.doe.k12.de.us/high-ed

Charles L. Hebner Memorial Scholarship

Type of award: Scholarship, renewable.
Intended use: For full-time undergraduate study at 4-year institution. Designated institutions: University of Delaware, Delaware State University.
Eligibility: Applicant must be high school senior. Applicant must be U.S. citizen or permanent resident residing in Delaware.
Basis for selection: Major/career interest in humanities/liberal arts; social/behavioral sciences or political science/government. Applicant must demonstrate high academic achievement.
Application requirements: Essay, transcript. FAFSA.

Additional information: Applicant must rank in top half of graduating class. Minimum combined score of 1350 on SAT. Preference given to political science majors. Award covers tuition, fees, room, board, and books. Visit Website for deadline information.

Amount of award:	Full tuition
Number of awards:	2
Number of applicants:	35

Contact:
Delaware Higher Education Office
John G. Townsend Building
401 Federal Street
Dover, DE 19901
Phone: 302-735-4000
Fax: 302-739-4654
Web: www.doe.k12.de.us/high-ed

Delaware Educational Benefits for Children of Deceased Veterans and Others

Type of award: Scholarship, renewable.
Intended use: For undergraduate study at postsecondary institution.
Eligibility: Applicant must be at least 16, no older than 24. Applicant must be U.S. citizen or permanent resident residing in Delaware.
Additional information: Must live in Delaware for at least three years before applying. Must apply at least six weeks before classes begin. Award prorated when major not available at a Delaware public college. Award for maximum of four years. Must be child of one of the following: member of armed forces whose death was service-related, who is or was a POW, or is officially MIA; state police officer whose death was service-related; or state employee of the Department of Transportation routinely employed in job-related activities on the state highway system whose death was job-related. Visit Website for deadline.

Amount of award:	Full tuition
Number of applicants:	2

Contact:
Delaware Higher Education Office
John G. Townsend Building
401 Federal Street
Dover, DE 19901
Phone: 302-735-4000
Fax: 302-739-4654
Web: www.doe.k12.de.us/high-ed

Delaware Scholarship Incentive Program

Type of award: Scholarship.
Intended use: For full-time undergraduate study at accredited 2-year or 4-year institution. Designated institutions: Nonprofit, regionally accredited institutions in Delaware or Pennsylvania.
Eligibility: Applicant must be U.S. citizen or permanent resident residing in Delaware.
Basis for selection: Applicant must demonstrate financial need and high academic achievement.
Application requirements: Transcript. FAFSA.
Additional information: Minimum 2.5 GPA. Full-time undergraduate and graduate students whose majors are not offered at a Delaware public college will be considered. Visit Website for deadline.

Amount of award:	$700-$2,200
Number of awards:	1,010
Number of applicants:	11,000
Total amount awarded:	$1,369,400

Contact:
Delaware Higher Education Office
John G. Townsend Buillding
401 Federal Street
Dover, DE 19901
Phone: 302-735-4000
Fax: 302-739-4654
Web: www.doe.k12.de.us/high-ed

Diamond State Scholarship

Type of award: Scholarship, renewable.
Intended use: For full-time freshman study at accredited vocational, 2-year or 4-year institution in United States. Designated institutions: Nonprofit, regionally accredited institutions.
Eligibility: Applicant must be high school senior. Applicant must be U.S. citizen or permanent resident residing in Delaware.
Basis for selection: Applicant must demonstrate high academic achievement.
Application requirements: Essay, transcript. SAT scores.
Additional information: Must rank in top 25 percent of high school class. Minimum combined score of 1800 on SAT. Visit Website for deadline.

Amount of award:	$1,250
Number of awards:	54
Number of applicants:	124
Total amount awarded:	$67,500

Contact:
Delaware Higher Education Office
John G. Townsend Building
401 Federal Street
Dover, DE 19901
Phone: 302-735-4000
Fax: 302-739-4654
Web: www.doe.k12.de.us/high-ed

Herman M. Holloway, Sr. Memorial Scholarship

Type of award: Scholarship, renewable.
Intended use: For full-time freshman study at 4-year institution. Designated institutions: Delaware State University.
Eligibility: Applicant must be high school senior. Applicant must be U.S. citizen or permanent resident residing in Delaware.
Basis for selection: Applicant must demonstrate high academic achievement.
Application requirements: Essay, transcript. FAFSA.
Additional information: Applicants must rank in upper half of class and have combined score of at least 1350 on SAT. Awards full tuition, fees, room, board, and books. Visit Website for deadline information.

Amount of award:	Full tuition
Number of awards:	1
Number of applicants:	60

Contact:
Delaware Higher Education Office
John G. Townsend Building
401 Federal Street
Dover, DE 19901
Phone: 302-735-4000
Fax: 302-739-4654
Web: www.doe.k12.de.us/high-ed

Demas Law Group

Demas Law Group Scholarship

Type of award: Scholarship.
Intended use: For undergraduate or graduate study at accredited 4-year institution.
Eligibility: Applicant must be high school senior. Applicant must be U.S. citizen or permanent resident.
Application requirements: If chosen as a finalist the applicant must be able to provide both unofficial school transcripts, current proof of enrollment, and photo identification.
Additional information: Minimum 3.0 GPA. Open to graduating high school seniors, students attending a community college with the intent of transferring to a university, or students currently attending a four-year university.

Number of awards:	1
Application deadline:	May 2
Notification begins:	June 15
Total amount awarded:	$1,000

Contact:
Web: www.injury-attorneys.com/scholarship/

Dental Insurance Shop

Dental Insurance Shop Merit Scholarship

Type of award: Scholarship.
Intended use: For freshman study at vocational, 2-year or 4-year institution.
Eligibility: Applicant must be high school senior. Applicant must be U.S. citizen.
Additional information: Must have a minimum 3.8 GPA or rank in the top 5% of your class.

Number of awards:	1
Application deadline:	June 30
Notification begins:	July 15
Total amount awarded:	$1,000

Contact:
Web: www.dentalinsuranceshop.com/scholarship.html

Denver Physical Medicine and Rehab

Denver Physical Medicine and Rehab Scholarship Opportunity

Type of award: Scholarship.
Intended use: For undergraduate study at accredited 2-year or 4-year institution in United States.

Eligibility: Applicant must be U.S. citizen, permanent resident or international student.
Application requirements: Essay. 400-600 word essay.
Additional information: Minimum 3.0 GPA. Application and essay topic can be found on website.

Number of awards:	1
Application deadline:	July 31
Notification begins:	August 31
Total amount awarded:	$500

Contact:
Denver Physical Medicine and Rehab
1780 South Bellaire Street
#140
Denver, CO 80222
Phone: 303-757-7280
Web: http://denverphysicalmedicine.com/scholarship-opportunity/

DiBella Law Offices, P.C.

DiBella Law Offices, P.C. Scholarship

Type of award: Scholarship.
Intended use: For undergraduate study at accredited 2-year or 4-year institution.
Eligibility: Applicant must be high school senior. Applicant must be U.S. citizen or permanent resident.
Application requirements: Essay. Essay is required in which we ask about your academic goals and plans for improving your local community.
Additional information: Applicant must be a high school senior or a college freshman, sophomore, junior, or senior.

Amount of award:	$500
Number of awards:	1
Application deadline:	May 4
Notification begins:	June 5
Total amount awarded:	$500

Contact:
DiBella Law Offices, P.C.
45 Osgood Street
Suite 302
Methuen, MA 01844
Phone: 978-327-5140
Fax: 978-849-5140
Web: http://www.dibellalawoffice.com/scholarship/

The Digital Entertainment Group

Hedy Lamarr Achievement Award for Emerging Leaders in Entertainment Technology

Type of award: Scholarship.
Intended use: For full-time undergraduate study at accredited 4-year institution in United States.
Eligibility: Applicant must be female. Applicant must be U.S. citizen.

Basis for selection: Applicant must demonstrate high academic achievement.
Application requirements: Recommendations, essay, proof of eligibility. Applicant's college major interest must be Entertainment Technology. Resume or Curriculum Vitae. Essay: Please describe in what way you have demonstrated excellence, leadership and initiative in the Entertainment and/or technology fields, and how you hope to do so in the future (Please limit the essay to 1000 words or less). Letter of Recommendation from Faculty Member. If you wish you may include a short summary of any additional factors or information you would like to have considered.
Additional information: More information about the scholarship can be found on the application file.

Amount of award:	$25,000
Number of awards:	1
Application deadline:	February 17
Notification begins:	May 1
Total amount awarded:	$25,000

Contact:
The Digital Entertainment Group
10635 Santa Monica boulevard
Los Angeles, CA 90025
Phone: 424-371-5573
Fax: 424-248-3816
Web: http://degonline.org/wp-content/uploads/2016/11/Hedy-Lamarr-Achievement-Award-Application.pdf

Digital Third Coast

Digital Third Coast's Digital Marketing Scholarship

Type of award: Scholarship.
Intended use: For full-time undergraduate study at accredited 2-year or 4-year institution in United States.
Basis for selection: Major/career interest in marketing; business or public relations.
Application requirements: Essay.
Additional information: Minimum 2.5 GPA. Applicant must be studying or planning to study the fields of marketing, advertising, and/or public relations. If the applicant or the applicant's parent/legal guardian is employed by Digital Third Coast Internet Marketing, the student is not eligible for the scholarship. Applicant must send a submission e-mail with the subject "DTC scholarship" including a 500+ essay and a photo image of themselves. Visit web site for the essay topic.

Amount of award:	$500
Number of awards:	1
Application deadline:	August 1
Notification begins:	August 15

Contact:
Digital Third Coast
2035 West Wabansia Avenue
Chicago, IL 60647
Web: www.digitalthirdcoast.net/blog/dtc-digital-marketing-scholarship

Direct Textbook

Direct Textbook "Shine" Photo Essay Contest

Type of award: Scholarship.
Intended use: For full-time undergraduate study at accredited 2-year, 4-year or graduate institution.
Application requirements: Submit your original photo that captures the essence of what the theme "Shine" means to you.
Additional information: Must have a minimum 2.0 GPA. Two awardees will be selected by Direct Textbook. Two scholarships will be awarded to the photos with the most votes. Two photo entries selected at random from all qualifying entries will also be chosen.

Amount of award:	$500
Number of awards:	6
Application deadline:	January 16
Notification begins:	January 30
Total amount awarded:	$3,000

Contact:
Direct Textbook
1525 Chemeketa Street NE
Salem, OR 97301
Web: www.directtextbook.com/photocontest

Haiku Scholarship contest

Type of award: Scholarship.
Intended use: For freshman study at 2-year or 4-year institution.
Eligibility: Applicant must be high school senior.
Additional information: Minimum 2.0 GPA. Applicants must submit an original haiku poem. See website for more details and to apply.

Amount of award:	$500
Number of awards:	6
Application deadline:	September 15
Notification begins:	September 30
Total amount awarded:	$3,000

Contact:
Web: www.directtextbook.com/haiku

Disability Attorneys of Michigan

Disability Attorneys of Michigan Scholarship

Type of award: Scholarship.
Intended use: For full-time freshman study at 2-year or 4-year institution in United States.
Eligibility: Applicant must be high school senior. Applicant must be U.S. citizen residing in Michigan. Applicant must be dependent of disabled veteran.
Application requirements: Transcript. 500 word minimum essay explaining the manner in which the applicant's parent(s) and/or guardian(s) disability has impacted their life, education, and/or future goals.
Additional information: Must have a minimum 3.0 GPA. Must have proof that student's parent of guardian is currently receiving disability benefits through the US Social Security

Administration and/or the US Department of Veterans Affairs. Must be a graduating High School senior in Michigan.

Amount of award:	$1,000
Number of awards:	3
Application deadline:	May 31
Notification begins:	July 15
Total amount awarded:	$3,000

Contact:
Disability Attorneys of Michigan
30500 Van Dyke Avenue
Suite 400
Warren, MI 48093
Phone: 800-949-2900
Web: http://www.damichigan.com/resources/scholarship/

Disability Care Center

Disability Care Center Special Education Scholarship

Type of award: Scholarship.
Intended use: For full-time undergraduate or graduate study at 2-year, 4-year or graduate institution in United States.
Eligibility: Applicant must be U.S. citizen or permanent resident.
Basis for selection: Major/career interest in education, special.
Application requirements: Recommendations, essay, transcript. College acceptance letter or college ID, upcoming fall class schedule to confirm full-time status, most recent transcript, and valid ID confirming legal residency (driver's license, passport, etc.). 500 to 1,500 word essay on the following subject: "Explain why you are pursuing a degree in special education and how you plan to make a difference in the lives of the disabled." One letter of recommendation required from a creditable source.
Additional information: Minimum GPA of 2.5. Applicant must be currently majoring in special education.

Number of awards:	1
Application deadline:	August 1
Notification begins:	August 29
Total amount awarded:	$500

Contact:
Disability Care Center
2875 South Orange Avenue
#500
Orlando, FL 32806
Phone: 888-504-0035
Fax: 877-570-0649
Web: www.disabilitycarecenter.org/giving-back/scholarships/

Disabled Student Scholarship

Type of award: Scholarship.
Intended use: For full-time undergraduate or graduate study at vocational, 2-year, 4-year or graduate institution in United States.
Eligibility: Applicant must be physically challenged or learning disabled. Applicant must be U.S. citizen or permanent resident.
Application requirements: Recommendations, essay. College acceptance letter or college ID, upcoming fall class schedule to confirm full-time status, most recent transcript, and valid ID confirming legal residency (driver's license, passport, etc.). 500 to 1,500 word essay on the following subject: "Describe an

obstacle or hardship that arose due to your condition and how you were able to overcome it. Explain the impact it has had on your life and how it will influence you in the future." One letter of recommendation required from a creditable source.

Additional information: Must have a minimum 2.5 GPA. This scholarship program is for students who are suffering from a debilitating condition(s) while continuing their education at a U.S. college institution. The condition can be any medically diagnosed impairment (physical or mental) that interferes with everyday activities and quality of life.

Number of awards:	1
Application deadline:	August 1
Notification begins:	August 29
Total amount awarded:	$500

Contact:
Disability Care Center
2875 South Orange Avenue
#500
Orlando, FL 32806
Phone: 888-504-0035
Fax: 877-570-0649
Web: www.disabilitycarecenter.org/giving-back/scholarships/

Discovery Education

Siemens Competition in Math, Science and Technology

Type of award: Scholarship.
Intended use: For full-time undergraduate or graduate study at accredited 4-year or graduate institution.
Eligibility: Applicant must be enrolled in high school. Applicant must be U.S. citizen or permanent resident.
Basis for selection: Competition/talent/interest in science project, based on originality, scientific importance, validity, creativity, academic rigor, clarity of expression, comprehensiveness, experimental work, field knowledge. Major/career interest in biology; chemistry; engineering; environmental science; materials science; mathematics; physics; computer/information sciences or medicine.
Application requirements: Proof of eligibility, research proposal. An 18-page (maximum) research report followed by poster and oral presentations for Regional Finalists. Confirmation page signed by school administrator. Project advisor or mentor comments form.
Additional information: Competition to encourage students to do research in math, science, or technology, giving young scientists the opportunity to present their research to leading scientists in their field. Regional Finalists awarded trip to compete at one of six regional competitions. At regional event, after presenting poster, oral presentation, and participating in Q&A session, student or team of students will qualify for $1,000 or $3,000 scholarship. National Finalists qualify for $10,000 to $100,000 scholarship. Individual applicants must be seniors; team applicants may be freshmen, sophomores, juniors, or seniors. Register at Website.

Amount of award:	$1,000-$100,000
Number of awards:	60
Number of applicants:	1,911
Application deadline:	September 30
Notification begins:	October 19
Total amount awarded:	$617,000

Contact:
Discovery Education, ATT: Siemens Competition c/o Discovery Education
One Discovery Place
Silver Spring, MD 20910
Phone: 800-222-6098
Web: siemenscompetition.discoveryeducation.com

Distinguished Young Women

California's Distinguished Young Woman Competition

Type of award: Scholarship.
Intended use: For undergraduate study at accredited 2-year or 4-year institution in United States.
Eligibility: Applicant must be single, female, high school junior. Applicant must be U.S. citizen residing in California.
Basis for selection: Competition/talent/interest in poise/talent/fitness. Applicant must demonstrate high academic achievement.
Additional information: Local competitions held from January to May; state competition held in late July or early August. Awards not limited to state Junior Miss finalists; winners of various judged categories also receive awards. Participants must never have been pregnant or married. Minimum 3.0 GPA. Check Website for details.
Contact:
Distinguished Young Women (Formerly California's Junior Miss)
P.O. Box 2719
Bakersfield, CA 93303
Web: www.distinguishedyw.org/ca

Distinguished Young Women Scholarship

Type of award: Scholarship.
Intended use: For undergraduate or graduate study.
Eligibility: Applicant must be single, female, high school junior or senior. Applicant must be U.S. citizen.
Basis for selection: Competition/talent/interest in poise/talent/fitness, based on scholastic evaluation, skill in creative and performing arts, physical fitness, presence and composure, and panel interview.
Additional information: Must compete in state of legal residence. State winners expected to compete at higher levels. Must never have been married or pregnant. Only high school seniors can compete in national finals but students are encouraged to begin application process during sophomore year. Scholarship funds can be used for undergraduate work or deferred for graduate and professional studies. Evaluation categories: scholastic (25%), interview (25%), talent (20%), fitness (15%), self expression (15%). Visit Website for application and deadline information, as it varies from state to state.

Amount of award:	$100-$50,000

Contact:
Distinguished Young Women
Participant Inquiry
751 Government Street
Mobile, AL 36602
Phone: 251-438-3621
Fax: 251-431-0063
Web: www.distinguishedyw.org

District of Columbia Higher Education Financial Services

DC Tuition Assistance Grant Program (DCTAG)

Type of award: Scholarship, renewable.
Intended use: For undergraduate study at 2-year or 4-year institution in United States. Designated institutions: DCTAG-eligible institutions that can participate in Title IV programs.
Eligibility: Applicant must be no older than 24. Applicant must be U.S. citizen or permanent resident residing in District of Columbia.
Application requirements: Transcript, proof of eligibility. Student Aid Report, FAFSA, current utility bill, certified DC Income Tax Report (D-40) or a twelve month income/benefit history statement.
Additional information: Parents or guardian of applicant must be DC resident for 12 months prior to enrollment and throughout college. Award may not be used at proprietary institutions. Awards and deadlines vary. Visit Website for details.

Amount of award:	$2,500-$10,000

Contact:
Higher Education Financial Services
810 First St. NE
Third Floor
Washington, DC 20002
Phone: 202-727-2824
Web: www.osse.dc.gov/service/higher-education-financial-services

Dog Fence DIY

Vet Tech AND Other Veterinary Support Careers Electric Dog Fence DIY Scholarship

Type of award: Scholarship.
Intended use: For full-time undergraduate or graduate study at accredited vocational, 2-year, 4-year or graduate institution.
Basis for selection: Major/career interest in veterinary medicine.
Application requirements: Essay. Submit a 1,000 word essay on when to recommend an electric wireless or wired dog fence.
Additional information: Must have a minimum 3.5 GPA. Must be part of a Vet Tech program, pre-veterinary studies program, vocational training program for veterinary studies, or graduate program focused on animal assisted therapy.

Application and additional information can be found here: www.dogfencediy.com/2016/03/21/vet-tech-other-veterinary-support-careers-electric-dog-fence-diy-scholarship/

Number of awards:	1
Application deadline:	September 1
Notification begins:	September 30
Total amount awarded:	$1,000

Dolphin Scholarship Foundation

Dolphin Scholarship

Type of award: Scholarship, renewable.
Intended use: For full-time undergraduate study at accredited 4-year institution.
Eligibility: Applicant must be single, no older than 24. Applicant must be U.S. citizen. Must be child/stepchild of member or former member of U.S. Navy who served in, or in support of, Submarine Force.
Basis for selection: Applicant must demonstrate financial need, high academic achievement and service orientation.
Application requirements: Recommendations, essay, transcript, proof of eligibility. SAT/ACT scores.
Additional information: Applicant must be high school senior or college student. Applicant must demonstrate commitment to extracurricular activities and community service.

Amount of award:	$3,400
Number of awards:	116
Number of applicants:	380
Application deadline:	March 15
Notification begins:	May 1
Total amount awarded:	$391,000

Contact:
Dolphin Scholarship Foundation
4966 Euclid Road
Suite 109
Virginia Beach, VA 23462
Phone: 757-671-3200 ext. 112
Fax: 757-671-3330
Web: http://www.dolphinscholarship.org/index.cfm/scholarships/

Laura W. Bush Scholarship

Type of award: Scholarship, renewable.
Intended use: For undergraduate study at accredited 4-year institution.
Eligibility: Applicant must be no older than 24. Must be child/stepchild of member or former member of U.S. Navy submarine force who served on the USS Texas (SSN775).
Basis for selection: Applicant must demonstrate financial need, high academic achievement, depth of character, leadership, seriousness of purpose and service orientation.
Application requirements: SAT/ACT scores.
Additional information: Applicant must be unmarried high school senior or college student. Sponsor must be qualified in submarines and have served on active duty in the Submarine Force for a minimum of 8 years or must have served on active duty in direct submarine support activities for a minimum of 10 years. Visit Website for application and details.

Amount of award:	$3,400
Number of awards:	3
Number of applicants:	3
Application deadline:	March 15
Notification begins:	May 15
Total amount awarded:	$10,200

Contact:
Dolphin Scholarship Foundation
4966 Euclid Road, Suite 109
Virginia Beach, VA 23462
Phone: 757-671-3200 ext. 112
Fax: 757-671-3330
Web: www.dolphinscholarship.org

DoSomething.org

DoSomething.org Scholarships

Type of award: Scholarship.
Intended use: For undergraduate study at postsecondary institution.
Eligibility: Applicant must be no older than 25, enrolled in high school.
Basis for selection: Applicant must demonstrate leadership and service orientation.
Application requirements: Recommendations, essay.
Additional information: DoSomething.org scholarships award young people, ages 13-25 for the social change they do in the community. Visit Website for more information.
Contact:
DoSomething.org
19 West 21st Street
8th Floor
New York, NY 10010
Phone: 212-254-2390
Web: www.dosomething.org/scholarships

Dotcom-Monitor

Women in Computing Scholarship

Type of award: Scholarship.
Intended use: For full-time undergraduate or graduate study at vocational, 2-year, 4-year or graduate institution in United States or Canada.
Eligibility: Applicant must be female.
Application requirements: Essay. Students currently enrolled at an accredited college or university in the U.S. or Canada. Applicants should have either already declared their major or have completed at least one academic year in computer science, computer engineering, or closely related technical field. Application includes 3 essays of max 500 words each. Prompts can be found on the application website.

Amount of award:	$1,000
Number of awards:	1
Application deadline:	March 1
Notification begins:	April 1
Total amount awarded:	$1,000

Contact:
Dotcom-Monitor
5125 County Road 101
Minnetonka, MN 55345
Phone: 952-513-4392
Web: https://www.loadview-testing.com/scholarship/

Downloadfreeapk.com

You Make me Happy Scholarship

Type of award: Scholarship, renewable.
Intended use: For full-time undergraduate study at vocational, 2-year, 4-year or graduate institution.
Application requirements: Essay.
Additional information: Must have a minimum GPA of 3.0. Must be able to verify enrollment. Essay prompt and full details available on website.

Number of awards:	1
Application deadline:	July 31
Notification begins:	August 14
Total amount awarded:	$500

Contact:
Web: www.downloadfreeapk.com/scholarship

Dr. Arthur A. Kezian DDS

Dr. Arthur A. Kezian DDS Science Scholarship

Type of award: Scholarship.
Intended use: For undergraduate or graduate study at vocational, 2-year, 4-year or graduate institution.
Eligibility: Applicant must be at least 16, no older than 28.
Basis for selection: Major/career interest in science, general. Applicant must demonstrate financial need.
Application requirements: Essay, transcript. One to two page essay on why you deserve the Dr. Arthur A. Kezian Scholarship. Resume. Official transcript. SAT score report, DAT, GRE, MCAT, PCAT score report. Optional one minute video clip introducing yourself. Applicant must be a resident of the US or Canada.
Additional information: Apply online. Major must be in a field of science. Must have a minimum 3.0 GPA. Scholarship deadline is 3/31/2017.

Number of awards:	1
Application deadline:	March 31
Total amount awarded:	$1,200

Contact:
443 N. Larchmont Boulevard
Los Angeles, CA 90004
Phone: 323-467-2777
Web: www.drkezian.com/science-scholarship/

Dr. C. Moorer and Associates

From Failure to Promise Essay Scholarship

Type of award: Scholarship.
Intended use: For undergraduate or graduate study at accredited 4-year institution.
Basis for selection: Competition/talent/interest in writing/journalism, based on originality, quality of research, and effectiveness of presentation. Applicant must demonstrate high academic achievement.
Application requirements: Essay, transcript. 1500+ word essay on the topic: From Failure to Promise: 360 Degrees:. Which track(s): (On Track, Off Track, New Track, Fast Track, Tenure Track, or Backtrack) of the book, From Failure to Promise - "360 Degrees", presented or reiterated the most important life lessons for you and why? (Cite at least 3-5 key examples from the book). The author reiterates the importance of (Faith, Education, Experience, and Effort) throughout the book, From Failure to Promise - "360 Degrees", Which factor(s) was/were most vital to his evolution in going from a "flunk-out" to a "professor" at the very same university and beyond? (Cite at least 3-5 examples from the book). How does the "Dr. C. Moorer's - 7 Spheres of Influence and Integration Model" from the book, From Failure to Promise - "360 Degrees" affect your world-view as related to civic responsibility and global citizenship? Explain.
Additional information: Minimum 2.5 GPA. First place wins $10,000. Three runners-up win $500 each. Competition for writing/journalism and all other disciplines based on originality, quality of research, and effectiveness of presentation.

Amount of award:	$500-$10,000
Number of awards:	4
Application deadline:	July 31
Notification begins:	September 1
Total amount awarded:	$11,500

Contact:
"From Failure to Promise: Scholarship Fund"
Attn: Dr. C Moorer
12750 S. Saginaw St., Ste. 206
Grand Blanc, MI 48439
Phone: 708-252-4380
Web: www.fromfailuretopromise.com/Essay-Scholarship-Contest-.html

DuctchCrafters Amish Furniture

Heritage Scholarship

Type of award: Scholarship.
Intended use: For full-time undergraduate study at accredited 4-year institution in United States.
Eligibility: Applicant must be enrolled in high school. Applicant must be U.S. citizen or permanent resident.
Basis for selection: Applicant must demonstrate financial need and high academic achievement.

Application requirements: Essay. Application must include a written statement of financial need. Application includes a 750 word essay,more information about the essay requirments on the website https://www.dutchcrafters.com/heritagescholarship/application.aspx .
Additional information: All scholarship recipients may be subject to a criminal background check.Excluded from consideration are employees and relatives of employees of JMX Brands, the company that owns DutchCrafters.

Amount of award:	$500-$500
Number of awards:	3
Number of applicants:	600
Application deadline:	May 1
Notification begins:	July 6
Total amount awarded:	$1,500

Contact:
DutchCrafters Amish Furniture
3709 N. Lockwood Ridge Road
Sarasota, FL 34234
Web: https://www.dutchcrafters.com/heritage-scholarship

Dudley Debosier Injury Lawyers

Dudley Debosier Scholarship Program

Type of award: Scholarship.
Intended use: For freshman study at vocational, 2-year or 4-year institution.
Eligibility: Applicant must be high school senior. Applicant must be residing in Louisiana.
Application requirements: 350 to 500 word essay.
Additional information: Application can be found on website.

Amount of award:	$1,000-$2,000
Number of awards:	9
Application deadline:	March 17
Notification begins:	April 22
Total amount awarded:	$10,000

Contact:
1075 Government Street
Baton Rouge, LA 70802
Web: www.dudleydebosier.com/scholarship_program

Dunkin' Donuts

Dunkin' Donuts Philadelphia Regional Scholarship Program

Type of award: Scholarship.
Intended use: For full-time undergraduate study at accredited vocational, 2-year or 4-year institution.
Eligibility: Applicant must be high school senior. Applicant must be U.S. citizen residing in Delaware, New Jersey or Pennsylvania.
Basis for selection: Scholarships will be awarded based on applicants' demonstration of "well rounded" character: positive academic record, demonstrated leadership, commitment to school and community activities and experience in a work

environment. Applicant must demonstrate high academic achievement.

Additional information: Residency in one of the following counties required: Kent or New Castle Counties, DE; Atlantic, Burlington, Camden, Cape May, Cumberland, Gloucester, Mercer, Salem or Warren Counties, NJ; Berks, Bucks, Chester, Delaware, Lehigh, Montgomery, Northampton or Philadelphia Counties, PA.

Amount of award:	$2,000
Number of awards:	25
Application deadline:	April 17
Total amount awarded:	$50,000

Contact:
Dunkin' Donuts
One Scholarship Way
St.Peter, MN 56082
Phone: 800-537-4180
Web: https://www.scholarsapply.org/dunkin/

Eastern Orthodox Committee on Scouting

Boy and Girl Scouts Scholarship

Type of award: Scholarship.
Intended use: For full-time freshman study at accredited 4-year institution in United States.
Eligibility: Applicant must be high school senior. Applicant must be Eastern Orthodox. Applicant must be U.S. citizen.
Basis for selection: Applicant must demonstrate depth of character and service orientation.
Application requirements: Four letters of recommendation with application, one from each of following groups: religious institution, school, community leader, and head of Scouting unit.
Additional information: Eligible applicant must be registered member of Boy or Girl Scouts unit; Eagle Scout or Gold Award recipient; active member of Eastern Orthodox Church; have received Alpha Omega Religious Scout Award; have demonstrated practical citizenship in his or her church, school, Scouting unit, and community. Offers one $1,000 scholarship and one $500 scholarship upon acceptance to four-year accredited college or university.

Amount of award:	$500-$1,000
Number of awards:	2
Number of applicants:	120
Application deadline:	May 1
Total amount awarded:	$1,500

Contact:
EOCS Scholarship Committee
862 Guy Lombardo Avenue
Freeport, NY 11520
Phone: 516-868-4050
Web: www.eocs.org

Edmund F. Maxwell Foundation

Edmund F. Maxwell Foundation Scholarship

Type of award: Scholarship, renewable.
Intended use: For full-time freshman study. Designated institutions: Private colleges and universities.

Eligibility: Applicant must be U.S. citizen or permanent resident residing in Washington.
Basis for selection: Applicant must demonstrate financial need, high academic achievement, depth of character, leadership, seriousness of purpose and service orientation.
Application requirements: Essay, transcript. Financial aid worksheet.
Additional information: Must be resident of western Washington. Combined reading and math SAT scores must be greater than 1200. Equivalent ACT scores also accepted. Applicants encouraged to apply early in year. Awards and amounts may vary. Visit Website for application and more information.

Amount of award:	$5,000
Number of applicants:	78
Application deadline:	April 30
Notification begins:	June 1
Total amount awarded:	$346,000

Contact:
The Edmund F. Maxwell Foundation
P.O. Box 55548
Seattle, WA 98155-0548
Web: www.maxwell.org

Education Northwest

Steven R. Nelson Native Educator Scholarship Program

Type of award: Scholarship, renewable.
Intended use: For master's study at accredited graduate institution in United States.
Eligibility: Applicant must be Alaskan native, American Indian or Native Hawaiian/Pacific Islander. Applicant must be residing in Oregon, Montana, Alaska, Idaho or Washington.
Basis for selection: Major/career interest in education.
Application requirements: Recommendations, essay, proof of eligibility. Three letters of reccomendation (excluding family members) with at least one community member who can attest to the candidate's Native heritage and commitment to the designated course of study and to serving rural and/or Native communities after attainment of the master's degree.
Additional information: Must be purusing a master's degree in education policy, leadership, technical assistance, research, or a related field. As many as five scholarships will be rewarded, one for each state in the organization's primary service region. Awardees must reapply to the scholarship yearly to request continued scholarship support.

Amount of award:	$5,000
Number of awards:	5
Application deadline:	December 31
Notification begins:	March 31

Contact:
Education Northwest - Nelson Scholarship Administrator
101 SW Main Street
Suite 500
Portland, OR 97204
Web: http://educationnorthwest.org/nelsonscholarship

Edward Hosharian Scholarship Fund

Edward Hosharian Scholarship

Type of award: Scholarship.
Intended use: For full-time sophomore, junior, senior or graduate study at accredited 4-year or graduate institution in United States.
Eligibility: Applicant must be Armenian. Applicant must be U.S. citizen.
Basis for selection: Major/career interest in music. Applicant must demonstrate financial need.
Application requirements: Recommendations, essay, transcript. Personal statement, official transcripts mailed directly from the institution, two letters of recommendation directly mailed/e-mailed from instructors or advisors. Performance majors - YouTube link of a performance or self-made video. Composition majors - Upload two scores of compositions.
Additional information: Must be a sophomore or above majoring in music performance or composition.

Number of awards:	1
Application deadline:	February 1
Total amount awarded:	$5,000

Contact:
Edward Hosharian Scholarship Fund
PO Box 2577
Montebello, CA 90640
Web: www.edwardhosharian.com/eh/Scholarship.html

The Edwards Law Firm

The Edwards Annual College Scholarship

Type of award: Scholarship, renewable.
Intended use: For full-time undergraduate study at accredited 4-year or graduate institution in United States.
Eligibility: Applicant must be residing in Oklahoma.
Application requirements: Essay. Essay: Explain in 500 words or more how Social Media can be used more effectively to help increase awareness about texting and driving accidents.
Additional information: Minimum 2.5 GPA. Application can be found online. Open to all Oklahoma students enrolled in any accredited state community college or university.

Number of awards:	1
Application deadline:	December 1
Notification begins:	January 16
Total amount awarded:	$1,500

Contact:
The Edwards Law Firm Prism Office Center
8282 S. Memorial Dr.
Suite 304
Tulsa, OK 74133
Phone: 800-304-9246
Web: www.edwardslawok.com/scholarship-college.html

eLearners

eLearners Scholarship

Type of award: Scholarship.
Intended use: For undergraduate or graduate study at accredited 2-year, 4-year or graduate institution in United States.
Application requirements: Essay. Student must be attending (or planning to attend) an accredited post-secondary institution of higher learning. Student must be participating in an online, for-credit degree program. Part-time and Full-time students eligible.
Additional information: Visit our For Online Students Scholarship page for more information, FAQs and most importantly on how to enter.

Amount of award:	$1,000
Number of awards:	1
Number of applicants:	65
Application deadline:	February 28
Notification begins:	May 31
Total amount awarded:	$1,000

Contact:
eLearners Scholarship
5 Marine View Plaza
Hoboken, NJ 07030
Phone: 201-377-3057
Web: https://www.elearners.com/scholarships/online-students/

Elie Wiesel Foundation for Humanity

Elie Wiesel Prize in Ethics

Type of award: Scholarship.
Intended use: For full-time junior or senior study at accredited 4-year institution in United States.
Basis for selection: Competition/talent/interest in writing/journalism.
Application requirements: Proof of eligibility. Letter from college/university verifying full-time junior or senior status. Sponsorship by faculty member. Submit essay concerning an ethical dilemma, issue, or question related to the contest's annual topic. In 3,000 to 4,000 words, students are encouraged to raise questions, single out issues, and identify dilemmas.
Additional information: First prize is $5,000; second prize is $2,500; third prize is $1,500; two honorable mentions are $500 each. Deadline is late December; Notification begins in May. See Website for more information and application.

Amount of award:	$500-$5,000
Number of awards:	5
Number of applicants:	300
Application deadline:	December 19
Notification begins:	May 31
Total amount awarded:	$10,000

Scholarships

Contact:
Elie Wiesel Prize in Ethics
The Elie Wiesel Foundation for Humanity
555 Madison Avenue, 20th Floor
New York, NY 10022
Phone: 212-490-7788
Fax: 212-490-6006
Web: apply.ethicsprize.org

The Elizabeth Greenshields Foundation

The Elizabeth Greenshields Foundation Grant

Type of award: Scholarship, renewable.
Intended use: For full-time undergraduate, graduate or non-degree study at accredited 2-year or 4-year institution.
Eligibility: Applicant must be at least 18.
Basis for selection: Major/career interest in arts, general.
Application requirements: Portfolio, recommendations, proof of eligibility. Career interest must be to become a full-time practicing artist engaged in figurative/representational painting, sculpture, drawing or printmaking. A list of necessary documents, including a Portfolio, Artistic Proposal, Artist Statement and Budget, can be found on the website under How To Apply.
Additional information: Award money will be issued in the form of Canadian Dollars. First grant is CAD $15000; second and third grants are CAD $18000. For art students and artists in the early or developmental stages of their career creating representational or figurative works through painting, drawing, printmaking, or sculpture. Applications are welcome throughout the year; There is no deadline to apply. All award amounts are in Canadian dollars. Funds are intended to assist applicants in the study or practice of their art, and related costs, such as tuition, travel and living expenses. Applications may only be accessed through the Foundation's website. Applications must be completed online, then printed, dated and signed by the applicant, and submitted by mail with all required supporting documentation. The Foundation does not accept applications from commercial artists, graphic designers and illustrators; photographers; cartoonists; animation artists; video artists, filmmakers and digital artists; craft-makers; or any artist or student whose work or course of study falls primarily into these categories; Studies or training in art education, art therapy, museology, art restoration or conservation, or in any of the artistic pursuits not otherwise funded by the Foundation, are not eligible. The Foundation does not provide funding for the pursuit of abstract or non-objective art. The Foundation awards 50-70 grants per year. The Award may be used for: Full-time art studies, Undergraduate art studies, Graduate and Post-Graduate art studies, Non-degree art studies (such as residencies, apprenticeships/internships and studio training).

Amount of award:	$15,000-$18,000
Number of awards:	70

Contact:
The Elizabeth Greenshields Foundation
1814 Sherbrooke Street West
Montreal
Quebec, Canada, H3H 1E4
Phone: 514-937-9225
Web: www.elizabethgreenshieldsfoundation.ca

Elks National Foundation

Elks Most Valuable Student Scholarship

Type of award: Scholarship.
Intended use: For full-time undergraduate study at accredited postsecondary institution in United States.
Eligibility: Applicant must be high school senior. Applicant must be U.S. citizen.
Basis for selection: Applicant must demonstrate financial need, high academic achievement and leadership.
Application requirements: Essay, transcript. Counselor report, SAT/ACT scores, income range.
Additional information: Applications available starting September 1 on Website. Application deadline is in December. Award is distributed over four years. Membership in Elks not required, but application must be endorsed by and submitted to local Elks Lodge for entry into competition. Judging occurs at lodge, district, and state level before reaching national competition.

Amount of award:	$4,000-$50,000
Number of awards:	500
Number of applicants:	20,000
Notification begins:	April 30
Total amount awarded:	$2,440,000

Contact:
Elks National Foundation
2750 North Lakeview Avenue
Chicago, IL 60614-2256
Phone: 773-755-4732
Fax: 773-755-4733
Web: www.elks.org/enf/scholars

Elks National Foundation Legacy Awards

Type of award: Scholarship.
Intended use: For full-time undergraduate study at accredited postsecondary institution in United States.
Eligibility: Applicant must be high school senior. Applicant must be U.S. citizen.
Basis for selection: Applicant must demonstrate high academic achievement and leadership.
Application requirements: Essay, transcript. SAT/ACT scores.
Additional information: Applicant must be child or grandchild of a current Elks member who has been paid-up and in good standing for two consecutive years. Application available September 1 from Website. Eligible applicants from Guam, Panama, Puerto Rico, and the Philippines may attend schools in those countries. Visit Website for additional information and application.

Amount of award:	$4,000
Number of awards:	250
Number of applicants:	1,800
Application deadline:	January 31
Notification begins:	April 30
Total amount awarded:	$1,000,000

Contact:
Elks National Foundation
2750 North Lakeview Avenue
Chicago, IL 60614-2256
Phone: 773-755-4732
Fax: 773-755-4733
Web: www.elks.org/enf/scholars

Scholarships

EMS Consulting

EMS Consulting Scholarship Fund

Type of award: Scholarship.

Intended use: For full-time undergraduate study at accredited 2-year or 4-year institution.

Eligibility: Applicant must be at least 18, enrolled in high school. Applicant must be U.S. citizen.

Basis for selection: Students with relation to any employee of EMS Consulting cannot apply. Major/career interest in business or computer/information sciences. Applicant must demonstrate high academic achievement.

Application requirements: Essay. Applicants must be a U.S. undergraduate seeking a degree in business, computer sciences, or a related field. Submit a 1000 - 1500 word essay entitled EMS Consulting Higher Education Scholarship. The paper must be signed with the student's full name and edu email address.

Additional information: Submit your essay to social@consultems.com with the subject : EMS Consulting Higher Education Scholarship Application.

Amount of award:	$1,000
Number of awards:	1
Application deadline:	July 1
Notification begins:	July 15
Total amount awarded:	$1,000

Contact:
EMS Consulting
7650 W. Courtney Campbell Causeway
Suite 1125
Tampa, FL 33607
Phone: 813-287-2486
Web: www.consultems.com/salesforce/industries/higher-education/scholarship/

Engineers Foundation of Ohio

Engineers Foundation of Ohio Scholarships

Type of award: Scholarship.

Intended use: For freshman study at accredited 4-year institution in United States. Designated institutions: ABET-accredited schools in Ohio and University of Notre Dame.

Eligibility: Applicant must be high school senior. Applicant must be U.S. citizen residing in Ohio.

Basis for selection: Major/career interest in engineering. Applicant must demonstrate high academic achievement.

Application requirements: Essay, transcript.

Additional information: Minimum 3.0 GPA. Must have minimum 600 SAT (Math) and 500 SAT (Reading or Composition) or 29 ACT Math and 25 ACT English. EFO offers scholarships per year with various requirements; see Website for specifics. Some awards renewable.

Amount of award:	$500-$2,500
Application deadline:	January 9

Contact:
Engineers Foundation of Ohio
400 South Fifth Street
Suite 300
Columbus, OH 43215-5430
Phone: 614-223-1177
Fax: 614-223-1131
Web: www.ohioengineer.com

Enhancedinsurance.com

Enhanced Insurance Scholarship Program

Type of award: Scholarship.

Intended use: For full-time undergraduate study at accredited 2-year or 4-year institution in United States.

Eligibility: Applicant must be U.S. citizen.

Application requirements: 750 to 1250 word essay on "Why Insurance is Important to Me"; More details on Enhanced Insurance website.

Additional information: One award for every 500 entries. Send essay to email address in the contact information. Essay should be in the body of the email. Employees of Upper Left, Inc not eligible. Current Applicant Status: Current Undergraduate Student. Must have parental consent if under 17.

Amount of award:	$2,500
Application deadline:	October 31
Notification begins:	November 15

Contact:
Enhanced Insurance
104 Garfield st
St Paul, MN 55102
Phone: 800-328-7198
Web: www.enhancedinsurance.com/scholarships/

The Entomological Foundation

Stan Beck Fellowship

Type of award: Scholarship, renewable.

Intended use: For undergraduate or graduate study at 4-year or graduate institution. Designated institutions: Colleges or universities in the United States, Mexico, or Canada.

Basis for selection: Major/career interest in entomology; biology or zoology. Applicant must demonstrate financial need.

Application requirements: Recommendations, essay, transcript, proof of eligibility. Letter of nomination, letters of support demonstrating applicant's need or challenge.

Additional information: Award amount varies. Need is based on physical limitations or economic, minority, or environmental conditions. Applications must be submitted electronically. See Website for additional information.

Application deadline:	July 1

Contact:
The Entomological Foundation
Phone: 301-731-4535
Web: www.entsoc.org/awards/student/beck

The Environmental Institute for Golf

GCSAA Legacy Awards

Type of award: Scholarship.
Intended use: For full-time undergraduate or graduate study at accredited postsecondary institution.
Eligibility: Applicant or parent must be member/participant of Golf Course Superintendents Association of America.
Basis for selection: Applicant must demonstrate high academic achievement, leadership and service orientation.
Application requirements: Essay, transcript, proof of eligibility. Letter of acceptance from college or university (high school seniors).
Additional information: Applicant's parent or grandparent must have been a Golf Course Superintendents Association of America (GCSAA) member for five or more consecutive years and must be current active member in one of the following classifications: A, Superintendent Member, C, Retired-A, Retired-B, or AA Life. Children or grandchildren of deceased members also eligible if member was active at time of death. Award limited to one student per family. Children of Syngenta Professional Products employees, The Environmental Institute for Golf's Board of Trustees, and GCSAA staff not eligible. Past winners are ineligible to apply the following year. They may re-apply after a one-year hiatus.

Amount of award:	$1,500
Application deadline:	April 15
Notification begins:	June 15

Contact:
Golf Course Superintendents Association of America
Scholarship Program
1421 Research Park Drive
Lawrence, KS 66049-3859
Phone: 785-832-4445
Web: www.gcsaa.org

GCSAA Scholars Competition

Type of award: Scholarship.
Intended use: For sophomore, junior or senior study at accredited 2-year or 4-year institution.
Eligibility: Applicant or parent must be member/participant of Golf Course Superintendents Association of America.
Basis for selection: Major/career interest in turf management. Applicant must demonstrate high academic achievement and leadership.
Application requirements: Recommendations, essay, transcript, proof of eligibility.
Additional information: Must be member of Golf Course Superintendents Association of America. Must have completed at least 24 credit hours or the equivalent of one year of full-time study in the appropriate major. Must be planning career in golf course management or closely related profession. First and second place winners receive all-expense paid trip to GCSAA-sponsored Golf Industry Show. Children of GCSAA Environmental Institute for Golf's Board of Trustees, GCSAA Board of Directors, and GCSAA staff not eligible. Visit Website for details and application.

Amount of award:	$500-$6,000
Number of awards:	28
Application deadline:	June 1
Notification begins:	August 1

Contact:
Golf Course Superintendents Association of America
Scholarship Program
1421 Research Park Drive
Lawrence, KS 66049-3859
Phone: 785-832-4445
Web: www.gcsaa.org

GCSAA Student Essay Contest

Type of award: Scholarship.
Intended use: For undergraduate or graduate study at postsecondary institution.
Basis for selection: Competition/talent/interest in writing/journalism, based on essay focusing on golf course management. Major/career interest in turf management.
Application requirements: Essay, proof of eligibility.
Additional information: Must be member of Golf Course Superintendents Association of America. Must be pursuing degree in turf grass science, agronomy, or any other field related to golf course management. First prize is $2000; second prize, $1500; third prize, $1000. Visit Website for details.

Amount of award:	$1,000-$2,000
Number of awards:	3
Application deadline:	March 31

Contact:
Golf Course Superintendents Association of America
Student Essay Contest
1421 Research Park Drive
Lawrence, KS 66049-3859
Phone: 800-472-7878 ext. 4445
Web: www.gcsaa.org

Environmental Litigation Group, P.C.

Environmental Litigation Group Scholarship Program

Type of award: Scholarship.
Intended use: For full-time undergraduate or graduate study at accredited 2-year, 4-year or graduate institution in United States.
Eligibility: Applicant must be U.S. citizen.
Application requirements: Essay, transcript. Applicant must be 18 years or older. Must be enrolled for the upcoming semester. Must be a student who witnessed a parent, sibling, immediate family member or close friend fighting cancer. Must write a 500-1000 word essay answering the following question: What It Takes to Fight Cancer?
Additional information: More information about the scholarship and the application can be found on the scholarship webpage.

Amount of award:	$2,000-$5,000
Number of awards:	3
Application deadline:	July 31
Notification begins:	August 31
Total amount awarded:	$10,000

Contact:
Environmental Litigation Group, P.C.
2160 Highland Avenue
Suite 200
Birmingham, AL 35205
Phone: 760-696-7959
Web: https://www.elglaw.com/scholarship/

Epilepsy Foundation of San Diego County

Epilepsy Foundation of San Diego County Scholarship

Type of award: Scholarship.
Intended use: For undergraduate study at vocational, 2-year or 4-year institution.
Eligibility: Applicant must be residing in California.
Basis for selection: Applicant must demonstrate financial need and high academic achievement.
Additional information: Two categories of eligibility: 1) Student being treated for epilepsy who is or will be enrolled in a college, university, or trade school in the Fall. 2) Full-time college or university student involved in an epilepsy research project in health or social science with minimum 3.0 GPA. All applicants must be residents of San Diego or Imperial counties, but may be attending school outside the area.

Amount of award:	$250-$3,000
Number of awards:	8
Number of applicants:	19
Application deadline:	May 1
Total amount awarded:	$9,750

Contact:
Epilepsy Foundation of San Diego County
2055 El Cajon Boulevard
San Diego, CA 92104
Phone: 619-296-0161
Fax: 619-296-0802
Web: www.epilepsysandiego.org

EqualityMaine Foundation

The Joel Abromson Memorial Scholarship

Type of award: Scholarship.
Intended use: For freshman study at postsecondary institution.
Eligibility: Applicant must be high school senior. Applicant must be U.S. citizen or permanent resident residing in Maine.
Basis for selection: Competition/talent/interest in gay/lesbian, based on involvement and leadership in promoting equality for lesbian, gay, bisexual, and transgender people in schools and community. Applicant must demonstrate depth of character and service orientation.
Application requirements: Recommendations, essay. Cover letter. Acceptance letter from chosen higher education institution.
Additional information: Visit Website for essay question and additional information.

Amount of award:	$3,000
Application deadline:	March 1

Contact:
EqualityMaine
P.O. Box 1951
Portland, ME 04104
Phone: 207-761-3732
Fax: 207-761-3752
Web: www.equalitymaine.org/the-joel-abromson-memorial-scholarship-fund

ESA Foundation

ESA Foundation Scholarship Program

Type of award: Scholarship, renewable.
Intended use: For undergraduate or graduate study at vocational, 2-year, 4-year or graduate institution.
Basis for selection: Applicant must demonstrate financial need, high academic achievement, leadership and service orientation.
Application requirements: $5 application fee. Recommendations, essay, transcript.
Additional information: Individual scholarships have specific requirements; visit Website for details and application form.

Amount of award:	$500-$7,500
Number of awards:	196
Number of applicants:	9,000
Application deadline:	February 1
Notification begins:	June 1
Total amount awarded:	$195,000

Contact:
ESA Foundation
Kathy Loyd
563 NW Hwy N
Blairstown, MO 64726
Phone: 660-441-3310
Web: www.epsilonsigmaalpha.org/scholarships-and-grants

ET Foundation

ET Foundation International Aluminum Extrusion Student Design Competition

Type of award: Scholarship.
Intended use: For undergraduate or graduate study at vocational, 2-year, 4-year or graduate institution in or outside United States or Canada.
Eligibility: Applicant must be at least 16, no older than 30. Applicant must be U.S. citizen, permanent resident or international student.
Basis for selection: Major/career interest in architecture; design; engineering, industrial; engineering, materials or engineering.
Application requirements: To enter, you must submit a design that: includes at least one aluminum extruded component designed by the student; demonstrates the manufacturing, design, and material advantages of extruded

aluminum; and addresses the competition judging criteria found on the web site.

Additional information: Application can be found online. Special consideration will be given to entries that also submit a printed 3D model of their extrusion design with their other materials. Student design and supporting materials can be submitted by e-mail or by post. First place: $3,000, Second Place: $2,000, Third Place: $1,000. A Separate $2,500 scholarship for the Bonnell Aluminum LED Lighting Design Award may be presented to the entry that best uses aluminum extrusions, addressing some of the material's excellent advantages for this application - Students must indicate on the entry form that they are entering their design in consideration for this award.

Amount of award:	$1,000-$3,000
Number of awards:	4
Application deadline:	March 27
Notification begins:	May 2
Total amount awarded:	$8,500

Contact:
ET Foundation
1000 North Rand Road
Suite 214
Wauconda, IL 60084
Phone: 847-526-2010
Fax: 847-526-3993
Web: www.aec.org/?page=iaedc_student

EWGA Foundation

EWGA Foundation Women on Par Scholarship Program

Type of award: Scholarship.
Intended use: For full-time undergraduate study at vocational, 2-year or 4-year institution.
Eligibility: Applicant must be female, at least 30. Applicant must be U.S. citizen or permanent resident.
Basis for selection: Applicant must demonstrate financial need.
Application requirements: Essay. US or Canadian Citizen, or legal resident of the US or Canada. Applicants chosen for phase two will be asked to provide transcripts, financial documentation, and three sealed letters of recommendation. Detailed instructions on web site.
Additional information: Candidates must be first time applicants to school, or must be returning to school after an absence to complete a degree. Eligibility is declined if a Bachelor's degree has already been obtained. Handwritten applications and personal essays will not be considered. See website for application and FAQ documents, in PDF or Word format.

Amount of award:	$500-$1,000
Number of awards:	2
Number of applicants:	55
Application deadline:	April 15
Notification begins:	May 15, June 1
Total amount awarded:	$1,500

Contact:
EWGA Foundation
300 Avenue of the Champions
Suite 140
Palm Beach Gardens, FL 33418
Phone: 800-407-1477 Ext 12
Fax: 561-691-0012
Web: www.ewgafoundation.com/women-on-par-scholarship

Executive Women International

Executive Women International Scholarship

Type of award: Scholarship, renewable.
Intended use: For full-time undergraduate study at accredited 4-year institution in United States.
Eligibility: Applicant must be high school senior.
Basis for selection: Applicant must demonstrate high academic achievement, depth of character, leadership, seriousness of purpose and service orientation.
Application requirements: Interview, recommendations, essay, transcript. Biographical Questionnaire, FAFSA, most recent federal tax form(s) (Form 1040, pages 1 & 2; Form 1040A, pages 1 & 2; Form 1040EZ, page 1) from person who claims applicant on their income tax return.
Additional information: Applicant must reside within boundaries of participating Executive Women International chapter. Minimum 3.0 GPA. Scholarship awarded each academic year, for up to five consecutive years, until student completes degree. Applicants must have sponsoring teacher at their school. Must have a major/career interest in a professional field.

Amount of award:	$1,000-$5,000
Number of awards:	6
Application deadline:	April 30
Notification begins:	May 30
Total amount awarded:	$15,000

Contact:
Executive Women International
3860 South 2300 East
Suite 211
Salt Lake City, UT 84109
Phone: 801-355-2800
Fax: 801-355-2852
Web: www.ewiconnect.com

Experimental Aircraft Association

David Alan Quick Scholarship

Type of award: Scholarship.
Intended use: For junior or senior study at accredited 4-year institution.
Basis for selection: Major/career interest in aerospace or engineering. Applicant must demonstrate financial need.
Application requirements: Recommendations, essay. Resume, financial information.

Additional information: Must be Experimental Aircraft Association member or recommended by EAA member. Awarded to student pursuing degree in aerospace or aeronautical engineering. Awards dependent on funding. Apply online.

Amount of award:	$500
Number of awards:	1
Application deadline:	February 28

Contact:
EAA Scholarship Department
P.O. 3086
Oshkosh, WI 54903-3086
Phone: 920-426-6823
Web: www.youngeagles.org/programs/scholarships

David Mineck Memorial Scholarship

Type of award: Scholarship.
Intended use: For undergraduate study at postsecondary institution.
Basis for selection: Major/career interest in aerospace.
Additional information: Must be an Experimental Aircraft Association member or recommended by an EAA member.

Amount of award:	$500
Application deadline:	February 28

Contact:
EAA Scholarship Department
P.O. 3086
Oshkosh, WI 54903-3086
Phone: 920-426-6823
Web: www.youngeagles.org/programs/scholarships

Hansen Scholarship

Type of award: Scholarship, renewable.
Intended use: For undergraduate study at accredited vocational, 2-year or 4-year institution.
Basis for selection: Major/career interest in aerospace; aviation or engineering. Applicant must demonstrate financial need, high academic achievement, depth of character, leadership and service orientation.
Application requirements: Recommendations, essay. Resume, financial information.
Additional information: Must be Experimental Aircraft Association member or recommended by EAA member. Student should be pursuing degree in aerospace engineering or aeronautical engineering. Awards dependent on funding. Visit Website for details and application.

Amount of award:	$1,000
Number of awards:	1
Application deadline:	February 28

Contact:
EAA Scholarship Department
P.O. 3086
Oshkosh, WI 54903-3086
Phone: 920-426-6823
Web: www.youngeagles.org/programs/scholarships

Harry E. Arcamuzi Aviation Scholarship

Type of award: Scholarship, renewable.
Intended use: For undergraduate study at postsecondary institution.
Basis for selection: Major/career interest in aviation.

Additional information: Must be an Experimental Aircraft Association member or recommended by EAA member. Must be inner city student with a 2.0 minimum GPA.

Amount of award:	$500
Application deadline:	February 28

Contact:
EAA Scholarship Department
P.O. 3086
Oshkosh, WI 54903-3086
Phone: 920-426-6823
Web: www.youngeagles.org/programs/scholarships

H.P. Bud Milligan Aviation Scholarship

Type of award: Scholarship, renewable.
Intended use: For undergraduate study at accredited vocational, 2-year or 4-year institution.
Basis for selection: Major/career interest in aviation. Applicant must demonstrate financial need, depth of character, leadership and service orientation.
Application requirements: Recommendations, essay. Resume, financial information.
Additional information: Must be Experimental Aircraft Association member or recommended by EAA member. Awards dependent on funding. Complete application online.

Amount of award:	$500
Number of awards:	1
Application deadline:	February 28
Total amount awarded:	$2,800

Contact:
EAA Scholarship Department
P.O. 3086
Oshkosh, WI 54903-3086
Phone: 920-426-6823
Web: http://www.studentscholarshipsearch.com/scholarships/hp-milligan-aviation-scholarship.php

Hudner Medal of Honor Scholarship

Type of award: Scholarship.
Intended use: For undergraduate study at postsecondary institution.
Basis for selection: Major/career interest in aviation; military science or public administration/service. Applicant must demonstrate financial need, leadership and service orientation.
Application requirements: Recommendations, essay. Resume, financial information.
Additional information: Must be an Experimental Aircraft Association member or recommended by EAA member and have strong record of involvement with Experimental Aircraft Association. Must express intent to serve the country through military or public service. Winner must attend award presentation dinner. Special consideration given to Wisconsin or nearby resident. Recommendation from Experimental Aircraft Association member strongly desired. Awards dependent on funding. Visit Website for additional information and application.

Amount of award:	$500
Number of awards:	1
Application deadline:	February 28

Contact:
EAA Scholarship Department
P.O. 3086
Oshkosh, WI 54903-3086
Phone: 920-426-6823
Web: www.youngeagles.org/programs/scholarships

Payzer Scholarship

Type of award: Scholarship.
Intended use: For undergraduate study at accredited postsecondary institution.
Basis for selection: Major/career interest in engineering; mathematics; physical sciences; biology or aviation. Applicant must demonstrate financial need, depth of character, leadership and service orientation.
Application requirements: Recommendations, essay. Resume, financial information.
Additional information: Must be current Experimental Aircraft Association member or recommended by EAA member. Applicant must intend to pursue career in engineering, mathematics, or physical/biological sciences. Awards dependent on funding. Complete application online.

Amount of award:	$5,000
Number of awards:	1
Application deadline:	February 28

Contact:
EAA Scholarship Department
P.O. 3086
Oshkosh, WI 54903-3086
Phone: 920-426-6823
Web: www.youngeagles.org/programs/scholarships

Richard Lee Vernon Aviation Scholarship

Type of award: Scholarship.
Intended use: For undergraduate study at postsecondary institution.
Basis for selection: Major/career interest in aviation. Applicant must demonstrate financial need and high academic achievement.
Application requirements: Recommendations, essay. Resume, financial information.
Additional information: Must be Experimental Aircraft Association member or recommended by EAA member. Awarded to a student pursuing training leading to professional aviation occupation. Awards dependent on funding. Apply online.

Amount of award:	$500
Number of awards:	1
Application deadline:	February 28

Contact:
EAA Scholarship Department
P.O. 3086
Oshkosh, WI 54903-3086
Phone: 920-426-6823
Web: www.youngeagles.org/programs/scholarships

Experts Exchange

Experts Exchange Scholarship Contest

Type of award: Scholarship.
Intended use: For undergraduate or graduate study at vocational, 2-year, 4-year or graduate institution.
Application requirements: Students will submit an original piece of work via an article or video on a technology topic of their choosing to the Experts Exchange website. The work must be helpful in nature, describing and/or solving a specific problem.

Amount of award:	$500-$1,500
Number of awards:	3
Application deadline:	June 30, December 31
Notification begins:	August 1, January 16
Total amount awarded:	$3,000

Contact:
Experts Exchange
2701 McMillan Avenue
Suite 160
San Luis Obispo, CA 93401
Phone: 805-787-0603
Web: pages.experts-exchange.com/scholarship

Explorers Club

Explorers Club Youth Activity Fund Grant

Type of award: Research grant.
Intended use: For full-time undergraduate study at postsecondary institution.
Basis for selection: Competition/talent/interest in research paper, based on proposal's scientific and practical merit, investigator's competence, and budget's appropriateness. Major/career interest in natural sciences. Applicant must demonstrate seriousness of purpose.
Application requirements: Recommendations, proof of eligibility, research proposal. One-page description of project, budget, copy of student ID.
Additional information: For research project in the natural sciences under supervision of qualified scientist or institution. Average award amount is approximately $1500. For high school students or undergraduates only. Recipients of grants must provide one- to two-page report on their exploration or research within year of receiving the grant. Request application form from club. Notifications begin April. See Website for more details and deadline.

Amount of award:	$500-$5,000
Number of applicants:	79
Total amount awarded:	$125,200

Contact:
The Explorers Club
Attn: Coleen Castillo
46 East 70th Street
New York, NY 10021
Phone: 212-628-8383
Fax: 212-628-8384
Web: www.explorers.org

Express Medical Supply

Express Medical Supply Scholarship

Type of award: Scholarship.
Intended use: For undergraduate study.
Eligibility: Applicant must be U.S. citizen.
Application requirements: We are asking potential recipients to tweet us a photo @Express_Medical that best represents the word EXPRESS and briefly explain why.
Additional information: Include #ExmedScholarship in your tweet, include the link to the website listed below in the contact information in your tweet and email the URL to the scholarships email address. Include your full name, Twitter name, address, phone number, date of birth and parent/guardian (if under 18). The scholarship will be paid to the financial aid department of your school.

Amount of award:	$500
Number of awards:	1
Application deadline:	June 30
Notification begins:	July 7
Total amount awarded:	$500

Contact:
Express Medical Supply
218 Seebold Spur
St Louis, MO 63026
Phone: 800-633-2139
Web: exmed.net/500

ExpressVPN

The ExpressVPN Future of Privacy Scholarship

Type of award: Scholarship, renewable.
Intended use: For full-time undergraduate or graduate study at vocational, 2-year, 4-year or graduate institution.
Application requirements: Essay. 300-400 words essay :It's 2027 and government surveillance on citizen's internet activities is legal, in force, and widespread, Governments worldwide are watching everything you're doing, What happens to art, culture, innovation, scientific research, freedom of expression, etc ?
Additional information: Applicants must be currently enrolled in either a high school, undergraduate school, or graduate school located in the United States or in the United Kingdom. Essays must be sent via email to this address scholarship@expressvpn.com including (your name, the name and address and contact details of your school, your current grade level).One entry per student,multiple entries per student will be disregarded.employees of ExpressVPN and their immediate family members are not eligible for this contest.The winning essay shall be determined using the following criteria: Level of creativity, originality, and detail of the submission ,Student's ability to formulate an opinion ,Clear and articulate writing . More information about the Scholarship at https://www.expressvpn.com/expressvpn-scholarship.

Amount of award:	$5,000
Number of awards:	1
Number of applicants:	800
Application deadline:	August 31
Notification begins:	October 13
Total amount awarded:	$5,000

Contact:
The ExpressVPN
Web: www.expressvpn.com/expressvpn-scholarship

ExtremeTerrain

ExtremeTerrain's Student Scholarship Program

Type of award: Scholarship.
Intended use: For full-time undergraduate or graduate study at 2-year, 4-year or graduate institution in United States.
Basis for selection: Major/career interest in environmental science.
Application requirements: Essay.
Additional information: One scholarship awarded in Fall and one in Spring. Deadlines are October 15th and June 15th. Students should submit a 700 to 1500 word essay by e-mail that describes who you are, why you feel it is important to maintain access to public lands for recreational use, and how you plan to use your degree to advocate for the recreational use of public lands. Essays should be submitted as a PDF or Microsoft Word document to be eligible for consideration and must also be accompanied with proof of current enrollment in an accredited United States college or university.

Amount of award:	$3,000
Number of awards:	2
Total amount awarded:	$6,000

Contact:
ExtremeTerrain
7 Lee Boulevard
Malvern, PA 19355
Phone: 610-251-1672 x208
Web: www.extremeterrain.com/scholarships.html

Farah & Farah

Farah & Farah Scholarship

Type of award: Scholarship.
Intended use: For undergraduate study at 2-year or 4-year institution.
Eligibility: Applicant must be U.S. citizen or permanent resident.
Application requirements: Essay.
Additional information: Must have a minimum 3.0 GPA. Application and 600-1200 word essay prompt found online.

Number of awards:	1
Application deadline:	September 15
Notification begins:	October 12
Total amount awarded:	$500

Contact:
Web: www.farahandfarah.com/scholarship/

Federal Criminal Lawyer Farral Haber

White Collar Defense Diversity Scholarship

Type of award: Scholarship.
Intended use: For undergraduate or graduate study at accredited vocational, 2-year, 4-year or graduate institution.
Eligibility: Applicant must be African American or Hispanic American. Applicant must be high school senior.
Basis for selection: Applicant must demonstrate financial need and high academic achievement.
Application requirements: Recommendations, essay, transcript. Unofficial transcript, application cover sheet, application essay, one letter of recommendation. Essay topic (1000 words): "Describe the applicant's personal situation as a minority with a single mother, the impact that it has had on their life, and how they have overcome those challenges. Applicants should also address their college, law school and/or career plans and how this scholarship will help him/her achieve those plans."
Additional information: Minimum 3.0 GPA required. Candidate must have a demonstrated financial need and come from a single-mother home.

Amount of award:	$500
Number of awards:	1
Number of applicants:	20
Application deadline:	September 1
Total amount awarded:	$500

Contact:
White Collar Criminal Defense Scholarship
409 7th Street NW
Washington, DC 20004
Phone: 202-517-0502
Fax: 202-664-1331
Web: whitecollarattorney.net/diversity-scholarship-2016

Federal Employee Education and Assistance Fund

Federal Employee Education and Assistance Fund Scholarship

Type of award: Scholarship.
Intended use: For undergraduate, master's or doctoral study at accredited 2-year, 4-year or graduate institution.
Eligibility: Applicant or parent must be employed by Federal/U.S. Government.
Basis for selection: Applicant must demonstrate high academic achievement.
Application requirements: Recommendations, essay, transcript. List of community service/extracurricular activities.
Additional information: Current civilian federal and postal employees with minimum three years' service by the end of August of the application year and their dependents are eligible. Applicant must have completed community service activities. Minimum 3.0 GPA. Employee applicants eligible for part-time study; dependents must enroll full-time. Visit Website for application materials beginning in January. Deadline is the last Friday of March every year. Notification date is Summer 2017.

Amount of award:	$1,000-$5,000
Number of applicants:	2,336
Application deadline:	March 27
Total amount awarded:	$400,000

Contact:
Federal Employee Education and Assistance Fund
3333 S. Wadsworth Blvd.
Suite 300
Lakewood, CO 80227
Phone: 202-554-0007 x102
Web: www.feea.org

Feeding Tomorrow, The Foundation of the Institute of Food Technologists

Institute of Food Technologists Freshman Scholarship

Type of award: Scholarship, renewable.
Intended use: For full-time freshman study at 4-year institution. Designated institutions: Educational institutions with approved programs in food science/technology.
Eligibility: Applicant must be high school senior.
Basis for selection: Major/career interest in food science/technology. Applicant must demonstrate high academic achievement.
Application requirements: Recommendations, essay, transcript.
Additional information: IFT Scholarship recipients must join IFT student association. Applicant must be high school senior or high school graduate entering college for first time. Minimum 3.0 GPA required. Must enroll in IFT-approved program. Program descriptions and application available on Website.

Amount of award:	$1,000
Application deadline:	April 15
Notification begins:	June 1

Contact:
Scholarship Department Institute of Food Technologists
525 W. Van Buren, Suite 1000
Chicago, IL 60607
Phone: 312-782-8424
Fax: 312-782-8348
Web: www.ift.org/scholarships

Institute of Food Technologists Undergraduate Scholarship

Type of award: Scholarship, renewable.
Intended use: For full-time sophomore, junior or senior study at 4-year institution. Designated institutions: Educational institutions with approved programs in food science/technology.
Basis for selection: Major/career interest in food science/technology. Applicant must demonstrate high academic achievement.
Application requirements: Recommendations, transcript.
Additional information: Applicant must have minimum 3.0 GPA and must be enrolled in IFT-approved program. Program

description and application available through Website. Applicants must be IFT members. Number of awards varies from year to year.

Amount of award:	$1,000-$2,000
Application deadline:	February 20
Notification begins:	April 1

Contact:
Scholarship Department
Institute of Food Technologists
525 W. Van Buren, Suite 1000
Chicago, IL 60601
Phone: 312-782-8424
Fax: 312-782-8348
Web: www.ift.org/scholarships

Feldman & Royle, Attorneys at Law

Autism Spectrum Scholarship

Type of award: Scholarship.
Intended use: For undergraduate or graduate study at vocational, 2-year, 4-year or graduate institution.
Application requirements: Fill out the online form. Upload a brief statement of up to 100 words telling the reader what educational plans you have if you are awarded the scholarship. (Optional) Upload an essay of not less than 650 words and not more than 1,000 words on the subject of how having ASD has affected your education.
Additional information: All those who have ASD (DSM-5) are eligible for the scholarships, which will be used to assist you in furthering your educational goals. We may request proof of your ASD diagnosis.

Amount of award:	$1,000
Number of awards:	2
Application deadline:	November 7
Notification begins:	December 6

Contact:
Feldman & Royle, Attorneys at Law
2828 North Central Avenue
Suite 1203
Phoenix, AZ 85004
Phone: 602-899-8000
Web: www.feldmanroyle.com/autism-scholarships/

Feldman Law Firm

Disabled Veterans Scholarship

Type of award: Scholarship.
Intended use: For undergraduate or graduate study at vocational, 2-year, 4-year or graduate institution.
Eligibility: Applicant must be disabled while on active duty.
Application requirements: Complete the online application form on the scholarship website. Upload a short statement of no more than 100 words explaining your educational goals. (Optional but recommended) Upload an essay (between 650 and 1,000 words) that discusses how your life has been affected by your military service and/or disability.
Additional information: Must be a disabled veteran of the United States Armed Forces with a disability rating of at least

30 percent. May be asked to provide proof of disability and status as a veteran.

Amount of award:	$1,000
Number of awards:	2
Application deadline:	November 10
Notification begins:	December 9

Contact:
Feldman Law Firm
1 East Washington Street, #500
Phoenix, AZ 85004
Phone: 602-540-7887
Web: www.afphoenixcriminalattorney.com/disabled-veterans-scholarship

Financial Service Centers of New York

MoneyGram FSCNY Scholarship

Type of award: Scholarship.
Intended use: For freshman study at accredited vocational, 2-year or 4-year institution.
Eligibility: Applicant must be high school senior. Applicant must be residing in New York.
Basis for selection: Applicants will be considered based on the following criteria: 1) Academic achievement; 2) Demonstrated leadership in their school; 3) Demonstrated involvement in their community, contributing at least 50 valuable hours of volunteer. Applicant must demonstrate high academic achievement, leadership and service orientation.
Application requirements: Essay, proof of eligibility. In 250 words or less students should explain their most rewarding experience through their community service involvement.
Additional information: Applicants must be seniors attending public high schools in New York City's five boroughs or surrounding New York counties.

Amount of award:	$2,000-$7,500
Application deadline:	March 4
Notification begins:	March 22

Contact:
Financial Service Centers of New York
Court Plaza South, East Wing, 21 Main Street
1st Floor
Hackensack, NJ 07602
Phone: 212-268-1911
Web: www.fscny.org/?controller=scholarshipprogram

Rewarding Young Leaders in Our Community Scholarship

Type of award: Scholarship.
Intended use: For freshman study at postsecondary institution.
Eligibility: Applicant must be U.S. citizen or permanent resident.
Basis for selection: Applicant must demonstrate high academic achievement, leadership and service orientation.
Application requirements: Essay, transcript. Written verification of community involvement.
Additional information: Applicant must have contributed at least 50 hours of volunteer service per year in high school.

Amount of award:	$500-$7,500
Number of awards:	16
Total amount awarded:	$40,000

Contact:
Financial Service Centers of New York
Mr. Sanford Herman, Chairman
21 Main Street, Suite 101, P.O. Box 647
Hackensack, NJ 07601-0647
Phone: 212-268-1911
Web: www.fscny.org/?controller=scholarshipprogram

FineAwards.com

Custom Award and Recognition Scholarship

Type of award: Scholarship.
Intended use: For undergraduate or graduate study at vocational, 2-year, 4-year or graduate institution.
Application requirements: Submit your video application explaining who deserves to be recognized. Create a video explaining someone who deserves to be recognized.
Additional information: Visit https://www.fineawards.com/scholarship to learn more and submit your application.

Amount of award:	$500
Number of awards:	2
Application deadline:	June 15
Notification begins:	June 30
Total amount awarded:	$1,000

Contact:
FineAwards.com
250 North Dixie Highway #13
Hollywood, FL 33020
Phone: 954-843-0850
Fax: 954-843-0851
Web: https://www.fineawards.com/scholarship

First Catholic Slovak Ladies Association

First Catholic Slovak Ladies Association Scholarship Program

Type of award: Scholarship.
Intended use: For full-time undergraduate or graduate study at accredited postsecondary institution in United States or Canada.
Eligibility: Applicant or parent must be member/participant of First Catholic Slovak Ladies Association.
Basis for selection: Applicant must demonstrate high academic achievement, leadership and service orientation.
Application requirements: Recommendations, essay, transcript, proof of eligibility. SAT/ACT scores. Photograph.
Additional information: Applicant must be member of First Catholic Slovak Ladies Association for at least three years prior to date of application, and on a $1,000 legal reserve certificate, a $5,000 term certificate, or have an annuity certificate. Visit Website for more information.

Amount of award:	$1,250-$1,750
Number of awards:	133
Number of applicants:	396
Application deadline:	March 1
Notification begins:	June 15
Total amount awarded:	$248,250

Contact:
First Catholic Slovak Ladies Association
Director of Fraternal Scholarship Aid
24950 Chagrin Boulevard
Beachwood, OH 44122
Phone: 800-464-4642
Web: www.fcsla.org

First Command Educational Foundation

Donaldson D. Frizzell Memorial Scholarship

Type of award: Scholarship, renewable.
Intended use: For undergraduate or graduate study at vocational, 4-year or graduate institution.
Eligibility: Applicant must be at least 17, high school senior. Applicant must be in military service or veteran; or dependent of active service person or veteran; or spouse of active service person or veteran.
Basis for selection: Applicant must demonstrate high academic achievement.
Application requirements: Recommendations, essay. Complete the application and essay questions. Provide up to two letters of recommendation (one must be from a teacher or supervisor; other can be personal or academic/employer). Complete our free e-learning course, Basic Finances 4 ALL and pass the corresponding test OR complete our free smartphone app, SavvySaver and upload the certificate of completion with your application.
Additional information: The Donaldson D Frizzell Scholarship is open to US uniformed services members (active, guard, reserve, retired, and veterans) and their families (spouses and dependents), First Command Financial Services' clients and their families, dependent family members of First Command Advisors and field office staff members, and non-contractual ROTC students. Minimum 3.0 GPA required.

Amount of award:	$10,000
Number of awards:	15
Number of applicants:	95
Application deadline:	April 14
Notification begins:	June 1
Total amount awarded:	$30,000

Contact:
First Command Educational Foundation
1 First Command Plaza
Fort Worth, TX 76109
Phone: 817-569-2032
Web: https://www.fcef.com/scholarships/donaldson-d-frizzell-scholarship-3/

Donaldson D. Frizzell Scholarship

Type of award: Scholarship.
Intended use: For full-time undergraduate or graduate study at accredited vocational, 2-year, 4-year or graduate institution.
Eligibility: Applicant must be at least 17. Applicant must be U.S. citizen.
Application requirements: Recommendations, essay. Provide up to 2 letters of recommendation: At least one letter must be from a teacher/professor (non traditional); Additional letter can be personal or academic. Complete our free e-learning course, Basic$4ALL (online) and pass the corresponding rest OR

complete our free smartphone app, Basic$4ALL (mobile), and upload the certificate of completion with your application.

Additional information: more information can be found on the scholarship website.

Amount of award:	$1,000-$10,000
Number of awards:	15
Number of applicants:	175
Application deadline:	April 7
Notification begins:	May 31
Total amount awarded:	$30,000

Contact:
First Command Educational Foundation
Web: http://app.smarterselect.com/programs/37514-First-Command-Educational-Foundation

First Tech Federal Credit Union

First Tech Federal Credit Union Scholarship Program

Type of award: Scholarship, renewable.
Intended use: For full-time undergraduate or graduate study at vocational, 2-year, 4-year or graduate institution in United States.
Basis for selection: Applicant must demonstrate high academic achievement.
Application requirements: Transcript.
Additional information: Minimum 3.5 GPA. Must be a member of First Tech Federal Credit Union. Must be enrolled full time in trade school, college, or graduate program in Fall.

Amount of award:	$5,000
Number of awards:	10
Number of applicants:	101
Application deadline:	March 31
Notification begins:	May 13
Total amount awarded:	$50,000

Contact:
First Tech Federal Credit Union
P.O. Box 2100
Beaverton, OR 97075
Phone: 503-350-3337
Web: https://firsttech.profits4purpose.com/external/login

Flight Network

Fly High Scholarship

Type of award: Scholarship.
Intended use: For full-time undergraduate study at 4-year institution in United States or Canada.
Eligibility: Applicant must be at least 17.
Application requirements: Essay.
Additional information: Minimum 3.0 GPA. Students must submit a 500-1000 word essay about a travel related experience or topic. The winning essay will be featured on the Flight Network blog and will also secure the winner a one-time scholarship of $1000. Once submission has been made, go to Twitter and mention @FlightNetwork, tweet a travel photo and use the hashtag #FNScholarship. You can also post a travel

photo using the hashtag #FNScholarship on Flight Network's Facebook page (facebook.com/DiscountFlights) or by e-mail.

Number of awards:	1
Application deadline:	December 31
Notification begins:	January 31
Total amount awarded:	$1,000

Contact:
Flight Network
2947-A Portland Drive
Oakville, ON
Phone: 877-496-4815
Web: www.flightnetwork.com/pages/scholarship/

Florida Department of Education

Access to Better Learning and Education (ABLE) Grant Program

Type of award: Research grant, renewable.
Intended use: For full-time undergraduate study. Designated institutions: Eligible private Florida Post-secondary private institutions.
Eligibility: Applicant must be U.S. citizen or permanent resident residing in Florida.
Application requirements: Undergraduate must be enrolled in a degree program.
Additional information: Each participating institution determines application procedures, deadlines, and student eligibility. Award amount specified in the General Appropriations Act. The amount of ABLE award plus all other scholarships and grants specifically designated for payment of tuition and fees cannot exceed the total amount of tuition and fees charged by the institution. Applications available from financial aid offices at participating institutions. May not be enrolled in program of study leading to degree in theology or divinity.

Contact:
Office of Student Financial Assistance
325 West Gaines Street
Suite 1314
Tallahassee, FL 32399-0400
Phone: 888-827-2004
Web: www.floridastudentfinancialaid.org

Florida Bright Futures Scholarship Program

Type of award: Scholarship.
Intended use: For at vocational, 2-year or 4-year institution. Designated institutions: Eligible Florida institutions.
Eligibility: Applicant must be high school senior. Applicant must be U.S. citizen or permanent resident residing in Florida.
Basis for selection: Applicant must demonstrate high academic achievement.
Application requirements: Transcript. Must complete the Initial Student Florida Financial Aid Application by high school graduation.
Additional information: Must be a Florida resident and U.S. citizen or eligible non-citizen as determined by student's postsecondary institution. Must apply during senior year, after December 1 and prior to high school graduation. Must not have been found guilty of or have plead nolo contendere to a

felony charge. Must meet specific academic requirements for individual awards. Award amount is based on a cost per credit hour. Levels include Florida Academic Scholars, Florida Medallion Scholars, Florida Gold Seal Vocational Scholars. Visit Website for more details.

Contact:
Florida Department of Education
325 West Gaines Street
Suite 1314
Tallahassee, FL 32399-0400
Phone: 888-827-2004
Fax: 850-487-1809
Web: www.floridastudentfinancialaid.org/SSFAD/home/uamain.htm

Florida Department of Education Florida Incentive Scholarship Program

Type of award: Scholarship, renewable.
Intended use: For full-time undergraduate study at accredited 4-year institution. Designated institutions: Eligible Florida postsecondary institution.
Eligibility: Applicant must be U.S. citizen residing in Florida.
Basis for selection: Applicant must demonstrate high academic achievement.
Application requirements: Must have received a national merit $2,500 scholarship, a national achievement $2,500 scholarship, a Corporate-sponsored Merit Scholarship, a college-sponsored Merit Scholarship.
Additional information: Awarded to students who achieved the National Merit or National Achievement finalist designation. Award amount is the cost of attendance minus the sum of the Bright Futures award and the National Merit/Achievement award. To be considered, enroll at an eligible postsecondary institution during the fall academic term following high school graduation. An initial application is not required. Visit web site for more details. To renew, awardees must have 3.0 on a 4.0 scale and earn credit for all hours enrolled by the drop/add period.

Contact:
Florida Department of Education Office of Student Financial Assistance
325 West Gaines Street
Suite 1314
Tallahassee, FL 32399-0400
Phone: 1-888-827-2004
Web: www.floridastudentfinancialaid.org

Florida First Generation Matching Grant Program

Type of award: Scholarship.
Intended use: For undergraduate study. Designated institutions: Florida state universities and colleges. Eligible Florida state post-secondary institutions.
Eligibility: Applicant must be U.S. citizen or permanent resident residing in Florida.
Basis for selection: Applicant must demonstrate financial need.
Application requirements: FAFSA.
Additional information: Open to currently enrolled first generation college students whose parents have not earned baccalaureate degrees or higher. Undergraduate study must be dedicated to a degree program. Funding may vary. Each participating institution determines application procedures,

deadlines, and student eligibility. Applications available from participating schools' financial aid offices.
Contact:
Office of Student Financial Assistance
325 West Gaines Street
Suite 1314
Tallahassee, FL 32399-0400
Phone: 888-827-2004
Web: www.floridastudentfinancialaid.org

Florida Public Postsecondary Career Education Student Assistance Grant Program

Type of award: Scholarship.
Intended use: For undergraduate study. Designated institutions: Eligible Florida colleges or career centers.
Eligibility: Applicant must be U.S. citizen or permanent resident residing in Florida.
Basis for selection: Applicant must demonstrate financial need.
Application requirements: FAFSA.
Additional information: Award amount specified in the General Appropriations Act. Each participating institution determines application procedures, deadlines, and student eligibility. Visit website for information.
Contact:
Office of Student Financial Assistance
325 West Gaines Street
Suite 1314
Tallahassee, FL 32399-0400
Phone: 888-827-2004
Web: www.floridastudentfinancialaid.org

Florida Scholarships for Children and Spouses of Deceased or Disabled Veterans

Type of award: Scholarship, renewable.
Intended use: For undergraduate study. Designated institutions: Eligible Florida postsecondary institutions.
Eligibility: Applicant must be at least 16, no older than 22. Applicant must be U.S. citizen or permanent resident residing in Florida. Applicant must be dependent of disabled veteran, deceased veteran or POW/MIA; or spouse of disabled veteran or deceased veteran.
Additional information: Child applicant must be between ages of 16 and 22. Spouse of deceased service member must not be remarried. Service members must be certified by Florida Department of Veterans Affairs. Award for students of eligible private schools based on average cost of Florida public tuition/fees. Award amount specified in the General Appropriations Act. Award amount varies. Visit Website for additional information.
Application deadline: April 1
Contact:
Office of Student Financial Assistance
325 West Gaines Street
Suite 1314
Tallahassee, FL 32399-0400
Phone: 888-827-2004
Web: www.floridastudentfinancialaid.org

Florida Student Assistance Grant (FSAG) Program

Type of award: Scholarship, renewable.
Intended use: For undergraduate study at 2-year or 4-year institution. Designated institutions: Eligible Florida postsecondary institutions.
Eligibility: Applicant must be U.S. citizen or permanent resident residing in Florida.
Basis for selection: Applicant must demonstrate financial need.
Application requirements: FAFSA.
Additional information: Award amount specified in the General Appropriations Act. Each participating institution determines application procedures, deadlines, student eligibility, and award amounts. Applications available from participating schools' financial aid offices. Visit Website for more information. Undergraduate study must be in a degree program.
Contact:
Office of Student Financial Assistance
325 West Gaines Street
Suite 1314
Tallahassee, FL 32399-0400
Phone: 888-827-2004
Web: www.floridastudentfinancialaid.org

Florida Work Experience Program

Type of award: Scholarship, renewable.
Intended use: For undergraduate study at vocational, 2-year or 4-year institution. Designated institutions: Eligible Florida postsecondary institutions.
Eligibility: Applicant must be U.S. citizen or permanent resident residing in Florida.
Basis for selection: Applicant must demonstrate financial need.
Application requirements: FAFSA.
Additional information: Minimum 2.0 GPA on a 4.0 scale. Provides students with opportunity to be employed off-campus in jobs related to their academic major or area of career interest. Applications available from participating schools' financial aid offices. Amount of award determined by institution and may not exceed student's financial need. Visit website for more information.
Contact:
Office of Student Financial Assistance
325 West Gaines Street
Suite 1314
Tallahassee, FL 32399-0400
Phone: 888-827-2004
Web: www.floridastudentfinancialaid.org

Jose Marti Scholarship Challenge Grant Fund

Type of award: Scholarship, renewable.
Intended use: For full-time undergraduate or graduate study at 2-year, 4-year or graduate institution. Designated institutions: Eligible public or private Florida institutions.
Eligibility: Applicant must be Mexican American, Hispanic American or Puerto Rican. Applicant must be U.S. citizen or permanent resident residing in Florida.
Basis for selection: Applicant must demonstrate financial need and high academic achievement.
Application requirements: FAFSA and Florida Financial Aid Application (FFAA).

Additional information: Minimum 3.0 GPA on a 4.0 scale. Must be a Hispanic-American or a person of Spanish culture, born in Mexico or Hispanic Country of the Caribbean, Central American, or South American regardless of race, or child of same. Award amount specified in the General Appropriations Act. Award number is limited to the amount of available funds. First priority to graduating high school seniors, second priority to graduate students. Visit Website for more information. Undergraduate study must be in a degree program.
   Application deadline:　　　April 1
Contact:
Office of Student Financial Assistance
325 West Gaines Street
Suite 1314
Tallahassee, FL 32399-0400
Phone: 888-827-2004
Web: www.floridastudentfinancialaid.org

Mary McLeod Bethune Scholarship

Type of award: Scholarship, renewable.
Intended use: For full-time undergraduate study at 4-year institution in United States. Designated institutions: Bethune-Cookman University, Edward Waters College, Florida A&M University, and Florida Memorial University.
Eligibility: Applicant must be U.S. citizen or permanent resident residing in Florida.
Basis for selection: Applicant must demonstrate financial need and high academic achievement.
Additional information: Minimum 3.0 high school GPA on a 4.0 scale. Award amount specified in the General Appropriations Act. Deadlines established by participating institutions. Award funds contingent upon matching contributions raised by the eligible institutions. Applications can be obtained from any of four designated institutions' financial aid offices. Visit Website for more information applying and renewal.
Contact:
Office of Student Financial Assistance
325 West Gaines Street
Suite 1314
Tallahassee, FL 32399-0400
Phone: 888-827-2004
Web: www.floridastudentfinancialaid.org

Minority Teacher Education Scholarship Program/Florida Fund for Minority Teachers, Inc.

Type of award: Scholarship, renewable.
Intended use: For junior study at postsecondary institution in United States. Designated institutions: Eligible Florida postsecondary institutions.
Eligibility: Applicant must be Alaskan native, Asian American, African American, Mexican American, Hispanic American, Puerto Rican, American Indian or Native Hawaiian/Pacific Islander. Be a member of one of the following racial groups: African American/Black, Hispanic/Latino, Asian American/Pacific Islander, or American Indian/Alaskan native. Applicant must be U.S. citizen or permanent resident residing in Florida.
Basis for selection: Major/career interest in education. Applicant must demonstrate high academic achievement.
Application requirements: Upon graduation, a recipient is required to teach one year in a Florida public school for each year the scholarship ($4,000) was received. See application for details.

Scholarships

Additional information: Must be a junior and not have exceeded 18 hours of upper division education courses, and be newly admitted into a teacher education program at any of the program's eligible postsecondary institutions. Special consideration given to Florida college (public community college) graduates. Award amount specified in the General Appropriations Act. A renewal application is not required. A recipient is automatically considered for a renewal award each semester (fall and spring).

   Application deadline: August 1, November 15
Contact:
Office of Student Financial Assistance
325 West Gaines Street
Suite 1314
Tallahassee, FL 32399-0400
Phone: 352-392-9196
Web: www.floridastudentfinancialaid.org

Rosewood Family Scholarship Program

Type of award: Scholarship, renewable.
Intended use: For undergraduate study at vocational, 2-year or 4-year institution. Designated institutions: Public Florida postsecondary institutions.
Eligibility: Applicant must be U.S. citizen or permanent resident.
Basis for selection: Applicant must demonstrate financial need.
Application requirements: Transcript, proof of eligibility. Applicants must submit a FAFSA and Florida Financial Aid Application (FFAA). If not Florida resident, copy of Student Aid Report (SAR) must be sent to OSFA and postmarked by May 15th. Applicants must show proof of ancestry.
Additional information: Applicant must be direct descendent of Rosewood families affected by the incidents of January, 1923; renewal applicants given priority. Award amount specified in the General Appropriations Act. Award covers annual cost of tuition and fees up to $6,100 per semester for up to eight semesters. Visit Website for more information. Undergraduate study must be in a degree, certificate or diploma program.
   Number of awards: 50
   Application deadline: April 1
Contact:
Office of Student Financial Assistance
325 West Gaines Street
Suite 1314
Tallahassee, FL 32399-0400
Phone: 888-827-2004
Web: www.floridastudentfinancialaid.org

William L. Boyd, IV, Florida Resident Access Grant (FRAG) Program

Type of award: Scholarship, renewable.
Intended use: For full-time undergraduate study at 4-year institution. Designated institutions: Eligible private, nonprofit Florida colleges and universities. Schools must be accredited by SACS.
Eligibility: Applicant must be U.S. citizen or permanent resident residing in Florida.
Additional information: Applicant must not have previously received bachelor's degree and may not use award for study of divinity or theology. Award amount specified in the General Appropriations Act. Amount of award plus all other scholarships and grants may not exceed total amount of tuition. Award amount may vary depending on institution. Contact financial aid office of eligible institutions for application and more information. Undergraduate study must be in a degree program.
Contact:
Office of Student Financial Assistance
325 West Gaines Street
Suite 1314
Tallahassee, FL 32399-0400
Phone: 888-827-2004
Web: www.floridastudentfinancialaid.org

Folds of Honor Foundation

Folds of Honor Foundation Scholarships

Type of award: Scholarship, renewable.
Intended use: For undergraduate study at postsecondary institution.
Eligibility: Applicant must be dependent of disabled veteran, deceased veteran or POW/MIA; or spouse of disabled veteran, deceased veteran or POW/MIA.
Application requirements: Proof of eligibility. Proof of enrollment.
Additional information: Scholarships available through the Immediate Use Scholarship program. Applicants are also eligible if they are a spouse or dependent of one or more of the following: a veteran who with an established MEB/PEB or VA rating for service-connected disability; service member missing in action or captured in line of duty; service member who received a Purple Heart Medal.
   Amount of award: $1-$5,000
   Number of awards: 1,200
   Number of applicants: 1,580
   Application deadline: April 30
   Notification begins: June 4
   Total amount awarded: $6,000,000
Contact:
Folds of Honor
5800 North Patriot Drive
Owasso, OK 74055
Phone: 918-272-5307
Fax: 918-274-4709
Web: www.foldsofhonor.org/scholarships

Foot Locker

Foot Locker Scholar Athletes

Type of award: Scholarship.
Intended use: For full-time freshman study at 4-year institution.
Eligibility: Applicant must be at least 13, no older than 22, high school senior. Applicant must be U.S. citizen or permanent resident.
Application requirements: Recommendations, essay. Two 500 word essays, one non-family recommendation required. Applicants can also submit optional supplementary materials such as photos and videos.

Additional information: Minimum 3.0 GPA. Students must be college-bound high school seniors. Must participate in a sports-related activity in their high school or community. The scholarship will be awarded in four equal annual payments of $5,000 throughout the winner's four-year college career. Application can be found on web site.

Amount of award:	$20,000-$25,000
Number of awards:	20
Number of applicants:	9,016
Application deadline:	December 17
Notification begins:	April 1
Total amount awarded:	$405,000

Contact:
19W 21st Street
8th Floor
New York, NY 10010
Phone: 22-254-2390 ext. 218
Fax: 212-254-2391
Web: www.footlockerscholarathletes.com

Foreclosure.com

Foreclosure.com Scholarship Contest

Type of award: Scholarship.
Intended use: For undergraduate study at 4-year institution.
Additional information: Must be a currently enrolled undergraduate student. First place: $5,000; second through fifth place: $1,000 each. See Website for essay topic.

Amount of award:	$1,000-$5,000
Number of awards:	5
Number of applicants:	10,000
Application deadline:	December 15
Notification begins:	February 1
Total amount awarded:	$9,000

Contact:
Foreclosure.com
Phone: 561-988-9669 ext. 7387
Web: www.foreclosure.com/scholarship

Foundation for Surgical Technology

Foundation for Surgical Technology Student Scholarship

Type of award: Scholarship.
Intended use: For undergraduate study in United States.
Basis for selection: Major/career interest in surgical technology. Applicant must demonstrate financial need and high academic achievement.
Application requirements: Recommendations, transcript, proof of eligibility.
Additional information: Applicant must be enrolled in surgical technology program accredited by CAAHEP or ABHES and be eligible to sit for the NBSTSA national surgical technologist certifying examination. Award amount varies. Visit Website for application.

Number of applicants:	200
Application deadline:	March 1
Notification begins:	June 15

Contact:
The Foundation for Surgical Technology
Attn: Scholarship Department
6 West Dry Creek Circle, Suite 200
Littleton, CO 80120
Phone: 303-694-9130
Fax: 303-694-9169
Web: www.ast.org/Members/Student_Members

Foundation of the National Student Nurses Association, Inc.

National Student Nurses Association Scholarship

Type of award: Scholarship.
Intended use: For full-time undergraduate study at accredited 2-year or 4-year institution. Designated institutions: State-approved schools of nursing or pre-nursing.
Eligibility: Applicant must be U.S. citizen or permanent resident.
Basis for selection: Major/career interest in nursing. Applicant must demonstrate financial need, high academic achievement and service orientation.
Application requirements: $10 application fee. Essay, transcript, proof of eligibility. National Student Nurses Association members must submit proof of membership.
Additional information: All applicants considered for following scholarships: General Scholarships, Career Mobility Scholarships, Breakthrough to Nursing Scholarships, Specialty Scholarships, and Promise of Nursing Scholarships. Applicants must be enrolled in nursing or pre-nursing program, and may hold alien registration. Awards granted for use in summer, fall of the same year and only spring of following academic year. Number of awards varies. Applications available from May through January. See Website for deadline and application.

Amount of award:	$1,000-$2,500
Number of applicants:	160
Application deadline:	January 14
Total amount awarded:	$410,000

Contact:
Foundation of the National Student Nurses Association, Inc.
45 Main Street
Suite 606
Brooklyn, NY 11201
Phone: 718-210-0705
Fax: 718-797-1186
Web: www.nsna.org

Francis Ouimet Scholarship Fund

The Ouimet Scholarship

Type of award: Scholarship, renewable.
Intended use: For full-time undergraduate study at accredited postsecondary institution.

Basis for selection: Competition/talent/interest in athletics/ sports. Applicant must demonstrate financial need, high academic achievement and leadership.
Application requirements: Interview, recommendations, essay, transcript. FAFSA and CSS Profile, SAT scores. Photo.
Additional information: Applicants must have worked on golf course in Massachusetts for at least two years in a golf-related position. Contact the Ouimet Fund office in June to be put on application mailing list for awards for following school year, or sign up for application online.

Amount of award:	$1,500-$8,000
Number of awards:	260
Number of applicants:	364
Application deadline:	December 1
Notification begins:	August 31
Total amount awarded:	$1,500,000

Contact:
Francis Ouimet Scholarship Fund
William F. Connell Golf House & Museum
300 Arnold Palmer Blvd.
Norton, MA 02766
Phone: 774-430-9093
Fax: 774-430-9091
Web: www.ouimet.org

Fred G. Zahn Foundation

Fred G. Zahn Scholarship Fund

Type of award: Scholarship, renewable.
Intended use: For undergraduate study at accredited 2-year or 4-year institution in United States. Designated institutions: Institutions in Washington state.
Eligibility: Applicant must be residing in Washington.
Basis for selection: Applicant must demonstrate financial need, high academic achievement and depth of character.
Application requirements: Essay, transcript. Student Aid Report.
Additional information: Must have graduated from Washington state high school. Preference to juniors and seniors with minimum 3.75 GPA. May obtain application and more information at eligible Washington state institutions.

Amount of award:	$1,500
Application deadline:	April 15
Notification begins:	June 15

Contact:
Fred G. Zahn Scholarship Fund
c/o US Trust/Bank of America
100 Westminster Street
Providence, RI 02903
Phone: 866-461-7287
Fax: 877-773-6292

The Frederic Whitaker and Eileen Monaghan Whitaker Foundation

The Whitaker Foundation Scholarship Fund

Type of award: Scholarship.
Intended use: For full-time undergraduate study at accredited 2-year or 4-year institution.

Eligibility: Applicant must be U.S. citizen or permanent resident.
Basis for selection: Major/career interest in art/art history or museum studies.
Application requirements: Essay, transcript.
Additional information: For the Fall 2016 scholarship the application opens March 1st and closes May 31st, Awarded in July. For the Spring 2017 scholarship the application opens September 9th and closes November 30th, Awarded in December. Minimum 3.0 GPA. Two Bachelors of Fine Art scholarships available. One Bachelors in Art History or Museum Studies scholarship available. Fine Art scholarship applicants must have an emphasis on watercolor and must submit photos of two original watercolor artworks done within the past couple years. Art History and Museum Studies applicants must write an essay. Selection is mostly based on these artworks, the submitted essays, and student statements. Transcripts, GPA, and other eligibility requirements will be approved before final selection. Apply online.

Amount of award:	$2,000
Number of awards:	3
Number of applicants:	27
Total amount awarded:	$6,000

Contact:
The Whitaker Foundation Scholarship Fund
725 Argyle Avenue
Friday Harbor, WA 98250
Phone: 360-378-1028
Web: whitakerwatercolors.org/the-foundation-scholarship-fund-and-application/

Freedom From Religion Foundation

Brian Bolton Graduate Student/ Older Student Essay Contest

Type of award: Scholarship, renewable.
Intended use: For undergraduate or graduate study at graduate institution.
Eligibility: Applicant must be at least 25, no older than 30.
Basis for selection: Competition/talent/interest in writing/ journalism.
Application requirements: Proof of eligibility. The topic is: Why God and Politics/Government Are a Dangerous Mix Especially in an Election Year. Write a persuasive essay between 600 to 800 words about the dangers of religion and politics/government mixing in this election year. Analyze current examples of religious pandering, church politicking or political religious litmus tests that concern you and threaten the Establishment Clause. You may wish to use examples of the harm created by religion in politics and government from a legal, topical or historic perspective, or discuss how it makes you feel excluded as a young secular voter. Submit essay both by mail and email by postmark deadline. No faxes. Essay must be typed, double-spaced, standard margins and stapled. Include word count. Place name and essay title on each page. Choose own title. Attach a one-paragraph biography on separate page at end of essay including name, age and birth date, hometown, university or college, year in school, major or intended major, degree being earned and interests. Do not include a résumé.
Additional information: Winners include; First Place Brian Bolton Memorial Award: $3,000, Second Place: $2,000, Third

Place: $1,000, Fourth Place: $750, Fifth Place: $500, Sixth Place: $400, Optional Honorable Mention(s): $200. See website for additional information regarding requirements and submission.

Number of awards:	10
Number of applicants:	75
Application deadline:	July 15
Total amount awarded:	$30,000

Contact:
Freedom From Religion Foundation
P.O. Box 750
Madison, WI 53701
Phone: 608-256-8900
Web: www.ffrf.org/outreach/ffrf-student-scholarship-essay-contests

Michael Hakeem Memorial Award

Type of award: Scholarship, renewable.
Intended use: For full-time undergraduate study at postsecondary institution. Designated institutions: North American institutions.
Eligibility: Applicant must be no older than 25.
Basis for selection: Competition/talent/interest in writing/journalism, based on best-written essays.
Application requirements: Essay, proof of eligibility. Essay should be 750-900 words, typed, stapled, double-spaced with standard margins. Include autobiographical paragraph giving both campus and permanent addresses, phone numbers, and e-mail. Identify college/university, major, and interests. Essay on free thought concerning religion; essay most suitable for atheistic and agnostic student.
Additional information: Applicant must be currently enrolled college student. Essay topics and requirements change annually and are announced in February. Check Website for current topic. Students are requested not to inquire before then. Visit Website for more information. First place receives $3,000; second place, $2,000; third place, $1000; fourth place, $750; fifth place, $500; sixth place, $400; honorable mention(s), $200. Essays must be submitted via postal mail and email.

Amount of award:	$200-$3,000
Number of applicants:	100
Application deadline:	June 15
Notification begins:	September 1

Contact:
Freedom From Religion Foundation
College Essay Competition
P.O. Box 750
Madison, WI 53701
Phone: 608-256-8900
Web: www.ffrf.org/outreach/ffrf-student-scholarship-essay-contests

William J. Schulz High School Essay Contest

Type of award: Scholarship.
Intended use: For freshman study at postsecondary institution.
Eligibility: Applicant must be high school senior.
Basis for selection: Competition/talent/interest in writing/journalism, based on best-written essays.
Application requirements: Essay, proof of eligibility. Essay should be 350-500 words, stapled, typed, double-spaced with standard margins. Include autobiographical paragraph giving both campus and permanent address, phone numbers, and e-mail. Identify high school and college/university to be attended. Include intended major and other interests.

Additional information: Applicant must be college-bound high school senior. Essay topics and requirements change annually and are announced in February. Students are requested not to inquire before then. Visit Website for more information. First place receives $3,000; second place, $2,000; third place, $1000; fourth place, $750; fifth place, $500; sixth place, $400; honorable mention(s), $200. Essays must be submitted via postal mail and email.

Amount of award:	$200-$3,000
Application deadline:	June 1
Notification begins:	August 1

Contact:
Freedom From Religion Foundation
High School Essay Contest
P.O. Box 750
Madison, WI 53701
Phone: 608-256-8900
Web: www.ffrf.org

Friends of Gumbo Limbo

Charles N Kurucz Memorial Scholarship

Type of award: Scholarship.
Intended use: For full-time freshman study at 2-year or 4-year institution.
Basis for selection: Major/career interest in environmental science. Applicant must demonstrate financial need.
Application requirements: Recommendations, essay, transcript. Transcript of high school curriculum. List and describe science and/or environmentally oriented extracurricular activities. Letter of reference from a science teacher or guidance counselor. 500 word or less essay describing the significance of your contributions to the mission of Gumbo Limbo Nature Center ("To increase public awareness of coastal and marine ecosystems through research, education, preservation and conservation."), and how you intend to use your education to further that mission in the future.
Additional information: Must apply online. Must be pursuing a degree that contributes towards marine/coastal conservation, education, or research. Typically awarded to marine biologists, but not restricted to just biology. Include planned college/university information including top three most likely colleges to attend and the degree sought. Cumulative GPA must be at least 3.2, and science GPA must be at least 3.5. Student must either be a 1st generation college student (immediate family such as parents, step-parents, or grandparents and/or be eligible for the Free & Reduced Price School Meals program (must provide a written confirmation from the student's guidance counselor). $2,500 for freshman year and $2,500 for sophomore year as long as student remains a full-time student with at least a 3.0 GPA.

Amount of award:	$2,500-$5,000
Number of awards:	1
Application deadline:	February 12

Contact:
1801 N. Ocean Boulevard
Boca Raton, FL 33432
Phone: 561-544-8608
Web: www.gumbolimbo.org/scholarship

Gordon J. Gilbert Scholarship

Type of award: Scholarship.
Intended use: For full-time freshman study at 2-year or 4-year institution.
Basis for selection: Major/career interest in environmental science.
Application requirements: Recommendations, essay, transcript. Transcript of high school curriculum. List and describe science and/or environmentally oriented extracurricular activities. Letter of reference from a science teacher or guidance counselor. 500 word or less essay describing the significance of your contributions to the mission of Gumbo Limbo Nature Center ("To increase public awareness of coastal and marine ecosystems through research, education, preservation and conservation."), and how you intend to use your education to further that mission in the future.
Additional information: Must apply online. Must be pursuing a degree that contributes towards marine/coastal conservation, education, or research. Typically awarded to marine biologists, but not restricted to just biology. Include planned college/university information including top three most likely colleges to attend and the degree sought. Cumulative GPA must be at least 3.2, and science GPA must be at least 3.5. Must present a summary of their research to the committee and commit to an additional public presentation for a more general audience.

Amount of award:	$2,500
Number of awards:	5
Application deadline:	February 12

Contact:
1801 North Ocean Boulevard
Boca Raton, FL 33432
Phone: 561-544-8608
Web: www.gumbolimbo.org/scholarship

Friends of the California State Fair Volunteer Group

Friends of the Fair Scholarship

Type of award: Scholarship.
Intended use: For undergraduate study at accredited 4-year institution.
Eligibility: Applicant must be high school senior. Applicant must be residing in California.
Basis for selection: Applicants will be evaluated on the basis of their personal commitment and goals established for their chosen field, leadership potential, civic accomplishments, as well as qualifications for the category entered and the completeness of the application packet. Top applicants will be asked to interview to be potentially awarded an additional scholarship. Major/career interest in agriculture; animal sciences; arts, general; business; culinary arts; education or international studies.
Application requirements: Recommendations, essay. Personal statement. Official transcript from school. Two current letters of recommendations. Two sets of all documents submitted with the application are required (one set can be copies of the original).
Additional information: Minimum 3.0 GPA. Applicants may only apply to one category. A total of twenty-five scholarships will be available: Three at $2,500, four at $1,500 each, seven at $1,000 each, four at $750, and six at $500 each. The overall outstanding candidate receives an additional $5,000 from the Ironstone Concours Foundation. Scholarships will be awarded in the following areas: agriculture, animal science, arts, business, culinary, education, enology, event planning, fair industry, international studies, teaching credential program, viticulture, and past exhibitors to the California State Fair. Must be a California resident with a valid ID. Must be enrolled in or planning to enroll in a four-year California accredited college, community college, university, or an accredited trade school.

Amount of award:	$1,000-$2,500
Number of awards:	25
Application deadline:	March 2
Total amount awarded:	$37,000

Contact:
California Exposition & State Fair
1600 Exposition Boulevard
Sacramento, CA 95815
Phone: 916-263-3000
Web: www.castatefair.org/friends-fair/

Fundera

Fundera Small Business & Technology Scholarship

Type of award: Scholarship.
Intended use: For undergraduate study at accredited 2-year or 4-year institution in United States.
Additional information: Record a 3 minute video responding to the question "How can technology change the way small businesses are run?" Publish the video to your Youtube channel with the title "Fundera Small Businesses & Technology Scholarship." E-mail your video to content@fundera.com from your school e-mail.

Number of awards:	2
Application deadline:	January 1, June 1
Notification begins:	January 15, June 15
Total amount awarded:	$2,000

Contact:
Fundera Attn: Content Team
123 William Street
Floor 21
New York, NY 10038
Web: www.fundera.com/resources/fundera-scholarship

Future Farmers of America

AGCO Scholarships

Type of award: Scholarship.
Intended use: For full-time undergraduate study at 2-year or 4-year institution in United States.
Eligibility: Applicant must be no older than 22.
Basis for selection: Major/career interest in agriculture; agribusiness; marketing; engineering; education; journalism; public relations; business/management/administration; economics or food production/management/services. Applicant must demonstrate financial need, high academic achievement and service orientation.
Application requirements: Essay. High school ranking, GPA, SAT/ACT scores.

Additional information: Additional majors also eligible. Must be FFA member. Must obtain FFA advisor's electronic approval on Signature Page. Signature Page must be mailed and postmarked by February 22. Must have valid mailing address in the U.S. Eligibility requirements vary. Visit Website for additional details.

Amount of award:	$1,000-$2,000
Number of awards:	134
Application deadline:	February 1
Notification begins:	May 7

Contact:
National FFA Organization Scholarship Office
P.O. Box 68960
Indianapolis, IN 46268-0960
Phone: 317-802-6099
Web: www.ffa.org/programs/grantsandscholarships/Scholarships/Pages/default.aspx

Alpha Gamma Rho Educational Foundation Scholarship

Type of award: Scholarship.
Intended use: For full-time undergraduate study at 4-year institution in United States. Designated institutions: Universities with Alpha Gamma Rho chapter.
Eligibility: Applicant must be male, no older than 22.
Basis for selection: Major/career interest in agriculture. Applicant must demonstrate leadership.
Application requirements: High school ranking, GPA, SAT/ACT scores.
Additional information: Must be a member of FFA. Must have valid mailing address in the U.S. Must obtain FFA advisor's electronic approval on Signature Page. Apply online. Visit www.agrs.org for a list of universities with Alpha Gamma Rho chapters.

Amount of award:	$1,000
Number of awards:	1
Application deadline:	February 1

Contact:
National FFA Organization Scholarship Office
P.O. Box 68960
Indianapolis, IN 46268-0960
Phone: 317-802-6099
Web: www.ffa.org/programs/grantsandscholarships/Scholarships/Pages/default.aspx

American Family Insurance Scholarship

Type of award: Scholarship.
Intended use: For full-time undergraduate study at 4-year institution in United States.
Eligibility: Applicant must be no older than 22. Applicant must be residing in Wisconsin, Minnesota or Missouri.
Application requirements: High school ranking, GPA, SAT/ACT scores.
Additional information: Must be a member of FFA. Must have valid mailing address in the U.S. Must obtain FFA advisor's electronic approval on Signature Page. Apply online.

Amount of award:	$1,000
Number of awards:	3
Application deadline:	February 1
Total amount awarded:	$3,000

Contact:
National FFA Scholarship Office
P.O. Box 68960
Indianapolis, IN 46268-0960
Phone: 317-802-6099
Web: https://www.ffa.org/participate/grants-and-scholarships

American Veterinary Medical Association Scholarship

Type of award: Scholarship.
Intended use: For full-time undergraduate study at 4-year institution in United States.
Eligibility: Applicant must be no older than 22.
Basis for selection: Major/career interest in animal sciences; dairy; equestrian/equine studies; biology or veterinary medicine.
Application requirements: High school ranking, GPA, SAT/ACT scores.
Additional information: Preference to applicants planning a career in veterinary medicine or veterinary food supply/public health. Must be a member of FFA. Must have valid mailing address in the U.S. Must obtain FFA advisor's electronic approval on Signature Page. Apply online.

Amount of award:	$1,000
Number of awards:	3
Application deadline:	February 1
Total amount awarded:	$3,000

Contact:
National FFA Organization Scholarship Office
P.O. Box 68960
Indianapolis, IN 46268-0960
Phone: 317-802-6099
Web: https://www.ffa.org/participate/grants-and-scholarships

Ameriprise Financial and AGSTAR Financial Services, Inc. Scholarship

Type of award: Scholarship.
Intended use: For full-time undergraduate study at 4-year institution in United States.
Eligibility: Applicant must be no older than 22.
Basis for selection: Major/career interest in agriculture.
Application requirements: High school ranking, GPA, SAT/ACT scores.
Additional information: Must be a member of one of the following Minnesota FFA chapters: Fillmore Central, Kingsland, Lanesboro, Lewiston, Mabel-Canton, Rushford-Peterson, St. Charles, Winona. Family must be involved in production agriculture. Must live on family farm. Must be a member of FFA. Must have valid mailing address in the U.S. Must obtain FFA advisor's electronic approval on Signature Page. Apply online.

Amount of award:	$1,000
Number of awards:	1
Application deadline:	February 1

Contact:
National FFA Organization Scholarship Office
P.O. Box 68960
Indianapolis, IN 68960-0960
Phone: 317-802-6099
Web: www.ffa.org/programs/grantsandscholarships/Scholarships/Pages/default.aspx

The Andersons, Inc. Scholarship

Type of award: Scholarship.
Intended use: For full-time undergraduate study at 4-year institution in United States. Designated institutions: Illinois, Indiana, Michigan, Ohio institutions.
Eligibility: Applicant must be no older than 22. Applicant must be residing in Wisconsin, Iowa, Michigan, Ohio, Minnesota, Florida, Indiana, Nebraska, Illinois or Alabama.
Basis for selection: Major/career interest in agriculture. Applicant must demonstrate service orientation.
Application requirements: High school ranking, GPA, SAT/ ACT scores.
Additional information: Social services concentrations not eligible. Must be a resident of one of the following counties: Montgomery in Alabama; Collier, Hendry, Highlands, Lee or Orange in Florida; Champaign, Fulton or Platt in Illinois; Carroll, Cass, Champaign, DeKalb, Delaware, Jay, Wabash or Wells in Indiana; Crawford in Iowa; Calhoun, Eaton, Hillsdale, Ingham, Ionia or Saint Joseph in Michigan; Winona in Minnesota; Buffalo, Keith, Fillmore in Nebraska; Dark, Fulton, Hamilton, Lucas, Sandusky, Seneca, Trumbuss, Wood or Wyandot in Ohio; Dane, Iowa, Outagamie or Wood in Wisconsin. Must be a member of FFA. Must have valid mailing address in the U.S. Must obtain FFA advisor's electronic approval on Signature Page. Apply online.

Amount of award:	$1,250
Number of awards:	2
Application deadline:	February 1
Total amount awarded:	$2,500

Contact:
National FFA Organization Scholarship Office
P.O. Box 68960
Indianapolis, IN 46268-0960
Phone: 317-802-6099
Web: www.ffa.org/programs/grantsandscholarships/Scholarships/ Pages/default.aspx

Animal Health International Scholarship

Type of award: Scholarship.
Intended use: For full-time undergraduate study at 4-year institution in United States.
Eligibility: Applicant must be no older than 22. Applicant must be residing in South Dakota, Kansas, Louisiana, Nevada, California, Mississippi, Montana, Nebraska, Alabama, Missouri, Iowa, Utah, Texas, Minnesota, Arkansas, Washington, Arizona, Florida, Georgia, Wyoming, Oklahoma, Oregon, New Mexico, Idaho, Colorado or North Dakota.
Basis for selection: Major/career interest in animal sciences or dairy.
Application requirements: High school ranking, GPA, SAT/ ACT scores.
Additional information: Must be a member of FFA. Must have valid mailing address in the U.S. Must obtain FFA advisor's electronic approval on Signature Page. Apply online.

Amount of award:	$1,000
Number of awards:	1
Application deadline:	February 1

Contact:
National FFA Organization Scholarship Office
P.O. Box 68960
Indianapolis, IN 46268-0960
Phone: 317-802-6099
Web: www.ffa.org/programs/grantsandscholarships/Scholarships/ Pages/default.aspx

Archer Daniels Midland Company Scholarships

Type of award: Scholarship.
Intended use: For full-time undergraduate study at 2-year or 4-year institution in United States.
Eligibility: Applicant must be no older than 22.
Basis for selection: Major/career interest in agriculture. Applicant must demonstrate high academic achievement, leadership and service orientation.
Application requirements: Essay. High school ranking, GPA, SAT/ACT scores.
Additional information: Must be current FFA member. Some residency requirements may apply. FDA chapter of each recipient will also receive a $250 FFA grant from ADM to assist in continued education excellence. Degree/Major interests: agriculture including communication, education, finance, sales, marketing, crop, animal, sustainable agriculture, plant, public service; and non-ag majors including welding, diesel mechanics, transportation, communication, engineering, politics, sales, marketing, finance, information technology, accounting, supply chain management, and business. Apply online at www.ffa.org.

Amount of award:	$1,000
Number of awards:	80
Application deadline:	February 1
Notification begins:	May 7
Total amount awarded:	$80,000

Contact:
National FFA Organization Scholarship Office
P.O. Box 68960
Indianapolis, IN 46268-0960
Phone: 317-802-6099
Web: https://www.ffa.org/participate/grants-and-scholarships

Arysta LifeScience North America Scholarship

Type of award: Scholarship.
Intended use: For full-time undergraduate study at 4-year institution in United States.
Eligibility: Applicant must be no older than 22. Applicant must be residing in Iowa, South Dakota, Washington, Kansas, Arizona, California, Oregon, New Mexico, Illinois or North Dakota.
Basis for selection: Major/career interest in public relations; agriculture; marketing or entomology. Applicant must demonstrate high academic achievement.
Application requirements: High school ranking, GPA, SAT/ ACT scores.
Additional information: Must be a member of FFA. Must have valid mailing address in the U.S. Must obtain FFA advisor's electronic approval on Signature Page. Minimum 3.0 GPA. Other majors also eligible. Apply online.

Amount of award:	$1,200
Number of awards:	3
Application deadline:	February 1

Contact:
National FFA Organization Scholarship Office
P.O. Box 68960
Indianapolis, IN 46268-0960
Phone: 317-802-6099
Web: https://www.ffa.org/participate/grants-and-scholarships

Scholarships

Behlen Mfg. Co./Walter and Ruby Behlen Memorial Scholarship

Type of award: Scholarship.

Intended use: For full-time undergraduate study at 2-year or 4-year institution in United States.

Eligibility: Applicant must be no older than 22. Applicant must be residing in Nebraska.

Basis for selection: Major/career interest in agriculture or science, general.

Application requirements: High school ranking, GPA, SAT/ACT scores.

Additional information: Social services majors not eligible. Must be a member of FFA. Must have valid mailing address in the U.S. Must obtain FFA advisor's electronic approval on Signature Page. Apply online.

Amount of award:	$1,000
Number of awards:	1
Application deadline:	February 1

Contact:
National FFA Organization Scholarship Office
P.O. Box 68960
Indianapolis, IN 46268-0960
Phone: 317-802-6099
Web: https://www.ffa.org/participate/grants-and-scholarships

Birdsong Peanuts Scholarship

Type of award: Scholarship.

Intended use: For full-time undergraduate study at 4-year institution in United States.

Eligibility: Applicant must be no older than 22. Applicant must be residing in Alabama, Georgia or Florida.

Basis for selection: Major/career interest in agriculture or agribusiness.

Application requirements: High school ranking, GPA, SAT/ACT scores.

Additional information: Applicant or applicant's family must be peanut producers. Must be a member of FFA. Must have valid mailing address in the U.S. Must obtain FFA advisor's electronic approval on Signature Page. Apply online.

Amount of award:	$1,000
Number of awards:	1
Application deadline:	February 1

Contact:
National FFA Organization Scholarship Office
P.O. Box 68960
Indianapolis, IN 46268-0960
Phone: 317-802-6099
Web: https://www.ffa.org/participate/grants-and-scholarships

BNSF Railway Company Scholarship

Type of award: Scholarship, renewable.

Intended use: For full-time undergraduate study at accredited 4-year institution in United States.

Eligibility: Applicant must be no older than 22. Applicant must be residing in Iowa, South Dakota, Texas, Minnesota, Kansas, California, Montana, Nebraska, Illinois or North Dakota.

Basis for selection: Major/career interest in agriculture; agricultural economics; agribusiness; marketing or finance/banking. Applicant must demonstrate high academic achievement.

Application requirements: Essay. High school ranking, GPA, SAT/ACT scores.

Additional information: Must be FFA member. Minimum 3.0 GPA. Marketing and finance majors must be related to agriculture. One scholarship will be awarded to an applicant from each eligible state. Award paid in yearly increments of $1250. Must maintain a 3.0 GPA and full-time status to renew scholarship. Must have valid mailing address in the U.S. Must obtain FFA advisor's electronic approval on Signature Page. Signature Page must be mailed and postmarked by February 22. Apply online at www.ffa.org.

Amount of award:	$1,250-$5,000
Number of awards:	10
Application deadline:	February 1
Notification begins:	May 7

Contact:
National FFA Organization Scholarship Office
P.O. Box 68960
Indianapolis, IN 46268-0960
Phone: 317-802-6099
Web: https://www.ffa.org/participate/grants-and-scholarships

Bunge North America Scholarship

Type of award: Scholarship.

Intended use: For full-time undergraduate study at 2-year or 4-year institution in United States.

Eligibility: Applicant must be no older than 22.

Basis for selection: Major/career interest in agribusiness; agricultural economics; agricultural education; agriculture; communications; science, general or engineering. Applicant must demonstrate high academic achievement and leadership.

Application requirements: High school ranking, GPA, SAT/ACT scores. Must be seeking a degree in: agricultural production, communication, education, management, finance, sales, marketing, science, equestrian science, sustainable agriculture, engineering or public service in agriculture.

Additional information: Must be a member of FFA. Must have valid mailing address in the U.S. and reside in one of the 48 contiguous states. Must obtain FFA advisor's electronic approval on Signature Page. Other majors also eligible. Apply online.

Amount of award:	$1,000
Number of awards:	8
Application deadline:	February 1

Contact:
National FFA Organization Scholarship Office
P.O. Box 68960
Indianapolis, IN 46268-0960
Phone: 317-802-6099
Web: https://www.ffa.org/participate/grants-and-scholarships

Case IH Future Farmer Scholarships

Type of award: Scholarship.

Intended use: For full-time undergraduate study at 4-year institution in United States.

Eligibility: Applicant must be no older than 22.

Basis for selection: Major/career interest in agriculture or agribusiness. Applicant must demonstrate high academic achievement.

Application requirements: High school ranking, GPA, SAT/ACT scores. Major/Degree in select areas of agriculture including agronomy, sciences, education, finance, management, engineering, conservation and genetics. Must have valid mailing address in the U.S. Student must live on a family farm and must be involved in beef or dairy cattle, corn, cotton, fruit or vegetable production, grain sorghum, peanuts, production agriculture, sheep, soybean, swine, or wheat. Must be member of FFA.

Additional information: Must obtain FFA advisor's electronic approval on Signature Page. Award amounts may vary. Apply online.

Amount of award:	$1,000
Number of awards:	3
Application deadline:	February 1

Contact:
National FFA Organization Scholarship Office
P.O. Box 68960
Indianapolis, IN 46268-0960
Phone: 317-802-6099
Web: https://www.ffa.org/participate/grants-and-scholarships

Chief Industries Scholarship

Type of award: Scholarship.
Intended use: For full-time undergraduate study at 4-year institution in United States.
Eligibility: Applicant must be no older than 22. Applicant must be residing in Nebraska or Indiana.
Basis for selection: Major/career interest in agriculture. Applicant must demonstrate service orientation.
Application requirements: High school ranking, GPA, SAT/ACT scores.
Additional information: Must be a member of FFA. Must have valid mailing address in the U.S. Must obtain FFA advisor's electronic approval on Signature Page. Apply online.

Amount of award:	$1,000
Number of awards:	1
Application deadline:	February 1

Contact:
National FFA Organization Scholarship Office
P.O. Box 68960
Indianapolis, IN 46268-0960
Phone: 317-802-6099
Web: https://www.ffa.org/participate/grants-and-scholarships

Church & Dwight Company, Inc. Scholarship

Type of award: Scholarship.
Intended use: For full-time undergraduate study at 4-year institution in United States.
Eligibility: Applicant must be no older than 22. Applicant must be U.S. citizen.
Basis for selection: Major/career interest in animal sciences; dairy; agribusiness; engineering, agricultural or agriculture. Applicant must demonstrate high academic achievement.
Application requirements: High school ranking, GPA, SAT/ACT scores.
Additional information: Preference given to applicants with a demonstrated interest in a dairy-related career. Must be a member of FFA. Minimum 3.0 GPA. Must have valid mailing address in the U.S. Must obtain FFA advisor's electronic approval on Signature Page. Apply online.

Amount of award:	$1,000
Number of awards:	3
Application deadline:	February 8
Total amount awarded:	$3,000

Contact:
National FFA Organization Scholarship Office
P.O. Box 68960
Indianapolis, IN 46268-0960
Phone: 317-802-6099
Web: www.ffa.org/programs/grantsandscholarships/Scholarships/Pages/default.aspx

CNH Capital Scholarship

Type of award: Scholarship.
Intended use: For full-time undergraduate study at 4-year institution in United States. Designated institutions: Penn State University, Purdue University, University of Illinois at Urbana-Champaign, or University of Wisconsin-Madison.
Eligibility: Applicant must be no older than 22.
Basis for selection: Major/career interest in agribusiness; agriculture; agricultural economics; education; journalism; public relations; business; economics; finance/banking or marketing. Applicant must demonstrate high academic achievement, leadership and service orientation.
Application requirements: High school ranking, GPA, SAT/ACT scores.
Additional information: Must be a member of FFA. Must have valid mailing address in the U.S. Must obtain FFA advisor's electronic approval on Signature Page. Minimum 3.5 GPA. Other majors also eligible. Apply online.

Amount of award:	$8,000
Number of awards:	4
Application deadline:	February 1

Contact:
National FFA Organization Scholarship Office
P.O. Box 68960
Indianapolis, IN 46268-0960
Phone: 317-802-6099
Web: https://www.ffa.org/participate/grants-and-scholarships

Dean Foods Company Scholarship

Type of award: Scholarship.
Intended use: For full-time undergraduate study at 4-year institution in United States.
Eligibility: Applicant must be no older than 22.
Basis for selection: Major/career interest in dairy; agriculture; food science/technology or veterinary medicine. Applicant must demonstrate financial need, leadership and service orientation.
Application requirements: High school ranking, GPA, SAT/ACT scores.
Additional information: Open to FFA members and non-members. Must have valid mailing address in the U.S. Other majors also eligible. Apply online.

Amount of award:	$1,000
Number of awards:	20
Application deadline:	February 1

Contact:
National FFA Organization Scholarship Office
P.O. Box 68960
Indianapolis, IN 46268-0960
Phone: 317-802-6099
Web: https://www.ffa.org/participate/grants-and-scholarships

Earl R. Sorensen Memorial Scholarships

Type of award: Scholarship.
Intended use: For full-time undergraduate study at 4-year institution in United States.
Eligibility: Applicant must be no older than 22. Applicant must be residing in Michigan or Iowa.
Basis for selection: Major/career interest in agriculture. Applicant must demonstrate service orientation.
Application requirements: High school ranking, GPA, SAT/ACT scores.
Additional information: Must not be pursuing degree in area of food service, parks and recreation studies or dietetics. Must be a member of FFA. Must have valid mailing address in the

U.S. Must obtain FFA advisor's electronic approval on
Signature Page. Apply online.

Amount of award:	$1,000
Number of awards:	2
Application deadline:	February 1
Total amount awarded:	$2,000

Contact:
National FFA Organization Scholarship Office
P.O. Box 68960
Indianapolis, IN 46268-0960
Phone: 317-802-6099
Web: www.ffa.org/programs/grantsandscholarships/Scholarships/
Pages/default.aspx

Farm Credit Services of Mid-America Scholarship

Type of award: Scholarship.
Intended use: For full-time undergraduate study at 4-year
institution in United States.
Eligibility: Applicant must be no older than 22. Applicant
must be residing in Ohio or Kentucky.
Basis for selection: Major/career interest in agribusiness;
economics; finance/banking or accounting.
Application requirements: High school ranking, GPA, SAT/
ACT scores.
Additional information: Must be a member of FFA. Must
have valid mailing address in the U.S. Must obtain FFA
advisor's electronic approval on Signature Page. Apply online.

Amount of award:	$2,000
Number of awards:	2
Application deadline:	February 1
Total amount awarded:	$4,000

Contact:
National FFA Organization Scholarship Office
P.O. Box 68960
Indianapolis, IN 46268-0960
Phone: 317-802-6099
Web: www.ffa.org/programs/grantsandscholarships/Scholarships/
Pages/default.aspx

Farmers Mutual Hail Insurance Company of Iowa Scholarship

Type of award: Scholarship.
Intended use: For full-time undergraduate study at 2-year or
4-year institution in United States.
Eligibility: Applicant must be no older than 22. Applicant
must be residing in Wisconsin, South Dakota, Ohio, Tennessee,
Kansas, Virginia, California, Mississippi, Montana, Nebraska,
Kentucky, Illinois, Missouri, Michigan, Texas, Minnesota,
Arkansas, Maryland, Pennsylvania, Oklahoma, New
Hampshire, Indiana, Idaho, North Carolina, Colorado or North
Dakota.
Basis for selection: Major/career interest in agribusiness;
agriculture or agricultural economics. Applicant must
demonstrate high academic achievement.
Application requirements: High school ranking, GPA, SAT/
ACT scores.
Additional information: Must be a member of FFA. Must
have valid mailing address in the U.S. Must obtain FFA
advisor's electronic approval on Signature Page. Major in
agronomy, crop science, farm and ranch management, general
agriculture, sustainable agriculture, agricultural
communications, education, journalism, extension, public
relations, business management, economics, finance,
agricultural policy, systems and natural resources management,

sales, marketing, computer systems in agriculture, plant
pathology or breeding/genetics, soil science, soil/water
conservation or public service and administration in agriculture.
Apply online.

Amount of award:	$1,500
Number of awards:	17
Application deadline:	February 1

Contact:
National FFA Organization Scholarship Office
P.O. Box 68960
Indianapolis, IN 46268-0960
Phone: 317-802-6099
Web: https://www.ffa.org/participate/grants-and-scholarships

Ford Fund and Ford Trucks Built Ford Tough FFA Scholarship Program

Type of award: Scholarship.
Intended use: For full-time undergraduate study at 2-year or
4-year institution in United States.
Eligibility: Applicant must be no older than 22.
Basis for selection: Applicant must demonstrate high academic
achievement.
Application requirements: Essay. High school ranking, GPA,
SAT/ACT scores.
Additional information: Must be FFA member. Must have a
Ford dealer signature and dealer code on the required Signature
Page. To find participating dealers, visit FFA Website. 500
scholarships available at $1,000 each awarded on behalf of
participating Ford dealers. Five additional scholarships at
$1,000 available to students without participating Ford Truck
dealer in the area that obtain signature and dealer code from
local Ford dealer. Must obtain FFA advisor's electronic
approval on Signature Page. Signature Page must be mailed
and postmarked by February 22. Must have a valid mailing
address in the U.S. Apply online at www.ffa.org.

Amount of award:	$1,000
Number of awards:	500
Application deadline:	February 1
Notification begins:	May 7
Total amount awarded:	$500,000

Contact:
National FFA Organization Scholarship Office
P.O. Box 68960
Indianapolis, IN 46268-0960
Phone: 317-802-6099
Web: https://www.ffa.org/participate/grants-and-scholarships

Foth Production Solutions, LLC Scholarship

Type of award: Scholarship.
Intended use: For full-time undergraduate study at 2-year or
4-year institution in United States.
Eligibility: Applicant must be no older than 22. Applicant
must be residing in Wisconsin.
Basis for selection: Major/career interest in biochemistry;
engineering, agricultural; computer/information sciences;
engineering, environmental; food science/technology or
biology. Applicant must demonstrate high academic
achievement.
Application requirements: High school ranking, GPA, SAT/
ACT scores.
Additional information: Must be a member of FFA. Must
have valid mailing address in the U.S. Must obtain FFA
advisor's electronic approval on Signature Page. Minimum 3.0

GPA. Other majors also eligible. Must be Wisconsin resident, preferably in following counties: Brown, Calumet, Dane, Dodge, Door, Kewaunee, Marinette, Oconto, or Outagamie. Preference given to applicants planning to attend University of Wisconsin-Madison, University of Wisconsin-Platteville, University of Wisconsin-Milwaukee School of Engineering, Madison Area Technical College, or Northeast Wisconsin Technical College. Apply online.

Amount of award:	$1,000
Number of awards:	2
Application deadline:	February 1

Contact:
National FFA Organization Scholarship Office
P.O. Box 68960
Indianapolis, IN 46268-0960
Phone: 317-802-6099
Web: https://www.ffa.org/participate/grants-and-scholarships

Hoard's Dairyman Scholarship

Type of award: Scholarship.
Intended use: For full-time undergraduate study at 4-year institution in United States.
Eligibility: Applicant must be no older than 22.
Basis for selection: Major/career interest in dairy or agriculture.
Application requirements: High school ranking, GPA, SAT/ACT scores.
Additional information: Must be a member of FFA. Must have valid mailing address in the U.S. Must obtain FFA advisor's electronic approval on Signature Page. Applicants must be pursuing a degree in dairy science or agricultural journalism. Preference given to applicants with agricultural communications emphasis. Apply online.

Amount of award:	$1,000
Number of awards:	1
Application deadline:	February 1

Contact:
National FFA Organization Scholarship Office
P.O. Box 68960
Indianapolis, IN 46268-0960
Phone: 317-802-6099
Web: https://www.ffa.org/participate/grants-and-scholarships

Hormel Foods Corporation Scholarship

Type of award: Scholarship.
Intended use: For full-time undergraduate study at 4-year institution in United States.
Eligibility: Applicant must be no older than 22. Applicant must be residing in Wisconsin, Michigan, Iowa, South Dakota, Minnesota, Kansas, Indiana, Nebraska, Illinois, North Dakota or Missouri.
Basis for selection: Major/career interest in agriculture; animal sciences; business/management/administration; economics; food production/management/services; food science/technology or hospitality administration/management. Applicant must demonstrate high academic achievement and leadership.
Application requirements: High school ranking, GPA, SAT/ACT scores.
Additional information: Minimum 3.0 GPA. Agronomy, animal nutrition, agricultural communications, agriculture policy/systems management/sales/marketing/engineering, food packaging majors also eligible. Must be a member of FFA. Must have valid mailing address in the U.S. Must obtain FFA advisor's electronic approval on Signature Page. Apply online.

Amount of award:	$1,500
Number of awards:	6
Application deadline:	February 1
Total amount awarded:	$9,000

Contact:
National FFA Organization Scholarship Office
P.O. Box 68960
Indianapolis, IN 46268-0960
Phone: 317-802-6099
Web: www.ffa.org/programs/grantsandscholarships/Scholarships/Pages/default.aspx

Iowa Interstate Railroad, Ltd. Scholarship

Type of award: Scholarship.
Intended use: For full-time undergraduate study at 4-year institution in United States. Designated institutions: Institutions in Iowa and Illinois.
Eligibility: Applicant must be no older than 22. Applicant must be residing in Iowa.
Basis for selection: Preference to expressed interest in transportation. Major/career interest in agriculture; agribusiness or agricultural economics. Applicant must demonstrate high academic achievement.
Application requirements: High school ranking, GPA, SAT/ACT scores. Pursuing a four-year degree in agronomy, crop science, nursery & landscape management, agricultural business management, economics or finance, pulp & paper technology or transportation.
Additional information: Open to FFA members and non-members. Must have valid mailing address in the U.S. Other majors also eligible. Preference given to applicants with expressed interest in transportation. Apply online.

Amount of award:	$1,000
Number of awards:	1
Application deadline:	February 1

Contact:
National FFA Organization Scholarship Office
P.O. Box 68960
Indianapolis, IN 46268-0960
Phone: 317-802-6099
Web: https://www.ffa.org/participate/grants-and-scholarships

Jerry Lake - Rain For Rent Scholarship

Type of award: Scholarship.
Intended use: For full-time sophomore, junior or senior study at 4-year institution in United States.
Eligibility: Applicant must be no older than 22. Applicant must be residing in California, Idaho or Arizona.
Basis for selection: Major/career interest in agriculture; agribusiness or engineering, agricultural. Applicant must demonstrate financial need, high academic achievement, leadership and service orientation.
Application requirements: High school ranking, GPA, SAT/ACT scores.
Additional information: Minimum 3.0 GPA. Those majoring in agriculture power and equipment or soil and water conservation also eligible. Must be a member of FFA. Must have valid mailing address in the U.S. Must obtain FFA advisor's electronic approval on Signature Page. Apply online.

Amount of award:	$1,500
Number of awards:	4
Application deadline:	February 1

Contact:
National FFA Organization Scholarship Office
P.O. Box 68960
Indianapolis, IN 46268-0960
Phone: 317-802-6099
Web: www.ffa.org/programs/grantsandscholarships/Scholarships/
Pages/default.aspx

John and Amy Rakestraw Scholarship

Type of award: Scholarship.
Intended use: For full-time undergraduate study at 2-year or 4-year institution in United States.
Eligibility: Applicant must be no older than 22. Applicant must be residing in Mississippi or Colorado.
Basis for selection: Major/career interest in agriculture. Applicant must demonstrate leadership and service orientation.
Application requirements: High school ranking, GPA, SAT/ACT scores.
Additional information: Must have preference in animal nutrition, animal science, farm/livestock or ranch management. Must be involved in beef cattle. Must be a member of FFA. Must have valid mailing address in the U.S. Must obtain FFA advisor's electronic approval on Signature Page. Apply online.

Amount of award:	$1,000
Number of awards:	2
Application deadline:	February 1
Total amount awarded:	$2,000

Contact:
National FFA Organization Scholarship Office
P.O. Box 68960
Indianapolis, IN 46268-0960
Phone: 317-802-6099
Web: www.ffa.org/programs/grantsandscholarships/Scholarships/
Pages/default.aspx

KenAG Scholarship

Type of award: Scholarship.
Intended use: For full-time undergraduate study at 4-year institution in United States.
Eligibility: Applicant must be no older than 22.
Basis for selection: Major/career interest in dairy.
Application requirements: High school ranking, GPA, SAT/ACT scores.
Additional information: Must be a member of FFA and pursuing a degree in dairy science. Must have valid mailing address in the U.S. Must obtain FFA advisor's electronic approval on Signature Page. Other majors also eligible. Apply online.

Amount of award:	$1,000
Number of awards:	1
Application deadline:	February 1

Contact:
National FFA Organization Scholarship Office
P.O. Box 68960
Indianapolis, IN 46268-0960
Phone: 317-802-6099
Web: https://www.ffa.org/participate/grants-and-scholarships

Kent Nutrition Group, Inc. Scholarship

Type of award: Scholarship.
Intended use: For full-time undergraduate study at 4-year institution in United States. Designated institutions: Eligible institutions in Connecticut, Delaware, Illinois, Indiana, Iowa, Kansas, Kentucky, Maine, Maryland, Massachusetts, Michigan, Missouri, Nebraska, New Hampshire, New Jersey, New York, Ohio, Pennsylvania, Rhode Island, Vermont, Virginia, or West Virginia.
Eligibility: Applicant must be no older than 22. Applicant must be residing in Ohio, New York, Delaware, Kansas, Massachusetts, Virginia, Connecticut, Nebraska, Illinois, Kentucky, Missouri, Vermont, Iowa, Michigan, Maine, Maryland, Pennsylvania, New Hampshire, West Virginia, Indiana, New Jersey or Rhode Island.
Basis for selection: Major/career interest in animal sciences; dairy; agriculture or agribusiness.
Application requirements: High school ranking, GPA, SAT/ACT scores.
Additional information: Must be a member of FFA. Must have valid mailing address in the U.S. Must obtain FFA advisor's electronic approval on Signature Page. Other majors also eligible. Apply online.

Amount of award:	$1,000
Number of awards:	2
Application deadline:	February 1

Contact:
National FFA Organization Scholarship Office
P.O. Box 68960
Indianapolis, IN 46268-0960
Phone: 317-802-6099
Web: https://www.ffa.org/participate/grants-and-scholarships

KeyBank Scholarship

Type of award: Scholarship.
Intended use: For full-time undergraduate study at accredited 2-year or 4-year institution in United States. Designated institutions: Idaho institutions.
Eligibility: Applicant must be no older than 22. Applicant must be residing in Idaho.
Basis for selection: Major/career interest in agriculture; communications; education; finance/banking; engineering; marketing; science, general; agricultural economics or business/management/administration. Applicant must demonstrate financial need and service orientation.
Application requirements: High school ranking, GPA, SAT/ACT scores.
Additional information: Must be a resident of Bannock, Bingham, Bonneville, Cassia, Fremont, Madison, Minidoka, Power, Teton, or Twin Falls counties in Idaho. Must be a member of FFA. Must have valid mailing address in the U.S. Must obtain FFA advisor's electronic approval on Signature Page. Apply online.

Amount of award:	$1,000
Number of awards:	1
Application deadline:	February 1

Contact:
National FFA Organization Scholarship Office
P.O. Box 68960
Indianapolis, IN 46268-0960
Phone: 317-802-6099
Web: www.ffa.org/programs/grantsandscholarships/Scholarships/
Pages/default.aspx

Kikkoman Foods, Inc. Scholarship

Type of award: Scholarship.
Intended use: For full-time undergraduate study at 2-year or 4-year institution in United States. Designated institutions: Wisconsin institutions.

Eligibility: Applicant must be no older than 22. Applicant must be residing in Wisconsin.
Basis for selection: Major/career interest in agribusiness; food science/technology; dietetics/nutrition or food production/management/services.
Application requirements: High school ranking, GPA, SAT/ACT scores.
Additional information: Must be a member of FFA. Must have valid mailing address in the U.S. Must obtain FFA advisor's electronic approval on Signature Page. Other majors also eligible. Apply online.

Amount of award:	$1,000
Number of awards:	1
Application deadline:	February 1

Contact:
National FFA Organization Scholarship Office
P.O. Box 68960
Indianapolis, IN 46268-0960
Phone: 317-802-6099
Web: https://www.ffa.org/participate/grants-and-scholarships

King Ranch Scholarship

Type of award: Scholarship.
Intended use: For full-time undergraduate study at 4-year institution in United States. Designated institutions: Texas A& M University-Kingsville, Texas Tech University, Texas A&M University-College Station, or University of Florida.
Eligibility: Applicant must be no older than 22. Applicant must be residing in Texas, New Mexico or Florida.
Basis for selection: Major/career interest in agriculture or wildlife/fisheries. Applicant must demonstrate high academic achievement, leadership and service orientation.
Application requirements: High school ranking, GPA, SAT/ACT scores.
Additional information: Must be a member of FFA. For students pursuing a degree in agronomy, animal/crop/range science, wildlife management. Must have valid mailing address in the U.S. Must obtain FFA advisor's electronic approval on Signature Page. Other majors also eligible. Apply online.

Amount of award:	$1,000
Number of awards:	1
Application deadline:	February 1

Contact:
National FFA Organization Scholarship Office
P.O. Box 68960
Indianapolis, IN 46268-0960
Phone: 317-802-6099
Web: https://www.ffa.org/participate/grants-and-scholarships

Mahindra USA Women in Ag Scholarship

Type of award: Scholarship.
Intended use: For full-time undergraduate study at 2-year or 4-year institution in United States.
Eligibility: Applicant must be female, no older than 22. Applicant must be residing in New York, Tennessee, Kansas, Louisiana, Massachusetts, Virginia, California, Connecticut, Mississippi, Illinois, Alabama, Kentucky, Missouri, Michigan, Iowa, Texas, , Maine, Arkansas, Maryland, Arizona, Georgia, Florida, Oklahoma, West Virginia or Indiana.
Basis for selection: Major/career interest in agriculture. Applicant must demonstrate financial need, high academic achievement, leadership and service orientation.
Application requirements: Essay. High school ranking, GPA, SAT/ACT scores.

Additional information: Must be member of FFA. Minimum 3.0 GPA. Food service, packaging, parks and recreation studies, public service, and dietetics majors not eligible. Must have valid mailing address in the U.S. Must obtain FFA advisor's electronic approval on Signature Page. Signature Page must be mailed and postmarked by February 22.

Amount of award:	$2,500
Number of awards:	4
Application deadline:	February 1
Notification begins:	May 7
Total amount awarded:	$10,000

Contact:
National FFA Organization Scholarship Office
P.O. Box 68960
Indianapolis, IN 46268-0960
Phone: 317-802-6099
Web: https://www.ffa.org/participate/grants-and-scholarships

MetLife Foundation Scholarship

Type of award: Scholarship.
Intended use: For full-time undergraduate study at 4-year institution in United States.
Eligibility: Applicant must be no older than 22. Applicant must be residing in Wisconsin, South Dakota, Ohio, Tennessee, Kansas, Louisiana, California, Mississippi, Montana, Nebraska, Kentucky, Alabama, Illinois, Missouri, Iowa, Michigan, Texas, Minnesota, Arkansas, Washington, South Carolina, Florida, Georgia, Wyoming, Oklahoma, Idaho, Indiana, North Carolina, Colorado or North Dakota.
Basis for selection: Major/career interest in agribusiness; agriculture; communications; education; journalism; public relations; finance/banking; economics; marketing or engineering.
Application requirements: High school ranking, GPA, SAT/ACT scores.
Additional information: Must be a member of FFA. Must have valid mailing address in the U.S. Must obtain FFA advisor's electronic approval on Signature Page. Other majors also eligible. Apply online.

Amount of award:	$2,000
Number of awards:	10
Application deadline:	February 1

Contact:
National FFA Organization Scholarship Office
P.O. Box 68960
Indianapolis, IN 46268-0960
Phone: 317-802-6099
Web: https://www.ffa.org/participate/grants-and-scholarships

NAPA Auto Parts Scholarship

Type of award: Scholarship.
Intended use: For full-time undergraduate study at 2-year or 4-year institution in United States.
Eligibility: Applicant must be no older than 22.
Basis for selection: Major/career interest in agribusiness; agricultural economics or agriculture.
Application requirements: High school ranking, GPA, SAT/ACT scores.
Additional information: Must be a member of FFA. Must have valid mailing address in the U.S. Must obtain FFA advisor's electronic approval on Signature Page. Preference given to applicants with interest in agricultural parts/aftermarket. Other majors also eligible. Apply online.

Amount of award:	$1,000
Number of awards:	10
Application deadline:	February 1

Contact:
National FFA Organization Scholarship Office
P.O. Box 68960
Indianapolis, IN 46268-0960
Phone: 317-802-6099
Web: https://www.ffa.org/participate/grants-and-scholarships

The National FFA Alumni Association Scholarship

Type of award: Scholarship.
Intended use: For full-time undergraduate study at 4-year institution in United States.
Eligibility: Applicant must be no older than 22.
Basis for selection: Major/career interest in agricultural education.
Application requirements: High school ranking, GPA, SAT/ ACT scores.
Additional information: Must be an alumni member or from an FFA chapter with an active alumni affiliate. Must be planning career as an agriculture teacher. Must be a member of FFA. Must have valid mailing address in the U.S. Must obtain FFA advisor's electronic approval on Signature Page. Apply online.

Amount of award:	$1,000
Number of awards:	1
Application deadline:	February 1

Contact:
National FFA Organization Scholarship Office
P.O. Box 68960
Indianapolis, IN 46268-0960
Phone: 317-802-6099
Web: www.ffa.org/programs/grantsandscholarships/Scholarships/ Pages/default.aspx

The National FFA Scholarship Funded by National FFA Staff, Board and Individual Contributors

Type of award: Scholarship.
Intended use: For full-time undergraduate study at 4-year institution in United States.
Eligibility: Applicant must be no older than 22.
Basis for selection: Major/career interest in agricultural education.
Application requirements: High school ranking, GPA, SAT/ ACT scores.
Additional information: Must be a member of FFA. Must have valid mailing address in the U.S. Must obtain FFA advisor's electronic approval on Signature Page. Apply online.

Amount of award:	$1,000
Number of awards:	1
Application deadline:	February 1

Contact:
National FFA Organization Scholarship Office
P.O. Box 68960
Indianapolis, IN 46268-0960
Phone: 317-802-6099
Web: https://www.ffa.org/participate/grants-and-scholarships

National Wild Turkey Federation Scholarship

Type of award: Scholarship.
Intended use: For full-time undergraduate study at 2-year or 4-year institution in United States.

Eligibility: Applicant must be no older than 22.
Basis for selection: Major/career interest in wildlife/fisheries. Applicant must demonstrate financial need, high academic achievement, leadership and service orientation.
Application requirements: High school ranking, GPA, SAT/ ACT scores.
Additional information: Minimum 3.0 GPA. Must be pursuing degree in wildlife management. Must support preservation of the hunting tradition, demonstrate a commitment to conservation, actively participate in hunting sports, and have work or volunteer-related experience in the hunting sport. Must be a member of FFA. Must have valid mailing address in the U.S. Must obtain FFA advisor's electronic approval on Signature Page. Apply online.

Amount of award:	$5,000
Number of awards:	1
Application deadline:	February 1

Contact:
National FFA Organization Scholarship Office
P.O. Box 68960
Indianapolis, IN 46268-0960
Phone: 317-802-6099
Web: www.ffa.org/programs/grantsandscholarships/Scholarships/ Pages/default.aspx

Norfolk Southern Foundation Scholarship

Type of award: Scholarship.
Intended use: For full-time undergraduate study at 4-year institution in United States. Designated institutions: Institutions in Alabama, Delaware, Georgia, Illinois, Indiana, Louisiana, Maryland, Michigan, Mississippi, Missouri, New York, North Carolina, Ohio, Pennsylvania, South Carolina, Tennessee, and Virginia.
Eligibility: Applicant must be no older than 22.
Basis for selection: Major/career interest in agriculture; communications; forestry; education; business/management/ administration; finance/banking; marketing; science, general or engineering.
Application requirements: High school ranking, GPA, SAT/ ACT scores.
Additional information: Must be a member of FFA. Must have valid mailing address in the U.S. Must obtain FFA advisor's electronic approval on Signature Page. Apply online.

Amount of award:	$1,000
Number of awards:	3
Application deadline:	February 1
Total amount awarded:	$3,000

Contact:
National FFA Organization Scholarship Office
P.O. Box 68960
Indianapolis, IN 46268-0960
Phone: 317-802-6099
Web: www.ffa.org/programs/grantsandscholarships/Scholarships/ Pages/default.aspx

Penton Farm Progress Scholarship

Type of award: Scholarship.
Intended use: For full-time undergraduate study at 4-year institution in United States.
Eligibility: Applicant must be no older than 22.
Basis for selection: Major/career interest in agriculture; communications; journalism or marketing. Applicant must demonstrate financial need.
Application requirements: High school ranking, GPA, SAT/ ACT scores.

Additional information: Must live on a family-owned farm. Minimum 50% of family income must come from production agriculture. Must be a member of FFA. Must have valid mailing address in the U.S. Must obtain FFA advisor's electronic approval on Signature Page. Apply online.

Amount of award:	$1,000
Number of awards:	1
Application deadline:	February 1

Contact:
National FFA Organization Scholarship Office
P.O. Box 68960
Indianapolis, IN 46268-0960
Phone: 317-802-6099
Web: www.ffa.org/programs/grantsandscholarships/Scholarships/Pages/default.aspx

Peterson Family Scholarship

Type of award: Scholarship.
Intended use: For full-time undergraduate study at 4-year institution in United States.
Eligibility: Applicant must be no older than 22. Applicant must be residing in Montana.
Basis for selection: Major/career interest in agriculture; communications; education; business/management/administration; finance/banking; marketing; science, general or engineering.
Application requirements: High school ranking, GPA, SAT/ACT scores.
Additional information: Must be a member of the Shields Valley FFA chapter (MT0017). Must be a member of FFA. Must have valid mailing address in the U.S. Must obtain FFA advisor's electronic approval on Signature Page. Apply online.

Amount of award:	$1,000
Number of awards:	1
Application deadline:	February 1

Contact:
National FFA Organization Scholarship Office
P.O. Box 68960
Indianapolis, IN 46268-0960
Phone: 317-802-6099
Web: www.ffa.org/programs/grantsandscholarships/Scholarships/Pages/default.aspx

PLANET Academic Excellence Foundation Scholarship

Type of award: Scholarship.
Intended use: For full-time undergraduate study at 2-year or 4-year institution in United States.
Eligibility: Applicant must be no older than 22.
Basis for selection: Major/career interest in horticulture; landscape architecture; environmental science or turf management. Applicant must demonstrate leadership and service orientation.
Application requirements: High school ranking, GPA, SAT/ACT scores.
Additional information: Must be a member of FFA. Must have valid mailing address in the U.S. Must obtain FFA advisor's electronic approval on Signature Page. Other majors also eligible. Apply online.

Amount of award:	$1,500
Number of awards:	1
Application deadline:	February 1

Contact:
National FFA Organization Scholarship Office
P.O. Box 68960
Indianapolis, IN 46268-0960
Phone: 317-802-6099
Web: https://www.ffa.org/participate/grants-and-scholarships

Ram Trucks Scholarship

Type of award: Scholarship.
Intended use: For full-time undergraduate study at 2-year or 4-year institution in United States.
Eligibility: Applicant must be no older than 22.
Basis for selection: Applicant must demonstrate financial need and high academic achievement.
Application requirements: Essay. High school ranking, GPA, SAT/ACT scores. Must be FFA member. Must have documented a strong supervised agricultural experience program (SAE). Must have valid mailing address in the U.S. Must obtain FFA advisor's electronic approval on Signature Page. Signature Page must be mailed and postmarked by February 22.
Additional information: One sc b Apply online.

Amount of award:	$1,000-$3,000
Number of awards:	92
Application deadline:	February 1
Notification begins:	May 7
Total amount awarded:	$50,000

Contact:
National FFA Organization Scholarship Office
P.O. Box 68960
Indianapolis, IN 46268-0960
Phone: 317-802-6099
Web: https://www.ffa.org/participate/grants-and-scholarships

Rose Acre Farms Scholarship

Type of award: Scholarship.
Intended use: For full-time undergraduate study at 4-year institution in United States.
Eligibility: Applicant must be no older than 22. Applicant must be residing in Iowa, Indiana, North Carolina, Illinois, Missouri or Georgia.
Basis for selection: Major/career interest in agriculture; animal sciences; food production/management/services or food science/technology.
Application requirements: High school ranking, GPA, SAT/ACT scores.
Additional information: FFA and non-FFA members eligible. Applicants majoring in nutrition, livestock management, breeding, genetics, pathology also eligible. Preference given to applicants majoring in food science or animal/poultry science. Must be resident of Clinton or Iroquois counties in Illinois; Adair, Guthrie, or Madison counties in Iowa; Johnson or Lincoln counties in Missouri; Clinton, Jackson, Jennings, Newton, Pulaski, or White counties in Indiana; Hart, Morgan, or Putnam counties in Georgia; and Hyde country in North Carolina. Must have valid mailing address in the U.S. Apply online.

Amount of award:	$1,000
Number of awards:	16
Application deadline:	February 1
Total amount awarded:	$12,000

Contact:
National FFA Organization Scholarship Office
P.O. Box 68960
Indianapolis, IN 46268-0960
Phone: 317-802-6099
Web: www.ffa.org/programs/grantsandscholarships/Scholarships/
Pages/default.aspx

TeeJet Technologies Scholarship

Type of award: Scholarship.
Intended use: For full-time undergraduate study at 4-year institution in United States.
Eligibility: Applicant must be no older than 22.
Basis for selection: Major/career interest in engineering, agricultural.
Application requirements: High school ranking, GPA, SAT/ACT scores.
Additional information: Agricultural mechanization and agriculture power and equipment majors also eligible. Must be a member of FFA. Must have valid mailing address in the U.S. Must obtain FFA advisor's electronic approval on Signature Page. Apply online.

Amount of award:	$1,000
Number of awards:	1
Application deadline:	February 1

Contact:
National FFA Organization Scholarship Office
P.O. Box 68960
Indianapolis, IN 46268-0960
Phone: 317-802-6099
Web: www.ffa.org/programs/grantsandscholarships/Scholarships/
Pages/default.aspx

Theisen's Home Farm Auto Scholarship

Type of award: Scholarship.
Intended use: For full-time undergraduate study at 2-year or 4-year institution in United States.
Eligibility: Applicant must be no older than 22. Applicant must be residing in Iowa.
Basis for selection: Major/career interest in animal sciences; dairy; agriculture; business/management/administration; economics; marketing or engineering.
Application requirements: High school ranking, GPA, SAT/ACT scores.
Additional information: Some other majors also eligible. Must be resident of Benton, Cedar, Chickasaw, Clinton, Delaware, Dubuque, Floyd, Hardin, Jackson, Jasper, Johnson, Jones, Linn, Marion, Marshall, Poweshiek, Story, or Warren counties. Must be a member of FFA. Must have valid mailing address in the U.S. Must obtain FFA advisor's electronic approval on Signature Page. Apply online.

Amount of award:	$1,000
Number of awards:	4
Application deadline:	February 1
Total amount awarded:	$4,000

Contact:
National FFA Organization Scholarship Office
P.O. Box 68960
Indianapolis, IN 46268-0960
Phone: 317-802-6099
Web: www.ffa.org/programs/grantsandscholarships/Scholarships/
Pages/default.aspx

Toyota Motor Sales, U.S.A. Inc. Scholarship

Type of award: Scholarship.
Intended use: For full-time undergraduate study at 4-year institution in United States.
Eligibility: Applicant must be no older than 22. Applicant must be residing in Michigan, Texas, California, West Virginia, Mississippi, Indiana, Alabama, Kentucky or Missouri.
Basis for selection: Major/career interest in engineering, agricultural. Applicant must demonstrate financial need.
Application requirements: High school ranking, GPA, SAT/ACT scores.
Additional information: Agricultural science/technology majors also eligible. Must have been active in extracurricular activities. Must be a member of FFA. Must have valid mailing address in the U.S. Must obtain FFA advisor's electronic approval on Signature Page. Apply online.

Amount of award:	$2,500
Number of awards:	10
Application deadline:	February 1
Total amount awarded:	$25,000

Contact:
National FFA Organization Scholarship Office
P.O. Box 68960
Indianapolis, IN 46268-0960
Phone: 317-802-6099
Web: www.ffa.org/programs/grantsandscholarships/Scholarships/
Pages/default.aspx

Tyrholm Big R Stores Scholarship

Type of award: Scholarship.
Intended use: For full-time undergraduate study at 4-year institution in United States.
Eligibility: Applicant must be no older than 22.
Basis for selection: Major/career interest in agriculture. Applicant must demonstrate financial need, high academic achievement, leadership and service orientation.
Application requirements: High school ranking, GPA, SAT/ACT scores.
Additional information: Minimum 3.0 GPA. FFA chapter must be located in Modoc or Siskiyou counties in California, or in Crook, Deschutes, Jackson, Jefferson, Klamath, or Josephine counties in Oregon. Must be a member of FFA. Must have valid mailing address in the U.S. Must obtain FFA advisor's electronic approval on Signature Page. Apply online.

Amount of award:	$1,000
Number of awards:	3
Application deadline:	February 1
Total amount awarded:	$3,000

Contact:
National FFA Organization Scholarship Office
P.O. Box 68960
Indianapolis, IN 46268-0960
Phone: 317-802-6099
Web: www.ffa.org/programs/grantsandscholarships/Scholarships/
Pages/default.aspx

Tyson Foods Inc. Scholarship

Type of award: Scholarship.
Intended use: For full-time undergraduate study at 2-year or 4-year institution in United States.
Eligibility: Applicant must be no older than 22.
Basis for selection: Major/career interest in agriculture or animal sciences.

Application requirements: High school ranking, GPA, SAT/ACT scores.

Additional information: Must be resident of a community in which a Tyson Foods processing facility is located. Other majors relating to agriculture also eligible. Must be a member of FFA. Must have valid mailing address in the U.S. Must obtain FFA advisor's electronic approval on Signature Page. Apply online.

Amount of award:	$1,000
Number of awards:	10
Application deadline:	February 1
Total amount awarded:	$10,000

Contact:
National FFA Organization Scholarship Office
P.O. Box 68960
Indianapolis, IN 46268-0960
Phone: 317-802-6099
Web: www.ffa.org/programs/grantsandscholarships/Scholarships/Pages/default.aspx

United Dairymen of Idaho Scholarship

Type of award: Scholarship.

Intended use: For full-time undergraduate study at 2-year or 4-year institution in United States.

Eligibility: Applicant must be no older than 22. Applicant must be residing in Idaho.

Basis for selection: Major/career interest in dairy or agricultural education.

Application requirements: High school ranking, GPA, SAT/ACT scores.

Additional information: Must have dairy cattle background. Must live on family farm and have dairy ownership/experience in supervised agricultural experience (SAE). Must be pursuing degree in dairy science, animal science as it relates to the dairy industry, agricultural education or extension, animal breeding and genetics, large animal nutrition or large animal veterinarian. Must be a member of FFA. Must have valid mailing address in the U.S. Must obtain FFA advisor's electronic approval on Signature Page. Apply online.

Amount of award:	$1,600
Number of awards:	3
Application deadline:	February 1
Total amount awarded:	$4,800

Contact:
National FFA Organization Scholarship Office
P.O. Box 68960
Indianapolis, IN 46268-0960
Phone: 317-802-6099
Web: https://www.ffa.org/participate/grants-and-scholarships

Virgil Eihusen Foundation Scholarship

Type of award: Scholarship.

Intended use: For full-time undergraduate study at 2-year or 4-year institution in United States.

Eligibility: Applicant must be no older than 22. Applicant must be residing in Nebraska.

Basis for selection: Major/career interest in agriculture.

Application requirements: High school ranking, GPA, SAT/ACT scores.

Additional information: Must be a member of FFA. Must have valid mailing address in the U.S. Must obtain FFA advisor's electronic approval on Signature Page. Apply online.

Amount of award:	$1,400
Number of awards:	1
Application deadline:	February 1

Contact:
National FFA Organization Scholarship Office
P.O. Box 68960
Indianapolis, IN 46268-0960
Phone: 317-802-6099
Web: www.ffa.org/programs/grantsandscholarships/Scholarships/Pages/default.aspx

Wells Fargo Scholarship

Type of award: Scholarship.

Intended use: For full-time sophomore, junior or senior study at 4-year institution in United States. Designated institutions: University of California-Davis, California Polytechnic State University-San Luis Obispo, University of California-Fresno.

Eligibility: Applicant must be no older than 22. Applicant must be residing in California.

Basis for selection: Major/career interest in agriculture; animal sciences; dairy; business; business/management/administration; economics or food science/technology. Applicant must demonstrate financial need, high academic achievement and leadership.

Application requirements: High school ranking, GPA, SAT/ACT scores.

Additional information: Minimum 3.25 GPA. Must be a member of FFA. Must have valid mailing address in the U.S. Must obtain FFA advisor's electronic approval on Signature Page. Apply online.

Amount of award:	$1,000
Number of awards:	2
Application deadline:	February 1
Total amount awarded:	$2,000

Contact:
National FFA Organization Scholarship Office
P.O. Box 68960
Indianapolis, IN 46268-0960
Phone: 317-802-6099
Web: www.ffa.org/programs/grantsandscholarships/Scholarships/Pages/default.aspx

Wilbur-Ellis Company High School Scholarship

Type of award: Scholarship.

Intended use: For full-time undergraduate study at 4-year institution in United States.

Eligibility: Applicant must be no older than 22. Applicant must be residing in South Dakota, New York, Ohio, Kansas, California, Montana, Nebraska, Michigan, Minnesota, Texas, Washington, Arizona, Oregon, Idaho, New Mexico, Colorado or North Dakota.

Basis for selection: Major/career interest in agriculture; turf management; horticulture; entomology or biology. Applicant must demonstrate high academic achievement.

Application requirements: High school ranking, GPA, SAT/ACT scores.

Additional information: Minimum 3.25 GPA. Minimum SAT of 1000 out of 1600 or ACT of 20. Must live on family farm. Other majors also eligible. Must be a member of FFA. Must have valid mailing address in the U.S. Must obtain FFA advisor's electronic approval on Signature Page. Apply online.

Amount of award:	$1,000-$5,000
Number of awards:	13
Application deadline:	February 8
Total amount awarded:	$19,000

Contact:
National FFA Organization Scholarship Office
P.O. Box 68960
Indianapolis, IN 46268-0960
Phone: 317-802-6099
Web: www.ffa.org/programs/grantsandscholarships/Scholarships/
Pages/default.aspx

Wix Filters Scholarship

Type of award: Scholarship.
Intended use: For full-time undergraduate study at 2-year or 4-year institution in United States.
Eligibility: Applicant must be no older than 22.
Basis for selection: Major/career interest in engineering, agricultural. Applicant must demonstrate financial need, high academic achievement and service orientation.
Application requirements: High school ranking, GPA, SAT/ACT scores.
Additional information: Minimum 3.0 GPA. Must live on a family farm. Two scholarships for students pursuing a four-year degree in agricultural engineering. Four scholarships for students pursuing a two-year degree in agricultural mechanization or agriculture power and equipment. Must be a member of FFA. Must have valid mailing address in the U.S. Must obtain FFA advisor's electronic approval on Signature Page. Apply online.

Amount of award:	$1,000-$2,000
Number of awards:	6
Application deadline:	February 1
Total amount awarded:	$8,000

Contact:
National FFA Organization Scholarship Office
P.O. Box 68960
Indianapolis, IN 46268-0960
Phone: 317-802-6099
Web: www.ffa.org/programs/grantsandscholarships/Scholarships/
Pages/default.aspx

Garden Club Federation of Massachusetts Scholarships

Garden Club Federation of Massachusetts

Type of award: Scholarship, renewable.
Intended use: For undergraduate or graduate study at accredited 2-year, 4-year or graduate institution. Designated institutions: For three of the eleven scholarships: one of the five campuses in the University of Massachusetts system.
Eligibility: Applicant must be U.S. citizen residing in Massachusetts.
Basis for selection: Major/career interest in horticulture; landscape architecture; forestry; environmental science; botany; biology or agriculture. Applicant must demonstrate financial need, high academic achievement and depth of character.
Application requirements: Recommendations, essay, transcript. List of activities, GCFM Financial Aid form.
Additional information: Must be legal resident of Massachusetts for at least one year. Minimum 3.0 GPA. Floriculture, landscape design, agronomy, sustainable food and farming, city planning, land management, and allied subjects are also eligible majors.

Amount of award:	$1,000
Number of awards:	11
Number of applicants:	40
Application deadline:	March 1
Total amount awarded:	$11,000

Contact:
Garden Club Federation of Massachusetts
Attn: Scholarship Secretary
219 Washington Street
Wellesley Hills, MA 02481
Phone: 781-237-0336
Web: www.gcfm.org

Garden Club of America

Caroline Thorn Kissel Summer Environmental Studies Scholarship

Type of award: Scholarship.
Intended use: For undergraduate, graduate, postgraduate or non-degree study at postsecondary institution.
Eligibility: Applicant must be U.S. citizen residing in New Jersey.
Basis for selection: Major/career interest in environmental science.
Application requirements: Recommendations, essay.
Additional information: Must be either New Jersey resident or non-resident studying in New Jersey. Visit Website for application and deadline.

Amount of award:	$3,000
Number of awards:	1
Application deadline:	February 10

Contact:
Garden Club of America
Magda Cruz
14 East 60th Street
New York, NY 10022-1006
Phone: 212-753-8287
Fax: 212-753-0134
Web: www.gcamerica.org

Clara Carter Higgins Scholarship and GCA Awards for Summer Environmental Studies

Type of award: Scholarship.
Intended use: For freshman, sophomore or junior study at 4-year institution.
Basis for selection: Major/career interest in environmental science or ecology.
Application requirements: Recommendations, essay, transcript.
Additional information: Awards for summer study in field of ecology and environmental studies. Application must be sent via mail.

Amount of award:	$2,000
Number of awards:	1
Application deadline:	February 10

Scholarships

Contact:
Garden Club of America Awards for Summer Environmental
Studies
Magda Cruz
14 East 60th Street
New York, NY 10022-1006
Phone: 212-753-8287
Fax: 212-753-0134
Web: www.gcamerica.org

Corliss Knapp Engle Scholarship in Horticulture

Type of award: Scholarship.
Intended use: For undergraduate, graduate, postgraduate or
non-degree study at accredited postsecondary institution in
United States.
Basis for selection: Major/career interest in horticulture.
Application requirements: Recommendations, essay.
Additional information: Award for research and
documentation in the field of horticulture. Non-degree seeking
applicants also eligible.

Amount of award:	$3,000
Application deadline:	February 1

Contact:
Garden Club of America
Magda Cruz
14 East 60th Street
New York, NY 10022-1006
Phone: 212-753-8287
Fax: 212-753-0134
Web: www.gcamerica.org

Elizabeth Gardner Norweb Summer Environmental Studies Scholarship

Type of award: Scholarship.
Intended use: For sophomore, junior or senior study at 4-year
institution in United States.
Basis for selection: Major/career interest in environmental
science.
Application requirements: Recommendations, essay,
transcript.
Additional information: Award funds summer studies in
environmental field.

Amount of award:	$2,000
Application deadline:	February 10

Contact:
Garden Club of America
Magda Cruz
14 East 60th Street
New York, NY 10022-1006
Phone: 212-753-8287
Fax: 212-753-0134
Web: www.gcamerica.org

Frances M. Peacock Native Bird Habitat Scholarship

Type of award: Scholarship.
Intended use: For senior or graduate study at postsecondary
institution.
Basis for selection: Major/career interest in ornithology.
Application requirements: Project proposal of no more than
five pages.
Additional information: Grant for advanced study of U.S.
winter/summer habitat of threatened or endangered native

birds. Awarded in cooperation with the Cornell Lab of
Ornithology. Second semester juniors may apply for senior
year. No phone calls. To apply, contact: www.birds.cornell.edu/
about/jobs.html.

Amount of award:	$4,500
Number of awards:	1
Application deadline:	January 15
Notification begins:	March 31
Total amount awarded:	$4,500

Contact:
Cornell Lab of Ornithology
Irby Lovette
159 Sapsucker Woods Road
Ithaca, NY 14850-1999
Fax: 212-753-8287
Web: www.gcamerica.org or www.birds.cornell.edu

GCA Award in Desert Studies

Type of award: Scholarship.
Intended use: For junior, senior or graduate study at
accredited postsecondary institution in United States.
Basis for selection: Major/career interest in horticulture;
botany; environmental science or landscape architecture.
Application requirements: Recommendations, essay. Resume,
research/project proposal.
Additional information: Projects must pertain to arid
environment, preference given to projects that generate
scientifically sound water and plant management. Visit
www.dbg.org for application information.

Amount of award:	$4,000
Application deadline:	January 15
Notification begins:	March 31

Contact:
Desert Botanical Garden
Kenny Zelov
1201 N. Galvin Parkway
Phoenix, AZ 85008
Phone: 480-481-8162
Web: www.gcamerica.org or www.dbg.org/educational-
programs/scholarships

GCA Summer Scholarship in Field Botany

Type of award: Scholarship.
Intended use: For undergraduate or graduate study at
accredited 4-year or graduate institution in United States.
Basis for selection: Major/career interest in botany.
Application requirements: Recommendations, essay,
transcript.
Additional information: Award for summer study in field
botany.

Amount of award:	$2,000
Number of awards:	1
Application deadline:	February 1

Contact:
Garden Club of America
Magda Cruz
14 East 60th Street
New York, NY 10022-1006
Phone: 212-753-8287
Fax: 212-753-0134
Web: www.gcamerica.org

GCA Zone VI Fellowship in Urban Forestry

Type of award: Scholarship.
Intended use: For junior, senior or graduate study at 4-year institution.
Basis for selection: Major/career interest in horticulture; environmental science or forestry.
Application requirements: Recommendations.
Additional information: Award funds research in urban forestry.

　　Amount of award:　　　　$5,000
　　Application deadline:　　January 31
Contact:
Casey Trees, Attn: Dr. Jessica Sanders
3030 12th Street NE
Washington, DC 20017
Phone: 202-833-4010
Web: https://gcamerica.org/index.cfm/scholarships/details/id/22

Joan K. Hunt and Rachel M. Hunt Summer Scholarship in Field Botany

Type of award: Scholarship.
Intended use: For undergraduate or graduate study at accredited postsecondary institution in United States.
Basis for selection: Major/career interest in botany or horticulture.
Application requirements: Recommendations, essay, transcript.
Additional information: Award for summer study in the field. Submit application via U.S. Mail. Preference given to undergraduate students. Visit Website for application.

　　Amount of award:　　　　$2,000
　　Application deadline:　　February 1
Contact:
Garden Club of America
Magda Cruz
14 East 60th Street
New York, NY 10022-1006
Phone: 212-753-8287
Fax: 212-753-0134
Web: www.gcamerica.org

Katharine M. Grosscup Scholarships in Horticulture

Type of award: Scholarship.
Intended use: For junior, senior or graduate study at accredited 4-year or graduate institution in United States.
Basis for selection: Major/career interest in horticulture. Applicant must demonstrate financial need and high academic achievement.
Application requirements: Interview, recommendations, essay, transcript.
Additional information: Minimum 3.5 GPA. Several scholarships available. Preference given to students who are residents of Pennsylvania, Ohio, West Virginia, Michigan, Indiana, and Kentucky. Major can be in related field. Please do not contact by phone. Application available on Website, and must be submitted via mail.

　　Amount of award:　　　　$3,500
　　Application deadline:　　January 10

Contact:
Katharine M. Grosscup Scholarship Committee
c/o Leslie Marting
2513 Marlboro Road
Cleveland Heights, OH 44118
Web: www.gcamerica.org

The Loy McCandless Marks Scholarship in Tropical Horticulture

Type of award: Scholarship.
Intended use: For sophomore, junior, senior or graduate study at accredited 4-year or graduate institution in United States.
Eligibility: Applicant must be U.S. citizen.
Basis for selection: Major/career interest in botany; horticulture or landscape architecture.
Application requirements: Recommendations, essay, transcript. Budget.
Additional information: For study and research at appropriate foreign institution specializing in study of tropical plants. Provides $5,000 each even-numbered year to student specializing in tropical horticulture, botany, or landscape architecture. Award meant to supplement student's pursuit of previously accepted program of study abroad. Visit Website for application. Award only given in even-numbered years.

　　Amount of award:　　　　$5,000
　　Number of awards:　　　1
　　Application deadline:　　February 1
Contact:
Garden Club of America
Magda Cruz Magda Cruz
14 East 60th Street
New York, NY 10022-1006
Phone: 212-753-8287
Fax: 212-753-0134
Web: www.gcamerica.org

Mary T. Carothers Environmental Studies Scholarship

Type of award: Scholarship.
Intended use: For sophomore, junior or senior study at 4-year institution.
Basis for selection: Major/career interest in environmental science.
Additional information: Funds summer studies in environmental field.

　　Amount of award:　　　　$2,000
　　Application deadline:　　February 10
Contact:
Garden Club of America
Magda Cruz
14 East 60th Street
New York, NY 10022-1006
Phone: 212-753-8287
Fax: 212-753-0134
Web: www.gcamerica.org

Sara Shallenberger Brown GCA National Parks Conservation Scholarship

Type of award: Scholarship.
Intended use: For undergraduate study in United States.
Eligibility: Applicant must be at least 19, no older than 20. Applicant must be U.S. citizen.

Application requirements: Recommendations, essay. Resume.
Additional information: Provides training, transportation, and $750 stipend to SCA apprentice crew leaders working under experienced leaders in three-week summer trail crew in one of America's national parks. Preference given to those with SCA experience. Application available on Website, and must be submitted via mail.

Amount of award:	$750
Application deadline:	February 23

Contact:
Garden Club of America Apprentice Crew Leader Program
P.O. Box 550
689 River Road
Charlestown, NH 03603
Phone: 603-543-1700
Fax: 603-543-1828
Web: www.gcamerica.org

Zeller Summer Scholarship in Medicinal Botany

Type of award: Scholarship.
Intended use: For undergraduate study at accredited postsecondary institution in United States.
Basis for selection: Major/career interest in botany.
Application requirements: Recommendations, essay, transcript.
Additional information: Mail all application materials together in one envelope. Award to be used for summer study.

Amount of award:	$2,000
Number of awards:	1
Application deadline:	February 1

Contact:
Garden Club of America
Magda Cruz
14 East 60th Street
New York, NY 10022-1006
Phone: 212-753-8287
Fax: 212-753-0134
Web: www.gcamerica.org

The Gates Millennium Scholars

Gates Millennium Scholars Program

Type of award: Scholarship, renewable.
Intended use: For full-time freshman study at accredited 4-year institution in United States.
Eligibility: Applicant must be Alaskan native, Asian American, African American, Mexican American, Hispanic American, Puerto Rican, American Indian or Native Hawaiian/Pacific Islander. Applicant must be U.S. citizen or permanent resident.
Basis for selection: Applicant must demonstrate financial need, high academic achievement, leadership and service orientation.
Application requirements: Recommendations, transcript, nomination by high school principal, teacher, counselor, college president, professor, or dean. Nominee Personal Information Form, FAFSA, GMS information sheet, admission letter.
Additional information: Must be eligible for Pell Grant. Must participate in community service, volunteer work, or extracurricular activities. Minimum 3.3 GPA. Scholarship

provides tuition, room, materials, and board not covered by existing financial aid. Eliminates loans, work-study, and outside jobs for scholarship recipients. Funded by Bill and Melinda Gates Foundation. Visit Website for application and deadline.

Number of awards:	1,000
Number of applicants:	13,350
Total amount awarded:	$61,415,141

Contact:
Gates Millenium Scholars
P.O. Box 10500
Fairfax, VA 22031
Phone: 877-690-4677
Web: www.gmsp.org

Generation Hope

Generation Hope Scholar Program

Type of award: Scholarship, renewable.
Intended use: For undergraduate study at 2-year or 4-year institution in United States.
Eligibility: Applicant must be no older than 25. Applicant must be U.S. citizen or permanent resident.
Application requirements: Interview, recommendations, transcript. Must be a resident of the DC Metro area (DC, Maryland, or Northern Virginia). Must be a teen parent (defined as having a child by the age of 19) and be age 25 or younger at the time of application submission. Submit a copy of SAR or FAFSA, two letters of recommendation, and a current transcript with submission.
Additional information: Minimum 2.5 GPA. Must be raising or actively involved in child's life (defined by regular support and care of your child). Must be attending or planning to attend college in the Washington DC Metro area. Must plan to take a minimum of 6 credits each semester. Residency is open to US Citizens, permanent legal residents, and individuals with Deferred Action for Childhood Arrivals (DACA) immigration.

Amount of award:	$1,200-$2,400
Number of awards:	33
Number of applicants:	65
Application deadline:	April 1
Notification begins:	June 15
Total amount awarded:	$92,000

Contact:
Generation Hope
415 Michigan Avenue NE
Suite 250
Washington, DC 20017
Phone: 202-642-5649
Web: www.supportgenerationhope.org

Georgia Student Finance Commission

Georgia Hope Grant - GED Recipient

Type of award: Scholarship.
Intended use: For undergraduate study at accredited vocational, 2-year or 4-year institution. Designated institutions: HOPE-eligible colleges and universities in Georgia.

311

Eligibility: Applicant must be U.S. citizen or permanent resident residing in Georgia.

Application requirements: Proof of eligibility.

Additional information: Must have received GED from Georgia Department of Technical and Adult Education after June 30, 1993. Submit HOPE voucher upon enrollment. Students receiving GED from DTAE receive voucher automatically. Visit Website for application, deadline, amount of award, and number of awards available.

Number of applicants:	3,664
Total amount awarded:	$1,801,678

Contact:
Georgia Student Finance Commission
2082 East Exchange Place
Suite 100
Tucker, GA 30084
Phone: 800-505-4732
Fax: 770-724-9004
Web: www.gacollege411.org

Georgia Hope Grant - Public Technical Institution

Type of award: Scholarship, renewable.

Intended use: For undergraduate study at accredited vocational, 2-year or 4-year institution. Designated institutions: Branches and affiliates of the Georgia Department of Technical and Adult Education and branches of the University System of Georgia.

Eligibility: Applicant must be U.S. citizen or permanent resident residing in Georgia. Applicant may also be dependent child of military personnel stationed in Georgia.

Additional information: Must be enrolled, matriculated technical certificate or diploma student. Visit Website for application, deadline, amount of award, and number of awards available.

Number of applicants:	85,219
Total amount awarded:	$71,516,394

Contact:
Georgia Student Finance Commission
2082 East Exchange Place
Suite 100
Tucker, GA 30084
Phone: 800-505-4732
Fax: 770-724-9004
Web: www.gacollege411.org

Georgia Hope Scholarship - Private Institution

Type of award: Scholarship, renewable.

Intended use: For undergraduate study at accredited 2-year or 4-year institution. Designated institutions: Eligible Georgia private colleges and universities.

Eligibility: Applicant must be U.S. citizen or permanent resident residing in Georgia.

Basis for selection: Applicant must demonstrate high academic achievement.

Additional information: Visit Website for application, deadline, amount of award, and number of awards available.

Number of applicants:	11,319
Total amount awarded:	$40,735,330

Contact:
Georgia Student Finance Commission
2082 East Exchange Place
Suite 100
Tucker, GA 30084
Phone: 800-505-4732
Fax: 770-724-9004
Web: www.gacollege411.org

Georgia Hope Scholarship - Public College or University

Type of award: Scholarship, renewable.

Intended use: For undergraduate study at accredited 2-year or 4-year institution. Designated institutions: Eligible Georgia public colleges and universities.

Eligibility: Applicant must be U.S. citizen or permanent resident residing in Georgia.

Basis for selection: Applicant must demonstrate high academic achievement.

Application requirements: Proof of eligibility.

Additional information: Minimum 3.0 GPA. Must be designated HOPE scholar. Visit Website for application, deadline, amount of award, and number of awards available.

Number of applicants:	84,002
Total amount awarded:	$368,191,111

Contact:
Georgia Student Finance Commission
2082 East Exchange Place
Suite 100
Tucker, GA 30084
Phone: 800-505-4732
Fax: 770-724-9004
Web: www.gacollege411.org

Georgia Student Finance Commission Public Safety Memorial Grant

Type of award: Scholarship, renewable.

Intended use: For full-time undergraduate study at accredited vocational, 2-year or 4-year institution. Designated institutions: Georgia colleges and public technical institutions.

Eligibility: Applicant must be U.S. citizen or permanent resident residing in Georgia. Applicant's parent must have been killed or disabled in work-related accident as firefighter, police officer or public safety officer.

Application requirements: Proof of eligibility.

Additional information: Must complete preliminary document that verifies claim with parent's former employer and doctors. Parent must have been permanently disabled or killed in the line of duty as Georgia police officer, firefighter, emergency medical technician, or corrections officer. Visit Website for application, deadline, amount of award, and number of awards available.

Amount of award:	$18,000
Number of applicants:	34
Total amount awarded:	$398,320

Contact:
Georgia Student Finance Commission
2082 East Exchange Place
Suite 100
Tucker, GA 30084
Phone: 800-505-4732
Fax: 770-724-9004
Web: www.gacollege411.org

Georgia Tuition Equalization Grant

Type of award: Scholarship, renewable.
Intended use: For full-time undergraduate study at accredited 2-year or 4-year institution. Designated institutions: GSFC approved institutions.
Eligibility: Applicant must be U.S. citizen or permanent resident residing in Georgia.
Application requirements: Proof of eligibility. Mileage affidavit (for out-of-state schools only).
Additional information: Must be enrolled at eligible private college or university in Georgia. Amount of award determined by Georgia General Assembly appropriations. Application deadlines set by schools. Visit Website for list of approved institutions, application, amount of award, and number of awards available.

Number of applicants:	33,215
Total amount awarded:	$19,467,731

Contact:
Georgia Student Finance Commission
2082 East Exchange Place
Suite 100
Tucker, GA 30084
Phone: 800-505-4732
Fax: 770 724-9000
Web: https://www.gafutures.org/scholarship-search/#scholarshipDetails

Move on When Ready

Type of award: Scholarship.
Intended use: For undergraduate study at accredited vocational, 2-year or 4-year institution.
Eligibility: Applicant must be high school junior or senior. Applicant must be U.S. citizen or permanent resident residing in Georgia.
Application requirements: Must submit completed application to high school for each participating term.
Additional information: Assistance for high school students to take college level coursework for credit in both high school and college. Must be approved by both high school and college as a dual credit enrollment student. Awards are pro-rated for students taking less than 12 hours per semester. Students must apply on or before the last day of school term or student's withdrawal date, whichever is first. Visit Website for application, deadline, amount of award, and number of awards available.

Number of applicants:	7,118
Total amount awarded:	$8,542,651

Contact:
Georgia Student Finance Commission
2082 East Exchange Place
Suite 100
Tucker, GA 30084
Phone: 800-505-4732
Fax: 770-724-9004
Web: www.gacollege411.org

Zell Miller Scholarship

Type of award: Scholarship, renewable.
Intended use: For full-time undergraduate study at accredited 2-year or 4-year institution.
Eligibility: Applicant must be U.S. citizen residing in Georgia.
Basis for selection: Applicant must demonstrate high academic achievement.
Additional information: Full Tuition for Georgia students to eligible colleges for students with a 3.75 GPA in Core classes.

Application deadline is Prior to the last day of college term for which the student applies. For more information: https://www.gafutures.org/hope-state-aid-programs/hope-zell-miller-scholarships/zell-miller-scholarship/
Contact:
Georgia Student Finance
2082 EAST Exchange Place
Tucker, GA 30084
Phone: 770-724-9071
Fax: 770-724-9099

GlobalAir.com

Calvin L. Carrithers Aviation Scholarship

Type of award: Scholarship.
Intended use: For full-time at accredited 2-year or 4-year institution in United States.
Eligibility: Applicant must be U.S. citizen.
Basis for selection: Major/career interest in aviation.
Application requirements: Applicants must be willing to write a 200-500 word blog post a minimum of once a week throughout the school year while at school. Posts can be about aircraft, flying, ground training, weekend activities, internships, or anything that the student finds interesting and pertains to life in their particular aviation program.
Additional information: Must be enrolled in a fully accredited university aviation program (Commercial Aviation, Professional Pilot, Aviation Management, Airport Management, etc.)

Amount of award:	$1,000
Number of awards:	4
Application deadline:	August 14
Total amount awarded:	$4,000

Contact:
GlobalAir.com
2700 Moran Avenue
Louisville, KY 40205
Phone: 888-236-4309
Web: webmaster@globalair.com

Goddard Systems, Inc.

The Goddard Systems, Inc Anthony A. Martino Memorial Scholarship

Type of award: Scholarship.
Intended use: For full-time undergraduate study at accredited vocational, 2-year or 4-year institution.
Eligibility: Applicant must be high school senior. Applicant must be U.S. citizen, permanent resident or international student.
Application requirements: Essay, transcript. Applicant must be a graduate of a Goddard School Pre-Kindergarten and/or Kindergarten program. Essay: 500-1000 words, what are your aspirations? How has your family, coach, or school prepared you for your next academic step? What do you consider your greatest achievement? Who is/are your role mode(s) and why? Why should you reveive Anthony A. Martino Scholarship? How has the Goddard School helped shape who you are today?

Additional information: Applicant must be a high school senior who is a US citizen, a permanent resident, or a non-US citizen living legally in the United States. Relatives of Goddard Systems, Inc employees or franchises and/or any Goddard School employees are not eligible. Applicant must submit a transcript from all high schools attended with his/her application. Transcripts must indicate a cumulative GPA. Send application by mail.

Amount of award:	$10,000
Number of awards:	1
Number of applicants:	15
Application deadline:	March 11
Notification begins:	May 10

Contact:
Goddard Systems, Inc.
1016 West 9th Avenue
Suite 140
King of Prussia, PA 19406
Phone: 610-265-8510
Web: www.goddardschool.com/approach-to-education/scholarship

Goldberg and Osborne

Don't Text and Drive Scholarship

Type of award: Scholarship.
Intended use: For undergraduate or graduate study at vocational, 2-year, 4-year or graduate institution in United States.
Additional information: The winner of each bimonthly Don't Text and Drive Scholarship is chosen at random. Apart from US residency eligibility rules, the applicant must pledge not to text and drive in order for the application to go through. Application on website.

Number of awards:	1
Total amount awarded:	$1,000

Contact:
Goldberg and Osborne
4423 East Thomas Road
Phoenix, AZ 85018
Web: https://1800theeagle.com/scholarships/

Golden Apple

Golden Apple Scholars of Illinois Program

Type of award: Scholarship.
Intended use: For undergraduate study at 4-year institution in United States. Designated institutions: Participating Illinois universities.
Eligibility: Applicant must be high school senior. Applicant must be U.S. citizen residing in Illinois.
Basis for selection: Major/career interest in education; education, early childhood; education, special or education, teacher. Applicant must demonstrate high academic achievement.
Application requirements: Transcript. ACT scores, eight essays.

Additional information: Must obtain teacher's certification and teach for five years in Illinois school of need. Must participate in Summer Institutes. Must be high school senior or college sophomore. Scholars receive $2,000 stipend for attending Summer Institute program. Recipients may receive a maximum of $23,000 over four years. Must demonstrate a passion for teaching. Visit Website for application, nomination forms and list of Golden Apple's partner universities.

Number of awards:	175
Number of applicants:	175
Application deadline:	December 1
Notification begins:	April 1
Total amount awarded:	$3,105,000

Contact:
Golden Apple
8 South Michigan Avenue
Suite 700
Chicago, IL 60603
Phone: 312-407-0006
Fax: 312-407-0344
Web: www.goldenapple.org

Golden Door Scholars

Golden Door Scholars

Type of award: Scholarship, renewable.
Intended use: For full-time freshman study at 4-year institution. Designated institutions: Queens University of Charlotte, Davidson College, Elon University, Guilford College, High Point University, Salem College, Wake Forest University, Wingate University, Wofford College, Oberlin College, Tufts University, Berea College, and Meredith College.
Eligibility: Applicant must be high school senior.
Application requirements: Essay, transcript. Must qualify for DACA: Deferred Action for Childhood Arrivals.
Additional information: Minimum 3.5 GPA. Selected applicants will be awarded full tuition scholarships to a Golden Door Scholar partner school (with many scholars receiving support for room, board, healthcare and books). Priority is given to students from states that charge out-of-state tuition to DACA students.

Amount of award:	$7,500
Number of awards:	90
Number of applicants:	1,300
Application deadline:	October 27
Notification begins:	December 5
Total amount awarded:	$3,000,000

Contact:
Web: www.goldendoorscholars.org

Golden Key International Honour Society

Achieving Success Awards: For Transfer Students Scholarship

Type of award: Scholarship.
Intended use: For junior or senior study at 4-year institution.

Application requirements: Essay, transcript. Resume, personal statement.

Additional information: Must be Golden Key member who transferred from a two-year school and is currently enrolled in a four-year school.

Amount of award:	$1,000
Number of awards:	3
Application deadline:	October 1

Contact:
Golden Key International Honour Society
Phone: 800-377-2401
Web: www.goldenkey.org

Golden Key Community Service Award

Type of award: Scholarship.

Intended use: For undergraduate or graduate study at accredited postsecondary institution.

Basis for selection: Applicant must demonstrate service orientation.

Application requirements: Recommendations, essay. List of extracurricular activities detailing community service, resume.

Additional information: Must have accumulated 100 hours of unpaid community service through a non-profit organization. Only Golden Key members who were enrolled as students during previous academic year eligible to apply. Winner and charity of winner's choice will each receive $1,000. Visit Website for application. Number of awards varies.

Amount of award:	$1,000
Number of awards:	2
Application deadline:	April 1

Contact:
1040 Crown Pointe Parkway Suite 900
Atlanta, GA 30338
Phone: 800-377-2401
Fax: 678-689-2297
Web: www.goldenkey.org

Golden Key Emerging Scholar Award

Type of award: Scholarship.

Intended use: For undergraduate or graduate study.

Basis for selection: Applicant must demonstrate high academic achievement.

Application requirements: Recommendations, essay, transcript. Resume. Letter from Golden Key chapter advisor stating your contributions. One-minute video submission stating what you plan to do after graduation.

Additional information: Open to Golden Key members only. Applicant must be active member in good standing. Visit Website for details and application.

Amount of award:	$1,000
Number of awards:	3
Application deadline:	April 1

Contact:
Golden Key International Honour Society
Phone: 800-377-2401
Web: www.goldenkey.org

Golden Key GEICO Life Award

Type of award: Scholarship.

Intended use: For undergraduate study at postsecondary institution.

Basis for selection: Applicant must demonstrate high academic achievement.

Application requirements: Recommendations, essay, transcript. Resume.

Additional information: Minimum 3.5 GPA. Open to Golden Key members only. Must be balancing academic achievement and other commitments such as work or family. Applicant must be active undergraduate member in good standing who has completed at least 12 credit hours since returning to university. Visit Website for details and application.

Amount of award:	$1,000
Number of awards:	5
Application deadline:	June 15

Contact:
Golden Key International Honour Society
Phone: 800-377-2401
Web: www.goldenkey.org

Golden Key Outstanding Alumni Member Award

Type of award: Scholarship.

Intended use: For undergraduate or graduate study at postsecondary institution.

Application requirements: Recommendations, essay, transcript. Resume. Letters from both Golden Key chapter advisor and community official stating how you have promoted Golden Key on campus and in the community. Video submission explaining Golden Key involvement.

Additional information: Open to Golden Key members only. Applicant must be active member in good standing. Visit Website for details and application.

Amount of award:	$1,000
Number of awards:	5
Application deadline:	April 1

Contact:
Golden Key International Honour Society
Phone: 800-377-2401
Web: www.goldenkey.org

Golden Key Research Grants

Type of award: Research grant.

Intended use: For undergraduate or graduate study at postsecondary institution.

Basis for selection: Applicant must demonstrate high academic achievement.

Application requirements: Transcript. Resume, budget summary and description of proposed research.

Additional information: Only Golden Key members eligible to apply. Grant for members to travel to professional conferences and student research symposia, or to conduct thesis research. Visit Website for details and application.

Amount of award:	$1,000
Number of awards:	10
Application deadline:	April 1

Contact:
Phone: 800-377-2401
Web: www.goldenkey.org

Golden Key Undergraduate Achievement Scholarship

Type of award: Scholarship.

Intended use: For undergraduate study at accredited postsecondary institution.

Basis for selection: Major/career interest in education. Applicant must demonstrate high academic achievement.

Application requirements: Recommendations, essay, transcript. Resume, essay detailing how you exemplify the Society's commitment to academics, leadership, and service.

Additional information: Minimum 3.5 GPA. Open to Golden Key members only. Visit Website for application.

Amount of award:	$5,000
Number of awards:	18
Application deadline:	June 15

Contact:
1040 Crown Pointe Parkway
Suit 900
Atlanta, GA 30338
Phone: 800-377-2401
Fax: 678-689-2297
Web: www.goldenkey.org

Joan Nelson Study Abroad Scholarship

Type of award: Scholarship.

Intended use: For undergraduate, graduate or postgraduate study at 4-year or graduate institution.

Application requirements: Recommendations, essay, transcript. Resume.

Additional information: Award for study abroad programs used for academic credit. Must be Golden Key member.

Amount of award:	$5,000
Number of awards:	1
Application deadline:	June 15
Notification begins:	December 15

Contact:
Golden Key International Honour Society
Phone: 800-377-2401
Web: www.goldenkey.org

Study Abroad Scholarships

Type of award: Scholarship.

Intended use: For undergraduate, graduate or postgraduate study at postsecondary institution.

Basis for selection: Competition/talent/interest in study abroad, based on relevance of study abroad program to major field of study. Applicant must demonstrate high academic achievement.

Application requirements: Transcript, proof of eligibility. Resume, description of planned academic program at host university, one-page statement of relevance of program to degree.

Additional information: Only Golden Key members eligible to apply. Number of awards varies. Visit Website for details and application.

Amount of award:	$1,000
Number of awards:	10
Application deadline:	April 1

Contact:
Phone: 800-377-2401
Web: www.goldenkey.org

Goldia.com

Goldia.com Scholarship

Type of award: Scholarship.

Intended use: For undergraduate or graduate study at vocational, 2-year, 4-year or graduate institution in or outside United States or Canada.

Eligibility: Applicant must be U.S. citizen, permanent resident or international student.

Application requirements: Essay.

Additional information: Fill out application online. Answer one of the last three essay questions with 750 words or less.

Number of awards:	1
Application deadline:	December 31
Total amount awarded:	$500

Contact:
Goldia.com
P.O. Box 5557
New York, NY 10185
Web: www.goldia.com/scholarship.html

Golf Course Superintendents Association of America

GCSAA Legacy Awards

Type of award: Scholarship.

Intended use: For full-time undergraduate study at accredited 2-year, 4-year or graduate institution.

Eligibility: Applicant or parent must be member/participant of Golf Course Superintendents Association of America.

Basis for selection: Applicant must demonstrate high academic achievement, leadership and service orientation.

Application requirements: Recommendations, essay, transcript.

Additional information: Applicants must be child or grandchild of GCSAA members active for at least five years. Must be enrolled full-time at accredited postsecondary institution or, if high school senior, must be accepted for following academic year. Must be studying field unrelated to golf course management. Award is funded by Syngenta Professional Products. Visit Website or contact via e-mail (ahoward@gcsaa.org) for more information.

Amount of award:	$1,500
Number of awards:	20
Application deadline:	April 15
Notification begins:	June 15
Total amount awarded:	$30,000

Contact:
Senior Manager of Development
Attn: Mischia Wright
1421 Research Park Drive
Lawrence, KS 66049
Phone: 800-472-7878 ext. 4445
Fax: 785-832-3673
Web: www.gcsaa.org

GCSAA Scholars Competition

Type of award: Scholarship.
Intended use: For sophomore, junior or senior study at accredited 2-year or 4-year institution.
Eligibility: Applicant or parent must be member/participant of Golf Course Superintendents Association of America.
Basis for selection: Major/career interest in turf management. Applicant must demonstrate high academic achievement.
Application requirements: Recommendations, essay, transcript.
Additional information: Applicant must be GCSAA member. Must be planning career as golf course superintendent and have successfully completed at least one year of full-time study in golf course management program. Employees of GCSAA and their children are ineligible. Visit Website for more information.

Amount of award:	$500-$6,000
Application deadline:	June 1

Contact:
Senior Manager of Development
Attn: Mischia Wright
1421 Research Park Drive
Lawrence, KS 66049-3859
Phone: 800-472-7878 ext. 4445
Fax: 785-832-3673
Web: www.gcsaa.org

GCSAA Student Essay Contest

Type of award: Scholarship.
Intended use: For undergraduate or graduate study at accredited 2-year, 4-year or graduate institution.
Eligibility: Applicant or parent must be member/participant of Golf Course Superintendents Association of America.
Basis for selection: Competition/talent/interest in writing/journalism, based on seven- to twelve-page essay focusing on golf-course management. Major/career interest in turf management.
Additional information: Applicant must be member of GCSAA. Applicant must be pursuing degree in turfgrass science, agronomy or other field related to golf-course management. First place award, $2,000; 2nd, $1,500; 3rd, $1,000. Visit Website or contact via e-mail ahoward@gcsaa.org for more information.

Amount of award:	$1,000-$2,000
Number of awards:	3
Application deadline:	March 31
Total amount awarded:	$4,500

Contact:
Senior Manager of Development
Attn: Mischia Wright
1421 Research Park Drive
Lawrence, KS 66049
Phone: 800-472-7878 ext. 4445
Fax: 785-832-3673
Web: www.gcsaa.org

Good Tidings

Good Tidings Community Service Scholarship

Type of award: Scholarship.
Intended use: For full-time undergraduate study at vocational, 2-year or 4-year institution.

Eligibility: Applicant must be high school senior. Applicant must be residing in California.
Basis for selection: Applicant must demonstrate service orientation.
Application requirements: Recommendations, essay. Must be a senior in high school residing in one of the following counties: Alameda, Contra Costa, Marin, Monterey, Napa, Sacramento, San Benito, San Francisco, San Joaquin, San Mateo, Santa Cruz, Santa Clara, Solano, Sonoma, Stanislaus, Yolo.
Additional information: Available to high school seniors based on the greatest public service and financial need. Application online.

Amount of award:	$10,000
Number of awards:	10
Number of applicants:	280
Application deadline:	October 26
Notification begins:	November 1
Total amount awarded:	$100,000

Contact:
Web: app.smarterselect.com/programs/29797-Good-Tidings-Foundation

Gordon Law Group

Gordon Law Group Need-Based Scholarship

Type of award: Scholarship.
Intended use: For full-time undergraduate study at accredited 2-year or 4-year institution in United States.
Eligibility: Applicant must be U.S. citizen or permanent resident.
Basis for selection: Major/career interest in law. Applicant must demonstrate financial need.
Application requirements: Essay. Submit an essay addressing the following topic: "Should the federal income tax code be changed to a flat tax of 18% with no deductions so that every person pays the same tax rate?"

Amount of award:	$1,500
Number of awards:	1
Application deadline:	June 1
Notification begins:	September 1
Total amount awarded:	$1,500

Contact:
Gordon Law Group
620B Academy Drive
Northbrook, IL 60062
Phone: 847-940-4000
Web: https://www.gordonlawltd.com/gordon-law-group-scholarship/

Grange Insurance Association

Grange Insurance Scholarship

Type of award: Scholarship.
Intended use: For full-time undergraduate or graduate study at accredited vocational, 2-year, 4-year or graduate institution.

Eligibility: Applicant must be U.S. citizen or permanent resident residing in Wyoming, California, Oregon, Idaho, Washington or Colorado.

Basis for selection: Applicant must demonstrate financial need, high academic achievement, depth of character, leadership, patriotism, seriousness of purpose and service orientation.

Application requirements: Essay, transcript. Cover letter.

Additional information: Applicant must be one of the following: current GIA policyholder (or child of GIA policyholder) or child of current GIA company employee. Previous recipients also eligible to apply. Application must be postmarked by deadline.

Amount of award:	$1,000-$1,500
Number of awards:	26
Number of applicants:	72
Application deadline:	March 1
Notification begins:	April 15
Total amount awarded:	$26,000

Contact:
Grange Insurance Association
Scholarship Committee
P.O. Box 21089
Seattle, WA 98111-3089
Phone: 800-247-2643 ext. 2200
Web: www.grange.com

Great Minds in STEM

HENAAC Scholars Program

Type of award: Scholarship, renewable.
Intended use: For full-time undergraduate or graduate study at 2-year, 4-year or graduate institution.
Eligibility: Applicant must be Hispanic American.
Basis for selection: Major/career interest in engineering; mathematics; science, general or technology. Applicant must demonstrate high academic achievement and leadership.
Application requirements: Recommendations, essay, transcript. Resume, photo.
Additional information: Minimum 3.0 GPA. Include SASE with application request, or download application from Website. Amount of award varies.

Amount of award:	$500-$10,000
Number of awards:	109
Application deadline:	April 30
Notification begins:	August 1
Total amount awarded:	$250,000

Contact:
Great Minds in STEM
Attn: HENAAC Scholars
602 Monterey Pass Road
Monterey Park, CA 91754
Phone: 323-262-0997
Fax: 323-262-0946
Web: www.greatmindsinstem.org

Greater Kanawha Valley Foundation

Greater Kanawha Valley Scholarship Program

Type of award: Scholarship, renewable.
Intended use: For full-time undergraduate or graduate study at 4-year or graduate institution.
Eligibility: Applicant must be residing in West Virginia.
Basis for selection: Applicant must demonstrate high academic achievement and depth of character.
Application requirements: Recommendations, transcript. First page of parents' federal income tax return.
Additional information: Minimum 20 ACT score and 2.5 GPA. Foundation offers more than 80 scholarships, each with specific eligibility criteria. Visit Website for complete listing, and to apply.

Amount of award:	$1,000
Number of awards:	450
Number of applicants:	719
Application deadline:	January 15
Notification begins:	May 15
Total amount awarded:	$475,000

Contact:
The Greater Kanawha Valley Foundation
900 Lee Street East
16th Floor
Charleston, WV 25301
Phone: 304-346-3620
Fax: 304-346-3640
Web: www.tgkvf.org

GreenAllies

GreenAllies Challenge

Type of award: Scholarship.
Intended use: For undergraduate study at vocational, 2-year or 4-year institution.
Eligibility: Applicant must be at least 12, no older than 19.
Additional information: Applicants will complete a self-designed environmental project over the course of the 2015/2016 school year, with the assistance of the GreenAllies organization. At the end of the competition, students will submit a visual, electronic presentation about their project to a panel of judges. In addition to the $1,000 educational scholarship, the winning student will receive $1,000 to use to continue their environmental project. Complete rules and guidelines on web site.

Number of awards:	1
Application deadline:	November 15
Total amount awarded:	$1,000

Contact:
GreenAllies
35 King Road
Green Lane, PA 18054
Phone: 267-371-2288
Web: greenalliesnetwork.org

Greenhouse Scholars

Greenhouse Scholars Program

Type of award: Scholarship, renewable.
Intended use: For full-time undergraduate study at 4-year institution.
Eligibility: Applicant must be high school senior. Applicant must be U.S. citizen or permanent resident residing in California, New York, Illinois, Colorado or Georgia.
Basis for selection: Based on commitment to community, ability to persevere through difficult circumstances, strong sense of accountability. Applicant must demonstrate financial need, high academic achievement, leadership and service orientation.
Application requirements: Recommendations, transcript. Three letters of recommendation, ACT scores.
Additional information: The Greenhouse Scholars Program is a scholarship and mentorship program for under-resourced, high-achieving students. The program uses a 'Whole Person' approach to address the intellectual, academic, professional, and financial needs of students. Minimum 3.5 GPA. Renewable for four years. Household annual income may not exceed $70,000. Visit Website for application and more information. Online applications must be subitted at greenhousescholars.fluidreview.com/ .

Amount of award:	$4,000-$20,000
Number of awards:	30
Number of applicants:	300
Application deadline:	December 10
Total amount awarded:	$90,000

Contact:
Greenhouse Scholars
1881 9th Street
Suite 200
Boulder, CO 80302
Phone: 720-449-7444
Web: www.greenhousescholars.org

Grill Tanks Plus

The Grill Tanks Plus Award

Type of award: Scholarship, renewable.
Intended use: For full-time undergraduate or graduate study at vocational, 2-year, 4-year or graduate institution.
Application requirements: Essay. We require an easy 1000 words minimum on why Grill Tanks Plus should give the award given applicant the reward.
Additional information: More information about the scholarship program can be found on the website.

Amount of award:	$500
Number of awards:	1
Number of applicants:	10
Application deadline:	June 1
Notification begins:	June 25
Total amount awarded:	$500

Contact:
Grill Tanks Plus Paul Ricard
5107 Oak Hill Road
Delray Beach, FL 33484
Phone: 561-244-2534
Web: https://www.grilltanksplus.com/gtp-scholarship-.html

Groth Law Firm

Groth Law Firm Scholarship

Type of award: Scholarship.
Intended use: For full-time undergraduate study at vocational, 2-year, 4-year or graduate institution.
Eligibility: Applicant must be U.S. citizen.
Basis for selection: Between May 1—May 8, the team at Groth Law Firm will choose the top ten submissions for voting. Voting via social media will open up on May 9 and will end on May 27. The submission with the most votes will win. Major/career interest in law.
Application requirements: Create a 30-second video (uploaded to YouTube or Vimeo) that creatively answers this question: How can we make driving safer?
Additional information: See website for official rules as well as resources for creating a video.

Amount of award:	$1,500
Number of awards:	1
Application deadline:	April 30
Notification begins:	June 1

Contact:
Groth Law Firm
1578 West National Avenue
Milwaukee, WI 53204
Phone: 414-455-6981
Web: www.grothlawfirm.com/video-scholarship-contest/

Guardian Debt Relief

Guardian Debt Relief Scholarship

Type of award: Scholarship.
Intended use: For full-time undergraduate or graduate study at accredited 4-year institution in United States.
Application requirements: Essay, transcript. 2,000 word essay on one of the following topics. Who do you consider to be a role model in your life? Why is this person your role model? What do you consider to be the most pressing societal problem we face today and why? Pick an experience from your own life and explain how it has influenced your development.
Additional information: Must have a minimum 3.0 GPA.

Amount of award:	$1,000
Number of awards:	5
Application deadline:	December 31
Notification begins:	March 31
Total amount awarded:	$5,000

Contact:
Web: https://www.guardiandebtrelief.com/guardian-debt-relief-scholarship/

Hallmark

Mahogany & Blues Babe Scholarship

Type of award: Scholarship.
Intended use: For undergraduate study at accredited 4-year institution.

Basis for selection: Applicant must demonstrate financial need, high academic achievement and service orientation.

Application requirements: Recommendations, essay, transcript. Copy of Student Aid Report. Writing sample two to four pages in length. Letter of recommendation. Current, complete transcript of grades.

Additional information: Open to all current postsecondary undergraduates pursuing a career in the writing arts.

Amount of award:	$10,000
Number of awards:	2
Application deadline:	October 30
Notification begins:	January 15
Total amount awarded:	$20,000

Contact:
Web: https://www.scholarsapply.org/mahogany/

Harness Tracks of America

Harness Tracks of America Scholarship Fund

Type of award: Scholarship.

Intended use: For full-time undergraduate or graduate study at accredited postsecondary institution.

Eligibility: Applicant or parent must be member/participant of Harness Racing Industry.

Basis for selection: Applicant must demonstrate financial need and high academic achievement.

Application requirements: Essay, transcript, proof of eligibility. FAFSA and U.S. or Canadian tax return.

Additional information: Must be child of licensed driver, trainer, breeder, owner or caretaker of harness horses or be personally active in harness racing industry. Children of deceased industry members also eligible. Recommendations not required but considered if included with application. Awards based on financial need, academic excellence, and active harness racing involvement. Visit Website for more information.

Amount of award:	$5,000
Number of awards:	3
Number of applicants:	23
Application deadline:	June 20
Notification begins:	September 15
Total amount awarded:	$15,000

Contact:
Harness Tracks of America
12025 East Dry Gulch Place
Tucson, AZ 85749
Phone: 520-529-2525
Web: www.harnesstracks.com

Harrington Family Foundation

Oregon Community Quarterback Scholarship

Type of award: Scholarship, renewable.

Intended use: For full-time undergraduate or graduate study at vocational, 2-year, 4-year or graduate institution.

Eligibility: Applicant must be U.S. citizen residing in Oregon.

Basis for selection: Applicant must demonstrate financial need.

Application requirements: Interview, recommendations, essay, proof of eligibility. Scholarship is a renewable four-year collegiate scholarship program for Oregon high school seniors who are emerging leaders, and plan to attend an Oregon trade school, college or university. Need based scholarship with criteria focusing on an individual's involvement in his or her community, rather than academic or athletic performance. Applicants must submit: personal/academic information, financial information, a one-page leadership essay, list of community service and extracurricular activities, and 2 letters of reference. 10 scholarship finalists will be asked to interview with the Harrington Family Foundation Scholarship Committee.

Additional information: Each scholarship is worth $2,500 per year, for a total of $10,000 per student. In addition to the scholarship, each recipient will have a board of mentors available to them throughout and following their schooling to help guide their path to a successful career and future.

Amount of award:	$2,500-$10,000
Number of awards:	4
Number of applicants:	300
Application deadline:	March 31
Notification begins:	February 27
Total amount awarded:	$10,000

Contact:
Madeline Guzzo
1355 NW 13th Avenue
Portland, OR 97209
Phone: 855-868-3549
Fax: 855-868-3549
Web: harringtonfamilyfoundation.slideroom.com

Harris Personal Injury Lawyers

Injury Scholarship

Type of award: Scholarship.

Intended use: For undergraduate or graduate study at vocational, 2-year, 4-year or graduate institution.

Application requirements: Must provide a letter stating 1: How has your injury or accident affected your education? 2: How has overcoming your injury or accident prepared you to meet the challenges of higher learning? 3: How will college attendance demonstrate your determination to rebuild your life following your injury?

Additional information: For college or university students who have experienced a serious injury. Apply online.

Number of awards:	1
Application deadline:	December 31
Total amount awarded:	$1,000

Contact:
Web: http://harrispersonalinjury.com/injury-scholarship/

Havana National Bank

McFarland Charitable Foundation Scholarship

Type of award: Scholarship, renewable.
Intended use: For full-time undergraduate study at accredited vocational, 2-year or 4-year institution in United States.
Basis for selection: Major/career interest in nursing. Applicant must demonstrate seriousness of purpose.
Application requirements: Interview, recommendations, transcript, proof of eligibility. Letter of acceptance to RN program.
Additional information: Award recipients must contractually obligate themselves to return to Havana, Illinois, and work as registered nurses for two years for each year of funding. Reverts to loan if work obligation is not met. Two co-signers are required. To fund RN programs only. Number of awards and amounts vary.

Application deadline:	May 15
Notification begins:	June 15

Contact:
Havana National Bank
112 South Orange
P.O. Box 200
Havana, IL 62644-0200
Phone: 309-543-3361
Web: www.havanabank.com

Hawaii Community Foundation

100th Infantry Battalion Memorial Scholarship Fund

Type of award: Scholarship.
Intended use: For full-time undergraduate or graduate study at accredited 2-year or 4-year institution in United States.
Eligibility: Applicant must be U.S. citizen or permanent resident. Applicant must be descendant of veteran. Must be direct descendant of a 100th Infantry Battalion World War II veteran.
Basis for selection: Applicant must demonstrate financial need, high academic achievement, depth of character and service orientation.
Application requirements: Recommendations, essay, transcript, proof of eligibility. SAR, FAFSA, Personal Statement, SAT/ACT scores. Essay on topic: "What is the legacy of the 100th Infantry Battalion of WWII and how will you contribute to forwarding this legacy?" Name of World War II 100th Battalion member you are descended from and your relationship to individual.
Additional information: Must be direct descendant of a 100th Infantry Battalion World War II veteran and be willing to promote its legacy. Minimum 3.5 GPA. Applicant does not have to be resident of Hawaii. Must apply online. Must be active in extracurricular activities and community service.

Application deadline: February 15

Contact:
Hawaii Community Foundation Scholarships
827 Fort Street Mall
Honolulu, HI 96813
Phone: 888-731-3863
Web: www.hawaiicommunityfoundation.org

A & B Ohana Scholarship

Type of award: Scholarship, renewable.
Intended use: For full-time undergraduate study at 2-year or 4-year institution in United States.
Eligibility: Applicant must be residing in Hawaii.
Basis for selection: Applicant must demonstrate financial need and high academic achievement.
Application requirements: Recommendations, essay, transcript. FAFSA, SAR, SAT/ACT scores. Name and title of parent who is Alexander & Baldwin employee.
Additional information: Minimum 2.7 GPA. Must be dependent child of full-time employee of Alexander & Baldwin, Inc. Employee must have completed one year of full-time continuous service by application deadline. Must attend college or university with 501c3 status. If attending community college, award amount will be lower.

Application deadline: February 15

Contact:
Hawaii Community Foundation
827 Fort Street Mall
Honolulu, HI 96813
Phone: 888-731-3863
Web: www.hawaiicommunityfoundation.org

ABC Stores Jumpstart Scholarship

Type of award: Scholarship.
Intended use: For undergraduate study at accredited 2-year, 4-year or graduate institution in United States.
Eligibility: Applicant must be residing in Hawaii or Nevada.
Basis for selection: Applicant must demonstrate financial need, high academic achievement and depth of character.
Application requirements: Recommendations, essay, transcript. SAR, FAFSA, SAT/ACT scores, Personal Statement. Name of ABC Stores Employee and relationship (i.e., mother).
Additional information: Applicant must be employee or dependent of ABC Stores or Company Island Gourmet Markets employee. Must be resident of Hawaii, Nevada, Guam, or Saipan. Minimum 2.7 GPA. Applicants must have permanent address in Hawaii. Amount of award may change yearly.

Application deadline: February 15

Contact:
Hawaii Community Foundation Scholarships
827 Fort Street Mall
Honolulu, HI 96813
Phone: 888-731-3863
Web: www.hawaiicommunityfoundation.org

Aiea General Hospital Association Scholarship

Type of award: Scholarship, renewable.
Intended use: For full-time undergraduate study at accredited 2-year, 4-year or graduate institution in United States.
Eligibility: Applicant must be U.S. citizen or permanent resident residing in Hawaii.
Basis for selection: Major/career interest in health-related professions. Applicant must demonstrate financial need, high academic achievement and depth of character.

Application requirements: Recommendations, essay, transcript. FAFSA, SAR, SAT/ACT scores.

Additional information: Minimum 2.7 GPA. Applicant must be resident of Leeward Oahu ZIP Codes: 96701, 96706, 96707, 96782, 96792, or 96797. Amount and number of awards vary.

Application deadline: February 15

Contact:
Hawaii Community Foundation Scholarships
827 Fort Street Mall
Honolulu, HI 96813
Phone: 888-731-3863
Web: www.hawaiicommunityfoundation.org

Allan Eldin & Agnes Sutorik Geiger Scholarship Fund

Type of award: Scholarship.

Intended use: For full-time undergraduate or graduate study at accredited 2-year or 4-year institution in United States.

Eligibility: Applicant must be U.S. citizen residing in Hawaii.

Basis for selection: Major/career interest in veterinary medicine. Applicant must demonstrate financial need, high academic achievement and depth of character.

Application requirements: Recommendations, essay, transcript. SAR, FAFSA, Personal Statement, SAT/ACT scores.

Additional information: Minimum 3.0 GPA. Applicants must have permanent address in Hawaii. Applicants taking up mainland residency must have relatives living in Hawaii. Amount of award may change yearly. Preference given to renewal applicants.

Application deadline: February 15

Contact:
Hawaii Community Foundation Scholarships
827 Fort Street Mall
Honolulu, HI 96813
Phone: 888-731-3863
Web: www.hawaiicommunityfoundation.org

Alma White-Delta Kappa Gamma Scholarship

Type of award: Scholarship.

Intended use: For full-time junior, senior or graduate study at accredited postsecondary institution in United States.

Eligibility: Applicant must be U.S. citizen or permanent resident residing in Hawaii.

Basis for selection: Major/career interest in education. Applicant must demonstrate financial need, high academic achievement and depth of character.

Application requirements: Recommendations, essay, transcript. FAFSA and SAR, SAT/ACT scores. Official letter confirming enrollment in education program.

Additional information: Minimum 2.7 GPA. Applicants must have permanent address in Hawaii. Applicants taking up mainland residency must have relatives living in Hawaii. Amount and number of awards vary and may change yearly.

Application deadline: February 15

Contact:
Hawaii Community Foundation Scholarships
827 Fort Street Mall
Honolulu, HI 96813
Phone: 888-731-3863
Web: www.hawaiicommunityfoundation.org

Ambassador Minerva Jean Falcon Hawaii Scholarship

Type of award: Scholarship.

Intended use: For full-time undergraduate or graduate study at 2-year, 4-year or graduate institution. Designated institutions: 2-year or 4-year colleges in Hawaii.

Eligibility: Applicant must be Native Hawaiian/Pacific Islander. Applicant must be residing in Hawaii.

Basis for selection: Applicant must demonstrate financial need and high academic achievement.

Application requirements: Recommendations, essay, transcript. FAFSA and SAR, SAT/ACT scores.

Additional information: Minimum 2.7 GPA. Must be graduate of Hawaii high school. Must be of Filipino ancestry.

Application deadline: February 15

Contact:
Hawaii Community Foundation
827 Fort Street Mall
Honolulu, HI 96813
Phone: 888-731-3863
Web: www.hawaiicommunityfoundation.org

American Institute of Graphic Arts (AIGA) Honolulu Chapter Scholarship Fund

Type of award: Scholarship.

Intended use: For full-time undergraduate or graduate study at 2-year, 4-year or graduate institution.

Eligibility: Applicant must be residing in Hawaii.

Basis for selection: Major/career interest in arts, general or graphic arts/design. Applicant must demonstrate financial need and high academic achievement.

Application requirements: Recommendations, essay, transcript. SAR, FAFSA, SAT/ACT scores.

Additional information: Minimum 2.7 GPA. Must major in graphic design, visual communication, or commercial arts.

Application deadline: February 15

Contact:
Hawaii Community Foundation
827 Fort Street Mall
Honolulu, HI 96813
Phone: 888-731-3863
Web: www.hawaiicommunityfoundation.org

Arthur Jackman Memorial Scholarship

Type of award: Scholarship.

Intended use: For full-time undergraduate study at vocational institution in United States. Designated institutions: Hawaii community colleges.

Eligibility: Applicant must be residing in Hawaii.

Basis for selection: Applicant must demonstrate financial need and high academic achievement.

Application requirements: Recommendations, essay, transcript. SAR, FAFSA, SAT/ACT scores.

Additional information: Minimum 2.7 GPA. Must be enrolled in AS or AAS career technical degree program at Hawaii community college. Must be resident of island of Hawaii.

Application deadline: February 15

Scholarships

Contact:
Hawaii Community Foundation
827 Fort Street Mall
Honolulu, HI 96813
Phone: 888-731-3863
Web: www.hawaiicommunityfoundation.org

Bal Dasa Scholarship Fund

Type of award: Scholarship.
Intended use: For full-time undergraduate or graduate study at accredited 2-year, 4-year or graduate institution in United States.
Eligibility: Applicant must be U.S. citizen or permanent resident residing in Hawaii.
Basis for selection: Applicant must demonstrate financial need, high academic achievement and depth of character.
Application requirements: Essay, transcript. FAFSA and SAR, SAT/ACT scores.
Additional information: Minimum 2.7 GPA. Must be graduate of Waipahu High School. Award amount varies yearly. Applicants taking up mainland residency must have relatives living in Hawaii.
Application deadline: February 15
Contact:
Hawaii Community Foundation Scholarships
827 Fort Street Mall
Honolulu, HI 96813
Phone: 888-731-3863
Web: www.hawaiicommunityfoundation.org

Bank of Hawaii Foundation Scholarship

Type of award: Scholarship.
Intended use: For full-time undergraduate study at accredited 2-year or 4-year institution in United States.
Eligibility: Applicant must be U.S. citizen residing in Hawaii.
Basis for selection: Applicant must demonstrate financial need and high academic achievement.
Application requirements: Essay, transcript. FAFSA/SAR, SAT/ACT scores.
Additional information: Minimum 2.0 GPA. Must be high school senior or graduate who is child or grandchild of active employee of Bank of Hawaii Corporation.
Application deadline: February 15
Contact:
Hawaii Community Foundation
827 Fort Street Mall
Honolulu, HI 96813
Phone: 888-731-3863
Web: www.hawaiicommunityfoundation.org

Bick Bickson Scholarship

Type of award: Scholarship, renewable.
Intended use: For full-time undergraduate or graduate study at accredited 2-year or 4-year institution in United States.
Eligibility: Applicant must be U.S. citizen residing in Hawaii.
Basis for selection: Major/career interest in marketing; law or tourism/travel. Applicant must demonstrate financial need, high academic achievement and depth of character.
Application requirements: Essay, transcript. FAFSA and SAR, SAT/ACT scores.
Additional information: Minimum 3.0 GPA.
Application deadline: February 15

Contact:
Hawaii Community Foundation
827 Fort Street Mall
Honolulu, HI 96813
Phone: 888-731-3863
Web: www.hawaiicommunityfoundation.org

Blossom Kalama Evans Memorial Scholarship

Type of award: Scholarship, renewable.
Intended use: For full-time junior, senior or graduate study at accredited 4-year or graduate institution in United States. Designated institutions: Schools in Hawaii.
Eligibility: Applicant must be Native Hawaiian/Pacific Islander. Applicant must be U.S. citizen or permanent resident residing in Hawaii.
Basis for selection: Major/career interest in Hawaiian studies. Applicant must demonstrate financial need, high academic achievement and depth of character.
Application requirements: Transcript. FAFSA and SAR, SAT/ACT scores. Personal essay stating how applicant's knowledge will be used to serve the needs of the Native Hawaiian community.
Additional information: Minimum 2.7 GPA. Students must be of Hawaiian ancestry. Preference given to students studying Hawaiian studies or language. Applicants must have permanent address in Hawaii. Applicants who take up mainland residency must have relatives living in Hawaii. Amount and number of awards vary.
Application deadline: February 15
Contact:
Hawaii Community Foundation Scholarships
827 Fort Street Mall
Honolulu, HI 96813
Phone: 888-731-3863
Web: www.hawaiicommunityfoundation.org

Booz Allen Scholarship

Type of award: Scholarship.
Intended use: For full-time undergraduate study at accredited 4-year institution.
Eligibility: Applicant must be residing in Hawaii.
Basis for selection: Applicant must demonstrate financial need and high academic achievement.
Application requirements: Recommendations, essay, transcript. SAR, FAFSA, SAT/ACT scores.
Additional information: Minimum 3.0 GPA.
Application deadline: February 15
Contact:
Hawaii Community Foundation
827 Fort Street Mall
Honolulu, HI 96813
Phone: 888-731-3863
Web: www.hawaiicommunityfoundation.org

Camille C. Chidiac Fund

Type of award: Scholarship.
Intended use: For full-time undergraduate or graduate study at accredited 2-year, 4-year or graduate institution in United States.
Eligibility: Applicant must be high school senior. Applicant must be U.S. citizen or permanent resident residing in Hawaii.
Basis for selection: Applicant must demonstrate financial need, high academic achievement and depth of character.

Application requirements: Essay, transcript. FAFSA and SAR, SAT/ACT scores. Essay must state why it is important for Hawaii students to be internationally aware.

Additional information: Minimum 2.7 GPA. Applicant must be student at Ka'u High School. Amount of scholarship varies yearly. Applicants taking up mainland residency must have relatives living in Hawaii.

> **Application deadline:** February 15

Contact:
Hawaii Community Foundation Scholarships
827 Fort Street Mall
Honolulu, HI 96813
Phone: 888-731-3863
Web: www.hawaiicommunityfoundation.org

Candon, Todd, & Seabolt Scholarship Fund

Type of award: Scholarship.

Intended use: For junior or senior study at 4-year institution in United States.

Eligibility: Applicant must be U.S. citizen residing in Hawaii.

Basis for selection: Major/career interest in accounting or finance/banking. Applicant must demonstrate high academic achievement.

Application requirements: Recommendations, essay, transcript. SAR, FAFSA, SAT/ACT scores.

Additional information: Minimum 3.2 GPA.

> **Application deadline:** February 15

Contact:
Hawaii Community Foundation Scholarships
827 Fort Street Mall
Honolulu, HI 96813
Phone: 808-537-6333
Fax: 808-521-6286
Web: www.hawaiicommunityfoundation.org

Castle & Cooke Mililani Technology Park Scholarship Fund

Type of award: Scholarship.

Intended use: For full-time undergraduate or graduate study at accredited 4-year or graduate institution in United States.

Eligibility: Applicant must be high school senior. Applicant must be U.S. citizen or permanent resident residing in Hawaii.

Basis for selection: Major/career interest in science, general; engineering; computer/information sciences or technology. Applicant must demonstrate financial need and high academic achievement.

Application requirements: Essay, transcript. FAFSA and SAR, SAT/ACT scores.

Additional information: Minimum 2.7 GPA. Applicants must be graduating senior from Leilehua, Mililani, or Waialua high schools. Preference given to majors in technology fields. Applicants must have permanent address in Hawaii. Applicants taking up mainland residency must have relatives living in Hawaii. Amount and number of awards vary and may change yearly.

> **Application deadline:** February 15

Contact:
Hawaii Community Foundation Scholarships
827 Fort Street Mall
Honolulu, HI 96813
Phone: 888-731-3863
Web: www.hawaiicommunityfoundation.org

Castle & Cooke W. Y. Yim Scholarship Fund

Type of award: Scholarship.

Intended use: For full-time undergraduate or graduate study at accredited 2-year or 4-year institution in United States.

Eligibility: Applicant must be U.S. citizen residing in Hawaii.

Basis for selection: Applicant must demonstrate financial need, high academic achievement and depth of character.

Application requirements: Recommendations, essay, transcript. SAR, FAFSA, Personal Statement, SAT/ACT scores. Castle & Cooke employee name, position, and relationship to applicant.

Additional information: Minimum 3.0 GPA. Must be a dependent of current employee with at least one year of service with Castle & Cooke Hawaii affiliated company. Applicants must have permanent address in Hawaii. Applicants taking up mainland residency must have relatives living in Hawaii. Amount of award may change yearly.

> **Application deadline:** February 15

Contact:
Hawaii Community Foundation Scholarships
827 Fort Street Mall
Honolulu, HI 96813
Phone: 888-731-3863
Web: www.hawaiicommunityfoundation.org

Community Scholarship Fund

Type of award: Scholarship, renewable.

Intended use: For full-time undergraduate or graduate study at accredited 4-year institution in United States.

Eligibility: Applicant must be U.S. citizen or permanent resident residing in Hawaii.

Basis for selection: Major/career interest in arts, general; architecture; education; humanities/liberal arts or social/behavioral sciences. Applicant must demonstrate financial need, high academic achievement, depth of character and service orientation.

Application requirements: Essay, transcript. FAFSA and SAR, SAT/ACT scores.

Additional information: Must have 3.3 to 3.8 GPA. Must show commitment to community in Hawaii. Must be first-generation college student. Preference given to sophomores. Must have permanent address in Hawaii. Applicants taking up mainland residency must have relatives living in Hawaii. Amount and number of awards vary and may change yearly.

> **Application deadline:** February 15

Contact:
Hawaii Community Foundation Scholarships
827 Fort Street Mall
Honolulu, HI 96813
Phone: 888-731-3863
Web: www.hawaiicommunityfoundation.org

Cora Aguda Manayan Fund

Type of award: Scholarship, renewable.

Intended use: For full-time undergraduate or graduate study at accredited 2-year, 4-year or graduate institution in United States.

Eligibility: Applicant must be of Filipino ancestry. Applicant must be U.S. citizen or permanent resident residing in Hawaii.

Basis for selection: Major/career interest in health-related professions. Applicant must demonstrate financial need, high academic achievement and depth of character.

Application requirements: Essay, transcript. FAFSA and SAR, SAT/ACT scores.

Additional information: Minimum 3.0 GPA. Supports students of Filipino ancestry. Preference given to students studying in Hawaii. Applicants must have permanent address in Hawaii. Applicants who take up mainland residency must have relatives living in Hawaii. Amount and number of awards vary.

Application deadline: February 15

Contact:
Hawaii Community Foundation Scholarships
827 Fort Street Mall
Honolulu, HI 96813
Phone: 888-731-3863
Web: www.hawaiicommunityfoundation.org

CPB Works For You Scholarship

Type of award: Scholarship.
Intended use: For undergraduate study at accredited 2-year or 4-year institution.
Eligibility: Applicant must be residing in Hawaii.
Basis for selection: Applicant must demonstrate financial need and high academic achievement.
Application requirements: Recommendations, essay, transcript. SAR, FAFSA, SAT/ACT scores, name and position of CPB employee.
Additional information: Minimum 2.7 GPA. Must be active status employee or dependent child (no older than 25) of active status employee of CPB or CPHL with minimum one year of service by application deadline. Part-time awards will be less than full-time awards.

Application deadline: February 15

Contact:
Hawaii Community Foundation
827 Fort Street Mall
Honolulu, HI 96813
Phone: 888-731-3863
Web: www.hawaiicommunityfoundation.org

Dan & Pauline Lutkenhouse & Hawaii Tropical Botanical Garden Scholarship

Type of award: Scholarship.
Intended use: For full-time undergraduate study at accredited postsecondary institution.
Eligibility: Applicant must be residing in Hawaii.
Basis for selection: Major/career interest in agriculture; science, general; medicine or nursing. Applicant must demonstrate financial need and high academic achievement.
Application requirements: Recommendations, essay, transcript. SAR, FAFSA, SAT/ACT scores.
Additional information: Minimum 2.7 GPA. Must be resident of Hilo Coast and Hamakua Coast, north of Wailuki River.

Application deadline: February 15

Contact:
Hawaii Community Foundation
827 Fort Street Mall
Honolulu, HI 96813
Phone: 888-731-3863
Web: www.hawaiicommunityfoundation.org

David L. Irons Memorial Scholarship Fund

Type of award: Scholarship.
Intended use: For full-time freshman study at accredited 2-year or 4-year institution in United States.

Eligibility: Applicant must be high school senior. Applicant must be U.S. citizen or permanent resident residing in Hawaii.
Basis for selection: Applicant must demonstrate financial need, high academic achievement and depth of character.
Application requirements: Essay, transcript. FAFSA and SAR, SAT/ACT scores.
Additional information: Minimum 2.7 GPA. Applicant must be graduating senior at Punahou School. Applicants taking up mainland residency must have relatives living in Hawaii. Amount of award may change yearly.

Application deadline: February 15

Contact:
Hawaii Community Foundation Scholarships
827 Fort Street Mall
Honolulu, HI 96813
Phone: 808-537-6333
Fax: 808-521-6286
Web: www.hawaiicommunityfoundation.org

Diamond Resort Scholarship

Type of award: Scholarship.
Intended use: For full-time freshman study at accredited 2-year or 4-year institution in United States.
Eligibility: Applicant must be U.S. citizen or permanent resident residing in Hawaii.
Basis for selection: Applicant must demonstrate financial need and high academic achievement.
Application requirements: Essay, transcript. FAFSA/SAR, SAT/ACT scores.
Additional information: Must be graduating senior from public high school in County of Maui. Minimum 3.0 GPA.

Application deadline: February 15

Contact:
Hawaii Community Foundation
827 Fort Street Mall
Honolulu, HI 96813
Phone: 888-731-3863
Web: www.hawaiicommunityfoundation.org

Dolly Ching Scholarship Fund

Type of award: Scholarship.
Intended use: For full-time undergraduate study at accredited postsecondary institution in United States. Designated institutions: Institutions in University of Hawaii system.
Eligibility: Applicant must be high school senior. Applicant must be U.S. citizen or permanent resident residing in Hawaii.
Basis for selection: Applicant must demonstrate financial need, high academic achievement, depth of character and service orientation.
Application requirements: Recommendations, essay, transcript. FAFSA and SAR, SAT/ACT scores.
Additional information: Minimum 2.7 GPA. Must be graduating senior from a high school on Kauai. Must be resident of Kauai. Amount and number of awards vary.

Application deadline: February 15

Contact:
Hawaii Community Foundation Scholarships
827 Fort Street Mall
Honolulu, HI 96813
Phone: 888-731-3863
Web: www.hawaiicommunityfoundation.org

Doris & Clarence Glick Classical Music Scholarship

Type of award: Scholarship.
Intended use: For full-time undergraduate study at accredited 2-year or 4-year institution in United States.
Eligibility: Applicant must be residing in Hawaii.
Basis for selection: Major/career interest in music. Applicant must demonstrate financial need, high academic achievement and depth of character.
Application requirements: Essay, transcript. FAFSA and SAR, SAT/ACT scores. Describe in personal statement how program of study relates to classical music.
Additional information: Minimum 2.7 GPA. Must major in music, with emphasis on classical music. Applicants must have permanent address in Hawaii. Applicants taking up mainland residency must have relatives living in Hawaii. Amount and number of awards vary and may change yearly.
   Application deadline: February 15
Contact:
Hawaii Community Foundation Scholarships
827 Fort Street Mall
Honolulu, HI 96813
Phone: 888-731-3863
Web: www.hawaiicommunityfoundation.org

Dr. Alvin and Monica Saake Scholarship

Type of award: Scholarship.
Intended use: For full-time junior, senior or graduate study at accredited 2-year, 4-year or graduate institution.
Eligibility: Applicant must be residing in Hawaii.
Basis for selection: Major/career interest in physical education; athletic training; sports/sports administration; physical therapy or occupational therapy. Applicant must demonstrate financial need, high academic achievement and depth of character.
Application requirements: Essay, transcript. FAFSA and SAR, SAT/ACT scores.
Additional information: Minimum 2.7 GPA. Must be majoring in kinesiology, leisure science, physical education, athletic training, exercise science, sports medicine, physical therapy, or occupational therapy. Applicant must have permanent Hawaii address. Applicants taking up mainland residency must have relatives living in Hawaii.
   Application deadline: February 15
Contact:
Hawaii Community Foundation Scholarships
827 Fort Street Mall
Honolulu, HI 96813
Phone: 888-731-3863
Web: www.hawaiicommunityfoundation.org

Dr. and Mrs. Moon Park Scholarship

Type of award: Scholarship.
Intended use: For full-time undergraduate or graduate study at accredited 4-year institution in United States.
Eligibility: Applicant must be U.S. citizen residing in Hawaii.
Basis for selection: Applicant must demonstrate financial need and high academic achievement.
Application requirements: Recommendations, essay, transcript. SAR, FAFSA, SAT/ACT scores, Personal Statement. Clinical Laboratories of Hawaii, LLC employee name and relationship to applicant.

Additional information: Minimum 3.0 GPA. Must be an employee or child dependent with minimum one year of service of Clinical Laboratories of Hawaii, LLP and/or Pan Pacific Pathologies, LLC. Applicants must have permanent address in Hawaii. Applicants taking up mainland residency must have relatives living in Hawaii. Amount of award may change yearly. Preference given to renewal applicants.
   Application deadline: February 15
Contact:
Hawaii Community Foundation Scholarships
827 Fort Street Mall
Honolulu, HI 96813
Phone: 888-731-3863
Web: www.hawaiicommunityfoundation.org

Dr. Edison and Sallie Miyawaki Scholarship

Type of award: Scholarship.
Intended use: For undergraduate study at accredited 2-year or 4-year institution.
Eligibility: Applicant must be residing in Hawaii.
Basis for selection: Applicant must demonstrate financial need and high academic achievement.
Application requirements: Recommendations, essay, transcript. FAFSA and SAR, SAT/ACT scores.
Additional information: GPA between 2.5 and 3.0. Must participate in extracurricular sports program. Amount and number of awards vary and may change yearly. Preference given to renewal applicants.
   Application deadline: February 15
Contact:
Hawaii Community Foundation
827 Fort Street Mall
Honolulu, HI 96813
Phone: 888-731-3863
Web: www.hawaiicommunityfoundation.org

Dr. Hans & Clara Zimmerman Foundation Education Scholarship

Type of award: Scholarship.
Intended use: For undergraduate or graduate study at accredited 2-year or 4-year institution in United States.
Eligibility: Applicant must be U.S. citizen or permanent resident residing in Hawaii.
Basis for selection: Major/career interest in education or education, teacher. Applicant must demonstrate financial need, high academic achievement, depth of character and leadership.
Application requirements: Recommendations, essay, transcript. FAFSA and SAR, SAT/ACT scores. Recommendations must include an evaluation of applicant's "classroom teaching effectiveness." Personal statement describing applicant's community service projects or activities. Essay must also answer question "What is your teaching philosophy and how is it applied in classroom today?" (with one example). Applicants disqualified if they fail to address essay topic in personal statement.
Additional information: Minimum 2.8 GPA. Must major in education with an emphasis on classroom teaching. Preference given to nontraditional students with at least two years of teaching experience. Preference given to students of Hawaiian ethnicity. Applicants must have permanent address in Hawaii. Amount and number of awards vary and may change yearly.
   Application deadline: February 15

Contact:
Hawaii Community Foundation Scholarships
827 Fort Street Mall
Honolulu, HI 96813
Phone: 808-537-6333
Fax: 808-521-6286
Web: www.hawaiicommunityfoundation.org

Dr. Hans and Clara Zimmerman Foundation Health Scholarship

Type of award: Scholarship, renewable.
Intended use: For full-time junior, senior or graduate study at accredited postsecondary institution in United States.
Eligibility: Applicant must be U.S. citizen or permanent resident residing in Hawaii.
Basis for selection: Major/career interest in health sciences; health-related professions or medicine. Applicant must demonstrate financial need, high academic achievement and depth of character.
Application requirements: Transcript. FAFSA and SAR, SAT/ACT scores. Personal statement including description of applicant's community service projects or activities.
Additional information: Minimum 3.0 GPA. Applicants must have permanent address in Hawaii. Applicants who take up mainland residency must have relatives living in Hawaii. Sports medicine and some psychology majors ineligible. Amount and number of awards vary.

  Application deadline: February 15
  Total amount awarded: $567,605
Contact:
Hawaii Community Foundation Scholarships
827 Fort Street Mall
Honolulu, HI 96813
Phone: 888-731-3863
Web: www.hawaiicommunityfoundation.org

Eastside & Northshore Kauai Scholarship Fund

Type of award: Scholarship.
Intended use: For full-time undergraduate or graduate study at accredited 2-year or 4-year institution in United States.
Eligibility: Applicant must be U.S. citizen residing in Hawaii.
Basis for selection: Applicant must demonstrate financial need, high academic achievement and depth of character.
Application requirements: Recommendations, essay, transcript. SAR, FAFSA, Personal Statement, SAT/ACT scores.
Additional information: Minimum 2.5 GPA. Must be resident of one of the following East and Northshore Kaua'i areas: Anahola (96703), Kapa'a (96746), Kilauea (96754), Hanalei (96714), Princeville (96722), Kealia (96751), Wailua (96746).

  Application deadline: February 15
Contact:
Hawaii Community Foundation Scholarships
827 Fort Street Mall
Honolulu, HI 96813
Phone: 888-731-3863
Web: www.hawaiicommunityfoundation.org

Edward J. and Norma Doty Scholarship

Type of award: Scholarship.
Intended use: For full-time junior, senior or graduate study at accredited 2-year or 4-year institution in United States.

Eligibility: Applicant must be U.S. citizen or permanent resident residing in Hawaii.
Basis for selection: Major/career interest in medicine. Applicant must demonstrate financial need, high academic achievement and depth of character.
Application requirements: Essay, transcript. FAFSA and SAR, SAT/ACT scores.
Additional information: Minimum 2.7 GPA. Preference given to students specializing in geriatric medicine or Alzheimer's care. Applicants must have permanent address in Hawaii. Applicants taking up mainland residency must have relatives living in Hawaii. Amount of award may change yearly.

  Application deadline: February 15
Contact:
Hawaii Community Foundation Scholarships
827 Fort Street Mall
Honolulu, HI 96813
Phone: 808-537-6333
Fax: 808-521-6286
Web: www.hawaiicommunityfoundation.org

Edward Payson and Bernice Pi'ilani Irwin Scholarship Trust Fund

Type of award: Scholarship.
Intended use: For full-time junior, senior or graduate study at accredited 4-year institution in United States.
Eligibility: Applicant must be U.S. citizen or permanent resident residing in Hawaii.
Basis for selection: Major/career interest in journalism or communications. Applicant must demonstrate financial need, high academic achievement and depth of character.
Application requirements: Essay, transcript. FAFSA and SAR, SAT/ACT scores.
Additional information: Minimum 2.7 GPA. Must have permanent address in Hawaii. Applicants who take up mainland residency must have relatives living in Hawaii. Amount and number of awards vary and may change yearly.

  Application deadline: February 15
Contact:
Hawaii Community Foundation Scholarships
827 Fort Street Mall
Honolulu, HI 96813
Phone: 888-731-3863
Web: www.hawaiicommunityfoundation.org

E.E. Black Scholarship

Type of award: Scholarship, renewable.
Intended use: For full-time undergraduate study at accredited postsecondary institution in United States.
Eligibility: Applicant must be U.S. citizen or permanent resident residing in Hawaii.
Basis for selection: Applicant must demonstrate financial need, high academic achievement and depth of character.
Application requirements: Essay, transcript. FAFSA and SAR, SAT/ACT scores. Name of Tesoro employee and relationship.
Additional information: Minimum 3.0 GPA. Must be dependent of an employee of Tesoro Hawaii or its subsidiaries. Applicants must have permanent address in Hawaii. Applicants who take up mainland residency must have relatives living in Hawaii. Amount and number of awards vary.

  Application deadline: February 15

Scholarships

Contact:
Hawaii Community Foundation Scholarships
827 Fort Street Mall
Honolulu, HI 96813
Phone: 888-731-3863
Web: www.hawaiicommunityfoundation.org

Elena Albano Maka'alohilohi Scholarship Fund

Type of award: Scholarship.
Intended use: For full-time undergraduate or graduate study at accredited 2-year or 4-year institution in United States.
Eligibility: Applicant must be U.S. citizen residing in Hawaii.
Basis for selection: Applicant must demonstrate financial need, high academic achievement and depth of character.
Application requirements: Recommendations, essay, transcript. SAR, FAFSA, SAT/ACT scores, personal statement. Two letters of recommendation from mentors, teachers, counselors, or other mental health professionals.
Additional information: Minimum 2.7 GPA. Must be in recovery from mental health/behavioral/psychological disability. Must be resident of Maui county. Preference given to students of Hawaiian ancestry and renewal applicants. Applicants must have permanent address in Hawaii. Applicants taking up mainland residency must have relatives living in Hawaii. Amount of award may change yearly.
  Application deadline: February 15
Contact:
Hawaii Community Foundation Scholarships
827 Fort Street Mall
Honolulu, HI 96813
Phone: 888-731-3863
Web: www.hawaiicommunityfoundation.org

Ellen Hamada Fashion Design Scholarship

Type of award: Scholarship.
Intended use: For full-time undergraduate study at 2-year institution in United States. Designated institutions: University of Hawaii community colleges.
Eligibility: Applicant must be residing in Hawaii.
Basis for selection: Major/career interest in fashion/fashion design/modeling. Applicant must demonstrate financial need and high academic achievement.
Application requirements: Recommendations, essay, transcript. SAR, FAFSA, SAT/ACT scores.
Additional information: Minimum 2.7 GPA. Must pursue an AS or AAS degree.
  Application deadline: February 15
Contact:
Hawaii Community Foundation
827 Fort Street Mall
Honolulu, HI 96813
Phone: 888-731-3863
Web: www.hawaiicommunityfoundation.org

Ellison Onizuka Memorial Scholarship

Type of award: Scholarship.
Intended use: For full-time undergraduate study at accredited 4-year institution in United States.
Eligibility: Applicant must be high school senior. Applicant must be U.S. citizen or permanent resident residing in Hawaii.
Basis for selection: Major/career interest in aerospace. Applicant must demonstrate financial need and depth of character.
Application requirements: Recommendations, transcript. SAT/ACT scores, FAFSA, SAR and personal statement describing extracurricular activities, club affiliations, and community service projects.
Additional information: Minimum 3.0 GPA. Applicants must have permanent address in Hawaii. Applicants who take up mainland residency must have relatives living in Hawaii. Amount and number of awards vary.
  Application deadline: February 15
Contact:
Hawaii Community Foundation Scholarships
827 Fort Street Mall
Honolulu, HI 96813
Phone: 888-731-3863
Web: www.hawaiicommunityfoundation.org

Esther Kanagawa Memorial Art Scholarship

Type of award: Scholarship.
Intended use: For full-time undergraduate or graduate study at accredited 2-year or 4-year institution in United States.
Eligibility: Applicant must be high school senior. Applicant must be U.S. citizen or permanent resident residing in Hawaii.
Basis for selection: Major/career interest in arts, general. Applicant must demonstrate financial need, high academic achievement and depth of character.
Application requirements: Essay, transcript. FAFSA and SAR, SAT/ACT scores.
Additional information: Minimum 2.7 GPA. Must major in fine art, drawing, painting, sculpture, ceramics, or photography. Applicants must have permanent address in Hawaii. Applicants taking up mainland residency must have relatives living in Hawaii. Amount of award varies yearly.
  Application deadline: February 15
Contact:
Hawaii Community Foundation Scholarships
827 Fort Street Mall
Honolulu, HI 96813
Phone: 888-731-3863
Web: www.hawaiicommunityfoundation.org

F. Koehnen Ltd. Scholarship Fund

Type of award: Scholarship.
Intended use: For full-time undergraduate or graduate study at accredited 4-year institution in United States.
Eligibility: Applicant must be U.S. citizen residing in Hawaii.
Basis for selection: Applicant must demonstrate financial need, high academic achievement and depth of character.
Application requirements: Recommendations, essay, transcript. SAR, FAFSA, SAT/ACT scores, Personal Statement. Name of employee, retail establishment and phone number of human resources department of retail establishment.
Additional information: Minimum 2.5 GPA. Must be graduate of high school on island of Hawaii. Must be son, daughter, or grandchild of employee of retail establishment on island of Hawaii.
  Application deadline: February 15
Contact:
Hawaii Community Foundation Scholarships
827 Fort Street Mall
Honolulu, HI 96813
Phone: 888-731-3863
Web: www.hawaiicommunityfoundation.org

Scholarships

Filipino Nurses' Organization of Hawaii Scholarship

Type of award: Scholarship.
Intended use: For full-time undergraduate or graduate study at accredited 2-year, 4-year or graduate institution in United States.
Eligibility: Applicant must be of Filipino ancestry. Applicant must be U.S. citizen or permanent resident residing in Hawaii.
Basis for selection: Major/career interest in nursing. Applicant must demonstrate financial need, high academic achievement, depth of character and service orientation.
Application requirements: Essay, transcript. FAFSA and SAR, SAT/ACT scores.
Additional information: Minimum 2.7 GPA. Must have permanent address in Hawaii. Applicants taking up mainland residency must have relatives living in Hawaii. Amount of award may vary yearly.
  Application deadline: February 15
Contact:
Hawaii Community Foundation Scholarships
827 Fort Street Mall
Honolulu, HI 96813
Phone: 888-731-3863
Web: www.hawaiicommunityfoundation.org

Financial Women International Scholarship

Type of award: Scholarship.
Intended use: For full-time junior, senior or graduate study at accredited 4-year institution in United States.
Eligibility: Applicant must be female. Applicant must be U.S. citizen or permanent resident residing in Hawaii.
Basis for selection: Major/career interest in business. Applicant must demonstrate financial need, high academic achievement and depth of character.
Application requirements: Essay, transcript. FAFSA and SAR, SAT/ACT scores.
Additional information: Minimum 3.5 GPA. Applicant must have permanent address in Hawaii. Applicants taking up mainland residency must have relatives living in Hawaii. Amount of award may change yearly.
  Application deadline: February 15
Contact:
Hawaii Community Foundation Scholarships
827 Fort Street Mall
Honolulu, HI 96813
Phone: 888-731-3863
Web: www.hawaiicommunityfoundation.org

Fletcher & Fritzi Hoffmann Education Fund

Type of award: Scholarship.
Intended use: For full-time undergraduate study at accredited vocational or 2-year institution. Designated institutions: Community colleges on island of Hawaii.
Eligibility: Applicant must be U.S. citizen or permanent resident residing in Hawaii.
Basis for selection: Applicant must demonstrate financial need, high academic achievement and depth of character.
Application requirements: Essay, transcript. FAFSA and SAR, SAT/ACT scores. Personal statement must include information on family's history and roots in the Hamakua area.
Additional information: Minimum 2.7 GPA. Preference given to Honoka'a high school graduates. Must be longtime resident

of Hamakua Coast in 96727 zip code in Hawaii. Amount of award may change yearly.
  Application deadline: February 15
Contact:
Hawaii Community Foundation Scholarships
827 Fort Street Mall
Suite 80
Honolulu, HI 96813
Phone: 888-731-3863
Web: www.hawaiicommunityfoundation.org

Frances S. Watanabe Memorial Scholarship

Type of award: Scholarship.
Intended use: For full-time undergraduate or graduate study at accredited 2-year institution in United States. Designated institutions: University of Hawaii community colleges.
Eligibility: Applicant must be U.S. citizen or permanent resident residing in Hawaii.
Basis for selection: Applicant must demonstrate financial need, high academic achievement and depth of character.
Application requirements: Essay, transcript. FAFSA, SAR, SAT/ACT scores.
Additional information: Minimum 2.7 GPA required. Must be member of Hawaii USA Federal Credit Union. Must be enrolled in AS or AAS career and technical degree in University of Hawaii community college system. Applicants must have permanent address in Hawaii. Applicants who take up mainland residency must have relatives living in Hawaii.
  Application deadline: February 15
Contact:
Hawaii Community Foundation Scholarships
827 Fort Street Mall
Honolulu, HI 96813
Phone: 888-731-3863
Web: www.hawaiicommunityfoundation.org

GEAR UP Scholars Scholarship

Type of award: Scholarship.
Intended use: For full-time undergraduate study at accredited 2-year or 4-year institution in United States.
Eligibility: Applicant must be residing in Hawaii.
Basis for selection: Applicant must demonstrate financial need and high academic achievement.
Application requirements: Essay, transcript. FAFSA and SAR, SAT/ACT scores.
Additional information: Minimum 2.7 GPA. Must be Gear Up scholar. Must have earned a State of Hawaii Board of Education Recognition Diploma.
  Application deadline: February 15
Contact:
Hawaii Community Foundation
827 Fort Street Mall
Honolulu, HI 96813
Phone: 888-731-3863
Web: www.hawaiicommunityfoundation.org

GEAR UP Tuition Assistance Trust Scholarship

Type of award: Scholarship.
Intended use: For full-time undergraduate study at accredited 2-year or 4-year institution in United States.
Eligibility: Applicant must be high school senior. Applicant must be U.S. citizen residing in Hawaii.

Basis for selection: Applicant must demonstrate financial need and high academic achievement.

Application requirements: Essay, transcript. FAFSA and SAR, ACT/SAT scores.

Additional information: Minimum 2.0 GPA. Must be a GEAR UP scholar who submitted a completed Step Up pledge from while attending a title 1 school. Must have earned a State of Hawaii Board of Education Recognition Diploma. Must be eligible for Pell Grant. Priority given to those studying in state of Hawaii. Amount and number of awards vary and may change yearly.

Application deadline: February 15

Contact:
Hawaii Community Foundation
827 Fort Street Mall
Honolulu, HI 96813
Phone: 888-731-3863
Web: www.hawaiicommunityfoundation.org

George & Augusta Rapozo Kama'aina Scholarship Fund

Type of award: Scholarship.

Intended use: For undergraduate study at accredited 2-year or 4-year institution.

Eligibility: Applicant must be residing in Hawaii.

Basis for selection: Applicant must demonstrate high academic achievement.

Application requirements: Recommendations, essay, transcript. FAFSA and SAR, SAT/ACT scores. Essay about family ties to Kauai or Ni'ihau and work, family, military and other commitments.

Additional information: Minimum 2.7 GPA. Must be graduate of Kauai or Ni'ihau high school or charter school. Preference given to Ni'ihau residents. Amount and number of awards vary and may change yearly.

Application deadline: February 15

Contact:
Hawaii Community Foundation
827 Fort Street Mall
Honolulu, HI 96813
Phone: 888-731-3863
Web: www.hawaiicommunityfoundation.org

George & Lucille Cushnie Scholarship

Type of award: Scholarship, renewable.

Intended use: For full-time undergraduate or graduate study at accredited 2-year, 4-year or graduate institution in United States.

Eligibility: Applicant must be U.S. citizen or permanent resident residing in Hawaii.

Basis for selection: Major/career interest in medicine. Applicant must demonstrate financial need, high academic achievement and depth of character.

Application requirements: Essay, transcript. FAFSA and SAR, SAT/ACT scores.

Additional information: Preference given to students from the island of Hawaii. Minimum 2.7 GPA.

Application deadline: February 15

Contact:
Hawaii Community Foundation
827 Fort Street Mall
Honolulu, HI 96813
Phone: 888-731-3863
Web: www.hawaiicommunityfoundation.org

George Mason Business Scholarship Fund

Type of award: Scholarship.

Intended use: For full-time senior study at accredited 4-year institution. Designated institutions: Universities and colleges in Hawaii.

Eligibility: Applicant must be residing in Hawaii.

Basis for selection: Major/career interest in business or business/management/administration. Applicant must demonstrate financial need, high academic achievement and depth of character.

Application requirements: Essay, transcript. FAFSA and SAR, SAT/ACT scores. Essay must state why you have chosen business as an intended career and how you expect to make a difference in the business world.

Additional information: Minimum 3.0 GPA. Applicant must have permanent Hawaii address.

Application deadline: February 15

Contact:
Hawaii Community Foundation Scholarships
827 Fort Street Mall
Honolulu, HA 96813
Phone: 888-731-3863
Web: www.hawaiicommunityfoundation.org

George S. Ishiyama Unicold Scholarship

Type of award: Scholarship, renewable.

Intended use: For full-time undergraduate or graduate study at accredited 2-year, 4-year or graduate institution in United States.

Eligibility: Applicant must be at least 17, no older than 24.

Basis for selection: Applicant must demonstrate financial need, high academic achievement and depth of character.

Application requirements: Essay, transcript. FAFSA and SAR, SAT/ACT scores.

Additional information: Must be child of Unicold Employee from the Oakland, Honolulu & Los Angeles offices with minimum one year of service by application deadline. Must maintain 2.7-3.5 GPA. Preference given to first-generation college students and renewal applicants.

Application deadline: February 15

Contact:
Hawaii Community Foundation
827 Fort Street Mall
Honolulu, HI 96813
Phone: 888-731-3863
Web: www.hawaiicommunityfoundation.org

Gerrit R. Ludwig Scholarship

Type of award: Scholarship.

Intended use: For full-time undergraduate or graduate study at accredited 4-year or graduate institution.

Eligibility: Applicant must be residing in Hawaii.

Basis for selection: Major/career interest in classics or arts, general. Applicant must demonstrate financial need, high academic achievement and depth of character.

Application requirements: Essay, transcript. FAFSA and SAR, SAT/ACT scores.

Additional information: Minimum 2.5 GPA. Preference given to applicants pursuing a degree in fine arts or classics. Must be graduate from East Hawaii public school: Hilo, Honoka'a, Ka'u, Kea'au, Laupahoehoe, Pahoa, Waiakea and Hawaii

Academy of Arts and Science. Applicants taking up mainland residency must have relatives living in Hawaii.

Application deadline: February 15

Contact:
Hawaii Community Foundation Scholarships
827 Fort Street Mall
Honolulu, HI 96813
Phone: 888-731-3863
Web: www.hawaiicommunityfoundation.org

Good Eats Scholarship Fund

Type of award: Scholarship.
Intended use: For full-time undergraduate or graduate study at accredited vocational, 2-year or 4-year institution in United States.
Eligibility: Applicant must be U.S. citizen residing in Hawaii.
Basis for selection: Major/career interest in culinary arts; agriculture or food production/management/services. Applicant must demonstrate financial need, high academic achievement and depth of character.
Application requirements: Recommendations, essay, transcript. SAR, FAFSA, SAT/ACT scores, personal statement discussing activities that demonstrate interest in food production and preparation.
Additional information: Minimum 2.7 GPA. Must pursue post high school studies in culinary arts or agriculture. Must demonstrate interest in food production and preparation through participation in related classes, clubs, and activities.

Application deadline: February 15

Contact:
Hawaii Community Foundation Scholarships
827 Fort Street Mall
Honolulu, HI 96813
Phone: 888-731-3863
Web: www.hawaiicommunityfoundation.org

Grace Pacific Outstanding Scholars Fund

Type of award: Scholarship.
Intended use: For full-time undergraduate or graduate study at accredited 2-year or 4-year institution in United States.
Eligibility: Applicant must be high school senior. Applicant must be U.S. citizen residing in Hawaii.
Basis for selection: Applicant must demonstrate financial need, high academic achievement and depth of character.
Application requirements: Recommendations, essay, transcript. SAR, FAFSA, personal statement, SAT/ACT scores.
Additional information: Minimum 2.7 GPA. Must be former participant of Grace Pacific Outstanding Keiki Scholars Program. Must be high school senior or previous recipient of scholarship. Applicants must have permanent address in Hawaii. Applicants taking up mainland residency must have relatives living in Hawaii. Amount of award may change yearly.

Application deadline: February 15

Contact:
Hawaii Community Foundation Scholarships
827 Fort Street Mall
Honolulu, HI 96813
Phone: 888-731-3863
Web: www.hawaiicommunityfoundation.org

Guy Marshall Scholarship Fund

Type of award: Scholarship.
Intended use: For full-time freshman study at accredited 4-year institution in United States.
Eligibility: Applicant must be high school senior. Applicant must be U.S. citizen residing in Hawaii.
Basis for selection: Applicant must demonstrate financial need, high academic achievement and depth of character.
Application requirements: Recommendations, essay, transcript. SAR, FAFSA, personal statement, SAT/ACT scores.
Additional information: Must have 3.3 to 3.5 GPA. Must plan to attend college in continental United States. Must be graduate of Hawaii high school.

Application deadline: February 15

Contact:
Hawaii Community Foundation Scholarships
827 Fort Street Mall
Honolulu, HI 96813
Phone: 888-731-3863
Web: www.hawaiicommunityfoundation.org

Guy Toyama Memorial Scholarship

Type of award: Scholarship.
Intended use: For full-time undergraduate study at accredited 2-year or 4-year institution.
Eligibility: Applicant must be U.S. citizen residing in Hawaii.
Basis for selection: Applicant must demonstrate financial need and high academic achievement.
Application requirements: Essay, transcript. FAFSA and SAR, ACT/SAT scores.
Additional information: Minimum 2.7 GPA. Must be interested in fields related to sustainability. Preference given to renewal applicants.

Application deadline: February 15

Contact:
Hawaii Community Foundation
827 Fort Street Mall
Honolulu, HI 96813
Phone: 888-731-3863
Web: www.hawaiicommunityfoundation.org

Haseko Training Fund

Type of award: Scholarship.
Intended use: For full-time undergraduate study at accredited 2-year institution. Designated institutions: University of Hawaii community colleges.
Eligibility: Applicant must be residing in Hawaii.
Basis for selection: Applicant must demonstrate financial need and high academic achievement.
Application requirements: Recommendations, essay, transcript. SAR, FAFSA, SAT/ACT scores.
Additional information: Minimum 2.7 GPA. Must be Ewa Beach resident. Must enroll in AS or AAS career and technical degree program within University of Hawaii community college system. Preference given to student in marine-related program.

Application deadline: February 15

Contact:
Hawaii Community Foundation
827 Fort Street Mall
Honolulu, HI 96813
Phone: 888-731-3863
Web: www.hawaiicommunityfoundation.org

Scholarships

Hawaii GEAR UP Scholars Program

Type of award: Scholarship.
Intended use: For full-time undergraduate or graduate study at accredited postsecondary institution.
Eligibility: Applicant must be residing in Hawaii.
Basis for selection: Applicant must demonstrate financial need and high academic achievement.
Application requirements: Recommendations, essay, transcript. SAR, FAFSA, SAT/ACT scores.
Additional information: Minimum 3.0 GPA. Must be 2009 high school graduate. Must be Gear Up scholar and earn State of Hawaii Board of Education Recognition Diploma. Must be eligible for Pell Grant.
  Application deadline: February 15
Contact:
Hawaii Community Foundation
827 Fort Street Mall
Honolulu, HI 96813
Phone: 888-731-3863
Web: www.hawaiicommunityfoundation.org

Hawaii Pacific Gerontological Society Nursing Scholarship Fund

Type of award: Scholarship.
Intended use: For full-time undergraduate or graduate study at accredited 2-year or 4-year institution in United States. Designated institutions: Two- or four-year colleges in Hawaii.
Eligibility: Applicant must be U.S. citizen residing in Hawaii.
Basis for selection: Major/career interest in nursing. Applicant must demonstrate financial need, high academic achievement and depth of character.
Application requirements: Recommendations, essay, transcript. SAR, FAFSA, SAT/ACT scores, essay explaining interest in geriatric nursing.
Additional information: Minimum 2.7 GPA. Must pursue an LN or RN degree with interest in geriatric nursing.
  Application deadline: February 15
Contact:
Hawaii Community Foundation Scholarships
827 Fort Street Mall
Honolulu, HI 96813
Phone: 888-731-3863
Web: www.hawaiicommunityfoundation.org

Hawaii Pizza Hut Scholarship Fund

Type of award: Scholarship.
Intended use: For full-time undergraduate study at accredited 2-year or 4-year institution in United States.
Eligibility: Applicant must be U.S. citizen residing in Hawaii.
Basis for selection: Applicant must demonstrate financial need, high academic achievement and depth of character.
Application requirements: Recommendations, essay, transcript. SAR, FAFSA, personal statement, SAT/ACT scores.
Additional information: GPA must be between 3.0 and 3.5. Preference given to renewals.
  Application deadline: February 15
Contact:
Hawaii Community Foundation Scholarships
827 Fort Street Mall
Honolulu, HI 96813
Phone: 888-731-3863
Web: www.hawaiicommunityfoundation.org

Hawaii Society of Certified Public Accountants Scholarship Fund

Type of award: Scholarship.
Intended use: For full-time junior, senior or graduate study at 4-year institution in United States. Designated institutions: Four-year colleges and universities in Hawaii.
Eligibility: Applicant must be U.S. citizen residing in Hawaii.
Basis for selection: Major/career interest in accounting. Applicant must demonstrate financial need, high academic achievement and depth of character.
Application requirements: Recommendations, essay, transcript. SAR, FAFSA, SAT/ACT scores, personal statement should include description of extracurricular activities, involvement in professional, civic and social organizations, and employment history.
Additional information: Minimum 3.0 GPA. Must have already completed two or more 300-level accounting courses. Preference given to students involved in Accounting Club.
  Application deadline: February 15
Contact:
Hawaii Community Foundation Scholarships
827 Fort Street Mall
Honolulu, HI 96813
Phone: 888-731-3863
Web: www.hawaiicommunityfoundation.org

H.C. Shipman Vocational Scholarship Fund

Type of award: Scholarship.
Intended use: For full-time undergraduate study at accredited vocational or 2-year institution in United States. Designated institutions: University of Hawaii community colleges.
Eligibility: Applicant must be residing in Hawaii.
Basis for selection: Applicant must demonstrate high academic achievement.
Application requirements: Recommendations, essay, transcript. FAFSA and SAR, SAT/ACT scores.
Additional information: Minimum 2.0 GPA. Must be graduate of Kea'au High School or KeKula 'O Nawahiokalani'opu'u, Iki Laboratory Public Charter School. Must enroll in AS or AA career and technical degree program in University of Hawaii Community College system. Amount and number of awards vary and may change yearly.
  Application deadline: February 15
Contact:
Hawaii Community Foundation
827 Fort Street Mall
Honolulu, HI 96813
Phone: 888-731-3863
Web: www.hawaiicommunityfoundation.org

Henry A. Zuberano Scholarship

Type of award: Scholarship.
Intended use: For full-time undergraduate study at accredited 2-year or 4-year institution.
Eligibility: Applicant must be residing in Hawaii.
Basis for selection: Major/career interest in political science/ government; international relations; business, international or public administration/service. Applicant must demonstrate financial need, high academic achievement and depth of character.
Application requirements: Essay, transcript. FAFSA and SAR, SAT/ACT scores.

Additional information: Minimum 2.7 GPA. Applicant must have permanent Hawaii address. Applicants taking up mainland residency must have relatives living in Hawaii. Preference given to previous recipients.

Application deadline: February 15

Contact:
Hawaii Community Foundation Scholarships
827 Fort Street Mall
Honolulu, HI 96813
Phone: 888-731-3863
Web: www.hawaiicommunityfoundation.org

Henry and Dorothy Castle Memorial Fund Scholarship

Type of award: Scholarship, renewable.
Intended use: For full-time undergraduate or graduate study at accredited 2-year, 4-year or graduate institution in United States.
Eligibility: Applicant must be U.S. citizen or permanent resident residing in Hawaii.
Basis for selection: Major/career interest in education, early childhood. Applicant must demonstrate financial need, high academic achievement and depth of character.
Application requirements: Essay, transcript. FAFSA and SAR, SAT/ACT scores. Essay stating interests and goals in early childhood education, and plans to contribute to field.
Additional information: Minimum 2.7 GPA required. Applicants must have permanent address in Hawaii. Applicants who take up mainland residency must have relatives living in Hawaii. Amount and number of awards vary and may change yearly.

Application deadline: February 15

Contact:
Hawaii Community Foundation Scholarships
827 Fort Street Mall
Honolulu, HI 96813
Phone: 888-731-3863
Web: www.hawaiicommunityfoundation.org

Herbert & Ollie Brook Fund

Type of award: Scholarship.
Intended use: For full-time undergraduate or graduate study at accredited 2-year, 4-year or graduate institution in United States.
Eligibility: Applicant must be high school senior. Applicant must be U.S. citizen residing in Hawaii.
Basis for selection: Applicant must demonstrate financial need, high academic achievement and depth of character.
Application requirements: Recommendations, essay, transcript. SAR, FAFSA, personal statement, SAT/ACT scores.
Additional information: Minimum 2.7 GPA. Must be high school senior in Maui County. Preference given to those who plan to return to Maui County after completing education to contribute to community.

Application deadline: February 15

Contact:
Hawaii Community Foundation Scholarships
827 Fort Street Mall
Honolulu, HI 96813
Phone: 888-731-3863
Web: www.hawaiicommunityfoundation.org

Hew-Shinn Scholarship Fund

Type of award: Scholarship.
Intended use: For full-time undergraduate study at accredited vocational or 2-year institution in United States. Designated institutions: University of Hawaii community colleges.
Eligibility: Applicant must be residing in Hawaii.
Basis for selection: Applicant must demonstrate financial need and high academic achievement.
Application requirements: Recommendations, essay, transcript. SAR, FAFSA, SAT/ACT scores.
Additional information: Minimum 2.7 GPA. Must be Maui county resident enrolled in vocational program in the University of Hawaii Community College system.

Application deadline: February 15

Contact:
Hawaii Community Foundation Scholarships
827 Fort Street Mall
Honolulu, HI 96813
Phone: 888-731-3863
Web: www.hawaiicommunityfoundation.org

Hideko & Zenzo Matsuyama Scholarship Fund

Type of award: Scholarship.
Intended use: For full-time undergraduate or graduate study at accredited 2-year or 4-year institution in United States.
Eligibility: Applicant must be U.S. citizen residing in Hawaii.
Basis for selection: Applicant must demonstrate financial need, high academic achievement and depth of character.
Application requirements: Recommendations, essay, transcript. SAR, FAFSA, personal statement, SAT/ACT scores.
Additional information: Minimum 3.0 GPA. Must be graduate of high school in Hawaii or have received GED in Hawaii. Preference given to students of Japanese ancestry born in Hawaii.

Application deadline: February 15

Contact:
Hawaii Community Foundation Scholarships
827 Fort Street Mall
Honolulu, HI 96813
Phone: 888-731-3863
Web: www.hawaiicommunityfoundation.org

Hilo Chinese School Scholarship

Type of award: Scholarship.
Intended use: For full-time undergraduate or graduate study at accredited 2-year or 4-year institution in United States.
Eligibility: Applicant must be U.S. citizen residing in Hawaii.
Basis for selection: Applicant must demonstrate financial need, high academic achievement and depth of character.
Application requirements: Recommendations, essay, transcript. SAR, FAFSA, personal statement, SAT/ACT scores.
Additional information: Minimum 2.5 GPA. Must be resident of Hawaii island. Preference given to descendants of Hilo Chinese School alumni and students of Chinese ancestry.

Application deadline: February 15

Contact:
Hawaii Community Foundation Scholarships
827 Fort Street Mall
Honolulu, HI 96813
Phone: 888-731-3863
Web: www.hawaiicommunityfoundation.org

Scholarships

Hoku Scholarship Fund

Type of award: Scholarship.
Intended use: For full-time undergraduate or graduate study at accredited 2-year or 4-year institution.
Eligibility: Applicant must be residing in Hawaii.
Basis for selection: Major/career interest in physics; astronomy; mathematics; engineering; technology or computer/information sciences. Applicant must demonstrate high academic achievement.
Application requirements: Recommendations, essay, transcript. FAFSA and SAR, SAT/ACT scores.
Additional information: Minimum 3.0 GPA. Must have stated interest in observatory career. Amount and number of awards vary and may change yearly.
  Application deadline: February 15
Contact:
Hawaii Community Foundation
827 Fort Street Mall
Honolulu, HI 96813
Phone: 888-731-3863
Web: www.hawaiicommunityfoundation.org

Hokulani Hawaii Fund

Type of award: Scholarship.
Intended use: For full-time undergraduate study at 4-year institution in United States. Designated institutions: Private institutions on U.S. mainland. Preference given to small, private institutions with strong core liberal arts and science programs.
Eligibility: Applicant must be U.S. citizen residing in Hawaii.
Basis for selection: Applicant must demonstrate financial need and high academic achievement.
Application requirements: Recommendations, essay, transcript. FAFSA and SAR, SAT/ACT scores.
Additional information: GPA must be between 2.9 and 3.4. Must be graduate of private high school in Hawaii within last three years. Preference given to first generation college students from middle income families. Amount and number of awards vary and may change yearly.
  Application deadline: February 15
Contact:
Hawaii Community Foundation
827 Fort Street Mall
Honolulu, HI 96813
Phone: 888-731-3863
Web: www.hawaiicommunityfoundation.org

Hokuli'a Foundation Scholarship Fund

Type of award: Scholarship.
Intended use: For full-time undergraduate or graduate study at accredited 2-year or 4-year institution in United States.
Eligibility: Applicant must be U.S. citizen residing in Hawaii.
Basis for selection: Major/career interest in health-related professions; education or social work. Applicant must demonstrate financial need, high academic achievement, depth of character and service orientation.
Application requirements: Recommendations, essay, transcript. SAR, FAFSA, SAT/ACT scores, personal statement should include record of community service and how future career will benefit Hawaii residents and state intentions to stay or return to Hawaii after graduation.
Additional information: Minimum 2.7 GPA. Must be resident of South or North Kona. Preference given to students demonstrating emphasis in advancing native Hawaiian culture.

  Application deadline: February 15
Contact:
Hawaii Community Foundation Scholarships
827 Fort Street Mall
Honolulu, HI 96813
Phone: 888-731-3863
Web: www.hawaiicommunityfoundation.org

Hon Chew Hee Scholarship Fund

Type of award: Scholarship.
Intended use: For full-time undergraduate or graduate study at accredited 2-year or 4-year institution in United States.
Eligibility: Applicant must be U.S. citizen residing in Hawaii.
Basis for selection: Major/career interest in art/art history. Applicant must demonstrate financial need, high academic achievement and depth of character.
Application requirements: Recommendations, essay, transcript. SAR, FAFSA, SAT/ACT scores, personal statement. Two letters of recommendation required. One must be from an art instructor.
Additional information: Minimum 2.7 GPA. Major in fine arts with preference given to students focusing on painting, drawing, sculpting, ceramics, printmaking, and textiles.
  Application deadline: February 15
Contact:
Hawaii Community Foundation Scholarships
827 Fort Street Mall
Honolulu, HI 96813
Phone: 888-731-3863
Web: www.hawaiicommunityfoundation.org

Ho'omaka Hou - A New Beginning Fund

Type of award: Scholarship.
Intended use: For full-time undergraduate or graduate study at accredited 2-year or 4-year institution in United States.
Eligibility: Applicant must be U.S. citizen residing in Hawaii.
Basis for selection: Applicant must demonstrate financial need, high academic achievement and depth of character.
Application requirements: Recommendations, essay, transcript. SAR, FAFSA, SAT/ACT scores, personal statement should describe substance abuse problems and how they were overcome.
Additional information: Minimum 2.7 GPA. Applicant must have overcome substance abuse.
  Application deadline: February 15
Contact:
Hawaii Community Foundation Scholarships
827 Fort Street Mall
Honolulu, HI 96813
Phone: 888-731-3863
Web: www.hawaiicommunityfoundation.org

Ian Doane Smith Memorial Scholarship Fund

Type of award: Scholarship.
Intended use: For full-time undergraduate or graduate study at accredited 2-year or 4-year institution in United States.
Eligibility: Applicant must be high school senior. Applicant must be U.S. citizen residing in Hawaii.
Basis for selection: Applicant must demonstrate financial need, high academic achievement, depth of character and service orientation.

Application requirements: Recommendations, essay, transcript. SAR, FAFSA, SAT/ACT scores, personal statement must detail community service and experiences with surfing or soccer.
Additional information: Minimum 2.7 GPA. Must be resident of island of Maui. Must be active in soccer and/or surfing.
  Application deadline: February 15
Contact:
Hawaii Community Foundation Scholarships
827 Fort Street Mall
Honolulu, HI 96813
Phone: 888-731-3863
Web: www.hawaiicommunityfoundation.org

Ichiro & Masako Hirata Scholarship

Type of award: Scholarship.
Intended use: For full-time junior, senior or graduate study at accredited postsecondary institution.
Eligibility: Applicant must be residing in Hawaii.
Basis for selection: Major/career interest in education. Applicant must demonstrate financial need and high academic achievement.
Application requirements: Recommendations, essay, transcript. SAR, FAFSA, SAT/ACT scores.
Additional information: Minimum 3.0 GPA. Preference given to past recipients.
  Application deadline: February 15
Contact:
Hawaii Community Foundation
827 Fort Street Mall
Honolulu, HI 96813
Phone: 888-731-3863
Web: www.hawaiicommunityfoundation.org

Ida M. Pope Memorial Scholarship

Type of award: Scholarship.
Intended use: For full-time undergraduate or graduate study at accredited 2-year or 4-year institution in United States.
Eligibility: Applicant must be Native Hawaiian/Pacific Islander. Applicant must be female. Applicant must be U.S. citizen residing in Hawaii.
Basis for selection: Major/career interest in health-related professions; science, general; education or mathematics. Applicant must demonstrate high academic achievement and depth of character.
Application requirements: Recommendations, essay, transcript. SAR, FAFSA, personal statement, SAT/ACT scores, birth certificate.
Additional information: Minimum 3.5 GPA. Must be of Hawaiian descent.
  Application deadline: February 15
Contact:
Hawaii Community Foundation Scholarships
827 Fort Street Mall
Honolulu, HI 96813
Phone: 888-731-3863
Web: www.hawaiicommunityfoundation.org

Isemoto Contracting Co., Ltd. Scholarship Fund

Type of award: Scholarship.
Intended use: For full-time sophomore, junior, senior or graduate study at accredited 2-year or 4-year institution in United States.
Eligibility: Applicant must be U.S. citizen residing in Hawaii.

Basis for selection: Major/career interest in engineering; nursing or education. Applicant must demonstrate financial need, high academic achievement and depth of character.
Application requirements: Recommendations, essay, transcript. SAR, FAFSA, personal statement, SAT/ACT scores.
Additional information: Minimum 2.7 GPA. Must be graduate of high school on island of Hawaii. Must be accepted as upper classman to a school of engineering, teacher education program, or nursing program.
  Application deadline: February 15
Contact:
Hawaii Community Foundation Scholarships
827 Fort Street Mall
Honolulu, HI 96813
Phone: 888-731-3863
Web: www.hawaiicommunityfoundation.org

Iwamoto Family Scholarship

Type of award: Scholarship, renewable.
Intended use: For full-time undergraduate or graduate study at accredited 2-year or 4-year institution in United States.
Eligibility: Applicant must be U.S. citizen or permanent resident residing in Hawaii.
Basis for selection: Applicant must demonstrate financial need, high academic achievement and depth of character.
Application requirements: Essay, transcript. FAFSA, SAR, SAT/ACT scores.
Additional information: Must have graduated from a Kauai high school within the last three years. Minimum 3.0 GPA.
  Application deadline: February 15
Contact:
Hawaii Community Foundation
827 Fort Street Mall
Honolulu, HI 96813
Phone: 888-731-3863
Web: www.hawaiicommunityfoundation.org

Iwamoto Family Vocational Scholarship

Type of award: Scholarship, renewable.
Intended use: For full-time undergraduate study at accredited 2-year institution in United States. Designated institutions: University of Hawaii community colleges.
Eligibility: Applicant must be U.S. citizen or permanent resident residing in Hawaii.
Basis for selection: Applicant must demonstrate financial need, high academic achievement and depth of character.
Application requirements: Essay, transcript. FAFSA and SAR, SAT/ACT scores.
Additional information: Minimum 2.8 GPA. Must be graduate of Kauai high school within last three years. Must be enrolled in vocational program in University of Hawaii community college system.
  Application deadline: February 15
Contact:
Hawaii Community Foundation
827 Fort Street Mall
Honolulu, HI 96813
Phone: 888-731-3863
Web: www.hawaiicommunityfoundation.org

Scholarships

Jean Estes Epstein Charitable Foundation Scholarship

Type of award: Scholarship, renewable.
Intended use: For full-time freshman study at accredited postsecondary institution in United States. Designated institutions: Schools in the continental United States.
Eligibility: Applicant must be residing in Hawaii.
Basis for selection: Applicant must demonstrate financial need and high academic achievement.
Application requirements: Recommendations, essay, transcript. SAR, FAFSA, SAT/ACT scores. Personal statement must include personal and career goals.
Additional information: Minimum 3.7 GPA. Must be graduate of Hawaii public high school. Must attend college in the continental United States.

> **Application deadline:** February 15

Contact:
Hawaii Community Foundation
827 Fort Street Mall
Honolulu, HI 96813
Phone: 888-731-3863
Web: www.hawaiicommunityfoundation.org

Jean Fitzgerald Scholarship Fund

Type of award: Scholarship, renewable.
Intended use: For full-time freshman study at accredited 2-year or 4-year institution in United States.
Eligibility: Applicant must be female, high school senior. Applicant must be U.S. citizen or permanent resident residing in Hawaii.
Basis for selection: Applicant must demonstrate financial need, high academic achievement and depth of character.
Application requirements: Essay, transcript. FAFSA and SAR, SAT/ACT scores.
Additional information: Minimum 2.7 GPA. Applicant must be active tennis player; preference may be given to USTA/ Hawaii Pacific Section members. Applicants must have permanent address in Hawaii. Applicants who take up mainland residency must have relatives living in Hawaii. Amount and number of awards vary.

> **Application deadline:** February 15
> **Total amount awarded:** $7,000

Contact:
Hawaii Community Foundation Scholarships
827 Fort Street Mall
Honolulu, HI 96813
Phone: 888-731-3863
Web: www.hawaiicommunityfoundation.org

Jean Ileialoha Beniamina Scholarship for Ni'ihau Students Fund

Type of award: Scholarship.
Intended use: For full-time undergraduate or graduate study at accredited postsecondary institution.
Eligibility: Applicant must be residing in Hawaii.
Basis for selection: Applicant must demonstrate financial need and high academic achievement.
Application requirements: Recommendations, essay, transcript. SAR, FAFSA, SAT/ACT scores. Essay describing family descent and connection to Ni'ihau and addressing proficiency in Hawaiian language and listing courses taken in Hawaiian.

Additional information: Minimum 2.7 GPA. Must be resident of Kauai or Ni'ihau Island. Preference given to current Ni'ihau residents or Kauai residents who are one or two generations removed from Ni'ihau Island. Preference given to students fluent in Hawaiian language.

> **Application deadline:** February 15

Contact:
Hawaii Community Foundation
827 Fort Street Mall
Honolulu, HI 96813
Phone: 888-731-3863
Web: www.hawaiicommunityfoundation.org

Johanna Drew Cluney Scholarship

Type of award: Scholarship.
Intended use: For undergraduate study at accredited vocational or 2-year institution in United States. Designated institutions: Community colleges in the University of Hawaii system.
Eligibility: Applicant must be residing in Hawaii.
Basis for selection: Applicant must demonstrate financial need and high academic achievement.
Application requirements: Recommendations, essay, transcript. SAR, FAFSA, SAT/ACT scores.
Additional information: Minimum 2.0 GPA. Must be enrolled in University of Hawaii Community College system.

> **Application deadline:** February 15

Contact:
Hawaii Community Foundation
827 Fort Street Mall
Honolulu, HI 96813
Phone: 888-731-3863
Web: www.hawaiicommunityfoundation.org

John & Anne Clifton Scholarship Fund

Type of award: Scholarship.
Intended use: For full-time undergraduate study at accredited vocational or 2-year institution in United States. Designated institutions: Community colleges in the University of Hawaii system.
Eligibility: Applicant must be residing in Hawaii.
Basis for selection: Applicant must demonstrate financial need and high academic achievement.
Application requirements: Recommendations, essay, transcript. SAR, FAFSA, SAT/ACT scores.
Additional information: Minimum 2.0 GPA. Must be enrolled in a vocational educational program in the University of Hawaii Community College system.

> **Application deadline:** February 15

Contact:
Hawaii Community Foundation
827 Fort Street Mall
Honolulu, HI 96813
Phone: 888-731-3863
Web: www.hawaiicommunityfoundation.org

John Dawe Dental Education Fund

Type of award: Scholarship, renewable.
Intended use: For full-time undergraduate or graduate study at accredited postsecondary institution in United States.
Eligibility: Applicant must be U.S. citizen or permanent resident residing in Hawaii.
Basis for selection: Major/career interest in dentistry; dental hygiene or dental assistant. Applicant must demonstrate

financial need, high academic achievement and depth of character.

Application requirements: Recommendations, essay, transcript, proof of eligibility. FAFSA and SAR, SAT/ACT scores. Letter from school confirming enrollment in the dental hygiene or dentistry program.

Additional information: Minimum 2.7 GPA. Applicants must have permanent address in Hawaii. Applicants taking up mainland residency must have relatives living in Hawaii. Amount and number of awards vary.

Application deadline: February 15

Contact:
Hawaii Community Foundation Scholarships
827 Fort Street Mall
Honolulu, HI 96813
Phone: 888-731-3863
Web: www.hawaiicommunityfoundation.org

John M. Ross Foundation Scholarship

Type of award: Scholarship.

Intended use: For full-time undergraduate or graduate study at 2-year, 4-year or graduate institution.

Eligibility: Applicant must be residing in Hawaii.

Basis for selection: Applicant must demonstrate financial need and high academic achievement.

Application requirements: Recommendations, essay, transcript. FAFSA and SAR, SAT/ACT scores.

Additional information: Minimum 2.7 GPA. Must be resident of Hawaii island. Amount and number of awards vary and may change yearly.

Application deadline: February 15

Contact:
Hawaii Community Foundation
827 Fort Street Mall
Honolulu, HI 96813
Phone: 888-731-3863
Web: www.hawaiicommunityfoundation.org

Joseph & Alice Duarte Memorial Fund

Type of award: Scholarship.

Intended use: For full-time undergraduate or graduate study at accredited 2-year or 4-year institution in United States.

Eligibility: Applicant must be U.S. citizen residing in Hawaii.

Basis for selection: Applicant must demonstrate financial need, high academic achievement and depth of character.

Application requirements: Recommendations, essay, transcript. SAR, FAFSA, personal statement, SAT/ACT scores.

Additional information: Minimum 2.7 GPA. Must be from North or South Kona districts of Hawaii. Preference given to graduates of Holualoa Elementary School.

Application deadline: February 15

Contact:
Hawaii Community Foundation Scholarships
827 Fort Street Mall
Honolulu, HI 96813
Phone: 888-731-3863
Web: www.hawaiicommunityfoundation.org

Juliette M. Atherton Scholarship - Minister's Sons and Daughters

Type of award: Scholarship.

Intended use: For full-time undergraduate study at accredited postsecondary institution.

Eligibility: Applicant must be Protestant. Applicant must be residing in Hawaii.

Basis for selection: Applicant must demonstrate financial need and high academic achievement.

Application requirements: Recommendations, essay, transcript. SAR, FAFSA, SAT/ACT scores. Personal statement must include minister's current position, name of church/parish, denomination, place/date of ordination, name of seminary attended.

Additional information: Minimum 2.7 GPA. Must be dependent son or daughter of ordained and active Protestant minister in established denomination in Hawaii.

Application deadline: February 15

Contact:
Hawaii Community Foundation
827 Fort Street Mall
Honolulu, HI 96813
Phone: 888-731-3863
Web: www.hawaiicommunityfoundation.org

Ka'iulani Home for Girls Trust Scholarship

Type of award: Scholarship, renewable.

Intended use: For full-time freshman or sophomore study at accredited postsecondary institution in United States.

Eligibility: Applicant must be Native Hawaiian/Pacific Islander. Applicant must be female. Applicant must be U.S. citizen or permanent resident residing in Hawaii.

Basis for selection: Applicant must demonstrate financial need, high academic achievement and depth of character.

Application requirements: Essay, transcript, proof of eligibility. FAFSA and SAR, SAT/ACT scores, birth certificate.

Additional information: Minimum 3.3 GPA. Must be of Hawaiian ancestry. First time applicants must be freshmen or sophomores. Juniors and seniors who are past recipients also eligible. Must have permanent address in Hawaii. Applicants taking up mainland residency must have relatives living in Hawaii. Amount and number of awards vary and may change yearly.

Application deadline: February 15

Contact:
Hawaii Community Foundation Scholarships
827 Fort Street Mall
Honolulu, HI 96813
Phone: 888-731-3863
Web: www.hawaiicommunityfoundation.org

Ka'a'awa Community Fund

Type of award: Scholarship.

Intended use: For full-time undergraduate or graduate study at accredited 2-year or 4-year institution in United States.

Eligibility: Applicant must be U.S. citizen or permanent resident residing in Hawaii.

Basis for selection: Applicant must demonstrate financial need, high academic achievement and depth of character.

Application requirements: Essay, transcript. FAFSA and SAR, SAT/ACT scores.

Additional information: Minimum 2.7 GPA. Must be resident of the Ka'a'awa area on Windward O'ahu. Preference given to long-time residents. Amount and number of awards vary and may change yearly.

Application deadline: February 15
Contact:
Hawaii Community Foundation Scholarships
827 Fort Street Mall
Honolulu, HI 96813
Phone: 888-731-3863
Web: www.hawaiicommunityfoundation.org

Kahala Nui Residents Scholarship Fund

Type of award: Scholarship.
Intended use: For undergraduate or graduate study at accredited 2-year or 4-year institution.
Eligibility: Applicant must be U.S. citizen residing in Hawaii.
Basis for selection: Applicant must demonstrate financial need, high academic achievement and depth of character.
Application requirements: Recommendations, essay, transcript. SAR, FAFSA, personal statement, SAT/ACT scores.
Additional information: Minimum 2.7 GPA. Applicant must be an employee or a dependent of an employee of Kahala Senior Living Community, Inc. for at least 6 months prior to application deadline. Amount of award varies.

Application deadline: February 15
Contact:
Hawaii Community Foundation Scholarships
827 Fort Street Mall
Honolulu, HI 96813
Phone: 888-731-3863
Web: www.hawaiicommunityfoundation.org

Kalihi Education Coalition Scholarship Fund

Type of award: Scholarship.
Intended use: For full-time undergraduate or graduate study at accredited postsecondary institution.
Eligibility: Applicant must be residing in Hawaii.
Basis for selection: Applicant must demonstrate financial need and high academic achievement.
Application requirements: Recommendations, essay, transcript. SAR, FAFSA, SAT/ACT scores.
Additional information: Minimum 3.0 GPA. Must either be a graduate or undergraduate student who is a resident of Kalihi-Palama with one of following zip codes: 96817, 96819.

Application deadline: February 15
Contact:
Hawaii Community Foundation
827 Fort Street Mall
Honolulu, HI 96813
Phone: 888-731-3863
Web: www.hawaiicommunityfoundation.org

Kapolei Business & Community Scholarship

Type of award: Scholarship.
Intended use: For full-time undergraduate study at accredited 2-year or 4-year institution in United States.
Eligibility: Applicant must be high school senior. Applicant must be U.S. citizen or permanent resident residing in Hawaii.
Basis for selection: Applicant must demonstrate financial need, high academic achievement and depth of character.

Application requirements: Essay, transcript. FAFSA and SAR, SAT/ACT scores.
Additional information: Minimum 2.7 GPA. Applicant must be a senior from Campbell, Kapolei, Nanakuli, or Waianae high schools. Applicants taking up mainland residency must have relatives living in Hawaii. Amount of award may vary yearly.

Application deadline: February 15
Contact:
Hawaii Community Foundation Scholarships
827 Fort Street Mall
Honolulu, HI 96813
Phone: 808-537-6333
Fax: 808-521-6286
Web: www.hawaiicommunityfoundation.org

Kawasaki-McGaha Scholarship Fund

Type of award: Scholarship.
Intended use: For full-time undergraduate study at postsecondary institution. Designated institutions: Hawaii Pacific University.
Eligibility: Applicant must be permanent resident residing in Hawaii.
Basis for selection: Major/career interest in computer/information sciences or international studies. Applicant must demonstrate financial need, high academic achievement and depth of character.
Application requirements: Essay, transcript. FAFSA and SAR, SAT/ACT scores.
Additional information: Minimum 2.7 GPA. Applicants must have permanent address in Hawaii. Applicants taking up mainland residency must have relatives living in Hawaii. Amount and number of awards vary and may change yearly.

Application deadline: February 15
Contact:
Hawaii Community Foundation Scholarships
827 Fort Street Mall
Honolulu, HI 96813
Phone: 888-731-3863
Web: www.hawaiicommunityfoundation.org

Kazuma and Ichiko Hisanaga Scholarship Fund

Type of award: Scholarship.
Intended use: For full-time undergraduate study at accredited 2-year or 4-year institution in United States. Designated institutions: NAIA or Division III school in the contiguous United States.
Eligibility: Applicant must be high school senior. Applicant must be U.S. citizen residing in Hawaii.
Basis for selection: Applicant must demonstrate financial need, high academic achievement, depth of character, leadership and service orientation.
Application requirements: Recommendations, essay, transcript. SAR, FAFSA, SAT/ACT scores, personal statement detailing sports involvement, leadership experience and community service. One recommendation letter must be from high school athletic director, or post-secondary counselor or administrator.
Additional information: Minimum 3.0 GPA. Amount of award varies. Applicant must be a graduating senior at Hilo High School; if Hilo has no eligible applicants from Hilo High School, seniors from other Hawai'i Island high schools will be considered in the following order: Waiakea High School, St.

Joseph High School, other Hawai'i Island high schools. Applicant must be an athlete that participated in a varsity high school sport. Preference given to those participating in more than one varsity sport. Must have served as the captain of a varsity sports team, a student government leader, or an officer of an extracurricular program.

Application deadline: February 15

Contact:
Hawaii Community Foundation Scholarships
827 Fort Street Mall
Honolulu, HI 96813
Phone: 888-731-3863
Web: www.hawaiicommunityfoundation.org

Kenneth Makinney & David T. Pietsch Familes Scholarship Fund

Type of award: Scholarship.
Intended use: For full-time undergraduate or graduate study at accredited postsecondary institution.
Eligibility: Applicant must be residing in Hawaii.
Basis for selection: Applicant must demonstrate financial need and high academic achievement.
Application requirements: Recommendations, essay, transcript. SAR, FAFSA, SAT/ACT scores, name and job title of Guaranty employee.
Additional information: Minimum 2.7 GPA. Must be full-time employee of at least one year or qualified dependent of Title Guaranty of Hawaii, Incorporated or Title Guaranty Escrow Services, Inc.

Application deadline: February 15

Contact:
Hawaii Community Foundation
827 Fort Street Mall
Honolulu, HI 96813
Phone: 888-731-3863
Web: www.hawaiicommunityfoundation.org

King Kekaulike High School Scholarship

Type of award: Scholarship.
Intended use: For full-time undergraduate study at accredited 2-year or 4-year institution in United States.
Eligibility: Applicant must be high school senior. Applicant must be U.S. citizen or permanent resident residing in Hawaii.
Basis for selection: Applicant must demonstrate financial need, high academic achievement, depth of character and service orientation.
Application requirements: Essay, transcript. FAFSA and SAR, SAT/ACT scores. Additional 500-word essay on how well Na Ali'I 3 R's (Respect, Relevance, and Rigor) relate to your future goals.
Additional information: Minimum 2.8 GPA and three or more hours of community service required. Applicant must be graduating senior at King Kekaulike High School. Children of KKHS staff members not eligible. Amount of award may change yearly. Applicants taking up mainland residency must have relatives living in Hawaii. Must have three or more hours of community service.

Application deadline: February 15

Contact:
Hawaii Community Foundation Scholarships
827 Fort Street Mall
Honolulu, HI 96813
Phone: 888-731-3863
Web: www.hawaiicommunityfoundation.org

K.M. Hatano Scholarship

Type of award: Scholarship, renewable.
Intended use: For full-time undergraduate study at accredited 4-year institution in United States. Designated institutions: Institutions in Hawaii.
Eligibility: Applicant must be high school senior. Applicant must be U.S. citizen or permanent resident residing in Hawaii.
Basis for selection: Applicant must demonstrate financial need, high academic achievement and depth of character.
Application requirements: Essay, transcript. FAFSA and SAR, SAT/ACT scores.
Additional information: Minimum 2.7 GPA. Applicant must be high school graduate of Maui, including Lanai or Molokai counties. Must attend college in Hawaii. Applicant must have permanent address in Hawaii. Applicants taking up mainland residency must have relatives living in Hawaii. Amount and number of awards vary and may change yearly.

Application deadline: February 15

Contact:
Hawaii Community Foundation Scholarships
827 Fort Street Mall
Honolulu, HI 96813
Phone: 888-731-3863
Web: www.hawaiicommunityfoundation.org

Kohala Ditch Education Fund

Type of award: Scholarship.
Intended use: For full-time undergraduate study at accredited 2-year or 4-year institution in United States.
Eligibility: Applicant must be high school senior. Applicant must be U.S. citizen or permanent resident residing in Hawaii.
Basis for selection: Applicant must demonstrate financial need, high academic achievement and depth of character.
Application requirements: Essay, transcript. FAFSA and SAR, SAT/ACT scores.
Additional information: Minimum 2.7 GPA. Applicant must be student at Kohala High School. Amount of award may change yearly. Applicants taking up mainland residency must have relatives living in Hawaii.

Application deadline: February 15

Contact:
Hawaii Community Foundation Scholarships
827 Fort Street Mall
Honolulu, HI 96813
Phone: 888-731-3863
Web: www.hawaiicommunityfoundation.org

Koloa Scholarship

Type of award: Scholarship, renewable.
Intended use: For full-time undergraduate or graduate study at accredited vocational, 2-year or 4-year institution in United States.
Eligibility: Applicant must be U.S. citizen or permanent resident residing in Hawaii.
Basis for selection: Applicant must demonstrate financial need, high academic achievement and depth of character.
Application requirements: Recommendations, transcript. FAFSA and SAR, SAT/ACT scores. Personal essay explaining personal understanding of meaning of "aloha," how it has played a part in personal development and how applicant hopes to use chosen field to further this meaning among family and community. Must include how long applicant has lived in Koloa area, list of books or other publications read on Hawaii's history, and list of relatives born in Koloa District,

including relationship to applicant, and place and approximate year of birth.

Additional information: Minimum 2.0 GPA. Applicant must be resident of one of the following Kauai areas in Hawaii: Koloa, including Omao and Poipu (96756), Lawai (96765), or Kalaheo (96741). Applicants taking up mainland residency must have relatives living in Hawaii. Amount of award varies and may change yearly.

  Application deadline:　　　February 15

Contact:
Hawaii Community Foundation Scholarships
827 Fort Street Mall
Honolulu, HI 96813
Phone: 888-731-3863
Web: www.hawaiicommunityfoundation.org

Korean University Club Scholarship Fund

Type of award: Scholarship.
Intended use: For full-time undergraduate or graduate study at accredited 2-year or 4-year institution in United States.
Eligibility: Applicant must be U.S. citizen residing in Hawaii.
Basis for selection: Applicant must demonstrate financial need, high academic achievement and depth of character.
Application requirements: Recommendations, essay, transcript. SAR, FAFSA, SAT/ACT scores, Personal Statement.
Additional information: Minimum 2.7 GPA. Must be of Korean ancestry.

  Application deadline:　　　February 15

Contact:
Hawaii Community Foundation Scholarships
827 Fort Street Mall
Honolulu, HI 96813
Phone: 888-731-3863
Web: www.hawaiicommunityfoundation.org

Korean War Veteran's Children's Scholarship

Type of award: Scholarship.
Intended use: For full-time undergraduate or graduate study at accredited postsecondary institution.
Eligibility: Applicant must be residing in Hawaii. Applicant must be descendant of veteran who served in the Army, Air Force, Marines or Navy.
Basis for selection: Applicant must demonstrate financial need and high academic achievement.
Application requirements: Recommendations, essay, transcript. FAFSA and SAR, SAT/ACT scores.
Additional information: Minimum 3.0 GPA. Must be direct descendant of Korean War veteran or soldier who served in foreign war. First preference given to descendants of those who died in combat, second preference to those who served in Korea. Amount and number of awards vary and may change yearly. Community service preferred.

  Application deadline:　　　February 15

Contact:
Hawaii Community Foundation
827 Fort Street Mall
Honolulu, HI 96813
Phone: 888-731-3863
Web: www.hawaiicommunityfoundation.org

Kurt W. Schneider Memorial Scholarship Fund

Type of award: Scholarship.
Intended use: For full-time undergraduate or graduate study at accredited 2-year, 4-year or graduate institution in United States.
Eligibility: Applicant must be high school senior. Applicant must be U.S. citizen or permanent resident residing in Hawaii.
Basis for selection: Major/career interest in tourism/travel. Applicant must demonstrate financial need, high academic achievement and depth of character.
Application requirements: Essay, transcript. FAFSA and SAR, SAT/ACT scores.
Additional information: Minimum 2.7 GPA. Applicant must be student at Lana'i High School. Preference given to travel industry management majors. Applicants taking up mainland residency must have relatives living in Hawaii. Amount of award may change yearly.

  Application deadline:　　　February 15

Contact:
Hawaii Community Foundation Scholarships
827 Fort Street Mall
Honolulu, HI 96813
Phone: 888-731-3863
Web: www.hawaiicommunityfoundation.org

Laura N. Dowsett Fund

Type of award: Scholarship, renewable.
Intended use: For full-time junior, senior or graduate study at accredited 2-year, 4-year or graduate institution in United States.
Eligibility: Applicant must be U.S. citizen or permanent resident residing in Hawaii.
Basis for selection: Major/career interest in occupational therapy. Applicant must demonstrate financial need, high academic achievement and depth of character.
Application requirements: Essay, transcript. FAFSA and SAR, SAT/ACT scores.
Additional information: Minimum 2.7 GPA. Applicants must have permanent address in Hawaii. Applicants who take up mainland residency must have relatives living in Hawaii. Amount and number of awards vary.

  Application deadline:　　　February 15

Contact:
Hawaii Community Foundation Scholarships
827 Fort Street Mall
Honolulu, HI 96813
Phone: 888-731-3863
Web: www.hawaiicommunityfoundation.org

Laura Rowe Burdick Scholarship Fund

Type of award: Scholarship.
Intended use: For full-time undergraduate study at accredited 2-year or 4-year institution in United States.
Eligibility: Applicant must be high school senior. Applicant must be U.S. citizen residing in Hawaii.
Basis for selection: Applicant must demonstrate financial need, high academic achievement, depth of character and service orientation.
Application requirements: Recommendations, essay, transcript. SAR, FAFSA, personal statement, SAT/ACT scores.
Additional information: Minimum 2.7 GPA. Amount of award varies. Applicant must be a high school senior in Maui

County. Preference given to applicants who want to return to Maui County after completing their education or training in order to contribute to the community that formed them.

Application deadline: February 15
Contact:
Hawaii Community Foundation Scholarships
827 Fort Street Mall
Honolulu, HI 96813
Phone: 888-731-3863
Web: www.hawaiicommunityfoundation.org

Lillian B. Reynolds Scholarship

Type of award: Scholarship, renewable.
Intended use: For full-time undergraduate or graduate study at accredited 2-year, 4-year or graduate institution in United States.
Eligibility: Applicant must be U.S. citizen or permanent resident residing in Hawaii.
Basis for selection: Major/career interest in medicine or nursing. Applicant must demonstrate depth of character.
Application requirements: Essay, transcript. FAFSA and SAR, SAT/ACT scores.
Additional information: Minimum 2.7 GPA. Must be medical or nursing student.

Application deadline: February 15
Contact:
Hawaii Community Foundation
827 Fort Street Mall
Honolulu, HI 96813
Phone: 888-731-3863
Web: www.hawaiicommunityfoundation.org

Logan Nainoa Fujimoto Memorial Scholarship

Type of award: Scholarship.
Intended use: For full-time undergraduate study at accredited vocational institution in United States. Designated institutions: Vocational schools with automotive technology programs.
Eligibility: Applicant must be residing in Hawaii.
Basis for selection: Applicant must demonstrate financial need and high academic achievement.
Application requirements: Recommendations, essay, transcript. SAR, FAFSA, SAT/ACT scores.
Additional information: Minimum 2.7 GPA. Preference given to students attending Universal Technical Institute. Must be concentrating in Automotive Technology.

Application deadline: February 15
Contact:
Hawaii Community Foundation
827 Fort Street Mall
Honolulu, HI 96813
Phone: 888-731-3863
Web: www.hawaiicommunityfoundation.org

March Taylor Educational Fund Scholarship

Type of award: Scholarship, renewable.
Intended use: For full-time undergraduate study at accredited vocational institution in United States.
Eligibility: Applicant must be U.S. citizen or permanent resident residing in Hawaii.
Basis for selection: Applicant must demonstrate financial need, high academic achievement and depth of character.

Application requirements: Essay, transcript. FAFSA and SAR, SAT/ACT scores.
Additional information: Minimum 2.7 GPA. Must be from island of Hawaii, with preference given to residents of West Hawaii. Must be enrolled in auto body repair and painting program.

Application deadline: February 15
Contact:
Hawaii Community Foundation
827 Fort Street Mall
Honolulu 96813-HI
Phone: 888-731-3863
Web: www.hawaiicommunityfoundation.org

Margaret Follett Haskins (Kansas) Scholarship

Type of award: Scholarship.
Intended use: For full-time junior or senior study at accredited 4-year institution in United States. Designated institutions: University of Kansas (Lawrence), Kansas State University (Manhattan).
Eligibility: Applicant must be U.S. citizen residing in Hawaii.
Basis for selection: Applicant must demonstrate financial need and high academic achievement.
Application requirements: Essay, transcript. FAFSA and SAR, SAT/ACT scores.
Additional information: Minimum 3.2 GPA. Must be current graduate of University of Hawaii community college.

Application deadline: February 15
Contact:
Hawaii Community Foundation
827 Fort Street Mall
Honolulu, HI 96813
Phone: 888-731-3863
Web: www.hawaiicommunityfoundation.org

Margaret Follett Haskins (Maui) Scholarship

Type of award: Scholarship.
Intended use: For full-time junior or senior study at accredited 4-year institution in United States. Designated institutions: Schools in the University of Hawaii system.
Eligibility: Applicant must be residing in Hawaii.
Basis for selection: Applicant must demonstrate financial need and high academic achievement.
Application requirements: Recommendations, essay, transcript. FAFSA and SAR, SAT/ACT scores.
Additional information: Minimum 3.0 GPA. Must be graduate of Maui Community College attending 4-year University of Hawaii school. Amount and number of awards vary and may change yearly. Preference given to previous recipients.

Application deadline: February 15
Contact:
Hawaii Community Foundation
827 Fort Street Mall
Honolulu, HI 96813
Phone: 888-731-3863
Web: www.hawaiicommunityfoundation.org

Scholarships

Margaret Follett Haskins Hawaii Scholarship

Type of award: Scholarship.
Intended use: For full-time junior or senior study at accredited 4-year institution in United States. Designated institutions: UH-Manoa, UH-Hilo, or UH-West Oahu.
Eligibility: Applicant must be residing in Hawaii.
Basis for selection: Applicant must demonstrate financial need and high academic achievement.
Application requirements: Recommendations, essay, transcript. FAFSA and SAR, SAT/ACT scores.
Additional information: Minimum 3.5 GPA. Must be current graduate of community college in University of Hawaii system transferring to UH-Manoa, UH-Hilo, or UH-West Oahu. Amount and number of awards vary and may change yearly.

   Application deadline: February 15
Contact:
Hawaii Community Foundation
827 Fort Street Mall
Honolulu, HI 96813
Phone: 888-731-3863
Web: www.hawaiicommunityfoundation.org

Margaret Jones Memorial Nursing Scholarship

Type of award: Scholarship, renewable.
Intended use: For full-time junior, senior or graduate study at accredited 4-year or graduate institution in United States. Designated institutions: University of Hawaii, Manoa; University of Hawaii, Hilo; Hawaii Pacific University; or PhD programs in Hawaii or mainland U.S.
Eligibility: Applicant must be U.S. citizen or permanent resident residing in Hawaii.
Basis for selection: Major/career interest in nursing. Applicant must demonstrate financial need, high academic achievement and depth of character.
Application requirements: Essay, transcript. FAFSA and SAR, SAT/ACT scores.
Additional information: Minimum 3.0 GPA. Applicants must be enrolled in BSN, MSN, or doctoral nursing program. Preference may be given to members of Hawaii Nurses Association. Applicants must have permanent address in Hawaii. Applicant taking up mainland residency must have relatives living in Hawaii. Amount and number of awards vary and change yearly.

   Number of awards: 13
   Application deadline: February 15
Contact:
Hawaii Community Foundation Scholarships
827 Fort Street Mall
Honolulu, HI 96813
Phone: 888-731-3863
Web: www.hawaiicommunityfoundation.org

Marion Maccarrell Scott Scholarship

Type of award: Scholarship, renewable.
Intended use: For full-time undergraduate or graduate study at accredited postsecondary institution in United States. Designated institutions: Institutions on U.S. mainland.
Eligibility: Applicant must be U.S. citizen or permanent resident residing in Hawaii.
Basis for selection: Applicant must demonstrate financial need, high academic achievement and depth of character.
Application requirements: Essay, transcript. FAFSA and SAR, SAT/ACT scores. Essay (2-3 typed pages, double-spaced) must demonstrate commitment to international understanding and world peace.
Additional information: Minimum 2.8 GPA. Must be graduate of Hawaii public high school and attend accredited mainland U.S. college or university. Applicant must have permanent address in Hawaii. Applicants taking up mainland residency must have relatives living in Hawaii. Amount and number of awards vary and may change yearly.

   Application deadline: February 15
Contact:
Hawaii Community Foundation Scholarships
827 Fort Street Mall
Honolulu, HI 96813
Phone: 888-731-3863
Web: www.hawaiicommunityfoundation.org

Mary Josephine Bloder Scholarship

Type of award: Scholarship.
Intended use: For full-time undergraduate study at accredited 2-year or 4-year institution in United States.
Eligibility: Applicant must be high school senior. Applicant must be U.S. citizen or permanent resident residing in Hawaii.
Basis for selection: Applicant must demonstrate financial need, high academic achievement and depth of character.
Application requirements: Recommendations, essay, transcript. FAFSA and SAR, SAT/ACT scores. One of the two letters of recommendation must be from Lahainaluna High School science teacher.
Additional information: Minimum 2.7 GPA. Must be graduating senior at Lahainaluna High School. Preference given to boarding students. Must have high GPA in sciences. Applicants taking up mainland residency must have relatives living in Hawaii. Amount and number of awards vary and may change yearly.

   Application deadline: February 15
Contact:
Hawaii Community Foundation Scholarships
827 Fort Street Mall
Honolulu, HI 96813
Phone: 888-731-3863
Web: www.hawaiicommunityfoundation.org

Mildred Towle Scholarship - Study Abroad

Type of award: Scholarship, renewable.
Intended use: For full-time junior, senior or graduate study at accredited postsecondary institution outside United States.
Eligibility: Applicant must be residing in Hawaii.
Basis for selection: Applicant must demonstrate financial need, high academic achievement and depth of character.
Application requirements: Essay, transcript. FAFSA and SAR, SAT/ACT scores. Essay must include intended country and semester of study.
Additional information: Minimum 3.0 GPA. Award for Hawaii residents studying abroad during regular academic year while enrolled at U.S. institution. Summer semester not included. Preference given to students pursuing social sciences pertaining to international understanding and interracial fellowship. Amount and number of awards vary and may change yearly.

   Application deadline: February 15

Contact:
Hawaii Community Foundation Scholarships
827 Fort Street Mall
Honolulu, HI 96813
Phone: 888-731-3863
Web: www.hawaiicommunityfoundation.org

Mildred Towle Scholarship for African-Americans

Type of award: Scholarship.
Intended use: For half-time undergraduate study at postsecondary institution. Designated institutions: Hawaii postsecondary institutions.
Eligibility: Applicant must be African American. Applicant must be U.S. citizen.
Basis for selection: Applicant must demonstrate financial need and high academic achievement.
Application requirements: Recommendations, essay, transcript. FAFSA and SAR, SAT/ACT scores.
Additional information: Minimum 3.0 GPA. Must attend school in Hawaii. Preference given to students pursuing studies in social sciences pertaining to international understanding and interracial fellowship. Hawaii residency not required.

  Application deadline: February 15
  Total amount awarded: $11,000
Contact:
Hawaii Community Foundation Scholarships
827 Fort Street Mall
Honolulu, HI 96813
Phone: 888-731-3863
Web: www.hawaiicommunityfoundation.org

Mitsuo Shito Public Housing Scholarship

Type of award: Scholarship, renewable.
Intended use: For full-time undergraduate or graduate study at accredited 2-year or 4-year institution in United States.
Eligibility: Applicant must be U.S. citizen or permanent resident residing in Hawaii.
Basis for selection: Applicant must demonstrate financial need, high academic achievement and depth of character.
Application requirements: Essay, transcript. Must include name of public housing unit in personal statement. FAFSA and SAR, SAT/ACT scores.
Additional information: Preference given to residents of public housing in Hawaii. Minimum 2.7 GPA.

  Application deadline: February 15
Contact:
Hawaii Community Foundation
827 Fort Street Mall
Honolulu 96813
Phone: 888-731-3863
Web: www.hawaiicommunityfoundation.org

Neil Tepper Scholarship

Type of award: Scholarship.
Intended use: For full-time undergraduate study at accredited 4-year institution.
Eligibility: Applicant must be U.S. citizen residing in Hawaii.
Basis for selection: Applicant must demonstrate financial need and high academic achievement.
Application requirements: Essay, transcript. FAFSA and SAR, SAT/ACT scores.
Additional information: Minimum 3.0 GPA.

  Application deadline: February 15
Contact:
Hawaii Community Foundation
827 Fort Street Mall
Honolulu, HI 96813
Phone: 888-731-3863
Web: www.hawaiicommunityfoundation.org

Nick Van Pernis Scholarship

Type of award: Scholarship.
Intended use: For full-time undergraduate or graduate study at accredited 2-year, 4-year or graduate institution in United States.
Eligibility: Applicant must be U.S. citizen or permanent resident residing in Hawaii.
Basis for selection: Major/career interest in oceanography/marine studies; bioengineering; health sciences or education, early childhood. Applicant must demonstrate financial need, high academic achievement, depth of character and service orientation.
Application requirements: Essay, transcript. FAFSA and SAR, SAT/ACT scores. Essay must include record of community service and description of how student's education and career will benefit Hawaii residents.
Additional information: Minimum 2.7 GPA. Must be graduate of public or private school in the North Kona, South Kona, North Kohala, South Kohala, or Ka'u districts. Applicants taking up mainland residency must have relatives living in Hawaii. Amount and number of awards may vary yearly.

  Application deadline: February 15
Contact:
Hawaii Community Foundation Scholarships
827 Fort Street Mall
Honolulu, HI 96813
Phone: 888-731-3863
Web: www.hawaiicommunityfoundation.org

Oahu Filipino Community Council Golf Scholarship

Type of award: Scholarship.
Intended use: For full-time undergraduate or graduate study at accredited 2-year, 4-year or graduate institution.
Eligibility: Applicant must be U.S. citizen residing in Hawaii.
Basis for selection: Applicant must demonstrate financial need and high academic achievement.
Application requirements: Essay, transcript. FAFSA and SAR, SAT/ACT scores.
Additional information: Must be of Filipino ancestry. Minimum 2.7 GPA.

  Application deadline: February 15
Contact:
Hawaii Community Foundation
827 Fort Street Mall
Honolulu, HI 96813
Phone: 888-731-3863
Web: www.hawaiicommunityfoundation.org

Office of Hawaiian Affairs Higher Education Scholarship Program

Type of award: Scholarship.
Intended use: For undergraduate or graduate study at accredited 2-year or 4-year institution in United States.

Eligibility: Applicant must be Native Hawaiian/Pacific Islander. Applicant must be U.S. citizen.
Basis for selection: Applicant must demonstrate financial need, high academic achievement and depth of character.
Application requirements: Recommendations, essay, transcript, proof of eligibility. SAR, FAFSA, personal statement, SAT/ACT scores.
Additional information: Minimum 2.0 GPA for undergraduate students, 3.0 GPA for graduate students. Applicant must be of Hawaiian ancestry; ancestry must be verified through OHA's Hawaiian Registry Program. Does not have to be resident of Hawaii. Amount of award varies.

  Application deadline: February 15
Contact:
Hawaii Community Foundation Scholarships
827 Fort Street Mall
Honolulu, HI 96813
Phone: 888-731-3863
Web: www.hawaiicommunityfoundation.org

Oscar and Rosetta Fish Fund

Type of award: Scholarship.
Intended use: For full-time undergraduate or graduate study at 2-year or 4-year institution. Designated institutions: Any University of Hawaii campus, excluding Manoa.
Eligibility: Applicant must be U.S. citizen or permanent resident residing in Hawaii.
Basis for selection: Major/career interest in business. Applicant must demonstrate financial need, high academic achievement and depth of character.
Application requirements: Essay, transcript. FAFSA and SAR, SAT/ACT scores.
Additional information: Minimum 2.7 GPA. Must have permanent address in Hawaii. Amount and number of awards vary and may change yearly.

  Application deadline: February 15
Contact:
Hawaii Community Foundation Scholarships
827 Fort Street Mall
Honolulu, HI 96813
Phone: 888-731-3863
Web: www.hawaiicommunityfoundation.org

Ouida Mundy Hill Memorial Fund

Type of award: Scholarship.
Intended use: For full-time undergraduate study at accredited vocational or 2-year institution in United States. Designated institutions: Community colleges in the University of Hawaii system.
Eligibility: Applicant must be residing in Hawaii.
Basis for selection: Applicant must demonstrate financial need and high academic achievement.
Application requirements: Recommendations, essay, transcript. SAR. FAFSA, SAT/ACT scores.
Additional information: Minimum 2.8 GPA. Must be enrolled in AS or AAS degree program.

  Application deadline: February 15
Contact:
Hawaii Community Foundation
827 Fort Street Mall
Honolulu, HI 96813
Phone: 888-731-3863
Web: www.hawaiicommunityfoundation.org

Paulina L. Sorg Scholarship

Type of award: Scholarship.
Intended use: For full-time junior, senior or graduate study at accredited 4-year institution in United States.
Eligibility: Applicant must be U.S. citizen residing in Hawaii.
Basis for selection: Major/career interest in physical therapy or nursing. Applicant must demonstrate financial need, high academic achievement and depth of character.
Application requirements: Recommendations, essay, transcript. SAR, FAFSA, personal statement, SAT/ACT scores.
Additional information: Minimum 2.7 GPA. Amount of award varies.

  Application deadline: February 15
Contact:
Hawaii Community Foundation Scholarships
827 Fort Street Mall
Honolulu, HI 96813
Phone: 888-731-3863
Web: www.hawaiicommunityfoundation.org

Perry & Sally Sorenson Scholarship for Dependents of Hospitality Workers

Type of award: Scholarship.
Intended use: For full-time undergraduate or graduate study at accredited 2-year or 4-year institution in United States.
Eligibility: Applicant must be U.S. citizen residing in Hawaii.
Basis for selection: Applicant must demonstrate financial need, high academic achievement and depth of character.
Application requirements: Recommendations, essay, transcript, proof of eligibility. SAR, FAFSA, SAT/ACT scores, personal statement, name of Outrigger employee/position at company.
Additional information: Minimum 2.7 GPA. Amount of award varies. Applicant must be a dependent of an employee currently employed by Outrigger Enterprises in Hawaii working in a hospitality industry position.

  Application deadline: February 15
Contact:
Hawaii Community Foundation Scholarships
827 Fort Street Mall
Honolulu, HI 96813
Phone: 888-731-3863
Web: www.hawaiicommunityfoundation.org

Perry & Sally Sorenson Scholarship for Foster Youth

Type of award: Scholarship.
Intended use: For full-time undergraduate or graduate study at accredited 2-year, 4-year or graduate institution in United States.
Eligibility: Applicant must be at least 18, no older than 25. Applicant must be U.S. citizen residing in Hawaii.
Basis for selection: Applicant must demonstrate financial need, high academic achievement and depth of character.
Application requirements: Recommendations, essay, transcript. SAR, FAFSA, personal statement, SAT/ACT scores.
Additional information: Minimum 2.0 GPA. Amount of award varies. Applicant must be permanently or temporarily separated from birth parent(s) and aged out of the foster care system in the state of Hawaii.

  Application deadline: February 15

Scholarships

Contact:
Hawaii Community Foundation Scholarships
827 Fort Street Mall
Honolulu, HI 96813
Phone: 888-731-3863
Web: www.hawaiicommunityfoundation.org

Peter R. Papworth Scholarship

Type of award: Scholarship.
Intended use: For full-time undergraduate or graduate study at accredited 2-year or 4-year institution in United States.
Eligibility: Applicant must be U.S. citizen residing in Hawaii.
Basis for selection: Applicant must demonstrate financial need, high academic achievement and depth of character.
Application requirements: Recommendations, essay, transcript. SAR, FAFSA, personal statement.
Additional information: Applicant must be a graduate of Campbell High School. Minimum 2.7 GPA. Amount of award varies.
   Application deadline: February 15
Contact:
Hawaii Community Foundation Scholarships
827 Fort Street Mall
Honolulu, HI 96813
Phone: 888-731-3863
Web: www.hawaiicommunityfoundation.org

Philippine Nurses' Association Scholarship

Type of award: Scholarship.
Intended use: For full-time undergraduate or graduate study at accredited 2-year, 4-year or graduate institution in United States.
Eligibility: Applicant must be Native Hawaiian/Pacific Islander. Applicant must be residing in Hawaii.
Basis for selection: Major/career interest in nursing. Applicant must demonstrate financial need and high academic achievement.
Application requirements: Recommendations, essay, transcript. FAFSA and SAR, SAT/ACT scores.
Additional information: Minimum 2.7 GPA. Must be of Filipino ancestry. Amount and number of awards vary and may change yearly.
   Application deadline: February 15
Contact:
Hawaii Community Foundation
827 Fort Street Mall
Honolulu, HI 96813
Phone: 888-731-3863
Web: www.hawaiicommunityfoundation.org

PRSA-Hawaii/Roy Leffingwell Public Relations Scholarship

Type of award: Scholarship.
Intended use: For full-time junior, senior or graduate study at accredited 2-year or 4-year institution in United States.
Eligibility: Applicant must be U.S. citizen or permanent resident residing in Hawaii.
Basis for selection: Major/career interest in public relations; communications or journalism. Applicant must demonstrate financial need, high academic achievement and depth of character.
Application requirements: Essay, transcript. FAFSA and SAR, SAT/ACT scores.

Additional information: Minimum 2.7 GPA. Must intend to pursue career in public relations. Award amount varies.
   Application deadline: February 15
Contact:
Hawaii Community Foundation Scholarships
827 Fort Street Mall
Honolulu, HI 96813
Phone: 888-731-3863
Web: www.hawaiicommunityfoundation.org

Ray Yoshida Kauai Fine Arts Scholarship

Type of award: Scholarship.
Intended use: For full-time undergraduate study at accredited 2-year or 4-year institution in United States.
Eligibility: Applicant must be high school senior. Applicant must be U.S. citizen residing in Hawaii.
Basis for selection: Major/career interest in arts, general. Applicant must demonstrate financial need, high academic achievement and depth of character.
Application requirements: Recommendations, essay, transcript. SAR, FAFSA, personal statement, SAT/ACT scores.
Additional information: Minimum 2.7 GPA. Amount of award varies. Applicant must be a high school senior from a school on the island of Kauai, and must pursue studies in Fine Arts.
   Application deadline: February 15
Contact:
Hawaii Community Foundation Scholarships
827 Fort Street Mall
Honolulu, HI 96813
Phone: 888-731-3863
Web: www.hawaiicommunityfoundation.org

Raymond F. Cain Scholarship Fund

Type of award: Scholarship.
Intended use: For full-time undergraduate or graduate study at accredited 2-year or 4-year institution in United States.
Eligibility: Applicant must be U.S. citizen residing in Hawaii.
Basis for selection: Major/career interest in landscape architecture. Applicant must demonstrate financial need, high academic achievement and depth of character.
Application requirements: Recommendations, essay, transcript. SAR, FAFSA, personal statement, SAT/ACT scores.
Additional information: Minimum 2.7 GPA. Amount of award varies.
   Application deadline: February 15
Contact:
Hawaii Community Foundation Scholarships
827 Fort Street Mall
Honolulu, HI 96813
Phone: 888-731-3863
Web: www.hawaiicommunityfoundation.org

Rich Meiers Health Administration Fund

Type of award: Scholarship.
Intended use: For full-time junior, senior or graduate study at accredited 2-year or 4-year institution in United States. Designated institutions: Hawaii institutions.
Eligibility: Applicant must be U.S. citizen residing in Hawaii.
Basis for selection: Major/career interest in health services administration. Applicant must demonstrate financial need, high academic achievement and depth of character.

Scholarships

Application requirements: Recommendations, essay, transcript. SAR, FAFSA, personal statement, SAT/ACT scores.
Additional information: Minimum 2.7 GPA. Amount of award varies. Majors may also include hospital administration, health care administration, and long-term care administration.
  Application deadline: February 15
Contact:
Hawaii Community Foundation Scholarships
827 Fort Street Mall
Honolulu, HI 96813
Phone: 888-731-3863
Web: www.hawaiicommunityfoundation.org

Richard Smart Scholarship

Type of award: Scholarship, renewable.
Intended use: For full-time undergraduate or graduate study at accredited 2-year or 4-year institution in United States.
Eligibility: Applicant must be U.S. citizen or permanent resident residing in Hawaii.
Basis for selection: Applicant must demonstrate financial need, high academic achievement and depth of character.
Application requirements: Essay, transcript. FAFSA and SAR, SAT/ACT scores.
Additional information: Minimum 2.7 GPA. Must be first-generation college student. Must be from Waimea area (zip code 96743). Vocational programs not eligible.
  Application deadline: February 15
Contact:
Hawaii Community Foundation
827 Fort Street Mall
Honolulu, HI 96813
Phone: 888-731-3863
Web: www.hawaiicommunityfoundation.org

Rise Up Scholarship

Type of award: Scholarship.
Intended use: For undergraduate or graduate study at accredited 2-year, 4-year or graduate institution in United States.
Eligibility: Applicant must be residing in Hawaii.
Basis for selection: Applicant must demonstrate financial need.
Application requirements: Recommendations, essay, transcript. FAFSA and SAR, SAT/ACT scores.
Additional information: Minimum 2.7 GPA. Must be resident of Kauai. Preference given to children of divorced parents. Amount and number of awards vary and may change yearly.
  Application deadline: February 15
Contact:
Hawaii Community Foundation
827 Fort Street Mall
Honolulu, HI 96813
Phone: 888-731-3863
Web: www.hawaiicommunityfoundation.org

Ritchie M. Gregory Fund

Type of award: Scholarship.
Intended use: For full-time undergraduate or graduate study at accredited 2-year or 4-year institution in United States.
Eligibility: Applicant must be U.S. citizen residing in Hawaii.
Basis for selection: Major/career interest in arts, general. Applicant must demonstrate financial need, high academic achievement and depth of character.
Application requirements: Recommendations, essay, transcript. SAR, FAFSA, personal statement, SAT/ACT scores.

Additional information: Minimum 2.7 GPA. Amount of award varies. Applicant must major in Art.
  Application deadline: February 15
Contact:
Hawaii Community Foundation Scholarships
827 Fort Street Mall
Honolulu, HI 96813
Phone: 888-731-3863
Web: www.hawaiicommunityfoundation.org

Robanna Fund

Type of award: Scholarship.
Intended use: For full-time undergraduate or graduate study at accredited 2-year, 4-year or graduate institution in United States.
Eligibility: Applicant must be U.S. citizen residing in Hawaii.
Basis for selection: Major/career interest in health-related professions. Applicant must demonstrate financial need, high academic achievement and depth of character.
Application requirements: Recommendations, essay, transcript. SAR, FAFSA, personal statement, SAT/ACT scores.
Additional information: Minimum 2.7 GPA. Amount of award varies.
  Application deadline: February 15
Contact:
Hawaii Community Foundation Scholarships
827 Fort Street Mall
Honolulu, HI 96813
Phone: 888-731-3863
Web: www.hawaiicommunityfoundation.org

Ron Bright Scholarship

Type of award: Scholarship.
Intended use: For full-time undergraduate study at accredited 2-year or 4-year institution in United States.
Eligibility: Applicant must be high school senior. Applicant must be U.S. citizen or permanent resident residing in Hawaii.
Basis for selection: Major/career interest in education. Applicant must demonstrate financial need, high academic achievement and depth of character.
Application requirements: Essay, transcript. FAFSA and SAR, SAT/ACT scores. Grades from first semester of 12th grade.
Additional information: Minimum 2.7 GPA. Must attend one of the following Windward Oahu high schools: Castle, Kahuku, Kailua, Kalaheo, or Olomana. Preference given to students with extracurricular activities in the performing arts. Must have permanent address in Hawaii. Applicants taking up mainland residency must have relatives living in Hawaii. Amount and number of awards vary and may change yearly.
  Application deadline: February 15
Contact:
Hawaii Community Foundation Scholarships
827 Fort Street Mall
Honolulu, HI 96813
Phone: 808-537-6333
Fax: 808-521-6286
Web: www.hawaiicommunityfoundation.org

Rosemary & Nellie Ebrie Fund

Type of award: Scholarship.
Intended use: For full-time undergraduate or graduate study at accredited 2-year or 4-year institution in United States.

Eligibility: Applicant must be Native Hawaiian/Pacific Islander. Applicant must be U.S. citizen or permanent resident residing in Hawaii.
Basis for selection: Applicant must demonstrate financial need, high academic achievement and depth of character.
Application requirements: Essay, transcript. FAFSA and SAR, SAT/ACT scores.
Additional information: Minimum 2.7 GPA. Must be of Hawaiian ancestry. Must be long-term resident born and currently living on the island of Hawaii. Applicants taking up mainland residency must have relatives living in Hawaii. Amount of award may change yearly.
  Application deadline: February 15
Contact:
Hawaii Community Foundation Scholarships
827 Fort Street Mall
Honolulu, HI 96813
Phone: 888-731-3863
Web: www.hawaiicommunityfoundation.org

Safeway Foundation Hawaii Scholarship Fund

Type of award: Scholarship.
Intended use: For full-time undergraduate or graduate study at accredited 2-year or 4-year institution in United States. Designated institutions: Hawaii institutions.
Eligibility: Applicant must be U.S. citizen residing in Hawaii.
Basis for selection: Applicant must demonstrate financial need, high academic achievement and depth of character.
Application requirements: Recommendations, essay, transcript. SAR, FAFSA, personal statement, SAT/ACT scores.
Additional information: Minimum 3.0 GPA. Amount of award varies. Preference for current and past employees of Safeway Hawaii and their dependents.
  Application deadline: February 15
Contact:
Hawaii Community Foundation Scholarships
827 Fort Street Mall
Honolulu, HI 96813
Phone: 888-731-3863
Web: www.hawaiicommunityfoundation.org

Sarah Rosenberg Teacher Education Scholarship

Type of award: Scholarship.
Intended use: For full-time senior study at accredited postsecondary institution.
Eligibility: Applicant must be residing in Hawaii.
Basis for selection: Major/career interest in education. Applicant must demonstrate financial need and high academic achievement.
Application requirements: Recommendations, essay, transcript. SAR, FAFSA, SAT/ACT scores.
Additional information: Minimum 2.7 GPA.
  Application deadline: February 15
Contact:
Hawaii Community Foundation
827 Fort Street Mall
Honolulu, HI 96813
Phone: 888-731-3863
Web: www.hawaiicommunityfoundation.org

Senator Richard M. & Dr. Ruth Matsuura Scholarship Fund

Type of award: Scholarship.
Intended use: For full-time undergraduate study at accredited 2-year or 4-year institution in United States.
Eligibility: Applicant must be U.S. citizen residing in Hawaii.
Basis for selection: Applicant must demonstrate financial need, high academic achievement and depth of character.
Application requirements: Recommendations, essay, transcript. SAR, FAFSA, personal statement, SAT/ACT scores.
Additional information: Applicant must be a graduate of Hilo High School or Waiakea High School and a resident of the island of Hawaii. Minimum 2.7 GPA. Amount of award varies.
  Application deadline: February 15
Contact:
Hawaii Community Foundation Scholarships
827 Fort Street Mall
Honolulu, HI 96813
Phone: 888-731-3863
Web: www.hawaiicommunityfoundation.org

Shirley McKown Scholarship Fund

Type of award: Scholarship.
Intended use: For full-time junior, senior or graduate study at accredited 4-year institution in United States.
Eligibility: Applicant must be U.S. citizen or permanent resident residing in Hawaii.
Basis for selection: Major/career interest in advertising; journalism or public relations. Applicant must demonstrate high academic achievement and depth of character.
Application requirements: Essay, transcript. FAFSA and SAR, SAT/ACT scores.
Additional information: Minimum 3.0 GPA. Applicants must have permanent address in Hawaii. Applicants taking up mainland residency must have relatives living in Hawaii.
  Application deadline: February 15
Contact:
Hawaii Community Foundation Scholarships
827 Fort Street Mall
Honolulu, HI 96813
Phone: 888-731-3863
Web: www.hawaiicommunityfoundation.org

Shuichi, Katsu and Itsuyo Suga Scholarship

Type of award: Scholarship.
Intended use: For full-time undergraduate or graduate study at accredited 2-year or 4-year institution in United States.
Eligibility: Applicant must be U.S. citizen or permanent resident residing in Hawaii.
Basis for selection: Major/career interest in mathematics; physics; science, general; computer/information sciences or technology. Applicant must demonstrate financial need, high academic achievement and depth of character.
Application requirements: Essay, transcript. FAFSA and SAR, SAT/ACT scores.
Additional information: Minimum 3.0 GPA. Applicants must have permanent address in Hawaii. Applicants taking up mainland residency must have relatives living in Hawaii. Amount of award may change yearly.
  Application deadline: February 15

Contact:
Hawaii Community Foundation Scholarships
827 Fort Street Mall
Honolulu, HI 96813
Phone: 888-731-3863
Web: www.hawaiicommunityfoundation.org

Takehiko Hasegawa Academic Scholarship

Type of award: Scholarship.
Intended use: For full-time undergraduate or graduate study at accredited 2-year or 4-year institution in United States.
Eligibility: Applicant must be U.S. citizen residing in Hawaii.
Basis for selection: Applicant must demonstrate financial need, high academic achievement and depth of character.
Application requirements: Recommendations, essay, transcript. SAR, FAFSA, personal statement, SAT/ACT scores.
Additional information: Minimum GPA of 3.5. Must be a resident of the Island of Kaua'i. Amount of award varies.
Application deadline: February 15
Contact:
Hawaii Community Foundation Scholarships
827 Fort Street Mall
Honolulu, HI 96813
Phone: 888-731-3863
Web: www.hawaiicommunityfoundation.org

Takehiko Hasegawa Kaua'i Community College Scholarship

Type of award: Scholarship, renewable.
Intended use: For full-time undergraduate study at accredited 2-year institution in United States. Designated institutions: Community college on island of Kauai.
Eligibility: Applicant must be U.S. citizen or permanent resident residing in Hawaii.
Basis for selection: Applicant must demonstrate financial need, high academic achievement and depth of character.
Application requirements: Essay, transcript. FAFSA and SAR, SAT/ACT scores.
Additional information: Minimum 2.7 GPA. Must be resident of Kauai and attend Kauai community college.
Application deadline: February 15
Contact:
Hawaii Community Foundation
827 Fort Street Mall
Honolulu, HI 96813
Phone: 888-731-3863
Web: www.hawaiicommunityfoundation.org

Thz Fo Farm Fund

Type of award: Scholarship.
Intended use: For full-time undergraduate or graduate study at accredited postsecondary institution in United States.
Eligibility: Applicant must be Chinese. Applicant must be U.S. citizen or permanent resident residing in Hawaii.
Basis for selection: Major/career interest in gerontology. Applicant must demonstrate financial need, high academic achievement and depth of character.
Application requirements: Recommendations, essay, transcript. FAFSA and SAR, SAT/ACT scores.
Additional information: Minimum 2.7 GPA. Must be of Chinese ancestry. Applicants must have permanent address in Hawaii. Applicants who take up mainland residency must have relatives living in Hawaii. Amount of award varies.

Application deadline: February 15
Contact:
Hawaii Community Foundation Scholarships
827 Fort Street Mall
Honolulu, HI 96813
Phone: 888-731-3863
Web: www.hawaiicommunityfoundation.org

Times Supermarket Shop & Score Scholarship

Type of award: Scholarship.
Intended use: For full-time undergraduate study at accredited postsecondary institution in United States.
Eligibility: Applicant must be high school senior. Applicant must be residing in Hawaii.
Basis for selection: Applicant must demonstrate financial need and high academic achievement.
Application requirements: Recommendations, essay, transcript. SAR, FAFSA, SAT/ACT scores.
Additional information: Minimum 2.7 GPA. Must be graduating senior of any high school on Oahu participating in Times Shop and Score program.
Application deadline: February 15
Contact:
Hawaii Community Foundation
827 Fort Street Mall
Honolulu, HI 96813
Phone: 888-731-3863
Web: www.hawaiicommunityfoundation.org

Tommy Lee Memorial Scholarship Fund

Type of award: Scholarship.
Intended use: For full-time undergraduate study at accredited 2-year or 4-year institution in United States.
Eligibility: Applicant must be high school senior. Applicant must be U.S. citizen or permanent resident residing in Hawaii.
Basis for selection: Applicant must demonstrate financial need, high academic achievement and depth of character.
Application requirements: Recommendations, essay, transcript. FAFSA and SAR, SAT/ACT scores.
Additional information: Minimum 2.7 GPA. Must be high school senior residing in the Waialua or Haleiwa area. Applicants taking up mainland residency must have relatives living in Hawaii. Amount of award may change yearly.
Application deadline: February 15
Contact:
Hawaii Community Foundation Scholarships
827 Fort Street Mall
Honolulu, HI 96813
Phone: 888-731-3863
Web: www.hawaiicommunityfoundation.org

Tongan Cultural Society Scholarship

Type of award: Scholarship.
Intended use: For full-time undergraduate or graduate study at accredited 2-year or 4-year institution in United States. Designated institutions: Hawaii institutions.
Eligibility: Applicant must be U.S. citizen residing in Hawaii.
Basis for selection: Applicant must demonstrate financial need, high academic achievement and depth of character.
Application requirements: Recommendations, essay, transcript. SAR, FAFSA, personal statement, SAT/ACT scores.

Additional information: Must be of primarily Tongan ancestry. Must attend school in Hawaii. Minimum 2.7 GPA. Amount of awards varies.

Application deadline: February 15

Contact:
Hawaii Community Foundation Scholarships
827 Fort Street Mall
Honolulu, HI 96813
Phone: 888-731-3863
Web: www.hawaiicommunityfoundation.org

Toraji & Toki Yoshinaga Scholarship

Type of award: Scholarship.
Intended use: For full-time sophomore study at accredited 2-year or 4-year institution. Designated institutions: Brigham Young University-Hawaii, Chaminade University, Hawaii Pacific University.
Eligibility: Applicant must be U.S. citizen or permanent resident residing in Hawaii.
Basis for selection: Applicant must demonstrate financial need, high academic achievement and depth of character.
Application requirements: Essay, transcript. FAFSA and SAR, SAT/ACT scores.
Additional information: Minimum 2.7 GPA. Applicants must have permanent address in Hawaii. Applicants taking up mainland residency must have relatives living in Hawaii. Amount of award may change yearly.

Application deadline: February 15

Contact:
Hawaii Community Foundation Scholarships
827 Fort Street Mall
Honolulu, HI 96813
Phone: 808-537-6333
Fax: 808-521-6286
Web: www.hawaiicommunityfoundation.org

Troy Barboza Educational Fund Scholarship

Type of award: Scholarship.
Intended use: For full-time undergraduate or graduate study at accredited postsecondary institution in United States.
Eligibility: Applicant must be residing in Hawaii. Applicant's parent must have been killed or disabled in work-related accident as firefighter, police officer or public safety officer.
Basis for selection: Applicant must demonstrate financial need and high academic achievement.
Application requirements: Recommendations, essay, transcript. SAR, FAFSA, SAT/ACT scores.
Additional information: Minimum 2.7 GPA. Must be public employee or dependent of public employee injured in line of duty or be a resident of Hawaii who has performed a heroic act.

Application deadline: February 15

Contact:
Hawaii Community Foundation
827 Fort Street Mall
Honolulu, HI 96813
Phone: 808-537-6333
Fax: 808-521-6286
Web: www.hawaiicommunityfoundation.org

Vicki Willder Scholarship Fund

Type of award: Scholarship.
Intended use: For full-time undergraduate or graduate study at accredited 2-year, 4-year or graduate institution in United States.
Eligibility: Applicant must be U.S. citizen or permanent resident residing in Hawaii.
Basis for selection: Major/career interest in culinary arts or tourism/travel. Applicant must demonstrate financial need, high academic achievement and depth of character.
Application requirements: Essay, transcript. FAFSA and SAR, SAT/ACT scores.
Additional information: Minimum 2.7 GPA. Applicant must graduate of Kamehameha Schools food services department. Preference given to students majoring in culinary arts or travel industry management. Applicants taking up mainland residency must have relatives living in Hawaii. Amount and number of awards vary and may change yearly.

Application deadline: February 15

Contact:
Hawaii Community Foundation Scholarships
827 Fort Street Mall
Honolulu, HI 96813
Phone: 808-537-6333
Fax: 808-521-6286
Web: www.hawaiicommunityfoundation.org

Victoria S. and Bradley L. Geist Foundation Scholarship

Type of award: Scholarship.
Intended use: For full-time undergraduate or graduate study at accredited postsecondary institution.
Eligibility: Applicant must be residing in Hawaii.
Basis for selection: Applicant must demonstrate financial need and high academic achievement.
Application requirements: Recommendations, essay, transcript, proof of eligibility. SAR, FAFSA, SAT/ACT scores, confirmation letter from DHS or Family Foster program case worker.
Additional information: Minimum 2.7 GPA. Must be currently or formerly placed in foster care in Hawaii. Deadlines are February 22nd for fall and spring; September 20th for spring only.

Application deadline: February 20, September 20

Contact:
Hawaii Community Foundation
827 Fort Street Mall
Honolulu, HI 96813
Phone: 888-731-3863
Web: www.hawaiicommunityfoundation.org

Walter H. Kupau Memorial Fund

Type of award: Scholarship.
Intended use: For full-time undergraduate study at accredited 2-year or 4-year institution in United States.
Eligibility: Applicant must be U.S. citizen or permanent resident residing in Hawaii.
Basis for selection: Applicant must demonstrate financial need and high academic achievement.
Application requirements: Essay, transcript, proof of eligibility. FAFSA and SAR, ACT/SAT scores, Name and member number of Local 745 member, along with relationship to applicant.
Additional information: Minimum 2.7 GPA. Applicant must be descendant of Hawaii Carpenter's Union Local 745 member

Scholarships

in good standing; preference given to descendants of retired members.

Application deadline: February 15

Contact:
Hawaii Community Foundation Scholarships
827 Fort Street Mall
Honolulu, HI 96813
Phone: 888-731-3863
Web: www.hawaiicommunityfoundation.org

Will J. Henderson Scholarship Fund in Hawaii

Type of award: Scholarship.
Intended use: For full-time undergraduate or graduate study at accredited 4-year institution in United States.
Eligibility: Applicant must be U.S. citizen residing in Hawaii.
Basis for selection: Applicant must demonstrate financial need, high academic achievement and depth of character.
Application requirements: Recommendations, essay, transcript. SAR, FAFSA, SAT/ACT scores, personal statement, name/job title of parent employed by Queen's Medical Center.
Additional information: Minimum 2.0 GPA. Amount of award varies. Applicant must be a child dependent of a current employee at Queen's Medical Center, and must attend community college in Hawaii.

Application deadline: February 15

Contact:
Hawaii Community Foundation Scholarships
827 Fort Street Mall
Honolulu, HI 96813
Phone: 888-731-3863
Web: www.hawaiicommunityfoundation.org

William James & Dorothy Bading Lanquist Fund

Type of award: Scholarship.
Intended use: For full-time undergraduate or graduate study at accredited 2-year or 4-year institution in United States.
Eligibility: Applicant must be U.S. citizen or permanent resident residing in Hawaii.
Basis for selection: Major/career interest in physical sciences. Applicant must demonstrate financial need, high academic achievement and depth of character.
Application requirements: Essay, transcript. FAFSA and SAR, SAT/ACT scores.
Additional information: Minimum 3.0 GPA. Must major in the physical sciences or related fields, excluding biological and social sciences. Must have permanent address in Hawaii. Applicants taking up mainland residency must have relatives living in Hawaii. Amount and number of awards vary and may change yearly.

Application deadline: February 15

Contact:
Hawaii Community Foundation Scholarships
827 Fort Street Mall
Honolulu, HI 96813
Phone: 888-731-3863
Web: www.hawaiicommunityfoundation.org

William Lew (Associate Degree) Scholarship

Type of award: Scholarship.
Intended use: For full-time undergraduate study at accredited 2-year or 4-year institution. Designated institutions: Culinary programs in Hawaii.
Eligibility: Applicant must be U.S. citizen residing in Hawaii.
Basis for selection: Major/career interest in culinary arts. Applicant must demonstrate financial need and high academic achievement.
Application requirements: Essay, transcript. FAFSA and SAR, SAT/ACT scores.
Additional information: Must be of Chinese ancestry. Must be accepted into culinary program in Hawaii. Minimum 2.7 GPA.

Application deadline: February 15

Contact:
Hawaii Community Foundation
827 Fort Street Mall
Honolulu, HI 96813
Phone: 888-731-3863
Web: www.hawaiicommunityfoundation.org

William Lew (Bachelor Degree) Scholarship

Type of award: Scholarship.
Intended use: For full-time junior or senior study at accredited 4-year institution in United States. Designated institutions: University of Hawaii schools.
Eligibility: Applicant must be U.S. citizen residing in Hawaii.
Basis for selection: Major/career interest in business. Applicant must demonstrate financial need and high academic achievement.
Application requirements: Essay, transcript. FAFSA and SAR, SAT/ACT scores.
Additional information: Must be of Chinese ancestry. Minimum 3.0 GPA. Must be junior or senior majoring in business at University of Hawaii campus.

Application deadline: February 15

Contact:
Hawaii Community Foundation
827 Fort Street Mall
Honolulu, HI 96813
Phone: 888-731-3863
Web: www.hawaiicommunityfoundation.org

HeadsetPlus.com

HeadsetPlus.com Annual College Scholarship Program

Type of award: Scholarship.
Intended use: For undergraduate or graduate study at vocational, 2-year, 4-year or graduate institution.
Eligibility: Applicant must be at least 16. Applicant must be U.S. citizen.
Basis for selection: The contest requires you to create a short YouTube video about yourself, your past achievements, how you can help shape the world around you, why college education is important, and what motivates you. Give us

examples what you have achieved in school and outside of school.

Application requirements: Transcript. Proof you're attending an accredited college or university or have been accepted to an accredited college or university.

Additional information: For full rules and instructions visit the web site.

Number of awards:	1
Application deadline:	December 31
Notification begins:	January 15
Total amount awarded:	$1,000

Contact:
HeadsetPlus.com
570 El Camino Real
Suite 150-421
Redwood City, CA 94063
Phone: 1-877-999-3838
Fax: 650-361-8922
Web: headsetplus.com/newsdesk95/newsdesk_info.html

Healthcare Administration Degree Program

Healthcare Administration and Management Scholarship

Type of award: Scholarship.
Intended use: For full-time undergraduate or graduate study at accredited 4-year or graduate institution in United States.
Eligibility: Applicant must be U.S. citizen.
Basis for selection: Major/career interest in health-related professions or health services administration.
Application requirements: Transcript.
Additional information: Minimum 3.0 GPA. One scholarship awarder per semester. Application deadlines are May 15th and October 15th. Complete rules,application, and guidelines on web site.

Amount of award:	$1,500
Number of awards:	2
Total amount awarded:	$3,000

Contact:
PO Box 454
Parker Ford, PA 19457
Web: www.healthcare-administration-degree.net

The Heart of America Foundation

The Christopher Reeve Award

Type of award: Scholarship.
Intended use: For freshman study at postsecondary institution.
Eligibility: Applicant must be enrolled in high school.
Basis for selection: Applicant must demonstrate depth of character and service orientation.
Application requirements: Recommendations, nomination by a person in the community not related to student.
Additional information: Student must have demonstrated compassion and caring service to community. Application must include information about nominee's service efforts, what sets

nominee apart from peers, why nominee should be considered for award, and any supporting documentation. Apply online. Upon request, award is mailed to awardee's institution of choice.

Amount of award:	$1,000
Number of awards:	1
Application deadline:	October 31
Notification begins:	March 1
Total amount awarded:	$1,000

Contact:
The Heart of America Foundation
c/o Rachel Martin
1625 K St. NW
Washington, DC 20006
Phone: 202-347-6278
Web: www.heartofamerica.org/scholarships.htm

Helen Diller Family Foundation

Diller Teen Tikkun Olam Awards

Type of award: Scholarship.
Eligibility: Applicant must be Jewish. Applicant must be U.S. citizen, Award is open to teens or age 13-19.
Basis for selection: Recipients are selected based upon their demonstrated leadership and impact in repairing the world. Applicant must demonstrate leadership and service orientation.
Application requirements: For details on the application process, and for application materials, please visit www.dillerteenawards.org/nominations-applications/process. Applicants can be nominated any community member who knows the value of their project except family members or may also nominate themselves.
Additional information: The award celebrates Jewish teens who have demonstrated impressive leadership and are actively engaged in community service projects that embody the value of tikkun olam (repair of the world). Up to fifteen selected teens from across the United States are acknowledged annually for their visionary actions with an award of $36,000, to be used to further their philanthropic work or their education. The award is open to Jewish teens who are residents of the US and are ages 13-19 at the time of nomination. Teens' projects can help either the Jewish community or the general community, so long as teens have not been compensated for their services.

Amount of award:	$36,000
Number of awards:	15
Application deadline:	January 11
Total amount awarded:	$540,000

Contact:
Diller Teen Tikkun Olam Awards
121 Steuart Street
San Francisco, CA 94105
Phone: 415-512-6432
Web: www.dillerteenawards.org/

Helicopter Foundation International

Bill Sanderson Aviation Maintenance Technician Scholarship Award

Type of award: Scholarship.
Intended use: For undergraduate or non-degree study at vocational institution. Designated institutions: U.S. helicopter airframe and engine manufacturers; aviation maintenance schools.
Basis for selection: Major/career interest in aviation repair.
Application requirements: Recommendations.
Additional information: For students who wish to study helicopter maintenance. Award includes full tuition to aviation maintenance program, stipend of $500-1600, three-year membership in HAI and free admission to HELI-EXPO. Applicant must be about to graduate from FAA-approved Part 147 Aviation Maintenance Technician School, or a recent recipient of Airframe and Powerplant (A&P) certificate or international equivalent. Applications and deadline information available on Website.

Amount of award:	$650-$1,600
Number of awards:	8
Number of applicants:	45
Application deadline:	November 30

Contact:
Bill Sanderson Aviation Maintenance Technician Scholarship
Helicopter Foundation International
1920 Ballenger Avenue
Alexandria, VA 22314-2898
Phone: 703-302-8463
Fax: 703-683-4745
Web: www.rotor.com

Helicopter Foundation International Commercial Helicopter Pilot Rating Scholarship

Type of award: Scholarship.
Intended use: For full-time undergraduate or non-degree study at vocational institution in or outside United States. Designated institutions: Certified FAA Part 141 training program.
Eligibility: Applicant must be U.S. citizen or international student.
Basis for selection: Major/career interest in aviation.
Application requirements: Recommendations, essay. Proof of enrollment in FAA Part 141 school helicopter pilot training program or international equivalent, copy of FAA or International Equivalent Certificate, resume, essay describing why you want to be a helicopter pilot, letter from school certifying they are FAA certified Part 141.Tuition upon program completion and certification.
Additional information: Must be enrolled in certified FAA Part 141 commercial helicopter course/ training. Foreign students must prove foreign citizenship. Recipients receive one-year membership to HAI and free entry to HELI-EXPO.

Amount of award:	$5,000
Number of awards:	4
Application deadline:	November 30

Contact:
Helicopter Foundation International
1920 Ballenger Avenue
Alexandria, VA 22314-2898
Phone: 703-683-4646
Fax: 703-683-4745
Web: www.rotor.com

Helicopter Foundation International Maintenance Technician Certificate Scholarship

Type of award: Scholarship.
Intended use: For full-time undergraduate or non-degree study at vocational institution in or outside United States. Designated institutions: Certified FAA Part 147 training program.
Eligibility: Applicant must be U.S. citizen or international student.
Basis for selection: Major/career interest in aviation repair.
Application requirements: Recommendations, essay. Proof of enrollment in certified FAA approved or international equivalent Part 147 maintenance technician program, essay describing why you want to be a helicopter maintenance technician.
Additional information: Must be enrolled in FAA Part 147 maintenance technician program or international equivalent. Foreign students must provide proof of foreign citizenship. Recipients receive one-year membership to HAI and free entry to HELI-EXPO.

Amount of award:	$2,500
Number of awards:	6
Application deadline:	November 30

Contact:
Helicopter Foundation International
1920 Ballenger Avenue
Alexandria, VA 22314-2898
Phone: 703-683-4646
Fax: 703-683-4745
Web: www.rotor.com

Henry David Thoreau Foundation

Henry David Thoreau Foundation

Type of award: Scholarship, renewable.
Intended use: For full-time undergraduate study at 4-year institution.
Eligibility: Applicant must be high school senior. Applicant must be residing in Massachusetts.
Basis for selection: Major/career interest in environmental science; engineering, environmental; ecology; energy research or hydrology. Applicant must demonstrate high academic achievement and leadership.
Additional information: Candidates for the Henry David Thoreau Scholarship must be residents of Massachusetts. The candidates must also be enrolled in and graduate from a Massachusetts high school in the year they apply for a scholarship and begin college studies. Students with strong academic qualifications and a commitment to the environmental field may apply for an undergraduate scholarship totaling up to $20,000 to the student's accredited institution of choice. Additional Information: This is an

environmental scholarship. After enrolling and choosing any major, Thoreau Scholars are required to carry 25 percent of their undergraduate course work in subjects related to the environment. To maintain scholarship assistance, Scholars are required to submit an annual report of their activities in the environmental field, including academic courses. Scholars must provide an official copy of their transcript at the end of each marking period and maintain more than a 2.5 grade point average on a 4.0 scale to remain eligible for scholarship support.

Number of awards:	10
Application deadline:	February 1
Total amount awarded:	$20,000

Contact:
Henry David Thoreau Foundation
265 Medford Street, Suite 102
Somerville, MA 02143
Phone: 617-666-6900
Web: www.thoreauscholar.org

Herschel C. Price Educational Foundation

Herschel C. Price Educational Scholarship

Type of award: Scholarship, renewable.
Intended use: For undergraduate or graduate study at accredited 2-year, 4-year or graduate institution in United States.
Eligibility: Applicant must be U.S. citizen.
Basis for selection: Applicant must demonstrate financial need and high academic achievement.
Application requirements: Interview, transcript.
Additional information: Applicant must reside in West Virginia or attend West Virginia college or university. Achievement in community activities also considered. Preference given to undergraduates. Limited number of applications available by written request in January and February for fall term or August and early September for spring term. Limited number of applications available.

Number of applicants:	100
Application deadline:	April 1, October 1
Notification begins:	May 15, November 15
Total amount awarded:	$190,000

Contact:
Herschel C. Price Educational Foundation
P.O. Box 412
Huntington, WV 25708-0412
Phone: 304-529-3852

HIE Help Center

HIE Help Center Scholarship

Type of award: Scholarship, renewable.
Intended use: For full-time undergraduate or graduate study at vocational, 2-year, 4-year or graduate institution.
Eligibility: Applicant must be U.S. citizen or permanent resident.

Application requirements: Essay, transcript. Must not be a past, present, or future client of Reiter & Walsh, PC. Must be currently enrolled in college or graduate program. Must submit an essay or creative project about your experience with birth injuries: examples include videos, photographs with explanations, or any other creative submission you'd like.
Additional information: Scholarship open to students studying: medical, nursing or rehabilitative medicine and therapy, special education teaching, policy or law, caregivers or social work, adaptive recreation specialists, or any other academic pursuit, goal, or experience that relates to neonatal injuries and/or disability.

Amount of award:	$1,000
Number of awards:	1
Application deadline:	July 31
Notification begins:	August 31
Total amount awarded:	$1,000

Contact:
HIE Help Center
122 Concord Road
Bloomfield Hills, MI 48304
Phone: 888-329-0122
Web: https://hiehelpcenter.org/hie-help-center-scholarship/

Highestcashoffer.com

Highestcashoffer.com Scholarship

Type of award: Scholarship.
Intended use: For undergraduate or graduate study at accredited 2-year or 4-year institution in United States.
Eligibility: Applicant must be at least 18.

Number of awards:	1
Application deadline:	May 27
Notification begins:	June 24
Total amount awarded:	$500

Contact:
Web: http://highestcashoffer.com/scholarship/

HighIncomeParents.com

Melissa Read Memorial Scholarship

Type of award: Scholarship.
Intended use: For undergraduate study at vocational, 2-year or 4-year institution.
Application requirements: Essay, transcript, proof of eligibility. Applicants must either be enrolled or actively be applying for enrollment to an undergraduate program. Students at technical, community and four-year colleges are welcome to apply. Must write an essay (600-1200 words) on the topic: What is the worst financial decision you have made and what did you learn from it?
Additional information: Send the essay with other information in a Microsoft Word document and email to the contact address. More information about the application details on the website.

Amount of award:	$1,000
Number of awards:	1
Application deadline:	August 1
Notification begins:	September 1
Total amount awarded:	$1,000

Contact:
HighIncomeParents.com
Web: http://www.highincomeparents.com/melissa-read-memorial-scholarship/

HireOwl

HireOwl Scholarship Program

Type of award: Scholarship, renewable.
Intended use: For full-time undergraduate or graduate study at vocational, 2-year, 4-year or graduate institution.
Eligibility: Applicant must be at least 18.
Additional information: Students need to work a minimum of one job for a HireOwl client and receive a positive review on their work. Jobs and scholarship information can be found on web site.

Amount of award:	$250-$10,000
Number of awards:	10
Number of applicants:	400
Notification begins:	October 1
Total amount awarded:	$25,000

Contact:
HireOwl
222 Broadway
New York, NY 10038
Phone: 646-559-0698
Web: www.hireowl.com/about#scholarship

Hispanic Association of Colleges and Universities

NASCAR/Wendell Scott Sr. Award

Type of award: Scholarship.
Intended use: For full-time undergraduate or graduate study at 2-year, 4-year or graduate institution. Designated institutions: HACU member institutions. Must attend school in Florida, Georgia, or North Carolina.
Basis for selection: Major/career interest in engineering; business; public relations; marketing or technology.
Application requirements: Essay, transcript. FAFSA, resume.
Additional information: Minimum 3.0 GPA.

Amount of award:	$2,200
Application deadline:	May 30

Contact:
Hispanic Association of Colleges and Universities
One Dupont Circle
Suite 430
Washington, WA 20036
Phone: 202-833-8361
Fax: 202-261-5082
Web: www.hacu.net

Hispanic Foundation of Silicon Valley

Latinos in Technology Scholarship

Type of award: Scholarship, renewable.
Intended use: For junior or senior study.
Eligibility: Applicant must be Hispanic American.
Basis for selection: Applicant must demonstrate financial need and high academic achievement.
Application requirements: Recommendations, essay, transcript.
Additional information: Minimum 2.5 GPA. Graduate of a high school in the Greater Silicon Valley (includes Santa Clara County, San Mateo County, San Francisco County; Fremont, Newark, and Union City in Alameda County and Scotts Valley in Santa Cruz County). Preference will be given to San Mateo and Santa Clara County high school graduates. Have a declared major in and been accepted into a STEM program.

Amount of award:	$30,000
Number of awards:	100
Application deadline:	February 24

Contact:
Phone: 650-450-5487

Hispanic Heritage Foundation

Hispanic Heritage Youth Awards Program

Type of award: Scholarship.
Intended use: For full-time undergraduate study at postsecondary institution.
Eligibility: Applicant must be Hispanic American. Applicant must be high school junior. Applicant must be U.S. citizen or permanent resident.
Basis for selection: Applicant must demonstrate high academic achievement, depth of character, leadership and service orientation.
Application requirements: Recommendations, essay, transcript, proof of eligibility.
Additional information: Applicant must have at least one parent of Hispanic/Latino ancestry. Foundation offers regional and national awards in a number of categories; amount of award and application deadlines vary by year. Awards may also be used for education related expenses, or to establish a community service effort in the student's community. Applications due in June or July. Visit Website for application and updates regarding Youth Awards Program.

Amount of award:	$1,000
Number of awards:	160
Number of applicants:	10,000
Application deadline:	October 2
Total amount awarded:	$210,000

Contact:
Hispanic Heritage Foundation
9675 Main Street Suite D
Fairfax, VA 22031
Phone: 202-558-9473
Web: www.hispanicheritage.org

Hollins, Raybin, & Weissman

Hollins, Raybin, & Weissman Stop Texting & Driving $1,000 Scholarship

Type of award: Scholarship.

Intended use: For undergraduate study at vocational, 2-year, 4-year or graduate institution.

Eligibility: Applicant must be high school junior or senior. Applicant must be U.S. citizen.

Application requirements: Essay. Essay Prompt: "If you had to convince just one friend not to text and drive, what would you say?" Essay must be 500 words in length.

Additional information: Three scholarships awarded: Williamson County Tennessee - deadline July 1st, Davidson County Tennessee - deadline July 15th, and a national winner - deadline August 1st.

Amount of award:	$1,000
Number of awards:	3
Application deadline:	August 1

Contact:

Web: www.hollinslegal.com/essay-scholarships-how-to-stop-texting-driving/

Homekitchenary

Homekitchenary Student Scholarship

Type of award: Scholarship, renewable.

Intended use: For undergraduate or graduate study at 4-year or graduate institution.

Eligibility: Applicant must be female. Applicant must be U.S. citizen.

Basis for selection: Applicant must demonstrate high academic achievement.

Application requirements: Essay. Must be attending a College or University in the Fall.

Additional information: Only applications by email will accepted. More information on the Website.

Amount of award:	$500-$1,000
Number of awards:	2
Application deadline:	June 30
Notification begins:	July 20
Total amount awarded:	$1,000

Contact:

Homekitchenary
1489 Walkers Ridge Way
West Chicago, IL 60185
Phone: 630-231-3968
Web: http://homekitchenary.com/share-story-with-homekitchenary/

Hometeam Care

Hometeam Homecare Scholarship

Type of award: Scholarship.

Intended use: For full-time undergraduate study at vocational, 2-year or 4-year institution in United States.

Eligibility: Applicant must be high school senior.

Basis for selection: Major/career interest in nursing.

Application requirements: Essay. Questions on application: Are you currently or have you ever provided support for an individual? For whom did you provide support for? How Long? Two essay questions (500 words or less): What do you believe is the greatest challenge of providing care or support for someone? What do you believe about homecare or nursing?

Additional information: Minimum 3.0 GPA. Eligible applicants must be admitted or enrolled in a nursing school or home care certification program. To be considered for the scholarship applicants will have to fill out the application form on the web site.

Number of awards:	1
Application deadline:	February 1
Total amount awarded:	$2,000

Contact:

Hometeam Care
525 Broadway
New York, NY 10012
Phone: 844-226-7407
Web: https://www.hometeamcare.com/scholarship

Hopi Tribe Grants and Scholarship Program

APS Scholarship

Type of award: Scholarship.

Intended use: For sophomore, junior or senior study at accredited 2-year or 4-year institution.

Eligibility: Applicant must be American Indian.

Basis for selection: Major/career interest in science, general; mathematics; technology; engineering; nursing or education. Applicant must demonstrate high academic achievement and service orientation.

Application requirements: Essay, transcript. Must be member of Hopi tribe.

Additional information: Minimum 2.5 GPA. Must be enrolled member of Hopi tribe. Must be majoring in science, technology, engineering and math. Secondary preference given to students majoring in education and nursing. Students must perform 20 hours of community service benefitting the Hopi community.

Amount of award:	$4,000
Number of awards:	10
Application deadline:	September 1

Contact:

Hopi Tribe Grants and Scholarship Program
P.O. Box 123
Kykotsmovi, AZ 86039
Phone: 800-762-9630
Fax: 928-734-9575
Web: www.hopieducationfund.org

Hopi BIA Higher Education Grant

Type of award: Scholarship, renewable.
Intended use: For full-time undergraduate or graduate study at accredited 2-year, 4-year or graduate institution.
Eligibility: Applicant must be American Indian. Must be enrolled member of the Hopi Tribe.
Basis for selection: Applicant must demonstrate financial need and high academic achievement.
Additional information: Entering freshmen must have minimum 2.0 GPA for high school coursework or minimum composite score of 50% on GED Exam. Continuing students must have minimum 2.0 GPA for all graduate coursework. Four deadlines per year: November 1st (for winter quarter), December 1st (for spring), May 1st (for summer), and July 1st (for fall). Must reapply each academic year or semester. Number and amount of awards vary.

Amount of award:	$5,000
Number of applicants:	140
Application deadline:	December 1, July 1

Contact:
Hopi Tribe Grants and Scholarship Program
P.O. Box 123
Kykotsmovi, AZ 86039
Phone: 800-762-9630
Fax: 928-734-9575

Hopi Education Award

Type of award: Scholarship, renewable.
Intended use: For undergraduate or graduate study at accredited 2-year, 4-year or graduate institution.
Eligibility: Applicant must be American Indian. Must be enrolled member of the Hopi Tribe.
Basis for selection: Applicant must demonstrate financial need and high academic achievement.
Application requirements: Essay, transcript. FAFSA.
Additional information: Entering freshmen must have minimum 2.5 GPA for high school coursework or minimum composite score of 50 percent on the GED Exam. Continuing students must have minimum 2.5 GPA for all college work. Four deadlines per year: November 1st (for winter quarter), December 1st (for spring), May 1st (for summer), and July 1st (for fall). Must reapply each academic year or semester.

Amount of award:	$5,000
Number of applicants:	140
Application deadline:	December 1, July 1

Contact:
Hopi Tribe Grants and Scholarship Program
P.O. Box 123
Kykotsmovi, AZ 86039
Phone: 800-762-9630
Fax: 928-734-9575

Hopi Tribal Priority Award

Type of award: Scholarship, renewable.
Intended use: For full-time junior, senior or graduate study at accredited 4-year or graduate institution.
Eligibility: Applicant must be American Indian. Must be enrolled member of the Hopi Tribe.
Basis for selection: Applicant must demonstrate high academic achievement, depth of character, leadership and seriousness of purpose.
Application requirements: Recommendations, transcript, proof of eligibility.
Additional information: Minimum 3.5 GPA. Award is based on amount of college cost. Student receives monthly stipend of $1500 plus cost of books and room and board, as well as tuition. Preference given to those majoring in fields considered to be of tribal priority. Applicant must have college submit financial needs analysis to determine amount of award.

Amount of award:	Full tuition
Number of applicants:	3

Contact:
Hopi Tribe Grants and Scholarship Program
P.O. Box 123
Kykotsmovi, AZ 86039
Phone: 800-762-9630
Fax: 928-734-9575

Horatio Alger Association

Horatio Alger Ak-Sar-Ben Scholarship Program

Type of award: Scholarship.
Intended use: For full-time undergraduate study at accredited 2-year or 4-year institution in United States.
Eligibility: Applicant must be high school senior. Applicant must be U.S. citizen residing in Iowa or Nebraska.
Basis for selection: Applicant must demonstrate financial need, high academic achievement, seriousness of purpose and service orientation.
Application requirements: Essay, transcript. Letter of support, income statement.
Additional information: Minimum 2.0 GPA. Program assists high school seniors in Nebraska or Western Iowa who have faced and overcome adversity and have participated in co-curricular and community activities. Must plan to pursue bachelor's degree. See Website for application and list of eligible Iowa counties.

Amount of award:	$6,000
Number of awards:	50
Application deadline:	October 30

Contact:
Horatio Alger Association
99 Canal Center Plaza, Suite 320
Alexandria, VA 22314
Phone: 703-684-9444
Fax: 703-548-3822
Web: www.horatioalger.org/scholarships

Horatio Alger Arizona Scholarship

Type of award: Scholarship.
Intended use: For full-time freshman study at 2-year or 4-year institution in United States.
Eligibility: Applicant must be high school senior. Applicant must be U.S. citizen residing in Arizona.
Basis for selection: Applicant must demonstrate financial need, high academic achievement, seriousness of purpose and service orientation.
Application requirements: Essay, transcript. Letter of support, income statement, certification form.
Additional information: Minimum 2.0 GPA. Program assists high school seniors in Arizona who have faced and overcome adversity and have participated in co-curricular and community activities. Must plan to pursue bachelor's degree.

Amount of award:	$6,000
Number of awards:	10
Application deadline:	October 25

Contact:
Horatio Alger Association
99 Canal Center Plaza, Suite 320
Alexandria, VA 22314
Phone: 703-684-9444
Fax: 703-684-9445
Web: www.horatioalger.org/scholarships

Horatio Alger California (Northern) Scholarship Program

Type of award: Scholarship.
Intended use: For full-time undergraduate study at accredited 2-year or 4-year institution in United States.
Eligibility: Applicant must be high school senior. Applicant must be U.S. citizen residing in California.
Basis for selection: Applicant must demonstrate financial need, high academic achievement, seriousness of purpose and service orientation.
Application requirements: Essay, transcript. Letter of support, income statement, certification form.
Additional information: Minimum 2.0 GPA. Program assists high school seniors in Northern California who have faced and overcome adversity and have participated in co-curricular and community activities. Applicant should have strong commitment to use college degree in service to others. Must plan to pursue bachelor's degree. See Website for application.

Amount of award:	$6,000
Number of awards:	38
Application deadline:	October 25

Contact:
Horatio Alger Association
99 Canal Center Plaza, Suite 320
Alexandria, VA 22314
Phone: 703-684-9444
Fax: 703-684-9445
Web: www.horatioalger.org/scholarships

Horatio Alger Cortopassi Family Foundation Vocational Scholarship

Type of award: Scholarship, renewable.
Intended use: For full-time at accredited vocational or 2-year institution. Designated institutions: Butte College, Yuba College, Woodland College, Folsom Lake College, American River College, Sacramento City College, Consumnes River College, San Joaquin Delta College, Modesto Junior College, Merced College, Fresno City College, Reedley College, West Hills Community College- Coalinga, West Hills Community College- Lemoore, College of the Sequoias, Porterville College, Bakersfield College.
Eligibility: Applicant must be no older than 35. Applicant must be residing in California.
Basis for selection: Applicant must demonstrate financial need.
Application requirements: Essay, transcript. Student Aid Report (SAR form).
Additional information: Must be enrolled in approved vocational program. Must reside in, or have graduated from high school in Madera, Merced, San Joaquin, or Stanislaus Counties. Family income must be below $55,000.

Amount of award:	$2,500-$40,000
Number of awards:	40
Number of applicants:	100
Total amount awarded:	$400,000

Contact:
99 Canal Center Plaza
Suite 320
Alexandria, VA 22314
Phone: 703-684-9444
Web: www.horatioalger.org

Horatio Alger Delaware Scholarship Program

Type of award: Scholarship.
Intended use: For full-time undergraduate study at accredited 2-year or 4-year institution in United States.
Eligibility: Applicant must be high school senior. Applicant must be U.S. citizen residing in Delaware.
Basis for selection: Applicant must demonstrate financial need, high academic achievement and service orientation.
Application requirements: Essay, transcript. Letter of support, income statement, certification form.
Additional information: Minimum 2.0 GPA. Program assists high school seniors in Delaware who have faced and overcome adversity and have participated in co-curricular and community activities. Must plan to pursue bachelor's degree. See Website for application.

Amount of award:	$6,000
Number of awards:	5
Application deadline:	October 25

Contact:
Horatio Alger Association
99 Canal Center Drive, Suite 320
Alexandria, VA 22314
Phone: 703-684-9444
Fax: 703-684-9445
Web: www.horatioalger.org/scholarships

Horatio Alger District of Columbia, Maryland and Virginia Scholarship Program

Type of award: Scholarship.
Intended use: For full-time undergraduate study at accredited 2-year or 4-year institution in United States.
Eligibility: Applicant must be high school senior. Applicant must be U.S. citizen residing in Virginia, District of Columbia or Maryland.
Basis for selection: Applicant must demonstrate financial need, high academic achievement, seriousness of purpose and service orientation.
Application requirements: Essay, transcript. Letter of support, income statement, certification form.
Additional information: Program assists high school seniors in the DC metro area who have faced and overcome adversity and have participated in co-curricular and community activities. See Website for list of eligible counties. Must plan to pursue bachelor's degree. See Website for application.

Amount of award:	$6,000
Number of awards:	20
Application deadline:	October 25

Contact:
Horatio Alger Association
99 Canal Center Plaza, Suite 320
Alexandria, VA 22314
Phone: 703-684-9444
Fax: 703-684-9445
Web: www.horatioalger.com/scholarships

Horatio Alger Georgia Scholarship Program

Type of award: Scholarship.
Intended use: For full-time undergraduate study at accredited 2-year or 4-year institution in United States.
Eligibility: Applicant must be high school senior. Applicant must be U.S. citizen residing in Georgia.
Basis for selection: Applicant must demonstrate financial need, high academic achievement, seriousness of purpose and service orientation.
Application requirements: Essay, transcript. Letter of support, income statement, certification form.
Additional information: Minimum 2.0 GPA. Program assists high school seniors in Georgia who have faced and overcome adversity and have participated in co-curricular and community activities. Must plan to pursue bachelor's degree. Visit Website for application.

Amount of award:	$6,000
Number of awards:	50
Application deadline:	October 25

Contact:
Horatio Alger Association
99 Canal Center Plaza, Suite 320
Alexandria, VA 22314
Phone: 703-684-9444
Fax: 703-684-9445
Web: www.horatioalger.org/scholarships

Horatio Alger Illinois Scholarship Program

Type of award: Scholarship.
Intended use: For full-time undergraduate study at accredited 2-year or 4-year institution in United States.
Eligibility: Applicant must be high school senior. Applicant must be U.S. citizen residing in Illinois.
Basis for selection: Applicant must demonstrate financial need, high academic achievement and service orientation.
Application requirements: Essay, transcript. Letter of support, income statement, certification form.
Additional information: Minimum 2.0 GPA. Program assists high school seniors in Illinois who have faced and overcome adversity and have participated in co-curricular and community activities. Must plan to pursue bachelor's degree. Visit Website for application.

Amount of award:	$6,000
Number of awards:	20
Application deadline:	October 25

Contact:
Horatio Alger Association
99 Canal Center Plaza, Suite 320
Alexandria, VA 22314
Phone: 703-684-9444
Fax: 703-684-9445
Web: www.horatioalger.org/scholarships

Horatio Alger John Hardin Hudiburg Scholarship Program

Type of award: Scholarship.
Intended use: For freshman study at accredited 2-year or 4-year institution in United States.
Eligibility: Applicant must be high school senior. Applicant must be residing in Texas.
Basis for selection: Applicant must demonstrate financial need and high academic achievement.

Application requirements: Essay, transcript. Letter of support, income statement, certification form.
Additional information: Minimum 2.0 GPA. Program assists high school seniors in eligible Texas counties who have faced and overcome adversity and have participated in co-curricular and community activities. Must plan to pursue bachelor's degree. Visit Website for application. Must be Texas resident who attends school in one of the following districts: Grapevine-Colleyville, Hurst-Euless-Bedford, Keller, and Birdville ISD's.

Amount of award:	$6,000
Number of awards:	1
Application deadline:	October 25

Contact:
Horatio Alger Association
99 Canal Center Plaza, Suite 320
Alexandria, VA 22314
Phone: 703-684-9444
Fax: 703-684-9445
Web: www.horatioalger.org/scholarships

Horatio Alger Louisiana Scholarship Program

Type of award: Scholarship.
Intended use: For full-time undergraduate study at accredited 2-year or 4-year institution in United States. Designated institutions: Louisiana colleges and universities.
Eligibility: Applicant must be high school senior. Applicant must be U.S. citizen residing in Louisiana.
Basis for selection: Applicant must demonstrate financial need, high academic achievement, seriousness of purpose and service orientation.
Application requirements: Essay, transcript. Letter of support, income statement, certification form.
Additional information: Minimum 2.0 GPA. Program assists high school seniors in Louisiana who have faced and overcome adversity and have participated in co-curricular and community activities. Must plan to pursue bachelor's degree in Louisiana. See Website for application.

Amount of award:	$10,500
Number of awards:	50
Application deadline:	April 15

Contact:
Horatio Alger Association
99 Canal Center Plaza, Suite 320
Alexandria, VA 22314
Phone: 703-684-9444
Fax: 703-684-9445
Web: www.horatioalger.org/scholarships

Horatio Alger Missouri Scholarship Program

Type of award: Scholarship.
Intended use: For full-time undergraduate study at accredited 2-year or 4-year institution in United States.
Eligibility: Applicant must be high school senior. Applicant must be U.S. citizen residing in Missouri.
Basis for selection: Applicant must demonstrate financial need, high academic achievement, seriousness of purpose and service orientation.
Application requirements: Essay, transcript. Letter of support, income statement, certification form.
Additional information: Minimum 2.0 GPA. Program assists high school seniors in Missouri who have faced and overcome adversity and have participated in co-curricular and community

activities. Must plan to pursue bachelor's degree. See Website for application.

Amount of award:	$6,000
Number of awards:	10
Application deadline:	October 25

Contact:
Horatio Alger Association
99 Canal Center Plaza, Suite 320
Alexandria, VA 22314
Phone: 703-684-9444
Fax: 703-684-9445
Web: www.horatioalger.org/scholarships

Horatio Alger Montana Scholarship Program

Type of award: Scholarship.
Intended use: For full-time undergraduate study in United States. Designated institutions: University of Montana institutions.
Eligibility: Applicant must be high school senior. Applicant must be U.S. citizen residing in Montana.
Basis for selection: Applicant must demonstrate financial need, high academic achievement and service orientation.
Application requirements: Essay, transcript. Letter of support, income statement, certification form.
Additional information: Minimum 2.0 GPA. Program assists high school seniors in Montana who have faced and overcome adversity and have participated in co-curricular and community activities. Must plan to pursue bachelor's degree at a University of Montana school. See Website for application.

Amount of award:	$6,000
Number of awards:	50
Application deadline:	April 15

Contact:
Horatio Alger Association
99 Canal Center Plaza, Suite 320
Alexandria, VA 22314
Phone: 703-684-9444
Fax: 703-684-9445
Web: www.horatioalger.org/scholarships

Horatio Alger National Scholarship

Type of award: Scholarship.
Intended use: For full-time undergraduate study at accredited 2-year or 4-year institution in United States.
Eligibility: Applicant must be high school senior. Applicant must be U.S. citizen.
Basis for selection: Based on co-curricular and community activities. Applicant must demonstrate financial need, high academic achievement, seriousness of purpose and service orientation.
Application requirements: Essay, transcript. Letter of support, income statement, certification form.
Additional information: Minimum 2.0 GPA. Program assists high school seniors who have faced and overcome adversity and have participated in co-curricular and community activities. Must plan to pursue bachelor's degree. Visit Website for application. Must have a family income of less than $55,000.

Amount of award:	$23,000
Number of awards:	106
Number of applicants:	4,000
Application deadline:	October 25
Notification begins:	January 31
Total amount awarded:	$2,500,000

Contact:
Horatio Alger Association
99 Canal Center Plaza
Suite 320
Alexandria, VA 22314
Phone: 703-684-9444
Web: www.horatioalger.org

Horatio Alger North Dakota Scholarship Program

Type of award: Scholarship.
Intended use: For full-time undergraduate study at accredited 2-year or 4-year institution in United States.
Eligibility: Applicant must be high school senior. Applicant must be U.S. citizen residing in North Dakota.
Basis for selection: Applicant must demonstrate financial need, high academic achievement, seriousness of purpose and service orientation.
Application requirements: Essay, transcript. Letter of support, income statement, certification form.
Additional information: Minimum 2.0 GPA. Program assists high school seniors in North Dakota who have faced and overcome adversity and have participated in co-curricular and community activities. Must plan to pursue bachelor's degree. Visit Website for application.

Amount of award:	$6,000
Number of awards:	28
Application deadline:	October 25

Contact:
Horatio Alger Association
99 Canal Center Plaza, Suite 320
Alexandria, VA 22314
Phone: 703-684-9444
Fax: 703-684-9445
Web: www.horatioalger.org/scholarships

Horatio Alger Pennsylvania Scholarship Program

Type of award: Scholarship.
Intended use: For full-time undergraduate study at accredited 2-year or 4-year institution in United States.
Eligibility: Applicant must be high school senior. Applicant must be U.S. citizen residing in Pennsylvania.
Basis for selection: Applicant must demonstrate financial need, high academic achievement and service orientation.
Application requirements: Essay, transcript. Letter of support, income statement, certification form.
Additional information: Minimum 2.0 GPA. Program assists high school seniors in Pennsylvania who have faced and overcome adversity and have participated in co-curricular and community activities. Must plan to pursue bachelor's degree. See Website for application.

Amount of award:	$6,000
Number of awards:	50
Application deadline:	October 25

Contact:
Horatio Alger Association
99 Canal Center Drive, Suite 320
Alexandria, VA 22314
Phone: 703-684-9444
Fax: 703-684-9445
Web: www.horatioalger.org/scholarships

Horatio Alger Ronald C. Waranch Scholarship Program

Type of award: Scholarship.
Intended use: For freshman study at accredited 2-year or 4-year institution in United States.
Eligibility: Applicant must be high school senior. Applicant must be U.S. citizen residing in Texas.
Basis for selection: Applicant must demonstrate financial need, high academic achievement, depth of character and seriousness of purpose.
Application requirements: Essay, transcript. Letter of support, income statement, certification form.
Additional information: Minimum 2.0 GPA. Program assists high school seniors in Texas who have faced and overcome adversity and have participated in co-curricular and community activities. Must plan to pursue bachelor's degree. Visit Website for application.

Amount of award:	$6,000
Number of awards:	5
Application deadline:	October 25

Contact:
Horatio Alger Association
99 Canal Center Plaza, Suite 320
Alexandria, VA 22314
Phone: 703-684-9444
Fax: 703-684-9445
Web: www.horatioalger.org/scholarships

Horatio Alger South Dakota Scholarship Program

Type of award: Scholarship.
Intended use: For full-time undergraduate study at accredited 2-year or 4-year institution in United States.
Eligibility: Applicant must be high school senior. Applicant must be U.S. citizen residing in South Dakota.
Basis for selection: Applicant must demonstrate financial need, high academic achievement, seriousness of purpose and service orientation.
Application requirements: Essay, transcript. Letter of support, income statement, certification form.
Additional information: Minimum 2.0 GPA. Program assists high school seniors in South Dakota who have faced and overcome adversity and have participated in co-curricular and community activities. Must plan to pursue bachelor's degree. See Website for application and more information.

Amount of award:	$6,000
Number of awards:	25
Application deadline:	October 25

Contact:
The Horatio Alger Association
99 Canal Center Plaza, Suite 320
Alexandria, VA 22314
Phone: 703-684-9444
Fax: 703-684-9445
Web: www.horatioalger.org/scholarships

Horatio Alger State Scholarship

Type of award: Scholarship.
Intended use: For full-time freshman study in United States.
Eligibility: Applicant must be high school senior. Applicant must be U.S. citizen.
Application requirements: Transcript. High school transcript, support form, certification form from school counselor, short essays, and adversity section.

Additional information: Minimum 2.0 GPA. Family income must be below $55,000. Must be involved in co-curricular and community service activities. Must display integrity and perseverance in overcoming adversity. Number of scholarships per state varies.

Amount of award:	$8,000
Number of awards:	772
Number of applicants:	5,000
Application deadline:	October 25
Notification begins:	January 30
Total amount awarded:	$6,000,000

Contact:
Horatio Alger Association
99 Canal Center Plaza
Suite 320
Alexandria, VA 22314
Phone: 703-684-9444
Web: www.horatioalger.org

Horatio Alger Texas Ft. Worth Scholarship Program

Type of award: Scholarship.
Intended use: For full-time undergraduate study at accredited 2-year or 4-year institution in United States.
Eligibility: Applicant must be high school senior. Applicant must be U.S. citizen residing in Texas.
Basis for selection: Applicant must demonstrate financial need, high academic achievement, seriousness of purpose and service orientation.
Application requirements: Essay, transcript. Letter of support, income statement.
Additional information: Minimum 2.0 GPA. Applicant must reside in Fort Worth, Texas. Program assists high school seniors who have faced and overcome adversity and have participated in co-curricular and community activities. Must plan to pursue bachelor's degree. Visit Website for application.

Amount of award:	$6,000
Number of awards:	12
Application deadline:	October 25

Contact:
Horatio Alger Association
99 Canal Center Plaza, Suite 320
Alexandria, VA 22314
Phone: 703-684-9444
Fax: 703-684-9445
Web: www.horatioalger.org/scholarships

Horatio Alger Texas Scholarship Program

Type of award: Scholarship.
Intended use: For full-time undergraduate study at accredited 2-year or 4-year institution in United States.
Eligibility: Applicant must be high school senior. Applicant must be U.S. citizen residing in Texas.
Basis for selection: Applicant must demonstrate financial need, high academic achievement, depth of character and service orientation.
Application requirements: Essay, transcript. Letter of support, income statement, certification form.
Additional information: Minimum 2.0 GPA required. Program assists high school seniors in Texas who have faced and overcome adversity and have participated in co-curricular and community activities. Must plan to pursue bachelor's degree. See Website for application.

Amount of award:	$6,000
Number of awards:	7
Application deadline:	October 25

Contact:
Horatio Alger Association
99 Canal Center Plaza, Suite 320
Alexandria, VA 22314
Phone: 703-684-9444
Fax: 703-684-9445
Web: www.horatioalger.org/scholarships

Horatio Alger Utah Scholarship Program

Type of award: Scholarship.
Intended use: For full-time undergraduate study at accredited 2-year or 4-year institution in United States.
Eligibility: Applicant must be high school senior. Applicant must be U.S. citizen residing in Utah.
Basis for selection: Applicant must demonstrate financial need, high academic achievement, seriousness of purpose and service orientation.
Application requirements: Essay, transcript. Letter of support, income statement, certification form.
Additional information: Minimum 2.0 GPA. Program assists high school seniors in Utah who have faced and overcome adversity and have participated in co-curricular and community activities. Must plan to pursue bachelor's degree. Visit Website for application.

Amount of award:	$6,000
Number of awards:	7
Application deadline:	October 25

Contact:
Horatio Alger Association
99 Canal Center Plaza, Suite 320
Alexandria, VA 22314
Phone: 703-684-9444
Fax: 703-684-9445
Web: www.horatioalger.org/scholarships

Horatio Alger Wyoming Scholarship Program

Type of award: Scholarship.
Intended use: For full-time undergraduate study at accredited 2-year or 4-year institution in United States.
Eligibility: Applicant must be high school senior. Applicant must be U.S. citizen residing in Wyoming.
Basis for selection: Applicant must demonstrate financial need, high academic achievement, seriousness of purpose and service orientation.
Application requirements: Essay, transcript. Letter of support, income statement, certification form.
Additional information: Minimum 2.0 GPA. Program assists high school seniors in Wyoming who have faced and overcome adversity and have participated in co-curricular and community activities. Must plan to pursue bachelor's degree. Visit Website for application.

Amount of award:	$6,000
Number of awards:	15
Application deadline:	October 25

Contact:
Horatio Alger Association
99 Canal Center Plaza, Suite 320
Alexandria, VA 22314
Phone: 703-684-9444
Fax: 703-684-9445
Web: www.horatioalger.org/scholarships

Horticultural Research Institute

Bryan A. Champion Scholarship

Type of award: Scholarship.
Intended use: For full-time sophomore, junior, senior or graduate study at accredited 2-year, 4-year or graduate institution in United States. Designated institutions: Institutions in Ohio.
Basis for selection: Major/career interest in horticulture or landscape architecture.
Application requirements: Recommendations, transcript. Resume, cover letter.
Additional information: Minimum 2.25 overall GPA and minimum 2.7 in major. Must be majoring in landscape, horticulture, or closely related field. Must have at least sophomore standing in four-year curriculum or senior standing in two-year curriculum. Preference given to applicants who plan to work within green industry following graduation. Students in vocational agriculture programs will be considered. Previous winners eligible for additional funding. Visit Website for application and more information.

Amount of award:	$1,000
Number of awards:	1
Application deadline:	May 31

Contact:
Horticultural Research Institute
1200 G Street NW
Suite 800
Washington, DC 20005
Phone: 202-695-2474
Fax: 888-761-7883
Web: www.hriresearch.org

Horticultural Research Institute Carville M. Akehurst Memorial Scholarship

Type of award: Scholarship.
Intended use: For full-time junior, senior or graduate study at accredited 2-year, 4-year or graduate institution.
Eligibility: Applicant must be residing in Virginia, West Virginia or Maryland.
Basis for selection: Major/career interest in horticulture or landscape architecture. Applicant must demonstrate high academic achievement.
Application requirements: Recommendations, essay, transcript. Resume, cover letter.
Additional information: Minimum 2.7 overall GPA and minimum 3.0 in major. Must be majoring in horticulture, landscape, or closely related field. Must have junior standing in four-year curriculum or senior standing in two-year curriculum. Preference given to applicants who plan to work within industry following graduation. Previous winners eligible for

additional funding. Visit Website for application and more information.

Amount of award:	$4,000
Number of awards:	1
Number of applicants:	10
Application deadline:	May 31
Total amount awarded:	$4,000

Contact:
Horticultural Research Institute
1200 G Street NW
Suite 800
Washington, DC 20005
Phone: 202-695-2474
Fax: 888-761-7883
Web: www.hriresearch.org

Horticultural Research Institute Spring Meadow Scholarship

Type of award: Scholarship.
Intended use: For full-time undergraduate or graduate study at accredited vocational, 2-year, 4-year or graduate institution.
Basis for selection: Major/career interest in horticulture or landscape architecture. Applicant must demonstrate high academic achievement.
Application requirements: Recommendations, essay, transcript. Resume, cover letter.
Additional information: Must have minimum 2.25 overall GPA, and minimum 2.7 in major. Must have at least sophomore standing in 4-year program or senior standing in 2-year program. Must be enrolled in accredited landscape, horticulture or closely related program. Must be interested in woody plant production, propagation, and breeding or horticulture sales and marketing. Preference given to those who plan to work in industry following graduation. Visit Website for application and more information.

Amount of award:	$3,000
Number of awards:	3
Number of applicants:	69
Application deadline:	May 31
Total amount awarded:	$1,500

Contact:
Horticultural Research Institute
1200 G Street NW
Suite 800
Washington, DC 20005
Phone: 202-695-2474
Fax: 888-761-7883
Web: www.hriresearch.org

Muggets Scholarship

Type of award: Scholarship, renewable.
Intended use: For undergraduate or graduate study at vocational, 2-year, 4-year or graduate institution in United States. Designated institutions: California state colleges and universities.
Basis for selection: Major/career interest in landscape architecture or horticulture. Applicant must demonstrate high academic achievement.
Application requirements: Recommendations, essay, transcript. Cover letter and resume.
Additional information: Students enrolled in vocational agricultural programs also eligible. Must be majoring in landscape, horticulture, or closely related field. Students in vocational agriculture programs will be considered. Must be a sophomore or above in 4-year program, or senior in 2-year program. Preference given to applicants who plan to work

within the industry after graduation. Minimum 2.25 GPA overall; minimum 2.7 GPA in major. Visit Website for application.

Amount of award:	$1,500
Number of awards:	1
Application deadline:	May 31
Total amount awarded:	$1,500

Contact:
Endowment Program Administrator, Horticultural Research Institute
1200 G Street NW
Suite 800
Washington, DC 20005
Phone: 202-695-2474
Fax: 888-761-7883
Web: www.hriresearch.org

Susie & Bruce Usrey Scholarship

Type of award: Scholarship.
Intended use: For full-time undergraduate or graduate study at accredited 4-year or graduate institution in United States. Designated institutions: Institutions in California.
Basis for selection: Major/career interest in horticulture or landscape architecture.
Application requirements: Recommendations, transcript. Resume, cover letter.
Additional information: Minimum 2.25 overall GPA and minimum 2.7 in major. Must be majoring in landscape, horticulture, or closely related field. Students in vocational agriculture programs will be considered. Preference given to applicants who plan to work within industry following graduation. Previous winners eligible for additional funding. Visit Website for application and more information.

Amount of award:	$500
Application deadline:	May 31

Contact:
Horticultural Research Institute
1200 G Street NW
Suite 800
Washington, DC 20005
Phone: 202-695-2474
Fax: 202-789-1893
Web: www.hriresearch.org

Timothy and Palmer W. Bigelow, Jr. Scholarship

Type of award: Scholarship.
Intended use: For full-time undergraduate or graduate study at accredited 2-year, 4-year or graduate institution.
Eligibility: Applicant must be residing in Vermont, New Hampshire, Connecticut, Maine, Massachusetts or Rhode Island.
Basis for selection: Major/career interest in landscape architecture or horticulture. Applicant must demonstrate financial need, high academic achievement, depth of character and seriousness of purpose.
Application requirements: Recommendations, essay, transcript. Resume and cover letter.
Additional information: Minimum GPA: 2.25 overall and 3.0 major for undergraduates; 3.0 for graduate students. Must be enrolled in accredited landscape, horticulture, or closely related program. Applicant must have senior standing in two-year program, junior standing in four-year program, or graduate standing. Applicant must be resident of one of the six New England states, but need not attend institution there. Preference given to applicants who plan to work in nursery industry after

graduation, including the desire to own one's own business. Preference also given to applicants who demonstrate financial need. Visit Website for application.

Amount of award:	$3,000
Number of awards:	1
Number of applicants:	8
Application deadline:	May 31
Notification begins:	July 1
Total amount awarded:	$3,000

Contact:
Horticultural Research Institute
1200 G Street NW
Suite 800
Washington, DC 20005
Phone: 202-695-2474
Fax: 888-761-7883
Web: www.hriresearch.org

The Usrey Family Scholarship

Type of award: Scholarship.
Intended use: For full-time undergraduate or graduate study at accredited vocational, 2-year, 4-year or graduate institution. Designated institutions: Institutions in California.
Basis for selection: Major/career interest in horticulture.
Application requirements: Recommendations, transcript. Resume, cover letter.
Additional information: Minimum 2.25 overall GPA and minimum 2.7 in major. Must be majoring in landscape, horticulture, or closely related field. Students in vocational agriculture programs will be considered. Preference given to applicants who plan to work within industry following graduation. Previous winners eligible for additional funding. Visit Website for application and more information.

Amount of award:	$1,000
Number of awards:	1
Application deadline:	May 31

Contact:
Horticultural Research Institute
1200 G Street NW
Suite 800
Washington, DC 20005
Phone: 202-695-2474
Fax: 888-761-7883
Web: www.hriresearch.org

Housing opportunities made equal

Joanne Champion Granger Scholarship

Type of award: Scholarship.
Intended use: For freshman study at 4-year institution.
Application requirements: Essay. Be a college-bound, high school senior with an average of B or greater. Complete an essay demonstrating community involvement and a commitment to human rights. Submit a nominating letter from school personnel or community leader. Attend HOME's 54th Annual Dinner on Thursday, April 20rd, 2017 to accept the $1,000 scholarship award.
Additional information: Applicants must be residents of Erie County.

Amount of award:	$1,000
Number of awards:	1
Number of applicants:	36
Application deadline:	February 10
Notification begins:	April 5
Total amount awarded:	$1,000

Contact:
Kibrett Facey
1542 Main Street
Buffalo, NY 14209
Phone: 716-854-1400
Fax: 716-854-1140
Web: www.homeny.org/events-updates/joannne-champion-granger-scholarship/

Houston Livestock Show and Rodeo

Area Go Texan Scholarships

Type of award: Scholarship.
Intended use: For undergraduate study at postsecondary institution. Designated institutions: Texas colleges and universities.
Eligibility: Applicant must be high school senior. Applicant must be U.S. citizen residing in Texas.
Basis for selection: Applicant must demonstrate financial need, high academic achievement, depth of character, leadership and service orientation.
Application requirements: Recommendations, essay, transcript, proof of eligibility. Class standing and photograph. SAT/ACT scores. FAFSA.
Additional information: Scholarships awarded to one eligible public high school student from each of 62 Area Go Texan counties. Minimum 1350 SAT combined score (reading and math), or minimum 19 ACT score. Applicant must attend public high school and be in top third of graduating class. Applicant cannot receive more than $40,000 from financial aid or other scholarships. Contact sponsor or visit Website for eligible counties, deadline, and application.

Amount of award:	$4,500
Number of awards:	78
Application deadline:	March 1
Total amount awarded:	$1,050,000

Contact:
Houston Livestock Show and Rodeo
Office of Education Programs
P.O. Box 20070
Houston, TX 77225-0070
Phone: 832-667-1113
Web: www.rodeohouston.com

Houston Livestock Show and Rodeo Metropolitan Scholarships

Type of award: Scholarship, renewable.
Intended use: For undergraduate study at accredited 4-year institution in United States. Designated institutions: Colleges and universities in Texas.
Eligibility: Applicant must be high school senior. Applicant must be U.S. citizen residing in Texas.
Basis for selection: Applicant must demonstrate financial need, high academic achievement, depth of character and leadership.

Scholarships

363

Application requirements: Recommendations, essay, transcript. SAT/ACT Scores. FAFSA.

Additional information: Must be graduating from Houston area public school districts in Brazoria, Chambers, Fort Bend, Galveston, Harris, Liberty, Montgomery, and Waller Counties. Must be in the top quarter of graduating class and have a minimum 950 SAT (reading and math sections only) or 19 ACT score.

Amount of award:	$4,500
Number of awards:	238
Application deadline:	March 1

Contact:
Houston Livestock Show and Rodeo
Educational Programs Department
P.O. Box 20070
Houston, TX 77225-0070
Phone: 832-667-1285
Web: www.rodeohouston.com/Scholarships/
ApplyforScholarships

Houston Livestock Show and Rodeo Opportunity Scholarship

Type of award: Scholarship, renewable.

Intended use: For full-time undergraduate study at 4-year institution. Designated institutions: Texas colleges and universities.

Eligibility: Applicant must be high school senior. Applicant must be U.S. citizen residing in Texas.

Basis for selection: Applicant must demonstrate financial need, high academic achievement, depth of character, leadership and service orientation.

Application requirements: Recommendations, transcript, proof of eligibility. Up to three references. FAFSA. Two-page essay must describe importance of college and career goals. Class standing and photograph. SAT/ACT scores.

Additional information: Must have minimum 1300 SAT (reading and math) or 18 ACT. Must be graduating in top half of class from specified Texas school districts in Brazoria, Chambers, Fort Bend, Galveston, Harris, Liberty, Montgomery, or Waller counties. Visit Website for list of eligible districts, application, and more information. For applications, contact guidance counselor or Office of Education Programs.

Amount of award:	$4,500
Number of awards:	114
Application deadline:	February 24
Total amount awarded:	$1,500,000

Contact:
Houston Livestock Show and Rodeo
Office of Education Programs
P.O. Box 20070
Houston, TX 77225-0070
Phone: 832-667-1113
Web: www.rodeohouston.com

Houston Livestock Show and Rodeo School Art Scholarships

Type of award: Scholarship, renewable.

Intended use: For undergraduate study at accredited 4-year institution in United States. Designated institutions: Colleges and universities in Texas.

Eligibility: Applicant must be high school senior. Applicant must be U.S. citizen residing in Texas.

Basis for selection: Applicant must demonstrate financial need, high academic achievement, depth of character and leadership.

Application requirements: Recommendations, essay, transcript, proof of eligibility. SAT/ACT scores. FAFSA.

Additional information: Must be a high school senior that participated in the HLSR School Art Competition and/or the Quick Draw Competition. Must be in the top quarter of graduating class and have a minimum 950 SAT (reading and math sections only) or 19 ACT score. Visit website for deadline.

Amount of award:	$4,500
Number of awards:	15
Application deadline:	March 1

Contact:
Houston Livestock Show and Rodeo
Educational Programs Department
P.O. Box 20070
Houston, TX 77225-0070
Phone: 832-667-1285
Web: www.rodeohouston.com/Scholarships/
ApplyforScholarships

Military Scholarship

Type of award: Scholarship.

Intended use: For full-time undergraduate study at accredited 4-year institution in United States. Designated institutions: Accredited, not-for-profit universities in Texas.

Eligibility: Applicant must be high school senior. Applicant must be U.S. citizen residing in Texas.

Basis for selection: Applicant must demonstrate financial need, high academic achievement, depth of character and leadership.

Application requirements: Transcript. FAFSA.

Additional information: Must be high school senior graduating from eligible Texas high school. Must be dependent of service member, either active, in reserves, or honorably discharged or in National Guard. Must be in top 25 percent of class. Minimum 950 SAT (reading and math only) or 19 ACT.

Amount of award:	$4,500
Number of awards:	5
Application deadline:	February 24

Contact:
Houston Livestock Show and Rodeo
Educational Programs Department
P.O. Box 20070
Houston, TX 77225-0070
Phone: 832-667-1285
Web: www.rodeohouston.com/Scholarships/
ApplyforScholarships

Technical Scholarship

Type of award: Scholarship.

Intended use: For full-time freshman or post-bachelor's certificate study at accredited 2-year institution in United States. Designated institutions: Accredited, not-for-profit universities in Texas.

Eligibility: Applicant must be high school senior. Applicant must be U.S. citizen residing in Texas.

Basis for selection: Applicant must demonstrate financial need and high academic achievement.

Application requirements: Transcript, proof of eligibility. FAFSA.

Additional information: Must be high school senior graduating from eligible Texas high school. Must pursue an associate's degree in approved technical field. Five awards go to students who have participated in Houston Livestock Show and Rodeo Agricultural Mechanics Project Show or Tractor Technician Contest Finals.

Amount of award:	$4,500
Number of awards:	5
Application deadline:	February 1

Contact:
Houston Livestock Show and Rodeo
Educational Programs Department
P.O. Box 20070
Houston, TX 77225-0070
Phone: 832-667-1285
Web: www.rodeohouston.com/Scholarships/
ApplyforScholarships

Hylan Dental Care

Hylan Family Scholarship

Type of award: Scholarship.
Intended use: For full-time undergraduate or graduate study at accredited 2-year, 4-year or graduate institution in United States.
Eligibility: Applicant must be high school senior.
Application requirements: 500-750 word essay on the following topic: "Pick an experience from your life and explain how it has influenced your educational and personal development."

Amount of award:	$2,500
Number of awards:	1
Number of applicants:	100
Application deadline:	June 30
Total amount awarded:	$2,500

Contact:
Hylan Dental Care
3447 West 117th Street
Cleveland, OH 44111
Web: https://www.drbradhylan.com/scholarship.html

ICMA Retirement Corporation

Vantagepoint Public Employee Memorial Scholarship Fund

Type of award: Scholarship.
Intended use: For full-time undergraduate or graduate study at accredited postsecondary institution.
Basis for selection: Applicant must demonstrate financial need, high academic achievement, leadership and service orientation.
Application requirements: Recommendations, essay, transcript, proof of eligibility. Statement of goals and aspirations, official letter from deceased employee's place of work certifying employee died in line of duty.
Additional information: High school seniors and graduates, as well as current undergraduate or graduate students eligible. Must be child or spouse of deceased local or state government employee who has died in the line of duty. Work experience, goals and aspirations, and unusual personal or family circumstances also factored into selection. Award amount varies; maximum is $10,000 (tuition and fees only). Visit Website for complete information and application.

Amount of award:	$10,000
Number of awards:	30
Application deadline:	March 15
Notification begins:	June 1

Contact:
Vantagepoint Public Employee Memorial Scholarship Program
c/o Scholarship America
One Scholarship Way
St. Peter, MN 56082
Phone: 507-931-1682
Web: www.vantagescholar.org

Idaho State Board of Education

Idaho GEAR UP Scholarship

Type of award: Scholarship, renewable.
Intended use: For full-time undergraduate study at accredited 2-year or 4-year institution in United States. Designated institutions: North Idaho College, Lewis-Clark State College, College of Southern Idaho, Eastern Idaho Technical College, University of Idaho, Boise State University, Idaho State University, BYU Idaho, Northwest Nazarene University, College of Idaho, College of Western Idaho.
Eligibility: Applicant must be no older than 21. Applicant must be U.S. citizen or permanent resident residing in Idaho.
Basis for selection: Applicant must demonstrate financial need.
Application requirements: FAFSA.
Additional information: Must be graduating senior from Idaho high school who participated in GEAR UP early intervention component (7th-10th grade).

Application deadline:	February 15

Contact:
Idaho State Board of Education
650 West State Street
P.O. Box 83720
Boise, ID 83720-0037
Phone: 208-334-2270
Web: www.boardofed.idaho.gov/scholarship/gear_up.asp

Idaho Governor's Cup Scholarship

Type of award: Scholarship, renewable.
Intended use: For full-time undergraduate study at postsecondary institution. Designated institutions: Idaho state-funded colleges and universities.
Eligibility: Applicant must be high school senior. Applicant must be residing in Idaho.
Basis for selection: Applicant must demonstrate high academic achievement, leadership and service orientation.
Application requirements: Recommendations, essay, transcript. SAT/ACT scores. Documentation of volunteer work, leadership, and public service.
Additional information: Minimum 2.8 GPA. Must be graduating senior from Idaho high school who has demonstrated commitment to public service. For more information, contact high school guidance counselor or Idaho State Board of Education.

Amount of award:	$3,000
Application deadline:	February 15

Contact:
Idaho State Board of Education
650 West State Street
P.O. Box 83720
Boise, ID 83720-0037
Phone: 208-334-2270
Web: www.boardofed.idaho.gov/scholarship/gov_cup.asp

Idaho Opportunity Scholarship

Type of award: Scholarship.
Intended use: For full-time undergraduate study at 2-year or 4-year institution in United States. Designated institutions: Eligible Idaho colleges and universities.
Eligibility: Applicant must be U.S. citizen or permanent resident residing in Idaho.
Basis for selection: Applicant must demonstrate financial need.
Application requirements: FAFSA.
Additional information: Must be graduate of Idaho high school or received GED in Idaho.

Amount of award:	$3,000
Application deadline:	March 1

Contact:
Idaho State Board of Education
650 West State Street
P.O. Box 83720
Boise, ID 83720-0037
Phone: 208-334-2270
Web: www.boardofed.idaho.gov/scholarship/opportunity.asp

Idaho State Board of Education Armed Forces and Public Safety Officer Dependent Scholarship

Type of award: Scholarship.
Intended use: For full-time undergraduate study at accredited 4-year institution in United States. Designated institutions: Idaho postsecondary institutions.
Eligibility: Applicant must be U.S. citizen or permanent resident residing in Idaho. Applicant's parent must have been killed or disabled in work-related accident as public safety officer.
Additional information: Must be graduate of Idaho high school or have taken GED in Idaho. Must be spouse or child of full-time or part-time Idaho public safety officer employed in Idaho that was killed or disabled in line of duty, or member of armed forces who was killed or listed missing in action. Provides tuition waiver and on-campus housing plus up to $500 for books per semester.

Amount of award:	Full tuition
Application deadline:	February 15

Contact:
Idaho State Board of Education
650 West State Street
P.O. Box 83720
Boise, ID 83720-0037
Phone: 208-334-2270
Web: www.boardofed.idaho.gov/scholarship/pub_safety.asp

Illinois Department of Veterans' Affairs

Illinois MIA/POW Scholarship

Type of award: Scholarship, renewable.
Intended use: For full-time undergraduate study at accredited postsecondary institution in United States. Designated institutions: Illinois state-supported schools.
Eligibility: Applicant must be U.S. citizen residing in Illinois. Applicant must be dependent of disabled veteran, deceased veteran or POW/MIA; or spouse of disabled veteran, deceased veteran or POW/MIA.
Application requirements: Proof of eligibility.
Additional information: Available to dependents of veterans who have been declared prisoners of war, missing in action, become permanently disabled, or have died due to service related disability. Veteran must have been Illinois resident within six months of entering service.

Amount of award:	Full tuition

Contact:
Illinois Department of Veterans' Affairs
833 South Spring Street
P.O. Box 19432
Springfield, IL 62794-9432
Phone: 217-782-6641
Web: www.veterans.illinois.gov/benefits

Illinois Student Assistance Commission

Illinois Grant Program for Dependents of Correctional Officers

Type of award: Scholarship, renewable.
Intended use: For freshman study at 2-year or 4-year institution in United States. Designated institutions: ISAC-approved institutions in Illinois.
Eligibility: Applicant must be U.S. citizen or permanent resident. Applicant's parent must have been killed or disabled in work-related accident as public safety officer.
Application requirements: Proof of eligibility.
Additional information: Must be child or spouse of Illinois corrections officer killed or at least 90 percent disabled in line of duty. Award is equal to full tuition and mandatory fees at public Illinois institutions; at private schools a corresponding amount is awarded. Applicant need not be Illinois resident at time of enrollment. Beneficiaries may receive the equivalent of eight semesters or 12 quarters of assistance. Contact ISAC or visit Website for additional information.

Amount of award:	Full tuition
Application deadline:	October 1

Contact:
Illinois Student Assistance Commission
ISAC College Zone Counselor
1755 Lake Cook Road
Deerfield, IL 60015
Phone: 800-899-ISAC
Web: www.isac.org/students/during-college

Illinois Grant Program for Dependents of Police or Fire Officers

Type of award: Scholarship, renewable.
Intended use: For undergraduate or graduate study at 2-year, 4-year or graduate institution. Designated institutions: ISAC-approved institutions in Illinois.
Eligibility: Applicant must be U.S. citizen or permanent resident. Applicant's parent must have been killed or disabled in work-related accident as firefighter or police officer.
Application requirements: Proof of eligibility.
Additional information: Grant for tuition and fees for spouses and children of Illinois policemen or firemen killed or at least 90 percent disabled in line of duty. Award amount adjusted annually. Applicant need not be Illinois resident at time of enrollment. Beneficiaries may receive the equivalent of eight semesters or 12 quarters of assistance. Contact ISAC or visit Website for additional information.

Amount of award:	Full tuition
Application deadline:	October 1, March 1
Total amount awarded:	$710,192

Contact:
Illinois Student Assistance Commission
ISAC College Zone Counselor
1755 Lake Cook Road
Deerfield, IL 60015
Phone: 800-899-ISAC
Web: www.isac.org/students/during-college

Illinois Higher Education License Plate (HELP) Program

Type of award: Scholarship.
Intended use: For undergraduate study at accredited postsecondary institution in United States. Designated institutions: Participating Illinois universities.
Eligibility: Applicant must be U.S. citizen.
Application requirements: FAFSA.
Additional information: Provides grants to students who attend Illinois colleges for which collegiate license plates are available. Contact your college to determine if it participates in the HELP program. Number and amount of awards contingent on number of license plates sold.
Contact:
Illinois Student Assistance Commission
1755 Lake Cook Road
Deerfield, IL 60015
Phone: 800-899-ISAC
Web: www.isac.org/students/during-college

Illinois Monetary Award Program (MAP)

Type of award: Scholarship, renewable.
Intended use: For undergraduate study at 2-year or 4-year institution. Designated institutions: ISAC/MAP-approved institutions in Illinois.
Eligibility: Applicant must be U.S. citizen or permanent resident residing in Illinois.
Basis for selection: Applicant must demonstrate financial need.
Application requirements: FAFSA.
Additional information: Must not have received bachelor's degree. Must reapply every year for renewal. Contact ISAC or visit Website for application, deadlines, and additional

information. Amount of award dependent on legislative action and available funding in any given year.
Contact:
Illinois Student Assistance Commission
ISAC College Zone Counselor
1755 Lake Cook Road
Deerfield, IL 60015
Phone: 800-899-ISAC
Web: www.isac.org/students/during-college

Illinois National Guard Grant

Type of award: Scholarship, renewable.
Intended use: For undergraduate or graduate study at 2-year or 4-year institution. Designated institutions: Approved Illinois institutions.
Eligibility: Applicant must be residing in Illinois. Applicant must be in military service in the Reserves/National Guard. Must have served at least one year of active duty in Illinois National Guard or Naval Militia.
Application requirements: Proof of eligibility.
Additional information: Available to enlisted and company grade officers up to rank of captain who have either served one year active duty; are currently on active duty status; or have been active for at least five consecutive years and have been called to federal active duty for at least six months and be within 12 months after discharge date. Applied toward tuition and certain fees. Recipients may use award for eight semesters or 12 quarters (or the equivalent). Award amount varies. Deadlines: 10/1 for full year, 3/1 for second/third term, 6/15 for summer term. Applications available from ISAC or National Guard units. Contact ISAC or National Guard units or visit Website for additional information.

Application deadline:	October 1

Contact:
Illinois Student Assistance Commission
ISAC College Zone Counselor
1755 Lake Cook Road
Deerfield, IL 60015
Phone: 800-899-ISAC
Web: www.isac.org/students/during-college

Illinois Special Education Teacher Tuition Waiver

Type of award: Scholarship, renewable.
Intended use: For undergraduate or graduate study at postsecondary institution in United States. Designated institutions: Eligible four-year institutions in Illinois: Chicago State University, Eastern Illinois University, Governors State University, Illinois State University, Northeastern Illinois University, Northern Illinois University, Southern Illinois University (Carbondale and Edwardsville), University of Illinois (Chicago, Springfield, Urbana), and Western Illinois University.
Eligibility: Applicant must be U.S. citizen or permanent resident residing in Illinois.
Basis for selection: Major/career interest in education, special.
Additional information: Must be Illinois high school graduate and rank in upper half of graduating class. Must not already hold valid teaching certificate in special education. Recipients must teach in Illinois for two years, or scholarship becomes loan. See Website for application and more details.

Amount of award:	Full tuition
Number of awards:	250
Application deadline:	March 1
Notification begins:	July 1

Contact:
Illinois Student Assistance Commission
1755 Lake Cook Road
Deerfield, IL 60015
Phone: 800-899-ISAC
Web: www.isac.org/students/during-college

Illinois Veteran Grant (IVG) Program

Type of award: Scholarship, renewable.
Intended use: For undergraduate or graduate study at postsecondary institution.
Eligibility: Applicant must be U.S. citizen or permanent resident residing in Illinois. Applicant must be veteran. Must have been Illinois resident or Illinois college student six months prior to entering service and must have returned to Illinois to reside within six months of leaving service. Must have served one year of federal active duty or have served in a foreign country in a time of hostilities in that country.
Application requirements: Proof of eligibility.
Additional information: Provides payment of tuition and mandatory fees to qualified Illinois veterans or military service members. Grant is available for equivalent of four academic years of full-time enrollment for undergraduate and graduate study. Recipient not required to enroll for minimum number of credit hours each term. One-time application only. See Website for additional information and application.

    Amount of award: Full tuition
Contact:
Illinois Student Assistance Commission
ISAC College Zone Counselor
1755 Lake Cook Road
Deerfield, IL 60015
Phone: 800-899-ISAC
Web: www.isac.org/students/during-college

Minority Teachers of Illinois Scholarship

Type of award: Scholarship, renewable.
Intended use: For undergraduate or graduate study at postsecondary institution. Designated institutions: ISAC-approved institutions in Illinois.
Eligibility: Applicant must be Alaskan native, Asian American, African American, Mexican American, Hispanic American, Puerto Rican, American Indian or Native Hawaiian/Pacific Islander. Applicant must be U.S. citizen or permanent resident residing in Illinois.
Basis for selection: Major/career interest in education, teacher or education. Applicant must demonstrate high academic achievement.
Application requirements: Teacher Education Program application.
Additional information: Minimum 2.5 GPA. Applicant should be in course of study leading to teacher certification. Recipient must sign commitment to teach one year in Illinois for each year assistance is received. Must teach at nonprofit Illinois preschool, elementary school, or secondary school with at least 30 percent minority enrollment. If teaching commitment is not fulfilled, scholarship converts to loan, and entire amount, plus interest, must be paid. Contact ISAC or visit Website for additional information.

    Amount of award: $5,000
    Application deadline: March 1

Contact:
Illinois Student Assistance Commission
ISAC College Zone Counselor
1755 Lake Cook Road
Deerfield, IL 60015
Phone: 800-899-ISAC
Web: www.isac.org/students/during-college

Immune Deficiency Foundation

Varun Bhaskaran Scholarship

Type of award: Scholarship.
Intended use: For undergraduate or graduate study at 2-year or 4-year institution.
Eligibility: Applicant must be U.S. citizen or permanent resident.
Application requirements: Recommendations, essay, proof of eligibility. FAFSA, letter from immunologist.
Additional information: Applicant must be living with Wiskott-Aldrich Syndrome.
    Application deadline: April 15
Contact:
Immune Deficiency Foundation
40 W. Chesapeake Avenue
Suite 308
Towson, MD 21204
Phone: 800-296-4433
Web: www.primaryimmune.org/services/idf-academic-scholarship-programs

Infinity Dental Web

Infinity Dental Web - Advances in Technology

Type of award: Scholarship.
Basis for selection: The award will be given to the student with the essay that is not only the most well written, but also is the most thoughtful and reveals the student with the most promise based on the judgement of the scholarship sponsor. Major/career interest in marketing.
Application requirements: Essay. Must provide documentation verifying that they will be a student for the Fall semester.
Additional information: Qualifying applicants will answer the essay question provided. The essay must be between 450-600 words. You may upload an essay in Word or PDF format, or you may copy and paste it into the application form. To be considered, you must submit the application and essay before the deadline. Student's major must be in the marketing field of study.

    Amount of award: $250
    Number of awards: 1
    Application deadline: June 30

Contact:
Infinity Dental Web - Advances in Technology
Phone: 480-273-8888 4#
Web: www.infinitydentalweb.com/infinity-scholarship.html

Insurance Accounting and Systems Association

Insurance Industry Collegiate Scholarship Program

Type of award: Scholarship.
Intended use: For full-time junior or senior study at 4-year institution.
Basis for selection: Major/career interest in insurance/actuarial science; finance/banking; accounting or technology.
Application requirements: Statement (max 500 words) describing short-term personal and career goals and objectives. Statement (max 500 words) describing how scholarship would help achieve goals.
Additional information: Minimum 3.0 GPA required. Must be pursuing degree in: Insurance, Risk Management, Finance, Accounting, Systems, Technology or related major. Current and former IASA members and their immediate family members are eligible to apply for this scholarship so long as the aforementioned eligibility requirements are met. Members of IASA Scholarship Selection Committee and their immediate families are not eligible.

Amount of award:	$500-$2,500
Number of awards:	21
Application deadline:	February 29
Total amount awarded:	$20,000

Contact:
Insurance Accounting and Systems Association
3511 Shannon Road
Suite 160
Durham, NC 27707
Phone: 919-489-0991 X206
Fax: 919-489-1994
Web: www.iasa.org/Scholarship

InsurTech

InsurTech Scholarship

Type of award: Scholarship.
Intended use: For undergraduate or graduate study at vocational, 2-year, 4-year or graduate institution.
Eligibility: Applicant must be at least 18.
Application requirements: Recommendations, essay, transcript. 1,500 word essay, current college transcript, letter of recommendation.
Additional information: Intended for students who are puruing a career in the insurance industry.

Number of awards:	1
Application deadline:	October 31
Notification begins:	November 30
Total amount awarded:	$1,000

Contact:
Web: https://www.getitc.com/scholarship/

International Association of Fire Fighters

W.H. McClennan Scholarship

Type of award: Scholarship, renewable.
Intended use: For full-time undergraduate study at accredited vocational, 2-year or 4-year institution.
Eligibility: Applicant's parent must have been killed or disabled in work-related accident as firefighter.
Basis for selection: Applicant must demonstrate financial need, depth of character, seriousness of purpose and service orientation.
Application requirements: Recommendations, essay, transcript, proof of eligibility. IA77 McClennan application.
Additional information: Open to children of firefighters who were killed in the line of duty and were members in good standing of IAFF at the time of deaths.

Amount of award:	$2,500
Number of applicants:	50
Application deadline:	February 1
Notification begins:	August 1
Total amount awarded:	$127,500

Contact:
W. H. McClennan Scholarship/International Association of Fire Fighters
1750 New York Ave., NW
3rd Floor, Dept. of Education
Washington, DC 20006
Phone: 202-737-8484
Fax: 202-737-8418
Web: www.iaff.org/scholarships

International Buckskin Horse Association, Inc.

Buckskin Horse Association Scholarship

Type of award: Scholarship, renewable.
Intended use: For full-time undergraduate study at accredited postsecondary institution in United States.
Eligibility: Applicant must be high school senior. Applicant must be U.S. citizen.
Basis for selection: Applicant must demonstrate financial need, high academic achievement, depth of character, leadership and seriousness of purpose.
Application requirements: Portfolio, recommendations, proof of eligibility.
Additional information: Available to children of association members. Parent must have been member for at least 2 years.

Amount of award:	$500-$1,000
Number of awards:	12
Number of applicants:	8
Application deadline:	March 15
Notification begins:	September 15
Total amount awarded:	$7,500

Scholarships

Contact:
International Buckskin Horse Association, Inc.
P.O. Box 268
Shelby, IN 46377
Phone: 219-552-1013
Fax: 219-552-1013
Web: www.ibha.net

International College Counselors

International College Counselors Scholarship

Type of award: Scholarship.
Intended use: For undergraduate study at vocational, 2-year, 4-year or graduate institution in United States.
Application requirements: High school freshmen, sophomores or juniors must write an essay that addresses the following topic: You have been invited to talk to the future U.S. Secretary of Education. What would you say?
Additional information: Two winners will be selected: One from Miami-Dade, Broward, or Palm Beach County; and one at large winner from anywhere in the world, domestic or international, including home schooled students. Each winner will receive a $250 check payable to the winner's college/ university or certified trade school in the United States. All submissions must be accompanied by a completed Official Student Registration form found on web site. Essays and forms must be submitted via mail.

Amount of award:	$250
Number of awards:	2
Application deadline:	March 1
Notification begins:	May 1
Total amount awarded:	$500

Contact:
International College Counselors
3107 Stirling Road
Suite 208
Ft. Lauderdale, FL 33312
Web: iccscholarship.com/

International Executive Housekeepers Association

IEHA Educational Foundation Scholarship

Type of award: Scholarship.
Intended use: For undergraduate or non-degree study at accredited postsecondary institution.
Basis for selection: Major/career interest in hospitality administration/management.
Application requirements: Essay, transcript. Letter from school official verifying enrollment. Class schedule and coursework curriculum. Original and three copies of prepared manuscript on housekeeping (maximum 2,000 words, double-spaced).

Additional information: Applicant must be member of International Executive Housekeepers Association. Scholarship will be awarded to student submitting best original manuscript on housekeeping within any industry segment (e.g., hospitality, healthcare, education, rehabilitation centers, government buildings). Other major/career interest: facilities management. Can be used for IEHA certification program. No set limit on number of awards granted.

Application deadline:	January 10
Notification begins:	June 1
Total amount awarded:	$8,000

Contact:
International Executive Housekeepers Association
Educational Foundation Scholarships
1001 Eastwind Drive, Suite 301
Westerville, OH 43081-7166
Phone: 800-200-6342
Fax: 614-895-7166
Web: www.ieha.org

International Foodservice Editorial Council

Scholarship for Foodservice Communication Careers

Type of award: Scholarship.
Intended use: For full-time undergraduate or master's study at accredited postsecondary institution in United States.
Basis for selection: Major/career interest in food science/ technology; food production/management/services; culinary arts; communications; public relations or journalism. Applicant must demonstrate financial need, high academic achievement, depth of character, leadership, seriousness of purpose and service orientation.
Application requirements: Recommendations, essay, transcript, proof of eligibility.
Additional information: Applicant must pursue academic study in editorial or public relations within the food service industry. Writing ability considered. Applications may be requested by e-mail or downloaded from Website.

Amount of award:	$500-$4,000
Number of awards:	8
Number of applicants:	85
Application deadline:	March 15
Notification begins:	July 1
Total amount awarded:	$17,000

Contact:
International Foodservice Editorial Council (IFEC)
P.O. Box 491
Hyde Park, NY 12538
Phone: 845-229-6973
Fax: 845-229-6973
Web: www.ifeconline.com

International Furnishings and Design Association Educational Foundation

Green/Sustainable Design Scholarship

Type of award: Scholarship.
Intended use: For undergraduate study in United States.
Basis for selection: Major/career interest in interior design.
Application requirements: Portfolio, recommendations, essay, transcript. Two to three examples of original design work, letter of recommendation from instructor on official school stationery, recommendation from current IFDA member.
Additional information: Student must be planning to seek LEED accreditation. See Website for further requirements and application.

Amount of award:	$1,500
Number of awards:	1
Application deadline:	March 31
Notification begins:	July 31
Total amount awarded:	$1,500

Contact:
IFDA Educational Foundation, Director of Grants/Scholarships
Earline Feldman
112 Hidden Lake Circle
Canton, GA 30114
Web: www.ifdaef.org

IFDA Leaders Commemorative Scholarship

Type of award: Scholarship.
Intended use: For undergraduate study at postsecondary institution in United States.
Eligibility: Applicant must be U.S. citizen or permanent resident.
Basis for selection: Major/career interest in design or interior design. Applicant must demonstrate depth of character, leadership and service orientation.
Application requirements: Portfolio, recommendations, essay, transcript. Two-three examples of original student design work, recommendation from professor on official school stationery, recommendation from IFDA member.
Additional information: Must have completed four courses in interior design (or related field) at post-secondary level. Student must be involved with volunteer or community service and held leadership positions during past five years. See Website for further requirements and application.

Amount of award:	$1,500
Number of awards:	1
Application deadline:	March 31
Notification begins:	July 31
Total amount awarded:	$1,500

Contact:
IFDA Educational Foundation, Director of Grants/Scholarships
Earline Feldman
112 Hidden Lake Circle
Canton, GA 30114
Web: www.ifdaef.org

International Furnishings and Design Association Educational Foundation Part-Time Student Scholarship

Type of award: Scholarship.
Intended use: For half-time undergraduate study at postsecondary institution in United States.
Basis for selection: Major/career interest in interior design.
Application requirements: Portfolio, recommendations, essay, transcript. Two to three examples of the student's original design work. Resume. Recommendations from instructor and current IFDA member.
Additional information: Applicants must have completed four courses in interior design or related field. Must be currently enrolled in at least two courses as part-time student. Visit Website for application and additional information.

Amount of award:	$1,500
Number of awards:	1
Application deadline:	March 31
Notification begins:	July 31
Total amount awarded:	$1,500

Contact:
IFDA Educational Foundation, Director of Grants/Scholarships
Earline Feldman
112 Hidden Lake Circle
Canton, GA 30114
Web: www.ifdaef.org

International Furnishings and Design Association Student Member Scholarships

Type of award: Scholarship.
Intended use: For full-time undergraduate study at accredited postsecondary institution in United States.
Basis for selection: Major/career interest in interior design. Applicant must demonstrate high academic achievement, depth of character, seriousness of purpose and service orientation.
Application requirements: Recommendations, essay, transcript. Two to three examples of student design work. Recommendation from IFDA member. Recommendation from professor or instructor on official school stationery.
Additional information: Must be member of IFDA. Must have completed four courses in interior design (or related field) at post-secondary level. Must have completed at least one semester of postsecondary school. Furniture design majors also eligible. See Website for further requirements and application.

Amount of award:	$2,000
Number of awards:	1
Application deadline:	March 31
Notification begins:	July 31
Total amount awarded:	$2,000

Contact:
IFDA Educational Foundation, Director of Grants/Scholarships
Earline Feldman
112 Hidden Lake Circle
Canton, GA 30114
Web: www.ifdaef.org

Scholarships

Ruth Clark Furniture Design Scholarship

Type of award: Scholarship.
Intended use: For undergraduate or graduate study at postsecondary institution in United States.
Eligibility: Applicant must be U.S. citizen or permanent resident.
Basis for selection: Major/career interest in design.
Application requirements: Portfolio, recommendations, essay, transcript. Letter from instructor on official school stationery. Five examples of original furniture designs.
Additional information: Must have completed four courses in interior design (or related field) at post-secondary level. Must be major in design with focus on residential upholstered and/or wood furniture design. See Website for further requirements and application.

Amount of award:	$3,000
Number of awards:	1
Application deadline:	March 31
Notification begins:	July 31
Total amount awarded:	$3,000

Contact:
IFDA Educational Foundation, Director of Grants/Scholarships
Earline Feldman
112 Hidden Lake Circle
Canton, GA 30114
Web: www.ifdaef.org

International Order of the King's Daughters and Sons

Health Career Scholarship

Type of award: Scholarship, renewable.
Intended use: For full-time junior, senior, master's or first professional study at accredited 4-year or graduate institution in United States or Canada.
Eligibility: Applicant must be U.S. citizen or Canadian citizen.
Basis for selection: Major/career interest in medicine; dentistry; pharmacy/pharmaceutics/pharmacology; nursing; health sciences; health-related professions; physical therapy or occupational therapy. Applicant must demonstrate financial need, high academic achievement, depth of character, leadership, seriousness of purpose and service orientation.
Application requirements: Recommendations, essay, transcript, proof of eligibility.
Additional information: To request application, student must email director stating field and present level of study and include business-size SASE. Pre-med students not eligible. R.N., M.D. and D.D.S. students must have completed first year. Number of scholarships varies year to year.

Amount of award:	$1,000
Application deadline:	April 1

Contact:
International Order of the King's Daughters and Sons
Director, Health Careers Department
P.O. Box 1040
Chautauqua, NY 14722-1040
Phone: 716-357-4951
Web: www.iokds.org

North American Indian Scholarship

Type of award: Scholarship, renewable.
Intended use: For full-time undergraduate study at accredited 2-year or 4-year institution in United States.
Eligibility: Applicant must be American Indian. Applicant must be U.S. citizen.
Basis for selection: Applicant must demonstrate financial need, depth of character, leadership, seriousness of purpose and service orientation.
Application requirements: Recommendations, essay, transcript, proof of eligibility. Written documentation of tribal registration and other requirements. Photo.
Additional information: Offers scholarships with no restrictions as to tribal affiliations or Indian blood quantum. For more information, send SASE to director of North American Indian Department.

Amount of award:	$500-$700
Application deadline:	April 1
Notification begins:	July 1

Contact:
International Order of the King's Daughters and Sons
Director, North American Indian Dept.
P.O. Box 1040
Chautauqua, NY 14722-1040
Phone: 716-357-4951
Web: www.iokds.org

The Internicola Law Firm

Franchisee University Young Entrepreneur Scholarship

Type of award: Scholarship.
Intended use: For full-time freshman study at vocational, 2-year or 4-year institution.
Eligibility: Applicant must be U.S. citizen.
Basis for selection: Major/career interest in business.
Application requirements: 500-600 essay based on these topics: What does being an entrepreneur mean to you? What does Success mean to you? How would becoming a future entrepreneur and building a business have a favorable impact for you and your community? Give specific, real world examples of entrepreneurs who have achieved success and overcame obstacles. How do you see yourself in ten years from now? Bonus questions: After reading Success for Teens, what are the most powerful principles and lessons that really stuck with you (maybe even surprised you) and how you will apply them in your life?
Additional information: Open to all high school seniors. After applying, you will get a copy of "Success for Teens: Real Teens Talk about Using the Slight Edge" provided free of charge. Application can be found on web site.

Number of awards:	1
Application deadline:	May 1
Total amount awarded:	$500

Contact:
The Internicola Law Firm
1000 South Avenue
Suite 104
Staten Island, NY 10314
Phone: 718-979-8688
Fax: 718-407-4835
Web: www.franchiselawsolutions.com/blog/win-500-franchisee-university-young-entrepreneur-scholarship/

Intertribal Timber Council

Truman D. Picard Scholarship

Type of award: Scholarship, renewable.
Intended use: For full-time undergraduate or graduate study at accredited 2-year, 4-year or graduate institution in United States.
Eligibility: Applicant must be Alaskan native or American Indian. Must be enrolled member of a federally recognized tribe. Applicant must be U.S. citizen.
Basis for selection: Major/career interest in natural resources/conservation; forestry; wildlife/fisheries or agriculture. Applicant must demonstrate financial need, high academic achievement, depth of character, leadership, seriousness of purpose and service orientation.
Application requirements: Recommendations, transcript, proof of eligibility. Resume, and two-page (maximum) letter of application.
Additional information: Applicants must be Native American and pursuing higher education in natural resources. Check Website for application deadline dates.

Amount of award:	$2,000-$2,500
Number of applicants:	58
Total amount awarded:	$71,500

Contact:
Intertribal Timber Council
Education Committee
1112 NE 21st Avenue, Ste. 4
Portland, OR 97232-2114
Phone: 503-282-4296
Fax: 503-282-1274
Web: www.itcnet.org

Inverters R Us

Inverters R Us Power Scholarship

Type of award: Scholarship.
Intended use: For full-time undergraduate or graduate study at accredited 2-year, 4-year or graduate institution in United States.
Eligibility: Applicant must be U.S. citizen or permanent resident.
Application requirements: Essay, transcript. Applicants must complete the application, upload transcript and complete a small writing project.
Additional information: Minimum 3.0 GPA required. May be used for study abroad.

Amount of award:	$1,000
Number of awards:	2
Application deadline:	June 30, January 1
Total amount awarded:	$2,000

Contact:
Inverters R Us
PO Box 33264
Reno, NV 89533
Phone: 866-419-2616 x4
Web: http://invertersrus.com/power-scholarships/

InvestmentZen

$1k Financial Future Scholarship

Type of award: Scholarship.
Intended use: For undergraduate or graduate study at vocational, 2-year, 4-year or graduate institution.
Eligibility: Applicant must be at least 18. Applicant must be U.S. citizen or permanent resident.
Application requirements: Essay. To enter, please submit an essay (500-1500 words) answering one of the following: how are you managing your money in college to prepare for a bright financial future; what financial challenges have you overcome in your life; what lesson(s) did they teach you; what are the most common financial pitfalls you see your peers making, and what advice do you have for them.

Number of awards:	1
Application deadline:	April 1
Notification begins:	June 15
Total amount awarded:	$1,000

Contact:
InvestmentZen
600 Congress Avenue
Austin, TX 78701
Phone: 415-867-2843
Web: www.investmentzen.com/scholarship

Iowa College Student Aid Commission

All Iowa Opportunity Scholarship

Type of award: Scholarship.
Intended use: For undergraduate study at accredited 2-year or 4-year institution in United States. Designated institutions: Eligible Iowa colleges and universities.
Eligibility: Applicant must be high school senior. Applicant must be U.S. citizen residing in Iowa.
Basis for selection: Applicant must demonstrate financial need and high academic achievement.
Application requirements: FAFSA. Iowa financial aid application.
Additional information: Minimum 2.5 GPA. Awards of up to average tuition and fee rate of Regents University for current academic year. Priority given to students who participated in federal TRIO programs, students who graduated from alternative high schools, and homeless youth.

Amount of award:	$8,118
Application deadline:	March 1

Contact:
Iowa College Student Aid Commission
430 East Grand Avenue, 3rd Floor
Des Moines, IA 50309
Phone: 877-272-4456 option 3
Fax: 515-725-3401
Web: www.iowacollegeaid.gov

Governor Terry E. Branstad Iowa State Fair Scholarship

Type of award: Scholarship.
Intended use: For undergraduate study at postsecondary institution in United States. Designated institutions: Iowa colleges and universities.
Eligibility: Applicant must be high school senior. Applicant must be U.S. citizen residing in Iowa.
Basis for selection: Applicant must demonstrate financial need.
Application requirements: Essay. FAFSA, proof of involvement in Iowa State Fair. Iowa financial aid application.
Additional information: Must be graduating senior from Iowa state high school who has been actively involved with the Iowa State Fair. Visit Website for application.

    Amount of award: $500-$5,000
    Number of awards: 10
    Application deadline: March 1
Contact:
Iowa College Student Aid Commission
430 East Grand Avenue, 3rd Floor
Des Moines, IA 50309
Phone: 877-272-4456
Fax: 515-725-3401
Web: www.iowacollegeaid.gov

Iowa Barber and Cosmetology Arts and Sciences Tuition Grant

Type of award: Scholarship.
Intended use: For undergraduate study at accredited vocational, 2-year or 4-year institution in United States. Designated institutions: Participating Iowa barber and cosmetology colleges.
Eligibility: Applicant must be U.S. citizen or permanent resident residing in Iowa.
Basis for selection: Major/career interest in cosmetology/hairdressing. Applicant must demonstrate financial need.
Application requirements: FAFSA.
Additional information: Must be Iowa resident studying at participating Iowa barber and cosmetology colleges.

    Amount of award: $1,200
    Application deadline: July 1
Contact:
Iowa College Student Aid Commission
430 East Grand Avenue, 3rd Floor
Des Moines, IA 50309
Phone: 877-272-4456 Option 3
Fax: 515-725-3401
Web: www.iowacollegeaid.gov

Iowa Grant

Type of award: Scholarship, renewable.
Intended use: For full-time undergraduate study at vocational, 2-year or 4-year institution. Designated institutions: Iowa colleges and universities.

Eligibility: Applicant must be U.S. citizen or permanent resident residing in Iowa.
Basis for selection: Applicant must demonstrate financial need.
Application requirements: FAFSA.
Additional information: Award amount adjusted for part-time study. Eligible colleges and universities receive Iowa grant allocations and award grants to students with greatest financial need. Priority given to students whose parent was a public safety officer killed in the line of duty.

    Amount of award: $1,000
    Total amount awarded: $791,177
Contact:
Iowa College Student Aid Commission
430 East Grand Avenue, 3rd Floor
Des Moines, IA 50309
Phone: 877-272-4456
Fax: 515-725-3401
Web: www.iowacollegeaid.gov

Iowa National Guard Educational Assistance Program

Type of award: Scholarship, renewable.
Intended use: For undergraduate study at accredited postsecondary institution. Designated institutions: Eligible Iowa colleges and universities.
Eligibility: Applicant must be U.S. citizen residing in Iowa. Applicant must be in military service in the Reserves/National Guard.
Application requirements: Iowa financial aid application.
Additional information: Applicant must be in military service in the Iowa Reserves/National Guard. Selection is based on National Guard designation. Award varies yearly. Maximum award is 100 percent of tuition for students at public institutions; for students at private institutions, award is equal to average tuition rate at Iowa Regents Universities.

    Amount of award: $6,658
    Application deadline: July 1
Contact:
Iowa College Student Aid Commission
430 East Grand Avenue, 3rd Floor
Des Moines, IA 50309
Phone: 877-272-4456
Fax: 515-275-3401
Web: www.iowacollegeaid.gov

Iowa Tuition Grant

Type of award: Scholarship, renewable.
Intended use: For undergraduate study at accredited 2-year or 4-year institution. Designated institutions: Private colleges in Iowa.
Eligibility: Applicant must be U.S. citizen or permanent resident residing in Iowa.
Basis for selection: Applicant must demonstrate financial need.
Application requirements: Proof of eligibility. FAFSA.

    Amount of award: $6,000
    Application deadline: July 1
Contact:
Iowa College Student Aid Commission
430 East Grand Avenue, 3rd Floor
Des Moines, IA 50309
Phone: 877-272-4456
Fax: 515-725-3401
Web: www.iowacollegeaid.gov

Iowa Vocational-Technical Tuition Grant

Type of award: Scholarship, renewable.
Intended use: For undergraduate study at vocational or 2-year institution. Designated institutions: Iowa community colleges.
Eligibility: Applicant must be U.S. citizen or permanent resident residing in Iowa.
Basis for selection: Applicant must demonstrate financial need.
Application requirements: Proof of eligibility. FAFSA.
Additional information: Only vocational-technical career majors considered.

Amount of award:	$1,200
Application deadline:	July 1

Contact:
Iowa College Student Aid Commission
430 East Grand Avenue, 3rd Floor
Des Moines, IA 50309
Phone: 877-272-4456
Fax: 515-725-3401
Web: www.iowacollegeaid.gov

Robert D. Blue Scholarship

Type of award: Scholarship.
Intended use: For undergraduate study at postsecondary institution in United States. Designated institutions: Iowa colleges and universities.
Eligibility: Applicant must be U.S. citizen residing in Iowa.
Basis for selection: Applicant must demonstrate financial need, high academic achievement, depth of character, leadership and seriousness of purpose.
Application requirements: Recommendations, essay, transcript. GPA.
Additional information: Visit Website for application.

Amount of award:	$500-$1,000
Application deadline:	May 10

Contact:
Robert D. Blue Scholarship
Michael L. Fitzgerald, Treasurer of State
State Capitol Building
Des Moines, IA 50319
Phone: 515-242-5270
Web: www.iowacollegeaid.gov

Iron Company

Fitness and Education Scholarship

Type of award: Scholarship.
Intended use: For freshman study at accredited 4-year institution in United States.
Eligibility: Applicant must be high school senior. Applicant must be U.S. citizen.
Application requirements: Essay. 500 word essay. Prompt can be found on the website.
Additional information: Minimum 3.0 GPA. Major must be fitness related. Must be a high school senior who will be attending a California institution.

Number of awards:	2
Application deadline:	August 1
Notification begins:	August 15
Total amount awarded:	$500

Contact:
IronCompany.com
7349 Millikin Avenue
140-332
Rancho Cucamonga, CA 91730-7435
Phone: 760-694-4502
Fax: 1-866-841-3875
Web: www.ironcompany.com/scholarship.aspx

iSeeCars

Future Entrepreneurs Scholarship

Type of award: Scholarship.
Intended use: For full-time undergraduate or graduate study at accredited 4-year or graduate institution.
Application requirements: Transcript. 500 to 600 word essay. Completed scholarship application from. College transcript.

Number of awards:	1
Application deadline:	December 31
Total amount awarded:	$1,000

Contact:
Web: www.iseecars.com/scholarship

Italian Catholic Federation

Italian Catholic Federation Scholarship

Type of award: Scholarship, renewable.
Intended use: For full-time freshman study at accredited 2-year or 4-year institution.
Eligibility: Applicant must be high school senior. Applicant must be Italian. Applicant must be Roman Catholic. Applicant must be U.S. citizen residing in California, Illinois, Arizona or Nevada.
Basis for selection: Applicant must demonstrate financial need and high academic achievement.
Application requirements: Recommendations, essay, transcript.
Additional information: Minimum 3.2 GPA. Residency restrictions do not apply if parent or grandparent is member of Federation. Also open to non-Italian students whose parents or grandparents are members of Federation. First year's scholarship award is $400. Larger amounts available for advanced scholarships.

Amount of award:	$400
Number of awards:	200
Number of applicants:	446
Application deadline:	March 15
Notification begins:	May 1
Total amount awarded:	$73,600

Contact:
Italian Catholic Federation
8393 Capwell Drive
Suite 110
Oakland, CA 94621
Phone: 510-633-9058
Fax: 510-633-9758
Web: www.icf.org

IUE-CWA

Bruce van Ess Scholarship

Type of award: Scholarship.

Intended use: For full-time undergraduate study at accredited vocational, 2-year or 4-year institution.

Eligibility: Applicant or parent must be member/participant of International Union of EESMF Workers, AFL-CIO.

Basis for selection: Applicant must demonstrate depth of character, leadership, seriousness of purpose and service orientation.

Application requirements: Proof of GPA, short statement on civic contributions. 500-word essay on importance of labor movement.

Additional information: Available to all IUE-CWA members and employees (including retired or deceased members and employees) and their children and grandchildren. Apply online.

Amount of award:	$2,500
Number of awards:	1
Application deadline:	March 31
Total amount awarded:	$2,500

Contact:
IUE Department of Education
Web: www.iue-cwa.org

James B. Carey Scholarship

Type of award: Scholarship.

Intended use: For full-time undergraduate study at accredited postsecondary institution in United States.

Eligibility: Applicant or parent must be member/participant of International Union of EESMF Workers, AFL-CIO.

Basis for selection: Applicant must demonstrate depth of character, leadership, seriousness of purpose and service orientation.

Application requirements: Recommendations, transcript, proof of eligibility. 150-word essay on civic contributions, 500-word essay on importance of labor movement.

Additional information: Available to children and grandchildren of all IUE-CWA members and employees (including retired or deceased members and employees) and their children and grandchildren. Must be accepted or enrolled in college, university, nursing school, or technical school. Apply online.

Amount of award:	$1,000
Number of awards:	9
Application deadline:	March 31
Total amount awarded:	$9,000

Contact:
IUE Department of Education
Web: www.iue-cwa.org

Paul Jennings Scholarship

Type of award: Scholarship.

Intended use: For full-time undergraduate study in United States.

Eligibility: Applicant must be high school senior.

Basis for selection: Applicant must demonstrate depth of character, leadership and service orientation.

Application requirements: Transcript, proof of eligibility. 150-word essay on civic contributions, 500-word essay on importance of labor movement.

Additional information: Award available to children and grandchildren of IUE-CWA members who are now or have been local union elected officials. Families of full-time union officers or employees not eligible. Must be accepted or enrolled in college, university, nursing school, or technical school. Apply online.

Amount of award:	$3,000
Number of awards:	1
Application deadline:	March 31
Total amount awarded:	$3,000

Contact:
IUE Department of Education
Web: www.iue-cwa.org

Robert L. Livingston Scholarship

Type of award: Scholarship.

Intended use: For full-time undergraduate study at accredited vocational, 2-year or 4-year institution.

Basis for selection: Applicant must demonstrate depth of character, leadership, seriousness of purpose and service orientation.

Application requirements: Proof of GPA, short statement which includes applicant's civic contributions, career objectives, and extracurricular activities.

Additional information: Open to dependents of IUE-CWA members or retired members. Dependents of IUE-CWA Division employees ineligible. Apply online.

Amount of award:	$1,500
Number of awards:	2
Application deadline:	February 28
Total amount awarded:	$3,000

Contact:
IUE Department of Education
Web: www.iue-cwa.org

Sal Ingrassia Scholarship

Type of award: Scholarship.

Intended use: For full-time undergraduate study at accredited vocational, 2-year or 4-year institution.

Eligibility: Applicant or parent must be member/participant of International Union of EESMF Workers, AFL-CIO.

Basis for selection: Applicant must demonstrate depth of character, leadership, seriousness of purpose and service orientation.

Application requirements: Proof of GPA, 150-word essay on civic contributions, 500-word essay on relationship to labor movement.

Additional information: Available to all IUE-CWA members and employees (including retired or deceased members and employees) and their children and grandchildren. Apply online.

Amount of award:	$2,500
Number of awards:	1
Application deadline:	February 28
Total amount awarded:	$2,500

Contact:
IUE Department of Education
Web: www.iue-cwa.org

Willie Rudd Scholarship

Type of award: Scholarship.

Intended use: For full-time undergraduate study at accredited vocational, 2-year or 4-year institution.

Eligibility: Applicant or parent must be member/participant of International Union of EESMF Workers, AFL-CIO.

Basis for selection: Applicant must demonstrate depth of character, leadership, seriousness of purpose and service orientation.

Application requirements: Proof of GPA, 150-word essay on civic contributions, 500-word essay on importance of labor movement.

Additional information: Available to all IUE-CWA members and employees and their children and grandchildren (including retired or deceased members and employees). Apply online.

Amount of award:	$1,000
Number of awards:	1
Application deadline:	February 28
Total amount awarded:	$1,000

Contact:
IUE Department of Education
Web: www.iue-cwa.org

Jack Kent Cooke Foundation

Jack Kent Cooke Foundation College Scholarship

Type of award: Scholarship.
Intended use: For full-time freshman study at 4-year institution.
Basis for selection: Applicant must demonstrate financial need, high academic achievement, leadership and service orientation.
Application requirements: Recommendations, essay.
Additional information: Minimum 3.5 GPA. Standardized test scores must be in top 15 percent. Minimum SAT score 1200 (reading and math) or ACT score 26 or above. Must be graduate of U.S. high school. Applications due in November.

Amount of award:	$40,000
Number of awards:	40

Contact:
Jack Kent Cooke Foundation
44325 Woodridge Parkway
Lansdowne, VA 20176
Phone: 703-723-8000
Fax: 703-723-8030
Web: www.jkcf.org

Jack Kent Cooke Foundation Undergraduate Transfer Scholarship

Type of award: Scholarship, renewable.
Intended use: For full-time sophomore study at accredited 4-year institution in United States.
Basis for selection: Applicant must demonstrate financial need.
Application requirements: Recommendations, transcript. Online application, transcripts from all colleges attended for the last 15 years, two recommendations from professors or instructors at the applicant's community college, student financial form, tax return, parent financial form including a copy of federal tax return in the applicant is under 30 years old.
Additional information: Application deadline in December, notification date in April. Must have sophomore status at a community college and be planning to transfer to a 4-year college or university the following fall.

Amount of award:	$40,000
Number of awards:	85
Application deadline:	December 1
Notification begins:	April 1

Contact:
Jack Kent Cooke Foundation
44325 Woodridge Parkway
Lansdowne, VA 20176
Phone: 703-723-8000 x276
Fax: 1-571-209-1776
Web: www.jkcf.org/scholarship-programs/undergraduate-transfer/

Jackie Robinson Foundation

Jackie Robinson Foundation Mentoring and Leadership Curriculum

Type of award: Scholarship, renewable.
Intended use: For full-time undergraduate study at accredited 4-year institution in United States.
Eligibility: Applicant must be Alaskan native, Asian American, African American, Mexican American, Hispanic American, Puerto Rican, American Indian or Native Hawaiian/Pacific Islander. Applicant must be high school senior. Applicant must be U.S. citizen.
Basis for selection: Applicant must demonstrate financial need, high academic achievement, leadership and service orientation.
Application requirements: Interview, recommendations, essay, transcript. SAR, SAT/ACT scores, list of extracurricular activities, parents' tax return, guidance counselor name and email address.
Additional information: Applicants must have minimum SAT score of 1000 or ACT score of 21. Award amount varies up to $7,500. Applications available online and must be submitted via website.

Amount of award:	$6,000
Number of awards:	60
Number of applicants:	3,000
Application deadline:	February 15
Notification begins:	June 15
Total amount awarded:	$1,800,000

Contact:
Jackie Robinson Foundation
Attn: Scholarship Programs
One Hudson Sq., 75 Varick Street, 2nd floor
New York, NY 10013-1917
Phone: 212-290-8600
Fax: 212-290-8081
Web: www.jackierobinson.org

JacksonWhite Attorneys At Law

The JacksonWhite Family Law Bi-Annual Scholarship

Type of award: Scholarship.
Intended use: For full-time undergraduate or graduate study at accredited vocational, 2-year, 4-year or graduate institution in United States.

Application requirements: Essay, transcript. Applicant must currently attend an accredited college or university in the US. Be a full-time student in undergraduate, graduate in Law or Medical school programs. Send your essay of 1,000 words or less as a PDF file, along with an unofficial transcript. Submission information and essay promt found on the website.

Amount of award:	$1,000
Number of awards:	1
Number of applicants:	20
Application deadline:	April 30
Notification begins:	June 1
Total amount awarded:	$1,000

Contact:
40 N Center Street
Mesa, AZ 85201
Phone: 480-464-1111
Fax: 480-464-5692
Web: www.jacksonwhitelaw.com/arizona-family-law/scholarship/

The JacksonWhite Labor Law Bi-Annual Scholarship

Type of award: Scholarship.
Intended use: For full-time undergraduate or graduate study at accredited vocational, 2-year, 4-year or graduate institution in United States.
Eligibility: Applicant must be enrolled in high school.
Basis for selection: Applicant must demonstrate high academic achievement.
Application requirements: Essay, transcript. Submit essay of 1,000 words or less as a PDF file, along with an unofficial transcript to scholarship@jacksonwhitelaw.com, Include JacksonWhite Scholarship in the subject line. Please include the following: Name, address, phone number, email address, School name and expected date of graduation.
Additional information: Scholarship applies for study abroad.

Amount of award:	$1,000-$1,000
Number of awards:	1
Application deadline:	April 30
Notification begins:	June 1
Total amount awarded:	$1,000

Contact:
JacksonWhite Attorneys At Law
40 North Center Street
Mesa, AZ 85201
Phone: 480-464-1111
Fax: 480-464-5692
Web: www.jacksonwhitelaw.com/az-labor-employment-law/scholarship/

The JacksonWhite Personal Injury Bi-Annual Scholarship

Type of award: Scholarship.
Intended use: For full-time undergraduate or graduate study at accredited vocational, 2-year, 4-year or graduate institution in United States.
Eligibility: Applicant must be enrolled in high school.
Basis for selection: Applicant must demonstrate high academic achievement.
Application requirements: Essay, transcript. Submit essay of 1000 words or less as a PDF file, along with an unofficial transcript to scholarship@jacksonwhitelaw.com . Include JacksonWhite Scholarship in the subject line.Please include: Name, address, phone number, email address, school name and expected date of graduation.

Additional information: Scholarship applies on abroad study.

Amount of award:	$1,000
Number of awards:	1
Application deadline:	April 30
Notification begins:	June 1
Total amount awarded:	$1,000

Contact:
JacksonWhite Attorneys At Law
40 North Center Street
Mesa, AZ 85201
Phone: 480-464-1111
Fax: 480-464-5692
Web: www.jacksonwhitelaw.com/az-personal-injury/jacksonwhite-scholarship/

JacksonWhite Criminal Law

The JacksonWhite Criminal Law Bi-Annual Scholarship

Type of award: Scholarship.
Intended use: For full-time undergraduate or graduate study at accredited vocational, 2-year, 4-year or graduate institution in United States.
Application requirements: Essay, transcript. Submit an essay of up to 1000 words or less as a PDF, along with an unofficial transcript to scholarship@jacksonwhitelaw.com, Include (JacksonWhite Scholarship) in the subject line including (Name, address, phone number, email address, School name and expected date of graduation).
Additional information: Applicants must Currently attend an accredited college or university in the US.

Amount of award:	$1,000
Number of awards:	1
Application deadline:	April 30
Notification begins:	June 1
Total amount awarded:	$1,000

Contact:
JacksonWhite Criminal Law
40 North Center Street
Mesa, AZ 85201
Phone: 480-464-1111
Fax: 480-464-5692
Web: www.jacksonwhitelaw.com/criminal-defense-law/scholarship/

Jain Foundation

LGMD Awareness Social Media Scholarship

Type of award: Scholarship, renewable.
Intended use: For undergraduate or graduate study at accredited postsecondary institution.
Eligibility: Applicant must be at least 17, no older than 30.
Basis for selection: Students may submit a post each week during the contest to improve their score, and the single highest one-week score for each applicant will be used to determine the winners. An applicants score is dependant on the number of votes received during a single week, Visit web site for complete rules and applications.

Application requirements: Applicant must demonstrate ability to teach others about rare muscle diseases called limb girdle muscular dystrophies (LGMDs) using social media. Write a post to teach your friends about LGMDs that includes one LGMD fact of your choice and post it on the Jain Foundation Facebook scholarship tab. Pictures are optional; you can use a picture from the gallery here with a fact already included on it or you can design your own.

Additional information: Social Media Scholarship entrants will post a message and a picture (optional) on the Jain Foundation Scholarship Facebook Tab with information about LGMDs to spread disease awareness. The contest will run weekly for 20 weeks starting and ending on a Wednesday. The first week will begin January 6th and the final week will end May 25th.

Amount of award:	$3,000
Number of awards:	2
Total amount awarded:	$6,000

Contact:
Jain Foundation
9725 Third Avenue Northeast
Suite 204
Seattle, WA 98115
Phone: 425-882-1492
Fax: 425-658-1703
Web: www.jain-foundation.org/scholarship

Merit-Based Scholarship

Type of award: Scholarship.
Intended use: For full-time undergraduate or graduate study at accredited vocational, 2-year, 4-year or graduate institution in United States.
Eligibility: Applicant must be at least 17, no older than 30.
Basis for selection: Applicant must demonstrate high academic achievement and leadership.
Application requirements: Essay, transcript. GPA, transcript, History of academic success, Participation in extracurricular activities and leadership experience, Proof of spreading awareness of rare muscle diseases called LGMDs to 25-100 individuals, Answers to two short essay (250 words max) questions.
Additional information: May be used for study abroad if money is paid to an accredited US institution; cannot be used if money goes directly to another institution. Scholarships will be paid directly to the student's post-secondary institution in late 2016 or early 2017 after the institution has confirmed that the student is enrolled and in good standing.

Amount of award:	$3,000
Number of awards:	12
Number of applicants:	5,000
Application deadline:	May 25
Notification begins:	June 30

Contact:
Jain Foundation
9725 3rd Avenue NE
Suite 204
Seattle, WA 98115
Phone: 425-882-1492
Fax: 425-658-1703
Web: www.jain-foundation.org/scholarship

James Beard Foundation

Allie's Cabin Scholarship

Type of award: Scholarship.
Intended use: For undergraduate study at accredited postsecondary institution. Designated institutions: Licensed or accredited culinary schools.
Eligibility: Applicant must be residing in Colorado.
Basis for selection: Major/career interest in culinary arts.
Application requirements: Transcript.
Additional information: Must be high school senior or graduate planning to attend a licensed or accredited culinary school. Applicants must be resident of or attending culinary school in Eagle County, Colorado.

Amount of award:	Full tuition
Number of awards:	1
Application deadline:	May 15

Contact:
Scholarship Management Services
One Scholarship Way
Saint Peter, MN 56082
Phone: 507-931-1682
Web: www.jamesbeard.org

American Restaurant Scholarship

Type of award: Scholarship.
Intended use: For undergraduate study in United States. Designated institutions: Licensed or accredited culinary schools.
Basis for selection: Major/career interest in culinary arts. Applicant must demonstrate financial need.
Application requirements: Recommendations, transcript. Financial statement, resume.
Additional information: Must plan to enroll in licensed or accredited culinary school.

Amount of award:	$5,000
Number of awards:	1
Application deadline:	May 15

Contact:
Scholarship America
One Scholarship Way
St. Peter, MN 56082
Phone: 507-931-1682
Web: www.jamesbeard.org

Andrew Michael Italian Kitchen Scholarship

Type of award: Scholarship.
Intended use: For undergraduate study. Designated institutions: Licensed or accredited culinary schools.
Basis for selection: Major/career interest in culinary arts.
Application requirements: Transcript.
Additional information: Must be high school senior or graduate planning to attend a licensed or accredited culinary school.

Amount of award:	$3,750
Number of awards:	1
Application deadline:	May 15

Contact:
Scholarship Management Services
One Scholarship Way
Saint Peter, MN 56082
Phone: 507-931-1682
Web: www.jamesbeard.org

Andrew Zimmern Second Chances Scholarship

Type of award: Scholarship.
Intended use: For undergraduate study at accredited postsecondary institution. Designated institutions: Licensed or accredited culinary schools.
Basis for selection: Major/career interest in culinary arts.
Application requirements: Essay, transcript. Essay describing extreme challenges applicant has faced and how scholarship will them get a second chance.
Additional information: Must be high school senior or graduate planning to attend a licensed or accredited culinary school.

Amount of award:	$10,000
Number of awards:	1
Application deadline:	May 15

Contact:
Scholarship Management Services
One Scholarship Way
Saint Peter, MN 56082
Phone: 507-931-1682
Web: www.jamesbeard.org

AnQi House of An - South Coast Plaza Scholarship

Type of award: Scholarship.
Intended use: For undergraduate study at accredited postsecondary institution. Designated institutions: Licensed or accredited culinary schools.
Basis for selection: Major/career interest in culinary arts.
Application requirements: Transcript.
Additional information: Must be high school senior or graduate planning to attend a licensed or accredited culinary school.

Amount of award:	$7,500
Number of awards:	1
Application deadline:	May 15

Contact:
Scholarship Management Services
One Scholarship Way
Saint Peter, MN 56082
Phone: 507-931-1682
Web: www.jamesbeard.org

Azurea at One Ocean Resort Hotel & Spa Scholarship

Type of award: Scholarship.
Intended use: For undergraduate study at postsecondary institution.
Application requirements: Transcript.
Additional information: Must be enrolled or plan to enroll in a licensed or accredited culinary or hospitality management program in Florida.

Amount of award:	$5,400
Number of awards:	1
Application deadline:	May 15

Contact:
James Beard Foundation Scholarship Program
One Scholarship Way
Saint Peter, MN 56082
Phone: 507-931-1682
Web: www.jamesbeard.org

Bern Laxer Memorial Scholarship

Type of award: Scholarship.
Intended use: For undergraduate study at accredited postsecondary institution. Designated institutions: Licensed or accredited culinary schools.
Eligibility: Applicant must be residing in Florida.
Basis for selection: Major/career interest in culinary arts; hospitality administration/management or food science/technology. Applicant must demonstrate financial need and high academic achievement.
Application requirements: Recommendations, essay, transcript, proof of eligibility. Proof of residency, financial statement, resume.
Additional information: Must have at least one year of culinary experience and have high school diploma or equivalent. One scholarship granted annually in one of the following categories: culinary studies, hospitality management, and viticulture/oenology. Recipients who reapply will be given priority consideration over new applicants. May be received for a maximum of four years, but applicant must maintain a B-GPA.

Amount of award:	$4,500
Number of awards:	2
Application deadline:	May 15
Total amount awarded:	$8,000

Contact:
Scholarship America
One Scholarship Way
St. Peter, MN 56082
Phone: 507-931-1682
Web: www.jamesbeard.org

Blackbird Scholarship

Type of award: Scholarship.
Intended use: For undergraduate study at accredited postsecondary institution. Designated institutions: Accredited culinary schools.
Basis for selection: Major/career interest in culinary arts.
Application requirements: Transcript.
Additional information: Must be enrolled or planning to enroll in accredited culinary program.

Amount of award:	$3,750
Number of awards:	1
Application deadline:	May 15

Contact:
James Beard Foundation Scholarship Program
One Scholarship Way
St. Peter, MN 56082
Phone: 507-931-1682
Web: www.jamesbeard.org

Bob Zappatelli Memorial Scholarship

Type of award: Scholarship.
Intended use: For undergraduate study at accredited postsecondary institution.
Basis for selection: Major/career interest in culinary arts; food production/management/services; food science/technology;

hospitality administration/management or hotel/restaurant management.

Application requirements: Recommendations, essay, transcript.

Additional information: Must plan to enroll in culinary school. Preference given to Benchmark employees or relatives of employees. Must have experience in food and beverage industry.

Amount of award:	$3,000
Number of awards:	1
Application deadline:	May 15
Total amount awarded:	$5,000

Contact:
Scholarship America
One Scholarship Way
St. Peter, MN 56082
Phone: 504-931-1682
Web: www.jamesbeard.org

Charleston Food & Wine Festival Scholarship

Type of award: Scholarship.

Intended use: For undergraduate study at accredited postsecondary institution. Designated institutions: Licensed or accredited culinary schools.

Basis for selection: Major/career interest in culinary arts.

Application requirements: Transcript.

Additional information: Must be high school senior or graduate planning to attend a licensed or accredited culinary school. Preference given to applicants who are residents of or attending school in South Carolina.

Amount of award:	$6,250
Number of awards:	1
Application deadline:	May 15

Contact:
Scholarship Management Services
One Scholarship Way
Saint Peter, MN 56082
Phone: 507-931-1682
Web: www.jamesbeard.org

Chefs of Louisiana Cookery Scholarship

Type of award: Scholarship.

Intended use: For undergraduate study at postsecondary institution. Designated institutions: Culinary schools in Louisiana.

Eligibility: Applicant must be U.S. citizen residing in Louisiana.

Basis for selection: Major/career interest in culinary arts; food production/management/services; food science/technology; hospitality administration/management or hotel/restaurant management. Applicant must demonstrate financial need.

Application requirements: Recommendations, essay, transcript.

Additional information: Must plan to enroll in Louisiana culinary school.

Amount of award:	$5,900
Number of awards:	1
Application deadline:	May 15

Contact:
Scholarship America
One Scholarship Way
St. Peter, MN 56082
Phone: 504-931-1682
Web: www.jamesbeard.org

Chelsea Market Sunday Supper Scholarship

Type of award: Scholarship.

Intended use: For undergraduate study at accredited postsecondary institution. Designated institutions: Licensed or accredited culinary schools.

Basis for selection: Major/career interest in culinary arts.

Application requirements: Transcript.

Additional information: Candidates will be recommended by NYC C-CAP. Must be high school senior or graduate planning to attend a licensed or accredited culinary school.

Amount of award:	$20,000
Number of awards:	1
Application deadline:	May 15

Contact:
Scholarship Management Services
One Scholarship Way
Saint Peter, MN 56082
Phone: 507-931-1682
Web: www.jamesbeard.org

Christian Wolffer Scholarship

Type of award: Scholarship.

Intended use: For undergraduate study at accredited postsecondary institution. Designated institutions: Licensed or accredited culinary schools.

Eligibility: Applicant must be residing in New York.

Basis for selection: Major/career interest in culinary arts; food production/management/services or food science/technology. Applicant must demonstrate high academic achievement.

Application requirements: Recommendations, essay, transcript, proof of eligibility. Proof of residency, financial statement, resume.

Additional information: Minimum 3.0 GPA. Must be enrolled or planning to enroll in accredited culinary or wine studies program.

Amount of award:	$2,000
Number of awards:	1
Application deadline:	May 15
Total amount awarded:	$5,000

Contact:
Scholarship America
One Scholarship Way
St. Peter, MN 56082
Phone: 507-931-1682
Web: www.jamesbeard.org

Cru Restaurant Scholarship

Type of award: Scholarship.

Intended use: For undergraduate study at accredited postsecondary institution. Designated institutions: Licensed or accredited culinary schools.

Eligibility: Applicant must be residing in Massachusetts.

Basis for selection: Major/career interest in culinary arts.

Application requirements: Transcript.

Additional information: Must be resident (part-time or full-time) of Nantucket, Massachusetts. Must be high school senior or graduate planning to attend a licensed or accredited culinary school.

Amount of award:	$3,750
Number of awards:	1
Application deadline:	May 15

Contact:
Scholarship Management Services
One Scholarship Way
Saint Peter, MN 56082
Phone: 507-931-1682
Web: www.jamesbeard.org

Dana Campbell Memorial Scholarship

Type of award: Scholarship.
Intended use: For undergraduate study at 4-year institution in United States.
Eligibility: Applicant must be residing in Texas, Arkansas, Delaware, Maryland, Louisiana, South Carolina, Georgia, Florida, Oklahoma, Virginia, West Virginia, Mississippi, Kentucky, Alabama, North Carolina or Missouri.
Basis for selection: Major/career interest in food production/management/services; culinary arts or journalism.
Application requirements: Transcript.
Additional information: Must have career interest in food journalism. Must be in second or third year of study in journalism or food-related curriculum.

Amount of award:	$2,000
Number of awards:	1
Application deadline:	May 15

Contact:
James Beard Foundation Scholarship Program
One Scholarship Way
St. Peter, MN 56082
Phone: 507-931-1682
Web: www.jamesbeard.org

Deseo at the Westin Scholarship

Type of award: Scholarship.
Intended use: For undergraduate study at postsecondary institution.
Eligibility: Applicant must be residing in Arizona.
Basis for selection: Major/career interest in culinary arts; food production/management/services or food science/technology. Applicant must demonstrate financial need.
Application requirements: Recommendations, essay, transcript, proof of eligibility. Proof of residency, financial statement, resume.
Additional information: Applicants must have participated in Arizona Careers Through Culinary Arts program and be recommended by Arizona C-CAP.

Amount of award:	$3,750
Number of awards:	1
Application deadline:	May 15
Total amount awarded:	$6,250

Contact:
Scholarship America
One Scholarship Way
St. Peter, MN 56082
Phone: 507-931-1682
Web: www.jamesbeard.org

Green Door Gourmet Scholarship

Type of award: Scholarship.
Intended use: For undergraduate study at accredited postsecondary institution. Designated institutions: Licensed or accredited culinary schools.
Basis for selection: Major/career interest in culinary arts.
Application requirements: Transcript.
Additional information: Applicant must indicate interest in sustainable farming, responsible, total use of ingredients, and creative cooking with fresh nutritious food. Must be high school senior or graduate planning to attend a licensed or accredited culinary school.

Amount of award:	$3,750
Number of awards:	1
Application deadline:	May 15

Contact:
Scholarship Management Services
One Scholarship Way
Saint Peter, MN 56082
Phone: 507-931-1682
Web: www.jamesbeard.org

James Beard Foundation School Scholarships

Type of award: Scholarship.
Intended use: For undergraduate study at postsecondary institution. Designated institutions: Participating culinary programs.
Basis for selection: Major/career interest in culinary arts.
Application requirements: Transcript.
Additional information: Scholarships are awarded as waivers to participating culinary programs. Eligibility and application requirements vary. Check Website for current list of participating programs and list of requirements.

Amount of award:	Full tuition
Application deadline:	May 15

Contact:
James Beard Foundation Scholarship Program
One Scholarship Way
Saint Peter, MN 56082
Phone: 507-931-1682
Web: www.jamesbeard.org

La Toque Scholarship in Wine Studies

Type of award: Scholarship.
Intended use: For undergraduate study at postsecondary institution. Designated institutions: Licensed or accredited culinary schools.
Basis for selection: Major/career interest in culinary arts or food production/management/services. Applicant must demonstrate financial need.
Application requirements: Recommendations, essay, transcript, proof of eligibility. Proof of residency, financial statement, resume.
Additional information: Applicants must be enrolled in or be planning to enroll in an accredited wine studies program.

Amount of award:	$3,000
Number of awards:	1
Application deadline:	May 15
Total amount awarded:	$6,000

Contact:
Scholarship America
One Scholarship Way
St. Peter, MN 56082
Phone: 507-931-1682
Web: www.jamesbeard.org

Lemaire Restaurant at the Jefferson Hotel Scholarship

Type of award: Scholarship.
Intended use: For undergraduate study at accredited postsecondary institution. Designated institutions: Accredited culinary schools.
Basis for selection: Major/career interest in culinary arts.
Application requirements: Transcript.
Additional information: Must be enrolled or planning to enroll in accredited culinary program.

Amount of award:	$4,000
Number of awards:	1
Application deadline:	May 15

Contact:
James Beard Foundation Scholarship Program
One Scholarship Way
St. Peter, MN 56082
Phone: 507-931-1682
Web: www.jamesbeard.org

Miljenko Mike Grgich's American Dream Scholarship

Type of award: Scholarship.
Intended use: For undergraduate study at accredited postsecondary institution. Designated institutions: Schools with accredited wine studies program.
Basis for selection: Major/career interest in culinary arts.
Application requirements: Transcript.
Additional information: Must be high school senior or graduate planning to attend a licensed or accredited Wine Studies program.

Amount of award:	$5,000
Number of awards:	1
Application deadline:	May 15

Contact:
Scholarship Management Services
One Scholarship Way
Saint Peter, MN 56082
Phone: 507-931-1682
Web: www.jamesbeard.org

MK The Restaurant Scholarship

Type of award: Scholarship.
Intended use: For undergraduate study at accredited postsecondary institution. Designated institutions: Licensed or accredited culinary schools.
Basis for selection: Major/career interest in culinary arts.
Application requirements: Transcript.
Additional information: Preference given to students attending culinary school or residing in Northern Illinois or northern Indiana. Must be high school senior or graduate planning to attend a licensed or accredited culinary school.

Amount of award:	$7,000
Number of awards:	1
Application deadline:	May 15

Contact:
Scholarship Management Services
One Scholarship Way
Saint Peter, MN 56082
Phone: 507-931-1682
Web: www.jamesbeard.org

M.Y. China Scholarship

Type of award: Scholarship.
Intended use: For undergraduate study at accredited postsecondary institution. Designated institutions: Licensed or accredited culinary schools.
Basis for selection: Major/career interest in culinary arts.
Application requirements: Transcript.
Additional information: Must be high school senior or graduate planning to attend a licensed or accredited culinary school.

Amount of award:	$11,000
Number of awards:	1
Application deadline:	May 15

Contact:
Scholarship Management Services
One Scholarship Way
Saint Peter, MN 56082
Phone: 507-931-1682
Web: www.jamesbeard.org

New Tang Dynasty Television Scholarship for Traditional Chinese Culinary Studies

Type of award: Scholarship.
Intended use: For undergraduate study at accredited postsecondary institution. Designated institutions: Licensed or accredited culinary schools.
Basis for selection: Major/career interest in culinary arts.
Application requirements: Transcript.
Additional information: Must be high school senior or graduate planning to attend a licensed or accredited program focusing on traditional Chinese culinary studies.

Amount of award:	$8,500
Number of awards:	1
Application deadline:	May 15

Contact:
Scholarship Management Services
One Scholarship Way
Saint Peter, MN 56082
Phone: 507-931-1682
Web: www.jamesbeard.org

Omaha Steaks Scholarship

Type of award: Scholarship.
Intended use: For undergraduate study at accredited postsecondary institution in United States. Designated institutions: Accredited culinary schools.
Basis for selection: Major/career interest in culinary arts.
Application requirements: Recommendations, transcript.
Additional information: Up to five scholarships will be awarded, with at least one scholarship awarded to applicant currently or planning to be enrolled in Culinary Arts Program of Omaha's Metropolitan Community College.

Amount of award:	$3,000
Number of awards:	5
Application deadline:	May 15

Scholarships

Contact:
James Beard Foundation Scholarship Program
One Scholarship Way
St. Peter, MN 56082
Phone: 507-931-1682
Web: www.jamesbeard.org

The Peter Cameron/Housewares Charity Foundation Scholarship

Type of award: Scholarship.
Intended use: For undergraduate study at accredited postsecondary institution. Designated institutions: Licensed or accredited culinary schools.
Eligibility: Applicant must be high school senior.
Basis for selection: Major/career interest in culinary arts; food production/management/services or food science/technology. Applicant must demonstrate financial need and high academic achievement.
Application requirements: Recommendations, essay, transcript, proof of eligibility. Financial statement, resume.
Additional information: Minimum 3.0 GPA. Must attend licensed or accredited culinary school.

Amount of award:	$4,000
Number of awards:	1
Application deadline:	May 15
Total amount awarded:	$4,000

Contact:
Scholarship America
One Scholarship Way
St. Peter, MN 56082
Phone: 507-931-1682
Web: www.jamesbeard.org

Peter Kump Memorial Scholarship

Type of award: Scholarship.
Intended use: For undergraduate study at accredited postsecondary institution. Designated institutions: Licensed or accredited culinary schools.
Eligibility: Applicant must be high school senior.
Basis for selection: Major/career interest in culinary arts; food production/management/services or food science/technology. Applicant must demonstrate financial need and high academic achievement.
Application requirements: Recommendations, essay, transcript, proof of eligibility. Proof of residency, financial statement, resume.
Additional information: Minimum 3.0 GPA. Minimum one year substantiated culinary experience.

Amount of award:	$5,000
Number of awards:	5
Application deadline:	May 15
Total amount awarded:	$12,000

Contact:
Scholarship America
One Scholarship Way
St. Peter, MN 56082
Phone: 507-931-1682
Web: www.jamesbeard.org

The Ranch House at Devil's Thumb Scholarship

Type of award: Scholarship.
Intended use: For undergraduate study at postsecondary institution.

Basis for selection: Major/career interest in culinary arts.
Application requirements: Transcript.
Additional information: Must be enrolled or plan to enroll in a licensed or accredited culinary school.

Amount of award:	$3,650
Number of awards:	1
Application deadline:	May 15

Contact:
James Beard Foundation Scholarship Program
One Scholarship Way
Saint Peter, MN 56082
Phone: 507-931-1682
Web: www.jamesbeard.org

Sanford D'Amato Scholarship

Type of award: Scholarship.
Intended use: For undergraduate study at accredited postsecondary institution. Designated institutions: Licensed or accredited culinary schools.
Basis for selection: Major/career interest in culinary arts.
Application requirements: Transcript.
Additional information: Must be high school senior or graduate planning to attend a licensed or accredited culinary school.

Amount of award:	$2,750
Number of awards:	1
Application deadline:	May 15

Contact:
Scholarship Management Services
One Scholarship Way
Saint Peter, MN 56082
Phone: 507-931-1682
Web: www.jamesbeard.org

Schnitzer Steel Racing to Stop Hunger Scholarship

Type of award: Scholarship.
Intended use: For undergraduate study at postsecondary institution.
Basis for selection: Major/career interest in culinary arts.
Application requirements: Transcript. Essay on topic "Fighting Hunger in Oregon: What I've done or Would Like to Do to Make a Difference."
Additional information: Must be resident of Oregon or be enrolled or plan to enroll in a licensed or accredited culinary school in Oregon.

Amount of award:	$4,500
Number of awards:	1
Application deadline:	May 15

Contact:
James Beard Foundation Scholarship Program
One Scholarship Way
Saint Peter, MN 56082
Phone: 507-931-1682
Web: www.jamesbeard.org

Spencer's Restaurant at the Mountain Scholarship

Type of award: Scholarship.
Intended use: For undergraduate study at accredited postsecondary institution. Designated institutions: Licensed or accredited culinary schools.
Basis for selection: Major/career interest in culinary arts.
Application requirements: Transcript.

Additional information: Must be high school senior or graduate planning to attend a licensed or accredited culinary school.

Amount of award:	$10,000
Number of awards:	1
Application deadline:	May 15

Contact:
Scholarship Management Services
One Scholarship Way
Saint Peter, MN 56082
Phone: 507-931-1682
Web: www.jamesbeard.org

Spiaggia Scholarship

Type of award: Scholarship.
Intended use: For undergraduate study at accredited postsecondary institution. Designated institutions: Licensed or accredited culinary schools.
Basis for selection: Major/career interest in culinary arts.
Application requirements: Transcript.
Additional information: Must be high school senior or graduate planning to attend a licensed or accredited culinary school.

Amount of award:	$4,000
Number of awards:	1
Application deadline:	May 15

Contact:
Scholarship Management Services
One Scholarship Way
Saint Peter, MN 56082
Phone: 507-931-1682
Web: www.jamesbeard.org

Steven Scher Memorial Scholarship for Aspiring Restaurateurs

Type of award: Scholarship.
Intended use: For undergraduate study at accredited postsecondary institution.
Basis for selection: Major/career interest in culinary arts. Applicant must demonstrate financial need.
Application requirements: Essay, transcript. Detail work experience; list of top three favorite restaurants and explaining why they have earned that ranking. Essay detailing ideal restaurant/hospitality concept and reasons for entering the field.
Additional information: Must be enrolled in culinary or hospitality management program. Must be high school graduate. One scholarship will be granted for study in restaurant management at the French Culinary Institute in New York City; the other to an institution of the applicant's choice.

Amount of award:	$5,000
Number of awards:	2
Application deadline:	May 15
Total amount awarded:	$10,000

Contact:
James Beard Foundation Scholarship Program
One Scholarship Way
St. Peter, MN 56082
Phone: 507-931-1682
Web: www.jamesbeard.org

Sunday Supper South Atlanta Scholarship

Type of award: Scholarship.
Intended use: For undergraduate study at accredited postsecondary institution.
Basis for selection: Major/career interest in culinary arts. Applicant must demonstrate financial need.
Application requirements: Transcript.
Additional information: Applicants must plan to enroll in accredited culinary school. Two scholarships awarded for $5,000, two for $4,000, and one for $2,000. Preference given to students who are residents of or attending school in one of the following states: Alabama, Florida, Georgia, North Carolina, South Carolina, Louisiana, Virginia, Arkansas, Texas, Mississippi, Kentucky, Maryland, Missouri, Oklahoma, or West Virginia.

Amount of award:	$2,000-$5,000
Number of awards:	5
Application deadline:	May 15
Total amount awarded:	$11,500

Contact:
James Beard Foundation Scholarship Program
One Scholarship Way
St. Peter, MN 56082
Phone: 507-931-1682
Web: www.jamesbeard.org

Sunday Supper Union Market, Washington, D.C. Scholarship

Type of award: Scholarship.
Intended use: For undergraduate, graduate or non-degree study at accredited postsecondary institution. Designated institutions: Licensed or accredited culinary schools or schools with accredited hospitality management or management/operations continuing education programs.
Eligibility: Applicant must be female, returning adult student.
Basis for selection: Major/career interest in culinary arts or hospitality administration/management.
Application requirements: Essay, transcript. Essay describing applicant's ideal restaurant concept and explaining their reasons for entering the field.
Additional information: Must be female who has attained a secondary degree with at least five years experience in restaurant or hotel.

Amount of award:	$10,000
Number of awards:	1
Application deadline:	May 15

Contact:
Scholarship Management Services
One Scholarship Way
Saint Peter, MN 56082
Phone: 507-931-1682
Web: www.jamesbeard.org

Union Center National Bank Scholarship

Type of award: Scholarship.
Intended use: For full-time undergraduate study. Designated institutions: Licensed or accredited culinary schools.
Basis for selection: Major/career interest in culinary arts.
Application requirements: Transcript.
Additional information: Must be resident of or attend school in New Jersey. Must be high school senior or graduate planning to attend a licensed or accredited culinary school.

Amount of award:	$4,250
Number of awards:	1
Application deadline:	May 15

Contact:
Scholarship Management Services
One Scholarship Way
Saint Peter, MN 56082
Phone: 507-931-1682
Web: www.jamesbeard.org

Visit Orlando/James Beard Scholarship

Type of award: Scholarship.
Intended use: For undergraduate study at accredited postsecondary institution. Designated institutions: University of Central Florida, Valencia College.
Eligibility: Applicant must be residing in Florida.
Basis for selection: Major/career interest in culinary arts or hospitality administration/management.
Application requirements: Transcript.
Additional information: Must be high school graduate planning to attend either University of Central Florida or Valencia college and attend the culinary program, hospitality management program, or food and wine studies program.

Amount of award:	$2,500
Number of awards:	5
Application deadline:	May 15

Contact:
Scholarship Management Services
One Scholarship Way
Saint Peter, MN 56082
Phone: 507-931-1682
Web: www.jamesbeard.org

Zov's Bistro Scholarship

Type of award: Scholarship.
Intended use: For undergraduate study at accredited postsecondary institution. Designated institutions: Licensed or accredited culinary schools.
Basis for selection: Major/career interest in culinary arts. Applicant must demonstrate financial need.
Application requirements: Recommendations, essay, transcript. Financial statement, resume.
Additional information: Must plan to enroll in licensed or accredited culinary school.

Amount of award:	$10,000
Number of awards:	1
Application deadline:	May 15
Total amount awarded:	$3,000

Contact:
Scholarship America
One Scholarship Way
St. Peter, MN 56082
Phone: 507-931-1682
Web: www.jamesbeard.org

James F. Byrnes Foundation

James F. Byrnes Scholarship

Type of award: Scholarship, renewable.
Intended use: For full-time freshman study at accredited 4-year institution.

Eligibility: Applicant must be high school senior. Applicant must be U.S. citizen residing in South Carolina.
Basis for selection: Applicant must demonstrate financial need, high academic achievement, depth of character, leadership, patriotism, seriousness of purpose and service orientation.
Application requirements: Interview, essay, transcript. SAT/ACT scores, photograph, autobiography (three typed pages maximum) describing home situation, death of parent/s, desire for college education, college ambitions, reasons financial assistance is needed, how college will be financed, etc. Two non-relative references (one from current guidance counselor or teacher).
Additional information: Applicant must be high school senior. Applicant must have minimum 2.5 GPA. One or both parents of applicant must be deceased. Visit Website for additional information.

Amount of award:	$3,250
Number of awards:	8
Number of applicants:	126
Application deadline:	February 10
Notification begins:	April 20
Total amount awarded:	$84,500

Contact:
James F. Byrnes Foundation
P.O. Box 6781
Columbia, SC 29260-6781
Phone: 803-254-9325
Fax: 803-254-9354
Web: www.byrnesscholars.org

Janet Logan Daily Foundation

Janet Logan Daily Foundation Scholarship

Type of award: Scholarship.
Intended use: For full-time freshman study at accredited vocational, 2-year or 4-year institution in United States.
Eligibility: Applicant must be at least 16, no older than 20, high school senior. Applicant must be U.S. citizen residing in New Jersey.
Additional information: Must have a minimum 2.5 GPA. Award is divided evenly over a four-year academic period. Applicants must actively participate in at least one extra-curricular activity. Must have worked an average of 30 hours per week during the summer since the age of 16.

Number of awards:	1
Application deadline:	April 1
Total amount awarded:	$10,000

Contact:
Janet Logan Daily Foundation
1105 Taylorsville Road
Suite 100
Washington Crossing, PA 18977
Phone: 215-305-8794
Web: janetlogandailyfoundation.org/application.asp

Jeannette Rankin Foundation

Jeanette Rankin Foundation Scholarship

Type of award: Scholarship.
Intended use: For undergraduate study at accredited vocational, 2-year or 4-year institution in United States.
Eligibility: Applicant must be female, at least 35. Applicant must be U.S. citizen or permanent resident.
Basis for selection: Applicant must demonstrate financial need, depth of character and seriousness of purpose.
Application requirements: Recommendations, essay.
Additional information: Applicant must be 35+ as of March 1 and meet low-income guidelines. Must display attainable goals and plan for reaching them, and understanding of how degree will benefit self and others. Download application from Website from November through mid-February, or send SASE with application request.

Amount of award:	$2,000
Number of applicants:	850
Application deadline:	March 17
Notification begins:	July 1
Total amount awarded:	$174,000

Contact:
Jeannette Rankin Foundation
1 Huntington Road, #701
Athens, GA 30606
Phone: 706-208-1211
Fax: 706-548-0202
Web: www.rankinfoundation.org

Jewish Family and Children's Services (JFCS)

JFCS Scholarship Fund

Type of award: Scholarship.
Intended use: For undergraduate or graduate study at accredited postsecondary institution.
Eligibility: Applicant must be Jewish. Applicant must be residing in California.
Basis for selection: Applicant must demonstrate financial need and high academic achievement.
Application requirements: FAFSA.
Additional information: Minimum 2.75 GPA for grants. Applicants must demonstrate connection to Jewish community. High school seniors, undergraduates, and graduate students may apply. Applicants may also be high school students traveling to Israel. Grants available for residents of Sonoma, Marin, San Francisco, San Mateo, or Santa Clara counties; loans available for all nine Bay area counties. Deadline is for consideration for school year; applicants for Israel travel, Holocaust study, and vocational study may apply any time. Organization has several scholarships and loans; see Website for more details.

Amount of award:	$1,500-$3,000
Number of awards:	100
Number of applicants:	110
Application deadline:	October 31
Total amount awarded:	$250,000

Contact:
Jewish Family and Children's Services
Attn: Michelle Lamphere
2150 Post Street
San Francisco, CA 94115
Phone: 415-449-1226
Fax: 415-848-7012
Web: www.jfcs.org

Jewish Vocational Service

Jewish Vocational Service Scholarship Program

Type of award: Scholarship, renewable.
Intended use: For full-time undergraduate or graduate study at accredited postsecondary institution in United States.
Eligibility: Applicant must be Jewish. Applicant must be U.S. citizen or permanent resident residing in California.
Basis for selection: Applicant must demonstrate financial need and high academic achievement.
Application requirements: Recommendations, essay, transcript. FAFSA and tax returns.
Additional information: Minimum 2.7 GPA for undergraduates, 3.0 for graduates. Must be Jewish and legal, permanent resident of Los Angeles County with verifiable financial need. Number of awards varies. Visit Website for electronic application.

Amount of award:	$500-$10,000
Number of applicants:	400
Application deadline:	March 31
Notification begins:	January 31
Total amount awarded:	$8,492,000

Contact:
JVS Scholarship Program
c/o Patricia Sills
6505 Wilshire Blvd., Suite 200
Los Angeles, CA 90048
Phone: 323-761-8888 ext. 8868
Fax: 323-761-8580
Web: www.jvsla.org

Jewish War Veterans of the United States of America

Charles Kosmutza Memorial Grant

Type of award: Scholarship.
Intended use: For undergraduate study at accredited vocational, 2-year or 4-year institution.
Eligibility: Applicant must be Jewish. Applicant must be U.S. citizen.
Application requirements: Essay, transcript. DD-214 form.

Scholarships

Additional information: Essay contest answering question "How will military experience help you pursue your academic goals?"

Amount of award:	$1,000-$2,500
Number of awards:	2
Application deadline:	May 30
Total amount awarded:	$3,500

Contact:
Jewish War Veterans of the United States of America
National Achievement Program
1811 R Street Northwest
Washington, DC 20009
Phone: 202-265-6280
Fax: 202-234-5662
Web: www.jwv.org/images/uploads/National_Achievement_Program_Application_030415.pdf

Edith, Louis and Max S. Millen Memorial Athletic Grant

Type of award: Scholarship.
Intended use: For freshman study at accredited 4-year institution.
Eligibility: Applicant must be high school senior.
Basis for selection: Applicant must demonstrate high academic achievement.
Application requirements: SAT/ACT scores.
Additional information: Must be a direct descendent of Jewish War Veterans Member. Must be in upper 25 percent of high school class. Must have participated in athletic activities. Visit Website for application and more information.

Amount of award:	$1,000
Number of awards:	1
Application deadline:	May 1

Contact:
Jewish War Veterans of the United States of America
National Scholarship Committee
1811 R Street Northwest
Washington, DC 20009
Phone: 202-265-6280
Fax: 202-234-5662
Web: www.jwv.org

Jewish War Veterans of the United States of America Bernard Rotberg Memorial Scholarship

Type of award: Scholarship.
Intended use: For freshman study at accredited 4-year institution.
Eligibility: Applicant must be high school senior. Applicant must be Jewish.
Basis for selection: Applicant must demonstrate financial need and high academic achievement.
Application requirements: SAT/ACT scores.
Additional information: Applicant must be direct descendant of Jewish War Veterans member. Must be in upper 25 percent of high school class; must have participated in extracurricular activities in school as well as in Jewish community. SAT scores and recommendations encouraged. Visit Website for application and more information.

Amount of award:	$1,000
Number of awards:	1
Application deadline:	May 1

Contact:
Jewish War Veterans of the United States of America
National Scholarship Committee
1811 R Street Northwest
Washington, DC 20009
Phone: 202-265-6280
Fax: 202-234-5662
Web: www.jwv.org

Leon Brooks Memorial Grant

Type of award: Scholarship.
Intended use: For undergraduate study at accredited vocational, 2-year or 4-year institution.
Eligibility: Applicant must be Jewish. Applicant must be U.S. citizen or permanent resident.
Application requirements: Transcript. Form DD-214.
Additional information: Essay contest answering question "How will military experience help you pursue your academic goals?"

Amount of award:	$1,000
Number of awards:	1
Application deadline:	May 30

Contact:
Jewish War Veterans of the United States of America
National Achievement Program
1811 R Street Northwest
Washington, DC 20009
Phone: 202-265-6280
Fax: 202-234-5662
Web: www.jwv.org/images/uploads/National_Achievement_Program_Application_030415.pdf

Max R. & Irene Rubenstein Memorial Grant

Type of award: Scholarship.
Intended use: For undergraduate study at accredited vocational, 2-year or 4-year institution.
Eligibility: Applicant must be Jewish. Applicant must be U.S. citizen or permanent resident.
Application requirements: Transcript. Form DD-214.
Additional information: Essay contest answering question "How will military experience help you pursue your academic goals?"

Amount of award:	$1,500
Number of awards:	1
Application deadline:	May 30

Contact:
Jewish War Veterans of the United States of America
National Achievement Program
1811 R Street NW
Washington, DC 20009
Phone: 202-265-6280
Fax: 202-234-5662
Web: www.jwv.org/images/uploads/National_Achievement_Program_Application_030415.pdf

Robert and Rebecca Rubin Memorial Grant

Type of award: Research grant.
Intended use: For freshman study at accredited 4-year institution.
Eligibility: Applicant must be high school senior. Applicant must be Jewish.

Basis for selection: Applicant must demonstrate high academic achievement.
Application requirements: SAT/ACT scores.
Additional information: Applicant must be direct descendant of JWV member. Must be in upper 25 percent of high school class; must have participated in extracurricular activities in school as well as in Jewish community. Visit Website for application and more information.

Amount of award:	$1,250
Number of awards:	1
Application deadline:	May 1

Contact:
Jewish War Veterans of the United States of America
National Scholarship Committee
1811 R Street Northwest
Washington, DC 20009
Phone: 202-265-6280
Fax: 202-234-5662
Web: www.jwv.org/images/uploads/National_Achievement_Program_Application_030415.pdf

Seymour and Phyllis Shore Memorial Grant

Type of award: Research grant.
Intended use: For freshman study at accredited vocational or 4-year institution.
Eligibility: Applicant must be high school senior. Applicant must be Jewish.
Basis for selection: Applicant must demonstrate high academic achievement.
Application requirements: SAT/ACT scores.
Additional information: Applicant must be direct descendant of JWV member. Must be in upper 25 percent of high school class; must have participated in extracurricular activities in school as well as in Jewish community. Visit Website for application and more information.

Amount of award:	$1,500
Number of awards:	1
Application deadline:	May 1

Contact:
Jewish War Veterans of the United States of America
National Scholarship Committee
1811 R Street Northwest
Washington, DC 20009
Phone: 202-265-6280
Fax: 202-234-5662
Web: www.jwv.org

Jim Dodson Law

Jim Dodson Law Scholarship for Brain Injury Victims & Their Caregivers

Type of award: Scholarship.
Intended use: For full-time undergraduate study at accredited 4-year institution in United States.
Eligibility: Applicant must be U.S. citizen residing in Florida.
Basis for selection: Applicant must demonstrate service orientation.
Application requirements: Transcript. Essay (should not exceed 500 words): Tell us how having a brain injury has

changed your life. If you are a caregiver or a family member of someone who has a brain injury, please write your essay on how it has impacted you and/or your family's life. Full rules and guidelines can be found on the web site.
Additional information: Must have completed at least 12 credit hours. Must be a florida resident.

Amount of award:	$1,000
Number of awards:	1
Application deadline:	June 30
Total amount awarded:	$1,000

Contact:
Jim Dodson Law
310 Wildwood Way
Clearwater, FL 33756
Phone: 727-446-0840
Fax: 727-446-0850
Web: https://www.jimdodsonlaw.com/library/the-jim-dodson-law-scholarship.cfm

The John Bayliss Foundation

John Bayliss Scholarship Award

Type of award: Scholarship.
Intended use: For full-time junior, senior or graduate study at 4-year or graduate institution. Designated institutions: BEA Member Institutions.
Basis for selection: Major/career interest in radio/television/film. Applicant must demonstrate high academic achievement, depth of character and seriousness of purpose.
Application requirements: Recommendations, essay, transcript.
Additional information: Award intended for study in radio only. Should be able to show evidence of potential to be outstanding electronic media professional. Application available from campus faculty or online.

Amount of award:	$2,500
Number of awards:	1
Application deadline:	October 10
Total amount awarded:	$2,500

Contact:
Broadcast Education Association (BEA)
1771 N Street, N.W.
Washington, DC 20036-2891
Phone: 202-429-3935
Web: www.beaweb.org

John M. O'Brien & Associates

John M. O'Brien & Associates Scholarship Program

Type of award: Scholarship.
Intended use: For full-time undergraduate or graduate study at 2-year, 4-year or graduate institution.
Eligibility: Applicant must be high school senior. Applicant must be U.S. citizen.

Application requirements: Essay, transcript. Applicant must be at least 18 years old. Must be a high school senior. Must write a 100-300 word essay.

Additional information: More information on how to apply and essay topics on scholarship webpage.

Amount of award:	$1,000
Number of awards:	1
Application deadline:	July 31
Notification begins:	August 31
Total amount awarded:	$1,000

Contact:
John M. O'Brien & Associates
717 K Street #530
Sacramento, CA 95814
Phone: 760-696-7959
Web: https://www.jobrienlaw.com/scholarship/

Johnson Scholarship Foundation

Children of Florida UPS Employees Scholarship

Type of award: Scholarship, renewable.
Intended use: For undergraduate study at accredited vocational, 2-year or 4-year institution in United States.
Eligibility: Applicant must be residing in Florida.
Basis for selection: Applicant must demonstrate financial need.
Application requirements: Recommendations, transcript, proof of eligibility. Parents' financial data.
Additional information: Must be a child of regular full-time or permanent part-time Florida UPS employee. UPS employee must currently reside in Florida. UPS employee must have a minimum of one year employment with the company as of application deadline and must be employed at UPS when awards are announced. Children of UPS retirees and deceased UPS employees who met the stated employee requirements at the time of retirement or death also eligible.

Amount of award:	$1,000-$10,000
Application deadline:	April 15
Notification begins:	January 1
Total amount awarded:	$1,040,000

Contact:
Johnson Scholarship Foundation Scholarship Program
Scholarship Management Services
One Scholarship Way, P.O. Box 297
Saint Peter, MN 56082
Phone: 507-931-1682
Web: www.jsf.bz

State University System of Florida Theodore R. and Vivian M. Johnson Scholarship

Type of award: Scholarship, renewable.
Intended use: For undergraduate study at 4-year institution in United States. Designated institutions: State University System of Florida Institutions: Florida A&M University, University of Central Florida, Florida Atlantic University, University of Florida, Florida Gulf Coast University, University of North Florida, Florida International University, University of South Florida, Florida State University, University of West Florida, New College of Florida, Florida Polytechnic University.
Eligibility: Applicant must be residing in Florida.
Basis for selection: Applicant must demonstrate financial need and high academic achievement.
Application requirements: Recommendations, essay, transcript, proof of eligibility. FAFSA. Must provide documentation of the nature and/or extent of disability. Must meet guidelines required by institution in which student is enrolled.
Additional information: Award is for students with disabilities. Minimum 2.0 GPA. Award amount varies and is dependent upon institution. Must meet specific qualifications to renew yearly. Apply directly to institution. Contact institution's financial aid office for more information.

Amount of award:	$1,500-$5,000
Application deadline:	May 15
Notification begins:	January 1
Total amount awarded:	$500,000

Contact:
Disability Resource Center of the pertinent state university.
Web: www.jsf.bz

JPG To PDF Online

JPGTOPDF College Scholarship

Type of award: Scholarship.
Intended use: For undergraduate study at accredited vocational, 2-year, 4-year or graduate institution in United States.
Eligibility: Applicant must be U.S. citizen.

Amount of award:	$1,000-$1,000
Number of awards:	1
Application deadline:	June 30
Total amount awarded:	$1,000

Contact:
Web: www.jpgtopdf.com/blog/college-scholarship-1000-open-to-any-student-at-an-accredited-us-college/

Jurewitz Law Group

Jurewitz Law Group San Diego Scholarship

Type of award: Scholarship.
Intended use: For undergraduate study at accredited 2-year or 4-year institution.
Eligibility: Applicant must be high school senior. Applicant must be U.S. citizen or permanent resident residing in California.
Application requirements: Essay.
Additional information: Minimum 3.0 GPA. Must be a graduating San Diego County high school senior. Application and essay can be found on website.

Number of awards:	1
Application deadline:	June 30
Notification begins:	July 29
Total amount awarded:	$500

Contact:
Phone: 619-452-0716
Fax: 888-233-3180
Web: www.jurewitz.com/scholarship-sd/

Jurewitz Law Group Scholarship

Type of award: Scholarship.
Intended use: For undergraduate study at accredited 2-year or 4-year institution.
Eligibility: Applicant must be high school senior. Applicant must be U.S. citizen or permanent resident.
Application requirements: Essay.
Additional information: Must have a minimum 3.0 GPA for the latest semester/grading period. Application and essay question can be found online.

Number of awards:	1
Application deadline:	August 24
Notification begins:	July 15
Total amount awarded:	$500

Contact:
Phone: 619-452-0716
Fax: 888-233-3180
Web: www.jurewitz.com/scholarship/

Kahn Roven, LLP

Kahn Roven, LLP Scholarship

Type of award: Scholarship.
Intended use: For full-time freshman study at accredited 4-year institution.
Eligibility: Applicant must be U.S. citizen or permanent resident.
Application requirements: Essay, transcript. Submit a 500 word essay on: What does post-secondary education mean to you? How is it going to help you achieve your future goals?
Additional information: Minimum 3.0 GPA. Available to High School seniors who are planning to attend an accredited 4-year college or university.

Number of awards:	1
Application deadline:	April 15
Notification begins:	May 15
Total amount awarded:	$500

Contact:
Kahn Roven, LLP
5550 Topanga Cyn. Boulevard
Suite 200
Woodland Hills, CA 90035
Phone: 213-738-0708
Web: www.kahnroven.com/scholarship.html

Kansas Board of Regents

Career Technical Workforce Grant

Type of award: Scholarship.
Intended use: For at accredited vocational, 2-year or 4-year institution. Designated institutions: Kansas schools offering technical or AAS degrees.
Eligibility: Applicant must be residing in Kansas.

Application requirements: $12 application fee. FAFSA.State of Kansas Student Aid application.
Additional information: Applicant must be Kansas resident and graduate of Kansas accredited high school. Must be pursuing technical or Associate of Applied Science degree in a high demand, critical industry employment field.. Students pursuing baccalaureate degrees not eligible.

Amount of award:	$250-$1,000
Application deadline:	May 1

Contact:
Kansas Board of Regents
1000 Southwest Jackson Street
Suite 520
Topeka, KS 66612-1368
Phone: 785-296-3421
Fax: 785-296-0983
Web: www.kansasregents.org

Kansas Ethnic Minority Scholarship

Type of award: Scholarship, renewable.
Intended use: For full-time undergraduate study at postsecondary institution. Designated institutions: Kansas postsecondary institutions.
Eligibility: Applicant must be Alaskan native, Asian American, African American, Mexican American, Hispanic American, Puerto Rican, American Indian or Native Hawaiian/Pacific Islander. Applicant must be U.S. citizen or permanent resident residing in Kansas.
Basis for selection: Applicant must demonstrate financial need and high academic achievement.
Application requirements: $12 application fee. Proof of eligibility. State of Kansas Student Aid Application. FAFSA.

Amount of award:	$1,850
Application deadline:	May 1

Contact:
Kansas Board of Regents
1000 SW Jackson Street
Suite 520
Topeka, KS 66612-1368
Phone: 785-296-3517
Fax: 785-296-0983
Web: www.kansasregents.org

Kansas Military Service Scholarship

Type of award: Scholarship.
Intended use: For undergraduate study at accredited 2-year or 4-year institution. Designated institutions: Institutions in Kansas.
Eligibility: Applicant must be residing in Kansas. Applicant must be veteran who served in the Army, Air Force, Marines or Navy during Middle East War. Must be honorably discharged veteran who has served at least 90 days in support of conflict in Iraq or Afghanistan or less than 90 days due to injury sustained in Iraq or Afghanistan.
Application requirements: $12 application fee. Form DD-214, FAFSA.State of Kansas Student Aid application.
Additional information: Applicant must be Kansas resident enrolled in Kansas school. Must be enrolled for minimum of 6 credit hours per semester.

Amount of award:	Full tuition
Application deadline:	May 1

Contact:
Kansas Board of Regents
1000 Southwest Jackson Street
Suite 520
Topeka, KS 66612-1368
Phone: 785-296-3421
Fax: 785-296-0983
Web: www.kansasregents.org

Kansas Nursing Service Scholarship

Type of award: Scholarship, renewable.
Intended use: For full-time undergraduate study at postsecondary institution. Designated institutions: Kansas postsecondary schools with approved nursing programs.
Eligibility: Applicant must be U.S. citizen or permanent resident residing in Kansas.
Basis for selection: Major/career interest in nursing. Applicant must demonstrate financial need.
Application requirements: $12 application fee. State of Kansas Student Aid Application. FAFSA.
Additional information: Must obtain sponsorship from adult-care home licensed under the Adult Care Home Licensure Act; state agency that employs LPNs or RNs; or state-licensed medical care facility, psychiatric hospital, home health agency or local health department. Must agree to work in Kansas one year for each year that scholarship is received. If recipient does not meet obligation, award becomes loan.

Amount of award:	$2,500-$3,500
Application deadline:	May 1

Contact:
Kansas Board of Regents
1000 SW Jackson Street
Suite 520
Topeka, KS 66612-1368
Phone: 785-296-3517
Fax: 785-296-0983
Web: www.kansasregents.org

Kansas ROTC Service Scholarship

Type of award: Scholarship.
Intended use: For full-time undergraduate study at postsecondary institution.
Eligibility: Applicant or parent must be member/participant of Reserve Officers Training Corps (ROTC). Applicant must be residing in Kansas.
Additional information: Applicant must be Kansas resident enrolled in Kansas ROTC program. Must be full-time undergraduate with at least 12 credit hours. Scholarship limited to eight semesters. Award amount may be up to tuition and costs of average four-year regents institution; average award is $1,650. Award may only be used at the following: Kansas State University, Pittsburg State University, University of Kansas and Washburn University.

Application deadline:	May 1

Contact:
Kansas Board of Regents, Director of Student Financial Assistance
1000 SW Jackson Street
Suite 520
Topeka, KS 66612-1368
Phone: 785-296-3517
Fax: 785-296-0983
Web: www.kansasregents.org

Kansas State Scholarship

Type of award: Scholarship, renewable.
Intended use: For full-time undergraduate study at postsecondary institution.
Eligibility: Applicant must be residing in Kansas.
Basis for selection: Applicant must demonstrate financial need and high academic achievement.
Application requirements: $12 application fee. Proof of eligibility. FAFSA.The State of Kansas Student Aid Application.
Additional information: Applicant must be Kansas resident, high school senior or undergraduate, and must be designated State Scholar in senior year of high school. Must be enrolled in Kansas school. Must have a high GPA and ACT score: the average profile of a designated scholars is 3.90 GPA and 30 ACT.

Amount of award:	$1,000
Application deadline:	May 1

Contact:
Kansas Board of Regents
1000 SW Jackson Street
Suite 520
Topeka, KS 66612-1368
Phone: 785-296-3517
Fax: 785-296-0983
Web: www.kansasregents.org

Kansas Teacher Service Scholarship

Type of award: Scholarship, renewable.
Intended use: For full-time junior or senior study at 4-year or graduate institution.
Eligibility: Applicant must be residing in Kansas.
Basis for selection: Major/career interest in education, teacher. Applicant must demonstrate high academic achievement.
Application requirements: $12 application fee. Recommendations, transcript, proof of eligibility. FAFSA. Personal statement.The State of Kansas Student Aid application. Personal statement of education goals.
Additional information: Applicant must be Kansas resident enrolled in Kansas school that offers education degree. Must plan to teach in a hard-to-fill discipline or underserved geographic area of the state. Scholarships are competitive; selection based on GPA, high school rank, transcript and recommendation. Preference given to juniors and seniors, or currently licensed teachers pursuing licensure or endorsement in hard-to-fill disciplines.

Amount of award:	$1,103-$5,514
Application deadline:	May 1

Contact:
Kansas Board of Regents
1000 Southwest Jackson Street
Suite 520
Topeka, KS 66612-1368
Phone: 785-296-3517
Fax: 785-296-0983
Web: www.kansasregents.org

National Guard Educational Assistance Program

Type of award: Scholarship, renewable.
Intended use: For undergraduate study at accredited 2-year or 4-year institution. Designated institutions: Kansas institutions.
Eligibility: Applicant must be U.S. citizen residing in Kansas.
Application requirements: $12 application fee. The State of Kansas Student Aid Application.

Additional information: Award amount varies. Requires service obligation.

Amount of award:	Full tuition
Application deadline:	May 1

Contact:
Kansas Board of Regents, Attn: Diane Lindeman
1000 Southwest Jackson Street
Suite 520
Topeka, KS 66612-1368
Phone: 785-296-3421
Fax: 785-296-0983
Web: www.kansasregents.org/scholarships_and_grants

Kappa Kappa Gamma Foundation

Kappa Kappa Gamma Scholarship

Type of award: Scholarship, renewable.
Intended use: For full-time undergraduate or graduate study at 4-year or graduate institution in United States.
Basis for selection: Applicant must demonstrate financial need and high academic achievement.
Application requirements: Recommendations, transcript.
Additional information: Applicant must be active member in good standing of Kappa Kappa Gamma fraternity, with minimum 3.0 GPA. Recipients must reapply each year. Must be U.S. citizen or permanent resident from Canada. Number of awards varies.

Amount of award:	$500-$3,000
Number of awards:	186
Number of applicants:	1,188
Application deadline:	February 1
Notification begins:	June 1
Total amount awarded:	$575,199

Contact:
Kappa Kappa Gamma Foundation
P.O. Box 38
Columbus, OH 43216-0038
Phone: 614-228-6515
Fax: 614-228-6303
Web: www.kappa.org

Karin Riley Porter Attorney at Law

Karin Riley Porter Good Works Scholarship

Type of award: Scholarship.
Intended use: For undergraduate or graduate study at accredited vocational, 2-year, 4-year or graduate institution.
Eligibility: Applicant must be high school senior.
Basis for selection: Applicant must demonstrate high academic achievement.
Application requirements: Recommendations, essay, transcript. Unofficial transcript, application cover sheet, application essay, one letter of recommendation. Essay topic (500 words): describe the applicant's leadership and dedication in giving back to his or her community through community

service projects, including projects involving criminal justice issues.
Additional information: Minimum 3.0 GPA required.

Amount of award:	$500
Number of awards:	1
Number of applicants:	20
Application deadline:	May 1
Total amount awarded:	$500

Contact:
Karin Riley Porter Attorney at Law Good Works Scholarship
10605 Judicial Drive
Suite 200
Fairfax, VA 22030
Phone: 202-517-0502
Fax: 703-991-0604
Web: www.virginia-criminallawyer.com/2016-good-works-scholarship.html

Keller Law Offices

Keller Law Offices Scholarship for Higher Education

Type of award: Scholarship.
Intended use: For full-time undergraduate study at accredited 2-year or 4-year institution in United States.
Eligibility: Applicant must be U.S. citizen or permanent resident.
Basis for selection: The scholarship committee will base the judging criteria on financial need and the quality of the essay. Major/career interest in law. Applicant must demonstrate financial need.
Application requirements: Submit a written essay on the topic: A 19¬ year¬ old is convicted of statutory rape with a 15¬ year¬ old. Should the 19¬ year old be required to register as a sex offender?

Amount of award:	$2,000
Number of awards:	1
Application deadline:	June 1
Notification begins:	September 1
Total amount awarded:	$2,000

Contact:
Keller Law Offices
620B Academy Drive
Northbrook, IL 60062
Phone: 847-940-4000
Web: http://kellerlawoffices.com/keller-higher-education-scholarship/

Kelly Law Team

Down Syndrome Scholarship

Type of award: Scholarship.
Intended use: For full-time undergraduate or graduate study at vocational, 2-year, 4-year or graduate institution.
Eligibility: Applicant must be U.S. citizen.
Application requirements: A statement of not more than 100 words indicating what the scholarship will do for you. (Optional) An essay (650 to 1,000 words) discussing how

Down syndrome has affected you in terms of your education; the essay must be original.

Additional information: Scholarships are open to US citizens with Down syndrome. Applicant may be asked for documentation that applicant has Down syndrome.

Amount of award:	$1,000
Number of awards:	2
Application deadline:	November 7
Notification begins:	December 7

Contact:
Kelly Law Team
1 East Washington Street
Suite 500
Phoenix, AZ 85004
Phone: 602-283-4122
Web: www.jkphoenixpersonalinjuryattorney.com/down-syndrome-scholarships/

Kelsey B. Diamantis TS Scholarship Family Foundation, INC.

Dollars 4 Tic Scholars

Type of award: Scholarship.

Intended use: For undergraduate study at accredited 2-year or 4-year institution in United States.

Application requirements: Recommendations, essay, transcript. Must provide an original letter on letterhead of your diagnosis of Chronic Tic Disorder or Tourette's Syndrome provided by and signed by your neurologist or psychiatrist. This will be verified for authenticity.

Additional information: Must have a minimum 2.5 GPA. 3 minute personal video about what you want to do after you graduate from college. Personal essay, 300 to 500 words, on what life has been like for you as a person with Tourette's Syndrome including one particularly meaningful or memorable occasion.

Amount of award:	$1,000
Number of awards:	4
Number of applicants:	28
Application deadline:	April 15
Total amount awarded:	$4,000

Contact:
The Kelsey B. Diamantis TS Scholarship Family Foundation, Inc.
21801 Little Bear Lane
Boca Raton, FL 33428
Phone: 561-487-9528
Web: www.dollars4ticscholars.org/

Kentucky Higher Education Assistance Authority (KHEAA)

Kentucky College Access Program Grant (CAP)

Type of award: Scholarship, renewable.

Intended use: For undergraduate study at postsecondary institution. Designated institutions: Kentucky institutions.

Eligibility: Applicant must be U.S. citizen or permanent resident residing in Kentucky.

Basis for selection: Applicant must demonstrate financial need.

Application requirements: FAFSA.

Additional information: Applicant ineligible if family contribution exceeds the maximum Pell EFC. May be used at eligible schools. Visit Website for additional information.

Amount of award:	$50-$1,900
Number of awards:	36,400
Number of applicants:	302,000
Total amount awarded:	$57,200,000

Contact:
Kentucky Higher Education Assistance Authority (KHEAA)
Grant Programs
P.O. Box 798
Frankfort, KY 40602-0798
Phone: 800-928-8926
Fax: 502-696-7373
Web: www.kheaa.com

Kentucky Early Childhood Development Scholarship

Type of award: Scholarship.

Intended use: For half-time undergraduate study at 2-year or 4-year institution. Designated institutions: Approved Kentucky institutions.

Eligibility: Applicant must be U.S. citizen or permanent resident residing in Kentucky.

Basis for selection: Major/career interest in education, early childhood. Applicant must demonstrate financial need.

Application requirements: FAFSA and ECDS application.

Additional information: Part-time students working at least twenty hours in childcare facility eligible. Must agree to service commitment. Must reapply for each term. Deadlines: July 15 for fall, November 15 for spring, April 15 for summer. Apply online.

Amount of award:	$1,800
Number of awards:	700
Number of applicants:	1,000
Application deadline:	July 15, November 15
Total amount awarded:	$850,000

Contact:
Kentucky Higher Education Assistance Authority
P.O. Box 798
Frankfort, KY 40602-0798
Phone: 800-928-8926
Fax: 502-696-7373
Web: www.kheaa.com

Kentucky Educational Excellence Scholarship (KEES)

Type of award: Scholarship, renewable.

Intended use: For undergraduate study at accredited vocational, 2-year or 4-year institution in United States. Designated institutions: Participating public and private postsecondary institutions in Kentucky and selected out-of-state institutions if program of study not offered in Kentucky.

Eligibility: Applicant must be enrolled in high school. Applicant must be U.S. citizen or permanent resident residing in Kentucky.

Basis for selection: Applicant must demonstrate high academic achievement.

Additional information: Scholarship is earned each year of high school. Minimum annual high school GPA of 2.5.

Supplemental award is given for highest ACT score (or SAT equivalent) achieved by high school graduation, based on minimum ACT score of 15. Recipient must be enrolled in postsecondary program at least half-time. Visit Website or contact via e-mail for additional information.

Amount of award:	$125-$2,500
Number of awards:	68,700
Number of applicants:	68,700
Total amount awarded:	$102,200,000

Contact:
Kentucky Higher Education Assistance Authority (KHEAA)
P.O. Box 798
Frankfort, KY 40602-0798
Phone: 800-928-8926
Fax: 502-696-7373
Web: www.kheaa.com

Kentucky Go Higher Grant

Type of award: Scholarship.
Intended use: For undergraduate study at postsecondary institution in United States. Designated institutions: Kentucky colleges and universities.
Eligibility: Applicant must be at least 24. Applicant must be U.S. citizen or permanent resident residing in Kentucky.
Basis for selection: Applicant must demonstrate financial need.
Application requirements: FAFSA and Go Higher Grant application.
Additional information: For less than half-time adult students who are at least 24 years old.

Amount of award:	$1,000
Number of awards:	190
Number of applicants:	640
Total amount awarded:	$190,000

Contact:
Kentucky Higher Education Assistance Authority (KHEAA)
P.O. Box 798
Frankfort, KY 40602-0798
Phone: 800-928-8926
Web: www.kheaa.com

Kentucky Teacher Scholarship

Type of award: Scholarship, renewable.
Intended use: For full-time undergraduate or graduate study at accredited 2-year or 4-year institution. Designated institutions: Participating Kentucky institutions.
Eligibility: Applicant must be U.S. citizen residing in Kentucky.
Basis for selection: Major/career interest in education, teacher; education, early childhood or education, special. Applicant must demonstrate financial need.
Application requirements: FAFSA and Kentucky teacher scholarship application.
Additional information: Must enroll in course of study leading to initial Kentucky teacher certification. Loan forgiveness for teaching in Kentucky schools: one semester for each semester of financial assistance, two semesters if service is in teacher shortage area. Scholarship becomes loan if recipient does not complete education program or fulfill teaching obligation. Visit Website for application (see ZipAccess) and additional information.

Amount of award:	$300-$5,000
Number of applicants:	1,000
Application deadline:	May 1
Notification begins:	May 30
Total amount awarded:	$412,300

Contact:
Kentucky Higher Education Assistance Authority (KHEAA)
Teacher Scholarship Program
P.O. Box 798
Frankfort, KY 40602-0798
Phone: 800-928-8926
Fax: 502-696-7373
Web: www.kheaa.com

Kentucky Tuition Grant

Type of award: Scholarship, renewable.
Intended use: For full-time undergraduate study at 2-year or 4-year institution. Designated institutions: Eligible private institutions in Kentucky.
Eligibility: Applicant must be U.S. citizen residing in Kentucky.
Basis for selection: Applicant must demonstrate financial need.
Application requirements: FAFSA.
Additional information: Visit Website for additional information.

Amount of award:	$200-$3,000
Number of awards:	11,200
Number of applicants:	56,900
Total amount awarded:	$29,800,000

Contact:
Kentucky Higher Education Assistance Authority
Grant Programs
P.O. Box 798
Frankfort, KY 40602-0798
Phone: 800-928-8926
Fax: 502-696-7373
Web: www.kheaa.com

The Kevin Dare Foundation

Life Back on Track Scholarship

Type of award: Scholarship, renewable.
Intended use: For full-time undergraduate study at 4-year institution.
Eligibility: Applicant must be physically challenged. Applicant must be at least 14, no older than 25, enrolled in high school. Applicant must be U.S. citizen.
Application requirements: Essay. Three letters of recommendation, physician verification of disability, current photograph.
Additional information: Back on Track scholarships are awarded to student athletes who have participated in organized competitive high school sports and subsequently have sustained a life changing accident or illness (e.g. traumatic brain or head injuries, paralysis, cancer, spine injuries, amputation). Past recipients may apply each year and have top consideration for future year's scholarships. Each year the recipient must maintain satisfactory progress toward their degree program (minimum of 12 credit hours per semester) and maintain a minimum grade point average of 3.0 on a 4.0 scale. In order to receive aid in subsequent years, recipients must also provide a copy of their cumulative transcript at the end of each academic year, as well as an application and letter requesting renewal of their scholarship.

Application deadline:	May 29
Notification begins:	August 1
Total amount awarded:	$20,000

Contact:
476 Rolling Ridge Drive
State College, PA 16801
Phone: 814-231-2249
Fax: 814-235-3500
Web: www.kevindare.com

KidGuard

KidGuard for Education Essay Scholarship Program

Type of award: Scholarship.
Intended use: For full-time undergraduate or graduate study at accredited vocational, 2-year, 4-year or graduate institution in United States.
Application requirements: Essay. Essay topic: Do you think parents should monitor their children's phones and online activities? More information about the essay on the website. Applicants have to provide a copy of verification of full-time enrollment at the school.
Additional information: Notification date is ASAP. More information available on the website.

Amount of award:	$500-$1,500
Number of awards:	2
Application deadline:	March 31
Total amount awarded:	$2,000

Contact:
KidGuard Jesse Frank
117 West 9th Street
Suite 1009
Los Angeles, CA 90015
Phone: 888-481-0881
Web: https://www.kidguard.com/nonprofits/scholarship/

KidGuard for Education Essay Scholarship Program

Type of award: Scholarship.
Intended use: For full-time undergraduate or graduate study at accredited vocational, 2-year, 4-year or graduate institution in United States.
Eligibility: Applicant must be high school junior or senior.
Application requirements: Essay, proof of eligibility. Essay topic: Statistics show that 42% of teenagers with tech access have been cyberbullied over the past year and that 1 in 4 have been bullied more than once, We believe that you as high school students can give us invaluable feedback,Choose one of the following to write your essay on:. How have you or your peers been affected by cyberbullying? Propose your solution for cyberbullying. How do you think schools can aid in stopping cyberbullying? Propose your solution for cyberbullying.
Additional information: Notification date is ASAP. Applicats must provide a copy of verification of full-time enrollment at the school. More information available on website.

Amount of award:	$500-$1,000
Number of awards:	3
Application deadline:	March 31
Total amount awarded:	$2,000

Contact:
KidGuard
117 West 9th Street
Suite 1009
Los Angeles, CA 90015
Phone: 888-481-0881
Web: https://www.kidguard.com/nonprofits/high-school-scholarship/

The Kim and Harold Louie Family Foundation

The Louie Foundation Scholarship

Type of award: Scholarship.
Intended use: For full-time undergraduate study at vocational, 2-year or 4-year institution.
Eligibility: Applicant must be permanent resident.
Basis for selection: Applicant must demonstrate high academic achievement.
Application requirements: Recommendations, transcript, proof of eligibility. Personal essays, SAR.
Additional information: Minimum 3.5 GPA; SAT score of 1800 or ACT score of 26. Special consideration will be noted for applicants whose parents did not attend college, whose parents are United States veterans, who have overcome significant adversity, or who are first-generation immigrants to the United States.

Number of awards:	25
Number of applicants:	500
Application deadline:	March 31
Total amount awarded:	$100,000

Contact:
The Kim and Harold Louie Family Foundation - Scholarship
1325 Howard Avenue, 949
Burlingame, CA 94010
Phone: 650-491-3434
Fax: 650-490-3153
Web: www.louiefamilyfoundation.org

Kirmar Foundation

Kirmar Foundation Student Scholarship

Type of award: Scholarship.
Intended use: For full-time undergraduate or graduate study at 2-year, 4-year or graduate institution.
Basis for selection: Applicant must demonstrate financial need.
Application requirements: Recommendations, transcript. A completed application form. A cover letter expressing the applicant's educational goals and aspirations describing how the Kirmar Foundation Scholarship can help the applicant to realize these goals financially and how his or her education will be used for the greater good as well as for the enrichment of his or her own life. High School Transcript and SATs and/ or ACT scores. College Transcript if the applicant is currently attending a college or university. Two letters of

recommendation (at least 1 by a teacher). A copy of parents' or guardians' most recent income tax return.

Additional information: Send your cover letter to kstewart@amcigroup.com to get the scholarship application. Award amount is on an individual basis. There are no deadlines for applying, year round Scholarship is available. There will be no application fee.

Contact:
Kirmar Foundation

Kitchen Cabinet Kings

Kitchen Cabinet Kings Entrepreneur Scholarship

Type of award: Scholarship.
Intended use: For undergraduate study at accredited 4-year or graduate institution in United States.
Eligibility: Applicant must be U.S. citizen.
Application requirements: Under 1,500 word essay about creating a business plan. View website for full details.
Additional information: Business major preferred, but not required. Only submissions via the scholarship page will be accepted.

Number of awards:	1
Application deadline:	August 15
Notification begins:	August 22
Total amount awarded:	$5,000

Contact:
Kitchen Cabinet Kings
380 Lexington Avenue
17th Floor
New York, NY 10168
Phone: 888-696-6454
Fax: 718-701-2527
Web: www.kitchencabinetkings.com/scholarship

kitchensGuides.com

Smart Kitchen Improvement Scholarship

Type of award: Scholarship, renewable.
Intended use: For full-time.
Eligibility: Applicant must be enrolled in high school.
Application requirements: Essay. Applicant needs to write 1000-1500 words on the given topics. All graduates or post graduates students can apply. Content must be unique and impressive.
Additional information: For more information feel free contact us info@kitchensguides.com and visit at: http://www.kitchensguides.com/kitchen-guides-scholarship.

Amount of award:	$500
Number of awards:	1
Application deadline:	October 15
Notification begins:	December 1
Total amount awarded:	$500

Contact:
KitchenGuides.com
3548 Wyatt Street
Boca Raton, FL 33432
Phone: 561-393-8087
Web: www.kitchensguides.com/kitchen-guides-scholarship/

Korean Ancestry Grants

The William Orr Dingwall Foundation

Type of award: Scholarship, renewable.
Intended use: For full-time undergraduate study at accredited 4-year institution in United States.
Eligibility: Applicant must be Asian American.
Basis for selection: There is a strong preference for applicants of Korean ancestry.
Application requirements: Recommendations, essay, transcript. Written statement in support of application not to exceed 1,000 words. 2 to 3 letters of recommendation from professors/teachers. An official, sealed transcript of the grades earned by the applicant at any undergraduate college or university he or she is currently attending or may have previously attended. In the case of an applicant who will be commencing his or her undergraduate education at the beginning of the next academic semester, a transcript of the grades he or she has earned in secondary school may be substituted. A CV/academic resume.
Additional information: Minimum 3.5 or greater GPA. Applicants must be of Asian ancestry, with at least one Asian grandparent, there is a strong preference for applicants of Korean ancestry. Mor informaition about grants can be found at www.dingwallfoundation.org/grants/.

Amount of award:	$750-$10,000
Number of awards:	50
Number of applicants:	393
Application deadline:	April 1
Notification begins:	June 30
Total amount awarded:	$150,000

Contact:
The William Orr Dingwall Foundation
P.O. Box 57088
Washington, DC 20037
Web: http://app.smarterselect.com/programs/38597-The-Dingwall-Foundation

Kosciuszko Foundation

Kosciuszko Foundation Year Abroad Program

Type of award: Scholarship, renewable.
Intended use: For junior or senior study at 4-year institution in Poland. Designated institutions: Center for Polish Language and Culture in Cracow, Poland. Institute of Polish Diaspora and Ethnic Studies (formerly the Polonia Institute, Krakow).
Eligibility: Applicant must be U.S. citizen.
Basis for selection: Competition/talent/interest in study abroad. Major/career interest in Polish language/studies. Applicant must demonstrate high academic achievement.

Application requirements: $50 application fee. Recommendations, essay, transcript. Two passport-sized photos with full name on reverse side of each. Graduates must submit copies of degree diplomas, Polish Ministry of Education application completed in English.

Additional information: Must have interest in Polish subjects and/or involvement in Polish-American community. Scholarship covers tuition and stipend for housing and living expenses for one academic year or semester. Airfare not included. Minimum 3.0 GPA. Visit Website for more information and application. Applications available from October 1 to January 5.

Amount of award:	Full tuition
Number of applicants:	5
Application deadline:	January 5
Total amount awarded:	$5,400

Contact:
Kosciuszko Foundation
Year Abroad Program
15 East 65th Street
New York, NY 10065
Phone: 212-734-2130 ext. 210
Fax: 212-628-4552
Web: www.thekf.org

Massachusetts Federation of Polish Women's Clubs Scholarships

Type of award: Scholarship.

Intended use: For full-time sophomore, junior or senior study at postsecondary institution in United States.

Eligibility: Applicant must be Polish. Applicant must be U.S. citizen or permanent resident residing in Massachusetts.

Basis for selection: Applicant must demonstrate financial need and high academic achievement.

Application requirements: $35 application fee. Recommendations, essay, transcript, proof of eligibility. Proof of Polish ancestry. Two passport-sized photos with full name printed on reverse side of each. SASE.

Additional information: Minimum 3.0 GPA. Selection based on academic excellence, motivation, and interest in Polish subjects and involvement in Polish-American community. Only one member per immediate family may receive Massachusetts Federation of Polish Women's Scholarship during any given academic year. Visit Website for more information and application.

Amount of award:	$1,250
Number of awards:	4
Number of applicants:	6
Application deadline:	January 16
Notification begins:	May 25
Total amount awarded:	$5,000

Contact:
Kosciuszko Foundation
15 East 65th Street
New York, NY 10065
Phone: 212-734-2130 ext. 210
Fax: 212-628-4552
Web: www.thekf.org

The Polish American Club of North Jersey Scholarships

Type of award: Scholarship, renewable.

Intended use: For full-time undergraduate study at accredited postsecondary institution in United States.

Eligibility: Applicant must be Polish. Applicant must be U.S. citizen or permanent resident.

Basis for selection: Applicant must demonstrate financial need and high academic achievement.

Application requirements: $35 application fee. Recommendations, essay, transcript, proof of eligibility. Proof of Polish ancestry. Two passport-sized photos with full name printed on reverse side of each. SASE.

Additional information: Applicant must be an active member of Polish American Club of North Jersey. Children and grandchildren of Polish American Club of North Jersey members also eligible. Minimum 3.0 GPA. Only one member per immediate family may receive a Polish American Club of North Jersey Scholarship during any given academic year. Selection based on academic excellence, motivation, and interest in Polish subjects and involvement in the Polish-American community. Number of awards varies. Applications available October 1 through January 16. Visit Website for application and more information.

Amount of award:	$200-$550
Number of applicants:	14
Application deadline:	January 16
Notification begins:	May 25
Total amount awarded:	$4,660

Contact:
Kosciuszko Foundation
15 East 65th Street
New York, NY 10065
Phone: 212-734-2130 ext. 210
Fax: 212-628-4552
Web: www.thekf.org

The Polish National Alliance of Brooklyn, USA, Inc. Scholarships

Type of award: Scholarship, renewable.

Intended use: For full-time undergraduate study at accredited postsecondary institution in United States.

Eligibility: Applicant or parent must be member/participant of Polish National Alliance of Brooklyn. Applicant must be Polish. Applicant must be U.S. citizen or permanent resident.

Basis for selection: Applicant must demonstrate financial need and high academic achievement.

Application requirements: $35 application fee. Recommendations, essay, transcript, proof of eligibility. Proof of Polish ancestry. Two passport-sized photos with full name printed on reverse side of each. SASE.

Additional information: Applicant must be member in good standing of Polish National Alliance of Brooklyn, USA, Inc Group #1903. Minimum 3.0 GPA. Only one member per immediate family may receive scholarship during any given academic year. Selection based on academic excellence, motivation, and interest in Polish subjects and involvement in the Polish-American community. Applications available October 1 through January 16. Visit Website for application and more information.

Amount of award:	$2,000
Number of awards:	1
Number of applicants:	7
Application deadline:	January 16
Notification begins:	May 25
Total amount awarded:	$2,000

Contact:
Kosciuszko Foundation
15 East 65th Street
New York, NY 10065
Phone: 212-734-2130 ext. 210
Fax: 212-628-4552
Web: www.thekf.org

Krist Law Firm

Krist Law Firm National Scholarship

Type of award: Scholarship.
Intended use: For undergraduate or graduate study at accredited 2-year, 4-year or graduate institution.
Eligibility: Applicant must be U.S. citizen or permanent resident.
Basis for selection: Applicant must demonstrate depth of character.
Application requirements: Recommendations, essay. Letter of recommendation, transcript, and typed essay of 300-500 words required. Essay prompt can be found on the application.
Additional information: Minimum 3.0 GPA.

Number of awards:	1
Application deadline:	December 1
Notification begins:	December 31
Total amount awarded:	$10,000

Contact:
Web: www.houstoninjurylawyer.com/the-krist-law-firm-national-scholarship/

Kush Arora Attorney At Law

Kush Arora Federal Justice Reform Scholarship

Type of award: Scholarship.
Intended use: For undergraduate or graduate study at accredited vocational, 2-year, 4-year or graduate institution.
Eligibility: Applicant must be high school senior.
Basis for selection: Essays will be judged on the best-reasoned response, not on the position of the applicant. Applicant must demonstrate high academic achievement.
Application requirements: Essay, transcript. Unofficial transcript, application cover sheet, application essay. Essay topic (1000 words): "Provide a well-reasoned argument about whether a specific policy in the criminal justice system (your choice) is unjust and requires reform, or is just and should stay the same."
Additional information: Minimum 3.0 GPA required.

Amount of award:	$500
Number of awards:	1
Number of applicants:	20
Application deadline:	May 1
Total amount awarded:	$500

Contact:
Kush Arora Federal Criminal Justice Reform Scholarship
409 7th Street NW
Suite 210
Washington, DC 20004
Phone: 202-517-0502
Fax: 202-664-1331
Web: maryland-criminallawyer.com/2016-federal-justice-reform-scholarship.html

LA Area Chamber of Commerce

World Trade Week College or University Scholarship

Type of award: Scholarship, renewable.
Intended use: For full-time undergraduate or graduate study at vocational, 2-year, 4-year or graduate institution.
Basis for selection: Major/career interest in business, international.
Application requirements: Recommendations. Two letters of recommendation - one must be from a faculty member.
Additional information: Must have a minimum 3.0 GPA. Must be in an academic program relating to international trade, if a student's major does not have and international dimension, an international trade internship will suffice. Those who apply for this scholarship will also be in the running to potentially receive another additional $500 through selection as the Global Trade Scholar Award.

Amount of award:	$1,000-$1,500
Number of awards:	10
Application deadline:	March 17
Notification begins:	April 17

Contact:
LA Area Chamber of Commerce
350 South Bixel Street
Los Angeles, CA 90017
Phone: 213-580-7569
Web: https://lachamber.com/forms/world-trade-week-2017-college-university-scholarship-application/

World Trade Week High School Scholarship

Type of award: Scholarship, renewable.
Intended use: For undergraduate study at vocational, 2-year or 4-year institution.
Eligibility: Applicant must be high school senior.
Application requirements: Transcript. Two letters of recommendation by mail. One recommendation may be from a high school faculty member or administrator and the second letter should be from a community service or work supervisor. A one-page, single-spaced essay discussing the student's future college and career goals OR a two minute video submission.
Additional information: Must have a minimum 3.0 GPA. Must have a demonstrated interest in international trade/business.

Amount of award:	$500-$1,000
Number of awards:	10
Application deadline:	March 17
Notification begins:	April 17

Contact:
LA Area Chamber of Commerce
350 South Bixel Street
Los Angeles, CA 90017
Phone: 213-580-7569
Web: https://lachamber.com/forms/world-trade-week-2017-high-school-scholarship-application/

LA Tutors

LA Tutors Innovation in Education Scholarship

Type of award: Scholarship.
Intended use: For full-time undergraduate or graduate study at accredited vocational, 2-year, 4-year or graduate institution in United States or Canada.
Eligibility: Applicant must be enrolled in high school. Applicant must be U.S. citizen, permanent resident or international student.
Application requirements: Essay. Must submit an essay describing the goal of the particular project and provide supporting documentation.
Additional information: One scholarship awarded every month. Application deadline is the 20th of each month. Notification date is the last day of the month. Minimum 3.0 GPA required. Must have designed an innovative project that makes a difference in the lives of others (could be a website, series of blogs, an app, fundraising event, etc).

Number of awards:	1
Number of applicants:	45
Total amount awarded:	$500

Contact:
LA Tutors
9454 Wilshire Boulevard
Suite 600
Beverly Hills, CA 90212
Phone: 866-608-8867
Fax: 866-666-9426
Web: www.latutors123.com/scholarship/

The Lagrant Foundation

The Lagrant Foundation Scholarship Program

Type of award: Scholarship, renewable.
Intended use: For full-time undergraduate study at accredited 4-year or graduate institution in United States.
Eligibility: Applicant must be Alaskan native, Asian American, African American, Mexican American, Hispanic American, Puerto Rican, American Indian or Native Hawaiian/Pacific Islander. Applicant must be U.S. citizen or permanent resident.
Basis for selection: Major/career interest in advertising; marketing or public relations.
Application requirements: Recommendations, essay, transcript. Applicants must complete application found on web site. Includes three essay questions as well as one optional question. Unofficial transcripts, resume, and letter of recommendation from internship or faculty required.

Additional information: 40 Ethnically diverse minority students will receive a grant. 20 undergraduates will receive $2,500 each. 20 Graduate students will receive $5,000 each.

Amount of award:	$2,500-$5,000
Number of awards:	40
Number of applicants:	350
Application deadline:	February 29
Total amount awarded:	$150,000

Contact:
The LAGRANT Foundation
600 Wilshire Boulevard
Suite 1520
Los Angeles, CA 90017
Phone: 323-469-8680 Ext. 240
Fax: 323-469-8683
Web: www.lagrantfoundation.org/Scholarship%20Program

Laine Gabriel

The Tenfold Initiative

Type of award: Scholarship.
Intended use: For full-time freshman study at accredited 4-year institution in United States.
Eligibility: Applicant must be at least 13, no older than 100. Applicant must be U.S. citizen residing in Ohio.
Basis for selection: Major/career interest in arts, general. Applicant must demonstrate financial need.
Application requirements: Portfolio, recommendations, essay. The sample should include four images of your artwork. The essay should consist of 500 words or less and clearly state why you are the most deserving candidate for the 2017 tenfold initiative Scholarship. Include two letters of recommendation. More information about the artwork, essay, and the recommendation letters is on the website http://lainegabriel.com/tenfold/
Additional information: Applicant must be resident of Central Ohio region. Please be sure to send all materials together in one package and clearly state your name on each piece.

Amount of award:	$1,500
Number of awards:	1
Number of applicants:	20
Application deadline:	June 16
Notification begins:	June 30
Total amount awarded:	$1,500

Contact:
Laine Gabriel
1266 Manning parkway
Powell, OH 43065
Phone: 614-441-4226
Web: http://lainegabriel.com/tenfold/

Lambda Alpha National Collegiate Honors Society for Anthropology

Lambda Alpha National Collegiate Honors Society Senior Scholarship

Type of award: Scholarship.
Intended use: For senior study in United States.

Eligibility: Applicant must be U.S. citizen or permanent resident.

Basis for selection: Major/career interest in anthropology. Applicant must demonstrate high academic achievement and seriousness of purpose.

Application requirements: Recommendations, transcript, nomination by faculty sponsor from department of anthropology. Curriculum vitae, writing sample.

Additional information: Applicant must be member of Lambda Alpha. Institution must have a chartered Lambda Alpha chapter. Apply in senior year.

Amount of award:	$5,000
Number of awards:	1
Number of applicants:	16
Application deadline:	March 1
Notification begins:	May 1
Total amount awarded:	$5,000

Contact:
Lambda Alpha National Collegiate Honors Society for Anthropology
Dept. of Anthropology, Attn: Mark Groover PhD
Ball State University
Muncie, IN 47306-0435
Phone: 765-285-5297
Web: cms.bsu.edu/Academics/CollegesandDepartments/Anthropology/LambdaAlpha.aspx

Lambda Theta Alpha Latin Sorority Inc. and Lambda Upsilon Lambda Fraternity Inc.

LTA/LUL Scholarship

Type of award: Scholarship.

Intended use: For undergraduate or graduate study at vocational, 2-year, 4-year or graduate institution.

Eligibility: Applicant must be high school senior. Applicant must be residing in North Carolina.

Application requirements: Essays, resume, college acceptances required.

Additional information: Open to students who study in North Carolina during their senior year and are of Latinx heritage, documented or undocumented.

Amount of award:	$500-$2,000
Number of awards:	1
Application deadline:	April 25, May 6

Contact:
Lambda Theta Alpha Latin Sorority Inc and Lambda Upsilon Lambda Fraternity Inc Duke Chapters
400 Chapel Drive
Durham, NC 27708
Phone: 650-335-5875

Lance Surety

Lance Surety's $1,500 College Scholarship

Type of award: Scholarship, renewable.

Intended use: For undergraduate or graduate study at accredited vocational, 2-year, 4-year or graduate institution in United States.

Application requirements: Essay of minimum 500 words on one of the following topics: 1: What would be your motivation to start a small business, if you could launch it right now? 2: How does the U.S. economy benefit from surety bonds? Write an essay on a topic of your choice about one of the following businesses: Auto Dealership, Freight Brokerage, Construction, or Mortgage Brokerage.

Additional information: Complete rules and guidelines on web site.

Number of awards:	1
Application deadline:	December 15
Notification begins:	January 15
Total amount awarded:	$1,500

Contact:
Lance Surety Bond Associates
4387 Swamp Road #287
Doylestown, PA 18902
Phone: 877-514-5146
Fax: 267-362-4817
Web: www.suretybonds.org/surety-bond-scholarship

Landscape Architecture Foundation

ASLA Council of Fellows Scholarship

Type of award: Scholarship.

Intended use: For junior or senior study at accredited 4-year institution in United States.

Eligibility: Applicant must be U.S. citizen or permanent resident.

Basis for selection: Major/career interest in landscape architecture. Applicant must demonstrate financial need.

Application requirements: $5 application fee. Recommendations, essay. Resume, 150-word bio, photo in jpg format; two letters of recommendation, at least one from a faculty member, 500-word essay about how applicant will contribute to the profession of landscape architecture; 250-word statement describing financial need; SAR, financial aid form.

Additional information: Must be student ASLA member. Must be a third, fourth, or fifth-year undergraduate in a Landscape Architecture Accreditation Board (LAAB) accredited program of landscape architecture. Two to three scholarships awarded; one specifically available to students of under-represented populations. Applicants seeking consideration for diversity scholarship should indicate specific cultural or ethnic group.

Amount of award:	$4,000
Number of awards:	3
Total amount awarded:	$8,000

Contact:
Landscape Architecture Foundation
1129 20th Street NW
Suite 202
Washington, DC 20036
Phone: 202-331-7070
Fax: 202-331-7079
Web: https://lafoundation.org/scholarship/scholarships-and-fellowships/awards-available/

Courtland Paul Scholarship

Type of award: Scholarship.
Intended use: For junior or senior study at accredited 4-year institution. Designated institutions: Schools accredited by the Landscape Architecture Accreditation Board.
Eligibility: Applicant must be U.S. citizen.
Basis for selection: Major/career interest in landscape architecture. Applicant must demonstrate financial need, high academic achievement and seriousness of purpose.
Application requirements: $5 application fee. Recommendations, essay. General Submission Form; photo; 150-word bio; resume; Financial Aid Form; 2 letters of recommendation; 500-word essay.
Additional information: Eligible applicants include United States citizens who are undergraduate students in the final two years of study in Landscape Architecture Accreditation Board accredited schools. Applicants must demonstrate financial need and a minimum grade point average of 'C'. This award must be used only to cover the costs of tuition and/or books within the school year of the award.

    Amount of award: $5,000
    Number of awards: 1

Contact:
Landscape Architecture Foundation
1129 20th Street NW
Suite 202
Washington, DC 20036
Phone: 202-331-7070
Fax: 202-331-7079
Web: https://lafoundation.org/scholarship/scholarships-and-fellowships/awards-available/

The EDSA Minority Scholarship

Type of award: Scholarship.
Intended use: For junior, senior or graduate study at 4-year or graduate institution.
Eligibility: Applicant must be Alaskan native, Asian American, African American, Mexican American, Hispanic American, Puerto Rican, American Indian or Native Hawaiian/Pacific Islander.
Basis for selection: Major/career interest in landscape architecture. Applicant must demonstrate financial need and seriousness of purpose.
Application requirements: $5 application fee. Recommendations, transcript. General Submission Form; photo; 150-word bio; resume; 2 letters of recommendation; 500-word essay; 3 8.5"x11" work samples.
Additional information: The EDSA Minority Scholarship was established to help African American, Hispanic, Native American and minority students of other cultural and ethnic backgrounds continue their landscape architecture education. Eligible candidates are in their final two years of undergraduate study or pursuing a graduate degree in landscape architecture.

    Amount of award: $5,000
    Number of awards: 1

Contact:
Landscape Architecture Foundation
1129 20th Street NW
Suite 202
Washington, DC 20036
Phone: 202-331-7070
Fax: 202-331-7079
Web: https://lafoundation.org/scholarship/scholarships-and-fellowships/awards-available/

Hawaii Chapter/David T. Woolsey Scholarship

Type of award: Scholarship.
Intended use: For full-time junior, senior or graduate study at accredited 4-year or graduate institution.
Eligibility: Applicant must be permanent resident residing in Hawaii.
Basis for selection: Major/career interest in landscape architecture. Applicant must demonstrate service orientation.
Application requirements: $5 application fee. Recommendations, essay. General Submission Form; photo; 150-word bio; resume; proof of Hawaii residency; 2 letters of recommendation; 500-word essay; 3 8.5"x11" work samples.
Additional information: The award provides funds for educational or professional development purposes exclusively. Eligible applicants are third-, fourth-, or fifth-year undergraduate or graduate students of landscape architecture at Landscape Architecture Accreditation Board (LAAB) accredited programs, whose permanent residence is Hawaii.

    Amount of award: $2,000
    Number of awards: 2

Contact:
Landscape Architecture Foundation
1129 20th Street NW
Suite 202
Washington, DC 20036
Phone: 202-331-7070
Fax: 202-331-7079
Web: https://lafoundation.org/scholarship/scholarships-and-fellowships/awards-available/

Landscape Forms Design for People Scholarship

Type of award: Scholarship.
Intended use: For full-time senior study at accredited 4-year institution. Designated institutions: Schools with LAAB-accredited program.
Basis for selection: Major/career interest in landscape architecture. Applicant must demonstrate financial need and seriousness of purpose.
Application requirements: $5 application fee. Portfolio, recommendations, transcript. General Submission Form; photo; 150-word bio; resume; 2 letters of recommendation; 300-word essay; 3 8.5"x11" work samples.
Additional information: Applicants must show a proven contribution to the design of public spaces that integrates landscape design and the use of amenities to promote social interaction. The scholarship will be awarded on the basis of academic accomplishment and creative ability.

    Amount of award: $3,000
    Number of awards: 1

Contact:
Landscape Architecture Foundation
1129 20th Street NW
Suite 202
Washington, DC 20036
Phone: 202-331-7070
Fax: 202-331-7079
Web: https://lafoundation.org/scholarship/scholarships-and-fellowships/awards-available/

Peridian International Inc./Rae L. Price FASLA Scholarship

Type of award: Scholarship.
Intended use: For junior or senior study at postsecondary institution. Designated institutions: UCLA Extension or Cal Poly Pomona.
Eligibility: Applicant must be U.S. citizen.
Basis for selection: Major/career interest in landscape architecture. Applicant must demonstrate financial need and high academic achievement.
Application requirements: $5 application fee. Recommendations, essay. Applicants must submit the following: General Submission Form; photo; 150-word bio; resume; Financial Aid Form; 2 letters of recommendation; 500-word essay.
Additional information: The use of funds is restricted to tuition, books, and program-required supplies within the school year of the award. Minimum 'B' GPA.

> Amount of award: $5,000
> Number of awards: 1

Contact:
Landscape Architecture Foundation
1129 20th Street NW
Suite 202
Washington, DC 20036
Phone: 202-331-7070
Fax: 202-331-7079
Web: https://lafoundation.org/scholarship/scholarships-and-fellowships/awards-available/

Rain Bird Intelligent Use of Water Scholarship

Type of award: Scholarship.
Intended use: For full-time junior or senior study at accredited 4-year institution.
Basis for selection: Major/career interest in landscape architecture; horticulture; hydrology or urban planning. Applicant must demonstrate high academic achievement.
Application requirements: $5 application fee. Essay. Applicants must submit the following: General Submission Form; photo; 150-word bio; resume; 300-word essay.
Additional information: This scholarship was established by the Rain Bird Corporation to recognize an outstanding landscape architecture, horticulture or irrigation science student. Eligible applicants include students in the final two years of undergraduate study (third-, fourth-, or fifth-year students) who have demonstrated commitment to these professions through participation in extracurricular activities and exemplary scholastic achievements.

> Amount of award: $2,500
> Number of awards: 1

Contact:
Landscape Architecture Foundation
1129 20th Street NW
Suite 202
Washington, DC 20036
Phone: 202-331-7070
Fax: 202-331-7079
Web: https://lafoundation.org/scholarship/scholarships-and-fellowships/awards-available/

Steven G. King Play Environments Scholarship

Type of award: Scholarship.
Intended use: For full-time junior, senior or graduate study at accredited 4-year or graduate institution. Designated institutions: LAAB-accredited schools.
Basis for selection: Major/career interest in landscape architecture. Applicant must demonstrate financial need and seriousness of purpose.
Application requirements: $5 application fee. Recommendations, essay, transcript. General Submission Form; photo; 150-word bio; resume; 2 letters of recommendation; 300-500 word essay; work sample showing a plan and details of a play environment of the applicant's design.
Additional information: This student must show an interest in the value of integrating playgrounds into parks, schools and other play environments and understand the significant social and educational value of play. Key qualities in the student receiving the Scholarship are creativity, openness to innovation, and a demonstrated interest in park and playground planning.

> Amount of award: $5,000
> Number of awards: 1

Contact:
Landscape Architecture Foundation
1129 20th Street NW
Suite 202
Washington, DC 20036
Phone: 202-331-7070
Fax: 202-331-7079
Web: https://lafoundation.org/scholarship/scholarships-and-fellowships/awards-available/

Las Vegas CyberKnife

Las Vegas CyberKnife Scholarship

Type of award: Scholarship.
Intended use: For undergraduate or graduate study at vocational, 2-year, 4-year or graduate institution.
Eligibility: Applicant must be high school senior.
Application requirements: Transcript. Finalists will be asked to provide a sealed copy of their transcript.
Additional information: Must have a minimum 3.0 GPA. Application can be found on web site.

> Number of awards: 1
> Application deadline: June 15
> Total amount awarded: $500

Contact:
Web: http://cyberknifeoflasvegas.com/las-vegas-cyberknife-scholarship/

Latin American Educational Foundation

Latin American Educational Scholarship

Type of award: Scholarship, renewable.
Intended use: For full-time undergraduate or non-degree study at accredited postsecondary institution in United States.
Eligibility: Applicant must be Mexican American, Hispanic American or Puerto Rican. Applicant must be residing in Colorado.
Basis for selection: Applicant must demonstrate financial need, high academic achievement, leadership and service orientation.
Application requirements: Recommendations, essay, transcript. Previous year's tax return.
Additional information: Minimum 3.0 GPA. SAT/ACT scores required for high school seniors. Must be Hispanic American or actively involved in Hispanic American community. Recipients must fulfill ten hours of community service during the award year. Applicants must reapply each year.

Amount of award:	$750-$2,000
Number of awards:	100
Number of applicants:	350
Application deadline:	March 15
Notification begins:	June 15
Total amount awarded:	$200,000

Contact:
Latin American Education Foundation
561 Santa Fe Drive
Denver, CO 80204
Phone: 303-446-0541 ext. 12
Fax: 303-446-0526
Web: www.laef.org

The Law Firm of Jack Tolliver

Tolliver Annual Nursing Scholarship

Type of award: Scholarship.
Intended use: For freshman study at accredited 2-year or 4-year institution.
Eligibility: Applicant must be residing in Kentucky.
Basis for selection: Major/career interest in nursing.
Application requirements: A completed application will include an essay on the following topic: Tell us about a specific time when you provided excellent care to someone within your family or community and how you anticipate personally improving the nursing field in the future. Essays should be between 400 and 600 words. Please single-space your essay and format in 12 point Times New Roman font. Essays can be uploaded as Microsoft Word or PDF files only.
Additional information: The Tolliver Annual Nursing Scholarship is open to current high school seniors living in Kentucky, currently attending a Kentucky high school, and interested in pursuing a nursing degree in college. Scholarship applicants must be applying for entry to a Kentucky college or

university that offers an accredited program of study in nursing.

Amount of award:	$1,000
Number of awards:	5
Application deadline:	January 15
Notification begins:	March 1
Total amount awarded:	$5,000

Contact:
The Law Firm of Jack Tolliver
13800 Lake Point Way
Suite 102
Louisville, KY 40223
Web: www.kymedicalmalpractice.com/scholarship

The Law Office of David P. Shapiro

Annual Leukemia Scholarship

Type of award: Scholarship.
Intended use: For full-time undergraduate or graduate study at vocational, 2-year, 4-year or graduate institution.
Application requirements: Online application. Short statement of not more than 100 words telling us how you intend to further your educational goals. Essay (optional) between 650 and 1000 words discussing how being diagnosed with and/or treated for leukemia has affected your day to day activities.
Additional information: Applicant must be diagnosed with leukemia. Complete information and application form may be found at website.

Amount of award:	$1,000
Number of awards:	2
Application deadline:	November 9
Notification begins:	December 8

Contact:
The Law Office of David P. Shapiro
1501 5th Avenue, #200
San Diego, CA 92101
Phone: 619-295-3555
Web: www.davidpshapirolaw.com/leukemia-scholarships/

The Law Office of Edward Tayter

Ed Tayter Outstanding Citizen Scholarship

Type of award: Scholarship.
Intended use: For undergraduate or graduate study at accredited vocational, 2-year, 4-year or graduate institution.
Eligibility: Applicant must be high school senior.
Basis for selection: Applicant must demonstrate high academic achievement.
Application requirements: Recommendations, essay, transcript. Unofficial transcript, application cover sheet, application essay, updated resume, one letter of reccomendation. Essay topic (500 words): "What is one of the most important ways an individual can serve her or his community, and how have you served your community in this way?"

Additional information: Minimum 3.0 GPA required. All candidates must possess a proven commitment to citizenry, as demonstrated by their essay and resume.

Amount of award:	$500
Number of awards:	1
Application deadline:	May 1
Total amount awarded:	$500

Contact:
Edward Tayter Outstanding Citizen Scholarship
5052 Dorsey Hall Drive
Suite 202
Ellicott City, MD 21042
Phone: 202-517-0502
Fax: 202-664-1331
Web: mdcriminalattorney.net/scholarship.html

Law Offices Of George T. Bochanis

George T. Bochanis Law Offices College Scholarship

Type of award: Scholarship.
Intended use: For full-time undergraduate study at accredited 2-year or 4-year institution in United States.
Eligibility: Applicant must be U.S. citizen or permanent resident.
Basis for selection: Major/career interest in law. Applicant must demonstrate financial need.
Application requirements: Essay. The student must complete an online application and submit an essay discussing how to make driving safer in our community.

Amount of award:	$5,000
Number of awards:	1
Application deadline:	June 1
Notification begins:	September 1
Total amount awarded:	$5,000

Contact:
Law Offices Of George T. Bochanis
620B Academy Drive
Northbrook, IL 60062
Phone: 847-940-4000
Web: http://lvaccident.com/scholarship/

Law Offices of Judd S. Nemiro

Annual Dyslexia Scholarship

Type of award: Scholarship.
Intended use: For full-time undergraduate or graduate study at vocational, 2-year, 4-year or graduate institution.
Application requirements: Essay. The completed online application, including the agreement to be bound by the terms of the scholarship program. A short statement (approximately 100 words) describing your educational goals. An optional essay (650 to 1,000 words), describing how Dyslexia has affected your formal education.

Additional information: Must be diagnosed with dyslexia, and may be asked for proof of diagnosis. Award may be used for study abroad.

Amount of award:	$1,000
Number of awards:	2
Application deadline:	November 4

Contact:
Law Offices of Judd S. Nemiro
2617 North 24th Street
Phoenix, AZ 85008
Phone: 602-237-5323
Web: www.jnphoenixfamilylawyer.com/dyslexia-scholarships/

The Law Offices of Michael L. Guisti

The Law Offices of Michael L. Guisti Scholarship

Type of award: Scholarship.
Intended use: For undergraduate study at accredited 2-year or 4-year institution.
Eligibility: Applicant must be U.S. citizen or permanent resident.
Application requirements: Essay. Essay question can be found online with the application.
Additional information: Minimum GPA of 3.0.

Number of awards:	1
Application deadline:	May 30
Notification begins:	June 30
Total amount awarded:	$500

Contact:
Web: www.topcalifornialawyer.com/scholarship/

Law Offices of Sheryl R. Rentz

Law Offices of Sheryl R. Rentz Scholarship

Type of award: Scholarship.
Intended use: For undergraduate study at accredited 2-year or 4-year institution.
Eligibility: Applicant must be U.S. citizen or permanent resident.
Application requirements: Application includes an essay section to tell us about your academic goals and how those goals will help you give back to the community.
Additional information: Additional information and applications can be found on our website. Scholarship is open to graduating high school seniors and current undergraduate college students who have demonstrated a commitment to bettering their community.

Amount of award:	$500
Number of awards:	1
Application deadline:	March 30
Notification begins:	April 26
Total amount awarded:	$500

Contact:
Law Offices of Sheryl R. Rentz
326 West Lancaster Avenue
#100
Ardmore, PA 19003
Web: www.srrentzlaw.com/scholarship/

LawnStarter.com

Lawntrepreneur Scholarship

Type of award: Scholarship.
Intended use: For full-time undergraduate or graduate study at 2-year, 4-year or graduate institution.
Eligibility: Applicant must be U.S. citizen.
Application requirements: Essay, transcript. Transcript, updated resume, and a 500-700 word essay on the topic: "What makes you passionate about building a business?"
Additional information: Must own a law care business, have run a lawn care business in the past, or plan on starting a business upon graduating college.

Amount of award:	$1,000
Number of awards:	2
Application deadline:	December 31, August 1
Notification begins:	January 15, August 15
Total amount awarded:	$2,000

Contact:
LawnStarter Lawn Care Service
2018 Bienville Street
New Orleans, LA 70119
Phone: 504-475-0538
Web: https://www.lawnstarter.com/new-orleans-la-lawn-care#scholarship

Lawsuit Legal

Advance Prevention Lawsuit Legal Scholarship

Type of award: Scholarship.
Intended use: For freshman study at accredited 4-year institution.
Eligibility: Applicant must be high school senior. Applicant must be U.S. citizen or permanent resident.
Application requirements: Transcript. High School transcripts, SAT or ACT scores, and any recommendations letters for the university you attend or are enrolled in for your freshman year.
Additional information: Must have a GPA of 3.0 or higher. Must be entering freshman year or attending freshman year in college.

Number of awards:	1
Application deadline:	December 5
Total amount awarded:	$1,000

Contact:
Lawsuit Legal
401 East Las Olas Boulevard
suite 130-484
Fort Lauderdale, FL 33301
Web: https://www.lawsuitlegal.com/giving-back/scholarship.php

League of United Latin American Citizens

GE Foundation/LULAC Scholarship Program

Type of award: Scholarship, renewable.
Intended use: For full-time sophomore study at accredited 2-year or 4-year institution in United States.
Eligibility: Applicant must be Alaskan native, Asian American, African American, Mexican American, Hispanic American, Puerto Rican, American Indian or Native Hawaiian/Pacific Islander. Applicant must be U.S. citizen or permanent resident.
Basis for selection: Major/career interest in business or engineering. Applicant must demonstrate high academic achievement, seriousness of purpose and service orientation.
Application requirements: Recommendations, essay, transcript, proof of eligibility.
Additional information: Must be minority student with minimum 3.25 GPA who is entering sophomore year in the fall. Recipients may be offered temporary summer or internship positions with GE businesses; however, the students are under no obligation to accept GE employment. Application available on Website.

Amount of award:	$5,000
Notification begins:	August 15

Contact:
League of United Latin American Citizens
Attn: GE Scholarship
1133 19th Street NW, Suite 1000
Washington, DC 20036
Phone: 202-835-9646
Fax: 202-835-9685
Web: www.lnesc.org

LULAC General Awards

Type of award: Scholarship.
Intended use: For undergraduate or graduate study at accredited vocational, 2-year, 4-year or graduate institution in United States.
Eligibility: Applicant must be U.S. citizen or permanent resident.
Basis for selection: Applicant must demonstrate financial need, high academic achievement, depth of character, leadership and service orientation.
Application requirements: Verification of admittance to institution.
Additional information: Academic performance considered, however motivation, sincerity, and integrity will also be considered in selection process. Students are ineligible for scholarship if related to scholarship committee member, council president, or individual contributor to the local funds of the council. Submit application to local participating LULAC council. See Website for application and list of participating councils. Local council may require additional information and personal interview.

Amount of award:	$250-$1,000
Application deadline:	March 31
Notification begins:	May 15

Contact:
League of United Latin American Citizens
2000 L Street NW, Suite 610
Washington, DC 20036
Phone: 202-835-9646
Fax: 202-835-9685
Web: www.lnesc.org

LULAC Honors Awards

Type of award: Scholarship.
Intended use: For full-time undergraduate or graduate study at accredited vocational, 2-year, 4-year or graduate institution in United States.
Eligibility: Applicant must be U.S. citizen or permanent resident.
Basis for selection: Applicant must demonstrate high academic achievement.
Application requirements: Essay, transcript, proof of eligibility. Verification of admittance to institution. SAT/ACT scores.
Additional information: Students are ineligible for scholarship if related to scholarship committee member, council president, or individual contributor to the local funds of the council. Minimum 3.0 GPA. Entering freshmen must have scored at least 23 on ACT or 1100 (reading and math) on SAT. Submit application to local participating LULAC council. See Website for application and list of participating LULAC councils. Local LULAC council may require additional information and personal interview.

Amount of award:	$500-$2,000
Application deadline:	March 31
Notification begins:	May 15

Contact:
League of United Latin American Citizens
2000 L Street NW, Suite 610
Washington, DC 20036
Phone: 202-835-9646
Fax: 202-835-9685
Web: www.lnesc.org

LULAC National Scholastic Achievement Awards

Type of award: Scholarship.
Intended use: For full-time undergraduate or graduate study at accredited 2-year, 4-year or graduate institution in United States.
Eligibility: Applicant must be U.S. citizen or permanent resident.
Basis for selection: Applicant must demonstrate high academic achievement.
Application requirements: Essay, transcript, proof of eligibility. Verification of admittance to institution. SAT/ACT scores.
Additional information: Students are ineligible for scholarship if related to scholarship committee member, council president, or individual contributor to the local funds of the council. Entering freshmen must have scored at least 29 on ACT or 1350 (reading and math) on SAT. Minimum 3.5 GPA. Minimum amount of award is $1,000. See Website for list of participating LULAC councils. Local LULAC council may require additional information and personal interview.

Amount of award:	$2,000
Application deadline:	March 31
Notification begins:	May 15

Contact:
League of United Latin American Citizens
2000 L Street NW, Suite 610
Washington, DC 20036
Phone: 202-835-9646
Fax: 202-835-9685
Web: www.lnesc.org

Learning Ally

Marion Huber Learning Through Listening Award

Type of award: Scholarship.
Intended use: For undergraduate study at vocational, 2-year or 4-year institution.
Eligibility: Applicant must be learning disabled. Applicant must be high school senior.
Basis for selection: Applicant must demonstrate high academic achievement, leadership and service orientation.
Application requirements: Recommendations, essay, transcript. List of honors, achievements, and activities.
Additional information: Must be registered as a Learning Ally member for at least one year. Must not have previously received award from Learning Ally, formerly Recording for the Blind and Dyslexic. Family members of Learning Ally staff or volunteers serving on local or national board not eligible. Winners may be asked to represent Learning Ally as spokesperson and advocate at various events, with costs funded by Learning Ally. Winners must be present at celebratory event to receive award. Must have 3.0 GPA or better in grades 10-12. Applications due in March.

Amount of award:	$2,000-$6,000
Number of awards:	6
Application deadline:	March 10
Total amount awarded:	$24,000

Contact:
NAA Awards
c/o Melissa Greenwald, Learning Ally
20 Roszel Road
Princeton, NJ 08540
Phone: 609-452-0606
Web: www.LearningAlly.org

Mary P. Oenslager Scholastic Achievement Award

Type of award: Scholarship.
Intended use: For senior, master's or doctoral study at accredited 4-year or graduate institution in United States.
Eligibility: Applicant must be visually impaired.
Basis for selection: Applicant must demonstrate high academic achievement, leadership and service orientation.
Application requirements: Recommendations, essay, transcript. List of honors, achievements, and community activities.
Additional information: Must be legally blind. Must have been registered as a Learning Ally member, formerly Recording for the Blind and Dyslexic, for at least one year. Must not have previously received an award from Learning Ally. Must receive degree during the current year. Minimum 3.0 GPA on 4.0 scale or equivalent. Winners may be asked to represent Learning Ally as spokesperson and advocate at various events, with cost funded by Learning Ally. Winners

must be present at celebratory event to receive award. Continuing education beyond bachelor's degree not required. Applications due in March.

Amount of award:	$1,000-$6,000
Number of awards:	9
Application deadline:	March 20
Total amount awarded:	$30,000

Contact:
SAA Awards
c/o Melissa Greenwald, Learning Ally
20 Roszel Road
Princeton, NJ 08540
Phone: 609-452-0606
Web: www.LearningAlly.org

Learning for Life

Captain James J. Regan Memorial Scholarship

Type of award: Scholarship.
Intended use: For full-time undergraduate study at accredited postsecondary institution.
Eligibility: Applicant or parent must be member/participant of Learning for Life. Applicant must be U.S. citizen or permanent resident.
Basis for selection: Major/career interest in criminal justice/law enforcement. Applicant must demonstrate high academic achievement, leadership and seriousness of purpose.
Application requirements: Essay, transcript, proof of eligibility. Certification from post advisor, head of participating organization, Learning for Life representative. Three letters of recommendation (two from outside of law enforcement). Additional essay (minimum of 250 words) on "How Will Technology Affect Law Enforcement in the 21st Century?" Black-and-white photo (preferably in uniform). Must submit original and four copies of all materials.
Additional information: Program open to Learning for Life's Law Enforcement Explorers. Visit Website for application and more information.

Amount of award:	$500
Number of awards:	2
Application deadline:	March 31
Total amount awarded:	$1,000

Contact:
National Law Enforcement Scholarships and Awards
1325 West Walnut Hill Lane
P.O. Box 152079
Irving, TX 75015
Phone: 972-580-2433
Fax: 972-580-2502
Web: www.learning-for-life.org/exploring

James E. Breining Scholarship

Type of award: Scholarship.
Intended use: For undergraduate study at accredited 2-year or 4-year institution in United States.
Eligibility: Applicant must be U.S. citizen or permanent resident.
Basis for selection: Applicant must demonstrate high academic achievement, depth of character and leadership.
Application requirements: Recommendations, essay, transcript. GPA, photo.

Additional information: Open to member of the Law Enforcement Explorers program.

Amount of award:	$1,500
Application deadline:	March 31

Contact:
Learning for Life James E. Breining Scholarship
1201 SW Wall
Des Moines, IA 50315
Phone: 972-580-2433
Web: www.learning-for-life.org/exploring

Sheryl A. Horak Law Enforcement Explorer Scholarship

Type of award: Scholarship.
Intended use: For full-time undergraduate study at accredited 2-year or 4-year institution.
Eligibility: Applicant or parent must be member/participant of Learning for Life. Applicant must be high school senior. Applicant must be U.S. citizen or permanent resident.
Basis for selection: Major/career interest in criminal justice/law enforcement. Applicant must demonstrate high academic achievement, leadership and service orientation.
Application requirements: Transcript. Certification from post advisor, head of participating organization, Learning for Life representative. Three letters of recommendation (two from outside of law enforcement). Essay (500 words minimum) on "Why I Want to Pursue a Career in Law Enforcement." Black-and-white photo (preferably in uniform). Must submit original and two copies of all materials.
Additional information: Program open to Learning for Life's Law Enforcement Explorers. Number of awards granted varies. Visit Website for application and more information.

Amount of award:	$1,000
Application deadline:	March 31

Contact:
National Law Enforcement Scholarships and Awards
1325 West Walnut Hill Lane
P.O. Box 152079
Irving, TX 75015
Phone: 972-580-2433
Fax: 972-580-2502
Web: www.learning-for-life.org/exploring

LendingTree

LendingTree Scholarship

Type of award: Scholarship.
Intended use: For full-time at 2-year or 4-year institution.
Eligibility: Applicant must be high school senior. Applicant must be U.S. citizen.
Application requirements: Students need only write a 200 word essay responding to the question "why, for you personally, is a college education worth the time, energy, and money?"
Additional information: Open to all high school seniors that are US citizens and that have a minimum 3.5 GPA.

Number of awards:	1
Application deadline:	July 15
Notification begins:	July 31
Total amount awarded:	$2,500

Contact:
LendingTree
11115 Rushmore Drive
Charlotte, NC 28277
Phone: 704-943-8714
Web: www.lendingtree.com/about/scholarship

Lendza

Lendza's Better Than a Loan Scholarship

Type of award: Scholarship.
Intended use: For full-time undergraduate study.
Eligibility: Applicant must be at least 18. Applicant must be U.S. citizen or permanent resident.
Basis for selection: Competition/talent/interest in writing/ journalism, Sponsor will consider all eligible Submissions. Submissions that follow directions and include essays that are well-written and clearly and creatively answer The Scholarship question have a greater likelihood of winning. Each Submission is judged as follows: overall quality (40%), creativity (40%), and grammar (20%). All decisions by Sponsor are final.
Application requirements: Essay. 1) Submit a Tweet: If the Applicant has a Twitter account, he or she must Tweet a condensed version of his or her answer to the scholarship question to @LendzaLoans along with the hashtag #BetterThanALoan in the Tweet. Then, submit a 500-word version. 2) Submit your Submission (Application and Essay): Whether or not the Applicant has a Twitter account, the Applicant must (also) submit an Application online, attaching a 500-word Essay explaining his or her answer to the scholarship question. In addition to your essay, your Submission must include your real name and contact information, background details and academic details. Essay topic: Pitch us a business plan for an exciting new venture you think would be profitable.

Amount of award:	$2,000
Number of awards:	1
Application deadline:	December 31
Total amount awarded:	$2,000

Contact:
Lendza
1146 North Central Avenue
Suite 403
Glendale, CA 91202
Phone: 212-213-2238
Web: https://lendza.com/scholarship

LEP Foundation

John Lepping Memorial Scholarship

Type of award: Scholarship.
Intended use: For undergraduate study at 4-year or graduate institution.
Eligibility: Applicant must be physically challenged or learning disabled. Applicant must be residing in New York, New Jersey or Pennsylvania.
Application requirements: Recommendations, transcript, proof of eligibility.

Additional information: Scholarship recipients must be able to provide proof of disability with letter of confirmation by a physician. All applicants must submit an application including a separate document providing a description of their condition and how it is a financial issue/challenge, and statement of goals, ambitions for the future. Applicants must also provide a transcripts of grades and three (3) letters of recommendation from non-family members, and a completed FAFSA.

Amount of award:	$5,000
Number of awards:	5
Number of applicants:	30
Application deadline:	May 1
Total amount awarded:	$25,000

Contact:
LEP Foundation for Youth Education
9 Whispering spring Drive
Millstone Township, NJ 08510
Web: www.lepfoundation.org

Lependorf and Silverstein P.C.

Lependorf and Silverstein P.C. Scholarship

Type of award: Scholarship.
Intended use: For freshman study at accredited 2-year or 4-year institution.
Eligibility: Applicant must be high school senior. Applicant must be U.S. citizen or permanent resident.
Application requirements: Essay. Short essay question can be found online with the application.
Additional information: Must have a minimum 3.0 GPA. Must be a graduating high school senior.

Number of awards:	1
Application deadline:	May 30
Notification begins:	June 30
Total amount awarded:	$500

Contact:
Web: www.lependorf.com/scholarship/

Lependorf and Silverstein, P.C

Lependorf & Silverstein, P.C. New Jersey Scholarship

Type of award: Scholarship.
Intended use: For undergraduate study at accredited 2-year or 4-year institution.
Eligibility: Applicant must be high school senior. Applicant must be U.S. citizen or permanent resident residing in New Jersey.
Basis for selection: Applicant must demonstrate high academic achievement.
Application requirements: Essay. This scholarship is open to graduating high school senior and current undergraduate students who have a 3.0 GPA and are residents of New Jersey. The application includes an essay in which you can tell us

about your academic goals and how your post-secondary education will help you in your pursuit to improve your New Jersey community.

Amount of award:	$500
Number of awards:	1
Application deadline:	May 29
Notification begins:	June 29
Total amount awarded:	$500

Contact:
Lependorf & Silverstein, P.C
4365 US Highway 1
Suite 104
Princeton, NJ 08540
Phone: 609-240-0040
Fax: 609-240-0044
Web: www.lependorf.com/nj-scholarship/

Levy Production Group

Levy Production Group's Rising Star in Production Scholarship

Type of award: Scholarship.
Basis for selection: Applicant must demonstrate financial need.
Application requirements: Essay.
Additional information: 3.0+ GPA. Pursuing a career in video production. Apply on website or download the PDF and send in. Deadline 6/15. Needs-based and small essays.

Amount of award:	$1,000
Number of awards:	1
Application deadline:	June 15

Contact:
5905 S Decatur Boulevard
Las Vegas, NV 89118
Phone: 702-739-3082
Web: www.levyproductiongroup.com/video-production-scholarship

Life Happens

Life Lessons Scholarship Program

Type of award: Scholarship.
Intended use: For undergraduate study at postsecondary institution in United States.
Eligibility: Applicant must be at least 17, no older than 24. Applicant must be U.S. citizen or permanent resident.
Basis for selection: Competition/talent/interest in writing/journalism, based on 500-word essay or 3-minute video describing how applicant has experienced personal and financial challenges caused by death of parent or legal guardian.
Application requirements: Proof of eligibility. Essay of 500 words or 3-minute video describing personal and financial challenges caused by death of a parent and how lack of life insurance impacted their college funding plans.
Additional information: Applicant must have experienced the death of a parent or legal guardian. Apply online. Deadline dates vary. Visit Website for exact dates.

Amount of award:	$2,000-$15,000
Number of applicants:	2,000
Application deadline:	March 1
Total amount awarded:	$250,000

Contact:
Life Happens
Attn: Life Lessons Scholarship
1530 Wilson Blvd, Suite 1060
Arlington, VA 22209
Phone: 202-464-5000 ext. 4446
Fax: 202-464-5011
Web: www.lifehappens.org/lifelessons

Lighthouse Guild

Lighthouse Guild Scholarships

Type of award: Scholarship.
Intended use: For full-time freshman or graduate study at accredited 2-year or 4-year institution.
Eligibility: Applicant must be visually impaired. Applicant must be high school senior. Applicant must be U.S. citizen.
Basis for selection: Applicant must demonstrate high academic achievement.
Application requirements: Recommendations, essay, transcript, proof of eligibility. SAT/ACT scores, proof of legal blindness. Three letters of recommendation. Two personal statements of 500 words or less.
Additional information: Must be U.S. citizen who is legally blind. Open to high school seniors as well as graduate students. All college admissions policies must be non-denominational and open to applicants of all religions, faiths, and beliefs.

Amount of award:	$10,000
Number of awards:	21
Number of applicants:	52
Application deadline:	March 31
Total amount awarded:	$160,000

Contact:
Lighthouse Guild
15 West 65th Street
New York, NY 10023
Phone: 212-769-7801
Web: www.lighthouseguild.org/programs-services/scholarships

Lighthouse International

Lighthouse Undergraduate Award

Type of award: Scholarship.
Intended use: For full-time undergraduate study at accredited postsecondary institution in United States.
Eligibility: Applicant must be visually impaired. Applicant must be U.S. citizen.
Basis for selection: Applicant must demonstrate high academic achievement.
Application requirements: Recommendations, transcript, proof of eligibility. Official documentation of visual impairment. ACT/SAT scores. Personal essay of 400-600 words.
Additional information: Applicant must be visually impaired. Must reside in United States or U.S. territory. Previous SCA recipients and Lighthouse members and employees are

ineligible. Application deadline in late February or early March; visit Website for exact dates.

Amount of award:	$10,000
Number of awards:	2
Number of applicants:	65
Application deadline:	March 15
Notification begins:	May 1
Total amount awarded:	$10,000

Contact:
Lighthouse International
Melissa Shorey, Scholarship and Career Awards
111 East 59 Street
New York, NY 10022-1202
Phone: 212-821-9227
Fax: 212-821-9702
Web: www.lighthouse.org

Lighthouse Lands

Vildeus "Jules" Jean-Baptiste Service Award and Scholarship

Type of award: Scholarship, renewable.
Intended use: For at 2-year or 4-year institution.
Eligibility: Applicant must be high school senior.
Application requirements: Essay, transcript. Two letters of recommendation from a high school teacher and member of your community, academic performance transcript, proof of college/university acceptance, answer to 500 word essay question.
Additional information: Must be a resident of the United States or Haiti. Must have a minimum 3.0 GPA. Must be a graduating high school senior. Application found on website. Special attention given to those who plan on majoring in agricultural/educational/environmental studies.

Amount of award:	$100-$1,000
Number of awards:	4
Application deadline:	April 3
Notification begins:	April 21
Total amount awarded:	$1,300

Contact:
Lighthouse Lands
290 Norwood Avenue
Suite 204
Deal, NJ 07723
Web: http://lighthouseland.org/scholarship/

Lint Center for National Security Studies

Scholarships for National Security Studies

Type of award: Scholarship.
Intended use: For full-time undergraduate or graduate study at accredited 4-year or graduate institution.
Eligibility: Applicant must be U.S. citizen.
Application requirements: Essay. The application process includes the submission of a short essay pertaining to counterintelligence, national security/defense, and/or alliance

building. This essay should reflect a student's ability to utilize innovative, creative and interdisciplinary thinking.
Additional information: Must have a major geared toward a career in national/homeland security.

Amount of award:	$500-$1,500
Application deadline:	January 31

Contact:
Lint Center for National Security Studies
737 Flowing Meadows Drive
Henderson, NV 89014
Web: www.lintcenter.org/scholarships/

Living the Dream

Living the Dream Scholarship

Type of award: Scholarship.
Intended use: For full-time junior or senior study at accredited 4-year institution in United States.
Eligibility: Applicant must be residing in Massachusetts.
Application requirements: Essay. Applicants are encouraged to tell your story. What makes you socially/economically challenged and how hard was it for you to get where you are? All household incomes and sizes are encouraged to apply. Individuals can and are challenged in many different ways.
Additional information: All applicants must be entering into their junior or senior year. Each student must have an average GPA of 3.5 or higher and currently attend an accredited four (4) year school. Each student must reside and/or attend a school within that criteria located in the state of Massachusetts. Individuals should be actively engaged/enrolled in an ongoing entrepreneurship class/program and/or currently own or starting their own business.

Amount of award:	$2,500
Number of awards:	6
Application deadline:	November 30
Notification begins:	December 30
Total amount awarded:	$15,000

Contact:
Living the Dream
161 Kuniholm Drive
Holliston, MA 01746
Phone: 508-922-6538
Fax: 508-321-1307

Los Padres Foundation

Los Padres Foundation College Tuition Assistance Program

Type of award: Scholarship, renewable.
Intended use: For full-time undergraduate or graduate study at accredited 4-year or graduate institution in United States.
Eligibility: Applicant must be Mexican American, Hispanic American or Puerto Rican. Applicant must be high school senior. Applicant must be U.S. citizen or permanent resident residing in New York or New Jersey.
Basis for selection: Applicant must demonstrate financial need, high academic achievement, seriousness of purpose and service orientation.

Application requirements: Recommendations, essay, transcript. Proof of income.

Additional information: Primarily for Latin American or Puerto Rican students in New York or New Jersey metropolitan area. Applicant must have minimum 3.0 GPA and proof of low income. Applicant must be first generation in family to attend college. Award is renewable up to four years. Must complete 100 hours of community service by June 1st of first college year. Application available at financial aid office, high school counselor's office, and online.

Amount of award:	$2,000
Number of applicants:	30
Application deadline:	January 15

Contact:
Los Padres Foundation
CTA Program
P.O. Box 305
Nassau, DE 19969
Phone: 800-528-4105
Fax: 866-810-1361
Web: www.lospadresfoundation.org

Los Padres Foundation Second Chance Program

Type of award: Scholarship.
Intended use: For undergraduate study at accredited postsecondary institution.
Eligibility: Applicant must be Mexican American, Hispanic American or Puerto Rican. Applicant must be U.S. citizen or permanent resident residing in New York, Puerto Rico or New Jersey.
Basis for selection: Applicant must demonstrate financial need.
Application requirements: Transcript, proof of eligibility. Proof of low income.
Additional information: Minimum 3.0 GPA. Applicant must have high school diploma or GED and be out of high school for more than a year prior to submitting and never attended a postsecondary institution. Awardees must complete 100 hours of non-faith-based community service by June 1 of the first year in program. Must meet low-income federal guidelines.

Amount of award:	$2,000
Application deadline:	June 1

Contact:
Los Padres Foundation
Second Chance Program
P.O. Box 305
Nassau, DE 19969
Phone: 800-528-4105
Fax: 866-810-1361
Web: www.lospadresfoundation.org

LostGolfBalls.com

LostGolfBalls.com Great Golf Tips Scholarship

Type of award: Scholarship.
Intended use: For freshman study at accredited 2-year or 4-year institution.
Eligibility: Applicant must be high school senior. Applicant must be U.S. citizen.

Application requirements: Recommendations, transcript. Applicant must be a high school senior. A 1 to 2 minute video demonstrating a fun golf tip, Camera phone videos are acceptable, as long as we can clearly see and understand your tip. Two letters of recommendation or support from teachers, coaches, counselors, or other academic professionals. An electronic copy of your high school transcript. Unofficial transcripts are permitted, but unofficial grade reports are not an acceptable alternative.

Amount of award:	$1,500
Number of awards:	1
Application deadline:	April 30
Total amount awarded:	$1,500

Contact:
LostGolfBalls.com
12505 Reed Road
Suite 200
Sugar Land, TX 77478
Phone: 866-639-4819
Web: https://www.lostgolfballs.com/scholarship

Louisiana Department of Veterans Affairs

Louisiana Veterans Affairs Survivors and Dependents Education Program

Type of award: Scholarship, renewable.
Intended use: For full-time undergraduate, graduate or non-degree study at vocational, 2-year, 4-year or graduate institution. Designated institutions: Louisiana public institutions.
Eligibility: Applicant must be residing in Louisiana. Applicant must be dependent of disabled veteran or deceased veteran. Deceased veteran must have died of wartime injuries.
Application requirements: Proof of eligibility. Certification of eligibility.
Additional information: Award is a tuition waiver at all Louisiana state-supported schools. Living veteran must be Louisiana resident for at least two years prior to child entering program. Deceased veteran must have been Louisiana resident for at least twelve months immediately preceding entry into service. Disability must be at least 90 percent as rated by U.S. Department of Veterans Affairs to qualify. Applicant also eligible if disability rating is 60 percent or more but employability rating is 100 percent unemployable. Waiver available for five year period before applicant turns 25. Award amounts vary.

Amount of award:	Full tuition

Contact:
Louisiana Department of Veterans Affairs
P.O. Box 94095
Baton Rouge, LA 70804-9095
Phone: 225-219-5000
Web: www.vetaffairs.la.gov

Louisiana Office of Student Financial Assistance

Chafee Educational and Training Voucher

Type of award: Scholarship, renewable.
Intended use: For undergraduate study at postsecondary institution.
Eligibility: Applicant must be at least 16, no older than 21. Applicant must be residing in Louisiana.
Application requirements: FAFSA.
Additional information: Awards for students who have been in foster care system.

Amount of award:	$5,000
Number of awards:	66
Number of applicants:	106
Total amount awarded:	$332,565

Contact:
Louisiana Office of Student Financial Assistance
602 North 5th Street
Baton Rouge, LA 70822
Phone: 800-259-5626 ext. 1012
Fax: 255-922-0790
Web: www.osfa.la.gov

Louisiana Go Grants

Type of award: Scholarship, renewable.
Intended use: For undergraduate study at postsecondary institution. Designated institutions: Louisiana institutions.
Eligibility: Applicant must be residing in Louisiana.
Basis for selection: Applicant must demonstrate financial need.
Application requirements: FAFSA.
Additional information: Financial aid for nontraditional and low to moderate income students. Must receive Pell grant to qualify.

Amount of award:	$300-$3,000
Number of awards:	33,231
Total amount awarded:	$25,982,911

Contact:
Louisiana Office of Student Financial Assistance
P.O. Box 91202
Baton Rouge, LA 70821-9202
Phone: 800-259-5626 ext 1012
Fax: 225-922-0790
Web: www.osfa.la.gov

Louisiana Rockefeller Wildlife Scholarship

Type of award: Scholarship, renewable.
Intended use: For full-time undergraduate or graduate study at 4-year or graduate institution. Designated institutions: Louisiana public colleges and universities.
Eligibility: Applicant must be U.S. citizen residing in Louisiana.
Basis for selection: Major/career interest in wildlife/fisheries; forestry or oceanography/marine studies. Applicant must demonstrate high academic achievement.
Application requirements: FAFSA, Rockefeller State Wildlife Application.
Additional information: Minimum 2.5 GPA for undergraduate students or 3.0 for graduate students. Undergraduate students must have earned at least 60 hours of college credit. Undergraduate award is $2,000; graduate award is $3,000.

Amount of award:	$2,000-$3,000
Number of awards:	30
Number of applicants:	45
Application deadline:	July 1
Total amount awarded:	$60,000

Contact:
Louisiana Office of Student Financial Assistance
P.O. Box 91202
Baton Rouge, LA 70821-9202
Phone: 800-259-5626 ext. 1012
Fax: 225-922-0790
Web: www.osfa.la.gov

Louisiana Taylor Opportunity Program for Students (TOPS) Award

Type of award: Scholarship, renewable.
Intended use: For full-time undergraduate study at postsecondary institution. Designated institutions: Eligible Louisiana postsecondary institutions.
Eligibility: Applicant must be U.S. citizen or permanent resident residing in Louisiana.
Basis for selection: Applicant must demonstrate high academic achievement.
Application requirements: FAFSA. SAT or ACT scores.
Additional information: Open to Louisiana residents who will be first-time, full-time freshmen at Louisiana public or LAICU private postsecondary institutions no later than fall following first anniversary of high school graduation. Must have no criminal convictions. Must have completed 19 units college-prep TOPS core curriculum. Individual requirements for awards below; please send one inquiry, only, for all award levels: TOPS OPPORTUNITY AWARD: Equal to tuition at public institution (or weighted average tuition at LAICU member institution). Must have minimum 2.5 core GPA, minimum ACT score based on state's prior year average (never below 20) or minimum SAT of 940. TOPS PERFORMANCE AWARDS: Equal to tuition at public institution (or weighted average tuition at LAICU member institution) plus $400/yr stipend. Minimum 3.0 core GPA, minimum ACT score of 23 or SAT score of 1050. TOPS HONORS AWARDS: Equal to tuition at public institution (or weighted average tuition at LAICU member institution) plus $800/yr stipend. Minimum 3.0 core GPA, ACT score of 27 or SAT score of 1210. Contact Public Information Rep for more details.

Amount of award:	Full tuition
Number of applicants:	28,182
Application deadline:	July 1
Notification begins:	June 1
Total amount awarded:	$165,620,684

Contact:
Louisiana Office of Student Financial Assistance
P.O. Box 91202
Baton Rouge, LA 70821-9202
Phone: 800-259-5626 ext. 1012
Fax: 225-922-0790
Web: www.osfa.la.gov

Scholarships

413

Louisiana TOPS Tech Early Start Program

Type of award: Scholarship.
Intended use: For half-time undergraduate study at postsecondary institution in United States. Designated institutions: Louisiana public colleges.
Eligibility: Applicant must be high school junior or senior. Applicant must be U.S. citizen or permanent resident residing in Louisiana.
Additional information: Full tuition for six credit hours per semester for juniors and seniors in public Louisiana public high schools who wish to concurrently enroll in public Louisiana college. Must be enrolled in vocational course leading to industry-based certification in a Top Demand Occupation. Minimum 2.0 GPA. Minimum 15 ACT score. Minimum passing score in English and math on GEE. Must have approved five-year education and career plan.

Amount of award:	$600

Contact:
Louisiana Office of Student Financial Assistance
602 North 5th Street
Baton Rouge, LA 70822
Phone: 800-259-5626 ext. 1012
Fax: 225-922-0790
Web: www.osfa.la.gov

Louisiana Tops Tech Program

Type of award: Scholarship, renewable.
Intended use: For full-time freshman study at postsecondary institution in United States. Designated institutions: Approved Louisiana institutions.
Eligibility: Applicant must be enrolled in high school. Applicant must be U.S. citizen or permanent resident residing in Louisiana.
Basis for selection: Applicant must demonstrate high academic achievement.
Application requirements: FAFSA.
Additional information: Minimum 2.5 GPA. Must have completed a certain number of Tech Core Units. Minimum 17 ACT score or SAT equivalent. Must enroll as first-time freshman. Full tuition to those attending community colleges and vocational schools. Partial tuition for students of schools where baccalaureate degrees are available.

Amount of award:	Full tuition
Application deadline:	July 1

Contact:
Louisiana Office of Student Financial Assistance
P.O. Box 91202
Baton Rouge, LA 70821
Phone: 800-259-5626 ext. 1012
Fax: 225-922-0790
Web: www.osfa.la.gov

Lowe's

The Carl Buchan Scholarship

Type of award: Scholarship.
Intended use: For full-time undergraduate study at accredited vocational, 2-year or 4-year institution in United States.
Eligibility: Applicant must be U.S. citizen.

Basis for selection: Applicant must demonstrate high academic achievement, leadership and service orientation.
Additional information: Minimum 3.25 GPA. Must be high school senior or current college undergraduate with at least one full semester completed. Must be full- or part-time Lowe's employee or qualified relative of employee with at least 90 days of service with Lowe's as of January 1 the year scholarship is awarded. Employee must still be employed at the time awards are announced. Must demonstrate history of commitment to community through leadership activities, community service, and/or work experience. Award not renewable, but students can reapply each year if eligibility requirements are met. Only available to Lowe's employees and their dependents.

Amount of award:	$5,000
Number of awards:	50
Application deadline:	February 28
Total amount awarded:	$250,000

Contact:
Lowe's
Web: www.lowes.com/scholarships

Lowe's Scholarship Program

Type of award: Scholarship.
Intended use: For full-time freshman study at accredited vocational, 2-year or 4-year institution in United States.
Eligibility: Applicant must be high school senior.
Basis for selection: Applicant must demonstrate high academic achievement, leadership and service orientation.
Additional information: Must maintain minimum 3.25 GPA. Must be residing in the United States. Lowe's employees and their children are also eligible. Must demonstrate a history of commitment to community through leadership activities, community service, and/or work experience. Award is not renewable, but students can reapply each year if they continue to meet eligibility requirements. Only available to Lowe's employees and their dependents.

Amount of award:	$2,500
Number of awards:	140
Application deadline:	February 28
Total amount awarded:	$350,000

Contact:
Lowe's
Web: www.lowes.com/scholarships

LRW Law Firm

Scholarship for Children of Police Officers

Type of award: Scholarship.
Intended use: For undergraduate study at accredited vocational, 2-year or 4-year institution.
Eligibility: Applicant must be at least 18.
Application requirements: 500+ word essay detailing how being the son or daughter of a police officer has influenced you as a college-bound student.
Additional information: Must have a minimum 3.0 GPA. Parent must be a police officer and be able to provide proof of employment.

Number of awards: 1
Application deadline: May 1
Notification begins: May 8
Total amount awarded: $2,000
Contact:
LRW Law Firm
315 Deaderick Street
Suite 1510
Nashville, TN 37219
Phone: 615-256-8880
Web: www.lrwlawfirm.com/scholarship-children-police-officers

LSP Association

LSP Association Scholarship Fund

Type of award: Scholarship.
Intended use: For full-time undergraduate study at accredited 4-year institution.
Eligibility: Applicant must be residing in Massachusetts.
Basis for selection: Major/career interest in biochemistry; biology; engineering, civil; engineering, chemical; geology/earth sciences; engineering, environmental; environmental science; epidemiology; forestry or hydrology.
Application requirements: Recommendations, transcript. Must be a current member of the LSP Association or an immediate family member.Have the school (High School or College) where he/she is enrolled send a transcript of all grades (including the latest 2016 - 2017 term) to the LSP Association Scholarship Fund, transfer students must also forward transcripts from previous schools. Presently be accepted in a degree program at an accredited New England College, University, Junior College, Technical Institute, or Community College and majoring in an approved curriculum as described in Appendix A, please provide a copy of a college acceptance letter.Include verification of enrollment or an indication of probable enrollment and major area of study.include three written letters of recommendation.
Additional information: College major interests: Biochemistry, Biology, Chemical Engineering, Chemistry, Civil Engineering, Earth Science, Environmental Engineering, Environmental Sciences, Epidemiology, Forestry, Geology, Hydrology, Hydrogeology, Geotechnical Engineering, Hazardous Waste Management, toxicology, microbiology, ecology, botany, zoology, Industrial Hygiene, Medicine, Physical Geography, Public Health (if technical in nature), Risk Assessment, Soil Science, Water Resources, Wetland Science.Complete and sign the application and submit it to the LSP Association Scholarship Fund.

Amount of award: $5,000-$5,000
Number of awards: 2
Number of applicants: 15
Application deadline: April 14
Notification begins: June 15
Total amount awarded: $10,000
Contact:
LSP Association Scholarship Fund
Brown & Caldwell Brown & Caldwell
1 Tech Drive, Suite 310
Andover, MA 01810
Phone: 978-983-2042
Fax: 978-794-0534
Web: www.lspa.org/lspa-scholarship-fund

LULAC National Education Services Centers, Inc.

Denny's Hungry for Education Scholarship

Type of award: Scholarship.
Intended use: For undergraduate study at accredited 2-year or 4-year institution in United States.
Eligibility: Applicant must be U.S. citizen or permanent resident residing in New York, Texas, Arizona, South Carolina, Nevada, Georgia, Florida, California, District of Columbia, New Mexico, Colorado or Illinois.
Application requirements: Essay.
Additional information: High school seniors and college students must submit essay about how Denny's can impact childhood hunger in the U.S. Three high school scholarships of $1,000 and five college scholarships of $1,000 available.

Amount of award: $1,000
Number of awards: 8
Application deadline: September 15
Contact:
LULAC National Education Services Centers, Inc.
1133 19th Street, NW
Suite 1000
Washington, DC 20036
Phone: 202-835-9646
Fax: 202-835-9685
Web: www.lnesc.org

Maine Division of Veterans Services

Maine Veterans Services Dependents Educational Benefits

Type of award: Scholarship.
Intended use: For undergraduate or master's study at vocational, 2-year or 4-year institution. Designated institutions: Public universities in Maine.
Eligibility: Applicant must be at least 16, no older than 22. Applicant must be residing in Maine. Applicant must be dependent of disabled veteran; or spouse of disabled veteran. Must apply for program prior to 22nd birthday, or before 26th birthday if applicant was enrolled in the U.S. Armed Forces. Age limits apply to child applicants only, not spouses.
Basis for selection: Applicant must demonstrate high academic achievement.
Application requirements: Proof of eligibility. Proof of veteran's disability, birth certificate. Stepchildren must provide parent's marriage certificate. Adopted children must provide adoption certificate or proof of paternity to natural parent. Spouse must provide marriage certificate.
Additional information: Applicant must have graduated from high school and must be dependent of permanently and totally disabled veteran. Veteran must have been resident of Maine prior to enlistment or resident of Maine for five years preceding application for aid. Provides tuition at all branches of University of Maine system, all State of Maine vocational-technical colleges, and Maine Maritime Academy for 120

415

credits to be used within six years. Must maintain "C" average to continue receiving benefits. Spouse award must be used within ten years.

Amount of award: Full tuition

Contact:
Maine Division of Veterans Services
117 State House Station
Augusta, ME 04333-0117
Phone: 207-430-6035
Fax: 207-626-4471
Web: www.mainebvs.org

Maine Innkeepers Association

Maine Innkeepers Association Scholarship

Type of award: Scholarship.
Intended use: For full-time undergraduate or graduate study at accredited vocational, 4-year or graduate institution in United States. Designated institutions: Institutions with fully accredited programs in hotel administration or culinary arts.
Eligibility: Applicant must be U.S. citizen or permanent resident residing in Maine.
Basis for selection: Major/career interest in culinary arts; hotel/restaurant management or hospitality administration/management. Applicant must demonstrate financial need and high academic achievement.
Application requirements: Recommendations, essay, transcript.
Additional information: Applicant must be Maine resident who is high school senior or college undergraduate. Deadline in early April; visit Website for exact date.

Amount of award:	$500-$3,000
Number of awards:	10
Number of applicants:	45
Application deadline:	April 4
Notification begins:	January 1
Total amount awarded:	$11,000

Contact:
Maine Innkeepers Association
45 Melville Street
Augusta, ME 04330
Phone: 207-213-2060
Fax: 207-213-2062
Web: www.maineinns.com

Maine Metal Products Association Education Fund

Maine Metal Products Association Scholarship

Type of award: Scholarship.
Intended use: For undergraduate study at postsecondary institution.
Eligibility: Applicant must be residing in Maine.

Basis for selection: Major/career interest in engineering; welding or manufacturing. Applicant must demonstrate financial need, high academic achievement, depth of character, leadership, seriousness of purpose and service orientation.
Application requirements: Recommendations, essay, transcript, proof of eligibility.
Additional information: Applicant must have career interest in Maine precision machining technology or manufacturing technology industry or related majors. Amount of award varies based on need and fund account. Visit Website for more information.

Amount of award:	$100-$1,000
Number of applicants:	50
Application deadline:	April 31
Total amount awarded:	$11,250

Contact:
Marion Sprague
Manufacturers Association of Maine
386 Bridgton Road
Westbrook, ME 04092
Phone: 207-854-2153
Fax: 207-854-3865
Web: www.mainemfg.com/students/scholarships

Maine Society of Professional Engineers

Maine Society of Professional Engineers Scholarship Program

Type of award: Scholarship.
Intended use: For freshman study at 4-year institution in United States. Designated institutions: ABET-accredited engineering schools.
Eligibility: Applicant must be high school senior. Applicant must be permanent resident residing in Maine.
Basis for selection: Major/career interest in engineering or engineering, civil.
Application requirements: Interview, recommendations, essay, transcript. SAT/ACT scores.
Additional information: Applicant must intend to earn a degree in engineering and to enter the practice of engineering after graduation. Must go to ABET-accredited school. Money awarded only after successful completion of first semester. Must be resident of Maine but awardees do not have to attend school in Maine. Application available on Website.

Amount of award:	$2,500
Number of awards:	2
Number of applicants:	40
Application deadline:	March 1
Notification begins:	May 30
Total amount awarded:	$5,000

Contact:
Colin C. Hewett
Maine Society of Professional Engineers
P.O. Box 318
Winthrop, ME 04364
Phone: 207-449-0339
Web: www.mespe.org

Maine State Society of Washington, D.C.

Maine State Society of Washington, D.C. Foundation Scholarship Program

Type of award: Scholarship.
Intended use: For full-time sophomore, junior or senior study at accredited 4-year institution. Designated institutions: Maine institutions.
Eligibility: Applicant must be no older than 25. Applicant must be U.S. citizen.
Basis for selection: Applicant must demonstrate high academic achievement and seriousness of purpose.
Application requirements: Portfolio, essay, transcript, proof of eligibility.
Additional information: Applicant must have been born in Maine or have been legal resident of Maine for at least four years or have at least one parent who was born in Maine or who has been legal resident of Maine for at least four years. Applicant must currently attend college in Maine, with a minimum GPA of 3.2 for latest academic year. Requests for applications must include SASE. Visit Website for application.

Amount of award:	$1,000
Number of applicants:	79
Application deadline:	March 15
Total amount awarded:	$12,500

Contact:
Maine State Society of Washington, D.C. Foundation Scholarship
4718 Columbia Road
Annandale, VA 22003
Phone: 703-256-4524
Fax: 703-941-4674
Web: www.mainestatesociety.org/MSSFoundation.htm

Mainor Wirth Injury Lawyers

Mainor Wirth Injury Lawyers Need-Based Scholarship

Type of award: Scholarship.
Intended use: For full-time undergraduate study at accredited 2-year or 4-year institution in United States.
Eligibility: Applicant must be U.S. citizen or permanent resident.
Basis for selection: Major/career interest in law. Applicant must demonstrate financial need.
Application requirements: The judging criteria is based on financial need and the quality of a PSA video focusing on distracted driving (maximum of 2 minutes).

Amount of award:	$1,000
Number of awards:	1
Application deadline:	June 1
Notification begins:	September 1
Total amount awarded:	$1,000

Contact:
Mainor Wirth Injury Lawyers
620B Academy Drive
Northbrook, IL 60062
Phone: 847-940-4000
Web: http://mainorwirth.com/mainor-wirth-injury-lawyers-scholarship/

Male Sense Pro

Male Sense Pro Marketing Scholarship

Type of award: Scholarship, renewable.
Intended use: For full-time undergraduate or graduate study at 2-year or 4-year institution.
Basis for selection: Major/career interest in business or marketing.
Application requirements: To enter this scholarship program you must research and create a piece of text between 500-1000 words on the subject: "Internet Marketing and its Importance in 2017". Please include these points: Why is e-marketing important? And, how do our websites/articles use this? Please only apply if currently enrolled as a student in a college, university or high school, as only these candidates will be considered.
Additional information: The $1,000 check will be sent directly to your college.

Amount of award:	$1,000
Number of awards:	1
Application deadline:	April 30
Notification begins:	May 15
Total amount awarded:	$1,000

Contact:
Male Sense Pro
Web: https://www.malesensepro.com/scholarship/

Malmstrom Spouses' Club

Malmstrom Spouses' Club Scholarship

Type of award: Scholarship.
Intended use: For full-time undergraduate or graduate study at accredited vocational, 2-year, 4-year or graduate institution.
Eligibility: Applicant must be high school senior. Applicant must be dependent of active service person, veteran or deceased veteran who serves or served in the Air Force.
Application requirements: Dependent family member of one of the following: A. Active Duty Personnel (USAF) B. Active Guard or Reserve Personnel (USAF) C. Retired Personnel (USAF) D. Deceased Active or Retired Member (USAF) E. 341MW DoD Civilian Personnel The applicant must be: a natural child, legally adopted child, dependent stepchild, or dependent spouse of a member classified in paragraph one, and must be either: A. A high school senior attending public, private, or parochial school, or attending a home-school program with the intent of continuing his/her education. B. A former high school graduate or equivalent with the intent of continuing his/her education. 3. Dependent children must be younger than 23-years-old. 4. Active Duty and Retired service

Scholarships

members are not eligible to apply. 5. Applicants must have a minimum 3.0 GPA to apply. GED and HiSET equivalency diploma test scores can be submitted in lieu of a GPA, and must be the minimum equivalent to a minimum 3.0 GPA to be eligible. (501 or higher for GED and an accumulative average score of 12 or higher for HiSET.) TASC is not accepted at this time. Proof of scores must be submitted with your package. HIGH SCHOOL SENIORS ONLY Please submit a copy of your SAT or ACT score. Applicant does not have to be residing with sponsor to be eligible. Sponsors must be stationed at or assigned to Malmstrom Air Force Base or 120AW at the time of award. Application and all required documents are subject to verification. Applicants must have a valid military identification card. Family Member of 341MW DoD Civilian Personnel verification from the employee's supervisor confirming the family member is a legal dependent. Applicant must also submit a copy of their driver's license or state-issued identification.

Additional information: Minimum 3.0 GPA. Award may be used for Study Abroad . Must be a dependent child or spouse. Provide a copy of high school/college unofficial/official transcript. A letter of recommendation completed by a person who is not related to you and who can attest to your leadership skills, motivation, integrity, and character. The letter must be signed and submitted in a sealed envelope with your package. Professional or faculty recommendation must be on letterhead.

Amount of award:	$750
Number of awards:	16
Number of applicants:	19
Application deadline:	April 1

Contact:
Malmstrom Spouses' Club
P.O. Box 6516
Great Falls, MT 59405
Phone: 406-823-0314
Web: https://www.facebook.com/malmstromspouses

Manuelgo Electronics

Manuelgo Electronics Scholarship

Type of award: Scholarship, renewable.
Intended use: For full-time undergraduate or graduate study in or outside United States or Canada.
Eligibility: Applicant must be high school senior.
Additional information: Must have a minimum 3.0 GPA.

Number of awards:	1
Application deadline:	July 31
Notification begins:	August 11
Total amount awarded:	$500

Contact:
Web: www.manualgo.com/scholarship

Marine Corps Scholarship Foundation

Marine Corps Scholarship

Type of award: Scholarship, renewable.
Intended use: For undergraduate study at accredited 2-year or 4-year institution in United States.

Eligibility: Applicant must be dependent of active service person or veteran in the Marines or Navy. Must be child of Marine or Navy corpsman; see website for additional requirements.
Basis for selection: Applicant must demonstrate financial need and high academic achievement.
Application requirements: Essay, transcript, proof of eligibility. FAFSA, tax return.
Additional information: Minimum 2.0 GPA. Financial need criteria must be met. Applications available online. Awards available to all who qualify.

Amount of award:	$1,500-$10,000
Application deadline:	March 1

Contact:
Marine Corps Scholarship Foundation
909 North Washington Street
Suite 400
Alexandria, VA 22314
Phone: 866-496-5462
Web: www.mcsf.org

Market Inspector

Market Inspector Scholarship

Type of award: Scholarship, renewable.
Intended use: For full-time undergraduate or graduate study at accredited vocational, 2-year, 4-year or graduate institution.
Application requirements: Essay, transcript, proof of eligibility. All the participants should be either currently enrolled or have been accepted at an accredited UK/US post-secondary educational institution. All the participants should have been born in one of the following countries: Iran, Libya, Somalia, Sudan, Syria and Yemen. The applicant must be able to provide A copy of a valid passport or birth certificate; Transcripts or similar documentation proving that the applicant is currently enrolled or has been accepted at an accredited UK or US university; An essay.
Additional information: Scholarship applies to abroad studies. The applicants should submit all the documents via email at scholarship@marketinspector.co.uk . Write Scholarship Application + Your Name in the subject line. More information about the essay on the Website www.market-inspector.co.uk/scholarship.

Amount of award:	$1,000
Number of awards:	1
Application deadline:	October 31
Notification begins:	December 1
Total amount awarded:	$1,000

Contact:
Market Inspector
Phone: +0330 828 0745
Web: www.market-inspector.co.uk/scholarship

Maryland Higher Education Commission Office of Student Financial Assistance

Edward T. Conroy Memorial Scholarship Program

Type of award: Scholarship, renewable.
Intended use: For undergraduate or graduate study at postsecondary institution. Designated institutions: Eligible Maryland institutions.

Eligibility: Applicant must be U.S. citizen residing in Maryland. Applicant must be veteran or disabled while on active duty; or dependent of veteran, disabled veteran or deceased veteran; or spouse of disabled veteran, deceased veteran or POW/MIA who served in the Army during Vietnam. If applicant is dependent of disabled US Armed Forces veteran, the veteran must be declared 100% disabled as direct result of military service. Applicant may also be dependent or surviving spouse of victim of September 11, 2001 attacks. Also open to dependent or surviving spouse (not remarried) of Maryland resident who was public safety employee or volunteer who died or was 100% disabled in the line of duty.

Additional information: Must be Maryland resident unless spouse or child of Maryland state or local public safety employee killed in line of duty. Parent, veteran, POW, public safety employee, or volunteer specified above must have been resident of Maryland at time of death or when declared disabled. Amount of award may be equal to tuition and fees, but may not exceed $9,000. Visit Website for more information and application.

Application deadline: July 15
Contact:
Contact financial aid office at individual institution
Web: www.mhec.state.md.us/financialaid

Howard P. Rawlings Guaranteed Access Grant

Type of award: Scholarship, renewable.
Intended use: For full-time undergraduate study at accredited postsecondary institution. Designated institutions: Maryland institutions.
Eligibility: Applicant must be high school senior. Applicant must be U.S. citizen or permanent resident residing in Maryland.
Basis for selection: Applicant must demonstrate financial need and high academic achievement.
Application requirements: Proof of eligibility. FAFSA.
Additional information: Applicant must be high school senior who has completed college preparatory program or has graduated prior to the academic year and provide written documentation explaining why he or she was unable to attend college within one year of graduation from high school. Minimum 2.5 GPA. Must meet Guaranteed Access Family Grant income requirements; award equals 100% of student's financial need. New applicants must apply through Website. Both applicant and parents must be Maryland residents.

Amount of award: $400-$16,100
Application deadline: March 1
Contact:
Maryland Higher Ed. Commission Office of Student Financial Assistance
Guaranteed Access Grant
6 North Liberty Street, Ground Suite
Annapolis, MD 21201
Phone: 800-974-0203
Fax: 410-332-0250
Web: www.mhec.state.md.us/financialaid/descriptions.asp

Maryland Delegate Scholarship

Type of award: Scholarship, renewable.
Intended use: For undergraduate or graduate study at vocational, 2-year, 4-year or graduate institution. Designated institutions: Institutions in Maryland.
Eligibility: Applicant must be high school senior. Applicant must be U.S. citizen or permanent resident residing in Maryland.

Application requirements: Proof of eligibility, nomination by local state delegate. FAFSA.
Additional information: Applicant's parents (if applicant is dependent) must be Maryland residents. Rolling application deadline. Certain vocational programs eligible. Out-of-state institutions eligible only if major not offered in Maryland. Each state delegate makes awards to students. If OSFA makes awards for delegates, applicant must demonstrate financial need. Non-U.S. citizens living in Maryland may be eligible. Applicants must reapply yearly for renewal and maintain satisfactory academic progress.

Amount of award: $200-$19,000
Application deadline: March 1
Notification begins: July 1
Contact:
Maryland Higher Ed. Commission Office of Student Financial Assistance
Delegate Scholarship
6 North Liberty Street, Ground Suite
Annapolis, MD 21201
Phone: 800-974-0203
Fax: 410-332-0250
Web: www.mhec.state.md.us/financialaid

Maryland Educational Assistance Grant

Type of award: Scholarship, renewable.
Intended use: For full-time undergraduate study at 2-year or 4-year institution. Designated institutions: Maryland institutions.
Eligibility: Applicant must be U.S. citizen or permanent resident residing in Maryland.
Basis for selection: Applicant must demonstrate financial need.
Application requirements: Proof of eligibility. FAFSA.
Additional information: Applicant's parents (if applicant is dependent) must be Maryland residents. Applicants are ranked by Expected Family Contribution (EFC); those with lowest EFC are awarded first. Award may be renewed if eligibility maintained and FAFSA is submitted by March 1 each year. Funds may not be available to award all eligible students each year.

Amount of award: $400-$3,000
Application deadline: March 1
Notification begins: April 15
Contact:
Maryland Higher Ed. Commission Office of Student Financial Assistance
Educational Assistance Grant
6 North Liberty Street, Ground Suite
Annapolis, MD 21201
Phone: 800-974-0203
Fax: 410-332-0250
Web: www.mhec.state.md.us/financialaid

Maryland Jack F. Tolbert Memorial Grant

Type of award: Scholarship, renewable.
Intended use: For full-time undergraduate study at vocational institution. Designated institutions: Private career schools in Maryland.
Eligibility: Applicant must be U.S. citizen or permanent resident residing in Maryland.
Basis for selection: Applicant must demonstrate financial need.

Application requirements: Nomination by financial aid counselor at private career school. FAFSA.

Additional information: Applicant's parents (if applicant is dependent) must be Maryland residents. Applicant must enroll for minimum of 18 hours per week. Award amount varies; maximum is $500.

Amount of award:	$500
Application deadline:	March 1

Contact:
Contact financial aid office at individual institutions.
Phone: 800-974-0203
Web: www.mhec.state.md.us/financialaid/descriptions.asp

Maryland Part-Time Grant Program

Type of award: Scholarship, renewable.
Intended use: For half-time undergraduate study at accredited postsecondary institution. Designated institutions: Accredited institutions in Maryland.
Eligibility: Applicant must be enrolled in high school. Applicant must be residing in Maryland.
Basis for selection: Applicant must demonstrate financial need.
Application requirements: FAFSA.
Additional information: Applicant's parents (if applicant is dependent) must be Maryland residents. Must be taking 6 to 11 semester credit hours. Apply through financial aid office of Maryland institution. Applicants simultaneously enrolled in secondary school and an institution of higher education are also eligible. To renew award, student must maintain satisfactory academic progress and submit FAFSA by March 1 each year; may receive award up to eight years.

Amount of award:	$200-$2,000
Application deadline:	March 1

Contact:
Maryland Higher Ed. Commission Office of Student Financial Assistance
Part-Time Grant Program
6 North Liberty Street, Ground Suite
Annapolis, MD 21201
Phone: 800-974-0203
Fax: 410-332-0250
Web: www.mhec.state.md.us/financialaid/descriptions.asp

Maryland Senatorial Scholarship

Type of award: Scholarship, renewable.
Intended use: For undergraduate or graduate study at postsecondary institution. Designated institutions: Maryland colleges and universities.
Eligibility: Applicant must be residing in Maryland.
Basis for selection: Applicant must demonstrate financial need and high academic achievement.
Application requirements: Nomination by local state senator. FAFSA.
Additional information: Applicant and parents (if applicant is dependent) must be Maryland residents. SAT or ACT required for freshmen at four-year institutions unless applicant graduated from high school five years prior to aid application or has earned 24 college credit hours. Out-of-state institutions eligible only if major not offered in Maryland. Contact state senator's office for more information. Award automatically renewed if satisfactory academic progress is maintained. Full-time students may be awarded four years total, part-time students eight years total.

Amount of award:	$400-$10,100
Application deadline:	March 1

Contact:
Maryland Higher Ed. Commission Office of Student Financial Assistance
Senatorial Scholarship Program
6 North Liberty Street, Ground Suite
Annapolis, MD 21201
Phone: 800-974-0203
Fax: 410-332-0250
Web: www.mhec.state.md.us/financialaid/descriptions.asp

Maryland Tuition Reduction for Non-Resident Nursing Students

Type of award: Scholarship, renewable.
Intended use: For undergraduate study at postsecondary institution.
Eligibility: Applicant must be U.S. citizen.
Basis for selection: Major/career interest in nursing.
Additional information: Must be resident of state other than Maryland and accepted into Maryland degree-granting nursing program at two- or four-year public institution. Awardees fulfill service obligation in Maryland following graduation; two years for two-year program, four years for four-year program. Service must begin within six months of graduation. Award amount varies; college may reduce tuition so that non-residents pay tuition charged to Maryland resident. New applicants must apply through Website.

Number of applicants:	51

Contact:
Maryland Higher Ed. Commission Office of Student Financial Assistance
Out-of-State Nursing Program
6 North Liberty Street, Ground Suite
Annapolis, MD 21201
Phone: 800-974-0203
Web: www.mhec.state.md.us/financialaid/descriptions.asp

Maryland Tuition Waiver for Foster Care Recipients

Type of award: Scholarship, renewable.
Intended use: For undergraduate study at 2-year or 4-year institution. Designated institutions: Eligible Maryland public institutions.
Eligibility: Applicant must be no older than 25. Applicant must be residing in Maryland.
Application requirements: FAFSA.
Additional information: Applicant must have resided in Maryland foster care home at time of high school graduation or completion of GED. Also open to applicants who resided in Maryland foster care home on 14th birthday and were subsequently adopted. The Department of Human Resources must confirm applicant's eligibility. Applicant must be enrolled as a degree-seeking student before age of 25. Award renewal possible if satisfactory academic progress and enrollment in eligible program maintained.

Amount of award:	Full tuition
Application deadline:	March 1

Contact:
Maryland Higher Ed. Commission Office of Student Financial Assistance
6 North Liberty Street, Ground Suite
Annapolis, MD 21201
Phone: 800-974-0203
Fax: 410-332-0250
Web: www.mhec.state.md.us/financialaid/descriptions.asp

Masergy Communications, Inc.

Masergy STEM College Scholarship Program

Type of award: Scholarship.
Intended use: For full-time undergraduate or graduate study at accredited 4-year or graduate institution in United States.
Eligibility: Applicant must be U.S. citizen.
Basis for selection: Major/career interest in science, general; technology; engineering or mathematics.
Application requirements: Essay, transcript. Students must submit:. Their official academic (high school or college) transcript and. A 500-word essay answering the following question: What actions will you take to evolve the sectors of technology and science once you graduate? Submissions are judged based on originality, creativity and quality of writing.
Additional information: The candidate must be attending an accredited college or university in the United States. The Candidate must have a declared major in one of the STEM fields. More information about this scholarship can be found at the web address listed.

Amount of award:	$5,000
Number of awards:	1
Number of applicants:	500
Application deadline:	August 15
Notification begins:	September 1
Total amount awarded:	$5,000

Contact:
Masergy Communications
2740 North Dallas PKWY
Suite 260
Plano, TX 75093
Phone: 866-588-5885
Web: https://www.masergy.com/2017-masergy-stem-scholarship-program

Massachusetts Board of Higher Education

Adopted Child Tuition Waiver and Fee Assistance Program

Type of award: Scholarship.
Intended use: For undergraduate, post-bachelor's certificate or non-degree study at accredited vocational, 2-year or 4-year institution in United States. Designated institutions: Massachusetts public institutions.
Eligibility: Applicant must be no older than 24. Applicant must be U.S. citizen or permanent resident.
Application requirements: FAFSA.
Additional information: Must be in custody of Department of Children and Families and have been adopted by Massachusetts resident or eligible Massachusetts state employee.

Amount of award:	Full tuition

Contact:
Office of Student Financial Assistance
454 Broadway, Suite 200
Revere, MA 02151
Phone: 617-391-6070
Fax: 617-727-0667
Web: www.osfa.mass.edu

Agnes M. Lindsey Scholarship

Type of award: Scholarship.
Intended use: For full-time undergraduate study at 2-year or 4-year institution in United States. Designated institutions: Public institutions of higher education in Massachusetts.
Eligibility: Applicant must be U.S. citizen or permanent resident residing in Massachusetts.
Basis for selection: Applicant must demonstrate financial need.
Application requirements: FAFSA.
Additional information: Must be resident of rural Massachusetts. Individual student awards for an award period may vary.
Contact:
Office of Student Financial Assistance
454 Broadway, Suite 200
Revere, MA 02151
Phone: 617-391-6070
Fax: 617-727-0667
Web: www.osfa.mass.edu

Categorical Tuition Waiver

Type of award: Scholarship.
Intended use: For undergraduate study at accredited 2-year or 4-year institution in United States. Designated institutions: Massachusetts public institutions.
Eligibility: Applicant must be U.S. citizen or permanent resident residing in Massachusetts.
Application requirements: Must present documentation of categorical waiver eligibility to the appropriate college officials.
Additional information: Applicants must be in one of the following categories: military veteran, Native American, senior citizen, active member of armed forces, or clients of Massachusetts Rehabilitation Commission or Commission for the Blind.

Amount of award:	Full tuition

Contact:
Contact finanical aid office at institution.
Phone: 617-391-6070
Fax: 617-727-0667
Web: www.osfa.mass.edu

DCF Foster Child Tuition Waiver and Fee Assistance Program

Type of award: Scholarship, renewable.
Intended use: For undergraduate or graduate study at postsecondary institution in United States. Designated institutions: Public colleges and universities.
Eligibility: Applicant must be no older than 24. Applicant must be U.S. citizen or permanent resident residing in Massachusetts.
Basis for selection: Applicant must demonstrate financial need.
Application requirements: FAFSA.
Additional information: Must be foster child who was placed in custody through a Care and Protection Petition. Must be

child whose guardianship was sponsored by the Department of Children and Families through age 18. Must have been in custody for at least six months before age 18.

Amount of award: Full tuition

Contact:
Office of Student Financial Assistance
454 Broadway, Suite 200
Revere, MA 02151
Phone: 617-391-6070
Fax: 617-727-0667
Web: www.osfa.mass.edu

Foster Child Grant Program

Type of award: Scholarship, renewable.
Intended use: For full-time undergraduate study at accredited 4-year institution in United States. Designated institutions: An eligible institution shall mean a public, private, independent, for profit or nonprofit institution in the Commonwealth of Massachusetts and the continental United States authorized to offer undergraduate degrees or certificate programs. The institution must be accredited and eligible to participate in the Federal Title IV programs.
Eligibility: Applicant must be no older than 24. Applicant must be U.S. citizen or permanent resident residing in Massachusetts.
Application requirements: FAFSA.
Additional information: Must be a permanent legal resident of Massachusetts. Be a U.S. Citizen or noncitizen eligible under Title IV regulations. Be placed in the custody of the Department of Children and Families through a Care and Protection Petition. Must have singed a voluntary agreement with the department of Social Services establishing terms and conditions for receiving such aid. Must be in compliance with Selective Service Registration. Must not be in default of any Federal or State Student Loans for attendance at any institution or owe a refund for any previous financial aid received. Must be enrolled full time (at least 12 credits or its equivalent) in an eligible institution.

Amount of award: $6,000

Contact:
Office of Student Financial Assistance
454 Broadway, Suite 200
Revere, MA 02151
Phone: 617-391-6070
Fax: 617-727-0667
Web: www.osfa.mass.edu

Gear Up Scholarship Program

Type of award: Scholarship.
Intended use: For undergraduate study at accredited 2-year or 4-year institution in United States. Designated institutions: Massachusetts public institutions.
Eligibility: Applicant must be no older than 21. Applicant must be U.S. citizen or permanent resident residing in Massachusetts.
Application requirements: FAFSA.
Additional information: Must be graduate of Massachusetts public high school. Must have participated in Early Intervention component of GEAR UP Massachusetts. Award is based on enrollment status.

Amount of award: $800-$1,000

Contact:
Office of Student Financial Assistance
454 Broadway, Suite 200
Revere, MA 02151
Phone: 617-391-6070
Fax: 617-727-0667
Web: http://www.mass.edu/gearup/

High Technology Scholar/Intern Tuition Waiver Program

Type of award: Scholarship.
Intended use: For undergraduate study at accredited 2-year or 4-year institution in United States. Designated institutions: Massachusetts public institutions.
Eligibility: Applicant must be U.S. citizen or permanent resident residing in Massachusetts.
Basis for selection: Major/career interest in engineering; technology or computer/information sciences.
Additional information: Student must be deemed eligible by participating company. Program encourages institutions to seek funding from business and industry for computer and information science, technology, and engineering scholarships that the Commonwealth will match with full waiver of student's annual tuition charges. Must not have received a prior bachelor's degree or its equivalent. Individual student awards will match industry scholarships up to the resident undergraduate tuition rate at the participating institution.

Amount of award: Full tuition

Contact:
Contact financial aid office at institution.
Phone: 617-391-6070
Web: www.osfa.mass.edu

Incentive Program for Aspiring Teachers

Type of award: Scholarship.
Intended use: For junior or senior study at accredited 2-year or 4-year institution in United States. Designated institutions: Massachusetts public institutions.
Eligibility: Applicant must be U.S. citizen or permanent resident residing in Massachusetts.
Basis for selection: Major/career interest in education.
Additional information: Minimum 3.0 GPA. Must be in his/her third and/or fourth year of college and enrolled in state approved teacher education program field with teacher shortages. Must commit to teaching for two years in Massachusetts. If work commitment is not completed, waiver reverts to loan.

Amount of award: Full tuition

Contact:
Office of Student Financial Assistance
454 Broadway, Suite 200
Revere, MA 02151
Phone: 617-391-6070
Fax: 617-727-0667
Web: www.osfa.mass.edu

John and Abigail Adams Scholarship

Type of award: Scholarship, renewable.
Intended use: For full-time undergraduate study at 4-year institution in United States. Designated institutions: Massachusetts public colleges and universities.

Eligibility: Applicant must be high school senior. Applicant must be U.S. citizen or permanent resident residing in Massachusetts.

Basis for selection: Applicant must demonstrate financial need and high academic achievement.

Application requirements: FAFSA.

Additional information: Students who are eligible will be notified in fall of senior year of high school. Must score in the Advanced Category in either the mathematics or language arts section of the grade 10 MCAS test and score in the proficient or advanced category on second subject. Must have MCAS score that ranks in top twenty-five percent of school district.

Contact:
Office of Student Financial Assistance
454 Broadway, Suite 200
Revere, MA 02151
Phone: 617-391-6070
Fax: 617-727-0667
Web: www.osfa.mass.edu

Joint Admissions Tuition Advantage Waiver Program

Type of award: Scholarship, renewable.

Intended use: For undergraduate study in United States. Designated institutions: Massachusetts public institutions.

Eligibility: Applicant must be residing in Massachusetts.

Basis for selection: Applicant must demonstrate high academic achievement.

Additional information: Program provides tuition waiver equal to 33 percent of resident tuition at state college or participating university. Open to graduates of Massachusetts public community colleges.

Contact:
Office of Student Financial Assistance
454 Broadway, Suite 200
Revere, MA 02151
Phone: 617-391-6070
Fax: 617-727-0667
Web: www.osfa.mass.edu

Massachusetts Cash Grant Program

Type of award: Scholarship.

Intended use: For undergraduate study at 2-year or 4-year institution in United States. Designated institutions: Public colleges and universities.

Eligibility: Applicant must be U.S. citizen or permanent resident residing in Massachusetts.

Basis for selection: Applicant must demonstrate financial need.

Additional information: Must be legal resident of Massachusetts for at least one year prior to application date. Those holding baccalaureate or professional degrees not eligible. Contact your financial aid office for application requirements and deadlines.

Contact:
Office of Student Financial Assistance
454 Broadway, Suite 200
Revere, MA 02151
Phone: 617-391-6070
Fax: 617-727-0667
Web: www.osfa.mass.edu

Massachusetts Christian A. Herter Memorial Scholarship Program

Type of award: Scholarship, renewable.

Intended use: For full-time undergraduate study at accredited vocational, 2-year or 4-year institution. Designated institutions: Massachusetts institutions.

Eligibility: Applicant must be high school sophomore or junior. Applicant must be U.S. citizen or permanent resident residing in Massachusetts.

Basis for selection: Applicant must demonstrate financial need, high academic achievement, depth of character and seriousness of purpose.

Application requirements: Interview, recommendations, essay, transcript, nomination by high school principal, counselor, teacher, or social service agency. Nominated students must also complete and submit the current year application form.

Additional information: Program provides grant assistance for students from low income or disadvantaged backgrounds who have had to overcome adverse circumstances. Selection made during sophomore and junior years in high school. Award amount is up to half of student's demonstrated financial need. Minimum 2.5 GPA.

Amount of award:	$15,000
Number of awards:	25
Number of applicants:	200
Application deadline:	February 6
Total amount awarded:	$900,000

Contact:
Office of Student Financial Assistance
Massachusetts Board of Higher Education
454 Broadway, Suite 200
Revere, MA 02151
Phone: 617-391-6070
Fax: 617-727-0667
Web: www.osfa.mass.edu

Massachusetts Gilbert Matching Student Grant

Type of award: Scholarship, renewable.

Intended use: For full-time undergraduate study at accredited 2-year or 4-year institution. Designated institutions: Independent colleges or hospital schools of nursing in Massachusetts.

Eligibility: Applicant must be U.S. citizen or permanent resident residing in Massachusetts.

Basis for selection: Major/career interest in nursing. Applicant must demonstrate financial need.

Additional information: Deadline depends on institution. Applicant must be dependent of parent who has been a Massachusetts resident for at least 12 months prior to start of academic year or an independent student who has been a permanent resident of the Commonwealth for the twelve months immediately preceding the opening of the academic year. Must not have received prior bachelor's degree.

Amount of award:	$200-$2,500

Contact:
Apply to college financial aid office.
Phone: 617-391-6070
Fax: 617-727-0667
Web: www.osfa.mass.edu

Massachusetts MASSgrant Program

Type of award: Scholarship, renewable.
Intended use: For full-time undergraduate study at accredited vocational, 2-year or 4-year institution. Designated institutions: Schools in Massachusetts.
Eligibility: Applicant must be U.S. citizen or permanent resident or Massachusetts.
Basis for selection: Applicant must demonstrate financial need.
Application requirements: FAFSA.
Additional information: Applicant must have expected family contribution of $5,081 or less and be eligible for Title IV financial aid. Applicant must maintain satisfactory academic progress. Must not have received prior bachelor's degree. Award amount varies.

Number of awards:	28,553
Number of applicants:	250,000
Application deadline:	May 1
Notification begins:	June 15
Total amount awarded:	$24,000,000

Contact:
Office of Student Financial Assistance
Massachusetts Board of Higher Education
454 Broadway, Suite 200
Revere, MA 02151
Phone: 617-391-6070
Fax: 617-727-0667
Web: www.osfa.mass.edu

Massachusetts Math and Science Teachers Scholarship

Type of award: Scholarship.
Intended use: For undergraduate or graduate study at accredited 4-year or graduate institution in United States. Designated institutions: Public colleges or universities in Massachusetts that have approved educator preparation programs.
Eligibility: Applicant must be U.S. citizen or permanent resident residing in Massachusetts.
Basis for selection: Major/career interest in education; mathematics or science, general.
Application requirements: FAFSA.
Additional information: Must be employed as educator in Massachusetts public school or school that has publicly-funded special education. Must be teaching math or science. Must sign agreement to continue teaching in Massachusetts public school or repay funds. Teachers in high-need districts are eligible to receive one-hundred percent of costs.
Contact:
Office of Student Financial Assistance
454 Broadway, Suite 200
Revere, MA 02151
Phone: 617-391-6070
Fax: 617-727-0667
Web: www.osfa.mass.edu

Massachusetts Part-Time Grant Program

Type of award: Scholarship.
Intended use: For half-time undergraduate study at 2-year or 4-year institution in United States. Designated institutions: Massachusetts colleges and universities.
Eligibility: Applicant must be U.S. citizen residing in Massachusetts.

Basis for selection: Applicant must demonstrate financial need.
Application requirements: FAFSA.
Additional information: Must be legal resident of Massachusetts for at least one year prior to application date. Those holding baccalaureate or professional degrees not eligible. Must be eligible for Title IV aid. Awards range from $200 to a maximum that depends on the type of institution that the student attends.

Amount of award:	$200

Contact:
Office of Student Financial Assistance
454 Broadway, Suite 200
Revere, MA 02151
Phone: 617-391-6070
Fax: 617-727-0667
Web: www.osfa.mass.edu

Massachusetts Public Service Grant Program

Type of award: Scholarship, renewable.
Intended use: For full-time undergraduate study at accredited 2-year or 4-year institution. Designated institutions: Massachusetts colleges and universities.
Eligibility: Applicant must be U.S. citizen or permanent resident residing in Massachusetts.
Application requirements: Proof of eligibility. FAFSA.
Additional information: Awards available for children or widowed spouse of deceased firefighters, police officers, or corrections officers who died from injuries received performing his or her duties. Children of veterans killed in action or Vietnam POWs also eligible. Award in form of entitlement grant. Applicant must be resident of Massachusetts at least one year prior to start of school. For recipients attending Massachusetts public college or university, award shall equal cost of tuition. Must not have received a prior bachelor's degree. Recipients attending Massachusetts independent college or university, award will be equivalent to highest tuition amount paid to public institution.

Amount of award:	$2,500
Application deadline:	May 1
Notification begins:	June 1
Total amount awarded:	$22,665

Contact:
Office of Student Financial Assistance
Massachusetts Board of Higher Education
454 Broadway, Suite 200
Revere, MA 02151
Phone: 617-391-6070
Fax: 617-727-0667
Web: www.osfa.mass.edu

Paul Tsongas Scholarship Program

Type of award: Scholarship, renewable.
Intended use: For undergraduate study at postsecondary institution. Designated institutions: Massachusetts state colleges.
Eligibility: Applicant must be U.S. citizen or permanent resident residing in Massachusetts.
Basis for selection: Applicant must demonstrate financial need and high academic achievement.
Application requirements: SAT/ACT scores.
Additional information: Minimum 3.75 GPA. Tuition waiver for full tuition and related fees. For renewal, must maintain 3.3 GPA. Each state college may provide five new Paul Tsongas Scholarship Tuition Waivers per academic year.

Amount of award: Full tuition
Number of awards: 45
Contact:
Contact state college financial aid office.
Phone: 617-391-6070
Fax: 617-727-0667
Web: www.osfa.mass.edu

September 11, 2001 Tragedy Tuition Waiver Program

Type of award: Scholarship.
Intended use: For undergraduate study at accredited 2-year or 4-year institution in United States. Designated institutions: Massachusetts public institutions.
Eligibility: Applicant must be U.S. citizen residing in Massachusetts.
Application requirements: Student's birth certificate, official documentation of death related to September 11, 2001.
Additional information: Must be Massachusetts resident who is spouse or dependent of victim of events of September 11, 2001. Eligible students will be entitled to a tuition waiver equal to 100 percent of the resident tuition rate for eligible state-supported courses offered at the participating public higher education institution.
Amount of award: Full tuition
Contact:
Office of Student Financial Assistance
454 Broadway, Suite 200
Revere, MA 02151
Phone: 617-391-6070
Fax: 617-727-0667
Web: www.osfa.mass.edu

Stanley Z. Koplik Certificate of Mastery Tuition Waiver Program

Type of award: Scholarship, renewable.
Intended use: For freshman study at accredited 2-year or 4-year institution in United States. Designated institutions: Massachusetts public institutions.
Eligibility: Applicant must be enrolled in high school. Applicant must be U.S. citizen residing in Massachusetts.
Additional information: Must be enrolled in Massachusetts public high school. Must score "Advanced" on at least one grade 10 MCAS test subject and score "Proficient" on remaining sections. Must fulfill one of the following criteria: two AP exams with a score of 3 or higher; 2 SAT II exams (minimum score dependent on subject area); SAT II exam and ACT I exam; SAT II exam and one other achievement; AP exam and one other achievement.
Amount of award: Full tuition
Contact:
Massachusetts Department of Elementary and Secondary Education
Phone: 781-338-3581
Web: www.osfa.mass.edu

Valedictorian Tuition Waiver Program

Type of award: Scholarship.
Intended use: For undergraduate study at accredited 2-year or 4-year institution in United States. Designated institutions: Massachusetts public institutions.
Eligibility: Applicant must be U.S. citizen or permanent resident residing in Massachusetts.

Additional information: Must be high school valedictorian. Must be a permanent legal resident of Massachusetts for at least one year prior to the opening of the academic year.
Amount of award: Full tuition
Contact:
Office of Student Financial Assistance
454 Broadway, Suite 200
Revere, MA 02151
Phone: 617-391-6070
Fax: 617-727-0667
Web: www.osfa.mass.edu

Matinee

Matinee Voice over scholarship

Type of award: Scholarship, renewable.
Intended use: For undergraduate or graduate study at accredited 2-year, 4-year or graduate institution in United States or Canada.
Eligibility: Applicant must be U.S. citizen.
Basis for selection: Applicant must demonstrate financial need.
Application requirements: 250+ blog post. Subject can be found on web site. Winner will be determined by quality of writing, blog views, and the number of retweets with a blog link.
Number of awards: 1
Application deadline: January 5
Notification begins: January 12
Total amount awarded: $1,000
Contact:
Web: https://www.matinee.co.uk/voice-over-agency/matinee-scholarship/

Matthew L Sharp Trial Lawyer

Law Office of Matthew L Sharp Need-Based Scholarship

Type of award: Scholarship.
Intended use: For full-time undergraduate study at accredited 4-year institution in United States.
Eligibility: Applicant must be U.S. citizen or permanent resident.
Basis for selection: Major/career interest in law. Applicant must demonstrate financial need.
Application requirements: This scholarship will be awarded to the student who demonstrates financial need and who submits the strongest PSA video focusing on the following topic: "Do you think an injured party should be entitled to a trial by jury?
Amount of award: $2,000
Number of awards: 1
Application deadline: June 1
Notification begins: September 1
Total amount awarded: $2,000

Contact:
Matthew L Sharp Trial Lawyer
620B Academy Drive
Northbrook, IL 60062, IL 60062
Phone: 847-940-4000
Web: http://mattsharplaw.com/law-office-matthew-l-sharp-need-based-scholarship/

MBA Insight

MBA Insight Scholarship

Type of award: Scholarship.
Intended use: For full-time graduate study at graduate institution.
Additional information: Applicant must be an MBA student. Application online, just leave a review of your GMAT test prep/admissions consulting company on the website.

Number of awards:	1
Application deadline:	September 1
Notification begins:	September 15
Total amount awarded:	$500

Contact:
Web: http://mbainsight.com/mba-scholarships/

McKee Scholars

John McKee Scholarship

Type of award: Scholarship, renewable.
Intended use: For full-time undergraduate study at 4-year institution.
Eligibility: Applicant must be male, no older than 18, enrolled in high school. Applicant must be U.S. citizen residing in Pennsylvania.
Basis for selection: Applicant must demonstrate financial need and high academic achievement.
Application requirements: Interview, transcript. SAT/ACT scores, SAR, application, evaluation.
Additional information: For male applicants whose fathers are deceased, missing, permanently absent, or dysfunctional. Applicant must be a resident of Philadelphia, Bucks, Chester, Montgomery or Delaware counties. Award allotment after initial award year is based on upheld academic standards. Application available on Website.

Amount of award:	$3,500-$7,500
Number of awards:	56
Number of applicants:	54
Application deadline:	March 1
Notification begins:	May 15
Total amount awarded:	$234,475

Contact:
John McKee Scholarship Committee
Attn: Robert J. Stern, Executive Secretary
P.O. Box 144
Merion Station, PA 19066
Phone: 484-323-1348
Fax: 610-640-1965
Web: www.mckeescholars.org

Medical Scrubs Collection

Medical Scrubs Collection Scholarship

Type of award: Scholarship.
Intended use: For undergraduate or graduate study at accredited vocational, 2-year, 4-year or graduate institution.
Eligibility: Applicant must be high school senior. Applicant must be U.S. citizen or permanent resident.
Application requirements: Applicant must be a high school senior or currently enrolled in an accredited U.S. college or university. Pursuing a degree in the medical field such as: therapy, nursing, medicine, nutrition, laboratory science, dentistry, etc.
Additional information: Applicant may choose to complete one of the following projects: Writing - up to 500 words (relevant pictures may be included); Image - up to 8.5" x 11", along with a short description.

Amount of award:	$1,000
Number of awards:	1
Application deadline:	December 15
Total amount awarded:	$1,000

Contact:
Medical Scrubs Collection LLC
1665 Corporate Road West
Lakewood, NJ 08701
Phone: 732-719-8600
Web: https://medicalscrubscollection.com/scholarship-program

Mendez Scholarships Non-Profit

Georgina S. Mendez Pharmacology Scholarship

Type of award: Scholarship.
Intended use: For postgraduate study at accredited postsecondary institution in United States.
Basis for selection: Major/career interest in pharmacy/pharmaceutics/pharmacology.
Application requirements: Recommendations, essay, transcript. FAFSA, servant leader career goals essay.
Additional information: Must be servant leader enrolled in accredited pharmacology program. Visit Website for application.

Amount of award:	$250-$1,000
Number of awards:	4
Number of applicants:	100
Total amount awarded:	$5,000

Contact:
Web: www.mendezscholars.org

John L. Mendez Business Scholarship

Type of award: Scholarship.
Intended use: For postgraduate study at accredited postsecondary institution in United States.
Basis for selection: Major/career interest in business.

Application requirements: Recommendations, essay, transcript. FAFSA. Servant leader career goals essay.
Additional information: Visit Website for application. Must be servant leader enrolled in accredited business program.

Amount of award:	$250-$1,000
Number of awards:	4
Number of applicants:	100
Total amount awarded:	$5,000

Contact:
Web: www.mendezscholars.org

Julio C. Mendez Engineering Scholarship

Type of award: Scholarship.
Intended use: For postgraduate study at accredited postsecondary institution in United States.
Basis for selection: Major/career interest in engineering.
Application requirements: Recommendations, essay, transcript. FAFSA. Servant leader career goals essay.
Additional information: Visit Website for application. Must be servant leader enrolled in accredited engineering program.

Amount of award:	$250-$1,000
Number of awards:	4
Number of applicants:	20
Total amount awarded:	$5,000

Contact:
Web: www.mendezscholars.org

Menominee Indian Tribe of Wisconsin

Menominee Adult Vocational Training Grant

Type of award: Scholarship, renewable.
Intended use: For undergraduate or non-degree study at accredited vocational, 2-year or 4-year institution in United States.
Eligibility: Applicant must be American Indian. Applicant must be enrolled member of Menominee Indian tribe of Wisconsin.
Basis for selection: Applicant must demonstrate financial need.
Application requirements: FAFSA and Menominee Tribal Grant Application.
Additional information: Award also applicable toward associate's degree. Must apply through college financial aid office.

Amount of award:	$550-$2,200
Number of applicants:	100
Application deadline:	October 30, March 1

Contact:
Menominee Indian Tribe of Wisconsin
P.O. Box 910
Keshena, WI 54135
Phone: 715-799-5118
Fax: 715-799-5102
Web: www.menominee-nsn.gov

Menominee Higher Education Grant

Type of award: Scholarship, renewable.
Intended use: For undergraduate study at accredited 2-year or 4-year institution in United States.
Eligibility: Applicant must be American Indian. Applicant must be enrolled member of Menominee Indian tribe.
Basis for selection: Applicant must demonstrate financial need.
Application requirements: FAFSA and Menominee Tribal Grant Application.
Additional information: Applications and deadline dates available through Tribal Education office.

Amount of award:	$550-$2,200
Number of applicants:	200
Application deadline:	October 30, March 1

Contact:
Menominee Indian Tribe of Wisconsin
P.O. Box 910
Keshena, WI 54135
Phone: 715-799-5118
Fax: 715-799-5102
Web: www.menominee-nsn.gov

The Merchants Exchange

The Merchants Exchange Scholarship Fund

Type of award: Scholarship, renewable.
Intended use: For junior, senior or graduate study at accredited postsecondary institution.
Basis for selection: Major/career interest in international relations. Applicant must demonstrate high academic achievement and depth of character.
Application requirements: Recommendations, transcript.
Additional information: Scholarship is for students studying maritime affairs/international trade. Minimum 2.5 GPA. Financial need may be considered if all other factors are equal. Visit Website for application.

Amount of award:	$1,500
Number of awards:	7
Number of applicants:	5
Application deadline:	May 31

Contact:
The Merchants Exchange
200 SW Market, Suite 190
Portland, OR 97201
Phone: 503-220-2092
Web: www.pdxmex.com

Michael and Susan Dell Foundation

Dell Scholars Program

Type of award: Scholarship.
Intended use: For freshman study at accredited 2-year or 4-year institution in United States.

Scholarships

Eligibility: Applicant must be high school senior. Applicant must be U.S. citizen or permanent resident.

Basis for selection: Applicant must demonstrate financial need, high academic achievement, depth of character and seriousness of purpose.

Application requirements: Recommendations, essay, transcript. Student Aid Report from FAFSA.

Additional information: Dell Scholars are students who demonstrate desire and ability to overcome barriers and to achieve their goals. Must have overcome obstacles to pursue education. Must have been participating in a Michael & Susan Dell Foundation approved college readiness program for a minimum of two years. Must be currently graduating from an accredited high school. Minimum 2.4 GPA. Must be entering into a bachelor's degree program in the fall directly after graduating high school. Recipients receive $20,000 over six years. Visit Website for more information.

Amount of award:	$5,000
Number of awards:	300
Application deadline:	January 15
Notification begins:	April 10

Contact:
Michael and Susan Dell Foundation
Phone: 800-294-2039
Web: www.dellscholars.org

Michael Moody Fitness

Michael Moody Fitness Scholarship

Type of award: Scholarship.

Intended use: For full-time undergraduate or graduate study at accredited 2-year or 4-year institution.

Eligibility: Applicant must be high school senior.

Basis for selection: Major/career interest in sports/sports administration; athletic training; physical education or physical therapy. Applicant must demonstrate leadership.

Application requirements: Transcript. Details of outstanding achievement in school, list of involvement in school and community activities, list of work experience, current high school or university cumulative grade point average (GPA) on a 4.0 scale.

Additional information: The program selects scholarship applications from October 1st until 1,000 scholarship applications are submitted or April 15th, whichever comes first.

Number of awards:	1
Application deadline:	April 15
Total amount awarded:	$1,500

Contact:
Web: www.michaelmoodyfitness.com/student-scholarship-chicago

Michael First Credit Union

Young & Free Michigan Scholarship

Type of award: Scholarship.

Intended use: For full-time undergraduate or graduate study at 2-year, 4-year or graduate institution.

Eligibility: Applicant must be at least 17, no older than 25, high school senior. Applicant must be U.S. citizen or permanent resident residing in Michigan.

Basis for selection: Scholarship winners will be determined by a combination of public vote and judging committee. The Top Ten scholarship candidates in each category will be determined by public vote on the YoungFreeMichigan.com Scholarship Competition page. The Top Ten finalists' submissions, in each category, will move forward for review by the Judging Committee to determine the three scholarship winners in each category. The final judging for the scholarships will be based upon the merit of the submissions.

Application requirements: Video (sixty seconds or less) or essay (300 to 500 words) answering the question: What invention do you think the world would be better off without and why? Creative thinking encouraged. If submitting a video, set it to public view.

Additional information: Minimum GPA of 2.8. Must be a member of Michigan First Credit Union in good standing. Study full-time(minimum 12 credit hours) in a college or university for the Fall. See website for full rules and details.

Amount of award:	$1,000-$10,000
Number of awards:	40
Number of applicants:	180
Application deadline:	February 1
Notification begins:	February 29
Total amount awarded:	$85,000

Contact:
Michigan First Credit Union
27000 Evergreen Road
Lathrup Village, MI 48076
Phone: 248-395-4089
Web: www.youngfreemichigan.com/2016-scholarship

Michigan Higher Education Assistance Authority

Children of Veterans Tuition Grant

Type of award: Scholarship, renewable.

Intended use: For undergraduate study at postsecondary institution. Designated institutions: Michigan institutions.

Eligibility: Applicant must be at least 16, no older than 25. Applicant must be U.S. citizen or permanent resident residing in Michigan. Applicant must be dependent of disabled veteran or deceased veteran.

Application requirements: Birth certificate, veteran's DD 214 certificate and casualty report.

Additional information: Veteran must have been killed in action, been listed as MIA, or been permanently disabled due to service-related injuries. Veteran must have been a Michigan resident before entering military service or must have established residency in Michigan after entering military service.

Amount of award:	$1,400-$2,800
Number of awards:	410
Total amount awarded:	$996,000

Contact:
Michigan Higher Education Assistance Authority
Office of Scholarships and Grants
P.O. Box 30462
Lansing, MI 48909-7962
Phone: 888-447-2687
Fax: 517-241-5835
Web: www.michigan.gov/osg

Michigan Tuition Grant

Type of award: Scholarship, renewable.
Intended use: For undergraduate, master's or doctoral study at 2-year, 4-year or graduate institution. Designated institutions: Participating Michigan institutions.
Eligibility: Applicant must be U.S. citizen or permanent resident residing in Michigan.
Basis for selection: Applicant must demonstrate financial need.
Application requirements: FAFSA.
Additional information: Theology or religious education students ineligible.

Amount of award:	$1,524
Number of awards:	22,000
Application deadline:	July 1
Total amount awarded:	$30,500,000

Contact:
Michigan Higher Education Assistance Authority
Office of Scholarships and Grants
P.O. Box 30462
Lansing, MI 48909-7962
Phone: 888-447-2687
Fax: 517-241-5835
Web: www.michigan.gov/osg

Michigan Tuition Incentive Program

Type of award: Scholarship, renewable.
Intended use: For undergraduate study at postsecondary institution. Designated institutions: Michigan institutions.
Eligibility: Applicant must be U.S. citizen or permanent resident residing in Michigan.
Basis for selection: Applicant must demonstrate financial need.
Application requirements: Proof of eligibility.
Additional information: Eligibility determined by Medicaid status. Provides tuition assistance for up to 24 semesters or 36 term credits for first two years. Up to $2,000 total assistance for third and fourth years.

Number of awards:	16,000
Total amount awarded:	$34,600,000

Contact:
Michigan Higher Education Assistance Authority
Office of Scholarships and Grants
P.O. Box 30462
Lansing, MI 48909-7962
Phone: 888-447-2687
Fax: 517-241-5835
Web: www.michigan.gov/osg

Michigan Society of Professional Engineers

Michigan Society of Professional Engineers Scholarships for High School Seniors

Type of award: Scholarship, renewable.
Intended use: For undergraduate study at accredited 4-year institution. Designated institutions: ABET-accredited schools in Michigan.

Eligibility: Applicant must be high school senior. Applicant must be U.S. citizen residing in Michigan.
Basis for selection: Major/career interest in engineering. Applicant must demonstrate high academic achievement, depth of character, leadership and service orientation.
Application requirements: Recommendations, essay, transcript. ACT scores. List of senior classes taken.
Additional information: Minimum 3.0 GPA and 26 ACT score. Application must be postmarked by first Friday of February. Contact guidance counselor or local MSPE chapter for application and specific eligibility requirements. Applications must be submitted to local MSPE chapter.
Contact:
Scholarship Coordinator Local MSPE Chapter
P.O. Box 15276
Lansing, MI 48901-5276
Phone: 517-487-9388
Fax: 517-487-0635
Web: www.michiganspe.org

Microscopy Society of America

Microscopy Society of America Undergraduate Research Scholarship

Type of award: Research grant.
Intended use: For full-time junior or senior study at postsecondary institution.
Basis for selection: Major/career interest in science, general; biology; physics; chemistry; natural sciences or engineering, materials. Applicant must demonstrate seriousness of purpose.
Application requirements: Recommendations. Resume, budget, research proposal, letter from laboratory supervisor, letter from MSA member (may be same as supervisor or professor). Four hard copies of all application materials if not submitting electronically.
Additional information: Award for students interested in pursuing microscopy as career or major research tool. Applicant should be sponsored by MSA member. Must supply abstract of research project. Funds must be spent within year of award date, but in special cases may be extended to cover additional research during summer semester following graduation. Visit Website for more information and application.

Amount of award:	$3,000
Number of awards:	6
Number of applicants:	20
Application deadline:	December 31
Notification begins:	April 1
Total amount awarded:	$9,000

Contact:
Microscopy Society of America
Undergraduate Research Scholarship
12100 Sunset Hills Road, Suite 130
Reston, VA 20190
Phone: 800-538-3672
Fax: 703-435-4390
Web: www.microscopy.org

Scholarships

Microsoft Corporation

Microsoft General Scholarship

Type of award: Scholarship.
Intended use: For full-time at 4-year institution. Designated institutions: Colleges and universities in the United States, Canada, and Mexico.
Basis for selection: Major/career interest in computer/information sciences; engineering, computer; mathematics or physics. Applicant must demonstrate financial need, high academic achievement and leadership.
Application requirements: Recommendations, essay, transcript. Resume.
Additional information: Minimum 3.0 GPA. Please refer to the website for information and to apply. Eligible majors include: Computer Science, Computer Engineering, Electrical Engineering, or other related STEM discipline. Must have demonstrated passion for technology.

Amount of award:	Full tuition
Application deadline:	January 27
Total amount awarded:	$500,000

Contact:
Microsoft Scholarship Program
Microsoft Corporation
One Microsoft Way
Redmond, WA 98052-8303
Web: www.microsoft.com/scholarship

Midwestern Higher Education Compact

Midwest Student Exchange Program

Type of award: Scholarship, renewable.
Intended use: For full-time undergraduate, master's, doctoral or first professional study at accredited 2-year, 4-year or graduate institution in United States. Designated institutions: Participating institutions in Illinois, Indiana, Kansas, Michigan, Minnesota, Missouri, Nebraska, North Dakota, and Wisconsin.
Eligibility: Applicant must be residing in Wisconsin, Michigan, Minnesota, Kansas, Indiana, Nebraska, Illinois, Missouri or North Dakota.
Application requirements: Proof of eligibility.
Additional information: Reduced tuition rate for Illinois, Indiana, Kansas, Michigan, Minnesota, Missouri, Nebraska, North Dakota, and Wisconsin residents attending participating out-of-state institutions in one of eight other states in designated institutions or programs of study. For information, contact high school counselor or college admissions officer. For list of participating institutions and programs, and for individual state contact information, visit Website.
Contact:
Contact campus administrator at participating MSEP institutions.
Phone: 612-677-2777
Fax: 612-767-3353
Web: msep.mhec.org

Military Officers Association of America

General John Paul Ratay Educational Fund Grants

Type of award: Scholarship.
Intended use: For undergraduate study at postsecondary institution.
Eligibility: Applicant must be U.S. citizen. Applicant must be dependent of veteran.
Additional information: Grants available to children of surviving spouse of retired officers. Must be seeking first undergraduate degree. Students cannot receive both an MOAA loan and Ratay grant.

Amount of award:	$5,000
Application deadline:	March 1
Notification begins:	May 1

Contact:
Military Officers Association of America
201 N. Washington Street
Alexandria, VA 22314
Phone: 703-549-2311
Web: www.moaa.org/education

MOAA American Patriot Scholarship Program

Type of award: Scholarship, renewable.
Intended use: For undergraduate study at accredited postsecondary institution.
Eligibility: Applicant must be no older than 23. Applicant must be dependent of active service person. Must be dependent of an active duty uniformed service member (including Drilling Reserve and National Guard). Military academy cadets are ineligible.
Basis for selection: Applicant must demonstrate financial need and high academic achievement.
Additional information: Minimum 3.0 GPA. Must be seeking first undergraduate degree. Amount and number of awards given vary.

Amount of award:	$2,500
Number of applicants:	50
Application deadline:	March 1
Notification begins:	May 1
Total amount awarded:	$300,000

Contact:
MOAA Scholarship Fun
American Patriot Scholarships
201 North Washington Street
Alexandria, VA 22314-2529
Phone: 800-234-6622
Web: www.moaa.org/education

Military Order of the Purple Heart

Military Order of the Purple Heart Scholarship

Type of award: Scholarship, renewable.
Intended use: For full-time undergraduate study at postsecondary institution.

Eligibility: Applicant must be U.S. citizen. Applicant must be descendant of veteran or disabled while on active duty; or dependent of disabled veteran or deceased veteran; or spouse of disabled veteran or deceased veteran. Applicant must either be a recipient of the Purple Heart who is a member of the Military Order of the Purple Heart (MOPH); spouse or descendant of MOPH member, or descendant or spouse of veteran killed in action or who died of wounds. Great grandchildren not eligible to apply.
Basis for selection: Applicant must demonstrate high academic achievement.
Application requirements: $15 application fee. Recommendations, essay, transcript, proof of eligibility.
Additional information: Must have minimum unweighted 2.75 GPA. Deadline in mid February. Application package available on MOPH Website. Call MOPH for details.

Amount of award:	$3,000
Number of awards:	83
Number of applicants:	300
Total amount awarded:	$250,000

Contact:
Military Order of the Purple Heart
Scholarship Coordinator
5413-B Backlick Road
Springfield, VA 22151
Phone: 703-642-5360
Fax: 703-642-2054
Web: www.purpleheart.org

Minnesota Department of Veterans Affairs

Minnesota Educational Assistance for Veterans

Type of award: Scholarship.
Intended use: For undergraduate or graduate study at postsecondary institution. Designated institutions: Approved Minnesota institutions.
Eligibility: Applicant must be U.S. citizen residing in Minnesota. Applicant must be veteran. Applicant must have been Minnesota resident at time of entry into active duty and for six months immediately preceding entry. Must have served 181 consecutive days of active duty.
Application requirements: Proof of eligibility. Military Service DD Form 214.
Additional information: Applicant must have exhausted eligible federal educational benefits prior to the delimiting date or within the eligibility period in which benefits were available. Grant is one-time award. Contact county veterans service officer or institution for more information.

Amount of award:	$750

Contact:
Minnesota Department of Veterans Affairs
Veterans Service Building, 2nd Floor
20 West 12 Street
St. Paul, MN 55155-2079
Phone: 651-296-2562
Fax: 651-296-3954
Web: www.mdva.state.mn.us/education

Minnesota Office of Higher Education

Minnesota Child Care Grant

Type of award: Scholarship, renewable.
Intended use: For undergraduate study at accredited postsecondary institution. Designated institutions: Eligible Minnesota schools.
Eligibility: Applicant must be residing in Minnesota.
Basis for selection: Applicant must demonstrate financial need.
Additional information: Apply at college's financial aid office. Award amount prorated upon enrollment. Award based on family income and size. Eligibility limited to applicants with children 12 years or younger; maximum of $2600 per eligible child per academic year. Applicant cannot be receiving Aid to Families With Dependent Children, Minnesota Family Investment Program, or tuition reciprocity, or be in default of loan. Those with bachelor's degree or eight semesters or 12 quarters of credit, or equivalent, are not eligible. Applicant must be enrolled at least half-time in nonsectarian program and must be in good academic standing. Deadlines established by individual institution.

Amount of award:	$2,800
Number of awards:	2,421
Number of applicants:	2,863
Total amount awarded:	$4,927,539

Contact:
Minnesota Office of Higher Education
1450 Energy Park Drive, Suite 350
St. Paul, MN 55108-5227
Phone: 800-657-3866
Web: www.ohe.state.mn.us

Minnesota Indian Scholarship Program

Type of award: Scholarship.
Intended use: For undergraduate or graduate study in United States. Designated institutions: Any accredited post-secondary institution located in Minnesota.
Eligibility: Applicant must be American Indian. Applicant must be residing in Minnesota.
Application requirements: Proof of one-fourth or more American Indian ancestry. FAFSA.
Additional information: Applicant must be at least one-quarter American Indian. Undergraduates must be enrolled at least three-quarters time and graduate students must be enrolled at least half-time. Undergraduates must be eligible for Pell grant or Minnesota state grant. Awards made on first-completed, first-served basis.

Amount of award:	$6,000
Number of awards:	1,058
Number of applicants:	1,930
Notification begins:	February 1
Total amount awarded:	$3,499,762

Contact:
Minnesota Office of Higher Education
1450 Energy Park Drive, Suite 350
St. Paul, MN 55108-5227
Phone: 800-657-3866
Web: www.ohe.state.mn.us/indianscholarship

Scholarships

Minnesota Public Safety Officers Survivors Grant

Type of award: Scholarship.
Intended use: For undergraduate study at accredited 2-year or 4-year institution. Designated institutions: Eligible Minnesota schools.
Eligibility: Applicant must be residing in Minnesota. Applicant's parent must have been killed or disabled in work-related accident as firefighter, police officer or public safety officer.
Application requirements: Proof of eligibility. Eligibility certificate.
Additional information: Must be enrolled in degree or certificate program at institution participating in Minnesota State Grant Program. Applicant must be the surviving spouse or dependent child of a public safety officer killed in the line of duty. Apply through financial aid office. Award covers tuition and fees up to $13,000 at four-year college and $5,808 at two-year college.

Amount of award:	$5,808-$13,000
Number of awards:	6
Number of applicants:	12
Total amount awarded:	$63,025

Contact:
Contact financial aid office at institution.
Phone: 800-657-3866
Web: www.ohe.state.mn.us

Minnesota State Grant Program

Type of award: Scholarship, renewable.
Intended use: For undergraduate study at accredited vocational, 2-year or 4-year institution.
Eligibility: Applicant must be residing in Minnesota.
Basis for selection: Applicant must demonstrate financial need.
Application requirements: Proof of eligibility. FAFSA.
Additional information: Applicant must not have completed four years of college. If not Minnesota high school graduate and parents not residents of Minnesota, applicant must be resident of Minnesota for at least one year without being enrolled half-time or more. Cannot be in default on loans or delinquent on child-support payments. FAFSA used as application for Minnesota State Grant. Application deadline is 30 days from term start date.

Amount of award:	$100-$10,745
Number of awards:	99,500
Total amount awarded:	$172,500,000

Contact:
Minnesota Office of Higher Education
1450 Energy Park Drive, Suite 350
St. Paul, MN 55108-5227
Phone: 800-657-3866
Web: www.ohe.state.mn.us

Miss America Organization

Allman Medical Scholarships

Type of award: Scholarship, renewable.
Intended use: For undergraduate or graduate study at postsecondary institution.
Eligibility: Applicant must be female.

Basis for selection: Major/career interest in medicine. Applicant must demonstrate financial need and high academic achievement.
Application requirements: Recommendations, essay, transcript, proof of eligibility. MCAT scores.
Additional information: Must be pursuing a degree in medicine. Must have competed in Miss America system at local, state, or national level after 1998. Notification begins in August.

Application deadline:	June 30

Contact:
Miss America Organization
222 New Road, Suite 700
Attn: Scholarships
Linwood, NJ 08221
Phone: 609-653-8700
Web: www.missamerica.org/scholarships

Eugenia Vellner Fischer Award for the Performing Arts

Type of award: Scholarship.
Intended use: For undergraduate or graduate study at postsecondary institution.
Eligibility: Applicant must be female.
Basis for selection: Major/career interest in performing arts. Applicant must demonstrate financial need and high academic achievement.
Application requirements: Recommendations, essay, transcript, proof of eligibility.
Additional information: Must be pursuing degree in the performing arts, such as dance or music. Must have competed in Miss America system in local, state, or national level after 1998. Visit Website for more information.

Application deadline:	June 30
Notification begins:	September 1

Contact:
Miss America Organization
Attn: Scholarships
222 New Road, Suite 700
Linwood, NJ 08221
Phone: 609-653-8700
Web: www.missamerica.org/scholarships

Miss America Competition Awards

Type of award: Scholarship.
Intended use: For undergraduate, graduate or non-degree study at accredited postsecondary institution.
Eligibility: Applicant must be single, female, at least 17, no older than 24. Applicant must be U.S. citizen.
Basis for selection: Competition/talent/interest in poise/talent/fitness. Applicant must demonstrate depth of character, leadership, patriotism, seriousness of purpose and service orientation.
Application requirements: Proof of eligibility.
Additional information: Local winners go on to compete at state level, and state winners compete for Miss America. Contestants will apply their talent, intelligence, and speaking ability, and demonstrate their commitment to community service. Cash and tuition-based scholarships available at every level of competition. Deadlines for local competitions vary. Contact the Miss America Organization for more information or visit Website.

Amount of award:	$1,000-$50,000
Total amount awarded:	$40,000,000

Contact:
Miss America Organization
Attn: Scholarships
222 New Road, Suite 700
Linwood, NJ 08221
Phone: 609-653-8700
Web: www.missamerica.org/scholarships

Mission Eurasia

Next Generation Christian Leaders Scholarship

Type of award: Scholarship, renewable.
Intended use: For full-time undergraduate study at accredited 4-year institution.
Eligibility: Applicant must be high school senior. Applicant must be Christian. Applicant must be U.S. citizen.
Basis for selection: Major/career interest in ministry. Applicant must demonstrate financial need, high academic achievement, depth of character and leadership.
Application requirements: Interview, recommendations, essay, transcript. High school seniors who have been accepted into a full-time undergraduate degree program, or full-time college undergraduates. All NGCLS winners must be active participants in a local church and/or ministry. All applicants must be able to speak Russian or Ukrainian at a conversational level. All applicants must display Christian character, leadership abilities, and achievements. All applicants must have demonstrated financial need. All applicants must submit an application packet, which must include a completed NGCLS application form (available on our website), a letter of recommendation from the pastor of the church that the applicant attends, a two-page essay on "The Ministry of Young Christian Leaders and the Future of Missions," an official transcript from their high school/college that includes their GPA, and their most recent federal tax return as proof of financial need. All application materials must be sent in one envelope to the Mission Eurasia office. All application materials must be sent in one envelope to the Mission Eurasia office.
Additional information: Applicants Nationality : US, Canadian, or Mexican. Must be Slavic descent. Scholarships, which are available for any field of study, are made as a lump sum and paid directly to the college or university where the recipient is studying. Scholarship funds may be used for tuition, housing, books, and other expenses related to the stuedent's studies.

Amount of award:	$5,000
Number of awards:	3
Application deadline:	April 1
Notification begins:	June 1
Total amount awarded:	$15,000

Contact:
Mission Eurasia
PO Box 496
Wheaton, IL 60187
Phone: 630-462-1739
Fax: 630-690-2976
Web: https://missioneurasia.org/next-generation-christian-leaders-scholarship/

Mississippi Office of Student Financial Aid

Mississippi Eminent Scholars Grant

Type of award: Scholarship, renewable.
Intended use: For full-time undergraduate study at accredited vocational, 2-year or 4-year institution. Designated institutions: Eligible Mississippi institutions.
Eligibility: Applicant must be residing in Mississippi.
Basis for selection: Applicant must demonstrate high academic achievement.
Application requirements: Transcript. State of Mississippi tax return. SAT/ACT scores. Copy of Mississippi driver's license.
Additional information: Applicant may be high school senior. Must be Mississippi resident for at least one year. Minimum 3.5 GPA or rank in top 25 percent of class. Must have minimum ACT score of 29, SAT score of 1290, or be National Merit or National Achievement finalist or semi-finalist.

Amount of award:	$2,500
Application deadline:	September 15

Contact:
Mississippi Office of Student Financial Aid
3825 Ridgewood Road
Jackson, MS 39211-6453
Phone: 800-327-2980
Web: www.mississippi.edu/riseupms

Mississippi Higher Education Legislative Plan

Type of award: Scholarship, renewable.
Intended use: For full-time freshman or sophomore study at accredited 2-year or 4-year institution. Designated institutions: Eligible Mississippi institutions.
Eligibility: Applicant must be U.S. citizen residing in Mississippi.
Basis for selection: Applicant must demonstrate financial need and high academic achievement.
Application requirements: FAFSA. Household verification form.
Additional information: Minimum 2.5 GPA. Minimum 20 ACT. Must have completed specific high school core curriculum. Must be legal resident of Mississippi for at least two years. Must have graduated from high school within two years of application. Preference given to early applicants. Covers tuition and fees up to ten semesters. Visit Website for application and more details.

Amount of award:	Full tuition
Application deadline:	March 31
Total amount awarded:	$1,753,252

Contact:
Mississippi Office of Student Financial Aid
3825 Ridgewood Road
Jackson, MS 39211-6453
Phone: 800-327-2980
Web: www.mississippi.edu/riseupms

Mississippi Tuition Assistance Grant

Type of award: Scholarship, renewable.
Intended use: For full-time undergraduate study at accredited vocational, 2-year or 4-year institution. Designated institutions: Eligible Mississippi institutions.

Eligibility: Applicant must be U.S. citizen residing in Mississippi.

Basis for selection: Applicant must demonstrate high academic achievement.

Application requirements: FAFSA and Student Aid Report, ACT score, state tax return, copy of Mississippi driver's license.

Additional information: Applicant must be resident of Mississippi for at least one year. Must be receiving less than full Federal Pell Grant. Minimum 15 ACT. Must have minimum 2.5 GPA. Award is up to $500 per year for freshmen and sophomores; up to $1,000 per year for juniors and seniors. Recipients must maintain minimum 2.5 GPA to reapply. Applicants must not be in default on an educational loan. Apply online.

    Amount of award: $500-$1,000

    Application deadline: September 15

Contact:
Mississippi Office of Student Financial Aid
3825 Ridgewood Road
Jackson, MS 39211-6453
Phone: 800-327-2980
Web: www.mississippi.edu/riseupms

Nissan Scholarship

Type of award: Scholarship, renewable.

Intended use: For full-time undergraduate study at 2-year or 4-year institution. Designated institutions: Mississippi public institutions.

Eligibility: Applicant must be high school senior. Applicant must be residing in Mississippi.

Basis for selection: Applicant must demonstrate financial need, high academic achievement, leadership, seriousness of purpose and service orientation.

Application requirements: Recommendations, essay, transcript. FAFSA, resume, SAT/ACT scores, Mississippi driver's license, state tax return.

Additional information: Must be graduating from Mississippi high school in current year. Must have 20 ACT score or 940 SAT score (reading and math). Minimum 2.5 GPA. Visit Website for more information and application. Number and amount of awards vary.

    Amount of award: Full tuition

    Application deadline: March 1

Contact:
Mississippi Office of Student Financial Aid
3825 Ridgewood Road
Jackson, MS 39211-6453
Phone: 800-327-2980
Web: www.mississippi.edu/riseupms

Missouri Department of Higher Education

A+ Scholarship Program

Type of award: Scholarship.

Intended use: For full-time undergraduate study at vocational or 2-year institution in United States. Designated institutions: Participating Missouri public community colleges or vocational/technical school or private 2-year vocational/technical schools.

Eligibility: Applicant must be U.S. citizen residing in Missouri.

Basis for selection: Applicant must demonstrate high academic achievement.

Application requirements: FAFSA, ACT scores.

Additional information: Applicant must attend A+ high school for three consecutive years immediately prior to graduation. Minimum 2.5 GPA. Must have 95 percent attendance overall for grades 9-12. Must perform at least 50 hours unpaid tutoring or mentoring. Not applicable to theology or divinity studies.

Contact:
Missouri Department of Higher Education
P.O. Box 1469
Jefferson City, MO 65102-1469
Phone: 800-473-6757, option 4
Fax: 573-751-6635
Web: www.dhe.mo.gov

Access Missouri Financial Assistance Program

Type of award: Scholarship, renewable.

Intended use: For full-time undergraduate study at vocational, 2-year or 4-year institution. Designated institutions: Approved Missouri institutions.

Eligibility: Applicant must be U.S. citizen or permanent resident residing in Missouri.

Basis for selection: Applicant must demonstrate financial need.

Application requirements: FAFSA.

Additional information: Must be used only toward first baccalaureate degree and may not be used towards theology or divinity studies. Eligibility based on Expected Family Contribution (EFC), with individuals with EFC of $12,000 or less eligible. Award amounts vary. No paper application. Students must apply for renewal each year.

    Amount of award: $300-$2,850

    Application deadline: April 1

    Total amount awarded: $59,226,259

Contact:
Missouri Department of Higher Education
P.O. Box 1469
Jefferson City, MO 65102-1469
Phone: 800-473-6757, option 4
Fax: 573-751-6635
Web: www.dhe.mo.gov

Advanced Placement Incentive Grant

Type of award: Scholarship.

Intended use: For full-time undergraduate study at vocational, 2-year or 4-year institution in United States. Designated institutions: Approved Missouri institutions.

Eligibility: Applicant must be U.S. citizen or permanent resident residing in Missouri.

Basis for selection: Applicant must demonstrate high academic achievement.

Application requirements: Advanced Placement scores.

Additional information: Must achieve two grades of three or higher on Advanced Placement exams in math or science while attending a Missouri public high school. Must receive an award under the Access Missouri Student Financial Assistance Program or A+ Scholarship program.

Amount of award:	$500
Application deadline:	June 1
Total amount awarded:	$29,500

Contact:
Missouri Department of Higher Education
P.O. Box 1469
Jefferson City, MO 65102-1469
Phone: 800-473-6757, option 4
Fax: 573-751-6635
Web: www.dhe.mo.gov

Marguerite Ross Barnett Memorial Scholarship

Type of award: Scholarship, renewable.
Intended use: For half-time undergraduate study at accredited vocational, 2-year or 4-year institution in United States. Designated institutions: Approved Missouri institutions.
Eligibility: Applicant must be at least 18. Applicant must be U.S. citizen or permanent resident residing in Missouri.
Basis for selection: Applicant must demonstrate financial need.
Application requirements: Proof of eligibility. FAFSA.
Additional information: May only be used for first baccalaureate degree. For students employed at least 20 hours per week while attending school part-time. Scholarship awarded on first-come, first-served basis. Maximum award is the lesser of the following: tuition charged at school of part-time enrollment or amount of tuition charged to Missouri undergraduate resident enrolled part-time in same class level at University of Missouri-Columbia. Employer must verify applicant's employment. Recipient may not be pursuing degree in theology or divinity.

Application deadline:	August 1
Total amount awarded:	$622,140

Contact:
Missouri Department of Higher Education
P.O. Box 1469
Jefferson City, MO 65102-1469
Phone: 800-473-6757, option 4
Fax: 573-751-6635
Web: www.dhe.mo.gov

Minority and Underrepresented Environmental Literacy Program

Type of award: Scholarship.
Intended use: For full-time undergraduate or master's study at accredited vocational, 2-year, 4-year or graduate institution in United States. Designated institutions: Missouri institutions with approved environmentally related programs.
Eligibility: Applicant must be Alaskan native, African American, Hispanic American, American Indian or Native Hawaiian/Pacific Islander. Applicant must be U.S. citizen or permanent resident residing in Missouri.
Basis for selection: Major/career interest in wildlife/fisheries; engineering, environmental; engineering, chemical; engineering, agricultural; biology; geology/earth sciences; natural resources/conservation; environmental science; engineering, mechanical or engineering, civil. Applicant must demonstrate high academic achievement.
Application requirements: Recommendations, essay, transcript. Resume, ACT/SAT scores.
Additional information: Minimum 3.0 GPA. Preference given to African-American, Hispanic, Native American, Alaska Native, Hawaiian and Pacific Islander applicants.

Amount of award:	$3,045
Application deadline:	June 1
Total amount awarded:	$27,982

Contact:
Missouri Department of Higher Education
P.O. Box 1469
Jefferson City, MO 65102-1469
Phone: 800-473-6757, option 4
Fax: 573-751-6635
Web: www.dhe.mo.gov

Minority Teaching Scholarship

Type of award: Scholarship, renewable.
Intended use: For full-time undergraduate or master's study at accredited vocational, 2-year or 4-year institution in United States. Designated institutions: Approved Missouri institutions with approved teacher education programs.
Eligibility: Applicant must be Asian American, African American, Hispanic American or American Indian. Applicant must be returning adult student. Applicant must be U.S. citizen or permanent resident residing in Missouri.
Basis for selection: Major/career interest in education. Applicant must demonstrate high academic achievement.
Application requirements: Recommendations, essay, transcript, proof of eligibility.
Additional information: Must rank in top 25 percent of class and score in top 25 percent on ACT or SAT. Minimum 24 ACT score and 1360 SAT score. If college graduate, may receive award if returning to a master's level math or science education program. Upon graduation, recipient must teach for five years in Missouri public schools or scholarship becomes loan. Applicant may be renewed for up to 4 years.

Amount of award:	$3,000
Number of awards:	100
Number of applicants:	20
Application deadline:	June 1
Total amount awarded:	$38,000

Contact:
Missouri Department of Higher Education
P.O. Box 1469
Jefferson City, MO 65102-1469
Phone: 800-473-6757, option 4
Fax: 573-751-6635
Web: www.dhe.mo.gov

Missouri Department of Higher Education Vietnam Veteran's Survivor Grant Program

Type of award: Scholarship, renewable.
Intended use: For full-time undergraduate study at accredited vocational, 2-year or 4-year institution in United States. Designated institutions: Approved Missouri institutions.
Eligibility: Applicant must be U.S. citizen or permanent resident. Applicant must be dependent of deceased veteran; or spouse of deceased veteran during Vietnam.
Application requirements: Proof of eligibility.
Additional information: May only be used for first baccalaureate degree. Veteran must have been resident of Missouri when entering service and at time of death. For children and spouses of Vietnam veterans whose death was attributed to or caused by exposure to toxic chemicals during Vietnam conflict. Applicant cannot pursue degree in theology or divinity. Applications accepted in January; end date based on fund availability. Amount of award varies. Maximum amount is the lesser of actual tuition charged for twelve credit

hours at school where applicant is enrolled, or the average amount of tuition charged for twelve credit hours to undergraduate Missouri resident enrolled full-time in same class level and academic major at regional four-year public Missouri institutions.

Number of awards:	12
Number of applicants:	3
Total amount awarded:	$15,053

Contact:
Missouri Department of Higher Education
P.O. Box 1469
Jefferson City, MO 65102-1469
Phone: 800-473-6757, option 4
Fax: 573-751-6635
Web: www.dhe.mo.gov

Missouri Higher Education Bright Flight Academic Scholarship

Type of award: Scholarship, renewable.
Intended use: For full-time undergraduate study at accredited vocational, 2-year or 4-year institution in United States. Designated institutions: Approved Missouri institutions.
Eligibility: Applicant must be U.S. citizen or permanent resident residing in Missouri.
Basis for selection: Applicant must demonstrate high academic achievement.
Application requirements: Proof of eligibility. SAT/ACT scores.
Additional information: May only be used for first baccalaureate degree. May not be used for theology or divinity studies. SAT/ACT composite scores must be in top three percent of state students. Must achieve qualifying scores by June assessment date of senior year. GED and home-schooled students may also qualify. Application deadline is June assessment date of senior year. No paper application needed. Check with high school counselor or financial aid administrator for additional information or see Website. Deadline in June.

Amount of award:	$1,000-$3,000
Total amount awarded:	$10,856,464

Contact:
Missouri Department of Higher Education
P.O. Box 1469
Jefferson City, MO 65102-1469
Phone: 800-473-6757, option 4
Fax: 573-751-6635
Web: www.dhe.mo.gov

Public Service Officer or Employee's Child Survivor Grant

Type of award: Scholarship, renewable.
Intended use: For full-time undergraduate study at accredited vocational, 2-year or 4-year institution in United States. Designated institutions: Approved Missouri public institutions.
Eligibility: Applicant must be U.S. citizen or permanent resident residing in Missouri.
Application requirements: Proof of eligibility.
Additional information: May only be used for first baccalaureate degree. For public safety officers who were permanently disabled in the line of duty or for children and spouses of Missouri public safety officers killed or permanently disabled in the line of duty. Children of Missouri Department of Highway and Transportation employees also eligible if parent died or was permanently disabled during performance of job. May not be used for theology or divinity studies. Award amounts vary; contact sponsor for information. Amount

awarded is the lesser of 12 credit tuition hours at chosen institution or 12 credit tuition hours at University of Missouri. Applications accepted in January; end date based on fund availability.

Total amount awarded:	$74,488

Contact:
Missouri Department of Higher Education
P.O. Box 1469
Jefferson City, MO 65102-1469
Phone: 800-473-6757, option 4
Fax: 573-751-6635
Web: www.dhe.mo.gov

Missouri League for Nursing

Missouri League for Nursing Scholarship

Type of award: Scholarship, renewable.
Intended use: For full-time sophomore, junior, senior or master's study at accredited postsecondary institution. Designated institutions: Eligible institutions in Missouri.
Eligibility: Applicant must be U.S. citizen residing in Missouri.
Basis for selection: Major/career interest in nursing. Applicant must demonstrate financial need and high academic achievement.
Application requirements: Recommendations.
Additional information: Minimum 3.0 GPA. Scholarship must be used for study in Missouri. Amount of award varies. Applications can be obtained from dean of nationally recognized accredited schools of nursing in Missouri.

Amount of award:	$2,000
Number of awards:	2
Number of applicants:	30

Contact:
Contact deans at accredited nursing schools in Missouri.
Phone: 573-635-5355
Fax: 573-635-7908
Web: www.mlnmonursing.org

Mobdro Download App

Scholarship For All Students

Type of award: Scholarship.
Intended use: For undergraduate study in United States or Canada.
Eligibility: Applicant must be at least 16, high school junior or senior.
Application requirements: Recommendations, essay. USA and Canadian citizens only. 300-500 word essay mentioning your personal achievement in a short and precise manner. Must show proof of age and residency. Must provide a letter from a professor.
Additional information: Must have a minimum 3.0 GPA. Must have enrolled, or is applying to be enrolled in a University or College.

Number of awards:	1
Application deadline:	July 31
Notification begins:	November 1
Total amount awarded:	$1,000

Contact:
Mobro Download App
2826 Rardin Drive
San Mateo, CA 94403
Web: http://mobdrodownloadapp.com/scholarship/

Moll Law Group

Moll Law Group College Scholarship Award

Type of award: Scholarship.
Intended use: For full-time undergraduate or graduate study at vocational, 2-year, 4-year or graduate institution.
Eligibility: Applicant must be U.S. citizen or permanent resident.
Application requirements: Submit an essay that provides a response to the selected topic found on the Application. You may find further information about the essay requirements, deadlines and complete application at http://www.molllawgroup.com/scholarship-contest.html.
Additional information: Maybe used for study abroad. Application, supporting documentation and essay must be received by 11:59 PM CT on March 31. For more information please visit website.

Amount of award:	$1,000-$1,000
Number of awards:	2
Number of applicants:	25
Application deadline:	March 31, September 30
Notification begins:	April 4, October 4

Contact:
Moll Law Group
401 North Michigan Avenue, 12th Floor
Chicago, IL 60611
Phone: 312-462-1700
Fax: 312-756-0045
Web: www.molllawgroup.com/scholarship-contest.html

Montana Trappers Association

MTA Doug Slifka Memorial Scholarship

Type of award: Scholarship.
Intended use: For undergraduate study at postsecondary institution.
Eligibility: Applicant must be at least 15, no older than 25.
Basis for selection: Major/career interest in environmental science; life sciences; natural resources/conservation or wildlife/fisheries. Applicant must demonstrate depth of character and seriousness of purpose.
Application requirements: Interview, transcript. Essay or story on trapping or conservation. Recommendations by MTA members, teachers, or other pertinent individuals. Endorsement of MTA District Director (or sub-director) where applicant

resides. Student involvement in activities that include MTA programs, trapping, school programs, and community service.
Additional information: Applicant must be member of MTA for at least one year or minor dependent of MTA member. Member must have been member of Association for one year prior to application. MTA members out of state and their families also eligible to apply. For application, complete request form on Website or contact local director, officer or committee member.

Amount of award:	$500
Number of awards:	2
Application deadline:	June 1
Total amount awarded:	$1,000

Contact:
Montana Trappers Association MTA Scholarship Committee
c/o Gary VanHaele
P.O. Box 264
Hysham, MT 59038
Phone: 406-342-5552
Web: www.montanatrappers.org/programs/scholarship.htm

Montana University System

Montana Governor's Best and Brightest Merit Scholarship

Type of award: Scholarship, renewable.
Intended use: For full-time undergraduate study at 2-year or 4-year institution. Designated institutions: Montana University system or tribal colleges.
Eligibility: Applicant must be residing in Montana.
Basis for selection: Applicant must demonstrate high academic achievement.
Application requirements: Transcript. SAT/ACT scores.
Additional information: Applications available on Website. Must have minimum 3.0 GPA or 20 ACT score or 1440 SAT score.

Amount of award:	$2,000
Application deadline:	March 15

Contact:
Governor's Best and Brightest Merit Scholarship
P.O. Box 203201
Helena, MT 59604-3101
Phone: 800-537-7508
Fax: 406-444-1469
Web: www.scholarship.mt.gov

Montana Governor's Best and Brightest Merit-at-Large Scholarship

Type of award: Scholarship, renewable.
Intended use: For full-time undergraduate study at 2-year or 4-year institution in United States. Designated institutions: Montana University System school or tribal college in Montana.
Eligibility: Applicant must be residing in Montana.
Basis for selection: Applicant must demonstrate high academic achievement.
Application requirements: Transcript. SAT/ACT score.
Additional information: Applications available on Website. Applicants must be Montana high school graduate. Must have minimum 3.0 GPA or 20 ACT score or 1440 SAT score.

Amount of award:	$2,000
Application deadline:	March 15

Contact:
Montana University System
P.O. Box 203201
Helena, MT 59604-3101
Phone: 800-537-7508
Fax: 406-444-1469
Web: www.scholarship.mt.gov

Montana Governor's Best and Brightest Need Based Scholarship

Type of award: Scholarship.
Intended use: For undergraduate study at 2-year institution in United States. Designated institutions: Montana University System schools or Montana tribal colleges.
Eligibility: Applicant must be residing in Montana.
Basis for selection: Applicant must demonstrate financial need.
Application requirements: FAFSA.
Additional information: Applications available through college financial aid office.

Amount of award:	$1,000
Application deadline:	March 15

Contact:
Montana University System
P.O. Box 203201
Helena, MT 59604-3101
Phone: 800-537-7508
Fax: 406-444-1469
Web: www.scholarship.mt.gov

Montana Higher Education Grant

Type of award: Scholarship.
Intended use: For undergraduate study at postsecondary institution. Designated institutions: Eligible Montana institutions.
Eligibility: Applicant must be residing in Montana.
Basis for selection: Applicant must demonstrate financial need.
Application requirements: FAFSA.

Amount of award:	$500-$600
Number of awards:	1,000
Total amount awarded:	$600,000

Contact:
Contact college financial aid office for application information.
Phone: 800-537-7508
Fax: 406-444-1469
Web: www.scholarship.mt.gov

Montana Honorably Discharged Veteran Fee Waiver

Type of award: Scholarship.
Intended use: For undergraduate or graduate study at postsecondary institution. Designated institutions: Montana University system institutions.
Eligibility: Applicant must be permanent resident residing in Montana. Applicant must be veteran.
Application requirements: Proof of eligibility.
Additional information: Must have been honorably discharged person who served with the United States forces during wartime. Must be pursuing his or her initial undergraduate degree. Must have used up all federal veterans educational assistance benefits. Contact college financial aid office.

Amount of award:	Full tuition

Contact:
Montana University System
P.O. Box 203201
Helena, MT 59620-3101
Phone: 800-537-7508
Fax: 406-444-1469
Web: www.scholarship.mt.gov

Montana University System Honor Scholarship

Type of award: Scholarship, renewable.
Intended use: For freshman study at 4-year institution. Designated institutions: Campuses in Montana University system, as well as Dawson, Flathead Valley, and Miles community colleges.
Eligibility: Applicant must be high school senior. Applicant must be U.S. citizen residing in Montana.
Basis for selection: Applicant must demonstrate high academic achievement.
Application requirements: Recommendations, transcript, proof of eligibility. College acceptance letter, SAT/ACT scores.
Additional information: Must be high school senior enrolled at accredited Montana high school for at least three years. Recipients ranked based on GPA and ACT or SAT score. Minimum 3.4 GPA. Must have met college preparatory requirements. Must submit completed application to high school guidance counselor. See Website for more details.

Amount of award:	Full tuition
Application deadline:	March 15

Contact:
Montana University System
P.O. Box 203201
Helena, MT 59620-3101
Phone: 800-537-7508
Fax: 406-444-1469
Web: www.scholarship.mt.gov

The Moody's Foundation

Moody's Mega Math M3 Challenge

Type of award: Scholarship.
Intended use: For junior or senior study at 2-year or 4-year institution.
Eligibility: Applicant must be high school junior or senior. Applicant must be residing in South Dakota, Ohio, Tennessee, Delaware, Kansas, Louisiana, Massachusetts, Connecticut, Mississippi, Nebraska, Kentucky, Iowa, Michigan, Minnesota, Florida, South Carolina, Indiana, New Jersey, North Dakota, Wisconsin, New York, Nevada, Virginia, Montana, Alabama, Illinois, Missouri, Vermont, Utah, Texas, Maine, Arkansas, Maryland, Pennsylvania, Arizona, Georgia, Wyoming, Oklahoma, District of Columbia, New Hampshire, West Virginia, New Mexico, North Carolina, Colorado or Rhode Island.
Basis for selection: Competition/talent/interest in academics, based on responses to the assigned modeling problem.
Application requirements: Must submit a viable solution paper by the deadline.
Additional information: Each school may enter up to two teams of three to five students. Team prizes range from $1,000 to $20,000. Visit Website for details and to register.

Amount of award:	$1,000-$20,000
Number of awards:	65
Number of applicants:	6,500
Application deadline:	February 20
Notification begins:	April 9
Total amount awarded:	$125,000

Contact:
Society for Industrial and Applied Mathematics
Attn: Frank Kunkle
3600 Market Street, 6th Floor
Philadelphia, PA 19104
Phone: 267-350-6388
Fax: 215-525-2756
Web: m3challenge.siam.org

Morgan Stanley

Morgan Stanley Richard B. Fisher Scholarship Program

Type of award: Scholarship.
Intended use: For sophomore or junior study at accredited 4-year institution.
Eligibility: Applicant must be African American, Mexican American, Hispanic American, Puerto Rican or American Indian.
Basis for selection: Major/career interest in finance/banking or technology. Applicant must demonstrate high academic achievement.
Application requirements: Interview.
Additional information: Program provides outstanding Black, Hispanic, Native American, and LGBT students with a financial award for exceptional academic achievement and a ten-week summer internship the summer prior to graduation. Must be currently enrolled as sophomore (for Institutional Securities, Investment Management, or Research Divisions) or junior (for the Finance, Operations, Technology, or Wealth Management Divisions). Applications due between December and February.
Contact:
Morgan Stanley
Web: www.morganstanley.com/about/careers/ischolarships_na.html

Moses & Rooth Attorneys at Law

Paralegal Scholarship

Type of award: Scholarship.
Intended use: For undergraduate or graduate study at vocational, 2-year, 4-year or graduate institution.
Eligibility: Applicant must be U.S. citizen.
Application requirements: In order to apply applicants will be required to write a short introduction (100-200 words) telling us who you are, why you are applying for the scholarship, your interests, or anything that makes you special and an essay (300-600) explaining if you think the criminal justice system adequately deals with America's War on Drugs.

Additional information: Minimum 3.0 GPA. MUST be a legal US resident. If you are a high school student, please provide an unofficial high school transcript. During the selection process you may be contacted to verify your academic status with an official transcript. You then must mail an official, unopened transcript to ultimately confirm previously sent academic status. Please do not initially send the official copies. Applicants must be pursuing a career in Paralegal Studies. Notification will be over the summer.

Amount of award:	$500
Number of awards:	1
Application deadline:	June 1
Total amount awarded:	$500

Contact:
Moses & Rooth Attorneys at Law
115 Granada Court
Orlando, FL 32803
Phone: 407-337-0150
Fax: 407-337-0160
Web: https://www.mosesandrooth.com/2016-paralegal-scholarship/

Motavis Learning

Aspiring Educator Scholarship Initiative

Type of award: Scholarship.
Intended use: For undergraduate or graduate study at accredited 4-year or graduate institution in United States or Canada.
Eligibility: Applicant must be at least 18.
Basis for selection: Major/career interest in education.
Application requirements: Transcript. Essay prompt: in no more than 800, and no fewer than 500 words, explain how you plan to change the world through education - more specifically, will you promote student success in the classroom and beyond, through community engagement, emerging instructional practices, and/or educational technology?
Additional information: Submissions must be sent as a PDF or Word document, and sent via e-mail.

Number of awards:	1
Application deadline:	February 28
Notification begins:	March 31
Total amount awarded:	$10,000

Contact:
Motavis Learning
25 Pelham Road
Suite 204
Salem, NH 03079
Web: https://motivislearning.com/aspiring-educator-scholarship/

Motivis Learning

Motivis Learning aspiring Educator Scholarship

Type of award: Scholarship.
Intended use: For full-time undergraduate or graduate study at accredited vocational, 2-year, 4-year or graduate institution.
Eligibility: Applicant must be at least 18.

Basis for selection: Major/career interest in education.
Application requirements: Essay, transcript. Applicants must be legal citizens/residents of US or Canada. Applicants must submit an essay (500-800 words) and a copy of unofficial transcript. Employees of Motivis Learning Systems (the Sponsor), suppliers of Sponsor as well as the immediate family (spouse, parents, siblings and children) and household members of employees of Sponsor are not eligible.
Additional information: More information on how to submit application and esay topic can be found on the scholarship website.

Amount of award:	$10,000
Number of awards:	1
Application deadline:	February 28
Notification begins:	March 31
Total amount awarded:	$10,000

Contact:
Motivis Learning
25 Pelham Road
Suite 204
Salem, NH 03079
Phone: 855-202-6500
Web: https://motivislearning.com/aspiring-educator-scholarship/

Mountain America Credit Union

Paul R. Ball Scholarship

Type of award: Scholarship.
Intended use: For undergraduate study at vocational, 2-year, 4-year or graduate institution in United States.
Eligibility: Applicant must be residing in Utah, New Mexico, Idaho, Arizona or Nevada.
Additional information: Available to any Mountain America Credit Union member, their child, or child for whom they serve as guardian, in all 5 states MACU does business(Utah, Arizona, Nevada, Idaho, New Mexico). Parent or guardian must be a MACU member if applicant is not.

Amount of award:	$2,000
Number of awards:	3
Application deadline:	April 21
Total amount awarded:	$6,000

Contact:
Web: https://www.macu.com/scholarships

Utah Public Employees Association Scholarship

Type of award: Scholarship.
Intended use: For undergraduate or graduate study at vocational, 2-year, 4-year or graduate institution.
Eligibility: Applicant must be residing in Utah.
Additional information: Must be a member of Mountain America Credit Union and the Utah Public Employees Association.

Amount of award:	$1,000
Number of awards:	3
Application deadline:	March 1
Total amount awarded:	$3,000

Contact:
Web: https://www.macu.com/scholarships

Movoto

Movoto Love Where You Live Scholarship Contest

Type of award: Scholarship.
Intended use: For full-time undergraduate or graduate study at vocational, 2-year, 4-year or graduate institution.
Basis for selection: Three winners will be selected based on two judging criteria, determined in the judges sole and absolute discretion, applied to the entered articles at the following weight: . How creative/original is it? . How much local in depth knowledge of your city does it exhibit? How much does it make us want to visit?
Application requirements: Must be currently enrolled at any high school, college, university, associates, JC, Vocational institution in the US for the Fall semester. Tell us, in 500 words or less, what you love about your neighborhood. If possible, include photos (selfie's welcome!).

Amount of award:	$1,000
Number of awards:	3
Application deadline:	December 31
Notification begins:	February 1, February 28
Total amount awarded:	$3,000

Contact:
Movoto
1900 S Norfolk Street
#310
San Mateo, CA 94403
Phone: 877-830-1538
Fax: 650-349-9900
Web: http://www.movoto.com/scholarship/2017/

MyBioSource

MyBioSource All Majors Scholarhip

Type of award: Scholarship.
Intended use: For undergraduate study at vocational, 2-year or 4-year institution.
Eligibility: Applicant must be high school senior.
Application requirements: Transcript. Complete the application along with your transcript and a 250 word response on why you have chosen to enter the field of science and why should receive the scholarship.
Additional information: Minimum 3.0. Must be enrolled as a freshman or undergraduate student at an accredited college or university for the fall semester. Must be majoring in a non-STEM field (STEM majors may apply for the MyBioSource STEM Scholarship).

Amount of award:	$1,000
Number of awards:	5
Application deadline:	May 31
Notification begins:	July 1
Total amount awarded:	$5,000

Contact:
MyBioSource
P.O. Box 153308
San Diego, CA 92195-3308
Phone: 1-858-633-0165 x135
Fax: 858-633-0166
Web: www.mybiosource.com/scholarship

MyBioSource STEM Scholarship

Type of award: Scholarship.

Intended use: For undergraduate study at accredited vocational, 2-year or 4-year institution.

Eligibility: Applicant must be high school senior.

Basis for selection: Major/career interest in biology; biochemistry; biomedical; chemistry or microbiology.

Application requirements: Transcript. Completed application, transcript, and 250 word response on why you have chosen to enter the field of science and why you should receive the scholarship.

Additional information: Must have at least a 3.0 GPA. Application can be found online.

Amount of award:	$1,000
Number of awards:	5
Application deadline:	May 31
Notification begins:	July 1
Total amount awarded:	$5,000

Contact:
MyBioSource
P.O. Box 153308
San Diego, CA 92195-3308
Phone: 858-633-0165 ex. 135
Fax: 1-858-633-0166
Web: www.mybiosource.com/scholarship

MyGolfInstructor.com

Get Girls Golfing Scholarship

Type of award: Scholarship.

Intended use: For full-time freshman study at 2-year or 4-year institution.

Eligibility: Applicant must be female, high school senior.

Basis for selection: The scholarship will be awarded based on a combination of golf accomplishments, personal achievement, and overall need.

Application requirements: Must have played High School Golf. Must intend to play on a college golf team.

Additional information: The Get Girls Golfing Scholarship will be granted annually to one female high school senior that plays golf competitively in high school and intends to play golf as a freshman at a 2 or 4 year college.

Amount of award:	$1,500
Number of awards:	1
Application deadline:	May 15
Notification begins:	June 15
Total amount awarded:	$1,500

Contact:
MyGolfInstructor.com
P.O. Box 616
Grover, MO 63040
Phone: 314-440-9082
Web: www.mygolfinstructor.com/scholarship/

NAACP Legal Defense and Education Fund, Inc.

Herbert Lehman Education Fund

Type of award: Scholarship, renewable.

Intended use: For full-time freshman study at accredited 4-year institution in United States.

Eligibility: Applicant must be African American. Applicant must be high school senior. Applicant must be U.S. citizen.

Basis for selection: Applicant must demonstrate financial need, high academic achievement and service orientation.

Application requirements: Essay, transcript. Standardized test scores. Two recommendation letters in signed and sealed envelopes. Copy of acceptance letter to college you will attend.

Additional information: Awards are $20,000 per year for four years (as long as scholars remain in good academic standing). Decisions are made by the end of August. Apply online. See Website for additional information.

Amount of award:	$8,000
Application deadline:	May 1

Contact:
The Herbert Lehman Fund
NAACP Legal Defense and Educational Fund, Inc
40 Rector Street
5th Floor, NY 10006
Phone: 212-965-2200
Fax: 212-219-1595
Web: www.naacpldf.org/herbert-lehman-education-fund-scholarship

Naqvi Injury Law

Naqvi Injury Law Scholarship

Type of award: Scholarship.

Intended use: For senior study at 2-year or 4-year institution.

Eligibility: Applicant must be residing in Nevada.

Basis for selection: Major/career interest in law. Applicant must demonstrate financial need.

Application requirements: Transcript. Student Aid Report and official transcript.

Additional information: Applicants must be a high school senior or high school graduate in the state of Nevada. Must be seeking a law-oriented degree at any university. A student aid report and official transcript must be attached to all applications.

Number of awards:	1
Application deadline:	March 31
Total amount awarded:	$2,000

Contact:
Naqvi Injury Law
9500 W Flamingo Rd.
#104
Las Vegas, NV 89147
Web: www.naqvilaw.com/scholarship-application/

NASA Alabama Space Grant Consortium

NASA Space Grant Undergraduate Scholarship

Type of award: Scholarship, renewable.
Intended use: For full-time junior or senior study at accredited 4-year institution. Designated institutions: Alabama Space Grant member universities: University of Alabama Huntsville, Alabama A&M, University of Alabama, University of Alabama Birmingham, University of South Alabama, Auburn University, Tuskegee University.
Eligibility: Applicant must be U.S. citizen residing in Alabama.
Basis for selection: Major/career interest in aerospace; engineering or science, general. Applicant must demonstrate high academic achievement.
Application requirements: Recommendations, essay, transcript, nomination by faculty advisor at Alabama Space Grant Consortium member institution. Resume.
Additional information: Applicants must have minimum 3.0 GPA and attend Alabama University. Must be in final term of sophomore year or later when applying. The Consortium actively encourages women, minority, and physically challenged students to apply, but others not excluded.

Amount of award:	$1,000
Number of awards:	52
Number of applicants:	74
Application deadline:	March 1
Notification begins:	May 15
Total amount awarded:	$265,500

Contact:
NASA Alabama Space Grant Consortium
University of Alabama in Huntsville
301 Sparkman Dr. Materials Science Bldg, 205
Huntsville, AL 35899
Phone: 256-824-6800
Fax: 256-824-6061
Web: www.uah.edu/ASGC

NASA Connecticut Space Grant Consortium

NASA Connecticut Space Grant Undergraduate Fellowship

Type of award: Research grant, renewable.
Intended use: For full-time undergraduate study at accredited 4-year institution in United States. Designated institutions: Connecticut Space Grant Consortium member institutions.
Eligibility: Applicant must be U.S. citizen.
Basis for selection: Major/career interest in aerospace; engineering or science, general. Applicant must demonstrate high academic achievement.
Application requirements: Recommendations, transcript, proof of eligibility, research proposal. Resume.
Additional information: Minimum 3.0 GPA. Consortium actively encourages women, minority, and disabled students to apply. Award amount varies; maximum is $5,000.

Amount of award:	$5,000
Number of awards:	2
Number of applicants:	20
Application deadline:	October 31
Total amount awarded:	$58,500

Contact:
NASA Connecticut Space Grant Consortium
University of Hartford
200 Bloomfield Ave.
West Hartford, CT 06117
Phone: 860-768-4813
Fax: 860-768-5073
Web: www.ctspacegrant.org

NASA Delaware Space Grant Consortium

Delaware Space Grant Undergraduate Tuition Scholarship

Type of award: Scholarship, renewable.
Intended use: For full-time sophomore, junior or senior study at postsecondary institution. Designated institutions: University of Delaware, Delaware Technical and Community College, Swarthmore College, Delaware State University at Dover, Villanova University, Wesley College, Wilmington University.
Eligibility: Applicant must be U.S. citizen.
Basis for selection: Major/career interest in aerospace; astronomy; mathematics; engineering; geography; geology/earth sciences; geophysics; physics; oceanography/marine studies or technology.
Application requirements: Recommendations, transcript, nomination by department chair, DESGC Consortium Representative, or advisor. Applicant statement; letter from Department Chairperson.
Additional information: Must have proven interest in space-related studies. Recipient must currently attend Delaware Space Grant Consortium member institution. Award amounts vary and are available pending funding. May be used at designated institutions only. Contact Consortium office for deadlines and additional information.

Amount of award:	$3,000
Number of awards:	9
Number of applicants:	15
Total amount awarded:	$25,000

Contact:
Delaware Space Grant Consortium Program Office
University of Delaware
212 Sharp Lab
Newark, DE 19716
Phone: 302-831-1094
Fax: 302-831-1843
Web: www.delspace.org

NASA Georgia Space Grant Consortium

NASA Space Grant Georgia Fellowship Program

Type of award: Scholarship, renewable.
Intended use: For full-time junior, senior, master's or doctoral study at accredited postsecondary institution in United States.

Designated institutions: Albany State University, Clark Atlanta University, Columbus State University, Fort Valley State University, Georgia Institute of Technology, Georgia State University, Kennesaw State University, Mercer University, Morehouse College, Spelman College, State University of West Georgia, University of Georgia.
Eligibility: Applicant must be U.S. citizen residing in Georgia.
Basis for selection: Major/career interest in engineering; science, general; aerospace; physics; atmospheric sciences/meteorology; computer/information sciences; education or chemistry. Applicant must demonstrate seriousness of purpose and service orientation.
Application requirements: Interview, recommendations, essay, transcript.
Additional information: Funding available for students in all areas of engineering and science, and many areas of social science.
Contact:
Georgia Space Grant Consortium
Attn: Wanda G. Pierson
Aerospace Engineering
Atlanta, GA 30332-0150
Phone: 404-894-0521
Fax: 404-894-2760
Web: www.gasgc.org

NASA Hawaii Space Grant Consortium

NASA Space Grant Hawaii Undergraduate Fellowship Program

Type of award: Scholarship.
Intended use: For full-time undergraduate study at accredited postsecondary institution in United States. Designated institutions: Consortium member schools: University of Hawaii at Manoa, Hilo, and Maui, community colleges in Hawaii.
Eligibility: Applicant must be U.S. citizen.
Basis for selection: Major/career interest in astronomy; geology/earth sciences; oceanography/marine studies; physics; zoology; engineering or geography.
Application requirements: Recommendations, transcript. Abstract, research proposal, budget, resume. Three copies of all application materials.
Additional information: Must be resident of Hawaii or attend school at one of the designated institutions. Must be sponsored by a faculty member willing to act as the student's mentor during the award period. Field of study must be relevant to NASA's goals, e.g. areas of math, science, engineering, computer science (concerned with utilizing or exploring space), and air transportation. Full-time undergraduates at Manoa, Hilo with major declared can apply for two-semester fellowships. Stipend up to $4,000 per semester. Fellows may be eligible for up to $500 for supplies or travel. Recipients expected to work 10-15 hours per week on space-related projects. Women, under-represented minorities (specifically Native Hawaiians, other Pacific Islanders, Native Americans, Blacks, Hispanics), and physically challenged students who have interest in space-related fields are encouraged to apply. Visit Website for more information and application.

Amount of award:	$2,000-$4,000
Number of applicants:	20
Application deadline:	June 15, December 1

Contact:
NASA Hawaii Space Grant Consortium
Phone: 808-956-3138
Fax: 808-956-6322
Web: www.spacegrant.hawaii.edu

NASA Idaho Space Grant Consortium

NASA Idaho Space Grant Undergraduate Scholarship

Type of award: Scholarship, renewable.
Intended use: For full-time undergraduate study at accredited 2-year or 4-year institution. Designated institutions: College of Idaho, Boise State University, College of Southern Idaho, Idaho State University, Lewis Clark State College, North Idaho College, Northwest Nazarene University, BYU-Idaho, and the University of Idaho.
Eligibility: Applicant must be U.S. citizen.
Basis for selection: Major/career interest in engineering; mathematics or science, general. Applicant must demonstrate high academic achievement.
Application requirements: Recommendations, essay. High school or college transcripts, SAT/ACT scores.
Additional information: Award is approximately $2000 per year with a chance to renew for a second year. Applicants must attend Idaho Space Grant Consortium member institution in Idaho and maintain a 3.0 GPA. Women, minority students, and disabled students encouraged to apply. Application includes several very short essays; please see the application for word limits. Applications available on Website.

Amount of award:	$2,000
Number of awards:	25
Number of applicants:	100
Application deadline:	March 21
Notification begins:	June 30

Contact:
NASA Idaho Space Grant Consortium
University of Idaho
875 Perimeter Drive, Mail Stop 1026
Moscow, ID 83844-1026
Phone: 208-885-6438
Fax: 208-885-1399
Web: www.idahospacegrant.org/#!scholarships/kws74

NASA Illinois Space Grant Consortium

NASA Space Grant Illinois Undergraduate Scholarship

Type of award: Scholarship, renewable.
Intended use: For full-time undergraduate study at postsecondary institution. Designated institutions: Illinois Space Grant Consortium member institutions.
Eligibility: Applicant must be U.S. citizen.

Scholarships

443

Basis for selection: Major/career interest in engineering; aerospace; astronomy or science, general. Applicant must demonstrate high academic achievement.

Application requirements: Recommendations, essay, transcript.

Additional information: Minimum 2.5 GPA. Contact sponsor for deadline information.

Amount of award:	$3,000
Number of applicants:	62
Total amount awarded:	$95,000

Contact:
Associate Director/Illinois Space Grant Consortium
U of Illinois-Urbana, 306 Talbot Lab
104 S. Wright Street
Urbana, IL 61801-2935
Phone: 217-244-8048
Fax: 217-244-0720
Web: isgc.aerospace.illinois.edu

NASA Kentucky Space Grant Consortium

NASA Space Grant Kentucky Undergraduate Scholarship

Type of award: Scholarship, renewable.

Intended use: For full-time undergraduate study at accredited 4-year institution in United States. Designated institutions: Consortium member institutions.

Eligibility: Applicant must be U.S. citizen.

Basis for selection: Major/career interest in aerospace; astronomy; education; engineering or physics. Applicant must demonstrate high academic achievement.

Application requirements: Interview, recommendations, essay, transcript, nomination by professor/mentor at participating institution. Research proposal, written with mentor.

Additional information: Stipend for materials and travel up to $1500. Preference given to schools that waive tuition for recipient. Consortium actively encourages women, minority students, and physically challenged students to apply. Applicants doing work related to space exploration may qualify for funding, whatever their field of study may be.

Amount of award:	$6,000
Number of applicants:	10

Contact:
NASA/Kentucky Space Grant Consortium
University of Kentucky- Coll. Of Eng.
112 Robotics Building
Lexington, KY 40506-0108
Phone: 859-218-6272
Fax: 859-257-3304
Web: nasa.engr.uky.edu

NASA Maine Space Grant Consortium

NASA Space Grant Maine Consortium Annual Scholarship and Fellowship Program

Type of award: Research grant, renewable.

Intended use: For full-time undergraduate or graduate study at accredited 4-year or graduate institution. Designated institutions: University of Maine (Orono), University of Maine (Presque Isle), University of Southern Maine, University of New England, Maine Maritime Academy, College of the Atlantic, Bowdoin College, Colby College, Bates College, Saint Joseph's College.

Eligibility: Applicant must be U.S. citizen.

Basis for selection: Major/career interest in astronomy; geology/earth sciences; geophysics; engineering; aerospace; biology or medicine.

Additional information: Applicants from out of state who attend one of the designated institutions are eligible. Research project must be in an aerospace-related field. Applications from academic institutions in Maine other than those designated will be reviewed for consideration. Visit Website for additional details.

Contact:
Maine Space Grant Consortium
87 Winthrop Street
Suite 200
Augusta, ME 04330
Phone: 877-397-7223
Fax: 207-622-4548
Web: www.msgc.org

NASA Michigan Space Grant Consortium

MSGC Undergraduate Underrepresented Minority Fellowship Program

Type of award: Research grant.

Intended use: For full-time undergraduate study at 4-year institution in United States. Designated institutions: Michigan Space Grant Consortium member institutions.

Eligibility: Applicant must be African American, Hispanic American, American Indian or Native Hawaiian/Pacific Islander. Applicant must be U.S. citizen residing in Michigan.

Basis for selection: Major/career interest in aerospace; engineering; science, general or mathematics. Applicant must demonstrate high academic achievement.

Application requirements: Recommendations, essay, transcript, research proposal. Description of project expectations and specifications; 150-word abstract.

Additional information: Offers support in form of undergraduate research and public service fellowships to students in aerospace, space science, Earth system science and other related science, engineering, or math fields. Students working on educational research topics in math, science, or technology also eligible to apply. Preference given to projects directly related to aerospace, space science, earth system science, and directly related educational efforts. Students required to identify a mentor with whom they intend to work. Underrepresented minority students who have a GPA below 3.0, but have strong mentorship, do qualify for an award. Visit Website for more information.

Amount of award:	$2,500
Application deadline:	November 20
Notification begins:	February 28
Total amount awarded:	$14,000

Contact:
NASA Michigan Space Grant Consortium
University of Michigan
1320 Beal Ave. - 1049 FXB
Ann Arbor, MI 48109-2140
Phone: 734-764-9508
Fax: 734-763-6904
Web: www.mi.spacegrant.org

NASA Space Grant Michigan Undergraduate Fellowship

Type of award: Research grant, renewable.
Intended use: For undergraduate study at accredited 4-year institution. Designated institutions: Michigan Space Grant Consortium member institutions.
Eligibility: Applicant must be U.S. citizen.
Basis for selection: Major/career interest in aerospace; engineering; science, general or mathematics. Applicant must demonstrate high academic achievement.
Application requirements: Essay, transcript. Two letters of recommendation; description of project expectations and specifications; 150-word abstract.
Additional information: Offers support in form of undergraduate research and public service fellowships to students in aerospace, space science, Earth system science and other related science, engineering, or math fields. Students working on educational research topics in math, science, or technology also eligible to apply. Preference given to projects directly related to aerospace, space science, Earth system science, and directly related educational efforts. Announcements for next funding interval can be found on Website.

Amount of award:	$2,500-$5,000
Application deadline:	November 20
Notification begins:	February 28
Total amount awarded:	$100,000

Contact:
NASA Space Grant Michigan Space Grant Consortium
University of Michigan
1320 Beal Ave. - 1049 FXB
Ann Arbor, MI 48109-2140
Phone: 734-764-9508
Fax: 734-763-6904
Web: www.mi.spacegrant.org

NASA Minnesota Space Grant Consortium

NASA Minnesota Space Grant Consortium Undergraduate Scholarship

Type of award: Scholarship, renewable.
Intended use: For full-time undergraduate study at accredited 2-year or 4-year institution in United States. Designated institutions: Augsburg College, Bethel University, Bemidji State University, Carleton College, Concordia College, Fond du Lac Tribal and Community College, Leech Lake Tribal College, Macalester College, Southwest Minnesota State University, St. Catherine University, University of Minnesota - Duluth, University of Minnesota - Twin Cities, University of St. Thomas.

Eligibility: Applicant must be U.S. citizen.
Basis for selection: Major/career interest in aerospace; astronomy; atmospheric sciences/meteorology; mathematics; engineering; chemistry; physics or geology/earth sciences. Applicant must demonstrate high academic achievement.
Application requirements: Recommendations, essay, transcript. Letter of intent.
Additional information: Minimum 3.0 GPA. Women, minority, and physically challenged students encouraged to apply. Applicant must be attending a Minnesota Space Grant Consortium school but does not have to be a resident of the state. Must major in aerospace, astronomy, physics, geology, chemistry, mathematics, computer science, or engineering. Students should contact Space Grant representative at their school. Application deadlines vary by school.
Contact:
NASA Minnesota Space Grant Consortium
U of M: Dept of Aerospace Engineering
107 Akerman Hall, 110 Union St. SE
Minneapolis, MN 55455
Phone: 612-626-9295
Web: www.aem.umn.edu/mnsgc

NASA Missouri Space Grant Consortium

NASA Missouri State Space Grant Undergraduate Scholarship

Type of award: Scholarship, renewable.
Intended use: For full-time undergraduate study at accredited 4-year institution in United States. Designated institutions: Participaing Missouri space grant member institutions.
Eligibility: Applicant must be U.S. citizen residing in Missouri.
Basis for selection: Major/career interest in aerospace; astronomy; engineering; geology/earth sciences; physics; mathematics or engineering, mechanical.
Application requirements: Recommendations, essay, transcript.
Additional information: Program encourages applications from eligible space science students. Awardees must attend Missouri Space Grant Consortium affiliate institution. Women, minority students, and physically challenged students are actively encouraged to apply. Deadline varies but is usually the first week in April. Check sponsor for exact date. Awards normally granted sometime in May.
Contact:
NASA Missouri Space Grant Consortium
Missouri University of Science and Technology
137 Toomey Hall
Rolla, MO 65409-0050
Phone: 573-341-4887
Fax: 573-341-4607
Web: www.mst.edu/~spaceg

NASA Montana Space Grant Consortium

NASA Space Grant Montana Undergraduate Scholarship Program

Type of award: Scholarship, renewable.
Intended use: For full-time undergraduate study at accredited 2-year or 4-year institution in United States. Designated

institutions: Montana Space Grant Consortium member institutions.

Eligibility: Applicant must be U.S. citizen.

Basis for selection: Major/career interest in aerospace; biology; chemistry; geology/earth sciences; physics; astronomy; computer/information sciences; engineering, chemical; engineering, civil or engineering, electrical/electronic. Applicant must demonstrate depth of character and leadership.

Application requirements: Recommendations, essay, transcript.

Additional information: Must attend Montana Space Grant Consortium member institution, but does not need to be Montana resident. Awards for one year, renewable on a competitive basis. Recipients must agree to provide MSGC with information about studies and employment beyond period of award. Visit Website for online application form.

Amount of award:	$1,500
Number of awards:	36
Number of applicants:	45
Application deadline:	April 1
Total amount awarded:	$28,500

Contact:
NASA Space Grant Montana Space Grant Consortium
Montana State University
416 Cobleigh Hall, P.O. Box 173835
Bozeman, MT 59717-3835
Phone: 406-994-4223
Fax: 406-994-4452
Web: www.spacegrant.montana.edu

NASA New Mexico Space Grant Consortium

NASA Space Grant New Mexico Undergraduate Scholarship

Type of award: Research grant, renewable.

Intended use: For full-time sophomore, junior, senior or graduate study at accredited 4-year institution in United States. Designated institutions: New Mexico Space Grant Consortium institutions.

Eligibility: Applicant must be U.S. citizen.

Basis for selection: Major/career interest in astronomy; biology; chemistry; computer/information sciences; engineering, chemical; engineering, civil; engineering, electrical/electronic; engineering, mechanical; physics or mathematics. Applicant must demonstrate high academic achievement.

Application requirements: Transcript, research proposal, nomination by faculty mentor.

Additional information: Minimum 3.0 GPA. Geology, earth science, environmental science, agriculture, range science, and fishery and wildlife science majors also eligible. Preference given to applicants who can show nonfederal matching funds. Women, minority students, and physically challenged students encouraged to apply. Visit Website for application and more information.

Amount of award:	$5,000
Application deadline:	April 15
Notification begins:	April 15

Contact:
NASA New Mexico Space Grant Consortium
Box 30001 MSC SG
Las Cruces, NM 88003
Phone: 575-646-6414
Fax: 575-646-7791
Web: www.nmspacegrant.com

NASA North Carolina Space Grant Consortium

NASA North Carolina Space Grant Consortium Undergraduate Research Scholarship

Type of award: Scholarship.

Intended use: For full-time undergraduate study at postsecondary institution. Designated institutions: North Carolina Space Grant Consortium member institutions.

Eligibility: Applicant must be returning adult student. Applicant must be U.S. citizen.

Basis for selection: Major/career interest in science, general; engineering; aerospace; mathematics or technology. Applicant must demonstrate high academic achievement and leadership.

Application requirements: Recommendations, transcript, research proposal.

Additional information: Minimum 3.0 GPA. Visit Website for more information and application.

Amount of award:	$4,000-$5,000
Number of awards:	25
Number of applicants:	40
Application deadline:	February 1
Notification begins:	April 15
Total amount awarded:	$50,000

Contact:
NASA North Carolina Space Grant
NCSU Box 7515
Raleigh, NC 27695-7515
Phone: 919-515-4240
Fax: 919-515-5934
Web: www.ncspacegrant.org

NASA North Carolina Space Grant Consortium Undergraduate Scholarship Program

Type of award: Scholarship, renewable.

Intended use: For full-time freshman or sophomore study at 4-year institution. Designated institutions: North Carolina Space Grant Consortium Member Institutions.

Eligibility: Applicant must be U.S. citizen.

Basis for selection: Major/career interest in science, general; engineering; aerospace; technology or mathematics. Applicant must demonstrate high academic achievement and leadership.

Application requirements: Recommendations, essay, transcript.

Additional information: Minimum 3.0 GPA. May be new or returning adult student. Visit Website for application and more information.

Amount of award:	$1,000
Application deadline:	February 15
Notification begins:	April 15

Contact:
NASA North Carolina Space Grant
NCSU Box 7515
Raleigh, NC 27695-7515
Phone: 919-515-4240
Fax: 919-515-5934
Web: www.ncspacegrant.org

NASA North Dakota Space Grant Consortium

NASA Space Grant North Dakota Consortium Lillian Goettler Scholarship

Type of award: Scholarship.
Intended use: For full-time undergraduate study at accredited postsecondary institution in United States. Designated institutions: North Dakota State University.
Eligibility: Applicant must be female. Applicant must be U.S. citizen.
Basis for selection: Major/career interest in engineering; mathematics; science, general; biology; chemistry; geology/earth sciences; computer/information sciences; information systems; astronomy or physics. Applicant must demonstrate high academic achievement.
Additional information: Applicant must be female. Must have minimum 3.5 GPA and ideally be involved in research project of interest to NASA. Must be enrolled on campus at NDSGC institution; long distance learning programs not eligible. Deadline in mid-February.

Amount of award:	$2,500

Contact:
North Dakota Space Grant Consortium
U of North Dakota, Space Studies Dept.
P.O. Box 9008
Grand Forks, ND 58202-9008
Phone: 701-777-4161
Web: ndspacegrant.und.edu

NASA Space Grant North Dakota Undergraduate Scholarship

Type of award: Scholarship, renewable.
Intended use: For full-time undergraduate study at 2-year or 4-year institution. Designated institutions: Tribal or public NDSGC member institutions.
Eligibility: Applicant must be U.S. citizen.
Basis for selection: Major/career interest in biology; chemistry; engineering; geology/earth sciences; computer/information sciences; mathematics; astronomy or physics. Applicant must demonstrate high academic achievement.
Application requirements: Recommendations, transcript, nomination by participating North Dakota Space Grant Consortium member institution.
Additional information: Minimum 3.0 GPA. Must be enrolled on campus at NDSGC institution; long distance learning programs not eligible. Consortium actively encourages women, minority students, and physically challenged students to apply. Deadlines vary. Contact financial aid office at institutions directly.

Amount of award:	$500-$2,500

Contact:
Financial Aid Office at eligible institutions.
Web: ndspacegrant.und.edu

Pearl I. Young Scholarship

Type of award: Scholarship.
Intended use: For full-time undergraduate or graduate study at accredited postsecondary institution in United States. Designated institutions: University of North Dakota.
Eligibility: Applicant must be female. Applicant must be U.S. citizen or permanent resident.
Basis for selection: Major/career interest in biology; chemistry; engineering; geology/earth sciences; computer/information sciences; mathematics; astronomy or physics. Applicant must demonstrate high academic achievement.
Additional information: Applicants must have minimum 3.5 GPA and ideally be involved in research project of interest to NASA. Deadline in mid-February. Applicants must be female.

Amount of award:	$2,500
Number of awards:	1
Application deadline:	March 1

Contact:
NASA Space Grant North Dakota Space Grant Consortium
U of North Dakota, Space Studies Dept.
P.O. Box 9008
Grand Forks, ND 58202-9008
Phone: 701-777-4161
Web: ndspacegrant.und.edu

NASA Ohio Space Grant Consortium

NASA Ohio Space Grant Senior Scholarship Program

Type of award: Scholarship, renewable.
Intended use: For full-time senior study at accredited 4-year institution. Designated institutions: Ohio Space Grant Consortium members.
Eligibility: Applicant must be U.S. citizen.
Basis for selection: Major/career interest in science, general; engineering; aerospace or mathematics.
Application requirements: Recommendations, essay, transcript. Proposal of research project.
Additional information: Applications available at OSGC office at Consortium member institutions. Awardees required to participate in research projects and present results at annual OSGC Research Symposium.

Amount of award:	$4,000
Number of awards:	60
Number of applicants:	75
Application deadline:	March 1
Notification begins:	April 30
Total amount awarded:	$130,000

Contact:
OSGC campus representative.
Phone: 800-828-6742
Web: www.osgc.org/scholarship.html

Scholarships

447

NASA Oregon Space Grant Consortium

NASA Oregon Space Grant Undergraduate Scholarship

Type of award: Scholarship.

Intended use: For undergraduate or graduate study at accredited 2-year or 4-year institution in United States. Designated institutions: Oregon State University, University of Oregon, Portland State University, Eastern Oregon University, Southern Oregon University, Oregon Institute of Technology, Western Oregon University, George Fox University, Portland Community Colleges (Sylvania, Rock Creek and Cascades Campuses), Lane Community College, Pacific University, Linn Benton Community College, University of Portland.

Eligibility: Applicant must be U.S. citizen.

Basis for selection: Major/career interest in science, general; engineering; aerospace; mathematics; physical sciences; education or technology. Applicant must demonstrate high academic achievement.

Application requirements: Recommendations, essay, transcript.

Additional information: Contact Space Grant Consortium representative on campus or see Website for application deadlines and more information.

Contact:
Oregon NASA Space Grant Consortium
Oregon State University
92 Kerr Administration Bldg.
Corvallis, OR 97331-2103
Phone: 541-737-2414
Fax: 541-737-9946
Web: spacegrant.oregonstate.edu/scholarships

NASA Pennsylvania Space Grant Consortium

NASA Pennsylvania Space Grant Undergraduate Scholarship

Type of award: Scholarship.

Intended use: For full-time junior or senior study at accredited 4-year institution in United States. Designated institutions: Pennsylvania universities and colleges.

Eligibility: Applicant must be U.S. citizen.

Basis for selection: Major/career interest in science, general; mathematics; engineering; education; aerospace or astronomy. Applicant must demonstrate high academic achievement.

Application requirements: Recommendations, essay, transcript, research proposal. Resume, SAT scores, description of research project and plan of study.

Additional information: Contact campus Space Grant Consortium representative for details. Consortium actively encourages women, minority, and physically challenged students to apply.

Amount of award:	$4,000
Number of awards:	4
Number of applicants:	12
Application deadline:	April 1
Total amount awarded:	$16,000

Contact:
NASA Pennsylvania Space Grant Consortium
Penn State, University Park
2217 Earth-Engineering Sciences Building
University Park, PA 16802
Phone: 814-865-2535
Fax: 814-863-9563
Web: www.pa.spacegrant.org

NASA Rhode Island Space Grant Consortium

NASA Rhode Island Space Grant Summer Undergraduate Scholarship

Type of award: Scholarship, renewable.

Intended use: For sophomore, junior or senior study at postsecondary institution. Designated institutions: Rhode Island Space Grant Consortium member institutions: Brown University, Bryant University, Community College of Rhode Island, Providence College, Roger Williams University, Rhode Island College, Rhode Island School of Design, Salve Regina University, University of Rhode Island, Wheaton College.

Eligibility: Applicant must be U.S. citizen.

Basis for selection: Major/career interest in aerospace; biology; engineering; geology/earth sciences or physics. Applicant must demonstrate high academic achievement.

Application requirements: Interview, recommendations, essay, transcript. Research proposal, resume.

Additional information: Awardees expected to devote four hours per week to science education outreach. Application deadline in late February; call sponsor for exact dates. Number of awards may vary. Topics of study in space sciences also funded. Students should contact their campus representative or the Rhode Island Space Grant office.

Amount of award:	$3,000
Number of awards:	3
Number of applicants:	5
Application deadline:	February 8

Contact:
NASA Rhode Island Space Grant Consortium
Brown University
Box 1846
Providence, RI 02912
Phone: 401-863-1151
Fax: 401-863-3978
Web: www.brown.edu/initiatives/ri-space-grant

NASA Space Grant Rhode Island Undergraduate Research Scholarship

Type of award: Scholarship.

Intended use: For sophomore, junior or senior study at postsecondary institution. Designated institutions: Rhode Island Space Grant Consortium member institutions.

Eligibility: Applicant must be U.S. citizen.

Scholarships

Basis for selection: Major/career interest in aerospace; biology; engineering; geology/earth sciences or physics. Applicant must demonstrate high academic achievement.

Application requirements: Interview, recommendations, essay, transcript. Research proposal, resume.

Additional information: Awardees expected to work full-time with 75 percent of time devoted to research and the other 25 percent to science education outreach. Applications due in February; call sponsor for exact dates. Number of awards may vary. Topics of study in space sciences also funded. Students should contact campus representative or the Rhode Island Space Grant office.

Contact:
NASA Rhode Island Space Grant Consortium
Brown University
Box 1846
Providence, RI 02912
Phone: 401-863-1151
Fax: 401-863-3978
Web: www.brown.edu/initiatives/ri-space-grant

NASA South Carolina Space Grant Consortium

NASA Space Grant South Carolina Undergraduate Student Research Fellowship

Type of award: Research grant, renewable.

Intended use: For full-time sophomore, junior or senior study at accredited 4-year institution in United States. Designated institutions: SCSGC member institutions.

Eligibility: Applicant must be U.S. citizen.

Basis for selection: Major/career interest in aerospace; astronomy; atmospheric sciences/meteorology; engineering; environmental science; geophysics; mathematics or science, general. Applicant must demonstrate high academic achievement.

Application requirements: Recommendations, essay, transcript, research proposal. Faculty sponsorship. Resume.

Additional information: Applicants must attend South Carolina Space Grant Consortium member institution. Applicants must have sponsorship from a faculty advisor. Applicants may have a field of study or interest related to any NASA enterprise. Presentation and written report on project findings due within one year of completion. Consortium actively encourages women, minority, and disabled students to apply. See Website for application and more information.

Amount of award:	$5,000

Contact:
NASA South Carolina Space Grant Consortium, Tara B. Scozzaro, MPA
College of Charleston
66 George Street
Charleston, SC 29424
Phone: 843-953-5463
Fax: 843-953-3411
Web: www.cofc.edu/~scsgrant/scholar/undergraduate.html

NASA Texas Space Grant Consortium

STEM Columbia Crew Memorial Scholarship

Type of award: Scholarship.

Intended use: For sophomore, junior or senior study at 2-year or 4-year institution in United States. Designated institutions: Texas Space Grant Consortium member institutions.

Eligibility: Applicant must be U.S. citizen.

Basis for selection: Major/career interest in science, general; technology; engineering or mathematics. Applicant must demonstrate high academic achievement.

Application requirements: Recommendations, transcript.

Additional information: First and second year medical students also eligible. Deadline in February or March. Check Website for details.

Amount of award:	$1,500
Number of awards:	30
Number of applicants:	100
Application deadline:	March 21
Total amount awarded:	$45,000

Contact:
NASA Texas Space Grant Consortium
University of Texas at Austin
3925 West Braker Lane
Austin, TX 78759-5321
Phone: 800-248-8742
Web: www.tsgc.utexas.edu

NASA Utah Space Grant Consortium

NASA Utah Space Grant Consortium Undergraduate Scholarship

Type of award: Scholarship, renewable.

Intended use: For full-time undergraduate or graduate study at accredited postsecondary institution in United States. Designated institutions: Brigham Young University, Dixie State College, Salt Lake Community College, Snow College, Southern Utah University, Utah College of Applied Technology, The Leonardo, Utah State University, Utah Valley University, University of Utah, Weaver State University, Weber State University, and Westminster College.

Eligibility: Applicant must be U.S. citizen.

Basis for selection: Major/career interest in science, general; mathematics; engineering or technology. Applicant must demonstrate high academic achievement.

Application requirements: Recommendations, transcript, research proposal. Resume.

Additional information: Award varies from year to year. Contact sponsor for deadline information. Must be used at Utah Space Grant Consortium member institution. Award amounts are per month during academic year. Deadlines vary; check Website for details.

Amount of award:	$3,000-$9,000
Number of awards:	15
Number of applicants:	60
Total amount awarded:	$180,000

Contact:
Rocky Mountain NASA Space Grant Consortium
Utah State University
4120 Old Main Hill
Logan, UT 84322-4120
Phone: 435-797-0496
Web: www.utahspacegrant.com

NASA Vermont Space Grant Consortium

NASA Space Grant Vermont Consortium Undergraduate Scholarships

Type of award: Scholarship, renewable.
Intended use: For full-time undergraduate study at accredited postsecondary institution in United States. Designated institutions: Vermont institutions.
Eligibility: Applicant must be high school senior. Applicant must be U.S. citizen residing in Vermont.
Basis for selection: Major/career interest in science, general; engineering; mathematics; aerospace or physics. Applicant must demonstrate high academic achievement.
Application requirements: Recommendations, essay, transcript.
Additional information: Open to high school seniors in Vermont who intend to be enrolled full-time in the following year. Applicant must be enrolled in program relevant to NASA's goals at a Vermont institution. Minimum 3.0 GPA. Three awards designated for Native American applicants; three scholarships designated for Burlington Technical Center Aviation & Technical Center, Aerospace Work Force Development, and Aviation Technical School. Can be used at any accredited Vermont institution of higher education. Application deadline in April. Must attend awards ceremony and provide a report detailing impact of scholarship. Check website for details.

Amount of award:	$5,000
Number of awards:	10
Number of applicants:	15
Application deadline:	April 12
Notification begins:	May 17
Total amount awarded:	$18,000

Contact:
Vermont Space Grant Consortium
Votey Hall, College of Engineering and Math
University of Vermont
Burlington, VT 05405-0156
Phone: 802-656-1429
Web: www.cems.uvm.edu/VSGC

NASA Virginia Space Grant Consortium

Aerospace Undergraduate STEM Research Scholarship Program

Type of award: Scholarship.
Intended use: For full-time junior or senior study at accredited 4-year institution in United States. Designated institutions: Space Grant Consortium schools.
Eligibility: Applicant must be U.S. citizen.
Basis for selection: Major/career interest in aerospace; astronomy; chemistry; computer/information sciences; engineering; geology/earth sciences; mathematics or physics. Applicant must demonstrate high academic achievement.
Application requirements: Recommendations, essay, transcript, research proposal. Resume. Budget proposal.
Additional information: Any undergraduate major that includes coursework related to an understanding of aerospace is eligible. Must have completed at least two years of a STEM undergraduate program. Minimum 3.0 GPA. Awards can include $3,000 stipend plus $1,000 travel/research during the academic year, and $3,500 stipend plus $1,000 travel/research during the summer (ten weeks). Awardees must attend a Virginia Space Grant Consortium member institution and participate in USGC's Annual Student Research Conference. The consortium actively encourages women, minorities, and students with disabilities to apply.

Amount of award:	$1,000-$3,500
Application deadline:	February 8
Notification begins:	April 15

Contact:
Virginia Space Grant Consortium
600 Butler Farm Road, Suite 2253
Hampton, VA 23666
Phone: 757-766-5210
Fax: 757-766-5205
Web: www.vsgc.odu.edu

NASA Space Grant Virginia Community College STEM Scholarship

Type of award: Scholarship.
Intended use: For full-time sophomore study at accredited 2-year institution in United States. Designated institutions: Virginia community colleges.
Eligibility: Applicant must be U.S. citizen.
Basis for selection: Major/career interest in aerospace; computer/information sciences; electronics; engineering; mathematics; science, general or technology. Applicant must demonstrate high academic achievement.
Application requirements: Recommendations, essay, transcript. Resume, biographical information.
Additional information: Must apply during freshman year and be majoring in STEM program of study. Must have completed at least one semester of coursework. Minimum 3.0 GPA. Scholarship is open to students at all community colleges in Virginia. Application deadline may vary. Women, minorities, and students with disabilities are encouraged to apply. Visit Website for application.

Amount of award:	$2,000
Application deadline:	February 8
Notification begins:	April 1

Scholarships

Contact:
Virginia Space Grant Consortium
600 Butler Farm Road, Suite 2253
Hampton, VA 23666
Phone: 757-766-5210
Fax: 757-766-5205
Web: www.vsgc.odu.edu

STEM Bridge Scholarship

Type of award: Scholarship, renewable.
Intended use: For full-time sophomore study at accredited 4-year institution in United States. Designated institutions: Virginia Space Grant Consortium member institutions.
Eligibility: Applicant must be Alaskan native, Asian American, African American, Mexican American, Hispanic American, Puerto Rican, American Indian or Native Hawaiian/Pacific Islander. Applicant must be U.S. citizen.
Basis for selection: Major/career interest in science, general; technology; engineering or mathematics.
Additional information: Minimum 3.0 GPA. Must be sophomore from federally recognized minority group with STEM major.

Amount of award:	$1,000

Contact:
NASA Virginia Space Grant Consortium
600 Butler Farm Road, Suite 2253
Hampton, VA 23666
Phone: 757-766-5210
Fax: 757-766-5205
Web: www.vsgc.odu.edu

NASA West Virginia Space Grant Consortium

NASA West Virginia Space Grant Undergraduate Research Fellowship

Type of award: Scholarship.
Intended use: For full-time undergraduate study at accredited 4-year institution in United States. Designated institutions: West Virginia Space Grant Consortium member institutions.
Eligibility: Applicant must be U.S. citizen.
Basis for selection: Major/career interest in aerospace; science, general; engineering or mathematics. Applicant must demonstrate high academic achievement and seriousness of purpose.
Application requirements: Recommendations, essay, research proposal. Resume. One recommendation must be from research advisor. Proposal must include statement of purpose, methodology, expected results, and timeline.
Additional information: Visit Website for more information and application. Female and minority students encouraged to apply.

Application deadline:	March 5
Notification begins:	April 1

Contact:
NASA West Virginia Space Grant Consortium, West Virginia University
G-68 Engineering Sciences Building
P.O. Box 6070
Morgantown, WV 26506-6070
Phone: 304-293-4099
Fax: 304-293-4970
Web: www.nasa.wvu.edu

NASA Wisconsin Space Grant Consortium

NASA Space Grant Wisconsin Consortium Undergraduate Research Program

Type of award: Research grant.
Intended use: For full-time undergraduate study at 2-year or 4-year institution. Designated institutions: WSGC colleges and universities.
Eligibility: Applicant must be U.S. citizen.
Basis for selection: Major/career interest in aerospace; astronomy; engineering; science, general; architecture; law; business or medicine. Applicant must demonstrate high academic achievement and seriousness of purpose.
Application requirements: Recommendations, transcript, research proposal. Project proposal with budget.
Additional information: Funding for qualified students to create and implement a research project related to aerospace, space science, or other interdisciplinary space-related studies. For academic year or summer term use. Minimum 3.0 GPA and above-average SAT/ACT scores required. Consortium encourages applications from women, minorities, and students with disabilities. For more information, see Website.

Amount of award:	$3,500
Number of awards:	8
Application deadline:	January 31
Notification begins:	March 15
Total amount awarded:	$28,000

Contact:
Wisconsin Space Grant Consortium
University of Wisconsin, Green Bay
2420 Nicolet Drive
Green Bay, WI 54311-7001
Phone: 608-785-8431
Fax: 608-785-8403
Web: www.uwgb.edu/wsgc

NASA Space Grant Wisconsin Consortium Undergraduate Scholarship

Type of award: Scholarship, renewable.
Intended use: For full-time undergraduate study at accredited 4-year institution in United States. Designated institutions: WSGC colleges and universities.
Eligibility: Applicant must be U.S. citizen.
Basis for selection: Major/career interest in aerospace; astronomy; engineering; physics or science, general. Applicant must demonstrate high academic achievement.

Application requirements: Recommendations, essay, transcript.

Additional information: Applicant must attend Wisconsin Space Grant Consortium member institution and reside in Wisconsin during school year. Minimum 3.0 GPA and above-average SAT/ACT scores required. Qualified students may also apply for summer session's Undergraduate Research Award. Consortium actively encourages women, minorities, and students with disabilities to apply. See Website for application and details.

Amount of award:	$1,500
Application deadline:	January 31
Notification begins:	March 15

Contact:
Wisconsin Space Grant Consortium
University of Wisconsin, Green Bay
2420 Nicolet Drive
Green Bay, WI 54311-7001
Phone: 920-465-2108
Web: www.uwgb.edu/wsgc

National Academy for Nuclear Training

NANT Educational Assistance Program

Type of award: Scholarship, renewable.
Intended use: For full-time junior or senior study at accredited 4-year institution in United States.
Eligibility: Applicant must be U.S. citizen.
Basis for selection: Major/career interest in engineering, chemical; engineering, mechanical; engineering, electrical/electronic or engineering, nuclear. Applicant must demonstrate high academic achievement, depth of character, leadership, seriousness of purpose and service orientation.
Application requirements: Recommendations, transcript, proof of eligibility, nomination by INPO member utility.
Additional information: Minimum 3.0 GPA. Must have work experience at INPO member utility. Renewal for eligible students. Additional field of study: power generation health physics. Study of chemical engineering must include nuclear or power option. Applicant should be considering career in nuclear utility industry. For additional information and application deadline, contact by e-mail or visit Website. Application deadline in mid-June.

Amount of award:	$2,500
Number of awards:	125
Notification begins:	August 1

Contact:
National Academy for Nuclear Training Scholarship Program
101 ACT Drive
P.O. Box 4030
Iowa City, IA 52243-4030
Phone: 800-294-7492
Fax: 319-337-1204
Web: www.nei.org/careersandeducation

The National AIDS Memorial Grove

Pedro Zamora Young Leaders Scholarship

Type of award: Scholarship.
Intended use: For full-time undergraduate study at vocational, 2-year or 4-year institution in United States.
Eligibility: Applicant must be no older than 27.
Application requirements: Recommendations, essay. PART 1:. A completed Application with Personal Statement (not to exceed 500 words) describing some of the ways that you provide service and/or leadership in the fight against HIV/AIDS and how your studies, career plans, or public service will contribute to the fight against HIV/AIDS. Application/Personal Statement due 5:00PM, PST May 1st. PART 2:. A written Essay, not to exceed 1,500 words, in which you:. Reflect on the ways in which your life has been impacted by HIV/AIDS. Explore and describe the ways in which you are providing public service or leadership that makes a difference in the lives of people with HIV/AIDS, or people at risk. Detail how the scholarship will help you in your career path and how that career will allow you to continue to fight HIV/AIDS in a way that makes a difference. In addition to the Essay, the following documents will also be required (to be uploaded):. At least one written Letter of Recommendation from a teacher, program coordinator, supervisor/ally/community leader or other adult who is directly involved in your HIV/AIDS-related service, leadership, or field of study. A Transcript from current high school or college that demonstrates a minimum 2.5 GPA overall, or in the immediate past two semesters or three trimesters. Essay/Letter(s) of Recommendation/Transcript due 5:00PM, PST, May 26th.
Additional information: Our Scholarship is open to all current high school seniors, and college freshman, sophomores and juniors (ages 27 and younger) who demonstrate an active commitment to fighting AIDS and taking on roles of public service and leadership (e.g. providing peer-based prevention and education; engaging in advocacy or grass-roots activism; raising public awareness; and/or delivering practical, emotional or treatment support to people living with HIV/AIDS), and who plan to continue to find ways to make a difference in the epidemic through their careers or through public service opportunities after their education is complete. Since 2009, we have awarded a total of $140,000 in scholarships to 48 emerging young leaders in the fight against HIV/AIDS. A total of $50,000 was awarded to ten students in 2016. Our goal is to award an additional ten $5,000 scholarships in 2017.

Amount of award:	$2,500-$5,000
Number of awards:	10
Number of applicants:	250
Application deadline:	May 1, May 26
Total amount awarded:	$50,000

Contact:
Matt Kennedy
870 Market Street
Suite 965
San Francisco, CA 94102
Phone: 415-765-0446
Web: www.aidsmemorial.org/events/2015-pedro-zamora-young-leaders-scholarship

National Amateur Baseball Federation, Inc.

National Amateur Baseball Federation Scholarship

Type of award: Scholarship, renewable.
Intended use: For undergraduate study at accredited postsecondary institution in United States or Canada.
Basis for selection: Competition/talent/interest in athletics/sports. Major/career interest in athletic training. Applicant must demonstrate financial need and high academic achievement.
Application requirements: Recommendations, transcript, proof of eligibility, nomination by National Amateur Baseball Federation member association. Written statement. Documentation of previous awards received from sponsoring association, nomination by president or director of franchised member team.
Additional information: Amount of award determined annually. Applicant must have participated in National Amateur Baseball Federation event in the current season and be sponsored by National Amateur Baseball Federation member association. See Website for application.

Amount of award:	$500-$1,000
Number of awards:	10
Number of applicants:	11
Application deadline:	October 1
Notification begins:	January 1
Total amount awarded:	$3,000

Contact:
National Amateur Baseball Federation
Attn: Chairman Awards Committee
P.O. Box 705
Bowie, MD 20718
Phone: 410-721-4727
Fax: 410-721-4940
Web: www.nabf.com

National Association of Black Accountants Inc.

NABA National Scholarship Program

Type of award: Scholarship.
Intended use: For full-time undergraduate or master's study at 4-year or graduate institution.
Eligibility: Applicant must be Alaskan native, Asian American, African American, Mexican American, Hispanic American, Puerto Rican, American Indian or Native Hawaiian/Pacific Islander.
Basis for selection: Major/career interest in accounting; business; finance/banking or technology. Applicant must demonstrate high academic achievement, depth of character, leadership and service orientation.
Application requirements: Recommendations, essay, transcript, proof of eligibility. Resume.
Additional information: Must be active National Association of Black Accountants member. Applicants must have minimum

2.5 GPA for some awards, 3.3 GPA for others. Applicants must join association by December 31.

Amount of award:	$1,000-$10,000
Number of awards:	50
Number of applicants:	350
Application deadline:	January 31
Notification begins:	April 30
Total amount awarded:	$242,830

Contact:
National Association of Black Accountants Inc.
National Scholarship Program
7474 Greenway Center Drive, Suite 1120
Greenbelt, MD 20770
Phone: 301-474-6222
Fax: 301-474-3114
Web: www.nabainc.org

National Association of Black Journalists

Allison E. Fisher Scholarship

Type of award: Scholarship.
Intended use: For undergraduate or graduate study at postsecondary institution.
Eligibility: Applicant must be U.S. citizen, permanent resident or international student.
Basis for selection: Major/career interest in journalism. Applicant must demonstrate high academic achievement and service orientation.
Application requirements: Recommendations, essay, transcript. Cover letter, resume. Applicants must submit minimum of five samples of published work in print, radio, television, photography, slideshows, website, or flash animation. Must send four copies of all application materials. Essay on topic: What are the top three reasons you would like to pursue a career in journalism and what do you hope your legacy as a journalist will be?"
Additional information: Minimum 3.0 GPA. Must be a print or broadcast journalism major and a member of NABJ. Deadline in March. Check Website for details.

Amount of award:	$2,500
Number of awards:	1
Total amount awarded:	$2,500

Contact:
National Association of Black Journalists
1100 Knight Hall, Suite 3100
College Park, MD 20742
Phone: 301-405-2573
Fax: 301-314-1714
Web: www.nabj.org

Carole Simpson Scholarship

Type of award: Scholarship.
Intended use: For undergraduate or graduate study at accredited 4-year or graduate institution.
Eligibility: Applicant must be African American. Applicant must be U.S. citizen, permanent resident or international student.
Basis for selection: Major/career interest in journalism or radio/television/film. Applicant must demonstrate high academic achievement.

Application requirements: Recommendations, essay, transcript. Resume, cover letter. Applicants must submit minimum of five samples of published work in print, radio, television, photography, slideshows, website, or flash animation. Essay topic: "How has Carole Simpson's career inspired you to pursue a career in broadcast journalism and what do you hope your legacy will be?"

Additional information: Minimum 2.5 GPA. Must be member of National Association of Black Journalists and major in broadcast journalism. Deadline in March. Check Website for details.

Amount of award:	$2,500
Number of awards:	1
Total amount awarded:	$2,500

Contact:
National Association of Black Journalists
1100 Knight Hall, Suite 3100
College Park, MD 20742
Phone: 301-405-2573
Fax: 301-314-1714
Web: www.nabj.org

DeWayne Wickham Founder's High School Scholarship

Type of award: Scholarship.
Intended use: For full-time freshman study at accredited 4-year institution in United States.
Eligibility: Applicant must be high school senior.
Basis for selection: Major/career interest in journalism or communications. Applicant must demonstrate financial need, high academic achievement and service orientation.
Application requirements: Portfolio, recommendations, essay, transcript. Resume, cover letter, work samples.
Additional information: GPA must be between 2.5 and 3.0 Must be high school senior and member of National Association of Black Journalists and major in broadcast journalism. Deadline in March. Check Website for details.

Amount of award:	$2,500
Number of awards:	1

Contact:
National Association of Black Journalists
1100 Knight Hall, Suite 3100
College Park, MD 20742
Phone: 301-405-0248
Fax: 301-314-1714
Web: www.nabj.org

Larry Whiteside Scholarship

Type of award: Scholarship.
Intended use: For junior, senior or graduate study at accredited 4-year institution.
Eligibility: Applicant must be African American.
Basis for selection: Major/career interest in journalism. Applicant must demonstrate high academic achievement.
Application requirements: Portfolio, recommendations, essay, transcript. Resume, cover letter. Must submit three samples of work. Essay must profile sports journalist and why that person inspired you to pursue sports journalism as a career.
Additional information: Minimum 2.5 GPA in major and 2.0 major overall. Must be member of National Association of Black Journalists and be pursuing career in sports journalism. Recipient will receive free trip to NABJ Convention in Orlando, Florida. Deadline in March. Check Website for details.

Amount of award:	$2,500
Number of awards:	1
Total amount awarded:	$2,500

Contact:
National Association of Black Journalists
1100 Knight Hall, Suite 3100
College Park, MD 20742
Phone: 301-405-2573
Fax: 301-314-1714
Web: www.nabj.org

NABJ Scholarship

Type of award: Scholarship.
Intended use: For full-time undergraduate study at accredited 4-year institution in United States.
Basis for selection: Major/career interest in journalism or communications. Applicant must demonstrate high academic achievement and service orientation.
Application requirements: Portfolio, recommendations, essay, transcript. Resume, cover letter, work samples.
Additional information: Minimum 2.5 GPA. Must be member of National Association of Black Journalists and major in journalism. Deadline in March. Check Website for details.

Amount of award:	$2,500
Number of awards:	1

Contact:
National Association of Black Journalists
1100 Knight Hall, Suite 3100
College Park, MD 20742
Phone: 301-405-0248
Fax: 301-314-1714
Web: www.nabj.org

NABJ Visual Task Force (VTF) Scholarship

Type of award: Scholarship.
Intended use: For undergraduate or graduate study at 4-year or graduate institution.
Eligibility: Applicant must be African American.
Basis for selection: Major/career interest in journalism. Applicant must demonstrate high academic achievement.
Application requirements: Portfolio, recommendations, essay, transcript. Resume, cover letter. Applicants must submit minimum of five samples of published work in print, radio, television, photography, slideshows, Website, or flash animation. Essay should answer question: "What are the top three reasons you would like to pursue a career in visual journalism and how do you use your visual skills to effectively and creatively tell the story?"
Additional information: Minimum 2.75 GPA. Must be member of National Association of Black Journalists and have declared a concentration in visual journalism. Must have experience working on campus newspaper or TV studio and have had one internship. Deadline in March. Check Website for details.

Amount of award:	$1,250
Number of awards:	2
Total amount awarded:	$1,500

Contact:
National Association of Black Journalists
1100 Knight Hall, Suite 3100
College Park, MD 20742
Phone: 301-405-2573
Fax: 301-314-1714
Web: www.nabj.org

National Association of Broadcasters Education Foundation

NABEF Freedom of Speech PSA Contest

Type of award: Scholarship.
Intended use: For full-time undergraduate or graduate study at vocational, 2-year, 4-year or graduate institution.
Eligibility: Applicant must be U.S. citizen.
Basis for selection: Applicant must demonstrate financial need.
Application requirements: All entries should highlight the importance of free speech. The closing line of each PSA must include these exact words: "This message is brought to you by the NAB Education Foundation and the Broadcast Education Association". Entries must be 30 seconds in length, including the closing line. Students must have the necessary authorization to use the images, audio, text, and other content contained in their PSA.
Additional information: Open to students enrolled for the upcoming academic year. Student's career/degree interest shoud be in: Broadcasting, Journalism, Multimedia, Radio, TV, Production, Audio/Video.

Amount of award:	$2,500-$2,500
Number of awards:	2
Number of applicants:	160
Application deadline:	April 30
Notification begins:	June 1
Total amount awarded:	$5,000

Contact:
NABEF
1771 N St NW
Washington, DC 20036
Phone: 202-429-3191
Web: freedomofspeechpsa.org

National Association of Letter Carriers

Costas G. Lemonopoulos Scholarship

Type of award: Scholarship, renewable.
Intended use: For full-time undergraduate study at accredited 4-year institution. Designated institutions: St. Petersburg Junior College or four-year public Florida university.
Basis for selection: Applicant must demonstrate high academic achievement.
Application requirements: Transcript. SAT/ACT scores and NALC form.
Additional information: Applicant must be child of National Association of Letter Carriers member in good standing (active, retired, or deceased). Preliminary application available on Website; required for further details and primary application form. Notification published in March issue of Postal Record magazine.

Number of awards:	20
Number of applicants:	150
Application deadline:	June 1

Contact:
National Association of Letter Carriers
Costas G. Lemonopoulos Scholarship Trust
100 Indiana Avenue NW
Washington, DC 20001-2144
Phone: 202-393-4695
Fax: 202-737-1540
Web: www.nalc.org/nalc/members/scholarships.html

William C. Doherty Scholarships

Type of award: Scholarship, renewable.
Intended use: For full-time undergraduate study at accredited 4-year institution.
Eligibility: Applicant must be high school senior.
Basis for selection: Applicant must demonstrate financial need and high academic achievement.
Application requirements: Recommendations, essay, transcript, proof of eligibility. SAT/ACT scores.
Additional information: Applicant must be child of National Association of Letter Carriers member in good standing (active, retired, or deceased) for at least one year. Preliminary application on Website due December 31; supporting materials due March 31. Notification published in July issue of Postal Record magazine.

Amount of award:	$4,000
Number of awards:	5
Number of applicants:	1,200
Application deadline:	December 31
Total amount awarded:	$21,000

Contact:
National Association of Letter Carriers
Scholarship Committee
100 Indiana Avenue NW
Washington, DC 20001-2144
Phone: 202-393-4695
Fax: 202-737-1540
Web: www.nalc.org/nalc/members/scholarships.html

National Association of Water Companies (NJ Chapter)

Water Companies (NJ Chapter) Scholarship

Type of award: Scholarship.
Intended use: For freshman, sophomore, junior, senior or graduate study at accredited 2-year, 4-year or graduate institution in United States. Designated institutions: New Jersey colleges and universities.
Eligibility: Applicant must be U.S. citizen residing in New Jersey.
Basis for selection: Major/career interest in hydrology; natural resources/conservation; science, general; engineering, environmental; finance/banking; communications; accounting; business; computer/information sciences or law. Applicant must demonstrate financial need, high academic achievement, depth of character, leadership, seriousness of purpose and service orientation.

Application requirements: Recommendations, essay, transcript. Essay must illustrate interest in water utility industry or related field.

Additional information: Applicant must have interest in fields of study related to water industry. Acceptable fields of study also include consumer affairs and human resources. At least five years residence in New Jersey required. Minimum 3.0 GPA.

Amount of award:	$2,500
Number of awards:	2
Number of applicants:	80
Application deadline:	April 1
Notification begins:	June 1
Total amount awarded:	$2,500

Contact:
Nat'l Assn. of Water Companies (NJ Chapter)
Gail P. Brady
49 Howell Drive
Verona, NJ 07044
Phone: 973-669-5807
Web: www.nwac.org

National Association of Women in Construction

NAWIC Founders' Construction Trades Scholarship

Type of award: Scholarship.
Intended use: For undergraduate study at postsecondary institution.
Basis for selection: Major/career interest in construction or construction management. Applicant must demonstrate financial need.
Application requirements: Essay. Resume, list of extracurricular activities.
Additional information: Must be currently enrolled in construction-related training program approved by the Bureau of Apprenticeship Training or home state's Postsecondary Education Commission. Visit Website for application.

Amount of award:	$500-$2,500
Application deadline:	February 28
Total amount awarded:	$25,000

Contact:
National Association of Women in Construction
327 South Adams Street
Fort Worth, TX 76104
Phone: 800-552-3506
Web: www.nawic.org

NAWIC Founders' Undergraduate Scholarship

Type of award: Scholarship.
Intended use: For full-time undergraduate study at accredited 2-year or 4-year institution in United States or Canada.
Eligibility: Applicant must be U.S. citizen.
Basis for selection: Major/career interest in construction; construction management; engineering, construction or architecture. Applicant must demonstrate financial need and high academic achievement.
Application requirements: Interview, recommendations, essay, transcript. Resume.

Additional information: Number and amount of awards vary. Interest in construction, extracurricular activities, and employment experience also taken into consideration. Applicants must be enrolled in construction-related field and have at least one term of study remaining. Minimum 3.0 GPA. Only semifinalists will be interviewed. Visit Website for additional information and application.

Amount of award:	$500-$2,500
Application deadline:	February 28
Notification begins:	April 1
Total amount awarded:	$25,000

Contact:
National Association of Women in Construction
327 South Adams Street
Fort Worth, TX 76104
Phone: 800-552-3506
Web: www.nawic.org

National Athletic Trainers' Association Research & Education Foundation

Athletic Trainers' Entry Level Scholarship

Type of award: Scholarship.
Intended use: For full-time junior, senior, master's or doctoral study at 4-year or graduate institution.
Basis for selection: Major/career interest in athletic training. Applicant must demonstrate high academic achievement.
Application requirements: Recommendations, essay, transcript, proof of eligibility, nomination by BOC certified trainer.
Additional information: Must be National Athletic Trainers' Association member. Minimum 3.2 GPA. Intention to pursue the profession of athletic training as career required. Must be sponsored by a certified athletic trainer. Must be enrolled in Commission on Accreditation of Athletic Training Education (CAATE)-accredited undergraduate or master's program. See complete guidelines on Website.

Amount of award:	$2,300
Application deadline:	February 4
Notification begins:	May 1

Contact:
National Athletic Trainers' Association
1620 Valwood Parkway
Suite 115
Dallas, TX 75006
Phone: 214-637-6282
Fax: 214-637-2206
Web: www.natafoundation.org

National Black Nurses Association

Black Nurses Scholarship

Type of award: Scholarship.
Intended use: For undergraduate or graduate study at postsecondary institution.

Eligibility: Applicant must be African American.
Basis for selection: Major/career interest in nursing or nurse practitioner. Applicant must demonstrate leadership, seriousness of purpose and service orientation.
Application requirements: Recommendations, essay, transcript. Evidence of participation in both student nursing activities and the African-American community, professional headshot.
Additional information: Must be member of National Black Nurses Association and member of local chapter if one exists. Must be currently enrolled in a nursing program and have at least one full year of school left. Must be in good academic standing. Call association for current information on program.

Amount of award:	$1,000-$6,000
Number of awards:	12
Application deadline:	April 15
Notification begins:	July 1

Contact:
National Black Nurses Association
8630 Fenton Street
Room 330
Silver Spring, MD 20910
Phone: 301-589-3200
Fax: 301-589-3223
Web: www.nbna.org

National Center For Learning Disabilities

Anne Ford and Allegra Ford Scholarship

Type of award: Scholarship, renewable.
Intended use: For undergraduate study at vocational, 2-year or 4-year institution.
Eligibility: Applicant must be learning disabled. Applicant must be high school senior. Applicant must be U.S. citizen.
Basis for selection: Applicant must demonstrate financial need, depth of character, leadership, seriousness of purpose and service orientation.
Application requirements: Recommendations, essay, transcript, proof of eligibility. Personal statement may be written or recorded (audio or video). Financial statements, SAT/ACT scores. Must provide current documentation of an identified learning disability. Three letters of reommendation (for the Anne Ford scholarship, one must be from a teacher).
Additional information: Applicants must have identifiable learning disability. Minimum 3.0 GPA for the Anne Ford scholarhsip. The Anne Ford scholarship: awards $10,000 over 4 years ($2,500 per year) to a graduating high school senior with a documented learning disability and/or ADHD who will be enrolled in a full-time bachelor's degree program in the fall. The Allegra Ford Scholarship: one-time $2,500 scholarship awarded to a graduating high school senior who will be enrolled in a two-year community college, a vocational or technical training program, or a specialized programs for students with LD and/or ADHD in the fall.

Amount of award:	$10,000
Number of awards:	2
Number of applicants:	400
Application deadline:	November 13
Notification begins:	April 1
Total amount awarded:	$12,500

Contact:
Anne Ford and Allegra Ford Scholarship
National Center for Learning Disabilities
381 Park Avenue South, Suite 1401
New York, NY 10016-8806
Phone: 212-545-7510
Fax: 212-545-9665
Web: www.ncld.org/scholarships-and-awards

National Center for Policy Analysis

Young Patriots Essay Contest

Type of award: Scholarship.
Intended use: For full-time at 2-year or 4-year institution.
Eligibility: Applicant must be enrolled in high school. Applicant must be U.S. citizen.
Application requirements: Essay. Students are asked to write an essay not to exceed 1,200 words. Topic is: "Should the emerging and ongoing threat of global terrorism change how we view government surveillance as it relates to the 4th Amendment? Why or Why Not?" Two short readings are required, and one additional reading is recommended. Incorporating outside sources is also encouraged. Essays will be judged on the quality of their writing, level of engagement with the topic, and the strengh of their reasoning.
Additional information: Essay Contest for middle and high school students.

Amount of award:	$1,500-$5,000
Number of awards:	3
Number of applicants:	281
Application deadline:	January 5
Total amount awarded:	$9,000

Contact:
National Center for Policy Analysis
14180 Dallas Parkway
Suite 350
Dallas, TX 75254
Phone: 972-386-6272
Fax: 972-239-9823
Web: debate-central.ncpa.org/young_patriots_essay_contest_scholarship_1516/

National Commission for Cooperative Education

National Co-op Scholarship

Type of award: Scholarship, renewable.
Intended use: For undergraduate study at postsecondary institution. Designated institutions: Clarkson University, Drexel University, Kettering University, Rochester Institute of Technology, SUNY Oswego, University of Cincinnati, University of Toledo, Wentworth Institute of Technology.
Eligibility: Applicant must be high school senior. Applicant must be U.S. citizen.
Basis for selection: Applicant must demonstrate high academic achievement.

Application requirements: One-page essay on decision to pursue a college cooperative education program.
Additional information: Applicants must be accepted to and attend one of the twelve participating institutions. Application deadlines vary by institution. Minimum 3.5 GPA. Visit Website for more information and application.

Amount of award:	$6,000
Number of awards:	160
Total amount awarded:	$4,100,000

Contact:
National Commission for Cooperative Education
600 Suffolk Street
Suite 125
Lowell, MA 01854
Phone: 978-934-1870
Web: www.co-op.edu

National Dairy Shrine

Dairy Student Recognition Program

Type of award: Scholarship.
Intended use: For senior study at postsecondary institution.
Eligibility: Applicant must be U.S. citizen or Canadian citizen.
Basis for selection: Major/career interest in agriculture; business; dairy; environmental science; food production/management/services; food science/technology; law; manufacturing; marketing or veterinary medicine. Applicant must demonstrate leadership.
Application requirements: Recommendations, essay, transcript, nomination by college or university dairy-science department.
Additional information: Applicant must be recommended by university department. Must be U.S. or Canadian citizen. Cash awards for graduating seniors planning career in dairy cattle. Two candidates eligible per institution. First-place winner receives $2,000; second, $1,500; third through seventh, $1,000. National Dairy Shrine chooses final winners. Students who placed in top five in previous years not eligible for further competition.

Amount of award:	$1,000-$2,000
Number of awards:	9
Number of applicants:	22
Application deadline:	April 15
Notification begins:	August 1
Total amount awarded:	$9,500

Contact:
National Dairy Shrine
P.O. Box 725
Denmark, WI 54208
Phone: 920-863-6333
Web: www.dairyshrine.org

DMI Milk Marketing Scholarships

Type of award: Scholarship.
Intended use: For sophomore or junior study at postsecondary institution.
Eligibility: Applicant must be U.S. citizen.
Basis for selection: Major/career interest in agriculture; animal sciences; dairy; dietetics/nutrition or marketing. Applicant must demonstrate high academic achievement.
Application requirements: Recommendations, essay, transcript.

Additional information: For students interested in careers marketing milk or dairy products. Minimum 2.5 GPA. Visit Website for more details.

Amount of award:	$1,000-$1,500
Number of awards:	8
Number of applicants:	24
Application deadline:	April 15
Notification begins:	August 1
Total amount awarded:	$8,500

Contact:
National Dairy Shrine
P.O. Box 725
Denmark, WI 54208
Phone: 920-863-6333
Fax: 920-863-6333
Web: www.dairyshrine.org

Iager Dairy Scholarship

Type of award: Scholarship.
Intended use: For undergraduate study at 2-year institution.
Eligibility: Applicant must be U.S. citizen.
Basis for selection: Major/career interest in food production/management/services; food science/technology or dairy. Applicant must demonstrate high academic achievement and leadership.
Application requirements: Recommendations, essay, transcript.
Additional information: Must be second-year college student in two-year agricultural college. Minimum 2.5 GPA. May request application from Website or National Dairy Shrine.

Amount of award:	$1,000
Number of awards:	2
Number of applicants:	9
Application deadline:	April 15
Notification begins:	August 1
Total amount awarded:	$2,000

Contact:
National Dairy Shrine
P.O. Box 725
Denmark, WI 54208
Phone: 920-863-6333
Web: www.dairyshrine.org

Kildee Scholarship

Type of award: Scholarship.
Intended use: For junior, senior or graduate study at postsecondary institution.
Eligibility: Applicant must be U.S. citizen.
Basis for selection: Major/career interest in animal sciences; dairy; food production/management/services; food science/technology or veterinary medicine. Applicant must demonstrate high academic achievement and leadership.
Application requirements: Recommendations, essay, transcript.
Additional information: Applicant must have placed in top 25 in National 4-H, FFA or National Intercollegiate Judging Contests. First or second place winners from National Dairy Challenge are eligible to compete for graduate study scholarships. Up to two $3,000 scholarships for graduate study and one $2,000 scholarship for undergraduate study awarded. May request application from Website.

Amount of award:	$2,000-$3,000
Number of awards:	9
Number of applicants:	10
Application deadline:	April 15
Notification begins:	August 1
Total amount awarded:	$8,000

Contact:
National Dairy Shrine
P.O. Box 725
Denmark, WI 54208
Phone: 920-863-6333
Web: www.dairyshrine.org

Klussendorf Scholarship

Type of award: Scholarship.
Intended use: For sophomore, junior or senior study at 2-year or 4-year institution.
Eligibility: Applicant must be U.S. citizen.
Basis for selection: Major/career interest in animal sciences or dairy.
Application requirements: Recommendations, essay, transcript.
Additional information: For dairy or animal science majors in second, third, or fourth year of college. Must plan to become dairy cattle breeder, owner, herdsperson, or fitter. May request application from Website or National Dairy Shrine. Applicant must be U.S. or Canadian citizen.

Amount of award:	$1,500
Number of awards:	6
Number of applicants:	44
Application deadline:	April 15
Notification begins:	August 1
Total amount awarded:	$9,000

Contact:
National Dairy Shrine
P.O. Box 725
Denmark, WI 54208
Phone: 920-863-6333
Web: www.dairyshrine.org

Marshall E. McCullough Undergraduate Scholarship

Type of award: Scholarship.
Intended use: For full-time undergraduate study at accredited 4-year institution in United States.
Eligibility: Applicant must be high school senior. Applicant must be U.S. citizen.
Basis for selection: Major/career interest in animal sciences; dairy; communications or journalism.
Application requirements: Recommendations, essay, transcript.
Additional information: Finalists will be asked to submit video responding to specific questions about the dairy industry. Two awards: one for $2,500; one for $1,000. Must major in dairy/animal science with communications emphasis or agricultural journalism with dairy/animal science emphasis.

Amount of award:	$1,000-$2,500
Number of awards:	2
Number of applicants:	7
Application deadline:	April 15
Notification begins:	August 1
Total amount awarded:	$3,500

Contact:
National Dairy Shrine
P.O. Box 725
Denmark, WI 54208
Phone: 920-863-6333
Web: www.dairyshrine.org

Maurice E. Core Scholarship

Type of award: Scholarship, renewable.
Intended use: For full-time freshman study at accredited 4-year institution.
Eligibility: Applicant must be U.S. citizen.
Basis for selection: Major/career interest in agriculture; animal sciences or dairy. Applicant must demonstrate high academic achievement, leadership and seriousness of purpose.
Application requirements: Recommendations, essay, transcript.
Additional information: Minimum 2.5 GPA. Student must have commitment to career in dairy.

Amount of award:	$1,000
Number of awards:	2
Number of applicants:	20
Application deadline:	April 15
Notification begins:	August 1
Total amount awarded:	$2,000

Contact:
National Dairy Shrine
P.O. Box 725
Denmark, WI 54208
Phone: 920-863-6333
Web: www.dairyshrine.org

National Eagle Scout Association

Hall/McElwain Merit Scholarship

Type of award: Scholarship.
Intended use: For undergraduate study at postsecondary institution.
Eligibility: Applicant must be male.
Basis for selection: Applicant must demonstrate leadership.
Application requirements: Recommendations, proof of eligibility. Applicants may begin applying 8/1.
Additional information: Applicant must be Eagle Scout. Must have strong record of participation in activities outside of scouting. Visit Website for more information and application.

Amount of award:	$5,000
Number of awards:	156
Application deadline:	October 31

Contact:
NESA, Sum 322
1325 West Walnut Hill Lane
P.O. Box 152079
Irving, TX 75015-2079
Phone: 972-580-2000
Web: www.nesa.org

NESA Academic Scholarships

Type of award: Scholarship.
Intended use: For undergraduate study at accredited postsecondary institution.

Eligibility: Applicant must be male, high school senior.

Basis for selection: Applicant must demonstrate financial need, high academic achievement and leadership.

Application requirements: Recommendations, transcript. Minimum 1800 SAT (old test administered before January, 2016), 1290 (new test administered after March, 2016), or 28 ACT.

Additional information: Applicant must be Eagle Scout. Award may not be used at military institution. Minimum 1800 SAT (old test administered before January, 2016) or Minimum 1290 (new test administered after March 2016) or 28 ACT score. Award may be used at approved programs.

Amount of award:	$2,500-$50,000
Number of awards:	150
Number of applicants:	6,000
Application deadline:	October 31
Notification begins:	July 15
Total amount awarded:	$670,000

Contact:
NESA, Sum 322
1325 West Walnut Hill Lane
P.O. Box 152079
Irving, TX 75015-2079
Phone: 972-580-2000
Web: www.nesa.org

National Environmental Health Association/ American Academy of Sanitarians

NEHA/AAS Scholarship

Type of award: Scholarship.

Intended use: For full-time junior, senior or graduate study at accredited 4-year or graduate institution.

Basis for selection: Major/career interest in environmental science or public health. Applicant must demonstrate financial need, high academic achievement and seriousness of purpose.

Application requirements: Transcript, proof of eligibility. Three letters of recommendation (one from active NEHA member, two from faculty members at applicant's school).

Additional information: Undergraduates must be enrolled in an Environmental Health Accreditation Council accredited school or National Environmental Health Association Institutional/Educational or sustaining member school (list available at sponsor Website). Graduates must be enrolled in environmental health science and/or public health program. Visit Website for further information and updates.

Amount of award:	$1,000-$1,500
Number of awards:	3
Number of applicants:	100
Application deadline:	March 15
Total amount awarded:	$3,500

Contact:
National Environmental Health Association
NEHA/AAS Scholarship, Att: Cindy Dimmitt
720 South Colorado Blvd., Suite 1000-N
Denver, CO 80246-1925
Phone: 303-756-9090
Fax: 303-691-9490
Web: http://neha.org/sites/default/files/
2017%20Scholarship%20Brochure.doc

National Federation of the Blind

National Federation of the Blind Scholarships

Type of award: Scholarship, renewable.

Intended use: For full-time undergraduate or graduate study at postsecondary institution.

Eligibility: Applicant must be visually impaired. Applicant must be U.S. citizen.

Basis for selection: Major/career interest in humanities/liberal arts. Applicant must demonstrate financial need, high academic achievement and service orientation.

Application requirements: Recommendations, essay, transcript. Interview with NFB affiliate president, SAT/ACT scores (high school seniors only), proof of legal blindness.

Additional information: Applicant must be legally blind in both eyes. Recipients of Federation scholarships need not be members of National Federation of the Blind. Visit Website for application.

Amount of award:	$3,000-$12,000
Number of awards:	30
Application deadline:	March 31
Notification begins:	June 1

Contact:
National Federation of the Blind Scholarship Committee
NFB at Jernigan Place
200 East Wells Street
Baltimore, MD 21230
Phone: 410-659-9314 ext. 2415
Fax: 410-685-5653
Web: www.nfb.org/scholarships

National FFA Organization

Accelerated Genetics Scholarship

Type of award: Scholarship.

Intended use: For full-time undergraduate study at postsecondary institution in United States.

Eligibility: Applicant must be no older than 22.

Basis for selection: Major/career interest in agriculture. Applicant must demonstrate leadership.

Application requirements: High school ranking, GPA, SAT/ACT scores, Accelerated Genetics customer ID number.

Additional information: Must be member of FFA. Must have valid mailing address in the U.S. Applicant must live on family farm and applicant and/or family must purchase semen or products from an authorized Accelerated Genetics representative. Must obtain FFA advisor's electronic approval on Signature Page. Apply online.

Amount of award:	$1,000
Number of awards:	2
Application deadline:	February 1

Contact:
National FFA Organization Scholarship Office
P.O. Box 68960
Indianapolis, IN 46268-0960
Phone: 317-802-6099
Web: www.ffa.org/programs/grantsandscholarships/Scholarships/Pages/default.aspx

Beck's Hybrids Scholarship

Type of award: Scholarship.
Intended use: For full-time undergraduate study at 4-year institution in United States.
Eligibility: Applicant must be no older than 22. Applicant must be residing in Iowa, Wisconsin, Michigan, Ohio, Tennessee, Indiana, Illinois, Kentucky or Missouri.
Basis for selection: Major/career interest in agriculture.
Application requirements: High school ranking, GPA, ACT/SAT test scores.
Additional information: One scholarship awarded per state (Illinois, Indiana, Iowa, Kentucky, Michigan, Missouri, Ohio, Tennessee and Wisconsin). Family must be a Beck's Hybrids Seed customer. Must be a member of FFA. Must have valid mailing address in the U.S. Must obtain FFA advisor's electronic approval on Signature Page. Apply online.

Amount of award:	$2,000
Number of awards:	9
Application deadline:	February 1

Contact:
National FFA Organization Scholarship Office
P.O. Box 68960
Indianapolis, IN 46268-0960
Phone: 317-802-6099
Web: www.ffa.org/programs/grantsandscholarships/Scholarships/Pages/default.aspx

Bill Kirk Scholarship Endowment Scholarship

Type of award: Scholarship.
Intended use: For full-time undergraduate study at 4-year institution in United States.
Eligibility: Applicant must be no older than 22.
Basis for selection: Major/career interest in agricultural education. Applicant must demonstrate high academic achievement and leadership.
Application requirements: High school ranking, GPA, SAT/ACT scores.
Additional information: Must be a member of FFA. Must have valid mailing address in the U.S. Preference given to applicants with local, state or national leadership experience. Minimum 3.5 GPA Must obtain FFA advisor's electronic approval on Signature Page. Award amounts may vary. Apply online.

Amount of award:	$1,000
Number of awards:	1
Application deadline:	February 1

Contact:
National FFA Organization Scholarship Office
P.O. Box 68960
Indianapolis, IN 46268-0960
Phone: 317-802-6099
Web: www.ffa.org/programs/grantsandscholarships/Scholarships/Pages/default.aspx

Casey's General Stores, Inc. Scholarship

Type of award: Scholarship.
Intended use: For full-time undergraduate study at 2-year or 4-year institution in United States.
Eligibility: Applicant must be no older than 22. Applicant must be residing in Wisconsin, Iowa, South Dakota, Tennessee, Minnesota, Arkansas, Kansas, Oklahoma, Indiana, Nebraska, Kentucky, Illinois, North Dakota or Missouri.
Basis for selection: Major/career interest in agribusiness; wildlife/fisheries; agriculture; food production/management/services; engineering; economics; finance/banking or entomology. Applicant must demonstrate leadership.
Application requirements: High school ranking, GPA, ACT/SAT test scores.
Additional information: Other eligible majors include: agricultural farm/food service/landscape/nursery/ranch or wildlife management, communications, sales, marketing, mechanization, power & equipment, conservation, plant or soil science, agricultural computer systems, agricultural public service or general agriculture with career path in agriculture or agribusiness. Must be a member of FFA. Must have valid mailing address in the U.S. Must obtain FFA advisor's electronic approval on Signature Page. Apply online.

Amount of award:	$1,000
Number of awards:	3
Application deadline:	February 1

Contact:
National FFA Organization Scholarship Office
P.O. Box 68960
Indianapolis, IN 46268-0960
Phone: 317-802-6099
Web: www.ffa.org/programs/grantsandscholarships/Scholarships/Pages/default.aspx

Cheryl Dant Hennesy Scholarship

Type of award: Scholarship, renewable.
Intended use: For full-time undergraduate study at 2-year or 4-year institution in United States.
Eligibility: Applicant must be female, no older than 22. Applicant must be residing in Tennessee, Kentucky or Georgia.
Basis for selection: Applicant must demonstrate financial need.
Application requirements: High school ranking, GPA, SAT/ACT scores.
Additional information: Must be member of FFA. Must have valid mailing address in the U.S. Must obtain FFA advisor's electronic approval on Signature Page. Award amounts may vary. Apply online.

Amount of award:	$5,000
Number of awards:	3
Application deadline:	February 1

Contact:
National FFA Organization Scholarship Office
P.O. Box 68960
Indianapolis, IN 46268-0960
Phone: 317-802-6099
Web: www.ffa.org/programs/grantsandscholarships/Scholarships/
Pages/default.aspx

Cooperative Credit Company Scholarship

Type of award: Scholarship.
Intended use: For full-time undergraduate study at postsecondary institution in United States.
Eligibility: Applicant must be no older than 22. Applicant must be residing in Wisconsin, Iowa, South Dakota, Ohio, Minnesota or Illinois.
Basis for selection: Major/career interest in agriculture or agribusiness. Applicant must demonstrate high academic achievement and leadership.
Application requirements: High school ranking, GPA, SAT/ACT scores.
Additional information: Must be member of FFA. Must have valid mailing address in the U.S. Student or immediate family must be involved in beef/dairy cattle, equine, corn, fruit/vegetable production, grain sorghum, peanuts, production agriculture, sheep, soybean, swine or wheat. Minimum 3.0 GPA. Must obtain FFA advisor's electronic approval on Signature Page. Apply online.

Amount of award:	$1,000
Number of awards:	5
Application deadline:	February 1

Contact:
National FFA Organization Scholarship Office
P.O. Box 68960
Indianapolis, IN 46268-0960
Phone: 317-802-6099
Web: www.ffa.org/programs/grantsandscholarships/Scholarships/
Pages/default.aspx

CSX Scholarship

Type of award: Scholarship, renewable.
Intended use: For full-time undergraduate study at 4-year institution in United States.
Eligibility: Applicant must be no older than 22. Applicant must be residing in Ohio, New York, Tennessee, Maryland, South Carolina, Georgia, Florida, West Virginia, Illinois or Kentucky.
Basis for selection: Applicant must demonstrate high academic achievement and leadership.
Application requirements: High school ranking, GPA, ACT/SAT test scores.
Additional information: Minimum 3.0 GPA. Award is renewable if minimum 3.0 GPA is maintained. Must be pursuing a four-year degree in the following areas of agriculture: business management, communications, economics, finance, sales and marketing, agricultural engineering, agricultural mechanization or agriculture power and equipment. Other eligible majors include communications, engineering and transportation - preferably in the fields of railroad, trucking or logistics. Must be a member of FFA. Must have valid mailing address in the U.S. Must obtain FFA advisor's electronic approval on Signature Page. Apply online.

Amount of award:	$4,000
Number of awards:	10
Application deadline:	February 1

Contact:
National FFA Organization Scholarship Office
P.O. Box 68960
Indianapolis, IN 46268-0960
Phone: 317-802-6099
Web: www.ffa.org/programs/grantsandscholarships/Scholarships/
Pages/default.aspx

Dupont Pioneer Scholarships

Type of award: Scholarship.
Intended use: For full-time undergraduate study at 2-year or 4-year institution in United States.
Eligibility: Applicant must be no older than 22.
Basis for selection: Major/career interest in agribusiness; agricultural economics; agriculture or entomology.
Application requirements: High school ranking, GPA, ACT/SAT test scores.
Additional information: Minimum 3.0 GPA. Other eligible majors include: agronomy; crop, plant or soil science; farm and ranch management; horticulture; general agriculture/agricultural sciences; sustainable agriculture, agricultural communications, journalism, education, extension or public relations; agricultural business management, economics, finance, policy and management, systems management or international agriculture; sales and marketing; agricultural engineering, mechanization, power and equipment; Agriscience technician; biochemistry; biotechnology; plant breeding and genetics and plant pathology. Must be a member of FFA. Must have valid mailing address in the U.S. Must obtain FFA advisor's electronic approval on Signature Page. Apply online.

Amount of award:	$1,000
Number of awards:	8
Application deadline:	February 1

Contact:
National FFA Organization Scholarship Office
P.O. Box 68960
Indianapolis, IN 46268-0960
Phone: 317-802-6099
Web: www.ffa.org/programs/grantsandscholarships/Scholarships/
Pages/default.aspx

DuPont/Delaware FFA Endowment Scholarship

Type of award: Scholarship.
Intended use: For full-time undergraduate study at 4-year institution in United States.
Eligibility: Applicant must be no older than 22. Applicant must be residing in Delaware.
Basis for selection: Major/career interest in agricultural education or agriculture. Applicant must demonstrate high academic achievement and leadership.
Application requirements: High school ranking, GPA, SAT/ACT scores.
Additional information: Must be member of FFA. Must have valid mailing address in the U.S. Preference given to applicants with local or state leadership experience. Minimum 3.5 GPA. Must obtain FFA advisor's electronic approval on Signature Page. Award amounts may vary. Apply online.

Amount of award:	$1,000
Number of awards:	1
Application deadline:	February 1

Contact:
National FFA Organization Scholarship Office
P.O. Box 68960
Indianapolis, IN 46268-0960
Phone: 317-802-6099
Web: www.ffa.org/programs/grantsandscholarships/Scholarships/
Pages/default.aspx

Elmer J. and Hester Jane Johnson Memorial Scholarship

Type of award: Scholarship.
Intended use: For full-time undergraduate study at 4-year institution in United States.
Eligibility: Applicant must be no older than 22.
Basis for selection: Major/career interest in agricultural education. Applicant must demonstrate financial need, high academic achievement and leadership.
Application requirements: High school ranking, GPA, SAT/ACT scores.
Additional information: Must be member of FFA. Must have valid mailing address in the U.S. Must obtain FFA advisor's electronic approval on Signature Page. Award amounts may vary. Apply online.

Amount of award:	$1,000
Number of awards:	1
Application deadline:	February 1

Contact:
National FFA Organization Scholarship Office
P.O. Box 68960
Indianapolis, IN 46268-0960
Phone: 317-802-6099
Web: www.ffa.org/programs/grantsandscholarships/Scholarships/
Pages/default.aspx

Fastline Publications Scholarship

Type of award: Scholarship.
Intended use: For full-time undergraduate study at vocational, 2-year or 4-year institution in United States.
Eligibility: Applicant must be no older than 22. Applicant must be residing in Wisconsin, South Dakota, New York, Ohio, Tennessee, Kansas, Louisiana, Virginia, Mississippi, Nebraska, Alabama, Illinois, Kentucky, Missouri, Iowa, Michigan, Minnesota, Texas, Arkansas, Pennsylvania, South Carolina, Georgia, Florida, Oklahoma, West Virginia, Oregon, Idaho, Indiana, North Carolina or North Dakota.
Basis for selection: Major/career interest in agribusiness.
Application requirements: High school ranking, GPA, ACT/SAT test scores.
Additional information: Other eligible majors include farm & ranch management, livestock management or agricultural sales and marketing. Must live on a family farm and demonstrate interest in managing a farm. Must be a member of FFA. Must have valid mailing address in the U.S. Must obtain FFA advisor's electronic approval on Signature Page. Apply online.

Amount of award:	$1,000
Number of awards:	23
Application deadline:	February 1

Contact:
National FFA Organization Scholarship Office
P.O. Box 68960
Indianapolis, IN 46268-0960
Phone: 317-802-6099
Web: www.ffa.org/programs/grantsandscholarships/Scholarships/
Pages/default.aspx

Fifth Third Bank of Central Indiana Scholarship

Type of award: Scholarship.
Intended use: For full-time undergraduate study at 2-year or 4-year institution in United States. Designated institutions: Indiana institutions.
Eligibility: Applicant must be Alaskan native, Asian American, African American, Mexican American, Hispanic American, Puerto Rican, American Indian or Native Hawaiian/Pacific Islander. Applicant must be no older than 22. Applicant must be residing in Indiana.
Basis for selection: Applicant must demonstrate financial need, high academic achievement, leadership and service orientation.
Application requirements: High school ranking, GPA, ACT/SAT test scores.
Additional information: Minimum 3.0 GPA. Must be a resident of Adams, Allen, Bartholomew, Benton, Brown, Clay, Dearborn, Decatur, Fayette, Hamilton, Hancock, Hendricks, Johnson, Marion, Monroe, Morgan, Orange, Parke, Ripley, Shelby, Sullivan, Tippecanoe, Vermillion or Vigo counties in Indiana. Must be a member of FFA. Must have valid mailing address in the U.S. Must obtain FFA advisor's electronic approval on Signature Page. Apply online.

Amount of award:	$1,025
Number of awards:	2
Application deadline:	February 1

Contact:
National FFA Organization Scholarship Office
P.O. Box 68960
Indianapolis, IN 46268-0960
Phone: 317-802-6099
Web: www.ffa.org/programs/grantsandscholarships/Scholarships/
Pages/default.aspx

Georgia M. Hellberg Memorial Scholarships

Type of award: Scholarship.
Intended use: For full-time undergraduate study at 4-year institution in United States.
Eligibility: Applicant must be no older than 22.
Application requirements: High school ranking, GPA, SAT/ACT scores.
Additional information: Must be member of FFA. Must be studying soil and water conservation. Must have valid mailing address in the U.S. Applicants may also major in discipline leading to employment in area of soil and water conservation. Must obtain FFA advisor's electronic approval on Signature Page. Award amounts may vary. Apply online.

Amount of award:	$1,000
Number of awards:	4
Application deadline:	February 1

Contact:
National FFA Organization Scholarship Office
P.O. Box 68960
Indianapolis, IN 46268-0960
Phone: 317-802-6099
Web: www.ffa.org/programs/grantsandscholarships/Scholarships/
Pages/default.aspx

Kenneth and Ellen Nielso Cooperative Scholarship

Type of award: Scholarship.
Intended use: For full-time undergraduate study at 4-year institution in United States.
Eligibility: Applicant must be no older than 22.
Basis for selection: Major/career interest in animal sciences; dairy; agricultural education; journalism; public relations; marketing or veterinary medicine.
Application requirements: High school ranking, GPA, ACT/ SAT test scores.
Additional information: Applicant or applicant's parents/ guardians must be members of an agricultural cooperative that is also a member of the Iowa Institute for Cooperatives. Must be a member of FFA. Must have valid mailing address in the U.S. Must obtain FFA advisor's electronic approval on Signature Page. Apply online.

Amount of award:	$1,000
Number of awards:	2
Application deadline:	February 1

Contact:
National FFA Organization Scholarship Office
P.O. Box 68960
Indianapolis, IN 46268-0960
Phone: 317-802-6099
Web: www.ffa.org/programs/grantsandscholarships/Scholarships/ Pages/default.aspx

KeyBank Scholarship

Type of award: Scholarship.
Intended use: For full-time undergraduate study at accredited 2-year or 4-year institution in United States. Designated institutions: Institutions in Idaho.
Eligibility: Applicant must be no older than 22. Applicant must be residing in Idaho.
Basis for selection: Major/career interest in agriculture; communications; education; economics; finance/banking; marketing; science, general or engineering. Applicant must demonstrate financial need and service orientation.
Application requirements: High school ranking, GPA, SAT/ ACT scores.
Additional information: Must be member of FFA. Must have valid mailing address in the U.S. Applicant must be a resident of Bannock, Bingham, Bonneville, Cassia, Fremont, Madison, Minidoka, Power, Teton or Twin Falls counties. Must obtain FFA advisor's electronic approval on Signature Page. Apply online.

Amount of award:	$1,000
Number of awards:	1
Application deadline:	February 1

Contact:
National FFA Organization Scholarship Office
P.O. Box 68960
Indianapolis, IN 46268-0960
Phone: 317-802-6099
Web: www.ffa.org/programs/grantsandscholarships/Scholarships/ Pages/default.aspx

Martin Sorkin Memorial Scholarship

Type of award: Scholarship.
Intended use: For full-time undergraduate study at postsecondary institution in United States.
Eligibility: Applicant must be no older than 22.

Basis for selection: Major/career interest in economics or public administration/service. Applicant must demonstrate high academic achievement, leadership and service orientation.
Application requirements: High school ranking, GPA, SAT/ ACT scores.
Additional information: Must be member of FFA. Must have valid mailing address in the U.S. Must obtain FFA advisor's electronic approval on Signature Page. Minimum 3.0 GPA. Award amounts may vary. Apply online.

Amount of award:	$1,000
Number of awards:	2
Application deadline:	February 1

Contact:
National FFA Organization Scholarship Office
P.O. Box 68960
Indianapolis, IN 46268-0960
Phone: 317-802-6099
Web: www.ffa.org/programs/grantsandscholarships/Scholarships/ Pages/default.aspx

Mills Fleet Farm Scholarship

Type of award: Scholarship.
Intended use: For full-time undergraduate study at 2-year or 4-year institution in United States.
Eligibility: Applicant must be no older than 22. Applicant must be residing in Iowa, Wisconsin, Minnesota or North Dakota.
Basis for selection: Major/career interest in agriculture; agribusiness; business/management/administration or engineering. Applicant must demonstrate high academic achievement.
Application requirements: High school ranking, GPA, ACT/ SAT test scores.
Additional information: Minimum 3.0 GPA. Other eligible majors include: agricultural sciences, breeding, genetics, pathology, biotechnology. Visit Website for full listing of eligible counties of residence. Must be a member of FFA. Must have valid mailing address in the U.S. Must obtain FFA advisor's electronic approval on Signature Page. Apply online.

Amount of award:	$1,000
Number of awards:	6
Application deadline:	February 1

Contact:
National FFA Organization Scholarship Office
P.O. Box 68960
Indianapolis, IN 46268-0960
Phone: 317-802-6099
Web: www.ffa.org/programs/grantsandscholarships/Scholarships/ Pages/default.aspx

Monty's Food Plant Company

Type of award: Scholarship.
Intended use: For full-time undergraduate study at 4-year institution in United States.
Eligibility: Applicant must be no older than 22. Applicant must be residing in Ohio, Tennessee, Arkansas, Maryland, South Carolina, Georgia, Virginia, Mississippi, Indiana, Alabama, Illinois, Kentucky, North Carolina, North Dakota or Missouri.
Basis for selection: Major/career interest in agriculture. Applicant must demonstrate high academic achievement, leadership and service orientation.
Application requirements: High school ranking, GPA, SAT/ ACT scores.
Additional information: Must be member of FFA. Must have valid mailing address in the U.S. Applicant must live on a

family farm and applicant and/or family must be involved in corn, soybean, tobacco or vegetable production. Minimum 3.25 GPA, 1280 SAT or 22 ACT required. Must obtain FFA advisor's electronic approval on Signature Page. Apply online.

Amount of award:	$1,000
Number of awards:	4
Application deadline:	February 1

Contact:
National FFA Organization Scholarship Office
P.O. Box 68960
Indianapolis, IN 46268-0960
Phone: 317-802-6099
Web: www.ffa.org/programs/grantsandscholarships/Scholarships/Pages/default.aspx

National FFA Collegiate Scholarship Program

Type of award: Scholarship.
Intended use: For undergraduate study at postsecondary institution.
Eligibility: Applicant must be no older than 22.
Basis for selection: Applicant must demonstrate financial need and high academic achievement.
Additional information: Must be FFA member. Visit Website for more information and application.

Amount of award:	$1,000-$10,000
Number of awards:	1,500
Number of applicants:	7,820
Application deadline:	February 1
Notification begins:	June 1
Total amount awarded:	$2,100,000

Contact:
National FFA
Attn: Scholarship Office
P.O. Box 68960
Indianapolis, IN 46268-0960
Phone: 317-802-6060
Web: www.ffa.org

National Mastis Council Scholarship

Type of award: Scholarship.
Intended use: For full-time undergraduate study at 2-year or 4-year institution in United States.
Eligibility: Applicant must be no older than 22.
Basis for selection: Major/career interest in animal sciences; dairy; education; journalism; marketing or veterinary medicine. Applicant must demonstrate service orientation.
Application requirements: High school ranking, GPA, ACT/SAT test scores.
Additional information: Available for FFA and non-FFA members. Must have a dairy background or plan to pursue a career related to dairy and have participated in community service. Must have valid mailing address in the U.S. Apply online.

Amount of award:	$1,000
Number of awards:	1
Application deadline:	February 1

Contact:
National FFA Organization Scholarship Office
P.O. Box 68960
Indianapolis, IN 46268-0960
Phone: 317-802-6099
Web: www.ffa.org/programs/grantsandscholarships/Scholarships/Pages/default.aspx

Paradise Tomato Kitchens Scholarship

Type of award: Scholarship.
Intended use: For full-time undergraduate study at 4-year institution in United States. Designated institutions: Institutions in Indiana, Kentucky, or Ohio.
Eligibility: Applicant must be no older than 22. Applicant must be residing in Ohio, Indiana or Kentucky.
Basis for selection: Major/career interest in food science/technology. Applicant must demonstrate leadership.
Application requirements: High school ranking, GPA, ACT/SAT test scores.
Additional information: Preference given to applicants competing in state or national FFA sponsored events. Must be a member of FFA. Must have valid mailing address in the U.S. Must obtain FFA advisor's electronic approval on Signature Page. Apply online.

Amount of award:	$3,500
Number of awards:	3
Application deadline:	February 1

Contact:
National FFA Organization Scholarship Office
P.O. Box 68960
Indianapolis, IN 46268-0960
Phone: 317-802-6099
Web: www.ffa.org/programs/grantsandscholarships/Scholarships/Pages/default.aspx

Pepsi-Cola Bottling of Eastern Oregon Scholarship

Type of award: Scholarship.
Intended use: For full-time undergraduate study at 2-year or 4-year institution in United States.
Eligibility: Applicant must be no older than 22. Applicant must be residing in Oregon.
Basis for selection: Applicant must demonstrate high academic achievement and service orientation.
Application requirements: High school ranking, GPA, ACT/SAT test scores.
Additional information: Minimum 3.5 GPA. Must not be pursuing major in agricultural education, hospitality, or other non-ag related majors. Must be a resident of Baker, Malhuer, Union, or Wallowa counties in Oregon. Must be a member of FFA. Must have valid mailing address in the U.S. Must obtain FFA advisor's electronic approval on Signature Page. Apply online.

Amount of award:	$1,000
Number of awards:	1
Application deadline:	February 1

Contact:
National FFA Organization Scholarship Office
P.O. Box 68960
Indianapolis, IN 46268-0960
Phone: 317-802-6099
Web: www.ffa.org/programs/grantsandscholarships/Scholarships/Pages/default.aspx

Rabo Agrifinance Scholarship

Type of award: Scholarship.
Intended use: For full-time undergraduate study at 2-year or 4-year institution in United States.
Eligibility: Applicant must be no older than 22.
Basis for selection: Major/career interest in agriculture; communications; education; business/management/

administration; science, general or technology. Applicant must demonstrate high academic achievement and leadership.

Application requirements: High school ranking, GPA, ACT/SAT test scores.

Additional information: Minimum 3.0 GPA. Must be in top 50% of class. Preference given to applicants whose families are Rabo AgriFinance customers residing within the contiguous 48 states excluding California. Must live on family farm with interest in farm management. Must be a member of FFA. Must have valid mailing address in the U.S. Must obtain FFA advisor's electronic approval on Signature Page. Apply online.

Amount of award:	$2,000
Number of awards:	9
Application deadline:	February 1

Contact:
National FFA Organization Scholarship Office
P.O. Box 68960
Indianapolis, IN 46268-0960
Phone: 317-802-6099
Web: www.ffa.org/programs/grantsandscholarships/Scholarships/Pages/default.aspx

Red Barn Media Group Scholarship

Type of award: Scholarship.

Intended use: For full-time undergraduate study at postsecondary institution in United States.

Eligibility: Applicant must be no older than 22. Applicant must be residing in Alabama.

Application requirements: High school ranking, GPA, ACT/SAT test scores.

Additional information: Preference given to member from one of the following chapters: Springville HS, St. Clair County HS, Ashville HS, Moody HS, or Ragland HS. Must be member of FFA. Must have valid mailing address in the U.S. Must obtain FFA advisor's electronic approval on Signature Page. Apply online.

Amount of award:	$1,000
Number of awards:	1
Application deadline:	February 1

Contact:
National FFA Organization Scholarship Office
P.O. Box 68960
Indianapolis, IN 46268-0960
Phone: 317-802-6099
Web: www.ffa.org/programs/grantsandscholarships/Scholarships/Pages/default.aspx

Seneca Foods Corporation Scholarship

Type of award: Scholarship.

Intended use: For undergraduate study at 2-year or 4-year institution.

Basis for selection: Major/career interest in agriculture; science, general; horticulture; business/management/administration; education; engineering; finance/banking; entomology; food production/management/services or technology. Applicant must demonstrate high academic achievement and leadership.

Application requirements: High school ranking, GPA, ACT/SAT test scores.

Additional information: Minimum 2.0 GPA. Must be involved in fruit or vegetable production or processing. Must be a member of FFA. Must have valid mailing address in the U.S. Must obtain FFA advisor's electronic approval on Signature Page. Apply online.

Amount of award:	$1,000
Number of awards:	11
Application deadline:	February 1

Contact:
National FFA Organization Scholarship Office
P.O. Box 68960
Indianapolis, IN 46268-0960
Phone: 317-802-6099
Web: www.ffa.org/programs/grantsandscholarships/Scholarships/Pages/default.aspx

Wilson W. Carnes Scholarship

Type of award: Scholarship.

Intended use: For full-time undergraduate study at 4-year institution in United States.

Eligibility: Applicant must be no older than 22.

Basis for selection: Major/career interest in agriculture or communications.

Application requirements: High school ranking, GPA, SAT/ACT scores.

Additional information: Must be member of FFA. Must have valid mailing address in the U.S. Must obtain FFA advisor's electronic approval on Signature Page. Award amounts may vary. Apply online.

Amount of award:	$300
Number of awards:	1
Application deadline:	February 1

Contact:
National FFA Organization Scholarship Office
P.O. Box 68960
Indianapolis, IN 46268-0960
Phone: 317-802-6099
Web: www.ffa.org/programs/grantsandscholarships/Scholarships/Pages/default.aspx

National Genealogical Society

Senior Rubincam Award

Type of award: Scholarship.

Intended use: For freshman study.

Eligibility: Applicant must be at least 16, no older than 18. Applicant must be U.S. citizen, permanent resident or international student.

Application requirements: Essay. Supportive evidence and documentation.

Additional information: Applicant must be in Grades 10-12. Submit a single-line genealogy in biographical format for five generations, starting with oneself. Must be in English and original unpublished work. Visit Website for exact specifications. NGS membership not required.

Amount of award:	$500
Number of awards:	1
Number of applicants:	6
Application deadline:	December 15
Notification begins:	April 1
Total amount awarded:	$500

Contact:
National Genealogical Society Attn: NGS Rubincam Award
3108 Columbia Pike, Suite 300
Arlington, VA 22204-4370
Phone: 800-473-0050
Fax: 703-525-0052
Web: www.ngsgenealogy.org

National Ground Water Research and Education Foundation

NGWREF Len Assante Scholarship Fund

Type of award: Scholarship.
Intended use: For full-time undergraduate study at accredited 2-year or 4-year institution.
Basis for selection: Applicant must demonstrate financial need, high academic achievement, depth of character, leadership, patriotism, seriousness of purpose and service orientation.
Application requirements: Essay, transcript, proof of eligibility. Essay should be one-page biography.
Additional information: Applicant must be studying in a ground water-related field. Students in two-year well drilling associate degree program also eligible. Minimum 2.5 GPA. Amount and number of awards vary annually. Application available on Website.

Amount of award:	$1,000-$5,000
Number of awards:	10
Number of applicants:	80
Application deadline:	January 15
Total amount awarded:	$20,000

Contact:
NGWREF Len Assante Scholarship Fund
601 Dempsey Road
Westerville, OH 43081
Phone: 800-551-7379
Fax: 614-898-7786
Web: www.ngwa.org

National Inventors Hall of Fame

Collegiate Inventors Competition

Type of award: Scholarship.
Intended use: For full-time undergraduate or graduate study at postsecondary institution in United States or Canada.
Basis for selection: Competition/talent/interest in science project, based on invention's potential for society and scope of use.
Application requirements: Advisor letter; four copies of application and any supplementary material; personal essay describing invention, including a title page and one-paragraph overview of invention.
Additional information: Amount of awards varies. Entry must include summary of current literature and patent search, test data and invention's benefit. Entry must be original idea that has not been made available to public as a commercial product/process. Must not have been patented or published more than one year prior to date of submission. Competition accepts individual and team entries. Students must be (or have been) enrolled full-time at least part of 12-month period prior to date entry submitted. For teams, at least one member must meet full-time eligibility criteria. Other team members must have been enrolled on part-time basis (at minimum) sometime during 24-month period prior to date entry submitted. Deadline varies. See Website for more information.

Amount of award:	$7,500-$15,000
Number of awards:	3
Application deadline:	June 15

Contact:
The Collegiate Inventors Competition
The National Inventors Hall of Fame
3701 Highland Park NW
North Canton, OH 64720
Phone: 800-968-4332 ext. 5
Web: www.collegiateinventors.org

National Italian American Foundation

National Italian American Foundation Scholarship Program

Type of award: Scholarship.
Intended use: For full-time undergraduate or graduate study at accredited 4-year or graduate institution in United States.
Eligibility: Applicant must be U.S. citizen or permanent resident.
Basis for selection: Applicant must demonstrate high academic achievement, depth of character, leadership, seriousness of purpose and service orientation.
Application requirements: Recommendations, transcript.
Additional information: Must be member of NIAF. Completed application and teacher evaluation submitted online. Awards in two categories. General Category I Awards: Open to Italian-American students who demonstrate outstanding potential and high academic achievement. General Category II Awards: Open to those students majoring or minoring in Italian Language, Italian studies, Italian American Studies, or related fields. Awards not applicable for summer study. Minimum 3.5 GPA. Review individual scholarship descriptions to be sure you qualify for any NIAF scholarships before applying, individual scholarships may have requirements that vary from the Foundation's.

Amount of award:	$2,500-$12,000
Number of awards:	150
Number of applicants:	5,500
Application deadline:	March 1
Notification begins:	May 2
Total amount awarded:	$340,000

Contact:
The National Italian American Foundation
1860 19th Street NW
Washington, DC 20009
Phone: 202-387-0600
Fax: 202-387-0800
Web: www.niaf.org/scholarships

National Jewish Committee on Scouting, Boy Scouts of America

Chester M. Vernon Memorial Eagle Scout Scholarship

Type of award: Scholarship, renewable.
Intended use: For full-time undergraduate study at accredited 2-year or 4-year institution.
Eligibility: Applicant must be male, high school senior. Applicant must be Jewish. Applicant must be U.S. citizen or permanent resident.
Basis for selection: Applicant must demonstrate financial need, depth of character, leadership and service orientation.
Application requirements: Recommendation from a volunteer or professional scout leader and from a religious leader. FAFSA.
Additional information: Applicant must be registered, active member of a Boy Scout troop, Varsity Scout team, or Venturing crew. Must have received Eagle Scout Award. Must be active member of synagogue and have received Ner Tamid or Etz Chaim emblem. Award renewable for four years. Visit National Jewish Committee on Scouting Website for information and application. Recipients receive $1,000 per year for four years.

Amount of award:	$4,000
Number of awards:	1
Number of applicants:	10
Application deadline:	February 28
Notification begins:	May 1
Total amount awarded:	$4,000

Contact:
National Jewish Committee on Scouting, BSA
1325 West Walnut Hill Lane
P.O. Box 152079
Irving, TX 75015-2079
Phone: 972-580-2130
Fax: 972-580-2540
Web: www.jewishscouting.org

Frank L. Weil Memorial Eagle Scout Scholarship

Type of award: Scholarship.
Intended use: For full-time undergraduate study at accredited 2-year or 4-year institution.
Eligibility: Applicant must be male, high school senior. Applicant must be Jewish. Applicant must be U.S. citizen or permanent resident.
Basis for selection: Applicant must demonstrate depth of character, leadership and service orientation.
Application requirements: Recommendations from volunteer or professional scout leader and a religious leader.
Additional information: Recipient of scholarship receives $1,000. Two $500 second-place scholarship awards also given. Applicant must be registered, active member of a Boy Scout troop, Varsity Scout team, or Venturing crew. Must have received Eagle Scout Award. Must be active member of synagogue and have received Ner Tamid or Etz Chaim emblem. Visit National Jewish Committee on Scouting Website for more information and application.

Amount of award:	$500-$1,000
Number of awards:	3
Number of applicants:	20
Application deadline:	January 31
Notification begins:	May 1
Total amount awarded:	$2,000

Contact:
National Jewish Committee on Scouting, BSA
1325 West Walnut Hill Lane
P.O. Box 152079
Irving, TX 75015-2079
Phone: 972-580-2130
Fax: 972-580-2000
Web: www.jewishscouting.org

Rick Arkans Eagle Scout Scholarship

Type of award: Scholarship.
Intended use: For undergraduate study at postsecondary institution.
Eligibility: Applicant must be high school senior.
Basis for selection: Applicant must demonstrate financial need.
Application requirements: Recommendation from a volunteer or professional scout leader and from a religious leader. FAFSA.
Additional information: Applicant must be registered, active member of a Boy Scout troop, Varsity Scout team, or Venturing crew. Must have received Eagle Scout Award. Must be active member of synagogue and have received Ner Tamid or Etz Chaim emblem. Visit National Jewish Committee on Scouting Website for more information and application.

Amount of award:	$1,000
Number of awards:	1
Number of applicants:	10
Application deadline:	February 28
Notification begins:	May 1
Total amount awarded:	$1,000

Contact:
National Jewish Committee on Scouting, BSA
1325 West Walnut Hill Lane
P.O. Box 152079
Irving, TX 75015-2079
Phone: 972-580-2130
Fax: 972-580-2540
Web: www.jewishscouting.org

National Junior Classical League

Latin Honor Society Scholarship

Type of award: Scholarship.
Intended use: For full-time freshman study at 2-year or 4-year institution.
Eligibility: Applicant must be high school senior.
Basis for selection: Major/career interest in classics or education. Applicant must demonstrate high academic achievement.
Application requirements: Recommendations, essay, transcript.
Additional information: Must have been member in good standing of NJCL for at least three years and must be member

of NJCL Latin Honor Society for current academic year and at least one preceding year. Must be planning to major in and teach Latin, Greek, or classics. Application available online.

Amount of award:	$2,000
Number of awards:	1
Number of applicants:	7
Application deadline:	May 1
Total amount awarded:	$2,000

Contact:
National Junior Classical League, Attn: Scholarships
Miami University
422 Wells Mill Drive
Oxford, OH 45056
Phone: 513-529-7741
Web: www.njcl.org

National Junior Classical League Scholarship

Type of award: Scholarship.
Intended use: For full-time freshman study at 2-year or 4-year institution.
Eligibility: Applicant must be high school senior.
Basis for selection: Major/career interest in classics; education or humanities/liberal arts. Applicant must demonstrate financial need, high academic achievement, leadership, seriousness of purpose and service orientation.
Application requirements: Recommendations, essay, transcript. List of awards and activities.
Additional information: Must be NJCL member. Preference given to applicants who intend to teach Latin, Greek, or classical humanities.

Amount of award:	$1,200-$2,500
Number of awards:	11
Application deadline:	May 1

Contact:
National Junior Classical League, Attn: Scholarships
Miami University
422 Wells Mill Drive
Oxford, OH 45056
Phone: 513-529-7741
Web: www.njcl.org

National Liberty Museum

Liberty Scholarship and Leadership Program

Type of award: Scholarship.
Intended use: For undergraduate study at accredited vocational, 2-year or 4-year institution.
Eligibility: Applicant must be no older than 25, high school senior. Applicant must be U.S. citizen or permanent resident.
Application requirements: 3-5 minute video speech on the topic: "How I intend to Make a Positive Difference in the Lives of Others."
Additional information: Must be a Liberty Scholar Member of the National Liberty Museum.

Amount of award:	$500-$7,500
Number of awards:	14
Application deadline:	July 15
Notification begins:	August 15
Total amount awarded:	$25,000

Contact:
National Liberty Museum
321 Chestnut Street
Philadelphia, PA 19106
Web: http://libertyscholars.libertymuseum.org/

National Poultry & Food Distributors Association

NPFDA Foundation Scholarship

Type of award: Scholarship, renewable.
Intended use: For full-time junior or senior study at 4-year institution in United States.
Basis for selection: Major/career interest in dietetics/nutrition; agriculture; agricultural economics; agribusiness; food science/technology or animal sciences. Applicant must demonstrate high academic achievement.
Application requirements: Essay, transcript, proof of eligibility. Recommendation by dean, department head or advisor.
Additional information: Poultry science, animal science, or related agricultural business majors also eligible.

Amount of award:	$1,500-$2,000
Number of awards:	4
Number of applicants:	80
Application deadline:	May 31
Notification begins:	January 1
Total amount awarded:	$6,500

Contact:
National Poultry & Food Distributors Association
2014 Osborne Road
St. Marys, GA 31558
Phone: 770-535-9901
Fax: 770-535-7385
Web: www.npfda.org

National Press Photographers Foundation

NPPF Career Expansion Scholarship

Type of award: Scholarship.
Intended use: For full-time undergraduate or graduate study at postsecondary institution in United States or Canada.
Eligibility: Applicant must be U.S. citizen or permanent resident.
Basis for selection: Major/career interest in journalism. Applicant must demonstrate financial need.
Application requirements: Recommendations, essay. Portfolio of 6-12 slides (digital formats also accepted), statement of financial need, GPA, resume, two faculty recommendations.
Additional information: Applicants must be studying photojournalism. Visit Website for more information and application. Must have at least three years experience and have been published in a newspaper, book, or magazine.

Amount of award:	$5,000
Number of awards:	5
Application deadline:	May 15

Contact:
National Press Photographers Foundation
C. Thomas Hardin
1622 Forest Hill Drive
Louisville, KY 40205
Web: www.nppf.org

National Restaurant Association Educational Foundation

Al Schulman Ecolab First-Time Freshman Entrepeneurial Scholarship

Type of award: Scholarship.
Intended use: For undergraduate study at vocational, 2-year or 4-year institution. Designated institutions: California Polytechnic University-Pomona, Cornell University, Culinary Institute of America, DePaul University, Johnson & Wales University, Kendall College, Lynn University, Michigan State University, New York University, Penn State University, Purdue University, University of Denver, University of Houston, University of Nevada-Las Vegas, University of Massachusetts-Amherst.
Eligibility: Applicant must be U.S. citizen or permanent resident.
Basis for selection: Major/career interest in food science/technology; hotel/restaurant management; food science/technology; culinary arts or marketing.
Application requirements: Transcript. One to three letters of recommendation verifying work hours, on business or school letterhead, from current or previous employer in the restaurant or food service industry, paystubs, two essays: one stating food service background and career goals, the other discussing what person or experience influenced you to select food industry and how this will help you reach your career goals.
Additional information: Minimum 3.0 GPA. Must be first-time freshman accepted into accredited culinary school, or in college or university majoring in food service related major. Must plan to enroll in minimum of two terms for following school year. Must have minimum 250 hours of food-service-related work experience. Deadline in July or August. Visit Website for application.

Amount of award:	$3,000-$5,000
Application deadline:	April 23

Contact:
National Restaurant Association Educational Foundation
Scholarships and Mentoring Initiative
2055 L Street
Washington, DC 20036
Phone: 800-424-5156
Web: www.nraef.org/scholarships

Al Schuman Ecolab Undergraduate Entrepeneurial Scholarship

Type of award: Research grant.
Intended use: For undergraduate study at postsecondary institution. Designated institutions: California State Polytechnic University-Pomona, Cornell University, Culinary Institute of America, DePaul University, Johnson & Wales University, Kendall College, Lynn University, Michigan State University, New York University, Pennsylvania State University, Purdue University, University of Denver, University of Houston, University of Nevada-Las Vegas, University of Massachusetts-Amherst.
Eligibility: Applicant must be U.S. citizen or permanent resident.
Basis for selection: Major/career interest in culinary arts or food production/management/services. Applicant must demonstrate high academic achievement.
Application requirements: Recommendations, essay, transcript. Verification of work experience: paycheck stub or letter from employer, supervisor, or educator that lists totat number of hours worked.
Additional information: Minimum 3.0 GPA. Targeted to students who show entrepreneurial spirit through written essay. Must be enrolled in food service related program. Must have completed at least one grading term of postsecondary program. Must be enrolled for at least two consecutive terms, but not entering last semester before graduating.

Amount of award:	$3,000-$5,500
Application deadline:	April 24

Contact:
National Restaurant Educational Foundation
2055 L Street
Attn: Scholarship Program
Washington, IL 20036
Phone: 800-424-5156
Web: www.nraef.org

National Rifle Association

Jeanne E. Bray Law Enforcement Dependents Scholarship

Type of award: Scholarship.
Intended use: For full-time undergraduate or graduate study at accredited 2-year, 4-year or graduate institution in United States.
Eligibility: Applicant must be U.S. citizen. Applicant's parent must have been killed or disabled in work-related accident as police officer.
Basis for selection: Applicant must demonstrate high academic achievement and service orientation.
Application requirements: Recommendations, transcript, proof of eligibility. Letter from employing law enforcement agency; 500-700 word essay on the Second Amendment.
Additional information: Number of awards varies. Parent must be member of National Rifle Association. Parent must be active, disabled, deceased, discharged, or retired peace officer. Award given for up to four years or until applicable monetary cap is reached, as long as student maintains eligibility. Applications accepted on continuous basis.

Amount of award:	$5,000
Number of applicants:	35
Application deadline:	November 15
Notification begins:	February 15

Contact:
National Rifle Association
Jeanne E. Bray Memorial Scholarship
11250 Waples Mill Road
Fairfax, VA 22030
Phone: 800-554-9498
Fax: 703-267-1083
Web: le.nra.org/law-enforcement-benefits.aspx

National Scholar Foundation

National Scholar Foundation Peer Tutoring Scholarship Competition

Type of award: Scholarship.
Intended use: For undergraduate study at accredited 2-year or 4-year institution.
Basis for selection: The Scholarship Committee will evaluate applicants based on the following criteria: Scholarship- A dedication to learning and a passion for sharing knowledge. Service- A commitment to serving the community through peer tutoring. Leadership- A relentless determination to go above and beyond the call of duty to impact change through peer tutoring. Character- A consistent demonstration of respect, empathy, humility, maturity, and generosity as a peer tutor. Applicant must demonstrate high academic achievement, depth of character, leadership, seriousness of purpose and service orientation.
Application requirements: Essay. Must participate in non-paid, academic peer tutoring for academic achievement. All applicants must be non-paid, academic peer tutors. All applicant essays must be verified by an educator reference (ex. school teacher, school counselor, school administrator, etc.) to be considered for recognition. Scholarship funds must be applied toward the tuition payment at any accredited college or university in the form of a payout (All scholarships will be held in an account until the scholarship winner has graduated high school; while the scholarship winner is enrolled at an accredited college or university, he or she can contact us and request a Scholarship Payout Request Form. The National Scholar Foundation will then write a check directly to the college indicating that funds may be applied toward the student's tuition, room/board, and/or book expenses. More details regarding the scholarship payout process will be provided to scholarship recipients after they have won the competition).
Additional information: All student tutors applying must be enrolled in middle or high school at the time of application.

Amount of award:	$250-$1,000
Number of awards:	4
Number of applicants:	100
Application deadline:	March 1
Notification begins:	April 1, June 1
Total amount awarded:	$2,000

Contact:
National Scholar Foundation
Phone: 908-295-7208
Web: www.nationalscholarfoundation.org/scholarship.html

National Science Teachers Association

Toshiba/NSTA ExploraVision Award

Type of award: Scholarship.
Intended use: For undergraduate or non-degree study at postsecondary institution in United States or Canada.
Eligibility: Applicant must be enrolled in high school.
Basis for selection: Competition/talent/interest in science project, based on scientific accuracy, creativity, communication and feasibility of vision. Major/career interest in science, general.
Application requirements: Essay. Abstract, written description of research and design project, five graphics simulating Web pages.
Additional information: Applicants must apply as teams of two, three, or four students and a coach. Applicant must attend public, private, or home school. Technology study project. Open to grades K-12. Members of first-place team receive $10,000 savings bond. Members of second-place team receive $5,000 savings bond. Regional winners receive Toshiba products. Contact sponsor for entry kit, and visit Website to download application.

Amount of award:	$5,000-$10,000
Number of applicants:	4,500
Application deadline:	January 30
Notification begins:	March 1
Total amount awarded:	$240,000

Contact:
Toshiba/NSTA ExploraVision Awards
1840 Wilson Boulevard
Arlington, VA 22201-3000
Phone: 800-EXPLOR9
Web: www.exploravision.org

National Sculpture Society

Sculpture Society Scholarship

Type of award: Scholarship.
Intended use: For undergraduate, master's or doctoral study at postsecondary institution in United States.
Eligibility: Applicant must be U.S. citizen or permanent resident.
Basis for selection: Competition/talent/interest in visual arts, based on images of figurative or representational sculpture created by applicant. Major/career interest in arts, general. Applicant must demonstrate financial need.
Application requirements: Recommendations, essay, proof of eligibility. Brief letter of application including biography and background in sculpture; ten to eighteen images of at least six sculptures submitted on CD; list of works shown on CD; proof of financial need; SASE.
Additional information: Must be studying figurative or representational sculpture. Work inspired by nature, or figurative or realistic sculpture, preferred.

Amount of award:	$2,000
Number of awards:	4
Number of applicants:	35
Application deadline:	May 30
Total amount awarded:	$8,000

Contact:
National Sculpture Society
c/o ANS
75 Varick Street, 11th Floor
New York, NY 10013
Phone: 212-764-5645
Fax: 212-764-5651
Web: www.nationalsculpture.org

National Security Agency

National Security Agency Stokes Educational Scholarship Program

Type of award: Scholarship, renewable.
Intended use: For full-time undergraduate study in United States.
Eligibility: Applicant must be high school senior. Applicant must be U.S. citizen.
Basis for selection: Major/career interest in computer/information sciences; engineering, computer or engineering, electrical/electronic. Applicant must demonstrate high academic achievement, depth of character, leadership, patriotism, seriousness of purpose and service orientation.
Application requirements: Recommendations, essay, transcript, proof of eligibility. Resume, SAT/ACT scores.
Additional information: Current applications available September 1st through November 15th of each year. Must submit online and hard copy applications. Preference given to those with minimum 3.0 GPA, 1600 SAT score (reading and math) and/or 25 ACT score. Must undergo polygraph and security screening. Freshmen must major in computer science or electrical or computer engineering. Awardees must work at NSA in area related to major for 12 weeks in summer and after graduation for at least one and a half times length of study. If work debt not repaid, scholarship reverts to debt. Tuition cap is $30,000 per year. See Website for current program information.

Amount of award:	$30,000
Number of awards:	20
Number of applicants:	800
Application deadline:	October 31
Notification begins:	May 1

Contact:
National Security Agency Stokes Scholars Program
9800 Savage Road
Suite 6779
Fort Meade, MD 20755-6779
Phone: 410-854-4725 or 866-NSA-HIRE
Fax: 410-854-3002
Web: intelligencecareers.gov/nsa vs www.nsa.gov

National Society of Accountants Scholarship Foundation

National Society of Accountants Scholarship

Type of award: Scholarship.
Intended use: For sophomore, junior or senior study at accredited vocational, 2-year or 4-year institution in United States.

Eligibility: Applicant must be U.S. citizen or Canadian citizen.
Basis for selection: Major/career interest in accounting. Applicant must demonstrate financial need, high academic achievement and leadership.
Application requirements: Transcript. Appraisal form.
Additional information: Minimum 3.0 GPA. Student must be enrolled in undergraduate accounting program at time of application. Visit Website for more information and application.

Amount of award:	$500-$2,000
Number of awards:	39
Number of applicants:	1,200
Application deadline:	March 10
Total amount awarded:	$32,700

Contact:
National Society of Accountants Scholarship Program
c/o Scholarship Management Services
One Scholarship Way, P.O. Box 297
St. Peter, MN 56082
Phone: 800-966-6679
Web: www.nsacct.org

National Society of Professional Surveyors

Berntsen International Scholarship in Surveying

Type of award: Scholarship, renewable.
Intended use: For undergraduate study at 4-year institution.
Basis for selection: Major/career interest in surveying/mapping. Applicant must demonstrate high academic achievement and seriousness of purpose.
Application requirements: Recommendations, essay, transcript, proof of eligibility.
Additional information: Applicant must be member of NSPS. Open to students in surveying or closely related programs such as geomatics or surveying engineering. Degree of financial need will be used, if necessary, to break ties after the primary criteria have been considered. Funded by Berntsen International Inc. of Madison, Wisconsin. Visit Website for deadlines and additional information.

Amount of award:	$2,000
Number of awards:	1
Total amount awarded:	$2,000

Contact:
NSPS and AAGS Scholarships
5119 Pegasus Court
Suite Q
Frederick, MD 21704
Phone: 240-439-4615
Fax: 240-439-4952
Web: www.nsps.us.com

Berntsen International Scholarship in Surveying Technology

Type of award: Scholarship, renewable.
Intended use: For undergraduate certificate study at 2-year institution.
Basis for selection: Major/career interest in surveying/mapping or cartography. Applicant must demonstrate high academic achievement and seriousness of purpose.

Application requirements: Recommendations, essay, transcript, proof of eligibility.

Additional information: Applicant must be member of NSPS. Funded by Berntsen International Inc. of Madison, Wisconsin. Visit Website for deadlines and additional information.

Amount of award:	$1,000
Number of awards:	1
Total amount awarded:	$1,000

Contact:
NSPS and AAGS Scholarships
5119 Pegasus Court
Suite Q
Frederick, MD 21704
Phone: 240-439-4615
Fax: 240-439-4952
Web: www.nsps.us.com

Cady McDonnell Memorial Scholarship

Type of award: Scholarship, renewable.

Intended use: For undergraduate study at 2-year or 4-year institution.

Eligibility: Applicant must be female. Applicant must be residing in Utah, Alaska, Washington, Arizona, Nevada, Wyoming, California, Montana, Oregon, New Mexico, Idaho, Colorado or Hawaii.

Basis for selection: Major/career interest in surveying/mapping or cartography. Applicant must demonstrate high academic achievement and seriousness of purpose.

Application requirements: Recommendations, essay, transcript, proof of eligibility. Proof of legal home residence.

Additional information: Applicant must be member of NSPS. Degree of financial need will be used, if necessary, to break ties after the primary criteria have been considered. Visit Website for deadlines and additional information.

Amount of award:	$1,000
Number of awards:	1
Total amount awarded:	$1,000

Contact:
NSPS and AAGS Scholarships
5119 Pegasus Court
Suite Q
Frederick, MD 21704
Phone: 240-439-4615
Fax: 240-439-4952
Web: www.nsps.us.com

The Lowell H. and Dorothy Loving Undergraduate Scholarship

Type of award: Scholarship.

Intended use: For junior or senior study at accredited postsecondary institution in United States.

Basis for selection: Major/career interest in surveying/mapping. Applicant must demonstrate high academic achievement and seriousness of purpose.

Application requirements: Recommendations, essay, transcript, proof of eligibility.

Additional information: Applicant must be NSPS member. In addition to basic surveying, applicant must take courses in at least two of the following: land surveying, geometric geodesy, photogrammetry/remote sensing; or analysis and design of spatial measurement. Visit Website for deadlines and additional information.

Amount of award:	$2,000
Number of awards:	1
Total amount awarded:	$2,000

Contact:
NSPS and AAGS Scholarships
5119 Pegasus Court
Suite Q
Frederick, MD 21704
Phone: 240-439-4615
Fax: 240-439-4952
Web: www.nsps.us.com

Nettie Dracup Memorial Scholarship

Type of award: Scholarship, renewable.

Intended use: For undergraduate study at accredited 4-year institution. Designated institutions: ABET-accredited colleges and universities.

Eligibility: Applicant must be U.S. citizen.

Basis for selection: Major/career interest in surveying/mapping. Applicant must demonstrate high academic achievement and seriousness of purpose.

Application requirements: Recommendations, essay, transcript, proof of eligibility.

Additional information: Applicant must be member of NSPS and enrolled in geodetic surveying program. Degree of financial need will be used, if necessary, to break ties after primary criteria have been considered. Visit Website for deadlines and additional information.

Amount of award:	$2,000
Number of awards:	2
Total amount awarded:	$4,000

Contact:
NSPS and AAGS Scholarships
5119 Pegasus Court
Suite Q
Frederick, MD 21704
Phone: 240-439-4615
Fax: 240-439-4952
Web: www.nsps.us.com

NSPS Board of Governors Scholarship

Type of award: Scholarship, renewable.

Intended use: For junior study at 4-year institution.

Basis for selection: Major/career interest in surveying/mapping. Applicant must demonstrate high academic achievement and seriousness of purpose.

Application requirements: Recommendations, essay, transcript, proof of eligibility.

Additional information: Applicant must be member of NSPS. Minimum 3.0 GPA. Degree of financial need will be used, if necessary, to break ties after the primary criteria have been considered. Visit Website for deadlines and additional information.

Amount of award:	$1,000
Number of awards:	1
Total amount awarded:	$1,000

Contact:
NSPS and AAGS Scholarships
5119 Pegasus Court
Suite Q
Frederick, MD 21704
Phone: 240-439-4615
Fax: 240-439-4952
Web: www.nsps.us.com

NSPS Fellows Scholarship

Type of award: Scholarship.
Intended use: For junior or senior study at 4-year institution.
Basis for selection: Major/career interest in surveying/mapping or cartography. Applicant must demonstrate high academic achievement and seriousness of purpose.
Application requirements: Recommendations, essay, transcript, proof of eligibility.
Additional information: Applicant must be NSPS member. Student may also study related disciplines including geomatics or surveying engineering. Visit Website for deadlines and additional information.

Amount of award:	$2,000
Number of awards:	1
Total amount awarded:	$2,000

Contact:
NSPS and AAGS Scholarships
5119 Pegasus Court
Suite Q
Frederick, MD 21704
Phone: 240-439-4615
Fax: 240-439-4952
Web: www.nsps.us.com

NSPS Scholarships

Type of award: Scholarship, renewable.
Intended use: For full-time undergraduate study at 4-year institution.
Basis for selection: Major/career interest in surveying/mapping. Applicant must demonstrate high academic achievement and seriousness of purpose.
Application requirements: Recommendations, essay, transcript, proof of eligibility.
Additional information: Applicant must be member of NSPS. Students may also be enrolled in related degree program such as geomatics or surveying engineering. Degree of financial need will be used, if necessary, to break ties after the primary criteria have been considered. Awarded by National Society of Professional Surveyors. Visit Website for deadlines and additional information.

Amount of award:	$1,000
Number of awards:	2
Total amount awarded:	$2,000

Contact:
NSPS and AAGS Scholarships
5119 Pegasus Court
Suite Q
Frederick, MD 21704
Phone: 240-439-4615
Fax: 240-439-4952
Web: www.nsps.us.com

Schonstedt Scholarships in Surveying

Type of award: Scholarship, renewable.
Intended use: For undergraduate study at 4-year institution.

Basis for selection: Major/career interest in surveying/mapping. Applicant must demonstrate high academic achievement and seriousness of purpose.
Application requirements: Recommendations, essay, transcript, proof of eligibility.
Additional information: Applicant must be member of NSPS. Preference given to applicants with junior or senior standing. Degree of financial need will be used, if necessary, to break ties after primary criteria have been considered. Funded by Schonstedt Instrument Company of Kearneysville, West Virginia. Schonstedt donates magnetic locator to surveying program at each recipient's school. Visit Website for deadlines and additional information.

Amount of award:	$1,500
Number of awards:	2
Total amount awarded:	$3,000

Contact:
NSPS and AAGS Scholarships
5119 Pegasus Court
Suite Q
Frederick, MD 21704
Phone: 240-439-4615
Fax: 240-439-4952
Web: www.nsps.us.com

Tri-State Surveying & Photogrammetry Kris M. Kunze Scholarship

Type of award: Scholarship.
Intended use: For undergraduate study at postsecondary institution in United States.
Basis for selection: Major/career interest in business; business/management/administration or surveying/mapping. Applicant must demonstrate high academic achievement and seriousness of purpose.
Additional information: Applicant must be NSPS member. First priority: Licensed professional land surveyors or certified photogrammetrists taking college business administration or management courses. Second priority: Certified land survey interns taking college business administration or management courses. Third priority: Full-time students in two or four-year surveying and mapping degree programs taking business administration or management courses. Visit Website for deadlines and additional information.

Amount of award:	$1,000
Number of awards:	1
Total amount awarded:	$1,000

Contact:
NSPS and AAGS Scholarships
5119 Pegasus Court
Suite Q
Frederick, MD 21704
Phone: 240-439-4615
Fax: 240-439-4952
Web: www.nsps.us.com

National Society of the Sons of the American Revolution

Arthur M. and Berdena King Eagle Scout Scholarship

Type of award: Scholarship.
Intended use: For undergraduate study at postsecondary institution.

Eligibility: Applicant must be male, no older than 18.
Basis for selection: Applicant must demonstrate depth of character, leadership and patriotism.
Application requirements: Essay, proof of eligibility. Essay should be 500 words on Revolutionary War, subject of applicant's choice. Four generation ancestor chart.
Additional information: Open to all Eagle Scouts currently registered in active unit who will not reach 19th birthday during year of application. Competition conducted in three phases: Chapter (local), Society (state), and National. Applicants need only apply at Chapter level. Winners at local level entered into state competition; state winners used in National contest. Number of awards varies. Awards may also be available at chapter and state level. See Website for more information and application.

Amount of award:	$4,000-$10,000
Number of awards:	3
Application deadline:	December 31
Total amount awarded:	$20,000

Contact:
National Society of the Sons of the American Revolution
809 West Main Street
Louisville, KY 40202-2619
Phone: 502-589-1776
Web: www.sar.org/youth/eagle.html

National Speakers Association

National Speakers Association Scholarship

Type of award: Scholarship.
Intended use: For full-time junior, senior or graduate study at 4-year or graduate institution.
Basis for selection: Applicant must demonstrate financial need, high academic achievement, leadership and seriousness of purpose.
Application requirements: Recommendations, essay, transcript.
Additional information: Applicant must have above-average academic record and desire to be professional speaker. Application available by requesting information via email.

Amount of award:	$5,000
Number of awards:	4
Number of applicants:	37
Application deadline:	June 1
Notification begins:	September 1
Total amount awarded:	$20,000

Contact:
National Speakers Association
1500 South Priest Drive
Tempe, AZ 85281
Phone: 480-968-2552
Fax: 480-968-0911
Web: http://www.chegg.com/scholarships/national-speakers-association-scholarships

National Stone, Sand & Gravel Association

Barry K. Wendt Commitment Award and Scholarship

Type of award: Scholarship.
Intended use: For full-time undergraduate study in United States. Designated institutions: Engineering schools.
Eligibility: Applicant must be U.S. citizen or permanent resident.
Basis for selection: Major/career interest in engineering. Applicant must demonstrate high academic achievement.
Application requirements: Recommendations, essay.
Additional information: Must be planning career in aggregate industry. Visit Website for details and application.

Amount of award:	$2,500
Number of awards:	1
Application deadline:	May 30

Contact:
Wendt Memorial Scholarship Committee
c/o NSSGA
1605 King Street
Alexandria, VA 22314
Phone: 703-525-8788
Web: www.nssga.org

Navy Supply Corps Foundation

Navy Supply Corps Foundation Scholarship

Type of award: Scholarship, renewable.
Intended use: For full-time undergraduate study at accredited 2-year or 4-year institution.
Eligibility: Applicant must be U.S. citizen. Applicant must be dependent of veteran who served in the Navy. Applicant must be family member of active duty or enlisted Navy Supply Corps Officer/Warrant Officer.
Basis for selection: Applicant must demonstrate financial need, high academic achievement, depth of character, leadership and service orientation.
Application requirements: Recommendations, transcript, proof of eligibility. FAFSA.
Additional information: Minimum 2.5 GPA. Any family member of Foundation member or enlisted member (active duty, reservist, or retired) is eligible for consideration. Number of awards varies. Visit Website for application and more information.

Amount of award:	$1,000-$5,000
Application deadline:	March 9
Notification begins:	May 23
Total amount awarded:	$163,000

Contact:
Navy Supply Corps Foundation
3651 Mars Hill Road
Suite 200B
Watkinsville, GA 30677
Phone: 706-354-4111
Web: www.usnscf.com

NCJWLA

NCJWLA Scholarship Program

Type of award: Scholarship.
Intended use: For full-time undergraduate or graduate study at accredited vocational, 2-year, 4-year or graduate institution in United States. Designated institutions: Those located in the greater Los Angeles area, including Los Angeles, Orange, Riverside, and Ventura Counties.
Eligibility: Applicant must be residing in California.
Application requirements: Recommendations, essay, transcript. Transcripts, two letters of recommendation, personal statement, proof of enrollment, employment and volunteer history, financial information, and proof of childcare if applying for Childcare Scholarship.

Amount of award:	$1,000-$2,000
Number of awards:	10
Number of applicants:	140
Application deadline:	November 1, May 1
Notification begins:	December 30, June 30
Total amount awarded:	$30,000

Contact:
NCJWLA
543 North Fairfax Avenue
Los Angeles, CA 90036
Phone: 323-556-3580
Web: www.ncjwla.org/our-programs/scholarship-program/

Nebraska Coordinating Commission for Postsecondary Education

Nebraska Opportunity Grant

Type of award: Scholarship.
Intended use: For undergraduate study at postsecondary institution in United States. Designated institutions: Colleges and universities in Nebraska.
Eligibility: Applicant must be residing in Nebraska.
Basis for selection: Applicant must demonstrate financial need.
Application requirements: FAFSA.
Additional information: Award amount, application deadline, and requirements determined by individual institutions. Awards made on rolling basis. Notification begins in January preceding award year.

Number of applicants:	46,185
Total amount awarded:	$16,419,718

Contact:
Contact financial aid office at eligible institution
Phone: 402-471-2847
Fax: 402-471-2886
Web: https://ccpe.nebraska.gov/

NEFCU

Making a Difference College Scholarship

Type of award: Scholarship.
Intended use: For full-time undergraduate or graduate study at accredited 4-year or graduate institution.
Eligibility: Applicant must be at least 18. Applicant must be U.S. citizen or international student.
Basis for selection: Applicant must demonstrate high academic achievement.
Application requirements: Essay, transcript, proof of eligibility. Student must:. Complete online application form via myNEFCU.org/scholarships. Complete essay on assigned topic (the essay topic is availdble online on the application page). Attach unofficial school transript (students must have a minimum GPA of 3.5). Attach resume. Application must be completed online, paper applications will not be accepted. Eligibility Requirements: The student applicant must be a member or the applicant must have a parent/guardian who is a NEFCU member to be an eligible candidate.
Additional information: Student must be enrolled in an accredited 4 year college/university for a Bachelor's Degree or an accredited graduate program for a Master's Degree to apply. Student applicant or parent/guardian must be a member of NEFCU.

Amount of award:	$1,500
Number of awards:	5
Number of applicants:	80
Application deadline:	February 15
Notification begins:	October 1
Total amount awarded:	$7,500

Contact:
NEFCU
1000 Corporate Drive
Westbury, NY 11590
Phone: 516-714-2923
Fax: 516-714-2833
Web: https://www.mynefcu.org/community/nefcu-scholarships-grant-opportunities#undergrad

Making A Difference Community College Scholarship

Type of award: Scholarship.
Intended use: For full-time undergraduate study at accredited 2-year or 4-year institution.
Eligibility: Applicant must be at least 18. Applicant must be U.S. citizen or international student.
Basis for selection: Applicant must demonstrate high academic achievement.
Application requirements: Essay, transcript, proof of eligibility. Student must:. Complete online application form via myNEFCU.org/scholarships. Complete essay on assigned topic (the essay topic is availdble online on the application page). Attach unofficial school transript (students must have a minimum GPA of 3.0). Attach resume. Elligibility

Requirements:. The student applicant must be a member or the applicant must have a parent/guardian who is a NEFCU member.

Additional information: Student must be enrolled in an accredited community college. Application must be completed online, paper application will not be accepted.

Amount of award:	$1,000-$1,000
Number of awards:	5
Number of applicants:	10
Application deadline:	February 15
Notification begins:	October 1
Total amount awarded:	$5,000

Contact:
NEFCU
1000 Corporate Drive
Westbury, NY 11590
Phone: 516-714-2923
Fax: 516-714-2833
Web: https://www.mynefcu.org/community/nefcu-scholarships-grant-opportunities#community-college

Negative Population Growth

NPG Essay Scholarship Contest

Type of award: Scholarship.

Intended use: For full-time freshman, sophomore or junior study at accredited 2-year or 4-year institution in United States.

Eligibility: Applicant must be at least 14, high school senior. Applicant must be U.S. citizen or permanent resident.

Application requirements: Essay. Applicants are requested to provide NPG with a 500-700 words essay, in 12-14 pt font in a MSWord document or a MS Word compatible file. The essay topic can be found on the NPG Essay Scholarship Contest application form.

Additional information: Essays will be judged based on the quality of writing, originality, relevance to topic, and evidence of critical thinking. Official Contest information is available on our website (www.NPG.org) . Entries must be submitted via Email to NPGEssayScholarship@gmail.com. No mail, fax, or other submissions will be accepted. Applicants must be enrolled in an official undergraduate program of study for the Fall.To be considered submission must be complete and include the entrant's name, address, email, and telephone number (Full criteria and submission instructions available at www.NPG.org.). Applicant must sign and date the Application Form (A parent or guardian signature is also required for all applicants under 18). Relatives of employees or directors of NPG are not eligible. All submissions are subject to the NPG Privacy Policy.

Amount of award:	$1,000-$2,000
Number of awards:	5
Number of applicants:	800
Application deadline:	April 21
Notification begins:	January 5
Total amount awarded:	$6,500

Contact:
NPG
2861 Duke Street
Suit 36
Alexandria, VA 22314
Phone: 703-370-9510
Fax: 703-370-9514
Web: www.npg.org/scholarships.html

Photography Scholarship

Type of award: Scholarship.

Intended use: For full-time freshman, sophomore or junior study at accredited 2-year or 4-year institution in United States.

Eligibility: Applicant must be at least 14. Applicant must be U.S. citizen or permanent resident.

Application requirements: Submit your photo of a threatened U.S. environmental treasure that you believe is worth protecting, along with an explanation (40-50 words) of how population growth has put this treasure at risk.

Additional information: Entries must be submitted by e-mail. Must be submitted in JPG or PDF file format, file size of 1MB to 2MB, in high resolution (250 to 300 dpi). Full requirements and instructions on web site.

Amount of award:	$500-$1,500
Application deadline:	April 7
Notification begins:	June 9
Total amount awarded:	$6,500

Contact:
Negative Population Growth
2861 Duke Street
Suite 36
Alexandria, VA 22314
Phone: 703-370-9510
Fax: 703-370-9514
Web: http://npg.org/scholarships.html

Written Advertisement Scholarship

Type of award: Scholarship.

Intended use: For freshman, sophomore or junior study at accredited 2-year or 4-year institution in United States.

Eligibility: Applicant must be at least 14, high school senior. Applicant must be U.S. citizen or permanent resident.

Application requirements: Create a Written Advertisement appropriate for a magazine or newspaper. Ads must be at least 100 words but not more than 200 words. Your ad should persuade the general public to support programs that are designed to slow, halt, and eventually reverse U.S. population growth. Full instructions online.

Additional information: E-mailed or faxed entries will not be accepted.

Amount of award:	$1,000-$2,000
Number of awards:	5
Application deadline:	April 22
Total amount awarded:	$6,500

Contact:
Negative Population Growth
2861 Duke Street
Suite 36
Alexandria, VA 22314
Phone: 703-370-9510
Web: http://npg.org/scholarships.html

New England Board of Higher Education

NEBHE's Tuition Break Regional Student Program

Type of award: Scholarship.

Intended use: For undergraduate or graduate study in United States. Designated institutions: New England public colleges and universities.

Eligibility: Applicant must be permanent resident residing in Vermont, New Hampshire, Connecticut, Maine, Massachusetts or Rhode Island.

Additional information: Regional Student Program provides tuition discount to New England residents who study majors not offered at public institutions in their own state at out-of-state public colleges in New England. See Website for list of approved majors. Deadline varies by institution. Scholarship average award is $7,000.

Number of applicants:	9,300
Total amount awarded:	$56,000,000

Contact:
New England Board of Higher Education
45 Temple Place
Boston, MA 02111
Phone: 857-284-4879
Web: www.nebhe.org/tuitionbreak

New England Employee Benefits Council

NEEBC Scholarship

Type of award: Scholarship, renewable.

Intended use: For sophomore, junior, senior or graduate study at accredited postsecondary institution in United States. Designated institutions: New England colleges and universities.

Basis for selection: Major/career interest in business/management/administration; human resources; insurance/actuarial science or health services administration. Applicant must demonstrate high academic achievement, depth of character, leadership, seriousness of purpose and service orientation.

Application requirements: Recommendations, transcript. 500-word essay; minimum of two references from college professors, NEEBC members or other benefits professionals, resume.

Additional information: Minimum 3.0 GPA. Applicants must aspire to career in employee benefits. Applicants must reside or attend college in New England.

Amount of award:	$1,000-$3,000
Number of awards:	4
Number of applicants:	2
Application deadline:	April 1
Notification begins:	May 1
Total amount awarded:	$5,000

Contact:
New England Benefits Council
240 Bear Hill Road
Suite 102
Waltham, MA 02451
Phone: 781-684-8700
Fax: 781-684-9200
Web: www.neebc.org

New Jersey Hall of Fame

Arete Scholarship Fund

Type of award: Scholarship.

Intended use: For full-time undergraduate study at vocational, 2-year or 4-year institution.

Eligibility: Applicant must be high school senior. Applicant must be U.S. citizen residing in New Jersey.

Application requirements: Recommendations, transcript. Letters of recommendation from teacher, coach or extracurricular activity moderator, and community leader.

Amount of award:	$5,000
Number of awards:	2
Application deadline:	February 28
Total amount awarded:	$10,000

Contact:
Web: NJHallofFame.org/arete

New Jersey Higher Education Student Assistance Authority

New Jersey Governor's Industry Vocations Scholarship

Type of award: Scholarship.

Intended use: For undergraduate certificate study at postsecondary institution in United States. Designated institutions: New Jersey County colleges.

Additional information: Awards for women and minority students pursuing non-degree programs in construction-related fields.

Amount of award:	$500-$2,000
Number of awards:	125
Number of applicants:	78
Application deadline:	October 1, March 1
Total amount awarded:	$2,567

Contact:
New Jersey Higher Education Student Assistance Authority
P.O. Box 540
Trenton, NJ 08625-0540
Phone: 609-584-4480
Web: www.hesaa.org

Scholarships

New Jersey Law Enforcement Officer Memorial Scholarship

Type of award: Scholarship.
Intended use: For full-time undergraduate study. Designated institutions: New Jersey colleges, universities, and proprietary institutions.
Eligibility: Applicant must be U.S. citizen residing in New Jersey. Applicant's parent must have been killed or disabled in work-related accident as police officer.
Application requirements: Proof of eligibility.
Additional information: Must be dependent of law enforcement officer killed in the line of duty. Award may cover up to the cost of attendance at any approved institution of higher education in New Jersey. Awards are renewable for up to four years.

Amount of award:	Full tuition
Number of applicants:	4
Application deadline:	October 1, March 1
Total amount awarded:	$91,386

Contact:
New Jersey Higher Education Student Assistance Authority
4 Quakerbridge Plaza
P.O. Box 540
Trenton, NJ 08625-0540
Phone: 609-584-4480
Fax: 609-588-2228
Web: www.hesaa.org

New Jersey Part-Time Tuition Aid Grant for County Colleges

Type of award: Scholarship, renewable.
Intended use: For half-time undergraduate study at postsecondary institution in United States. Designated institutions: New Jersey county colleges.
Eligibility: Applicant must be U.S. citizen or permanent resident residing in New Jersey.
Basis for selection: Applicant must demonstrate financial need.
Application requirements: FAFSA.
Additional information: Must be enrolled part-time (6-11 credits). Must be legal New Jersey resident for at least 12 months prior to enrollment. Must maintain satisfactory academic progress. Renewals due June 1; new applications due October 1.

Amount of award:	$546-$1,900
Number of applicants:	10,272
Application deadline:	June 1, October 1
Total amount awarded:	$8,379,551

Contact:
New Jersey Higher Education Student Assistance Authority
4 Quakerbridge Plaza
P.O. Box 540
Trenton, NJ 08625-0540
Phone: 609-584-4480
Fax: 609-588-2228
Web: www.hesaa.org

New Jersey STARS II

Type of award: Scholarship, renewable.
Intended use: For full-time undergraduate study at accredited 4-year institution in United States. Designated institutions: Approved New Jersey 4-year institutions.
Eligibility: Applicant must be U.S. citizen or permanent resident residing in New Jersey.

Basis for selection: Applicant must demonstrate financial need and high academic achievement.
Application requirements: FAFSA.
Additional information: Must be successful NJ STARS scholar receiving associate's degree with a minimum 3.25 GPA. Awards determined after all other state and federal grants and scholarships are applied to charges, not to exceed $1,250 per year.

Amount of award:	$2,500
Number of applicants:	1,258
Application deadline:	June 1, October 1
Total amount awarded:	$3,005,879

Contact:
New Jersey Higher Education Student Assistance Authority
4 Quakerbridge Plaza
P.O. Box 540
Trenton, NJ 08625-0540
Phone: 609-584-4480
Fax: 609-588-2228
Web: www.hesaa.org

New Jersey Student Tuition Assistance Reward Scholarship (NJSTARS)

Type of award: Scholarship, renewable.
Intended use: For full-time undergraduate study in United States. Designated institutions: New Jersey county colleges.
Eligibility: Applicant must be U.S. citizen or permanent resident residing in New Jersey.
Basis for selection: Applicant must demonstrate high academic achievement.
Application requirements: FAFSA.
Additional information: Must be resident of New Jersey for 12 months prior to high school graduation. Provides tuition for up to 18 credits per semester for up to five semesters at a county college for students graduating in top 15 percent of high school class. To be eligible for renewal, students must have minimum 3.0 GPA.

Number of awards:	2,001
Application deadline:	March 1, October 1
Total amount awarded:	$5,074,308

Contact:
New Jersey Higher Education Student Assistance Authority
4 Quakerbridge Plaza
P.O. Box 540
Trenton, NJ 08625-0540
Phone: 609-584-4480
Fax: 609-588-2228
Web: www.hesaa.org

New Jersey Survivor Tuition Benefits Program

Type of award: Scholarship, renewable.
Intended use: For undergraduate study at accredited 2-year or 4-year institution in United States. Designated institutions: Approved New Jersey colleges, universities, and degree-granting institutions.
Eligibility: Applicant's parent must have been killed or disabled in work-related accident as firefighter, police officer or public safety officer.
Application requirements: Proof of eligibility.
Additional information: Parent or spouse must have been New Jersey firefighter, law enforcement officer, or emergency service worker killed in line of duty. Applications available on agency's website or by calling toll-free hotline. Grants pay cost

of tuition up to highest amount charged at a New Jersey public postsecondary school. Eligibility limited to eight years from date of child's high school graduation or date of spouse's death.

Amount of award:	Full tuition
Number of applicants:	3
Application deadline:	October 1, March 1
Total amount awarded:	$22,064

Contact:
New Jersey Higher Education Student Assistance Authority
4 Quakerbridge Plaza
P.O. Box 540
Trenton, NJ 08625-0540
Phone: 609-584-4480
Fax: 609-558-2228
Web: www.hesaa.org

New Jersey Tuition Aid Grants (TAG)

Type of award: Scholarship, renewable.
Intended use: For full-time undergraduate study in United States. Designated institutions: Approved New Jersey colleges, universities, and degree-granting proprietary institutions.
Eligibility: Applicant must be U.S. citizen or permanent resident residing in New Jersey.
Basis for selection: Applicant must demonstrate financial need.
Application requirements: FAFSA.
Additional information: Applicant must be legal New Jersey resident for at least 12 consecutive months immediately prior to enrollment. Students must maintain satisfactory academic progress. Deadline is June 1 for renewal students; October 1 for new applicants. Notification begins in March.

Amount of award:	$1,092-$11,550
Number of awards:	70,702
Number of applicants:	548,439
Application deadline:	June 1, October 1
Total amount awarded:	$332,724,424

Contact:
New Jersey Higher Education Student Assistance Authority
4 Quakerbridge Plaza
P.O. Box 540
Trenton, NJ 08625-0540
Phone: 800-584-4480
Fax: 609-558-2228
Web: www.hesaa.org

New Jersey World Trade Center Scholarship

Type of award: Scholarship, renewable.
Intended use: For full-time undergraduate study at postsecondary institution in United States. Designated institutions: Title IV eligible colleges or universities.
Eligibility: Applicant must be residing in New Jersey.
Additional information: Must be child of New Jersey resident who was killed or is presumed dead as a result of the terrorist attacks of September 11, 2001. This includes first responders and rescue workers who died as a result of illness caused by exposure to attack sites.

Amount of award:	$5,000
Number of applicants:	70
Application deadline:	October 1, March 1
Total amount awarded:	$366,930

Contact:
New Jersey Higher Education Student Assistance Authority
4 Quakerbridge Plaza
P.O. Box 540
Trenton, NJ 08625-0540
Phone: 609-584-4480
Fax: 609-588-2228
Web: www.hesaa.org

New Jersey Office of the Secretary of Higher Education

New Jersey Educational Opportunity Fund Grant

Type of award: Scholarship, renewable.
Intended use: For full-time undergraduate or graduate study at accredited 2-year or 4-year institution. Designated institutions: Participating New Jersey community colleges and four-year colleges and universities.
Eligibility: Applicant must be U.S. citizen or permanent resident residing in New Jersey.
Basis for selection: Applicant must demonstrate financial need.
Application requirements: FAFSA.
Additional information: For students from educationally disadvantaged backgrounds with demonstrated financial need. Must be New Jersey resident for at least 12 consecutive months prior to enrollment. Eligible students are admitted into EOF program by the college where they are enrolled. Program includes summer sessions, tutoring, counseling, and student leadership development. Award amounts vary by institutional sector. Contact EOF director at institution for specific application requirements.

Amount of award:	$200-$4,350
Number of awards:	12,197
Application deadline:	October 1
Notification begins:	April 1
Total amount awarded:	$17,715,650

Contact:
Office of the Secretary of Higher Education
P.O. Box 542
Trenton, NJ 08625-0542
Phone: 609-292-4310
Fax: 609-292-7225
Web: www.nj.gov/highereducation/EOF/EOF_programs.shtml

New Jersey State Golf Association

Caddie Scholarship

Type of award: Scholarship, renewable.
Intended use: For full-time undergraduate study at accredited 2-year or 4-year institution in United States. Designated institutions: Members of Association of American Colleges and Universities.

Basis for selection: Applicant must demonstrate financial need and high academic achievement.
Application requirements: Proof of eligibility. Recommendation from golf club.
Additional information: Applicants must have been a caddie for at least two seasons at a participating member club of New Jersey State Golf Association. Must be in top half of class and have minimum 900 SAT and 2.5 GPA. Awards renewable for up to four years. Foundation also offers one full scholarship award at Rutgers University.

Amount of award:	$3,500-$7,500
Number of awards:	225
Number of applicants:	219
Application deadline:	March 1
Notification begins:	June 15
Total amount awarded:	$713,600

Contact:
New Jersey State Golf Association
Caddie Scholarship Foundation
P.O. Box 6947
Freehold, NJ 07728
Phone: 848-863-6481
Web: www.njsga.org

New Mexico Higher Education Department

New Mexico Competitive Scholarships

Type of award: Scholarship.
Intended use: For full-time undergraduate study at 4-year institution in United States. Designated institutions: Public New Mexico institutions.
Basis for selection: Applicant must demonstrate high academic achievement.
Additional information: Minimum 3.5 GPA and 20 ACT score. Awards to encourage out-of-state students who have demonstrated high academic achievement in high school to enroll in public institutions in New Mexico. Recipients of at least $100 in competitive scholarships per semester eligible for resident tuition and fees. Applicants must meet GPA/ACT score requirements, which vary by institution. Contact financial aid office of any New Mexico public postsecondary institution or see Website.
Contact:
Contact financial aid office at institution.
Web: www.hed.state.nm.us

New Mexico Legislative Lottery Scholarship

Type of award: Scholarship.
Intended use: For full-time undergraduate study at postsecondary institution. Designated institutions: Eligible New Mexico public colleges and universities.
Eligibility: Applicant must be high school senior. Applicant must be residing in New Mexico.
Basis for selection: Applicant must demonstrate high academic achievement.
Additional information: During the first regular semester immediately following high school completion the student must complete 12 credit hours at a two-year institution or 15 credit

hours at a four year institution with a minimum 2.5 GPA. Deadlines vary according to institution. See Website or apply through financial aid office.

Amount of award:	Full tuition

Contact:
Contact financial aid office at institution.
Phone: 505-476-8400
Web: www.hed.state.nm.us

New Mexico Scholars Program

Type of award: Scholarship, renewable.
Intended use: For full-time undergraduate study at accredited 2-year or 4-year institution. Designated institutions: Public or private institutions in New Mexico.
Eligibility: Applicant must be no older than 21. Applicant must be U.S. citizen or permanent resident residing in New Mexico.
Basis for selection: Applicant must demonstrate financial need and high academic achievement.
Application requirements: FAFSA.
Additional information: Award includes books and required fees. Number of awards based on availability of funds. Must be graduate of New Mexico high school. Must have 25 ACT score, 1140 SAT score, or be in top five percent of class. Must attend eligible university by end of 21st birthday. Combined family income may not exceed $30,000 per year. Contact financial aid office of New Mexico postsecondary institution of choice for information and application. Application deadline set by institution.

Amount of award:	Full tuition

Contact:
Contact financial aid office at institution.
Phone: 505-476-8400
Web: www.hed.state.nm.us

New Mexico Student Incentive Grant

Type of award: Scholarship, renewable.
Intended use: For undergraduate study at accredited postsecondary institution. Designated institutions: Public or private colleges in New Mexico.
Eligibility: Applicant must be U.S. citizen or permanent resident residing in New Mexico.
Basis for selection: Applicant must demonstrate financial need.
Application requirements: FAFSA.
Additional information: Must demonstrate exceptional financial need. Contact financial aid office of designated institutions for information, application, and deadline. Part-time students eligible for pro-rated awards.

Amount of award:	$200-$2,500

Contact:
Contact financial aid office at institution.
Phone: 505-476-8400
Web: www.hed.state.nm.us

New York State Education Department

New York State Arthur O. Eve Higher Education Opportunity Program (HEOP)

Type of award: Scholarship.
Intended use: For undergraduate study at 2-year or 4-year institution. Designated institutions: Independent New York State colleges and universities.

Eligibility: Applicant must be residing in New York.
Basis for selection: Applicant must demonstrate financial need.
Additional information: Applicant must be resident of New York State for one year preceding entry into HEOP and be academically and economically disadvantaged. Contact college or university of interest for application and additional information, and apply at time of admission. Support services include pre-session summer program and tutoring, counseling, and special coursework during academic year. Award amounts vary; contact sponsor for information. For general information, contact New York State Education Department.

    Number of applicants: 5,368
Contact:
New York State Education Department
Room 505W
Education Building
Albany, NY 12234
Phone: 518-486-5202
Fax: 518-474-7468
Web: www.highered.nysed.gov/kiap/colldev/HEOP

New York State Grange

Caroline Kark Scholarship

Type of award: Scholarship.
Intended use: For undergraduate study at postsecondary institution.
Eligibility: Applicant or parent must be member/participant of New York State Grange. Applicant must be residing in New York.
Basis for selection: Major/career interest in deafness studies.
Additional information: Award available to Grange members preparing for a career working with the deaf or hearing impaired and to non-members who are deaf and want to further their education beyond high school. Hearing applicants must have been a Grange member for one year prior to applying. Deaf applicants must show sufficient hearing loss to receive full-time amplification.

    Application deadline: April 15
    Notification begins: June 15
Contact:
New York State Grange
100 Grange Place
Cortland, NY 13045
Phone: 607-756-7553
Fax: 607-756-7757
Web: www.nysgrange.org

Grange Denise Scholarship

Type of award: Scholarship, renewable.
Intended use: For full-time undergraduate study at 2-year or 4-year institution.
Eligibility: Applicant or parent must be member/participant of New York State Grange. Applicant must be residing in New York.
Basis for selection: Major/career interest in agriculture; agribusiness; agricultural education; agricultural economics or natural resources/conservation. Applicant must demonstrate financial need.
Application requirements: Recommendations, transcript.
Additional information: Send SASE for application.

    Amount of award: $1,000
    Number of awards: 3
    Number of applicants: 4
    Application deadline: April 15
    Notification begins: June 15
    Total amount awarded: $4,000
Contact:
New York State Grange
100 Grange Place
Cortland, NY 13045
Phone: 607-756-7553
Fax: 607-756-7757
Web: www.nysgrange.org

Grange Susan W. Freestone Education Award

Type of award: Scholarship, renewable.
Intended use: For full-time undergraduate or graduate study at 2-year or 4-year institution in United States. Designated institutions: Approved institutions in New York state.
Eligibility: Applicant or parent must be member/participant of New York State Grange. Applicant must be residing in New York.
Basis for selection: Applicant must demonstrate financial need, depth of character and service orientation.
Application requirements: Transcript.
Additional information: Applicant must be current New York State Grange member. Must have been Junior Grange member to qualify for maximum award. Send SASE for application. Activity in Grange work considered.

    Amount of award: $1,000
    Number of awards: 2
    Number of applicants: 2
    Application deadline: April 15
    Notification begins: June 15
    Total amount awarded: $4,000
Contact:
New York State Grange
100 Grange Place
Cortland, NY 13045
Phone: 607-756-7553
Fax: 607-756-7757
Web: www.nysgrange.org

June Gill Nursing Scholarship

Type of award: Scholarship, renewable.
Intended use: For undergraduate study at postsecondary institution.
Eligibility: Applicant or parent must be member/participant of New York State Grange. Applicant must be residing in New York.
Basis for selection: Major/career interest in nursing. Applicant must demonstrate financial need and high academic achievement.
Application requirements: Transcript, proof of eligibility. Career statement.
Additional information: Grandchild of member of the New York State Grange also eligible. Award amounts vary.

    Amount of award: $1,000
    Number of awards: 1
    Number of applicants: 1
    Application deadline: April 15
    Notification begins: June 1

Contact:
New York State Grange
100 Grange Place
Cortland, NY 13045
Phone: 607-756-7553
Fax: 607-756-7757
Web: www.nysgrange.org

New York State Higher Education Services Corporation

City University SEEK/College Discovery Program

Type of award: Scholarship.
Intended use: For undergraduate study at 2-year or 4-year institution. Designated institutions: City University of New York campuses.
Eligibility: Applicant must be U.S. citizen or permanent resident residing in New York.
Basis for selection: Applicant must demonstrate financial need.
Application requirements: Proof of eligibility. FAFSA, TAP.
Additional information: Applicant must be both academically and economically disadvantaged. Available at CUNY and community college campuses. Apply to CUNY financial aid office. For SEEK, student must have resided in New York State for at least one year; for College Discovery, student must have resided in New York City for at least one year.
Contact:
City University of New York
Office of Admission Services
1114 Avenue of the Americas
New York, NY 10036
Phone: 212-997-CUNY
Web: www.cuny.edu

Flight 587 Memorial Scholarships

Type of award: Scholarship, renewable.
Intended use: For full-time undergraduate study at postsecondary institution. Designated institutions: Approved New York state institutions.
Eligibility: Applicant must be residing in New York.
Application requirements: FAFSA. TAP. Scholarship supplement. Proof of applicant's relationship to the deceased (birth certificate, marriage license, etc.)
Additional information: Provides financial aid to children, spouses, and financial dependents of individuals killed as a direct result of American Airlines Flight 587's crash in the Belle Harbor neighborhood of Queens, New York, on the morning of November 12, 2001. Award is full tuition for students attending public colleges and universities in New York State, and the monetary equivalent for students attending private New York schools.

Amount of award:	Full tuition
Application deadline:	June 30

Contact:
New York State Higher Education Services Corporation
HESC Scholarship Unit
99 Washington Avenue, Room 1430A
Albany, NY 12255
Phone: 888-NYS-HESC
Web: www.hesc.com

New York Military Service Recognition Scholarship (MSRS)

Type of award: Scholarship, renewable.
Intended use: For full-time undergraduate study at 2-year or 4-year institution. Designated institutions: Approved New York State institutions.
Eligibility: Applicant must be residing in New York. Applicant must be disabled while on active duty; or dependent of disabled veteran, deceased veteran or POW/MIA; or spouse of disabled veteran, deceased veteran or POW/MIA. Must be child, spouse, or financial dependent of member of the U.S. armed forces or state-organized militia who, at any time after August 2, 1990, while New York State resident, (1) died or became permanently disabled as a result of injury or illness in a combat theater or combat zone or during military training operations in preparation for duty in a combat theater or (2) is classified as MIA in a combat theater or combat zone of operations.
Application requirements: FAFSA, TAP application.
Additional information: At public colleges and universities (CUNY or SUNY), award covers actual tuition and mandatory educational fees; actual room and board for living on campus (or an allowance for commuters); and allowances for books, supplies, and transportation. At private institutions, award amount equals SUNY four-year college tuition and fees and allowances for room and board, books, supplies, and transportation. New York State resident family members who were enrolled in undergraduate programs at U.S. colleges or universities outside of New York State on September 11, 2001, are also eligible. See Website for more details.

Amount of award:	Full tuition
Application deadline:	June 30

Contact:
New York State Higher Education Services Corporation
Scholarships and Grants
99 Washington Avenue
Albany, NY 12255
Phone: 888-NYS-HESC
Web: www.hesc.com

New York State Aid for Part-Time Study Program

Type of award: Scholarship, renewable.
Intended use: For half-time undergraduate study at postsecondary institution. Designated institutions: Participating New York state institutions.
Eligibility: Applicant must be U.S. citizen or permanent resident residing in New York.
Basis for selection: Applicant must demonstrate financial need and high academic achievement.
Application requirements: Proof of eligibility.
Additional information: Must fall within income limits. Campus-based program; recipients selected and award amount determined by school. Maximum award is $2,000. Must not have used up TAP eligibility or be in default on Federal Family Education Loan. Student must maintain minimum 2.0 GPA. Applications available from individual colleges.

Amount of award: $2,000
Contact:
New York State Higher Education Services Corporation
Scholarships and Grants
99 Washington Avenue
Albany, NY 12255
Phone: 888-NYS-HESC
Web: www.hesc.com

New York State Math and Science Teaching Incentive Program

Type of award: Scholarship.
Intended use: For full-time undergraduate or graduate study at 4-year or graduate institution in United States. Designated institutions: New York institutions.
Eligibility: Applicant must be U.S. citizen or permanent resident.
Basis for selection: Major/career interest in mathematics; education, teacher or science, general. Applicant must demonstrate high academic achievement.
Application requirements: FAFSA. Must apply for NYS Tuition Assistance Program.
Additional information: Award is for exchange of five years full-time employment as secondary education math or science teacher. Must be U.S. citizen or eligible non-citizen. Minimum 2.5 GPA. Must be matriculated in approved undergraduate or graduate program in New York State leading to career as secondary education math or science teacher. Program pays for student's annual tuition, up to the price of an undergraduate program at State University of New York, or actual tuition charged; whichever is less. Must retain 2.5 GPA, full-time attendance, and earn at least 27 credit hours yearly to retain award. May not have service obligation under another program. May not be in default on federally guaranteed student loan. Visit Website to apply.
Amount of award: $5,895
Application deadline: March 15
Contact:
New York State Higher Education Services Corporation
Phone: 888-697-4372
Web: www.hesc.com

New York State Memorial Scholarship for Families of Deceased Police/Volunteer Firefighters/Peace Officers and Emergency Medical Service Workers

Type of award: Scholarship, renewable.
Intended use: For full-time undergraduate study at 2-year or 4-year institution. Designated institutions: Approved New York institutions.
Eligibility: Applicant must be U.S. citizen residing in New York. Applicant's parent must have been killed or disabled in work-related accident as firefighter, police officer or public safety officer.
Application requirements: Proof of eligibility. Memorial Scholarship Supplement, FAFSA, and Express TAP Application.
Additional information: Spouse and/or children of police officer/firefighter/peace officer/EMS worker who died as result of injuries sustained in line of duty in service to New York State are eligible. Award will equal applicant's actual tuition cost or SUNY undergraduate tuition cost, whichever is less. Also provides funds to meet non-tuition costs, such as room

and board, books, supplies, and transportation. Visit Website for additional information.
Amount of award: Full tuition
Application deadline: June 30
Contact:
New York State Higher Education Services Corporation
Scholarships and Grants
99 Washington Avenue
Albany, NY 12255
Phone: 888-NYS-HESC
Web: www.hesc.com

New York State Regents Awards for Children of Deceased and Disabled Veterans

Type of award: Scholarship.
Intended use: For full-time undergraduate or non-degree study at 2-year or 4-year institution.
Eligibility: Applicant must be residing in New York. Applicant must be dependent of veteran, disabled veteran or deceased veteran during Korean War, Persian Gulf War, WW I, WW II or Vietnam. Student's parent must have been disabled or deceased veteran or POW, or classified as MIA. Student whose parent is a veteran of Afghanistan conflict also eligible. Student whose parent has received Armed Forces, Navy, or Marine Corps expeditionary medal for participation in operations in Lebanon, Grenada, and Panama also eligible, as are students born with spina bifida whose parent(s) served in Vietnam between 12/22/61 and 5/7/75.
Application requirements: Proof of eligibility. FAFSA and Express TAP Application.
Additional information: Student must initially establish eligibility by submitting a Child of Veteran Award Supplement before applying. Veteran must be a resident of New York state. Visit Website for additional information.
Amount of award: $450
Application deadline: June 30
Contact:
New York State Higher Education Services Corporation
Scholarships and Grants
99 Washington Avenue
Albany, NY 12255
Phone: 888-NYS-HESC
Web: www.hesc.com

New York State Tuition Assistance Program

Type of award: Scholarship, renewable.
Intended use: For full-time undergraduate or graduate study at accredited postsecondary institution in United States. Designated institutions: TAP-eligible schools in New York.
Eligibility: Applicant must be U.S. citizen or permanent resident residing in New York.
Basis for selection: Applicant must demonstrate financial need.
Application requirements: Proof of eligibility. FAFSA.
Additional information: Must fall within income limits. Must be charged at least $200 tuition per year. Submit FAFSA to receive prefilled Express TAP Application (ETA) to review, sign, and return. Award subject to budget appropriations. Must maintain at least C average. Must not be in default on a HESC-guaranteed loan. Part-time, first-time freshmen attending CUNY, SUNY, or not-for-profit independent degree-granting colleges also eligible. Visit Website for additional information.

| Amount of award: | $5,000 |
| Application deadline: | May 1 |

Contact:
New York State Higher Education Services Corporation
Grants and Scholarships
99 Washington Avenue
Albany, NY 12255
Phone: 888-NYS-HESC
Web: www.hesc.com

New York State Veterans Tuition Award

Type of award: Scholarship, renewable.
Intended use: For undergraduate or graduate study at accredited vocational, 2-year, 4-year or graduate institution in United States. Designated institutions: Approved postsecondary schools in New York.
Eligibility: Applicant must be returning adult student. Applicant must be U.S. citizen or permanent resident residing in New York. Applicant must be veteran during Persian Gulf War or Vietnam. Must have served in armed forces in hostilities in Indochina between December 1961 and May 1975, or in Persian Gulf on or after August 2, 1990. Veterans of the conflict in Afghanistan also eligible. Must not have been dishonorably discharged.
Application requirements: Proof of eligibility. FAFSA. Express Tap Application (ETA). Documentation of Indochina, Persian Gulf, or Afghanistan service.
Additional information: Students must have also applied for TAP and Federal Pell Grant awards. Visit Website for additional information.

| Amount of award: | $5,895 |
| Application deadline: | June 30 |

Contact:
New York State Higher Education Services Corporation
Scholarships and Grants
99 Washington Avenue
Albany, NY 12255
Phone: 888-NYS-HESC
Web: www.hesc.com

New York State World Trade Center Memorial Scholarship

Type of award: Scholarship, renewable.
Intended use: For full-time undergraduate study at 2-year or 4-year institution. Designated institutions: Approved New York colleges and universities.
Application requirements: Proof of eligibility. FAFSA, Express TAP Application.
Additional information: Must be child, spouse, or financial dependent of person who died or became severely and permanently disabled due to the September 11th attacks or rescue and recovery operation. At public colleges and universities (CUNY or SUNY), award covers actual tuition and mandatory educational fees; actual room and board for living on campus (or an allowance for commuters); and allowances for books, supplies, and transportation. At private institutions, award amount equals SUNY four-year college tuition and fees, and allowances for room and board, books, supplies, and transportation. New York State resident family members who were enrolled in undergraduate programs at U.S. colleges or universities outside of New York State on September 11, 2001, are also eligible. See Website for details.

| Amount of award: | Full tuition |
| Application deadline: | June 30 |

Contact:
New York State Higher Education Services Corporation
Grants and Scholarships
99 Washington Avenue
Albany, NY 12255
Phone: 888-NYS-HESC
Web: www.hesc.com

New York State Office of Adult Career and Educational Services

New York State Readers Aid Program

Type of award: Scholarship, renewable.
Intended use: For undergraduate, master's or doctoral study at 2-year, 4-year or graduate institution.
Eligibility: Applicant must be visually impaired or hearing impaired. Applicant must be residing in New York.
Application requirements: Proof of eligibility.
Additional information: Applicant must be legally blind or deaf. Number of awards varies. Applications available at degree-granting institutions. Award provides funds for note-takers, readers, or interpreters. Applicant may be attending out-of-state institution.

Amount of award:	$1,000
Number of applicants:	411
Application deadline:	March 15, June 30
Total amount awarded:	$300,000

Contact:
New York State Education Department
ACCES-VR, attn: Dennis Barlow
89 Washington Avenue, EBA 5th Floor
Albany, NY 12234
Phone: 518-474-7343
Web: www.acces.nysed.gov

New York Women in Communications Foundation

New York Women in Communications Foundation Scholarship

Type of award: Scholarship, renewable.
Intended use: For undergraduate or graduate study at accredited postsecondary institution.
Eligibility: Applicant must be U.S. citizen.
Basis for selection: Major/career interest in communications. Applicant must demonstrate financial need, high academic achievement, leadership and service orientation.
Application requirements: Interview, recommendations, essay, transcript, proof of eligibility. Resume.
Additional information: Minimum 3.2 GPA. Applicant must be majoring in a communications-related field or a high school

senior intending to declare a major in a communications-related field. Must be attending school in New York City or be a resident of New York, New Jersey, Connecticut, or Pennsylvania. Finalists will be required to attend an in-person interview in New York City in March. Visit Website for application and additional requirements.

Amount of award:	$2,500-$10,000
Number of awards:	15
Number of applicants:	500
Application deadline:	January 24
Notification begins:	April 1
Total amount awarded:	$100,000

Contact:
New York Women in Communications Foundation Scholarship Program
355 Lexington Avenue, 15th Floor
New York, NY 10017-6603
Phone: 212-297-2133
Fax: 212-370-9047
Web: www.nywici.org

Next Steps Digital

$5,000 Next Steps Digital Scholarship

Type of award: Scholarship.
Intended use: For full-time undergraduate or graduate study in United States.
Eligibility: Applicant must be U.S. citizen.
Basis for selection: Major/career interest in marketing.
Application requirements: Transcript. Essay of no more than two pages double spaced on one of the following topics: describe an accomplishment you have been recognized for and its influence on you; who has been most influential in you life and why; what are your career aspirations and why.
Additional information: Must have a cumulative college grade point average of at least 3.5 and be working towards a degree in Marketing.

Number of awards:	1
Application deadline:	December 15
Notification begins:	December 31
Total amount awarded:	$5,000

Contact:
Web: https://www.nextstepsdigital.com/scholarship/

Nicodemus Wilderness Project

Apprentice Ecologist Initiative

Type of award: Scholarship.
Intended use: For undergraduate study at postsecondary institution.
Eligibility: Applicant must be at least 13, no older than 21.
Basis for selection: Applicant must demonstrate leadership, seriousness of purpose and service orientation.
Application requirements: Essay.
Additional information: Scholarships awarded annually to the authors of the top three Apprentice Ecologist essays.

Applicants must be in primary (middle school), secondary (high school), or accredited post-secondary (undergraduate at college or university) educational institution. Visit Website for details.

Amount of award:	$250-$1,000
Number of awards:	3
Number of applicants:	112
Application deadline:	December 31
Notification begins:	April 22
Total amount awarded:	$850

Contact:
Nicodemus Wilderness Project
P.O. Box 40712
Albuquerque, NM 87196-0712
Web: www.wildernessproject.org/volunteer_apprentice_ecologist

Nikko Cosmetic Surgery Center

Breast Cancer Survivor Scholarship

Type of award: Scholarship.
Intended use: For full-time undergraduate or graduate study at vocational, 2-year, 4-year or graduate institution.
Eligibility: Applicant must be U.S. citizen.
Application requirements: Tell us briefly (100 words or less) about your educational goals. (Optional) Write an original 650 to 1,000 word essay on the subject of how being diagnosed with breast cancer has affected your life.
Additional information: Must be a US citizen who has been diagnosed with breast cancer. May be asked for documentation showing breast cancer diagnosis or treatment. Award may be used for study abroad.

Amount of award:	$1,000
Number of awards:	2
Application deadline:	September 30
Notification begins:	October 31

Contact:
Nikko Cosmetic Surgery Center
1001 West Loop South
813
Houston, TX 77027
Phone: 713-960-1311
Web: www.drnikko.com/breast-cancer-survivor-scholarships

Nisei Student Relocation Commemorative Fund

Nisei Student Relocation Commemorative Fund Scholarship

Type of award: Scholarship.
Intended use: For freshman study at vocational, 2-year or 4-year institution in United States.
Eligibility: Applicant must be Southeast Asian (Vietnamese, Cambodian, Hmong, Laotian, Amerasian) refugee or immigrant. Applicant must be high school senior.
Basis for selection: Applicant must demonstrate financial need, high academic achievement and service orientation.

Application requirements: Recommendations, essay, transcript.

Additional information: Applicant must be high school senior living in city/area/region of the U.S. where scholarships are awarded, as determined annually by organization's board of directors. Location changes yearly; contact group for information. Number of awards varies.

Amount of award:	$250-$2,000
Number of awards:	60
Number of applicants:	175
Application deadline:	April 1
Total amount awarded:	$50,000

Contact:
Nisei Student Relocation Commemorative Fund Scholarship
Web: www.nsrcfund.org

Nitro

Nitro College Scholarship

Type of award: Scholarship.
Intended use: For full-time undergraduate or graduate study at 2-year, 4-year or graduate institution in United States.
Additional information: Apply online for the Nitro $5,000 scholarship. If you recommend a friend to apply, they provide you as a reference and they win, you will win a $1,000 scholarship. Upcoming Application Deadlines: 6/30, 9/30, 12/31. Notification Dates: 8/1, 11/1, 2/1. Winner announcements will be made 1 month after the deadline.

Amount of award:	$1,000-$5,000
Number of awards:	2
Application deadline:	June 30, December 31
Notification begins:	August 1, February 1
Total amount awarded:	$6,000

Contact:
Web: https://www.nitrocollege.com/nitro-scholarship-application

NMIA Ohio

NMIA Ohio Scholarship Program

Type of award: Scholarship, renewable.
Intended use: For junior, senior or graduate study at accredited 4-year or graduate institution in United States.
Eligibility: Applicant must be U.S. citizen residing in Ohio.
Basis for selection: Applicant must demonstrate high academic achievement.
Additional information: Applicant must be interested in a career in Intelligence. Funds awarded may be used for tuition, room, board, and/or laboratory fees and will be payable to the student's institution. Size and number of awards depends on funding; one to six awards will be given each year. Scholarships for full-time students will be greater than scholarships for part-time students. Applicant must not be relative of NMIA scholarship committee members. Preference is given to students attending Ohio colleges and universities. The decision of the Scholarship Committee is final and not subject to external review.

Amount of award:	$500-$2,000
Number of applicants:	11
Application deadline:	March 31
Notification begins:	April 1
Total amount awarded:	$3,000

Contact:
NMIA Ohio
c/o Deanne Otto
P.O. Box 341508
Beavercreek, OH 45434
Fax: 937-431-3811
Web: www.nmiaohio.org

Non Commissioned Officers Association

Non Commissioned Officers Association Scholarship for Children of Members

Type of award: Scholarship, renewable.
Intended use: For full-time undergraduate study in United States.
Application requirements: Transcript. Autobiography, ACT/SAT scores, and minimum 200-word essay on Americanism. Include two recommendation letters from school and one personal recommendation letter from adult who is not a relative.
Additional information: Applicant's parent must be member of Non Commissioned Officers Association.

Amount of award:	$900
Number of applicants:	127
Application deadline:	March 31
Notification begins:	June 1

Contact:
Non Commissioned Officers Association
P.O. Box 33790
San Antonio, TX 78265
Phone: 210-653-6161
Fax: 210-637-3337
Web: www.ncoausa.org

Non Commissioned Officers Association Scholarship for Spouses of Members

Type of award: Scholarship, renewable.
Intended use: For full-time undergraduate study in United States.
Application requirements: Transcript. Copy of high school diploma or GED, brief biographical background, and certificates for any training courses completed. Letter of intent describing degree course of study, plans for completion of program, and a closing paragraph on "What a College Degree Means to Me."
Additional information: Must be spouse of member of Non Commissioned Officers Association. Recipient must apply for auxiliary membership in Non Commissioned Officers Association.

Amount of award:	$900
Application deadline:	March 31
Notification begins:	June 1

Contact:
Non Commissioned Officers Association
P.O. Box 33790
San Antonio, TX 78265
Phone: 210-653-6161
Fax: 210-637-3337
Web: www.ncoausa.org

Noodle

Noodle College Scholarship Sweepstakes

Type of award: Scholarship.
Intended use: For undergraduate or graduate study at accredited 2-year, 4-year or graduate institution in United States.
Eligibility: Applicant must be at least 18. Applicant must be U.S. citizen or permanent resident.
Application requirements: Register on Noodle to receive one entry. See scholarship website for opportunities to earn more entries.
Additional information: Must be currently enrolled in an accredited college located in the United States. Employees and immediate families of Noodle are not eligible.

Amount of award:	$1,000
Number of awards:	1
Number of applicants:	5,737
Application deadline:	March 31
Total amount awarded:	$1,000

Contact:
Noodle
59 Chelsea Piers
Suite 200
New York, NY 10011
Phone: 646-289-7800
Web: https://www.noodle.com/scholarships/college

North American Limousin Foundation

Limi Boosters National Educational Grant

Type of award: Scholarship.
Intended use: For undergraduate study at vocational, 2-year or 4-year institution.
Basis for selection: Major/career interest in agriculture. Applicant must demonstrate financial need, high academic achievement, depth of character, leadership, patriotism, seriousness of purpose and service orientation.
Application requirements: Recommendations, proof of eligibility. Recent photo. One of the three recommendations must be from active NALF member other than relative or guardian, two must be from the following: school superintendent, school principal, minister, 4-H leader, FFA instructor, county agent, or teacher.
Additional information: Experience with Limousin cattle preferred. Proven excellence in Limousin activities as well as leadership skills demonstrated in NALJA, 4-H, and FFA. Must be NALF Junior member.

Amount of award:	$500-$750
Application deadline:	May 16

Contact:
Marci Hicks
PO Box 791
Elk Point, SD 57025
Phone: 605-310-0791
Web: www.nalf.org

Limi Boosters Scholarship

Type of award: Scholarship.
Intended use: For undergraduate study at 4-year institution.
Basis for selection: Applicant must demonstrate financial need, high academic achievement, depth of character, leadership, patriotism, seriousness of purpose and service orientation.
Application requirements: Transcript, proof of eligibility. Three recommendations, one of which must be from active NALF member other than relative or guardian.
Additional information: Must be NALF member and be active in 4H and FFA work. Must rank in top third of class.

Amount of award:	$500-$750
Number of awards:	2
Application deadline:	May 16
Total amount awarded:	$3,000

Contact:
Marci Hicks
P.O. Box 4253
Midway, KY 40347
Phone: 859-576-2602
Web: www.nalf.org

North Carolina Community Colleges Foundation

North Carolina Community Colleges Wells Fargo Technical Scholarship

Type of award: Scholarship.
Intended use: For full-time sophomore study at vocational or 2-year institution.
Eligibility: Applicant must be residing in North Carolina.
Basis for selection: Applicant must demonstrate financial need and high academic achievement.
Additional information: Scholarships distributed through the 58 community colleges in the system; apply through financial aid office of institution where enrolled.

Amount of award:	$500

Contact:
North Carolina Community Colleges Foundation
5016 Mail Service Center
Raleigh, NC 27699
Phone: 919-807-7195
Fax: 919-807-7173
Web: www.nccommunitycolleges.edu

Rodney E. Powell Memorial Scholarship

Type of award: Scholarship.
Intended use: For full-time undergraduate study at 2-year institution. Designated institutions: Community colleges in Progress Energy's service area.
Eligibility: Applicant must be residing in North Carolina.
Basis for selection: Major/career interest in engineering, electrical/electronic; electronics or technology. Applicant must demonstrate financial need and high academic achievement.
Application requirements: Essay.
Additional information: Minimum 3.0 GPA. Scholarship for students of electronic technology. Applicant must be enrolled full-time or must intend to enroll as new student at designated institution. Number of awards varies.

Amount of award:	$1,000
Number of awards:	1

Contact:
North Carolina Department of Community Colleges
Attn: Lee McCollum
410 S. Wilmington Street PEB 7
Raleigh, NC 27601
Phone: 919-546-7585
Fax: 919-546-7652
Web: www.nccommunitycolleges.edu

North Carolina Division of Veterans Affairs

North Carolina Scholarships for Children of War Veterans

Type of award: Scholarship, renewable.
Intended use: For undergraduate or graduate study at accredited postsecondary institution.
Eligibility: Applicant must be no older than 24. Applicant must be residing in North Carolina. Applicant must be dependent of disabled veteran, deceased veteran or POW/MIA who served in the Army, Air Force, Marines, Navy or Coast Guard. Parent must have served during a period of war.
Basis for selection: Applicant must demonstrate financial need.
Application requirements: Interview, transcript, proof of eligibility. Birth certificate.
Additional information: Must be natural child or adopted child prior to age 15. For state schools, award is tuition waiver plus a room and board allowance for up to four years. For private schools, award is up to $4,500 per year. Parent must have been North Carolina resident at time of enlistment or child must have been born in and reside permanently in North Carolina. See Website for deadline information.

Amount of award:	Full tuition
Number of applicants:	555

Contact:
North Carolina Division of Veterans Affairs
1315 Mail Service Center
Raleigh, NC 27699-1315
Web: www.ncveterans.com

North Carolina Division of Vocational Rehabilitation Services

North Carolina Vocational Rehabilitation Award

Type of award: Scholarship, renewable.
Intended use: For full-time undergraduate study at accredited vocational, 2-year or 4-year institution.
Eligibility: Applicant must be physically challenged or learning disabled. Applicant must be residing in North Carolina.
Basis for selection: Applicant must demonstrate financial need.
Application requirements: Interview, proof of eligibility. Proof of mental, physical, or learning disability that is an impediment to employment.
Additional information: Award varies with need and eligibility. Applicant must have a physical, emotional, or learning disability and be eligible for Vocational Rehabilitation Services. This program provides educational assistance for individuals who meet eligibility requirements and require training to reach their vocational goals. Visit Website for full eligibility requirements.

Contact:
North Carolina Division of Vocational Rehabilitation Services
2801 Mail Service Center
Raleigh, NC 27699-2801
Phone: 919-855-3500
Fax: 919-715-0616
Web: https://bigfuture.collegeboard.org/scholarships/north-carolina-vocational-rehabilitation-award

North Carolina State Board of Refrigeration Examiners

North Carolina State Board of Refrigeration Examiners Scholarship

Type of award: Scholarship.
Intended use: For undergraduate study at 2-year institution.
Eligibility: Applicant must be residing in North Carolina.
Basis for selection: Major/career interest in air conditioning/heating/refrigeration technology. Applicant must demonstrate financial need and high academic achievement.
Application requirements: Essay.
Additional information: Number of awards varies. Must enroll in Associate of Applied Science degree of study in commercial refrigeration or HVAC/R technology. Must maintain GPA at or above level required for graduation. Must continue for duration of scholarship at the college where he or she was enrolled at the time of the scholarship award.

Number of awards:	2
Application deadline:	April 15

Contact:
North Carolina State Board of Refrigeration Examiners
1027 US 70 Hwy W
Suit 221
Garner, NC 27529
Phone: 919-779-4711
Fax: 919-779-4733
Web: www.refrigerationboard.org/wp

North Carolina State Education Assistance Authority

Golden LEAF Scholars Program - Two-Year Colleges

Type of award: Scholarship.
Intended use: For undergraduate study at 2-year institution. Designated institutions: Member institutions of North Carolina Community College system.
Eligibility: Applicant must be residing in North Carolina.
Basis for selection: Applicant must demonstrate financial need, high academic achievement, depth of character, leadership and service orientation.
Application requirements: Disclosure of other financial aid awards. FAFSA.
Additional information: Applicant must demonstrate need under federal TRIO formula. Award is up to $750 per semester (including summer) for curriculum students; up to $250 per semester for occupational education students. Finalist will undergo merit competition and be judged on academics, leadership, community service, and the effect of the economy's decline on his/her family. Must be permanent resident of one of 73 eligible counties. Visit Website for more information. Contact financial aid office for application.

Amount of award:	$500-$1,500

Contact:
Contact financial aid office at local community college.
Phone: 888-684-8404
Fax: 919-549-8481
Web: www.cfnc.org

Golden LEAF Scholarship - Four-Year University Program

Type of award: Scholarship, renewable.
Intended use: For undergraduate study at 4-year institution. Designated institutions: Public universities.
Eligibility: Applicant must be residing in North Carolina.
Basis for selection: Applicant must demonstrate financial need.
Application requirements: FAFSA.
Additional information: Must be incoming freshman, transfer student from a North Carolina community college, or previous recipient applying for renewal. New applicants must be permanent resident of economically distressed and/or tobacco-dependent rural county. Recipients of other aid amounting to 75 percent or more of total education costs will be given low priority. Visit Website for application and more information.

Amount of award:	$3,000
Number of awards:	215
Application deadline:	March 15

Contact:
North Carolina State Education Assistance Authority
Phone: 888-684-8404
Web: www.cfnc.org

Jagannathan Scholarship

Type of award: Scholarship, renewable.
Intended use: For full-time freshman study at 4-year institution in United States. Designated institutions: Constituent institutions of the University of North Carolina.
Eligibility: Applicant must be high school senior. Applicant must be U.S. citizen or permanent resident residing in North Carolina.
Basis for selection: Applicant must demonstrate financial need, high academic achievement and leadership.
Application requirements: Proof of eligibility, nomination by high school guidance counselor, financial office of UNC institution, or Tolaram Polymers, Cookson Fibers, or related company. SAT scores, College Scholarship Service's PROFILE (register and file by February 8), and documented proof of financial need. FAFSA.
Additional information: Special consideration given to students whose parents are employees of Tolaram Polymers, Cookson Fibers, or related companies. Applications available at all North Carolina public high schools. Minimum SAT 1200 score (reading and math) or ACT equivalent. Check Website for specific details. Apply online.

Amount of award:	$2,000
Number of awards:	4
Number of applicants:	4
Application deadline:	February 1
Notification begins:	May 1
Total amount awarded:	$14,000

Contact:
North Carolina State Education Assistance Authority
Phone: 919-549-8614
Web: www.cfnc.org/jag

Latino Diamante Scholarship Fund

Type of award: Scholarship.
Intended use: For freshman or sophomore study at postsecondary institution. Designated institutions: North Carolina institutions.
Eligibility: Applicant must be Hispanic American. Applicant must be residing in North Carolina.
Basis for selection: Applicant must demonstrate high academic achievement.
Application requirements: Recommendations, essay, transcript.
Additional information: Minimum 2.5 GPA. Visit Website for application and more information.

Application deadline:	August 15
Notification begins:	September 15

Contact:
Diamante, Inc.
315 North Academy Street
Suite 256
Cary, NC 27513
Phone: 919-852-0075
Web: www.cfnc.org

NC Sheriff's Association Criminal Justice Scholarship

Type of award: Scholarship.
Intended use: For full-time undergraduate study in United States. Designated institutions: Appalachian State University, East Carolina University, Elizabeth City State University, Fayetteville State University, North Carolina Central University, North Carolina State University, University of North Carolina at Charlotte, University of North Carolina at Pembroke, University of North Carolina at Wilmington, Western Carolina University.
Eligibility: Applicant must be residing in North Carolina.
Basis for selection: Major/career interest in criminal justice/law enforcement. Applicant must demonstrate financial need.
Application requirements: Recommendations, essay, transcript.
Additional information: Application available at financial aid offices of eligible institutions. Application and supplemental material should be submitted to sheriff of county where applicant resides. First priority given to child of sheriff/law enforcement officer killed in the line of duty; second priority given to child of retired or deceased sheriff/law enforcement officer; third priority given to criminal justice students.

Amount of award:	$2,000
Number of awards:	10
Number of applicants:	50
Total amount awarded:	$20,000

Contact:
North Carolina State Education Assistance Authority
Phone: 919-549-8614
Web: www.cfnc.org

North Carolina Aubrey Lee Brooks Scholarship

Type of award: Scholarship, renewable.
Intended use: For full-time undergraduate study at 4-year institution in United States. Designated institutions: North Carolina State University, University of North Carolina at Chapel Hill, University of North Carolina at Greensboro.
Eligibility: Applicant must be high school senior. Applicant must be U.S. citizen residing in North Carolina.
Basis for selection: Applicant must demonstrate financial need, depth of character, leadership and seriousness of purpose.
Application requirements: Proof of eligibility. FAFSA.
Additional information: Award amount varies; maximum $11,100 per year, plus one-time computer award up to $2,500. Scholarship pays additional amounts for approved summer study or internships. Applications available through high school. Applicants must reside and attend high school in one of the following counties: Alamance, Bertie, Caswell, Durham, Forsyth, Granville, Guilford, Orange, Person, Rockingham, Stokes, Surry, Swain, or Warren. One additional scholarship awarded to student from cities of Greensboro and High Point and to eligible senior at North Carolina School of Science and Mathematics. Apply online.

Amount of award:	$11,100
Number of awards:	17
Application deadline:	January 31

Contact:
North Carolina State Education Assistance Authority
Phone: 919-549-8614
Web: www.cfnc.org

North Coast Financial

North Coast Financial $500 Scholarship

Type of award: Scholarship, renewable.
Intended use: For full-time undergraduate study at 2-year, 4-year or graduate institution.
Eligibility: Applicant must be U.S. citizen.
Basis for selection: Major/career interest in real estate; accounting; finance/banking; business or business/management/administration.
Application requirements: Essay. 500 to 750 word essay.
Additional information: Must have a minimum 3.2 GPA.

Number of awards:	1
Application deadline:	April 30
Notification begins:	May 19
Total amount awarded:	$500

Contact:
North Coast Financial
2424 Vista Way
Suite 202
Oceanside, CA 92054
Web: www.northcoastfinancialinc.com/scholarship/

North Coast Financial, Inc.

North Coast Financial Scholarship

Type of award: Scholarship, renewable.
Intended use: For full-time at 2-year, 4-year or graduate institution.
Eligibility: Applicant must be U.S. citizen.
Basis for selection: Major/career interest in real estate; finance/banking or business.
Application requirements: Essay, transcript, proof of eligibility. Must submit an essay of at least 500 words (maximum of 750) to scholarship@northcoastfinancialinc.com on the following topic: How do you envision your studies in business will prepare you for your desired career choice upon graduation?. Use the subject line North Coast Financial Scholarship Application.

Amount of award:	$500-$500
Number of awards:	1
Application deadline:	April 30
Notification begins:	May 19
Total amount awarded:	$500

Contact:
North Coast Financial, Inc.
2424 Vista Way
#202
Oceanside, CA 92054
Phone: 760-212-5900
Fax: 760-721-9400
Web: www.northcoastfinancialinc.com/scholarship/

Scholarships

Northeast Credit Union

Northeast Credit Union Peter J. Kavalauskas Scholarship

Type of award: Scholarship.

Intended use: For freshman study at accredited 2-year institution.

Eligibility: Applicant must be high school senior.

Basis for selection: Judging will be based on both subjective criteria and weighted, objective criteria. Applicant must demonstrate high academic achievement.

Application requirements: Recommendations, essay, transcript. Must be in top 50% of his/her class. Must be member in good standing at Northeast Credit Union for at least one year prior. 300-500 word essay on the following: "How do you plan to make a difference in the world?".

Additional information: Applicants should submit a high school transcript documenting the GPA for grades 9 to 11, an SAT/PSAT/ACT transcript, letters of recommendation from two organizations the applicant volunteers with, and a letter of acceptance from the accredited community college.

Amount of award:	$5,000
Number of awards:	1
Application deadline:	March 15
Notification begins:	May 13
Total amount awarded:	$5,000

Contact:
Northeast Credit Union
100 Borthwich Ave
Portsmouth, NH 03801
Phone: 603-422-9815
Fax: 603-436-9154
Web: www.necu.org/scholarships

Northeast Credit Union Roger G. Marois and Bart M. DallaMura Scholarship Program

Type of award: Scholarship.

Intended use: For undergraduate study at accredited vocational, 2-year or 4-year institution.

Eligibility: Applicant must be high school senior.

Basis for selection: Judging will be based on both subjective criteria and weighted, objective criteria. These include academic achievements, extracurricular and community activities, essays, etc. Applicant must demonstrate high academic achievement and service orientation.

Application requirements: Recommendations, essay, transcript. Must be in top 50% of his or her class. Must be a member in good standing at Northeast Credit Union for at least one year prior. 300-500 word essay on subject: "how has your volunteering benefited the community?"

Additional information: Must provide a high school transcript documenting GPA for grades 9 to 11, SAT/PSAT/ACT transcript, and letters of recommendation from two organizations the applicant volunteers with, and a letter of acceptance from the accredited community college. Judging will be based on both subjective criteria and weighted, objected criteria.

Amount of award:	$2,000
Number of awards:	2
Number of applicants:	100
Application deadline:	March 15
Notification begins:	May 13
Total amount awarded:	$4,000

Contact:
Northeast Credit Union
100 Borthwich Ave
Portsmouth, NH 03801
Phone: 603-422-9815
Fax: 603-436-9154
Web: www.necu.org/scholarships

Northeast Credit Union Scholarship

Type of award: Scholarship.

Intended use: For freshman study at accredited vocational, 2-year or 4-year institution.

Eligibility: Applicant must be high school senior.

Basis for selection: Judging will be based on both subjective criteria and weighted, objective criteria. Applicant must demonstrate high academic achievement.

Application requirements: Essay, transcript. Must be in top 50% of his/her class. Must be a member in good standing at Northeast Credit Union for at least one year prior. The applicant must also submit a 300-500 word essay. Visit the application on the Northeast Credit Union website for the topic of the essay.

Additional information: Applicants must submit a high school transcript documenting the GPA for grades 9 to 11, an SAT/PSAT/ACT transcript, letters of recommendation from two teachers, and a letter of acceptance from the accredited community college.

Amount of award:	$500-$1,500
Number of awards:	20
Application deadline:	March 15
Notification begins:	May 13
Total amount awarded:	$18,000

Contact:
Northeast Credit Union
100 Borthwich Ave
Portsmouth, NH 03801
Phone: 603-422-9815
Fax: 603-436-9154
Web: www.necu.org/scholarships

Northern Cheyenne Tribal Education Department

Northern Cheyenne Higher Education Program

Type of award: Scholarship, renewable.

Intended use: For undergraduate study at postsecondary institution.

Eligibility: Applicant must be American Indian. Must be enrolled with Northern Cheyenne Tribe. Applicant must be U.S. citizen.

Basis for selection: Applicant must demonstrate financial need.

Application requirements: Recommendations, essay, transcript, proof of eligibility. FAFSA.

Scholarships

Additional information: Award amount varies, depends on unmet need. Deadlines: October 1 for spring, April 1 for summer, and March 1 for fall.

Amount of award:	$6,000
Number of awards:	54
Number of applicants:	68
Application deadline:	March 1, April 1
Notification begins:	January 1
Total amount awarded:	$195,617

Contact:
Northern Cheyenne Tribal Education Department
Attn: Norma Bixby
P.O. Box 307
Lame Deer, MT 59043
Phone: 406-477-6602
Fax: 406-477-8150
Web: www.cheyennenation.com

Northwest Danish Association

The Kaj Christensen Scholarship for Vocational Training

Type of award: Scholarship, renewable.
Intended use: For undergraduate or graduate study at postsecondary institution in or outside United States.
Eligibility: Applicant must be at least 17. Applicant must be U.S. citizen or permanent resident residing in Oregon or Washington.
Basis for selection: Applicant must demonstrate depth of character and service orientation.
Application requirements: Recommendations, transcript. Personal essay on educational goals, two references.
Additional information: Must be member of Northwest Danish Association. Must demonstrate some connection to Denmark via life experience, travel, heritage, etc. Must be resident of Oregon or Washington. Must have interest in vocational training. Available to students aged 17 and up.

Amount of award:	$500
Number of awards:	1
Application deadline:	April 30
Notification begins:	June 1
Total amount awarded:	$500

Contact:
Northwest Danish Association
1833 North 105th Street
Suite 101
Seattle, WA 98133-8973
Phone: 206-523-3263
Fax: 206-729-6997
Web: www.northwestdanish.org

Northwest Danish Association Scholarship

Type of award: Scholarship.
Intended use: For undergraduate or graduate study at postsecondary institution in United States.
Eligibility: Applicant must be U.S. citizen or permanent resident residing in Oregon or Washington.
Basis for selection: Applicant must demonstrate service orientation.

Application requirements: Recommendations, essay, transcript.
Additional information: Studies must be related to Danish community. Must be of Danish descent or married to someone of Danish descent, who actively participates in Danish community. Current family membership is OK if applicant is under 18 years old. Consideration given to those of non-Danish descent who show exceptional involvement with and service orientation related to Danish community. Must be resident of Oregon or Washington. Those training for artistic careers also considered.

Amount of award:	$500-$1,000
Number of awards:	6
Application deadline:	April 30
Notification begins:	June 1

Contact:
Northwest Danish Association
1833 North 105th Street
Suite 101
Seattle, WA 98133-8973
Phone: 206-523-3263
Fax: 206-729-6997
Web: www.northwestdanish.org

Nurse.org

Healthcare Leader Scholarship

Type of award: Scholarship.
Intended use: For undergraduate or graduate study at accredited 2-year, 4-year or graduate institution.
Eligibility: Applicant must be at least 17, high school senior.
Basis for selection: Major/career interest in nurse practitioner; nursing; medical assistant; medical emergency; pediatric nurse practitioner or health-related professions.
Application requirements: 600 to 1,000 word essay explaining what you hope to accomplish during your career in the medical field.
Additional information: Minimum 3.0 GPA.

Number of awards:	1
Application deadline:	January 29
Notification begins:	March 15
Total amount awarded:	$1,000

Contact:
Web: http://nurse.org/healthcare-leaders/

OCA

OCA-AXA Achievement Scholarships

Type of award: Scholarship.
Intended use: For freshman study at postsecondary institution.
Eligibility: Applicant must be Asian American or Native Hawaiian/Pacific Islander. Applicant must be U.S. citizen or permanent resident.
Basis for selection: Applicant must demonstrate high academic achievement, leadership and service orientation.
Application requirements: Recommendations, essay. Resume.

Scholarships

Additional information: Minimum 3.0 GPA. Number of awards varies. Visit Website for more information and deadline.

Amount of award:	$2,000
Number of awards:	10
Number of applicants:	250
Application deadline:	January 15
Notification begins:	May 1
Total amount awarded:	$20,000

Contact:
OCA
1322 18th Street, NW
Washington, DC 20036
Phone: 202-223-5500
Fax: 202-296-0540
Web: www.ocanational.org

OCA/UPS Foundation Gold Mountain College Scholarship

Type of award: Scholarship.
Intended use: For full-time freshman study in United States.
Eligibility: Applicant must be Asian American or Native Hawaiian/Pacific Islander. Applicant must be U.S. citizen or permanent resident.
Basis for selection: Applicant must demonstrate financial need and high academic achievement.
Application requirements: Recommendations, essay. Resume, FAFSA.
Additional information: Minimum 3.0 GPA. Applicant must be Asian Pacific American and first person in family to go to college in the United States. Visit Website for deadline.

Amount of award:	$2,000
Number of awards:	15
Number of applicants:	250
Application deadline:	January 15
Notification begins:	May 1
Total amount awarded:	$30,000

Contact:
OCA
1322 18th Street, NW
Washington, DC 20036
Phone: 202-223-5500
Fax: 202-296-0540
Web: www.ocanational.org

Odyssey Teams, INC.

Odyssey Teams Scholarship

Type of award: Scholarship, renewable.
Intended use: For undergraduate study at accredited vocational, 2-year or 4-year institution.
Eligibility: Applicant must be high school freshman, sophomore or junior. Applicant must be U.S. citizen or permanent resident.
Application requirements: Essay. Plan to enroll Part-time or Full-Time in an accredited not-for-profit OR for-profit 2- or 4-year college or university during SPRING or FALL of scholarship cycle year. U.S Citizen, Permanent Legal Resident, DACA or Eligible Non-Citizen (as defined by FAFSA). Essay : What are your educational goals? How do you see a communications degree impacting your future? How do you see a communications degree impacting your community or the world in general? Please keep this essay to a maximum of two pages, double-spaced, there is no minimum length, so long as you fully answer the question.
Additional information: Scholarship for major interest : Social Science.

Amount of award:	$2,500
Number of awards:	1
Application deadline:	April 1
Notification begins:	May 1
Total amount awarded:	$2,500

Contact:
Odyssey Teams, INC.
173 East 3rd Avenue
Chico, CA 95926
Phone: 800-342-1650
Web: https://odysseyteams.com/scholarship/

Ohio Department Higher Education

Ohio College Opportunity Grant

Type of award: Research grant, renewable.
Intended use: For freshman study at accredited 2-year or 4-year institution. Designated institutions: Ohio and select Pennsylvania schools.
Eligibility: Applicant must be residing in Ohio.
Basis for selection: Applicant must demonstrate financial need.
Application requirements: FAFSA.
Additional information: Must be pursuing associates degree, bachelor's degree, or nursing diploma at an eligible institution. Amount of award varies. Visit Website for more information.

Number of awards:	76,171
Application deadline:	October 1
Total amount awarded:	$93,472,188

Contact:
Web: www.ohiohighered.org/ocog

Ohio Department of Higher Education

Ohio Safety Officers College Memorial Fund

Type of award: Scholarship, renewable.
Intended use: For undergraduate study at accredited 2-year or 4-year institution. Designated institutions: Ohio institutions.
Eligibility: Applicant must be U.S. citizen or permanent resident residing in Ohio. Applicant's parent must have been killed or disabled in work-related accident as firefighter, police officer or public safety officer.
Application requirements: Proof of eligibility.
Additional information: Applicant whose spouse was killed in the line of duty as a firefighter, police officer, or public safety officer also eligible. Visit Website for more information.
Award is for full instructional and general fee charges at public institutions and partial instructional and general fee charges at private institutions.

Number of awards: 43

Number of applicants: 43

Total amount awarded: $324,457

Contact:

Web: www.ohiohighered.org/safety-officers-college-fund

Ohio War Orphans Scholarship

Type of award: Scholarship, renewable.

Intended use: For full-time undergraduate study at accredited 2-year or 4-year institution. Designated institutions: Ohio institutions.

Eligibility: Applicant must be no older than 25. Applicant must be U.S. citizen or permanent resident residing in Ohio. Applicant must be dependent of veteran, disabled veteran, deceased veteran or POW/MIA. Child of disabled veteran who has combined disability rating of 60% or more.

Application requirements: Proof of eligibility.

Additional information: The Ohio Ear Orphans Scholarship Program awards tuition assistance to the children of deceased or severly disables Ohio veterans who served in the armed forces during a period of declared war or conflict. Visit Website for more information.

Number of awards: 928

Application deadline: May 1

Notification begins: August 1

Total amount awarded: $6,880,794

Contact:

Phone: 614-752-9528

Web: www.ohiohighered.org/ohio-war-orphans

Ohio National Guard

Ohio National Guard Scholarship Program

Type of award: Scholarship, renewable.

Intended use: For undergraduate study at accredited postsecondary institution. Designated institutions: Degree-granting institutions in Ohio approved by Ohio Board of Regents.

Eligibility: Applicant must be residing in Ohio. Applicant must be in military service in the Reserves/National Guard. Must enlist, re-enlist, or extend current enlistment to equal six years with Ohio National Guard. Must remain in good standing.

Application requirements: Proof of eligibility.

Additional information: Minimum three credit hours per semester or quarter. Award covers 100 percent of instructional and general fees for state-assisted institutions; average of state-assisted university fees for proprietary/private institutions. Application deadlines: July 1 (fall), November 1 (winter quarter/spring semester), February 1 (spring quarter), April 1 (summer). Must not already possess bachelor's degree. Lifetime maximum of 12 full-time quarters or eight full-time semesters. Number of awards varies.

Amount of award: Full tuition

Number of awards: 6,400

Number of applicants: 5,940

Total amount awarded: $16,200,000

Contact:

Adjutant General's Department

Ohio National Guard Scholarship Program

2825 West Dublin Granville Road

Columbus, OH 43235

Phone: 888-400-6484 or 614-336-7053

Fax: 614-336-7318

Web: www.ongsp.org

Ohio New Media Foundation

The Harold K. Douthit Scholarship

Type of award: Scholarship.

Intended use: For sophomore, junior or senior study at postsecondary institution. Designated institutions: Ohio institutions.

Eligibility: Applicant must be U.S. citizen residing in Ohio.

Basis for selection: Major/career interest in communications; journalism; advertising or marketing. Applicant must demonstrate financial need and high academic achievement.

Application requirements: Essay, transcript. Applicant must have graduated form a high school in Cuyahoga, Lorain, Huron, Erie, Wood, Geauga, Sandusky, Ottawa, or Lucas County. Minimum 3.0 GPA. Student may provide up to two published writing samples.Two letters of recommendation from faculty members.

Amount of award: $1,500

Number of awards: 1

Number of applicants: 14

Application deadline: March 31

Notification begins: May 15

Total amount awarded: $1,500

Contact:

Ohio Newspapers Foundation Douthit Scholarship

1335 Dublin Road

Suite 216-B

Columbus, OH 43215

Phone: 614-486-6677

Web: www.ohionews.org/aws/ONA/pt/sp/scholarships

Ohio News Media Foundation

Minority Scholarship

Type of award: Scholarship.

Intended use: For full-time freshman study at accredited postsecondary institution. Designated institutions: Ohio institutions.

Eligibility: Applicant must be Asian American, African American, Hispanic American or American Indian. Applicant must be high school senior.

Basis for selection: Major/career interest in journalism; communications; advertising or marketing. Applicant must demonstrate high academic achievement.

Application requirements: Recommendations, essay, transcript, proof of eligibility. Applicant must be a graduating senior at an Ohio high school. Up to two writing samples or published articles.

Amount of award:	$1,500
Number of awards:	1
Number of applicants:	8
Application deadline:	March 31
Notification begins:	May 15
Total amount awarded:	$1,500

Contact:
Ohio Newspapers Foundation Minority Scholarship
1335 Dublin Road
Suite 216-B
Columbus, OH 43215
Phone: 614-486-6677
Web: www.ohionews.org/aws/ONA/pt/sp/scholarships

ONWA Annual Scholarship

Type of award: Scholarship.
Intended use: For junior or senior study at postsecondary institution. Designated institutions: Ohio institutions.
Eligibility: Applicant must be residing in Ohio.
Basis for selection: Major/career interest in communications; journalism; advertising or marketing.
Application requirements: Recommendations, transcript. Three or four newspaper clippings demonstrating applicant's writing skills. Answers to questions: Who or what was your inspiration to get involved in the field of journalism and why did you select print journalism as your area of interest? Why do you need a scholarship? What do you think qualifies you for a scholarship? What do you hope to accomplish during your career as a newspaper industry professional?
Additional information: Applicants may be male or female.

Amount of award:	$2,000
Number of awards:	1
Application deadline:	March 31

Contact:
Ohio Newspaper Foundation
1335 Dublin Road
Suite 216-B
Columbus, OH 43215
Phone: 614-486-6677
Web: www.ohionews.org

University Journalism Scholarship

Type of award: Scholarship.
Intended use: For sophomore, junior or senior study at 2-year or 4-year institution. Designated institutions: Ohio institutions.
Eligibility: Applicant must be residing in Ohio.
Basis for selection: Major/career interest in communications; journalism; advertising or marketing. Applicant must demonstrate high academic achievement.
Application requirements: Recommendations, essay, transcript. Two letters of recommendation from faculty members and published writing samples.
Additional information: Minimum 2.5 GPA. Preference given to applicants demonstrating career commitment to newspaper journalism.

Amount of award:	$2,000
Number of awards:	2
Number of applicants:	6
Application deadline:	March 31
Notification begins:	May 15
Total amount awarded:	$4,000

Contact:
Ohio Newspaper Foundation University Journalism Scholarship
1335 Dublin Road
Suite 216-B
Columbus, OH 43215
Phone: 614-486-6677
Web: www.ohionews.org

Oklahoma Engineering Foundation

Oklahoma Engineering Foundation Scholarship

Type of award: Scholarship, renewable.
Intended use: For undergraduate study at accredited 4-year institution in United States. Designated institutions: Oklahoma Christian University of Science & Arts, Oklahoma State University, University of Oklahoma, University of Central Oklahoma, Oral Roberts University, University of Tulsa.
Eligibility: Applicant must be high school senior. Applicant must be U.S. citizen residing in Oklahoma.
Basis for selection: Major/career interest in engineering. Applicant must demonstrate high academic achievement, depth of character, leadership and service orientation.
Application requirements: Interview, essay, transcript.
Additional information: Minimum 3.0 GPA, ACT composite score of 24-29, and ACT Math component score of 28 or above. Applicants eligible for National Merit or Oklahoma Regents Scholarships not eligible for this award. Visit Website for pre-qualification form. Award is $500/semester for a total of $4,000 per student.

Amount of award:	$1,000
Number of awards:	12
Number of applicants:	52
Application deadline:	February 15
Notification begins:	May 15
Total amount awarded:	$12,000

Contact:
Oklahoma Engineering Foundation Executive Director
201 Northeast 27th Street
Suite 125
Oklahoma City, OK 73105
Phone: 405-528-1435
Web: www.oef.org/scholarships

Oklahoma State Regents for Higher Education

George and Donna Nigh Public Service Scholarship

Type of award: Scholarship.
Intended use: For full-time undergraduate study at 4-year institution in United States.
Eligibility: Applicant must be U.S. citizen or permanent resident residing in Oklahoma.

Basis for selection: Major/career interest in public administration/service. Applicant must demonstrate high academic achievement.
Application requirements: Nomination by presidents of Oklahoma colleges and universities.
Additional information: Scholarship provides opportunities to outstanding students preparing for careers in public service. Winners must participate in seminars on public service offered by Nigh Institute. Eligible colleges may nominate one scholarship per year. For information, contact the Nigh Institute.

    Amount of award: $1,000
Contact:
Nigh Institute, Attn: Carl F. Reherman
Kilpatrick Bank
3001 E. Memorial Road
Edmond, OK 73013
Phone: 405-818-0414
Web: www.okcollegestart.org

Independent Living Act (Department of Human Services Tuition Waiver)

Type of award: Scholarship.
Intended use: For undergraduate study at vocational, 2-year or 4-year institution.
Eligibility: Applicant must be no older than 21. Applicant must be residing in Oklahoma.
Application requirements: Proof of eligibility.
Additional information: Awards tuition waivers to eligible individuals who have been or are in the Oklahoma Department of Human Services foster care program. Applicant must have been in DHS custody for at least nine months between the ages of 16 and 18. Within last three years, applicant must have graduated from State Board of Education-accredited high school, the Oklahoma School of Science and Mathematics, or approved school in a bordering state, or have attained GED. Tuition waivers available to eligible students up to age 26 or completion of baccalaureate degree or program certificate, whichever comes first.

    Amount of award: Full tuition
Contact:
Oklahoma State Regents for Higher Education
P.O. Box 108850
Oklahoma City, OK 73101-8850
Phone: 800-858-1840
Web: www.okhighered.org

National Guard Tuition Waiver

Type of award: Scholarship.
Intended use: For undergraduate study at 2-year or 4-year institution.
Eligibility: Applicant must be residing in Oklahoma. Applicant must be bona fide member in good standing of Oklahoma National Guard.
Application requirements: Proof of eligibility. Statement of Understanding and Certificate of Basic Eligibility.
Additional information: Applicant must be enrolled in degree-granting program. Applicant cannot currently have a bachelor's or graduate degree. Waivers not awarded for certificate-granting courses, continuing education courses, or career technology courses.

    Amount of award: Full tuition

Contact:
Oklahoma State Regents for Higher Education
P.O. Box 108850
Oklahoma City, OK 73101-8850
Phone: 800-858-1840
Web: www.okhighered.org

Oklahoma Academic Scholars Program

Type of award: Scholarship, renewable.
Intended use: For full-time undergraduate study at postsecondary institution. Designated institutions: Oklahoma institutions.
Eligibility: Applicant must be residing in Oklahoma.
Basis for selection: Applicant must demonstrate high academic achievement.
Application requirements: Transcript, proof of eligibility.
Additional information: Applicant must be National Merit Scholar or Finalist; Presidential Scholar; have SAT/ACT in 99.5 percentile for Oklahoma residents. Out-of-state National Merit Scholars, National Merit Finalists, and United States Presidential Scholars may qualify. Application deadline varies.

    Amount of award: $1,800-$5,500
Contact:
Oklahoma State Regents for Higher Education
P.O. Box 108850
Oklahoma City, OK 73101-8850
Phone: 800-858-1840
Web: www.okhighered.org

Oklahoma Future Teachers Scholarship

Type of award: Scholarship, renewable.
Intended use: For undergraduate or graduate study at accredited 2-year or 4-year institution.
Eligibility: Applicant must be U.S. citizen or permanent resident residing in Oklahoma.
Basis for selection: Major/career interest in education, early childhood or education. Applicant must demonstrate high academic achievement.
Application requirements: Essay, transcript, proof of eligibility, nomination by college. SAT/ACT scores.
Additional information: Application deadline varies; visit Website for more information. Priority given to full-time students. Must maintain minimum 2.5 GPA. Recipient must agree to teach in shortage area in Oklahoma public schools for at least three years after graduation and licensure. Must apply for renewal. Visit Website for list of shortage areas.

    Amount of award: $500-$1,500
    Number of awards: 85
Contact:
Oklahoma State Regents for Higher Education
P.O. Box 108850
Oklahoma City, OK 73101-8850
Phone: 800-858-1840
Web: www.okhighered.org

Oklahoma Tuition Aid Grant

Type of award: Scholarship, renewable.
Intended use: For undergraduate study at vocational, 2-year or 4-year institution. Designated institutions: Approved Oklahoma institutions.
Eligibility: Applicant must be residing in Oklahoma.

Basis for selection: Applicant must demonstrate financial need.
Application requirements: Proof of eligibility. FAFSA.
Additional information: Award is $1,000 for public schools and $1,300 for private non-profit institutions. For best consideration, apply as soon as possible after October 1.

Amount of award:	$1,000-$1,300
Number of awards:	22,000
Number of applicants:	65,000
Total amount awarded:	$18,677,062

Contact:
Oklahoma Tuition Aid Grant Program
P.O. Box 108850
Oklahoma City, OK 73101-8850
Phone: 800-858-1840
Web: www.okcollegestart.org

Oklahoma's Promise - Oklahoma Higher Learning Access Program

Type of award: Scholarship.
Intended use: For undergraduate study at 2-year or 4-year institution.
Eligibility: Applicant must be residing in Oklahoma.
Basis for selection: Applicant must demonstrate financial need, high academic achievement and seriousness of purpose.
Additional information: Scholarship for students in families earning less than $50,000 per year. Student must enroll in the program in eighth, ninth, or tenth grade and demonstrate commitment to academic success in high school; homeschooled students must be age 13, 14, or 15. Deadline for homeschooled students must occur before student's 16th birthday. Minimum 2.5 GPA. Award amount varies; full tuition at public institutions or portion of tuition at private institutions in OK. See counselor or visit Website for details.

Number of awards:	19,000
Number of applicants:	9,649
Application deadline:	June 30
Total amount awarded:	$61,200,000

Contact:
Oklahoma State Regents for Higher Education
P.O. Box 108850
Oklahoma City, OK 73101-8850
Phone: 800-858-1840
Web: www.okpromise.org

Regional University Baccalaureate Scholarship

Type of award: Scholarship.
Intended use: For full-time undergraduate study at postsecondary institution. Designated institutions: Participating Oklahoma regional universities.
Eligibility: Applicant must be residing in Oklahoma.
Basis for selection: Applicant must demonstrate high academic achievement.
Additional information: Must have ACT score of at least 30 or be National Merit Semifinalist or Commended Student. Award is $3,000 plus resident tuition waiver. Application deadlines vary by institution.

Amount of award:	$3,000

Contact:
Oklahoma State Regents for Higher Education
P.O. Box 108850
Oklahoma City, OK 73101-8850
Phone: 800-858-1840
Web: www.okhighered.org

SREB Academic Common Market

Type of award: Scholarship, renewable.
Intended use: For at 4-year or graduate institution in United States.
Eligibility: Applicant must be U.S. citizen or permanent resident residing in Oklahoma.
Application requirements: Proof of eligibility. Copy of letter of acceptance into specific program, completed application and residency certification form, curricular information about the program.
Additional information: Academic Common Market allows Oklahoma residents to pay in-state tuition rates at a non-Oklahoma college or university in the South while studying in select programs not available at Oklahoma public institutions. Award may be used for selected baccalaureate programs. Visit Website for eligible programs, application, more information.
Contact:
ACM State Coordinator for Oklahoma, Academic Common Market Program
Oklahoma State Regents for Higher Education
P.O. Box 108850
Oklahoma City, OK 73101-8850
Phone: 405-225-9170
Web: www.okcollegestart.org

Omaha Storm Chasers

Robinson Athletic Scholarship

Type of award: Scholarship.
Intended use: For freshman study at accredited postsecondary institution.
Eligibility: Applicant must be African American. Applicant must be high school senior. Applicant must be U.S. citizen or permanent resident.
Application requirements: Transcript. Applications require : Current, complete transcript of grades. Letter of support from current supervising principal, coach or guidance counselor. Statement of how and why sports have been important in your life.
Additional information: Minimum 2.5 GPA. The scholarship award will go out to one male and female student. Applicants must be participating in athletics. Applicants must reside in the counties of Sarpy, Douglas, Cass, Lancaster, and Pottawattamie. Applicants must be a high school senior or graduate planning to enroll in a full time undergraduate course of study at an accredited postsecondary institution. Sponsored by Weitz.

Amount of award:	$1,000
Number of awards:	2
Application deadline:	March 25
Notification begins:	April 1
Total amount awarded:	$2,000

Contact:
Home Run Foundation of Greater Omaha c/o Omaha Storm Chasers Baseball Club
12356 Ballpark Way
Papillion, NE 68046
Phone: 402-738-2181
Web: www.milb.com/content/page.jsp?ymd=20150219&content_id=109730196&f ext=.jsp&sid=t541&vkey=

Why I Want to go to College Essay Contest

Type of award: Research grant.
Basis for selection: All entries will be judged based on the following criteria: Creativity 40%, Theme 40% (including relevance to theme and adherence to these Official Rules), and Well-written Content 20%.
Application requirements: Entries must be postmarked by March 18. Entries must be submitted by mail and include a cover sheet with the following information: the entrant's name, address, phone number, and email address (if available), the entrant's school, and the entrant's U.S. Congressional District if a Nebraska resident. Must be no more than 750 words. Must be submitted on 8 1/2 X 11 paper, double-spaced.
Additional information: Participation is open only to individual, legal residents of the fifty (50) United States and the District of Columbia who are enrolled in 7th or 8th Grade (public, private, or home school) as of the date of entry. The awards take the form of a NEST savings account set up in the applicant's name.

Amount of award:	$500-$2,000
Number of awards:	12
Application deadline:	March 17
Notification begins:	April 28
Total amount awarded:	$14,000

Contact:
Omaha Storm Chasers
12356 Ballpark Way
Papillion, NE 68046
Web: https://treasurer.nebraska.gov/csp/scholarships/

OMNE/Nursing Leaders of Maine

OMNE/Nursing Leaders of Maine Scholarship

Type of award: Scholarship.
Intended use: For undergraduate or graduate study at accredited 4-year or graduate institution. Designated institutions: Maine institutions.
Eligibility: Applicant must be U.S. citizen residing in Maine.
Basis for selection: Major/career interest in nursing. Applicant must demonstrate high academic achievement, seriousness of purpose and service orientation.
Application requirements: Recommendations, transcript, proof of eligibility. Brief note explaining how scholarship would help applicant.
Additional information: Applicant must be enrolled in baccalaureate or graduate nursing program. Minimum 2.0 GPA. Applications must be sent to current OMNE chairperson. Visit Website for more information.

Amount of award:	$500
Number of awards:	2
Number of applicants:	30
Application deadline:	May 1
Notification begins:	June 30
Total amount awarded:	$1,000

Contact:
OMNE
Web: www.omne.org

One Family

One Family Scholars Program

Type of award: Scholarship.
Intended use: For undergraduate study at accredited 2-year or 4-year institution in United States.
Eligibility: Applicant must be U.S. citizen residing in Massachusetts.
Application requirements: Recommendations, transcript. Tax return, FAFSA, SAR.
Additional information: Applicants must be endorsed by partnering community organization. Must be single head of household with children under 18 with family income 200 percent below Federal Poverty Level. Must be endorsed by a partnering community organization from One Family's network or referred by two organizations with which the applicant is currently affiliated.

Application deadline:	July 1, October 28

Contact:
One Family
Fax: 617-588-0441
Web: www.onefamilyscholars.org

One Love Foundation

Pets Vs. Partners Scholarship Contest

Type of award: Scholarship.
Intended use: For undergraduate or graduate study at 2-year, 4-year or graduate institution.
Eligibility: Applicant must be at least 18, no older than 26.
Application requirements: Create a meme in the spirit of the campaign using the Pets vs Partners meme generator on the website. Provide your email address in he "subscribe to our newsletter" box. Share your meme submission on Facebook, Twitter or Instagram. Email a screenshot of your shared photo submission along with your name, e-mail address, and telephone number.

Amount of award:	$500
Number of awards:	3
Application deadline:	December 31
Total amount awarded:	$1,500

Contact:
One Love Foundation
PO Box 368
Bronxville, NY 10708
Web: www.petsvspartners.com/scholarship-rules

Online Medical Coding

Medical Horizon Scholarship

Type of award: Scholarship.
Intended use: For undergraduate or graduate study at vocational, 2-year, 4-year or graduate institution.
Application requirements: Essay prompt: "How will you use your education to create a stronger local economy?"

499

Additional information: Minimum 3.0 GPA. Application can be found on web site.

Number of awards:	1
Total amount awarded:	$500

Contact:
Web: www.onlinemedicalbillingcodingschools.com/medical-horizon-scholarship/

ONS Foundation

ONS Foundation Bachelor's Scholarships

Type of award: Scholarship.
Intended use: For undergraduate study at accredited 4-year institution in United States. Designated institutions: Schools accredited by National League for Nursing or Commission on Collegiate Nursing Education.
Basis for selection: Major/career interest in nursing or oncology. Applicant must demonstrate high academic achievement, depth of character, leadership and service orientation.
Application requirements: $5 application fee. Essay, transcript, proof of eligibility.
Additional information: Must be currently enrolled in bachelor's nursing degree program. At the end of each year of scholarship participation, recipient shall submit a summary of education activities in which he/she participated.

Amount of award:	$2,000
Number of applicants:	39
Application deadline:	February 1
Notification begins:	April 15
Total amount awarded:	$24,000

Contact:
ONS Foundation
125 Enterprise Drive
Pittsburgh, PA 15275-1214
Phone: 866-257-4667, option 4
Web: www.onsfoundation.org/apply/ed/Bachelors

OppLoans

Finance Your Future Student Scholarship

Type of award: Scholarship, renewable.
Intended use: For full-time undergraduate study at accredited 2-year or 4-year institution in United States.

Number of awards:	1
Application deadline:	September 30
Notification begins:	October 14
Total amount awarded:	$2,500

Contact:
Web: www.opploans.com/scholarship/

Oregon Student Assistance Commission

Ahmad-Sehar Saleha Ahmad and Abrahim Ekramullah Zafar Foundation

Type of award: Scholarship, renewable.
Intended use: For undergraduate study at accredited 4-year institution in United States. Designated institutions: Public and nonprofit Oregon institutions.
Eligibility: Applicant must be female, high school senior. Applicant must be U.S. citizen or permanent resident residing in Oregon.
Basis for selection: Major/career interest in mathematics or science, general. Applicant must demonstrate high academic achievement.
Application requirements: Essay, transcript. FAFSA.
Additional information: Must be graduating from Oregon high school. GED recipients and home-schooled seniors in Oregon are also eligible. Visit Website for details and application.

Application deadline:	March 1

Contact:
Oregon Student Assistance Commission
Grants and Scholarship Division
1500 Valley River Drive, Suite 100
Eugene, OR 97401
Phone: 800-452-8807
Web: www.osac.state.or.us

Albina Fuel Company Scholarship

Type of award: Scholarship.
Intended use: For undergraduate study in United States.
Eligibility: Applicant must be enrolled in high school.
Application requirements: Essay, transcript.
Additional information: Applicant must be dependent child of current Albina Fuel Company employee who has been employed by Albina for at least one year by October 1 prior to application deadline. Early bird deadline mid-February. Visit Website for more details.

Application deadline:	March 1

Contact:
Oregon Student Assistance Commission
Grants and Scholarship Division
1500 Valley River Drive, Suite 100
Eugene, OR 97401
Phone: 800-452-8807
Web: www.osac.state.or.us

Allcott/Hunt Share It Now II Scholarship

Type of award: Scholarship.
Intended use: For undergraduate study in United States.
Eligibility: Applicant must be residing in Oregon.
Basis for selection: Applicant must demonstrate financial need.
Application requirements: Essay, transcript. Names, addresses, and phone numbers of two community or school references. FAFSA strongly recommended.

Additional information: Preference given to first- or second-generation immigrants to the U.S. Early bird deadline mid-February. Visit Website for details.

Application deadline: March 1

Contact:
Oregon Student Assistance Commission
Grants and Scholarship Division
1500 Valley River Drive, Suite 100
Eugene, OR 97401
Phone: 800-452-8807
Web: www.osac.state.or.us

American Federation of State, County, and Municipal Employees (AFSCME) Oregon Council #75

Type of award: Scholarship, renewable.
Intended use: For undergraduate or graduate study at 4-year or graduate institution in United States.
Eligibility: Applicant must be U.S. citizen or permanent resident.
Application requirements: Transcript. FAFSA. Essay: What is the importance of organizing political action and contract bargaining for workers?
Additional information: Applicant, spouse (including life partner), parent, or grandparent must be member (active, laid-off, retired, or disabled) of Oregon AFSCME Council. Must have been member for at least one year prior to scholarship deadline or for one year prior to death, layoff, disability, or retirement. Part-time enrollment (minimum six credit hours) considered for active members and spouses or laid-off members. Early bird deadline mid-February. Visit Website for application and details.

Application deadline: March 1

Contact:
Oregon Student Assistance Commission
Grants and Scholarship Division
1500 Valley River Drive, Suite 100
Eugene, OR 97401
Phone: 800-452-8807
Web: www.osac.state.or.us

Bandon Submarine Cable Council Scholarship

Type of award: Scholarship, renewable.
Intended use: For undergraduate or graduate study at postsecondary institution in United States.
Eligibility: Applicant must be residing in Oregon.
Basis for selection: Applicant must demonstrate financial need.
Application requirements: Essay, transcript. Essay: How does using seafood as a sustainable resource affect local and global communities? Length: 1 page.
Additional information: First preference given to members of the Bandon Submarine Cable Council or their dependent children. Second preference given to commercial fishermen or their family members residing in Coos County. Third preference given to any commercial fishermen or family member. Fourth preference given to postsecondary students residing in Clatsop, Coos, Curry, Lane, Lincoln, or Tillamook counties. Fifth preference to any postsecondary student in Oregon. Early bird deadline mid-February. Visit Website for essay topic.

Application deadline: March 1

Contact:
Oregon Student Assistance Commission
Grants and Scholarship Division
1500 Valley River Drive, Suite 100
Eugene, OR 97401
Phone: 800-452-8807
Web: www.osac.state.or.us

Ben Selling Scholarship

Type of award: Scholarship, renewable.
Intended use: For sophomore, junior or senior study at postsecondary institution in United States. Designated institutions: Public and nonprofit institutions.
Eligibility: Applicant must be U.S. citizen or permanent resident residing in Oregon.
Basis for selection: Applicant must demonstrate financial need and high academic achievement.
Application requirements: Essay, transcript. FAFSA.
Additional information: Minimum 3.5 GPA. Early bird deadline in mid-February. Visit Website for details and application.

Amount of award: $500
Application deadline: March 1

Contact:
Oregon Student Assistance Commission
Grants and Scholarship Division
1500 Valley River Drive, Suite 100
Eugene, OR 97401
Phone: 800-452-8807
Fax: 541-687-7414
Web: www.osac.state.or.us

Benjamin Franklin/Edith Green Scholarship

Type of award: Scholarship.
Intended use: For full-time undergraduate study at accredited 4-year institution. Designated institutions: Oregon public colleges.
Eligibility: Applicant must be high school senior. Applicant must be U.S. citizen or permanent resident residing in Oregon.
Basis for selection: Applicant must demonstrate financial need and high academic achievement.
Application requirements: Essay, transcript. FAFSA.
Additional information: Must show graduate from Oregon high school. Early bird deadline mid-February. Visit Website for details and application.

Application deadline: March 1

Contact:
Oregon Student Assistance Commission
Grants and Scholarship Division
1500 Valley River Drive, Suite l00
Eugene, OR 97401
Phone: 800-452-8807
Web: www.osac.state.or.us

Bertha P. Singer Scholarship

Type of award: Scholarship, renewable.
Intended use: For full-time sophomore, junior, senior or graduate study at accredited postsecondary institution. Designated institutions: Oregon institutions.
Eligibility: Applicant must be U.S. citizen or permanent resident residing in Oregon.
Basis for selection: Major/career interest in nursing. Applicant must demonstrate financial need and high academic achievement.

Scholarships

501

Application requirements: Essay, transcript, proof of eligibility. FAFSA.

Additional information: Employees of U.S. Bank, their children, or near relatives not eligible. Minimum 3.0 GPA. Must be a graduate of Oregon high school. Must be enrolling as a second-year student in two-year program or third-year student in a four-year program. Visit Website for details and application.

    Application deadline: March 1

Contact:
Oregon Student Assistance Commission
Grants and Scholarship Division
1500 Valley River Drive, Suite 100
Eugene, OR 97401
Phone: 800-452-8807
Web: www.osac.state.or.us

Chafee Education and Training Grant

Type of award: Scholarship, renewable.

Intended use: For undergraduate or graduate study in United States.

Eligibility: Applicant must be at least 14, no older than 20. Applicant must be residing in Oregon.

Basis for selection: Applicant must demonstrate financial need and service orientation.

Application requirements: Transcript. Two essays, FAFSA.

Additional information: Applicant must currently be in or previously been in foster care placement with the Oregon Department of Human Services or federally recognized Oregon Tribes; be a former foster youth with 180 days of substitute care after age 14 with Oregon DHS or an Oregon Tribe; and exited substitute care at age 16 or older. Deadline for fall, August 1; spring, February 1; summer, May 1; winter, November 1. Students may continue receiving award until age 23, but first-time recipients must be no older than 20. May apply for fall after deadline, but all funds may already be allocated. Visit Website for details and supplemental information form.

    Amount of award: $3,000
    Application deadline: August 1, February 1

Contact:
Oregon Student Assistance Commission
Chafee Program
1500 Valley River Drive, Suite 100
Eugene, OR 97401
Phone: 800-452-8807
Fax: 541-687-7414
Web: www.osac.state.or.us/chafeetv.html

Clark-Phelps Scholarship

Type of award: Scholarship.

Intended use: For undergraduate or graduate study at 4-year or graduate institution. Designated institutions: Oregon public institutions.

Eligibility: Applicant must be U.S. citizen or permanent resident residing in Oregon or Alaska.

Basis for selection: Major/career interest in dentistry; medicine or nursing. Applicant must demonstrate financial need.

Application requirements: Essay, transcript. FAFSA.

Additional information: Preference given to Oregon Health and Science University students and graduates of Oregon and Alaskan high schools. Award amount varies. Early bird application deadline is mid-February. Visit Website for details and application.

    Application deadline: March 1

Contact:
Oregon Student Assistance Commission
Grants and Scholarship Division
1500 Valley River Drive, Suite 100
Eugene, OR 97401
Phone: 800-452-8807
Web: www.osac.state.or.us

Darlene Hooley for Oregon Veterans Scholarship

Type of award: Scholarship.

Intended use: For undergraduate or graduate study at postsecondary institution in United States. Designated institutions: Oregon institutions.

Eligibility: Applicant must be U.S. citizen or permanent resident residing in Oregon. Applicant must be veteran who served in the Army, Air Force, Marines, Navy, Coast Guard or Reserves/National Guard. Must have served in armed services during Global War on Terror.

Basis for selection: Applicant must demonstrate financial need.

Application requirements: Essay, transcript, proof of eligibility. FAFSA. Specify relationship to veteran, dates served, and type of document you will provide (length: 1 page). Submit copy of DD214 showing service during the correct time frame.

Additional information: Award amount varies. Early bird application deadline is mid-February. Visit Website for details and application. Preference to active duty oregon reserves or Oregon National Guard who deployed to an overseas conflict. Must have actively served in the military post 9/11/2001.

    Application deadline: March 1

Contact:
Oregon Student Assistance Commission
Grants and Scholarship Division
1500 Valley River Drive, Suite 100
Eugene, OR 97401
Phone: 800-452-8807
Web: www.osac.state.or.us

David Family Scholarship

Type of award: Scholarship, renewable.

Intended use: For sophomore, junior, senior or graduate study at postsecondary institution in United States. Designated institutions: Public or nonprofit institutions.

Eligibility: Applicant must be U.S. citizen or permanent resident residing in Oregon.

Basis for selection: Major/career interest in health-related professions; health education; health sciences; education or health services administration. Applicant must demonstrate financial need and high academic achievement.

Application requirements: Essay, transcript. FAFSA. Essay: If you were given $1 million to be used for something in your area of specialty (health or education related). How would you use that money and why? Length: 1 page.

Additional information: Minimum 3.4 GPA. Intended for residents of Benton, Clackamas, Lane, Multnomah, and Washington counties. Preference given to applicants enrolling at least half-time in upper-division or graduate health- or education-related programs at four-year colleges. Visit Website for details and application.

    Application deadline: March 1

Contact:
Oregon Student Assistance Commission
Grants and Scholarship Division
1500 Valley River Drive, Suite 100
Eugene, OR 97401
Phone: 800-452-8807
Web: www.osac.state.or.us

Dorothy Campbell Memorial Scholarship

Type of award: Scholarship, renewable.
Intended use: For full-time undergraduate study at accredited 4-year institution. Designated institutions: Oregon institutions.
Eligibility: Applicant must be female, high school senior. Applicant must be U.S. citizen or permanent resident residing in Oregon.
Basis for selection: Applicant must demonstrate financial need and high academic achievement.
Application requirements: Transcript. FAFSA. Essay (one page): Describe strong continuing interest in golf and contribution the sport has made to applicant's development.
Additional information: Must have strong interest in golf. Preference given to applicants participating on high school golf team (including intramural team). Minimum 2.75 GPA. Early bird deadline in mid-February. Visit Website for details and application.
   Application deadline: March 1
Contact:
Oregon Student Assistance Commission
Grants and Scholarship Division
1500 Valley River Drive, Suite 100
Eugene, OR 97401
Phone: 800-452-8807
Web: www.osac.state.or.us

Eugene Bennet Visual Arts Scholarship

Type of award: Scholarship.
Intended use: For undergraduate or graduate study in United States. Designated institutions: Public and nonprofit institutions.
Eligibility: Applicant must be residing in Oregon.
Basis for selection: Major/career interest in arts, general. Applicant must demonstrate financial need and high academic achievement.
Application requirements: Interview, essay, transcript. FAFSA.
Additional information: Applicants must be graduates of a Jackson County high school, or GED recipients or home-schooled graduates from Jackson County. Minimum 2.75 GPA. Career interest should be in fine/visual arts, not performing arts. Early bird deadline mid-February. Visit Website for details.
   Application deadline: March 1
Contact:
Oregon Student Assistance Commission
Grants and Scholarship Division
1500 Valley River Drive, Suite 100
Eugene, OR 97401
Phone: 800-452-8807
Web: www.osac.state.or.us

Ford Opportunity Program

Type of award: Scholarship, renewable.
Intended use: For full-time undergraduate study at accredited 2-year or 4-year institution. Designated institutions: Public or nonprofit Oregon institutions.
Eligibility: Applicant must be single. Applicant must be U.S. citizen or permanent resident residing in California or Oregon.
Basis for selection: Applicant must demonstrate financial need and high academic achievement.
Application requirements: Interview, essay, transcript. FAFSA. Must have no felony convictions, or will have satisfied the terms of any felony convictions by August 1 of the application year.
Additional information: Minimum 3.0 GPA or 2650 GED score, unless application is accompanied by special recommendation form from counselor or OSAC. Must be single head of household with custody of dependent child/children without the support of a domestic partner. Interviews required of all semifinalists. Visit Website for details and application.
   Application deadline: March 1
Contact:
Oregon Student Assistance Commission
Grants and Scholarship Division
1500 Valley River Drive, Suite 100
Eugene, OR 97401
Phone: 800-452-8807
Web: www.osac.state.or.us

Ford Scholars Program

Type of award: Scholarship, renewable.
Intended use: For full-time undergraduate study at accredited 2-year or 4-year institution. Designated institutions: Public or nonprofit Oregon institutions.
Eligibility: Applicant must be U.S. citizen or permanent resident residing in Oregon.
Basis for selection: Applicant must demonstrate financial need and high academic achievement.
Application requirements: Interview, essay, transcript. FAFSA.
Additional information: Minimum 3.0 GPA or 2650 GED score, unless application accompanied by special recommendation form from counselor or OSAC. Intended for high school graduates who have not yet been full-time undergraduates, or for individuals who have completed two years at Oregon community college and are entering junior year at Oregon four-year college. Visit Website for details and application.
   Application deadline: March 1
Contact:
Oregon Student Assistance Commission
Grants and Scholarship Division
1500 Valley River Drive, Suite 100
Eugene, OR 97401
Phone: 800-452-8807
Web: www.osac.state.or.us

Frank Stenzel M.D. and Kathryn Stenzel II Scholarship

Type of award: Scholarship, renewable.
Intended use: For undergraduate or graduate study at postsecondary institution in United States.
Eligibility: Applicant must be U.S. citizen or permanent resident residing in Oregon.

Scholarships

Basis for selection: Applicant must demonstrate financial need and high academic achievement.

Application requirements: Transcript. FAFSA.

Additional information: Not open to graduating high school seniors. Not open to medicine, nursing, or physician assistant majors. Preference given to nontraditional students, first-generation college students, and students approaching final year of program. Minimum GPA for first-time freshmen: 2.75. Minimum 2.5 GPA for current college students. Award amount varies. Early bird application deadline mid-February. Visit Website for details and application.

Application deadline: March 1

Contact:
Oregon Student Assistance Commission
Grants and Scholarship Division
1500 Valley River Drive, Suite 100
Eugene, OR 97401
Phone: 800-452-8807
Web: www.osac.state.or.us

Glenn Jackson Scholars

Type of award: Scholarship, renewable.

Intended use: For full-time undergraduate study at postsecondary institution in United States. Designated institutions: Public and nonprofit institutions.

Eligibility: Applicant must be high school senior. Applicant must be U.S. citizen or permanent resident residing in Oregon.

Basis for selection: Applicant must demonstrate financial need.

Application requirements: Essay, transcript. FAFSA.

Additional information: For dependents of employees/retirees of Oregon Department of Transportation or Parks and Recreation Department. Parent must have been employed by their department at least three years. Financial need not required, but considered. Early bird deadline mid-February. Visit Website for details and application.

Application deadline: March 1

Contact:
Oregon Student Assistance Commission
Grants and Scholarship Division
1500 Valley River Drive, Suite 100
Eugene, OR 97401
Phone: 800-452-8807
Fax: 514-687-7414
Web: www.osac.state.or.us

Ida M. Crawford Scholarship

Type of award: Scholarship, renewable.

Intended use: For full-time undergraduate study at accredited postsecondary institution in United States.

Eligibility: Applicant must be U.S. citizen or permanent resident residing in Oregon.

Basis for selection: Applicant must demonstrate financial need and high academic achievement.

Application requirements: Essay, transcript, proof of eligibility. FAFSA.

Additional information: Minimum 3.5 GPA. Must be graduate of accredited Oregon high school. Not available to students majoring in law, medicine, music, theology, or education. U.S. Bank employees, their children, and near relatives not eligible. Visit Website for details and application.

Application deadline: March 1

Contact:
Oregon Student Assistance Commission
Grants and Scholarship Division
1500 Valley River Drive, Suite 100
Eugene, OR 97401
Phone: 800-452-8807
Web: www.osac.state.or.us

Jackson Foundation Journalism Scholarship

Type of award: Scholarship, renewable.

Intended use: For full-time undergraduate study at postsecondary institution. Designated institutions: Public and nonprofit Oregon institutions.

Eligibility: Applicant must be U.S. citizen or permanent resident residing in Oregon.

Basis for selection: Major/career interest in journalism. Applicant must demonstrate financial need and high academic achievement.

Application requirements: Essay, transcript. FAFSA.

Additional information: Must be graduate of an Oregon high school. Preference given to applicants who have strong SAT writing scores. Early bird deadline mid-February. Visit Website for details and application.

Application deadline: March 1

Contact:
Oregon Student Assistance Commission
Grants and Scholarship Division
1500 Valley River Drive, Suite 100
Eugene, OR 97401
Phone: 800-452-8807
Web: www.osac.state.or.us

James Carlson Memorial Scholarship

Type of award: Scholarship.

Intended use: For full-time senior or graduate study at accredited 4-year institution in United States.

Eligibility: Applicant must be U.S. citizen or permanent resident residing in Oregon.

Basis for selection: Major/career interest in education; education, teacher; education, special or education, early childhood. Applicant must demonstrate financial need and high academic achievement.

Application requirements: Essay, transcript. FAFSA.

Additional information: Available to elementary or secondary education majors entering senior year or fifth year of study, or to graduate students in fifth year for elementary or secondary certificate. Preference given to students with experience living or working in diverse environments (250-350 word essay describing this experience required for applicants qualifying under this preference); dependents of Oregon Education Association members; and students committed to teaching autistic children. Early bird deadline in mid-February. Visit Website for details and application.

Application deadline: March 1

Contact:
Oregon Student Assistance Commission
Grants and Scholarship Division
1500 Valley River Drive, Suite 100
Eugene, OR 97401
Phone: 800-452-8807
Web: www.osac.state.or.us

Jeffrey Alan Scoggins Memorial Scholarship

Type of award: Scholarship.
Intended use: For junior or senior study at 4-year institution. Designated institutions: Oregon public and nonprofit institutions.
Eligibility: Applicant must be U.S. citizen or permanent resident residing in Oregon.
Basis for selection: Major/career interest in engineering. Applicant must demonstrate financial need and high academic achievement.
Application requirements: Essay, transcript. FAFSA.
Additional information: Minimum 3.0 GPA. Preference given to applicants attending Oregon State University and to members of Sigma Chi fraternity. Award amount varies. Early bird application deadline mid-February. Visit Website for details and application.
    Application deadline: March 1
Contact:
Oregon Student Assistance Commission
Grants and Scholarship Division
1500 Valley River Drive, Suite 100
Eugene, OR 97401
Phone: 800-452-8807
Web: www.osac.state.or.us

Jerome B. Steinbach Scholarship

Type of award: Scholarship.
Intended use: For full-time sophomore, junior or senior study at accredited postsecondary institution in United States.
Eligibility: Applicant must be U.S. citizen residing in Oregon.
Basis for selection: Applicant must demonstrate financial need and high academic achievement.
Application requirements: Essay, transcript, proof of eligibility. FAFSA.
Additional information: Minimum 3.5 GPA. Must be U.S. citizen by birth. Must specify state of birth. U.S. Bank employees, their children, and near relatives not eligible. Early bird deadline in mid-February. Visit Website for details and application.
    Application deadline: March 1
Contact:
Oregon Student Assistance Commission
Grants and Scholarship Division
1500 Valley River Drive, Suite 100
Eugene, OR 97401
Phone: 800-452-8807
Fax: 541-687-7414
Web: www.osac.state.or.us

Laurence R. Foster Memorial Scholarship

Type of award: Scholarship, renewable.
Intended use: For undergraduate or graduate study at accredited 4-year institution in United States. Designated institutions: Public and nonprofit institutions.
Eligibility: Applicant must be U.S. citizen or permanent resident residing in Oregon.
Basis for selection: Major/career interest in nursing; medical specialties/research; physician assistant; public health; medical assistant; health-related professions or nurse practitioner. Applicant must demonstrate financial need and service orientation.

Application requirements: Essay, transcript. FAFSA. Two additional essays.
Additional information: Applicant must be seeking career in public health, not private practice. General preference given to applicants of diverse cultures. Preference also given to persons working in (or graduate students majoring in) public health and to undergraduates entering junior/senior-year health programs. Early bird deadline in mid-February. Visit Website for essay topic and application.
    Application deadline: March 1
Contact:
Oregon Student Assistance Commission
Grants and Scholarship Division
1500 Valley River Drive, Suite 100
Eugene, OR 97401
Phone: 800-452-8807
Fax: 541-687-7414
Web: www.osac.state.or.us

Maria C. Jackson-General George A. White Scholarship

Type of award: Scholarship, renewable.
Intended use: For full-time undergraduate or graduate study at postsecondary institution. Designated institutions: Oregon institutions.
Eligibility: Applicant must be U.S. citizen or permanent resident residing in Oregon. Applicant must be veteran; or dependent of active service person or veteran in the Army, Air Force, Marines, Navy or Coast Guard. Must have been Oregon resident at time of enlistment.
Basis for selection: Applicant must demonstrate financial need and high academic achievement.
Application requirements: Essay, transcript, proof of eligibility. FAFSA.
Additional information: Minimum 3.75 GPA for undergraduates; no GPA requirement for graduate students or students at technical schools. U.S. Bank employees, children, and near relatives not eligible. Early bird deadline in mid-February. Visit Website for details and application.
    Application deadline: March 1
Contact:
Oregon Student Assistance Commission
Grants and Scholarship Division
1500 Valley River Drive, Suite 100
Eugene, OR 97401
Phone: 800-452-8807
Fax: 541-687-7414
Web: www.osac.state.or.us

One World Scholarship Essay

Type of award: Scholarship.
Intended use: For undergraduate study in United States. Designated institutions: Public and nonprofit institutions.
Eligibility: Applicant must be no older than 21. Applicant must be residing in Oregon.
Basis for selection: Competition/talent/interest in writing/journalism, based on 500-word essay analyzing the inter-relationships of policy, programs, and personal responsibility on hunger and the stability of the food supply. Must be original work with outside sources identified.
Application requirements: Transcript.
Additional information: Early bird deadline mid-February. Visit Website for more details.
    Application deadline: March 1

Contact:
Oregon Student Assistance Commission
Grants and Scholarship Division
1500 Valley River Drive, Suite 100
Eugene, OR 97401
Phone: 800-452-8807
Web: www.osac.state.or.us

Oregon Alpha Delta Kappa Scholarship

Type of award: Scholarship, renewable.
Intended use: For full-time senior or graduate study at accredited postsecondary institution in United States. Designated institutions: Oregon institutions.
Eligibility: Applicant must be U.S. citizen or permanent resident residing in Oregon.
Basis for selection: Major/career interest in education. Applicant must demonstrate financial need and high academic achievement.
Application requirements: Transcript. FAFSA. Two essays.
Additional information: Applicants must be elementary or secondary education majors. Visit Website for details and application.

    Application deadline: March 1
Contact:
Oregon Student Assistance Commission
Grants and Scholarship Division
1500 Valley River Drive, Suite 100
Eugene, OR 97401
Phone: 800-452-8807
Web: www.osac.state.or.us

Oregon Dungeness Crab Commission

Type of award: Scholarship.
Intended use: For full-time undergraduate study at postsecondary institution in United States.
Eligibility: Applicant must be no older than 23. Applicant must be U.S. citizen or permanent resident residing in Oregon.
Basis for selection: Major/career interest in wildlife/fisheries or environmental science. Applicant must demonstrate high academic achievement.
Application requirements: Essay, transcript.
Additional information: Major/career interest restrictions do not apply to high school seniors. For dependents of licensed Oregon Dungeness Crab fishermen or crew. Early bird deadline in mid-February. Visit Website for details and application.

    Application deadline: March 1
Contact:
Oregon Student Assistance Commission
Grants and Scholarship Division
1500 Valley River Drive, Suite 100
Eugene, OR 97401
Phone: 800-452-8807
Web: www.osac.state.or.us

Oregon Foundation for Blacktail Deer Scholarship

Type of award: Scholarship.
Intended use: For undergraduate study at postsecondary institution. Designated institutions: Oregon institutions.
Eligibility: Applicant must be residing in Oregon.

Basis for selection: Major/career interest in forestry; biology; wildlife/fisheries or zoology. Applicant must demonstrate financial need and seriousness of purpose.
Application requirements: Transcript. FAFSA. Essay (250 words) discussing the challenges of wildlife management in the coming ten years. Copy of previous year's hunting license.
Additional information: Must have serious commitment to career in wildlife management. Early bird deadline mid-February. Visit Website for details.

    Application deadline: March 1
Contact:
Oregon Student Assistance Commission
Grants and Scholarship Division
1500 Valley River Drive, Suite 100
Eugene, OR 97401
Phone: 800-452-8807
Web: www.osac.state.or.us

Oregon Occupational Safety and Health Division Workers Memorial Scholarship

Type of award: Scholarship, renewable.
Intended use: For full-time undergraduate or graduate study at postsecondary institution in United States.
Eligibility: Applicant must be U.S. citizen or permanent resident residing in Oregon.
Basis for selection: Applicant must demonstrate financial need and high academic achievement.
Application requirements: Essay, transcript. FAFSA. Additional 500-word essay: "How has the injury or death of your parent or spouse affected or influenced your decision to further your education?" Must provide name, last four digits of social security number, or workers' compensation claim number of worker permanently disabled or fatally injured; date of death or injury; location of incident; and exact relationship to applicant.
Additional information: Applicant must be dependent or spouse of Oregon worker permanently disabled on the job or be the recipient of fatality benefits as dependent or spouse of worker fatally injured in Oregon. Early bird deadline in mid-February. Visit Website for details and application.

    Application deadline: March 1
Contact:
Oregon Student Assistance Commission
Grants and Scholarship Division
1500 Valley River Drive, Suite l00
Eugene, OR 97401
Phone: 800-452-8807
Web: www.osac.state.or.us

Oregon Scholarship Fund Community College Student Award Programs

Type of award: Scholarship, renewable.
Intended use: For undergraduate study at accredited 2-year institution. Designated institutions: Oregon community colleges.
Eligibility: Applicant must be high school senior. Applicant must be U.S. citizen or permanent resident residing in Oregon.
Basis for selection: Applicant must demonstrate financial need.
Application requirements: Essay, transcript. FAFSA.
Additional information: Early bird deadline in mid-February. Visit Website for details and application.

Application deadline: March 1

Contact:
Oregon Student Assistance Commission
Grants and Scholarship Division
1500 Valley River Drive, Suite 100
Eugene, OR 97401
Phone: 800-452-8807
Web: www.osac.state.or.us

Peter Connacher Memorial Scholarship

Type of award: Scholarship, renewable.
Intended use: For full-time undergraduate or graduate study at postsecondary institution in United States.
Eligibility: Applicant must be U.S. citizen or permanent resident residing in Oregon. Must be former American prisoner of war or descendant.
Basis for selection: Applicant must demonstrate financial need and high academic achievement.
Application requirements: Transcript, proof of eligibility. FAFSA, fifty character specifying relationship to POW, copy of POW's military discharge papers and proof of POW status, if selected as a semifinalist.
Additional information: Preference given to Oregon residents and their dependents. Visit Website for details and application.

Application deadline: March 1

Contact:
Oregon Student Assistance Commission
Grants and Scholarship Division
1500 Valley River Drive, Suite 100
Eugene, OR 97401
Phone: 800-452-8807
Web: www.osac.state.or.us

Professional Land Surveyors of Oregon Scholarship

Type of award: Scholarship, renewable.
Intended use: For full-time undergraduate study at 2-year or 4-year institution. Designated institutions: Public and nonprofit Oregon institutions.
Eligibility: Applicant must be U.S. citizen or permanent resident residing in Oregon.
Basis for selection: Major/career interest in surveying/mapping. Applicant must demonstrate financial need.
Application requirements: Essay, transcript. FAFSA. Names, addresses, and phone numbers of two references (do not submit letters).
Additional information: Students must be enrolled in curricula leading to land-surveying career. Community college applicants must intend to transfer to eligible four-year schools. Four-year applicants must intend to take Fundamentals of Land Surveying (FLS) exam. Maximum award based on year in school. Early bird deadline mid-February. Visit Website for details and application.

Application deadline: March 1

Contact:
Oregon Student Assistance Commission
Grants and Scholarship Division
1500 Valley River Drive, Suite 100
Eugene, OR 97401
Phone: 800-452-8807
Web: www.osac.state.or.us

Richard F. Brentano Memorial Scholarship

Type of award: Scholarship, renewable.
Intended use: For full-time undergraduate study at postsecondary institution in United States.
Eligibility: Applicant must be U.S. citizen or permanent resident.
Basis for selection: Applicant must demonstrate high academic achievement.
Application requirements: Essay, transcript.
Additional information: Intended for children or IRS-legal dependents of employees of Waste Control Systems, Inc., and subsidiaries. Parent must have been employed by Waste Control Systems one year as of deadline. Early bird deadline mid-February. Visit Website for details and application.

Application deadline: March 1

Contact:
Oregon Student Assistance Commission
Grants and Scholarship Division
1500 Valley River Drive, Suite 100
Eugene, OR 97401
Phone: 800-452-8807
Web: www.osac.state.or.us

Roger W. Emmons Memorial Scholarship

Type of award: Scholarship, renewable.
Intended use: For full-time undergraduate study at accredited postsecondary institution in United States. Designated institutions: Public and nonprofit institutions.
Eligibility: Applicant must be high school senior. Applicant must be U.S. citizen or permanent resident.
Basis for selection: Applicant must demonstrate high academic achievement.
Application requirements: Essay, transcript, proof of eligibility.
Additional information: Parent(s) or grandparent(s) must have been solid waste company owner(s) or employee(s) for at least three years and member(s) of Oregon Refuse & Recycling Association. Early bird deadline in mid-February. Visit Website for details and application.

Application deadline: March 1

Contact:
Oregon Student Assistance Commission
Grants and Scholarship Division
1500 Valley River Drive, Suite 100
Eugene, OR 97401
Phone: 800-452-8807
Web: www.osac.state.or.us

Teamsters Clyde C. Crosby/Joseph M. Edgar and Thomas J. Malloy Memorial Scholarship

Type of award: Scholarship, renewable.
Intended use: For full-time undergraduate study at postsecondary institution in United States.
Eligibility: Applicant must be high school senior. Applicant must be U.S. citizen or permanent resident residing in Oregon.
Basis for selection: Applicant must demonstrate financial need and high academic achievement.
Application requirements: Essay, transcript. FAFSA.
Additional information: Minimum 3.0 cumulative GPA. Must be child or dependent stepchild of active, retired, disabled, or

deceased member of local unions affiliated with Joint Council of Teamsters #37. Qualifying members must have been active at least one year. Early bird deadline in mid-February. Visit Website for details and application.

Application deadline: March 1

Contact:
Oregon Student Assistance Commission
Grants and Scholarship Division
1500 Valley River Drive, Suite 100
Eugene, OR 97401
Phone: 800-452-8807
Fax: 541-687-7414
Web: www.osac.state.or.us

Teamsters Council #37 Federal Credit Union Scholarship

Type of award: Scholarship.
Intended use: For undergraduate or graduate study at postsecondary institution in United States.
Eligibility: Applicant must be U.S. citizen or permanent resident residing in Oregon.
Basis for selection: Applicant must demonstrate financial need and high academic achievement.
Application requirements: Essay, transcript. FAFSA.
Additional information: For members (or dependents) of Council #37 credit union. Members must have been active in local affiliated with the Joint Council of Teamsters #37 for at least one year. Applicant must have cumulative GPA between 2.0 and 3.0. Early bird deadline mid-February. Visit Website for details and application.

Application deadline: March 1

Contact:
Oregon Student Assistance Commission
Grants and Scholarship Division
1500 Valley River Drive, Suite 100
Eugene, OR 97401
Phone: 800-452-8807
Web: www.osac.state.or.us

Teamsters Local 305 Scholarship

Type of award: Scholarship, renewable.
Intended use: For full-time undergraduate study at postsecondary institution in United States.
Eligibility: Applicant must be high school senior. Applicant must be U.S. citizen or permanent resident.
Basis for selection: Applicant must demonstrate high academic achievement.
Application requirements: Essay, transcript.
Additional information: Must be child or dependent stepchild of active, retired, disabled, or deceased member of Local 305 of the Joint Council of Teamsters #37. Member must have been active at least one year. Early bird deadline in mid-February. Visit Website for details and application.

Application deadline: March 1

Contact:
Oregon Student Assistance Commission
Grants and Scholarship Division
1500 Valley River Drive, Suite 100
Eugene, OR 97401
Phone: 800-452-8807
Web: www.osac.state.or.us

Walter and Marie Schmidt Scholarship

Type of award: Scholarship, renewable.
Intended use: For undergraduate study at postsecondary institution in United States.
Eligibility: Applicant must be U.S. citizen or permanent resident residing in Oregon.
Basis for selection: Major/career interest in nursing or gerontology. Applicant must demonstrate financial need and high academic achievement.
Application requirements: Essay, transcript. FAFSA. Additional essay describing desire to pursue nursing career in geriatric healthcare.
Additional information: Available to students enrolling in programs to become registered nurses and intending to pursue careers in geriatric healthcare. Priority given to students: 1) attending Lane Community College; 2) enrolled in another two-year nursing program. U.S. Bank employees, children, and near relatives not eligible. Early bird deadline in mid-February. Visit Website for details and application.

Application deadline: March 1

Contact:
Oregon Student Assistance Commission
Grants and Scholarship Division
1500 Valley River Drive, Suite 100
Eugene, OR 97401
Phone: 800-452-8807
Fax: 541-687-7414
Web: www.osac.state.or.us

Organization for Autism Research

Lisa Higgins Hussman Scholarship Program

Type of award: Scholarship.
Intended use: For undergraduate study at postsecondary institution.
Application requirements: Recommendations, essay. Documentation of original autism diagnosis by physician.
Additional information: Award is for qualified individuals with more severe autism spectrum diagnoses (DSM-IV or later criteria). Awards given to students in 4 categories: 4-year undergraduate attendants; 2-year undergraduate attendants; trade, technical, or vocational school attendants; and post-secondary cooperative life skills or transition program attendants. Apply online. Visit Website for more information.

Amount of award: $3,000
Application deadline: April 25
Notification begins: July 20
Total amount awarded: $51,000

Contact:
Organization for Autism Research
2000 14th Street North
Suite 240
Arlington, VA 22201
Phone: 703-243-9710
Fax: 703-243-9751
Web: www.researchautism.org/news/otherevents/scholarship.asp

Schwallie Family Scholarship Program

Type of award: Scholarship.
Intended use: For full-time undergraduate study at accredited postsecondary institution in United States.
Eligibility: Applicant must be U.S. citizen or permanent resident.
Application requirements: Recommendations, essay, proof of eligibility. Documentation by physician of applicant's autism or Asperger Syndrome, original diagnosis.
Additional information: Award is for qualified individuals with autism or Asperger's Syndrome (DSM-IV or later criteria). One-time awards of $3,000 will be given to students in each of the following categories: 1) four-year undergraduate attendants; 2) two-year undergraduate attendants; and 3) trade, technical, or vocational school attendants. Apply online. Visit Website for more information.

Amount of award:	$3,000
Number of applicants:	425
Application deadline:	April 25
Notification begins:	July 20
Total amount awarded:	$42,000

Contact:
Organization for Autism Research
2000 14th Street North
Suite 240
Arlington, VA 22201
Phone: 703-243-9710
Fax: 703-243-9751
Web: www.researchautism.org/news/otherevents/scholarship.asp

The Orthotic and Prosthetic Education and Development Fund

Chester Haddan Scholarship Program

Type of award: Scholarship.
Intended use: For undergraduate or post-bachelor's certificate study at accredited 2-year or 4-year institution in United States.
Eligibility: Applicant must be U.S. citizen.
Basis for selection: Major/career interest in orthotics/prosthetics or medical specialties/research. Applicant must demonstrate financial need, depth of character, leadership, seriousness of purpose and service orientation.
Application requirements: Recommendations, transcript. A 200-word essay on why student wants to work in orthotics or prosthetics. Recent W-2 or letter from current employer.
Additional information: Students may apply directly or professors may nominate them. Applicants must be willing to financially contribute to their education.

Amount of award:	$1,000
Number of awards:	1
Application deadline:	January 31

Contact:
The Orthotic and Prosthetic Education and Development Fund
The Academy
1331 H Street, NW, Suite 501
Washington, DC 20005
Phone: 202-380-3663 ext. 212
Web: www.oandp.org/education

Dan McKeever Scholarship Program

Type of award: Scholarship.
Intended use: For senior or master's study at accredited 4-year institution in United States. Designated institutions: American Academy of Orthotists and Prosthetists-accredited institutions.
Eligibility: Applicant must be U.S. citizen.
Basis for selection: Major/career interest in orthotics/prosthetics or medical specialties/research. Applicant must demonstrate financial need, high academic achievement, leadership, seriousness of purpose and service orientation.
Application requirements: Recommendations, transcript. A 200-word essay on why student wants to work in orthotics or prosthetics. Recent W-2 or letter from current employer.
Additional information: Students may apply directly or professors may nominate them. Must maintain minimum 3.0 GPA. Applicants must be willing to financially contribute to their education.

Amount of award:	$1,000
Number of awards:	3
Application deadline:	May 30

Contact:
The Orthotic and Prosthetic Education and Development Fund
The Academy
1331 H Street, NW, Suite 501
Washington, DC 20005
Phone: 202-380-3663 ext. 212
Web: www.oandp.org/education

Ken Chagnon Scholarship

Type of award: Scholarship.
Intended use: For undergraduate study at accredited 2-year or 4-year institution in United States.
Eligibility: Applicant must be U.S. citizen.
Basis for selection: Major/career interest in orthotics/prosthetics or medical specialties/research. Applicant must demonstrate financial need, leadership and seriousness of purpose.
Application requirements: Recommendations, transcript. A 200-word essay on why student wants to work in orthotics or prosthetics. Recent W-2 or letter from current employer.
Additional information: Students may apply directly or professors may nominate them. Applicants must be willing to financially contribute to their education. Applicants must be enrolled in technician program and show exceptional technical aptitude.

Amount of award:	$500
Number of awards:	1
Application deadline:	January 31

Contact:
The Orthotic and Prosthetic Education and Development Fund
The Academy
1331 H Street, NW, Suite 501
Washington, DC 20005
Phone: 202-380-3663 ext. 212
Web: www.oandp.org/education

Scholarships

509

Osage Tribal Education Committee

Osage Tribal Education Scholarship

Type of award: Scholarship, renewable.
Intended use: For undergraduate or graduate study at accredited postsecondary institution in United States.
Eligibility: Applicant must be American Indian. Must be a member of the Osage Nation. Applicant must be U.S. citizen.
Basis for selection: Applicant must demonstrate high academic achievement.
Application requirements: Proof of Osage Indian blood.
Additional information: Must maintain 2.0 GPA. Award amount varies.

   Application deadline: July 1, December 31
Contact:
Osage Tribal Education Committee
Oklahoma Area Education Office
200 Northwest 4th, Suite 4049
Oklahoma City, OK 73102
Phone: 405-605-6051 ext. 313
Fax: 405-605-6057

Ovid

The Ovid Scholarship

Type of award: Scholarship.
Intended use: For undergraduate or graduate study at vocational, 2-year, 4-year or graduate institution in United States.
Application requirements: Essay, transcript. Application will ask the student to answer the following question using a max of 500 words: Why should someone follow you?
Additional information: Minimum 3.0 GPA. Download application online. Apply via email.

   Amount of award: $500-$1,500
   Number of awards: 6
   Application deadline: April 30
   Notification begins: June 1
Contact:
Web: https://www.ovidlife.com/scholarship

Pacific Medical Training

Pacific Medical Training Essay Contest

Type of award: Scholarship.
Intended use: For full-time undergraduate or graduate study at vocational, 2-year, 4-year or graduate institution. Designated institutions: Pacific Medical Training.
Basis for selection: Major/career interest in medicine; nursing; dentistry or physical therapy.
Application requirements: Essay, transcript, proof of eligibility. Proof of enrollment in a qualifying degree program may be required for eligibility. Your submission will be a 750 to 1,000 word essay discussing emergency medical care from the perspective of a medical student, more details of the essay subject on the Website. This includes, but is not limited to, degree programs and courseware supporting the following professions: AthleticTrainer, Cardiac Sonographer, Cardiovascular Technologist, Dental Assistant, Dentist, Diagnostic Medical Sonographer, Electrocardiographic Technician, Emergency Medical Technician, Exercise Scientist/ Specialist, Mammographer, Medical Assistant, Nuclear Medicine Technologist, Nurse Anesthetists, Nurse Assistant, Nurse Practitioner, Nursing Assistant, Paramedic, Pharmacist, Phlebotomist, Physical Therapist, Physician Assistant,Physician, Practical Nurse, Registered Nurse, Respiratory Therapist.Pre-professional programs such as pre-nursing and pre-medicine students are qualified as well. Students begin their coursework but ultimately transfer to another institution to complete their degree.
Additional information: Career major interest : Medicine, Nursing, Dentistry, Physical Therapy, Phlebotomy, Radiology. visit program url eligibility requirements.Employees and Pacific Medical Training, and their family members, are not eligible to participate in this program. All entries become the sole property of Pacific Medical Training. Employees and Pacific Medical Training, and their family members, are not eligible to participate in this program.

   Amount of award: $1,000
   Number of awards: 1
   Application deadline: August 20
   Total amount awarded: $1,000
Contact:
Pacific Medical Training
1100 E Hector Street
Suite 101
Conshohocken, PA 19428
Phone: 800-417-1748
Web: http://pacificmedicaltraining.net/

Pali Adventures

Pali Adventures College Scholarship Program

Type of award: Scholarship.
Intended use: For full-time undergraduate or graduate study at 2-year, 4-year or graduate institution.
Eligibility: Applicant must be at least 16, no older than 22. Applicant must be U.S. citizen.
Additional information: Applicant must have attended an overnight summer camp for at least one week between the ages of 8-16, and provide a minimum 300 word essay answering the following question: "What difference did summer camp make in your life? What are the core values that you learned at summer camp of which you are most proud?" Essay must be at least 300 words, no maximum limit on length.

   Number of awards: 1
   Application deadline: June 15
   Notification begins: July 15
   Total amount awarded: $1,500
Contact:
Pali Adventures
PO Box 2237
Running Springs, CA 92382
Phone: 909-867-5743
Fax: 909-867-1964
Web: www.paliadventures.com/college-scholarship-program

Scholarships

PanHellenic Scholarship Foundation

PanHellenic Scholarship Awards

Type of award: Scholarship.
Intended use: For undergraduate study at accredited 4-year institution in United States.
Eligibility: Applicant must be at least 18. Applicant must be Greek. Applicant must be U.S. citizen or permanent resident.
Basis for selection: Applicant must demonstrate financial need and high academic achievement.
Application requirements: Recommendations, essay, transcript.
Additional information: Must have a minimum 3.5 GPA. Must have at least one great grandparent with Hellenic roots. All scholarship award recipients are required to attend the Foundation's Awards Ceremony & Gala in June.

Amount of award:	$2,500-$10,000
Number of awards:	40
Application deadline:	January 31
Notification begins:	April 28
Total amount awarded:	$250,000

Contact:
PanHellenic Scholarship Foundation
17 North Wabash
Suite 600
Chicago, IL 60602
Phone: 312-357-6432
Web: www.panhellenicscholarships.org/

Papercheck.com

Papercheck.com Charles Shafae' Scholarship Fund

Type of award: Scholarship.
Intended use: For undergraduate study at accredited 4-year institution in United States.
Eligibility: Applicant must be U.S. citizen or permanent resident.
Basis for selection: Competition/talent/interest in writing/journalism. Applicant must demonstrate high academic achievement.
Application requirements: Transcript. Minimum 1,000-word essay in MLA format. Include "works cited" page with at least two sources.
Additional information: Minimum 3.2 GPA. Applicant must be in good standing at institution. Visit Website for essay questions, guidelines, and deadline. Complete entry form online. Contact via e-mail.

Amount of award:	$500
Number of awards:	2
Number of applicants:	200
Application deadline:	May 1, December 1
Notification begins:	June 1, January 1
Total amount awarded:	$1,000

Contact:
Papercheck.com
Web: www.papercheck.com

Par Aide

Par Aide's Joseph S. Garske Collegiate Grant Program

Type of award: Scholarship, renewable.
Intended use: For undergraduate study at vocational, 2-year or 4-year institution.
Eligibility: Applicant must be high school senior.
Basis for selection: Applicant must demonstrate high academic achievement, leadership and service orientation.
Application requirements: Transcript. A 500-word essay evaluating a significant experience, achievement, or risk and its effect on the student.
Additional information: Minimum 2.0 GPA. Applicant's parent or stepparent must be Golf Course Superintendents Association of America member for five or more consecutive years in one of the following classifications: A, Superintendent Member, C, Retired-A, Retired-B, or AA life. Children or stepchildren of deceased members eligible if member was active for five years at time of death. Children of Par Aide employees, the Environmental Institute for Golf's Board of Trustees, the GCSAA Board of Directors, and GCSAA staff not eligible. First-place awardees eligible for one-year renewal.

Amount of award:	$1,000-$2,500
Number of awards:	3
Application deadline:	March 15
Notification begins:	May 15
Total amount awarded:	$7,500

Contact:
Golf Course Superintendents Association of America
Phone: 800-472-7878, ext. 4445
Web: www.gcsaa.org

Pasadena CyberKnife

Pasadena CyberKnife Future in Medicine Scholarship

Type of award: Scholarship.
Intended use: For undergraduate or graduate study at vocational, 2-year, 4-year or graduate institution.
Eligibility: Applicant must be high school senior.
Application requirements: Essay prompt: "How will you use your education to create a stronger local economy?"
Additional information: Minimum 3.0 GPA. Application can be found on web site.

Number of awards:	1
Application deadline:	June 15
Total amount awarded:	$3,000

Contact:
Web: http://pasadenacyberknife.com/pasadena-cyberknife-scholarship

Patient Advocate Foundation

Patient Advocate Foundation Scholarships for Survivors

Type of award: Scholarship.
Intended use: For full-time undergraduate or graduate study at accredited 2-year, 4-year or graduate institution.
Eligibility: Applicant must be no older than 25.
Basis for selection: Applicant must demonstrate financial need, high academic achievement, depth of character, leadership and service orientation.
Application requirements: Recommendations, essay, transcript, proof of eligibility. Previous year's tax returns. Written documentation from physician stating medical history.
Additional information: Must be survivor of life-threatening, chronic, or debilitating disease. Must maintain 3.0 overall GPA. Must complete 20 hours of community service in year scholarship will be dispensed. Check Website for application deadline.

Amount of award:	$3,000
Number of awards:	12
Number of applicants:	150
Total amount awarded:	$36,000

Contact:
Patient Advocate Foundation
421 Butler Farm Road
Hapmton
VA 23666
Phone: 800-532-5274
Fax: 757-873-8999
Web: www.patientadvocate.org

Peacock Productions, Inc.

Audria M. Edwards Scholarship Fund

Type of award: Scholarship, renewable.
Intended use: For full-time undergraduate study at accredited vocational, 2-year or 4-year institution in United States.
Eligibility: Applicant must be U.S. citizen residing in Oregon or Washington.
Basis for selection: Major/career interest in arts, general. Applicant must demonstrate financial need, depth of character and leadership.
Application requirements: Recommendations, essay, transcript, proof of eligibility.
Additional information: Applicant must be gay, lesbian, bisexual, or transgendered; or the child of gay, lesbian, bisexual, or transgendered parents. Applicant must be pursuing degree in academic field, trade, vocation, or the arts. Applicants living in Washington must reside in Clark, Cowlitz, Skamania, or Wahkiakum counties. Visit Website for application information.

Amount of award:	$1,000-$10,000
Application deadline:	May 1
Total amount awarded:	$5,000

Contact:
Peacock Productions, Inc.
Audria M. Edwards Scholarship Fund
P.O. Box 8854
Portland, OR 97207-8854
Web: www.peacockinthepark.com

Pearson Foundation

Pearson Prize for Higher Education

Type of award: Scholarship.
Intended use: For sophomore or junior study at accredited 2-year or 4-year institution.
Eligibility: Applicant must be U.S. citizen or permanent resident.
Basis for selection: Applicant must demonstrate high academic achievement, leadership and service orientation.
Application requirements: Recommendations.
Additional information: Minimum 2.5 GPA. Must have demonstrated leadership in community service. If applicant is graduating from a 2-year college, they must be transferring to 4-year program to be eligible. Must have at least 30 credits accumulated. Cannot have won Pearson Prize in the past. Cannot be related to someone from Pearson or Pearson Foundation. Apply online. Deadline in April. Semi-finalists notified in June. Winners notified in late July.

Amount of award:	$1,000
Number of awards:	100

Contact:
Pearson Foundation
Web: www.pearsonfoundation.org/pearsonprize

Peck Law Firm

Peck Law Firm Scholarship

Type of award: Scholarship.
Intended use: For full-time freshman, sophomore, junior, senior or graduate study at accredited 2-year, 4-year or graduate institution.
Eligibility: Applicant must be high school senior. Applicant must be U.S. citizen.
Basis for selection: Major/career interest in law.
Additional information: Minimum 3.0 GPA required.

Amount of award:	$2,000
Number of awards:	1
Application deadline:	May 31
Notification begins:	July 1
Total amount awarded:	$2,000

Contact:
Peck Law Firm
Charleston, SC 29401
Phone: 843-631-7117
Web: www.thepeckfirm.com/peck-law-firm-scholarship

Scholarships

Penguin Putnam, Inc.

Signet Classic Student Scholarship Essay Contest

Type of award: Scholarship.
Intended use: For undergraduate study at postsecondary institution.
Eligibility: Applicant must be high school junior or senior. Applicant must be U.S. citizen or permanent resident.
Basis for selection: Competition/talent/interest in writing/journalism, based on style, content, grammar, and originality; judges look for clear, concise writing that is articulate, logically organized, and well-supported. Major/career interest in English or literature.
Application requirements: Proof of eligibility, nomination by high school English teacher. Entrant must read designated book and answer one of several book-related questions in two- to three-page essay. Cover letter on school letterhead from teacher. Only one junior and one senior essay may be submitted per teacher. Parent or legal guardian must submit essay for home-schooled students.
Additional information: Home-schooled entrants must be between ages of 16 and 18. Immediate relatives of employees of Penguin Group (USA) Inc. and its affiliates ineligible. Visit Website for details and application. Winner also receives Signet Classic library for school (or for public library in the case of home-schooled winner). Deadline in mid-April.

Amount of award:	$1,000
Number of awards:	5
Notification begins:	June 15
Total amount awarded:	$5,000

Contact:
Penguin Group Signet Classic Student Scholarship Essay Contest
Academic Marketing Department
375 Hudson Street
New York, NY 10014
Web: www.us.penguingroup.com/static/pages/services-academic/essayhome.html

Pennsylvania Higher Education Assistance Agency

Blind or Deaf Beneficiary Grant Program

Type of award: Scholarship, renewable.
Intended use: For undergraduate study at postsecondary institution.
Eligibility: Applicant must be visually impaired or hearing impaired. Applicant must be residing in Pennsylvania.
Basis for selection: Applicant must demonstrate high academic achievement.
Additional information: Award is up to $500. Student must be blind or deaf. Must qualify to receive benefits through the PA Office of Vocational Rehabilitation. Must maintain satisfactory academic progress. Award can replace student's EFC but cannot exceed cost of attendance. Awards are given on a first-come, first-served basis.

Amount of award:	$500
Application deadline:	December 31

Contact:
PHEAA State Grant and Special Programs
P.O. Box 8157
Harrisburg, PA 17105-8157
Phone: 800-692-7392
Web: www.pheaa.org

Chafee Education and Training Grant (ETG) Program

Type of award: Scholarship, renewable.
Intended use: For undergraduate study at accredited vocational, 2-year or 4-year institution. Designated institutions: Institutions approved by U.S. Department of Education for Title IV student assistance programs.
Eligibility: Applicant must be residing in Pennsylvania.
Basis for selection: Applicant must demonstrate financial need.
Application requirements: FAFSA.
Additional information: Must be eligible for services under the Commonwealth's Chafee Foster Care Independence Program. Must be in foster care or adopted from foster care after age 16. Must participate in ETG program on 21st birthday until age 23. Must maintain satisfactory academic progress. Visit Website for details and application. Maximum awards are determined each year.

Amount of award:	$4,000

Contact:
PHEAA State Grant and Special Programs
P.O. Box 8157
Harrisburg, PA 17105-8157
Phone: 800-692-7392
Web: www.pheaa.org

Pennsylvania Higher Education Assistance Agency Partnership for Access to Higher Education (PATH)

Type of award: Scholarship, renewable.
Intended use: For undergraduate study at postsecondary institution in United States. Designated institutions: Pennsylvania State Grant-approved postsecondary institutions in Pennsylvania.
Eligibility: Applicant must be U.S. citizen residing in Pennsylvania.
Basis for selection: Applicant must demonstrate financial need and high academic achievement.
Application requirements: Nomination by participating PATH organization (visit PHEAA Website for list). FAFSA.
Additional information: Must receive a scholarship or grant from participating PHEAA PATH organization for the academic year that PATH aid is requested. Amount of award varies, and is up to $2,500 per academic year.

Amount of award:	$2,500

Contact:
PHEAA State Grant and Special Programs
P.O. Box 8157
Harrisburg, PA 17105-8157
Phone: 800-443-0646
Web: www.pheaa.org

Pennsylvania Higher Education Assistance Agency Postsecondary Educational Gratuity Program

Type of award: Scholarship, renewable.
Intended use: For full-time undergraduate study at 2-year or 4-year institution. Designated institutions: Pennsylvania public institutions.
Eligibility: Applicant must be no older than 25. Applicant must be residing in Pennsylvania. Applicant must be dependent of deceased veteran. Applicant's parent must have been killed or disabled in work-related accident as firefighter, police officer or public safety officer.
Application requirements: Record of application for other financial aid. Certified copy of birth certificate or adoption record. FAFSA.
Additional information: Applicant must be child by birth or adoption of deceased police officer, firefighter, rescue or ambulance squad member, corrections facility employee, or active National Guard member who died after January 1, 1976 as direct result of performing official duties; or child by birth or adoption of deceased sheriff, deputy sheriff, National Guard member, or certain other individual on federal or state active military duty who died since September 11, 2001 as direct result of performing official duties. Award may include waiver of tuition, fees, and room and board costs. Must apply for other available financial aid prior to application to this program. Visit Website for application.
   Amount of award: Full tuition
Contact:
PHEAA State Grant and Special Programs
P.O. Box 8157
Harrisburg, PA 17105-8157
Phone: 800-692-7392
Web: www.pheaa.org

Pennsylvania State Grant Program

Type of award: Scholarship, renewable.
Intended use: For undergraduate study at accredited vocational, 2-year or 4-year institution in United States.
Eligibility: Applicant must be residing in Pennsylvania.
Basis for selection: Applicant must demonstrate financial need.
Application requirements: Proof of eligibility. FAFSA.
Additional information: Applicant must be high school graduate or GED recipient enrolled in PHEAA-approved program. Applicant must not already have four-year undergraduate degree. Grants are portable to approved institutions in other states. Number and amount of awards vary. Deadlines: May 1 for first-time applicants in a degree program or college-transferable program at a junior college or other college or university (excludes community colleges); May 1 for renewal applicants; August 1 for first-time applicants in a community college, business, trade, technical school, or hospital school of nursing, or a 2-year program that is not transferable to another institution; August 15 for summer-term applicants.
   Application deadline: May 1, August 1
Contact:
PHEAA State Grant and Special Programs Division
P.O. Box 8157
Harrisburg, PA 17105-8157
Phone: 800-692-7392
Web: www.pheaa.org

Pennsylvania Targeted Industry Program (PA-TIP)

Type of award: Scholarship, renewable.
Intended use: For undergraduate study at postsecondary institution. Designated institutions: PHEAA approved institutions.
Basis for selection: Major/career interest in energy research; materials science or agriculture. Applicant must demonstrate financial need.
Application requirements: FAFSA.
Additional information: Must be domiciled in Pennsylvania. Provides need-based awards to students pursuing eligible courses of study that are greater than 10 weeks but less than 2 years in length (diploma or certificate programs) at approved schools. Awards for students enrolled in the following programs: Energy, Advanced Materials and Diversified Manufacturing, Agriculture and Food Production. Amount of award is up to equivalent maximum Pennsylvania State Grant award or 75 percent of the allowable program cost, whichever is less, per award year. Awards cover tuition, books, supplies, and specific living expenses.
   Amount of award: $500-$4,011
Contact:
Pennsylvania Higher Education Assistance Agency
P.O. Box 8157
Harrisburg, PA 17105-8157
Phone: 800-692-7392
Fax: 717-720-3786
Web: www.pheaa.org/pa-tip

Pennsylvania Work-Study Program

Type of award: Scholarship, renewable.
Intended use: For undergraduate, master's, doctoral or first professional study at accredited postsecondary institution. Designated institutions: PHEAA-approved institutions.
Eligibility: Applicant must be U.S. citizen or permanent resident residing in Pennsylvania.
Basis for selection: Applicant must demonstrate financial need.
Application requirements: Interview, proof of eligibility. Proof of state grant or subsidized Stafford loan.
Additional information: Student must demonstrate ability to benefit from career-related high-tech or community service work experience. Applicant must be state grant or subsidized federal loan recipient and not owe state grant refund or be in default on student loan. Recipient must secure a job with PHEAA-approved on or off-campus SWSP employer. Amount and number of awards vary. Deadlines: Fall term only and academic year, October 1; spring term only, January 31; summer, June 30.
   Application deadline: October 1, January 31
Contact:
PHEAA State Grant and Special Programs Division
P.O. Box 8157
Harrisburg, PA 17105-8157
Phone: 800-692-7392
Web: www.pheaa.org

Ready-to-Succeed Scholarship Program (RTSS)

Type of award: Scholarship.
Intended use: For undergraduate study at 2-year or 4-year institution.

Application requirements: Nomination. The student must meet all other Pennsylvania State Grant eligibility requirements to qualify for RTSS. This included the submission of a FAFSA and a Pennsylvania State Grant Form (SGF). Must also have a family income that does not exceed $110,000.

Additional information: Minimum 3.25 GPA. Must have completed at least one academic year; defined as having earned at least 24 semester credits or the equivalent by the time that the student's school checks academic progress for the Pennsylvania State Grant program- this may be at the end of the Spring or Summer term of 2014 for the 2014-15 Academic Year. Students must be nominated by their post-secondary institution for participation in the program.

Amount of award:	$500-$2,000

Contact:
Pennsylvania Higher Education Assistance Agency
1200 North 7th Street
Harrisburg, PA 17102
Phone: 800-692-7392
Web: www.pheaa.org/funding-opportunities/rtss/index.shtml

Teacher Education Assistance for College and Higher Education (TEACH) Grant

Type of award: Scholarship, renewable.
Intended use: For undergraduate study at 4-year institution. Designated institutions: Participating institutions.
Basis for selection: Major/career interest in education.
Additional information: Award is for students who intend to teach in a public or private elementary or secondary school that serves low-income families. Award is up to $4,000 per year. Must agree to work full-time as a teacher in high-need field for at least 4 academic years within 8 calendar years from the date program of study is completed, for which TEACH Grant was received. If service is not completed, TEACH Grant will convert to Direct Unsubsidized Stafford Loan that must be repaid, charged interest from the date TEACH Grant is disbursed.

Amount of award:	$4,000
Application deadline:	April 1

Contact:
Pennsylvania Higher Education Assistance Agency
P.O. Box 8157
Harrisburg, PA 17105-8157
Phone: 800-692-7392
Fax: 717-720-3786
Web: www.studentaid.ed.gov

Pennsylvania's State System of Higher Education

Highmark Healthcare Scholarship for Rising Juniors

Type of award: Scholarship.
Intended use: For full-time junior study in United States. Designated institutions: 14 Pennsylvania's State System of Higher Education universities.
Eligibility: Applicant must be residing in Pennsylvania.
Basis for selection: Applicant must demonstrate financial need.

Application requirements: Recommendations, essay, transcript. College Major interest: any major in the field of healthcare. Must be a junior in college. Must have completed 60 credits with a GPA of 3.0 or higher.
Additional information: This is a two year award, $1000 for the fall 2017 semester and $1000 for the fall 2018 semester.

Amount of award:	$2,000
Number of awards:	100
Application deadline:	May 26
Total amount awarded:	$200,000

Contact:
PA's State System of Higher Education
2986 N. 2nd Street
Harrisburg, PA 17110
Phone: 717-720-4065
Fax: 717-720-4211
Web: www.thepafoundation.org/scholarship.php

Pennsylvania's State System of Higher Education Foundation

Dr. & Mrs. Arthur William Phillips Scholarship

Type of award: Scholarship.
Intended use: For full-time freshman study at 4-year institution in United States. Designated institutions: Pennsylvania's State System of Higher Education universities.
Eligibility: Applicant must be residing in Pennsylvania.
Basis for selection: Applicant must demonstrate financial need and high academic achievement.
Additional information: Must be resident of Butler, Clarion, Forest, Jefferson, Lawrence, Mercer, or Venango counties. Visit Website for deadline and other information. Universities select recipients.

Amount of award:	$500-$1,000
Number of awards:	8
Application deadline:	June 2

Contact:
Pennsylvania's State System of Higher Education Foundation
2896 N. 2nd Street
Harrisburg, PA 17110
Phone: 717-720-4065
Fax: 717-720-4211
Web: www.thepafoundation.org

Fitz Dixon Memorial Scholarship

Type of award: Scholarship.
Intended use: For undergraduate or graduate study at 4-year or graduate institution in United States. Designated institutions: Pennsylvania's State System of Higher Education universities.
Basis for selection: Applicant must demonstrate financial need, high academic achievement and service orientation.
Application requirements: Recommendations, essay. Community/University service form.
Additional information: Undergraduate applicants must have passed 45 credits at a PASSHE university with a minimum GPA of 3.0. Graduate students must have passed nine credits at a PASSHE university with a minimum GPA of 3.5.

Amount of award:	$500
Number of awards:	2
Number of applicants:	16
Application deadline:	May 19

Contact:
Pennsylvania's State System of Higher Education Foundation
2896 N. 2nd Street
Harrisburg, PA 17110
Phone: 717-720-4065
Fax: 717-720-4211
Web: www.thepafoundation.org

Hershey Entertainment & Resorts Hospitality Scholarship

Type of award: Scholarship.
Intended use: For full-time junior or senior study at 4-year institution. Designated institutions: Pennsylvania's State System of Higher Education institutions.
Eligibility: Applicant must be high school junior or senior. Applicant must be residing in Pennsylvania.
Basis for selection: Major/career interest in hospitality administration/management; marketing; human resources; information systems or criminal justice/law enforcement.
Application requirements: Transcript. Cover letter.
Additional information: Must have passed 60 college credits. Minimum GPA is 3.0. Application can be found on web site.

Amount of award:	$1,000
Number of awards:	5
Application deadline:	May 19
Total amount awarded:	$5,000

Contact:
Pennsylvania's State System of Higher Education Foundation
2986 North 2nd Street
Harrisburg, PA 17110
Phone: 717-720-4065
Fax: 717-720-4211
Web: www.thepafoundation.org

M&T Bank Scholarship

Type of award: Scholarship.
Intended use: For full-time undergraduate study at 4-year institution in United States. Designated institutions: 14 Pennsylvania's State System of Higher Education universities.
Eligibility: Applicant must be residing in Pennsylvania.
Basis for selection: Applicant must demonstrate financial need.
Application requirements: Essay. Applicant must reside in Cumberland, Dauphin, or Franklin counties. Demonstrate financial needbased on need analysis from application for federal student aid.

Amount of award:	$1,000
Number of awards:	15
Application deadline:	June 9
Total amount awarded:	$15,000

Contact:
PA 'sState System of Higher Education Foundation
2986 North 2nd Street
Harrisburg, PA 17110
Phone: 717-720-4065
Fax: 717-720-4211
Web: http://www.thepafoundation.org/scholarship.php

Momentum, Inc. Healthcare Award

Type of award: Scholarship.
Intended use: For full-time junior or senior study at 4-year institution in United States. Designated institutions: Pennsylvania's State System of Higher Education 14 universities.
Eligibility: Applicant must be residing in Pennsylvania.
Basis for selection: Major/career interest in health-related professions. Applicant must demonstrate high academic achievement.
Application requirements: Transcript. Completed application, transcript, Power Point and cover letter.
Additional information: Minimum 3.0 GPA. Must be majoring in a healthcare-related field, including biology and healthcare informatics. Must have completed 60 credits.

Amount of award:	$1,000
Number of awards:	1
Application deadline:	May 26

Contact:
Pennsylvania's State System of Higher Education Foundation
2896 North 2nd Street
Harrisburg, PA 17110
Phone: 717-720-4065
Fax: 717-720-4211
Web: www.thepafoundation.org

PSECU International Education Scholarship

Type of award: Scholarship.
Intended use: For full-time undergraduate study at 4-year institution. Designated institutions: Pennsylvania's State System of Higher Education institutions.
Eligibility: Applicant must be residing in Pennsylvania.
Basis for selection: Applicant must demonstrate high academic achievement.
Additional information: Must be in good academic and judicial standing at university. Must be Pell or PHEAA grant qualified.

Amount of award:	$2,000
Number of awards:	10
Number of applicants:	16
Application deadline:	June 9
Total amount awarded:	$20,000

Contact:
Pennsylvania's State System of Higher Education Foundation
2896 N. 2nd Street
Harrisburg, PA 17110
Phone: 717-720-4086
Fax: 717-720-4211
Web: www.thepafoundation.org

Quido and Anna Pichini Merit Scholarships

Type of award: Scholarship.
Intended use: For full-time undergraduate study at 4-year institution in United States. Designated institutions: Pennsylvania's State System of Higher Education universities.
Eligibility: Applicant must be residing in Pennsylvania.
Basis for selection: Applicant must demonstrate high academic achievement and service orientation.
Application requirements: Recommendations, essay, transcript. Voluntary services verification form.

Scholarships

Additional information: Minimum 3.5 GPA. First preference given to Berks County residence of Polish or Italian descent. Preference given to PA residents of Polish or Italian descent.

Amount of award:	$1,000
Number of awards:	17
Number of applicants:	20
Application deadline:	May 19

Contact:
Pennsylvania's State System of Higher Education Foundation
2896 N. 2nd Street
Harrisburg, PA 17110
Phone: 717-720-4065
Fax: 717-720-4211
Web: www.thepafoundation.org

State System Board of Governors Chair, Guido M. Pichini, Endowed Scholarship

Type of award: Scholarship.
Intended use: For full-time undergraduate study at 4-year institution in United States. Designated institutions: Pennsylvania's State System of Higher Education 14 universities.
Eligibility: Applicant must be residing in Pennsylvania.
Basis for selection: Applicant must demonstrate financial need, high academic achievement and leadership.
Application requirements: Essay, transcript. Completed Application, transcript and essay. Demonstrated leadership aspirations at the university or in the community.
Additional information: Minimum 3.2 GPA required.

Amount of award:	$800
Number of awards:	1
Application deadline:	May 20

Contact:
Pennsylvania's State System of Higher Education Foundation
2896 North 2nd Street
Harrisburg, PA 17110
Phone: 717-720-4065
Fax: 717-720-4211
Web: www.thepafoundation.org

Wells Fargo Endowed Scholarship for Academic Excellence

Type of award: Scholarship.
Intended use: For full-time freshman study at 4-year institution in United States. Designated institutions: Pennsylvania's State System of Higher Education institutions.
Eligibility: Applicant must be high school senior. Applicant must be residing in Pennsylvania.
Basis for selection: Applicant must demonstrate financial need and high academic achievement.
Additional information: Must reside in Allegheny, Berks, Bucks, Carbon, Chester, Cumberland, Dauphin, Delaware, Lackawanna, Lancaster, Lebanon, Lehigh, Luzerne, Monroe, Montgomery, Northampton, Philadelphia, Pike, or York counties in Pennsylvania. Must be in top 25% of high school graduating class with a GPA of 3.2 or better. Number of awards varies yearly.

Amount of award:	$1,000
Number of awards:	11
Number of applicants:	143
Application deadline:	May 12

Contact:
Pennsylvania's State System of Higher Education Foundation
2896 N. 2nd Street
Harrisburg, PA 17110
Phone: 717-720-4065
Fax: 717-720-4211
Web: www.thepafoundation.org

William D. Greenlee Scholarship

Type of award: Scholarship.
Intended use: For full-time junior or senior study at 4-year institution in United States. Designated institutions: Pennsylvania's State System of Higher Education 14 universities.
Eligibility: Applicant must be residing in Pennsylvania.
Basis for selection: Major/career interest in political science/government; journalism or communications. Applicant must demonstrate financial need and high academic achievement.
Application requirements: Recommendations, essay, transcript. Completed Application, transcript, work/internship history and essay.
Additional information: Must have a minimum of 60 credits and GPA of 3.0 or higher.

Amount of award:	$2,500
Number of awards:	2
Number of applicants:	16
Application deadline:	May 26
Total amount awarded:	$5,000

Contact:
Pennsylvania's State System of Higher Education Foundation
2896 N. 2nd Street
Harrisburg, PA 17110
Phone: 717-720-4065
Fax: 717-720-4211
Web: www.thepafoundation.org

Pennsylvania State System of Higher Education Foundation

PPL Community Scholarship Award

Type of award: Scholarship.
Intended use: For junior or senior study at 4-year institution in United States. Designated institutions: 14 universities of Pennsylvania's State System of Higher Education.
Eligibility: Applicant must be residing in Pennsylvania.
Basis for selection: Major/career interest in energy research. Applicant must demonstrate financial need.
Application requirements: Transcript. Applicant must reside in: Berks, Bucks, Carbon, Chester, Clinton, Columbia, Cumberland, Dauphin, Juniata, Lackawanna, Lancaster, Lebanon, Lehigh, Luzerne, Lycoming, Monroe, Montgomery, Montour, Northampton, Northumberland, Perry, Pike, Schuylkill, Snyder, Susquehanna, Union Wayne, Wyomig or York. College Major interest: Energy and related fields. Must have completed 60 credits.

Amount of award:	$1,000
Application deadline:	May 26
Total amount awarded:	$50,000

Contact:
PA State System of Higher Education Foundation
2986 North 2nd Street
Harrisburg, PA 17110
Phone: 717-720-4065
Fax: 717-720-4211
Web: http://www.thepafoundation.org/scholarship.php

Pennsylvania Women's Press Association

Pennsylvania Women's Press Association Scholarship

Type of award: Scholarship.
Intended use: For junior, senior or graduate study at 4-year or graduate institution in United States. Designated institutions: Pennsylvania institutions.
Eligibility: Applicant must be U.S. citizen or permanent resident residing in Pennsylvania.
Basis for selection: Major/career interest in journalism.
Application requirements: Essay, transcript. Clippings of published work from school newspapers or other publications; a list of siblings, including their ages and educational status; an optional statement of financial need.
Additional information: Winner is chosen on basis of proven journalistic ability, dedication to a newspaper career, and general merit. Men and women are eligible. Deadline in mid-April.

Amount of award:	$1,500
Number of awards:	1

Contact:
Pennsylvania Women's Press Association
Web: www.pwpa.us/scholarship

Pennsylvania's State System of Higher Education Foundation

AT&T STEM Award

Type of award: Scholarship.
Intended use: For full-time junior or senior study at 4-year institution in United States. Designated institutions: Pennsylvania's State System of Higher Education 14 universities.
Eligibility: Applicant must be residing in Pennsylvania.
Basis for selection: Applicant must demonstrate financial need and high academic achievement.
Application requirements: Essay, transcript. Completed application, transcript and essay.
Additional information: Must be majoring in a STEM related field. Minimum 3.0 GPA required. Must have completed at least 60 credits. The purpose of this award is to improve PA's future workforce for the computer technology, advanced manufacturing and energy industries.

Amount of award:	$1,000
Number of awards:	25
Number of applicants:	57
Application deadline:	June 2
Total amount awarded:	$20,000

Contact:
Pennsylvania's State System of Higher Education Foundation
2986 North 2nd Street
Harrisburg, PA 17110
Phone: 717-720-4065
Fax: 717-720-4211
Web: www.thepafoundation.org

PSECU Credit Union Industry Scholarship for Rising Juniors and Seniors

Type of award: Scholarship.
Intended use: For full-time junior or senior study at 4-year institution in United States. Designated institutions: Pennsylvania's State System of Higher Education 14 universities.
Eligibility: Applicant must be residing in Pennsylvania.
Basis for selection: Major/career interest in finance/banking; business; marketing; human resources; information systems or criminal justice/law enforcement. Applicant must demonstrate financial need and high academic achievement.
Application requirements: Essay, transcript. Completed application, transcript and essay.
Additional information: Minimum 3.0 GPA required. Must have completed at least 60 credits.

Amount of award:	$1,000
Number of awards:	20
Application deadline:	June 2
Total amount awarded:	$20,000

Contact:
Pennsylvania's State System of Higher Education Foundation
2986 North 2nd Street
Harrisburg, PA 17110
Phone: 717-720-4065
Fax: 717-720-4211
Web: www.thepafoundation.org

Scott Electric Environmental Sustainability Scholarship

Type of award: Scholarship.
Intended use: For full-time junior or senior study at 4-year institution in United States. Designated institutions: Pennsylvania's State System of Higher Education 14 universities.
Eligibility: Applicant must be residing in Pennsylvania.
Basis for selection: Applicant must demonstrate financial need and high academic achievement.
Application requirements: Essay, transcript. Completed Application, transcript and essay.
Additional information: Minimum 3.0 GPA required. Must have completed at least 60 credits. Residents of the following PA counties are NOT eligible to apply: Bradford, Bucks, Carbon, Chester, Delaware, Lackawanna, Lehigh, Luzerne, Monroe, Montgomery, Northampton, Philadelphia, Pike, Sullivan, Susquehanna, Wayne and Wyoming.

Amount of award:	$1,000
Number of awards:	11
Application deadline:	June 9
Total amount awarded:	$10,000

Contact:
Pennsylvania's State System of Higher Education Foundation
2986 North 2nd Street
Harrisburg, PA 17110
Phone: 717-720-4065
Fax: 717-720-4211
Web: www.thepafoundation.org

Peters Foundation

Peters Foundation Scholarship Program

Type of award: Scholarship.
Intended use: For freshman study at accredited 4-year institution in United States. Designated institutions: Applicants must attend colleges located in Illinois, Wisconsin, Michigan, Arizona or Colorado.
Eligibility: Applicant must be high school senior.
Basis for selection: Major/career interest in environmental science; forestry or education. Applicant must demonstrate financial need and high academic achievement.
Application requirements: Essay, transcript.
Additional information: The scholarships are a total award that range from $10,000 to $20,000 over a four-year period ($2,500 to $5,000 per year). Selected applicants will be invited to complete a Phase II application. Selected applicants may be required to attend an interview. High School transcript (unofficial accepted), SAT scores, and one writing sample required with application. Send in application via e-mail or fax.

Amount of award:	$2,500-$5,000
Application deadline:	April 1

Contact:
Fax: 1-866-847-2922
Web: www.petersfoundation.org/scholarshipapplication.html

PFLAG National Office

PFLAG National Scholarship Program

Type of award: Scholarship.
Intended use: For full-time freshman study at 2-year or 4-year institution.
Eligibility: Applicant must be high school senior.
Basis for selection: Competition/talent/interest in gay/lesbian.
Additional information: Applicants who graduated within last year also eligible. Must self-identify as gay, lesbian, bisexual, transgender, or ally/supporter of LGBT people who has worked on behalf of the LGBT community or overcome odds because of identity. Applications and full details available online in December. Number of awards vary.

Amount of award:	$1,000-$5,000
Number of applicants:	300
Application deadline:	April 15
Notification begins:	May 15
Total amount awarded:	$35,000

Contact:
PFLAG National Office
1828 L. St. NW, Suite 660
Washington, DC 20036
Phone: 202-467-8180
Web: www.pflag.org

PG&E

Better Together STEM Scholarship

Type of award: Scholarship, renewable.
Intended use: For undergraduate study at accredited 4-year institution. Designated institutions: California Polytechnic State University, CSU Chico, CSU East Bay, CSU Fresno, CSU Sacramento, San Jose State University, San Francisco State University Stanford University, UC Berkeley, UC Davis, UC Irvine, UC Los Ángeles, UC Merced, UC Riverside, UC San Diego, UC Santa Barbara, UC Santa Cruz.
Eligibility: Applicant must be high school senior. Applicant must be U.S. citizen residing in California.
Basis for selection: Major/career interest in engineering; computer/information sciences or environmental science. Applicant must demonstrate financial need, high academic achievement and leadership.
Additional information: Must be a PG&E costumer at the time of application.

Amount of award:	$5,000
Number of awards:	20
Application deadline:	March 31
Total amount awarded:	$100,000

Contact:
PG&E Better Together STEM Scholarship Program
One Scholarship Way
St. Peter, MN 56082
Phone: 800-537-4180
Fax: 507-931-9168
Web: pge.com/educationprograms

Phillips University Legacy Foundation

Undergraduate Scholarship and Leadership Development Program

Type of award: Scholarship.
Intended use: For undergraduate study at 4-year institution in Any of the 17 colleges or universities currently or historically affiliated with the Christian Church (Disciples of Christ).
Eligibility: Applicant must be high school senior.
Basis for selection: Recipients are chosen based on their academic achievements, their present and potential leadership in the church, their chosen vocation, and their community. Applicant must demonstrate high academic achievement and leadership.
Application requirements: Recommendations. Three references.
Additional information: It is not a requirement that recipients attend a church that is affiliated with the Christian Church (Disciples of Christ).

Scholarships

Amount of award:	$5,000
Application deadline:	March 10
Notification begins:	April 20

Contact:
Phillips University, Inc.
P.O. Box 2127
Enid, OK 73702-2127
Phone: 580-237-4433
Web: www.pulf.org/scholarshipforms

Phoenix CyberKnife

Future Oncologist Scholarship

Type of award: Scholarship.
Intended use: For undergraduate or graduate study at vocational, 2-year, 4-year or graduate institution.
Eligibility: Applicant must be high school senior.
Basis for selection: Major/career interest in oncology.
Application requirements: Essay prompt: "How will you use your education to create a stronger local economy?"
Additional information: Minimum 3.0 GPA. Application can be found on web site.

Number of awards:	1
Application deadline:	June 15
Total amount awarded:	$500

Contact:
Web: http://phoenixcyberknifecenter.com/phoenix-cyberknife-scholarship/

Plaintiff Relief

Plaintiff Relief Scholarship

Type of award: Scholarship.
Intended use: For full-time undergraduate study at vocational, 2-year or 4-year institution.
Eligibility: Applicant must be high school senior. Applicant must be U.S. citizen or permanent resident.
Basis for selection: Applicant must demonstrate financial need, high academic achievement and leadership.
Application requirements: Essay, transcript. Applicants must excel academically, show exceptional leadership potential and have a track record of bettering the community around them.Applicants should demonstrate academic achievement, exhibit leadership ability, participate in community service activities and demonstrate financial need.Students should include: .Cover Letter (750 words)Tell us about yourself, your achievements, and your aspirations, Explain how this scholarship would help you achieve the latter,Include SAT / ACT Scores. High School Transcript, College Transcript if Applicable.

Amount of award:	$1,000
Number of awards:	1
Application deadline:	November 1
Total amount awarded:	$1,000

Contact:
Plaintiff Relief
3379 Peachtree Road NE
Suite 555
Atlanta, GA 30326
Phone: 866-301-0084
Web: www.plaintiffrelief.com

PLAY (Pet Lifestyle and You)

Scholars Helping Collars PLAY Scholarship

Type of award: Scholarship.
Intended use: For freshman study at postsecondary institution.
Eligibility: Applicant must be high school junior or senior. Applicant must be U.S. citizen.
Application requirements: Essay (500-1000 words) with 2-3 photos of volunteer efforts to help animals in need and how that involvement has changed your life or shaped your perceptions on the importance of animal welfare.
Additional information: Immediate family of P.L.A.Y. employees ineligible. Visit the Website for additional information.

Amount of award:	$1,000
Number of awards:	1
Number of applicants:	26
Application deadline:	December 3

Contact:
PLAY (Pet Lifestyle and You)
246 Second Street
Unit A
San Francisco, CA 94105
Phone: 855-300-7529
Web: www.petplay.com/scholarship

Plumbing-Heating-Cooling Contractors Educational Foundation

A.O. Smith Scholarship

Type of award: Scholarship.
Intended use: For full-time undergraduate study at accredited vocational, 2-year or 4-year institution in United States.
Eligibility: Applicant must be U.S. citizen or Canadian citizen.
Basis for selection: Major/career interest in air conditioning/ heating/refrigeration technology; business/management/ administration; construction management or engineering, mechanical. Applicant must demonstrate high academic achievement.
Application requirements: Recommendations, essay, transcript. SAT/ACT scores. List of extracurricular activities.
Additional information: Students enrolled or planning to enroll in PHCC-approved apprenticeship program also eligible. Other eligible majors include mechanical CAD design, plumbing or HVACR installation, and others directly related to

the plumbing-heating-cooling profession. Must be working full-time for an active member of PHCC National Association. Minimum 2.0 GPA. Can be US or Canadian citizen. Visit Website for details and application.

Amount of award:	$2,500
Number of awards:	2
Application deadline:	May 1

Contact:
PHCC-EF Scholarships
180 South Washington St.
Suite 100
Falls Church, VA 22046
Phone: 800-533-7694
Fax: 703-237-7442
Web: www.phccfoundation.org

Bradford White Corporation Scholarship

Type of award: Scholarship.
Intended use: For full-time undergraduate study at accredited vocational, 2-year or 4-year institution in United States.
Eligibility: Applicant must be U.S. citizen or Canadian citizen.
Basis for selection: Major/career interest in air conditioning/heating/refrigeration technology; business/management/administration; construction management or engineering, mechanical. Applicant must demonstrate high academic achievement.
Application requirements: Recommendations, essay, transcript. List of extracurricular activities. SAT/ACT scores.
Additional information: Students enrolled or planning to enroll in PHCC-approved apprenticeship program also eligible. Other eligible majors include mechanical CAD design, plumbing or HVACR installation, and others directly related to the plumbing-heating-cooling profession. Must be sponsored by active member of PHCC National Association. Minimum 2.0 GPA. Visit Website for details and application. Can be US or Canadian citizen.

Amount of award:	$2,500
Number of awards:	3
Application deadline:	May 1

Contact:
PHCC-EF Scholarships
180 South Washington St.
Suite 100
Falls Church, VA 22046
Phone: 800-533-7694
Fax: 703-237-7442
Web: www.phccfoundation.org

Delta Faucet Company Scholarship

Type of award: Scholarship.
Intended use: For full-time undergraduate study at accredited vocational, 2-year or 4-year institution in United States.
Eligibility: Applicant must be U.S. citizen or Canadian citizen.
Basis for selection: Major/career interest in air conditioning/heating/refrigeration technology; business/management/administration; construction management or engineering, mechanical. Applicant must demonstrate high academic achievement.
Application requirements: Recommendations, essay, transcript. SAT/ACT scores, list of extracurricular activities.
Additional information: Applicants must pursue studies in major related to plumbing-heating-cooling industry or apprentice in a PHCC-approved program. Must be sponsored by active member of PHCC National Association. Minimum

2.0 GPA. Can be a US or Canadian citizen. Visit Website for application.

Amount of award:	$2,500
Number of awards:	6
Number of applicants:	45
Application deadline:	May 1
Total amount awarded:	$15,000

Contact:
PHCC-EF Scholarships
180 South Washington St.
Suite 100
Falls Church, VA 22046
Phone: 800-533-7694
Fax: 703-237-7442
Web: www.phccfoundation.org

Fran Williams Memorial Scholarship

Type of award: Scholarship.
Intended use: For full-time undergraduate study at accredited vocational, 2-year or 4-year institution in United States.
Eligibility: Applicant must be U.S. citizen or Canadian citizen.
Basis for selection: Major/career interest in business/management/administration; air conditioning/heating/refrigeration technology; construction or engineering. Applicant must demonstrate high academic achievement.
Application requirements: Recommendations, essay, transcript. SAT/ACT scores, list of extracurricular activities.
Additional information: Applicants must pursue studies in major related to plumbing-heating-cooling industry or apprentice in a PHCC-approved program. Must be sponsored by active member of PHCC National Association. Minimum 2.0 GPA. Must be a US or Canadian citizen. Visit Website for application.

Amount of award:	$1,000
Number of awards:	1
Application deadline:	May 1

Contact:
PHCC-EF Scholarships
180 South Washington Street
Suite 100
Falls Church, VA 22046
Phone: 800-533-7694
Fax: 703-237-7442
Web: www.phccfoundation.org

PHCC Auxiliary of Texas Scholarship

Type of award: Scholarship.
Intended use: For full-time undergraduate study at accredited 2-year or 4-year institution in United States.
Eligibility: Applicant must be high school senior. Applicant must be U.S. citizen residing in Texas.
Basis for selection: Applicant must demonstrate high academic achievement.
Application requirements: Recommendations, essay, transcript. SAT/ACT scores. List of extracurricular activities.
Additional information: Must be sponsored by active member of PHCC National Auxiliary residing in Texas. Minimum 2.0 GPA. Can be a US or Canadian citizen. Visit Website for details and application.

Amount of award:	$1,500
Number of awards:	1
Application deadline:	May 1

Contact:
PHCC Educational Foundation
180 South Washington Street
Suite 100
Falls Church, VA 22046
Phone: 800-533-7694
Fax: 703-237-7442
Web: www.foundation.phccweb.org

PHCC Educational Foundation Scholarships

Type of award: Scholarship.
Intended use: For full-time undergraduate study at accredited vocational, 2-year or 4-year institution in United States.
Eligibility: Applicant must be U.S. citizen or Canadian citizen.
Basis for selection: Major/career interest in air conditioning/heating/refrigeration technology; business/management/administration; construction management or engineering, mechanical. Applicant must demonstrate financial need and high academic achievement.
Application requirements: Recommendations, essay, transcript. SAT/ACT scores. List of extracurricular activities.
Additional information: Students enrolled or planning to enroll in PHCC-approved apprenticeship program also eligible. Other eligible majors include mechanical CAD design, plumbing or HVACR installation, and others directly related to the plumbing-heating-cooling profession. Must be sponsored by active member of PHCC National Association. Minimum 2.0 GPA. Can be US or Canadian citizen. Visit Website for details and application.

Amount of award:	$2,500-$5,000
Number of awards:	5
Application deadline:	May 1
Total amount awarded:	$15,000

Contact:
PHCC Educational Foundation
180 South Washington Street
Suite 100
Falls Church, VA 22040
Phone: 800-533-7694
Fax: 703-237-7442
Web: www.foundation.phccweb.org

PHCC of Massachusetts Auxiliary Scholarship

Type of award: Scholarship.
Intended use: For full-time undergraduate study at accredited vocational, 2-year or 4-year institution in United States.
Eligibility: Applicant must be high school senior. Applicant must be U.S. citizen residing in Massachusetts.
Basis for selection: Applicant must demonstrate high academic achievement.
Application requirements: Recommendations, essay, transcript. SAT/ACT scores. List of extracurricular activities.
Additional information: Students enrolled or planning to enroll in PHCC-approved apprenticeship program also eligible. Other eligible majors include mechanical CAD design, plumbing or HVACR installation, and others directly related to the plumbing-heating-cooling profession. Must be sponsored by active member of PHCC National Association. Minimum 2.0 GPA. Can be a US or Canadian citizen. Visit Website for details and application.

Amount of award:	$1,500
Number of awards:	1
Application deadline:	May 1

Contact:
PHCC Educational Foundation
180 South Washington Street
Suite 100
Falls Church, VA 22046
Phone: 800-533-7694
Fax: 703-237-7442
Web: www.phccfoundation.org

PHCC Past National Officers Scholarship

Type of award: Scholarship, renewable.
Intended use: For full-time undergraduate study at accredited vocational, 2-year or 4-year institution in United States.
Eligibility: Applicant must be U.S. citizen or Canadian citizen.
Basis for selection: Major/career interest in air conditioning/heating/refrigeration technology; architecture; business; engineering, construction or construction management. Applicant must demonstrate high academic achievement.
Application requirements: Recommendations, essay, transcript. SAT/ACT scores, list of extracurricular activities.
Additional information: Applicants must pursue studies in major related to plumbing-heating-cooling industry or apprentice in a PHCC-approved program. Must be sponsored by active member of PHCC National Association. Must maintain minimum 2.0 GPA. Can be a US or Canadian citizen. Visit Website for application.

Amount of award:	$2,500
Number of awards:	1
Application deadline:	May 1

Contact:
PHCC-EF Scholarships
180 South Washington Street
Suite 100
Falls Church, VA 22046
Phone: 800-533-7694
Fax: 703-237-7442
Web: www.phccfoundation.org

RIDGID Tool Company Scholarship

Type of award: Scholarship.
Intended use: For full-time undergraduate study at accredited vocational, 2-year or 4-year institution in United States.
Eligibility: Applicant must be U.S. citizen or Canadian citizen.
Basis for selection: Major/career interest in air conditioning/heating/refrigeration technology; business/management/administration; construction or engineering. Applicant must demonstrate high academic achievement.
Application requirements: Recommendations, essay, transcript. SAT/ACT scores, list of extracurricular activities.
Additional information: Applicants must pursue studies in major related to plumbing-heating-cooling industry or apprentice in a PHCC-approved program. Must be sponsored by active member of PHCC National Association. Minimum 2.0 GPA. Can be a US or Canadian citizen. Visit Website for application.

Amount of award:	$1,000
Number of awards:	4
Application deadline:	May 1

Contact:
PHCC-EF Scholarships
180 South Washington Street
Suite 100
Falls Church, VA 22046
Phone: 800-533-7694
Fax: 703-237-7442
Web: www.phccfoundation.org

State Water Heaters Scholarship

Type of award: Scholarship.
Intended use: For full-time undergraduate study at accredited vocational, 2-year or 4-year institution in United States.
Eligibility: Applicant must be U.S. citizen or Canadian citizen.
Basis for selection: Major/career interest in engineering, mechanical or business/management/administration. Applicant must demonstrate high academic achievement.
Application requirements: Recommendations, essay, transcript. SAT/ACT scores. List of extracurricular activities.
Additional information: Students enrolled or planning to enroll in PHCC-approved apprenticeship program also eligible. Other eligible majors include mechanical CAD design, plumbing or HVACR installation, and others directly related to the plumbing-heating-cooling profession. Minimum 2.0 GPA. Can be a US or Canadian citizen. Visit Website for details and application.

Amount of award:	$2,500
Number of awards:	1
Application deadline:	May 1

Contact:
PHCC-EF Scholarships
180 South Washington Street
Suite 100
Falls Church, VA 22046
Phone: 800-533-7694
Fax: 703-737-7442
Web: www.phccfoundation.org

Point Foundation

Point Scholarship

Type of award: Scholarship.
Intended use: For undergraduate or graduate study at accredited 4-year institution in United States.
Basis for selection: Competition/talent/interest in gay/lesbian. Applicant must demonstrate financial need, high academic achievement, depth of character, leadership, seriousness of purpose and service orientation.
Application requirements: Essay, transcript. Two or three letters of recommendation, two of them from a teacher or professor. Applicants who have been out of school five years or more may substitute a reference from a supervisor for one letter.
Additional information: Applicants should have a history of leadership in the lesbian, gay, bisexual, and transgendered community and plan to be a LGBT leader in the future (not necessarily in a career). Award amount varies based on available funds; average award $10,000. Scholars must be willing to speak publicly at Foundation events, provide the Foundation with transcripts, remain in contact with Foundation, and do an individual community service project with the LGBT community. Deadline occurs in February; visit Website for exact date and application.

Number of awards:	28

Contact:
Point Foundation
5757 Wilshire Blvd., Suite #370
Los Angeles, CA 90036
Phone: 323-933-1234
Web: www.pointfoundation.org

Positive Coaching Alliance

Triple-Impact Competitor Scholarship Program

Type of award: Scholarship.
Intended use: For full-time freshman study at vocational, 2-year or 4-year institution.
Eligibility: Applicant must be high school junior. Applicant must be U.S. citizen.
Basis for selection: Winners will be selected based on their essays explaining how they meet the standard defined in Elevating Your Game: Becoming a Triple-Impact Competitor by PCA Founder Jim Thompson: 1) Personal Mastery: Making oneself better; 2) Leadership: Making one's teammates better; 3) Honoring the Game: Making the game better.
Application requirements: Triple-Impact competitor scholarship application. Testimonial from school administrator, coach, and one other individual familiar with the student-athlete.
Additional information: Application can be found online. Must be a High School Junior with a GPA of 2.5 or above. Must participate in individual or team sport sponsored by the school or local club.

Amount of award:	$1,000-$2,000
Number of applicants:	1,710
Application deadline:	May 31

Contact:
Positive Coaching Alliance
1001 North Rengstorff Avenue
Suite 100
Mountain View, CA 94043
Phone: 650-210-1815
Web: www.positivecoach.org/our-awards/triple-impact-competitor-scholarships/

Power Over Life

Gaining Power Over Life Scholarship

Type of award: Scholarship, renewable.
Intended use: For full-time undergraduate or graduate study at accredited vocational, 2-year, 4-year or graduate institution in United States.
Eligibility: Applicant must be U.S. citizen or international student.
Application requirements: Essay. Applicant must be US citizen or hold a current valid student visa. Student must currently be enrolled at an accredited college or univeristy in the United States. Essay question and guidelines can be found on the scholarship web page. Essay must be a minimum of 1,000 words; there is no maximum word count.

Additional information: How to apply can be found on scholarship web page.Scholarship is available for US Resident or hold a current valid student visa.

Amount of award:	$500-$500
Number of awards:	1
Application deadline:	May 31
Notification begins:	August 1
Total amount awarded:	$500

Contact:
Power Over Life
3010 E Bonanza Road
Gilbert, AZ 85297
Web: www.poweroverlife.com/scholarship/

PreJax Foundation

PreJax Foundation Scholarship

Type of award: Scholarship.
Intended use: For full-time undergraduate study at accredited vocational, 2-year or 4-year institution.
Eligibility: Applicant must be U.S. citizen.
Application requirements: Scholarship recipients will be selected on the basis of academic record, participation in school or community activities, personal recommendations, goals and aspirations, and an essay (written by the applicant) regarding the impact of multiple sclerosis (MS) on his/her life. The selection process will not be influenced or affected by the actual or perceived race, religion, color, national origin, ancestry, level of disability, gender, age, or sexual orientation of any applicant.

Amount of award:	$1,000-$1,000
Application deadline:	April 30, May 15

Contact:
PreJax Foundation
1761 Travertime Terrance
Sanford, FL 32771
Phone: 407-734-3114
Web: www.theprejaxfoundation.com/The_PreJax_Foundation/Apply.html

Prephound

PrepHound College Coaching Scholarship

Type of award: Scholarship.
Intended use: For undergraduate study at 2-year, 4-year or graduate institution.
Application requirements: Essay.
Additional information: Minimum 3.0 GPA. Application found online.

Number of awards:	1
Application deadline:	September 30
Notification begins:	December 1
Total amount awarded:	$7,500

Contact:
Web: https://scholarships360.org/prephound-college-coaching-scholarship/

Presbyterian Church (U.S.A.)

Financial Aid for Service

Type of award: Scholarship, renewable.
Intended use: For undergraduate study at 4-year institution.
Designated institutions: Presbyterian-affiliated colleges.
Eligibility: Applicant must be Presbyterian.
Basis for selection: Applicant must demonstrate financial need and service orientation.
Application requirements: Recommendation from church pastor, biographical questionnaire, and record from high school guidance counselor.
Additional information: Application deadline varies.

Number of awards:	500
Number of applicants:	750
Total amount awarded:	$1,120,000

Contact:
Presbyterian Church (U.S.A.)
Financial Aid for Studies
100 Witherspoon Street
Louisville, KY 40202-1396
Phone: 800-728-7228 ext. 5224
Fax: 502-569-8766
Web: www.pcusa.org/financialaid

National Presbyterian College Scholarship

Type of award: Scholarship, renewable.
Intended use: For full-time undergraduate study in United States. Designated institutions: Presbyterian-affiliated colleges.
Eligibility: Applicant must be high school senior. Applicant must be Presbyterian.
Basis for selection: Applicant must demonstrate financial need and high academic achievement.
Application requirements: Transcript. Recommendation from church pastor, biographical questionnaire, and record from high school guidance counselor.
Additional information: Must re-apply annually. Award is up to $2000.

Number of awards:	30
Number of applicants:	30
Application deadline:	May 15
Notification begins:	May 1
Total amount awarded:	$45,000

Contact:
Presbyterian Church (U.S.A.)
Financial Aid for Studies
100 Witherspoon Street
Louisville, KY 40202-1396
Phone: 800-728-7228 ext. 5224
Fax: 502-569-8766
Web: www.pcusa.org/financialaid

Presbyterian Student Opportunity Scholarship

Type of award: Scholarship, renewable.
Intended use: For full-time sophomore, junior or senior study at accredited 4-year institution in United States.
Eligibility: Applicant must be Presbyterian. Applicant must be U.S. citizen or permanent resident.

Basis for selection: Applicant must demonstrate financial need and high academic achievement.

Application requirements: Recommendations, essay, transcript, proof of eligibility.

Additional information: Preference given to students of African American, Asian American, Hispanic American, Alaskan Native, and Native American descent. Minimum 2.5 GPA. Award is up to $2,000. Must reapply annually for renewal.

Number of awards:	80
Number of applicants:	42
Application deadline:	June 15
Notification begins:	August 1
Total amount awarded:	$99,100

Contact:
Presbyterian Church (U.S.A.)
Financial Aid for Studies
100 Witherspoon Street
Louisville, KY 40202-1396
Phone: 800-728-7228 ext. 5224
Fax: 502-569-8766
Web: www.pcusa.org/financialaid

Samuel Robinson Award

Type of award: Scholarship.

Intended use: For full-time junior or senior study at 4-year institution. Designated institutions: One of 69 colleges affiliated with Presbyterian Church (USA).

Eligibility: Applicant must be Presbyterian.

Application requirements: A 2,000-word essay on assigned topic related to the Catechism.

Additional information: Applicant must successfully recite answers of the Westminster Shorter Catechism. Award is up to $5,000. Amount of award based on annual funds.

Number of awards:	16
Number of applicants:	13
Application deadline:	April 1
Notification begins:	May 15
Total amount awarded:	$40,000

Contact:
Presbyterian Church (U.S.A.)
Financial Aid for Studies
100 Witherspoon Street
Louisville, KY 40202-1396
Phone: 800-728-7228 ext. 5224
Fax: 502-569-8766
Web: www.pcusa.org/financialaid

Price Benowitz LLP

Price Benowitz Social Justice Scholarship

Type of award: Scholarship.

Intended use: For undergraduate or graduate study at accredited vocational, 2-year, 4-year or graduate institution.

Eligibility: Applicant must be high school senior.

Basis for selection: Applicant must demonstrate high academic achievement.

Application requirements: Unofficial transcript, application cover sheet, application essay, updated resume. Essay topic (750 words): "What are some significant challenges people with disabilities encounter on a regular basis? What are some practicable public policies that could address these challenges? Feel free to speak about the challenges you have experienced or witnessed in a loved-one's life."

Additional information: Minimum 3.0 GPA required. The scholarship candidate must possess an interest in social justice, as demonstrated by past and present volunteer, professional, and educational experiences.

Amount of award:	$500
Number of awards:	1
Number of applicants:	20
Application deadline:	May 1
Total amount awarded:	$500

Contact:
Price Benowitz LLP
409 7th Street NW
Washington, DC 20004
Phone: 202-517-0502
Fax: 202-664-1331
Web: pricebenowitz.com/2016-student-opportunities

Pride of the Greater Lehigh Valley

Diversity Essay Contest

Type of award: Scholarship.

Intended use: For undergraduate study at accredited postsecondary institution in United States.

Eligibility: Applicant must be residing in New Jersey or Pennsylvania.

Basis for selection: Competition/talent/interest in writing/journalism, based on essay contest.

Application requirements: Recommendations, transcript.

Additional information: Essay contest open to all students regardless of sexual orientation or gender identity. Applicant's high school or accredited institution or both must be located in: Berks, Bucks, Carbon, Lehigh, Monroe, Montgomery, Northampton, Schuylkill counties in Pennsylvania or Warren County in New Jersey. Students from diverse backgrounds encouraged to apply. Visit Website for more information and application.

Amount of award:	$200-$500
Number of awards:	1
Application deadline:	July 31
Total amount awarded:	$1,200

Contact:
Pride of the Greater Lehigh Valley
c/o Diversity Essay Contest
1101 West Hamilton Street
Allentown, PA 18101-1043
Phone: 610-770-6200
Web: www.prideglv.org

Rainbow Scholarship and LGBT Student of the Year Scholarship

Type of award: Scholarship.

Intended use: For undergraduate study at accredited postsecondary institution in United States.

Eligibility: Applicant must be residing in New Jersey or Pennsylvania.

Basis for selection: Applicant must demonstrate high academic achievement.

Application requirements: Recommendations, transcript.

Additional information: Rainbow Award Scholarship is awarded to GLBT (gay, lesbian, bisexual, transgender) student based on academic excellence. The GLBT Student of the Year Scholarship is awarded to GLBT student who is a leader in community activities. Applicant's high school or accredited institution or both must be located in: Berks, Bucks, Carbon, Lehigh, Monroe, Montgomery, Northampton, Schuylkill counties in Pennsylvania and Warren County in New Jersey. Students from diverse backgrounds encouraged to apply. Visit Website for more information and application.

Amount of award:	$500
Number of awards:	2
Number of applicants:	2
Application deadline:	July 1
Total amount awarded:	$1,200

Contact:
The Rainbow Scholarship
522 W Maple St Allentown
Allentown, PA 18101-1043
Phone: 610-770-6200
Fax: 610-903-4880
Web: www.prideglv.org

The Princess Grace Foundation USA

Princess Grace Award for Dance

Type of award: Scholarship.
Intended use: For sophomore, junior or senior study in United States. Designated institutions: Non-profit institutions.
Eligibility: Applicant must be U.S. citizen or permanent resident.
Basis for selection: Major/career interest in dance.
Application requirements: Nomination by dean or department head. Resume, 1-page biography, 8 x 10 glossy photo, compilation of solos on DVD.
Additional information: Award amount varies.

Amount of award:	$7,500-$30,000
Number of awards:	6
Application deadline:	April 30
Notification begins:	July 31

Contact:
The Princess Grace Foundation USA
150 E. 58th Street
25th Floor
New York, NY 10155
Phone: 212-317-1470
Fax: 212-317-1473
Web: www.pgfusa.org

Princess Grace Award For Film

Type of award: Scholarship.
Intended use: For senior or graduate study at accredited 4-year or graduate institution. Designated institutions: Eligible film schools.
Eligibility: Applicant must be U.S. citizen or permanent resident.
Basis for selection: Major/career interest in film/video.
Application requirements: Nomination by dean or department head.

Additional information: Award amount varies. Scholarships to help produce thesis projects. Only students of invited film schools are eligible to apply.

Number of awards:	6
Application deadline:	June 1

Contact:
The Princess Grace Foundation USA
150 E. 58th Street
25th Floor
New York, NY 10155
Phone: 212-317-1470
Fax: 212-317-1473
Web: www.pgfusa.org

Princess Grace Award For Playwriting

Type of award: Scholarship.
Intended use: For undergraduate study in United States.
Eligibility: Applicant must be U.S. citizen or permanent resident.
Basis for selection: Competition/talent/interest in writing/journalism. Major/career interest in playwriting/screenwriting.
Application requirements: Recommendations, essay. Resume. One published, unproduced play.
Additional information: Award given directly to individual through residency at New Dramatists, Inc. in New York. Applicant must not have had any professional productions. Readings, workshops, and Equity showcases are admissible. See Website for application.

Amount of award:	$7,500
Number of awards:	1
Application deadline:	April 1

Contact:
The Princess Grace Playwriting Grant
c/o New Dramatists
424 W. 44th St.
New York, NY 10036
Phone: 212-757-6960
Web: www.pgfusa.org

Princess Grace Award For Theater

Type of award: Scholarship.
Intended use: For senior or master's study at accredited 4-year or graduate institution.
Eligibility: Applicant must be U.S. citizen or permanent resident.
Basis for selection: Major/career interest in theater arts or theater/production/technical.
Application requirements: Essay, nomination by dean or department head. Resume, 8 x 10 glossy photo, 1-page biography, DVD with 2-3 pieces of work.
Additional information: Scholarships awarded to students for their last year (undergraduate or graduate) of professional training in acting, directing, scenic, lighting, sound, costume design or projection design. Award amount varies.

Amount of award:	$7,500-$30,000
Number of awards:	6
Application deadline:	March 31

Contact:
The Princess Grace Foundation USA
150 E. 58th Street
25th Floor
New York, NY 10155
Phone: 212-317-1470
Fax: 212-317-1473
Web: www.pgfusa.org

Print and Graphics Scholarship Foundation

PGSF Annual Scholarship Competition

Type of award: Scholarship, renewable.
Intended use: For full-time undergraduate study at 2-year or 4-year institution in United States.
Eligibility: Applicant must be U.S. citizen.
Basis for selection: Major/career interest in graphic arts/design; printing or publishing. Applicant must demonstrate high academic achievement.
Application requirements: Recommendations, transcript. Biographical information including extracurricular activities and academic honors. Photocopy of intended course of study. High school students must submit SAT, PSAT/NMSQT, or ACT scores.
Additional information: To renew, recipients must maintain 3.0 GPA and continue as graphic arts/printing technology major. Application requirements and criteria may vary by trust fund member institution. Applicants must promote the scholarship and post on PGSF Facebook. The application must be submitted online at PGSF website.

Amount of award:	$1,000-$5,000
Number of awards:	200
Number of applicants:	800
Application deadline:	April 1
Notification begins:	June 30
Total amount awarded:	$400,000

Contact:
Print and Graphics Scholarship Foundation
301 Brush Creek Road
Warrendale, PA 15086
Phone: 800-910-4283 or 412-259-1740
Web: www.pgsf.org

Procter & Gamble

Secret Mean Stinks Scholarship

Type of award: Scholarship.
Intended use: For undergraduate study.
Eligibility: Applicant must be at least 17.
Application requirements: Essay. Students are asked to share how they will bring an end to bullying once and for all while living the Mean Stinks mantra of spreading nice to make a positive impact on those around them. Judges will base entries on four categories. Purpose and Support: Exhibits a good understanding of the issues of girl-to-girl bullying and supports it with examples that he/she has witnessed or endured personally (25%). Organization and Logic of Idea: Develops a sound plan to end girl-to-girl bullying in his/her community or school; this can be something he/she has already executed or a plan he/she will execute in the future (45%). Leadership and Results: Articulates ways in which his/her plan has impacted his/her community. If the plan hasn't been executed yet, describes ways that he/she will measure success (20%). Grammar and Spelling (10%).
Additional information: Apply online.

Amount of award:	$10,000
Number of awards:	3
Application deadline:	December 14
Notification begins:	December 30

Contact:
Phone: 212-485-1694
Web: https://meanstinksscholarship.com/pages/registration.php

Professional Association of Georgia Educators Foundation, Inc.

PAGE Foundation Scholarships

Type of award: Scholarship.
Intended use: For junior, senior or post-bachelor's certificate study at accredited 4-year or graduate institution in United States.
Eligibility: Applicant must be U.S. citizen or permanent resident residing in Georgia.
Basis for selection: Major/career interest in education. Applicant must demonstrate high academic achievement and service orientation.
Application requirements: Recommendations, essay, transcript.
Additional information: Minimum 3.0 GPA. Must be PAGE or SPAGE member. Intended for future teachers and certified teachers seeking advanced degrees. Must agree to teach in Georgia for three years. Applications available from October to April. The application deadline is April 30. Visit Website for additional information, deadline, and application procedures.

Amount of award:	$1,000
Number of awards:	16
Number of applicants:	75
Application deadline:	April 30
Notification begins:	July 1
Total amount awarded:	$16,000

Contact:
PAGE Foundation
P.O. Box 942270
Atlanta, GA 31141-2270
Phone: 800-334-6861
Fax: 770-216-9672
Web: www.pagefoundation.org

Prompt

Prompt's $20,000 Scholarship Essay Contest

Type of award: Scholarship.
Intended use: For full-time freshman study at accredited vocational, 2-year or 4-year institution in United States or Canada.
Application requirements: Submit ANY college application essay. May be for any prompt, length, topic, or any school.
Additional information: Full rules and guidelines on the web site. Also based on online recommendations. Monthly $2000 scholarship with deadlines on the 15th of every month. $10,000 grand prize application deadline is January 15th.

Amount of award:	$200-$10,000
Number of awards:	14
Application deadline:	January 15
Notification begins:	April 1
Total amount awarded:	$20,000

Contact:
Web: https://prompt.com/scholarship/

Proof-Reading.com

Proof-Reading.com Scholarship Program

Type of award: Scholarship.
Intended use: For full-time undergraduate study at postsecondary institution in United States.
Eligibility: Applicant must be U.S. citizen or permanent resident.
Basis for selection: Applicant must demonstrate high academic achievement.
Application requirements: Minimum 1,500-word essay in MLA format answering topical question. Include work cited page with at least two sources.
Additional information: Must maintain a minimum 3.5 GPA. Visit Website for essay topic and online application.

Amount of award:	$1,500
Number of awards:	1
Number of applicants:	30
Application deadline:	January 23
Notification begins:	February 23
Total amount awarded:	$1,500

Contact:
Proof-Reading.com Scholarship Program
Web: www.proof-reading.com/proof-reading_scholarship_program.asp

Prospanica Foundation

The Prospanica Foundation Scholarship

Type of award: Scholarship.
Intended use: For full-time junior, senior or master's study at accredited 4-year or graduate institution in United States. Designated institutions: AACSB.
Eligibility: Applicant must be Hispanic American or Puerto Rican. Hispanic/Latino only. Applicant must be high school junior or senior. Applicant must be U.S. citizen or permanent resident.
Basis for selection: Major/career interest in business. Applicant must demonstrate financial need, high academic achievement and service orientation.
Application requirements: Recommendations, essay. Applicant must be of Hispanic.Lantino heritage. Must have a Prospanica membership (Member ID required). Graduate award applicant must be enrolled or planning to enroll, not later than the upcoming fall, in a Master's Degree program in the business school at a college/university in the US or Puerto Rico accredited by AACSB. Undergraduate award applicant must be a junior or senior, no later than the upcoming fall, pursuing a bachelor's degree within the business school at a

college/university in the US or Puerto Rico accredited by AACSB. Scholarship recipients are selected on the basis of academic achievement, work experience, personal statement of goals and aspirations, Prospanica participation, community service, recommendations, and a Prospanica essay.
Additional information: Undergraduate Awards are $1,500 and the Graduate Awards range from $2,000-$5,000.

Amount of award:	$1,500-$5,000
Number of awards:	8
Number of applicants:	346
Application deadline:	May 15
Notification begins:	June 19
Total amount awarded:	$20,000

Contact:
Prospanica Foundation
c/o Prospanica 2711 LBJ Freeway
Suite 800
Dallas, TX 75234
Phone: 877-467-4622
Web: www.prospanica.org/page/Scholarships

Public Relations Foundation of Houston

Public Relations Foundation of Houston Scholarship

Type of award: Scholarship.
Intended use: For full-time undergraduate or graduate study at 2-year, 4-year or graduate institution.
Basis for selection: Applications will be graded on: 1) Writing Sample - 25%; 2) Student and professional organizations participation and leadership (preference given to PRSSA) - 25%; 3) GPA - 20%; 4) Community involvement, collegiate activities, letters of recommendation - 10%; 5) Work experience - 10%; 6) Financial need - 10%. Finalists will be invited to an in-person interview. The final decision will be based on the combined application (50%) and interview scored (50%). Major/career interest in communications; public relations; journalism or marketing. Applicant must demonstrate financial need and high academic achievement.
Application requirements: Recommendations, essay, transcript. Transcript (unofficial okay as long as GPA is included on transcript, but selected applicant must submit official transcript), application form, writing assignment, recommendation letter.
Additional information: One award for a freshman or sophomore, one award for a junior or senior, and one award for graduate students. Recipient must be seeking a degree in communications, public relations, journalism or marketing and have a desire to practice the public relations profession. Undergraduates must be full-time; graduate students may be part-time or full-time. Preferred minimum GPA: 3.25 major and 3.0 overall for undergraduate students. Preferred minimum GPA: 3.25 for graduate students. Preference given to students attending University of Houston, Sam Houston State University, Stephen F Austin University, & Texas A&M University; students attending other institutions are still encouraged to apply. May also submit a resume and/or sample of work. Entire application package should be submitted electronically with samples saved in separate PDF document and no longer than five printed pages (not including transcript).

Amount of award:	$1,000-$3,000
Number of awards:	3
Number of applicants:	15
Application deadline:	March 5, March 30

Contact:
Public Relations Foundation of Houston
5120 Woodway Drive
Suite 6000
Houston, TX 77056
Phone: 713-960-1990
Web: www.prsahouston.org/foundation

Pumphrey Law Firm

Pumphrey Law Scholarship

Type of award: Scholarship.
Intended use: For full-time undergraduate study at accredited 2-year or 4-year institution.
Eligibility: Applicant must be high school senior. Applicant must be U.S. citizen residing in Florida.
Application requirements: 800-1000 word essay on a designated topic and unofficial high school or college transcript/enrollment verification.
Additional information: One scholarship each semester.

Number of awards:	1
Application deadline:	December 1
Notification begins:	December 12
Total amount awarded:	$1,500

Contact:
Web: www.pumphreylawfirm.com/resources/pumphrey-law-scholarship/

QualityBath.com

QualityBath.com Scholarship Program

Type of award: Scholarship.
Intended use: For undergraduate or graduate study at accredited 2-year, 4-year or graduate institution in United States.
Eligibility: Applicant must be high school senior. Applicant must be U.S. citizen or permanent resident.
Basis for selection: Major/career interest in design; arts management; arts, general or art/art history.
Application requirements: Convey the beauty of humanity, e.g. a good deed you witnessed or envision, in a way that will inspire others. Original, unpublished content only. Submit one of the following: Essay up to 1,500 words; Image up to 8.5" x 11" with description; Video up to 90 seconds long in one of the following formats: .mov, .mp4, .m4v, .flv, .3gp, .avi, .wmv.
Additional information: Must have a minimum 3.0 GPA.

Number of awards:	1
Application deadline:	March 1
Total amount awarded:	$1,500

Contact:
Scholarship Contest c/o Qualuty Bath
1144 East County Line Road
Unit 200
Lakewood, NJ 08701
Web: www.qualitybath.com/scholarship

Quanta Aesthetic lasers

Quanta Picosecond Laser Annual Scholarship

Type of award: Scholarship.
Intended use: For full-time undergraduate study at accredited vocational, 2-year or 4-year institution.
Eligibility: Applicant must be high school senior.
Basis for selection: Major/career interest in engineering; physics; biology; medicine; nursing or science, general. Applicant must demonstrate high academic achievement.
Application requirements: Transcript.
Additional information: Applicants must be currently in High school senior, college freshman, college sophomore, college junior.Interested students can download the application form and send their completed application and documents to scholarship@quantausa.com.

Amount of award:	$1,000-$1,000
Number of awards:	1
Application deadline:	July 31
Notification begins:	August 4
Total amount awarded:	$1,000

Contact:
Quanta Aesthetic lasers
611 Corporate Circle
Suite A
Golden, CO 80401
Phone: 844-694-1064
Web: https://quantausa.com/quanta-picosecond-laser-annual-scholarship/

Quill and Scroll Foundation

Edward J. Nell Memorial Scholarship

Type of award: Scholarship.
Intended use: For full-time freshman study at accredited 2-year or 4-year institution in United States.
Eligibility: Applicant must be high school senior. Applicant must be U.S. citizen.
Basis for selection: Major/career interest in journalism. Applicant must demonstrate seriousness of purpose.
Application requirements: Recommendations, essay, transcript. Statement of intent to major in journalism. Three selections of student's journalistic work. One color photo of applicant.
Additional information: Open only to winners of Quill and Scroll's Annual National Yearbook Excellence or International Writing/Photo Contests at any time during high school career.

Amount of award: $500-$1,500
Number of awards: 6
Number of applicants: 50
Application deadline: May 10
Notification begins: June 1
Total amount awarded: $5,000
Contact:
Scholarship Committee Quill and Scroll Foundation
E346 Adler Journalism Building
University of Iowa
Iowa City, IA 52242-1401
Phone: 319-335-3457
Fax: 319-335-3989
Web: www.quillandscroll.org

Radio Television Digital News Association (RTDNA)

Carole Simpson Scholarship

Type of award: Scholarship.
Intended use: For full-time sophomore, junior or senior study at 4-year institution.
Basis for selection: Major/career interest in communications; film/video; journalism or radio/television/film. Applicant must demonstrate depth of character and seriousness of purpose.
Application requirements: Recommendations, essay, proof of eligibility. Cover letter. Three to five links to online work samples. Link to personal Website recommended.
Additional information: Must be preparing for career in electronic journalism. Preference given to minority students. Visit Website for deadline and application.

Amount of award: $2,000
Number of awards: 1
Number of applicants: 20
Total amount awarded: $2,000
Contact:
RTDNA Scholarships
Phone: 202-536-8356
Web: www.rtdna.org

Ed Bradley Scholarship

Type of award: Scholarship.
Intended use: For full-time sophomore, junior or senior study at 4-year institution.
Basis for selection: Major/career interest in communications; film/video; journalism or radio/television/film. Applicant must demonstrate seriousness of purpose.
Application requirements: Recommendations, essay, proof of eligibility. Cover Letter. Three to five links of online relevant work samples. Link to personal Website recommended.
Additional information: Must have at least one full year of school remaining. Must be preparing for career in electronic journalism. Preference given to minority students. Visit Website for deadline and application.

Amount of award: $10,000
Number of awards: 1
Number of applicants: 47
Total amount awarded: $10,000
Contact:
RTDNA Scholarships
Phone: 202-536-8356
Web: www.rtdna.org

The George Foreman Tribute to Lyndon B. Johnson Scholarship

Type of award: Scholarship.
Intended use: For full-time sophomore, junior or senior study at 4-year institution in United States. Designated institutions: University of Texas at Austin.
Eligibility: Applicant must be U.S. citizen or permanent resident residing in Texas.
Basis for selection: Major/career interest in communications; film/video; journalism or radio/television/film.
Application requirements: Recommendations, essay, proof of eligibility. Cover Letter. Three to five links to relevant online work samples. Link to personal website recommended.
Additional information: Must be preparing for career in electronic journalism. Visit Website for deadline and application.

Amount of award: $6,000
Number of awards: 1
Number of applicants: 9
Total amount awarded: $6,000
Contact:
RTDNA Scholarships
Phone: 202-536-8356
Web: www.rtdna.org

Lou and Carole Prato Sports Reporting Scholarship

Type of award: Scholarship.
Intended use: For full-time sophomore, junior or senior study at postsecondary institution.
Basis for selection: Major/career interest in communications; film/video; journalism; radio/television/film or sports/sports administration.
Application requirements: Recommendations, essay, proof of eligibility. Cover Letter. Three to five links to relevant online work samples. Link to personal website recommended.
Additional information: Must be planning career as sports reporter in television or radio. Visit Website for deadline and application.

Amount of award: $1,000
Number of awards: 1
Number of applicants: 15
Total amount awarded: $1,000
Contact:
RTDNA Scholarships
Phone: 202-536-8356
Web: www.rtdna.org

Mike Reynolds Scholarship

Type of award: Scholarship.
Intended use: For full-time sophomore, junior or senior study at 4-year institution in United States.
Basis for selection: Major/career interest in communications; film/video; journalism or radio/television/film. Applicant must demonstrate financial need and high academic achievement.
Application requirements: Recommendations, essay, proof of eligibility. Cover letter. Three to five links to relevant online work. Link to personal Website recommended.
Additional information: Applicant should indicate media-related jobs held and contribution made to funding of education. Must be preparing for career in electronic journalism. Visit Website for deadline and application.

Amount of award:	$1,000
Number of awards:	1
Total amount awarded:	$1,000

Contact:
RTDNA Scholarships
Phone: 202-536-8356
Web: www.rtdna.org

Pete Wilson Journalism Scholarship

Type of award: Scholarship.
Intended use: For full-time sophomore, junior, senior or graduate study at accredited 4-year or graduate institution. Designated institutions: San Francisco Bay area institutions.
Eligibility: Applicant must be residing in California.
Basis for selection: Major/career interest in communications; film/video; journalism or radio/television/film.
Application requirements: Recommendations, essay, proof of eligibility. Cover Letter. Three to five links to relevant online work samples. Link to personal Website recommended.
Additional information: Must be preparing for career in electronic journalism. Must have one full year of school left to be eligible. Alternates yearly between graduate and undergraduate award winner. Visit Website for deadline and application.

Amount of award:	$2,000
Number of awards:	1
Total amount awarded:	$2,000

Contact:
RTDNA Scholarships
Phone: 202-536-8356
Web: www.rtdna.org

Presidents Scholarships

Type of award: Scholarship.
Intended use: For full-time junior or senior study at 2-year or 4-year institution.
Basis for selection: Major/career interest in communications; film/video; journalism or radio/television/film. Applicant must demonstrate high academic achievement and seriousness of purpose.
Application requirements: Recommendations, essay, proof of eligibility. Cover letter. Three to five links to relevant online work samples. Link to personal website recommended.
Additional information: Must be preparing for career in electronic journalism. Visit Website for deadline and application.

Amount of award:	$1,000
Number of awards:	2
Number of applicants:	79
Total amount awarded:	$2,000

Contact:
RTDNA Scholarships
Phone: 202-536-8356
Web: www.rtdna.org

Raj Cheritable Foundation

Raj Cheritable Foundation Texas Scholarships

Type of award: Scholarship, renewable.
Intended use: For full-time undergraduate study at accredited 4-year institution in United States.

Eligibility: Applicant must be at least 17, no older than 19, high school senior. Applicant must be residing in Texas.
Basis for selection: Applicant must demonstrate financial need, high academic achievement and leadership.
Application requirements: Recommendations, essay, transcript. Transcript, two letters of recommendation. Must have financial need.
Additional information: Must have a minimum 3.5 GPA. Must be in the top 30% of his/her class for both sophomore and junior years. Must have been involved in extra curricular activities and demonstrate leadership abilities while attending high school.

Amount of award:	$2,000
Number of awards:	2
Application deadline:	March 25
Total amount awarded:	$4,000

Contact:
Raj Charitable Foundation
P.O. Box 23078
Beaumont, TX 77720
Web: http://rajreddyfoundation.org/application

RealMoney.co.uk

Emily Woodward Scholarship

Type of award: Scholarship.
Intended use: For undergraduate or graduate study at vocational, 2-year, 4-year or graduate institution in or outside United States or Canada.
Eligibility: Applicant must be at least 18. Applicant must be U.S. citizen, permanent resident or international student.
Application requirements: Essay. 1,000 word essay on the following topic: "what does the future hold for money?" Must be written in English.
Additional information: Must have a minimum 3.0 GPA. Apply via e-mail, subject line "Emily Woodward Scholarship," with the following information: full name, university name, major, essay, and brief personal info (50-100 words).

Amount of award:	$2,000
Number of awards:	1
Application deadline:	May 31
Notification begins:	July 31
Total amount awarded:	$2,000

Contact:
Web: www.realmoney.co.uk/scholarship/

Recycling Research

Veteran's Stipend

Type of award: Scholarship, renewable.
Intended use: For at accredited vocational, 2-year or 4-year institution in United States.
Eligibility: Applicant must be U.S. citizen. Applicant must be veteran.
Application requirements: Essay, proof of eligibility. Copy of DD form 214 (please black out your social security number). 2 letters of recommendation. Resume detailing military duty and awards, volunteer activities, community services and jobs held during the past 5 years. Two essay questions with no length requirement.

531

Additional information: Must have a minimum 2.5 GPA. Must have served a minimum 2 years active duty or 4 years reserve in a branch of the US military and have been honorably discharged. The stipends covers $2,000 per year and is renewable for up to four years or the length of study.

Number of awards:	1
Application deadline:	June 1
Total amount awarded:	$2,000

Contact:
ISRI
1615 L Street, NW
Suite 600
Washington, DC 20036
Phone: 202-662-8524
Fax: 202-626-0924
Web: www.isri.org/rrf

Red River Valley Fighter Pilots Association

Red River Valley Fighter Pilots Association (RRVA) Scholarship Program

Type of award: Scholarship, renewable.
Intended use: For undergraduate or graduate study at accredited vocational, 2-year, 4-year or graduate institution in United States.
Eligibility: Applicant must be U.S. citizen.
Basis for selection: Applicant must demonstrate financial need, high academic achievement and service orientation.
Application requirements: Transcript, proof of eligibility. SAT/ACT scores.
Additional information: Kinship eligibility is as follows: Must be immediate dependent (legal son, daughter, or spouse) of 1) A U.S. aircrew member listed as Killed in Action (KIA) or Missing in Action (MIA) from any combat situation involving U.S. military from August 1964 (Vietnam Era) through the present; 2) a military aircrew member killed as the result of performing aircrew duties during a non-combat mission; 3) an RRVA member who is currently in good standing or was in good standing at the time of their death. Also eligible are those pursuing a career in field related to aviation/space (kinship not required). See Website for application and more information.

Amount of award:	$500-$3,500
Number of awards:	32
Number of applicants:	42
Application deadline:	May 15
Total amount awarded:	$80,000

Contact:
Red River Valley Fighter Pilots Association
P.O. Box 1553
Front Royal, VA 22630
Phone: 540-636-9798
Fax: 540-636-9776
Web: www.river-rats.org

Regeneration Center of Thailand

The Regen Center Scholarship

Type of award: Scholarship.
Intended use: For undergraduate or graduate study at accredited 2-year, 4-year or graduate institution in or outside United States or Canada.
Eligibility: Applicant must be Asian American. Applicant must be high school senior. Applicant must be U.S. citizen, permanent resident or international student.
Application requirements: Essay. Essay must be between 500 and 1000 words on the following topic: "How will this scholarship help you in your career goals?"
Additional information: Must be of ASEAN ancestry. ASEAN countries include Runei Darussalem, Cambodia, Indonesia, Lao PDR, Malaysia, Myanmar, Singapore, Thailand, Philippines, and Vietnam. Winner will be selected exactly one week after scholarship deadline. Required documents to confirm eligibility will be requested from winner.

Number of awards:	1
Application deadline:	December 31
Total amount awarded:	$1,500

Contact:
Web: stemcellthailand.org/scholarship/

RehabMart.com

RehabMart.com Scholarship Fund

Type of award: Scholarship.
Intended use: For undergraduate or graduate study at vocational, 2-year, 4-year or graduate institution.
Eligibility: Applicant must be physically challenged.
Basis for selection: Major/career interest in education, special; medicine; biomedical; nursing; physician assistant; surgical technology; rehabilitation/therapeutic services or health-related professions.
Application requirements: Essay. Short essay as well as a biography.
Additional information: Scholarship is available for the following: any medical major; a major in special needs education; or a disabled student of any major. Application and essay prompt can be found on website. Applications received after the deadline will be considered for the following year.

Amount of award:	$250-$2,500
Application deadline:	May 31
Total amount awarded:	$25,000

Contact:
Phone: 800-827-8283
Web: www.rehabmart.com/scholarship/

Renee B. Fisher Foundation

Milton Fisher Scholarship for Innovation and Creativity

Type of award: Scholarship, renewable.
Intended use: For undergraduate study at vocational or 4-year institution in United States.

Eligibility: Applicant must be high school junior or senior. Applicant must be U.S. citizen.

Application requirements: Recommendations, essay, transcript. Completion of a unique and/or innovative personal project, 2 letters of support, Online application available at www.rbffoundation.org which includes 2 short essays, 1 official high school transcript, IRS 1040/FAFSA, Supporting information about the project.

Additional information: Scholarship is open to a student graduating from a Connecticut or New York City metropolitan area high school planning to attend or attending an educational institution anywhere in the United States; OR a student graduating from a U.S. high school planning to attend or attending an educational institution in Connecticut or the New York City metropolitan area. The student's project must fall into one of the following categories: have solved an artistic, scientific, or technical problem in a new or unusual way. Have come up with a distinctive solution to problems faced by their school, community, or family. Have created a new group, organization, or institution that serves an important need. Financial need does not affect chances of winning; only the dollar amount of the scholarship. Honorable mentions are also awarded.

Amount of award:	$500-$20,000
Number of awards:	12
Number of applicants:	102
Application deadline:	April 30
Total amount awarded:	$110,000

Contact:
Milton Fisher Scholarship
Community Foundation for Greater New Haven
70 Audubon Street
New Haven, CT 06510
Phone: 203-777-2386
Fax: 203-787-6584
Web: www.rbffoundation.org

RentHop

RentHop Apartment Scholarship

Type of award: Scholarship.

Intended use: For full-time undergraduate study at 4-year institution.

Eligibility: Applicant must be at least 15, no older than 26.

Application requirements: Send an essay in under 1000 words that explains where you see yourself 5 years after finishing school and how those goals are aligned with the RentHop values and those of your school and degree program.

Additional information: Apply via e-mail (you must apply using your school e-mail address). Three prizes a year. Deadlines Dec 1st, April 30th, and August 31st. Winner is awarded an optional part-time or full-time Renthop internship.

Number of awards:	1
Total amount awarded:	$1,000

Contact:
RentHop
101 Avenue of the Americas
18th Floor
New York, NY 10013
Web: www.renthop.com/college_scholarship

Respshop.com

Respshop.com Scholarship Prize

Type of award: Scholarship, renewable.

Intended use: For undergraduate study.

Application requirements: Essay.

Additional information: Submit 500-750 word essay. Selection based on quality of submitted essay . Essay must be submitted by 01/31.

Amount of award:	$1,500-$5,000
Number of awards:	6

Contact:
RespShop.com
17521 NE 67th Court
Redmond, WA 98052
Phone: 866-936-3754
Web: https://www.respshop.com/respshop_scholarship.php

Restaurant Association of Maryland Education Foundation

Applebee's/The Rose Group Hospitality Scholarship

Type of award: Scholarship.

Intended use: For freshman study at 4-year institution in United States.

Eligibility: Applicant must be U.S. citizen residing in Maryland.

Basis for selection: Major/career interest in hospitality administration/management. Applicant must demonstrate high academic achievement and service orientation.

Application requirements: Interview, recommendations, essay.

Additional information: Must have minimum of 150 hours of documented industry experience. Minimum 3.0 GPA. Visit Website for essay topic.

Amount of award:	$1,100
Number of awards:	1

Contact:
Restaurant Association of Maryland Education Foundation
6301 Hillside Court
Columbia, MD 21046
Phone: 410-290-6800
Fax: 410-290-6882
Web: www.marylandrestaurants.com

Letitia B. Carter Scholarship

Type of award: Scholarship.

Intended use: For undergraduate study in United States.

Eligibility: Applicant must be enrolled in high school. Applicant must be U.S. citizen residing in Maryland.

Basis for selection: Major/career interest in hospitality administration/management. Applicant must demonstrate high academic achievement.

Application requirements: Recommendations, essay. Paystub from most recent employer in industry-related work. One typed and double-spaced essay: Describe any personal skills and characteristics that will help you meet the future challenges of the food service/hospitality industry.

Additional information: Applicant must have applied to an RAMEF-recognized professional development program in hospitality or enrolled in a RAMEF-recognized food service/hospitality program. Any high school or college student applying for scholarship must have a minimum 3.0 cumulative GPA and a minimum of 400 hours documented industry experience. Any teachers or instructors applying must have a minimum of 1,500 hours documented industry experience. Visit Website for more information.

Amount of award:	$500-$2,000
Number of applicants:	10
Notification begins:	May 11
Total amount awarded:	$5,000

Contact:
Restaurant Association of Maryland Education Foundation
6301 Hillside Court
Columbia, MD 21046
Phone: 410-290-6800
Fax: 410-290-6882
Web: www.marylandrestaurants.com

Marcia S. Harris Legacy Fund Scholarship

Type of award: Scholarship.
Intended use: For full-time undergraduate or graduate study at postsecondary institution.
Eligibility: Applicant must be U.S. citizen residing in Maryland.
Basis for selection: Applicant must demonstrate financial need and high academic achievement.
Application requirements: Interview, essay, transcript. The award decision is based on several factors including the essay required. School transcripts. Work experience. Volunteer experience. An interview may be required for finalists.
Additional information: Selection based on grades in food service coursework. Number and amount of award varies.Must be pursuing hospitality related coursework.

Amount of award:	$500-$2,000
Number of awards:	3
Number of applicants:	7
Notification begins:	May 26

Contact:
Restaurant Association of Maryland Education Foundation
6301 Hillside Court
Columbia, MD 21046
Phone: 410-290-6800
Fax: 410-290-6882
Web: www.marylandrestaurants.com/scholarships

Michael Birchenall Scholarship Fund

Type of award: Scholarship.
Intended use: For full-time undergraduate or graduate study at accredited vocational, 2-year, 4-year or graduate institution in United States.
Eligibility: Applicant must be U.S. citizen residing in Virginia, District of Columbia, Delaware or Maryland.
Basis for selection: Major/career interest in hospitality administration/management or culinary arts.
Application requirements: Interview, essay, transcript. The essay required. School transcripts. Work experience. Volunteer experience. An interview may be required for finalists.

Additional information: More information about the Scholarship on the Website.

Amount of award:	$500-$2,500
Number of awards:	2
Notification begins:	May 12

Contact:
Restaurant Association of Maryland Education Foundation
6301 Hillside Court
Columbia, MD 21046
Phone: 410-290-6800
Fax: 410-290-6882
Web: www.marylandrestaurants.com/scholarships

Rhine law firm, P.C.

Rhine Law Firm, P.C. Scholarship

Type of award: Scholarship.
Intended use: For undergraduate study at accredited 2-year or 4-year institution.
Eligibility: Applicant must be high school senior. Applicant must be U.S. citizen or permanent resident.
Basis for selection: Applicant must demonstrate high academic achievement.
Application requirements: Essay. In your essay, please tell us about the goals you have for your post-secondary education and how your education will help you better your community.
Additional information: The online application, GPA from previous grading period (3.0 GPA), and essay are all that is required to apply for this scholarship. Applicants must be either graduating high school seniors or currently-enrolled college students.

Amount of award:	$500
Number of awards:	1
Application deadline:	April 24
Notification begins:	May 24
Total amount awarded:	$500

Contact:
Joel Rhine
1612 Military Cutoff Road, Suite 300
Wilmington, NC 28403
Phone: 910-772-9960
Fax: 910-772-9062
Web: www.carolinaaccidentattorneys.com/scholarship/

Rhode Island Higher Education Assistance Authority

Rhode Island State Grant

Type of award: Scholarship, renewable.
Intended use: For undergraduate study at vocational, 2-year or 4-year institution in or outside United States or Canada. Designated institutions: U.S., Canadian, or Mexican institutions that participate in at least one federal financial aid program.
Eligibility: Applicant must be U.S. citizen or permanent resident residing in Rhode Island.
Basis for selection: Applicant must demonstrate financial need.

Application requirements: FAFSA.

Additional information: Must meet all Title IV eligibility requirements. Dependent applicant's parent must reside in Rhode Island. Award notification begins in late spring.

Amount of award:	$250-$750
Number of awards:	19,000
Number of applicants:	65,583
Application deadline:	March 1
Total amount awarded:	$12,134,726

Contact:
Rhode Island Higher Education Assistance Authority
560 Jefferson Boulevard
Warwick, RI 02886
Phone: 401-736-1170
Fax: 401-736-1178
Web: www.riheaa.org

Richard Console

Diagnosis Delayed Scholarship

Type of award: Scholarship.

Intended use: For undergraduate study.

Eligibility: Applicant must be U.S. citizen.

Application requirements: Proof of enrollment (acceptance letter, class schedule, etc.); unofficial transcript; and a word document containing your name, address, birthdate, program/school, GPA, and a short essay (500 words) describing why you deserve to win the scholarship.

Additional information: Scholarship for students with majors related to the legal or medical field. Submit all materials by e-mail.

Number of awards:	1
Application deadline:	August 1
Total amount awarded:	$500

Contact:
Web: www.diagnosisdelayed.com/scholarship/

The Richard Eaton Foundation

Richard Eaton Foundation Award

Type of award: Scholarship.

Intended use: For full-time junior, senior or graduate study at 4-year or graduate institution. Designated institutions: BEA Institutional Member schools.

Basis for selection: Major/career interest in radio/television/film. Applicant must demonstrate high academic achievement, depth of character and seriousness of purpose.

Application requirements: Recommendations, essay, transcript.

Additional information: Must show evidence of potential in electronic media. Application available from campus faculty or on Website.

Amount of award:	$2,500
Number of awards:	1
Application deadline:	October 10
Total amount awarded:	$2,500

Contact:
Broadcast Education Association (BEA)
1771 N Street, NW
Washington, DC 20036-2891
Phone: 202-429-3935
Web: www.beaweb.org

Richard Harris Law Firm

Richard Harris Law Firm Students with a Cause PSA

Type of award: Scholarship.

Intended use: For full-time undergraduate or graduate study.

Eligibility: Applicant must be high school freshman, sophomore, junior or senior. Applicant must be residing in Nevada.

Additional information: Students with a cause is a video scholarship for students in Nevada. The Richard Harris Law Firm encourages students to creatively express true stories and life experiences to illustrate important issues with a 30 second video PSA.

Amount of award:	$500-$1,500
Number of awards:	2
Number of applicants:	30
Application deadline:	May 3
Notification begins:	May 22
Total amount awarded:	$2,000

Contact:
Richard Harris Law Firm
801 S 4th St.
Las Vegas, NV 89101
Phone: 702-444-4444
Fax: 702-444-4455
Web: www.richardharrislaw.com/community/students-cause/

The Richmond Defense Firm

Michael Kiely Strong Roots and Scholarship

Type of award: Scholarship.

Intended use: For undergraduate or graduate study at accredited vocational, 2-year, 4-year or graduate institution.

Eligibility: Applicant must be high school senior.

Basis for selection: Applicant must demonstrate high academic achievement.

Application requirements: Essay, transcript. Unofficial transcript, application cover sheet, application essay, updated resume. Essay topic (500 words): "How is the meaning of the word 'community' changing in today's world, and what does that mean for people who wish to build strong, healthy communities?"

Additional information: Minimum 3.0 GPA required. All candidates must possess an interest in community building, as demonstrated by their essay and resume.

Amount of award: $500
Number of awards: 1
Application deadline: May 1
Total amount awarded: $500
Contact:
Michael Kiely Strong Roots Scholarship
4124 East Parham Road
Suite 250
Richmond, VA 23228
Phone: 202-517-0502
Fax: 804-265-1451
Web: virginialawfirm.net/healthy-communities-scholarship/

Rittgers & Rittgers

Rittgers & Rittgers Annual Scholarship

Type of award: Scholarship.
Intended use: For undergraduate study.
Eligibility: Applicant must be high school senior. Applicant must be residing in Ohio.
Application requirements: Essay.
Additional information: The law firm of Rittgers & Rittgers is giving back to Warren County community. Through an annual high school essay contest, four scholarships are awarded totaling $10,000 to deserving high school seniors in Warren County, Ohio. Apply between January and April.

Amount of award: $1,000-$5,000
Number of awards: 4
Application deadline: April 20
Total amount awarded: $10,000
Contact:
Rittgers & Rittgers Attorneys at Law
12 East Warren Street
Lebanon, OH 45036
Phone: 513-932-2115
Web: www.rittgers.com/Firm-Overview/Scholarships

RoadRunner

RoadRunner Auto Transport Annual Scholarship

Type of award: Scholarship.
Intended use: For full-time undergraduate study at 4-year institution in United States.
Eligibility: Applicant must be at least 17, no older than 22. Applicant must be U.S. citizen.
Application requirements: Take a photo of a car, edit it to include the RoadRunner logo (found on the top right corner of the web site), and create a RoadRunner Auto Transport banner. The most creative and artistic submission will be chosen as the winner. Send submission by e-mail, include first and last name, age and birthdate, phone number, e-mail address, name of College or University, transcript or school schedule including name, and custom banner.
Additional information: Must be enrolled full-time in any US college or university. Cannot be, or be related to, a RoadRunner Auto Transport employee or partner.

Number of awards: 1
Application deadline: January 1
Total amount awarded: $1,500
Contact:
1055 Stewart Avenue
Bethpage, NY 11714
Phone: 516-605-2665 ext. 538
Fax: 516-605-2663
Web: www.roadrunnerautotransport.com/

Robert Reeves Law

The Reeves Law Group Scholarship

Type of award: Scholarship.
Intended use: For undergraduate or graduate study at 4-year or graduate institution.
Basis for selection: Major/career interest in law.
Application requirements: Essay, transcript. Unofficial transcript (official transcript if selected as a finalist), letter from admissions confirming deposit on school letterhead, official enrollment verification form, acceptance letter, readable copy of your entry, and a headshot no smaller than 300 pixels (width) of yourself. Must be in .PNG or .JPG format.
Additional information: Also required: brief personal statement, detailing who you are, your interests, or anything else about you, as well as a 750-1000 word essay (or PowerPoint/Prezi presentation). Essay topic is as follows: Tell us about contributions you may have made or are currently making to help a non-profit institution, a specific group, your local community, or the public at large; and tell us also how you intend to use your legal training to advance those goals.

Number of awards: 1
Application deadline: December 15
Total amount awarded: $3,000
Contact:
Robert Reeves Law
200 W Santa Ana Boulevard
#630
Santa Ana, CA 92701
Web: www.robertreeveslaw.com/scholarship/

Robinson and Henry, P.C.

Robinson and Henry, P.C. Family Law Scholarship

Type of award: Scholarship.
Intended use: For full-time undergraduate study at accredited 2-year or 4-year institution in United States.
Eligibility: Applicant must be high school senior. Applicant must be U.S. citizen or permanent resident.
Application requirements: Essay, transcript. Must be enrolled for upcoming Fall Semester. Scholarship is available for high school seniors and current college students nationwide. A 500-word minimum essay explaining yourparents divorce andhow it changed your everyday outlook, or why you are pursuing a career in family law. Although not required, applicants are encouraged to submit recommendation letters and/or resumes to substantiate their application for consideration. Any incomplete or late scholarship applications will not be accepted.

Additional information: Funds will be sent to the college you plan on attending/currently attend. Scholarship is a one-time award of $1,000.

Amount of award:	$1,000
Number of awards:	1
Application deadline:	May 31
Notification begins:	July 23
Total amount awarded:	$1,000

Contact:
Robinson and Henry, P.C.
7535 East Hampden Avenue
Suite 250
Denver, CO 80231
Phone: 208-670-0921
Web: https://www.robinsonandhenry.com/denver-divorce-lawyer#scholarship

Robinson and Henry, P.C. Injury Scholarship

Type of award: Scholarship.
Intended use: For full-time undergraduate study at accredited 2-year or 4-year institution in United States.
Eligibility: Applicant must be high school senior. Applicant must be U.S. citizen or permanent resident.
Application requirements: Essay, transcript. Students should apply if you or your family was involved in a personal injury accident. Scholarship is available for high school seniors and current college students nationwide. Must be enrolled for upcoming Fall Semester. A 500-word minimum essay explaining you or your family's personal injury accident and how it changed your everyday outlook and possible future plans. Special preferences will be given to members of a family that has recently been injured in a car accident. Although not required, applicants are encouraged to submit recommendation letters and/or resumes to substantiate their application for consideration. Any incomplete or late scholarship applications will not be accepted.
Additional information: Funds will be sent to the college you plan on attending/currently attend. Scholarship is a one-time award of $1,500.

Amount of award:	$1,500
Number of awards:	1
Application deadline:	May 31
Notification begins:	July 23
Total amount awarded:	$1,500

Contact:
Robinson and Henry, P.C.
7535 East Hampden Avenue
Suite 250
Denver, CO 80231
Phone: 208-670-0921
Web: https://www.robinsonandhenry.com/denver-personal-injury-lawyer/#scholarship

Rocky Mountain Coal Mining Institute

RCMI Technical/Trade School Scholarship

Type of award: Scholarship.
Intended use: For sophomore study at vocational or 2-year institution.

Eligibility: Applicant must be U.S. citizen residing in Wyoming, Utah, Texas, Montana, New Mexico, Colorado, North Dakota or Arizona.
Basis for selection: Major/career interest in engineering, mining or geology/earth sciences.
Additional information: Applicant must be first-year student at a two-year technical school in good standing. Must be studying an applicable trade and be interested in coal as a career path.

Amount of award:	$1,000
Number of awards:	8
Number of applicants:	7
Application deadline:	February 1
Notification begins:	March 1
Total amount awarded:	$7,000

Contact:
Rocky Mountain Coal Mining Institute
3500 S. Wadsworth Blvd., Ste. 211
Lakewood, CO 80235
Phone: 303-948-3300
Fax: 303-954-9004
Web: www.rmcmi.org

Rocky Mountain Coal Mining Institute Scholarship

Type of award: Scholarship, renewable.
Intended use: For full-time junior or senior study in United States. Designated institutions: Mining schools approved by Rocky Mountain Coal Mining Institute.
Eligibility: Applicant must be U.S. citizen residing in Wyoming, Utah, Texas, Montana, New Mexico, Colorado, Arizona or North Dakota.
Basis for selection: Major/career interest in engineering; engineering, mining or geology/earth sciences. Applicant must demonstrate high academic achievement.
Application requirements: Interview, recommendations.
Additional information: Must have career interest in western coal mining. Recommended 3.0 GPA or higher. One new award per Rocky Mountain Coal Mining Institute member state per year. Can be renewed as senior or post-graduate.

Amount of award:	$2,750
Number of awards:	8
Number of applicants:	32
Application deadline:	February 1
Notification begins:	March 1
Total amount awarded:	$40,000

Contact:
Rocky Mountain Coal Mining Institute
3500 S. Wadsworth Blvd., Ste. 211
Lakewood, CO 80235
Phone: 303-948-3300
Fax: 303-954-9004
Web: www.rmcmi.org

Roller Skating Foundation

Roller Skating Foundation College Scholarship

Type of award: Scholarship.
Intended use: For undergraduate study.
Basis for selection: Major/career interest in sports/sports administration; food production/management/services or hotel/

restaurant management. Applicant must demonstrate high academic achievement and leadership.

Application requirements: Recommendations, essay, transcript. Copy of current Federal Income Tax return.

Additional information: Must have cumulative 3.4 GPA and 3.5 GPA in major. Two scholarships available: one for $4,000 and one for $3,000. Contact Roller Skating Foundation for official application.

Amount of award:	$4,000
Number of awards:	2
Application deadline:	April 2

Contact:
Roller Skating Foundation
6905 Corporate Drive
Indianapolis, IN 46278
Phone: 317-347-2626
Fax: 317-347-2636
Web: www.rollerskating.org/about/foun.html

Roller Skating Foundation High School Senior Scholarship

Roller Skating Foundation

Type of award: Scholarship.
Intended use: For freshman study at 4-year institution.
Eligibility: Applicant must be high school senior.
Basis for selection: Applicant must demonstrate high academic achievement.
Additional information: Minimum 3.4 GPA. Must have composite score on the SAT/ACT in the 85th percentile or higher. Student does not have to be a member of Roller Skating Foundation, but preferably has skated in a member rink. Contact RSF for official application.

Amount of award:	$4,000
Number of awards:	1
Application deadline:	April 1
Total amount awarded:	$4,000

Contact:
Roller Skating Foundation
6905 Corporate Drive
Indianapolis, IN 46278
Phone: 317-347-2626
Fax: 317-347-2636
Web: www.rollerskating.org/about/scho.html

Ron Brown Scholar Fund

Ron Brown Scholar Program

Type of award: Scholarship, renewable.
Intended use: For full-time undergraduate study at accredited 4-year institution in United States.
Eligibility: Applicant must be African American. Applicant must be high school senior. Applicant must be U.S. citizen or permanent resident.
Basis for selection: Applicant must demonstrate financial need, high academic achievement, depth of character, leadership, seriousness of purpose and service orientation.

Application requirements: Recommendations, essay, transcript.

Additional information: In addition to financial assistance, scholars get other benefits: summer internships, career guidance, placement opportunities, mentors, and leadership training. Scholarships may be used to pursue any academic discipline. Award is $10,000 per year for four years. 10 - 20 awards given yearly. Earlier deadline is for those who wish to have their information forwarded to select colleges and scholarship programs.

Amount of award:	$40,000
Number of awards:	20
Number of applicants:	6,000
Application deadline:	November 1, January 9
Notification begins:	April 1
Total amount awarded:	$760,000

Contact:
Ron Brown Scholar Program
1160 Pepsi Place, Suite 206
Charlottesville, VA 22901
Phone: 434-964-1588
Fax: 434-964-1589
Web: www.ronbrown.org

Ronald McDonald House Charities (RMHC)

RMHC U.S. Scholarship Program

Type of award: Scholarship.
Intended use: For full-time undergraduate study at accredited vocational, 2-year or 4-year institution.
Eligibility: Applicant must be high school senior. Applicant must be U.S. citizen or permanent resident.
Basis for selection: Applicant must demonstrate financial need, high academic achievement, leadership and service orientation.
Application requirements: Recommendations, essay, transcript, proof of eligibility. IRS Form 1040, other valid financial documents.
Additional information: Must be a legal U.S. resident. Intended for those who live within geographic boundaries of RMHC Chapter that offers scholarships. Geographic areas listed on Website. Some requirements include: RMHC/ASIA: Applicant must have at least one parent of Asian heritage; RMHC/Future African American Achievers: Applicant must have at least one parent of African American or Black/Caribbean heritage; RMHC/HACER: Applicant must have at least one parent of Hispanic heritage; RMHC/Scholars: All students may apply regardless of ethnic heritage. Number of awards varies. Minimum award $1000. Award notification begins in May. See Website for contact information and application. Deadline in January.

Number of applicants:	29,430
Application deadline:	January 1
Notification begins:	May 1
Total amount awarded:	$4,100,000

Contact:
Ronald McDonald House Charities Scholarship Program
Administrators
One Kroc Drive
Oak Brook, IL 60523
Phone: 630-623-7048
Fax: 630-623-7488
Web: www.rmhc.org

Rosengren Kohlmeyer And Hagen Law Office

Rosengren Kohlmeyer Law Office Scholarship

Type of award: Scholarship.
Intended use: For full-time undergraduate study at accredited
2-year or 4-year institution in United States.
Eligibility: Applicant must be U.S. citizen or permanent
resident.
Basis for selection: Major/career interest in law. Applicant
must demonstrate financial need.
Application requirements: Recommendations, essay,
transcript. A transcript must be attached with counselor or
school representative signature for application to be considered.
Although not required, applicants are encouraged to submit
recommendation letters and/or resumes to substantiate their
application.

Amount of award:	$1,500
Number of awards:	1
Application deadline:	June 30
Notification begins:	September 1
Total amount awarded:	$1,500

Contact:
Rosengren Kohlmeyer And Hagen Law Office
620B Academy Drive
Northbrook, IL 60062
Phone: 847-940-4000
Web: https://rokolaw.com/scholarship-application/

Sachs Foundation

Sachs Foundation Undergraduate Grant

Type of award: Scholarship, renewable.
Intended use: For full-time undergraduate study at accredited
2-year or 4-year institution.
Eligibility: Applicant must be African American. Applicant
must be high school senior. Applicant must be U.S. citizen or
permanent resident residing in Colorado.
Basis for selection: Applicant must demonstrate financial
need, high academic achievement, depth of character and
leadership.
Application requirements: Interview, recommendations,
transcript, proof of eligibility. Financial statement and parents'
tax returns. Small recent photo. One-page personal biography.
FAFSA. A copy of Colorado School Enrollment form.
Additional information: Must have been resident of Colorado
for at least five years.

Amount of award:	$5,000
Number of awards:	35
Application deadline:	March 15

Contact:
Sachs Foundation
Phone: 719-633-2353
Web: www.sachsfoundation.org

SAE International

BMW/SAE Engineering Scholarships

Type of award: Scholarship, renewable.
Intended use: For full-time freshman study at accredited
4-year institution in United States. Designated institutions:
ABET-accredited engineering schools.
Eligibility: Applicant must be high school senior. Applicant
must be U.S. citizen.
Basis for selection: Major/career interest in engineering or
computer/information sciences. Applicant must demonstrate
high academic achievement, depth of character and leadership.
Application requirements: Transcript. SAT or ACT scores.
Additional information: Must have 3.75 GPA and rank in
90th percentile on ACT composite or SAT I (Math and
Reading). Must maintain 3.0 GPA to renew scholarship.
Renewable for four years. Visit Website for more information.
For list of ABET-accredited schools, visit www.abet.org.

Amount of award:	$1,500
Number of awards:	1
Application deadline:	January 15
Notification begins:	June 30

Contact:
SAE International
SAE Engineering Scholarships
400 Commonwealth Drive
Warrendale, PA 15096-0001
Phone: 724-776-4841
Web: www.sae.org/scholarships

Edward D. Hendrickson/SAE Engineering Scholarship

Type of award: Scholarship, renewable.
Intended use: For undergraduate study at accredited
postsecondary institution. Designated institutions: ABET-
accredited institutions.
Eligibility: Applicant must be high school senior. Applicant
must be U.S. citizen.
Basis for selection: Major/career interest in engineering.
Applicant must demonstrate high academic achievement.
Application requirements: Essay, transcript. SAT or ACT
scores.
Additional information: Minimum 3.75 GPA. Must rank in
90th percentile on SAT (Math and Reading) or composite
ACT. Award renewable for three years if student maintains 3.0
GPA. Visit Website for application. For list of ABET-
accredited schools, visit www.abet.org.

Amount of award:	$1,000
Number of awards:	1
Application deadline:	January 15
Notification begins:	June 30

Contact:
SAE International
SAE Engineering Scholarships
400 Commonwealth Drive
Warrendale, PA 15096-0001
Phone: 724-776-4841
Web: www.sae.org/scholarships

Fred M. Young, Sr./SAE Engineering Scholarship

Type of award: Scholarship, renewable.
Intended use: For undergraduate study at accredited postsecondary institution. Designated institutions: ABET-accredited institutions.
Eligibility: Applicant must be high school senior. Applicant must be U.S. citizen.
Basis for selection: Major/career interest in engineering. Applicant must demonstrate high academic achievement.
Application requirements: Transcript. SAT or ACT scores.
Additional information: Minimum 3.75 GPA. Applicants must rank in the 90th percentile on SAT (Math and Reading) or ACT. Award renewable for three years if student maintains 3.0 GPA. Visit Website for application. For list of ABET-accredited schools, visit www.abet.org.

Amount of award:	$1,000
Number of awards:	1
Application deadline:	January 15
Notification begins:	June 30

Contact:
SAE International
SAE Engineering Scholarships
400 Commonwealth Drive
Warrendale, PA 15096-0001
Phone: 724-776-4841
Web: www.sae.org/scholarships

SAE Long-Term Member Sponsored Scholarship

Type of award: Scholarship.
Intended use: For full-time senior study at 4-year institution. Designated institutions: ABET-accredited engineering schools.
Basis for selection: Major/career interest in engineering. Applicant must demonstrate leadership.
Application requirements: Recommendations.
Additional information: Applicant must be active SAE student member. Must demonstrate support for SAE activities and programs. Must be junior in college at time of application. Number of awards varies. Apply online.

Amount of award:	$1,000
Application deadline:	February 15
Notification begins:	June 30

Contact:
SAE International
SAE Engineering Scholarships
400 Commonwealth Drive
Warrendale, PA 15096-0001
Phone: 724-776-4841
Web: www.sae.org/scholarships

SAE/David Hermance Hybrid Technologies Scholarship

Type of award: Scholarship.
Intended use: For junior study at accredited 2-year or 4-year institution in United States. Designated institutions: ABET-accredited engineering schools.
Eligibility: Applicant must be U.S. citizen.
Basis for selection: Major/career interest in engineering. Applicant must demonstrate high academic achievement.
Application requirements: High school and college transcripts. SAT/ACT scores.
Additional information: Minimum 3.5 GPA. For list of ABET-accredited schools, visit www.abet.org.

Amount of award:	$2,500
Number of awards:	1
Application deadline:	February 15
Notification begins:	June 30

Contact:
SAE International
SAE Engineering Scholarships
400 Commonwealth Drive
Warrendale, PA 15096-0001
Phone: 724-776-4841
Web: www.sae.org/scholarships

SAE/Ford Partnership for Advanced Studies Scholarship

Type of award: Scholarship.
Intended use: For full-time freshman study at accredited 4-year institution in United States. Designated institutions: ABET-accredited engineering schools.
Eligibility: Applicant must be high school senior. Applicant must be U.S. citizen.
Basis for selection: Major/career interest in engineering. Applicant must demonstrate high academic achievement.
Application requirements: Recommendations, transcript. SAT/ACT scores.
Additional information: Minimum 3.0 GPA. Must rank in the 90th percentile in both math and critical reading on SAT I or the composite ACT scores. Must be past or present student of Ford PAS program at their high school or in a Ford PAS afterschool/weekend/summer/college program. For list of ABET-accredited schools, visit www.abet.org.

Amount of award:	$5,000
Number of awards:	1
Application deadline:	January 15
Notification begins:	June 30

Contact:
SAE International
SAE Engineering Scholarships
400 Commonwealth Drive
Warrendale, PA 15096-0001
Phone: 724-776-4841
Web: www.sae.org/scholarships

Tau Beta Pi/SAE Engineering Scholarship

Type of award: Scholarship.
Intended use: For freshman study at accredited postsecondary institution. Designated institutions: ABET-accredited engineering schools.
Eligibility: Applicant must be high school senior. Applicant must be U.S. citizen.

Basis for selection: Major/career interest in engineering. Applicant must demonstrate high academic achievement.
Application requirements: Transcript. SAT or ACT scores.
Additional information: Minimum 3.75 GPA. Applicant must rank in 90th percentile on SAT (Math and Reading) or composite ACT. Visit Website for application. For list of ABET-accredited schools, visit www.abet.org.

Amount of award:	$1,000
Number of awards:	6
Application deadline:	January 15
Notification begins:	June 30
Total amount awarded:	$6,000

Contact:
SAE International
SAE Engineering Scholarships
400 Commonwealth Drive
Warrendale, PA 15096-0001
Phone: 724-776-4841
Fax: 724-776-0790
Web: www.sae.org/scholarships

TMC/SAE Donald D. Dawson Technical Scholarship

Type of award: Scholarship, renewable.
Intended use: For undergraduate study. Designated institutions: ABET-accredited engineering schools.
Eligibility: Applicant must be U.S. citizen.
Basis for selection: Major/career interest in engineering. Applicant must demonstrate high academic achievement.
Application requirements: Transcript. Essay showing evidence of hands-on automotive experience or activity, SAT or ACT scores.
Additional information: Graduating high school seniors must have minimum 3.25 GPA, 600 SAT (Math) and 550 SAT (Reading), 27 ACT. Transfer students from four-year schools with 3.0 GPA, and students/graduates of technical/vocational schools with 3.5 GPA also eligible. Award renewable for four years as long as a 3.0 GPA maintained. Visit Website for application. For list of ABET-accredited schools, visit www.abet.org.

Amount of award:	$1,500
Number of awards:	1
Application deadline:	January 15
Notification begins:	June 30

Contact:
SAE International
SAE Engineering Scholarships
400 Commonwealth Drive
Warrendale, PA 15096-0001
Phone: 724-776-4841
Web: www.sae.org/scholarships

Yanmar/SAE Scholarship

Type of award: Scholarship, renewable.
Intended use: For full-time senior or graduate study at accredited 4-year institution. Designated institutions: ABET-accredited engineering schools.
Eligibility: Applicant must be U.S. citizen or Canadian or Mexican citizen.
Basis for selection: Major/career interest in engineering. Applicant must demonstrate high academic achievement and leadership.
Application requirements: College transcript.
Additional information: Must pursue course of study or research related to conservation of energy in transportation, agriculture and construction, or power generation. Emphasis

placed on research or study related to internal combustion engine. Must be junior in college or post-graduate at time of application. Scholarship renewable for one additional year if in good standing with university and minimum 2.5 GPA. Visit Website for application. For list of ABET-accredited schools, visit www.abet.org.

Amount of award:	$1,000
Number of awards:	1
Application deadline:	February 15
Notification begins:	June 30

Contact:
SAE International
SAE Scholarship & Award Program
400 Commonwealth Drive
Warrendale, PA 15096-0001
Phone: 724-776-4841
Web: www.sae.org/scholarships

Salute to Education, Inc.

Salute to Education Scholarship

Type of award: Scholarship.
Intended use: For undergraduate study at postsecondary institution.
Eligibility: Applicant must be high school senior. Applicant must be U.S. citizen residing in Florida.
Basis for selection: Applicant must demonstrate financial need, high academic achievement, depth of character, leadership, seriousness of purpose and service orientation.
Additional information: Minimum 3.0 GPA. Number of total scholarships varies. Winners of this one-time grant also receive laptop computer. Applicant must be a resident of and attend an accredited public or private high school in Miami-Dade or Broward County. Scholarships in following categories: athletics, language arts and foreign languages, leadership/service, mathematics/computer science, natural science, and performing arts & visual arts. Visit Website for application and deadline. Application deadline in late January. Notification begins mid-April.

Amount of award:	$1,500
Number of applicants:	1,500
Total amount awarded:	$120,000

Contact:
Salute to Education, Inc.
P.O. Box 833425
Miami, FL 33283
Phone: 305-799-6726
Fax: 786-515-9864
Web: www.stescholarships.org

Scarlett Family Foundation Scholarship Program

Scarlett Family Foundation Scholarship

Type of award: Scholarship, renewable.
Intended use: For full-time undergraduate study at postsecondary institution. Designated institutions: Not-for-profit institutions.

Eligibility: Applicant must be residing in Tennessee.
Basis for selection: Major/career interest in accounting; business; business, international; business/management/ administration or finance/banking. Applicant must demonstrate financial need and high academic achievement.
Application requirements: Essay, transcript. FAFSA.
Additional information: Minimum award is $2500. Amount of award varies based on need. Minimum of 2.5 GPA preferred. Must have demonstrated entrepreneurial interests or leadership. Applicant must be from one of 40 counties in Tennessee. Visit Website for details. Majors include: Business, Business-related, and STEM majors.

Amount of award:	$2,500-$15,000
Number of awards:	35
Number of applicants:	432
Application deadline:	December 15
Notification begins:	March 15
Total amount awarded:	$293,000

Contact:
Scarlett Family Foundation Scholarship Program
c/o ISTS, Inc.
1321 Murfreesboro Rd., Ste. 800
Nashville, TN 37217
Phone: 615-777-3750
Fax: 615-320-3151
Web: www.scarlettfoundation.org

Schechter, McElwee, Shaffer and Harris, LLP.

Schechter, McElwee, Shaffer and Harris Aspiring Law Student Scholarship

Type of award: Scholarship, renewable.
Intended use: For full-time undergraduate or graduate study at accredited 4-year or graduate institution.
Basis for selection: Major/career interest in law.
Application requirements: Essay. Write an argumentation about whether a specific policy (of your choosing) in the personal injury system is unjust and requires reform, or is just and should stay the same. Please provide your personal information and upload your essay.
Additional information: Scholarship program Website:https:// www.smslegal.com/schechter-mcelwee-shaffer-harris-offering-aspiring-law-student-chance-receive-1000-scholarship/ . More information at : http://maintenanceandcure.com/maintenance-cure-offering-aspiring-law-student-chance-receive-1000-scholarship/ .

Amount of award:	$1,000
Number of awards:	2
Application deadline:	May 1, November 1
Notification begins:	May 15, November 15
Total amount awarded:	$2,000

Contact:
Schechter, McElwee, Shaffer & Harris
3700 Travis Street
#300
Houston, TX 77006
Phone: 713-337-8321
Fax: 713-751-0412

Scholarship America

Scholarship America Dream Award

Type of award: Scholarship, renewable.
Intended use: For full-time sophomore, junior or senior study at accredited vocational, 2-year or 4-year institution in United States.
Eligibility: Applicant must be at least 17. Applicant must be U.S. citizen.
Basis for selection: Applicant must demonstrate financial need.
Additional information: Apply online. Notifications in April. Emphasis will be on financial need and the ability to overcome challenges and barriers.

Amount of award:	$5,000-$15,000
Number of awards:	21
Number of applicants:	3,015
Application deadline:	December 15

Contact:
Phone: 1-800-537-4180
Web: https://www.scholarsapply.org/dreamaward

Scholarship America Dream Award

Type of award: Scholarship, renewable.
Intended use: For full-time sophomore, junior or senior study at accredited vocational, 2-year or 4-year institution.
Eligibility: Applicant must be U.S. citizen or permanent resident.
Basis for selection: Applicant must demonstrate financial need.
Additional information: Must have a minimum 3.0 GPA. For students entering their second year or higher of education beyond high school. Renewable for three years or until a bachelor's degree is earned. Each year of renewal the award will increase by $1,000.

Amount of award:	$5,000-$15,000
Application deadline:	December 15

Contact:
Scholarship America Dream Award
One Scholarship Way
Saint Peter, MN 56082
Phone: 800-537-4180
Fax: 507-931-9168
Web: https://www.scholarsapply.org/dreamaward

Scholarship America Scholarships

Type of award: Scholarship.
Intended use: For undergraduate or graduate study at postsecondary institution.
Additional information: Scholarship America awards scholarships through multiple national, regional, and local scholarship programs for various levels of study. Eligibility criteria, award amounts, and deadlines vary by scholarship and sponsor. Students who register with Scholarship America can be matched with scholarships for which they may be eligible.

Amount of award:	$100-$30,000
Number of awards:	106,500
Number of applicants:	400,000
Total amount awarded:	$203,000,000

Contact:
Scholarship America
One Scholarship Way
Saint Peter, MN 56082
Phone: 507-931-1682
Web: www.scholarshipamerica.org

ScholarshipOwl

"You Deserve It" Scholarship

Type of award: Scholarship.
Intended use: For undergraduate or graduate study at accredited vocational, 2-year, 4-year or graduate institution in United States.
Eligibility: Applicant must be at least 16. Applicant must be U.S. citizen or permanent resident.
Additional information: ScholarshipOwl is giving away a $1,000 "You Deserve It!" Scholarship once in a month. The award cycle expires on the 29th of each month and immediately restarts a new selection session. A winner will be chosen at random. The scholarship winner will have the funds go towards their tuition and fees.

Number of awards:	1
Application deadline:	March 29, April 29
Total amount awarded:	$1,000

Contact:
Web: https://scholarshipowl.com/awards/you-deserve-it-scholarship

School Furniture Depot

Teachers Make Teachers Scholarship

Type of award: Scholarship.
Intended use: For full-time undergraduate study at vocational, 2-year, 4-year or graduate institution.
Eligibility: Applicant must be at least 17, no older than 25, high school senior. Applicant must be U.S. citizen.
Basis for selection: Major/career interest in education.
Additional information: Minimum 3.0 GPA. See all requirements on scholarship webpage.

Amount of award:	$1,000-$1,000
Number of awards:	1
Application deadline:	April 28
Notification begins:	May 31
Total amount awarded:	$1,000

Contact:
School Furniture Depot
230 Springview Commerce Drive
Suite 300
DeBary, FL 32713
Phone: 407-299-0896
Fax: 407-299-0895
Web: www.schoolfurnituredepot.com/scholarship-application

Screen Actors Guild Foundation

John L. Dales Standard Scholarship

Type of award: Scholarship, renewable.
Intended use: For full-time undergraduate or graduate study at accredited 2-year, 4-year or graduate institution in United States.
Eligibility: Applicant or parent must be member/participant of Screen Actor's Guild.
Basis for selection: Applicant must demonstrate financial need.
Application requirements: Recommendations, essay, transcript, proof of eligibility. Most recent federal income tax return and additional financial information. SAT/ACT scores.
Additional information: Member under the age of 22 must have been a member for five years and have lifetime earnings of $30,000. Parent of applicant must have ten vested years of pension credits or lifetime earnings of $150,000. Consult office or Website for more information. Number and amount of awards vary.

Number of awards:	81
Number of applicants:	135
Application deadline:	March 15
Notification begins:	July 7
Total amount awarded:	$282,000

Contact:
Screen Actors Guild Foundation
John L. Dales Scholarship Fund
5757 Wilshire Boulevard, Suite 124
Los Angeles, CA 90036
Phone: 323-549-6708
Fax: 323-549-6710
Web: www.sagfoundation.org

John L. Dales Transitional Scholarship

Type of award: Scholarship, renewable.
Intended use: For full-time undergraduate or graduate study at accredited postsecondary institution in United States.
Eligibility: Applicant or parent must be member/participant of Screen Actor's Guild.
Basis for selection: Applicant must demonstrate financial need.
Application requirements: Recommendations, essay, transcript, proof of eligibility. Most recent federal income tax return and additional financial information. SAT/ACT scores.
Additional information: Must be member of Screen Actors Guild. Applicant must have ten vested years of pension credits with SAG or lifetime earnings of $150,000. Consult office or visit Website for more information. Number and amount of awards vary.

Number of awards:	7
Number of applicants:	15
Application deadline:	March 15
Notification begins:	July 7
Total amount awarded:	$24,000

Contact:
Screen Actors Guild Foundation
John L. Dales Scholarship Fund
5757 Wilshire Boulevard, Suite 124
Los Angeles, CA 90036
Phone: 323-549-6649
Fax: 323-549-6710
Web: www.sagfoundation.org

Scrub Shopper, LLC.

Greta James Memorial Scholarship

Type of award: Scholarship.
Intended use: For undergraduate or graduate study at accredited 2-year, 4-year or graduate institution.
Eligibility: Applicant must be high school senior. Applicant must be U.S. citizen or permanent resident.
Basis for selection: Major/career interest in nursing; medicine; dentistry or veterinary medicine.
Application requirements: Essay, transcript. Students must be enrolled in medical degree seeking programs (ex: AND or BSN) at an accredited university. Scholarship is open to all legal residents, who reside and attend school in the United States. Fill out 2 short essays highlighting financial need and leadership within their community.

Amount of award:	$500-$500
Number of awards:	4
Application deadline:	April 18
Notification begins:	July 1
Total amount awarded:	$500

Contact:
Scrub Shopper, LLC.
1 West Center St
Fayetteville, AR 72701
Phone: 800-490-8919
Web: https://www.scrubshopper.com/pages/scholarship

Seabee Memorial Scholarship Association, Inc.

Seabee Memorial Scholarship

Type of award: Scholarship, renewable.
Intended use: For full-time undergraduate study at accredited 2-year or 4-year institution in United States.
Eligibility: Applicant must be U.S. citizen. Applicant must be descendant of veteran who served in the Navy. Applicant must be child or grandchild of a currently enlisted, honorably discharged, or deceased member of Naval Construction FORCE (Seabees) or Navy CEC (Civil Engineer Corps).
Basis for selection: Applicant must demonstrate financial need, high academic achievement, depth of character, leadership, patriotism, seriousness of purpose and service orientation.
Application requirements: Essay, transcript, proof of eligibility. IRS Form 1040. Official document (DD214, reenlistment certificate, transfer orders, etc.) that verifies rate/rank of sponsor.

Additional information: Not available for part-time or graduate students. Not available for great-grandchildren of members of Seabees or Navy CEC. Award is renewable for up to four years. Download application from Website.

Amount of award:	$2,800
Number of awards:	100
Number of applicants:	235
Application deadline:	April 15
Notification begins:	June 15

Contact:
Scholarship Committee
P.O. Box 6574
Silver Spring, MD 20916
Phone: 301-570-2850
Fax: 301-570-2873
Web: www.seabee.org

Sebring Services

Sebring Scholarship

Type of award: Scholarship, renewable.
Intended use: For full-time undergraduate or graduate study at accredited vocational, 2-year, 4-year or graduate institution in United States.
Eligibility: Applicant must be at least 18. Applicant must be U.S. citizen.
Basis for selection: Applicant must demonstrate high academic achievement.
Application requirements: Essay. All US citizens from all US States and Territories eligible to apply. Record a 1-2 Minute Video Describing What You Plan to Do With Your Degree. Application must include a 1-2 minute video describing what you plan to do with your degree. Videos should be posted to YouTube publicly with a link to Sebring Services included in the video descroption.
Additional information: Fill Out the Online Form www.sebringservices.com/sebring-scholarship-application/

Amount of award:	$500-$500
Number of awards:	1
Application deadline:	May 28
Notification begins:	June 11
Total amount awarded:	$500

Contact:
Sebring Services
424 Fort Hill Drive
Naperville, IL 60540
Phone: 630-369-6829
Web: http://www.sebringservices.com/scholarship/

Second Marine Division Association

Second Marine Division Association Scholarship Fund

Type of award: Scholarship, renewable.
Intended use: For full-time undergraduate study at accredited vocational, 2-year or 4-year institution.

Eligibility: Must be dependent child or grandchild of person who serves or served in Second Marine Division, U.S. Marine Corps, or unit attached to the division.

Basis for selection: Applicant must demonstrate financial need and high academic achievement.

Application requirements: Essay, transcript, proof of eligibility. Income verification.

Additional information: Family's adjusted gross income should not exceed $75,000 for the taxable year prior to application. Exceptions may be made for larger families. Minimum 2.5 GPA. Must reapply for renewal. Include SASE when requesting application. Parent or grandparent who served in the Second Marine Division must join SMDA, if not already a member, once scholarship is awarded.

Amount of award:	$1,500
Number of awards:	40
Number of applicants:	25
Application deadline:	April 1, July 1
Notification begins:	September 15
Total amount awarded:	$37,500

Contact:
Second Marine Division Association Memorial Scholarship Fund
Second Marine Division Association
Box 8180
Camp Lejeune, NC 28547
Phone: 910-265-9588
Web: www.2Dmardiv.com

SelectBlinds.com

SelectBlinds.com College Scholarship

Type of award: Scholarship.

Intended use: For undergraduate or graduate study at accredited vocational, 2-year, 4-year or graduate institution in United States.

Eligibility: Applicant must be U.S. citizen, permanent resident or international student.

Application requirements: Applicants must submit one idea(Video photo, image, infograph, etc) an one of the following items: What's the most creative thing you can do with window coverings? OR come up with new technology for window coverings. They must also submit a 250-750 word essay answering one of the following questions: What do you want to do to make the world a better place? What's the importance of your major/area of study in today's society? What are your most meaningful achievements, and how do they relate to your field of study? Why did you choose your field of study, and where do you see yourself in 10 years? Why are you a good candidate to receive this scholarship?

Additional information: Must have a minimum 2.5 GPA. Submit application via e-mail.

Application deadline:	June 15
Notification begins:	July 15

Contact:
Select Blinds
1910 S Stapley Drive
Suite 137
Mesa, AZ 85204
Web: www.SelectBlinds.com/Scholarship.html

SelfScore

SelfScore International Student Scholarship

Type of award: Scholarship.

Intended use: For undergraduate or graduate study at 2-year, 4-year or graduate institution in United States.

Eligibility: Applicant must be international student.

Application requirements: Must submit a valid I-20 or DS-2019 form.

Additional information: Must have a minimum 3.0 GPA. Intended for students studying in the US on a F1, J1, or M1 visa. Must score in the top 15% on a standardized US college entrance exam (SAT, ACT, GRE, or GMAT). Six scholarships will be awarded to undergrads, and six will be awarded to graduate students. All applicants are enrolled in a free financial literacy program.

Amount of award:	$5,000
Number of awards:	12
Application deadline:	December 15
Total amount awarded:	$60,000

Contact:
Web: www.selfscore.com/scholarship/

SEMA

SEMA Memorial Scholarship Fund

Type of award: Scholarship.

Intended use: For full-time undergraduate or graduate study at accredited vocational, 2-year, 4-year or graduate institution in United States.

Eligibility: Applicant must be U.S. citizen.

Basis for selection: Major/career interest in automotive technology; transportation; engineering; manufacturing; marketing; design or advertising.

Application requirements: Recommendations, essay, transcript. Provide unofficial school transcripts. One letter of recommendation from a post-secondary teacher, administrator, guidance counselor; someone who is familiar with your academic performance. Provide two 250-word essays on the following questions: a) Why do you want to pursue a career in the automotive aftermarket? What do you feel you can contribute to this industry? b) The automotive aftermarket is driven by the passion of the people in it. What drives you? What inspires you? Why should you be awarded a SEMA Memorial Scholarship?

Additional information: Must have minimum 2.5 GPA. Must be pursuing studies leading to a career in the automotive industry or related field. Apply online. If attending a four-year university you must have completed a minimum of 50 credit hours. If attending a two-year community college or vocational/technical program you must have completed a minimum of 25 credit hours. If attending an accredited automotive training certification program, you must have half of total requirements completed. If pursuing a master's, post-baccalaureate, or doctorate degree, provide proof of acceptance or proof of enrollment in a graduate program.

Amount of award:	$2,000-$5,000
Number of awards:	40
Application deadline:	March 1

Contact:
Web: www.sema.org/scholarships

Senator George J. Mitchell Scholarship Research Institute

Senator George J. Mitchell Scholarship

Type of award: Scholarship, renewable.
Intended use: For freshman study at accredited 2-year or 4-year institution in United States.
Eligibility: Applicant must be high school senior. Applicant must be U.S. citizen residing in Maine.
Basis for selection: Applicant must demonstrate financial need, high academic achievement and service orientation.
Application requirements: Essay, transcript, proof of eligibility. Letter from guidance counselor, SAR, copy of financial aid award from college student plans to attend.
Additional information: One award made to graduating senior from every public high school in Maine. Renewable for up to four years. Award total is $6,000 ($1,500 per year for four years). Scholarship to be applied to spring semester bill. Application due April 1, supporting materials due May 1.

Amount of award:	$2,250-$9,000
Number of awards:	127
Number of applicants:	1,200
Application deadline:	May 1
Notification begins:	June 1
Total amount awarded:	$750,000

Contact:
Senator George J. Mitchell Scholarship Research Institute
75 Washington Avenue
Suite 2E
Portland, ME 04101
Phone: 207-773-7700
Fax: 207-773-1133
Web: www.mitchellinstitute.org

Seneca Nation and BIA

Seneca Nation Higher Education Program

Type of award: Scholarship, renewable.
Intended use: For undergraduate or graduate study at accredited 2-year, 4-year or graduate institution.
Eligibility: Applicant must be American Indian. Must be an enrolled member of Seneca Nation of Indians. Applicant must be U.S. citizen.
Basis for selection: Applicant must demonstrate financial need.
Application requirements: Essay, transcript, proof of eligibility. Proof of tribal enrollment, letter of reference from non-relative. FAFSA. NYS Tuition Assistance Program Application, NYS Indian Aid Application (for NY residents).
Additional information: Amount and number of awards vary. Residency requirements: Level 1- New York State residents living on reservation; Level 2- New York State residents living in New York; Level 3- Enrolled members living outside New York. Application deadlines: fall, July 1; spring, December 1; summer, May 1. Contact sponsor or see Website for more information.

Application deadline:	July 1, December 1

Contact:
Seneca Nation of Indians
Higher Education Program
12861 Route 438
Irving, NY 14081
Phone: 716-532-4900
Fax: 716-532-3269
Web: www.sni.org/hep

Sertoma

Sertoma Scholarships for Students Who are Hard of Hearing or Deaf

Type of award: Scholarship, renewable.
Intended use: For full-time undergraduate study at 4-year institution in United States.
Eligibility: Applicant must be hearing impaired. Applicant must be U.S. citizen.
Basis for selection: Applicant must demonstrate high academic achievement, depth of character, seriousness of purpose and service orientation.
Application requirements: Transcript. Statement of purpose, two letters of recommendation, documentation of hearing impairment in form of recent audiogram or signed statement by hearing-health professional.
Additional information: Applicant must have minimum of 40 dB bilateral hearing loss as evidenced by an audiogram. Must demonstrate how their hearing loss has shaped their lives to become the person they are today. Must have minimum 3.2 GPA. Visit Website for application and more information.

Amount of award:	$1,000
Number of awards:	45
Number of applicants:	220
Application deadline:	May 1
Notification begins:	June 15
Total amount awarded:	$45,000

Contact:
Sertoma, Inc.
Attn: Scholarships
1912 East Meyer Boulevard
Kansas City, MO 64132-1174
Phone: 816-333-8300
Fax: 816-333-4320
Web: www.sertoma.org/scholarship

ServiceMaster by Glenn's

Disaster Preparation Scholarship

Type of award: Scholarship, renewable.
Intended use: For freshman study at vocational, 2-year or 4-year institution.

Eligibility: Applicant must be at least 13, no older than 20, high school senior. Applicant must be U.S. citizen residing in Florida.

Basis for selection: The video will be judged of the following: Content, originality, creativity, and the ServiceMaster Restore branding.

Application requirements: This scholarship will be awarded to the high school or college student that demonstrates knowledge in how to properly prepare for hurricanes or flooding disasters. ServiceMaster By Glenn's will award a grand prize scholarship of $1,500 and $500 to the runner up that submits a 2-5 minute video on disaster preparation. The video must use visual aids and proper citation of research on how a business can properly prepare for a disaster. Upload the video to your YouTube account and send the link of your video to along with your application to the scholarship website (below in contact information) and we will add it to our submissions playlist.

Additional information: May not be a current employee. All video submissions will be property of ServiceMaster by Glenn's and used accordingly. Scholarship will be awarded after 6 weeks of enrollment into university or trade school classes.

Amount of award:	$500-$1,500
Number of awards:	2
Application deadline:	May 1
Notification begins:	May 15

Contact:
ServiceMaster by Glenn's
1505 10th Avenue
Vero Beach, FL 32960
Phone: 772-567-4435
Web: http://waterdamagespecialists.com/scholarship

Seth Okin Attorney at Law

Seth Okin Good Deeds Scholarship

Type of award: Scholarship.
Intended use: For undergraduate or graduate study at accredited vocational, 2-year, 4-year or graduate institution.
Eligibility: Applicant must be high school senior.
Basis for selection: Applicant must demonstrate high academic achievement.
Application requirements: Essay, transcript. Unofficial transcript, application cover sheet, application essay, updated resume. Essay topic (500 words): "With so many people and organizations in today's world in need of volunteers and financial assistance, how should people decide where to direct their time and donations?"
Additional information: Minimum 3.0 GPA required. Applicants must be both interested and engaged in serving their community.

Amount of award:	$500
Number of awards:	1
Application deadline:	May 1
Total amount awarded:	$500

Contact:
Seth Okin Good Deeds Scholarship
108 West Timonium Road
Suite 333
Lutherville-Timonium, MD 21093
Phone: 202-517-0502
Fax: 443-740-9295
Web: criminallawyermaryland.net/good-deeds-scholarship.html

Sexner and Associates LLC

Mitchell S. Sexner and Associates LLC Scholarship

Type of award: Scholarship.
Intended use: For undergraduate study at accredited 2-year or 4-year institution.
Eligibility: Applicant must be high school senior. Applicant must be U.S. citizen or permanent resident.
Application requirements: Essay, transcript. Unofficial and official transcripts, current proof of enrollment, and photo identification.
Additional information: Must have a minimum 3.0 GPA. Essay prompt can be found in the online application.

Number of awards:	1
Application deadline:	April 30
Notification begins:	May 30
Total amount awarded:	$500

Contact:
Sexner and Associates LLC
2126 West Van Buren Street
Chicago, IL 60612
Phone: 312-644-0444
Fax: 847-690-9998
Web: www.sexner.com/personal-injury/scholarship/

Shoshone Tribe

Shoshone Tribal Scholarship

Type of award: Scholarship, renewable.
Intended use: For undergraduate or graduate study at accredited vocational, 2-year or 4-year institution in United States.
Eligibility: Applicant must be American Indian. Must be enrolled member of Eastern Shoshone Tribe.
Basis for selection: Applicant must demonstrate financial need and high academic achievement.
Application requirements: Transcript, proof of eligibility. FAFSA. Letter of Acceptance from school attending. Formal personal letter. Certificate of Indian Blood from Shoshone Enrollment.
Additional information: Must first apply for Pell Grant and appropriate campus-based aid. Minimum 2.5 GPA. Award renewable for maximum ten semesters. Application deadlines: academic year, June 15; winter, November 15; spring, February 15; summer, April 15. Number of awards varies.

Amount of award:	$50-$15,000
Number of awards:	60
Number of applicants:	100
Application deadline:	June 15, November 15
Total amount awarded:	$300,000

Contact:
Eastern Shoshone Tribe
PL102-447 Program
104 Washakie Street, P.O. Box 628
Fort Washakie, WY 82514
Phone: 307-335-8000
Fax: 307-335-8004
Web: www.easternshoshoneeducation.com

Sid Richardson Memorial Fund

Sid Richardson Scholarship

Type of award: Scholarship, renewable.
Intended use: For full-time undergraduate or graduate study at accredited postsecondary institution.
Basis for selection: Applicant must demonstrate financial need and high academic achievement.
Application requirements: Essay, transcript, proof of eligibility. SAT or ACT scores.
Additional information: Those eligible to apply for a Sid Richardson Memorial Fund scholarship are direct descendants (children or grandchildren) of persons who qualified for Early Retirement, Normal Retirement, Disability Retirement, or Death Benefits from The Bass Retirement Plan (formerly The Retirement Plan For Employees of Bass Enterprises Production Co.), Retirement Plan for Employees of Barbnet / San Jose Cattle Co., Retirement Plan for Employees of City Center Development Co., City Club Retirement Plan, Retirement Plan for Employees of Richardson Aviation, G.P., Retirement Plan for Employees of Sid W. Richardson Foundation, or Retirement Plan for Employees of Sundance Square. Those eligible also include direct descendants (children or grandchildren) of persons presently employed with a minimum of three years' full-time service (as of March 31) with any of the following employers: Barbnet Investment Co. (tax ID #75-2033355), BEPCO, L.P. (tax ID #75-1076930), BOPCO, L.P. (tax ID #37-1483123), City Club of Ft. Worth (tax ID #75-2035506), Richardson Aviation (tax ID #75-2125310), San Jose Cattle Co. (tax ID #75-1018369), Sid Richardson Carbon Co. (SRCE, L.P.) (tax ID #75-2468081), Sid W. Richardson Foundation (tax ID #75-6015828), and Sundance Square Management, L.P. (tax ID #20-1942332).

Amount of award:	$500-$9,000
Number of applicants:	95
Application deadline:	March 31
Notification begins:	May 31
Total amount awarded:	$344,500

Contact:
Sid Richardson Memorial Fund
Attn: Shanda Ranelle
309 Main Street
Fort Worth, TX 76102
Phone: 817-336-0494
Fax: 817-332-2176

Sidney B. Meadows Scholarship Endowment Fund

Southern Nursery Association Sidney B. Meadows Scholarship

Type of award: Scholarship.
Intended use: For full-time junior, senior, master's or doctoral study at accredited 4-year or graduate institution.
Eligibility: Applicant must be U.S. citizen residing in Tennessee, Louisiana, Virginia, Mississippi, Alabama, Kentucky, Missouri, Texas, Arkansas, Maryland, Florida, Georgia, South Carolina, Oklahoma, West Virginia or North Carolina.
Basis for selection: Major/career interest in horticulture. Applicant must demonstrate high academic achievement.
Application requirements: Recommendations, transcript. Resume, cover letter.
Additional information: Must be enrolled in ornamental horticulture or related discipline in good standing. Minimum 2.75 GPA for undergraduates, 3.0 for graduates. Must be resident of one of 16 states in Southern Nursery Organization, but matriculation in these states is not mandatory. Preference given to applicants who plan to work in the horticulture industry after graduation, and for those who demonstrate financial need. Visit Website for application and additional information.

Amount of award:	$1,500
Number of awards:	12
Application deadline:	May 30
Notification begins:	July 1
Total amount awarded:	$18,000

Contact:
Sidney B. Meadows Scholarship Endowment Fund
P.O. Box 801513
Acworth, GA 30101
Phone: 678-813-1880
Fax: 678-813-1881
Web: www.sbmsef.org

Siemens Foundation

Siemens We Can Change the World Challenge

Type of award: Scholarship, renewable.
Intended use: For freshman study at postsecondary institution.
Eligibility: Applicant must be enrolled in high school.
Basis for selection: Competition/talent/interest in academics, based on identification of environmental issue or problem and research, scientific approach, sharing and replication to a larger audience, global impact, creativity and innovation.
Additional information: Competition to encourage K-12 students to develop innovative green solutions for environmental issues. High school 1st, 2nd, and 3rd place teams could win $50,000, $25,000, and $10,000 respectively, to be shared equally among team members. Deadline in March.

Amount of award:	$10,000-$50,000
Number of awards:	3
Number of applicants:	300
Total amount awarded:	$85,000

Contact:
Siemens Foundation
Web: www.wecanchange.com

Silicon Valley Community Foundation

AIASCV William R. Hawley Scholarship

Type of award: Scholarship.
Intended use: For undergraduate or graduate study.

Eligibility: Applicant must be residing in California.
Basis for selection: Major/career interest in architecture.
Application requirements: Interview, portfolio, recommendations, essay.
Additional information: Must be a legal resident of Santa Clara County. Previous recipients of this scholarship are eligible. Undergraduate students must have completed a minimum of two years of college work in required major at the end of the current academic year.

Amount of award:	$5,000
Number of awards:	2
Application deadline:	April 18
Notification begins:	May 6

Contact:
Phone: 408-298-0611
Web: www.siliconvalleycf.org/scholarships/aiascv-william-r-hawley-scholarship

Anthony Narigi Hospitality Scholarship Fund

Type of award: Scholarship.
Intended use: For at vocational, 2-year, 4-year or graduate institution.
Basis for selection: Major/career interest in hospitality administration/management or hotel/restaurant management.
Additional information: Minimum GPA of 2.5. Must reside in Monterey County, San Francisco County, Sonoma County, Napa County, Contra Costa County or Santa Clara County. Applicants must be currently employed in the hospitality profession or applying for or enrolled in an educational program pursuing a degree or certificate designed for the hospitality industry, such as ; which includes: hotel/motel spas, restaurant, and winery. Must have worked a minimum of 250 hours if currently employed in the hospitality industry or 100 hours if a current student. Applicants must hold a high school diploma.

Amount of award:	$5,000
Number of awards:	5

Contact:
Phone: 831-645-4002
Web: www.siliconvalleycf.org/scholarships/anthony-narigi-hospitality-scholarship-fund

The BAC Local 3 Sullivan Kraw Scholarship

Type of award: Scholarship.
Intended use: For undergraduate study.
Eligibility: Applicant must be high school senior. Applicant must be U.S. citizen.
Basis for selection: Applicant must demonstrate high academic achievement.
Additional information: The BAC Local 3 Sullivan Kraw Scholarship is for employees and/or family members of current employees of the Bricklayers and Allied Craftworkers Local 3 CA who plan to attend an accredited college or university. Qualifying member must have been a member in good standing of BAC 3 CA for at least five years immediately preceding the date of application. Minimum 3.0 GPA required. Must be a current graduating high school senior, high school graduate or undergraduate planning to attend a college or university in California on a full-time basis.

Amount of award:	$2,500
Number of awards:	19

Contact:
Web: www.siliconvalleycf.org/scholarships/bac-local-3-sullivan-kraw-scholarship

Bobette Bibo Gugliotta Memorial Scholarship for Creative Writing

Type of award: Scholarship.
Intended use: For full-time freshman study at 4-year institution.
Eligibility: Applicant must be high school senior.
Basis for selection: Competition/talent/interest in writing/journalism.
Application requirements: Demonstrated passion for creative writing (two writing samples are required with student's application).
Additional information: Must be current graduating senior or graduate of a public or private high school in San Mateo County or Santa Clara County. Must be United States citizen or eligible non-citizen (eligible non-citizens include United States legal residents and A.B. 540 students).

Amount of award:	$1,000
Number of awards:	2

Contact:
Phone: 650-450-5487
Web: www.siliconvalleycf.org/scholarships/

The Bright Futures Scholarship

Type of award: Scholarship.
Intended use: For full-time undergraduate study at 4-year institution.
Basis for selection: The selection committee will take into consideration the overall quality of the personal statement. Applicant must demonstrate financial need and high academic achievement.
Application requirements: Recommendations, essay, transcript.
Additional information: Cumulative GPA between 3.3 and 3.8 required. Must have applied for, but was not awarded, a community foundation managed scholarship and/or was awarded a scholarship, but can demonstrate unmet need after all other forms of college financial aid are secured. Special consideration will be given to working students and those pursuing a teaching or master's degree with an emphasis in the teaching of mathematics.

Amount of award:	$10,000
Number of awards:	20
Application deadline:	February 24
Notification begins:	May 6

Contact:
Phone: 650-450-5487
Web: www.siliconvalleycf.org/scholarships/bright-futures-scholarship

Crain Educational Grants Program

Type of award: Scholarship.
Intended use: For full-time undergraduate study at 4-year institution.
Eligibility: Applicant must be high school senior. Applicant must be U.S. citizen residing in California.
Basis for selection: Applicant must demonstrate financial need, high academic achievement and service orientation.
Application requirements: Interview.
Additional information: Minimum 3.5 GPA. Must be current graduating senior, or graduate of a public or private high school in San Mateo County or Santa Clara County.

| Amount of award: | $5,000 |
| Number of awards: | 10 |

Contact:
Phone: 650-450-5487
Web: www.siliconvalleycf.org/scholarships/crain-educational-grants-program

Curry Award for Girls and Young Women

Type of award: Scholarship.
Intended use: For full-time undergraduate study at 2-year or 4-year institution.
Eligibility: Applicant must be female, at least 18, no older than 26, high school senior. Applicant must be residing in California.
Basis for selection: Applicant must demonstrate financial need.
Additional information: Maximum 3.3 GPA. Must be current resident of San Mateo County; preference given to residents of East Palo Alto, East Menlo Park, Redwood City and San Mateo. Must graduating high school senior, graduate or GED. Certificate holder: preference given to students who attend(ed) East Palo Alto Academy, East Side College Prep, Menlo Atherton, Sequoia, Carlmont and San Mateo high schools.

| Amount of award: | $1,000 |
| Number of awards: | 10 |

Contact:
Phone: 650-450-5487
Web: www.siliconvalleycf.org/scholarships/curry-award-girls-and-young-women

Cynthia Kuo Scholarship

Type of award: Scholarship.
Intended use: For full-time undergraduate study at 4-year institution in United States.
Eligibility: Applicant must be high school senior. Applicant must be Chinese. Applicant must be Christian.
Basis for selection: Applicant must demonstrate financial need and high academic achievement.
Additional information: Minimum 3.0 GPA . Must be actively involved in the Christian faith or Christian youth group. Applicants must be Chinese students who are either first-generation in the U.S. or born overseas, planning to attend a four-year college in the U.S. on a full-time basis.

| Amount of award: | $5,000 |
| Number of awards: | 5 |

Contact:
Web: www.siliconvalleycf.org/scholarships/cynthia-kuo-scholarship

Dr. James L. Hutchinson and Evelyn Ribbs Hutchinson Medical School Scholarship

Type of award: Scholarship.
Intended use: For full-time senior or graduate study.
Eligibility: Applicant must be U.S. citizen.
Basis for selection: Applicant must demonstrate depth of character, leadership, patriotism, seriousness of purpose and service orientation.

| Amount of award: | $2,000 |
| Total amount awarded: | $2,000 |

Contact:
Phone: 650-450-5487
Web: www.siliconvalleycf.org

Ehrlich Rominger Scholarship

Type of award: Scholarship.
Intended use: For undergraduate study.
Eligibility: Applicant must be U.S. citizen or permanent resident residing in California.
Basis for selection: Major/career interest in architecture.
Application requirements: Interview, portfolio, recommendations, essay.
Additional information: Must be a current resident of Santa Clara County and legal resident of the United States.

Amount of award:	$5,000
Number of awards:	2
Application deadline:	April 18
Notification begins:	May 6

Contact:
Phone: 408-298-0611
Web: www.aiascv.org

Eustace-Kwan Family Foundation Scholarship

Type of award: Scholarship.
Intended use: For full-time undergraduate study at 4-year institution.
Eligibility: Applicant must be high school senior. Applicant must be residing in California.
Basis for selection: Applicant must demonstrate financial need and high academic achievement.
Application requirements: Interview, recommendations, essay, transcript. Demonstrated school and/or extra-curricular activities (volunteer or paid). Special consideration will be given to working students.
Additional information: Minimum 3.0-3.70 GPA for high school seniors and 2.5-3.60 for college students. Must have permanently resided in Redwood City, San Carlos, Belmont, East Palo Alto or Menlo Park during high school.

Amount of award:	$10,000
Number of awards:	10
Application deadline:	February 24

Contact:
Phone: 650-450-5487
Web: www.siliconvalleycf.org

The Harold Johnson Law Enforcement Scholarship

Type of award: Scholarship, renewable.
Intended use: For full-time undergraduate study at vocational, 2-year or 4-year institution.
Eligibility: Applicant must be high school senior. Applicant must be U.S. citizen residing in California.
Basis for selection: Major/career interest in criminal justice/law enforcement. Applicant must demonstrate financial need, high academic achievement, leadership and service orientation.
Application requirements: Interview, recommendations, essay, transcript.
Additional information: Minimum 2.5 GPA required. Must have a demonstrated desire and a plan to pursue a career in police work, corrections or other criminal justice fields; law school students are not eligible. Must be a current graduating senior or graduate of a public or private high school in the greater San Francisco Bay Area (includes San Francisco, San Mateo, Marin, Alameda, Contra Costa, Santa Clara, Napa, Solano, Sonoma, Monterey Bay, Santa Cruz, Monterey and San Benito counties).

Amount of award:	$5,000
Number of awards:	7
Application deadline:	February 24
Notification begins:	May 6

Contact:

Phone: 650-450-5487

Web: www.siliconvalleycf.org/scholarships/harold-johnson-law-enforcement-scholarship

Hazel Reed Baumeister Scholarship Program

Type of award: Scholarship.

Intended use: For full-time undergraduate study at 4-year institution.

Eligibility: Applicant must be high school senior. Applicant must be U.S. citizen residing in California.

Basis for selection: Applicant must demonstrate financial need, high academic achievement, leadership and service orientation.

Additional information: Minimum GPA 3.5. Must be graduating high school senior or graduate of a public or private high school in San Mateo County or Santa Clara County.

Amount of award:	$5,000
Total amount awarded:	$15

Contact:

Phone: 650-450-5487

Web: www.siliconvalleycf.org/scholarships/hazel-reed-baumeister-scholarship-program

Honmyo Nguyen Family Trust Scholarship

Type of award: Scholarship.

Intended use: For full-time undergraduate study at 4-year institution. Designated institutions: California public college (Cal State) or university (UC).

Eligibility: Applicant must be high school senior. Applicant must be residing in California.

Basis for selection: Applicant must demonstrate financial need and high academic achievement.

Application requirements: Recommendations, essay, transcript.

Additional information: Minimum 3.3 GPA. Must be current graduating senior or graduate of a public or private high school in Santa Clara County.

Amount of award:	$1,500
Number of awards:	2
Application deadline:	April 20

Contact:

Phone: 408-859-2613

Web: www.siliconvalleycf.org/scholarships/honmyo-nguyen-family-trust-scholarship-0

Huang Leadership Development Scholarship

Type of award: Scholarship, renewable.

Intended use: For full-time undergraduate study at 4-year institution.

Basis for selection: Applicant must demonstrate high academic achievement, leadership and service orientation.

Additional information: Applicant must be a current employee or past employee, or a legal dependent or grandchild of a current or past employee of SYNNEX Corporation, or its subsidiaries who left the company in good standing, that worked for SYNNEX Corporation or its subsidiaries for a minimum of three years at the time of the application deadline. Applicant must attend or plan to attend a top ranked-university according to US News & World Report; lists available on scholarship's website.

Amount of award:	$34,000
Number of awards:	10

Contact:

Phone: 650-450-5487

Web: http://www.siliconvalleycf.org/scholarships/huang-leadership-development-scholarship

The Juniper Networks Engineering Scholarship

Type of award: Scholarship.

Intended use: For full-time freshman study at 4-year institution.

Eligibility: Applicant must be high school senior.

Basis for selection: Applicant must demonstrate financial need, high academic achievement and service orientation.

Application requirements: Recommendations, essay, transcript.

Additional information: Must be a current graduating high school senior residing in San Mateo County or Santa Clara County in California; Fairfax County, Loudoun County, or Prince Williams County in Virginia; Middlesex County or Worcester County in Massachusetts; New Jersey, or Ottawa West (Kanata, Nepean, Bell's Corners, Stittsville, Dunrobin, Richmond, Fitzroy) in Ontario, Canada. Minimum 3.5 GPA required for US students. Minimum 70% for Ontario students. Must have demonstrated success in STEM education courses (science, technology, engineering and math). Must be planning to major in engineering; preference will be given to students pursuing majors in computer science, computer engineering, electrical engineering and computer networking.

Amount of award:	$5,000
Number of awards:	10
Application deadline:	February 24
Notification begins:	May 6

Contact:

Phone: 650-450-5487

Web: www.siliconvalleycf.org/scholarships/juniper-networks-engineering-scholarship

Krishnan Shah Scholarship

Type of award: Scholarship.

Intended use: For full-time undergraduate study at 4-year institution.

Eligibility: Applicant must be high school senior. Applicant must be residing in California.

Basis for selection: Applicant must demonstrate financial need and high academic achievement.

Application requirements: Recommendations, essay, transcript.

Additional information: Minimum 3.0 GPA. Must be graduating high school senior or current community college student planning to attend a four-year college or university in the fall. Must have demonstrated involvement in activities (extracurricular, volunteer, paid, etc).

Number of awards:	5
Application deadline:	February 24
Total amount awarded:	$40,000

Contact:

Phone: 650-450-5487

Web: http://www.siliconvalleycf.org/scholarships/krishnan-shah-scholarship

The Marie A. Calderilla Scholarship

Type of award: Scholarship, renewable.
Intended use: For undergraduate study. Designated institutions: College in the San Mateo County Community College District (Calfnada College, College of San Mateo and Skyline Community College).
Eligibility: Applicant must be female.
Basis for selection: Applicant must demonstrate financial need and seriousness of purpose.
Application requirements: Interview, recommendations, essay, transcript, proof of eligibility.
Additional information: The selection committee looks for academic promise, women who have demonstrated a commitment to completing a degree or certificate program or to increasing their work skills, and personal characteristics such as honesty, good judgment and perseverance. Recipients are eligible for up to three years of funding; however, students must meet renewal requirements to continue to receive the award.

Amount of award:	$20,000
Number of awards:	20
Application deadline:	March 23

Contact:
Phone: 650-450-5487
Web: www.siliconvalleycf.org/scholarships/marie-calderilla-scholarship

The Peninsula Regent Charitable Foundation Educational Grant Program

Type of award: Scholarship, renewable.
Eligibility: Applicant must be U.S. citizen or permanent resident.
Basis for selection: Applicant must demonstrate financial need.
Application requirements: Recommendations, essay, transcript, proof of eligibility.
Additional information: Must be current employee of the Peninsula Regent for at least 90 days as of the application deadline or dependents of an employee who has worked at the Peninsula Regent for at least 90 days as of the application deadline. Preference will be given to applicants with strong educational motivation, perseverance, involvement outside the classroom and personal characteristics such as honesty and good judgment. The selection committee will also strongly consider applicants who have dropped out of school for reasons beyond their control or have undergone unusual hardships to remain in school.

Amount of award:	$1,000-$10,000
Number of awards:	12
Application deadline:	March 23

Contact:
Phone: 650-450-5487
Web: www.siliconvalleycf.org/scholarships/peninsula-regent

The Roshan Rahbari Scholarship Fund

Type of award: Scholarship.
Intended use: For at 4-year institution.
Eligibility: Applicant must be residing in California.
Basis for selection: Applicant must demonstrate financial need, high academic achievement, depth of character and service orientation.

Application requirements: Recommendations, essay, transcript.
Additional information: Minimum 3.0 GPA required. Must be a current community college student transferring to a four-year college or university on a part-time or full-time basis.

Application deadline:	June 3

Contact:
Web: www.siliconvalleycf.org/scholarships/roshan-rahbari-scholarship-fund

Sabre Passport to Freedom Survivor Scholarship

Type of award: Scholarship, renewable.
Intended use: For undergraduate study in United States.
Eligibility: Applicant must be high school senior.
Basis for selection: Applicant must demonstrate financial need and high academic achievement.
Application requirements: Recommendations, essay, transcript, proof of eligibility.
Additional information: Must be a human trafficking survivor. Minimum 2.75 GPA (If a graduating high school senior or current college student; not applicable if out of school for more than 10 years),

Amount of award:	$2,500
Number of awards:	5

Contact:
Sabre
Attn: Passport to Freedom Program Manager
3150 Sabre Drive
Southlake, TX 76092
Web: www.sabre.com/about/corporate-responsibility/passport-to-freedom/scholarships/

Sand Hill Scholars Program

Type of award: Scholarship, renewable.
Intended use: For full-time freshman study at 4-year institution.
Eligibility: Applicant must be high school senior. Applicant must be residing in California.
Basis for selection: Applicant must demonstrate financial need and high academic achievement.
Application requirements: Interview, recommendations, essay, transcript, proof of eligibility. In addition to a personal statement: Please write (in no more than 350 words) about a previous or current mentoring relationship. Include what you learned from the relationship and how you benefited from it. If you haven't had a mentoring experience, describe why you would like a mentoring relationship and how you would hope to benefit from it. This essay can be submitted on the online application.
Additional information: Must be a current graduating senior attending a high school in San Mateo County. Special considerations are given to students who graduated from the Ravenswood City School District. Minimum 3.0 GPA required. Award recipients must be willing to participate actively in workshop and mentoring activities throughout their undergraduate careers.

Amount of award:	$3,000
Number of awards:	2
Application deadline:	February 24
Notification begins:	May 6

Contact:
Phone: 650-450-5487
Web: www.siliconvalleycf.org/scholarships/sand-hill-scholars-program

The SanDisk Scholars Program

Type of award: Scholarship, renewable.
Intended use: For full-time freshman or sophomore study at accredited 2-year or 4-year institution in United States.
Eligibility: Applicant must be high school senior. Applicant must be U.S. citizen or permanent resident.
Basis for selection: Major/career interest in computer/information sciences or engineering. Applicant must demonstrate financial need, high academic achievement, leadership and service orientation.
Application requirements: Essay.
Additional information: Minimum 3.0 GPA required. Must be majoring or plan to major in Computer Science and Engineering or related field.

    Amount of award: $2,500
    Application deadline: March 31
Contact:
Phone: 855-670-4787
Web: https://www.sandisk.com/about/corp-responsibility/scholars-program

The Stephanie Brown Cadet Memorial Scholarship

Type of award: Scholarship, renewable.
Intended use: For undergraduate study at vocational, 2-year or 4-year institution.
Eligibility: Applicant must be high school senior.
Basis for selection: Applicant must demonstrate high academic achievement and service orientation.
Application requirements: Interview, recommendations, essay, transcript. Max 500 word essay on your volunteerism.
Additional information: Must have volunteered in community service for a significant number of hours within the last 18 months. Minimum 3.0 GPA required.

    Amount of award: $1,000
    Application deadline: February 5
Contact:
The Stephanie Brown Cadet Memorial Foundation
Attention: Scholarship Award Committee
PO Box 610103
Redwood City, CA 94061
Phone: 650-257-0722
Web: www.sbcfoundation.org/scholarship-program

The Tang Scholarship

Type of award: Scholarship, renewable.
Intended use: For full-time undergraduate study at vocational, 2-year, 4-year or graduate institution.
Eligibility: Applicant must be Asian American or Native Hawaiian/Pacific Islander. Applicant must be at least 17, no older than 25, high school senior. Applicant must be U.S. citizen or permanent resident.
Basis for selection: Applicant must demonstrate financial need and high academic achievement.
Application requirements: Interview, recommendations, transcript, proof of eligibility.
Additional information: Must be self-identified as Asian/Pacific Islander and gay, lesbian, bisexual or transgender; (at least 25% API ancestry); and involved in the GLBT community. Must have graduated from a high school in one of the nine Bay Area counties; Alameda, Contra Costa, Marin, San Francisco, San Mateo, Santa Clara County, Napa, Sonoma or Solano. Minimum 3.0 GPA required.

    Amount of award: $15,000
    Number of awards: 4
    Application deadline: April 30
    Total amount awarded: $60,000
Contact:
Edward Tang
PO Box 6961
San Carlos, CA 94070-6961
Web: https://sites.google.com/site/tangscholarship/

The Wine Group Scholarship

Type of award: Scholarship.
Intended use: For full-time undergraduate study at 2-year or 4-year institution.
Eligibility: Applicant must be high school senior.
Basis for selection: Applicant must demonstrate high academic achievement and leadership.
Additional information: Minimum 3.0 GPA required. Must be child or legal dependent of a full-time employee of The Wine Group; employee must have at least three years of continuous service with The Wine Group and must be employed with The Wine Group at the time scholarship award selections are made.

    Amount of award: $10,000
    Number of awards: 10
Contact:
Web: www.siliconvalleycf.org/scholarships/wine-group-scholarship

Simplilearn Americas LLC

Simplilearn Student Ambassador Scholarship Program

Type of award: Scholarship.
Intended use: For full-time undergraduate or graduate study at vocational, 2-year, 4-year or graduate institution.
Eligibility: Applicant must be at least 18, no older than 25. Applicant must be U.S. citizen.
Additional information: More information about the program can be found on the website.

    Amount of award: $1,000-$1,000
    Number of awards: 3
    Application deadline: March 17
    Notification begins: March 24
    Total amount awarded: $3,000
Contact:
Simplilearn Americas LLC
201 Spear Street
#1100
San Francisco, CA 94105
Phone: +1-844-532-7688 x1025
Web: https://www.simplilearn.com/student-ambassador-scholarship-program

SitterSwitch.com

SitterSwitch.com Scholarship

Type of award: Scholarship.
Intended use: For full-time undergraduate or graduate study at vocational, 2-year or 4-year institution.

Application requirements: Essay. GPA, SAT or ACT. Class rank if available. Brief application essay.

Amount of award:	$250
Number of awards:	1
Application deadline:	March 1
Notification begins:	May 1
Total amount awarded:	$250

Contact:
Sitter Switch
16810 104th Avenue SE
Renton, WA 98055
Phone: 216-848-8001
Web: www.SitterSwitch.com

Six Star Pro Nutrition

Six Star Greatness is Earned Scholarship Award

Type of award: Scholarship.
Intended use: For undergraduate study at vocational, 2-year or 4-year institution.
Eligibility: Applicant must be at least 17, no older than 22. Applicant must be U.S. citizen.
Basis for selection: Applicant must demonstrate high academic achievement.
Application requirements: Essay. Must be currently attending or planning to attend a college or university during the fall academic year. Applications must be submitted in essay format (max 1000 words) or through creative video (no longer than 3 minutes). Demonstrates achievements as the all-around student; athletics, academics and community involvement.
Additional information: Entries are encouraged to have a sports/fitness focus. All submissions should be submitted at http://sixstarpro.com/scholarship/. 1 male and 1 female will be picked as winners.

Amount of award:	$15,000-$15,000
Number of awards:	2
Application deadline:	April 30
Total amount awarded:	$30,000

Contact:
Six Star Pro Nutrition
381 North Service Road
Oakville, ON
Phone: 647-500-2863
Web: www.sixstarpro.com/scholarship/

Slovak Gymnastic Union Sokol, USA

Milan Getting Scholarship

Type of award: Scholarship, renewable.
Intended use: For full-time undergraduate study at accredited 4-year institution.
Eligibility: Applicant must be high school junior or senior. Applicant must be U.S. citizen.
Basis for selection: Applicant must demonstrate high academic achievement, depth of character, leadership, patriotism and seriousness of purpose.

Application requirements: Recommendations, transcript.
Additional information: Applicant must be member in good standing of Slovak Gymnastic Union Sokol, USA, for at least three years. Minimum scholastic average of C+ or equivalent required. Award renewable for four years. Number of awards varies. Deadline in March. Contact sponsor for application form and more information.

Amount of award:	$500
Number of applicants:	6
Total amount awarded:	$6,000

Contact:
Slovak Gymnastic Union Sokol, USA
P.O. Box 189
East Orange, NJ 07019
Phone: 888-253-0362
Web: www.sokolusa.org

Slovenian Women's Union of America

Slovenian Women's Union Scholarship Foundation

Type of award: Scholarship.
Intended use: For full-time undergraduate study at accredited 2-year or 4-year institution in United States.
Eligibility: Applicant must be returning adult student.
Basis for selection: Applicant must demonstrate financial need, depth of character, leadership and service orientation.
Application requirements: Recommendations, essay, transcript. FAFSA, resume, and photograph.
Additional information: Applicants must be members of the Slovenian Women's Union or apply for a one year membership in the Slovenian Women's Union prior to application. Applicant must be an adult returning to college or a technical school part time. Open to women and men with interest in promoting Slovene culture. Letters of recommendation are required from a high school or college educator, and a letter from either a branch officer of the Slovenian Union, a pastor,or a priest. Applicants must have one ancestor of Slovene origin. Number of awards varies. Contact Mary Turvey at SWUA for more information. All Materials must be sent through postal mail; Emailed materials will not be accepted.

Amount of award:	$2,000
Number of awards:	12
Number of applicants:	14
Application deadline:	March 1
Notification begins:	April 1
Total amount awarded:	$18,500

Contact:
Slovenian Women's Union of America
4 Lawrence Drive
Marquette, MI 49855
Phone: 906-249-4288
Web: www.swusf.org

SLS Consulting

SLS Consulting Marketing Scholarship

Type of award: Scholarship.

Intended use: For full-time undergraduate or graduate study at accredited 2-year, 4-year or graduate institution.

Eligibility: Applicant must be at least 16, high school senior. Applicant must be U.S. citizen.

Basis for selection: Major/career interest in marketing; business/management/administration; design or engineering, computer.

Additional information: Minimum 3.0 GPA. All applicants must currently hold or anticipate earning a high school diploma within the 2014-2015 school year, currently be attending an accredited four-year university or college, or currently be attending a two-year institution with the intent of transferring to a four-year university or college. Visit web site for application and complete guidelines.

Amount of award:	$500
Application deadline:	April 15
Notification begins:	May 15

Contact:
SLS Consulting
1030 S. Arroyo Parkway
Suite 216
Pasadena, CA 91105
Phone: 323-254-1510
Fax: 323-254-1588
Web: www.legalinternetmarketing.com/scholarship.html

Smart Paper Help

Smart Paper Help Scholarship Contest

Type of award: Scholarship.

Intended use: For full-time undergraduate study at vocational, 2-year, 4-year or graduate institution.

Eligibility: Applicant must be high school senior.

Application requirements: Essay. Must submit a maximum 1,000 word essay via e-mail. Prompt can be found online. Applicant must also follow Smart Paper on Twitter as well as like Smart Paper Help on Facebook.

Amount of award:	$400-$1,000
Number of awards:	3
Application deadline:	January 10
Notification begins:	January 15
Total amount awarded:	$2,100

Contact:
Web: www.smartpaperhelp.com/blog/scholarship-program-for-students

SME Education Foundation

Albert E. Wischmeyer Memorial Scholarship Award

Type of award: Scholarship, renewable.

Intended use: For full-time undergraduate study at accredited 4-year institution. Designated institutions: Institutions located in the state of New York.

Eligibility: Applicant must be U.S. citizen or permanent resident residing in New York.

Basis for selection: Major/career interest in manufacturing; engineering or technology. Applicant must demonstrate high academic achievement.

Application requirements: Recommendations, essay, transcript. Resume, SAT or ACT scores for current high school students.

Additional information: Applicants must reside in New York State west of Interstate 81. Must be graduating high school seniors or current undergraduate students enrolled in a manufacturing engineering, manufacturing engineering technology, or mechanical technology accredited degree program at a college or university in New York State. Must reapply for renewal. Application available on Website. Awards vary.

Application deadline:	February 1

Contact:
SME Education Foundation
One SME Drive, P.O. Box 930
Dearborn, MI 48121-0930
Phone: 313-425-3300
Web: www.smeef.org

Allen and Loureena Weber Scholarship

Type of award: Scholarship.

Intended use: For sophomore, junior or senior study at 2-year or 4-year institution in United States.

Eligibility: Applicant must be U.S. citizen or permanent resident residing in Kentucky.

Basis for selection: Major/career interest in manufacturing; engineering, mechanical; engineering, industrial or technology. Applicant must demonstrate high academic achievement.

Application requirements: Recommendations, transcript. Resume.

Additional information: Minimum 3.0 GPA. First preference given to students who are graduates of Dayton High School (Dayton, KY). Second preference given to other high schools in Dayton, KY area. Third preference will be given, but not limited to, students attending colleges or universities in the state of Kentucky. Applicants must have completed a minimum of 30 college credit hours. Must have technical aptitude and desire for education and practical learning. Scholarship may be used toward books, fees, or tuition.

Application deadline:	February 1

Contact:
SME Education Foundation
One SME Drive, P.O. Box 930
Dearborn, MI 48121-0930
Phone: 313-425-3300
Web: www.smeef.org

Alvin and June Sabroff Manufacturing Engineering Scholarship

Type of award: Scholarship.
Intended use: For undergraduate study at accredited 4-year institution in United States or Canada.
Eligibility: Applicant must be U.S. citizen.
Basis for selection: Major/career interest in manufacturing; engineering or technology. Applicant must demonstrate high academic achievement.
Application requirements: Recommendations, transcript. Resume.
Additional information: Minimum 3.0 GPA. Must be seeking degree in manufacturing engineering, technology, or closely related field. First preference given to applicants attending college or university in Ohio. Award amount varies.

   Application deadline: February 1
Contact:
SME Education Foundation
One SME Drive, P.O. Box 930
Dearborn, MI 48121-0930
Phone: 313-425-3300
Web: www.smeef.org

Arthur and Gladys Cervenka Scholarship

Type of award: Scholarship, renewable.
Intended use: For full-time sophomore, junior or senior study at accredited 4-year institution in United States or Canada.
Basis for selection: Major/career interest in manufacturing; engineering or technology. Applicant must demonstrate high academic achievement.
Application requirements: Recommendations, essay, transcript. Resume.
Additional information: Must be residing in the U.S. or Canada. Applicant must have completed minimum of 30 college credit hours. Minimum 3.0 GPA. Must be full-time undergraduate students enrolled in a degree program in manufacturing engineering/technology or a closely related field. Preference given to students attending institutions in Florida. Awards vary.

   Application deadline: February 1
Contact:
SME Education Foundation
One SME Drive, P.O. Box 930
Dearborn, MI 48121-0930
Phone: 313-425-3300
Web: www.smeef.org

Chapter 17 - St. Louis Scholarship

Type of award: Scholarship, renewable.
Intended use: For sophomore, junior or senior study at accredited 2-year or 4-year institution.
Basis for selection: Major/career interest in manufacturing; engineering; engineering, mechanical or technology. Applicant must demonstrate high academic achievement, depth of character and seriousness of purpose.
Application requirements: Recommendations, essay, transcript. Resume.
Additional information: Must be residing in the U.S. or Canada. Applicants must be enrolled in manufacturing engineering, industrial technology, or related degree program. Preference given to applicants residing in boundaries of St. Louis Chapter 17. Second preference given to applicants living

in Missouri. Minimum 2.5 GPA. Must reapply for renewal. Application available on Website. Awards vary.

   Application deadline: February 1
Contact:
SME Education Foundation
One SME Drive, P.O. Box 930
Dearborn, MI 48121-0930
Phone: 313-425-3300
Web: www.smeef.org

Chapter 198 - Downriver Detroit Scholarship

Type of award: Scholarship.
Intended use: For full-time undergraduate or graduate study at accredited 2-year, 4-year or graduate institution.
Basis for selection: Major/career interest in manufacturing; engineering, mechanical; engineering; technology or mathematics. Applicant must demonstrate high academic achievement.
Application requirements: Recommendations, essay, transcript. Resume, SAT or ACT scores for current high school students. Must be seeking an associate's degree, bachelor's degree or graduate degree in manufacturing, mechanical, or industrial engineering, engineering technology, or industrial technology at an accredited public or private college or university in the state of Michigan.
Additional information: Must be residing in the U.S. or Canada. First preference given to children or grandchildren of current SME Downriver Chapter 198 members. Second preference given to members of student SME chapters sponsored by Chapter 198 or Ann Arbor Area Chapter 079. Third preference given to residents of Michigan. Fourth preference given to applicants planning to attend college/ university in Michigan. Not restricted to Michigan. Minimum 2.5 GPA. Awards vary.

   Application deadline: February 1
Contact:
SME Education Foundation
One SME Drive, P.O. Box 930
Dearborn, MI 48121-0930
Phone: 313-425-3300
Web: www.smeef.org

Chapter 23 - Quad Cities Iowa/ Illinois Scholarship

Type of award: Scholarship.
Intended use: For undergraduate study at accredited 4-year institution.
Basis for selection: Major/career interest in manufacturing or engineering, industrial. Applicant must demonstrate high academic achievement.
Application requirements: Recommendations, transcript. Resume. Scholarship applicants must be seeking a Bachelor's degree in manufacturing engineering, industrial engineering, manufacturing technology or integrated fg systems.
Additional information: Minimum 2.5 GPA. Scholarship may be used toward books, fees, or tuition. First preference given to applicant who is a child, grandchild, or stepchild of registered SME member or student member. Second preference given to applicant who is resident of Iowa or Illinois and attending an Iowa or Illinois college or university. Third preference given to students who are residents of Iowa or Illinois. Fourth preference will be given to applicants who attend a college or university located in Iowa or Illinois. Award amount varies.

   Application deadline: February 1

Scholarships

Contact:
SME Education Foundation
One SME Drive, P.O. Box 930
Dearborn, MI 48121-0930
Phone: 313-425-3300
Web: www.smeef.org

Chapter 311 - Tri City Scholarship

Type of award: Scholarship.

Intended use: For undergraduate study at accredited 4-year institution.

Basis for selection: Major/career interest in manufacturing; engineering or engineering, industrial. Applicant must demonstrate high academic achievement.

Application requirements: Recommendations, transcript. Resume.

Additional information: Must be seeking a bachelor's degree in manufacturing engineering, industrial engineering, manufacturing technology or integrated manufacturing systems degree program. Minimum 3.0 GPA. First preference given to scholarship applicants who are residents of Michigan. Second preference given to applicants seeking education from college or university in Michigan. Award amount varies.

Application deadline: February 1

Contact:
SME Education Foundation
One SME Drive, P.O. Box 930
Dearborn, MI 48121-0930
Phone: 313-425-3300
Web: www.smeef.org

Chapter 4 - Lawrence A. Wacker Memorial Scholarship

Type of award: Scholarship, renewable.

Intended use: For undergraduate study at accredited 4-year institution in United States. Designated institutions: Wisconsin institutions.

Basis for selection: Major/career interest in manufacturing; engineering, industrial or engineering, mechanical. Applicant must demonstrate high academic achievement.

Application requirements: Recommendations, essay, transcript. Resume, SAT or ACT scores for current high school students.

Additional information: Applicants must be seeking bachelor's degree in manufacturing, mechanical, or industrial engineering. Minimum 3.0 GPA. One scholarship granted to graduating high school senior, one to current undergraduate. First preference given to SME Chapter 4 members or spouses, children, or grandchildren of members. Second preference given to residents of Milwaukee, Ozaukee, Washington, and Waukesha counties. Third preference given to Wisconsin residents. Application available on Website. Award amounts vary.

Application deadline: February 1

Contact:
SME Education Foundation
One SME Drive, P.O. Box 930
Dearborn, MI 48121-0930
Phone: 313-425-3300
Web: www.smeef.org

Chapter 52 - Wichita Scholarship

Type of award: Scholarship.

Intended use: For sophomore, junior, senior or graduate study at accredited 2-year, 4-year or graduate institution in United States. Designated institutions: Kansas institutions.

Eligibility: Applicant must be residing in Kansas.

Basis for selection: Major/career interest in engineering; engineering, mechanical; engineering, industrial; manufacturing or technology. Applicant must demonstrate high academic achievement.

Application requirements: Recommendations, essay, transcript. Resume. All applicants must be seeking an associate's degree, bachelor's degree or graduate degree in manufacturing, mechanical, or industrial engineering, engineering technology, or industrial technology at an accredited public or private college or university in Kansas.

Additional information: Must be residing in the U.S. or Canada. First preference given to children, grandchildren, or other relatives of current SME Wichita Chapter 52 members. Second preference given to residents of Kansas, Oklahoma, and Missouri. Third preference given to applicants attending colleges or universities in Kansas. Minimum 2.5 GPA. Awards vary.

Application deadline: February 1

Contact:
SME Education Foundation
One SME Drive, P.O. Box 930
Dearborn, MI 48121-0930
Phone: 313-425-3300
Web: www.smeef.org

Chapter 56 - Fort Wayne Scholarship

Type of award: Scholarship.

Intended use: For undergraduate or graduate study at 2-year, 4-year or graduate institution. Designated institutions: Indiana institutions.

Eligibility: Applicant must be residing in Indiana.

Basis for selection: Major/career interest in engineering or engineering, mechanical. Applicant must demonstrate high academic achievement.

Application requirements: Recommendations, essay, transcript. Resume, SAT or ACT scores for high school students. All applicants must be seeking an associate's degree, bachelor's degree or graduate degree in manufacturing, mechanical, or industrial engineering, engineering technology, or industrial technology at an accredited public or private college or university located in the state of Indiana.

Additional information: Must be residing in the U.S. or Canada. First preference given to children or grandchildren of current members of SME Fort Wayne Chapter 56. Second preference given to members of SME student chapters sponsored by Chapter 56. Third preference given to residents of Indiana. Fourth preference given to applicants attending or planning to attend Indiana institutions. Minimum 2.5 GPA. Awards vary.

Application deadline: February 1

Contact:
SME Education Foundation
One SME Drive, P.O. Box 930
Dearborn, MI 48121-0930
Phone: 313-425-3300
Web: www.smeef.org

Scholarships

Chapter 6 - Fairfield County Scholarship

Type of award: Scholarship.
Intended use: For full-time undergraduate study in United States or Canada.
Basis for selection: Major/career interest in engineering; manufacturing or technology. Applicant must demonstrate high academic achievement.
Application requirements: Recommendations, essay, transcript. Resume, SAT or ACT scores for current high school students.
Additional information: Scholarship applicants must be an undergraduate student enrolled in a degree program in manufacturing engineering, technology, or a closely related field. Must be residing in the U.S. or Canada. Minimum 3.0 GPA. Preference given to residents of the eastern United States. Award amount varies.

  Application deadline: February 1
Contact:
SME Education Foundation
One SME Drive, P.O. Box 930
Dearborn, MI 48121-0930
Phone: 313-425-3300
Web: www.smeef.org

Chapter 67 - Phoenix Scholarship

Type of award: Scholarship, renewable.
Intended use: For full-time undergraduate study. Designated institutions: Arizona institutions.
Eligibility: Applicant must be residing in Arizona.
Basis for selection: Major/career interest in engineering; manufacturing or technology. Applicant must demonstrate high academic achievement.
Application requirements: Recommendations, essay, transcript. Resume, SAT or ACT scores for current high school students.
Additional information: Applicants may either be high school seniors who plan on enrolling in a manufacturing engineering .industrial engineering or manufacturing technology program, or current undergraduate students enrolled in a manufacturing engineering/technology, industrial engineering/technology or closely related program at an accredited college or university in Arizona. Minimum 3.0 overall GPA; maintain 3.0 in manufacturing courses to continue eligibility in future years. Awards vary.

  Application deadline: February 1
Contact:
SME Education Foundation
One SME Drive, P.O. Box 930
Dearborn, MI 48121-0930
Phone: 313-425-3300
Web: www.smeef.org

Chapter 93 - Albuquerque Scholarship

Type of award: Scholarship.
Intended use: For undergraduate study at accredited 2-year or 4-year institution in United States. Designated institutions: Colleges and universities in New Mexico.
Basis for selection: Major/career interest in engineering. Applicant must demonstrate high academic achievement.
Application requirements: Recommendations, transcript. Resume.

Additional information: Minimum 2.5 GPA. Must be pursuing manufacturing engineering or manufacturing technology. Scholarship may be used toward books, fees, or tuition. First preference goes to applicant who is child/grandchild/stepchild of current Chapter 93 member. Second preference given to SME student member attending a New Mexico university. Third preference given to applicants residing in New Mexico. Fourth preference given to scholarship applicants planning to attend engineering college or university in New Mexico. Fifth preference given to applicants pursuing associate's degree. Award amount varies.

  Application deadline: February 1
Contact:
SME Education Foundation
One SME Drive, P.O. Box 930
Dearborn, MI 48121-0930
Phone: 313-425-3300
Web: www.smeef.org

Chapter One - Detroit Associate Scholarship Award

Type of award: Scholarship, renewable.
Intended use: For undergraduate or graduate study at accredited 2-year, 4-year or graduate institution. Designated institutions: Wayne State University, Lawrence Technological University, University of Detroit Mercy, Focus: HOPE Center for Advanced Technologies, Henry Ford Community College, Macomb Community College, University of Michigan.
Basis for selection: Major/career interest in manufacturing or engineering. Applicant must demonstrate high academic achievement, depth of character and leadership.
Application requirements: Recommendations, essay, transcript. Resume.
Additional information: Awarded to one student each at associate, baccalaureate, and graduate levels. Applicants must be enrolled in manufacturing engineering, manufacturing engineering technology, or closely related degree or certificate program. Student must be member of SME student chapter sponsored by Detroit Chapter 1. Minimum 3.0 GPA. Applicants must reapply for renewal. Financial need considered only between two otherwise equal applicants. Application available on Website. Awards vary.

  Number of awards: 3
  Application deadline: February 1
Contact:
SME Education Foundation
One SME Drive, P.O. Box 930
Dearborn, MI 48121-0930
Phone: 313-425-3300
Web: www.smeef.org

Clarence & Josephine Myers Scholarship

Type of award: Scholarship.
Intended use: For undergraduate or graduate study at 2-year, 4-year or graduate institution. Designated institutions: Indiana institutions.
Eligibility: Applicant must be residing in Indiana.
Basis for selection: Major/career interest in engineering, mechanical; engineering; manufacturing or engineering, industrial. Applicant must demonstrate high academic achievement.
Application requirements: Recommendations, essay, transcript. Resume, SAT or ACT scores for current high school students.

Additional information: Scholarship applicants must be seeking an associate, bachelor, or graduate degree in manufacturing, mechanical, or industrial engineering in the state of Indiana. Preference given to students planning to attend or currently attending college or university in Indiana, students who attend Arsenal Technological High School in Indianapolis, members of SME student chapters sponsored by SME Chapter 37, and children or grandchildren of current SME Chapter 37 members. Minimum 3.0 GPA. Award varies.

Application deadline: February 1

Contact:
SME Education Foundation
One SME Drive, P.O. Box 930
Dearborn, MI 48121-0930
Phone: 313-425-3300
Web: www.smeef.org

Clinton J. Helton Manufacturing Scholarship Award

Type of award: Scholarship.
Intended use: For full-time sophomore, junior or senior study at accredited 4-year institution. Designated institutions: Colorado State University and all University of Colorado campuses.
Eligibility: Applicant must be residing in Colorado.
Basis for selection: Major/career interest in manufacturing; engineering or technology. Applicant must demonstrate high academic achievement and depth of character.
Application requirements: Recommendations, essay, transcript. Resume.
Additional information: Applicants must be enrolled in manufacturing engineering or technology degree program and must have completed at least 30 credit hours. Preference will be given, but not limited to, students attending Colorado State University or the University of Colorado. Minimum 3.0 GPA. Applicants must reapply for renewal. Application available on Website. Awards vary.

Application deadline: February 1

Contact:
SME Education Foundation
One SME Drive, P.O. Box 930
Dearborn, MI 48121-0930
Phone: 313-425-3300
Web: www.smeef.org

Connie and Robert T. Gunter Scholarship

Type of award: Scholarship.
Intended use: For full-time sophomore, junior or senior study at accredited 4-year institution. Designated institutions: Georgia Institute of Technology, Georgia Southern College, Southern College of Technology.
Basis for selection: Major/career interest in manufacturing; engineering or technology. Applicant must demonstrate high academic achievement, depth of character and seriousness of purpose.
Application requirements: Recommendations, essay, transcript. Resume.
Additional information: Must be residing in the U.S. or Canada. Applicants must be enrolled in manufacturing engineering degree program and must have completed at least 30 credit hours. Minimum 3.5 GPA. Applicants must reapply for renewal. Application available on Website. Award amount varies.

Application deadline: February 1

Contact:
SME Education Foundation
One SME Drive, P.O. Box 930
Dearborn, MI 48121-0930
Phone: 313-425-3300
Web: www.smeef.org

E. Wayne Kay Co-op Scholarship

Type of award: Scholarship, renewable.
Intended use: For full-time sophomore, junior or senior study at accredited postsecondary institution in United States or Canada.
Basis for selection: Major/career interest in manufacturing; engineering or technology. Applicant must demonstrate high academic achievement.
Application requirements: Essay, transcript, proof of eligibility. Letter of recommendation from employer and letter of support from faculty member at college or university.
Additional information: Must be residing in the U.S. or Canada. Applicants must be enrolled in manufacturing engineering or technology degree program and working through co-op program in a manufacturing-related environment. Applicants must have completed minimum 30 college credit hours. Must provide evidence of demonstrated excellence related to manufacturing engineering or technology which may include project completed for employer. Minimum 3.0 GPA. Applicants must reapply for renewal. Application available on Website. Awards vary.

Application deadline: February 1

Contact:
SME Educational Foundation
One SME Drive, P.O. Box 930
Dearborn, MI 48121-0930
Phone: 313-425-3300
Web: www.smeef.org

E. Wayne Kay Community College Scholarship

Type of award: Scholarship, renewable.
Intended use: For full-time freshman or sophomore study at accredited vocational or 2-year institution in United States or Canada. Designated institutions: Community colleges and trade schools.
Basis for selection: Major/career interest in manufacturing or technology. Applicant must demonstrate high academic achievement.
Application requirements: Recommendations, essay, transcript. Resume, SAT or ACT scores.
Additional information: Must be residing in the U.S. or Canada. Applicants must be enrolled in manufacturing engineering or closely related degree program at a two-year community college or trade school in the U.S. or Canada. Entering freshman or sophomore students with 60 or fewer college credits are also eligible. Minimum 3.0 GPA. Must reapply for renewal. Application available on Website. Awards vary.

Application deadline: February 1

Contact:
SME Education Foundation
One SME Drive, P.O. Box 930
Dearborn, MI 48121-0930
Phone: 313-425-3300
Web: www.smeef.org

E. Wayne Kay Scholarship

Type of award: Scholarship, renewable.
Intended use: For full-time undergraduate study at accredited 4-year institution in United States or Canada.
Basis for selection: Major/career interest in manufacturing or engineering. Applicant must demonstrate high academic achievement.
Application requirements: Recommendations, essay, transcript. Resume.
Additional information: Must be residing in the U.S. or Canada. Applicants must be enrolled in manufacturing engineering or technology degree program or closely related field. Minimum 3.0 GPA. Must reapply for renewal. Application available on Website. Awards vary.

   Application deadline: February 1
Contact:
SME Education Foundation
One SME Drive, P.O. Box 930
Dearborn, MI 48121-0930
Phone: 313-425-3300
Web: www.smeef.org

Edward S. Roth Manufacturing Engineering Scholarship

Type of award: Scholarship, renewable.
Intended use: For full-time undergraduate or graduate study at accredited 4-year institution in United States. Designated institutions: California State Polytechnic University; University of Miami, FL; Bradley University, IL; Central State University, OH; Miami University, OH; Boston University; Worcester Polytechnic Institute, MA; University of Massachusetts; St. Cloud State University, MN; University of Texas-Pan American; Brigham Young University, UT; Utah State University.
Eligibility: Applicant must be U.S. citizen.
Basis for selection: Major/career interest in manufacturing or engineering. Applicant must demonstrate high academic achievement, depth of character and seriousness of purpose.
Application requirements: Recommendations, essay, transcript. Resume.
Additional information: Applicants must be enrolled in manufacturing engineering degree program. Minimum 3.0 GPA. Preference given to students demonstrating financial need, minority students, and students participating in co-op program. Must reapply for renewal. Application available on Website. Award amount varies.

   Application deadline: February 1
Contact:
SME Education Foundation
One SME Drive, P.O. Box 930
Dearborn, MI 48121-0930
Phone: 313-425-3300
Web: www.smeef.org

Giuliano Mazzetti Scholarship

Type of award: Scholarship, renewable.
Intended use: For full-time sophomore, junior or senior study at accredited 4-year institution in United States or Canada.
Basis for selection: Major/career interest in manufacturing; engineering or technology. Applicant must demonstrate high academic achievement.
Application requirements: Recommendations, essay, transcript. Resume.
Additional information: Must be residing in the U.S. or Canada. Applicants must be enrolled in manufacturing

engineering, technology, or closely related degree program and must have completed minimum 30 college credit hours. Minimum 3.0 GPA. Must reapply for renewal. Application available on Website. Awards vary.

   Application deadline: February 1
Contact:
SME Education Foundation
One SME Drive, P.O. Box 930
Dearborn, MI 48121-0930
Phone: 313-425-3300
Web: www.smeef.org

Lucile B. Kaufman Women's Scholarship

Type of award: Scholarship, renewable.
Intended use: For full-time sophomore, junior or senior study at 4-year institution in United States or Canada.
Eligibility: Applicant must be female.
Basis for selection: Major/career interest in manufacturing or engineering. Applicant must demonstrate high academic achievement.
Application requirements: Recommendations, essay, transcript. Resume.
Additional information: Must be residing in the U.S. or Canada. Applicants must be enrolled in manufacturing engineering or manufacturing engineering technology degree program and must have completed minimum 30 credits. Minimum 3.0 GPA. Must reapply for renewal. Application available on Website. Awards vary.

   Application deadline: February 1
Contact:
SME Education Foundation
One SME Drive, P.O. Box 930
Dearborn, MI 48121-0930
Phone: 313-425-3300
Web: www.smeef.org

Myrtle and Earl Walker Scholarship

Type of award: Scholarship, renewable.
Intended use: For full-time undergraduate study at accredited 4-year institution in United States or Canada.
Basis for selection: Major/career interest in manufacturing or engineering. Applicant must demonstrate high academic achievement.
Application requirements: Recommendations, essay, transcript. Resume.
Additional information: Must be residing in the U.S. or Canada. Applicants must be enrolled in manufacturing engineering degree or technology program and must have completed minimum 15 credits. Minimum 3.0 GPA. Must reapply for renewal. Application available on Website. Awards vary.

   Amount of award: $2,500
   Application deadline: February 1
Contact:
SME Education Foundation
One SME Drive, P.O. Box 930
Dearborn, MI 48121-0930
Phone: 313-425-3300
Web: www.smeef.org

North Central Region 9 Scholarship

Type of award: Scholarship.
Intended use: For full-time undergraduate study at 2-year or 4-year institution. Designated institutions: Institutions in Iowa,

Minnesota, Nebraska, North Dakota, South Dakota, Wisconsin, or the upper peninsula of Michigan.

Eligibility: Applicant must be residing in Michigan, Wisconsin, Iowa, South Dakota, Minnesota, Nebraska or North Dakota.

Basis for selection: Major/career interest in manufacturing; engineering or engineering, mechanical. Applicant must demonstrate high academic achievement.

Application requirements: Recommendations, essay, transcript. Resume, SAT or ACT scores for current high school students.

Additional information: Must be residing in the U.S. or Canada. First preference given to applicants from the North Central Region who are SME members, spouses of members, or children or grandchildren of members. Second preference given to residents of Iowa, Minnesota, Nebraska, North Dakota, South Dakota, Wisconsin, and the upper peninsula of Michigan. Minimum 3.0 GPA. Awards vary.

Application deadline: February 1

Contact:
SME Education Foundation
One SME Drive, P.O. Box 930
Dearborn, MI 48121-0930
Phone: 313-425-3300
Web: www.smeef.org

SME Directors Scholarship

Type of award: Scholarship, renewable.

Intended use: For full-time sophomore, junior or senior study at accredited 4-year institution in United States or Canada.

Basis for selection: Major/career interest in manufacturing. Applicant must demonstrate high academic achievement and leadership.

Application requirements: Recommendations, essay, transcript. Resume.

Additional information: Must be full-time undergraduate students enrolled in a manufacturing degree or closely related field. Must be residing in the U.S. or Canada. Applicants must have completed minimum 30 college credit hours. Minimum 3.5 GPA. Applicants must reapply for renewal. Preference given to applicants who demonstrate leadership skills in a community, academic, or professional environment. Application available on Website. Awards vary.

Application deadline: February 1

Contact:
SME Education Foundation
One SME Drive, P.O. Box 930
Dearborn, MI 48121-0930
Phone: 313-425-3300
Web: www.smeef.org

SME Education Foundation Family Scholarship

Type of award: Scholarship.

Intended use: For full-time undergraduate study in United States or Canada.

Basis for selection: Major/career interest in engineering or manufacturing. Applicant must demonstrate high academic achievement.

Application requirements: Recommendations, essay, transcript. Resume. High school seniors must submit SAT/ACT scores.

Additional information: Must be residing in the U.S. or Canada. Applicant must have parent or grandparent who has been SME member in good standing for at least two years. Must pursue a degree in manufacturing engineering, manufacturing engineering technology, or a closely related engineering field of study. Graduating high school seniors and current undergraduates with fewer than 30 credit hours are eligible. Minimum 3.0 GPA. Minimum 1000 SAT or 21 ACT. Awards vary.

Application deadline: February 1

Contact:
SME Education Foundation
One SME Drive, P.O. Box 930
Dearborn, MI 48121-0930
Phone: 313-425-3300
Web: www.smeef.org

SME-EF Future Leaders of Manufacturing Scholarships

Type of award: Scholarship.

Intended use: For full-time undergraduate or graduate study at accredited postsecondary institution in United States.

Basis for selection: Major/career interest in manufacturing; engineering or technology.

Application requirements: Recommendations, transcript, nomination by SME student chapter faculty advisor. Resume.

Additional information: Students must be enrolled in a manufacturing engineering, engineering technology, industrial technology, technical, or related engineering major at an accredited college or university. Must be residing in the U.S. or Canada. Applicant must be current SME student member. Visit Website for nomination form and application. Awards vary.

Application deadline: February 1

Contact:
SME Education Foundation
One SME Drive, P.O. Box 930
Dearborn, MI 48121-0930
Phone: 313-425-3300
Web: www.smeef.org

Walt Bartram Memorial Education Award (Region 12 and Chapter 119)

Type of award: Scholarship, renewable.

Intended use: For full-time undergraduate study at accredited 2-year or 4-year institution. Designated institutions: Schools with manufacturing engineering programs within the areas of Arizona, New Mexico, or Southern California.

Eligibility: Applicant must be high school senior.

Basis for selection: Major/career interest in manufacturing or engineering. Applicant must demonstrate high academic achievement, depth of character and seriousness of purpose.

Application requirements: Recommendations, essay, transcript. Resume, SAT or ACT scores for current high school students.

Additional information: Applicant must be enrolled in manufacturing engineering or closely related degree program. Minimum 2.5 GPA. Application available on Website. Award varies. Must reside within the Desert Pacific states and be members of SME, except high school students who may apply without any SME member relationship.

Application deadline: February 1

Contact:
SME Foundation
One SME Drive, P.O. Box 930
Dearborn, MI 48121-0930
Phone: 313-425-3300
Web: www.smeef.org

William E. Weisel Scholarship

Type of award: Scholarship, renewable.
Intended use: For full-time sophomore, junior or senior study at 4-year institution in United States or Canada.
Basis for selection: Major/career interest in manufacturing; engineering; robotics or technology. Applicant must demonstrate high academic achievement.
Application requirements: Recommendations, essay, transcript. Resume.
Additional information: Must be residing in the U.S. or Canada. Applicant must be enrolled in manufacturing engineering degree program and must have completed minimum 30 credits. Preference given to applicants seeking career in robotics or automated systems used in manufacturing. Consideration given to students who intend to apply knowledge to career in medical robotics. Minimum 3.0 GPA. Applicants must reapply for renewal. Financial need considered only between two otherwise equal applicants. Application available on Website. Awards vary.

    Application deadline: February 1
Contact:
SME Education Foundation
One SME Drive, P.O. Box 930
Dearborn, MI 48121-0930
Phone: 313-425-3300
Web: www.smeef.org

SocialSEO

SocialSEO Digital Marketing and SEO Scholarship

Type of award: Scholarship.
Intended use: For full-time undergraduate or graduate study at accredited 4-year or graduate institution in United States.
Eligibility: Applicant must be enrolled in high school.
Basis for selection: Major/career interest in business; marketing; advertising; finance/banking or accounting.
Application requirements: Transcript, proof of eligibility. Applicants must be already accepted to or attending a United States accredited college or university and can be in any year of their college career. Scan or image of high school transcript or current college/university transcript . Scan or image of letter of acceptance to an accredited US college or university.
Additional information: Interested applicants can find more information at https://www.socialseo.com/socialseo-digital-marketing-and-seo-scholarship . All material submitted to scholarship@socialseo.com.

    Amount of award: $1,000
    Number of awards: 1
    Application deadline: August 1
    Notification begins: August 7
    Total amount awarded: $1,000
Contact:
SocialSEO
5475 Mark Dabling Boulevard
Suit 210
Colorado Springs, CO 80918
Phone: 719-725-6408
Web: https://www.socialseo.com/socialseo-digital-marketing-and-seo-scholarship

Sociedad Honoraria Hispanica

Joseph Adams Senior Scholarship

Type of award: Scholarship.
Intended use: For full-time freshman study in United States.
Eligibility: Applicant must be high school senior.
Basis for selection: Applications will be judged on the following criteria. Applicant's proficiency in Spanish or Portuguese. Applicant's special contribution to and for the SHH and the community. Specific teacher recommendations. General academic standing and performance. All achievements and contributions pertaining to Spanish or Portuguese (These should be specific, as they are of special interest to the judges.) Major/career interest in Latin American studies.
Application requirements: Recommendations, essay, transcript, proof of eligibility, nomination by local high school chapter sponsor. Completed application form including the signatures. List of honors and extracurricular activities. Signed letter from teacher/sponsor. Signed letter of recommendation from principal, counselor or another teacher. Video.
Additional information: The applicant must be a high school senior and member of the SHH who is currently enrolled in a Spanish or Portuguese class. If a student has already completed the highest level of Spanish or Portuguese offered prior to the senior year, and as a result is not enrolled in a Spanish or Portuguese class, he/she may still apply. A letter from a school counselor or administrator must be included to verify that there were no Spanish classes available to the student. The chapter sponsor must certify that he/she is a member in good standing of the American Association of Teachers of Spanish and Portuguese at the time of application. Only one application per chapter is allowed. Receipt of more than one application per chapter will disqualify all candidates from the chapter. Incomplete applications will not be considered. Career interests must include Latin American Studies or World Languages. 48 Award scholarships are worth 1000. 12 Award scholarships are worth 2000.

    Number of awards: 60
    Number of applicants: 200
    Application deadline: December 1
    Notification begins: March 1
    Total amount awarded: $72,000
Contact:
Sociedad Honoraria Hispanica
Phone: 248-960-2180
Web: www.aatsp.org

Society for Range Management

Masonic Range Science Scholarship

Type of award: Scholarship, renewable.
Intended use: For full-time freshman or sophomore study at postsecondary institution. Designated institutions: Colleges or universities with range science programs.
Basis for selection: Major/career interest in range science. Applicant must demonstrate high academic achievement and leadership.

Application requirements: Recommendations, essay, transcript, nomination by member of Society for Range Management, National Association of Conservation Districts, or Soil and Water Conservation Society. SAT/ACT scores.

Additional information: Home-schooled applicants also welcome to apply. Award amount varies. Renewable for maximum of eight semesters. Student must maintain 2.5 GPA first two semesters, 3.0 GPA any subsequent semesters. Applications due in January. Visit Website for more information and application.

Number of awards:	1
Number of applicants:	16
Notification begins:	March 1
Total amount awarded:	$5,000

Contact:
Society for Range Management
Paul Loeffler
P.O. Box 1407
Alpine, TX 79831-1407
Phone: 303-986-3309
Fax: 303-986-3892
Web: www.rangelands.org

Society for Science & the Public

Intel International Science and Engineering Fair

Type of award: Scholarship.

Intended use: For undergraduate study at postsecondary institution.

Eligibility: Applicant must be enrolled in high school.

Basis for selection: Competition/talent/interest in science project, based on merit at Intel ISEF-affiliated regional or state fair. Major/career interest in science, general or engineering.

Additional information: World's largest precollege science competition. Over 1,600 students in grades 9 to 12 from 70 countries compete for awards and prizes at the Intel ISEF held mid-May. Students must be selected by their Intel ISEF-affiliated regional or state fair to advance to Intel ISEF. Visit website for more information.

Amount of award:	$100-$50,000
Number of awards:	800
Number of applicants:	1,594
Total amount awarded:	$4,000,000

Contact:
Intel ISEF
Society for Science and the Public
1719 N Street NW
Washington, DC 20036
Phone: 202-785-2255
Web: www.societyforscience.org/isef

Intel Science Talent Search

Type of award: Scholarship.

Intended use: For undergraduate study at postsecondary institution.

Eligibility: Applicant must be high school senior.

Basis for selection: Competition/talent/interest in science project, based on research paper and overall potential as a scientist as evidenced by essays, test scores, coursework, grades, and recommendations. Major/career interest in biology; science, general; physics or mathematics.

Application requirements: Recommendations, transcript, proof of eligibility. Twenty-page research paper on independent research in science, math, or engineering; standardized test scores.

Additional information: Any students attending their last year of US secondary school or US citizens attending a Department of Defense school, accredited overseas American or International School, or a temporary foreign exchange program are eligible. See Rules and Entry Instructions for complete eligibility requirements. Highly competitive program for college-bound students. Visit Website for more information.

Amount of award:	$1,000-$100,000
Number of awards:	300
Number of applicants:	1,839
Application deadline:	November 12
Total amount awarded:	$1,250,000

Contact:
Intel Science Talent Search
Society for Science and the Public
1719 N Street NW
Washington, DC 20036
Phone: 202-785-2255
Web: www.societyforscience.org/sts

Society of Daughters of the United States Army

Society of Daughters of United States Army Scholarship Program

Type of award: Scholarship, renewable.

Intended use: For full-time undergraduate study at accredited postsecondary institution.

Eligibility: Applicant must be female. Applicant must be daughter or granddaughter (including step or adopted) of a career warrant (WO 1-5) or commissioned officer (2nd & 1st LT, CPT, MAJ, LTC, COL, or General) of U.S. Army who (1) is currently on active duty; (2) retired from active duty after at least 20 years of service; (3) was medically retired before 20 years of active service; (4) died while on active duty; or (5) died after retiring from active duty with 20 or more years of service.

Basis for selection: Applicant must demonstrate high academic achievement, depth of character, leadership, patriotism and seriousness of purpose.

Additional information: Minimum 3.0 GPA. Scholarships cover academic expenses only. Request for application must include parent or grandparent's name, rank, component (Active, Regular, Reserve), inclusive dates of active service, and relationship to applicant. Number of awards varies annually. Send business-size SASE and one letter of request only. Do not send birth certificate or original documents. Do not use registered/certified mail. All application submissions become property of DUSA. Application request deadline is March 1. Completed applications due from March 15 to March 31.

Amount of award:	$1,000
Number of applicants:	100
Application deadline:	March 31
Notification begins:	June 1
Total amount awarded:	$10,000

Contact:
Society of Daughters of the United States Army
Mary P. Maroney, Scholarship Chairman
11804 Grey Birch Place
Reston, VA 20191-4223

Society of Exploration Geophysicists

Society of Exploration Geophysicists Scholarship

Type of award: Scholarship, renewable.
Intended use: For full-time undergraduate or graduate study at accredited 4-year or graduate institution.
Basis for selection: Major/career interest in geophysics; geology/earth sciences; physics or environmental science. Applicant must demonstrate high academic achievement.
Application requirements: Recommendations, essay, transcript. SAT or ACT scores for high school and undergraduate students, GRE or TOEFL scores for graduate students.
Additional information: Number of scholarships available yearly depends on the number of sponsors and the amount they contribute. Applicants must intend to pursue career in exploration geophysics (graduate students in operations, teaching, or research). Visit Website for more information.

Amount of award:	$1,000-$10,000
Application deadline:	June 15
Notification begins:	May 1

Contact:
SEG Foundation
Phone: 918-497-5500
Web: http://seg.org/scholarships

Society of Physics Students

Association of Women in Science Kirsten R. Lorentzen Award

Type of award: Scholarship.
Intended use: For sophomore or junior study in United States.
Eligibility: Applicant must be female. Applicant must be U.S. citizen or permanent resident.
Basis for selection: Major/career interest in physics.
Additional information: Applicants must be undergraduate members of the SPS national organization. The Kirsten R Lorentzen Award is an AWIS Educational Foundation program for female college sophomores and juniors studying physics, including space physics and geophysics, or geoscience. The award in the amount of $2,000 is given annually to an exceptionally well-rounded student who excels in her studies as well as outdoor activities, service, sports, music, or other non-academic pursuits or who has overcome significant obstacles.

Amount of award:	$5,000
Number of awards:	12
Number of applicants:	60
Application deadline:	February 1

Contact:
Society of Physics Students
1 Physics Ellipse
College Park, MD 20740
Phone: 301-209-3007
Web: https://www.spsnational.org/awards/scholarships

Aysen Tunca Memorial Scholarship

Type of award: Scholarship.
Intended use: For sophomore or junior study in United States.
Eligibility: Applicant must be female. Applicant must be U.S. citizen or permanent resident.
Basis for selection: Major/career interest in physics.
Additional information: Applicants must be female students in the sophomore or junior year of college who are majoring in a STEM field. Applicants must be undergraduate members of the SPS national organization. Preferably for a student with a disadvantaged economic background or someone who overcame significant obstacles in her life, or someone who is the first person in her family to go to college or major in a STEM field.

Amount of award:	$2,000
Number of awards:	12
Number of applicants:	60
Application deadline:	February 1

Contact:
Society of Physics Students
1 Physics Ellipse
College Park, MD 20740
Phone: 301-209-3007
Web: https://www.spsnational.org/awards/scholarships

Herbert Levy Memorial Scholarship

Type of award: Scholarship.
Intended use: For full-time junior or senior study at 4-year institution.
Eligibility: Applicant or parent must be member/participant of Society of Physics Students.
Basis for selection: Major/career interest in physics. Applicant must demonstrate financial need.
Application requirements: Recommendations, transcript. Statement of financial need. Completed W-9 Federal Tax Form.
Additional information: Applicants must be undergraduate members of the SPS national organization. Applicants must demonstrate financial need through a written statement. Students who expect to complete their bachelor's degree in physics in the spring or summer following the February 1 deadline are not eligible).

Amount of award:	$2,000
Number of awards:	12
Number of applicants:	60
Application deadline:	March 22

Contact:
Society of Physics Students
One Physics Ellipse
College Park, MD 20740
Phone: 301-209-3007
Fax: 301-209-0839
Web: https://www.spsnational.org/awards/scholarships

Peggy Dixon Two-Year Scholarship

Type of award: Scholarship.
Intended use: For full-time junior or senior study at 2-year or 4-year institution.

Eligibility: Applicant or parent must be member/participant of Society of Physics Students.
Basis for selection: Major/career interest in physics. Applicant must demonstrate high academic achievement.
Application requirements: Recommendations, transcript. Completed W-9 Federal Tax Form.
Additional information: Awarded to undergraduate students that have attended a two-year college, on the basis of scholarship and SPS participation. Intended for students transitioning from a two-year college into a physics bachelor's degree program.

Amount of award:	$2,000
Number of awards:	12
Number of applicants:	60
Application deadline:	March 22

Contact:
Society of Physics Students
One Physics Ellipse
College Park, MD 20740
Phone: 301-209-3007
Fax: 301-209-0839
Web: https://www.spsnational.org/awards/scholarships

Science Systems and Applications, Inc. (SSAI) Academic Scholarship

Type of award: Scholarship.
Intended use: For sophomore or junior study in United States.
Eligibility: Applicant must be U.S. citizen or permanent resident.
Basis for selection: Major/career interest in physics.
Additional information: For students interested in atmospheric sciences and related science. Applicants must be students in their sophomore or junior year of college who are majoring in physics or a related science. Applicants must be undergraduate members of the SPS national organization.

Amount of award:	$2,000
Number of awards:	12
Number of applicants:	60
Application deadline:	February 1

Contact:
Society of Physics Students
1 Physics Ellipse
College Park, MD 20740
Phone: 301-209-3007
Web: https://www.spsnational.org/awards/scholarships

Science Systems and Applications, Inc. (SSAI) Underrepresented Student Scholarship

Type of award: Scholarship.
Intended use: For sophomore or junior study in United States.
Eligibility: Applicant must be high school sophomore or junior. Applicant must be U.S. citizen or permanent resident.
Basis for selection: Major/career interest in physics.
Additional information: Applicants must be students in their sophomore or junior year of college who are majoring in physics or a related science. Applicants must be undergraduate members of the SPS national organization. Applicants must be from a group that is underrepresented in science and engineering. For students interested in atmospheric and related sciences.

Amount of award:	$5,000
Number of awards:	12
Number of applicants:	60
Application deadline:	February 1

Contact:
Society of Physics Students
1 Physics Ellipse
College Park, MD 20740
Phone: 301-209-3007
Web: https://www.spsnational.org/awards/scholarships

Society of Physics Students and Association of Physics Teachers Mary Beth Monroe Memorial Scholarship

Type of award: Scholarship.
Intended use: For junior study at 2-year institution.
Basis for selection: Major/career interest in physics or education.
Application requirements: Transcript.
Additional information: Applicants must be students in their junior year of college who are majoring in physics or physics education. Applicants must have started their education at a regionally accredited community college (this must be evident on their official transcripts). Applicants must demonstrate intent to pursue a career in education. Applicants must be undergraduate members of the SPS national organization.

Amount of award:	$5,000
Number of awards:	12
Number of applicants:	60
Application deadline:	February 1

Contact:
Society of Physics Students
1 Physics Ellipse
College Park, MD 20740
Phone: 301-209-3007
Web: https://www.spsnational.org/awards/scholarships

Society of Physics Students Award for Outstanding Undergraduate Research

Type of award: Scholarship.
Intended use: For undergraduate study.
Basis for selection: Major/career interest in physics.
Application requirements: Recommendations.
Additional information: Two or more awards may be made each year to individuals who meet the criteria. Winners receive a free trip to attend and present their research at the International Conference of Physics Students (ICPS), usually held in Europe; are encouraged to give a presentation in an SPS research session at a national physics meeting; and receive a $500 honorarium for themselves and a $500 honorarium for their SPS chapter. Awarded to undergraduates on the basis of their research, letters of recommendation, and SPS participation. Applicants must be members of the SPS national organization. Applicants must be undergraduate students at the time the application is due.

Amount of award:	$500
Number of awards:	2
Number of applicants:	60
Application deadline:	February 1

Contact:
Society of Physics Students
1 Physics Ellipse
College Park, MD 20740
Phone: 301-209-3007
Web: https://www.spsnational.org/awards/scholarships

Scholarships

Society of Physics Students Future Teacher Scholarship

Type of award: Scholarship.
Intended use: For full-time junior or senior study at 4-year institution.
Eligibility: Applicant or parent must be member/participant of Society of Physics Students.
Basis for selection: Major/career interest in physics or education.
Application requirements: Recommendations, transcript. Statement from SPS Advisor certifying participation in teacher education program. W-9 Federal Tax Form.
Additional information: Applicants must be undergraduate members of the SPS national organization. Applicants must be participating in a teacher education program. Students who expect to complete their bachelor's degree in physics in the spring or summer following the February 1 deadline are not eligible).The intern will support the Physics Teaching Resource Agents (PTRAs) as they develop and test activities associated with heliophysics topics in coordination with NASA-Goddard. Also, support eMentoring and online learning by assisting with pairings of mentors and mentees, program evaluation, arranging for a webinar series, and streamlining online resources. In addition, the intern will have the opportunity to develop documents and publications associated with the role of physics in the Next Generation Science Standards.

Amount of award:	$5,000
Number of awards:	12
Number of applicants:	60
Application deadline:	February 1

Contact:
Society of Physics Students
One Physics Ellipse
College Park, MD 20740
Phone: 301-209-3007
Fax: 301-209-0839
Web: https://www.spsnational.org/awards/scholarships

Society of Physics Students Leadership Scholarship

Type of award: Scholarship.
Intended use: For full-time junior or senior study at 2-year or 4-year institution.
Eligibility: Applicant or parent must be member/participant of Society of Physics Students.
Basis for selection: Major/career interest in physics. Applicant must demonstrate high academic achievement and seriousness of purpose.
Application requirements: Transcript. Letters of recommendation from at least two full-time faculty members.
Additional information: Awarded on the basis of academic performance and leadership in Society of Physics Students. Applicants must have junior level standing. The purpose of the Society of Physics Students scholarship program is to encourage the study of physics and the pursuit of high scholarship. Several awards may be made each year.

Amount of award:	$2,000-$5,000
Number of applicants:	60
Application deadline:	March 22

Contact:
Society of Physics Students
One Physics Ellipse
College Park, MD 20740
Phone: 301-209-3007
Fax: 301-209-0839
Web: https://www.spsnational.org/awards/scholarships

Society of Plastics Engineers

Extrusion Division/Lew Erwin Memorial Scholarship

Type of award: Scholarship.
Intended use: For full-time senior or master's study at 4-year or graduate institution.
Basis for selection: Major/career interest in chemistry; engineering; engineering, chemical; engineering, materials; engineering, mechanical or physics. Applicant must demonstrate financial need.
Application requirements: Research proposal. One- to two-page typed statement explaining reasons for application, qualifications, and educational/career goals in the plastics industry. Recommendation letter from faculty adviser associated with project.
Additional information: All applicants must be in good academic standing and have a demonstrated interest in the plastics industry. Applicants must be Ph.D. candidate or working on senior or MS research project in polymer extrusion that the scholarship will help support. The project must be described in writing, including background, objective, and proposed experiments. Recipient will be expected to furnish final research summary report. Visit Website for more information.

Amount of award:	$2,500
Number of awards:	1
Application deadline:	March 1
Total amount awarded:	$2,500

Contact:
Society of Plastics Engineers
13 Church Hill Road
Newtown, CT 06470
Phone: 203-740-5447
Fax: 203-775-8490
Web: www.4spe.org/spe-foundation

Fleming/Blaszcak Scholarship

Type of award: Scholarship.
Intended use: For full-time undergraduate or graduate study at 4-year or graduate institution.
Eligibility: Applicant must be Mexican American. Applicant must be U.S. citizen or permanent resident.
Basis for selection: Major/career interest in chemistry; engineering; engineering, chemical; engineering, materials; engineering, mechanical or physics. Applicant must demonstrate financial need.
Application requirements: Transcript. One- to two-page typed statement explaining reasons for application, qualifications, and educational/career goals in the plastics industry. Three recommendation letters: two from teachers or school officials and one from an employer or non-relative.

Additional information: All applicants must be in good standing and have a demonstrated interest in the plastics industry. Visit Website for more information.

Amount of award:	$2,000
Number of awards:	1
Application deadline:	March 30
Total amount awarded:	$2,000

Contact:
Society of Plastics Engineers
13 Church Hill Road
Newtown, CT 06470
Phone: 203-740-5447
Fax: 203-775-8490
Web: www.4spe.org/spe-foundation

Gulf Coast Hurricane Scholarships

Type of award: Scholarship.
Intended use: For full-time undergraduate or graduate study at 2-year, 4-year or graduate institution in United States. Designated institutions: Florida, Alabama, Mississippi, Louisiana, Texas institutions.
Eligibility: Applicant must be residing in Texas, Mississippi, Alabama, Louisiana or Florida.
Basis for selection: Major/career interest in chemistry; engineering; engineering, chemical; engineering, materials; engineering, materials or physics. Applicant must demonstrate financial need and high academic achievement.
Application requirements: Recommendations, essay, transcript, proof of eligibility. A listing of employment history, including description of work with plastics/polymers. A list of current and past school activities and community activities and honors.
Additional information: Applicants must have a demonstrated or expressed interest in the plastics industry. Applicants must be majoring in or taking courses that are beneficial to a career in the plastics/polymer industry. One four-year university scholarship of $6,000 (funds distributed on a yearly basis) and one two-year junior or technical institute scholarships of $2,000 (funds distributed on a yearly basis) are available. Applicants must be a resident of, and attending college in, a Gulf Coast State (Florida, Alabama, Mississippi, Louisiana, and Texas).

Amount of award:	$2,000-$6,000
Number of awards:	2
Application deadline:	March 30
Notification begins:	March 30

Contact:
Society of Plastics Engineers
13 Church Hill Road
Newtown, CT 06470
Phone: 203-740-5447
Fax: 203-775-8490
Web: www.4spe.org/spe-foundation

K. K. Wang Scholarship

Type of award: Scholarship.
Intended use: For full-time undergraduate or graduate study at 2-year, 4-year or graduate institution.
Basis for selection: Major/career interest in chemistry; engineering; engineering, chemical; engineering, materials; engineering, mechanical or physics. Applicant must demonstrate financial need and high academic achievement.
Application requirements: Recommendations, essay, transcript. A listing of employment history, including description of work in the plastics/polymers industry. A list of

current and past school activities, community activities, and honors.
Additional information: Applicants must have a demonstrated or expressed interest in the plastics industry, and must be majoring or taking courses that are beneficial to a career in the plastics/polymer industry. Applicants must have experience in injection molding and computer-aided engineering (CAE), such as courses taken, research conducted, or jobs held.

Amount of award:	$2,000
Number of awards:	1
Application deadline:	March 30
Notification begins:	March 30
Total amount awarded:	$2,000

Contact:
Society of Plastics Engineers
13 Church Hill Road
Newtown, CT 06470
Phone: 203-740-5447
Fax: 203-775-8490
Web: www.4spe.org/spe-foundation

Pittsburgh Scholarship

Type of award: Scholarship, renewable.
Intended use: For full-time undergraduate or graduate study at 2-year, 4-year or graduate institution.
Eligibility: Applicant must be residing in Pennsylvania.
Basis for selection: Major/career interest in chemistry; engineering, chemical; engineering, mechanical; physics or engineering, industrial. Applicant must demonstrate financial need.
Application requirements: Recommendations, essay, transcript, proof of eligibility. List of current and past school and community activities and honors. List of employment history with detailed description of any involvement in plastics/polymers.
Additional information: All applicants must be in good standing with their colleges and must have a demonstrated or expressed interest in the plastics industry. Plastics engineering and polymer science majors also eligible. Must have graduated from a high school in Pennsylvania.

Amount of award:	$2,000
Number of awards:	2
Application deadline:	March 30
Notification begins:	March 30
Total amount awarded:	$4,000

Contact:
Society of Plastics Engineers
13 Church Hill Road
Newtown, CT 06470
Phone: 203-740-5447
Fax: 203-775-8490
Web: www.4spe.org/spe-foundation

Plastics Pioneers Scholarships

Type of award: Scholarship, renewable.
Intended use: For full-time undergraduate study at 2-year or 4-year institution.
Eligibility: Applicant must be U.S. citizen.
Basis for selection: Major/career interest in chemistry; engineering, chemical; engineering, mechanical; physics or engineering, industrial. Applicant must demonstrate financial need.
Application requirements: Recommendations, essay, transcript. List of current and past school activities and community activities and honors. List of employment history

with detailed description of any involvement in plastics/polymers.

Additional information: All applicants must be in good standing with their colleges and must have a demonstrated or expressed interest in the plastics industry. Must be committed to becoming "hands-on" worker in the plastics industry as plastics technician or engineer. Plastics engineering and polymer science majors also eligible. Visit Website for more information.

Amount of award:	$3,000
Number of awards:	10
Application deadline:	March 30
Notification begins:	March 30
Total amount awarded:	$30,000

Contact:
Society of Plastics Engineers
13 Church Hill Road
Newtown, CT 06470
Phone: 203-740-5447
Fax: 203-775-8490
Web: www.4spe.org/spe-foundation

Society of Plastics Engineers General Scholarships

Type of award: Scholarship, renewable.
Intended use: For full-time undergraduate or graduate study at vocational, 2-year, 4-year or graduate institution.
Basis for selection: Major/career interest in chemistry; engineering; engineering, chemical; engineering, mechanical; engineering, materials or physics. Applicant must demonstrate financial need and seriousness of purpose.
Application requirements: Transcript. One- to two-page typed statement explaining reasons for application, qualifications, and educational/career goals in the plastics industry. Three recommendation letters: two from teachers or school officials and one from an employer or non-relative.
Additional information: All applicants must be in good standing with their colleges and must have a demonstrated interest in the plastics industry. Recipients must re-apply for renewal, for up to three additional years. Visit Website for more information.

Amount of award:	$1,000-$4,000
Application deadline:	March 30
Total amount awarded:	$107,500

Contact:
Society of Plastics Engineers
13 Church Hill Road
Newtown, CT 06470
Phone: 203-740-5447
Fax: 203-775-8490
Web: www.4spe.org/spe-foundation

The SPE Foundation Blow Molding Division Memorial Scholarships

Type of award: Scholarship.
Intended use: For junior study at 4-year institution.
Basis for selection: Major/career interest in engineering. Applicant must demonstrate financial need.
Application requirements: Recommendations, transcript. Essay on the importance of blow molding to the technical parts and packing industries.
Additional information: Applicants must be members of a Society of Plastics Engineers Student Chapter and be in second year of four-year undergraduate plastics engineering program. Award is $6,000, payable over two years.

Amount of award:	$6,000
Number of awards:	2
Application deadline:	March 30
Notification begins:	March 30
Total amount awarded:	$12,000

Contact:
Society of Plastics Engineers
13 Church Hill Road
Newtown, CT 06470
Phone: 203-740-5447
Fax: 203-775-8490
Web: www.4spe.org/spe-foundation

Thermoforming Division Memorial Scholarship

Type of award: Scholarship.
Intended use: For full-time undergraduate or graduate study at vocational, 2-year, 4-year or graduate institution.
Basis for selection: Major/career interest in chemistry; engineering; engineering, chemical; engineering, materials; engineering, mechanical or physics. Applicant must demonstrate financial need.
Application requirements: Transcript. One- to two-page typed statement explaining reasons for application, qualifications, and educational/career goals. Statement detailing exposure to the thermostat industry, including courses, research conducted, or jobs held. Three recommendation letters: two from teachers or school officials, and one from an employer or other non-relative.
Additional information: All applicants must be in good standing and have a demonstrated interest in the plastics industry. Visit Website for more information.

Amount of award:	$5,000
Number of awards:	2
Application deadline:	March 30
Total amount awarded:	$10,000

Contact:
Society of Plastics Engineers
13 Church Hill Road
Newtown, CT 06470
Phone: 203-740-5447
Fax: 203-775-8490
Web: www.4spe.org/spe-foundation

Thermoset Division/James I. MacKenzie Memorial Scholarship

Type of award: Scholarship.
Intended use: For full-time undergraduate or graduate study at vocational, 2-year or 4-year institution.
Basis for selection: Major/career interest in chemistry; engineering; engineering, chemical; engineering, materials; engineering, mechanical or physics. Applicant must demonstrate financial need.
Application requirements: Transcript. One- to two-page typed statement explaining reasons for application, qualifications, and educational/career goals. Statement detailing exposure to the thermoset industry. Three recommendation letters: two from teachers or school officials and one from an employer or non-relative.
Additional information: All applicants must be in good academic standing and have a demonstrated interest in the plastics industry. Must have experience in the thermoset industry, such as courses taken, research conducted, or jobs held. Visit Website for more information.

Amount of award: $2,500
Number of awards: 2
Application deadline: March 30
Total amount awarded: $5,000

Contact:
Society of Plastics Engineers
13 Church Hill Road
Newtown, CT 06470
Phone: 203-740-5447
Fax: 203-775-8490
Web: www.4spe.org/spe-foundation

Western Plastics Pioneers Scholarship

Type of award: Scholarship, renewable.
Intended use: For full-time undergraduate study at 2-year or 4-year institution. Designated institutions: Institutions in Arizona, California, Oregon, or Washington state.
Basis for selection: Major/career interest in chemistry; engineering, chemical; engineering, mechanical; physics or engineering, industrial. Applicant must demonstrate financial need.
Application requirements: Recommendations, essay, transcript. List of current and past school activities and community activities and honors. List of employment history with detailed description of any involvement in plastics/polymers.
Additional information: All applicants must be in good standing with their colleges and must have a demonstrated or expressed interest in the plastics industry. Plastics engineering and polymer science majors also eligible. Visit Website for more information.

Amount of award: $2,000
Number of awards: 1
Application deadline: March 30
Total amount awarded: $2,000

Contact:
Society of Plastics Engineers
13 Church Hill Road
Newtown, CT 06470
Phone: 203-740-5447
Fax: 203-775-8490
Web: www.4spe.org/spe-foundation

The Society of the Descendants of the Signers of the Declaration of Independence

The Society of the Descendants of the Signers of the Declaration of Independence Annual Scholarship

Type of award: Scholarship, renewable.
Intended use: For full-time undergraduate or graduate study at accredited vocational, 2-year, 4-year or graduate institution in or outside United States.
Basis for selection: Applicant must demonstrate high academic achievement, depth of character, leadership, patriotism, seriousness of purpose and service orientation.

Application requirements: Recommendations, essay, transcript, proof of eligibility. Resume.
Additional information: Applicant must be member of the Society of the Descendants of the Signers of the Declaration of Independence. Applicant must reapply for renewal. Number and amount of awards vary. See Website for application deadline and more information.

Number of applicants: 56
Application deadline: March 18
Notification begins: July 4
Total amount awarded: $200,000

Contact:
Descendants of the Signers of the Declaration of Independence
Web: www.dsdi1776.com

Society of Women Engineers

SWE Detroit Section Scholarship

Type of award: Scholarship.
Intended use: For freshman study at accredited 4-year institution.
Eligibility: Applicant must be female, high school senior. Applicant must be residing in Michigan.
Basis for selection: Major/career interest in engineering.
Application requirements: Essay, transcript. Include transcript with application. Essay is one page, single or double spaced, on the following topic: Tell us why you want to be an engineer and how this scholarship would help you.
Additional information: Application can be found online. Must be a female in her senior year of high school in Michigan. Must pursue an engineering degree at an ABET accredited engineering program.

Amount of award: $1,000-$3,000
Number of awards: 3
Number of applicants: 88
Application deadline: March 1
Notification begins: May 30
Total amount awarded: $7,000

Contact:
Society of Women Engineers, Detroit
PO Box 2978
Southfield, MI 48037
Web: www.swedetroit.org/outreach—scholarships.html

SWE Scholarships

Type of award: Scholarship.
Intended use: For full-time undergraduate or graduate study at accredited 4-year or graduate institution in United States.
Eligibility: Applicant or parent must be member/participant of Society of Women Engineers. Applicant must be female. Applicant must be U.S. citizen or permanent resident.
Basis for selection: Major/career interest in engineering or engineering, computer. Applicant must demonstrate high academic achievement.
Application requirements: Recommendations, essay, transcript, proof of eligibility.
Additional information: Must not be receiving full education funding from another organization. Applicants must be enrolled in ABET- or CSAB-accredited program or SWE-approved school. Preference given to computer-related engineering

Scholarships

majors. Visit www.abet.org for list of ABET-accredited schools. Visit Website for application. Award amount varies.

Amount of award:	$1,000-$10,000
Number of awards:	198
Application deadline:	February 15, May 15
Notification begins:	September 15
Total amount awarded:	$577,000

Contact:
Society of Women Engineers
130 East Randolph Street
Suit 3500
Chicago, IL 60601
Phone: 877-793-4636
Web: www.societyofwomenengineers.swe.org

Sodexo Stop Hunger Foundation

Stephen J. Brady Stop Hunger Scholarships

Type of award: Scholarship.
Intended use: For undergraduate, graduate, postgraduate or non-degree study at accredited postsecondary institution in United States.
Eligibility: Applicant must be U.S. citizen or permanent resident.
Basis for selection: Applicant must demonstrate service orientation.
Application requirements: Recommendations.
Additional information: Awards open to applicants who have performed unpaid, U.S. hunger-related volunteer services within the last 12 months. Open to students age 5-25 (kindergarten through graduate school). Added consideration for applicants fighting childhood hunger. Employees of Sodexo and previous recipients not eligible to apply, but previous regional Stop Hunger Honorees may apply. Award recipients will receive a $5,000 scholarship and a $5,000 grant to the local hunger-related charity of their choice. Visit Website for application and details.

Amount of award:	$5,000
Number of awards:	5
Number of applicants:	7,000
Application deadline:	December 5
Notification begins:	March 1
Total amount awarded:	$25,000

Contact:
Sodexo Stop Hunger Foundation
9801 Washingtonian Boulevard
Gaithersburg, MD 20878
Phone: 800-763-3946 ext.44848
Web: www.sodexofoundation.org/hunger_us/scholarships/scholarships.asp

Soil and Water Conservation Society

Donald A. Williams Soil Conservation Scholarship

Type of award: Scholarship.
Intended use: For undergraduate study at postsecondary institution.

Eligibility: Applicant or parent must be member/participant of Soil and Water Conservation Society.
Basis for selection: Major/career interest in natural resources/conservation. Applicant must demonstrate financial need, depth of character and seriousness of purpose.
Application requirements: Recommendations, essay.
Additional information: Applicant must have been member of Soil and Water Conservation Society for at least one year at time of application. Must demonstrate competence in line of work. Must have completed at least one year of full-time employment and be currently employed in a natural resource conservation endeavor. Number of awards varies. Visit Website for application and deadline.

Amount of award:	$1,000
Number of awards:	1
Application deadline:	February 29

Contact:
SWCS-Scholarship
945 SW Ankeny Road
Ankeny, IA 50023
Phone: 515-289-2331
Fax: 515-289-1227
Web: www.swcs.org

Melville H. Cohee Student Leader Conservation Scholarship

Type of award: Scholarship.
Intended use: For full-time junior, senior or graduate study at accredited 4-year or graduate institution.
Eligibility: Applicant or parent must be member/participant of Soil and Water Conservation Society.
Basis for selection: Major/career interest in natural resources/conservation.
Additional information: Must have been member of SWCS for at least 1 year. Family members of the Professional Development Committee not eligible. Visit Website for application and deadline.

Amount of award:	$500
Number of awards:	1
Application deadline:	February 29

Contact:
SWCS-Scholarship
945 SW Ankeny Road
Ankeny, IA 50023
Phone: 515-289-2331
Fax: 515-289-1227
Web: www.swcs.org

Sons of Italy Foundation

Henry Salvatori Scholarship

Type of award: Scholarship.
Intended use: For full-time undergraduate study.
Eligibility: Applicant must be high school senior. Applicant must be Italian. Applicant must be U.S. citizen.
Basis for selection: Applicant must demonstrate high academic achievement, depth of character, leadership, patriotism, seriousness of purpose and service orientation.
Application requirements: $30 application fee. Essay, transcript, proof of eligibility. SAT/ACT scores. Cover letter, resume. Two letters of recommendation from public figures

who have demonstrated the ideals of liberty, freedom, and equality in their work.

Additional information: Must have at least one Italian or Italian-American grandparent. Visit Website for application.

Amount of award:	$5,000
Number of awards:	1
Number of applicants:	200
Application deadline:	February 28
Notification begins:	April 15
Total amount awarded:	$5,000

Contact:
Sons of Italy Foundation
219 E Street NE
Washington, DC 20002
Phone: 202-547-2900
Web: www.osia.org

Sant'Anna Institute-Sorrento Lingue Scholarship

Type of award: Scholarship.
Intended use: For junior, senior or graduate study at accredited postsecondary institution outside United States.
Eligibility: Applicant must be Italian. Applicant must be U.S. citizen.
Basis for selection: Major/career interest in Italian.
Application requirements: $30 application fee. Recommendations, essay, transcript. Essay must be submitted in Italian. SAT/ACT scores. Resume, cover letter.
Additional information: Scholarship for study abroad in Sorrento, Italy from January to June. Must have at least one Italian or Italian-American grandparent. Basic knowledge of Italian language preferred. Visit Website for application and more information.

Application deadline:	February 28

Contact:
Sons of Italy Foundation
219 E Street NE
Washington, DC 20002
Phone: 202-547-2900
Web: www.osia.org

Sons of Italy General Scholarship

Type of award: Scholarship.
Intended use: For undergraduate or graduate study at accredited 4-year institution.
Eligibility: Applicant must be Italian. Applicant must be U.S. citizen.
Application requirements: $30 application fee. Recommendations, essay, transcript. Resume, cover letter. SAT/ACT scores.
Additional information: Must have at least one Italian or Italian-American grandparent. Visit Website for application.

Application deadline:	February 28

Contact:
Sons of Italy Foundation
219 E Street NE
Washington, DC 20002
Phone: 202-547-2900
Web: www.osia.org

Sons of Italy Italian Language Scholarship

Type of award: Scholarship.
Intended use: For junior or senior study.

Eligibility: Applicant must be Italian. Applicant must be U.S. citizen.
Basis for selection: Major/career interest in Italian.
Application requirements: $30 application fee. Recommendations, essay, transcript. Resume, cover letter. SAT/ACT scores. Essay must be in Italian.
Additional information: Must have at least one Italian or Italian-American grandparent. Visit Website for application.

Application deadline:	February 28

Contact:
Sons of Italy Foundation
219 E Street NE
Washington, DC 20002
Phone: 202-547-2900
Web: www.osia.org

Sons of Italy National Leadership Grant

Type of award: Scholarship.
Intended use: For full-time undergraduate, master's, doctoral or first professional study at accredited 4-year or graduate institution in United States.
Eligibility: Applicant must be Italian. Applicant must be U.S. citizen.
Basis for selection: Applicant must demonstrate high academic achievement, depth of character, leadership, seriousness of purpose and service orientation.
Application requirements: $30 application fee. Recommendations, essay, transcript, proof of eligibility. SAT/ACT scores, resume.
Additional information: Must have at least one Italian or Italian-American grandparent. Amount and number of awards vary. Visit Website for application.

Amount of award:	$4,000-$25,000
Number of awards:	12
Number of applicants:	600
Application deadline:	February 28
Notification begins:	April 15

Contact:
Sons of Italy Foundation
219 E Street NE
Washington, DC 20002
Phone: 202-547-2900
Fax: 202-546-8168
Web: www.osia.org

Sons of Norway Foundation

Astrid G. Cates Scholarship Fund and Myrtle Beinhauer Scholarship

Type of award: Scholarship.
Intended use: For undergraduate study at postsecondary institution.
Eligibility: Applicant or parent must be member/participant of Sons of Norway. Applicant must be U.S. citizen.
Basis for selection: Applicant must demonstrate financial need, high academic achievement, depth of character and service orientation.
Application requirements: Recommendations, essay, transcript, proof of eligibility. Headshot.
Additional information: Applicant, parent, or grandparent must be current member of Sons of Norway District 1-6.

Scholarships

Student must include the following information with application: GPA, what type of study is intended, where and when. Related fees must be specified, as well as long-term career goals, Sons of Norway involvement, extracurricular activities and financial need. The Cates Scholarship is $1,000; Beinhauer Scholarship awards $3,000 to the most qualified of all candidates. Student can be awarded maximum two scholarships within five-year period. Visit Website for application. Apply online.

Amount of award:	$1,000-$3,000
Number of awards:	8
Number of applicants:	99
Application deadline:	March 1
Notification begins:	May 1

Contact:
Sons of Norway Foundation
1455 West Lake Street
Minneapolis, MN 55408
Phone: 800-945-8851
Fax: 612-827-0658
Web: www.sonsofnorway.com/foundation

King Olav V Norwegian-American Heritage Fund

Type of award: Scholarship.
Intended use: For full-time undergraduate or graduate study at accredited postsecondary institution in United States.
Eligibility: Applicant or parent must be member/participant of Sons of Norway. Applicant must be at least 18.
Basis for selection: Major/career interest in Scandinavian studies/research. Applicant must demonstrate financial need, high academic achievement, depth of character, leadership and service orientation.
Application requirements: Recommendations, transcript, proof of eligibility. SAT or ACT scores. Essay of maximum 500 words about reasons for application; course of study to be pursued; length of the course; name, tuition, and other costs of institution; amount of financial assistance desired; and how the applicant's course of study will benefit his or her community and accord with the goals and objectives of the Sons of Norway Foundation, headshot.
Additional information: Open to Americans who have demonstrated keen and sincere interest in Norwegian heritage or Norwegians who have demonstrated interest in American heritage and have desire to further study heritage (arts, crafts, literature, history, music, folklore, etc.) at recognized educational institution. Number and amount of awards varies. Visit Website for application.

Amount of award:	$1,000-$1,500
Number of applicants:	100
Application deadline:	March 1
Notification begins:	May 1

Contact:
Sons of Norway Foundation
Phone: 800-945-8851
Web: www.sonsofnorway.com/foundation

Nancy Lorraine Jensen Memorial Scholarship

Type of award: Scholarship, renewable.
Intended use: For full-time undergraduate study.
Eligibility: Applicant or parent must be member/participant of Sons of Norway. Applicant must be female, at least 17, no older than 35. Applicant must be U.S. citizen.

Basis for selection: Major/career interest in chemistry; physics; engineering, electrical/electronic; engineering, mechanical or engineering, chemical. Applicant must demonstrate high academic achievement, depth of character and seriousness of purpose.
Application requirements: Recommendations, essay, transcript, proof of eligibility. SAT/ACT scores, headshot.
Additional information: Applicant or applicant's parent or grandparent must have been a member of Sons of Norway for at least three years. Must have completed at least one semester of undergraduate study in current program. Award is no less than 50 percent of one semester's tuition and no more than full tuition for one year. Minimum 1800 SAT (or at least 600 Math) or 26 ACT. Must apply each year. Visit Website for application. Apply online.

Number of awards:	6
Application deadline:	April 1

Contact:
Sons of Norway Foundation
1455 West Lake Street
Minneapolis, MN 55408
Phone: 800-945-8851
Fax: 612-827-0658
Web: www.sonsofnorway.com/foundation

Sons of the Republic of Texas

Texas History Essay Contest

Type of award: Scholarship.
Intended use: For freshman study at 4-year institution.
Eligibility: Applicant must be high school senior.
Basis for selection: Competition/talent/interest in research paper, based on depth of research in Texas history, originality of thought and expression, and organization.
Application requirements: Four photocopies of essay (total of 5 copies) including a CD copy with contestant's name, address, phone number and year of contest.
Additional information: Graduating seniors of any high school or home school may enter. Must follow Chicago Manual of Style or Turabian's Manual for Writers. Visit Website for yearly topic and more information.

Amount of award:	$1,000-$3,000
Number of awards:	3
Application deadline:	January 31
Total amount awarded:	$6,000

Contact:
Sons of the Republic of Texas
1717 8th Street
Bay City, TX 77414
Phone: 979-245-6644
Web: www.srttexas.org

South Asian American Association, Inc

SAAAI Scholarship

Type of award: Scholarship, renewable.
Intended use: For full-time undergraduate or graduate study at accredited vocational, 2-year or 4-year institution in United States.

Eligibility: Applicant must be U.S. citizen residing in New York or New Jersey.

Basis for selection: Major/career interest in engineering; architecture or surveying/mapping.

Application requirements: Transcript. Any letters of recommendation, if any, may be attached. Transcript of scholastic records, letter of acceptance, and statement as to goals in pursuing engineering, architecture, or land surveying required. A copy of household tax returns must be attached (household income cannot be over $85,000). Include a passport sized photo of yourself.

Additional information: Application can be found on the web site. Applicant need not be of Asian ancestry to apply for scholarship. Must be available to attend dinner in Queens held in October.

Amount of award:	$3,000-$5,000
Number of awards:	5
Application deadline:	October 10
Notification begins:	October 12
Total amount awarded:	$25,000

Contact:
SAAAI
40 Wall Street, 11th Floor
New York, NY 10005
Phone: 212-747-1997 ext. 519
Fax: 212-747-1947
Web: www.saaai.org/scholorship.htm

South Carolina Commission on Higher Education

Palmetto Fellows Scholarship Program

Type of award: Scholarship, renewable.

Intended use: For full-time undergraduate study at 4-year institution. Designated institutions: Eligible South Carolina institutions.

Eligibility: Applicant must be high school senior. Applicant must be U.S. citizen or permanent resident residing in South Carolina.

Basis for selection: Applicant must demonstrate high academic achievement.

Application requirements: Transcript. ACT/SAT scores. Must apply through guidance counselor.

Additional information: Minimum 1200 SAT (Math and Reading) or 27 ACT, 3.5 GPA on the SC Uniform Grading Policy, and rank in top six percent of class. Class ranking requirement waived for students with 1400 SAT (Math and Reading) or 32 ACT and 4.0 GPA. High school graduates or students who have completed home-school program as prescribed by law may be eligible. For more information, contact guidance counselor or S.C. Commission.

Amount of award:	$6,700-$7,500
Application deadline:	December 15, June 15
Notification begins:	February 15, August 15
Total amount awarded:	$44,035,892

Contact:
South Carolina Commission on Higher Education
1122 Lady Street, Suite 300
Columbia, SC 29201
Phone: 805-737-2262
Fax: 803-737-3610
Web: www.che.sc.gov

South Carolina Dayco Scholarship Program

Type of award: Scholarship, renewable.

Intended use: For full-time freshman study at 4-year institution in United States. Designated institutions: South Carolina institutions.

Eligibility: Applicant must be high school senior. Applicant must be U.S. citizen or permanent resident residing in South Carolina.

Basis for selection: Applicant must demonstrate financial need and high academic achievement.

Application requirements: Transcript, proof of eligibility. Need analysis, affidavit documenting that student has never been convicted of felonies or alcohol- or drug-related misdemeanor offenses.

Additional information: Must be either an employee or dependent of an employee of a branch of Dayco Products, Inc. in South Carolina. Employee must be employed by Dayco for at least four calendar years. In the event that there are no eligible dependents meeting above criteria, the award will be given to a resident of one of the counties of Walterboro, Williston, or Easley. Minimum 3.25 GPA. Must rank in top 20% of graduating high school class. Must have completed 12 credit hours at time of scholarship disbursement. Must not owe refund or repayment to a grant program or be under default on a loan. Must not have criminal record. Must reapply and meet eligibility requirements annually. Amount of award varies.

Contact:
South Carolina Commission on Higher Education
1122 Lady Street, Suite 300
Columbia, SC 29201
Phone: 803-737-8348
Fax: 803-737-3610
Web: www.che.sc.gov

South Carolina HOPE Scholarships

Type of award: Scholarship.

Intended use: For freshman study at 4-year institution. Designated institutions: Eligible South Carolina institutions.

Eligibility: Applicant must be U.S. citizen or permanent resident residing in South Carolina.

Basis for selection: Applicant must demonstrate high academic achievement.

Application requirements: Transcript, proof of eligibility.

Additional information: No application necessary. College or university will determine eligibility based on official high school transcript and will notify students directly. Minimum 3.0 cumulative GPA upon high school graduation. Student must certify that he/she has not been convicted of any felonies or any second drug/alcohol misdemeanors within past academic year. Contact institution's financial aid office for more information.

Amount of award:	$2,800
Number of awards:	2,724
Total amount awarded:	$7,037,260

Contact:
South Carolina Commission on Higher Education
1122 Lady Street, Suite 300
Columbia, SC 29201
Phone: 803-737-4397
Fax: 803-737-3610
Web: www.che.sc.gov

South Carolina LIFE Scholarship Program

Type of award: Scholarship, renewable.
Intended use: For full-time freshman study at vocational, 2-year or 4-year institution. Designated institutions: Eligible institutions in South Carolina.
Eligibility: Applicant must be U.S. citizen or permanent resident residing in South Carolina.
Basis for selection: Applicant must demonstrate high academic achievement.
Application requirements: Transcript. SAT/ACT scores.
Additional information: First-time entering freshmen at four-year institutions must meet two of three criteria: 3.0 high school GPA on Uniform Grading Policy (UGP); minimum 1100 SAT or 24 ACT; rank in top 30 percent of graduating class. First-time entering freshmen at two-year institution must have 3.0 high school GPA on UGP. Applicant must graduate from high school as South Carolina resident. No application required; college/university will determine eligibility based on transcript and will notify student directly. Maximum award $5,000 for four-year schools, average in-state tuition for two-year schools, and up to full in-state tuition at technical schools, not to exceed $5,000. Students in approved math and science programs could earn an additional $2,500.

Amount of award:	$5,000
Number of awards:	31,004
Total amount awarded:	$150,595,333

Contact:
South Carolina Commission on Higher Education
1122 Lady Street, Suite 300
Columbia, SC 29201
Phone: 803-737-4397
Fax: 803-737-3610
Web: www.che.sc.gov

South Carolina Lottery Tuition Assistance Program

Type of award: Scholarship, renewable.
Intended use: For undergraduate study at vocational or 2-year institution. Designated institutions: Eligible South Carolina institutions.
Eligibility: Applicant must be U.S. citizen or permanent resident residing in South Carolina.
Application requirements: FAFSA or FAFSA waiver.
Additional information: Award may not exceed cost of tuition. Award based on lottery revenue and number of applicants. Amount varies by semester. All federal grants and need-based grants must be awarded first before determining amount for which student is eligible. Student must be degree-seeking and enrolled in minimum six credit hours. Visit Website for more information.

Number of awards:	45,628
Number of applicants:	59,486
Total amount awarded:	$47,641,997

Contact:
South Carolina Commission on Higher Education
1122 Lady Street, Suite 300
Columbia, SC 29201
Phone: 803-737-2262
Fax: 803-737-3610
Web: www.che.sc.gov

South Carolina Need-Based Grants Program

Type of award: Scholarship.
Intended use: For undergraduate study at vocational, 2-year or 4-year institution. Designated institutions: Eligible South Carolina public institutions.
Eligibility: Applicant must be U.S. citizen or permanent resident residing in South Carolina.
Basis for selection: Applicant must demonstrate financial need.
Application requirements: FAFSA.
Additional information: May receive award for maximum eight full-time equivalent terms or until degree is earned, whichever is less. Must enroll in at least 12 credit hours per semester if full-time or six if part-time. Visit Website for more information.

Amount of award:	$1,250-$2,500
Number of awards:	28,051
Number of applicants:	28,507
Total amount awarded:	$26,989,583

Contact:
South Carolina Commission on Higher Education
1122 Lady Street, Suite 300
Columbia, SC 29201
Phone: 803-737-2262
Fax: 803-737-3610
Web: www.che.sc.gov

South Carolina Federal Credit Union

South Carolina Federal Credit Union Annual Competition

Type of award: Scholarship.
Intended use: For full-time undergraduate study at accredited 2-year or 4-year institution.
Eligibility: Applicant must be U.S. citizen.
Application requirements: Recommendations, essay, transcript. Member of South Carolina Federal Credit Union in good standing or U.S. residents who are eligible to apply for membership at South Carolina Federal at the time of scholarship application. Must include a letter of reccomendation from a teacher or counselor at your current school, a transcript from your current school, and a recent photo sample.
Additional information: Minimum 3.0 GPA. Essay is 500 words or less on how you have personally demonstrated the credit union's cooperative philosophy of People Helping People. Rewards are as follows: 1st place: $4,000 2nd place $2,500 3rd place $1,000. Complete the online application to be considered. View complete requirements on web site.

Amount of award: $1,000-$4,000
Number of awards: 3
Number of applicants: 160
Application deadline: March 14
Total amount awarded: $7,500
Contact:
South Carolina Federal Credit Union
PO Box 190012
N. Charleston, SC 29419
Phone: 843-797-8300
Fax: 843-797-3368
Web: smplsc.com/scholarship

South Carolina Higher Education Tuition Grants Commission

South Carolina Tuition Grants

Type of award: Scholarship, renewable.
Intended use: For full-time undergraduate study at accredited 2-year or 4-year institution in United States. Designated institutions: Participating South Carolina private, nonprofit institutions (visit Website for list).
Eligibility: Applicant must be U.S. citizen residing in South Carolina.
Basis for selection: Applicant must demonstrate financial need and high academic achievement.
Application requirements: FAFSA.
Additional information: Award amount varies. Recipient may reapply for up to four years. Incoming freshmen must score 900 SAT (Math and Reading) or 19 ACT, graduate in top three-fourths of high school class, or graduate from South Carolina high school with 2.0 GPA. Upperclassmen must complete 24 semester hours and meet college's satisfactory progress requirements. Application is automatic with FAFSA; submit to federal processor and list eligible college in college choice section. All eligible applicants funded if deadline is met. Contact campus financial aid office for details.
Amount of award: $2,500-$2,900
Number of awards: 14,200
Number of applicants: 27,206
Application deadline: June 30
Total amount awarded: $37,948,782
Contact:
South Carolina Higher Education Tuition Grants Commission
115 Atrium Way, Suite 102
Columbia, SC 29223-731
Phone: 803-896-1120
Fax: 803-896-1126
Web: www.sctuitiongrants.com

South Dakota Board of Regents

Dakota Corps Scholarship Program

Type of award: Scholarship.
Intended use: For freshman study at 4-year institution in United States. Designated institutions: Participating South Dakota institutions.

Eligibility: Applicant must be U.S. citizen or permanent resident.
Basis for selection: Applicant must demonstrate high academic achievement and service orientation.
Application requirements: Essay. Certification from high school counselor, principal, or other official.
Additional information: Must have graduated from accredited South Dakota high school with minimum 2.8 GPA. Minimum ACT score of 24 or SAT equivalent. Must agree in writing to stay in South Dakota and work in a critical need occupation after graduation for as many years as the scholarship was received plus one year. Must apply for Dakota Corps Scholarship for school period that begins within one year of high school graduation or within one year of release from active duty in armed forces.
Application deadline: February 1
Contact:
South Dakota Board of Regents
Attn: Dakota Corps Scholarship Program
306 East Capitol Ave., Suite 200
Pierre, SD 57501
Phone: 800-874-9033
Web: www.sdbor.edu

Jump Start Scholarship Program

Type of award: Scholarship.
Intended use: For freshman study at postsecondary institution in United States. Designated institutions: Participating South Dakota institutions.
Eligibility: Applicant must be U.S. citizen residing in South Dakota.
Additional information: Award is for South Dakota students who meet high school graduation requirements in three years. Must have attended public high school full-time for at least two years, and must attend postsecondary institution within one year of high school graduation. All students that meet criteria are awarded.
Amount of award: $1,866
Application deadline: September 1
Total amount awarded: $17,713
Contact:
South Dakota Board of Regents
Scholarship Committee
306 E. Capitol Ave., Suite 200
Pierre, SD 57501-2545
Phone: 605-773-3345
Web: www.sdbor.edu

South Dakota Annis I. Fowler/ Kaden Scholarship

Type of award: Scholarship.
Intended use: For freshman study at postsecondary institution. Designated institutions: University of South Dakota, Black Hills State University, Dakota State University, and Northern State University.
Eligibility: Applicant must be high school senior. Applicant must be U.S. citizen residing in South Dakota.
Basis for selection: Major/career interest in education, early childhood. Applicant must demonstrate high academic achievement, depth of character, leadership, seriousness of purpose and service orientation.
Application requirements: Recommendations, essay, transcript, proof of eligibility. ACT scores.
Additional information: Open to high school seniors who have a cumulative GPA of 3.0 after three years. Applicants must select elementary education as major field. Special

consideration given to applicants with demonstrated motivation or disability, or who are self-supporting. Transcript must include class rank, cumulative GPA, and list of courses to be taken during senior year. Deadline in late February.

Amount of award:	$1,000
Number of awards:	2
Number of applicants:	30
Notification begins:	April 15

Contact:
South Dakota Board of Regents
Scholarship Committee
306 E. Capitol Avenue, Suite 200
Pierre, SD 57501-3159
Phone: 605-773-3455
Web: www.sdbor.edu

South Dakota Ardell Bjugstad Scholarship

Type of award: Scholarship.
Intended use: For freshman study at postsecondary institution in United States.
Eligibility: Applicant must be American Indian. Must be member of federally recognized Indian tribe whose reservation is in North Dakota or South Dakota. Applicant must be high school senior. Applicant must be U.S. citizen residing in South Dakota or North Dakota.
Basis for selection: Major/career interest in agribusiness; agriculture; natural resources/conservation or environmental science. Applicant must demonstrate high academic achievement, depth of character, leadership and seriousness of purpose.
Application requirements: Recommendations, transcript. Verification of tribal enrollment.
Additional information: Transcript must include class rank and cumulative GPA.

Amount of award:	$500
Number of awards:	1
Number of applicants:	3
Notification begins:	April 15

Contact:
South Dakota Board of Regents
Scholarship Committee
306 E. Capitol Avenue, Suite 200
Pierre, SD 57501-3159
Phone: 605-773-3455
Web: www.sdbor.edu

South Dakota Marlin R. Scarborough Memorial Scholarship

Type of award: Scholarship.
Intended use: For full-time junior study at accredited 4-year institution in United States. Designated institutions: Public institutions in South Dakota.
Eligibility: Applicant must be residing in South Dakota.
Basis for selection: Applicant must demonstrate high academic achievement, depth of character, leadership, seriousness of purpose and service orientation.
Application requirements: Nomination by participating South Dakota public university. Essay explaining leadership and academic qualities, career plans, and educational interests.
Additional information: Students at all public universities in South Dakota eligible to apply. Applicants are to be of junior standing at public university in South Dakota when they receive funding. Submit application to school financial aid office. Minimum 3.5 GPA. Must have completed three full semesters at same university. Each South Dakota public university may nominate one student. Application deadlines vary by university; visit Website for dates and application.

Amount of award:	$1,500
Number of awards:	1
Notification begins:	April 15

Contact:
South Dakota Board of Regents
Scholarship Committee
306 East Capitol Avenue, Suit 200
Pierre, SD 57501-3159
Phone: 605-773-3455
Web: www.sdbor.edu

South Dakota Opportunity Scholarship Program

Type of award: Scholarship.
Intended use: For undergraduate study at accredited vocational, 2-year or 4-year institution in United States. Designated institutions: Augustana College, Colorado Technical University, Dakota Wesleyan University, Lake Area Technical Institute, Mitchell Technical Institute, Northern State University, South Dakota School of Mines & Technology, Southeast Technical Institute, University of Sioux Falls, Black Hills State University, Dakota State University, Kilian Community College, Mount Mary College, National American University, Presentation College, South Dakota State University, University of South Dakota, Western Dakota Technical Institute.
Eligibility: Applicant must be U.S. citizen or permanent resident residing in South Dakota.
Basis for selection: Applicant must demonstrate high academic achievement.
Application requirements: Transcript. SAT/ACT scores.
Additional information: Award is distributed bi-annually over four academic years. Minimum 1090 SAT (Verbal and Math) and 24 ACT. Minimum 3.0 GPA. See Website for specific high school curriculum requirements, which must be completed with no final grade below a 2.0. Completed applications must be submitted directly to the institution to which applicant is applying. Visit Website for detailed credit hour requirements.

Amount of award:	$6,500
Number of applicants:	3,975
Application deadline:	September 1, January 15
Total amount awarded:	$4,000,000

Contact:
South Dakota Board of Regents
c/o Dr. Paul D. Turman
306 E. Capitol Ave., Suite 200
Pierre, SD 57501-2545
Phone: 605-773-3455
Web: www.sdbor.edu

Southern Regional Education Board

Academic Common Market

Type of award: Scholarship.
Intended use: For undergraduate, master's, doctoral or first professional study at accredited 2-year, 4-year or graduate institution in United States. Designated institutions: Participating institutions in Alabama, Arkansas, Delaware,

Florida, Georgia, Kentucky, Louisiana, Maryland, Mississippi, Oklahoma, South Carolina, Tennessee, Texas, Virginia, West Virginia.

Eligibility: Applicant must be residing in Texas, Tennessee, Arkansas, Delaware, Maryland, Louisiana, Florida, South Carolina, Georgia, Virginia, Oklahoma, West Virginia, Mississippi, Alabama or Kentucky.

Application requirements: Proof of eligibility.

Additional information: The Academic Common Market is a tuition-savings program for college students in the SREB member states who want to pursue degrees that are not offered by their in-state institutions. The program is not competitive or merit-based, but applicants must meet state residency and college program requirements. Students must be accepted into their program of choice prior to certification. Florida and Texas participate at the graduate level only. For list of participating institutions and programs, and for individual state contact information, visit Website.

Contact:
Phone: 404-875-9211 ext. 217
Fax: 404-872-1477
Web: www.sreb.org/page/1304/academic_common_market.html

Southern Scholarship Foundation

Southern Scholarship Foundation Scholarships

Type of award: Scholarship, renewable.

Intended use: For undergraduate or graduate study in United States. Designated institutions: Florida State University, Florida A&M, University of Florida, Florida Gulf Coast University, Tallahassee Community College, Santa Fe College.

Basis for selection: Applicant must demonstrate financial need, high academic achievement, depth of character and service orientation.

Application requirements: Interview, recommendations, essay, transcript, proof of eligibility. Resume, FAFSA, SAR, recent color photograph.

Additional information: Number of awards varies. Minimum 3.0 GPA. Applicants encouraged to submit early in spring and fall semesters. Applications accepted year-round. Graduating high school students and students currently attending community college and universities are eligible to apply. Awards given in the form of housing at one of 27 Florida-based scholarship houses. The rent-free scholarship housing is equal to $12,000 per year. Awardees do not pay rent, but are responsible for basic household expenses. Each student contributes approximately $950/semester. Florida Gulf Coast University awards are for females only. Deadlines for applications are March 1, and October 31.

Number of awards:	100
Number of applicants:	1,000
Application deadline:	March 1, October 31

Contact:
Southern Scholarship Foundation
Admissions
322 Stadium Drive
Tallahassee, FL 32304
Phone: 850-222-3833
Fax: 850-222-6750
Web: www.southernscholarship.org

Southwestern Rugs Depot Scholarship

Southwestern Rugs Depot

Type of award: Scholarship.

Intended use: For undergraduate or graduate study at vocational, 2-year, 4-year or graduate institution.

Eligibility: Applicant must be at least 18.

Application requirements: Minimum 300 word essay on why decor matters.

Number of awards:	1
Application deadline:	January 2
Notification begins:	January 31
Total amount awarded:	$500

Contact:
Southwestern Rugs Depot
22773 Teppert Avenue
Eastpointe, MI 48021
Web: https://www.southwesternrugsdepot.com/scholarship

SpanishDict

SpanishDict Scholarship

Type of award: Scholarship.

Intended use: For undergraduate or graduate study at vocational, 2-year, 4-year or graduate institution in or outside United States or Canada.

Eligibility: Applicant must be at least 13. Applicant must be U.S. citizen, permanent resident or international student.

Application requirements: Short essay prompt in application.

Number of awards:	1
Application deadline:	August 31
Notification begins:	September 21
Total amount awarded:	$1,000

Contact:
SpanishDict
1400 Key Boulevard
Arlington, VA 22209
Phone: 305-505-4667
Web: www.spanishdict.com/traductor

SPIE - The International Society for Optical Engineering

SPIE Optics and Photonics Education Scholarships

Type of award: Scholarship, renewable.

Intended use: For undergraduate, graduate or non-degree study at accredited postsecondary institution in or outside United States.

Basis for selection: Major/career interest in engineering or physics. Applicant must demonstrate seriousness of purpose.

Application requirements: Recommendations, essay.

Scholarships

Additional information: Open only to SPIE student members; nonmembers may submit SPIE student membership application and dues with scholarship application. High school and pre-university students may receive one-year complimentary membership. Applicant must be enrolled in optics, photonics, imaging, optoelectronics, or related program at accredited institution for year in which award will be used (unless high school student). Award amount and number of awards varies. Students must reapply for renewal. Visit Website for application and deadline.

Amount of award:	$2,000-$11,000
Number of applicants:	360
Application deadline:	February 15
Notification begins:	May 1

Contact:
SPIE Scholarship Committee
PO Box 10
Phone: 360-676-3290
Fax: 360-647-1445
Web: www.spie.org/scholarships

SpinLife.com

SpinLife.com Innovation in Motion Scholarship Program

Type of award: Scholarship.
Intended use: For undergraduate study at accredited 4-year institution.
Eligibility: Applicant must be physically challenged. Applicant must be at least 17. Applicant must be U.S. citizen or permanent resident.
Additional information: Minimum 3.0 GPA. For users of a manual or power wheelchair. Visit website for application and full details.

Amount of award:	$500-$1,000
Number of awards:	2
Application deadline:	June 30
Notification begins:	July 31
Total amount awarded:	$2,000

Contact:
SpinLife
330 West Spring Street
Suite 303
Columbus, OH 43215
Phone: 614-564-1400
Web: www.spinlife.com/scholarship/

Spokane CyberKnife

Science and Medicine Scholarship

Type of award: Scholarship.
Intended use: For undergraduate study at vocational, 2-year, 4-year or graduate institution.
Eligibility: Applicant must be high school senior.
Application requirements: Essay. Essay: "How will you use your education to create a stronger local economy?"
Additional information: Minimum 3.0 GPA. Application on web site.

Number of awards:	1
Application deadline:	June 15
Total amount awarded:	$500

Contact:
Web: http://spokanecyberknife.com/spokane-cyberknife-scholarship

Stadium Managers Association

Stadium Managers Association Foundation Scholarship

Type of award: Scholarship, renewable.
Intended use: For full-time junior, senior or graduate study at 4-year institution.
Application requirements: Recommendations, transcript. Writing samples. Career and/or college major interests must be Sports/Facilities Management. Materials needed with the application include; Current transcript, letters of reference, writing sample, resume, completion of application form.
Additional information: Scholarship is intended for students who have expressed a strong interest in attending graduate school to prepare for a career in Stadium Management or related fields. Visit web site for more details.

Amount of award:	$3,000
Number of awards:	2
Number of applicants:	20
Application deadline:	April 15
Notification begins:	May 15
Total amount awarded:	$6,000

Contact:
Stadium Managers Association
7960 E Kiowa Circle
Mesa, AZ 85209
Phone: 480-358-1791
Fax: 480-358-1866
Web: www.stadiummanagers.org

Staples

Staples Associates Annual Scholarships Plan

Type of award: Scholarship, renewable.
Intended use: For undergraduate, graduate or non-degree study at vocational, 2-year, 4-year or graduate institution.
Application requirements: Proof of eligibility.
Additional information: Applicants must have worked at Staples for 90 days, averaging at least 18 hours per week. Contact Human Resources for complete details and application. Number of awards granted depends on funding.

Amount of award:	$750-$2,000
Number of applicants:	3,000
Application deadline:	September 30
Notification begins:	November 15
Total amount awarded:	$2,500,000

Contact:
Staples
500 Staples Drive
Framingham, MA 01702
Phone: 888-490-4747

Starbucks

Starbucks College Achievement Plan

Type of award: Scholarship, renewable.
Intended use: For undergraduate study. Designated institutions: Arizona State University.
Eligibility: Applicant must be at least 16.
Additional information: Must be employed by Starbucks and be benefits eligible. Award is for full tuition coverage for each term in order to earn a bachelor's degree. Must be admitted to Arizona State University through their normal application process.
Contact:
Web: www.starbucks.com/collegeplan

State Council of Higher Education for Virginia

Virginia Academic Common Market

Type of award: Scholarship.
Intended use: For at 4-year or graduate institution. Designated institutions: Participating public institutions in 15 southeastern states.
Eligibility: Applicant must be U.S. citizen or permanent resident residing in Virginia.
Application requirements: Institution acceptance letter, verification documents.
Additional information: Awards Virginia residents in-state tuition at participating out-of-state institutions in the South. Institution must offer program unavailable at Virginia public institutions, view list on provided website. Applicant must be domiciled in Virginia. Deadlines vary by institution. Additional information and program application available on Website.
Contact:
State Council of Higher Education for Virginia
Academic Common Market
101 N. 14th Street, 10th Fl. Monroe Bldg.
Richmond, VA 23219
Phone: 804-225-2600
Fax: 804-225-2604
Web: http://www.schev.edu/index/tuition-aid/academic-common-market

Virginia Tuition Assistance Grant

Type of award: Scholarship, renewable.
Intended use: For full-time undergraduate study at accredited 4-year or graduate institution. Designated institutions: Participating private nonprofit institutions in Virginia.
Eligibility: Applicant must be residing in Virginia.
Additional information: Must be in eligible degree program in participating Virginia private college. Graduate students

must be enrolled in health-related major. Applicant must be domiciled in Virginia. Theology and divinity majors not eligible. Maximum award is $3,100 for undergraduates. Awards depend on available funding. If funding is insufficient, priority given first to renewals, then to new applicants who apply prior to deadline. Interested students should contact financial aid office of qualifying postsecondary institution. School must be accredited by SACS. For more information about the scholarship visit link http://www.schev.edu/index/tuition-aid/financialaid/state-student-aid/tuition-assistance-grant-program.

Amount of award:	$3,300
Application deadline:	July 31
Total amount awarded:	$68,000,000

Contact:
Contact representative at participating private institutions.
Web: www.schev.edu

State of Alabama

Alabama Scholarship for Dependents of Blind Parents

Type of award: Scholarship, renewable.
Intended use: For undergraduate study at vocational, 2-year or 4-year institution. Designated institutions: Alabama public institutions.
Eligibility: Parent must be visually impaired. Applicant must be U.S. citizen or permanent resident residing in Alabama.
Basis for selection: Applicant must demonstrate financial need.
Application requirements: Proof of eligibility.
Additional information: Award waives instructional fees and tuition costs and pays for portion of books. Parent must be head of household and legally blind, and family income must be at or below 1.3 times the federal poverty guidelines. Applicant must have been Alabama resident for five years prior to application. Must reapply for renewal. Award available for all eligible applicants.

Amount of award:	Full tuition
Application deadline:	June 30, September 30

Contact:
Alabama Department of Rehabilitation Services
Attn: Debra Culver
31 Arnold Street
Talladega, AL 35160
Phone: 256-362-0638

State Student Assistance Commission of Indiana

Frank O'Bannon Grant

Type of award: Scholarship, renewable.
Intended use: For full-time undergraduate study at 2-year or 4-year institution. Designated institutions: Eligible Indiana schools.
Eligibility: Applicant must be U.S. citizen or permanent resident residing in Indiana.

Basis for selection: Applicant must demonstrate financial need.
Application requirements: FAFSA.
Additional information: Submitting FAFSA automatically fulfills application requirement. All eligible students offered an award. Amount of award varies. Visit Website for list of eligible schools.

Number of awards:	50,000
Number of applicants:	54,554
Application deadline:	March 10
Notification begins:	July 1
Total amount awarded:	$196,838,902

Contact:
State Student Assistance Commission of Indiana
W462 Indiana Government Center South
402 West Washington Street
Indianapolis, IN 46204
Phone: 888-528-4719
Web: www.in.gov/sfa

Indiana Minority Teacher & Special Education Services Scholarship

Type of award: Scholarship, renewable.
Intended use: For full-time undergraduate or graduate study at accredited 4-year or graduate institution.
Eligibility: Applicant must be African American, Mexican American, Hispanic American or Puerto Rican. Applicant must be U.S. citizen or permanent resident residing in Indiana.
Basis for selection: Applicant must demonstrate financial need and high academic achievement.
Application requirements: Proof of eligibility. FAFSA.
Additional information: Minimum 2.0 GPA. Applicant must be black or Hispanic. Graduate students must be seeking a teaching certificate. Number of awards varies. Application deadline established by school. Schools responsible for selecting and notifying eligible applicants. Applications available online. Contact college financial aid office for more information.

Amount of award:	$1,000-$4,000
Number of applicants:	214
Total amount awarded:	$240,000

Contact:
State Student Assistance Commission of Indiana
101 West Ohio Street
Suite 300
Indianapolis, IN 46204
Phone: 888-528-4719
Web: www.in.gov/sfa

Indiana National Guard Supplemental Grant

Type of award: Scholarship, renewable.
Intended use: For undergraduate study at 2-year or 4-year institution. Designated institutions: Indiana state-funded colleges and universities.
Eligibility: Applicant must be residing in Indiana. Applicant must be member of Indiana Air and Army National Guard. Applicant must be in active drilling status and be certified by Indiana National Guard (ING).
Application requirements: FAFSA.
Additional information: Room, board, and textbooks not covered. Contact unit commander with eligibility and certification questions.

Amount of award:	Full tuition
Number of applicants:	726
Application deadline:	March 10
Notification begins:	September 1
Total amount awarded:	$2,509,489

Contact:
State Student Assistance Commission of Indiana
W462 Indiana Government Center
402 West Washington Street
Indianapolis, IN 46204
Phone: 888-528-4719
Web: www.in.gov/sfa

Indiana Twenty-First Century Scholars Program

Type of award: Scholarship.
Intended use: For full-time undergraduate study at accredited 2-year or 4-year institution. Designated institutions: Participating Indiana schools.
Eligibility: Applicant must be high school senior. Applicant must be U.S. citizen or permanent resident residing in Indiana.
Basis for selection: Applicant must demonstrate financial need and high academic achievement.
Application requirements: FAFSA.
Additional information: Minimum 2.0 high school GPA. Must enroll in 7th or 8th grade by taking pledge to remain drug, alcohol, and crime free. Must file affirmation that pledge was fulfilled in high school senior year. Full tuition waiver after other financial aid applied. Must meet income eligibility requirements. Number and amount of awards varies. Visit Website for details.

Number of awards:	9,875
Number of applicants:	9,875
Notification begins:	July 1
Total amount awarded:	$22,787,104

Contact:
State Student Assistance Commission of Indiana
Web: www.in.gov/21stcenturyscholars

The Mitch Daniels Early Graduation Scholarship

Type of award: Scholarship.
Intended use: For freshman study at 4-year institution in United States. Designated institutions: SSACI-eligible Indiana colleges.
Eligibility: Applicant must be U.S. citizen residing in Indiana.
Application requirements: FAFSA. Application must be signed by principal or superintendent.
Additional information: Must graduate one year early from a publicly supported high school, after December 31, 2010. Must have attended publicly supported high school full-time for at least the last two semesters before graduating. See Website for additional criteria.

Amount of award:	$4,000

Contact:
State Student Assistance Commission of Indiana
Attn: Mitch Daniels Early Graduation
402 W. Washington Street W462
Indianapolis, IN 46204
Web: www.in.gov/sfa

Staver Law Group

Staver Law Group National Scholarship

Type of award: Scholarship.

Intended use: For undergraduate study at accredited 4-year or graduate institution in United States.

Eligibility: Applicant must be U.S. citizen or permanent resident.

Application requirements: Essay, transcript. Essay question and application can be found online.

Additional information: Must have a minimum GPA of 3.0.

Number of awards:	1
Number of applicants:	100
Application deadline:	December 1
Notification begins:	December 31
Total amount awarded:	$5,000

Contact:
Staver Law Group, P.C.
120 West Madison Street
Suite 520
Chicago, IL 60602-4302
Phone: 312-236-2900
Web: www.chicagolawyer.com/staver-law-group-personal-injury-scholarship/

STDcheck.com

HIV-Positive Scholarship

Type of award: Scholarship.

Intended use: For full-time undergraduate or graduate study at 2-year, 4-year or graduate institution.

Eligibility: Applicant must be U.S. citizen.

Application requirements: Essay, transcript. Applicants must be HIV-positive and submit their 400 word minimum essay answering the prompt: "How the applicant contracted HIV, how it has affected the applicant's life, and what they wish those living without HIV knew about living with the virus." Applicants must be HIV-positive and willing to submit to a free-of-charge STDcheck.com HIV test as proof of HIV-positive status.

Amount of award:	$250-$5,000

Contact:
STDcheck.com
5821 Southwest Freeway
Suite 600
Houston, TX 77057
Phone: 832-251-7221
Web: https://www.stdcheck.com/scholarship-application.php

Stephen T. Marchello Scholarship Foundation

Legacy of Hope

Type of award: Scholarship.

Intended use: For undergraduate study at accredited vocational, 2-year or 4-year institution in United States.

Eligibility: Applicant must be high school senior. Applicant must be U.S. citizen residing in Montana or Colorado.

Application requirements: Interview, recommendations, essay, transcript, proof of eligibility. SAT/ACT scores (when available).

Additional information: Some awards renewable depending on fund availability; all others are one-time grants. Applicant must be survivor of childhood cancer. Visit Website for more information. Application available online. Number and amount of awards vary.

Amount of award:	$400-$1,500
Number of awards:	6
Number of applicants:	20
Application deadline:	March 15
Total amount awarded:	$9,500

Contact:
Stephen T. Marchello Scholarship Foundation
1170 East Long Place
Centennial, CO 80122
Phone: 303-886-5018
Web: www.stmfoundation.org

Strom And Associates Attorneys at Law

Strom And Associates Need-Based Scholarship

Type of award: Scholarship.

Intended use: For full-time undergraduate study at accredited 2-year or 4-year institution in United States.

Eligibility: Applicant must be U.S. citizen or permanent resident.

Basis for selection: Major/career interest in law. Applicant must demonstrate financial need.

Application requirements: Submit PSA video focusing on the following topic: "What does it take to be a good American?"

Amount of award:	$1,500
Number of awards:	1
Application deadline:	June 1
Notification begins:	September 1
Total amount awarded:	$1,500

Contact:
Strom And Associates Attorneys at Law
620B Academy Drive
Northbrook, IL 60062
Phone: 847-940-4000
Web: http://stromlawyers.com/strom-associates-need-based-scholarship/

Student Veterans of America

Accenture Student Veterans Scholarship

Type of award: Scholarship.

Intended use: For full-time sophomore, junior, senior or graduate study at accredited 4-year institution in United States.

Eligibility: Applicant must be veteran.
Basis for selection: Applicant must demonstrate leadership, seriousness of purpose and service orientation.
Application requirements: Essay, transcript, proof of eligibility. Two essays, online application, resume or CV, unofficial transcript, DD 214 or Certificate of Discharge.
Additional information: Applicant must be a veteran who has received an honorable discharge or is in good standing with his/her branch of service.

Amount of award:	$10,000
Number of awards:	4
Application deadline:	April 4

Contact:
Student Veterans of America
1012 14th Street NW
Suite 1200
Washington, DC 20005
Phone: 202-223-4710
Web: www.studentveterans.org/index.php/programs/scholarships?layout=edit&id=494

Raytheon Patriot Scholarship

Type of award: Scholarship.
Intended use: For full-time sophomore, junior, senior or graduate study at accredited 4-year institution in United States.
Eligibility: Applicant must be veteran who served in the Army.
Basis for selection: Applicant must demonstrate leadership, seriousness of purpose and service orientation.
Application requirements: Recommendations, essay, transcript, proof of eligibility. Three essays, online application, one letter of reference, resume or CV, unofficial transcript, DD 214 or Certificate of Discharge.
Additional information: Applicant must be a US Army veteran who has received an honorable discharge or is in good standing with his/her branch of service.

Amount of award:	$10,000
Number of awards:	2
Application deadline:	April 4

Contact:
Student Veterans of America
1012 14th Street NW
Suite 1200
Washington, DC 20005
Phone: 202-223-4710
Web: www.studentveterans.org/index.php/programs/scholarships?layout=edit&id=127

Raytheon SVA Scholarship

Type of award: Scholarship.
Intended use: For full-time sophomore, junior, senior or graduate study at accredited 4-year institution in United States.
Eligibility: Applicant must be veteran.
Basis for selection: Major/career interest in engineering, computer; engineering, electrical/electronic; aerospace or engineering, mechanical. Applicant must demonstrate leadership, seriousness of purpose and service orientation.
Application requirements: Recommendations, essay, transcript, proof of eligibility. Two essays, online application, one letter of reference, resume or CV, unofficial transcript, DD 214 or Certificate of Discharge.
Additional information: Applicant must be a veteran who has received an honorable discharge or is in good standing with his/her branch of service. Must be pursuing an engineering degree or a degree in a closely-related field (Software Engineering/Computer Science/IT; Computer Engineering;

Cyber Security/Network Security; Electrical Engineering; Systems Engineering; Aerospace Engineering; Mechanical Engineering).

Amount of award:	$10,000
Number of awards:	5
Application deadline:	April 4

Contact:
Student Veterans of America
1012 14th Street NW
Suite 1200
Washington, DC 20005
Phone: 202-223-4710
Web: www.studentveterans.org/index.php/programs/scholarships?layout=edit&id=16

Students of History

Students of History Scholarship

Type of award: Scholarship.
Intended use: For undergraduate study at accredited vocational, 2-year or 4-year institution.
Eligibility: Applicant must be high school senior.
Additional information: Must have completed at least three social studies or history classes in high school. Must have a recommendation of a social studies/history teacher.

Amount of award:	$1,000
Number of awards:	1
Application deadline:	May 1
Notification begins:	June 1
Total amount awarded:	$1,000

Contact:
Students of History
PO Box 4644
Broadlands, VA 20148
Web: https://studentsofhistory.org/scholarship/

Studio Art Centers International

Anna K. Meredith Fund Scholarship

Type of award: Scholarship.
Intended use: For undergraduate study in Florence, Italy. Designated institutions: Studio Art Centers International (SACI).
Basis for selection: Competition/talent/interest in study abroad. Major/career interest in arts, general or art/art history. Applicant must demonstrate financial need and high academic achievement.
Application requirements: Portfolio. SAR/FAFSA.
Additional information: Must demonstrate artistic talent. Must be accepted to study with Studio Art Centers International. Number of awards varies depending on budget.

Amount of award:	$2,000
Application deadline:	March 15, October 15
Notification begins:	April 15, November 15

Contact:
Studio Art Centers International
50 Broad Street
Suite 1617
New York, NY 10004-2372
Phone: 212-248-7225
Web: www.saci-florence.org

Clare Brett Smith Scholarship

Type of award: Scholarship.
Intended use: For undergraduate or graduate study in Florence, Italy. Designated institutions: Studio Art Centers International (SACI).
Basis for selection: Competition/talent/interest in study abroad. Major/career interest in arts, general. Applicant must demonstrate financial need.
Application requirements: Portfolio. SAR/FAFSA.
Additional information: Must be accepted to study with Studio Art Centers International. Applicant must be studying photography.

Amount of award:	$1,000
Number of awards:	2
Application deadline:	March 15, October 15
Notification begins:	April 15, November 15

Contact:
Studio Art Centers International
50 Broad Street
Suite 1617
New York, NY 10004-2372
Phone: 212-248-7225
Web: www.saci-florence.org

Florence Travel Stipend

Type of award: Scholarship.
Intended use: For undergraduate study. Designated institutions: Studio Art Centers International (SACI) institutions.
Basis for selection: Major/career interest in arts, general or art/art history.
Application requirements: $60 application fee. Portfolio. FAFSA.
Additional information: Award is two free roundtrip tickets to SACI Florence, Italy. Must be attending SACI in the spring term. Valid only on SACI's spring term group flight from New York.

Number of awards:	2
Application deadline:	October 15

Contact:
Studio Art Centers International
50 Broad Street
Suite 1617
New York, NY 10004-2372
Phone: 212-248-7225
Web: www.saci-florence.org

The Gillian Award

Type of award: Scholarship.
Intended use: For undergraduate study. Designated institutions: Studio Art Centers International (SACI).
Eligibility: Applicant must be female.
Basis for selection: Major/career interest in arts, general.
Application requirements: $60 application fee. Portfolio. FAFSA.
Additional information: Award is open to a female artist with demonstrated artistic achievement who will be attending in

both fall and spring terms. Award offers opportunity for aspiring fine artist to live and work in Florence, utilizing all the resources of SACI.

Amount of award:	$3,000
Number of awards:	1
Application deadline:	March 15, October 15

Contact:
Studio Art Centers International
50 Broad Street
Suite 1617
New York, NY 10004-2372
Phone: 212-248-7225
Web: www.saci-florence.org

International Incentive Awards

Type of award: Scholarship.
Intended use: For junior or senior study in Florence, Italy. Designated institutions: Studio Art Centers International (SACI).
Basis for selection: Competition/talent/interest in study abroad. Major/career interest in arts, general or art/art history. Applicant must demonstrate financial need and high academic achievement.
Application requirements: Portfolio. SAR/FAFSA.
Additional information: Must be accepted to study with Studio Art Centers International. Minimum 3.0 GPA. Special efforts made to encourage applications from minorities and underrepresented groups. Number of awards varies depending on budget.

Amount of award:	$1,500
Application deadline:	March 15, October 15
Notification begins:	April 15, November 15

Contact:
Studio Art Centers International
50 Broad Street
Suite 1617
New York, NY 10004-2372
Phone: 212-248-7225
Web: www.saci-florence.org

Jules Maidoff Scholarship

Type of award: Scholarship.
Intended use: For undergraduate or graduate study in Florence, Italy. Designated institutions: Studio Art Centers International (SACI).
Basis for selection: Competition/talent/interest in study abroad. Major/career interest in arts, general or art/art history. Applicant must demonstrate financial need.
Application requirements: Portfolio. FAFSA/SAR.
Additional information: Must be accepted to study with Studio Art Centers International. Awarded to students exhibiting both exceptional artistic talent and financial need. Number of awards varies depending on budget.

Amount of award:	$2,500
Application deadline:	March 15, October 15
Notification begins:	April 15, November 15

Contact:
Studio Art Centers International
50 Broad Street
Suite 1617
New York, NY 10004-2372
Phone: 212-248-7225
Web: www.saci-florence.org

Lele Cassin Scholarship

Type of award: Scholarship.
Intended use: For undergraduate or graduate study in Florence, Italy. Designated institutions: Studio Art Centers International (SACI).
Basis for selection: Competition/talent/interest in study abroad. Major/career interest in film/video. Applicant must demonstrate financial need.
Application requirements: Video (no longer than 15 minutes) of own work. SAR/FAFSA.
Additional information: Must be accepted to study with Studio Art Centers International. Number of awards offered varies yearly according to budget.

Amount of award:	$1,000
Application deadline:	March 15, October 15
Notification begins:	April 15, November 15

Contact:
Studio Art Centers International
50 Broad Street
Suite 1617
New York, NY 10004-2372
Phone: 212-248-7225
Web: www.saci-florence.org

SACI Alumni Heritage Scholarship

Type of award: Scholarship.
Intended use: For undergraduate or graduate study at postsecondary institution in Florence, Italy. Designated institutions: Studio Art Centers International (SACI).
Basis for selection: Major/career interest in arts, general or art/art history. Applicant must demonstrate financial need and high academic achievement.
Application requirements: Portfolio. FAFSA/SAR. Statement indicating the name of parent who attended SACI and dates of attendance.
Additional information: Must be accepted to study with Studio Art Centers International and have a parent who attended SACI. Applicants for late spring or summer terms must submit materials by the admissions deadline of the term they wish to enroll. Number of awards varies depending on budget.

Amount of award:	$1,500
Application deadline:	March 15, October 15
Notification begins:	April 15, November 15

Contact:
Studio Art Centers International
50 Broad Street
Suite 1617
New York, NY 10004-2372
Phone: 212-248-7225
Web: www.saci-florence.com

SACI Consortium Scholarship

Type of award: Scholarship.
Intended use: For undergraduate or graduate study in Florence, Italy. Designated institutions: Studio Art Centers International (SACI) consortium institutions.
Basis for selection: Competition/talent/interest in study abroad. Major/career interest in arts, general or art/art history. Applicant must demonstrate financial need.
Application requirements: Portfolio, nomination by SACI consortium school. FAFSA/SAR.
Additional information: Must be accepted to study with Studio Art Centers International. Each consortium school may submit one nominee. Award for one semester; one award

available per semester. See Website for list of eligible institutions.

Amount of award:	Full tuition
Number of awards:	2
Application deadline:	March 15, October 15
Notification begins:	April 15, November 15

Contact:
Studio Art Centers International
50 Broad Street
Suite 1617
New York, NY 10004-2372
Phone: 212-248-7225
Web: www.saci-florence.org

StyleWe

StyleWe Scholarship

Type of award: Scholarship.
Intended use: For full-time undergraduate or graduate study at vocational, 2-year, 4-year or graduate institution.
Eligibility: Applicant must be high school senior.
Basis for selection: Applicant must demonstrate leadership and service orientation.
Additional information: Must have a minimum 3.0 GPA. Must have demonstrated creative abilities or leadership abilities through participation in community service, extracurricular, or other activities.

Amount of award:	$500
Number of awards:	2
Application deadline:	December 31
Notification begins:	January 31
Total amount awarded:	$1,000

Contact:
Web: www.stylewe.com/scholarship

Sunkist Growers

A.W. Bodine Sunkist Memorial Scholarship

Type of award: Scholarship, renewable.
Intended use: For full-time undergraduate study at accredited 2-year or 4-year institution.
Basis for selection: Applicant must demonstrate financial need, high academic achievement, depth of character, leadership, seriousness of purpose and service orientation.
Application requirements: Recommendations, essay, transcript, proof of eligibility. SAT or ACT scores, tax return (or parents' tax return for applicants younger than 21).
Additional information: Applicant or someone in immediate family must have derived majority of income from California- or Arizona-based agriculture. All majors eligible. Award renewable up to four years based on annual review. Must maintain 2.7 GPA and carry 12 credits per semester to qualify for renewal. Number of awards varies. Visit Website for application.

Amount of award:	$2,000
Number of applicants:	300
Application deadline:	April 30

Contact:
A.W. Bodine Sunkist Memorial Scholarship
Sunkist Growers
P.O. Box 7888
Van Nuys, CA 91409-7888
Phone: 818-379-7510
Web: www.sunkist.com/about/bodine_scholarship.aspx

Supreme Guardian Council, International Order of Job's Daughters

The Grotto Scholarships

Type of award: Scholarship.
Intended use: For full-time undergraduate study at 2-year or 4-year institution.
Eligibility: Applicant must be single, female, no older than 30.
Basis for selection: Major/career interest in dentistry.
Applicant must demonstrate financial need, high academic achievement, depth of character, leadership and seriousness of purpose.
Application requirements: Recommendations, transcript, proof of eligibility. Personal letter.
Additional information: Applicant must be member of Job's Daughters. Job's Daughters activities, financial self-help, and achievements outside of Job's Daughters are also factors in awarding scholarships. Training in the handicapped field is preferred. Visit Website for more information.

Amount of award:	$1,500
Application deadline:	April 30

Contact:
International Order of Job's Daughters
233 W. 6th Street
Papillion, NE 68046
Phone: 402-592-7987
Fax: 402 592-2177
Web: www.jobsdaughtersinternational.org

Supreme Guardian Council, International Order of Job's Daughters Scholarship

Type of award: Scholarship.
Intended use: For full-time undergraduate study at vocational, 2-year or 4-year institution.
Eligibility: Applicant must be single, female, no older than 30.
Basis for selection: Applicant must demonstrate financial need, high academic achievement, depth of character, leadership, seriousness of purpose and service orientation.
Application requirements: Recommendations, transcript, proof of eligibility. Personal letter.
Additional information: Applicant must be member of Job's Daughters. Job's Daughters activities, applicant's financial self-help, and achievements outside of Job's Daughters are also factors in awarding scholarships. Number of awards varies. Visit Website for more information.

Amount of award:	$750
Number of applicants:	100
Application deadline:	April 30

Contact:
Supreme Guardian Council
233 W. 6th Street
Papillion, NE 68046
Phone: 402-592-7987
Fax: 402 592-2177
Web: www.jobsdaughtersinternational.org

Susie Holmes Memorial Scholarship

Type of award: Scholarship.
Intended use: For full-time undergraduate study at vocational, 2-year or 4-year institution.
Eligibility: Applicant must be single, female, no older than 30.
Basis for selection: Applicant must demonstrate financial need, high academic achievement, depth of character and seriousness of purpose.
Application requirements: Recommendations, transcript, proof of eligibility. Personal letter.
Additional information: Applicant must be member of Job's Daughters. Must be high school graduate with 2.5 GPA; show dedicated, continuous, joyful service to Job's Daughters; and regularly attend Grand and/or Supreme Session and participate in competitions. Job's Daughter's activities, applicant's financial self-help, and achievements outside of Job's Daughters are also factors in awarding scholarships. Visit Website for more details.

Amount of award:	$1,000
Application deadline:	April 30

Contact:
Supreme Guardian Council, International Order of Job's Daughters
233 W. 6th Street
Papillion, NE 68046
Phone: 402-592-7987
Fax: 402 592-2177
Web: www.jobsdaughtersinternational.org

Suretybonds.com

SuretyBonds.com Small Business Student Scholarship Program

Type of award: Scholarship.
Intended use: For full-time undergraduate study at 4-year institution.
Eligibility: Applicant must be U.S. citizen or permanent resident.
Application requirements: Essay. 500- to 1,000-word essay about how small business ownership (personal, parent, grandparent, or legal guardian) has shaped you into the person you are today.
Additional information: Apply online.

Amount of award:	$1,500
Number of awards:	3
Number of applicants:	500
Application deadline:	March 31
Total amount awarded:	$4,500

Contact:
SuretyBonds.com
3514 I-70 Dr. SE
Suite 102
Columbia, MO 65201
Phone: 800-308-4358, ext. 210
Fax: 573-303-0131
Web: www.suretybonds.com/scholarships

Swiss Benevolent Society of New York

Sonia Streuli Maguire Outstanding Scholastic Achievement Award

Type of award: Scholarship.
Intended use: For full-time senior, post-bachelor's certificate, master's, doctoral or first professional study at accredited 4-year or graduate institution in United States.
Eligibility: Applicant must be Swiss. Applicant must be permanent resident residing in New York, Connecticut, Delaware, New Jersey or Pennsylvania.
Basis for selection: Applicant must demonstrate high academic achievement.
Application requirements: Recommendations, transcript, proof of eligibility. SAT/GRE results.
Additional information: Applicant or parent must be Swiss national. Must have minimum 3.8 GPA. Visit Website for application.

Application deadline:	March 31
Notification begins:	July 1

Contact:
Swiss Benevolent Society Scholarship Committee
500 Fifth Avenue
Room 1800
New York, NY 10110
Phone: 212-246-0655
Fax: 212-246-1366
Web: www.sbsny.org/sbs_scholarships.html

Swiss Benevolent Society Medicus Student Exchange

Type of award: Scholarship.
Intended use: For full-time junior, senior or graduate study at accredited 4-year or graduate institution in universities and polytechnic institutes in Switzerland.
Eligibility: Applicant must be Swiss. Applicant must be U.S. citizen or permanent resident.
Basis for selection: Competition/talent/interest in study abroad. Applicant must demonstrate financial need and high academic achievement.
Application requirements: Recommendations, transcript, proof of eligibility. SAT or GRE scores. Letter of acceptance from Swiss institution. Statement of funding. Proof of fluency in language of instruction.
Additional information: Provides partial financial support for U.S. students accepted to Swiss post-secondary institutions. Applicant or parent must be Swiss national. Visit Website for application.

Application deadline:	March 31
Notification begins:	July 1

Contact:
Swiss Benevolent Society Scholarship Committee
500 Fifth Avenue
Room 1800
New York, NY 10110
Phone: 212-246-0655
Fax: 212-246-1366
Web: www.sbsny.org/sbs_scholarships.html

Swiss Benevolent Society Pellegrini Scholarship

Type of award: Scholarship, renewable.
Intended use: For undergraduate, graduate or non-degree study at accredited postsecondary institution in United States.
Eligibility: Applicant must be Swiss. Applicant must be permanent resident residing in New York, Connecticut, Delaware, New Jersey or Pennsylvania.
Basis for selection: Applicant must demonstrate financial need and high academic achievement.
Application requirements: Recommendations, transcript, proof of eligibility. SAT or GRE scores. Proof of Swiss parentage and tax return. Copy of bursar's bill. Incoming freshmen should provide figures of anticipated cost.
Additional information: Applicant or parent must be Swiss national. Minimum 3.0 GPA. Visit Website for application.

Application deadline:	March 31
Notification begins:	July 1

Contact:
Swiss Benevolent Society Scholarship Committee
500 Fifth Avenue
Room 1800
New York, NY 10110
Phone: 212-246-0655
Fax: 212-246-1366
Web: www.sbsny.org/sbs_scholarships.html

TAG Education Collaborative

TAG Education Collaborative Web Challenge Contest

Type of award: Scholarship.
Intended use: For full-time undergraduate study.
Eligibility: Applicant must be enrolled in high school. Applicant must be U.S. citizen or permanent resident residing in Georgia.
Basis for selection: Competition/talent/interest in web-site design, based on use of technology to create a theme-based project. Major/career interest in computer/information sciences or computer graphics. Applicant must demonstrate seriousness of purpose.
Application requirements: Proof of eligibility.
Additional information: Applicants work in teams of up to four members to create projects using free and/or open source technologies. Team must be sponsored by faculty adviser. Total amount awarded varies. Visit Website for registration information, deadline, and contest information and theme.

Number of awards:	25
Number of applicants:	100
Total amount awarded:	$21,100

Contact:
TAG Education Collaborative
Web: www.tagedonline.org

Taglit-Birthright Israel

Taglit-Birthright Israel Gift

Type of award: Scholarship.

Intended use: For undergraduate or graduate study at postsecondary institution.

Eligibility: Applicant must be at least 18, no older than 26. Applicant must be Jewish.

Application requirements: Proof of eligibility. Passport.

Additional information: Applicant must be out of high school. All eligible applicants receive free trip to Israel under the auspices of Aish HaTorah, Hillel, and other organizations. Round-trip airfare and ten days of program activity (including hotel, transportation, and most meals) are funded. Must not have visited Israel previously on an educational peer-group trip or study program. Must not have lived in Israel past age 12. Visit Website or contact sponsor for current offerings.

Number of awards:	20,000

Contact:
Phone: 888-994-7723
Web: www.birthrightisrael.com

Taiwanese American Scholarship Fund

Taiwanese American Scholarship Fund Program

Type of award: Scholarship, renewable.

Intended use: For full-time freshman or sophomore study at accredited 2-year or 4-year institution in United States.

Eligibility: Applicant must be U.S. citizen or permanent resident.

Basis for selection: Applicant must demonstrate financial need and high academic achievement.

Application requirements: Three references are required.

Additional information: Applicant's ethnic background must beTaiwanese Descent. Must have a household income at or below the federal/state/county low income level. After receiving an award, awardees must submit a short YouTube video. Submit application online.

Amount of award:	$2,500
Number of awards:	20
Number of applicants:	100
Application deadline:	March 29
Notification begins:	June 30
Total amount awarded:	$50,000

Contact:
Asian Pacific Community Fund
1145 Wilshire Boulevard
Suit 105
Los Angeles, CA 90017
Phone: 213-624-6400 ext.6
Fax: 213-624-6406
Web: http://tascholarshipfund.org/2017-tasf-scholarship-overview/

Tall Clubs International

TCI Student Scholarships

Type of award: Scholarship.

Intended use: For freshman study at accredited 2-year or 4-year institution.

Eligibility: Applicant must be no older than 20.

Basis for selection: Applicant must demonstrate high academic achievement.

Application requirements: Recommendations, essay, transcript, nomination by local Tall Clubs. College entry test scores, photograph for publication, release form to publish essay and/or photo of applicant.

Additional information: Must meet height requirement: 5'10'' for women and 6'2'' for men. Number of awards available varies. Contact local TCI Member Club and request their sponsorship as candidate for scholarship.

Amount of award:	$1,000
Number of applicants:	400
Application deadline:	March 1
Notification begins:	July 15
Total amount awarded:	$4,000

Contact:
Tall Clubs International
Web: www.tall.org/scholarships.cfm

Taradash Workers' Comp and Injury Lawyers

Taradash Law Firm Scholarship

Type of award: Scholarship.

Intended use: For full-time undergraduate study at accredited 2-year or 4-year institution in United States.

Eligibility: Applicant must be U.S. citizen or permanent resident.

Basis for selection: The scholarship committee will base the judging criteria on financial need and the quality of a written essay. Major/career interest in law. Applicant must demonstrate financial need.

Application requirements: Essay. Submit written essay on the topic: Describe what contributions you plan on making to society over the next ten years.

Amount of award:	$1,500
Number of awards:	1
Application deadline:	June 1
Notification begins:	September 1
Total amount awarded:	$1,500

Contact:
Taradash Workers' Comp and Injury Lawyers
620B Academy Drive
Northbrook, IL 60062
Phone: 847-940-4000
Web: http://taradashlaw.com/taradash-law-firm-scholarship/

Targeting Excellence

Targeting Excellence Scholarship

Type of award: Scholarship, renewable.
Intended use: For full-time undergraduate or graduate study at 2-year, 4-year or graduate institution.
Basis for selection: Major/career interest in agribusiness; animal sciences; food production/management/services or food science/technology.
Additional information: Preference will be given to students enrolled in a food animal production curriculum. Preference will also be given to students enrolled in regions where fund-raising events are held (award areas include Iowa, Minnesota, North Carolina, and Pennsylvania). Additional consideration will be given to students participating in the the fund-raising event. Applicant must be accepted or enrolled in a College of Agriculture which offers courses in food animal production. Applicant must be enrolled in classes effective September 1. Applicant must have a strong desire to pursue a career, upon graduation, in some aspect of food animal production. Scholarship applications open January 15.

Amount of award:	$1,000-$3,000
Number of awards:	45
Number of applicants:	70
Application deadline:	March 15
Notification begins:	May 1
Total amount awarded:	$120,000

Contact:
Targeting Excellence
P.O. Box 759
Rose Hill, NC 28458
Web: www.targetingexcellence.org

Teacher.org

Teacher.org's Inspire our Future Scholarship

Type of award: Scholarship.
Intended use: For full-time undergraduate or graduate study at accredited 2-year, 4-year or graduate institution in United States.
Eligibility: Applicant must be at least 18. Applicant must be U.S. citizen or permanent resident.
Basis for selection: Major/career interest in education; education, early childhood; education, special or education, teacher.
Application requirements: Essay, transcript. Entrants must go to the web site to fill out the entry form and answer the question in the space allotted with a 500-700 word response.
Additional information: Minimum 3.5 GPA. Winner will be required to submit an official transcript.

Number of awards:	1
Application deadline:	April 1
Total amount awarded:	$2,500

Contact:
Teacher.org
7120 Hayvenhurst Avenue
Van Nuys, CA 91406
Web: www.teacher.org/scholarship-entry-rules/

TechChecks

TechChecks Business Leadership Scholarship

Type of award: Scholarship.
Intended use: For undergraduate study at vocational, 2-year, 4-year or graduate institution in United States.
Eligibility: Applicant must be Asian American, African American, Mexican American, Hispanic American, Puerto Rican, American Indian or Native Hawaiian/Pacific Islander. Applicant must be female, high school senior. Applicant must be U.S. citizen.
Basis for selection: Major/career interest in business; marketing or business/management/administration.
Application requirements: Recommendations. Letter of referral from a professor, faculty member, or academic advisor. Copy of official transcript, or copy of upcoming Fall enrollment schedule if a high school senior. 600-800 word essay topic can be found online.
Additional information: Minimum 3.5 GPA. Must be working toward MBA or any field that emphasizes business or marketing. Must have a minimum SAT score of 1070, or Math ACT score of 26. Preference will be given to female students. Preference will also be given to all students of the following origins: Hispanic, African American, Asian/Pacific Islander, or Native American.

Amount of award:	$1,000
Number of awards:	4
Application deadline:	June 15
Total amount awarded:	$4,000

Contact:
TechChecks
138 Daniel Drive
Lakewood, NJ 08701
Phone: 866-laser58
Fax: 866-527-8883
Web: www.techchecks.net/techchecks-business-leadership-scholarship

Ted Rollins

Ted Rollins Eco Scholarship

Type of award: Scholarship.
Intended use: For undergraduate study at vocational, 2-year or 4-year institution in United States.
Eligibility: Applicant must be high school senior. Applicant must be U.S. citizen or permanent resident.
Basis for selection: Major/career interest in natural resources/conservation; energy research; engineering, environmental or wildlife/fisheries.

Application requirements: Must plan to take at least 10 credit hours per semester . 500 word essay, questions found on the application.

Additional information: Major (or plans to major) in a field related to sustainability. Must plan to take at least 10 credit hours during the spring semester. Submit the application form below, along with your essay, by November 15th, 2016. Use the "Your Story And Goals" field to share your interests, experience and goals related to sustainability and ecopreneurism.

Number of awards:	1
Application deadline:	June 15
Notification begins:	July 1
Total amount awarded:	$1,000

Contact:
Ted Rollins
9101 Southern Pine Boulevard
Charlotte, NC 28273
Web: www.tedrollinsecoscholars.com/apply-now/

Templeton Press

The State of the American Mind Essay & Video Contest

Type of award: Scholarship.
Intended use: For undergraduate study at accredited vocational, 2-year or 4-year institution.
Eligibility: Applicant must be at least 18, high school senior. Applicant must be U.S. citizen.
Application requirements: Essay must be between 1500 and 2000 words in length. Video must be up to 3 minutes in length.
Additional information: Stuents may submit an essay OR a video. Subject will be on one of three prompts. Complete rules for submission, prompts, and the application can be found on the website.

Amount of award:	$2,000-$5,000
Number of awards:	6
Application deadline:	December 31
Total amount awarded:	$20,000

Contact:
Templeton Press
300 Conshohocken State Road
Suite 665
West Conshohocken, PA 19428
Web: www.soamcontest.com

Tennessee Promise

Tennessee Promise Scholarship

Type of award: Scholarship, renewable.
Intended use: For full-time at vocational, 2-year or 4-year institution.
Eligibility: Applicant must be high school senior. Applicant must be U.S. citizen or permanent resident residing in Tennessee.
Application requirements: Students must attend mandatory meetings and participate in the mentoring program, and

perform 8 hours community service prior to each term the award is receiving.
Additional information: Award amount varies based on amount of remaining tuition and mandatory fees after all other gifts aid has been applied.

Number of awards:	8,830
Application deadline:	November 1
Total amount awarded:	$15,200,000

Contact:
Tennessee Promise Scholarship
404 James Robertson Parkway
Suite 1510
Nashville, TN 37243
Phone: 615-532-3503
Web: http://tnpromise.gov/parents.shtml

Tennessee Student Assistance Corporation

Helping Heroes Grant

Type of award: Scholarship, renewable.
Intended use: For undergraduate study at 2-year or 4-year institution.
Eligibility: Applicant must be residing in Tennessee. Applicant must be veteran who served in the Army, Air Force, Marines, Navy or Reserves/National Guard. Must be a veteran who was honorably discharged and was awarded the Iraq Campaign Medal, Afghanistan Campaign Medal, or Global War on Terrorism Expeditionary Medal.
Additional information: Award amount is up to $2,000. Fall application deadline is September 1; spring deadline is February 1; summer deadline is May 1. Scholarships are given on a first-come, first-served basis, with up to $750,000 awarded per academic year.

Amount of award:	$2,000
Number of awards:	486
Application deadline:	September 1, February 1
Total amount awarded:	$734,000

Contact:
Tennessee Student Assistance Corporation
Parkway Towers, Suite 1510
404 James Robertson Parkway
Nashville, TN 37243-0820
Phone: 800-342-1633
Fax: 615-741-6101
Web: www.tn.gov/collegepays

Hope Foster Child Tuition Grant

Type of award: Scholarship, renewable.
Intended use: For undergraduate study at 2-year or 4-year institution.
Eligibility: Applicant must be residing in Tennessee.
Application requirements: FAFSA.
Additional information: Must meet the academic requirements for the HOPE Scholarship or HOPE Access Grant. Must have been in custody of Tennessee Department of Children's Services for at least one year after age 14.

Amount of award:	Full tuition
Number of awards:	78
Application deadline:	September 1
Notification begins:	January 1
Total amount awarded:	$463,000

Contact:
Tennessee Student Assistance Corporation
Parkway Towers, Suite 1510
404 James Robertson Parkway
Nashville, TN 37243-0820
Phone: 800-342-1663
Fax: 615-741-6101
Web: www.tn.gov/collegepays

HOPE-Aspire Award

Type of award: Scholarship.
Intended use: For undergraduate study at postsecondary institution. Designated institutions: Eligible Tennessee institutions.
Eligibility: Applicant must be residing in Tennessee.
Basis for selection: Applicant must demonstrate financial need and high academic achievement.
Application requirements: FAFSA.
Additional information: Applicant must be eligible for HOPE. Entering freshman must have a minimum 21 ACT or 980 SAT or 3.0 GPA. Parent's or student's income must be $36,000 or less. Applicant must be a Tennessee resident for one year prior to enrollment.

Amount of award:	$2,250
Number of awards:	18,028
Application deadline:	June 30
Notification begins:	January 1
Total amount awarded:	$82,500,000

Contact:
Tennessee Student Assistance Corporation
Parkway Towers, Suite 1510
404 James Robertson Parkway
Nashville, TN 37243-0820
Phone: 800-342-1663
Fax: 615-741-6101
Web: www.tn.gov/collegepays

Hope-General Assembly Merit Scholarship

Type of award: Scholarship, renewable.
Intended use: For undergraduate study at postsecondary institution. Designated institutions: Eligible Tennessee institutions.
Eligibility: Applicant must be residing in Tennessee.
Basis for selection: Applicant must demonstrate high academic achievement.
Application requirements: FAFSA.
Additional information: Supplement to HOPE Scholarship. Entering freshman must have minimum 3.75 weighted GPA and 29 ACT or 1280 SAT. Applicant must be a resident of Tennessee for one year prior to enrollment.

Amount of award:	$1,500
Number of awards:	6,724
Application deadline:	September 1
Notification begins:	January 1
Total amount awarded:	$32,100,000

Contact:
Tennessee Student Assistance Corporation
Parkway Towers, Suite 1510
404 James Robertson Parkway
Nashville, TN 37243-0820
Phone: 800-342-1663
Fax: 614-741-6101
Web: www.tn.gov/collegepays

Nontraditional HOPE Scholarship

Type of award: Scholarship.
Intended use: For undergraduate study at 4-year institution in United States.
Eligibility: Applicant must be at least 25. Applicant must be U.S. citizen residing in Tennessee.
Basis for selection: Applicant must demonstrate high academic achievement.
Additional information: Must be at least 25 and have adjusted gross income of $36,000 or less. Must enroll as entering freshman or have at least two years break in enrollment. Must maintain continuous enrollment and attempt at least 12 credit hours with a 2.75 GPA or greater before becoming eligible. Applicant is ineligible to receive the Aspire Award or General Assembly Scholarship.

Amount of award:	$3,000-$6,000
Number of awards:	2,182
Application deadline:	September 1
Total amount awarded:	$5,700,000

Contact:
Tennessee Student Assistance Corporation
Parkway Towers, Suite 1510
404 James Robertson Parkway
Nashville, TN 37724-0820
Phone: 800-342-1663
Fax: 615-741-6101
Web: www.tn.gov/collegepays

Step-Up Scholarship

Type of award: Scholarship, renewable.
Intended use: For full-time at 4-year institution. Designated institutions: Lipscomb University, University of Memphis, University of Tennessee, or Vanderbilt University.
Eligibility: Applicant must be at least 18. Applicant must be residing in Tennessee.
Application requirements: Must enroll in an eligible post secondary program no later than 16 months after completing high school and apply for the Tennessee Step-Up scholarship.
Additional information: Must complete high school in Tennessee in accordance with the requirements of the student's individualized education program and receive a high school diploma or certificate, special education diploma, a transition certificate, or an IED certificate. Student will receive $1,750 per semester. Application can be found on web site.

Amount of award:	$3,500
Number of awards:	65
Number of applicants:	51
Application deadline:	September 1
Total amount awarded:	$229,000

Contact:
Tennessee Student Assistance Corporation
404 James Robertson Parkway
Suite 1510
Nashville, TN 37243
Phone: 615-753-5517
Fax: 615-741-6106
Web: https://www.tn.gov/collegepays/article/tennessee-step-up-scholarship

TCAT Reconnect Scholarship

Type of award: Scholarship.
Intended use: For full-time at vocational institution. Designated institutions: Any Tennessee College of Applied Technology (TCAT).
Eligibility: Applicant must be residing in Tennessee.

Basis for selection: Applicant must demonstrate financial need.

Additional information: Award amount varies based on amount of remaining tuition and mandatory fees after all other gift aid has first been applied. Scholarship is terminated after student earns a diploma. Or no longer maintains continuous enrollment or satisfactory academic progress. Or is not longer enrolled full-time or in a certificate or diploma. See more at: www.tn.gov/collegepays/article/tcat-reconnect-scholarship.

Number of awards:	1,547
Application deadline:	January 1
Total amount awarded:	$1,400,000

Contact:
Tennessee Student Assistance Corporation
404 James Robertson Parkway
Suite 1510
Nashville, TN 37243
Phone: 615-532-3503
Fax: 615-741-6106
Web: http://tnreconnect.gov/PayForCollege/
TennesseeReconnectTCATGrant/tabid/5252/Default.aspx

Tennessee Dependent Children Scholarship Program

Type of award: Scholarship, renewable.
Intended use: For full-time undergraduate study at accredited postsecondary institution.
Eligibility: Applicant must be U.S. citizen residing in Tennessee. Applicant's parent must have been killed or disabled in work-related accident as firefighter or police officer.
Basis for selection: Applicant must demonstrate financial need.
Application requirements: Proof of eligibility. FAFSA.
Additional information: Applicant must be enrolled in a degree-granting program. Applicant's parent may also be emergency medical technician killed or disabled in work-related accident. Award based on student's financial aid package.

Amount of award:	Full tuition
Number of awards:	26
Number of applicants:	42
Application deadline:	July 15
Total amount awarded:	$290,000

Contact:
Tennessee Student Assistance Corporation
Parkway Towers, Suite 1510
404 James Robertson Parkway
Nashville, TN 37243-0820
Phone: 800-342-1663
Fax: 615-741-6101
Web: www.tn.gov/collegepays

Tennessee Dual Enrollment Grant

Type of award: Scholarship, renewable.
Intended use: For undergraduate study at postsecondary institution.
Eligibility: Applicant must be high school junior or senior. Applicant must be residing in Tennessee.
Additional information: Award is up to $1,200 per year. Student must meet dual enrollment requirements for high school and postsecondary institution. Must be a Tennessee resident for at least one year prior to enrollment. Visit Website for designated institutions. Application deadline is September 15 for fall; February 1 for spring; May 1 for summer. Apply online.

Amount of award:	$1,200
Number of awards:	24,671
Application deadline:	September 15, February 1
Total amount awarded:	$15,900,000

Contact:
Tennessee Student Assistance Corporation
Parkway Towers, Suite 1510
404 James Robertson Parkway
Nashville, TN 37243-0820
Phone: 800-342-1663
Fax: 615-741-6101
Web: www.tn.gov/collegepays

Tennessee HOPE Access Grant

Type of award: Scholarship.
Intended use: For freshman study at 2-year or 4-year institution. Designated institutions: Eligible Tennessee institutions.
Eligibility: Applicant must be residing in Tennessee.
Basis for selection: Applicant must demonstrate financial need and high academic achievement.
Application requirements: FAFSA.
Additional information: Award amount is up to $4,125 for four-year institutions or up to $2,625 for two-year institutions. Minimum 2.75 GPA. Minimum 18 ACT, 860 SAT. Parents' or independent student and spouse's adjusted gross income must be $36,000 or less on IRS tax form. Applicant must be a Tennessee resident for one year prior to enrollment.

Amount of award:	$2,625-$4,125
Number of awards:	382
Application deadline:	September 1
Notification begins:	January 1
Total amount awarded:	$662,500

Contact:
Tennessee Student Assistance Corporation
Parkway Towers, Suite 1510
404 James Robertson Parkway
Nashville, TN 37243-0820
Phone: 800-342-1663
Fax: 615-741-6101
Web: www.tn.gov/collegepays

Tennessee HOPE Scholarship

Type of award: Scholarship.
Intended use: For undergraduate study at postsecondary institution. Designated institutions: Eligible Tennessee institutions.
Eligibility: Applicant must be residing in Tennessee.
Basis for selection: Applicant must demonstrate high academic achievement.
Application requirements: FAFSA.
Additional information: Applicant must be a Tennessee resident for one year prior to enrollment. Award amount is up to $6,000 for four-year institutions, up to $3,000 for two-year institutions. Minimum 3.0 GPA or 21 ACT/980 SAT.

Amount of award:	$3,000-$6,000
Number of awards:	45,951
Application deadline:	September 1
Notification begins:	January 1
Total amount awarded:	$154,100,000

Contact:
Tennessee Student Assistance Corporation
Parkway Towers, Suite 1510
404 James Robertson Parkway
Nashville, TN 37243-0820
Phone: 800-342-1663
Fax: 615-741-6101
Web: www.tn.gov/collegepays

Tennessee Ned McWherter Scholars Program

Type of award: Scholarship, renewable.
Intended use: For full-time freshman study at accredited 2-year or 4-year institution.
Eligibility: Applicant must be high school senior. Applicant must be U.S. citizen residing in Tennessee.
Basis for selection: Applicant must demonstrate high academic achievement and leadership.
Application requirements: Transcript, proof of eligibility. List of leadership activities.
Additional information: Applicant must score at 95th percentile on ACT/SAT. Minimum 3.5 cumulative GPA. Difficulty of high school courses considered.

Amount of award:	$6,000
Number of awards:	192
Number of applicants:	1,208
Application deadline:	February 15
Total amount awarded:	$564,000

Contact:
Tennessee Student Assistance Corporation
Parkway Towers, Suite 1510
404 James Robertson Parkway
Nashville, TN 37243-0820
Phone: 800-342-1663
Fax: 615-741-6101
Web: www.tn.gov/collegepays

Tennessee STEP UP Scholarship

Type of award: Scholarship, renewable.
Intended use: For full-time undergraduate study at 4-year institution in United States. Designated institutions: Lipscomb University, University of Memphis, University of Tennessee, Vanderbilt University, Union University.
Eligibility: Applicant must be learning disabled. The Tennessee STEP UP Scholarship is a program designed to assist students with intellectual disabilities who have completed high school and enroll in an individualized program of study of up to four yours at an eligible postsecondary institution. Applicant must be at least 18. Applicant must be residing in Tennessee.
Application requirements: Must be a Tennessee resident as defined by regulations promulgates by the board of regents under 59-8-104 for one year immediately preceding the date pf application for a scholarship or the renewal of the scholarship. Complete high School in a Tennessee high School in accordance with the requirements of the student's individualized education program and receive a high school diploma, occupational diploma or certificate, a special education diploma, a transition certificate, or an IEP certificate.be admitted to and enroll in an eligible postsecondary institution in an eligible postsecondary program no later than sixteen months after completing high school.
Additional information: Application Deadlines for Fall Sept 1, for Spring Feb 1, for Summer May 1. For entering students beginning with fall students will receive $1750 per semester. For students who first received the STEP UP scholarship in fall

2012 through 2015 students will continue to receive $2000 per semester.

Amount of award:	$3,500
Number of awards:	98
Application deadline:	September 1, February 1
Total amount awarded:	$339,000

Contact:
Tennessee Student Assistance Corporation
404 James Robertson Parkway
Suit 1510
Nashville, TN 37243
Phone: 615-253-7460
Fax: 615-741-6106
Web: https://www.tn.gov/collegepays/article/tennessee-step-up-scholarship

Tennessee Student Assistance Award Program

Type of award: Scholarship, renewable.
Intended use: For undergraduate study at postsecondary institution.
Eligibility: Applicant must be U.S. citizen residing in Tennessee.
Basis for selection: Applicant must demonstrate financial need.
Application requirements: FAFSA.
Additional information: Applicant's expected family contribution must be $2,100 or less. Award is up to $4,000 for private institutions; up to $2,000 for public, based on funding.

Number of awards:	34,308
Number of applicants:	460,721
Total amount awarded:	$62,200,000

Contact:
Tennessee Student Assistance Corporation
Parkway Towers, Suite 1510
404 James Robertson Parkway
Nashville, TN 37243-0820
Phone: 800-342-1663
Fax: 615-741-6101
Web: www.tn.gov/collegepays

Wilder-Naifeh Technical Skills Grant

Type of award: Scholarship.
Intended use: For freshman or sophomore study at vocational institution. Designated institutions: Tennessee College of Applied Technology.
Eligibility: Applicant must be residing in Tennessee.
Application requirements: FAFSA.
Additional information: Applicant must be Tennessee resident for one year prior to enrollment. Application deadline varies. See Website for details.

Amount of award:	$2,000
Number of awards:	11,576
Application deadline:	July 1
Notification begins:	January 1
Total amount awarded:	$14,900,000

Contact:
Tennessee Student Assistance Corporation
Parkway Towers, Suite 1510
404 James Robertson Parkway
Nashville, TN 37243-0820
Phone: 800-342-1663
Fax: 615-741-6101
Web: www.tn.gov/collegepays

Tennessee Valley Interstellar Workshop

Tennessee Valley Interstellar Workshop Scholarship Program

Type of award: Scholarship.
Intended use: For full-time undergraduate study at accredited 4-year institution in United States.
Eligibility: Applicant must be high school senior. Applicant must be U.S. citizen residing in Tennessee, Louisiana, South Carolina, Georgia, Florida, Virginia, Mississippi, Alabama, Kentucky or North Carolina.
Basis for selection: Major/career interest in engineering; mathematics; science, general; physics; chemistry or biology.
Application requirements: Recommendations, essay, transcript. Applicants must submit the following items:. Completed application form. A brief (one page) explanation of career goals and biographical (background) information. A 1000-2000 word essay. High School Transcripts (for rising freshmen) or College Transcripts (for rising upperclassmen). A one-page letter of recommendation from a teacher, professor, or supervisor familiar with the applicants work. The 1000-2000 word essay should be on one of the following topics:. The rationale for humanity to become an interstellar species. A near-term plan (within 20 years) for building advocacy toward interstellar space exploration. Space Development is important because,,,
Additional information: Applicant must be a current High School Senior or Undergraduate student enrolled in an accredited college or university. Student must have a declared major in Engineering, Math, or Sciences. The scholarship may be used at any college or university in the United States.

Amount of award:	$2,500
Number of awards:	2
Application deadline:	May 15
Notification begins:	July 7
Total amount awarded:	$5,000

Contact:
Martha Knowles Tennessee Valley Interstellar Workshop
P.O. Box 4171
Oak Ridge, TN 37831
Web: https://tviw.wordpress.com/scholarships/

Texas 4-H Club

Texas 4-H Opportunity Scholarships

Type of award: Scholarship, renewable.
Intended use: For undergraduate study at accredited 4-year institution in United States. Designated institutions: Colleges and universities in Texas.
Eligibility: Applicant must be high school senior. Applicant must be U.S. citizen residing in Texas.
Basis for selection: Applicant must demonstrate financial need and high academic achievement.
Application requirements: Recommendations, essay, transcript. SAT/ACT scores.
Additional information: Must be current Texas 4-H member in good standing. Must graduate from Texas public/private high school or home school in top fourth of class or upper half of class, depending on scholarship. Must have minimum 1350

SAT or 19 ACT score. Cannot have applied for scholarship through state FFA or state FCCLA.

Amount of award:	$1,000-$20,000
Number of awards:	225
Number of applicants:	350
Application deadline:	January 31
Notification begins:	June 1
Total amount awarded:	$2,250,000

Contact:
Texas 4-H and Youth Development Foundation
Scholarship Selection Committee
4180 S Highway 6
College Station, TX 77845
Phone: 979-845-1211
Fax: 979-845-6495
Web: texas4-h.tamu.edu

Texas Association, Family Career and Community Leaders of America

Blue Bell Scholarship

Type of award: Scholarship.
Intended use: For full-time undergraduate study at accredited postsecondary institution in United States. Designated institutions: Colleges and universities in Texas.
Eligibility: Applicant must be high school senior. Applicant must be U.S. citizen residing in Texas.
Basis for selection: Applicant must demonstrate financial need, high academic achievement, depth of character and leadership.
Application requirements: Recommendations, essay, transcript. SAT/ACT scores.
Additional information: Must be active member of Family Career and Community Leaders of America in good standing. Must have passed TAKS Mastery/Exit Level exam and be in top fourth of graduating class. Scholarship recipient required to attend the FCCLA State Leadership Conference.

Amount of award:	$1,000
Number of awards:	5
Application deadline:	March 1
Notification begins:	April 1

Contact:
Texas Association, Family Career and Community Leaders of America
1107 W. 45th St.
Austin, TX 78756
Phone: 512-306-0099
Fax: 512-442-7100
Web: www.texasfccla.org

C. J. Davidson Scholarship

Type of award: Scholarship, renewable.
Intended use: For undergraduate study at accredited postsecondary institution in United States. Designated institutions: Texas colleges with family and consumer sciences departments.
Eligibility: Applicant must be high school senior. Applicant must be U.S. citizen residing in Texas.
Basis for selection: Applicant must demonstrate financial need and high academic achievement.

Application requirements: Recommendations, essay, transcript. SAT/ACT scores.
Additional information: Must graduate from a Texas high school with 85 average. Must be active member of Family Career and Community Leaders of America for at least one year. Must major in family/consumer sciences. Scholarship recipient required to attend the FCCLA State Leadership Conference.

Amount of award:	$4,500
Number of awards:	10
Application deadline:	March 1
Notification begins:	April 1

Contact:
Texas Association, Family Career and Community Leaders of America
1107 W. 45th St.
Austin, TX 78756
Phone: 512-306-0099
Fax: 512-442-7100
Web: www.texasfccla.org

FCCLA Regional Scholarship

Type of award: Scholarship.
Intended use: For full-time undergraduate study at accredited postsecondary institution in United States. Designated institutions: Texas colleges and universities with family and consumer sciences departments.
Eligibility: Applicant must be high school senior. Applicant must be U.S. citizen residing in Texas.
Basis for selection: Applicant must demonstrate financial need, high academic achievement, depth of character and leadership.
Application requirements: Recommendations, essay, transcript. SAT/ACT scores, two copies of autobiography.
Additional information: Must be active Family Career and Community Leaders of America member in good standing for at least one year. Must be FFCLA regional or state officer. Must be a graduate of Texas high school with minimum 85 average. Must major in family/consumer sciences. Scholarship recipient required to attend the FCCLA Leadership Conference.

Amount of award:	$1,000
Number of awards:	1
Number of applicants:	5
Application deadline:	March 1
Notification begins:	April 1
Total amount awarded:	$1,000

Contact:
Texas Association, Family Career and Community Leaders of America
1107 W. 45th St.
Austin, TX 78756
Phone: 512-306-0099
Fax: 512-442-7100
Web: www.texasfccla.org

Houston Livestock Show and Rodeo Scholarships

Type of award: Scholarship, renewable.
Intended use: For full-time undergraduate study at accredited 4-year institution in United States. Designated institutions: Colleges and universities in Texas.
Eligibility: Applicant must be high school senior. Applicant must be U.S. citizen residing in Texas.
Basis for selection: Applicant must demonstrate financial need, high academic achievement, depth of character and leadership.

Application requirements: Recommendations, essay, transcript. SAT/ACT scores.
Additional information: Must be current member of Family Career and Community Leaders of America in good standing. Must graduate from Texas public high school in top fourth of class and have minimum 1350 SAT or 19 ACT score. Cannot have applied for scholarship through Texas 4-H or FFA. Scholarship recipient required to attend the FCCLA State Leadership Conference.

Amount of award:	$4,500
Number of awards:	10
Application deadline:	March 1
Notification begins:	April 1

Contact:
Texas Association, Family Career and Community Leaders of America
1107 W. 45th St.
Austin, TX 78756
Phone: 512-306-0099
Fax: 512-442-7100
Web: www.texasfccla.org

Texas Department of Transportation

Don't Mess with Texas Scholarship Contest

Type of award: Scholarship.
Intended use: For undergraduate study at accredited 2-year or 4-year institution in United States.
Eligibility: Applicant must be high school senior. Applicant must be residing in Texas.
Application requirements: Essay. Applications will be judged based on student essays detailing creative and sustainable solutions to litter problems in their school and/or community.
Additional information: Available to any Texas high School senior who is planning to pursue a two or four year degree at an accredited Texas college or university next year. Application can be found online.

Amount of award:	$2,000
Number of awards:	3
Number of applicants:	1,456
Application deadline:	March 26
Notification begins:	May 31
Total amount awarded:	$6,000

Contact:
Texas Department of Transportation
200 South Congress Avenue
Austin, TX 78704
Web: www.dontmesswithtexas.org/education/scholarships/

Texas Future Farmers of America

FFA Scholarships

Type of award: Scholarship, renewable.
Intended use: For undergraduate study at accredited 4-year institution in United States. Designated institutions: Colleges and universities in Texas.

Eligibility: Applicant must be high school senior. Applicant must be U.S. citizen residing in Texas.
Basis for selection: Applicant must demonstrate financial need, high academic achievement and leadership.
Application requirements: Interview, recommendations, essay, transcript. SAT/ACT scores.
Additional information: Must be current member of and have participation in Texas FFA and be in good standing. Must have graduated from Texas public high school in top half of class. Must have minimum 1350 SAT or 19 ACT score. Cannot have applied for scholarship through Texas 4-H or FCCLA. Preliminary deadlines vary based on area. Visit Website for more information.

Amount of award:	$2,000-$18,000
Number of awards:	135
Number of applicants:	700
Total amount awarded:	$2,000,000

Contact:
Texas FFA Association
614 East 12th Street
Austin, TX 78701
Phone: 512-480-8045
Fax: 512-476-2894
Web: www.texasffa.org

Texas Higher Education Coordinating Board

Texas $1,000 Tuition Rebate for Certain Undergraduates

Type of award: Scholarship.
Intended use: For full-time undergraduate study at postsecondary institution in United States. Designated institutions: Texas public colleges and universities.
Eligibility: Applicant must be residing in Texas.
Additional information: Program provides tuition rebates for students who efficiently acquire their bachelor's degrees. Students must graduate in a timely manner to receive rebate: within four years for four-year degree, five years for five-year degree. Student must have taken all coursework at Texas public institutions, and must have been entitled to pay in-state tuition at all times while pursuing degree. Student must complete bachelor's degree with no more than 3 hours in excess of degree plan, excluding up to 9 hours of credit by examination. Students must apply for tuition rebate prior to receiving bachelor's degree. Contact business office at college/university for more information.

Amount of award:	$1,000

Contact:
Texas Higher Education Coordinating Board
Phone: 800-242-3062
Web: www.collegeforalltexans.com

Texas Armed Services Scholarship Program

Type of award: Scholarship.
Intended use: For freshman study at 4-year institution.
Eligibility: Applicant must be high school senior. Applicant must be U.S. citizen or permanent resident residing in Texas.
Basis for selection: Applicant must demonstrate high academic achievement.

Application requirements: Nomination by the governor, lieutenant governor, state senator, or state representative.
Additional information: Must meet two of four following criteria: Minimum 3.0 GPA. Minimum 1590 (SAT) or 23 (ACT). Must be ranked in top third of high school graduating class or be on track to graduate high school with the Distinguished Achievement Program (DAP) or the International Baccalaureate Program (IB). Must enroll in Reserve Officers' Training Corps, agree to four years of ROTC training, and graduate no later than five years after date first enrolled. After graduation, must enter into four-year commitment to Texas Army or Texas Air Force National Guard, contract to serve as commissioned officer in branch in the U.S., or repay scholarship if requirements not met. See Website for additional criteria.

Amount of award:	$10,000

Contact:
Texas Higher Education Coordinating Board
Phone: 800-242-3062
Web: www.collegeforalltexans.com

Texas Competitive Scholarship Waiver

Type of award: Scholarship.
Intended use: For undergraduate study at 4-year institution in United States. Designated institutions: Public institutions in Texas.
Eligibility: Applicant must be U.S. citizen, permanent resident or international student residing in Texas.
Additional information: Program enables public institutions to grant waiver of nonresident tuition charges to individuals who receive scholarships totaling at least $1,000 awarded by their institution in competition open both to residents and to nonresidents. Students must have competed with other students, including Texas residents, for the award. Student may receive a waiver of nonresident tuition for the period of time covered by the scholarship, not to exceed 12 months. Process for applying for waivers varies from college to college.

Contact:
Texas Higher Education Coordinating Board
Phone: 800-242-3062
Web: www.collegeforalltexans.com

Texas Concurrent Enrollment Waiver (Enrollment in Two Texas Community Colleges)

Type of award: Scholarship.
Intended use: For undergraduate study at 2-year or 4-year institution in United States. Designated institutions: Texas public colleges or universities.
Eligibility: Applicant must be residing in Texas.
Application requirements: Proof of eligibility. Proof of concurrent enrollment.
Additional information: Waiver provides a break in tuition charges to students enrolled at two public Texas community colleges at the same time. Award is reduced tuition at second institution of enrollment (student pays minimum tuition rate at second institution). Must meet GPA requirement and hourly limit requirement set by institution. No funds may be used to pay tuition for continuing education classes for which the college receives no state tax support. For more information, contact registrar at second college in which you are enrolled.

Contact:
Texas Higher Education Coordinating Board
Phone: 800-242-3062
Web: www.collegeforalltexans.com

Texas Exemption for Peace Officers Disabled in the Line of Duty

Type of award: Scholarship.
Intended use: For undergraduate study at postsecondary institution in United States. Designated institutions: Texas public colleges and universities.
Eligibility: Applicant must be residing in Texas.
Application requirements: Proof of eligibility. Satisfactory evidence of status as a disabled peace officer as required by institution.
Additional information: Award for persons injured in the line of duty while serving as peace officers in Texas. Must enroll in classes for which college receives tax support. Maximum award is exemption from payment of tuition and fees for not more than 12 semesters or sessions. Must meet GPA requirement and hourly limit requirement set by institution for renewal. Contact college for additional information.

    Amount of award: Full tuition

Contact:
Texas Higher Education Coordinating Board
Phone: 800-242-3062
Web: www.collegeforalltexans.com

Texas Exemption for Students Under Conservatorship of the Department of Family & Protective Services

Type of award: Scholarship, renewable.
Intended use: For undergraduate or graduate study at accredited vocational, 2-year or 4-year institution in United States. Designated institutions: Texas public colleges and universities.
Eligibility: Applicant must be U.S. citizen or permanent resident residing in Texas.
Application requirements: Proof of eligibility from the Department of Family and Protective Services.
Additional information: Applicants must have been either in the care or conservatorship of Texas Department of Family and Protective Services on the day before their 18th birthday, the day of their graduation from high school, or the day of receipt of GED or the day preceding; or in the care or conservatorship of the TDFS on 14th birthday and then adopted. Must enroll in college before 25th birthday. Program awards tuition and fees; once student determined eligible for the benefit, it continues indefinitely. Contact college's financial aid office for application.

    Amount of award: Full tuition

Contact:
Texas Higher Education Coordinating Board
Phone: 800-242-3062
Web: www.collegeforalltexans.com

Texas Exemption for the Surviving Spouse and Dependent Children of Certain Deceased Public Servants (Employees)

Type of award: Scholarship.
Intended use: For full-time undergraduate study at postsecondary institution in United States. Designated institutions: Texas public colleges and universities.
Eligibility: Applicant must be residing in Texas.
Application requirements: Proof of eligibility.
Additional information: Exemption for surviving spouse and/or minor dependent children of certain public employees (defined by Texas Government Code 615.003) killed in the line of duty. Public employee must have died on or after September 1, 2000. Program covers cost of tuition and fees, textbooks, and possibly room and board. Must meet GPA requirement and hourly limit requirement set by institution for renewal. Visit Website for link to list of eligible public servants. Contact registrar's office at college/university for information on claiming this exemption.

    Amount of award: Full tuition

Contact:
Texas Higher Education Coordinating Board
Phone: 800-242-3062
Web: www.collegeforalltexans.com

Texas Exemptions for Texas Veterans (Hazelwood Exemption)

Type of award: Scholarship, renewable.
Intended use: For undergraduate or graduate study at accredited 2-year, 4-year or graduate institution. Designated institutions: Texas public colleges and universities.
Eligibility: Applicant must be U.S. citizen residing in Texas. Applicant must be veteran; or dependent of disabled veteran or deceased veteran. Must have served at least 181 days of active military duty, excluding basic training. Must have received honorable discharge or general discharge under honorable conditions. If dependent of disabled veteran, parent must be totally disabled for purposes of employability as result of service-related injury or illness.
Application requirements: Proof of eligibility.
Additional information: Must have tuition and fee charges that exceed all federal education benefits. Veteran must have been resident of Texas prior to enlistment. Award amount includes all dues, fees, and charges, excluding property deposit, student services, and lodging/board/clothing fees. Must be enrolled in courses receiving state tax support. For a child of eligible veteran to receive benefits, child must be 25 or younger on first day of semester that exemption is claimed, must make satisfactory progress, must be biological, stepchild, adopted or claimed as dependent in current or previous tax year. If a child to whom hours have been delegated fails to use all of the assigned hours, a veteran may re-assign available unused hours to another dependent child. If the veteran has died prior to this transfer request, another legally designated caretaker may re-assign unused hours to an eligible child. Applicants should contact specific school's financial aid office for more information.

    Amount of award: Full tuition

Contact:
Texas Higher Education Coordinating Board
Phone: 800-242-3062
Web: www.collegeforalltexans.com

Texas Federal Supplemental Educational Opportunity Grant

Type of award: Scholarship.
Intended use: For undergraduate study at vocational, 2-year, 4-year or graduate institution in United States.
Eligibility: Applicant must be U.S. citizen or permanent resident.
Basis for selection: Applicant must demonstrate financial need and high academic achievement.
Application requirements: FAFSA.
Additional information: Must have valid Social Security Number. Expected Family Contribution must be lower than the federal cut-off rate set each year. Must have high school diploma, GED Certificate, pass test approved by the U.S. Department of Education or meet other standards approved by U.S. Department of Education. Must register for the Selective Service.

Amount of award: $100-$4,000
Contact:
Texas Higher Education Coordinating Board
Phone: 800-242-3062
Web: www.collegeforalltexans.com

Texas Fifth-Year Accounting Student Scholarship Program

Type of award: Scholarship.
Intended use: For senior, post-bachelor's certificate or master's study at accredited postsecondary institution in United States. Designated institutions: Texas institutions.
Eligibility: Applicant must be residing in Texas.
Basis for selection: Major/career interest in accounting. Applicant must demonstrate financial need and high academic achievement.
Application requirements: Proof of eligibility. Signed statement of intent to take CPA exam in Texas. FAFSA.
Additional information: Must be enrolled as fifth-year accounting student who has completed at least 120 credit hours, including 15 hours of accounting. Must register for selective service or be exempt from this requirement. Contact college financial aid office for application.

Amount of award: $5,000
Contact:
Texas Higher Education Coordinating Board
Phone: 800-242-3062
Web: www.collegeforalltexans.com

Texas Good Neighbor Scholarship

Type of award: Scholarship.
Intended use: For undergraduate or graduate study at accredited 2-year, 4-year or graduate institution in United States. Designated institutions: Texas public colleges and universities.
Eligibility: Applicant must be native-born citizen of any Western Hemisphere country other than Cuba.
Application requirements: Proof of eligibility.
Additional information: Must plan to return to native country. Contact institution's financial aid office or the international student affairs office for application. Must meet GPA requirement and hourly limit requirement set by institution for renewal. Award covers one year of tuition.

Amount of award: Full tuition

Contact:
Texas Higher Education Coordinating Board
Phone: 800-242-3062
Web: www.collegeforalltexans.com

TEXAS Grant (Toward Excellence, Access, and Success)

Type of award: Scholarship, renewable.
Intended use: For undergraduate study at vocational, 2-year or 4-year institution. Designated institutions: Texas public colleges or universities.
Eligibility: Applicant must be U.S. citizen or permanent resident residing in Texas.
Basis for selection: Applicant must demonstrate financial need and high academic achievement.
Application requirements: Selective Service registration or exemption from requirement. FAFSA.
Additional information: Applicant must have completed Recommended High School Program or Distinguished Achievement Program, enroll in college at least 3/4-time (unless granted hardship waiver) within 16 months of high school graduation, and must receive first award prior to completing 30 hours on campus. Also eligible are students with associate degrees from public technical or community colleges in Texas, who enroll in public Texas universities within 12 months of receiving associate's. Expected Family Contribution (EFC) to education must be less than $4,620. Minimum 2.5 GPA required to renew award. Applicant must not have been convicted of felony or crime involving controlled substance. Award not to exceed student's need or public institution tuition and fees. Must register for Selective Service or be exempt from this requirement. Contact financial aid office at specific college/university for application deadline and procedures.

Amount of award: Full tuition
Contact:
Texas Higher Education Coordinating Board
Phone: 800-242-3062
Web: www.collegeforalltexans.com

Texas Highest Ranking High School Graduate Tuition Exemption

Type of award: Scholarship.
Intended use: For freshman study at accredited postsecondary institution. Designated institutions: Texas public colleges and universities.
Eligibility: Applicant must be residing in Texas.
Basis for selection: Applicant must demonstrate high academic achievement.
Application requirements: Proof of eligibility. Valedictorian certificate issued by Texas Education Agency.
Additional information: Must be highest-ranking graduate of accredited public or private Texas high school. Award covers tuition during both semesters of first regular session immediately following the student's high school graduation; fees not included. Deadline varies. Contact college/university financial aid office to apply.

Amount of award: Full tuition
Contact:
Texas Higher Education Coordinating Board
Phone: 800-242-3062
Web: www.collegeforalltexans.com

Texas Public Educational Grant

Type of award: Scholarship.
Intended use: For undergraduate or graduate study at accredited vocational, 2-year or 4-year institution. Designated institutions: Texas public colleges and universities.
Eligibility: Applicant must be residing in Texas.
Basis for selection: Applicant must demonstrate financial need.
Application requirements: FAFSA.
Additional information: Award amount varies; may not exceed student's financial need. Deadline varies. Applicant must register for Selective Service, unless exempt. Contact financial aid office at college/university for more information.
Contact:
Texas Higher Education Coordinating Board
Phone: 800-242-3062
Web: www.collegeforalltexans.com

Texas Senior Citizen, 65 or Older, Free Tuition for Up to 6 Credit Hours

Type of award: Scholarship.
Intended use: For half-time undergraduate or graduate study at 2-year or 4-year institution in United States. Designated institutions: Participating Texas public colleges and universities.
Eligibility: Applicant must be at least 65, returning adult student. Applicant must be residing in Texas.
Application requirements: Proof of eligibility.
Additional information: Program allows senior citizens to take up to 6 credit hours per semester, tuition-free. Texas institutions not required to offer program; applicants should check with registrar. Classes must not already be filled with students paying at full price and must use tax support for some of their cost. Must meet GPA requirement and hourly limit requirement set by institution for renewal. Contact college for additional information.
Contact:
Texas Higher Education Coordinating Board
Phone: 800-242-3062
Web: www.collegeforalltexans.com

Texas Tuition Equalization Grant (TEG)

Type of award: Scholarship.
Intended use: For full-time undergraduate or graduate study at accredited 2-year or 4-year institution in United States. Designated institutions: Private, non-profit Texas colleges and universities.
Eligibility: Applicant must be U.S. citizen or permanent resident residing in Texas.
Basis for selection: Applicant must demonstrate financial need.
Application requirements: Proof of eligibility. Selective Service registration or exemption from requirement. FAFSA.
Additional information: Non-resident National Merit Finalists also eligible. Not open to athletic scholarship recipients. Must maintain 2.5 GPA and complete 24 credit hours per year. Award cannot exceed difference between applicant's tuition at private institution and what applicant would pay at public institution. Award amount varies; maximum is $3,364, but students with exceptional need may receive up to $5,046. Applicants should contact the financial aid office at the Texas

private college/university they plan to attend for more information.

Amount of award:	$3,364-$5,046
Number of awards:	28,000

Contact:
Texas Higher Education Coordinating Board
Phone: 800-242-3062
Web: www.collegeforalltexans.com

Texas Tuition Exemption for Blind or Deaf Students

Type of award: Scholarship, renewable.
Intended use: For undergraduate or graduate study at accredited 2-year or 4-year institution in United States. Designated institutions: Texas public colleges and universities.
Eligibility: Applicant must be visually impaired or hearing impaired. Applicant must be U.S. citizen or permanent resident residing in Texas.
Basis for selection: Applicant must demonstrate depth of character.
Application requirements: Recommendations, transcript, proof of eligibility. Certification of disability. Written statement indicating which certificate, degree program, or professional enhancement applicant intends to pursue.
Additional information: Must be certified by Texas Department of Assistive and Rehabilitative Services and have high school diploma or equivalent. Applicant must enroll in classes for which the college receives tax support. Award does not include fees or charges for lodging, board, or clothing. Must meet GPA requirement and hourly limit requirement set by institution for renewal. Application deadline varies. Contact financial aid office at college/university for more information.

Amount of award:	Full tuition

Contact:
Texas Higher Education Coordinating Board
Phone: 800-242-3062
Web: www.collegeforalltexans.com

Texas Tuition Exemption for Children of Disabled or Deceased Firefighters, Peace Officers, Game Wardens, and Employees of Correctional Institutions

Type of award: Scholarship, renewable.
Intended use: For undergraduate or graduate study at 2-year or 4-year institution in United States. Designated institutions: Texas public colleges and universities.
Eligibility: Applicant must be no older than 21. Applicant must be residing in Texas. Applicant's parent must have been killed or disabled in work-related accident as firefighter, police officer or public safety officer.
Application requirements: Proof of eligibility.
Additional information: Applicant must be child of paid or volunteer firefighter; paid municipal, county or state peace officer; custodial employee of Department of Corrections; or game warden disabled or killed in Texas in the line of duty. Must meet GPA requirement and hourly limit requirement set by institution. Persons eligible to participate in a school district's special education program under section 29.003 at age 22 may also apply. Applicant must enroll in courses that use tax support to cover some of their cost. Applicant must obtain certification form from Texas Higher Education Coordinating Board, have parent's former employer complete it, and submit to Texas Higher Education Coordinating Board. The Board will

notify applicant's institution of eligibility. Students may be exempted from tuition and fees for the first 120 semester credits or until age 26, whichever comes first.

Amount of award: Full tuition

Contact:
Texas Higher Education Coordinating Board
Phone: 800-242-3062
Web: www.collegeforalltexans.com

Texas Tuition Reduction for Students Taking More Than 15 Hours

Type of award: Scholarship.
Intended use: For full-time undergraduate study at postsecondary institution. Designated institutions: Texas public colleges and universities.
Eligibility: Applicant must be residing in Texas.
Application requirements: Proof of eligibility.
Additional information: Applicant must be enrolled in at least 15 credit hours at institution during semester/term for which reduction is offered. Must be making satisfactory progress toward completion of a degree program. Must meet GPA requirement and hourly limit requirement set by institution for renewal. Contact registrar's office at college/university to inquire whether they offer reduction.

Contact:
Texas Higher Education Coordinating Board
Phone: 800-242-3062
Web: www.collegeforalltexans.com

Tuition Exemption for Children of U.S. Military POW/MIAs from Texas

Type of award: Scholarship, renewable.
Intended use: For undergraduate study at accredited 2-year or 4-year institution. Designated institutions: Texas public colleges or universities.
Eligibility: Applicant must be no older than 25. Applicant must be U.S. citizen or permanent resident residing in Texas. Applicant must be dependent of POW/MIA.
Application requirements: Proof of eligibility. Documentation from Department of Defense that a parent, classified as Texas resident, is MIA or a POW. FAFSA.
Additional information: Applicants 22 to 25 years of age must receive most of their support from a parent. Applicant must enroll in courses that use tax support to cover some of their cost. Award does not include room, board, clothing, or property deposits. Must meet GPA requirement and hourly limit requirement set by institution for renewal. Applicants should contact the registrar at the college/university they plan to attend for more information.

Amount of award: Full tuition

Contact:
Texas Higher Education Coordinating Board
Phone: 800-242-3062
Web: www.collegeforalltexans.com

ThePennyHoarder.com

ThePennyHoarder.com Frugal Student Scholarship

Type of award: Scholarship.
Intended use: For at accredited vocational, 2-year, 4-year or graduate institution.
Application requirements: Essay topic: "In 150 words, tell us the most unique or interesting thing you've ever done to make or save extra money."
Additional information: Must be enrolled in a college or university and have an active class schedule. Application can be found online.

Number of awards:	1
Application deadline:	December 31
Notification begins:	March 1
Total amount awarded:	$2,000

Contact:
661 Central Avenue
Saint Petersburg, FL 33601
Phone: 727-480-0602
Web: www.thepennyhoarder.com/frugal-student-scholarship/

Thermo Fisher Scientific

Thermo Fisher Scientific Antibody Scholarship

Type of award: Scholarship.
Intended use: For undergraduate or graduate study at accredited 2-year, 4-year or graduate institution.
Eligibility: Applicant must be at least 16. Applicant must be U.S. citizen or permanent resident.
Basis for selection: Major/career interest in biology; chemistry; biochemistry or life sciences.
Application requirements: Students must complete the application form on our website, including the essay question. Students are encouraged to include additional information, such as a CV or resume that outlines complete education background, work experience, extra-curricular activities and volunteer work, as well as letters of recommendation, posters, presentations and/or publications.
Additional information: Minimum 3.0 GPA. The Scholarship Committee seeks well-rounded students in biology, chemistry, bio-chemistry or related life science fields who best embody one or more of Thermo Fisher Scientific's values of Integrity, Intensity, Innovation or Involvement, as demonstrated by the application. Thermo Fisher Scientific, its subsidiaries, affiliates, distributors, sales representatives, and each of their respective officers, directors and employees (collectively, the Program Entities), as well as the immediate family members and/or those persons living in the same households of the foregoing are not eligible to apply or win a scholarship in this Program.

Amount of award:	$5,000-$10,000
Number of awards:	6
Number of applicants:	3,388
Application deadline:	June 15
Notification begins:	August 4
Total amount awarded:	$40,000

Contact:
Thermo Fisher Scientific
3747 N Meridian Road
Rockford, IL 61101
Phone: 815-668-4973
Fax: 815-968-8148
Web: www.thermofisher.com/antibodyscholarship

Third Marine Division Association

Third Marine Division Memorial Scholarship Fund

Type of award: Scholarship, renewable.
Intended use: For undergraduate study at accredited 2-year or 4-year institution in United States or Canada.
Eligibility: Applicant must be at least 16, no older than 23. Applicant must be U.S. citizen. Must be unmarried dependent child of qualified member or deceased member (Marine or Navy Corpsman) of the Third Marine Division Association, or dependent child of any military personnel who served in any Third Marine Division (Reinf) unit and who died as result of combat actions while serving in Vietnam between March 8, 1965 and November 27, 1969, or in operations Desert Shield, Desert Storm, or any other qualified Persian Gulf operations after August 2, 1990. Dependent children of deceased Third Marine Division personnel who served in above operations whose post-service deaths have been certified by the Department of Veterans Affairs to have been the result of combat-related wounds or other disabilities incurred during the period of eligible combat service, and were not the result of any misconduct by the veteran, are also eligible.
Basis for selection: Applicant must demonstrate financial need and high academic achievement.
Application requirements: Proof of eligibility. Financial aid form.
Additional information: Minimum 2.0 GPA. Number of awards varies. Eligible dependent children participating automatically receive renewal application forms.

Amount of award:	$500-$1,500
Number of applicants:	12
Application deadline:	April 15
Notification begins:	June 15
Total amount awarded:	$9,300

Contact:
GySgt. Don H Gee, USMC (Ret)
Secretary, Memorial Scholarship Fund
P.O. Box 254
Chalfont, PA 18914-0254
Web: www.caltrap.com

Thomas Soldan Attorney At Law

Thomas Soldan Healthy Communities Scholarship

Type of award: Scholarship.
Intended use: For undergraduate or graduate study at accredited vocational, 2-year, 4-year or graduate institution.

Eligibility: Applicant must be high school senior.
Basis for selection: Applicant must demonstrate high academic achievement.
Application requirements: Unofficial transcript, application cover sheet, application essay, updated resume. Essay topic (500 words): "Candidate should describe her or his past and future dedication to healthy communities and sustainable initiatives. The personal statement should make clear how the candidate would use his or her continued education to champion accessible health- and local-activities programs."
Additional information: Minimum 3.0 GPA required. The scholarship candidate must possess a proven record of interest in healthy communities through past and present volunteer, professional, or educational experiences.

Amount of award:	$500
Number of awards:	1
Number of applicants:	20
Application deadline:	May 1
Total amount awarded:	$500

Contact:
Thomas Soldan Healthy Communities Scholarship
20 West Market Street
Suite B
Leesburg, VA 20176
Phone: 202-517-0502
Fax: 703-940-9145
Web: virginialawfirm.net/healthy-communities-scholarship/

Thurgood Marshall College Fund

Thurgood Marshall Scholarship Award

Type of award: Scholarship, renewable.
Intended use: For full-time undergraduate or graduate study at 4-year or graduate institution in United States. Designated institutions: One of 47 designated historically black public universities.
Eligibility: Applicant must be U.S. citizen or permanent resident.
Basis for selection: Applicant must demonstrate financial need, high academic achievement, leadership and service orientation.
Application requirements: Recommendations, essay, transcript. Resume, headshot or personal photograph. FAFSA.
Additional information: Must have high school or current GPA of 3.0 or higher, and must maintain throughout duration of scholarship. Contact university's Thurgood Marshall College Fund campus coordinator directly for more information, or visit Website.

Amount of award:	$3,100
Number of awards:	200
Number of applicants:	2,270
Total amount awarded:	$1,200,000

Contact:
Thurgood Marshall College Fund
901 F Street
Suite 300
Washington, DC 20004
Phone: 202-507-4851
Fax: 202-652-2934
Web: www.thurgoodmarshallfund.net/scholarship/about-scholarships-program

Titan Web Agency

Titan Web Agency Scholarship Program

Type of award: Scholarship, renewable.
Intended use: For full-time undergraduate or graduate study at accredited 2-year, 4-year or graduate institution.
Eligibility: Applicant must be U.S. citizen.
Application requirements: Must be attending a two year community college or a four year accredited university. Minorities are encouraged to apply. To apply, please submit an essay (1000 word minimum) detailing why you want to be an entrepreneur, as well as a creative photo that you feel represents you best.
Additional information: When submitting your essays make sure you include:. Full Name. Address. Email Address. Phone Number. Proof of registration for school. The check will be made out to the school you are attending.

Amount of award:	$500
Number of awards:	1
Application deadline:	June 1
Notification begins:	June 15
Total amount awarded:	$500

Contact:
Titan Web Agency
P.O. Box 1262
Riverton, UT 84065
Phone: 801-783-3101
Web: https://titanwebagency.com/scholarship/

Toptal

Toptal Scholarships for Female Developers

Type of award: Scholarship.
Intended use: For undergraduate or graduate study at vocational, 2-year, 4-year or graduate institution in or outside United States or Canada.
Eligibility: Applicant must be female. Applicant must be U.S. citizen, permanent resident or international student.
Basis for selection: Major/career interest in engineering, computer.
Application requirements: Essay. Essay.
Additional information: One award every month. Must make or have made a meaningful contribution to open source. Publish a post on a personal blog explaining the open source project you chose, your contributions, the biggest challenges you faced, what you learned from your work, etc. After

completing the previous steps, complete the application online using the link below.

Amount of award:	$5,000
Number of awards:	12
Total amount awarded:	$60,000

Contact:
Toptal Scholarships
548 Market Street
San Francisco, CA 36879
Web: www.toptal.com/scholarships

Tortuga Backpacks

Tortuga Backpacks Study Abroad Scholarship

Type of award: Scholarship.
Intended use: For full-time undergraduate study at 4-year institution in United States in Applied or accepted into study abroad program eligible for credit by your college or university for study abroad.
Eligibility: Applicant must be U.S. citizen or permanent resident.
Basis for selection: Competition/talent/interest in study abroad.
Application requirements: Essay.
Additional information: 1 award per semester (Fall, Spring). Deadline for the Spring semester scholarship is December 20. Deadline for the Fall semester scholarship is May 20. Selection based on eligibility and strength of 500-word essay.

Amount of award:	$1,000
Number of awards:	5
Number of applicants:	350
Application deadline:	December 20, May 20
Total amount awarded:	$6,000

Contact:
Tortuga Backpacks Study Abroad Scholarship
340 S. Lemon Ave. #7616
Walnut, CA 91789
Web: www.tortugabackpacks.com/pages/study-abroad-scholarship

Tourism Cares

ASTA Alaska Airlines Scholarship

Type of award: Scholarship.
Intended use: For sophomore, junior or senior study at accredited 2-year or 4-year institution in United States or Canada.
Eligibility: Applicant must be U.S. citizen, permanent resident or Canadian citizen or resident.
Basis for selection: Major/career interest in tourism/travel or hospitality administration/management. Applicant must demonstrate high academic achievement.
Application requirements: Essay, transcript. Resume, copy of U.S. or Canadian Passport or Alien Registration Card. Two evaluations and letters of recommendation (one from hospitality/tourism-related faculty member, one from hospitality/tourism professional).
Additional information: Minimum 3.0 GPA. Must be entering the second year of a two-year school, third year of a three-year

school (for Quebec), junior or senior year of a four-year school, any year of graduate study. Check Website for deadline and additional criteria.

Amount of award: $1,000
Number of awards: 1

Contact:
Tourism Cares
275 Turnpike Street
Suite 307
Canton, MA 02021
Phone: 781-821-5990
Fax: 781-821-8949
Web: www.tourismcares.org/student-programs

ASTA American Express Travel Scholarship

Type of award: Scholarship, renewable.
Intended use: For full-time freshman study at accredited 2-year or 4-year institution in United States or Canada.
Eligibility: Applicant must be high school senior. Applicant must be U.S. citizen or permanent resident.
Basis for selection: Major/career interest in hospitality administration/management or tourism/travel. Applicant must demonstrate high academic achievement.
Application requirements: Essay, transcript. Resume. U.S. Passport or U.S. Alien Registration Card. Two evaluations and letters of recommendation (one from hospitality/tourism-related faculty member, one from hospitality/tourism professional).
Additional information: Minimum 3.0 GPA. Applicant must be high school senior attending high school with the Academy of Hospitality & Tourism (AOHT) Program, graduating at end of semester or term. Visit Website for deadline, application, additional criteria.

Amount of award: $1,000
Number of awards: 1

Contact:
Tourism Cares
275 Turnpike Street
Suite 307
Canton, MA 02021
Phone: 781-821-5990
Fax: 781-821-8949
Web: www.tourismcares.org/student-programs

ASTA Arizona Scholarship

Type of award: Scholarship, renewable.
Intended use: For sophomore, junior or senior study at accredited 2-year or 4-year institution in United States. Designated institutions: Colleges and universities in Arizona.
Eligibility: Applicant must be U.S. citizen, permanent resident or Canadian citizen/resident.
Basis for selection: Major/career interest in tourism/travel. Applicant must demonstrate high academic achievement.
Application requirements: Essay, transcript. Resume. U.S. or Canadian passport or U.S. or Canadian Alien Registration Card. Two evaluations and letters of recommendation (one from hospitality/tourism-related faculty member, one from hospitality/tourism professional).
Additional information: Minimum 3.0 GPA. Applicants attending two-year schools must be entering second year of program; students attending four-year schools must be entering junior or senior years. Visit Website for application, deadline, additional criteria.

Amount of award: $2,000
Number of awards: 1

Contact:
Tourism Cares
275 Turnpike Street
Suite 307
Canton, MA 02021
Phone: 781-821-5990
Fax: 781-821-8949
Web: www.tourismcares.org/student-programs

ASTA Northern California Chapter - Richard Epping Scholarship

Type of award: Scholarship, renewable.
Intended use: For sophomore, junior or senior study at accredited 2-year or 4-year institution in United States. Designated institutions: Colleges and universities in California.
Eligibility: Applicant must be U.S. citizen or permanent resident residing in California.
Basis for selection: Major/career interest in hospitality administration/management or tourism/travel. Applicant must demonstrate high academic achievement.
Application requirements: Essay, transcript. Resume. U.S. passport or Alien Registration Card, California driver's license. Two evaluations and letters of recommendation (one from hospitality/tourism-related faculty member, one from hospitality/tourism professional).
Additional information: Minimum 3.0 GPA. Must be entering second year at two-year school, junior or senior year at four-year school. Visit Website for application, deadline, additional criteria.

Amount of award: $1,000
Number of awards: 1

Contact:
Tourism Cares
275 Turnpike Street
Suite 307
Canton, MA 02021
Phone: 781-821-5990
Fax: 781-821-8949
Web: www.tourismcares.org/student-programs

ASTA Pacific Northwest Chapter/ William Hunt Scholarship

Type of award: Scholarship.
Intended use: For sophomore, junior or senior study at accredited 2-year or 4-year institution in United States or Canada.
Eligibility: Applicant must be U.S. citizen or permanent resident residing in Oregon, Montana, Alaska, Idaho or Washington.
Basis for selection: Major/career interest in tourism/travel or hospitality administration/management. Applicant must demonstrate high academic achievement.
Application requirements: Essay, transcript. Resume. U.S. Passport or U.S. Alien Registration card. U.S. driver's license as proof of state residency. Two evaluations and letters of recommendation (one from hospitality/tourism-related faculty member, one from hospitality/tourism professional).
Additional information: Minimum 3.0 GPA. Must be entering the second year of a two-year school, or junior or senior year of a four-year school. Submit all items in electronic form except transcript, which should be sent directly from school. Visit Website for deadline and additional eligibility criteria.

Amount of award: $1,000
Number of awards: 1

Contact:
Tourism Cares
275 Turnpike Street
Suite 307
Canton, MA 02021
Phone: 781-821-5990
Fax: 781-821-8949
Web: www.tourismcares.org/student-programs

ASTA Princess Cruises Scholarship

Type of award: Scholarship, renewable.
Intended use: For sophomore, junior or senior study at accredited 2-year or 4-year institution in United States or Canada.
Eligibility: Applicant must be U.S. citizen, permanent resident or Canadian citizen/resident.
Basis for selection: Major/career interest in hospitality administration/management or tourism/travel. Applicant must demonstrate high academic achievement.
Application requirements: Recommendations, essay, transcript. Resume. U.S. or Canadian passport or U.S. or Canadian Alien Registration Card. Two evaluations and letters of recommendation (one from hospitality/tourism-related faculty member, one from hospitality/tourism professional).
Additional information: Minimum 3.0 GPA. Must be entering the second year of a two-year school, third year of a three-year school (Quebec), junior or senior year of a four-year school. Visit Website for application, deadline, additional criteria.

Amount of award:	$2,500
Number of awards:	1

Contact:
Tourism Cares
275 Turnpike Street
Suite 307
Canton, MA 02021
Phone: 781-821-5990
Fax: 781-821-8949
Web: www.tourismcares.org/student-programs

IATAN Ronald A. Santana Memorial Scholarship

Type of award: Scholarship.
Intended use: For sophomore, junior or senior study at 2-year or 4-year institution in United States.
Eligibility: Applicant must be U.S. citizen, permanent resident or Guam or Puerto Rico citizens/residents.
Basis for selection: Major/career interest in tourism/travel or hospitality administration/management. Applicant must demonstrate high academic achievement.
Application requirements: Essay, transcript. Resume. U.S. passport or Alien Registration Card. Two evaluations and letters of recommendation (one from hospitality/tourism-related faculty member, one from hospitality/tourism professional).
Additional information: Minimum 3.0 GPA. Applicants attending two-year schools must be entering second year of program; students attending four-year schools must be entering junior or senior year. Visit Website for application, deadline, additional criteria.

Amount of award:	$1,000
Number of awards:	5
Total amount awarded:	$5,000

Contact:
Tourism Cares
275 Turnpike Street
Suite 307
Canton, MA 02021
Phone: 781-821-5990
Fax: 781-821-8949
Web: www.tourismcares.org/student-programs

NTA Canada Scholarship

Type of award: Scholarship.
Intended use: For full-time sophomore, junior, senior or graduate study at accredited 2-year or 4-year institution in United States or Canada.
Eligibility: Applicant must be permanent resident of Canada.
Basis for selection: Major/career interest in tourism/travel or hospitality administration/management. Applicant must demonstrate high academic achievement.
Application requirements: Essay, transcript. Resume. Canadian passport or Canadian Alien Registration Card. Two evaluations and letters of recommendation from hospitality/tourism-related faculty, one from a professional in the hospitality/tourism industry.
Additional information: Minimum 3.0 GPA. Must demonstrate focus and commitment to tourism. Must be entering the second year of a two-year school, third year of a three-year school (Quebec), senior year of a four-year school, any year of graduate school. Visit Website for application, deadline, additional criteria.

Amount of award:	$1,000
Number of awards:	1

Contact:
Tourism Cares
275 Turnpike Street
Suite 307
Canton, MA 02021
Phone: 781-821-5990
Fax: 781-821-8949
Web: www.tourismcares.org/student-programs

NTA Connecticut Scholarship

Type of award: Scholarship.
Intended use: For junior or senior study at accredited 4-year institution in United States.
Eligibility: Applicant must be U.S. citizen or permanent resident residing in Connecticut.
Basis for selection: Major/career interest in hospitality administration/management or tourism/travel. Applicant must demonstrate high academic achievement.
Application requirements: Essay, transcript. Resume. U.S. passport or Alien Registration Card, Connecticut driver's license. Two evaluations and letters of recommendation (one from hospitality/tourism-related faculty member, one from hospitality/tourism professional).
Additional information: Minimum 3.0 GPA. Visit Website for application, deadline, additional criteria.

Amount of award:	$1,000
Number of awards:	1

Contact:
Tourism Cares
275 Turnpike Street
Suite 307
Canton, MA 02021
Phone: 781-821-5990
Fax: 781-821-8949
Web: www.tourismcares.org/student-programs

NTA Florida Scholarship

Type of award: Scholarship.
Intended use: For sophomore, junior or senior study at accredited 2-year or 4-year institution in United States.
Eligibility: Applicant must be U.S. citizen or permanent resident residing in Florida.
Basis for selection: Major/career interest in hospitality administration/management or tourism/travel. Applicant must demonstrate high academic achievement.
Application requirements: Essay, transcript. Resume. U.S. passport or Alien Registration Card, Florida driver's license. Two evaluations and letters of recommendation (one from hospitality/tourism-related faculty member, one from hospitality/tourism professional).
Additional information: Minimum 3.0 GPA. Must be entering the second year of a two-year school, junior or senior year of a four-year school. Visit Website for application, deadline, additional criteria.

Amount of award:	$1,500
Number of awards:	1

Contact:
Tourism Cares
275 Turnpike Street
Suite 307
Canton, MA 02021
Phone: 781-821-5990
Fax: 781-821-8949
Web: www.tourismcares.org/student-programs

NTA LaMacchia Family Scholarship

Type of award: Scholarship.
Intended use: For full-time junior or senior study at 4-year institution. Designated institutions: Wisconsin institutions.
Eligibility: Applicant must be U.S. citizen or permanent resident.
Basis for selection: Major/career interest in tourism/travel or hospitality administration/management. Applicant must demonstrate high academic achievement.
Application requirements: Essay, transcript. Resume. U.S. passport or Alien Registration Card. Two evaluations and letters of recommendation (one from hospitality/tourism-related faculty member, one from hospitality/tourism professional).
Additional information: Must have minimum 3.0 GPA. Visit Website for application, deadline, additional criteria.

Amount of award:	$1,000
Number of awards:	1

Contact:
Tourism Cares
275 Turnpike Street
Suite 307
Canton, MA 02021
Phone: 781-821-5990
Fax: 781-821-8949
Web: www.tourismcares.org/student-programs

NTA Massachusetts Scholarship

Type of award: Scholarship.
Intended use: For sophomore, junior or senior study at accredited 2-year or 4-year institution in United States.
Eligibility: Applicant must be U.S. citizen or permanent resident residing in Massachusetts.
Basis for selection: Major/career interest in hospitality administration/management or tourism/travel. Applicant must demonstrate high academic achievement.

Application requirements: Essay, transcript. Resume. U.S. passport or Alien Registration Card, Massachusetts driver's license. Two evaluations and letters of recommendation (one from hospitality/tourism-related faculty member, one from hospitality/tourism professional).
Additional information: Minimum 3.0 GPA. Applicants attending two-year schools must be entering second year of program; students attending four-year schools must be entering junior or senior years. Visit Website for application, deadline, additional criteria.

Amount of award:	$1,000
Number of awards:	1

Contact:
Tourism Cares
275 Turnpike Street
Suite 307
Canton, MA 02021
Phone: 781-821-5990
Fax: 781-821-8949
Web: www.tourismcares.org/student-programs

NTA New Horizons - Kathy LeTarte Scholarship

Type of award: Scholarship.
Intended use: For junior or senior study at accredited 4-year institution in United States or Canada.
Eligibility: Applicant must be U.S. citizen or permanent resident residing in Michigan.
Basis for selection: Major/career interest in tourism/travel or hospitality administration/management. Applicant must demonstrate high academic achievement.
Application requirements: Essay, transcript. Resume. U.S. passport or U.S. Alien Registration Card. Michigan driver's license. Two evaluations and letters of recommendation (one from hospitality/tourism-related faculty and one from a professional in hospitality/tourism industry).
Additional information: Minimum 3.0 GPA. Must be entering third year of three-year school (Quebec), or junior, senior year of four-year school. Visit Website for application, deadline, additional criteria.

Amount of award:	$1,000
Number of awards:	1

Contact:
Tourism Cares
275 Turnpike Street
Suite 307
Canton, MA 02021
Phone: 781-821-5990
Fax: 781-821-8949
Web: www.tourismcares.org/student-programs

NTA New Jersey Scholarship

Type of award: Scholarship.
Intended use: For sophomore, junior or senior study at accredited 2-year or 4-year institution in United States.
Eligibility: Applicant must be U.S. citizen or permanent resident residing in New Jersey.
Basis for selection: Major/career interest in hospitality administration/management or tourism/travel. Applicant must demonstrate high academic achievement.
Application requirements: Essay, transcript. Resume. U.S. passport or U.S. Alien Registration Card. New Jersey driver's license. Two evaluations and letters of recommendation (one from hospitality/tourism-related faculty member, one from hospitality/tourism professional).

Additional information: Minimum 3.0 GPA. Applicant must be entering the second year of a two-year school, or junior or senior year of a four-year school. Visit Website for application, deadline, additional criteria.

>   **Amount of award:** $1,000
>   **Number of awards:** 1

Contact:
Tourism Cares
275 Turnpike Street
Suite 307
Canton, MA 02021
Phone: 781-821-5990
Fax: 781-821-8949
Web: www.tourismcares.org/student-programs

NTA New York Scholarship

Type of award: Scholarship.

Intended use: For full-time sophomore, junior or senior study at accredited 2-year or 4-year institution in United States.

Eligibility: Applicant must be U.S. citizen or permanent resident residing in New York.

Basis for selection: Major/career interest in hospitality administration/management or tourism/travel. Applicant must demonstrate high academic achievement.

Application requirements: Essay, transcript. Resume. U.S. passport or U.S. Alien Registration Card. New York driver's license. Two evaluations and letters of recommendation (one from hospitality/tourism-related faculty member, one from hospitality/tourism professional).

Additional information: Minimum 3.0 GPA. Applicants attending two-year schools must be entering second year of program; students at four-year schools must be entering junior or senior years. Visit Website for application, deadline, additional criteria.

>   **Amount of award:** $1,000
>   **Number of awards:** 1

Contact:
Tourism Cares
275 Turnpike Street
Suite 307
Canton, MA 02021
Phone: 781-821-5990
Fax: 781-821-8949
Web: www.tourismcares.org/student-programs

NTA North America Scholarship

Type of award: Scholarship.

Intended use: For sophomore, junior, senior or graduate study at 2-year, 4-year or graduate institution in United States or Canada.

Eligibility: Applicant must be U.S. citizen, permanent resident or Canadian citizen/resident.

Basis for selection: Major/career interest in tourism/travel or hospitality administration/management. Applicant must demonstrate high academic achievement.

Application requirements: Essay, transcript. Resume. U.S. or Canadian passport or U.S. or Canadian Alien Registration Card. Two evaluations and letters of recommendation (one from hospitality/tourism-related faculty member, one from hospitality/tourism professional).

Additional information: Minimum 3.0 GPA. Applicants attending two-year schools must be entering second year of program; students attending four-year schools must be entering junior or senior year. Visit Website for application, deadline, additional criteria.

>   **Amount of award:** $1,000
>   **Number of awards:** 13
>   **Total amount awarded:** $13,000

Contact:
Tourism Cares
275 Turnpike Street
Suite 307
Canton, MA 02021
Phone: 781-821-5990
Fax: 781-821-8949
Web: www.tourismcares.org/student-programs

NTA Ohio Scholarship

Type of award: Scholarship.

Intended use: For sophomore, junior or senior study at accredited 2-year or 4-year institution in United States.

Eligibility: Applicant must be U.S. citizen or permanent resident residing in Ohio.

Basis for selection: Major/career interest in hospitality administration/management or tourism/travel. Applicant must demonstrate high academic achievement.

Application requirements: Essay, transcript. Resume. U.S. passport or Alien Registration Card, Ohio driver's license. Two evaluations and letters of recommendation (one from hospitality/tourism-related faculty member, one from hospitality/tourism professional).

Additional information: Minimum 3.0 GPA. Applicants attending two-year schools must be entering second year of program; students at four-year schools must be entering junior or senior years. Visit Website for application, deadline, additional criteria.

>   **Amount of award:** $1,000
>   **Number of awards:** 1

Contact:
Tourism Cares
275 Turnpike Street
Suite 307
Canton, MA 02021
Phone: 781-821-5990
Fax: 781-821-8949
Web: www.tourismcares.org/student-programs

NTA Pat & Jim Host Scholarship

Type of award: Scholarship.

Intended use: For full-time sophomore, junior, senior or graduate study at accredited 4-year institution in United States.

Eligibility: Applicant must be U.S. citizen or permanent resident residing in Kentucky.

Basis for selection: Major/career interest in tourism/travel or hospitality administration/management. Applicant must demonstrate high academic achievement.

Application requirements: Essay, transcript. Resume. U.S. passport or U.S. Alien Registration Card. Copy of Kentucky driver's license. Two evaluations and letters of recommendation (one from hospitality/tourism-related faculty member; other from hospitality/tourism industry professional).

Additional information: Minimum 3.0 GPA. Must demonstrate a clear focus on and commitment to tourism. Visit Website for application, deadline, additional criteria.

>   **Amount of award:** $1,000
>   **Number of awards:** 1

Contact:
Tourism Cares
275 Turnpike Street
Suite 307
Canton, MA 02021
Phone: 781-821-5990
Fax: 781-821-8949
Web: www.tourismcares.org/student-programs

NTA Rene Campbell - Ruth McKinney Scholarship

Type of award: Scholarship.
Intended use: For sophomore, junior or senior study at accredited 4-year institution in United States or Canada.
Eligibility: Applicant must be U.S. citizen or permanent resident residing in North Carolina.
Basis for selection: Major/career interest in tourism/travel or hospitality administration/management. Applicant must demonstrate high academic achievement.
Application requirements: Essay, transcript. Resume. U.S. Passport or U.S. Alien Registration Card, North Carolina driver's license. Two evaluations and letters of recommendation (one from hospitality/tourism-related faculty member, one from hospitality/tourism professional).
Additional information: Minimum 3.0 GPA. Must be entering the second year of a two-year school, third year of a three-year school (Quebec), junior or senior year of a four-year school. Visit Website for application, deadline, additional criteria.

Amount of award:	$1,000
Number of awards:	1

Contact:
Tourism Cares
275 Turnpike Street
Suite 307
Canton, MA 02021
Phone: 781-821-5990
Fax: 781-821-8949
Web: www.tourismcares.org/student-programs

NTA Utah Keith Griffall Scholarship

Type of award: Scholarship.
Intended use: For sophomore, junior or senior study at accredited 2-year or 4-year institution in United States.
Eligibility: Applicant must be U.S. citizen or permanent resident residing in Utah.
Basis for selection: Major/career interest in hospitality administration/management or tourism/travel. Applicant must demonstrate high academic achievement.
Application requirements: Essay, transcript. Resume. U.S. Passport or Alien Registration Card, Utah driver's license. Two evaluations and letters of recommendation (one from hospitality/tourism-related faculty member, one from hospitality/tourism professional).
Additional information: Minimum 3.0 GPA. Must be entering the second year of a two-year school, junior or senior year of a four-year school. Visit Website for application, deadline, additional criteria.

Amount of award:	$1,000
Number of awards:	1

Contact:
Tourism Cares
275 Turnpike Street
Suite 307
Canton, MA 02021
Phone: 781-821-5900
Fax: 781-821-8949
Web: www.tourismcares.org/student-programs

TransCanada

TransCanada Trades Scholarship

Type of award: Scholarship, renewable.
Intended use: For full-time undergraduate study at accredited postsecondary institution.
Eligibility: Applicant must be high school senior.
Basis for selection: Priority given to first year students.
Application requirements: Essay, proof of eligibility. Applicant must be a US/Canadian citizen or permanent resident of either country. Student must be enrolled in this calendar year. Career/College Major Interest: must be in trades relevant to the energy industry, including: electrical, instrumentation, welding, millwright, pipefitter, machinist, heavy equiptment operator, power operator, heavy duty mechanic, etc. The school must be accredited to award trades certificates/diplomas. The scholarship is open to students from the communities where we do business across the US (and Canada). A map of our operating area can be found at www.tcscholarships.com.
Additional information: The award is renewable, however, students must apply/reapply annually.

Amount of award:	$1,000-$1,000
Number of awards:	75
Application deadline:	April 15
Notification begins:	June 1
Total amount awarded:	$75,000

Contact:
TransCanada Corp.
Web: www.transcanada.com/7109.html

TransCanada Corp.

TransCanada Community Leaders Scholarship

Type of award: Scholarship, renewable.
Intended use: For full-time at vocational, 2-year or 4-year institution.
Application requirements: Essay. Applicant must be a US/Canadian citizen or permanent resident of either country. Student must be enrolled in this calendar year. The school must be accredited to award trades certificates/diplomas. Students must demonstrate a strong commitment to their community. Students must maintain satisfactory academic standing throughout their program. The scholarship is open to students from the communities near TransCanada's proposed projects, projects under construction and/or operating assets across the US (and Canada). A map of our operating area can be found at www.tcscholarships.com.
Additional information: The TransCanada Community Leader Scholarship rewards those students who demonstrate a strong

commitment to their communities through volunteer work, community participation, leadership or other activities.

Amount of award:	$1,000-$1,000
Number of awards:	100
Application deadline:	April 15
Notification begins:	June 1
Total amount awarded:	$100,000

Contact:
TransCanada Corp.
Web: www.transcanada.com/7111.html

TransCanada Indigenous Legacy Scholarship

Type of award: Scholarship, renewable.
Intended use: For full-time undergraduate or graduate study at accredited vocational, 2-year, 4-year or graduate institution.
Eligibility: Applicant must be American Indian. Applicant must be U.S. citizen.
Application requirements: Essay. Applicant must identify as Native American, Indigenous, Tribal Member, First Nations, Métis, or Inuit. Applicant must be a US/Canadian citizen or permanent resident of either country. Student must be enrolled in this calendar year. The school must be accredited to award trades certificates/diplomas. The scholarship is open to students from the communities where we do business across the US (and Canada). A map of our operating area can be found at www.tcscholarships.com.
Additional information: The award is renewable, however, students must apply/reapply annually.

Amount of award:	$5,000-$5,000
Number of awards:	25
Application deadline:	April 15
Notification begins:	June 1
Total amount awarded:	$125,000

Contact:
TransCanada Corp.
Web: www.transcanada.com/7110.html

Transtutors

Transtutors Scholarship

Type of award: Scholarship.
Intended use: For full-time undergraduate or graduate study at vocational, 2-year, 4-year or graduate institution.
Application requirements: Essay of no more than 500 words on the question: "What do you expect out of college?"
Additional information: Open to college students in USA and Australia. Applicants should be a full-time college student as of May 31st. Application on web site.

Number of awards:	1
Application deadline:	May 31
Total amount awarded:	$10,000

Contact:
Transtutors
187 Wolf Road
Albany, NY 12205
Phone: 617-933-5480
Web: www.transtutors.com/scholarship

Treacy Foundation

Treacy Foundation Scholarship

Type of award: Scholarship, renewable.
Intended use: For full-time freshman or sophomore study at postsecondary institution.
Eligibility: Applicant must be residing in Montana, Idaho or North Dakota.
Basis for selection: Applicant must demonstrate financial need, leadership, seriousness of purpose and service orientation.
Application requirements: Transcript. Letter stating reason for applying.
Additional information: Student may attend school outside of ND, ID, and MT. Applications available online from January to end of April.

Amount of award:	$2,000
Number of awards:	50
Number of applicants:	90
Application deadline:	May 1
Notification begins:	May 15
Total amount awarded:	$180,000

Contact:
Treacy Foundation
P.O. Box 1479
Helena, MT 59624
Phone: 406-443-3549
Fax: 406-443-6183
Web: www.treacyfoundation.org

Tri-Community Coalition

Tri-Community Coalition Scholarship

Type of award: Scholarship.
Intended use: For undergraduate study at vocational, 2-year or 4-year institution.
Eligibility: Applicant must be high school senior. Applicant must be residing in Michigan.
Application requirements: Recommendations. Applicant must be a full-time student with twelfth grade credits (verified by the high school contact) who resides in or attends school in Berkley, Oak Park, or Huntington Woods, Michigan. Must provide two letters of recommendation from non-related adults.
Additional information: Candidate must complete an application and a project titled "Why I Am Drug and Alcohol Free". Options to complete the project include a written essay, art project, or video project. Details and instructions for each option are available on the downloadable application on the Tri-community Coalition website.

Amount of award:	$1,000
Number of awards:	6
Number of applicants:	6
Application deadline:	May 29
Notification begins:	June 3
Total amount awarded:	$6,000

Contact:
Tri-Community Coalition
14700 West Lincoln Street
Oak Park, MI 48237
Phone: 248-837-8008
Fax: 248-544-5835
Web: www.tricommunitycoalition.org

Number of awards:	1
Application deadline:	August 31
Notification begins:	September 1
Total amount awarded:	$500

Contact:
Triangle Pest Control
230 Fayetteville Street
Suite 202
Raleigh, NC 27601
Web: www.trianglepest.com/trianglepestcontrolscholarshipfund

Triangle Community Foundation

GSK Opportunity Scholarship

Type of award: Scholarship.
Intended use: For undergraduate or graduate study at vocational, 2-year, 4-year or graduate institution in United States. Designated institutions: Must be a public institution in North Carolina.
Eligibility: Applicant must be U.S. citizen residing in North Carolina.
Basis for selection: Applicant must demonstrate depth of character and seriousness of purpose.
Additional information: Applicant must have been a permanent resident of Durham, Orange, or Wake county for one year prior to application. Must demonstrate: potential to succeed despite adversity, exceptional desire to improve him or herself. GlaxoSmithKline and Triangle Community Foundation employees or their families not eligible. Awards granted per year: 1-5. Maximum individual award amount: $20,000 ($5,000 per year for up to 4 years). Visit Website for application.

Amount of award:	$20,000
Application deadline:	March 15

Contact:
Triangle Community Foundation
Attn: GSK Opportunity Scholarship
PO Box 12729
Durham, NC 27709
Phone: 919-474-8370
Fax: 919-941-9208
Web: www.trianglecf.org/award/gsk-opportunity-scholarship/

Triangle Pest Control

The Triangle Pest Control Scholarship Fund

Type of award: Scholarship.
Intended use: For undergraduate or graduate study at vocational, 2-year, 4-year or graduate institution in United States.
Eligibility: Applicant must be residing in North Carolina or South Carolina.
Basis for selection: Major/career interest in business.
Application requirements: Recommendations, essay. Letter of recommendation and personal letter of intent.
Additional information: Any student attending a school within North or South Carolina.

Trinity Episcopal Church

Shannon Scholarship

Type of award: Scholarship, renewable.
Intended use: For undergraduate study at postsecondary institution.
Eligibility: Applicant must be female. Applicant must be Episcopal. Applicant must be residing in Pennsylvania.
Basis for selection: Applicant must demonstrate financial need.
Application requirements: Proof of eligibility.
Additional information: Only open to daughters of Episcopal clergy who are canonical residents in the state of Pennsylvania. Must apply for state and federal financial assistance first. Previous recipients may reapply. Number of awards varies. For more information, contact church office.

Amount of award:	$500-$4,000
Number of applicants:	8
Application deadline:	April 30
Notification begins:	June 30

Contact:
Trinity Episcopal Church
200 South Second Street
Pottsville, PA 17901
Phone: 570-622-8720

Truck Accident Attorneys Roundtable

Truck Accident Injury Scholarship

Type of award: Scholarship, renewable.
Intended use: For full-time undergraduate or graduate study at accredited 2-year, 4-year or graduate institution in United States.
Eligibility: Applicant must be U.S. citizen or permanent resident.
Application requirements: Essay, transcript, proof of eligibility. Applicant must be a survivor of a truck accident. Must submit a copy of the police report or other proof of your accident. Must write an essay (up to 3 pages) describing the truck accident, your injury, and how you have worked to overcome your injury while pursuing an education.
Additional information: Information on how to apply on scholarship webpage.

Amount of award:	$500
Number of awards:	1
Application deadline:	June 1
Notification begins:	July 30
Total amount awarded:	$500

Contact:
Truck Accident Attorneys Roundtable
30101 Northwestern Hwy
Farmington Hills, MI 48334
Phone: 877-999-8227
Web: www.truckaccidentattorneysroundtable.com/scholarship/

True&Co.

The Future is Female Scholarship

Type of award: Scholarship.
Intended use: For full-time undergraduate or graduate study at 2-year, 4-year or graduate institution.
Eligibility: Applicant must be female. Applicant must be U.S. citizen or permanent resident.
Application requirements: 200 word essay, topics can be found in application online.
Additional information: Must have a minimum 3.0 GPA. Winners also receive a $300 True&Co brand product and full feature on the True&Co Journal.

Amount of award:	$3,000
Number of awards:	1
Application deadline:	March 31
Notification begins:	April 3
Total amount awarded:	$3,000

Contact:
Web: https://www.trueandco.com/scholarship

Trusts and Estates Attorney Kerri Castellini

Kerri Castellini Women's Leadership Scholarship

Type of award: Scholarship.
Intended use: For undergraduate or graduate study at accredited vocational, 2-year, 4-year or graduate institution in United States.
Eligibility: Applicant must be female, high school senior.
Basis for selection: Applicant must demonstrate high academic achievement.
Application requirements: Recommendations, essay, transcript. Unofficial transcript, one letter of recommendation, application cover sheet, application essay. Essay topic (500 words): "Describe an ideal woman leader in the 21st century. How do you believe that you exemplify this role in your daily life and career aspirations?"
Additional information: Minimum 3.0 GPA required. Candidates must exhibit strong leadership skills, as demonstrated by past and present educational, professional, and volunteer experiences.

Amount of award:	$500
Number of awards:	1
Application deadline:	May 1
Total amount awarded:	$500

Contact:
Kerri Castellini Women's Leadership Scholarship
409 7th Street NW
Suite 218
Washington, DC 20004
Phone: 202-517-0502
Fax: 410-749-5917
Web: trustandestateslawyers.com/scholarship/

Truth Initiative

Dr. Alma S. Adams Scholarship for Outreach and Health Communications to Reduce Tobacco Use Among Priority Populations

Type of award: Scholarship.
Intended use: For undergraduate or graduate study at accredited 4-year or graduate institution in United States.
Basis for selection: Applicant must demonstrate financial need, high academic achievement and service orientation.
Application requirements: Recommendations, essay, transcript. Must provide evidence of community service activities in an underserved community setting. Must submit sample of applicant's originally developed health communication material.
Additional information: Must submit the Student Aid Report received as result of filing FAFSA. Awards primarily granted based on student's commitment to community service in an underserved community, preferably related to tobacco prevention; and the best use of visual arts, media, creative writing, or other creative endeavor to convey health messages aimed at raising tobacco awareness. Number of awards varies. Website application: https://www.grantinterface.com/Home/Logon?urlkey=legacyforhealthscholarship.

Amount of award:	$5,000
Number of awards:	2
Number of applicants:	80
Application deadline:	April 30
Notification begins:	June 30
Total amount awarded:	$10,000

Contact:
American Legacy Foundation
Attn: Dr. Alma S. Adams Scholarship Fund
1724 Massachusetts Ave., NW
Washington, DC 20036
Phone: 202-454-5920
Fax: 202-454-5775
Web: https://truthinitiative.org/Adams-Scholarship

Two Ten Footwear Foundation

Two Ten Footwear Design Scholarship

Type of award: Scholarship, renewable.
Intended use: For undergraduate or graduate study in or outside United States.

Eligibility: Applicant must be U.S. citizen or permanent resident.
Basis for selection: Based on design talent. Major/career interest in design. Applicant must demonstrate financial need.
Application requirements: Portfolio, recommendations, essay, transcript.
Additional information: Individual must be attending recognized design program. Must be interested in pursuing career in footwear design.

Amount of award:	$1,000-$5,000
Application deadline:	March 2

Contact:
ISTS
Phone: 855-670-4787
Web: www.twoten.org

Two Ten Footwear Foundation Scholarship

Type of award: Scholarship, renewable.
Intended use: For undergraduate study at accredited vocational, 2-year or 4-year institution.
Eligibility: Applicant or parent must be employed by Footwear/Leather Industry. Applicant must be U.S. citizen or permanent resident.
Basis for selection: Applicant must demonstrate financial need and high academic achievement.
Application requirements: Recommendations, essay, transcript, proof of eligibility.
Additional information: Must have two years and 1,000 hours of work experience in footwear/leather industry. Additional information and application available on Website.

Amount of award:	$210-$3,000
Application deadline:	March 2
Notification begins:	June 15
Total amount awarded:	$700,000

Contact:
ISTS
Phone: 855-670-4787
Web: www.twoten.org

UCB Pharma Inc.

UCB Family Epilepsy Scholarship

Type of award: Scholarship.
Intended use: For undergraduate or graduate study at vocational, 2-year, 4-year or graduate institution in United States.
Eligibility: Applicant must be U.S. citizen or permanent resident.
Basis for selection: Applicant must demonstrate high academic achievement, leadership and service orientation.
Application requirements: Transcript. Essay or artistic presentation explaining why applicant should be selected for scholarship (awards received, community involvement, etc.) and how epilepsy has impacted his or her life. Photograph. Three letters of recommendation: one from a school official, one from a community member, and one from applicant's epilepsy healthcare team.
Additional information: Scholarships are awarded to people with epilepsy, and to caregivers and family members of epilepsy patients. Visit Website for deadline and application.

Amount of award:	$5,000
Number of awards:	30
Application deadline:	March 4
Total amount awarded:	$150,000

Contact:
UCB Family Epilepsy Scholarship Program
c/o Summit Medical Communications
1421 E. Broad St., Suite 340
Furquay-Varina, NC 27526
Phone: 866-825-1920
Web: www.ucbepilepsyscholarship.com

The Ulman Cancer Fund

Lisa Higgins-Hussman Foundation Scholarship

Type of award: Scholarship.
Intended use: For undergraduate study at 4-year institution.
Eligibility: Applicant must be at least 15, no older than 35. Applicant must be U.S. citizen residing in Virginia, District of Columbia or Maryland.
Additional information: Must have been affected by cancer through their own diagnosis or through the diagnosis of a parent/guardian or sibling.

Amount of award:	$2,500
Application deadline:	March 1

Contact:
The Ulman Cancer Fund
1215 East Fort Avenue, Suite 104
Baltimore, MD 21230
Web: www.ulmanfund.org

The Ulman Cancer Fund Scholarship

Type of award: Scholarship.
Intended use: For undergraduate study at 4-year institution.
Eligibility: Applicant must be U.S. citizen.
Basis for selection: Applicant must demonstrate financial need, leadership and service orientation.
Application requirements: Recommendations, essay, proof of eligibility. Physician verification form or copy of death certificate (if applicable), signed agreement to complete 40 hours of community service.
Additional information: Must be a young adult cancer survivor or patient diagnosed between the ages of 15-35 or a young adult who has lost a parent/guardian to cancer or must have a parent/guardian diagnosed or undergoing treatment for cancer or must have sibling diagnosed or undergoing treatment or must have lost a sibling due to cancer.

Amount of award:	$2,500
Application deadline:	March 1

Contact:
The Ulman Cancer Fund, Attn: Scholarship
1215 East Fort Avenue, Suite 104
Baltimore, MD 21230
Web: www.ulmanfund.org

Ultra Bright Lightz

Firest Responder Scholarship

Type of award: Scholarship.
Intended use: For undergraduate or graduate study at vocational, 2-year, 4-year or graduate institution.
Eligibility: Applicant must be at least 18.
Application requirements: Submit a 500 word essay explaining why you deserve the scholarship and the most defining moment you've experienced while responding to an emergency.
Additional information: Must have a minimum 3.0 GPA. Must be a volunteer first responder.

Number of awards:	1
Application deadline:	December 31
Notification begins:	January 15
Total amount awarded:	$250

Contact:
Web: www.ultrabrightlightz.com/scholarships/

UNICO Foundation

Bernard and Carolyn Torraco Memorial Nursing Scholarship

Type of award: Scholarship, renewable.
Intended use: For full-time undergraduate or graduate study in United States.
Eligibility: Applicant must be U.S. citizen.
Basis for selection: Major/career interest in nursing. Applicant must demonstrate depth of character, leadership and service orientation.
Application requirements: Applicant must reside in a state with an active UNICO Chapter. Must be currently enrolled in an accredited campus based nursing degree program in the United States, completing core nuring courses at one of the following: An Associate Degree School of Nursing; A Collegiate School of Nursing; A Diploma School of Nursing. Proof of enrollment must be provided prior to issuing the scholarship. In addition to the criteria previously listed, applications will be judged on citizenship, leadership, character, community service and commitment. Exhibits evidencing notable achievements in these areas may be attached.

Amount of award:	$2,500
Number of awards:	10
Application deadline:	April 15
Notification begins:	September 1
Total amount awarded:	$25,000

Contact:
UNICO Foundation
271 US Highway 46 West
Suite F-103
Fairfield, NJ 07004
Phone: 973-808-0035
Web: http://www.unico.org/scholarships.asp

Louise Torraco Memorial Scholarship for Science

Type of award: Scholarship.
Intended use: For full-time undergraduate study at accredited 4-year institution in United States.
Eligibility: Applicant must be U.S. citizen.
Basis for selection: Major/career interest in physical sciences or life sciences.
Application requirements: Applicant must reside in a state with an active UNICO Chapter. Student must be pursuing study in the Physical Sciences or Life Sciences.
Additional information: Applications may be aqurited from and submitted through a state chapter, the District Governor, or the UNICO National Office. Online degree programs are not eligible for UNICO scholarships. To fine a local chapter, please visit http://unico.org/search.asp or contact UNICO National at 973-808-0035.

Amount of award:	$2,500
Number of awards:	2
Total amount awarded:	$2,500

Contact:
UNICO Foundation
271 US Highway 46 West
Suite F-103
Fairfield, NJ 07004
Phone: 973-808-0035
Web: http://www.unico.org/scholarships.asp

Maria and Paolo Alessio Southern Italy Scholarship

Type of award: Scholarship.
Intended use: For full-time undergraduate study at accredited 4-year institution in United States.
Eligibility: Applicant must be Italian. Applicant must be U.S. citizen.
Application requirements: Applicant must reside in a state with an active UNICO chapter. A candidate must be currently enrolled in an accredited campus degree program in the United States. An applicant must be a United States citizen of Southern Italian heritage, specifically the regions of: Abruzzo, Basilicata, Campania, Calabria, Latium, Molise, Puglia, Sardinia, Sicilia.
Additional information: Applications may be aqurited from and submitted through a state chapter, the District Governor, or the UNICO National Office. Online degree programs are not eligible for UNICO scholarships. To fine a local chapter, please visit http://unico.org/search.asp or contact UNICO National at 973-808-0035.

Amount of award:	$1,000
Number of awards:	1
Application deadline:	April 15
Total amount awarded:	$1,000

Contact:
UNICO Foundation
271 US Highway 46 West
Suite F-103
Fairfield, NJ 07004
Phone: 973-808-0035
Web: www.unico.org/scholarships.asp

Scholarships

Ralph J. Torraco Fine Arts Scholarship

Type of award: Scholarship.
Intended use: For full-time undergraduate study at accredited 4-year institution in United States.
Eligibility: Applicant must be U.S. citizen.
Application requirements: Applicant must reside in a stae with an active UNICO Chapter. Must be pursuing a degree in the Fine Arts.
Additional information: Applications may be aqurited from and submitted through a state chapter, the District Governor, or the UNICO National Office. Online degree programs are not eligible for UNICO scholarships. To fine a local chapter, please visit http://unico.org/search.asp or contact UNICO National at 973-808-0035.

Amount of award:	$2,500
Number of awards:	2
Application deadline:	April 15
Total amount awarded:	$2,500

Contact:
UNICO Foundation
271 US Highway 46 West
Suite F-103
Fairfield, NJ 07004
Phone: 973-808-0035
Web: www.unico.org/scholarships.asp

UNICO Foundation, Inc.

Alphonse A. Miele Scholarship

Type of award: Scholarship.
Intended use: For undergraduate study at postsecondary institution.
Eligibility: Applicant must be high school senior. Applicant must be Italian. Applicant must be U.S. citizen.
Basis for selection: Applicant must demonstrate financial need, high academic achievement, depth of character and leadership.
Application requirements: Recommendations, essay, transcript, proof of eligibility. SAT/ACT scores.
Additional information: Candidates must be of Italian heritage and must reside in the home state of an active UNICO Chapter. Applications may be acquired from and submitted through a State Chapter, the District Governor or the UNICO National Office. Award is $1,500 per year for four years.

Amount of award:	$6,000
Number of awards:	1
Application deadline:	April 15

Contact:
Unico Foundation, Inc.
271 US Highway, 46 #F-103
Fairfield, NJ 07004
Phone: 973-808-0035
Fax: 973-808-0043
Web: www.unico.org

DiMattio Celli Family Study Abroad Scholarship

Type of award: Scholarship.
Intended use: For full-time undergraduate study at accredited 4-year institution in United States.

Eligibility: Applicant must be Italian. Applicant must be U.S. citizen.
Additional information: Award is for studying abroad in Italy. The study abroad program must be eligible for credit by student's college or university. Candidates must be of Italian heritage and must reside in the home state of an active UNICO Chapter. Applications may be acquired from and submitted through a State Chapter, the District Governor or the UNICO National Office.

Number of awards:	2
Application deadline:	March 1
Total amount awarded:	$1,250

Contact:
UNICO Foundation, Inc.
271 US Highway 46 #F-103
Fairfield, NJ 07004-2458
Phone: 973-808-0035
Web: www.unico.org

Ella T. Grasso Literary Scholarship

Type of award: Scholarship.
Intended use: For sophomore, junior or senior study at 4-year institution.
Eligibility: Applicant must be Italian. Applicant must be U.S. citizen.
Basis for selection: Competition/talent/interest in writing/journalism, quality of story or essay.
Application requirements: Essay. An original short story or essay celebrating Italian heritage.
Additional information: Candidates must be of Italian heritage and must reside in the home state of an active UNICO Chapter. Applications may be acquired from and submitted through a State Chapter, the District Governor or the UNICO National Office.

Amount of award:	$1,000
Number of awards:	2
Application deadline:	April 15

Contact:
UNICO Foundation, Inc.
271 US Highway 46 #F-103
Fairfield, NJ 07004-2458
Phone: 973-808-0035
Web: www.unico.org

Major Don S. Gentile Scholarship

Type of award: Scholarship.
Intended use: For undergraduate study at postsecondary institution.
Eligibility: Applicant must be high school senior. Applicant must be Italian. Applicant must be U.S. citizen.
Basis for selection: Applicant must demonstrate financial need, high academic achievement, depth of character and leadership.
Application requirements: Recommendations, essay, transcript, proof of eligibility. SAT/ACT scores.
Additional information: Candidates must be of Italian heritage and reside in the home state of an active UNICO Chapter. Applications may be acquired from and submitted through a State Chapter, the District Governor or the UNICO National Office. Award is $1,500 per year for four years.

Amount of award:	$6,000
Number of awards:	1
Application deadline:	April 15

Contact:
Unico Foundation, Inc.
271 US Highway 46 #F-103
Fairfield, NJ 07004-2458
Phone: 973-808-0035
Fax: 973-808-0043
Web: www.unico.org

Theodore Mazza Scholarship

Type of award: Scholarship.
Intended use: For undergraduate study at postsecondary institution.
Eligibility: Applicant must be high school senior. Applicant must be Italian. Applicant must be U.S. citizen.
Basis for selection: Applicant must demonstrate financial need, high academic achievement, depth of character and leadership.
Application requirements: Recommendations, essay, transcript, proof of eligibility. SAT/ACT scores.
Additional information: Candidates must be of Italian heritage and reside in the home state of an active UNICO Chapter. Applications may be acquired from and submitted through a State Chapter, the District Governor or the UNICO National Office. Award is $1,500 per year for four years.

Amount of award:	$6,000
Number of awards:	1
Application deadline:	April 15

Contact:
Unico Foundation, Inc.
271 US Highway 46 #F-103
Fairfield, NJ 07004-2458
Phone: 973-808-0035
Web: www.unico.org

William C. Davini Scholarship

Type of award: Scholarship.
Intended use: For undergraduate study at postsecondary institution.
Eligibility: Applicant must be high school senior. Applicant must be Italian. Applicant must be U.S. citizen.
Basis for selection: Applicant must demonstrate financial need, high academic achievement, depth of character and leadership.
Application requirements: Recommendations, essay, transcript, proof of eligibility. SAT/ACT scores.
Additional information: Candidates must be of Italian heritage and reside in the home state of an active UNICO Chapter. Applications may be acquired from and submitted through a State Chapter, the District Governor or the UNICO National Office. Award is $1,500 per year for four years.

Amount of award:	$6,000
Number of awards:	1
Application deadline:	April 15

Contact:
Unico Foundation, Inc.
271 US Highway 46 #F-103
Fairfield, NJ 07004-2458
Phone: 973-808-0035
Fax: 973-808-0043
Web: www.unico.org

Union Plus

Union Plus Scholarship

Type of award: Scholarship.
Intended use: For undergraduate or graduate study at accredited vocational, 2-year, 4-year or graduate institution.
Basis for selection: Applicant must demonstrate financial need, high academic achievement, depth of character and leadership.
Application requirements: Recommendations, essay, proof of eligibility.
Additional information: Open to current or retired members, and dependents and spouses of current or retired members, of unions that participate in Union Plus programs. Minimum 3.0 GPA preferred.

Amount of award:	$500-$4,000
Number of awards:	108
Number of applicants:	4,237
Application deadline:	January 31
Notification begins:	May 31
Total amount awarded:	$150,000

Contact:
Union Plus Education Foundation c/o Union Privilege
1100 1st St. NE, Ste. 850
Washington, DC 20002
Web: www.unionplus.org

Unitarian Universalist Association

Children of Unitarian Universalist Ministers College Stipend

Type of award: Scholarship.
Intended use: For undergraduate study at 4-year institution.
Application requirements: Proof of college enrollment.
Additional information: Must be child of Unitarian Universalist Minister. Priority given to applicants whose family income does not exceed $50,000. Visit Website for deadlines.

Application deadline:	October 15

Contact:
UUA Office of Church Staff Finances
c/o Joyce Stewart
25 Beacon Street
Boston, MA 02108-2800
Phone: 617-742-2100
Fax: 617-742-2875
Web: www.uua.org

Stanfield and D'Orlando Art Scholarships

Type of award: Scholarship.
Intended use: For full-time undergraduate or graduate study in United States.
Eligibility: Applicant must be Unitarian Universalist.
Basis for selection: Major/career interest in arts, general. Applicant must demonstrate financial need, depth of character and service orientation.
Application requirements: Portfolio, recommendations, essay, transcript, proof of eligibility.

Additional information: Number of awards varies; on average, five are given. Applicant must be preparing for fine arts career in fields such as painting, drawing, sculpture, or photography. Art therapy and performing arts majors not eligible. Returning adult students also eligible. See Website for application and more information.

Amount of award:	$1,000-$5,000
Number of awards:	5
Number of applicants:	15
Application deadline:	February 15
Notification begins:	May 1
Total amount awarded:	$20,000

Contact:
Unitarian Universalist Funding Program
P.O. Box 301149
Jamaica Plain, MA 02130
Phone: 617-971-9600
Fax: 617-971-0029
Web: www.uua.org/giving/awardsscholarships/

United Federation of Teachers

Albert Shanker College Scholarship Fund

Type of award: Scholarship.
Intended use: For freshman study.
Eligibility: Applicant must be high school senior. Applicant must be residing in New York.
Basis for selection: Applicant must demonstrate financial need, high academic achievement, leadership and service orientation.
Application requirements: Recommendations, essay, transcript, proof of eligibility. Valid proof of family income.
Additional information: Award is $5,000 over 4 years. Award is for New York City public high school seniors who will graduate from vocational, academic, or alternative school, night school, or New York City Board of Education alternative educational program. Must apply for and be eligible to receive federal financial aid. Must submit official documentation of income from all sources. Visit Website to determine financial eligibility and for more information.

Amount of award:	$1,250
Number of awards:	200
Application deadline:	January 31

Contact:
United Federation of Teachers
Web: www.uft.org/scholarship-fund

United Food and Commercial Workers International Union

United Food and Commercial Workers International Union Plus Scholarship Program

Type of award: Scholarship.
Intended use: For undergraduate or graduate study at accredited postsecondary institution in United States.

Basis for selection: Applicant must demonstrate high academic achievement and service orientation.
Application requirements: Essay, transcript. Complete biographical questionnaire.
Additional information: Minimum 3.0 GPA. Applicant or applicant's parent must be member of United Food and Commercial Workers International Union for one year prior to application. Dependents of members must be under age 20.

Amount of award:	$500-$4,000
Number of awards:	14
Number of applicants:	3,500
Application deadline:	January 31
Total amount awarded:	$56,000

Contact:
United Food and Commercial Workers International Union
Web: www.ufcw.org/scholarship

United Methodist Church General Board of Higher Education and Ministry

United Methodist Scholarships

Type of award: Scholarship, renewable.
Intended use: For full-time undergraduate or graduate study at accredited 2-year, 4-year or graduate institution in United States.
Eligibility: Applicant must be United Methodist.
Basis for selection: Applicant must demonstrate high academic achievement and seriousness of purpose.
Application requirements: Recommendations, essay, transcript. Online application.
Additional information: All recipients must be full active members of United Methodist Church for minimum of one year prior to application and maintain minimum 2.5 GPA. Awards vary. Some scholarships are renewable. Visit Website for more information. Deadline in March.

Notification begins:	June 1

Contact:
United Methodist Church General Board of Higher Education and Ministry
Office of Loans and Scholarships
P.O. Box 340007
Nashville, TN 37203-0007
Phone: 615-340-7344
Web: www.gbhem.org

United Methodist Communications

Leonard M. Perryman Communications Scholarship for Ethnic Minority Students

Type of award: Scholarship.
Intended use: For full-time junior or senior study at accredited 4-year institution in United States.

Eligibility: Applicant must be Alaskan native, Asian American, African American, Mexican American, Hispanic American, Puerto Rican, American Indian or Native Hawaiian/Pacific Islander. Applicant must be United Methodist.
Basis for selection: Major/career interest in journalism; communications; radio/television/film or religion/theology. Applicant must demonstrate seriousness of purpose.
Application requirements: Recommendations, essay, transcript. Three examples of journalistic work in any medium; photograph (appropriate for publicity purposes).
Additional information: Must plan to pursue career in religious journalism or religious communication. Application forms may be downloaded from Website.

Amount of award:	$2,500
Number of awards:	1
Number of applicants:	6
Application deadline:	March 15
Total amount awarded:	$2,500

Contact:
United Methodist Communications
Communications Ministry Team
P.O. Box 320, 810 12th Avenue South
Nashville, TN 37202-0320
Phone: 888-278-4862
Web: www.umcom.org

United Methodist Higher Education Foundation

Hoover-Lee Scholars Program

Type of award: Scholarship.
Intended use: For full-time undergraduate study at accredited 4-year or graduate institution in United States. Designated institutions: United Methodist-related institutions.
Eligibility: Applicant must be United Methodist. Applicant must be from Southeast Asia and Fukien Province.
Basis for selection: Applicant must demonstrate high academic achievement and service orientation.
Application requirements: Recommendations, essay, transcript. A copy of TOEFL score report, a recent photograph.
Additional information: Priority also given to students who wish to dedicate their lives to serving humankind as demonstrated by scholarship benefactors. Must agree to return to native country following graduation. Must be starting school in Fall semester. Must be comfortable with English language. Minimum TOEFL scores: 500 paper or 173 computer for undergraduates; 600 paper or 250 for graduates. Minimum 3.0 GPA.

Amount of award:	$15,000
Application deadline:	March 1

Contact:
United Methodist Higher Education Foundation
P.O. Box 340005
Nashville, TN 37203-0005
Phone: 800-811-8110
Web: www.umhef.org

September 11 Memorial Scholarship

Type of award: Scholarship.
Intended use: For full-time undergraduate or graduate study at 4-year or graduate institution in United States.

Eligibility: Applicant must be United Methodist. Applicant must be U.S. citizen or permanent resident.
Basis for selection: Applicant must demonstrate high academic achievement.
Application requirements: Transcript, proof of eligibility. A letter from pastor of United Methodist Church verifying membership in that church if attending non-United Methodist school. Copy of institution's billing statement for period applicant is requesting assistance. Physician's letter attesting to applicant's disability or disability of applicant's parent/guardian as a result of 9/11 terrorist attacks. Birth certificate if applicant is dependent of a direct victim of 9/11 terrorist attacks. Financial Statement.
Additional information: Must have lost a parent or guardian or have had a parent or guardian disabled as a result of the September 11, 2001 terrorist attacks or be a direct victim disabled as a result of the September 11, 2001 terrorist attacks. Must be attending one of the 123 United Methodist-related institutions in the United States or be United Methodist student attending higher-education institution in the United States. Visit Website for more information.
Contact:
United Methodist Higher Education Foundation
60 Music Square East
Suite 350
Nashville, TN 37203
Phone: 800-811-8110
Web: www.umhef.org

United Negro College Fund

UNCF Merck Science Initiative

Type of award: Scholarship.
Intended use: For full-time junior study at 4-year institution in United States.
Eligibility: Applicant must be African American. Applicant must be U.S. citizen or permanent resident.
Basis for selection: Major/career interest in life sciences; physical sciences or engineering. Applicant must demonstrate high academic achievement.
Additional information: Minimum 3.3 GPA. Must be committed to and eligible for 10- to 12-week summer internship at a Merck facility. Summer internship includes stipend of at least $5,000. Apply online.

Amount of award:	$25,000-$30,000
Number of awards:	15
Application deadline:	December 1

Contact:
United Negro College Fund
Web: umsi.uncf.org

United States Army/ROTC

United States Army/ROTC Four-Year Scholarship

Type of award: Scholarship, renewable.
Intended use: For freshman study at accredited 4-year institution in United States.

Scholarships

615

Eligibility: Applicant must be at least 17, no older than 26. Applicant must be U.S. citizen. Must enlist in Army on active duty or in Army Reserve or Army National Guard for minimum eight years.
Basis for selection: Major/career interest in military science. Applicant must demonstrate high academic achievement and depth of character.
Application requirements: Interview, recommendations, transcript. SAT/ACT scores. Proof of high school class rank.
Additional information: Recipient receives living allowance (increasing each year) for each year of scholarship, plus allowance for books and other educational items. Minimum 920 SAT (Math and Reading) or 19 ACT. Minimum 2.5 GPA. Limited number of three- and two-year scholarships available once student is on campus; check with professor of military science once enrolled. Contact local Army ROTC recruiter or visit Website for application.

Amount of award:	Full tuition

Contact:
U.S. Army ROTC
Phone: 888-550-ARMY
Web: www.goarmy.com/rotc/high-school-students/four-year-scholarship.html

U.S. Army/ROTC Nursing Scholarship

Type of award: Scholarship.
Intended use: For undergraduate study at accredited 4-year institution in United States.
Eligibility: Applicant must be at least 17, no older than 26. Applicant must be U.S. citizen.
Basis for selection: Major/career interest in military science or nursing. Applicant must demonstrate high academic achievement and depth of character.
Application requirements: Interview, transcript.
Additional information: Must enlist to serve in the Army on Active Duty or in a Reserve Component for eight years. Minimum 920 SAT (Math and Reading) or 19 ACT. Must maintain minimum 2.5 GPA in college. Scholarships offered at different levels, providing college tuition and educational fees. All applicants considered for each level. Includes living allowance (increasing each year) for each year of scholarship, plus allowance for books and other educational items. Travel expenses not included. Limited number of three- and two-year scholarships available once student is on campus; check with school's professor of military science or contact local Army ROTC recruiter.

Amount of award:	Full tuition

Contact:
U.S. Army ROTC
Phone: 888-550-ARMY
Web: www.goarmy.com/rotc/nurse_program.jsp

United States Association of Blind Athletes

Arthur and Helen Copeland Scholarship

Type of award: Scholarship.
Intended use: For full-time undergraduate study at 2-year or 4-year institution.

Eligibility: Applicant must be visually impaired. Applicant must be female. Applicant must be U.S. citizen.
Basis for selection: Applicant must demonstrate high academic achievement and service orientation.
Application requirements: Transcript, proof of eligibility. Autobiographical sketch outlining community service, USABA involvement, academic goals, and objective for which scholarship funds will be used.
Additional information: Applicants must be legally blind. Preference given to applicants who are members of the United States Association of Blind Athletes. Must be a high school senior or in college. $500 award may be split into two $250 scholarships if there are two qualified applicants.

Amount of award:	$500
Number of awards:	2
Application deadline:	June 30
Notification begins:	July 31
Total amount awarded:	$500

Contact:
United States Association of Blind Athletes
c/o Courtney Patterson
1 Olympic Plaza
Colorado Springs, CO 80909
Phone: 719-866-3019
Fax: 719-866-3400
Web: www.usaba.org

I C You Foundation Valor Achievement Award

Type of award: Scholarship.
Intended use: For full-time undergraduate study at 2-year or 4-year institution.
Eligibility: Applicant or parent must be member/participant of United States Association of Blind Athletes. Applicant must be visually impaired. Applicant must be U.S. citizen.
Application requirements: Essay. Brief cover letter. personal biography including your involvement with sport and US Association of Blind Athletes. Essay of no more than 300 words about the role and importance of sport in your life.
Additional information: Applicant must be a member of U.S Association of Blind Athletes. Applicant must be current high school or college or technical school student enrolled on two or four-year college.

Amount of award:	$250-$500
Number of awards:	2
Number of applicants:	4
Application deadline:	July 31
Notification begins:	August 15

Contact:
United States Association of Blind Athletes
1 Olympic Plaza
Colorado Springs, CO 80909
Phone: 719-866-3019
Fax: 719-866-3400
Web: http://usaba.org/index.php/membership/copeland-scholarship/USABA_Scholarship_Programs/

United States Institute of Peace

National Peace Essay Contest

Type of award: Scholarship.
Intended use: For undergraduate study at postsecondary institution.

Eligibility: Applicant must be enrolled in high school. Applicant must be U.S. citizen or permanent resident.
Basis for selection: Competition/talent/interest in writing/journalism.
Application requirements: 1500-word essay on topic chosen by the Institute. Student form and coordinator form.
Additional information: All high school students, including home-schooled students, foreign exchange students, or those enrolled in correspondence programs are eligible. All information regarding essay topic and online submission process can be found on Website. State-level winners receive $1,000 and will compete for national awards of $10,000, $5,000, and $2,500 (national amount includes state award). Also invited to attend awards program in Washington, DC. Visit Website for more information, including essay topic and study guide.

Amount of award:	$1,000-$10,000
Number of awards:	53
Number of applicants:	1,200
Application deadline:	February 9
Notification begins:	May 1
Total amount awarded:	$67,500

Contact:
United States Institute of Peace
2301 Constitution Ave. NW
Washington, DC 20037
Phone: 202-457-1700
Fax: 202-429-6063
Web: www.usip.org/npec

United Transportation Union Insurance Association

United Transportation Union Insurance Association Scholarship

Type of award: Scholarship, renewable.
Intended use: For full-time undergraduate study at accredited vocational, 2-year or 4-year institution in or outside United States.
Eligibility: Applicant or parent must be member/participant of United Transportation Union. Applicant must be no older than 25. Applicant must be permanent resident.
Application requirements: Proof of eligibility.
Additional information: Must own a UTUIA policy. Scholarships awarded by lottery. Applicant must be accepted to or enrolled in an eligible institution. Members and direct descendants of living or deceased members eligible. Notification takes place prior to fall enrollment. Deadline is last business day in March.

Amount of award:	$500
Number of awards:	50
Number of applicants:	900

Contact:
United Transportation Union Insurance Association
24950 Country Club Blvd., Ste. 340
North Olmsted, OH 44070-5333
Phone: 216-228-9400
Web: www.utuia.org/scholarship/utuiasch.htm

University Consortium For Liberia

University Consortium for Liberia

Type of award: Scholarship, renewable.
Intended use: For full-time undergraduate or graduate study at accredited vocational, 2-year, 4-year or graduate institution in United States.
Eligibility: Applicant must be African American. African or African/American from the black race.
Basis for selection: Applicant must demonstrate high academic achievement, depth of character and leadership.
Application requirements: Recommendations. Copy of Passport must accompany application for international students and identify what type of visa you currently have or will be applying for. Provide 2 letters of Recommendation from any of the following: College Professor, Community Member/Faith Leader, Current/Former Employer or Government Leader, your letter(s) of recommendation should address Leadership Abilities and Potential. Letters of Recommendation should be e-mailed by recommendation person to UCLSCHOLARSHIP@GMAIL.COM with their name, contact info, the students name, and the students school, The subject line should be : Student Name Reference Letter.
Additional information: Applicant's Ethnic background: Liberian. Complete the UCL Scholarship Application submit at UCLSCHOLARSHIP@GMAIL.COM.

Amount of award:	$500-$1,000
Number of awards:	8
Application deadline:	March 27
Notification begins:	February 27
Total amount awarded:	$5,000

Contact:
University Consortium for Liberia
225 Peachtree Street NE
Suite 515
Atlanta, GA 30303
Phone: 404-590-1655
Web: UCLIBERIA.COM/SCHOLARSHIPS/

University Film and Video Association

Carole Fielding Video Grant

Type of award: Research grant.
Intended use: For undergraduate or graduate study at accredited 2-year or 4-year institution.
Basis for selection: Major/career interest in film/video.
Application requirements: Resume, budget, research/production proposal.
Additional information: Project categories include narrative, documentary, experimental, multimedia/installation, animation, and research. Applicant must be sponsored by faculty member who is active member of University Film and Video Association. Number of awards varies. Visit Website for application. This is a project based production or research award and may not be used for other general academic expenses.

Scholarships

Amount of award:	$500-$1,000
Application deadline:	December 15
Notification begins:	March 31
Total amount awarded:	$5,000

Contact:
University Film and Video Association
Web: www.ufva.org

Unpakt

Unpakt College Scholarship

Type of award: Scholarship.
Intended use: For full-time undergraduate or graduate study at 2-year or 4-year institution.
Eligibility: Applicant must be at least 18, high school freshman, sophomore, junior or senior. Applicant must be U.S. citizen or permanent resident.
Application requirements: Essay. Essay: In no more than 500 words tell us where you plan to move once you finish your education and why.
Additional information: Applicant must be a current college student or recent college graduate (within one year) at time of award announcement. Apply online at http://www.unpakt.com/ .Additional information available at application link.

Amount of award:	$1,000-$1,000
Number of awards:	1
Application deadline:	December 15
Notification begins:	December 31
Total amount awarded:	$1,000

Contact:
Unpakt
555 W 25th Street
Floor 3
New York, NY 10001
Phone: 646-863-7004
Fax: 917-398-1404
Web: www.unpakt.com/scholarship

Unplag

Student Scholarship From Unplag

Type of award: Scholarship.
Intended use: For full-time undergraduate study at 2-year or 4-year institution in or outside United States.
Eligibility: Applicant must be at least 18.
Application requirements: Essay. 500 word minimum essay on plagiarism in academia. List of possible topics available on web site. Scholarship winner should also submit scanned copy of a document certifying that he or she is a student of a particular educational institution.

Number of awards:	1
Application deadline:	March 1
Notification begins:	March 9
Total amount awarded:	$2,000

Contact:
Web: unplag.com/scholarship-for-students/

Upakar

Indian American Scholarship

Type of award: Scholarship, renewable.
Intended use: For freshman study.
Eligibility: Applicant must be Asian American. Applicant must be U.S. citizen or permanent resident.
Basis for selection: Applicant must demonstrate financial need and high academic achievement.
Application requirements: Recommendations, essay.
Additional information: Applicant must have either been born or have one parent who was born in the Republic of India. Applicant must have cumulative, unadjusted GPA over 3.6. Applicant's family must have Adjusted Gross Income of less than $75,000. Must have green card or be American citizen.

Amount of award:	$2,000
Number of awards:	20
Number of applicants:	250
Application deadline:	April 30
Notification begins:	June 1
Total amount awarded:	$40,000

Contact:
Upakar c/o M. Mukunda
10237 Nolan Drive
Rockville, MD 20850
Web: www.upakarfoundation.org

uPONICS

Hydroponics/Aquaponics Scholarship

Type of award: Scholarship.
Intended use: For undergraduate study at vocational, 2-year or 4-year institution.
Eligibility: Applicant must be U.S. citizen.
Application requirements: Applicant must be a US citizen currently attending US College or University with an interest in hyrdroponics and/or aquaponics. Students must write a well-researched and original essay (1000-3500 words). Chose a topic that relates to how hyrdroponics and/or aquaponics is a sustainable method of agriculture.
Additional information: More information on the essay and the application found on the website.

Amount of award:	$1,000
Number of awards:	1
Application deadline:	November 1
Notification begins:	November 8
Total amount awarded:	$1,000

Contact:
uPONICS
Web: http://uponics.com/aquaponics-scholarship/

U.S. Army Recruiting Command

Montgomery GI Bill (MGIB)

Type of award: Scholarship.
Intended use: For undergraduate or graduate study at accredited postsecondary institution in United States.
Eligibility: Applicant must be at least 17, no older than 35. Applicant must be U.S. citizen. Applicant must be in military service in the Army.
Basis for selection: Applicant must demonstrate depth of character, leadership, patriotism, seriousness of purpose and service orientation.
Application requirements: Interview. Armed Services Vocational Aptitude Battery.
Additional information: Award amount varies depending on type of service. Contact local recruiter or Army job counselor for more information.
Contact:
U.S. Army Recruiting Command
Phone: 888-550-ARMY
Web: www.goarmy.com

Montgomery GI Bill (MGIB) Kicker

Type of award: Scholarship.
Intended use: For full-time undergraduate study at 2-year or 4-year institution.
Eligibility: Applicant must be at least 17, no older than 35. Applicant must be U.S. citizen or permanent resident.
Basis for selection: Applicant must demonstrate high academic achievement and depth of character.
Additional information: Student can add up to $695/month to Montgomery GI Bill for up to 36 months (total up to $25,020) with the GI Bill Kicker. Amounts vary according to job and rank. Visit Website to request more information.
Contact:
U.S. Army Recruiting Command
Phone: 888-550-ARMY
Web: www.goarmy.com

Selected Reserve Montgomery GI Bill

Type of award: Scholarship.
Intended use: For undergraduate or graduate study at accredited postsecondary institution.
Eligibility: Applicant must be at least 17, no older than 35. Applicant must be U.S. citizen. Applicant must be veteran who served in the Army or Reserves/National Guard.
Basis for selection: Applicant must demonstrate depth of character, leadership, patriotism, seriousness of purpose and service orientation.
Application requirements: Interview. Armed Services Vocational Aptitude Battery.
Additional information: Award amount varies. Contact local recruiter or Army job counselor for more information.
Contact:
U.S. Army Recruiting Command
Phone: 888-550-ARMY
Web: www.goarmy.com

U.S. Army Recruiting Command Student Loan Repayment Program

Type of award: Scholarship.
Intended use: For undergraduate study at 2-year or 4-year institution.
Eligibility: Applicant must be at least 17, no older than 35. Applicant must be U.S. citizen or permanent resident.
Basis for selection: Applicant must demonstrate high academic achievement and depth of character.
Additional information: Offered to qualified applicants at the time of enlistment. Visit Website for more information.
Contact:
U.S. Army Recruiting Command
Phone: 888-550-ARMY
Web: www.goarmy.com

U.S. Department of Agriculture

USDA/1890 National Scholars Program

Type of award: Scholarship, renewable.
Intended use: For full-time freshman, sophomore or junior study at 4-year institution in United States. Designated institutions: One of the 1890 Historically Black Land-Grant Institutions: Alabama A&M University, Alcorn State University (MS), Delaware State University, Florida A&M University, Fort Valley State University (GA), Kentucky State University, Lincoln University (MO), Langston University (OK), North Carolina A&T University, Prairie View A&M University (TX), South Carolina State University, Southern University (LA), Tennessee State University, Tuskegee University (AL), University of Arkansas at Pine Bluff, University of Maryland at Eastern Shore, Virginia State University, and West Virginia State University.
Eligibility: Applicant must be U.S. citizen.
Basis for selection: Major/career interest in agriculture; agribusiness; agricultural education; agricultural economics; animal sciences; botany; food science/technology; wildlife/fisheries; forestry or horticulture. Applicant must demonstrate high academic achievement, leadership and service orientation.
Application requirements: Transcript. SAT/ACT scores. Current high school seniors: One recommendation from school counselor and one recommendation from high school teacher. Current college students: Recommendation from Department Head, Dean of College, or University Vice President and recommendation from college professor. 500- to 800-word essay.
Additional information: Must be seeking bachelor's degree in agriculture, food, natural resource sciences, or related disciplines. Scholarship covers full tuition and fees, plus room and board, for four years, up to $120,000. Upon completion of academic degree program, recipient has obligation of one year of service to USDA for each year of financial support. Number of awards varies depending on funding. Minimum 1000 SAT (Math and Reading; 1500 Math/Reading/Writing) or minimum 21 ACT and 3.0 GPA. Program includes summer employment. Upon successful completion of summer program, students are eligible for non-competitive transition as permanent employees. Contact designated institutions for more information and application.

Scholarships

619

Amount of award: Full tuition
Number of applicants: 421
Notification begins: May 1
Total amount awarded: $2,280,000
Contact:
U.S. Department of Agriculture
Web: www.outreach.usda.gov/education/1890/index.htm

U.S. Department of Education

Federal Pell Grant Program

Type of award: Scholarship, renewable.
Intended use: For undergraduate study at 2-year or 4-year institution.
Eligibility: Applicant must be U.S. citizen or permanent resident.
Basis for selection: Applicant must demonstrate financial need.
Application requirements: Proof of eligibility. FAFSA.
Additional information: Grant based on financial need, costs to attend school, and enrollment status. Must not have previously earned baccalaureate or professional degree. Amount of award varies; the maximum amount is $5,550. Visit Website for more information.
Application deadline: June 30
Contact:
Federal Student Aid Information Center
Phone: 800-4-FED-AID
Web: www.studentaid.ed.gov

Federal Supplemental Educational Opportunity Grant Program

Type of award: Scholarship, renewable.
Intended use: For undergraduate study at accredited vocational, 2-year or 4-year institution in United States.
Eligibility: Applicant must be U.S. citizen or permanent resident.
Basis for selection: Applicant must demonstrate financial need.
Application requirements: Proof of eligibility. FAFSA.
Additional information: Priority given to Federal Pell Grant recipients with exceptional financial need. Must not have defaulted on federal grant or educational loan. Awards not generally made to students enrolled less than half-time. Check with institution's financial aid office for deadline.
Amount of award: $100-$4,000
Contact:
Federal Student Aid Information Center
Phone: 800-4-FED-AID
Web: www.studentaid.ed.gov

Federal Work-Study Program

Type of award: Scholarship.
Intended use: For undergraduate or graduate study at accredited postsecondary institution in United States.
Eligibility: Applicant must be U.S. citizen or permanent resident.
Basis for selection: Applicant must demonstrate financial need.
Application requirements: Proof of eligibility. FAFSA.

Additional information: Part-time on-campus and off-campus jobs based on class schedule and academic progress. Students earn at least federal minimum wage. Visit Website for more information.
Application deadline: June 30
Contact:
Federal Student Aid Information Center
Phone: 800-4-FED-AID
Web: www.studentaid.ed.gov

Iraq and Afghanistan Service Grant

Type of award: Scholarship.
Intended use: For undergraduate study at 4-year institution in United States.
Eligibility: Applicant must be no older than 24. Applicant must be U.S. citizen or permanent resident. Applicant must be dependent of deceased veteran.
Additional information: Grant is for students whose parent or guardian was a member of the U.S. Armed Forces and died as a result of service performed in Iraq or Afghanistan after September 11, 2001. Must not be eligible for Pell Grant on the basis of Expected Family Contribution but meet the remaining Federal Pell Grant eligibility requirements. Must be enrolled in college at least part-time at time of parent's or guardian's death.
Contact:
Federal Student Aid Information Center
Phone: 800-4-FED-AID
Web: www.studentaid.ed.gov

U.S. Department of Education Rehabilitation Services Administration

U.S. Department of Education Rehabilitation Vocational Rehabilitation Assistance

Type of award: Scholarship, renewable.
Intended use: For undergraduate or graduate study at postsecondary institution in United States.
Additional information: Number of awards varies; amount varies depending on institution. Applicant must have a disability. Award applicable to many fields/majors, but must be consistent with applicant's abilities, interest, and informed choice. Must contact state vocational rehabilitation agency to become eligible. See Website for more information.
Contact:
U.S. Dept. of Education, OSERS, Rehabilitation Services Administration
Potomac Center Plaza
500 12th St. S.W., Rm. 5032
Washington, DC 20202-2800
Phone: 202-245-7325
Web: www.ed.gov

U.S. Department of Health and Human Services

National Health Service Corps Scholarship

Type of award: Scholarship.
Intended use: For full-time undergraduate or graduate study at accredited 4-year or graduate institution in United States.
Eligibility: Applicant must be U.S. citizen.
Basis for selection: Major/career interest in dentistry; nursing; nurse practitioner; physician assistant or midwifery. Applicant must demonstrate depth of character, seriousness of purpose and service orientation.
Application requirements: Interview, recommendations, essay, transcript, proof of eligibility. Resume, tuition bill, W-4.
Additional information: Students pursuing degree in allopathic or osteopathic medicine also eligible. Doctorate nurse training and "pre-professional" students ineligible. Awardees commit to providing health-care services in a National Health Service Corps approved site. One year of service owed for every year of scholarship support. Minimum service commitment two years; maximum four years. Award includes monthly stipend. Must be in training program. Number of awards varies. Visit Website for deadline and application.

Amount of award:	Full tuition
Number of applicants:	1,400

Contact:
Web: www.nhsc.hrsa.gov

U.S. Environmental Protection Agency

EPA Greater Research Opportunities Undergraduate Student Fellowships

Type of award: Scholarship.
Intended use: For full-time junior or senior study at accredited 4-year institution in United States.
Eligibility: Applicant must be U.S. citizen or permanent resident.
Basis for selection: Major/career interest in life sciences; environmental science; engineering; social/behavioral sciences; physical sciences; mathematics; computer/information sciences or economics. Applicant must demonstrate financial need, high academic achievement and seriousness of purpose.
Application requirements: Recommendations, essay, transcript, proof of eligibility. Pre-application form. Resident Aliens must include green card number. EPA may verify number with the Immigration and Naturalization Service.
Additional information: Award provides funding for last two years of four-year education. Students must apply before beginning of junior year. Applicant must attend a four-year institution or be in the second year at a two-year school at the time of applying, with the intent of transferring to a four-year institution. Minimum 3.0 GPA. Fellowship provides up to $19,700 per year for two years to cover tuition and fees as well as $9,500 of internship support for a three month period. Stipends and expense allowance also provided. Recipient must complete summer internship at EPA facility between funded junior and senior years. Preference given to applicants attending academic institutions that are not highly funded for development of environmental research. See Website for link to list. Applicants must submit preapplication form first; following a merit review, top-ranked applicants will be asked to submit formal application. See Website for application and deadline.

Amount of award:	$50,000
Number of awards:	40
Total amount awarded:	$2,000,000

Contact:
U.S. Environmental Protection Agency
Peer Review Division (8725F)
1200 Pennsylvania Avenue, NW
Washington, DC 20460
Phone: 800-490-9194
Web: www.epa.gov/ncer/fellow

U.S. Navy/Marine NROTC College Scholarship Program

ROTC/Navy Nurse Corps Scholarship Program

Type of award: Scholarship.
Intended use: For full-time freshman study at accredited 4-year institution in United States. Designated institutions: NROTC-approved nursing schools.
Eligibility: Applicant must be at least 17, no older than 23. Applicant must be U.S. citizen.
Basis for selection: Major/career interest in nursing. Applicant must demonstrate high academic achievement and leadership.
Application requirements: Interview, recommendations, transcript, proof of eligibility. Applicant must be US citizen, or in process of becoming a Naturalized US Citizen.
Additional information: Scholarships are highly competitive and based on individual merit. Scholarships pay for college tuition, fees, books, uniforms, and offer $250 monthly allowance, which increases yearly. Electronic application is first step in application process. Number of awards varies. Applicant must be medically qualified for the NROTC Scholarship Program. Minimum 530 SAT (Reading), 520 (Math); minimum 22 ACT (English), 21 (Math). Participation in extracurricular activities and work experience required. Applicants must have fewer than 30 hours college credit. Obligation of eight years commissioned service, four of which must be active duty. Contact local recruiter for more details.

Amount of award:	Full tuition
Number of awards:	19
Number of applicants:	375
Application deadline:	January 31

Contact:
Contact local recruitment officer.
Phone: 800-NAV-ROTC
Web: www.nrotc.navy.mil

Scholarships

ROTC/Navy/Marine Four-Year Scholarship

Type of award: Scholarship.
Intended use: For full-time freshman study at accredited 4-year institution in United States. Designated institutions: Colleges and universities hosting NROTC program.
Eligibility: Applicant must be at least 17, no older than 23. Applicant must be U.S. citizen. Navy Option: Minimum 530 SAT (Reading), 520 (Math); minimum 22 ACT (English), 21 (Math). Marine Option: SAT: 1000 Combination of Math and Critical Reading Only ACT minimum composite score of 22 Armed Forces Qualification Test: 74.
Basis for selection: Applicant must demonstrate high academic achievement and leadership.
Application requirements: Interview, recommendations, transcript, proof of eligibility. Applicant must be US citizen, or in process of becoming a Naturalized US Citizen.
Additional information: Scholarships are highly competitive and based on individual merit. Provide full tuition, fees, book allowance, and $250 monthly allowance, which increases annually. Number of awards varies between 1728 for the Navy Options and 300 for the Marine option. Applicant must be medically qualified for NROTC Scholarship. Minimum 530 SAT (Reading), 520 (Math); minimum 22 ACT (English), 21 (Math). Participation in extracurricular activities and work experience required. Applicant must have fewer than 30 hours college credit. Obligation of eight years commissioned service, five of which must be active duty for Navy Option and 4 years for the Marine Option. Contact nearest NROTC unit for more information. Visit Website to fill out electronic application.

Amount of award:	Full tuition
Number of applicants:	5,500
Application deadline:	January 31
Notification begins:	September 15

Contact:
Contact local recruitment officer.
Phone: 800-NAV-ROTC
Web: www.nrotc.navy.mil

ROTC/Navy/Marine Two and Three-Year Scholarship

Type of award: Scholarship.
Intended use: For full-time junior or senior study at 4-year institution in United States. Designated institutions: Colleges and universities hosting NROTC programs.
Eligibility: Applicant must be at least 17, no older than 23. Applicant must be U.S. citizen.
Basis for selection: Applicant must demonstrate high academic achievement and leadership.
Application requirements: Interview, recommendations, transcript, proof of eligibility.
Additional information: Scholarships are highly competitive and based on individual merit. Scholarships open to students who have completed freshman (2-yr) or sophomore (3-yr) year, or third year in a five-year curriculum. NROTC scholarships pay for college tuition, fees, book allowance, uniforms, and $350 monthly allowance, which increases annually. Navy Option: Minimum GPA 2.5. Marine Option: Minimum 1000 SAT score (combination of Math and Critical Reading.) ACT minimum score of 22. Armed Forces Qualification Test: 74. Participation in extracurricular activities and work experience required. Total military service obligation is eight years, five of which must be active duty for Navy Option and four years for Marine Option. Contact local NROTC unit of university you wish to attend for more information. Number of awards varies with 94 for the Navy option and 50 for the Marine option.

Amount of award:	Full tuition
Number of applicants:	500
Application deadline:	January 31

Contact:
Contact local recruitment officer.
Phone: 800-NAV-ROTC
Web: www.nrotc.navy.mil

US News and World Report

Path to College Scholarship

Type of award: Scholarship.
Intended use: For full-time undergraduate study at accredited 4-year institution in United States.
Eligibility: Applicant must be enrolled in high school. Applicant must be U.S. citizen.
Additional information: Must have a minimum 3.0 GPA. Must plan to enroll in full-time undergraduate study at an accredited four-year college or university in the United States immediately following high school graduation.

Amount of award:	$2,500
Number of awards:	4
Application deadline:	January 31
Total amount awarded:	$10,000

Contact:
Web: www.usnews.com/education/scholarship

USAttorneys

USAttorneys Scholarship Program

Type of award: Scholarship.
Intended use: For undergraduate or graduate study at accredited vocational, 2-year, 4-year or graduate institution in United States.
Eligibility: Applicant must be U.S. citizen.
Application requirements: Essay. 800-1000 word essay on one of the following topics: deportation, how to apply for a work visa H1B, the importance of having an immigration lawyer, investment visas, explain the different types of visas.

Number of awards:	1
Application deadline:	February 1
Total amount awarded:	$2,500

Contact:
USAttorneys
240 NW 32nd Court
Fort Lauderdale, FL 33309
Web: http://immigration.usattorneys.com/usattorneyscom-immigration-scholarship-essay-contest/

USEPEC

Think Positive Be Positive No Essay Scholarship

Type of award: Scholarship.
Intended use: For undergraduate or graduate study at vocational, 2-year, 4-year or graduate institution in or outside United States.
Eligibility: Applicant must be enrolled in high school. Applicant must be U.S. citizen, permanent resident or international student.
Basis for selection: Entries will be judged on overall impact, effectiveness of conveying theme, and creativity.
Application requirements: The video file must be submitted as either a CD, DVD or on a memory stick (no submissions via email). Entrants must be planning on attending college classes, full or part time, between Sept. 1, 2015 and Mar. 1st, 2016.
Additional information: Submit a video 5 minutes or less in length. Video should be things in your local area, city, and neighborhood that make you feel positive and optimistic about the condition of the environment. Describe or show things that have been carefully preserved, or improved and describe how. Shoot the short video on your phone, tablet, computer, or video camera. Entries can express the theme in any genre or shooting style. Complete scholarship information on the website.

Amount of award:	$1,000
Application deadline:	April 30
Notification begins:	October 1

Contact:
USEPEC
716 County Road 10 NE
#316
Blaine, MN 55434
Web: www.usepec.org/scholarships.html

USTA Tennis and Education Foundation

USTA Scholarships

Type of award: Scholarship, renewable.
Intended use: For full-time undergraduate study at accredited 2-year or 4-year institution.
Eligibility: Applicant must be high school senior.
Basis for selection: Applicant must demonstrate financial need, high academic achievement, leadership and seriousness of purpose.
Application requirements: Interview, recommendations, essay, transcript. Photograph, FAFSA or SAR, ACT/SAT scores.
Additional information: Minimum 3.0 GPA. Applicant must have participated in USTA or other organized youth tennis program. The USTA offers seven scholarship programs. Amount and number of awards vary. Applications available online and must be mailed to local USTA Section office. Visit Website for application, deadline, and individual scholarship requirements. Deadline in February.

Amount of award:	$1,000-$15,000
Number of awards:	76
Total amount awarded:	$379,000

Contact:
United States Tennis Association
Phone: 914-696-7000
Web: www.ustaserves.com/grants_scholarships/college_scholarships_/

Utah Higher Education Assistance Authority (UHEAA)

Higher Education Success Stipend Program

Type of award: Scholarship, renewable.
Intended use: For undergraduate study at accredited postsecondary institution.
Eligibility: Applicant must be residing in Utah.
Basis for selection: Applicant must demonstrate financial need.
Application requirements: FAFSA.
Additional information: Allocations are made to participating Utah institutions. Contact participating institution's financial aid office.Award may be used at any public or private non-profit, regionally accredited, post-secondary institution in Utah.

Amount of award:	$300-$5,000
Number of awards:	7,028
Number of applicants:	4,163
Total amount awarded:	$3,483,958

Contact:
Utah Higher Education Assistance Authority (UHEAA)
Web: www.uheaa.org

Utilities Employees Credit Union

UECU Student Scholarship Program

Type of award: Scholarship.
Intended use: For undergraduate or graduate study at accredited postsecondary institution.
Basis for selection: Applicant must demonstrate high academic achievement.
Application requirements: Essay or video on current year's scholarship contest topic. GPA, list of honors and activities.
Additional information: Award is for students who qualify for UECU membership by having an eligible family member in the utility/energy industry who works for a UECU partner sponsor company (see uecu.org for list) and has become a UECU member. Student must be a UECU member in good standing with a UECU Share Savings Account in his/her own name. Cannot be an employee of UECU, its affiliates, a UECU board member, a supervisory committee member, or family member and/or living in the same household. Minimum 3.0 GPA. Student must follow submission guidelines and meet requirements provided online at www.uecu.org/scholarship.

Amount of award:	$1,000
Number of awards:	2
Number of applicants:	30
Application deadline:	April 30
Notification begins:	June 1
Total amount awarded:	$2,000

Contact:
Utilities Employees Credit Union, Attn: Marketing Department
P.O. Box 14864
Reading, PA 19612
Phone: 800-288-6423
Web: www.uecu.org/scholarship

Vacuum Cleaner Hub

Vacuum Cleaner Hub Scholarship

Type of award: Scholarship.
Intended use: For full-time undergraduate or graduate study at vocational, 2-year, 4-year or graduate institution.
Basis for selection: Applicant must demonstrate financial need and high academic achievement.
Application requirements: Essay. This is an open scholarship for all the students of University, College and High school. Every student can take part of this offer. Must be in good academic standing with your current educational institution. Must apply to the contest via email and provide your name, address and the name of your institution you are attending or plan to attend. Must provide your written article. Just write a decent informative and guide type article on the topic and submit it for the evaluation. All article submission should be sent to scholarshipinfo@vacuumcleanerhub.com.
Additional information: scholarship page url: https://www.vacuumcleanerhub.com/scholarship/ .

Amount of award:	$1,000
Number of awards:	1
Application deadline:	March 10
Notification begins:	March 30
Total amount awarded:	$1,000

Contact:
Vacuum Cleaner Hub
Shatabdi Center, 292 Inner Circular Road
Suit #8/C/2
Dhaka-1000, Bangladesh 1000
Phone: 347-927-8122
Web: https://www.vacuumcleanerhub.com/scholarship/

ValuePenguin

ValuePenguin Scholarship

Type of award: Scholarship.
Intended use: For undergraduate study at accredited 4-year institution.
Application requirements: Answer two questions with a response of 500 to 750 words each.
Additional information: Submit via e-mail.

Amount of award:	$2,000
Application deadline:	November 10
Notification begins:	February 1

Contact:
Web: www.valuepenguin.com/scholarship

Van Winkle's

Van Winkle's Scholarship Program

Type of award: Scholarship.
Intended use: For full-time freshman study at accredited vocational, 2-year or 4-year institution.
Eligibility: Applicant must be high school senior.
Basis for selection: Major/career interest in journalism. Applicant must demonstrate high academic achievement.
Application requirements: High School academic records and GPA, SAT or ACT scores, and acceptance or admission offer from your school.
Additional information: Minimum SAT score of 1180 or ACT score of 26. Minimum GPA of 3.5. Must have a major/career interest in sleep or journalism. Application and complete requirements available on web site.

Number of awards:	1
Application deadline:	March 5
Total amount awarded:	$1,500

Contact:
Web: http://vanwinkles.com/scholarships

Vectorworks

Vectorworks Design Scholarship

Type of award: Scholarship.
Intended use: For full-time at vocational, 2-year, 4-year or graduate institution.
Basis for selection: Major/career interest in design.
Additional information: Design submissions will be judged on design, technology, concept & originality, presentation, and written questions. For rules, guidelines, and application visit web site.

Amount of award:	$3,000-$10,000
Number of awards:	20
Application deadline:	August 31

Contact:
Web: www.vectorworks.net/scholarship/en/about

The Vegetarian Resource Group

The Vegetarian Resource Group College Scholarships

Type of award: Scholarship.
Intended use: For freshman study at postsecondary institution in United States.
Eligibility: Applicant must be high school senior. Applicant must be U.S. citizen.
Application requirements: Recommendations, essay, transcript.
Additional information: Award for graduating high school students who have promoted vegetarianism or veganism in their schools or communities. Students will be judged on having shown compassion, courage and a strong commitment

to promoting a peaceful world through a vegetarian or vegan diet/lifestyle. Visit Website for application information.

Amount of award:	$5,000-$10,000
Number of awards:	3
Number of applicants:	20,000
Application deadline:	February 20
Notification begins:	May 1
Total amount awarded:	$20,000

Contact:
The Vegetarian Resource Group
P.O. Box 1463
Baltimore, MD 21203
Phone: 410-366-8343
Fax: 410-366-8804
Web: www.vrg.org

Vegetarian Video Scholarship

Type of award: Scholarship.
Intended use: For undergraduate study.
Eligibility: Applicant must be U.S. citizen.
Additional information: Create and submit a video about what you want others to know about vegetarianism and/or veganism. Use of humor and feelings encouraged. See Website for full video submission guidelines.

Amount of award:	$250-$500
Number of awards:	3
Application deadline:	July 15

Contact:
The Vegetarian Resource Group
P.O. Box 1463
Baltimore, MD 21203
Phone: 410-336-8343
Fax: 410-366-8804
Web: www.vrg.org/videoscholarship.php

Velvet Jobs

Resume Template Design Scholarship

Type of award: Scholarship.
Intended use: For at vocational, 2-year, 4-year or graduate institution.
Eligibility: Applicant must be U.S. citizen or permanent resident.
Application requirements: Must create a unique resume template in Microsoft Word format. Also must submit a 1,500 word or less mock job interview for a job position of your choice. E-mail your essay and template to apply. Include your full name, phone number, college or university where you are enrolled, and current school year.

Number of awards:	1
Application deadline:	December 31
Notification begins:	January 30
Total amount awarded:	$1,000

Contact:
Velvet Jobs
1400 N. Martel
Suite 108
Los Angeles, CA
Phone: 877-370-7552
Web: https://www.velvetjobs.com/scholarship/resume-template-design-scholarship

Ventura County Japanese-American Citizens League

Ventura County Japanese-American Citizens League Scholarships

Type of award: Scholarship.
Intended use: For freshman study at vocational, 2-year, 4-year or graduate institution in United States.
Eligibility: Applicant must be high school senior. Applicant must be Japanese. Applicant must be U.S. citizen residing in California.
Application requirements: Recommendations, essay, transcript, proof of eligibility. SAT scores.
Additional information: Applicant must be a Ventura County high school senior and a member of the Japanese American Citizens League. Amount and number of awards depend on available funding. Visit Website for application.

Application deadline:	April 1
Total amount awarded:	$10,000

Contact:
Ventura County JACL Scholarship Committee
2686 Velarde Drive
Thousand Oaks, CA 91360
Phone: 805-405-5098
Web: www.vcjacl.org

Vermont Golf Association Scholarship Fund, Inc.

Vermont Golf Association Scholarship

Type of award: Scholarship, renewable.
Intended use: For full-time undergraduate study at 2-year or 4-year institution.
Eligibility: Applicant must be residing in Vermont.
Basis for selection: Applicant must demonstrate high academic achievement.
Application requirements: Interview, recommendations, transcript. FAFSA. GPA and SAT scores.
Additional information: Must be graduate of Vermont high school and in top 40 percent of class or have GPA of 3.0 and 1500 SAT. Applicant must have valid connection to golf.

Amount of award:	$1,000
Number of awards:	10
Number of applicants:	14
Application deadline:	May 1
Notification begins:	May 25
Total amount awarded:	$14,000

Contact:
Vermont Golf Association Scholarship Fund
P.O. Box 1612
Station A
Rutland, VT 05701
Phone: 802-775-7837
Fax: 802-773-7182
Web: www.vtga.org

Veterans of Foreign Wars

Voice of Democracy Scholarship

Type of award: Scholarship.
Intended use: For undergraduate or graduate study at postsecondary institution in United States.
Eligibility: Applicant must be no older than 19, enrolled in high school.
Application requirements: USB drive (with audio file) or audio CD of essay. Participants are judged by audio file, not written essay script.
Additional information: Student must be 19 or younger to apply. Must apply through high school or local Veterans of Foreign Wars post. Not all VFW posts participate in program. Any entry submitted to VFW National Headquarters will be returned to sender. Selection based on interpretation of assigned patriotic theme, content, and presentation of recorded 3-5 minute audio-essay. Visit Website for additional information and application form. Award is non-renewable.

Amount of award:	$1,000-$30,000
Number of awards:	54
Number of applicants:	35,000
Application deadline:	October 31
Total amount awarded:	$154,000

Contact:
Veterans of Foreign Wars National Headquarters
Voice of Democracy Program
406 West 34 Street
Kansas City, MO 64111
Phone: 816-756-3390 x6117
Fax: 816-968-1149
Web: https://www.vfw.org/VOD/

Villa

I Matter Scholarship

Type of award: Scholarship.
Intended use: For full-time freshman study at accredited 2-year or 4-year institution.
Eligibility: Applicant must be high school senior. Applicant must be U.S. citizen residing in Wisconsin, Michigan, New York, Ohio, Minnesota, Texas, Delaware, Pennsylvania, New Jersey or Illinois.
Basis for selection: Applicant must demonstrate service orientation.
Application requirements: Recommendations, essay, transcript. High school transcripts. Two letters of recommendation (not from relatives). One to two page essay (prompt can be found on web site).
Additional information: Minimum 3.0 GPA. Available to graduating seniors enrolling in an accredited undergraduate program. Must be in metro area of a Villa store.

Amount of award:	$250-$1,000
Number of awards:	50
Application deadline:	May 30
Notification begins:	June 15
Total amount awarded:	$50,000

Contact:
1926 Arch Street
Floor 3R
Philadelphia, PA 19139
Phone: 212-579-5600
Web: www.RuVilla.com/Scholarships

Virgin Islands Board of Education

Virgin Islands Music Scholarship

Type of award: Scholarship, renewable.
Intended use: For full-time undergraduate study at accredited 2-year or 4-year institution in United States.
Eligibility: Applicant must be U.S. citizen or permanent resident residing in Virgin Islands.
Basis for selection: Major/career interest in music. Applicant must demonstrate high academic achievement.
Application requirements: Transcript. Acceptance letter from college or university if first-time applicant.
Additional information: Minimum 2.0 GPA. Deadline in early May.

Amount of award:	$2,000

Contact:
Virgin Islands Board of Education Financial Aid Office
P.O. Box 11900
St. Thomas, VI 00801
Phone: 340-774-4546
Web: www.myviboe.com

Virginia Beach Law Group

Tatiana Mendez Future Resources Scholarship

Type of award: Scholarship.
Intended use: For undergraduate or graduate study at accredited vocational, 2-year, 4-year or graduate institution.
Eligibility: Applicant must be high school senior.
Basis for selection: Applicant must demonstrate high academic achievement.
Application requirements: Essay, transcript. Unofficial transcript, application cover sheet, application essay, updated resume. Essay topic (500 words): "What do you believe is the biggest issue that currently threatens our nation's natural resources, and what are at least two ways we can begin working to fix this issue?"
Additional information: Minimum 3.0 GPA required. Candidates must demonstrate a continued interest in environmental stewardship and the protection of natural resources, based on volunteer, professional, and academic experience.

Amount of award:	$500
Number of awards:	1
Application deadline:	May 1
Total amount awarded:	$500

Contact:
Tatiana Mendez Future Resources Scholarship
440 Monticello Avenue
Suite 1811A
Norfolk, VA 23510
Phone: 202-517-0502
Fax: 571-222-0034
Web: criminallawsvirginia.com/scholarship.html

Virginia Department of Education

Virginia Lee-Jackson Scholarship

Type of award: Scholarship.
Intended use: For full-time freshman study at accredited
2-year or 4-year institution in United States.
Eligibility: Applicant must be high school junior or senior.
Applicant must be residing in Virginia.
Basis for selection: Competition/talent/interest in writing/
journalism.
Application requirements: Essay demonstrating appreciation
for virtues exemplified by General Robert E. Lee or General
"Stonewall" Jackson.
Additional information: Award amount varies depending on
essay. Additional awards for exceptional essays. Students must
submit essay and application form to high school principal or
guidance counselor. Application deadline is generally in mid-
February. Community college awardees must plan to enroll in
their college's transfer program. See Website for more
information.

Amount of award:	$1,000-$10,000
Number of awards:	18
Total amount awarded:	$44,000

Contact:
The Lee-Jackson Foundation
P.O. Box 8121
Charlottesville, VA 22906
Web: www.lee-jackson.org

Virginia Department of Health

Mary Marshall Nursing RN Scholarship

Type of award: Scholarship.
Intended use: For undergraduate study at postsecondary
institution in United States. Designated institutions: Virginia
institutions.
Eligibility: Applicant must be residing in Virginia.
Basis for selection: Major/career interest in nursing.
Additional information: Award amount varies. Provides
awards to students who agree to work in nursing profession in
Virginia at rate of one month for every $100 of aid received.
Must be eligible for in-state tuition at the time award is
distributed. Recipient may reapply for up to four succeeding
years. Applications and guidelines available from dean or
financial aid office at applicant's nursing school, or from
address listed.

Amount of award:	$600-$2,000
Number of awards:	95
Number of applicants:	58
Application deadline:	June 30
Notification begins:	December 15
Total amount awarded:	$61,000

Contact:
Virginia Department of Health
109 Governor Street
Suite 1016-E
Richmond, VA 23219
Phone: 804-864-7422
Fax: 804-864-7440
Web: www.vdh.virginia.gov

Mary Marshall Nursing Scholarship Program (LPN)

Type of award: Scholarship.
Intended use: For undergraduate study. Designated
institutions: Virginia nursing schools.
Basis for selection: Major/career interest in nursing. Applicant
must demonstrate financial need.
Application requirements: Recommendations, transcript.
FAFSA.
Additional information: Applicant must be eligible for
Virginia in-state tuition at the time of award distribution.
Award amount varies. Provides awards to students who agree
to work in nursing practice in Virginia at rate of one month for
every $100 of aid received. Recipient may reapply for up to
four succeeding years. Applications and guidelines available
from dean or financial aid office at applicant's nursing school,
or from address listed.

Amount of award:	$600-$1,200
Number of awards:	88
Number of applicants:	34
Application deadline:	June 30
Notification begins:	December 15
Total amount awarded:	$22,800

Contact:
Virginia Department of Health
109 Governor Street
Suite 1016-E
Richmond, VA 23219
Phone: 804-864-7435
Fax: 804-864-7440
Web: www.vdh.virginia.gov

Virginia's Nurse Practitioner Nurse Midwife Scholarship

Type of award: Scholarship.
Intended use: For full-time undergraduate study at
postsecondary institution. Designated institutions: Institutions in
Virginia.
Basis for selection: Major/career interest in nurse practitioner.
Applicant must demonstrate high academic achievement and
depth of character.
Application requirements: Recommendations, transcript.
Additional information: Virginia resident preferred. Applicant
must commit to post-graduate employment in a medically
underserved area of Virginia, in a setting that provides services
to persons unable to pay and participates in all government-
sponsored insurance programs. Employment must last for
number of years equal to the number of annual scholarships
received. If work commitment is not fulfilled or student does
not complete studies, the award amount converts to loan. 3.0

GPA minimum preferred. Award amount and number of awards varies.

Amount of award:	$8,000
Number of awards:	5
Number of applicants:	9
Application deadline:	June 30
Notification begins:	December 15
Total amount awarded:	$24,000

Contact:
Virginia Department of Health
109 Governor Street
Suite 1016-E
Richmond, VA 23219
Phone: 804-864-7422
Fax: 804-864-7440
Web: www.vdh.virginia.gov

Virginia Museum of Fine Arts

Virginia Museum of Fine Arts Visual Arts and Art History Fellowship

Type of award: Scholarship, renewable.
Intended use: For full-time undergraduate or graduate study at accredited graduate institution.
Eligibility: Applicant must be at least 17, high school senior. Applicant must be U.S. citizen or permanent resident residing in Virginia.
Basis for selection: Major/career interest in arts, general; film/video or art/art history. Applicant must demonstrate financial need.
Application requirements: Portfolio, transcript. Eight images on CD representing recent work or three of the following: 16mm or video format films, videos, DVD, research papers, or published articles. References.
Additional information: May apply in one of the following categories on the undergraduate or graduate level: mixed media, new/emerging media, crafts, drawing, sculpture, filmmaking, painting, photography, printmaking. Candidates in art history may apply on the graduate level only. Visit Website for guidelines and application.

Amount of award:	$2,000-$8,000
Number of awards:	27
Number of applicants:	725
Application deadline:	November 4
Notification begins:	February 1
Total amount awarded:	$162,000

Contact:
Virginia Museum of Fine Arts Fellowships
Art and Education Division
200 N. Boulevard
Richmond, VA 23220-4007
Phone: 804-204-2685 or 804-204-2685
Fax: 804-204-2675
Web: www.vmfa.museum/fellowships

Vision Tech

Vision Tech Caps Scholarship

Type of award: Scholarship.
Intended use: For undergraduate study at 2-year or 4-year institution.
Eligibility: Applicant must be U.S. citizen or permanent resident.
Basis for selection: Major/career interest in technology; engineering, computer; engineering; graphic arts/design or science, general.
Application requirements: Transcript. Optional: up to three letters of recommendation, optional submission describing your work or a Youtube video showcasing your work (2 minutes or shorter).

Amount of award:	$500-$1,000
Number of awards:	3
Application deadline:	August 1
Notification begins:	August 15

Contact:
Vision Tech
117 Town and Country Drive
Suite B
Danville, CA 94526
Web: https://www.visiontechcamps.com/scholarship

Visionary Integration Professionals

Women In Technology Scholarship

Type of award: Scholarship.
Intended use: For undergraduate study at 2-year, 4-year or graduate institution.
Eligibility: Applicant must be female.
Basis for selection: The scholarship is based on three important criteria, thought other factors may be considered. 1) Academic performance 3.0 GPA or higher. 2) Essay: thoughtful answer to the essay question. 3) Level of participation in community service and/or extracurricular activities. Major/career interest in information systems; computer/information sciences; engineering, computer or technology.
Application requirements: Essay, transcript. After reviewing the second page of the application, students should provide the below information on a separate sheet of paper - failure to submit all requested information will result in disqualification. Personal information. Unofficial transcripts. Response to essay question. Major relevancy explanation. Community service/extracurricular activities. Applications can be sent by mail or email.
Additional information: Minimum 3.0 GPA.

Amount of award:	$1,000-$2,500
Number of awards:	10
Number of applicants:	275
Application deadline:	March 1
Total amount awarded:	$120,000

Contact:
Visionary Integration Professionals
80 Iron Point Circle
Suite 100
Folsom, CA 95630
Phone: 916-985-9625
Fax: 916-985-9632
Web: http://learn.trustvip.com/rs/975-YWK-747/images/2017_
WITS_ScholarshipApplication.pdf

VueVille

Future Technology Scholarship

Type of award: Scholarship.
Intended use: For full-time undergraduate or graduate study at accredited 4-year or graduate institution in or outside United States or Canada. Designated institutions: Must be enrolled full-time as an undergraduate or postgraduate student at accredited colleges or universities in the United States, Canada, Australia, New Zealand, the United Kingdom, Singapore, or India.
Basis for selection: Major/career interest in engineering; engineering, computer; information systems; business/management/administration or social/behavioral sciences.
Application requirements: Essay. 500-1000 word essay on the subject posted on the VueVulle scholarship page.
Additional information: Submit application and essay by e-mail.

Number of awards:	1
Application deadline:	January 31
Total amount awarded:	$1,000

Contact:
Web: www.vueville.com/scholarship/

Wal-Mart Foundation

Wal-Mart Dependent Scholarship

Type of award: Scholarship, renewable.
Intended use: For full-time undergraduate study at accredited 2-year or 4-year institution in United States.
Eligibility: Applicant or parent must be employed by Wal-Mart Stores, Inc. Applicant must be high school senior. Applicant must be U.S. citizen or permanent resident.
Basis for selection: Applicant must demonstrate financial need and high academic achievement.
Application requirements: Transcript, proof of eligibility. SAT/ACT scores and financial data.
Additional information: Award for dependents of Wal-Mart associates. Employee must have been working at Wal-Mart for at least six consecutive months. Visit Website for application and deadline information. Minimum 2.0 GPA.

Amount of award:	$3,250
Number of awards:	26
Number of applicants:	2,600
Application deadline:	March 13

Contact:
Wal-Mart Dependent Scholarship
Phone: 877-333-0284
Web: walmart.scholarsapply.org/dependent

Wallaroo

Wallaroo Scholarship

Type of award: Scholarship.
Intended use: For undergraduate or graduate study at vocational, 2-year, 4-year or graduate institution.
Application requirements: Essay prompt: "Give an example of a time where marketing or advertising significantly impacted your life. How will marketing play an important part in your professional career?"

Number of awards:	1
Total amount awarded:	$750

Contact:
Web: http://wallaroomedia.com/wallaroo-scholarship/

Washington Crossing Foundation

Washington Crossing Foundation Scholarship

Type of award: Scholarship.
Intended use: For full-time undergraduate study at accredited 4-year institution.
Eligibility: Applicant must be high school senior. Applicant must be U.S. citizen.
Basis for selection: Major/career interest in political science/government or public administration/service. Applicant must demonstrate high academic achievement, depth of character, leadership, patriotism, seriousness of purpose and service orientation.
Application requirements: Recommendations, transcript. Essay on why student is planning a career in government service, including any inspiration derived from Washington's famous crossing of the Delaware. SAT/ACT scores.
Additional information: Number of awards varies. Visit Website for more information.

Amount of award:	$500-$5,000
Application deadline:	January 15
Notification begins:	June 30
Total amount awarded:	$58,500

Contact:
Washington Crossing Foundation
Attn: Vice Chairman
P.O. Box 503
Levittown, PA 19058
Phone: 215-949-8841
Fax: 215-949-8843
Web: www.gwcf.org

Washington Media Scholars Foundation

Media Fellow Program - Fall Application Period

Type of award: Scholarship.
Intended use: For junior or senior study at 4-year institution.

Basis for selection: Applicant must demonstrate high academic achievement.

Application requirements: Recommendations, essay. 500-word proposal in which student articulates career goals, course load, and financial need.

Additional information: Minimum 3.0 GPA. Must be pursuing career in public policy advertising industry. Additional opportunity to apply for the popular Media Fellows Program scholarship. Finalists also participate in phone interview. Distributions made prior to spring semester.

Amount of award:	$1,000-$5,000
Number of awards:	10
Number of applicants:	350
Application deadline:	November 10
Total amount awarded:	$15,000

Contact:
Washington Media Scholars Foundation
815 Slaters Lane, Suite 201
Alexandria, VA 22314
Phone: 703-299-4399
Web: www.mediascholars.org

Media Plan Case Competition

Type of award: Scholarship.

Intended use: For undergraduate study at 4-year institution in United States.

Eligibility: Applicant must be at least 18.

Basis for selection: Competition/talent/interest in academics, based on creation of an in-depth media plan.

Additional information: The Media Plan Case Competition is made up of three rounds. The Qualification Round, the Case Competition semi-finals, and the Case Competition finals. Teams who reach the finals earn an all-expense-paid trip to Washington, D.C. to compete in the presentation round and network with media industry professionals. See Website for details. Deadline in February.

Amount of award:	$2,000-$3,000
Number of awards:	4
Number of applicants:	250
Application deadline:	February 10
Notification begins:	February 27
Total amount awarded:	$10,000

Contact:
Washington Media Scholars Foundation
815 Slaters Lane
Alexandria, VA 22314
Web: www.mediascholars.org/case-competition

Washington Media Scholars Media Fellows Program

Type of award: Scholarship.

Intended use: For junior or senior study at 4-year institution.

Eligibility: Applicant must be U.S. citizen.

Basis for selection: Applicant must demonstrate high academic achievement.

Application requirements: Recommendations, essay. Must submit written proposal in which student articulates career goals, course load, and financial need in 500 words or less. Proposal should include biographical information, statement of financial need, planned course load, career goals.

Additional information: Minimum 3.0 GPA in major concentration. Letter of recommendation may be from a professor, adviser, other home university official, a mentor, or previous employer.

Amount of award:	$1,000-$5,000
Number of awards:	20
Number of applicants:	1,500
Application deadline:	July 14
Notification begins:	August 18
Total amount awarded:	$35,000

Contact:
Washington Media Scholars Foundation
815 Slaters Lane
Alexandria, VA 22314
Phone: 703-299-4399
Web: www.mediascholars.org

Washington State Association For Justice

WSAJ American Justice Scholarship

Type of award: Scholarship.

Intended use: For full-time freshman study at vocational, 2-year or 4-year institution.

Eligibility: Applicant must be high school senior. Applicant must be residing in Washington.

Additional information: Application can be found on website. Notifications will be in mid-April.

Amount of award:	$3,750
Number of awards:	2
Application deadline:	March 17
Total amount awarded:	$7,500

Contact:
Web: https://www.washingtonjustice.org/index.cfm?pg=Scholarship

Washington State Higher Education Coordinating Board

Washington State Need Grant

Type of award: Scholarship, renewable.

Intended use: For undergraduate study at accredited vocational, 2-year or 4-year institution. Designated institutions: Eligible postsecondary institutions in Washington.

Eligibility: Applicant must be U.S. citizen or permanent resident residing in Washington.

Basis for selection: Applicant must demonstrate financial need.

Application requirements: Proof of eligibility. FAFSA.

Additional information: Grants are given only to students from low-income families. Family income must be equal to or less than 70 percent of the state median. Must meet qualifications every year for renewal, up to five years. Contact institution's financial aid office for additional requirements and deadlines. Must not be pursuing a degree in theology. Number of awards varies. Visit Website for family income requirements and more information. Grant amounts vary by school.

Total amount awarded:	$182,735,778

Contact:
Washington State Higher Education Coordinating Board
917 Lakeridge Way
P.O. Box 43430
Olympia, WA 98504-3430
Phone: 360-753-7850
Web: www.wsac.wa.gov

Washington State PTA

Washington State Scholarship Program

Type of award: Scholarship.
Intended use: For full-time freshman study at accredited vocational, 2-year or 4-year institution.
Eligibility: Applicant must be residing in Washington.
Basis for selection: Applicant must demonstrate financial need, high academic achievement, depth of character, leadership, seriousness of purpose and service orientation.
Application requirements: Recommendations, essay, transcript, proof of eligibility.
Additional information: Minimum 3.0 GPA. Must be graduate of a Washington State public high school. Grant administered according to college's determination. Not transferable to another institution if already enrolled in classes. Visit Website for additional information and application.

Amount of award:	$1,000-$2,000
Number of awards:	60
Number of applicants:	2,000
Application deadline:	May 1
Total amount awarded:	$65,000

Contact:
Washington State Scholarship Program
Phone: 800-562-3804
Web: www.wastatepta.org

Washington Student Achievement Council

Washington State American Indian Endowed Scholarship

Type of award: Scholarship, renewable.
Intended use: For full-time undergraduate or graduate study at accredited vocational, 2-year, 4-year or graduate institution. Designated institutions: Washington colleges and universities.
Eligibility: Applicant must be U.S. citizen residing in Washington.
Basis for selection: Applicant must demonstrate financial need, high academic achievement and service orientation.
Application requirements: Recommendations, essay, transcript, proof of eligibility. FAFSA.
Additional information: Must have close social and cultural ties to American Indian community within Washington State and strong commitment to return service to state's American Indian community. Awards and amounts may vary. Applicants pursuing degree in theology not eligible.

Amount of award:	$500-$2,000
Application deadline:	February 1
Notification begins:	March 1

Contact:
American Indian Endowed Scholarship Program
Washington Student Achievement Council
917 Lakeridge Way
Olympia, WA 98502
Phone: 360-753-7843
Fax: 360-704-6243
Web: www.hecb.wa.gov

Washington Women in Need

Washington Women in Need Education Grant

Type of award: Scholarship.
Intended use: For full-time undergraduate study at accredited vocational, 2-year or 4-year institution in United States. Designated institutions: Washington colleges and universities (see full list at www.wwin.org/eligibility).
Eligibility: Applicant must be female, at least 18. Applicant must be residing in Washington.
Basis for selection: Applicant must demonstrate financial need.
Additional information: Must be female, low-income, over 18, and a Washington resident for 12 months or more. Visit www.wwin.org/eligibility for full requirements.

Amount of award:	$250-$5,000
Number of awards:	50
Application deadline:	April 30
Notification begins:	June 15
Total amount awarded:	$250,000

Contact:
232 5th Avenue South
Suite 201
Kirkland, WA 98033
Phone: 425-451-8838 x1
Fax: 425-451-8845
Web: www.wwin.org/apply

Wattpad

Tell us your Story $1500 Wattpad Scholarship

Type of award: Scholarship.
Intended use: For undergraduate study at accredited 4-year institution in United States or Canada.
Eligibility: Applicant must be at least 13.
Application requirements: Essay. 1000-2000 word essay telling a true story about something that has impacted your life (and helped shape who you are today). Essays are to be submitted on Wattpad's platform and entrants must complete the application form found in the scholarship details on Web Site.
Additional information: Minimum 2.5 GPA. Transcripts will be asked of finalists.

Amount of award:	$1,500
Number of awards:	5
Application deadline:	August 15
Notification begins:	August 30
Total amount awarded:	$7,500

Contact:
Web: www.wattpad.com/143240652-tell-us-your-story-wattpad-scholarship-wattpad

Wells Fargo

Wells Fargo Scholarship Program for People With Disabilities

Type of award: Scholarship, renewable.
Intended use: For full-time at accredited 2-year or 4-year institution.
Eligibility: Applicant must be visually impaired, hearing impaired, physically challenged or learning disabled. Applicant must be high school senior.
Application requirements: Must have an identified disability (defined as someone who has, or considers themselves to have, a long-term or recurring issue that impacts one or more major life activity).
Additional information: Full-time student awards may be renewed for up to three (3) additional years at $2,500 and half-time student awards may be renewed for up to seven (7) years at $1,250 or until a bachelor's degree is earned, whichever occurs first. Renewal is contingent upon satisfactory academic performance (maintaining a cumulative grade point average of 2.5 on a 4.0 scale or the equivalent).

Number of awards:	25
Application deadline:	January 17
Total amount awarded:	$2,500

Contact:
Web: https://scholarsapply.org/pwdscholarship

Wells Fargo Veterans Scholarship Program

Type of award: Scholarship, renewable.
Intended use: For full-time undergraduate or graduate study at accredited vocational, 2-year, 4-year or graduate institution in United States.
Eligibility: Applicant must be U.S. citizen. Applicant must be spouse of disabled veteran. Honorably-discharged veterans or spouses of disabled veterans.
Additional information: Each award renewal will increase by $1,000 over the previous year to encourage progam completion.More information for how to apply is at www.scholarsapply.org/wellsfargoveterans.

Amount of award:	$7,000
Number of awards:	15
Application deadline:	February 28

Contact:
Wells Fargo Veterans Scholarship Program
One Scholarship Way
Saint Peter, MN 56082
Phone: 800-537-4180
Fax: 507-931-9168
Web: www.scholarsapply.org/wellsfargoveterans

Welsh Society of Philadelphia

Welsh Heritage Scholarship

Type of award: Scholarship, renewable.
Intended use: For full-time undergraduate study at accredited 2-year or 4-year institution.
Eligibility: Applicant must be Welsh.
Basis for selection: Applicant must demonstrate high academic achievement and seriousness of purpose.
Application requirements: Recommendations, essay, transcript. Statement of purpose.
Additional information: Applicant must be of Welsh descent. Applicant must live or attend college within 100 miles of Philadelphia. Participation in Welsh/Welsh-American organizations or events preferred.

Amount of award:	$500-$1,000
Number of awards:	5
Number of applicants:	50
Application deadline:	May 1
Total amount awarded:	$5,000

Contact:
Welsh Society of Philadelphia Scholarship Committee
c/o Dr. Donald Marcus
P.O. Box 7287
St. David's, PA 19087-7287
Web: www.philadelphiawelsh.org

Welsh Society of Philadelphia Undergraduate Scholarship

Type of award: Scholarship.
Intended use: For full-time undergraduate study at accredited 2-year or 4-year institution in United States.
Eligibility: Applicant must be Welsh. Applicant must be residing in Delaware, New Jersey, Maryland or Pennsylvania.
Basis for selection: Applicant must demonstrate high academic achievement, leadership, seriousness of purpose and service orientation.
Application requirements: Recommendations, essay, transcript, proof of eligibility.
Additional information: Applicant must be of Welsh descent. Must live or attend school within 100 miles of Philadelphia. Applicants studying in Wales with a primary residence within 100 miles of Philadelphia also eligible. Must rank in top third of class.

Amount of award:	$500-$1,000
Number of awards:	7
Number of applicants:	40
Application deadline:	May 1
Total amount awarded:	$5,000

Contact:
Welsh Society of Philadelphia Scholarship Committee
c/o Dr. Donald Marcus
P.O. Box 7287
St. Davids, PA 19087-7287
Web: www.philadelphiawelsh.org

Wendy's

Wendy's High School Heisman

Type of award: Scholarship, renewable.
Intended use: For full-time freshman study at accredited vocational, 2-year or 4-year institution.
Eligibility: Applicant must be high school senior.
Basis for selection: Applicant must demonstrate service orientation.
Application requirements: Transcript. Applicants must perform in at least one of the 43 school sponsored sports recognized by the International Olympic Committee in the Summer and Winter Olympic Games or the National Federation of State High School Associations.
Additional information: Minimum 3.0 GPA. Application can be found online.

Amount of award:	$1,000-$10,000
Number of awards:	100
Application deadline:	October 3
Total amount awarded:	$150,000

Contact:
Web: www.wendyshighschoolheisman.com

West Pharmaceutical Services, Inc.

Herman O. West Foundation Scholarship Program

Type of award: Scholarship, renewable.
Intended use: For full-time undergraduate study at accredited 2-year or 4-year institution.
Eligibility: Applicant or parent must be employed by West Pharmaceutical Services, Inc. Applicant must be high school senior. Applicant must be U.S. citizen.
Basis for selection: Applicant must demonstrate high academic achievement.
Application requirements: Recommendations, essay, transcript, proof of eligibility. List of extracurricular activities.
Additional information: Parent must be employee of West Pharmaceutical Services, Inc. Award is renewable annually for maximum of four years.

Amount of award:	$3,000
Number of awards:	7
Number of applicants:	33
Application deadline:	February 28
Notification begins:	May 1
Total amount awarded:	$70,000

Contact:
H.O. West Foundation
530 Herman O. West Drive
Exton, PA 19341
Phone: 610-594-2945

West Virginia Department of Veterans Assistance

West Virginia War Orphans Educational Assistance

Type of award: Scholarship, renewable.
Intended use: For undergraduate, graduate or non-degree study in United States.
Eligibility: Applicant must be at least 16, no older than 25. Applicant must be U.S. citizen residing in West Virginia. Applicant must be dependent of deceased veteran who served in the Army, Air Force, Marines, Navy, Coast Guard or Reserves/National Guard. Applicant's parent must be veteran who was killed while on active duty during wartime or who died of injury or illness resulting from wartime service.
Application requirements: Proof of eligibility.
Additional information: Award is waiver of tuition and registration fees for West Virginia residents attending a West Virginia school. If attending a private school in West Virginia or out of state college, may only receive a maximum of $2,000 for academic year. Non-West Virginia residents exempt.

Amount of award:	Full tuition
Number of applicants:	5
Application deadline:	August 1, December 1
Notification begins:	July 15, December 15
Total amount awarded:	$11,000

Contact:
West Virginia Department of Veterans Assistance
Attn: Angela S. Meadows
1514 B. Kanawha Blvd. East
Charleston, WV 25311
Phone: 304-558-3661 or 866-984-8387
Fax: 304-558-3662
Web: www.veterans.wv.gov

West Virginia Higher Education Policy Commission

PROMISE Scholarship

Type of award: Scholarship, renewable.
Intended use: For undergraduate study at 2-year or 4-year institution.
Eligibility: Applicant must be U.S. citizen or permanent resident residing in West Virginia.
Basis for selection: Applicant must demonstrate high academic achievement.
Application requirements: FAFSA. "Promise application"
Additional information: Merit-based scholarship; all eligible applicants will receive award up to $4,750. Minimum 22 composite ACT, with scores of at least 20 in math, science, English, and reading, or 1100 SAT (Math and Reading) with minimum 510 Math and 540 Evidence Based Reading and Writing. Minimum 3.0 GPA. GED/home-schooled students must maintain a 550 minimum score on the TASC. Students attending private institutions will receive tuition assistance based on average cost of public college tuition and fees. See Website for more information.

Amount of award:	$4,750
Number of awards:	10,000
Number of applicants:	11,400
Application deadline:	March 1
Notification begins:	April 1
Total amount awarded:	$47,500,000

Contact:
West Virginia Higher Education Policy Commission
PROMISE Scholarship Program Staff
1018 Kanawha Boulevard East, Suite 700
Charleston, WV 25301-2800
Phone: 304-558-4618
Web: www.cfwv.com

West Virginia Engineering, Science, and Technology Scholarship

Type of award: Scholarship, renewable.
Intended use: For full-time undergraduate study at 2-year or 4-year institution in United States. Designated institutions: Eligible West Virginia institutions.
Eligibility: Applicant must be U.S. citizen or permanent resident residing in West Virginia.
Basis for selection: Major/career interest in science, general; engineering; engineering, civil; engineering, computer; engineering, electrical/electronic; engineering, mechanical; computer/information sciences; life sciences; physical sciences or natural sciences. Applicant must demonstrate high academic achievement and seriousness of purpose.
Application requirements: Transcript.
Additional information: Recipients should obtain degree/ certificate in engineering, science, or technology and pursue career in West Virginia. Recipient must, within one year after ceasing to be a full-time student, work full-time in engineering, science, or technology field in West Virginia, or begin a program of community service relating to these fields in West Virginia for a duration of one year for each year scholarship was received. If work requirement fails to be met, recipient must repay scholarship plus interest and any required collection fees. Interested high school students should apply through high school counselor; currently enrolled college/university students should apply through their institution. Minimum 3.0 GPA. Application available on Website.

Amount of award:	$3,000
Number of awards:	217
Number of applicants:	851
Application deadline:	March 1
Total amount awarded:	$548,300

Contact:
West Virginia Higher Education Policy Commission
Financial Aid Program Staff
1018 Kanawha Boulevard East, Suite 700
Charleston, WV 25301-2800
Phone: 304-558-4618 or 877-987-7664
Web: www.cfwv.com

West Virginia Higher Education Adult Part-time Student (HEAPS) Grant Program

Type of award: Scholarship, renewable.
Intended use: For half-time undergraduate certificate, freshman, sophomore, junior or senior study at postsecondary institution. Designated institutions: West Virginia institutions.
Eligibility: Applicant must be returning adult student. Applicant must be U.S. citizen or permanent resident residing in West Virginia.

Basis for selection: Applicant must demonstrate financial need and high academic achievement.
Application requirements: FAFSA and any supplemental materials required by individual institutions.
Additional information: Applicant must plan to continue education on part-time basis. Must either be enrolled in college with cumulative 2.0 GPA (for renewal applicants), or be accepted for enrollment by intended institution (for first-time applicants); must have complied with Military Selective Service Act; must not be in default on higher education loan; and must not be incarcerated in correctional facility. At public colleges/universities, award is actual amount of tuition and fees. At independent colleges/universities and vocational/ technical schools, award is based upon average per credit/term hours tuition and fee charges assessed by all public undergraduate institutions. Contact school's financial aid office, or visit Website for additional information.
Contact:
West Virginia Higher Education Policy Commission
1018 Kanawha Boulevard East, Suite 700
Charleston, WV 25301-2800
Phone: 304-558-4618 or 877-987-7664
Web: www.cfwv.com

West Virginia Higher Education Grant

Type of award: Scholarship, renewable.
Intended use: For full-time undergraduate study at accredited 2-year or 4-year institution. Designated institutions: West Virginia or Pennsylvania institutions.
Eligibility: Applicant must be U.S. citizen residing in West Virginia.
Basis for selection: Applicant must demonstrate financial need and high academic achievement.
Application requirements: Transcript. FAFSA.
Additional information: Applicants must fill out the FAFSA only.

Amount of award:	$600-$2,700
Number of awards:	19,000
Number of applicants:	34,000
Application deadline:	April 15
Total amount awarded:	$41,000,000

Contact:
West Virginia Higher Education Grant Program
Office of Financial Aid and Outreach Services
1018 Kanawha Boulevard East, Suite 700
Charleston, WV 25301-2800
Phone: 304-558-4618
Fax: 304-558-4622
Web: www.cfwv.com

West Virginia Underwood-Smith Teacher Scholarship

Type of award: Scholarship, renewable.
Intended use: For full-time undergraduate or graduate study at 4-year or graduate institution.
Eligibility: Applicant must be U.S. citizen or permanent resident residing in West Virginia.
Basis for selection: Major/career interest in education; education, early childhood; education, special or education, teacher. Applicant must demonstrate high academic achievement.
Application requirements: Proof of eligibility.
Additional information: Recipients must agree to teach at the public school level in West Virginia for two years for each

year the scholarship is received or be willing to repay the scholarship on a pro rata basis. Visit Website for details and application.

Amount of award:	$5,000
Number of awards:	33
Number of applicants:	446
Total amount awarded:	$122,500

Contact:
West Virginia Higher Education Policy Commission
Underwood-Smith Teacher Scholarship Program
1018 Kanawha Boulevard East, Suite 700
Charleston, WV 25301-2800
Phone: 304-558-4614
Web: www.cfwv.com

Westcoast Landscape and Lawns, Inc.

Landscaping and Horticultural Science Scholarship

Type of award: Scholarship.
Intended use: For undergraduate study at vocational, 2-year or 4-year institution in United States.
Basis for selection: Major/career interest in horticulture or landscape architecture.
Application requirements: Transcript.
Additional information: Must have a minimum 3.25 GPA.

Number of awards:	1
Application deadline:	January 31
Notification begins:	March 15
Total amount awarded:	$1,000

Contact:
Westcoast Landscape & Lawns, Inc. Attn: Scholarship Application
3880 76th Avenue N
Pinellas Park, FL 33781
Web: http://westcoastlawns.com/scholarship/

Western European Architecture Foundation

Gabriel Prize

Type of award: Research grant.
Intended use: For non-degree study at postsecondary institution.
Eligibility: Applicant must be U.S. citizen.
Basis for selection: Major/career interest in architecture. Applicant must demonstrate seriousness of purpose.
Application requirements: Portfolio, recommendations, research proposal. Resume.
Additional information: Award to encourage personal investigative and critical studies of French architectural compositions completed between 1630 and 1930. Work is expected to be executed in France under supervision of foundation's European representative. Winner is required to begin studies in France by May 1, keep a traveling sketchbook, and prepare three large colored drawings within three months.

Must use stipend for travel and study. Send SASE for return of materials. Visit Website for application and deadline.

Amount of award:	$20,000
Number of awards:	1
Number of applicants:	24
Total amount awarded:	$20,000

Contact:
Western European Architecture Foundation
306 West Sunset, Suite 115
San Antonio, TX 78209
Phone: 210-829-4040
Fax: 210-829-4049
Web: www.gabrielprize.org

Western Golf Association/ Evans Scholars Foundation

Chick Evans Caddie Scholarship

Type of award: Scholarship, renewable.
Intended use: For full-time undergraduate study at accredited 4-year institution in United States. Designated institutions: Visit Website for comprehensive list of designated institutions.
Eligibility: Applicant must be high school senior.
Basis for selection: Competition/talent/interest in athletics/ sports, based on consistent caddie record at Western Golf Association-affiliated club. Applicant must demonstrate financial need, high academic achievement, depth of character and leadership.
Application requirements: Recommendations, essay, transcript, proof of eligibility. Tax returns, financial aid profile.
Additional information: Scholarship for full tuition, plus housing. Must have caddied minimum two years at Western Golf Association-affiliated club and maintain at least B average in college prep classes. Must have strong caddie record and work at sponsoring club during summer of application. Most recipients attend one of 14 universities where Evans Scholars Foundation owns and operates chapter house. Approximately 200 new Evans Scholarships awarded each year. Renewable up to four years. See Website for designated institutions.

Amount of award:	Full tuition
Number of awards:	200
Number of applicants:	678
Application deadline:	September 30
Notification begins:	March 1
Total amount awarded:	$8,000,000

Contact:
Scholarship Committee
Western Golf Assoc./Evans Scholars Foundation
1 Briar Road
Golf, IL 60029
Phone: 224-260-3726
Web: www.evansscholarsfoundation.com

Western Interstate Commission for Higher Education

Western Undergraduate Exchange

Type of award: Scholarship.
Intended use: For full-time undergraduate study at accredited 2-year or 4-year institution in United States. Designated

institutions: Participating institutions in Alaska, Arizona, California, Colorado, Hawaii, Idaho, Montana, Nevada, New Mexico, North Dakota, Oregon, South Dakota, Utah, Washington, Wyoming.

Application requirements: Proof of eligibility.

Additional information: Students who are residents of Western Interstate Commission for Higher Education states are eligible to request a reduced tuition rate of 150% of resident tuition at participating two- and four-year college programs outside of their home state. The WUE reduced tuition rate is not automatically awarded to all eligible candidates. For list of participating institutions and programs, and for individual state contact information, visit Website. Residents from Commonwealth of the Northern Mariana Islands and Guam are now eligible.

Contact:
Student Exchange Programs - WICHE
3035 Center Green Drive
Boulder, CO 80301
Phone: 303-541-0270
Web: www.wiche.edu/wue

Western Reserce Herb Society

Western Reserve Herb Society Scholarship

Type of award: Scholarship, renewable.
Intended use: For junior or senior study at accredited 2-year or 4-year institution in United States.
Eligibility: Applicant must be U.S. citizen.
Basis for selection: Major/career interest in horticulture.
Application requirements: Recommendations, essay, transcript. Applicant must be enrolled in a horticulture degree or related field (landscapte architecture or horticultural therapy) whose horticulture carer goals involved teaching/research, sustainable agriculture or work in the public or nonprofit sector. Applicants must have completed two fulls years of college.
Additional information: Scholarship available to students entering their 3rd, 4th, or 5th year of program.

Amount of award:	$9,500
Number of applicants:	41
Application deadline:	April 1
Notification begins:	May 1
Total amount awarded:	$9,500

Contact:
Western Reserve Herb Society
11030 East Boulevard
Cleveland, OH 44106
Web: www.westernreserveherbsociety.org/scholarship-programs/whrs-online-scholarship-application/

Western Reserve Herb Society

Frances Sylvia Zverina Scholarship

Type of award: Scholarship, renewable.
Intended use: For junior or senior study at accredited 2-year or 4-year institution in United States.

Eligibility: Applicant must be U.S. citizen.
Basis for selection: Major/career interest in horticulture. Applicant must demonstrate financial need.
Application requirements: Recommendations, essay, transcript. Applicant must be enrolled in a horticulture degree or related field (landscapte architecture or horticultural therapy) whose horticulture career goals involved teaching/research, sustainable agriculture or work in the public or nonprofit sector. Complete WHRS Online Application and Attach Essays. All correspondence should have the applicant's name in the subject line.
Additional information: Scholarship available to students entering their 3rd, 4th, or 5th year of program. For more information please contact :
scholarship@westernreserveherbsociety.org.

Amount of award:	$12,500
Number of awards:	1
Number of applicants:	41
Application deadline:	April 1
Notification begins:	May 1
Total amount awarded:	$12,500

Contact:
Western Reserve Herb Society
11030 East Boulevard
Cleveland, OH 44106
Web: www.westernreserveherbsociety.org/scholarship-programs/

Western Union

Western Union Foundation Global Scholarship Program

Type of award: Scholarship.
Intended use: For undergraduate study at accredited 2-year or 4-year institution.
Eligibility: Applicant must be at least 18, no older than 26.
Basis for selection: Major/career interest in science, general; technology; engineering; mathematics or business.
Application requirements: Recommendations, essay, transcript. Application includes biographical and academic information and short essays. Students must submit a letter of recommendation and an academic transcript.
Additional information: Students must be seeking an undergraduate degree in one of the following categories: science, technology, engineering, mathematics, and business/entrepreneurship.

Amount of award:	$2,500
Number of awards:	100
Application deadline:	April 12
Notification begins:	July 1
Total amount awarded:	$2,500

Contact:
Western Union
1400 K Street NW
Suite 700
Washington, DC 20005
Phone: 202-686-8652
Web: https://foundation.westernunion.com/wuscholars/index.html

WIIT

The WIIT Scholarship Program

Type of award: Scholarship.
Intended use: For undergraduate or graduate study at accredited 2-year, 4-year or graduate institution.
Eligibility: Applicant must be female.
Basis for selection: Major/career interest in international relations; international studies or business, international.
Application requirements: Essay. A completed application includes a 3 to 5 page essay, applicant information, and proof of acceptance or current enrollment in an accredited U.S. college or university. All materials should be submitted by e-mail only with the subject line: "Submission for WIIT TRUST Essay Writing Contest."
Additional information: One award each for undergraduate student and graduate student. Must have demonstrated interest in international development, international relations, international trade, international economics, or international business. Visit web site for essay question and application.

Amount of award:	$1,500
Number of awards:	2
Application deadline:	March 16, July 16
Total amount awarded:	$3,000

Contact:
Web: https://www.wiit.org/wiit-charitable-trust

The Willa Cather Foundation

Antonette Willa Skupa Turner Scholarship

Type of award: Scholarship.
Intended use: For full-time freshman study at accredited 4-year institution.
Eligibility: Applicant must be high school senior. Applicant must be residing in Nebraska.
Basis for selection: Major/career interest in English or history. Applicant must demonstrate depth of character.
Application requirements: Recommendations, essay, transcript. Applicants must be high school seniors who are prospective first year college students.The four-page application is required at : https://www.willacather.org/learn/scholarships. Essay must be 1500 word of your own choosing on Cather's novel My Antonia or her short story Neighbour Rosicky , you may comment on what impresses you in the work(s) such as various scenes, characters, theme, style, language, or the like, it is also permissible to use a previous essay you might have written on Cather and that you can adapt to the guidelines.
Additional information: Applicants must be residents of Nebraska. Scholarship applies to institutions located in Nebraska. Selection is based on intellectual promise, creativity and character of the applicant.

Amount of award:	$500-$500
Number of awards:	1
Number of applicants:	5
Application deadline:	February 28
Notification begins:	May 1
Total amount awarded:	$500

Contact:
Willa Cather Foundation
413 North Webster street
Red Cloud, NE 68970
Phone: 402-746-2653
Fax: 402-746-2652
Web: https://www.willacather.org/learn/scholarships

Norma Ross Walter Scholarship

Type of award: Scholarship.
Intended use: For full-time freshman study at accredited 4-year institution.
Eligibility: Applicant must be female, high school senior. Applicant must be residing in Nebraska.
Basis for selection: Major/career interest in English or journalism.
Application requirements: Recommendations, essay, transcript. Please write an approximately 1500 word essay of your own choosing on several of Cather's short stories (3) or on one of Cather's novels, you may comment on what impresses you in the work(s) such as various scenes, characters, theme, style, languages, or the like, it is also permissible to use a previous essay you might have written on Cather and one that you can adapt to the guidelines. Three letters of recommendation are required. Complete five-page application at https://www.willacather.org/learn/scholarships .
Additional information: Applicants must be residents of Nebraska. Scholarship applies to institutions located in Nebraska.Selection is based on intellectual promise, creativity and character of the applicant.

Amount of award:	$1,250-$2,500
Number of awards:	3
Number of applicants:	6
Application deadline:	January 31
Notification begins:	May 1
Total amount awarded:	$5,500

Contact:
Willa Cather Foundation
413 North Webster Street
Red Cloud, NE 68970
Phone: 402-746-2653
Fax: 402-746-2652
Web: https://www.willacather.org/learn/scholarships

William Randolph Hearst Foundation

Hearst Journalism Award

Type of award: Scholarship.
Intended use: For undergraduate study at accredited 4-year institution. Designated institutions: Institutions accredited by Accrediting Council on Education in Journalism and Mass Communication.
Basis for selection: Competition/talent/interest in writing/journalism, based on newsworthiness, research, excellence of journalistic writing, photojournalism, or broadcast news. Major/career interest in journalism; radio/television/film or communications.
Additional information: Field of study may also include photojournalism or broadcast news. Applicants must be actively involved in campus media and submit work that has been published or aired. Competition consists of monthly

contests and one championship. Scholarships awarded to student winners with matching grants awarded to their departments of journalism. Entries must be submitted by journalism department. For additional information and deadlines, applicants should contact journalism department chair or visit Website. Only two applicants per competition per school.

Amount of award:	$1,000-$2,600
Number of awards:	14
Total amount awarded:	$500,000

Contact:
Hearst Journalism Awards Program
90 New Montgomery Street
Suite 1212
San Francisco, CA 94105-4504
Phone: 415-908-4560
Web: www.hearstfdn.org

United States Senate Youth Program

Type of award: Scholarship.
Intended use: For undergraduate study at accredited 2-year or 4-year institution in United States.
Eligibility: Applicant must be high school junior or senior. Applicant must be U.S. citizen or permanent resident.
Basis for selection: Applicant must demonstrate leadership and service orientation.
Application requirements: Nomination by high school principal or teacher.
Additional information: Applicant must be permanent resident of and currently enrolled in public or private secondary school located in the state (including District of Columbia) in which parent or guardian legally resides. Must be currently serving in elected capacity as student body officer, class officer, student council representative, or student representative to district, regional, or state-level civic or educational organization. Selection process managed by state-level department of education. Scholarship includes all-expenses-paid week in Washington, D.C., in March. Application deadline is in early fall for most states; application available from high school principal or teacher. Visit Website for more information.

Amount of award:	$5,000
Number of awards:	104
Notification begins:	December 1
Total amount awarded:	$520,000

Contact:
Rayne Guilford, Program Director
William Randolph Hearst Foundation
90 New Montgomery Street, Suite 1212
San Francisco, CA 94105-4504
Phone: 800-841-7048 ext. 4540
Fax: 415-243-0760
Web: www.ussenateyouth.org

Wilson Ornithological Society

George A. Hall/Harold F. Mayfield Award

Type of award: Research grant.
Intended use: For non-degree study at postsecondary institution.
Basis for selection: Major/career interest in ornithology.

Application requirements: Recommendations, research proposal. Budget. Research proposal must be no longer than three pages.
Additional information: Research proposal must not exceed three pages. Award restricted to amateur researchers, including high school students, without access to funds and facilities of academic institutions or governmental agencies. Willingness to report research results as oral or poster paper is condition of award. Award should be used for equipment, supplies, travel, or living expenses. Visit Website for contact information and application.

Amount of award:	$1,000
Number of awards:	1
Number of applicants:	4
Application deadline:	February 1
Total amount awarded:	$1,000

Contact:
Wilson Ornithological Society
Web: www.wilsonsociety.org/awards

Paul A. Stewart Award

Type of award: Research grant.
Intended use: For undergraduate, master's, doctoral, postgraduate or non-degree study at postsecondary institution.
Basis for selection: Major/career interest in ornithology.
Application requirements: Recommendations, research proposal. Research budget.
Additional information: Research proposal should not exceed three pages. Preference given to proposals studying bird movements based on banding, analysis of recoveries, and returns of banded birds, with an emphasis on economic ornithology. Willingness to report research results as oral or poster paper is condition of award. Visit Website for contact information and application.

Amount of award:	$1,000
Number of awards:	8
Number of applicants:	18
Application deadline:	February 1
Total amount awarded:	$8,000

Contact:
Wilson Ornithological Society
Web: www.wilsonsociety.org/awards

Wisconsin Department of Veterans Affairs

Wisconsin Veterans Affairs Retraining Grant

Type of award: Scholarship.
Intended use: For undergraduate study at accredited vocational institution. Designated institutions: Wisconsin technical colleges; occupational/technical schools approved by the Wisconsin Educational Approval Board; Wisconsin on-the-job training programs.
Eligibility: Applicant must be residing in Wisconsin. Applicant must be veteran. Must have served two years of continuous active duty during peacetime or 90 days of active duty during designated wartime period.
Basis for selection: Applicant must demonstrate financial need.
Additional information: Applicant must be recently unemployed or underemployed and registered for or enrolled in

education program that will lead to re-employment and be completed within two years. Must have been involuntarily laid off within a period beginning one year before WDVA receives application. Must have been employed for six consecutive months with same employer or in the same or similar occupation. Must have been a resident of Wisconsin on entry into military service or a continuous resident of Wisconsin for at least five years after separation from military service. Apply year-round at local county Veterans Service Office to establish eligibility.

| Amount of award: | $3,000 |

Contact:
Wisconsin Department of Veterans Affairs
201 W. Washington Ave.
P.O. Box 7843
Madison, WI 53707-7843
Phone: 800-947-8387
Web: www.dva.state.wi.us/retraininggrants

Wisconsin Veterans Education GI Bill Tuition Remission Program

Type of award: Scholarship, renewable.
Intended use: For undergraduate study at vocational, 2-year or 4-year institution. Designated institutions: University of Wisconsin system schools, Wisconsin Technical College system schools.
Eligibility: Applicant must be residing in Wisconsin. Applicant must be veteran; or dependent of veteran, disabled veteran or deceased veteran; or spouse of veteran, disabled veteran or deceased veteran.
Basis for selection: Applicant must demonstrate financial need.
Application requirements: Proof of eligibility. Federal tax return or proof of annual income.
Additional information: Veteran must have been Wisconsin resident at time of entry into active duty; children of veterans must be between ages 17-25; widowed spouse of veteran must not be remarried. Veterans and spouses of veterans rated by the federal VA with a combined service-connected disability rating of 30% or greater are also eligible. Family income limit of $50,000; limit increases by $1,000 for each independent child. Veterans may receive up to 100 percent reimbursement of cost of tuition and fees. May receive reimbursement for up to eight semesters of full-time study. Visit Website for list of eligible schools, further requirements, and deadlines.
Contact:
Wisconsin Department of Veterans Affairs
201 W. Washington Ave.
P.O. Box 7843
Madison, WI 53707-7843
Phone: 800-947-8387
Web: www.dva.state.wi.us/wisgibill

Wisconsin Higher Educational Aids Board

Wisconsin Academic Excellence Scholarship

Type of award: Scholarship, renewable.
Intended use: For full-time undergraduate study at vocational, 2-year or 4-year institution. Designated institutions: Wisconsin non-profit colleges or universities.

Eligibility: Applicant must be high school senior. Applicant must be residing in Wisconsin.
Basis for selection: Applicant must demonstrate high academic achievement.
Application requirements: Nomination by high school guidance counselor.
Additional information: Awarded to Wisconsin high school seniors who have the highest grade point average in each public and private high school throughout Wisconsin. Must be registered with Selective Service, unless exempt. 3.0 GPA must be maintained for renewal.

Amount of award:	$2,250
Number of awards:	2,670
Application deadline:	March 1
Total amount awarded:	$2,894,469

Contact:
Higher Educational Aids Board
Attn: Nancy Wilkison
P.O. Box 7885
Madison, WI 53707-7885
Phone: 608-267-2213
Web: www.heab.state.wi.us

Wisconsin Hearing & Visually Handicapped Student Grant

Type of award: Scholarship, renewable.
Intended use: For undergraduate study at postsecondary institution. Designated institutions: Non-profit Wisconsin institutions; some out-of-state schools.
Eligibility: Applicant must be visually impaired or hearing impaired. Applicant must be residing in Wisconsin.
Basis for selection: Applicant must demonstrate financial need.
Application requirements: Proof of eligibility. FAFSA.

Amount of award:	$250-$1,800
Number of awards:	54
Total amount awarded:	$85,910

Contact:
Higher Educational Aids Board
Attn: Cindy Cooley
P.O. Box 7885
Madison, WI 53707-7885
Phone: 608-266-0888
Web: www.heab.state.wi.us

Wisconsin Higher Education Grant

Type of award: Scholarship, renewable.
Intended use: For undergraduate study at vocational or 4-year institution. Designated institutions: University of Wisconsin, Wisconsin Technical College, tribal institutions.
Eligibility: Applicant must be residing in Wisconsin.
Basis for selection: Applicant must demonstrate financial need.
Application requirements: Proof of eligibility. FAFSA.
Additional information: Apply with FAFSA through high school guidance counselor or financial aid office of institution. Must be registered with Selective Service, unless exempt. Rolling deadline.

Amount of award:	$250-$3,000
Number of awards:	37,172
Total amount awarded:	$35,060,586

Contact:
Higher Educational Aids Board
Attn: Cindy Cooley
P.O. Box 7885
Madison, WI 53707-7885
Phone: 608-266-0888
Web: www.heab.state.wi.us

Wisconsin Indian Student Assistance Grant

Type of award: Scholarship, renewable.
Intended use: For undergraduate or graduate study at postsecondary institution. Designated institutions: University of Wisconsin, Wisconsin Technical College, independent colleges and universities, tribal colleges, proprietary institutions in Wisconsin.
Eligibility: Applicant must be American Indian. Must be at least one-quarter Native American. Applicant must be residing in Wisconsin.
Basis for selection: Applicant must demonstrate financial need.
Application requirements: Proof of eligibility. FAFSA.
Additional information: Must be at least 25% Native American. Must be registered with Selective Service, unless exempt.

Amount of award:	$250-$1,100
Number of awards:	837
Total amount awarded:	$784,857

Contact:
Higher Educational Aids Board
Attn: Cindy Cooley
P.O. Box 7885
Madison, WI 53707-7885
Phone: 608-266-0888
Web: www.heab.state.wi.us

Wisconsin Talent Incentive Program Grant

Type of award: Scholarship, renewable.
Intended use: For freshman study at postsecondary institution. Designated institutions: Non-profit Wisconsin institutions.
Eligibility: Applicant must be residing in Wisconsin.
Basis for selection: Applicant must demonstrate financial need.
Application requirements: Nomination by financial aid department or Wisconsin Educational Opportunity Programs. FAFSA.
Additional information: Applicant must meet at least one of non-traditional/economically disadvantaged criteria. Visit Website for list. Eligibility cannot exceed ten semesters.

Amount of award:	$250-$1,800
Number of awards:	4,146
Total amount awarded:	$5,489,498

Contact:
Higher Educational Aids Board
Attn: Colette Brown
P.O. Box 7885
Madison, WI 53707-7885
Phone: 608-266-1665
Web: www.heab.state.wi.us

Women Grocers of America

Mary Macey Scholarship

Type of award: Scholarship, renewable.
Intended use: For sophomore, junior, senior or graduate study at accredited 2-year, 4-year or graduate institution in United States.
Basis for selection: Major/career interest in food production/management/services. Applicant must demonstrate high academic achievement.
Application requirements: Recommendations, essay, transcript.
Additional information: Must plan on a career in the independent sector of the grocery industry. Majors in public health and hotel management are not eligible. Minimum 2.0 GPA. Minimum of two $1500 awards each year. Deadline in mid-April.

Amount of award:	$1,500
Number of awards:	5
Number of applicants:	15
Application deadline:	April 19
Notification begins:	May 14
Total amount awarded:	$3,000

Contact:
Women Grocers of America
1005 North Glebe Road
Suite 250
Arlington, VA 22201-5758
Phone: 703-516-0700
Fax: 703-516-0115
Web: www.nationalgrocers.org

Women in Aerospace Foundation

Women in Aerospace Foundation Scholarship

Type of award: Scholarship.
Intended use: For senior study at accredited 4-year institution in United States.
Eligibility: Applicant must be female.
Basis for selection: Major/career interest in aerospace.
Application requirements: Recommendations, transcript. High school and college transcripts. Two letters of recommendation from a professor, or a supervisor of summer or Co-op work experience, or a supervisor of research work.
Recommendations from relatives will not be accepted. 500-1000 word essay on why the applicant is interested in aerospace, what she wants to accomplish in her career, and why she deserves the scholarship.
Additional information: Minimum 3.0 GPA. Notifications will be made in late April. Must be female student with a STEM major with Aerospace/Astrophysics focus. Must have completed at least two and a half academic years of full-time college work at the time of application. Application can be found on website.

Amount of award:	$2,000
Number of awards:	3
Application deadline:	March 23
Total amount awarded:	$6,000

Contact:
204 E Street NE
Washington DC, DC 20002
Phone: 202-547-0229
Fax: 202-547-6348
Web: www.womeninaerospacefoundation.org/foundation/

Women in Defense

Horizons-Michigan Scholarship

Type of award: Scholarship.
Intended use: For junior or senior study.
Eligibility: Applicant must be female. Applicant must be U.S. citizen residing in Michigan.
Basis for selection: Major/career interest in governmental public relations; engineering; computer/information sciences; business; law; international relations; political science/government or economics.
Application requirements: Recommendations, transcript. Must submit completed application, proof of U.S. citizenship, attached narrative responses, official transcripts, and two letters of recommendation.
Additional information: Minimum 3.25 GPA. Field of study must have relevance to a career in the areas of national security or defense. Must have completed at least 60 credits. Notification date in November. Complete rules and guidelines available on web site.

Amount of award:	$1,500-$3,500
Number of awards:	3
Application deadline:	September 15
Total amount awarded:	$7,000

Contact:
Women in Defense
PO Box 4744
Troy, MI 48099
Web: www.wid-mi.org/index.php/programs/horizons-scholarship

Women in Defense, A National Security Organization

Horizons Scholarship

Type of award: Scholarship.
Intended use: For junior, senior or graduate study at accredited 4-year institution in United States.
Eligibility: Applicant must be female. Applicant must be U.S. citizen.
Basis for selection: Major/career interest in science, general; engineering; mathematics; computer/information sciences; physics; business; law; international relations or political science/government. Applicant must demonstrate financial need and high academic achievement.
Application requirements: Recommendations, essay, transcript. Proof of citizenship.
Additional information: Scholarship intended to provide financial assistance to women either employed or planning careers in defense or national security areas. Minimum 3.25 GPA. Studies must be aimed at national defense/national

security. Visit Website for details and application (no phone calls). Award amount varies.

Number of awards:	5
Number of applicants:	40
Application deadline:	July 15
Total amount awarded:	$31,000

Contact:
Women in Defense
2111 Wilson Blvd., Suite 400
Arlington, VA 22201-3061
Phone: 703-522-1820
Fax: 703-522-1885
Web: www.wid.ndia.org

Women's Transportation Seminar Greater New York Chapter

Trade School and Community College Scholarship

Type of award: Scholarship.
Intended use: For undergraduate study at vocational or 2-year institution.
Eligibility: Applicant must be female.
Basis for selection: Major/career interest in transportation. Applicant must demonstrate high academic achievement.
Application requirements: Recommendations.
Additional information: Minimum 3.0 GPA. Must be female enrolled in a transportation-related field in New York or New Jersey.

Amount of award:	$1,000
Application deadline:	May 15
Total amount awarded:	$10,000

Contact:
Women's Transportation Seminar Greater New York Chapter
P.O. Box 989
New York, NY 10116-0989
Phone: 646-595-6571
Web: www.wtsinternational.org/greaternewyork/scholarships

Women's Transportion Seminar Greater New York Chapter

Miliotoris Leadership Scholarship

Type of award: Scholarship.
Intended use: For undergraduate study at accredited 2-year or 4-year institution.
Eligibility: Applicant must be female.
Basis for selection: Major/career interest in transportation. Applicant must demonstrate high academic achievement and leadership.
Application requirements: Recommendations.
Additional information: Minimum 3.0 GPA. Must be female enrolled in a transportation-related field in New York or New Jersey.

Amount of award:	$3,500
Number of awards:	6
Number of applicants:	31
Application deadline:	May 15
Total amount awarded:	$10,000

Contact:
Women's Transportion Seminar Greater New York Chapter
P.O. Box 989
New York, NY 10116-0989
Phone: 646-595-6571
Web: www.wtsinternational.org/greaternewyork/scholarships

Susan Miszkowicz Memorial Undergraduate Scholarship

Type of award: Scholarship.
Intended use: For undergraduate study at accredited 2-year or 4-year institution in United States.
Eligibility: Applicant must be female.
Basis for selection: Major/career interest in transportation. Applicant must demonstrate high academic achievement.
Application requirements: Recommendations. FAFSA and SAR, SAT/ACT scores.
Additional information: Minimum 3.0 GPA. Must be female enrolled in a transportation-related field in New York or New Jersey.

Amount of award:	$3,500
Number of awards:	1
Number of applicants:	31
Application deadline:	May 15
Total amount awarded:	$10,000

Contact:
Women's Transportion Seminar Greater New York Chapter
P.O. Box 989
New York, NY 10116-0989
Phone: 646-595-6571
Web: www.wtsinternational.org/greaternewyork/scholarships

Women's Western Golf Foundation

Women's Western Golf Foundation Scholarship

Type of award: Scholarship, renewable.
Intended use: For full-time freshman study at accredited 4-year institution in United States.
Eligibility: Applicant must be female, high school senior. Applicant must be U.S. citizen.
Basis for selection: Competition/talent/interest in athletics/sports. Applicant must demonstrate financial need, high academic achievement, depth of character, leadership and seriousness of purpose.
Application requirements: Essay, transcript, proof of eligibility. SAT/ACT scores, FAFSA. Personal recommendation required from high school teacher or counselor. List of high school activities.
Additional information: Must be in top 15 percent of class. Must demonstrate involvement in golf, but skill not criterion. Deadline to request application is March 1; SASE required. Awards renew for each of four years, assuming scholarship terms are fulfilled (financial need, GPA above 3.0, activeness

in school programs). About 20 new awards each year, plus 50 renewals. Applicant must be going to a 4 year university.

Amount of award:	$2,000
Number of awards:	22
Number of applicants:	500
Application deadline:	April 5
Notification begins:	May 20
Total amount awarded:	$150,000

Contact:
Director of Scholarship
Women's Western Golf Foundation
393 Ramsay Road
Deerfield, IL 60015
Web: www.wwga.org/WWGA.org/Scholarship_Information.html

Woodrow Wilson National Fellowship Foundation

Thomas R. Pickering Foreign Affairs Fellowship

Type of award: Scholarship.
Intended use: For full-time senior or graduate study at accredited 4-year or graduate institution in United States. Designated institutions: Institutions affiliated with Association of Professional Schools of International Affairs (graduate portion of fellowship).
Eligibility: Applicant must be U.S. citizen.
Basis for selection: Major/career interest in international relations; communications; history; economics; political science/government; foreign languages or business/management/administration. Applicant must demonstrate financial need, high academic achievement, depth of character, leadership, seriousness of purpose and service orientation.
Application requirements: Recommendations, essay, transcript, proof of eligibility. Resume, SAT or ACT scores, SAR, if applicable.
Additional information: Award is up to $40,000 toward tuition, mandatory fees, books, travel, and living stipend. Undergraduates must apply as juniors; applicants for graduate fellowship must be seeking admission to graduate school for the following academic year. Must have interest in career as Foreign Service officer. Number of fellowships determined by available funding. Finalists will attend interview session in Washington, D.C.; transportation to interview site paid. Orientation in Washington, D.C. Medical and security clearances required for program participation. Applicants must have minimum 3.2 GPA at time of application and maintain GPA throughout fellowship. Women and members of minority groups historically underrepresented in the Foreign Service encouraged to apply. Successful applicants obligated to a minimum of three years as a Foreign Service officer. Must register and apply online. Deadline varies; visit Website for details.
Contact:
Dr. Caryl Loney-McFarlane, Pickering Foreign Affairs Fellowship
Woodrow Wilson National Fellowship Foundation
P.O. Box 2437
Princeton, NJ 08543-2437
Phone: 609-452-7007
Web: www.woodrow.org

Worgul Law Firm

Worgul Law Firm Scholarship

Type of award: Scholarship.
Intended use: For undergraduate or graduate study at accredited 2-year, 4-year or graduate institution in United States.
Eligibility: Applicant must be U.S. citizen or permanent resident.
Basis for selection: Applicant must demonstrate service orientation.
Application requirements: Transcript. 300-500 word essay. Topic: there have been many public service campaigns about the dangers of drinking and driving; however, people continue to make the unfortunate decision to drink and get behind the wheel. Write an essay about the reasons why people continue to drink and drive and what initiatives could be executed to address those reasons.
Additional information: Must have a minimum 3.0 GPA.

Amount of award:	$10,000
Number of awards:	1
Application deadline:	March 31
Notification begins:	April 30
Total amount awarded:	$10,000

Contact:
Worgul Law Firm
428 Forbes Avenue
Suite 2300
Pittsburgh, PA 15219
Web: www.pittsburghcriminalattorney.com/worgul-law-firm-scholarship/

Worldstudio Foundation

Worldstudio AIGA Scholarship

Type of award: Scholarship.
Intended use: For full-time undergraduate or graduate study at accredited 2-year or 4-year institution in United States.
Eligibility: Applicant must be U.S. citizen or permanent resident.
Basis for selection: Major/career interest in graphic arts/design or arts, general. Applicant must demonstrate financial need, high academic achievement, seriousness of purpose and service orientation.
Application requirements: Portfolio, recommendations, transcript. Statement of purpose and self-portrait.
Additional information: Eligible majors are: fine art, graphic design, illustration, interactive design/motion graphics, and photography. The foundation's primary aim is to increase diversity in the creative professions and to foster social and environmental responsibility in the artists, designers, and studios of tomorrow. Applicants must be enrolled in courses related to or planning a career in design arts professions, and must demonstrate a social agenda in their work. Students with minority status given preference. Visit Website for guidelines and application. Awards not offered for performing arts.

Amount of award:	$500-$5,000
Number of awards:	20
Number of applicants:	500
Application deadline:	May 1

Contact:
Worldstudio Foundation AIGA Scholarships
233 Broadway
New York, NY 10279
Phone: 212-710-3111
Web: www.scholarships.worldstudioinc.com

Worthy

Women's Professional Studies Scholarship

Type of award: Scholarship, renewable.
Intended use: For in United States.
Eligibility: Applicant must be female, at least 30. Applicant must be U.S. citizen or permanent resident.
Application requirements: Essay.
Additional information: Scholarship is for female students over 30 enrolled in a continuing education professional studies program. Application and writing prompts found online.

Amount of award:	$1,000-$2,500
Number of awards:	3
Application deadline:	December 15
Total amount awarded:	$5,000

Contact:
Web: https://www.worthy.com/about/scholarship

Writers' Square

Writers' Square Scholarship Program

Type of award: Scholarship.
Intended use: For full-time undergraduate or graduate study at vocational, 2-year, 4-year or graduate institution.
Eligibility: Applicant must be enrolled in high school.
Application requirements: Essay. Essay information is on the website : www.writerssquare.org.
Additional information: Session 1 deadline: March 31st, Session 2 deadline: June 30th, Session 3 deadline September 30th. Two contests (English language and Chinese language). There is potential to win multiple awards per session. Money award may be received via check. Application and complete guidelines can be found on the web site.

Amount of award:	$100-$1,000
Number of awards:	319
Number of applicants:	3,166
Application deadline:	March 31, June 30
Notification begins:	April 22, July 22
Total amount awarded:	$67,300

Contact:
Writers' Square
Phone: 909-803-4506
Web: www.writerssquare.org

Wyland Foundation

Wyland National Art Challenge

Type of award: Scholarship.
Intended use: For undergraduate study at accredited 4-year institution.
Eligibility: Applicant must be high school junior or senior.
Additional information: Nationwide environmental mural, individual art, and photography contest. Complete rules, regulations, and application can be found online.

Number of awards:	2
Application deadline:	December 1
Notification begins:	January 31
Total amount awarded:	$1,500

Contact:
Web: www.wylandfoundation.org/artchallenge/

Wyzant Tutoring

Wyzant College Scholarship

Type of award: Scholarship.
Intended use: For undergraduate study at 4-year institution.
Basis for selection: Competition/talent/interest in writing/journalism.
Application requirements: 150 to 300-word essay on assigned topic: "Describe one way in which your education has empowered you?"
Additional information: First place winner receives $10,000 to school of choice; second place, $3,000; third place, $2,000. Anyone who plans to be enrolled in a United States college or university sometime between August 1st 2016 and November 1, 2018 is encouraged to apply. See Website for application and details.

Amount of award:	$2,000-$10,000
Number of awards:	3
Application deadline:	May 1
Notification begins:	June 10
Total amount awarded:	$15,000

Contact:
Wyzant College Scholarship
1714 N. Damen Ave
3rd floor
Chicago, IL 60647
Phone: 877-999-2681
Fax: 773-345-5525
Web: www.wyzant.com/scholarships

Xerox

Technical Minority Scholarship

Type of award: Scholarship.
Intended use: For full-time undergraduate or graduate study in United States.
Eligibility: Applicant must be Alaskan native, Asian American, African American, Mexican American, Hispanic American, Puerto Rican, American Indian or Native Hawaiian/Pacific Islander. Applicant must be U.S. citizen or permanent resident.

Basis for selection: Major/career interest in chemistry; engineering; science, general; information systems; physics or computer/information sciences. Applicant must demonstrate high academic achievement, leadership, patriotism and seriousness of purpose.
Application requirements: Resume and cover letter.
Additional information: Minimum 3.0 GPA. Spouses and children of Xerox employees not eligible. Visit Website for application and more information.

Amount of award:	$1,000-$10,000
Number of awards:	99
Number of applicants:	1,524
Application deadline:	September 30
Notification begins:	December 31
Total amount awarded:	$160,000

Contact:
Xerox
Web: www.xeroxstudentcareers.com

Yakama Nation Higher Education Program

Yakama Nation Tribal Scholarship

Type of award: Scholarship.
Intended use: For undergraduate, master's or doctoral study at accredited 2-year, 4-year or graduate institution.
Eligibility: Must be enrolled member of Yakama Nation.
Application requirements: Transcript. High school or GED score sheet. Tribal ID card copy. Enrollment verification, FAFSA, college acceptance letter.
Additional information: Maximum $3,000 awarded to undergraduate students; maximum $6,000 awarded to graduate students. Recipients notified two weeks prior to the start of semester to which aid will be applied.

Amount of award:	$3,000-$6,000
Number of awards:	300
Number of applicants:	299
Application deadline:	July 1
Notification begins:	July 10
Total amount awarded:	$200,000

Contact:
Yakama Nation Higher Education Program
P.O. Box 151
Toppenish, WA 98948
Phone: 509-865-5121
Fax: 509-865-6994

Young Christian Leaders

Young Christian Leaders Scholarship

Type of award: Scholarship.
Intended use: For full-time undergraduate study at accredited 2-year or 4-year institution in United States.
Eligibility: Applicant must be at least 18, no older than 25, high school senior. Applicant must be Christian. Applicant must be U.S. citizen residing in Connecticut, New York, New Jersey or Pennsylvania.

Basis for selection: Applicant must demonstrate service orientation.
Application requirements: Recommendations, essay. GPA, letters of recommendation, accomplishments, service, personal statement.
Additional information: Minimum 3.0 GPA. Two Scholarships awarded each month. Awarded based on both online votes as well as votes from a panel of judges. Must be active member of local church. Applications due on the 15th of every month. Complete rules and guidelines can be found online.

Amount of award:	$1,000
Number of awards:	24

Contact:
9 Broadman Parkway
Jersey City, NJ 07305
Phone: 201-432-7300
Web: http://yclscholarship.org

Zaner Harden Law

Auto Accident Scholarship

Type of award: Scholarship.
Intended use: For undergraduate or graduate study at 2-year or 4-year institution in United States.
Eligibility: Applicant must be U.S. citizen.
Basis for selection: Major/career interest in law.
Additional information: Must be affected by or know someone affected by a car accident.

Number of awards:	1
Application deadline:	December 30
Total amount awarded:	$2,000

Contact:
Zaner Harden Law
1610 Wynkoop Street
Suite 120
Denver, CO 80202
Phone: 303-563-5354
Web: www.zanerhardenlaw.com/denver-auto-accident-lawyer#accident-scholarship

Zelus Recovery

Zelus Recovery Scholarship

Type of award: Scholarship, renewable.
Intended use: For full-time undergraduate or graduate study at accredited vocational, 2-year, 4-year or graduate institution.
Application requirements: Essay. Applicant must be 18 years or older. Employees of Zelus Recovery are not eligible to participate. Must been currently enrolled or enrolled in the upcoming semester. Write a 500-1000 word essay on how substance abuse has affected your life.
Additional information: More information on how to apply on the scholarship webpage.

Amount of award:	$1,000
Number of awards:	1
Application deadline:	August 1
Notification begins:	September 1
Total amount awarded:	$1,000

Contact:
Zelus Recovery
1965 S. Eagle Rd.
Suite 140
Meridian, ID 83642
Phone: 208-957-6514
Fax: 208-957-6506
Web: www.zelusrecovery.com/zelus-recovery-college-scholarship/

ZendyHealth

ZendyHealth Med Tech Scholarship

Type of award: Scholarship.
Intended use: For undergraduate or graduate study at accredited 4-year or graduate institution in or outside United States or Canada.
Eligibility: Applicant must be U.S. citizen.
Basis for selection: Major/career interest in public health; engineering, computer; information systems; psychology or nursing.
Application requirements: Essay. 1,000 word essay explaining a startup idea for either a new company, application, or innovation in the field of healthcare technology.
Additional information: Apply via e-mail. Complete rules and instructions can be found on website.

Number of awards:	1
Application deadline:	December 31, May 15
Total amount awarded:	$2,000

Contact:
Web: https://zendyhealth.com/scholarship/

Zinda Law Group

Zinda Law Group Scholarship

Type of award: Scholarship.
Intended use: For undergraduate study at accredited 4-year institution.
Eligibility: Applicant must be high school senior. Applicant must be U.S. citizen or permanent resident residing in Texas or Colorado.
Basis for selection: Major/career interest in criminal justice/law enforcement; law; political science/government or sociology.
Application requirements: Essay. Must submit resume and 500-1000 word essay on topic of your choosing.
Additional information: Applicants should be pursuing an associate's or bachelor's degree related to government service, such as; criminal justice, law enforcement, political science, government, homeland security, sociology with a law/criminal emphasis, or forensic psychology. Applicants should have a desire to attend law school.

Number of awards:	1
Application deadline:	December 1
Total amount awarded:	$1,000

Contact:
Zinda Law Group
8834 North Capitol of Texas Highway
#304
Austin, TX 78759
Web: www.zdfirm.com/scholarships/

Zinus

Better Sleep Better Grades Scholarship

Type of award: Scholarship.
Intended use: For undergraduate or graduate study at accredited 2-year, 4-year or graduate institution.
Eligibility: Applicant must be at least 16. Applicant must be U.S. citizen or permanent resident.
Additional information: Must have a minimum 2.0 GPA. Create a photo or video wchich includes both a Zinus mattress and some form of school pride. A Zinus mattress must be shown in the photo/video and proof of purchase must be provided. Four runner-up awards of a MacBook Air 13" 128 GB will also be given. Complete the online application including original photo or video and link to Zinus.com with the hashtag #BetterSleepBetterGrades.

Number of awards:	1
Application deadline:	October 1
Notification begins:	October 14
Total amount awarded:	$10,000

Contact:
Web: https://www.zinus.com/back-to-school/

ZipRecruiter

ZipRecruiter Scholarship

Type of award: Scholarship.
Intended use: For undergraduate or graduate study at accredited 4-year or graduate institution in United States.
Eligibility: Applicant must be at least 18, returning adult student. Applicant must be U.S. citizen or permanent resident.
Basis for selection: Entries will be judged based upon content, style, creativity and effectiveness in attracting attention from an employer.
Application requirements: Proof of eligibility. A cover letter in the form of: a 130-500 word essay, video, song, or other medium of applicant's choosing. Proof of enrollment (such as college acceptance letter or transcript).
Additional information: Minimum 2.5 GPA required.
Monthly contest: one scholarship will be awarded each month. Applicant must craft a unique, engaging, creative, and effective cover letter.

Amount of award:	$1,000

Contact:
ZipRecruiter
401 Wilshire Boulevard
11th Floor
Santa Monica, CA 90401
Web: https://www.ziprecruiter.com/jobs/college-scholarship

Internships

Academy of Television Arts & Sciences Foundation

Academy of Television Arts & Sciences Student Internship Program

Type of award: Internship.
Intended use: For full-time undergraduate or graduate study in United States.
Eligibility: Applicant must be U.S. citizen, permanent resident or international student.
Basis for selection: Major/career interest in film/video or radio/television/film.
Application requirements: Recommendations, essay, transcript. Resume.
Additional information: Designed to expose students to professional TV production, techniques, and practices. Opportunities available in many fields; see Website for categories and special requirements. Internships are full-time for eight weeks. Interns responsible for housing, transportation, and living expenses. Interns must have car for transportation in Los Angeles. International students must be authorized to work in the United States. Apply online.

Amount of award:	$4,000
Number of awards:	41
Number of applicants:	1,200
Application deadline:	March 15
Notification begins:	May 15

Contact:
Academy of Television Arts & Sciences Foundation
Nancy Robinson, Student Internship Program
5220 Lankershim Boulevard
North Hollywood, CA 91601-3109
Phone: 818-754-2800
Web: www.emmysfoundationintern.org

Allstate

Allstate Internships

Type of award: Internship, renewable.
Intended use: For full-time undergraduate study at accredited 4-year institution.
Basis for selection: Major/career interest in insurance/actuarial science; accounting; marketing; business; business/management/administration; computer/information sciences; finance/banking; mathematics or statistics. Applicant must demonstrate high academic achievement.
Application requirements: Resume and cover letter.
Additional information: In addition to salary, eligible interns may receive subsidized transportation to and from Allstate Home Office in Northbrook, IL, at beginning and end of internship; daily transportation; and housing stipend. Please respond directly to position posted on Website.
Contact:
Allstate Insurance Company
2775 Sanders Road
Northbrook, IL 60062
Web: www.allstate.jobs

American Association of Advertising Agencies

American Association of Advertising Agencies Multicultural Advertising Intern Program

Type of award: Internship, renewable.
Intended use: For full-time senior or graduate study at accredited 4-year or graduate institution.
Eligibility: Applicant must be Alaskan native, Asian American, African American, Mexican American, Hispanic American, Puerto Rican, American Indian or Native Hawaiian/Pacific Islander. Applicant must be U.S. citizen or permanent resident.
Basis for selection: Major/career interest in advertising. Applicant must demonstrate high academic achievement and seriousness of purpose.
Application requirements: $25 application fee. Recommendations, essay, transcript. Resume, work samples (if applying for creative internship).
Additional information: Applicants must have completed at least junior year of college and have strong interest in advertising. Minimum 3.0 GPA. Students are placed in member agency offices for ten weeks during the summer. $10/hour. MAIP interns requesting travel/housing assistance will be responsible for paying $1,000 to the 4A's toward summer housing and transportation cost. Can apply for following departments: account management, digital/interactive design, media planning/buying, broadcast production, traffic, art direction, copywriting, public relations, internet marketing, project management, social media, or strategic/account planning. Agency professionals interview semifinalists before selection. Application deadline is second Friday in November; notification in late December. Number of awards varies. See Website for more information.

Number of applicants:	325

Contact:
American Association of Advertising Agencies
1065 Avenue of the Americas
16th Floor
New York, NY 10018
Phone: 212-850-0731
Fax: 212-682-8391
Web: maipmatters.aaaa.org

American Bar Foundation

American Bar Foundation Summer Research Diversity Fellowships in Law and Social Sciences for Undergraduate Students

Type of award: Internship.
Intended use: For junior or senior study at 4-year institution.
Eligibility: Applicant must be U.S. citizen or permanent resident.
Basis for selection: Major/career interest in law; social/behavioral sciences; criminal justice/law enforcement; public administration/service or humanities/liberal arts. Applicant must demonstrate high academic achievement.
Application requirements: Recommendations, essay, transcript.
Additional information: Interns work eight 35-hour weeks as research assistants at American Bar Foundation in Chicago. Fellowships are intended for, but not limited to, persons who are African American, Hispanic/Latino, Native American, Asian, or Puerto Rican. Applicants must have minimum 3.0 GPA and intend to pursue academic major in social sciences or humanities. See Website for program specifics.

Amount of award:	$3,600
Number of awards:	4
Number of applicants:	200
Application deadline:	February 15
Notification begins:	April 15

Contact:
American Bar Foundation - Summer Diversity Fellowships
750 North Lake Shore Drive
Chicago, IL 60611
Phone: 312-988-6515
Fax: 312-988-6579
Web: www.americanbarfoundation.org/fellowships/Call_for_Summer_Research_Diversity_Fellows.html

American City Business Journals and Dow Jones News Fund

American City Business Journals Reporting Program

Type of award: Scholarship.
Intended use: For full-time junior, senior or graduate study at 4-year or graduate institution in or outside United States.
Application requirements: Essay, transcript. Complete online application form. Submit proctored business reporting test created by Dow Jones News Fund. Resume. Required essay. Attach three to five recent clips. Unofficial transcript or list of courses and grades.
Additional information: Seriousness, commitment to journalism as a career, interest in and demonstrated ability in reporting, business journalism and proficiency in digital media. Program includes salary of no less than $400 per week for up to 12 weeks, transportation, pre-internship training including on-campus housing and meals.

Amount of award:	$1,000-$30,000
Number of awards:	10
Number of applicants:	144
Application deadline:	November 1
Notification begins:	December 25

Contact:
American City Business Journals
PO Box 300
Princeton, NJ 08543
Phone: 609-452-2820
Fax: Fax: 609-520-5804
Web: https://dowjonesnewsfund.org/PageText/Prg_HomePages.aspx?Page_ID=Prg_CollegeIntern

American Conservatory Theater

American Conservatory Theater Production Fellowships

Type of award: Internship.
Intended use: For undergraduate, graduate or non-degree study.
Eligibility: Applicant must be U.S. citizen or permanent resident.
Basis for selection: Major/career interest in performing arts; theater arts or theater/production/technical.
Application requirements: Recommendations, essay. Resume. Writing sample and/or portfolio, if required by specific fellowship.
Additional information: Provides fellow with practical experience in many areas of theater production. Departments include costume rentals, costume shop, properties, stage management, and production. Fellowships are full-time for duration of entire season (September to June). A weekly stipend is available. Visit Website for more information.

Number of awards:	6
Number of applicants:	120
Application deadline:	March 31
Notification begins:	May 10

Contact:
American Conservatory Theater
Fellowship Coordinator
30 Grant Avenue, 6th Floor
San Francisco, CA 94108-5834
Phone: 415-834-3200
Web: www.act-sf.org/fellowships

Artistic and Administrative Fellowships

Type of award: Internship.
Intended use: For undergraduate, graduate or non-degree study.
Eligibility: Applicant must be U.S. citizen or permanent resident.
Basis for selection: Major/career interest in theater arts; theater/production/technical; arts management; performing arts; public relations; marketing; English or literature.
Application requirements: Recommendations, essay. Resume. Writing sample and/or portfolio if required by specific fellowship.

Additional information: Provides fellow with opportunity to work in artistic, development, dramaturgy, general management, graphic design, marketing/public relations, education/publications, or web development departments. Fellowship is full-time for duration of entire season (September to June). A weekly stipend is available. Visit Website for more information.

Number of awards:	8
Number of applicants:	120
Application deadline:	March 31
Notification begins:	May 10

Contact:
American Conservatory Theater
Fellowship Coordinator
30 Grant Avenue, 6th Floor
San Francisco, CA 94108-5834
Phone: 415-834-3200
Web: www.act-sf.org/fellowships

American Federation of State, County and Municipal Employees

AFSCMA/UNCF Union Scholars Program

Type of award: Internship.
Intended use: For sophomore or junior study at 4-year institution.
Eligibility: Applicant must be Alaskan native, Asian American, African American, Mexican American, Hispanic American, Puerto Rican, American Indian or Native Hawaiian/Pacific Islander.
Basis for selection: Major/career interest in ethnic/cultural studies; women's studies; sociology; anthropology; history; political science/government; psychology; social work; economics or public administration/service. Applicant must demonstrate high academic achievement.
Application requirements: Recommendations, essay, transcript.
Additional information: Labor studies and American studies majors also eligible. Minimum 2.5 GPA. Must demonstrate interest in working for social and economic justice through the labor movement. Must have a driver's license. Award is a ten-week summer field placement to participate in union organizing campaign in one of several U.S. locations. Includes on-site housing and week-long orientation and training. Scholars receive up to $4,000 stipend and up to $5,000 academic scholarship for upcoming school year.

Amount of award:	$4,000-$9,000
Application deadline:	February 28

Contact:
AFSCME
Attn: Department of Education
1625 L Street, NW
Washington, DC 20036-5687
Phone: 703-205-2052
Web: www.afscme.org or www.uncf.org

American Museum of Natural History

Anthropology Internship Program

Type of award: Internship.
Intended use: For undergraduate or graduate study.
Basis for selection: Major/career interest in anthropology; archaeology or museum studies.
Application requirements: Essay, transcript. Resume, contact information of academic advisor.
Additional information: Must specify whether applying for paid academic credit, or unpaid internship. Deadlines: April 1 for summer; August 27 for fall; December 1 for spring. Recent graduates also eligible. Number of awards varies.

Application deadline:	December 1, August 27

Contact:
American Museum of Natural History
Attn: Anita Caltabiano
Central Park West at 79th Street
New York, NY 10024-5192
Phone: 212-769-5375
Web: www.research.amnh.org/anthropology/about/internship

Research Experiences for Undergraduates in the Physical Sciences

Type of award: Internship.
Intended use: For undergraduate study at accredited postsecondary institution in United States.
Eligibility: Applicant must be U.S. citizen or permanent resident.
Basis for selection: Major/career interest in physical sciences; astronomy or geophysics. Applicant must demonstrate high academic achievement and seriousness of purpose.
Application requirements: Essay, transcript. List of courses. List of references. Ranking of first two choices among summer projects listed on Website and explanation of why applicant chose them.
Additional information: Nearby university dormitory housing or housing stipend provided, as well as travel to and from New York City, as per need. Visit Website for updated list of projects offered and application. Application must be submitted electronically. Contact Dr. James Webster (jdw@amnh.org) for more information on the Earth and Planetary Science program or Dr. Charles Liu (cliu@amnh.org) for the Astrophysics program. Amount and number of awards vary. Deadline in early February. Visit Website for exact date.

Amount of award:	$5,100

Contact:
Richard Gilder Graduate School, REU Program in Physical Sciences
American Museum of Natural History
Central Park West at 79th Street
New York, NY 10024-5192
Phone: 212-769-5055
Web: www.research.amnh.org/physsci/reu.html

Internships

American Society of International Law

American Society of International Law Internships

Type of award: Internship.
Intended use: For undergraduate or graduate study at accredited postsecondary institution.
Basis for selection: Major/career interest in accounting; communications; international relations; law; public administration/service or public relations.
Application requirements: Cover letter, resume.
Additional information: Positions are based in Washington, D.C. and require a minimum commitment of 15 hours per week during fall and spring semesters. Summer semester positions may require a commitment of more than 15 hours per week. All internships unpaid; students may arrange academic credit. Visit Website for application requirements. Applications accepted on rolling basis.
Contact:
American Society of International Law
Internship Coordinator
2223 Massachusetts Avenue, NW
Washington, DC 20008
Phone: 202-939-6000
Fax: 202-797-7133
Web: www.asil.org/about/asil-internships

Applied Materials

Applied Materials Internship and Co-op Program

Type of award: Internship.
Intended use: For undergraduate or graduate study at accredited postsecondary institution.
Basis for selection: Major/career interest in accounting; business; business/management/administration; computer/information sciences; engineering, chemical; engineering, electrical/electronic; engineering, mechanical; finance/banking; materials science or physics. Applicant must demonstrate high academic achievement.
Application requirements: Resume.
Additional information: Applicant should have interest in semi-conductor industry. Summer and year-round internships and co-op positions available. Visit Website to submit resume and to find out when internship interviews will be held at college campuses. Internships are paid and may also include relocation assistance, medical insurance, and additional benefits.
Contact:
Applied Materials, Attn: Global College Programs
3050 Bowers Avenue
P.O. Box 58039
Santa Clara, CA 95054-3299
Web: www.appliedmaterials.com/careers

Arts and Business Council of New York

Arts and Business Council of New York Multicultural Arts Management Internship Program

Type of award: Internship.
Intended use: For sophomore, junior or senior study at 2-year or 4-year institution.
Basis for selection: Major/career interest in arts management.
Application requirements: Interview, recommendations, essay, transcript. Resume, cover letter.
Additional information: Interns spend ten weeks (June-August) working full-time at a New York City arts organization. Preference given to African-American, Asian-American, Latino/a, and Native American students. Must have taken arts, business, or marketing courses, or been involved in similar extracurricular activities. Interviews take place February/March; phone interviews may be arranged. Deadline in February. Visit Website for exact date and application.
  Amount of award: $2,500
Contact:
Americans for the Arts
Attn: Internship Program
One East 53rd Street, 3rd Floor
New York, NY 10022
Phone: 212-223-2787
Fax: 212-980-4857
Web: www.artsandbusiness-ny.org

Asian American Journalists Association

AAJA/NBC Summer Partnership

Type of award: Internship.
Intended use: For sophomore, junior, senior or graduate study at 4-year or graduate institution in United States.
Eligibility: Applicant must be at least 18.
Basis for selection: Major/career interest in journalism.
Application requirements: Recommendations, essay, transcript. Resume, work samples, and photo copy of ID or drivers' license.
Additional information: Internship lasts 10 weeks in New York City and includes stipend and AAJA mentor. AAJA membership is encouraged for applicants and required for recipients. Preference given to applicants with production experience. Deadline varies each year.
  Number of awards: 4
Contact:
Asian American Journalists Association
AAJA/NBC Summer Partnership
5 Third Street, Suite 1108
San Francisco, CA 94103
Phone: 415-346-2051 ext. 107
Fax: 415-346-6343
Web: www.aaja.org

Bernstein-Rein Advertising

Advertising Internship

Type of award: Internship.
Intended use: For junior study.
Basis for selection: Major/career interest in advertising; communications or marketing.
Application requirements: Interview, portfolio. Resume, cover letter, three reference names.
Additional information: Internship runs for eight weeks in summer. Applicant must have one or two semesters left before graduation. Pay is $10 per hour. Two positions each in account management, media, and creative. One position available in social media. Application available online.

Number of awards:	7
Number of applicants:	250
Application deadline:	March 15
Notification begins:	May 1

Contact:
Bernstein-Rein
Human Resources
4600 Madison, Suite 1500
Kansas City, MO 64112
Phone: 816-756-0640
Fax: 816-399-6000
Web: internships.b-r.com

Black & Veatch Corporation

Black & Veatch Summer Internship Program

Type of award: Internship.
Intended use: For full-time junior or senior study in United States.
Eligibility: Applicant must be U.S. citizen or permanent resident.
Basis for selection: Major/career interest in architecture; engineering, nuclear; engineering, civil; engineering, electrical/electronic; engineering, mechanical; technology or construction management. Applicant must demonstrate high academic achievement.
Application requirements: Resume.
Additional information: Internship compensation varies by discipline. Additional acceptable majors/career interests include construction management and mechanical, electrical or civil technicians. Minimum 2.75 GPA. Positions offered across the U.S. Positions will be posted online until filled.
Contact:
Web: www.bv.com/collegecareers

Board of Governors of the Federal Reserve System

Economic Research Division Project Internships

Type of award: Internship, renewable.
Intended use: For undergraduate or graduate study at postsecondary institution.

Eligibility: Applicant must be U.S. citizen or permanent resident.
Basis for selection: Major/career interest in economics; statistics; computer/information sciences; mathematics or finance/banking. Applicant must demonstrate high academic achievement.
Application requirements: Recommendations, transcript. Resume, cover letter.
Additional information: Paid internship lasts from June to September. Submit application by e-mail.

Application deadline:	April 1

Contact:
Board of Governors of the Federal Reserve System
20th Street and Constitution Avenue NW
Washington, DC 20551
Phone: 202-452-3880
Web: www.federalreserve.gov/careers/intern_research.htm

Boeing Company

Boeing Internships

Type of award: Internship.
Intended use: For undergraduate or graduate study in United States.
Eligibility: Applicant must be U.S. citizen or permanent resident.
Basis for selection: Major/career interest in aerospace; computer/information sciences; statistics; human resources; manufacturing; economics; science, general; engineering; mathematics or business.
Application requirements: Resume.
Additional information: Internships available in Alabama, Arizona, California, Florida, Illinois, Kansas, Missouri, Oklahoma, Pennsylvania, Texas, Washington, D.C. (Metro) and Washington state. Deadlines, eligibility requirements, and compensation vary depending on position. See Website for detailed information on available positions and to submit resume.

Number of awards:	1,200

Contact:
Web: www.boeing.com/careers

Boston Globe

Boston Globe Summer Internship

Type of award: Internship.
Intended use: For junior, senior or graduate study at 4-year or graduate institution.
Basis for selection: Major/career interest in journalism.
Application requirements: Interview, recommendations. Writing samples/clips, resume.
Additional information: Full-time, paid 12-week summer internship. Current undergraduate students in any major may apply, as well as journalism graduate students without professional experience as newspaper reporter. A previous internship at a daily newspaper is recommended. Application available online in September.

Number of awards: 10
Number of applicants: 500
Application deadline: November 1
Notification begins: December 31
Contact:
The Boston Globe
Attn: Paula Bouknight
P.O. Box 55819
Boston, MA 02205-5819
Phone: 617-929-3120
Web: www.bostonglobe.com/newsintern

Citizens for Global Solutions

Citizens for Global Solutions Internship

Type of award: Internship, renewable.
Intended use: For undergraduate or graduate study at postsecondary institution.
Basis for selection: Major/career interest in international relations; international studies; information systems; journalism; nonprofit administration; political science/government or web design.
Application requirements: Resume, cover letter, three- to five-page writing sample.
Additional information: Internship terms run from January through May (spring), June through August (summer), and September through December (fall). Applications are accepted until positions are filled. Recent graduates also eligible. Internship includes $15 per day stipend. Visit Website for more information.
Contact:
Citizens for Global Solutions
420 7th Street SE
Washington, DC 20003-2796
Phone: 202-546-3950 ext. 100
Fax: 202-546-3749
Web: www.globalsolutions.org/jobs

Congressional Hispanic Caucus Institute

CHCI Congressional Internship

Type of award: Internship.
Intended use: For full-time undergraduate study at accredited 2-year or 4-year institution.
Eligibility: Applicant must be U.S. citizen or permanent resident.
Basis for selection: Applicant must demonstrate high academic achievement, leadership and service orientation.
Application requirements: Recommendations, transcript. Three personal essays, resume.
Additional information: Spring (12 week), fall (12 week) and summer (eight week) internship in Washington, D.C. congressional offices. Transportation, housing, and stipend provided; $2,500 for eight week program, and $3,750 for 12 week program. Must have excellent writing and analytical

skills and active participation in community service activities. Work experience is complemented by leadership development sessions. Minimum 3.0 GPA preferred. Visit Website for deadline information and application.
Amount of award: $2,500-$3,750
Number of awards: 60
Number of applicants: 1,000
Application deadline: April 21
Contact:
CHCI Internship Program
300 M Street, SE
5th Floor, Suite 510
Washington, DC 20003
Phone: 202-543-1771
Fax: 202-546-2143
Web: www.chci.org/internships

Congressional Institute, Inc.

Congressional Institute Internships

Type of award: Internship.
Intended use: For undergraduate study at accredited 2-year or 4-year institution in United States.
Eligibility: Applicant must be U.S. citizen.
Basis for selection: Major/career interest in political science/ government; public administration/service; law or communications. Applicant must demonstrate high academic achievement.
Application requirements: Recommendations. Resume and writing samples.
Additional information: Paid internships available throughout the year on flexible terms. Must have interest in public policy or legislative policy issues. Visit Website for application and additional information.
Contact:
Congressional Institute, Inc.
1700 Diagonal Road
Suite 730
Alexandria, VA 22314
Phone: 703-837-8812
Fax: 703-837-8817
Web: www.conginst.org

Cushman School

Cushman School Internship

Type of award: Internship, renewable.
Intended use: For undergraduate or graduate study.
Basis for selection: Major/career interest in education.
Application requirements: Resume, cover letter.
Additional information: Internship is 17 weeks on Cushman School campus for fall and spring semesters. Interns assist staff in grading papers, supervising students, and performing administrative work. Internships are full-time, 8 a.m. to 4 p.m., Monday to Friday. Stipend of $2,000 for U.S. students and $3,000 for international students awarded each semester. International students must have J1 visa. Rolling application deadline. Number of internships varies.
Amount of award: $2,000-$3,000

Internships

Contact:
Cushman School
Arvi Balseiro
592 Northeast 60th Street
Miami, FL 33137
Phone: 305-757-1966
Fax: 305-757-1632
Web: www.cushmanschool.org

Denver Rescue Mission

Denver Rescue Mission Center for Mission Studies Internships

Type of award: Internship.
Intended use: For junior, senior or graduate study at postsecondary institution in United States.
Basis for selection: Major/career interest in social work; religion/theology; ministry; nonprofit administration; health services administration; public relations; marketing or information systems. Applicant must demonstrate service orientation.
Application requirements: Interview. Background check.
Additional information: Denver Rescue Mission is a nondenominational Christian charity offering internships in the following areas: child development, family studies, human services, management information systems, medical office administration, public relations/marketing, social work, volunteer relations, counseling, family therapy, shelter management, and nonprofit administration. Interns must be at least 21 years of age or have completed at least one year of post-secondary education. Internships vary in length, and some may have gender, age, level-of-study, or other requirements. Housing included. See Website for details and to apply.
Contact:
Denver Rescue Mission
3501 E. 46th Ave.
Denver, CO 80216
Phone: 303-953-3951
Web: www.denverrescuemission.org

Dominion

Dominion Diversity Scholarship

Type of award: Internship.
Intended use: For full-time undergraduate study.
Eligibility: Applicant must be high school senior.
Application requirements: High school seniors will need to show proof of acceptance. Applicants selected for interview will be required to provide an unofficial transcript.
Additional information: Must have a minimum 3.0 GPA. Must be enrolled/registered as a full-time student for the Fall Semester at an accredited 4-year or 2-year college or university. Acceptance of a scholarship requires that the applicant commit to a paid 10-12 week intern work session during the summer session - this work session is contingent upon satisfactory completion of normal pre-employment requirements.

Amount of award:	$5,000
Number of awards:	30

Contact:
Web: https://www.dom.com/corporate/careers/students/scholarships-and-awards

Explore Dominion Program

Type of award: Internship.
Intended use: For full-time freshman or sophomore study at accredited 2-year or 4-year institution.
Eligibility: Applicant must be high school senior.
Application requirements: Requires two paid 10-12 week work sessions over two summers.
Additional information: Must have a minimum 3.0 GPA. At the time of applying, applicants must be a graduating high school senior, college freshman, or sophomore. Must be enrolled/registered as a full-time student for the Fall Semester following the summer session at an accredited 4-year or 2-year college or university. If currently enrolled in a 2-year college program, students must be pursuing a transfer degree such as an Associate of Arts (AA), Associate of Science (AS), and Associate of Arts and Sciences (AA&S). These transfer programs are designed for students who plan to transfer to a 4-year college or university to complete a baccalaureate degree program.

Amount of award:	$5,000
Number of awards:	10

Contact:
Web: https://www.dom.com/corporate/careers/students/scholarships-and-awards

Dow Jones News Foundation

Data Journalism Intern Program

Type of award: Scholarship.
Intended use: For full-time junior, senior or graduate study at 4-year or graduate institution in United States.
Basis for selection: Applicant must demonstrate high academic achievement and seriousness of purpose.
Application requirements: Essay, transcript. Complete online application form, submit resume, proctored data journalism test created by Dow Jones News Fund, required essay, unofficial transcript or list of courses and grades.
Additional information: Seriousness, commitment to journalism as a career, interest in and demonstrated ability in investigative and data journalism. Program includes salary of no less than $400 per week, transportation, pre-internship training including on-campus housing and meals.

Amount of award:	$1,000-$18,000
Number of awards:	18
Number of applicants:	144
Application deadline:	November 1
Notification begins:	December 25

Contact:
Dow Jones News Foundation
PO Box 300
Princeton, NJ 08543
Phone: 609-452-2820
Fax: 609-520-5804
Web: https://dowjonesnewsfund.org/PageText/Prg_HomePages.aspx?Page_ID=Prg_CollegeIntern

Dow Jones News Fund

Digital Media Intern Program

Type of award: Internship.
Intended use: For full-time junior, senior or graduate study in United States.
Eligibility: Applicant must be U.S. citizen, permanent resident or international student.
Basis for selection: Major/career interest in journalism. Applicant must demonstrate high academic achievement and seriousness of purpose.
Application requirements: Essay, transcript. Resume, exam.
Additional information: May have any major but must intend to pursue journalism career. Common application form for all editing programs available online starting in August. Must take editing test administered by designated professor on applicant's campus. Finalists undergo telephone interview. Paid 10 to 12-week summer internships as editors at daily newspapers, online newspapers, or news services. Must attend one-week pre-internship training at Arizona State University. Interns returning to school receive scholarship. International students must have work visa.

Amount of award:	$1,000
Number of awards:	12
Number of applicants:	600
Application deadline:	November 1
Notification begins:	December 15
Total amount awarded:	$12,000

Contact:
Dow Jones News Fund
Digital Intern Program
P.O. Box 300
Princeton, NJ 08543-0300
Phone: 609-452-2820
Web: www.newsfund.org

Dow Jones Business Reporting Intern Program

Type of award: Internship.
Intended use: For full-time junior, senior or graduate study.
Eligibility: Applicant must be U.S. citizen, permanent resident or international student.
Basis for selection: Major/career interest in journalism or business. Applicant must demonstrate high academic achievement and seriousness of purpose.
Application requirements: Interview, essay, transcript. Resume, three to five recently published clips, reporting test.
Additional information: May have any major, but must plan to pursue journalism career. Special interest in business a plus. Applications available online August to November 1. All applicants notified by January 31. Applicants must take reporting test administered by designated professor on applicant's campus. Telephone interview required for finalists. Paid summer internships as business reporters at news media companies last at least 10 weeks. Interns returning to school receive scholarship at end of summer to apply toward following year. All interns attend pre-internship training that lasts one week. International students must have work visa.

Amount of award:	$1,000
Number of awards:	12
Number of applicants:	100
Application deadline:	November 1
Notification begins:	December 15
Total amount awarded:	$12,000

Contact:
Dow Jones News Fund
Business Reporting Intern Program
P.O. Box 300
Princeton, NJ 08543-0300
Phone: 609-452-2820
Web: www.newsfund.org

Multimedia Editing Intern Program

Type of award: Internship.
Intended use: For full-time junior, senior or graduate study in United States.
Eligibility: Applicant must be U.S. citizen, permanent resident or international student.
Basis for selection: Major/career interest in journalism. Applicant must demonstrate high academic achievement and seriousness of purpose.
Application requirements: Essay, transcript. Resume, editing test.
Additional information: May have any major but must plan to pursue journalism career. Common application form for all editing programs available online starting in August. All applicants notified by December 31. Editing test administered by designated professor on applicant's campus. Telephone interview required for finalists. Paid summer internships, as editors at daily newspapers, online newspapers, or real-time financial news services, last 10 to 12 weeks. Interns returning to school receive scholarship at end of summer to apply toward following year. All interns attend pre-internship training that lasts one week. International students must have work visa.

Amount of award:	$1,000
Number of awards:	50
Number of applicants:	600
Application deadline:	November 1
Notification begins:	December 15
Total amount awarded:	$40,000

Contact:
Dow Jones News Fund
News Editing Intern Program
P.O. Box 300
Princeton, NJ 08543-0300
Phone: 609-452-2820
Web: www.newsfund.org

DuPont Company

DuPont Internships

Type of award: Internship.
Intended use: For full-time sophomore, junior, senior or master's study at accredited 4-year institution in United States.
Eligibility: Applicant must be U.S. citizen or permanent resident.
Basis for selection: Major/career interest in accounting; finance/banking; marketing or information systems. Applicant must demonstrate high academic achievement.
Application requirements: Resume and cover letter.
Additional information: Interns normally work in summer between junior and senior years at DuPont company sites throughout U.S. May apply for extended internship. Minimum 3.0 GPA. Number and amount of awards vary. Must apply through Website.

Contact:
Phone: 302-774-1000
Web: www.dupont.com/careers

Eastman Kodak Company

Eastman Kodak Cooperative Internship Programs

Type of award: Internship.
Intended use: For full-time sophomore, junior, senior or graduate study.
Basis for selection: Major/career interest in accounting; business; chemistry; computer/information sciences; engineering; finance/banking; manufacturing; marketing; physics or graphic arts/design. Applicant must demonstrate high academic achievement.
Application requirements: Resume and cover letter.
Additional information: Internship must be minimum ten consecutive weeks during summer. Positions offered in Rochester, NY, Windsor, CO, and Dayton, OH. Internship includes competitive salary based upon discipline and education level, travel expenses, assistance locating housing, mentoring, and student activities. Applicant must be drug-screened as condition of employment. Apply online. Number of available internships varies.
Contact:
Web: www.kodak.com/go/careers

Entergy

Entergy Jumpstart Co-ops and Internships

Type of award: Internship, renewable.
Intended use: For full-time undergraduate or graduate study at accredited 4-year or graduate institution in United States.
Eligibility: Applicant must be U.S. citizen or permanent resident.
Basis for selection: Major/career interest in engineering, civil; business; accounting; human resources; finance/banking; engineering, electrical/electronic; engineering, mechanical; engineering, nuclear or information systems. Applicant must demonstrate high academic achievement and depth of character.
Additional information: Paid co-ops and internships available. Minimum 3.0 GPA. Apply online. Visit Website for application deadline and current openings. Must have work experience and give graduation date.
Contact:
Phone: 504-576-4000
Web: https://mycollegedollars.hyfnrsx1.com/scholarships/27181

Entertainment Weekly

Entertainment Weekly Internship Program

Type of award: Internship.
Intended use: For junior, senior or postgraduate study at postsecondary institution.

Application requirements: Resume, cover letter, and five clips/writing samples.
Additional information: Internships in editorial department last 12-18 weeks and pay $10 per hour. Application deadlines are February 15 for summer, June 15 for fall, and October 15 for winter. Number of internships varies.

Number of applicants:	200
Application deadline:	February 15, June 15
Notification begins:	March 1, July 1

Contact:
Entertainment Weekly Internship Program
Attn: Tina Jordan
135 W. 50th Street, 3rd Floor
New York, NY 10020
Phone: 212-522-4098
Fax: 212-522-6104
Web: www.entertainmentweekly.tumblr.com

ESPN Inc.

ESPN Internship

Type of award: Internship.
Intended use: For full-time junior study.
Eligibility: Applicant must be U.S. citizen or permanent resident.
Basis for selection: Major/career interest in sports/sports administration; communications; computer/information sciences; statistics; graphic arts/design; journalism; marketing or radio/television/film.
Application requirements: Resume and cover letter.
Additional information: Applicants should be current students within 12 months of graduation during the internship. Other majors welcome to apply. Internships last ten weeks at 40 hours per week. Most positions based in Bristol, CT or New York, NY, with limited opportunities at other locations. CT and NY interns may qualify for subsidized housing. Previous internship experience a plus. Competitive pay. Course credit offered based on college requirements. Limited internships offered in spring and fall; majority of internships offered in summer. Applications processed on rolling basis; apply online. Check Website for available positions and deadline.

Number of applicants:	10,000

Contact:
ESPN Inc.
Web: www.espncareers.com/campus

Essence Magazine

Essence Summer Internship

Type of award: Internship, renewable.
Intended use: For undergraduate or graduate study at accredited 4-year institution in United States.
Basis for selection: Major/career interest in advertising; business; fashion/fashion design/modeling; graphic arts/design; journalism; marketing; public relations or publishing.
Application requirements: Resume and writing sample or digital portfolio.
Additional information: Must be authorized to work in U.S. Nine-week summer internships available in several departments: sales and marketing, Essence.com, fashion and

beauty, art/photo, public relations, business office, and editorial. Interns responsible for finding their own housing. Receive bi-weekly paycheck. Must have appreciation for magazine industry; be self-motivated and detail-oriented. Visit Website for application and more information. Number of internships varies.

Number of applicants:	300
Application deadline:	January 31
Notification begins:	March 31

Contact:
Essence Internship Program, Attn: Human Resources
1271 Avenue of the Americas
7th Floor
New York, NY 10020
Phone: 212-522-1212
Fax: 212-467-2357
Web: www.essence.com/internships

Federal Reserve Bank of New York

Federal Reserve Bank of New York Undergraduate Summer Internship

Type of award: Internship.
Intended use: For full-time junior or senior study at postsecondary institution.
Basis for selection: Major/career interest in finance/banking; economics; business; computer/information sciences; accounting or public administration/service. Applicant must demonstrate high academic achievement.
Application requirements: Interview, transcript. Cover letter, resume.
Additional information: Paid internships begin in late May/early June. Applicants must have completed sophomore year of college before beginning internship. Applicants must be available for in-person interviews in March/April. Housing not provided. International students must be legally authorized to work in U.S. on a multi-year basis for other than practical training purposes. Submit resume online. Deadline varies. Visit Website for exact date.
Contact:
Federal Reserve Bank of New York
Summer Internship Coordinator
33 Liberty Street
New York, NY 10045
Phone: 212-720-5000
Web: www.ny.frb.org/careers/summerintern.html

Feminist Majority Foundation

Feminism & Leadership Internship

Type of award: Internship.
Intended use: For undergraduate study at accredited 4-year institution.
Basis for selection: Major/career interest in women's studies or political science/government. Applicant must demonstrate high academic achievement and leadership.

Application requirements: Resume, cover letter, writing sample.
Additional information: Recent graduates may also apply. Full-time or part-time internships for a minimum of two months available year-round in the Washington, D.C., area and Los Angeles. Interns have various responsibilities, such as monitoring press conferences and coalition meetings, researching, attending rallies, and organizing events. Internships unpaid, but students may be able to earn small stipend in exchange for administrative work. Applicants with experience working on women's issues preferred. People of color, people with disabilities, and math/science majors encouraged to apply. Applications processed on rolling basis. See Website for more information.
Contact:
Feminist Majority Foundation
Attn: Internship Coordinator
1600 Wilson Boulevard, Suite 801
Arlington, VA 22209
Phone: 703-522-2214
Fax: 703-522-2219
Web: www.feminist.org/intern

Filoli

Filoli Garden Internships and Apprenticeships

Type of award: Internship.
Intended use: For undergraduate, graduate or non-degree study at postsecondary institution. Designated institutions: Filoli.
Basis for selection: Major/career interest in horticulture; landscape architecture or botany. Applicant must demonstrate high academic achievement, depth of character, leadership and seriousness of purpose.
Application requirements: Recommendations, transcript. Resume and cover letter outlining interests.
Additional information: Also for students pursuing careers in public garden management and landscape maintenance. Students paid $10.50 per hour and may earn college credit for ten-week internship program or six-month apprenticeship program. Applicants must have at least 12 units of horticulture classes and 3.0 GPA. Ability to work well with public and work teams essential. Maximum five students per internship. Visit Website for deadlines and application.

Amount of award:	$4,200-$10,900
Number of awards:	10
Number of applicants:	12
Total amount awarded:	$48,000

Contact:
Filoli
Jim Salyards/Filoli Garden Internships
86 Canada Road
Woodside, CA 94062
Phone: 650-364-8300 ext. 223
Fax: 650-366-7836
Web: www.filoli.org/education/garden-internships.html

Fox Group

Fox Internship

Type of award: Internship.
Intended use: For junior, senior or graduate study at accredited 4-year or graduate institution.
Eligibility: Applicant must be International student eligible to work in United States.
Application requirements: Resume.
Additional information: Paid internships are available in all departments within Film, Television and Digital Media. Applicants must be current students. College credit available. Apply via Website.
Contact:
Web: www.foxcareers.com

Franklin D. Roosevelt Library

Roosevelt Archival Internships

Type of award: Internship.
Intended use: For undergraduate or graduate study at postsecondary institution.
Basis for selection: Major/career interest in library science; computer/information sciences; museum studies; history; political science/government or education.
Application requirements: Transcript.
Additional information: Interns work at FDR library with other interns and staff organizing and automating archival materials, making indices, finding aids and databases, digitizing documents and photographs, and assisting with other projects. Internship can last up to eight weeks and must take place during summer break (mid-May through end of August). Housing not provided. Work Monday through Friday, 9 a.m. to 5 p.m. Stipend of $3200 for eight weeks (two payments; first payment after Week 1 and second after Week 8). Number of awards depends on funding. Familiarity with FDR presidency helpful. Visit Website for application.

Number of awards:	3
Number of applicants:	75
Application deadline:	April 1
Notification begins:	April 15

Contact:
Franklin D. Roosevelt Library
Roosevelt Archival Internship Program
4079 Albany Post Road
Hyde Park, NY 12538
Phone: 845-486-7745
Fax: 845-486-1147
Web: www.fdrlibrary.marist.edu/getinvolved.html

Garden Club of America

GCA Internship in Garden History and Design

Type of award: Internship.
Intended use: For undergraduate or graduate study at postsecondary institution.
Basis for selection: Major/career interest in botany; horticulture; landscape architecture or museum studies.
Application requirements: Recommendations, essay, transcript. Two letters of recommendation (one from professor in major, one from adviser).
Additional information: May apply to Archives of American Gardens in Washington, D.C., or at other eligible institutions (contact sponsor to verify). Stipend provided; GCA funds act as supplement.

Amount of award:	$2,000
Number of awards:	1
Application deadline:	February 15

Contact:
Garden Club of America
Magda Cruz
14 East 60th Street
New York, NY 10022-1006
Phone: 212-753-8287
Fax: 212-753-0134
Web: www.gcamerica.org

Genentech, Inc.

Genentech, Inc. Internship Program

Type of award: Internship, renewable.
Intended use: For full-time undergraduate or graduate study at accredited 4-year or graduate institution.
Basis for selection: Major/career interest in biology; business; chemistry; computer/information sciences; engineering; engineering, biomedical; engineering, chemical; law; life sciences or medicine. Applicant must demonstrate high academic achievement.
Application requirements: Resume and cover letter.
Additional information: Paid summer internships last 9-12 weeks and are available in various research and business areas. Must have already completed one year of study. International students must have work authorization. Applications accepted January through April. Internships take place in South San Francisco, Vacaville, and Oceanside, California and Hillsboro, Oregon. Apply online or check Website for campus recruiting schedule.
Contact:
Genentech, Inc.
1 DNA Way
South San Francisco, CA 94080-4990
Phone: 650-225-1000
Fax: 650-225-6000
Web: www.gene.com/careers/academic-programs

Hannaford Bros. Co.

Hannaford Internships

Type of award: Internship.
Intended use: For undergraduate or master's study at postsecondary institution.
Eligibility: Applicant must be U.S. citizen, permanent resident or international student.
Basis for selection: Major/career interest in pharmacy/pharmaceutics/pharmacology. Applicant must demonstrate high academic achievement.

Application requirements: Cover letter and resume.
Additional information: Twelve-week paid summer internship, beginning early June. Interns at Hannaford are exposed to a multicultural organization with support systems and training opportunities. Internships available at Hannaford's corporate office, distribution centers, and retail locations. Pharmacy internships also available. Inquire at campus placement office to schedule recruiting interview or e-mail for additional information. Minimum 3.0 GPA. Must be legally authorized to work in United States. Amount of payment or course credit awarded varies. International students must have work authorization. Visit Website for more information. Applications accepted online only.
Contact:
Hannaford Brothers Company Employment Department
Web: www.hannaford.com

Hispanic Association of Colleges and Universities

HACU National Internship Program

Type of award: Internship.
Intended use: For sophomore, junior, senior or graduate study at 2-year, 4-year or graduate institution. Designated institutions: Institutions with significant number of Hispanic students.
Eligibility: Applicant must be U.S. citizen or permanent resident.
Basis for selection: Applicant must demonstrate high academic achievement and service orientation.
Application requirements: Essay, transcript. Resume, enrollment verification.
Additional information: Paid internships provide opportunities for students from institutions with significant numbers of Hispanic students to explore potential careers with federal agencies and private corporations. Interns work in Washington, D.C., area and field sites throughout country. Some internships require U.S. citizenship to participate. Applicants must have 3.0 GPA and have completed freshman year of college before internship begins. Weekly pay varies according to class level: $470 for sophomores and juniors, $500 for seniors and $570 for graduates. Must be active in college and community service. Fall and spring internships last 15 weeks; summer internships last ten weeks. Deadlines: November for spring, February for summer, June for fall. Visit Website for more information.
   Application deadline: June 9, March 1
Contact:
Hispanic Association of Colleges and Universities
One Dupont Circle, NW
Suite 430
Washington, DC 20036
Phone: 202-467-0893
Fax: 202-496-9177
Web: www.hacu.net

Hoffman-La Roche Inc.

Hoffman-La Roche Inc. Student Internship

Type of award: Internship.
Intended use: For full-time freshman, sophomore, junior or graduate study at postsecondary institution.

Basis for selection: Major/career interest in pharmacy/pharmaceutics/pharmacology; engineering; computer/information sciences; science, general; business; business/management/administration; biology; chemistry or biochemistry.
Application requirements: Interview. Cover letter, resume.
Additional information: Applicant must be authorized to work in the United States. Internship fields, topics, and amount of compensation vary. Send materials to address provided. If deadline is missed, application will be considered after those students who have met deadline. Visit Website for more information and internship descriptions.
Contact:
University Relations Department
Hoffman-La Roche, Inc.
340 Kingsland Street
Nutley, NJ 07110-1199
Phone: 973-235-4035 or 973-235-5000
Web: careers.roche.com/en/campus

IBM

IBM Co-op and Intern Program

Type of award: Internship.
Intended use: For full-time sophomore, junior, senior or graduate study at accredited 4-year or graduate institution in United States.
Basis for selection: Major/career interest in computer/information sciences; engineering, computer; engineering, electrical/electronic; information systems; accounting or finance/banking. Applicant must demonstrate high academic achievement and leadership.
Application requirements: Interview.
Additional information: Applicants chosen on competitive basis, based on relevant work or research experience, communication, team skills, and high evaluation during interview process. Most awardees are undergraduate juniors or first year master's students. Competitive salary based on number of credits completed towards degree. Applicants hired on semester basis. Must submit resume via IBM Website.
Contact:
IBM Co-op and Intern Program
Web: www-03.ibm.com/employment/students.html

The Indianapolis Star

Pulliam Journalism Fellowship

Type of award: Internship.
Intended use: For junior, senior, graduate or postgraduate study at postsecondary institution.
Basis for selection: Competition/talent/interest in writing/journalism. Major/career interest in humanities/liberal arts or journalism. Applicant must demonstrate high academic achievement, depth of character, leadership and seriousness of purpose.
Application requirements: Recommendations, transcript, proof of eligibility. Writing samples. Recent photograph.
Additional information: Paid fellowship lasts ten weeks during summer. Ten recipients work for The Indianapolis Star, ten for The Arizona Republic in Phoenix. Early deadline in

November. Some candidates may be accepted post-deadline. Visit Website for application and more information.

Amount of award:	$6,500
Number of awards:	20
Number of applicants:	175
Application deadline:	November 1

Contact:
Russell B. Pulliam, Director
The Pulliam Fellowship
P.O. Box 145
Indianapolis, IN 46206-0145
Phone: 317-444-6001
Web: www.indystar.com/pjf

INROADS, Inc.

INROADS Internship

Type of award: Internship, renewable.
Intended use: For full-time freshman, sophomore or junior study.
Eligibility: Applicant must be Alaskan native, Asian American, African American, Mexican American, Hispanic American, Puerto Rican, American Indian or Native Hawaiian/Pacific Islander. Applicant must be high school senior. Applicant must be U.S. citizen or permanent resident.
Basis for selection: Major/career interest in engineering; business; computer/information sciences; communications; retailing/merchandising; health-related professions or accounting. Applicant must demonstrate high academic achievement, leadership and service orientation.
Application requirements: Interview, transcript. Resume. National College Component Application.
Additional information: Applicant must have minimum 3.0 GPA or college 2.8 GPA. Must be full-time undergraduate with at least two summers or 54 credit hours remaining. Internship duration and compensation varies, and deadlines vary according to local affiliate office. Visit Website for additional information.

Number of awards:	4,000
Number of applicants:	20,000
Application deadline:	May 31

Contact:
INROADS, Inc.
10 S. Broadway
Suite 300
St. Louis, MO 63102
Phone: 314-241-7488
Fax: 314-241-9325
Web: www.inroads.org

Institute of Human Studies

Harper Internship Program

Type of award: Internship.
Intended use: For undergraduate or graduate study at postsecondary institution.
Additional information: Internships available in all departments. Competitive daily stipend offered. Available to all ages and experience levels.

Contact:
Institute of Human Studies
3434 Washington Blvd, MS IC5
Arlington, VA 22201
Phone: 703-993-4880
Web: www.theihs.org

International Radio and Television Society Foundation

International Radio and Television Society Foundation Summer Fellowship Program

Type of award: Internship.
Intended use: For full-time junior, senior or graduate study at postsecondary institution.
Basis for selection: Major/career interest in communications. Applicant must demonstrate high academic achievement.
Additional information: Nine week internship. Applicants must have prior internship experience and demonstrated interest in the field of communications. Fellows are awarded travel and housing expenses as well as an allowance. Visit Website for deadlines, information, and application.

Number of awards:	25
Application deadline:	November 1

Contact:
International Radio and Television Society Foundation
1697 Broadway
10th Floor
New York, NY 10019
Phone: 212-867-6650
Web: www.irts.org

J. Paul Getty Trust

J. Paul Getty Multicultural Undergraduate Summer Internships at the Getty Center

Type of award: Internship.
Intended use: For full-time undergraduate study at 4-year institution.
Eligibility: Applicant must be Asian American, African American, Mexican American, Hispanic American, Puerto Rican, American Indian or Native Hawaiian/Pacific Islander. Applicant must be U.S. citizen.
Basis for selection: Major/career interest in arts management; communications; humanities/liberal arts; architecture; museum studies/administration or art/art history.
Application requirements: Interview, recommendations. Supplemental application (plus three copies), all official transcripts (plus three copies), and SASE.
Additional information: Ten-week internship in specific departments of Getty Museum and other programs located at the Getty Center in Los Angeles. Interns receive $4,000 stipend. Limited to students attending school in or residing in

Los Angeles County. Intended for outstanding students who are members of groups currently underrepresented in museum professions and fields related to visual arts and humanities. Applicants must have completed at least one semester of college by June and not be graduating before December. Housing and transportation not included. Applications accepted in December, and applicants notified of acceptance in early May.

Amount of award:	$4,000
Number of awards:	20
Number of applicants:	124
Application deadline:	February 1

Contact:
Multicultural Undergraduate Internships at the Getty Center
The Getty Foundation
1200 Getty Center Dr., Suite 800
Los Angeles, CA 90049-1685
Phone: 310-440-7320
Fax: 310-440-7703
Web: www.getty.edu/foundation/initiatives/current/mui

The John F. Kennedy Center for the Performing Arts

Kennedy Center Arts Management Internship

Type of award: Internship.
Intended use: For junior, senior or post-bachelor's certificate study at accredited 4-year or graduate institution.
Basis for selection: Major/career interest in arts management.
Application requirements: Interview, transcript. Cover letter stating career goals. Two letters of recommendation. Resume and writing sample.
Additional information: Arts education majors also eligible. Three- to four-month part-time or full-time internship in many Kennedy Center departments. College credit may be available. Interns attend weekly sessions led by executives of Kennedy Center and other major arts institutions in Washington, D.C. Interns may attend performances, workshops, classes, and courses presented by center, free of charge (space available), during their internship. Visit Website for application, deadline, and more information.

Number of awards:	60
Number of applicants:	800

Contact:
Vilar Institute for Arts Management/Internships
2700 F Street NW
Washington, DC 20566
Phone: 202-416-8874
Web: www.kennedy-center.org/education/artsmanagement/internships

John F. Kennedy Library Foundation

Kennedy Library Archival Internship

Type of award: Internship.
Intended use: For undergraduate or graduate study at postsecondary institution. Designated institutions: John F. Kennedy Presidential Library.

Eligibility: Applicant must be U.S. citizen or permanent resident.
Basis for selection: Major/career interest in history; political science/government; library science; English; journalism; communications or museum studies. Applicant must demonstrate high academic achievement.
Application requirements: Interview, recommendations, transcript.
Additional information: Minimum 16 hours per week. Monthly stipend varies from $560-$1,400 depending on number of hours worked. Provides intern with opportunity to work on projects such as digitizing papers of Kennedy and his administration. Interns given career-relevant archival experience. Internships open up as vacancies occur. Library considers proposals for unpaid internships, independent study, work-study, and internships undertaken for academic credit. See Website for application and more information.

Amount of award:	$560-$1,400

Contact:
Archival Internships c/o Intern Coordinator
John F. Kennedy Presidential Library & Museum
Columbia Point
Boston, MA 02125-3313
Phone: 617-514-1629
Fax: 617-514-1625
Web: www.jfklibrary.org

John Wiley and Sons, Inc.

John Wiley and Sons, Inc. Internship Program

Type of award: Internship.
Intended use: For full-time junior or senior study at 4-year institution.
Basis for selection: Major/career interest in marketing; publishing; information systems or public relations.
Application requirements: Resume. Letter addressing why applicant would like to be selected for the program and listing areas of interest.
Additional information: Summer internship programs available for students who have completed junior year; program runs from mid-June through mid-August. Internships available in marketing, editorial, production, information technology, new media, and publicity; based at corporate offices in Hoboken and Somerset in NJ, Indianapolis, San Francisco, and Malden, MA. Interns receive weekly stipend. Those interested in interning in Hoboken, NJ, Somerset, NJ, San Francisco, CA, Indianapolis, IN, and Malden, MA should visit www.wiley.com for more information. Application address varies by city. See Website for details.

Application deadline:	April 1

Contact:
John Wiley and Sons, Inc. Attn: Internship Program
Human Resources Department
111 River Street
Hoboken, NJ 07030-5774
Fax: 201-748-6049
Web: www.wiley.com

Johnson Controls

Johnson Controls Co-op and Internship Programs

Type of award: Internship, renewable.
Intended use: For full-time undergraduate or graduate study at accredited 4-year institution in United States.
Basis for selection: Major/career interest in engineering; law; business/management/administration; manufacturing or automotive technology. Applicant must demonstrate high academic achievement.
Application requirements: Proof of eligibility. Resume, cover letter.
Additional information: Johnson Controls offers several co-op and internship programs in locations throughout the U.S. and abroad. The Engineering Co-op Program develops and trains students in all aspects of the Automotive Systems Group at Johnson Controls. Over a period of two to five years, mechanical and design engineering students alternate between work terms at Johnson Controls and school terms at college or university. Paid summer internships and positions in most other company divisions also available. Visit Website for complete program descriptions and application.
Contact:
Johnson Controls
Human Resources
5757 N. Green Bay Ave.
Milwaukee, WI 53209
Phone: 414-524-1200
Web: www.johnsoncontrols.com

Kentucky Higher Education Assistance Authority (KHEAA)

Kentucky Work-Study Program

Type of award: Internship, renewable.
Intended use: For undergraduate study at 2-year or 4-year institution. Designated institutions: Approved Kentucky institutions.
Eligibility: Applicant must be U.S. citizen residing in Kentucky.
Application requirements: Interview, proof of eligibility.
Additional information: Job must be related to major course of study. Work-study wage is at least federal minimum wage. May also be enrolled in technical schools. Visit Website for additional information.

Number of awards:	540
Number of applicants:	540
Total amount awarded:	$401,300

Contact:
Kentucky Higher Education Assistance Authority (KHEAA)
KHEAA Work-Study Program
P.O. Box 798
Frankfort, KY 40602-0798
Phone: 800-928-8926
Fax: 502-696-7373
Web: www.kheaa.com

Louis Carr Internship Foundation (LCIF)

Louis Carr Summer Internship

Type of award: Internship.
Intended use: For full-time freshman, sophomore or junior study in United States.
Eligibility: Applicant must be Asian American, African American, Mexican American, Hispanic American, Puerto Rican, American Indian or Native Hawaiian/Pacific Islander. Applicant must be U.S. citizen.
Basis for selection: Major/career interest in advertising; marketing; communications or public relations. Applicant must demonstrate high academic achievement, depth of character, leadership and seriousness of purpose.
Application requirements: Recommendations, essay, transcript. Resume.
Additional information: Paid, ten-week summer internship in New York, Chicago, Detroit, or Washington D.C.

Amount of award:	$4,000
Number of awards:	10
Number of applicants:	16
Application deadline:	March 31
Notification begins:	April 15
Total amount awarded:	$84,000

Contact:
Louis Carr Internship Foundation
P.O. Box 81859
Chicago, IL 60681-0589
Phone: 312-819-8617
Fax: 312-540-1109
Web: www.louiscarrfoundation.org

Macy's, Inc.

Internships at Macy's and Bloomingdale's

Type of award: Internship, renewable.
Intended use: For full-time undergraduate study.
Basis for selection: Applicant must demonstrate high academic achievement.
Application requirements: Resume.
Additional information: Eight- to ten-week paid internships offered in buying, planning, store management, product development, design, and macys.com. Apply online or visit Website for campus recruiting schedule.

Number of awards:	350

Contact:
Macy's, Inc.
Web: www.macysjobs.com/college/internships

Makovsky & Company Inc.

Makovsky & Company Inc. Public Relations Internship

Type of award: Internship.
Intended use: For junior or senior study at 4-year institution in United States or Canada.
Basis for selection: Major/career interest in public relations; communications; English or political science/government. Applicant must demonstrate high academic achievement.
Application requirements: Interview. Resume, cover letter, writing sample.
Additional information: Two to four full- or part-time (20 hours minimum) paid positions offered in summer. Must major in public relations or related subject. Applicant must be responsible, diligent, and energetic. Provides opportunity to receive hands-on experience in all facets of public relations under direction of forums staff.

Number of awards:	4
Number of applicants:	200
Application deadline:	March 15

Contact:
Makovsky & Company, Inc. Internship Coordinator
16 East 34th Street
15th Floor
New York, NY 10016
Phone: 212-508-9670
Fax: 212-751-9710
Web: www.makovsky.com

MCC Theater

MCC Theater Internships

Type of award: Internship.
Intended use: For undergraduate study at vocational institution.
Eligibility: Applicant must be residing in New York.
Basis for selection: Major/career interest in theater arts; theater/production/technical; performing arts; design; business/management/administration or arts management.
Application requirements: Resume.
Additional information: Rolling application deadlines, negotiable schedule. Internships available in general management/theater administration, development, marketing, production, and literary and arts education. College credit available. E-mail resume to apply.

Contact:
MCC Theater
311 West 43rd Street, Suite 302
New York, NY 10036
Phone: 212-727-7722
Fax: 212-727-7780
Web: www.mcctheater.org/education/internships.html

Metropolitan Museum of Art

The Cloisters Summer Internship Program

Type of award: Internship.
Intended use: For sophomore, junior or senior study at postsecondary institution.
Basis for selection: Major/career interest in art/art history; history; museum studies or museum studies/administration.
Application requirements: $50 application fee. Recommendations, essay, transcript. Resume and list of art history courses taken.
Additional information: Must be currently enrolled college student at time of internship. First- and second-year students especially encouraged to apply. Interns receive $3,150 stipend. Interest in medieval history appreciated. Nine-week full-time internship from mid-June to mid-August. Five-day, 35-hour work week.

Amount of award:	$3,150
Number of awards:	8
Application deadline:	January 15
Notification begins:	April 10

Contact:
The Cloisters
College Internship Program
Fort Tryon Park
New York, NY 10040
Phone: 212-650-2280
Web: www.metmuseum.org/education

Metropolitan Museum of Art Mentoring Program for College Juniors

Type of award: Internship.
Intended use: For sophomore or junior study at postsecondary institution.
Application requirements: $35 application fee. Recommendations, transcript.
Additional information: Interns work full-time for 6 weeks over the summer. Designed to encourage college juniors from diverse backgrounds to pursue museum careers. Participants work in one of the Museum's departments (curatorial, administrative, or educational). Includes a two-week orientation of the Museum, meetings with Museum professionals, a Museum mentor, and field trips to other institutions. Visit Website for deadline and application details.

Amount of award:	$3,250

Contact:
Metropolitan Museum of Art
1000 Fifth Avenue
New York, NY 10028-0198
Phone: 212-570-3710
Web: www.metmuseum.org/education

Metropolitan Museum of Art MuSe Summer Internship Program

Type of award: Internship.
Intended use: For senior, graduate or non-degree study at postsecondary institution.

Internships

Eligibility: Applicant must be U.S. citizen or international student.

Basis for selection: Major/career interest in art/art history; arts management or museum studies/administration. Applicant must demonstrate seriousness of purpose.

Application requirements: $50 application fee. Typed paper indicating desired internship, including name, home and school addresses and phone numbers. Resume. Two academic recommendations. Transcripts. Separate list with art history or relevant courses taken and knowledge of foreign languages. 500-word (maximum) essay describing career goals, interest in museum work, specific areas of interest within the museum, and reason for applying.

Additional information: Ten-week program for college students, recent college graduates who have not yet entered graduate school, and graduate students who have completed less than two years of graduate-level study. In addition to 10 week placements, the MuSe program also includes 6 month, 9 month, and 12 month internship positions. Interns work full-time. International students must have permission to work in U.S. Applicants should have broad background in art history. Program begins in June with two-week orientation, ends in August, and includes $3,500 honorarium for college interns and recent graduates and $4,000 for graduate interns. Visit Website for more information.

Amount of award:	$3,500-$4,000
Number of awards:	40

Contact:
Attn: Internship Programs
Metropolitan Museum of Art
1000 Fifth Avenue
New York, NY 10028-0198
Phone: 212-570-3710
Web: www.metmuseum.org/education

Minnesota Office of Higher Education

Minnesota Work-Study Program

Type of award: Internship.

Intended use: For undergraduate or graduate study.

Eligibility: Applicant must be residing in Minnesota.

Basis for selection: Applicant must demonstrate financial need.

Application requirements: Interview.

Additional information: This is a work-study program, but it may be applied to internships. Work placement must be approved by school or nonprofit agency. Must be used at Minnesota college or for internship with nonprofit or private sector employer located in Minnesota. Must be enrolled for at least six credit hours. Apply to financial aid office of school. Award maximum set at cost of attendance minus EFC and other financial aid.

Number of awards:	10,442
Number of applicants:	11,073
Total amount awarded:	$14,164,757

Contact:
Minnesota Office of Higher Education
1450 Energy Park Drive
Suite 350
St. Paul, MN 55108-5227
Phone: 800-657-3866
Web: www.ohe.state.mn.us

Morris Arboretum of the University of Pennsylvania

Arboriculture Internship

Type of award: Internship.

Intended use: For undergraduate or graduate study at postsecondary institution.

Basis for selection: Major/career interest in horticulture; forestry or landscape architecture.

Application requirements: Recommendations, transcript. Letter of intent, resume.

Additional information: Applicant should have interest in arboriculture. Internships train students in most up-to-date tree care techniques. Interns work 40 hours per week at hourly rate of $10.90 for full year. Intern works with Chief Arborist in all aspects of tree care, including tree assessment, pruning, cabling, and removal. Safety-conscious techniques are emphasized, and recent innovations in climbing and rigging are demonstrated and put into practice. Other opportunities include assisting with outreach activities including workshops and off-site consulting. Benefits include health, vision, and dental plan. Must have solid academic background in arboriculture and horticulture. Tree climbing ability helpful. Driver's license required. Academic credit given.

Application deadline: February 15

Contact:
Morris Arboretum of the University of Pennsylvania
Jan McFarlan, Education Coordinator
100 Northwestern Avenue
Philadelphia, PA 19118
Phone: 215-247-5777 ext. 156
Web: www.upenn.edu/arboretum

Morris Arboretum Education Internship

Type of award: Internship.

Intended use: For undergraduate or graduate study at postsecondary institution.

Basis for selection: Major/career interest in education; botany; horticulture; ecology or education, teacher.

Application requirements: Recommendations, transcript. Letter of intent, resume.

Additional information: Interns work 40 hours/week at hourly wage of $10.90 for full year. Interns develop workshops for experienced guides, training sessions for new guides, occasionally lead tours. Other responsibilities include supervising the school tour program, running special programs for the public, helping to prepare the adult education course brochure, and writing promotional copy including a newsletter for volunteer guides. Benefits include health, vision, and dental plan, and tuition benefits. Academic background or experience in education or educational programming preferred. Knowledge of plant-related subjects helpful. Strong writing and interpersonal skills essential. Academic credit given.

Application deadline: February 15

Contact:
Morris Arboretum of the University of Pennsylvania
Jan McFarlan, Education Coordinator
100 Northwestern Avenue
Philadelphia, PA 19118
Phone: 215-247-5777 ext. 156
Web: wwwupenn.edu/arboretum

Morris Arboretum Horticulture Internship

Type of award: Internship.

Intended use: For undergraduate or graduate study at postsecondary institution.

Basis for selection: Major/career interest in horticulture.

Application requirements: Recommendations, transcript. Letter of intent, resume.

Additional information: Intern assists in all phases of garden development and care of collections. Specific emphasis on refining practical horticultural skills. Supervisory skills are developed by directing activities of volunteers and part-time staff. Other activities include developing Integrated Pest Management skills, arboricultural techniques, and the operation and maintenance of garden machinery. Special projects will be assigned to develop individual skills in garden planning and management. Must have strong academic background in horticulture or closely related field. Interns work 40 hours per week at hourly wage of $10.90 for full year. Benefits include health, vision, and dental plan, and tuition benefits. Some internships require travel. Driver's license required. Academic credit given.

    Application deadline: February 15

Contact:
Morris Arboretum of the University of Pennsylvania
Jan McFarlan, Education Coordinator
100 Northwestern Avenue
Philadelphia, PA 19118
Phone: 215-247-5777 ext. 156
Web: www.upenn.edu/arboretum

Plant Propagation Internship

Type of award: Internship.

Intended use: For undergraduate or graduate study at postsecondary institution.

Basis for selection: Major/career interest in botany or horticulture.

Application requirements: Recommendations, transcript. Letter of intent, resume.

Additional information: Strong background in woody landscape plants, plant propagation, nursery management, and plant physiology required. Interns work 40 hours/week at hourly rate of $10.90 for full year. Benefits include health, vision, and dental plan and tuition benefits. Academic credit given. Intern assists propagator in the development of plant propagation and production schemes for arboretum. Emphasis is placed on the refinement of skills in traditional methods of plant propagation, nursery production, and greenhouse management. Other duties include management of the field nursery and data collection for ongoing research projects.

    Application deadline: February 15

Contact:
Morris Arboretum of the University of Pennsylvania
Jan McFarlan, Education Coordinator
100 Northwestern Avenue
Philadelphia, PA 19118
Phone: 215-247-5777 ext. 156
Web: www.upenn.edu/arboretum

Plant Protection Internship

Type of award: Internship.

Intended use: For undergraduate or graduate study at postsecondary institution.

Basis for selection: Major/career interest in horticulture; entomology or botany.

Application requirements: Recommendations, transcript. Letter of intent, resume.

Additional information: Interns work 40 hours per week at hourly wage of $10.90 for full year. Course work in entomology or plant pathology required. Intern assists arboretum's plant pathologist with the Integrated Pest Management program, which includes regular monitoring of the living collection and communicating information on pests and diseases to staff members. Related projects include establishing threshold levels for specific plant pests and evaluating the effectiveness of control measures. Modern laboratory facilities are available for identifying plant pests and pathogens. Intern also participates in Plant Clinic's daily operations, providing diagnostic services to the public about horticultural problems. Benefits include health, vision, and dental plan and tuition benefits. Strong writing skills essential. Academic credit given.

    Application deadline: February 15

Contact:
Morris Arboretum of the University of Pennsylvania
Jan McFarlan, Education Coordinator
100 Northwestern Avenue
Philadelphia, PA 19118
Phone: 215-247-5777 ext. 156
Web: www.upenn.edu/arboretum

Rose and Flower Garden Internship

Type of award: Internship.

Intended use: For undergraduate or graduate study at postsecondary institution.

Basis for selection: Major/career interest in horticulture. Applicant must demonstrate seriousness of purpose.

Application requirements: Recommendations, transcript. Letter of intent, resume.

Additional information: Intern assists Rosarian in garden development, management, and care of collections. Emphasis on mastering skills used in the culture of modern and antique roses, developing pest management skills, and refining horticulture skills including formal garden maintenance. Other duties include plant record keeping, support for volunteer gardeners, operation of garden machinery, and supervision of part-time staff. Interns work 40-hour week at hourly rate of $10.90 for full year. Benefits include health, vision, and dental plan, and tuition benefits. Applicant should have strong academic background in horticulture with course work in herbaceous and woody landscape plants. Driver's license required. Academic credit given.

    Application deadline: February 15

Contact:
Morris Arboretum of the University of Pennsylvania
Jan McFarlan, Education Coordinator
100 Northwestern Avenue
Philadelphia, PA 19118
Phone: 215-247-5777 ext. 156
Web: www.upenn.edu/arboretum

Urban Forestry Internship

Type of award: Internship.

Intended use: For undergraduate study at postsecondary institution.

Basis for selection: Major/career interest in forestry; horticulture; landscape architecture or ecology.

Application requirements: Recommendations, transcript. Letter of intent, resume.

Additional information: Intern will engage in urban forestry and natural resources programs and strategies for public

Internships

gardens, government agencies, and educational and community organizations; learn and teach stewardship concepts and practical applications through riparian and woodland restoration projects; develop community partnership, urban vegetation analysis, and management planning skills. Interns work 40 hours per week at hourly wage of $10.90 for full year. Benefits include health, vision, and dental plan and tuition benefits. Academic background in urban forestry, horticulture, landscape design, or related field. Communication skills essential. Car required; mileage reimbursed. Academic credit given.

Application deadline: February 15
Contact:
Morris Arboretum of the University of Pennsylvania
Jan McFarlan, Education Coordinator
100 Northwestern Avenue
Philadelphia, PA 19118
Phone: 215-247-5777 ext. 156
Web: www.upenn.edu/arboretum

Museum of Modern Art

Museum of Modern Art Internship

Type of award: Internship.
Intended use: For junior, senior, graduate or non-degree study at postsecondary institution.
Eligibility: Applicant must be U.S. citizen, permanent resident or international student.
Application requirements: Interview, essay, transcript. Resume and one recommendation.
Additional information: Course credit available, but not required. Fall, spring, summer, and 12-month internships. Twelve-month internships are paid, full-time programs for recent college graduates. Fall, spring, and summer internships are part-time and unpaid. Fields of study encompass broad spectrum of topics. Visit Website for complete list of departments, applications, and deadline information.

Number of awards: 130
Number of applicants: 2,500
Contact:
The Museum of Modern Art
Internship Coordinator, Human Resources
11 W. 53rd Street
New York, NY 10019
Web: www.moma.org/learn/courses/internships

NASA Arizona Space Grant Consortium

NASA Space Grant Arizona Undergraduate Research Internship

Type of award: Internship, renewable.
Intended use: For full-time sophomore, junior or senior study at accredited 2-year or 4-year institution in United States. Designated institutions: Arizona Space Grant Consortium (AZSGC) colleges and universities.
Eligibility: Applicant must be U.S. citizen residing in Arizona.

Basis for selection: Major/career interest in aerospace; astronomy; engineering; physics; geology/earth sciences; science, general; journalism or education.
Additional information: Approximately 100 students will be employed for 10-20 hours per week for the academic year in research programs, working alongside upper-level graduate students and practicing scientists. Hourly wage offered. Awardees must attend Arizona Space Grant Consortium member institution. Availability of internships varies. Some internships are renewable. Current announcements/application posted on Website.

Number of applicants: 350
Application deadline: July 6
Contact:
NASA Space Grant Arizona Space Grant Consortium
Lunar and Planetary Laboratory, Room 349
U of Arizona, 1629 E. University Blvd.
Tucson, AZ 85721-0092
Phone: 520-621-8556
Web: spacegrant.arizona.edu

NASA Delaware Space Grant Consortium

Delaware Space Grant Undergraduate Summer Research Internship

Type of award: Internship, renewable.
Intended use: For full-time sophomore, junior or senior study at postsecondary institution. Designated institutions: University of Delaware, Delaware Technical and Community College, Swarthmore College, Delaware State University at Dover, Villanova University, Wesley College, Wilmington University.
Eligibility: Applicant must be U.S. citizen.
Basis for selection: Major/career interest in geography; mathematics; science, general; technology or engineering.
Application requirements: Recommendations, transcript. Description of proposed research project from faculty mentor. Research mentor applies for student.
Additional information: Must have proven interest in space-related studies. Recipient must attend a Delaware Space Grant Consortium member institution. Stipend offered. May be used at designated institutions only. Contact Consortium office for deadlines and additional information.

Amount of award: $3,500
Number of awards: 6
Number of applicants: 13
Total amount awarded: $17,500
Contact:
Delaware Space Grant Consortium Program Office
University of Delaware
212 Sharp Lab
Newark, DE 19716
Phone: 302-831-1094
Fax: 302-831-1843
Web: www.delspace.org

NASA New Jersey Space Grant Consortium

NASA New Jersey Space Grant Consortium Undergraduate Summer Fellowships in Engineering and Science

Type of award: Internship, renewable.
Intended use: For junior or senior study at accredited 4-year institution in United States. Designated institutions: Georgian Court University, New Jersey Institute of Technology, Princeton University, Raritan Valley Community College, Rutgers University, Stevens Institute of Technology, University of Medicine and Dentistry of NJ, New Jersey City University, Rowan University, Seton Hall, College of New Jersey.
Eligibility: Applicant must be U.S. citizen.
Basis for selection: Major/career interest in aerospace; biology; computer/information sciences; engineering, computer; engineering, chemical; engineering, electrical/electronic; engineering, mechanical; materials science; natural sciences or physical sciences.
Application requirements: Recommendations, essay. Biographical sketch, statement that describes career goals and what applicant hopes to accomplish as Space Grant Fellow, plan for immediate future and reference letter from faculty adviser.
Additional information: Applicants must have completed at least two but preferably three years of college. Open to all science and engineering majors, but preference given to aerospace majors. Consortium actively encourages women, minority students, and physically challenged students to apply. Preference given to students attending NJSGC member institutions. Academic year ($2,000 stipend) and summer fellowships ($4,000 stipend) offered. Summer fellowship deadline in April. Academic year fellowship has ongoing deadline, although applications preferred by September. Visit Website for important dates and additional information.

  Application deadline: April 1
Contact:
Program Director, New Jersey Space Grant Consortium
Rutgers University, College of Engineering
Room B134, 98 Brett Road
Piscataway, NJ 08854
Phone: 848-445-2410
Fax: 732-445-7067
Web: njsgc.rutgers.edu

National Association of Black Journalists

NABJ Internships

Type of award: Internship.
Intended use: For full-time sophomore or junior study at postsecondary institution.
Eligibility: Applicant must be African American. Applicant must be at least 18.
Basis for selection: Major/career interest in journalism or radio/television/film.

Application requirements: Portfolio, recommendations, essay. Resume, cover letter. Applicants must submit minimum of five samples of published work in print, radio, television, photography, slideshows, website, or flash animation.
Additional information: Ten-week paid internship in print, broadcast, or multimedia journalism. Must be current NABJ member. Must have prior experience in collegiate or professional media. Must be member of National Association of Black Journalists. Weekly stipend varies between $400 and $600. Some internships are unpaid. Visit Website for more information.
Contact:
National Association of Black Journalists
1100 Knight Hall, Suite 3100
College Park, MD 20742-0248
Phone: 301-405-0248
Fax: 301-314-1714
Web: www.nabj.org

National Geographic Society

National Geographic Society Geography Students Internship

Type of award: Internship.
Intended use: For junior, senior or master's study at 4-year or graduate institution in United States.
Basis for selection: Major/career interest in geography or cartography.
Application requirements: Recommendations, essay, transcript. Resume.
Additional information: Spring, summer, and fall internships for 14 to 16 weeks in Washington, D.C., at $400 per week. Application deadline for all internships in the fall. Emphasis on editorial and cartographic research. Students should contact their school's geography department chair or call internship hotline for more information.

  Number of awards: 30
  Number of applicants: 100
Contact:
National Geographic Society
Robert E. Dulli
1145 17 Street, NW
Washington, DC 20036-4688
Phone: 202-857-7134
Web: www.nationalgeographic.com

National Museum of the American Indian

National Museum of the American Indian Internship

Type of award: Internship.
Intended use: For undergraduate, graduate or non-degree study at postsecondary institution.
Basis for selection: Major/career interest in museum studies. Applicant must demonstrate high academic achievement.

Application requirements: Recommendations, essay, transcript. Resume.

Additional information: Provides educational work/research experience for students in museum practice and related programming using resources of museum and other Smithsonian offices. Internships available at NMAI in Suitland, MD; Washington, DC; and New York City. Applicants must have minimum 3.0 GPA. Four 10-week internships, deadlines as follows: February 6 for summer; July 12 for fall; October 10 for winter; and November 20 for spring. Selection based on professional and educational goals of student; needs of museum. Students receiving stipends must work full-time; other interns must work at least 20 hours per week. Museum will grant academic credit if student makes arrangements with school. Visit Website or contact via e-mail for more information and application.

Number of awards:	20
Number of applicants:	40
Application deadline:	November 20, February 6

Contact:
Internship Program, National Museum of the American Indian
Cultural Resources Center-Community Services
4220 Silver Hill Road
Suitland, MD 20746-2863
Phone: 202-633-6645
Web: www.nmai.si.edu

National Museum of Women in the Arts

Elizabeth Stafford Hutchinson Endowed Internship

Type of award: Internship.

Intended use: For junior, senior, graduate or postgraduate study at 4-year or graduate institution in United States.

Basis for selection: Major/career interest in museum studies.

Application requirements: Recommendations, transcript. Cover letter, resume, writing sample.

Additional information: Minimum 3.25 GPA. Twelve-week internship in Washington D.C. Stipend of $1325 provided. Open to residents of Texas or students attending school in Texas. Must be pursuing career in museum studies and have finished sophomore year of college.

Amount of award:	$1,325
Number of awards:	1
Number of applicants:	5
Application deadline:	March 15

Contact:
National Museum of Women in the Arts
1250 New York Avenue, NW
Washington, DC 20005-3970
Phone: 800-222-7270
Web: www.nmwa.org

Museum Coca-Cola Internship

Type of award: Internship.

Intended use: For junior, senior, graduate or non-degree study in United States.

Basis for selection: Major/career interest in public relations; advertising; library science; journalism; museum studies; art/art history; museum studies/administration; accounting; education or retailing/merchandising. Applicant must demonstrate high academic achievement and seriousness of purpose.

Application requirements: Recommendations, transcript. Resume, cover letter, and one- to two-page writing sample.

Additional information: Internship available to students interested in pursuing careers in museum environments. Minimum 3.25 GPA. Interns receive $1500 stipend. Full-time internship lasts 12 weeks; application deadline for spring is October 15; summer is March 15; fall is June 15.

Amount of award:	$1,500
Number of awards:	3
Number of applicants:	25
Application deadline:	October 15, March 15
Total amount awarded:	$4,500

Contact:
National Museum of Women in the Arts
Assistant Educator
1250 New York Avenue, NW
Washington, DC 20005-3970
Phone: 800-222-7270
Fax: 202-393-3234
Web: www.nmwa.org

National Science Foundation

Research Experiences for Undergraduates - Maria Mitchell Observatory

Type of award: Internship.

Intended use: For undergraduate study at 4-year institution.

Eligibility: Applicant must be U.S. citizen or permanent resident.

Basis for selection: Major/career interest in astronomy. Applicant must demonstrate high academic achievement.

Application requirements: Recommendations, essay, transcript.

Additional information: Positions provide chance for students to conduct independent research and to participate in common project. Students expected to develop their ability to communicate with the public. Furnished housing is available at no cost. Partial travel funds available. Internship runs from June through August, with $1,800 monthly stipend. Applicant must demonstrate motivation in research. Minimum of one year undergraduate physics required.

Number of awards:	6
Number of applicants:	100
Application deadline:	February 1
Notification begins:	March 1

Contact:
Maria Mitchell Observatory
4 Vestal Street
Nantucket, MA 02554
Phone: 508-228-9273
Fax: 508-228-1031
Web: www.mariamitchell.org/get-involved/internships/reu

NCR Corporation

NCR Summer Internships

Type of award: Internship.

Intended use: For full-time undergraduate study at accredited 4-year institution.

Basis for selection: Major/career interest in accounting; computer/information sciences; engineering, computer; finance/banking; human resources; information systems or marketing. Applicant must demonstrate high academic achievement.

Application requirements: Interview, proof of eligibility. Resume.

Additional information: Minimum 3.0 GPA. Must have at least one semester or two quarters remaining before graduation. Interns paid hourly wage. Applicants must complete personal profile including resume on Website before applying for positions. Applicants encouraged to visit Website frequently during spring to review newly added offerings and important information.

Contact:
Visit Website for more information.
Web: www.ncr.com/careers

New Dramatists

Bernard B. Jacobs Internship Program

Type of award: Internship.

Intended use: For undergraduate or graduate study at postsecondary institution.

Basis for selection: Major/career interest in theater arts; performing arts or arts management.

Application requirements: Interview, recommendations, essay. Resume, statement of purpose.

Additional information: Must have passion for new plays and playwrights. Twelve- to twenty-week internships, three to five days per week. Internships run September to December, January to May, and June to August. Stipend is $25 per week for three days, $50 per week for five days. College credit may be available. Computer and writing skills essential. Applications must be filled out online.

Application deadline: August 1, November 8

Contact:
New Dramatists
Internship Coordinator
424 West 44th Street
New York, NY 10036
Phone: 212-757-6960
Fax: 212-265-4738
Web: www.newdramatists.org

New Mexico Higher Education Department

New Mexico Work-Study Program

Type of award: Internship, renewable.

Intended use: For undergraduate or graduate study at postsecondary institution. Designated institutions: St. John's College, University of the Southwest, Institute of American Indian Art, Crownpoint Institute of Technology, Diné College, Southwestern Indian Polytechnic Institute.

Eligibility: Applicant must be U.S. citizen or permanent resident residing in New Mexico.

Basis for selection: Applicant must demonstrate financial need.

Application requirements: FAFSA.

Additional information: Awards vary. Limit of 20 hours per week, on-campus or off-campus in federal, state, or local public agency. New Mexico residents receive state portion of funding. Contact financial aid office of New Mexico public postsecondary institutions for information, deadlines, and application.

Contact:
Contact financial aid office at institution.
Phone: 505-476-8400
Web: www.hed.state.nm.us

The New Republic

The New Republic Internships

Type of award: Internship.

Intended use: For undergraduate, graduate or non-degree study at postsecondary institution.

Eligibility: Applicant must be U.S. citizen.

Basis for selection: Major/career interest in journalism. Applicant must demonstrate depth of character and seriousness of purpose.

Application requirements: Cover letter, resume.

Additional information: Visit Website for list of available internships. Past internships include social media, literary, reporter-researcher, editorial web, and business associate. Provides intern with opportunity to gain editorial experience at leading opinion magazine located in Washington, D.C.

Contact:
The New Republic
Web: www.tnr.com

New York State Assembly

New York State Assembly Session Internship Program

Type of award: Internship, renewable.

Intended use: For full-time junior, senior or graduate study at accredited postsecondary institution in United States.

Basis for selection: Applicant must demonstrate high academic achievement.

Application requirements: Recommendations, essay, transcript, proof of eligibility. Writing sample. Letter from college endorsing candidate and outlining course credit arrangements.

Additional information: All majors eligible. Interns assigned to work with assembly members or assembly staff. Program runs from January to May. Undergraduate interns receive $4,140 stipend. Graduate interns receive $11,500 stipend. Applications accepted on an ongoing basis until deadline. Extensions granted upon request. Housing not provided, but

Internships

assistance offered in finding apartments and roommates. Visit Website for deadline information.

Amount of award:	$4,500-$11,500
Number of awards:	150
Number of applicants:	200
Application deadline:	November 1

Contact:
Kathleen McCarty, Director New York State Assembly
Assembly Intern Committee
Legislative Office Building, Room 104A
Albany, NY 12248
Phone: 518-455-4704
Fax: 518-455-4705
Web: www.assembly.state.ny.us/internship/

New York Times

David E. Rosenbaum Reporting Internship in Washington, D.C.

Type of award: Internship.
Intended use: For senior or graduate study at postsecondary institution.
Basis for selection: Major/career interest in journalism.
Application requirements: Essay. Cover letter, resume, 6 clips from daily professional or college media organizations, essay about interest in Washington reporting. Do not submit a Website link if it shows more than 6 clips.
Additional information: Ten-week summer internship at the Washington Bureau for aspiring reporters with interest in government and policy. Portion of first week spent in New York for orientation. Salary is $960/week. Applications via Website only. No telephone calls.

Number of awards:	1
Number of applicants:	150
Application deadline:	October 30

Contact:
New York Times
Web: www.nytimes-internship.com/internships/david-rosenbaum-reporting-fellow

NY Times Internships

Type of award: Internship.
Intended use: For undergraduate study at postsecondary institution.
Additional information: Variety of internships offered for undergraduates. Visit Website for current offerings and to apply.
Contact:
New York Times
Web: www.nytco.com/careers

NextEra Energy

NextEra Energy Internship Program

Type of award: Internship, renewable.
Intended use: For full-time undergraduate study at accredited vocational, 2-year or 4-year institution in United States.
Eligibility: Applicant must be U.S. citizen or permanent resident.

Basis for selection: Major/career interest in engineering; engineering, nuclear; engineering, mechanical; engineering, electrical/electronic; engineering, civil; engineering, industrial; finance/banking; accounting; computer/information sciences or business. Applicant must demonstrate high academic achievement.
Application requirements: Resume.
Additional information: Positions are paid. Minimum 3.0 GPA. Apply online or check Website for campus recruiting calendar.
Contact:
NextEra Energy
Web: www.nexteraenergy.com/careers/college.shtml

Ohio News Media Foundation

AdOhio Advertising Internship

Type of award: Internship.
Intended use: For junior or senior study at postsecondary institution. Designated institutions: Ohio institutions.
Eligibility: Applicant must be residing in Ohio.
Basis for selection: Major/career interest in journalism or advertising.
Application requirements: Resume, writing samples, and cover letter.
Additional information: Ten-week internship in Columbus office of this trade association, which represents 83 daily newspapers, more than 180 weekly newspapers, and more than 150 Websites in Ohio. Duties include writing and layout for sales presentation sheets and client mailings, assistance with newspaper ad bid sheets, newspaper tear sheets, and research. Internship lasts 10 weeks. Negotiable start date after June 1. Salary is $350 per week. Finalists will be contacted for interviews.

Application deadline:	March 31
Notification begins:	May 1

Contact:
Ohio Newspapers Foundation
Walt Dozier, AdOhio
1335 Dublin Road, Suite 216-B
Columbus, OH 43215
Web: www.ohionews.org/aws/ONA/pt/sp/foundation_internship

Ohio Newspaper Assiociation Publications/Public Relations Internship

Type of award: Internship.
Intended use: For junior or senior study at postsecondary institution. Designated institutions: Ohio institutions.
Eligibility: Applicant must be residing in Ohio.
Basis for selection: Major/career interest in communications; journalism; marketing or advertising.
Application requirements: Resume, writing samples, and cover letter.
Additional information: Ten-week internship at trade association, which represents 83 daily newspapers, more than 180 weekly newspapers, and more than 150 Websites in Ohio. Duties include writing and assisting in production of newsletter, miscellaneous flyers and mailings, meeting planning, and research. Internship lasts ten weeks. Negotiable

Internships

669

start date after June 1. Salary of $350 per week. Finalists will be contacted for interviews.

Application deadline:	March 31
Notification begins:	May 1

Contact:
Ohio Newspapers Foundation
Dennis Hetzel, Executive Director
1335 Dublin Road, Suite 216-B
Columbus, OH 43215
Web: www.ohionews.org/aws/ONA/pt/sp/foundation_internship

Oracle Corporation

Oracle Product Development Summer Internship Program

Type of award: Internship.
Intended use: For full-time sophomore, junior, senior or graduate study at accredited 4-year or graduate institution in United States.
Basis for selection: Major/career interest in computer/information sciences. Applicant must demonstrate high academic achievement.
Application requirements: Resume.
Additional information: Foreign student must have unrestricted permission to work in United States. Interns are offered excellent compensation and fully furnished corporate apartments are provided. Car/bike rentals and round-trip travel expenses are paid for, as well as a helicopter ride under the Golden Gate Bridge. Visit Website to submit resume and sign up to search for current openings.

Application deadline:	January 1
Notification begins:	February 28

Contact:
Oracle Corporation
500 Oracle Parkway
Redwood Shores, CA 94065
Phone: 800-633-0738
Web: www.oracle.com/us/corporate/careers/college/internships/index.html

Owens Corning

Owens Corning Internships

Type of award: Internship.
Intended use: For full-time junior, senior, master's or doctoral study at accredited 4-year institution.
Eligibility: Applicant must be U.S. citizen or permanent resident.
Basis for selection: Major/career interest in engineering; accounting; environmental science; information systems; marketing; materials science; technology or finance/banking. Applicant must demonstrate high academic achievement and leadership.
Application requirements: Proof of eligibility.
Additional information: Variety of internships offered with housing assistance, competitive salary. Summer programs last twelve weeks. Positions throughout the U.S. See Website for more information.

Contact:
Owens Corning
One Owens Corning Parkway
Toledo, OH 43659
Phone: 1-800-GET-PINK
Web: www.owenscorningcareers.com

Pacific Gas and Electric Company

Pacific Gas and Electric Summer Intern Program

Type of award: Internship.
Intended use: For full-time undergraduate or graduate study in United States.
Eligibility: Applicant must be U.S. citizen or permanent resident.
Basis for selection: Major/career interest in business; chemistry; statistics; computer/information sciences; economics; engineering; geology/earth sciences; marketing; engineering, mechanical or public administration/service. Applicant must demonstrate high academic achievement and seriousness of purpose.
Application requirements: Interview. Resume, cover letter.
Additional information: Paid internships available throughout northern and central California, including company headquarters in San Francisco. Deadline is rolling, but early applications are encouraged. Resume may be submitted online; format specifications available online. Visit Website or call sponsor for openings and campus recruitment dates. Must be eligible to work in the United States. Number and amount of awards vary. Most internships are summer only and typically last ten to twelve weeks. Internships include a competitive salary and paid company holidays.

Contact:
Pacific Gas and Electric Company
Phone: 877-660-6789
Web: www.pge.com/about/careers/college/intern

PBS

PBS Internships

Type of award: Internship.
Intended use: For undergraduate or graduate study at postsecondary institution.
Application requirements: Resume and cover letter.
Additional information: Various internships are available in different departments. All paid, except for internship in General Counsel's office. Internships also offered for graduate students seeking an MBA. Internships change on a semester basis. Recruitment starts in July for fall; November for winter and spring; February for summer. Visit Website for internship listings, application forms, and more information.

Contact:
PBS Internship Program
2100 Crystal Dr.
Arlington, VA 22202
Phone: 703-739-5088
Web: www.pbs.org/jobs

PGA Tour

PGA Tour Diversity Intern Program

Type of award: Internship.
Intended use: For sophomore, junior, senior or graduate study at postsecondary institution.
Eligibility: Applicant must be U.S. citizen.
Basis for selection: Major/career interest in marketing; business/management/administration; communications; information systems; journalism; radio/television/film; sports/sports administration or public relations. Applicant must demonstrate high academic achievement, depth of character, leadership, seriousness of purpose and service orientation.
Application requirements: Interview, recommendations, essay, transcript.
Additional information: Non-citizens eligible to work in U.S. may also apply. Internship lasts ten weeks and is paid. Internship sites located in Florida. Minimum 3.0 GPA. Visit Website to apply. Deadline in February.

Amount of award:	$4,400
Number of awards:	18
Number of applicants:	1,450
Notification begins:	May 1
Total amount awarded:	$132,000

Contact:
PGA Tour Diversity Intern Program
Web: www.pgatour.com

Phipps Conservatory and Botanical Gardens

Phipps Conservatory and Botanical Gardens Internships

Type of award: Internship.
Intended use: For junior, senior or graduate study at accredited 2-year or 4-year institution.
Eligibility: Applicant must be U.S. citizen.
Basis for selection: Major/career interest in horticulture; landscape architecture; environmental science or botany. Applicant must demonstrate high academic achievement.
Application requirements: Recommendations. Resume and cover letter.
Additional information: Interns paid $8 per hour. Related majors, such as environmental education, also eligible. Internships may be full- or part-time. Seven positions available in summer; one to two positions available during academic year. Application deadline is rolling. Contact sponsor or visit Website for more information.

Number of awards:	8
Number of applicants:	8
Application deadline:	January 31
Notification begins:	February 15

Contact:
Phipps Conservatory and Botanical Gardens Human Resources
One Schenley Park
Pittsburgh, PA 15213
Phone: 412-622-6915 ext. 3229
Fax: 412-622-7363
Web: www.phipps.conservatory.org

Princeton Plasma Physics Laboratory

Plasma Physics National Undergraduate Fellowship Program

Type of award: Internship.
Intended use: For junior study at 4-year institution in United States.
Eligibility: Applicant must be U.S. citizen or permanent resident.
Basis for selection: Major/career interest in engineering; physics; mathematics or computer/information sciences. Applicant must demonstrate high academic achievement, depth of character, leadership, seriousness of purpose and service orientation.
Application requirements: Recommendations, essay, transcript.
Additional information: Minimum 3.5 GPA. Internship paid and lasts nine weeks in the summer. Housing and travel costs provided. Application due in February.

Amount of award:	$4,800
Number of awards:	25
Number of applicants:	100
Notification begins:	March 15

Contact:
Princeton Plasma Physics Laboratory
P.O. Box 451
Princeton, NJ 08543-0451
Phone: 609-243-2000
Web: www.pppl.gov/education/science-education

Rhode Island State Government

Rhode Island State Government Internship Program

Type of award: Internship, renewable.
Intended use: For undergraduate or postgraduate study at postsecondary institution.
Eligibility: Applicant must be residing in Rhode Island.
Basis for selection: Major/career interest in governmental public relations or public administration/service. Applicant must demonstrate high academic achievement, depth of character, leadership, seriousness of purpose and service orientation.

Internships

Application requirements: Interview, recommendations, transcript, proof of eligibility. Writing sample (for law students only).

Additional information: Minimum 2.5 GPA. Summer program lasts eight weeks; spring and fall programs last entire semester. Fall application deadline is rolling. Compensation for summer interns only, at $20 per hour day for 7-hour days. Spring and fall interns earn academic credit or work-study, if eligible. All placements in Rhode Island.

Number of awards:	243
Number of applicants:	450

Contact:
Rhode Island State Government
State Capitol, Room 8AA
Providence, RI 02903
Phone: 401-222-6782
Fax: 401-222-4447
Web: webserver.rilin.state.ri.us/internoffice

Simon and Schuster Inc.

Simon and Schuster Internship Program

Type of award: Internship, renewable.
Intended use: For full-time undergraduate or graduate study at accredited vocational, 4-year or graduate institution.
Basis for selection: Major/career interest in publishing. Applicant must demonstrate high academic achievement and leadership.
Application requirements: Interview. Resume. Cover letter.
Additional information: Internship program is designed to train and recruit a diverse group of students interested in exploring careers in publishing. Summer, spring, fall, and year-round programs are available. Student must register for academic credit with their college or university and provide official documentation confirming this information. During spring/fall semesters, intern works a minimum 16 hours to a maximum 20 hours per week. During summer semester, office hours are 9 to 5 p.m. Applicants must have well-rounded extracurricular interests and work experience. Visit Website for application.
Contact:
Simon and Schuster, Inc.
Web: www.simonandschuster.biz/careers/internships

Smithsonian Environmental Research Center

Smithsonian Environmental Research Center Internship Program

Type of award: Internship, renewable.
Intended use: For undergraduate or master's study at 4-year or graduate institution.
Basis for selection: Major/career interest in biology; chemistry; environmental science; physics; mathematics or education. Applicant must demonstrate seriousness of purpose.
Application requirements: Recommendations, essay, transcript. Resume.

Additional information: Internship provides professional training in the environmental sciences. Projects are 40 hours per week, lasting from twelve to sixteen weeks. Stipend is $500 per week and available winter/spring, summer, and fall. Dorm space is available for $105 per week on limited basis. Several application deadlines: spring, November 15; summer, February 1; fall, June 1. Applicants should demonstrate academic credentials, relevant experience, and the congruence of expressed goals with those of internship program. Open to all undergraduates, recent college graduates (within six months), and beginning Master's students.

Number of awards:	40
Number of applicants:	350
Application deadline:	November 15, February 1
Notification begins:	December 15, April 15
Total amount awarded:	$245,000

Contact:
Smithsonian Environmental Research Center
Phone: 443-428-2217
Web: www.serc.si.edu/internship/index.htm

Smithsonian Institution

James E. Webb Internship Program for Minority Undergraduate Seniors and Graduate Students in Business and Public Administration

Type of award: Internship.
Intended use: For senior or graduate study at 4-year or graduate institution. Designated institutions: Smithsonian Institution.
Eligibility: Applicant must be Alaskan native, Asian American, African American, Mexican American, Hispanic American, Puerto Rican, American Indian or Native Hawaiian/Pacific Islander. Applicant must be U.S. citizen or permanent resident.
Basis for selection: Major/career interest in business/management/administration or public administration/service. Applicant must demonstrate high academic achievement.
Application requirements: Recommendations, essay, transcript. Resume.
Additional information: Minimum 3.0 GPA. Applicant must be minority student enrolled as undergraduate senior or graduate student in business or public administration program. Selection based on relevance of internship at the Smithsonian to student's academic and career goals. Internships are full-time, 40 hours per week for ten weeks. Stipend is $550 per week, with additional travel allowances offered in some cases. Deadlines: February 1 for summer and fall; October 1 for spring. Contact sponsor or visit Website for more information and application.

Application deadline:	February 1, October 1

Contact:
Smithsonian Institution Office of Fellowships
470 L'Enfant Plaza, SW, Suite 7102, MRC 902
P.O. Box 37012
Washington, DC 20013-7012
Phone: 202-633-7070
Web: www.si.edu/ofi

Smithsonian Minority Internship

Type of award: Internship.

Intended use: For undergraduate or graduate study at postsecondary institution. Designated institutions: Smithsonian Institution.

Basis for selection: Major/career interest in anthropology; archaeology; ecology; environmental science; art/art history; museum studies; zoology or natural sciences. Applicant must demonstrate high academic achievement.

Application requirements: Recommendations, essay, transcript. Resume.

Additional information: Research internships at Smithsonian Institution in anthropology/archaeology; astrophysics and astronomy; earth sciences/paleontology; ecology; environmental, behavioral (tropical animals), evolutionary, and systematic biology; history of science and technology; history of art (including American contemporary, African, Asian); 20th-century American crafts; social and cultural history and folk life of America. Applicants must have major/career interest in research or museum-related activity pursued by the Smithsonian Institution. Stipend of $550 per week for ten weeks. February 1 deadline for summer session and for fall; October 1 deadline for spring. Intended for U.S. minority groups under-represented in Smithsonian scholarly programs. Contact sponsor for minority requirements. Minimum 3.0 GPA. Visit Website for more information.

Application deadline: February 1, October 1

Contact:
Smithsonian Institution Office of Fellowships
470 L'Enfant Plaza, SW, Suite 7102, MRC 902
P.O. Box 37012
Washington, DC 20013-7012
Phone: 202-633-7070
Web: www.si.edu/ofi

Smithsonian Native American Internship

Type of award: Internship.

Intended use: For undergraduate or graduate study at postsecondary institution. Designated institutions: Smithsonian Institution.

Eligibility: Applicant must be Alaskan native or American Indian.

Basis for selection: Major/career interest in Native American studies.

Application requirements: Recommendations, essay, transcript. Resume.

Additional information: Internship at Smithsonian Institution in research or museum activities related to Native American studies. Stipend of $550 a week for ten weeks. Deadline for summer and fall is February 1; spring is October 1. American Indian students encouraged to apply. Contact Office of Fellowships for application procedures or visit Website.

Application deadline: February 1, October 1

Contact:
Smithsonian Institution Office of Fellowships
470 L'Enfant Plaza, SW, Suite 7102, MRC 902
P.O. Box 37012
Washington, DC 20013-7012
Phone: 202-633-1000
Web: www.si.edu/ofi

Society of Physics

Society of Physics Students Science Outreach Catalyst Kit Intern

Type of award: Internship.

Intended use: For undergraduate study.

Basis for selection: Must have: interest in public outreach and education; ability to work well with pre-college students; ability to effectively communicate scientific topics to non-scientists; excellent writing skills. Experience with science outreach or education preferred. Major/career interest in physics.

Additional information: Must have completed at least two years of college physics. SPS Science Outreach Catalyst Kits (SOCKs) are self-contained kits that feature creative, informative, and hands-on physics activities for SPS chapters nationwide to use in outreach programs in their communities. The SOCK intern and the SOCK/NIST intern will take the 2016-17 SOCK from inception to completion by brainstorming, testing, designing, and refining activities. The interns will participate in several physics outreach events over the course of the summer, and will write up lesson outlines and reflections on their experiences for a manual that will accompany the SOCK. Kits are different every year.

Amount of award:	$5,000
Number of awards:	12
Number of applicants:	60
Application deadline:	February 1

Contact:
Society of Physics
1 Physics Ellipse
College Park, MD 20740
Phone: 301-209-3007
Web: https://www.spsnational.org/programs/internships

Society of Physics Students

American Association of Physics Teachers Teacher Professional Development Programs Intern

Type of award: Internship.

Intended use: For undergraduate study.

Basis for selection: Must have: demonstrated writing skills; interest in teaching, particularly at the high school level; excellent communication skills. Some experience as a teaching or learning assistant or other classroom teaching, experience using technology in physics education, and familiarity with the Next Generation Science Standards preferred. Experience with engineering or project-based learning will be a plus. Major/career interest in physics.

Additional information: Must have completed at least two years of college physics. The intern will support the Physics Teaching Resource Agents (PTRAs) as they develop and test activities associated with heliophysics topics in coordination with NASA-Goddard. The intern will also support eMentoring and online learning by assisting with pairings of mentors and mentees, program evaluation, arranging for a webinar series, and streamlining online resources. In addition, the intern will have the opportunity to develop documents and publications

Internships

673

associated with the role of physics in the Next Generation Science Standards.

Amount of award:	$5,000
Number of awards:	12
Number of applicants:	60
Application deadline:	February 1

Contact:
Society of Physics Students
1 Physics Ellipse
College Park, MD 20740
Phone: 301-209-3007
Web: https://www.spsnational.org/programs/internships

American Institute of Physics History of Women and African-Americans in the Physical Sciences Intern

Type of award: Internship.
Intended use: For undergraduate study.
Basis for selection: Must have: nterest in public outreach and informal education; ability to effectively communicate scientific topics to pre-college students; strong writing skills. Experience with HTML a plus. Major/career interest in physics.
Additional information: Must have completed at least two years of college physics. The American Institute of Physics' (AIP) Center for History of Physics seeks two undergraduate physics students with an interest in the history of physics to contribute new lesson plans and other resources for the AIP Teachers Guides to the History of Women and African Americans in the Physical Sciences, and to test and revise existing materials in response to feedback from teachers. The interns will utilize materials in the collections of the Niels Bohr Library & Archives at AIP related to the designated topics—oral histories, autobiographies, photos, etc. The interns will work with the director of the Center for History of Physics, two graduate research assistants, and library specialists to refine the historical narratives and the web resources.

Amount of award:	$5,000
Number of awards:	12
Number of applicants:	60
Application deadline:	February 1

Contact:
Society of Physics Students
1 Physics Ellipse
College Park, MD 20740
Phone: 301-209-3007
Web: https://www.spsnational.org/programs/internships

American Institute of Physics Mather Policy Intern

Type of award: Internship.
Intended use: For undergraduate study.
Eligibility: Applicant must be U.S. citizen.
Basis for selection: Must have: interest in science policy; basic understanding of how Congress and the US government works; excellent communication skills; ability to work independently. Major/career interest in physics.
Additional information: Must have completed at least two years of college physics. The primary purpose of the AIP Mather policy internship program (supported by the John and Jane Mather Foundation for Science and the Arts) is to promote awareness of and interaction with the policy process in Washington DC for undergraduate physics students. This is

accomplished through direct engagement in science policy issues and efforts in the nation's capital, as AIP Mather policy interns work in Congressional offices on Capitol Hill. Previous AIP Mather policy interns have worked in member offices and committee offices. Specific placements are arranged on an individual basis after the AIP Mather policy interns are selected. As part of the larger SPS Internship program, the AIP Mather policy interns will introduce other SPS interns to the public policy process through one or more field trips to appropriate science policy events or locales—Congressional hearings, governmental agencies and/or facilities, for example.

Amount of award:	$5,000
Number of awards:	12
Number of applicants:	60
Application deadline:	February 1

Contact:
Society of Physics Students
1 Physics Ellipse
College Park, MD 20740
Phone: 301-209-3007
Web: https://www.spsnational.org/programs/internships

Society of Physics Students Internship Program at the National Institute of Standards and Technology

Type of award: Internship.
Intended use: For undergraduate study.
Eligibility: Applicant must be U.S. citizen.
Basis for selection: Must have: interest in physics research; previous laboratory/measurement experience, especially in the area of electronics or materials. Programming skills a plus. Major/career interest in physics.
Additional information: Must have completed at least two years of college physics. Two research positions to work at the National Institute of Standards and Technology are available each year. The science topics vary each year.

Amount of award:	$5,000
Number of awards:	12
Number of applicants:	60
Application deadline:	February 1

Contact:
Society of Physics Students
1 Physics Ellipse
College Park, MD 20740
Phone: 301-209-3007
Web: https://www.spsnational.org/programs/internships

Society of Physics Students NASA Goddard Research Intern

Type of award: Internship.
Intended use: For undergraduate study.
Eligibility: Applicant must be U.S. citizen.
Basis for selection: Previous research experience preferred. Must meet the eligibility requirements for the NASA internship program (see NASA OSSI intern website). Major/career interest in physics.
Additional information: Must have completed at least two years of college physics. Two research positions to work at NASA's Goddard Space Center are available each year. The science topics, which could be form cosmology to earth science, vary each year.

Amount of award:	$5,000
Number of awards:	12
Number of applicants:	60
Application deadline:	February 1

Contact:
Society of Physics Students
1 Physics Ellipse
College Park, MD 20740
Phone: 301-209-3007
Web: https://www.spsnational.org/programs/internships

Society of Physics Students SOCK & the National Institute of Standards and Technology Summer Institute Intern

Type of award: Internship.

Intended use: For undergraduate study.

Basis for selection: Must have: interest in public outreach and education; ability to work well with students and teachers; ability to effectively communicate scientific topics to non-scientists. Experience with science outreach or teaching preferred. Major/career interest in physics.

Additional information: Must have completed at least two years of college physics. The SOCK/NIST intern is responsible for creating a set of engaging and educational activities for the 2016-17 SOCK, together with the SOCK intern (see previous), during the first half of the internship. The intern will spend the second half of the internship at the National Institute for Standards and Technology (NIST), assisting with a two-week summer institute for about 20 middle school science teachers from across the country. The intern will incorporate some of the SOCK lessons into the Summer Institute, and will support the camp through preparing materials for activities, helping to facilitate activities, leading tour groups, and more. The intern will spend the last 1-2 weeks putting the final touches on the SPS SOCK.

Amount of award:	$5,000
Number of awards:	12
Number of applicants:	60
Application deadline:	February 1

Contact:
Society of Physics Students
1 Physics Ellipse
College Park, MD 20740
Phone: 301-209-3007
Web: https://www.spsnational.org/programs/internships

Society of Physics Students Summer Internship Program

Type of award: Internship.

Intended use: For full-time undergraduate study.

Eligibility: Applicant or parent must be member/participant of Society of Physics Students.

Basis for selection: Major/career interest in physics. Applicant must demonstrate high academic achievement.

Application requirements: Transcript. Resume and cover letter. Two letters of recommendation (one should be written by SPS advisor).

Additional information: Offers nine-and-a-half-week internships in science policy and research for undergraduate physics majors. Internships include $4,500 stipend, paid housing, and transportation supplement. Internships are based in Washington, D.C. Applicants must be active SPS members with excellent scholastic record and experience in science outreach events or science research. See Website for application and deadline.

Amount of award:	$4,500
Number of awards:	12
Number of applicants:	483
Application deadline:	February 15
Notification begins:	March 15
Total amount awarded:	$33,300

Contact:
SPS Summer Internship Program
One Physics Ellipse
College Park, MD 20740
Phone: 301-209-3007
Fax: 301-209-0839
Web: www.spsnational.org/programs/internships

Society of Physics Students/ American Physical Society Internship Program

Type of award: Internship.

Intended use: For undergraduate study.

Basis for selection: Must have: demonstrated writing skills; interest in public outreach and informal education; excellent communication skills. Major/career interest in physics.

Additional information: Must have completed at least two years of college physics. APS is looking for a creative and fun SPS summer intern with a passion for engaging the public in science to expand its outreach efforts. The APS Public Outreach intern will work with APS staff to develop and put into motion a new informational education effort. The intern will work alongside APS Outreach, Art, and Media Relations departments to come up with an outreach idea, define an audience and develop strategy to carry it out. The intern will be encouraged to think beyond "regular" demo shows and classroom activities; for example, the project could be a video contest for middle school students, a citizen science project targeted at people in retirement communities, or a guide for bringing science to street festivals.

Amount of award:	$5,000
Number of awards:	12
Number of applicants:	60
Application deadline:	February 1

Contact:
Society of Physics Students
1 Physics Ellipse
College Park, MD 20740
Phone: 301-209-3007
Web: https://www.spsnational.org/programs/internships

Solomon R. Guggenheim Museum

Guggenheim Museum Internship

Type of award: Internship.

Intended use: For junior, senior or graduate study at postsecondary institution.

Basis for selection: Major/career interest in art/art history; arts, general; arts management; communications; education; finance/banking; graphic arts/design; library science; museum studies or museum studies/administration. Applicant must demonstrate high academic achievement.

Application requirements: Interview, recommendations. Cover letter, resume, writing sample.
Additional information: Potential internships available in conservation, curatorial, education, development, director's office, exhibition design, exhibition management, finance, graphic design, human resources, information technology, legal, library archives, marketing, photography, public affairs, publications and digital media, registration, visitor services, and more. International students must have J-1 visa. Internships during academic year are for college credit; some stipends available in summer. Application deadlines are January 18 for summer, May 1 for fall and academic year, October 18 for spring. Spring, fall, and academic year internships are full- or part-time, with minimum commitment of 16 hours/week for three months. Summer internships are full-time.

Number of awards:	40
Number of applicants:	300
Application deadline:	November 1, January 30

Contact:
Solomon R. Guggenheim Museum
Internship Program
1071 Fifth Avenue
New York, NY 10128-0173
Phone: 212-423-3637
Web: www.guggenheim.org

Peggy Guggenheim Internship

Type of award: Internship.
Intended use: For undergraduate or graduate study at postsecondary institution.
Basis for selection: Major/career interest in arts, general; art/art history; education; museum studies or museum studies/administration. Applicant must demonstrate high academic achievement, depth of character, leadership and seriousness of purpose.
Application requirements: Recommendations, essay, transcript. Resume.
Additional information: One- to three-month internship at Peggy Guggenheim Collection in Venice, Italy. Must be fluent in English with knowledge of spoken Italian. Interns receive a monthly stipend. Visit Website for details.

Number of applicants:	1,400

Contact:
Peggy Guggenheim Collection, Internship Coodinator
701 Dorsoduro
30123 Venice, Italy
Phone: 39-041-240-5401
Web: www.guggenheim.org or www.guggenheim-venice.it

Sony Music Entertainment

Sony Credited Internship

Type of award: Internship.
Intended use: For undergraduate or graduate study at accredited postsecondary institution.
Eligibility: Applicant must be U.S. citizen or permanent resident.
Basis for selection: Major/career interest in accounting; business; finance/banking; communications; computer/information sciences; law; music; music management or marketing.
Application requirements: Interview, transcript, proof of eligibility. Resume and cover letter.

Additional information: Unpaid internship. Applicant must be available to work at least 15 hours a week. Internships are available in various departments throughout company. Must possess excellent computer skills (Word, Excel and Outlook) and strong organizational skills. Applicant must be enrolled at accredited university and provide verification of course credit. Visit Website for available internship listings. Apply online.

Number of awards:	60
Number of applicants:	200

Contact:
Phone: 212-833-8000
Web: www.sonymusic.com

Southface Energy Institute

Southface Internship

Type of award: Internship.
Intended use: For undergraduate or graduate study at accredited 2-year, 4-year or graduate institution in United States.
Eligibility: Applicant must be U.S. citizen, permanent resident or international student.
Basis for selection: Major/career interest in architecture; business/management/administration; engineering, civil; engineering, environmental; engineering, mechanical; environmental science; graphic arts/design; landscape architecture; public relations or urban planning. Applicant must demonstrate high academic achievement.
Application requirements: Names of references with contact information. Resume and cover letter.
Additional information: Internships cover variety of interests: sustainable building, community design, water-efficient landscaping, smart growth, environmental event planning, energy policy and tech assistance, non-profit marketing, and public relations. Six- to twelve-month positions available. Students work 40 hours per week; weekly stipend of $100. Shared housing available if space permits. Transportation assistance available. Applications accepted year-round. International students must have work authorization.
Contact:
241 Pine Street NE
Atlanta, GA 30308
Phone: 404-872-3549
Fax: 404-872-5009
Web: www.southface.org

Spoleto Festival USA

Spoleto Festival USA Apprenticeship Program

Type of award: Internship, renewable.
Intended use: For undergraduate, graduate or non-degree study in United States.
Basis for selection: Major/career interest in arts management; arts, general; music; public relations or theater/production/technical. Applicant must demonstrate seriousness of purpose.
Application requirements: Recommendations. Writing sample (media applicants only). Resume, cover letter.

Additional information: Four-week full-time apprenticeship with arts professionals producing and operating international arts festival from May 13 to June 9. Posts available in media relations, development, box office, production, orchestra management, finance and accounting, artist services/facilities management, and office administration. Weekly stipend may be provided; housing and travel allowance provided. See Website for details and deadlines. Deadline in mid-February.

Number of awards:	50
Application deadline:	January 30

Contact:
Spoleto Festival USA
Apprentice Program
14 George Street
Charleston, SC 29401
Phone: 843-579-3100
Web: www.spoletousa.org

Sports Journalism Institute

Aspiring Sports Journalist Internship

Type of award: Internship.
Intended use: For sophomore or junior study at postsecondary institution.
Basis for selection: Major/career interest in journalism; communications; publishing; English or sports/sports administration. Applicant must demonstrate high academic achievement and seriousness of purpose.
Application requirements: Recommendations, essay, transcript. Professional-style photo, up to seven writing samples.
Additional information: The Sports Journalism Institute is a nine-week, paid summer training and internship program for undergraduates interested in sports journalism. Applicants need not be journalism majors. A $500 scholarship is available for students returning to college upon successful completion of program. Visit Website for more information, application, and deadline.

Amount of award:	$500
Number of awards:	10

Contact:
Gregory Lee, Executive Sports Editor
South Florida Sun Sentinel
500 E. Broward Blvd.
Ft. Lauderdale, FL 33394
Web: www.sportsjournalisminstitute.org

Student Conservation Association

SCA Conservation Internships

Type of award: Internship, renewable.
Intended use: For undergraduate or graduate study at accredited postsecondary institution in United States.
Basis for selection: Major/career interest in archaeology; ecology; forestry; natural resources/conservation; history; education; wildlife/fisheries; biology or communications.

Application requirements: Resume.
Additional information: Travel and housing is provided, and a weekly stipend is given for food. Positions at various locations in United States. Applicants are advised to apply three months prior to position start date. Rolling admissions process—seven application deadlines per year. Applicants with interest in environmental education, interpretation, marine biology, and wilderness preservation also eligible. See Website for application.
Contact:
Admissions Department Student Conservation Association
Web: www.thesca.org

Texas Historical Commission

Diversity Internship Program

Type of award: Internship.
Intended use: For junior, senior or graduate study at 2-year, 4-year or graduate institution in United States.
Eligibility: Applicant must be Alaskan native, Asian American, African American, Mexican American, Hispanic American, Puerto Rican, American Indian or Native Hawaiian/Pacific Islander. Applicant must be U.S. citizen.
Basis for selection: Applicant must demonstrate high academic achievement.
Application requirements: Recommendations, transcript. Resume or CV, list of previous experience with the Texas Historical Commission, if any.
Additional information: Minimum 3.0 GPA. Applicants must either attend institutions in Texas, or be Texas residents attending school out-of-state. Preservation Fellows receive a $5,000 stipend for eight weeks of 40-hour-week employment under the supervision of the THC, either at its headquarters in Austin or "in the field" with an associated preservation organization. Apply online. Deadline in March.

Amount of award:	$5,000
Number of awards:	2
Number of applicants:	5
Notification begins:	September 1
Total amount awarded:	$10,000

Contact:
Texas Historical Commission
Phone: 512-936-0857
Web: www.thcfriends.org/special-projects/thc-diversity-internship

Time Inc.

Time Inc. Internship Program

Type of award: Internship.
Intended use: For undergraduate or graduate study at accredited 4-year or graduate institution.
Basis for selection: Major/career interest in finance/banking; advertising; communications; graphic arts/design; information systems; journalism or marketing. Applicant must demonstrate high academic achievement.
Application requirements: Essay. Cover letter and resume.

Internships

Additional information: Spring and fall academic year internships are offered on an as-needed basis, with available positions and magazines/Websites varying each semester. Most positions require a minimum of 14 hours per week and are based in NYC. Nine- to ten-week paid summer internship programs are also available.
Contact:
Time Inc.
Phone: 212-522-1212
Web: www.timeinc.com/careers

Tyson Foods, Inc.

Tyson Foods Intern Program

Type of award: Internship.
Intended use: For full-time undergraduate study at accredited vocational, 2-year or 4-year institution.
Basis for selection: Major/career interest in agribusiness; agriculture; computer/information sciences; engineering; food production/management/services; food science/technology; health-related professions; law; marketing or science, general. Applicant must demonstrate high academic achievement.
Application requirements: Proof of eligibility. Resume and cover letter.
Additional information: Various paid internships include but not limited to computer programming, industrial engineering, livestock procurement, quality assurance, carcass sales, and production. Program locations across the United States. Must be eligible to work in the U.S. Visit Website for job descriptions and list of campus recruiting events, or to submit resume and cover letter. Summer and academic-year internships available.
>   **Number of awards:**   50
Contact:
Tyson Foods, Inc.
Web: www.tysonfoodscareers.com

United States Holocaust Memorial Museum

United States Holocaust Memorial Museum Internship

Type of award: Internship, renewable.
Intended use: For freshman, sophomore, junior, senior or graduate study at postsecondary institution.
Eligibility: Applicant must be U.S. citizen, permanent resident or international student.
Basis for selection: Major/career interest in museum studies/administration; history; English; foreign languages; communications; geography; graphic arts/design or communications.
Additional information: Semester-long internships available during summer, fall, and spring in Holocaust research and museum studies. Phone interviews conducted with top qualified candidates. Most positions unpaid. Applicants interested in German or Eastern European studies also eligible. Application deadline is March 1 for summer; July 1 for fall; October 15 for winter/spring. Apply online. All applicants subject to criminal background check. International students must have work authorization. Award notification begins at the end of March.
>   **Number of awards:**   70
>   **Number of applicants:**   500
>   **Application deadline:**   March 1
>   **Notification begins:**   April 1
Contact:
Internship Coordinator, Office of Volunteer and Intern Services
United States Holocaust Memorial Museum
100 Raoul Wallenburg Place, SW
Washington, DC 20024-2150
Phone: 202-488-0400
Web: www.ushmm.org

United States Senate

U.S. Senate Member Internships

Type of award: Internship.
Intended use: For full-time undergraduate study at accredited 4-year institution.
Eligibility: Applicant must be U.S. citizen or permanent resident.
Basis for selection: Major/career interest in political science/government; law; communications; public relations; public administration/service or economics. Applicant must demonstrate high academic achievement.
Application requirements: Resume, cover letter, writing sample.
Additional information: Senate member interns generally reside or attend college in senator's state. Positions available in Washington, D.C., or member's state. Internships may be unpaid or paid (less common), but generally offer assistance obtaining college credit. Term of service, eligibility vary. Some internships restricted to upper-level undergraduates. Senators administer their own internship programs. Contact individual senator's office directly. Visit Website for links to member sites, e-mail addresses, and telephone numbers.
Contact:
Office of (name of senator)
United States Senate
Washington, DC 20510
Web: www.senate.gov

U.S. Department of State

U.S. Department of State Internship

Type of award: Internship.
Intended use: For junior, senior or graduate study at accredited 4-year or graduate institution.
Eligibility: Applicant must be U.S. citizen.
Basis for selection: Major/career interest in political science/government; foreign languages; governmental public relations; business; public administration/service; social work; economics; information systems; journalism or science, general. Applicant must demonstrate high academic achievement.
Application requirements: Transcript. Statement of interest.
Additional information: Must have a minimum of 60 credit hours. Undergraduate seniors must be intending to go to graduate school. Provides opportunities working in varied administrative branches of the Department of State, both

abroad and in Washington, D.C. Internships are generally unpaid, but many institutions provide academic credit and/or financial assistance for overseas assignments. Paid internships primarily granted to students in financial need. Must be able to work a minimum of ten weeks. Selected students must undergo background investigation to receive security clearance. Random drug testing performed. Internships available year-round. Visit Website for more information.

Contact:
U.S. Department of State
Web: www.careers.state.gov/students

U.S. House of Representatives

House Member Internships

Type of award: Internship, renewable.
Intended use: For full-time undergraduate study.
Eligibility: Applicant must be U.S. citizen or permanent resident.
Basis for selection: Major/career interest in political science/government; public administration/service; public relations or communications. Applicant must demonstrate high academic achievement.
Additional information: Members of the United Stated House of Representatives use undergraduate interns for a variety of jobs including constituent contact, research, and correspondence. Positions are based in Congressional District Offices and in Washington, D.C. Internships generally facilitate course credit, but offer no stipend. Some paid internships are funded through private nonprofit organizations. Information about the individual House member intern programs can usually be found online. A complete set of links to representatives' sites is available at www.house.gov. In general, applicants residing in the member's home district and enrolled in the same political party are favored. Typically, many Washington, D.C.-based internships are filled by students from outside the member district. Applicants may also be interested in working for congressperson serving on committee (i.e. Agriculture, Financial Services) relevant to their major. Interested parties should contact the representative with whom they are interested in working.

Contact:
Contact individual congressman/congresswoman's office.
Phone: 202-224-3121
Web: www.house.gov

U.S. National Arboretum

U.S. National Arboretum Horticultural Internship

Type of award: Internship.
Intended use: For undergraduate or graduate study at postsecondary institution.
Basis for selection: Major/career interest in botany; horticulture or landscape architecture.
Application requirements: Transcript. Resume, cover letter.

Additional information: Interns work on independent projects supervised by arboretum staff. Hourly wage or stipend is available. Full-time and part-time positions available, usually between 7 a.m. and 3:30 p.m. College credit available. Must have completed course work or have acquired practical experience in horticulture or related field. Must have basic gardening or laboratory skills, interest in plants, and ability to work independently. Visit Website for more information and application.

Contact:
Internship Coordinator
U.S. National Arboretum
3501 New York Avenue, NE
Washington, DC 20002-1958
Phone: 202-245-4563
Fax: 202-245-4575
Web: www.usna.usda.gov

U.S. National Arboretum National Herb Garden Year-Long Internship

Type of award: Internship.
Intended use: For full-time undergraduate or graduate study at postsecondary institution.
Eligibility: Applicant must be U.S. citizen.
Basis for selection: Major/career interest in agriculture; botany; education; forestry; horticulture or public administration/service.
Application requirements: Transcript. Resume and cover letter.
Additional information: Average workday for most interns: Monday through Friday, 7 a.m. to 3:30 p.m. Provides opportunity to gain experience in plant research in premier horticultural collection. Basic gardening or laboratory skills, interest in plants, strong communication skills, and ability to work independently preferred. See Website for deadline, application, and more information.

Contact:
Internship Coordinator
U.S. National Arboretum
3501 New York Avenue, NE
Washington, DC 20002-1958
Phone: 202-245-4563
Fax: 202-245-4575
Web: www.usna.usda.gov

The Wall Street Journal

The Wall Street Journal Asia Internship

Type of award: Internship.
Intended use: For undergraduate or graduate study at postsecondary institution.
Basis for selection: Major/career interest in journalism.
Application requirements: Cover letter, resume and up to six writing samples.
Additional information: Internships available in the U.S., Europe, and Asia. Selection process strongly emphasizes submitted clips and journalistic experience. Roundtrip airfare allowance included. Pay is $700 per week. Candidate should be fluent in one or more Asian languages—preferably Mandarin, Japanese or Korean—a strong interest in business reporting in

Internships

Asia, and experience living or working in the region. Apply online.

Number of awards:	1
Application deadline:	November 1

Contact:
The Wall Street Journal Asia
Web: www.dowjones.com/djcom/careers/wsj-interns.asp

The Wall Street Journal Internships

Type of award: Internship.
Intended use: For undergraduate or graduate study at postsecondary institution.
Basis for selection: Major/career interest in journalism.
Application requirements: Cover letter, resume, and up to six writing samples.
Additional information: Interns work in one of news bureaus. Previous journalism or college newspaper experience required. All majors encouraged to apply. Currently enrolled students only. Apply online.

Number of awards:	15
Number of applicants:	335

Contact:
The Wall Street Journal
Web: www.dowjones.com/careers-interns.asp

The Wall Street Journal London Internship

Type of award: Internship.
Intended use: For undergraduate or graduate study at postsecondary institution.
Basis for selection: Major/career interest in journalism.
Application requirements: Cover letter, resume and up to six writing samples. Proof of health insurance.
Additional information: Apply online.

Number of awards:	1

Contact:
The Wall Street Journal
Web: www.dowjones.com/djcom/careers/wsj-interns.asp

Walt Disney Company

Disney College Program

Type of award: Internship.
Intended use: For undergraduate study at postsecondary institution.
Eligibility: Applicant must be U.S. citizen, permanent resident or students studying in the U.S. under an F-1 visa.
Application requirements: Interview. Online application and Web-based interview required.
Additional information: Disney College Program is a semester-long paid internship at the Walt Disney World® Resort near Orlando, FL or the Disneyland® Resort in Anaheim, CA, in which students work in a front-line role at theme parks and resorts, participate in college-level coursework, and live in company-sponsored housing with other students from around the globe. Applicant must be enrolled in a college/university during the spring/fall semester prior to participation. Work schedules and pay rates vary by role. College credit may be available. Must have strong communication skills, understanding of guest service principles, ability to work independently and/or with large team. Program

terms vary; are at least one semester in length. See Website for application and more information.

Number of awards:	10,000

Contact:
Disney College Recruiting
Phone: 800-722-2930
Web: www.disneycollegeprogram.com

Disney Theme Parks & Resorts Professional Internships

Type of award: Internship.
Intended use: For junior or senior study at 2-year or 4-year institution in United States.
Eligibility: Applicant must be U.S. citizen, permanent resident or currently studying in the U.S. under an F-1 visa.
Basis for selection: Major/career interest in animal sciences; architecture; construction management; engineering; finance/banking; communications; human resources; hospitality administration/management; marketing or computer/information sciences. Applicant must demonstrate high academic achievement, seriousness of purpose and service orientation.
Application requirements: Interview. Resume and cover letter.
Additional information: Internships available in a variety of fields. Offerings vary by season. Certain roles only open to alumni participants of the Disney College Program. For most positions, applicants must be enrolled in college/university during spring/fall semester prior to participation. Pay rates and schedules vary by location. Must have valid driver's license. Housing may be available, with the exception of management internships. Visit Website for more information, application deadline, and to search for openings.

Contact:
Disney Professional Recruiting
P.O. Box 10000
Lake Buena Vista, FL 32830
Phone: 800-722-2930
Web: www.disneyinterns.com

Washington Internships for Students of Engineering

Washington Internships for Students of Engineering

Type of award: Internship.
Intended use: For junior, senior or graduate study at postsecondary institution.
Eligibility: Applicant must be U.S. citizen or permanent resident.
Basis for selection: Major/career interest in computer/information sciences; engineering; engineering, chemical; engineering, electrical/electronic or engineering, mechanical.
Application requirements: Recommendations, essay, transcript. Reference forms.
Additional information: Nine-week summer internship learning about technological issues and public policy available to students who have completed three years of study. Internship located in Washington, D.C. Interns write required research paper as part of process. Lodging expenses covered. Must be member of and sponsored by ANS, ASCE, ASME, IEEE, or SAE. IEEE will sponsor computer science majors.

Graduate students beginning Masters study in technology policy-related degree also eligible. $2,100 stipend provided to assist with intern's living and travel expenses. Apply directly to sponsoring organization; application forms and sponsor contact information available on Website.

Amount of award:	$2,100
Number of awards:	13
Application deadline:	December 31
Total amount awarded:	$25,200

Contact:
Washington Internships for Students of Engineering
Web: www.wise-intern.org

Wells Fargo

Wells Fargo Undergraduate Internships

Type of award: Internship.

Intended use: For full-time junior or senior study at accredited 4-year institution.

Eligibility: Applicant must be U.S. citizen or permanent resident.

Basis for selection: Major/career interest in finance/banking; accounting; business/management/administration; economics or real estate. Applicant must demonstrate high academic achievement and leadership.

Application requirements: Resume and cover letter.

Additional information: Ten- to twelve-week program consists of work assignments and professional development opportunities related to corporate and investment banking. Number of awards varies. Locations in major cities throughout the U.S. Visit Website to search for internships and to create a profile and apply online.

Contact:
Wells Fargo
Web: www.wellsfargo.com

Wolf Trap Foundation for the Performing Arts

Wolf Trap Foundation for the Performing Arts Internship

Type of award: Internship.

Intended use: For sophomore, junior, senior or graduate study in United States.

Eligibility: Applicant must be U.S. citizen, permanent resident or international student.

Basis for selection: Major/career interest in performing arts or arts management. Applicant must demonstrate seriousness of purpose.

Application requirements: Recommendations. Resume. Cover letter outlining career goals and specifying internship desired. Two writing samples (except technical, scenic painting, costuming, stage management, accounting, graphic design, photography, or information systems applicants). Graphic Design, Web Communications, and Multimedia applicants must submit three design samples. Refer to individual internship descriptions for additional required materials.

Additional information: Deadline for summer is March 1, deadline for fall is July 1, deadline for spring is November 1. All positions paid. College credit available. Applicant must have own car. Public transit not available. Internships are offered in: Ticket Services, Planning and Initiatives, Accounting, Information Services, Technical Theater, Costuming, Scenic/prop painting, Stage Management, Administrative, Directing, Programming and Production, Photography, Marketing, Ad Sales/Group Sales, Graphic Design, Web Communications, Creative Copywriting, Public Relations, Multimedia, Special Events, Major Gifts, Annual Fund, Education. International students must have J-1 or F-1 visa. Also available to recent college graduates. Internships vary by season. Visit Website for more details.

Number of awards:	30
Number of applicants:	712
Application deadline:	March 1, July 1
Notification begins:	April 1, August 1

Contact:
Wolf Trap Foundation for the Performing Arts
Attn: Anjali Lalani
1645 Trap Road
Vienna, VA 22182
Phone: 703-255-1933
Fax: 703-255-1924
Web: www.wolftrap.org/internships

Internships

Loans

American Legion Kentucky Auxiliary

Mary Barrett Marshall Student Loan Fund

Type of award: Loan, renewable.
Intended use: For undergraduate study at vocational, 2-year or 4-year institution. Designated institutions: Eligible postsecondary institutions in Kentucky.
Eligibility: Applicant or parent must be member/participant of American Legion Auxiliary. Applicant must be female. Applicant must be residing in Kentucky. Applicant must be descendant of veteran; or dependent of veteran; or spouse of veteran or deceased veteran during Grenada conflict, Korean War, Lebanon conflict, Panama conflict, Persian Gulf War, WW I, WW II or Vietnam.
Basis for selection: Applicant must demonstrate financial need.
Application requirements: SASE.
Additional information: Maximum $800 per year, payable monthly without interest after graduation or upon securing employment; 6% interest after five years.

    Amount of award: $800
    Application deadline: April 1

Contact:
American Legion Auxiliary, Department of Kentucky
P.O. Box 5435
Frankfort, KY 40602
Phone: 502-352-2380
Fax: 502-352-2381
Web: www.kyamlegionaux.org

American Legion South Dakota

American Legion South Dakota Educational Loan

Type of award: Loan, renewable.
Intended use: For undergraduate study at vocational, 2-year or 4-year institution. Designated institutions: South Dakota institutions.
Eligibility: Applicant must be residing in South Dakota. Applicant must be veteran or descendant of veteran; or dependent of veteran.
Additional information: Up to $1,500 per year; $3,000 maximum; 3% interest on unpaid balance.

    Amount of award: $1,500-$3,000
    Application deadline: November 1, May 1

Contact:
American Legion South Dakota
Department Adjutant
P.O. Box 67
Watertown, SD 57201-0067
Phone: 605-886-3604
Web: www.sdlegion.org

ASME Auxiliary, Inc.

ASME Auxiliary Student Loan Fund

Type of award: Loan.
Intended use: For junior, senior or graduate study at accredited 4-year or graduate institution in United States. Designated institutions: Schools with ABET-accredited mechanical engineering or engineering technology curricula.
Eligibility: Applicant must be U.S. citizen.
Basis for selection: Major/career interest in engineering, mechanical. Applicant must demonstrate financial need and high academic achievement.
Application requirements: Recommendations.
Additional information: Loans are interest-free until graduation. Maximum award is $3,000 per year; or $9,000 for each borrower. Applications accepted on a rolling basis. Must be American Society of Mechanical Engineers member. Number of loans available varies. Apply online.

    Amount of award: $9,000

Contact:
ASME Foundation
Roseann Piccoli
22 Law Drive
Fairfield, NJ 07007-2900
Phone: 202-785-7499
Web: www.asme.org/career-education/scholarships-and-grants/scholarship-and-loans

Delaware Higher Education Office

Christa McAuliffe Teacher Incentive Program

Type of award: Loan, renewable.
Intended use: For undergraduate study at accredited 4-year institution.
Eligibility: Applicant must be U.S. citizen or permanent resident residing in Delaware.
Basis for selection: Major/career interest in education. Applicant must demonstrate high academic achievement.
Application requirements: Essay, transcript. SAT scores.
Additional information: Applicant must be high school senior with combined score of 1570 on the SAT and rank in top half

of class, or undergraduate with minimum 2.75 GPA. Preference given to applicants planning to teach in critical need area as defined by DE Department of Education. Though award is for full-time students, it may be prorated for part-time students in a qualifying program. Loan not to exceed cost of tuition, fees, and other direct educational expenses. Loan forgiveness provision at rate of one year of teaching in a DE public school for one year of loan. Visit Website for deadline information.

Number of applicants: 69

Contact:
Delaware Higher Education Office
John G. Townsend Building
401 Federal Street
Dover, DE 19901
Phone: 302-735-4000
Fax: 302-739-4654
Web: www.doe.k12.de.us/high-ed

Delaware Nursing Incentive Program

Type of award: Loan, renewable.
Intended use: For undergraduate study at accredited vocational, 2-year or 4-year institution in United States. Designated institutions: Colleges with accredited nursing programs that lead to RN, LPN, or BSN certification.
Eligibility: Applicant must be U.S. citizen or permanent resident residing in Delaware.
Basis for selection: Major/career interest in nursing. Applicant must demonstrate high academic achievement.
Application requirements: Essay, transcript.
Additional information: Loan-forgiveness for practicing nursing at state-owned hospital or clinic, one year for each year of loan. High school seniors must rank in top half of class and have at least 2.5 GPA. Though award generally for full-time students who are residents of DE, current state employees do not have to be DE residents and may be considered for part-time enrollment. RNs with five or more years of state service may enroll in BSN program full or part time. Loan not to exceed cost of tuition, fees, and other direct educational expenses. Visit Website for deadline information.

Number of applicants: 84
Total amount awarded: $35,000

Contact:
Delaware Higher Education Office
John G. Townsend Building
401 Federal Street
Dover, DE 19901
Phone: 302-735-4000
Fax: 302-739-4654
Web: www.doe.k12.de.us/high-ed

Franklin Lindsay Student Aid Fund

Franklin Lindsay Student Aid Loan

Type of award: Loan, renewable.
Intended use: For full-time sophomore, junior, senior or graduate study at accredited 4-year or graduate institution in United States. Designated institutions: Texas colleges accredited by the Southern Association of Colleges and Schools Commission on Colleges.
Eligibility: Applicant must be U.S. citizen.

Basis for selection: Applicant must demonstrate financial need and high academic achievement.
Application requirements: Interview, recommendations, transcript. Copy of driver's license or ID and proof of school enrollment.
Additional information: Minimum 2.0 GPA for undergraduates and 3.0 for graduates. Must have co-signer who is U.S. citizen. Upon graduation or termination from school, loan goes to repayment structure at four percent, with maximum payment term of seven years. Visit Website for application and more information.

Amount of award: $10,000
Number of applicants: 97
Application deadline: June 1
Total amount awarded: $723,550

Contact:
The Franklin Lindsay Student Aid Fund
c/o JPMorgan Chase Bank, N.A.
P.O. Box 227237
Dallas, TX 75222-7237
Phone: 866-300-6222
Web: www.franklinlindsay.org

Grand Encampment of Knights Templar of the USA

Knights Templar Educational Foundation Loan

Type of award: Loan, renewable.
Intended use: For undergraduate study at accredited vocational, 4-year or graduate institution in United States.
Basis for selection: Applicant must demonstrate high academic achievement and depth of character.
Application requirements: Recommendations.
Additional information: Student should request application from Grand Encampment of Knights Templar in state of residence. Available loan amount varies by state division.

Contact:
Grand Encampment of Knights Templar of the USA
5909 West Loop South
Suite 495
Belaire, TX 77401-2402
Phone: 713-349-8700
Fax: 713-349-8710
Web: www.knightstemplar.org

Maine Educational Loan Authority

The Maine Loan

Type of award: Loan.
Intended use: For undergraduate or graduate study at accredited vocational, 2-year, 4-year or graduate institution in United States or Canada.
Eligibility: Applicant must be U.S. citizen or permanent resident residing in Maine.

Application requirements: Proof of eligibility. Income information/credit analysis.

Additional information: Loans available to Maine residents attending approved schools and out-of-state students attending Maine schools. May borrow full cost of education at fixed interest rate of 7.25%, minus other financial aid. May be used to pay prior balance up to one academic year. Applicant has 5-15 years to repay, depending on amount owed. See Website for interest rates, payment options, and additional information. Applications accepted year round. Minimum loan amount is $1,000.

Number of applicants:	2,510
Total amount awarded:	$30,000,000

Contact:
Maine Educational Loan Authority
131 Presumpscot Street
Portland, ME 04103
Phone: 800-922-6352
Fax: 207-791-3616
Web: www.mela.net

Massachusetts Board of Higher Education

Massachusetts No Interest Loan

Type of award: Loan.
Intended use: For full-time undergraduate study at accredited vocational, 2-year or 4-year institution.
Eligibility: Applicant must be U.S. citizen or permanent resident residing in Massachusetts.
Basis for selection: Applicant must demonstrate financial need.
Application requirements: FAFSA.
Additional information: No Interest Loan (NIL) Program offers no interest loans to those who meet requirements; students have 10 years to repay NIL loans; the borrowing limit is $20,000 ($4,000/year). Must not have received prior bachelor's degree.

Amount of award:	$1,000-$4,000
Number of applicants:	2,200
Total amount awarded:	$6,000,000

Contact:
Office of Student Financial Assistance
Massachusetts Board of Higher Education
454 Broadway, Suite 200
Revere, MA 02151
Phone: 617-391-6070
Fax: 617-727-0667
Web: www.osfa.mass.edu

Military Officers Association of America

MOAA Interest-Free Loan and Grant Program

Type of award: Loan, renewable.
Intended use: For full-time undergraduate study at accredited 2-year or 4-year institution in United States.

Eligibility: Applicant must be no older than 23. Applicant must be U.S. citizen. Applicant must be dependent of active service person, veteran or deceased veteran who serves or served in the Army, Air Force, Marines, Navy, Coast Guard or Reserves/National Guard. Applicant must be child of MOAA member or active-duty, Reserve, National Guard, or retired enlisted military personnel.

Basis for selection: Applicant must demonstrate financial need, high academic achievement, depth of character, leadership, patriotism, seriousness of purpose and service orientation.

Application requirements: Essay, transcript, proof of eligibility. SAT/ACT score. Parent or sponsor's military status and/or MOAA number.

Additional information: Minimum 3.0 GPA. Applicant must be child of active-duty or retired officer or enlisted personnel. Must be under 24; however, if applicant served in Uniformed Service before completing college, maximum age for eligibility increases by number of years served, up to five years. Parent must sign promissory note before funds can be disbursed. Military academy cadets not eligible. Application available on Website.

Amount of award:	$5,500
Number of awards:	1,600
Application deadline:	March 1
Notification begins:	May 1

Contact:
MOAA Scholarship Fund
Educational Assistance Program
201 North Washington Street
Alexandria, VA 22314
Phone: 800-234-6622
Web: www.moaa.org/education

Minnesota Office of Higher Education

Minnesota Student Educational Loan Fund (SELF)

Type of award: Loan.
Intended use: For undergraduate or graduate study at vocational, 2-year, 4-year or graduate institution. Designated institutions: Minnesota and eligible out-of-state institutions.
Additional information: Applicant must be enrolled at least half-time in eligible Minnesota school, or be Minnesota resident enrolled in eligible school outside Minnesota. Must seek aid from certain other sources before applying, except federal unsubsidized and subsidized Stafford loans, National Direct Student loans, HEAL loans, and other private loans. Institution must approve application. Must have a creditworthy cosigner.

Amount of award:	$500-$20,000
Number of awards:	8,350
Number of applicants:	12,082
Total amount awarded:	$54,448,352

Contact:
Minnesota Office of Higher Education
1450 Energy Park Drive
Suite 350
St. Paul, MN 55108-5227
Phone: 800-657-3866
Web: selfloan.state.mn.us

Loans

Mississippi Office of Student Financial Aid

Critical Needs Teacher Loan/Scholarship

Type of award: Loan, renewable.
Intended use: For junior or senior study at 4-year institution in United States. Designated institutions: Mississippi institutions.
Eligibility: Applicant must be U.S. citizen residing in Mississippi.
Basis for selection: Major/career interest in education; education, early childhood; education, special or education, teacher. Applicant must demonstrate high academic achievement.
Application requirements: Signed CNTP Rules and Regulations.
Additional information: Minimum 2.5 GPA. Must have ACT score of 21 or higher or Praxis 1 passing score. Must be enrolled in program of study leading to Class "A" teacher educator license. Must agree to full-time employment in Mississippi public school located in critical teacher shortage or subject area. Must participate in Entrance Counseling. Award covers tuition, fees, and housing plus book allowance. Students at private institutions receive award equivalent to costs at nearest comparable public institution. Interested non-Mississippi residents may apply if they have been accepted to Mississippi school. See Website for application and more information.

Application deadline:	March 31

Contact:
Mississippi Office of Student Financial Aid
3825 Ridgewood Road
Jackson, MS 39211-6453
Phone: 800-327-2980
Web: www.mississippi.edu/riseupms

Mississippi Health Care Professions Loan/Scholarship

Type of award: Loan, renewable.
Intended use: For full-time junior, senior or graduate study at accredited 4-year or graduate institution. Designated institutions: Mississippi institutions.
Eligibility: Applicant must be residing in Mississippi.
Basis for selection: Major/career interest in speech pathology/audiology or psychology. Applicant must demonstrate high academic achievement.
Application requirements: Transcript, proof of eligibility. Mississippi tax return, copy of Mississippi driver's license, letter of college acceptance.
Additional information: Loan forgiveness for service in Mississippi health care institution: one year for each year of financial assistance, with a maximum of two years. Undergraduates must major in speech pathology/audiology, psychology, or occupational therapy; graduates must major in physical therapy or occupational therapy at University of Mississippi Medical Center. Visit Website for application and further information.

Amount of award:	$1,500
Application deadline:	March 31
Notification begins:	August 1

Contact:
Susan Eckels, Program Manager
Mississippi Office of Student Financial Aid
3825 Ridgewood Road
Jackson, MS 39211-6453
Phone: 601-432-6997
Fax: 601-432-6527
Web: www.mississippi.edu/riseupms

Mississippi William Winter Teacher Scholar Loan Program

Type of award: Loan, renewable.
Intended use: For full-time junior or senior study at 4-year institution. Designated institutions: Mississippi institutions.
Eligibility: Applicant must be U.S. citizen residing in Mississippi.
Basis for selection: Major/career interest in education; education, early childhood; education, special or education, teacher. Applicant must demonstrate high academic achievement.
Application requirements: Proof of eligibility. Praxis 1/ACT score, copy of Mississippi driver's license, state tax return.
Additional information: Must be studying towards a Class A teacher educator license. Must have Praxis 1 or Praxis Core passing score or ACT score of 21 or higher. Minimum 2.5 GPA or must rank in top 50 percent of class. Loan forgiveness for teaching service in Mississippi public school or public school district: one year for each year of financial assistance, for a maximum of two years. Apply online.

Amount of award:	$4,000
Application deadline:	March 31
Notification begins:	August 1
Total amount awarded:	$1,921,658

Contact:
Mississippi Office of Student Financial Aid
3825 Ridgewood Road
Jackson, MS 39211-6453
Phone: 800-327-2980
Fax: 601-432-6527
Web: www.mississippi.edu/riseupms

Navy-Marine Corps Relief Society

Navy-Marine Corps Relief Society Education Assistance

Type of award: Scholarship.
Intended use: For full-time at accredited vocational, 2-year or 4-year institution in United States.
Eligibility: Applicant must be no older than 22. Applicant must be descendant of veteran; or dependent of active service person; or spouse of active service person or veteran in the Marines or Navy.
Basis for selection: Applicant must demonstrate financial need.
Additional information: Minimum 2.7 GPA. Must be a child or spouse of an active duty or retired sailor or marine. Additional Criteria on website.

Amount of award:	$500-$3,000
Application deadline:	May 1, June 1

Loans

Contact:
Navy-Marine Corps Relief Society
875 N Randolph St.
Suite 225
Arlington, VA 22203
Phone: 703-696-4960
Web: www.nmcrs.org/education

NMCRS Education Assistance

Type of award: Loan, renewable.
Intended use: For full-time undergraduate study in United States.
Eligibility: Applicant must be U.S. citizen. Applicant must be dependent of active service person; or spouse of active service person in the Marines or Navy.
Basis for selection: Applicant must demonstrate financial need and high academic achievement.
Application requirements: Proof of eligibility. Current military ID of service member, FAFSA.
Additional information: Minimum 3.0 GPA. Applicant must be dependent child or spouse of an active duty or retired service member of Navy or Marine Corp (including Reservists on active duty) or a spouse of active duty service member. Loan must be repaid in allotments over 24-month period (minimum monthly repayment is $50). Must reapply to renew.

Amount of award:	$500-$3,000
Number of applicants:	1,200
Application deadline:	May 1
Total amount awarded:	$800,000

Contact:
Navy-Marine Corps Relief Society
875 North Randolph Street, Suite 225
Arlington, VA 22203
Phone: 703-696-4960
Web: www.nmcrs.org/education

New Jersey Higher Education Student Assistance Authority

New Jersey Class Loan Program

Type of award: Loan.
Intended use: For undergraduate or graduate study at accredited vocational, 2-year, 4-year or graduate institution in United States. Designated institutions: Approved institutions. Proprietary institutions also eligible.
Eligibility: Applicant must be U.S. citizen or permanent resident.
Application requirements: Proof of eligibility. Income and credit history, FAFSA, school certification.
Additional information: All New Jersey residents may apply, as may out-of-state students attending school in New Jersey. Must demonstrate credit-worthiness or provide co-signer. Parent or other eligible family member may borrow on behalf of student. Maximum loan amount may not exceed education cost less all other financial aid. Minimum loan amount $500. Low fixed interest rate loans available for both undergraduate and graduate students. Three percent administrative fee deducted from approved loan amount. Apply online for instant credit pre-approval. Must meet minimum income requirements and have clear credit history.

Number of applicants:	13,300
Total amount awarded:	$201,746,555

Contact:
New Jersey Higher Education Student Assistance Authority
4 Quakerbridge Plaza
P.O. Box 538
Trenton, NJ 08625-0540
Phone: 800-792-8670
Fax: 609-631-6730
Web: www.hesaa.org or njclass.org

New Mexico Higher Education Department

New Mexico Allied Health Student Loan-for-Service Program

Type of award: Loan, renewable.
Intended use: For undergraduate or graduate study at accredited postsecondary institution. Designated institutions: Public postsecondary institutions in New Mexico.
Eligibility: Applicant must be U.S. citizen or permanent resident residing in New Mexico.
Basis for selection: Major/career interest in health-related professions; occupational therapy; mental health/therapy; physical therapy; pharmacy/pharmaceutics/pharmacology; dietetics/nutrition or speech pathology/audiology. Applicant must demonstrate financial need.
Application requirements: FAFSA.
Additional information: Loan forgiveness offered to those who practice in medically underserved areas in New Mexico. Must be accepted by or enrolled in approved programs at accredited New Mexico public postsecondary institution. Call sponsor number or visit Website for application and more information.

Amount of award:	$12,000
Application deadline:	July 1

Contact:
New Mexico Higher Education Department
Financial Aid and Student Services
2048 Galisteo Street
Santa Fe, NM 87505
Phone: 505-476-8400
Web: www.hed.state.nm.us

New Mexico Nursing Student Loan-for-Service

Type of award: Loan, renewable.
Intended use: For undergraduate or graduate study at accredited 2-year or 4-year institution. Designated institutions: New Mexico public colleges and universities.
Eligibility: Applicant must be U.S. citizen or permanent resident residing in New Mexico.
Basis for selection: Major/career interest in nursing. Applicant must demonstrate financial need.
Application requirements: FAFSA.
Additional information: Must have official acceptance into nursing program in New Mexico. Loan forgiveness for New Mexico resident to practice in medically underserved areas in New Mexico. Part-time students eligible for prorated awards.

Amount of award:	$12,000
Application deadline:	July 1

Contact:
New Mexico Higher Education Department
Financial Aid Division
2048 Galisteo Street
Santa Fe, NM 87505
Phone: 505-476-8400
Web: www.hed.state.nm.us

New Mexico Teacher's Loan-for-Service

Type of award: Loan.
Intended use: For undergraduate or graduate study at accredited postsecondary institution. Designated institutions: Public college or university with teaching programs in New Mexico.
Eligibility: Applicant must be physically challenged. Applicant must be U.S. citizen or permanent resident residing in New Mexico.
Basis for selection: Major/career interest in education, teacher. Applicant must demonstrate financial need.
Application requirements: FAFSA.
Additional information: Must have official acceptance by undergraduate, graduate, or alternative licensure teacher preparation program approved by State Board of Education. Must provide one year of teaching service for each year of award at a public school in New Mexico.

Amount of award:	$4,000
Application deadline:	July 1

Contact:
New Mexico Higher Education Department
Financial Aid Division
2048 Galisteo Street
Santa Fe, NM 87505
Phone: 505-476-8400
Web: www.hed.state.nm.us

New York State Grange

Grange Student Loan Fund

Type of award: Loan, renewable.
Intended use: For full-time undergraduate or graduate study at postsecondary institution.
Eligibility: Applicant or parent must be member/participant of New York State Grange. Applicant must be residing in New York.
Basis for selection: Applicant must demonstrate financial need.
Additional information: Must have been member of New York State Grange for at least 6 months at time of application. Must send SASE for application. Loanee may borrow a maximum of $11,000. May apply for less than the maximum award. Loan repayment at 2.5%

Amount of award:	$11,000
Number of awards:	8
Number of applicants:	8
Application deadline:	April 15
Notification begins:	June 15
Total amount awarded:	$88,000

Contact:
New York State Grange
100 Grange Place
Cortland, NY 13045
Phone: 607-756-7553
Fax: 607-756-7757
Web: www.nysgrange.org

Ohio Department of Higher Education

Ohio Nurse Education Assistance Loan Program

Type of award: Loan, renewable.
Intended use: For post-bachelor's certificate or master's study at 4-year or graduate institution. Designated institutions: Eligible Ohio institutions.
Eligibility: Applicant must be U.S. citizen or permanent resident residing in Ohio.
Basis for selection: Major/career interest in nursing. Applicant must demonstrate financial need.
Application requirements: Proof of eligibility. FAFSA.
Additional information: Future nurse applicants must demonstrate financial need. Future nurse instructor applicants awarded on first-come, first-served basis. Award amount varies; up to $3,000 for future nurses, and at least $5,000 for future nurse instructors. Must not be in default or owe refund to any federal financial aid programs. Number of awards varies. Study must be devoted to RN or Nurse Instructor. Student may be eligible for loan forgiveness. Visit Website for application and more information.

Number of awards:	458
Application deadline:	July 15
Notification begins:	August 31
Total amount awarded:	$598,750

Contact:
Phone: 614-466-3561
Web: www.ohiohighered.org/nealp

Pickett and Hatcher Educational Fund, Inc.

Pickett and Hatcher Educational Loan

Type of award: Loan, renewable.
Intended use: For full-time undergraduate study at 4-year institution.
Eligibility: Applicant must be U.S. citizen.
Basis for selection: Applicant must demonstrate financial need and high academic achievement.
Additional information: Not available to law, medicine, or ministry students. Loans renewed up to $40,000. Applications accepted year-round.

Amount of award: $1,000-$10,000
Number of awards: 520
Number of applicants: 413
Application deadline: May 29
Total amount awarded: $3,376,752
Contact:
Pickett and Hatcher Educational Fund, Inc.
Loan Program
P.O. Box 8169
Columbus, GA 31908-8169
Phone: 800-864-8308 ext 0
Fax: 706-324-6788
Web: www.phef.org

Presbyterian Church (U.S.A.)

Presbyterian Undergraduate and Graduate Loan

Type of award: Loan, renewable.
Intended use: For full-time undergraduate or graduate study at accredited 2-year, 4-year or graduate institution in United States.
Eligibility: Applicant must be Presbyterian. Applicant must be U.S. citizen or permanent resident.
Basis for selection: Applicant must demonstrate financial need and high academic achievement.
Additional information: Must establish and maintain minimum 2.0 GPA. Contact office for current interest rates and deferment policies. Must give evidence of financial reliability. Award is up to $3,000. Undergraduates and graduates can apply for up to $15,000, spread out over length of undergraduate and graduate studies.

Number of awards: 150
Number of applicants: 52
Application deadline: July 30
Notification begins: August 15
Total amount awarded: $153,500
Contact:
Presbyterian Church (U.S.A.)
Financial Aid for Studies
100 Witherspoon Street
Louisville, KY 40202-1396
Phone: 800-728-7228 ext. 5224
Fax: 502-569-8766
Web: www.pcusa.org/financialaid

South Carolina Student Loan Corporation

South Carolina Teacher Loans

Type of award: Loan, renewable.
Intended use: For undergraduate or graduate study at accredited 2-year, 4-year or graduate institution.
Eligibility: Applicant must be U.S. citizen or permanent resident residing in South Carolina.
Basis for selection: Major/career interest in education; education, early childhood; education, special or education,

teacher. Applicant must demonstrate high academic achievement.
Additional information: Freshmen and sophomores may borrow up to $2,500 per year; juniors, seniors, and graduate students may borrow up to $5,000 per year. Graduate study eligible only if required for initial teacher certification. Entering freshmen must have SAT score equal to South Carolina state average for year of high school graduation, and rank in top 40 percent of high school class. Undergraduate and entering graduate applicants must have 2.75 GPA and have passed PRAXIS 1 Examination. Graduate applicants who have completed at least one semester must have 3.5 GPA. Applicants with SAT score of 1100 or greater (1650 or greater for exams taken on or after March 1, 2005) or ACT score of 24 or greater are exempt from PRAXIS 1 requirement. Loan forgiveness for service in teacher shortage area in South Carolina public schools: 20 percent or $3,000, whichever is greater, for each year of service, 33 percent or $5,000, whichever is greater, if service in geographic and subject shortage area. Apply early.

Amount of award: $2,500-$5,000
Application deadline: April 15
Notification begins: July 15
Total amount awarded: $5,000,000
Contact:
South Carolina Student Loan Corporation
P.O. Box 102405
Columbia, SC 29224
Phone: 803-798-0916 or 800-347-2752
Web: www.scstudentloan.org

Student Aid Foundation

Student Aid Foundation Loan

Type of award: Loan, renewable.
Intended use: For full-time undergraduate, master's, doctoral or first professional study at accredited vocational, 2-year, 4-year or graduate institution in United States.
Eligibility: Applicant must be female. Applicant must be U.S. citizen residing in Georgia.
Basis for selection: Applicant must demonstrate financial need, high academic achievement and seriousness of purpose.
Application requirements: Recommendations, essay, transcript.
Additional information: Non-Georgia residents attending Georgia institutions can qualify. Loan not forgivable. Must have financially responsible endorser. Minimum 2.5 GPA. Send SASE with request for application, or download it from Website.

Amount of award: $3,500-$7,500
Number of awards: 40
Number of applicants: 89
Application deadline: April 15
Notification begins: June 1
Contact:
Student Aid Foundation
1266 West Paces Ferry Rd
#577
Atlanta, GA 30327
Phone: 770-973-7077
Fax: 770-973-2220
Web: www.studentaidfoundation.org

Loans

Tennessee Student Assistance Corporation

Math And Science Teachers Loan Forgiveness Program

Type of award: Loan, renewable.
Intended use: For undergraduate certificate, graduate or postgraduate study at postsecondary institution.
Eligibility: Applicant must be residing in Tennessee.
Basis for selection: Major/career interest in mathematics; science, general or education.
Additional information: Must be admitted to post-secondary institution seeking advanced degree in math/science, or a certificate to teach math/science, and be a tenured Tennessee public school teacher. Application deadline is September 1 for students beginning the academic year in the fall, February 1 for spring, and May 1 for summer. Apply online.

Amount of award:	$2,000
Number of awards:	2
Application deadline:	September 1, February 1
Total amount awarded:	$4,000

Contact:
Tennessee Student Assistance Corporation
404 James Robertson Parkway
Parkway Towers, Suite 1510
Nashville, TN 37243-0820
Phone: 800-342-1663
Web: www.tn.gov/collegepays

Tennessee Minority Teaching Fellows Program

Type of award: Loan, renewable.
Intended use: For full-time undergraduate study at accredited 2-year or 4-year institution.
Eligibility: Applicant must be Alaskan native, Asian American, African American, Hispanic American, American Indian or Native Hawaiian/Pacific Islander. Applicant must be U.S. citizen residing in Tennessee.
Basis for selection: Major/career interest in education. Applicant must demonstrate high academic achievement.
Application requirements: Recommendations, essay, transcript. List of extracurricular activities.
Additional information: Entering freshmen applicants have priority and must have minimum 2.75 GPA, rank in top 25 percent of class, or score at least 18 on ACT (860 SAT). Undergraduate applicants must have minimum 2.5 GPA. Must make commitment to teaching. Loan can be forgiven by teaching in Tennessee public pre K-12 schools, one year for each year of funding.

Amount of award:	$5,000
Number of awards:	62
Number of applicants:	244
Application deadline:	April 15
Total amount awarded:	$287,000

Contact:
Tennessee Student Assistance Corporation
404 James Robertson Parkway
Parkway Towers, Suite 1510
Nashville, TN 37243-0820
Phone: 800-342-1663
Fax: 615-741-6101
Web: www.tn.gov/collegepays

Tennessee Teaching Scholars Program

Type of award: Loan, renewable.
Intended use: For junior, senior, post-bachelor's certificate or master's study at accredited 4-year or graduate institution.
Eligibility: Applicant must be U.S. citizen residing in Tennessee.
Basis for selection: Major/career interest in education; education, teacher; education, special or education, early childhood. Applicant must demonstrate high academic achievement.
Application requirements: Recommendations, transcript, proof of eligibility. Verification of standardized test score and acceptance into Teacher Licensure Program.
Additional information: Loan can be forgiven for teaching in Tennessee public schools, K-12. Minimum 2.75 cumulative GPA and a standardized test score adequate for admission to the Teacher Education Program in Tennessee schools. Amount of award based on funding.

Amount of award:	$5,000
Number of awards:	143
Number of applicants:	349
Application deadline:	April 15
Total amount awarded:	$642,000

Contact:
Tennessee Student Assistance Corporation
404 James Robertson Parkway
Parkway Towers, Suite 1510
Nashville, TN 37243-0820
Phone: 800-342-1663
Fax: 615-741-6101
Web: www.tn.gov/collegepays

Texas Higher Education Coordinating Board

Texas College Access Loan (CAL)

Type of award: Loan.
Intended use: For undergraduate or graduate study at 2-year, 4-year or graduate institution in United States. Designated institutions: Texas institutions.
Eligibility: Applicant must be U.S. citizen or permanent resident residing in Texas.
Additional information: Texas colleges and universities have a limited number of CAL loans. Applicants need not show financial need. The loan may be used to cover the family's expected contribution (EFC). Co-signers must have good credit and meet other program criteria. Loans will not be sold to another lender and will be serviced by the THECB until paid in full. Apply online.
Contact:
Texas Higher Education Coordinating Board
Phone: 800-242-3062
Web: www.collegeforalltexans.com and www.hhloans.com

William D. Ford Direct Student Loans

Type of award: Loan.
Intended use: For undergraduate study at vocational, 2-year or 4-year institution in United States.

Loans

Eligibility: Applicant must be U.S. citizen or permanent resident residing in Texas.

Basis for selection: Applicant must demonstrate financial need and high academic achievement.

Application requirements: FAFSA.

Additional information: Borrowers must not be in default or delinquent on any federal student loan. Contact college financial aid office for more information.

    Amount of award: $2,625-$18,500

Contact:

Texas Higher Education Coordinating Board

Phone: 800-242-3062

Web: www.collegeforalltexans.com

United Methodist Church

United Methodist Loan Program

Type of award: Loan, renewable.

Intended use: For undergraduate or graduate study at accredited postsecondary institution in United States.

Eligibility: Applicant must be United Methodist.

Basis for selection: Applicant must demonstrate high academic achievement.

Additional information: Must be active member of United Methodist Church one year prior to application. Must maintain 2.5 GPA. May reapply for loan to maximum of $20,000. Interest rate 5 percent; cosigner required. Ten years permitted to repay loan after graduation or withdrawal from school. Qualified applicants are chosen on a first-come, first-served basis.

    Amount of award: $5,000

Contact:

United Methodist Church/Board of Higher Education and Ministry

Office of Loans and Scholarships

P.O. Box 340007

Nashville, TN 37203-0007

Phone: 615-340-7346

Web: www.gbhem.org

UPS

United Parcel Service Earn & Learn Program Loans

Type of award: Loan.

Intended use: For undergraduate study at accredited vocational, 2-year or 4-year institution in United States.

Application requirements: Proof of eligibility.

Additional information: Must be UPS employee. Award for part-time employees is $3,000 per year in student loans with $15,000 lifetime maximum. Award for part-time management employees is $4,000 per year with a $20,000 lifetime maximum. Visit Website for participating locations and job listings.

    Amount of award: $3,000-$20,000

Contact:

UPS

Phone: 888-WORK-UPS

Web: www.upsjobs.com

U.S. Department of Education

Federal Direct Loans

Type of award: Loan, renewable.

Intended use: For undergraduate or graduate study at postsecondary institution.

Eligibility: Applicant must be U.S. citizen or permanent resident.

Basis for selection: Applicant must demonstrate financial need.

Application requirements: Proof of eligibility. FAFSA and promissory note.

Additional information: Some loans subsidized, based on need eligibility. Loan amount depends on grade level in school and student type. Telecommunications Device for the Deaf at 800-730-8913. FAFSA available online. Visit Website for interest rates.

    Amount of award: $5,500-$20,500

Contact:

Federal Student Aid Information Center

Phone: 800-4-FED-AID

Web: www.studentaid.ed.gov

Federal Perkins Loan

Type of award: Loan, renewable.

Intended use: For undergraduate or graduate study at accredited postsecondary institution in United States.

Eligibility: Applicant must be U.S. citizen or permanent resident.

Basis for selection: Applicant must demonstrate financial need.

Application requirements: Proof of eligibility. FAFSA.

Additional information: Maximum annual loan amount: $5,500 for undergraduates, $8,000 for graduates. Five percent interest rate. Applicant must demonstrate exceptional financial need. Repayment begins nine months after graduation, leaving school, or dropping below half-time status. Visit Website for more information.

    Application deadline: June 30

Contact:

Federal Student Aid Information Center

Phone: 800-4-FED AID

Web: www.studentaid.ed.gov

Federal Plus Loan

Type of award: Loan.

Intended use: For undergraduate or graduate study at accredited postsecondary institution in or outside United States or Canada.

Eligibility: Applicant must be U.S. citizen or permanent resident.

Basis for selection: Applicant must demonstrate financial need.

Application requirements: PLUS loan application and promissory note. FAFSA.

Additional information: Unsubsidized loans for parents of undergraduate students, or for graduate students. Must pass credit check. Interest rate is 7.9 percent. Award amount varies. Loan is equal to cost of attendance minus any other financial aid. Generally, repayment must begin 60 days after the loan is fully disbursed. Visit Website for more information.

    Application deadline: June 30

Loans

Contact:
Federal Student Aid Information Center
Phone: 800-4-FED-AID
Web: www.studentaid.ed.gov

Utah State Office of Education

Utah Career Teaching Scholarship/ T.H. Bell Teaching Incentive Loan

Type of award: Loan, renewable.
Intended use: For full-time undergraduate study at accredited 4-year institution. Designated institutions: Utah institutions.
Eligibility: Applicant must be high school junior or senior. Applicant must be U.S. citizen residing in Utah.
Basis for selection: Major/career interest in education, teacher; education; education, early childhood or education, special.
Application requirements: Transcript. SAT/ACT score sheet.
Additional information: Must have completed requirements for Early Graduation Program (including ACT). Awardees at public institutions receive a waiver for tuition and fees. Awardees at private institutions receive $995 per semester. Awardees must teach in Utah public school for term equal to number of years loan was received in order to have loans forgiven. Visit Website for application.

Amount of award:	Full tuition
Number of applicants:	110
Application deadline:	March 28

Contact:
Utah State Office of Education Teaching and Learning
Linda Alder, Teaching & Learning - Licensing
250 East 500 South/P.O. Box 144200
Salt Lake City, UT 84114-4200
Web: www.schools.utah.gov/cert/loans-and-scholarships.aspx

Virgin Islands Board of Education

Virgin Islands Territorial Grants/ Loans Program

Type of award: Loan, renewable.
Intended use: For full-time undergraduate or graduate study at accredited postsecondary institution.
Eligibility: Applicant must be U.S. citizen or permanent resident residing in Virgin Islands.
Basis for selection: Applicant must demonstrate high academic achievement.
Application requirements: Transcript. Acceptance letter from institution for first-time applicants or transfer students.
Additional information: Minimum 2.0 GPA. Six percent interest on repayment, additional 2 percent if delinquent. Number and amount of award varies. Deadline in early May.

Contact:
Virgin Islands Board of Education
Scholarship Committee
P.O. Box 11900
St. Thomas, VI 00801
Phone: 340-774-4546
Web: www.myviboe.com

Wisconsin Higher Educational Aids Board

Wisconsin Minority Teacher Loan Program

Type of award: Loan, renewable.
Intended use: For junior, senior or graduate study at accredited 4-year institution. Designated institutions: Wisconsin colleges and universities offering teaching degree.
Eligibility: Applicant must be Asian American, African American, Mexican American, Hispanic American, Puerto Rican or American Indian. Asian American applicants must be either former citizens or descendants of former citizens of Laos, Vietnam, or Cambodia admitted to the U.S. after 12/31/1975. Applicant must be residing in Wisconsin.
Basis for selection: Major/career interest in education; education, special or education, teacher. Applicant must demonstrate financial need.
Application requirements: Nomination by financial aid office. FAFSA.
Additional information: Recipient must agree to teach in Wisconsin school district where minority students constitute at least 29 percent of enrollment or in school district participating in the inter-district pupil transfer (Chapter 220) program. For each year student teaches in eligible district, 25 percent of loan is forgiven; otherwise loan must be repaid at interest rate of 5 percent. Must be registered with Selective Service, unless exempt.

Amount of award:	$250-$2,500
Number of awards:	109
Total amount awarded:	$238,662

Contact:
Higher Educational Aids Board
Attn: Deanna Schulz
P.O. Box 7885
Madison, WI 53707-7885
Phone: 608-267-2212
Web: www.heab.state.wi.us

Loans

Sponsor Index

Sponsor Index

Program Index

Take learning to new heights.

With 38 courses in everything from Computer Science to Art History, AP® gives high school students the opportunity to earn college credit and stand out on college applications.

collegeboard.org/ap

Get credit for knowing.

CLEP® exams help you earn college credit for what you already know, for a fraction of the cost of a college course. CLEP offers 33 exams that cover what's taught in introductory college courses, saving you time and money toward a degree.

clep.org

Show up ready on test day.

Now, the best way to get ready for the SAT is free for everyone. The College Board partnered with Khan Academy® to create Official SAT® Practice. It's free, personalized, and the only online practice tool from the makers of the test. It's simply the best way to prepare. Sign up today.

satpractice.org

Registered and ready?

The SAT® tests what students are already learning in class. Preparing for it is easier than ever with free, personalized practice on Khan Academy®. Encourage your students to register today.

SAT® 🍎 CollegeBoard